CERT® Resilience Management Model

The SEI Series in Software Engineering

♦Addison-Wesley

Visit **informit.com/sei** for a complete list of available publications.

The **SEI Series in Software Engineering** is a collaborative undertaking of the Carnegie Mellon Software Engineering Institute (SEI) and Addison-Wesley to develop and publish books on software engineering and related topics. The common goal of the SEI and Addison-Wesley is to provide the most current information on these topics in a form that is easily usable by practitioners and students.

Books in the series describe frameworks, tools, methods, and technologies designed to help organizations, teams, and individuals improve their technical or management capabilities. Some books describe processes and practices for developing higher-quality software, acquiring programs for complex systems, or delivering services more effectively. Other books focus on software and system architecture and product-line development. Still others, from the SEI's CERT Program, describe technologies and practices needed to manage software and network security risk. These and all books in the series address critical problems in software engineering for which practical solutions are available.

PEARSON

♦Addison-Wesley | Cisco Press | EXAM/CRAM | IBM Press | QUE | PRENTICE HALL | SAMS | Safari

CERT® Resilience Management Model
A Maturity Model for Managing Operational Resilience

Richard A. Caralli
Julia H. Allen
David W. White

◆◆Addison-Wesley

Upper Saddle River, NJ • Boston • Indianapolis • San Francisco
New York • Toronto • Montreal • London • Munich • Paris • Madrid
Capetown • Sydney • Tokyo • Singapore • Mexico City

Software Engineering Institute | Carnegie Mellon

The SEI Series in Software Engineering

Many of the designations used by manufacturers and sellers to distinguish their products are claimed as trademarks. Where those designations appear in this book, and the publisher was aware of a trademark claim, the designations have been printed with initial capital letters or in all capitals.

CMM, CMMI, Capability Maturity Model, Capability Maturity Modeling, Carnegie Mellon, CERT, and CERT Coordination Center are registered in the U.S. Patent and Trademark Office by Carnegie Mellon University.

ATAM; Architecture Tradeoff Analysis Method; CMM Integration; COTS Usage-Risk Evaluation; CURE; EPIC; Evolutionary Process for Integrating COTS Based Systems; Framework for Software Product Line Practice; IDEAL; Interim Profile; OAR; OCTAVE; Operationally Critical Threat, Asset, and Vulnerability Evaluation; Options Analysis for Reengineering; Personal Software Process; PLTP; Product Line Technical Probe; PSP; SCAMPI; SCAMPI Lead Appraiser; SCAMPI Lead Assessor; SCE; SEI; SEPG; Team Software Process; and TSP are service marks of Carnegie Mellon University.

Special permission to reproduce in this book portions of "CERT® Resilience Management Model, Version 1.0," CMU/SEI-2010-TR-012/ESC-TR-2010-012, © 2010 Carnegie Mellon University; "CERT® Resilience Management Model, Version 1.0–Process Areas, Generic Goals and Practices, and Glossary," © 2010 Carnegie Mellon University; and "CERT® Resilience Management Model, Version 1.1," © 2010 Carnegie Mellon University, is granted by the Software Engineering Institute.

The authors and publisher have taken care in the preparation of this book, but make no expressed or implied warranty of any kind and assume no responsibility for errors or omissions. No liability is assumed for incidental or consequential damages in connection with or arising out of the use of the information or programs contained herein.

The publisher offers excellent discounts on this book when ordered in quantity for bulk purchases or special sales, which may include electronic versions and/or custom covers and content particular to your business, training goals, marketing focus, and branding interests. For more information, please contact:

   U.S. Corporate and Government Sales
   (800) 382-3419
   corpsales@pearsontechgroup.com

For sales outside the United States, please contact:

   International Sales
   international@pearsoned.com

Visit us on the Web: informit.com/aw

Library of Congress Cataloging-in-Publication Data is on file.

Copyright © 2011 Pearson Education, Inc.

All rights reserved. Printed in the United States of America. This publication is protected by copyright, and permission must be obtained from the publisher prior to any prohibited reproduction, storage in a retrieval system, or transmission in any form or by any means, electronic, mechanical, photocopying, recording, or likewise. For information regarding permissions, write to:

   Pearson Education, Inc.
   Rights and Contracts Department
   501 Boylston Street, Suite 900
   Boston, MA 02116
   Fax: (617) 671-3447

ISBN-13: 978-0-13-454506-6
ISBN-10:   0-13-454506-0

This product is printed digitally on demand. This book is the paperback version of an original hardcover book.
First Printing: January 2016

CONTENTS

LIST OF FIGURES	xi
LIST OF TABLES	xiii
PREFACE	xv
ACKNOWLEDGMENTS	xxi

PART ONE—ABOUT THE CERT RESILIENCE MANAGEMENT MODEL   1

1 INTRODUCTION   7
    1.1 The Influence of Process Improvement and Capability Maturity Models   8
    1.2 The Evolution of CERT-RMM   10
    1.3 CERT-RMM and CMMI Models   15
    1.4 Why CERT-RMM Is Not a *Capability Maturity* Model   18

2 UNDERSTANDING KEY CONCEPTS IN CERT-RMM   21
    2.1 Foundational Concepts   21
       2.1.1 Disruption and Stress   21
       2.1.2 Convergence   23
       2.1.3 Managing Operational Resilience   25
    2.2 Elements of Operational Resilience Management   27
       2.2.1 Services   27
       2.2.2 Business Processes   29

	2.2.3 Assets	30
	2.2.4 Resilience Requirements	33
	2.2.5 Strategies for Protecting and Sustaining Assets	35
	2.2.6 Life-Cycle Coverage	36
	2.3 Adapting CERT-RMM Terminology and Concepts	39
3	**MODEL COMPONENTS**	**41**
	3.1 The Process Areas and Their Categories	41
	3.1.1 Process Area Icons	42
	3.2 Process Area Component Categories	42
	3.2.1 Required Components	44
	3.2.2 Expected Components	44
	3.2.3 Informative Components	44
	3.3 Process Area Component Descriptions	44
	3.3.1 Purpose Statements	44
	3.3.2 Introductory Notes	44
	3.3.3 Related Process Areas Section	45
	3.3.4 Summary of Specific Goals and Practices	45
	3.3.5 Specific Goals and Practices	45
	3.3.6 Generic Goals and Practices	46
	3.3.7 Typical Work Products	46
	3.3.8 Subpractices, Notes, Example Blocks, Generic Practice Elaborations, References, and Amplifications	47
	3.4 Numbering Scheme	47
	3.5 Typographical and Structural Conventions	49
4	**MODEL RELATIONSHIPS**	**53**
	4.1 The Model View	54
	4.1.1 Enterprise Management	54
	4.1.2 Engineering	56
	4.1.3 Operations	56
	4.1.4 Process Management	57
	4.2 Objective Views for Assets	59
	4.2.1 People	59
	4.2.2 Information	59
	4.2.3 Technology	60
	4.2.4 Facilities	60

PART TWO—PROCESS INSTITUTIONALIZATION AND IMPROVEMENT 65

5 INSTITUTIONALIZING OPERATIONAL RESILIENCE MANAGEMENT PROCESSES 67
- 5.1 Overview 67
- 5.2 Understanding Capability Levels 68
- 5.3 Connecting Capability Levels to Process Institutionalization 69
    - 5.3.1 Capability Level 0: Incomplete 70
    - 5.3.2 Capability Level 1: Performed 70
    - 5.3.3 Capability Level 2: Managed 70
    - 5.3.4 Capability Level 3: Defined 72
    - 5.3.5 Other Capability Levels 72
- 5.4 CERT-RMM Generic Goals and Practices 73
    - 5.4.1 CERT-RMM Elaborated Generic Goals and Practices 74
- 5.5 Applying Generic Practices 74
- 5.6 Process Areas That Support Generic Practices 74

6 USING CERT-RMM 77
- 6.1 Examples of CERT-RMM Uses 78
    - 6.1.1 Supporting Strategic and Operational Objectives 78
    - 6.1.2 A Basis for Evaluation, Guidance, and Comparison 78
    - 6.1.3 An Organizing Structure for Deployed Practices 79
    - 6.1.4 Model-Based Process Improvement 80
- 6.2 Focusing CERT-RMM on Model-Based Process Improvement 80
    - 6.2.1 Making the Business Case 81
    - 6.2.2 A Process Improvement Process 82
- 6.3 Setting and Communicating Objectives Using CERT-RMM 83
    - 6.3.1 Organizational Scope 85
    - 6.3.2 Model Scope 87
    - 6.3.3 Capability Level Targets 90
- 6.4 Diagnosing Based on CERT-RMM 92
    - 6.4.1 Formal Diagnosis Using the CERT-RMM Capability Appraisal Method 92
    - 6.4.2 Informal Diagnosis 94
- 6.5 Planning CERT-RMM–Based Improvements 95
    - 6.5.1 Analyzing Gaps 95
    - 6.5.2 Planning Practice Instantiation 95

7 CERT-RMM PERSPECTIVES — 99

Using CERT-RMM in the Utility Sector,
 by Darren Highfill and James Stevens — 99

Addressing Resilience as a Key Aspect of Software Assurance Throughout the Software Life Cycle,
 by Julia Allen and Michele Moss — 104

Raising the Bar on Business Resilience,
 by Nader Mehravari, PhD — 110

Measuring Operational Resilience Using CERT-RMM,
 by Julia Allen and Noopur Davis — 115

PART THREE—CERT-RMM PROCESS AREAS — 119

ASSET DEFINITION AND MANAGEMENT — 121

ACCESS MANAGEMENT — 149

COMMUNICATIONS — 175

COMPLIANCE — 209

CONTROLS MANAGEMENT — 241

ENVIRONMENTAL CONTROL — 271

ENTERPRISE FOCUS — 307

EXTERNAL DEPENDENCIES MANAGEMENT — 341

FINANCIAL RESOURCE MANAGEMENT — 381

HUMAN RESOURCE MANAGEMENT — 411

IDENTITY MANAGEMENT — 447

INCIDENT MANAGEMENT AND CONTROL — 473

KNOWLEDGE AND INFORMATION MANAGEMENT — 513

MEASUREMENT AND ANALYSIS — 551

MONITORING — 577

ORGANIZATIONAL PROCESS DEFINITION — 607

ORGANIZATIONAL PROCESS FOCUS — 629

ORGANIZATIONAL TRAINING AND AWARENESS	653
PEOPLE MANAGEMENT	685
RISK MANAGEMENT	717
RESILIENCE REQUIREMENTS DEVELOPMENT	747
RESILIENCE REQUIREMENTS MANAGEMENT	771
RESILIENT TECHNICAL SOLUTION ENGINEERING	793
SERVICE CONTINUITY	831
TECHNOLOGY MANAGEMENT	869
VULNERABILITY ANALYSIS AND RESOLUTION	915

PART FOUR—THE APPENDICES 943

A	GENERIC GOALS AND PRACTICES	945
B	TARGETED IMPROVEMENT ROADMAPS	957
C	GLOSSARY OF TERMS	965
D	ACRONYMS AND INITIALISMS	989
E	REFERENCES	993

BOOK CONTRIBUTORS 997

INDEX	1001

LIST OF FIGURES

Figure 1.1:	The Three Critical Dimensions	9
Figure 1.2:	Bodies of Knowledge Related to Security Process Improvement	11
Figure 1.3:	CERT-RMM Influences	13
Figure 2.1:	Convergence of Operational Risk Management Activities	24
Figure 2.2:	Relationships Among Services, Business Processes, and Assets	28
Figure 2.3:	Relationship Between Services and Operational Resilience Management Processes	29
Figure 2.4:	Impact of Disrupted Asset on Service Mission	31
Figure 2.5:	Putting Assets in Context	32
Figure 2.6:	Driving Operational Resilience Through Requirements	34
Figure 2.7:	Optimizing Information Asset Resilience	35
Figure 2.8:	Generic Asset Life Cycle	36
Figure 2.9:	Software/System Asset Life Cycle	37
Figure 2.10:	Services Life Cycle	38
Figure 3.1:	Examples of Process Area Icons	43
Figure 3.2:	A Specific Goal and Specific Goal Statement	45
Figure 3.3:	A Specific Practice and Specific Practice Statement	46
Figure 3.4:	A Generic Goal and Generic Goal Statement	46
Figure 3.5:	A Generic Practice and Generic Practice Statement	46
Figure 3.6:	Summary of Major Model Components	48
Figure 3.7:	Format of Model Components	50

Figure 4.1:	Relationships That Drive Resilience Activities at the Enterprise Level	55
Figure 4.2:	Relationships That Drive Threat and Incident Management	58
Figure 4.3:	Relationships That Drive the Resilience of People	60
Figure 4.4:	Relationships That Drive Information Resilience	61
Figure 4.5:	Relationships That Drive Technology Resilience	62
Figure 4.6:	Relationships That Drive Facility Resilience	63
Figure 5.1:	Structure of the CERT-RMM Continuous Representation	69
Figure 6.1:	The IDEAL Model for Process Improvement	82
Figure 6.2:	Organizational Unit, Subunit, and Superunit on an Organization Chart	86
Figure 6.3:	Alternate Organizational Unit Designation on an Organization Chart	87
Figure 6.4:	Model Scope Options	90
Figure 6.5:	CERT-RMM Targeted Improvement Profile	91
Figure 6.6:	CERT-RMM Targeted Improvement Profile with Scope Caveats	92
Figure 6.7:	Capability Level Ratings Overlaid on Targeted Improvement Profile	94
Figure 6.8:	Alternate Locations for Organizational Process Assets	96

LIST OF TABLES

Table 1.1:	Process Areas in CERT-RMM and CMMI Models	16
Table 1.2:	Other Connections Between CERT-RMM and the CMMI Models	18
Table 3.1:	Process Areas by Category	41
Table 3.2:	CERT-RMM Components by Category	43
Table 3.3:	Process Area Tags	48
Table 5.1:	Capability Levels in CERT-RMM	69
Table 5.2:	Capability Levels Related to Goals and Process Progression	70
Table 5.3:	CERT-RMM Generic Practices Supported by Process Areas	75
Table 6.1:	Classes of Formal CERT-RMM Capability Appraisals	93
Table 7.1:	Examples of Metrics in Selected CERT-RMM Process Areas	117
Table B.1:	Targeted Improvement Roadmap for FISMA Compliance	957
Table B.2:	Targeted Improvement Roadmap for Cloud Computing	961
Table B.3:	Targeted Improvement Roadmap for Managing Insider Threat	963

PREFACE

> Resilience (*noun*): the physical property of a material by which it can return to its original shape or position after deformation that does not exceed its elastic limit[1]

We hear the word *resilience* everywhere these days. People are described as resilient when they bounce back from adversity. Things are described as resilient when they can withstand unusual wear and tear and still perform adequately. Organizations are described as resilient when they can meet their mission in the face of adversity and an ever-changing risk environment.

For something or somebody to be described as resilient, a few basic conditions must be met. First, a physical or logical impact must be able to be tolerated for some period of time. Second, the object or person must be able to continue its purpose or mission while impacted. And third, the object or person must be able, in some reasonable time, to return to a "normal" state.

The authors of this book have often struggled with finding the right metaphor for describing resilience. But we always seem to come back to something that everyone understands: a childhood toy called a "Slinky."

Nearly everyone growing up either had a Slinky or knew someone who did. There wasn't much to it—a coiled piece of wire that could do some basic tricks—but for the most part, it just kept us amused until we found something else to which to direct our attention. That is, until we tested the limits of the Slinky. Slinkys were mostly forgiving of our attempts to make them do things that weren't intended by the designers, but there was always that one thing we did that pushed the Slinky

---

1. See http://wordnet.princeton.edu.

to its limits. And the result? The spring became a mere wire, unable to bounce back to its original shape and never again to magically crawl down the stairs on its own.

People, things, and especially organizations can be very much like Slinkys. Most organizations can manage to expand and contract as necessary to absorb the "punch" of disruption. But when the expansion is beyond sustainable limits, in either impact or duration, the organization transforms from a Slinky to a mere wire—unable to spring back to a normal operating condition. Organizations that do not operate with a conscious eye to what their Slinky looks like do so to their own peril. Consider:

- In 2007 the Economist Intelligence Unit surveyed 181 executives from around the world about business resilience. Not surprisingly, 47% of respondents said that they could endure less than *one day* of downtime from IT systems before the disruption would seriously jeopardize the survival of *the entire company* [Economist 2007].
- A National Archives and Records Administration survey cites that 25% of companies that experienced an IT outage of two to six days went bankrupt *immediately* [Economist 2007]. This same study found that 93% of companies that lost their data center for ten days or more *filed for bankruptcy within a year*.

And it isn't as though organizations don't understand the necessity of improving their operational resilience capabilities. In a 2008 Carnegie Mellon CyLab report on Enterprise Security Governance, nearly 50% of survey respondents indicated that risk and crisis oversight is important, but only 37% responded that it was a critical governance issue. Thus, board of directors members recognize the importance of operational resilience but don't feel it's important enough to do anything about (or don't know what to do to address it) [Westby 2008].

In its 2007 report *The Resilient Economy: Integrating Competitiveness and Security*, the Council on Competitiveness makes a compelling argument that the ability of an organization to actively manage resilience will become a key competitive differentiator in the twenty-first century [van Opstal 2007]. The Council's conclusions frame a business- and economics-centric argument that supports the theories we posed in 2003 about the transformation of the security discipline into one that supports a larger business-driven purpose. Clearly, today that purpose is to ensure the organization is operationally resilient and able to carry out operational risk management activities in a coordinated way, liberated from traditional silos and organizational structures.

The CERT Resilience Management Model was developed to help organizations do this and, in the end, to help them be better Slinkys.

Introducing the CERT Resilience Management Model

The CERT Resilience Management Model (CERT-RMM) is an innovative and transformative way to approach the challenge of managing operational resilience in complex, risk-evolving environments. It is the result of years of research into the ways that organizations manage the security and survivability of the assets that ensure mission success: people, information, technology, and facilities. It incorporates concepts from an established process improvement community to create a model that transcends mere practice implementation and compliance—one that can be used to mature an organization's capabilities and improve predictability and success in sustaining operations whenever disruption occurs.

The ability to manage operational resilience at a level that supports mission success is the focus of CERT-RMM. By improving its operational resilience management system—the plan, program, processes, procedures, practices, and people that are necessary to manage operational resilience—the organization in turn improves the mission assurance of high-value services. The success of high-value services in meeting their missions consistently over time and in particular under stressful conditions is vital to meeting organizational goals and objectives.

Purpose

CERT-RMM v1.1 is a capability-focused maturity model for process improvement that comprehensively reflects best practices from industry and government for managing operational resilience across the disciplines of security management, business continuity management, and IT operations management. Through CERT-RMM these best practices are integrated into a single model that provides an organization with a transformative path from a silo-driven approach for managing operational risk to one that is focused on achieving resilience management goals and supporting the organization's strategic direction.

CERT-RMM incorporates many proven concepts and approaches from the Software Engineering Institute's process improvement experience in software and systems engineering and acquisition. Foundational concepts from CMMI (Capability Maturity Model Integration) are integrated into CERT-RMM to elevate operational resilience management to a process approach and to provide an evolutionary path for improving capability. Practices in the model focus on improving the organization's management of key operational resilience processes. The effect of this improvement is realized through improving the ability of high-value services to meet their mission consistently and with high quality, particularly during times of stress.

It should be noted that CERT-RMM is not based on the CMMI Model Foundation (CMF), which is a set of model components that are common to all CMMI models and constellations. In addition, CERT-RMM does not form an additional CMMI constellation or directly intersect with existing constellations. However,

CERT-RMM makes use of several CMMI components, including core process areas and process areas from CMMI-DEV. It incorporates the Generic Goals and Practices of CMMI models, and it expands the resilience concept for services found in CMMI-SVC. Section 1.4 of this book provides a detailed explanation of the connections between CERT-RMM and the CMMI models.

Audience

The audience for CERT-RMM is anyone interested in improving the mission assurance of high-value services through improving operational resilience processes. Simply stated, CERT-RMM can help improve the ability of an organization to meet its commitments and objectives with consistency and predictability in the face of changing risk environments and potential disruptions. CERT-RMM will be useful to you if you manage a large enterprise or organizational unit, are responsible for security or business continuity activities, manage large-scale IT operations, or help others to improve their operational resilience. CERT-RMM is also useful for anyone who wants to add a process improvement dimension or who wants to make more efficient and effective use of an installed base of codes of practice, such as ISO 27000, COBIT, or ITIL.

If you are a member of an established process improvement community, particularly one centered on CMMI models, CERT-RMM can provide an opportunity to extend your process improvement knowledge to the operations phase of the asset life cycle. Thus, process improvement need not end when an asset is put into production—it can instead continue until the asset is retired.

Organization of This Book

This book is organized into three main parts:

- Part One: About the CERT Resilience Management Model
- Part Two: Process Institutionalization and Improvement
- Part Three: CERT-RMM Process Areas

Part One, About the CERT Resilience Management Model, consists of four chapters:

- Chapter 1, Introduction, provides a summary view of the advantages and influences of a process improvement approach and capability maturity models on CERT-RMM.
- Chapter 2, Understanding Key Concepts in CERT-RMM, describes all the model conventions used in CERT-RMM process areas and how they are assembled into the model.

- Chapter 3, Model Components, addresses the core operational risk and resilience management principles on which the model is constructed.
- Chapter 4, Model Relationships, describes the model in two virtual views to ease adoption and usability.

Part Two, Process Institutionalization and Improvement, focuses on the capability dimension of the model and its importance in establishing a foundation on which an operational resilience management system can be sustained in complex environments and evolving risk landscapes. The effect of increased levels of capability in managing operational resilience on the mission success of high-value services is discussed. Part Two addresses the use of the model's Generic Goals and Practices, which are sourced from CMMI and tailored for institutionalizing operational resilience management processes. Part Two also describes various approaches for using CERT-RMM, as well as considerations when applying a Plan, Do, Check, Act model for process improvement. In the last chapter of Part Two, CERT-RMM Perspectives, several invited contributing authors share their thoughts about how CERT-RMM can be applied for different purposes. Another describes how his company evaluated CERT-RMM and found it to be "a comprehensive and flexible framework" for helping to meet business resilience objectives.

Part Three, CERT-RMM Process Areas, is a detailed view of the 26 CERT-RMM process areas. They are organized alphabetically by process area acronym. Each process area contains descriptions of goals, practices, and examples.

The appendices of the book provide a detailed treatment of the model's Generic Goals and Practices, book references, a list of commonly used acronyms, and a reference glossary.

How to Use This Book

Part One of this book provides a foundational understanding of CERT-RMM, whether or not you have previous experience with process improvement models.

If you have process improvement experience, particularly using models in the CMMI family, you should start with Section 1.4 in the Introduction, which describes the relationship between CERT-RMM and CMMI models. Reviewing Part Three will provide you with a baseline understanding of the process areas covered in CERT-RMM and how they may be similar to or different from those in CMMI. Next, you should examine Part Two to understand how generic goals and practices are used in CERT-RMM. Pay particular attention to the example blocks in the generic goals and practices; they provide an illustration of how the capability dimension can be implemented in the CERT-RMM model.

If you have no process improvement experience, you should begin with the Introduction in Part One and continue sequentially through the book. The chapters are arranged to build understanding before you reach Part Three, the process areas.

Additional Information and Reader Feedback

CERT-RMM continues to evolve as more organizations use it to improve their operational resilience management processes. You can always find up-to-date information about the CERT-RMM model, including new process areas as they are developed and added, at www.cert.org/resilience. There, you can also learn how CERT-RMM is being used for critical infrastructure protection and how it forms the basis for exciting research in the area of resilience measurement and analysis.

Your suggestions for improving CERT-RMM are welcome. For information on how to provide feedback, see the CERT website at www.cert.org/resilience/request-comment. If you have comments or questions about CERT-RMM, send email to rmm-comments@cert.org.

ACKNOWLEDGMENTS

This book is the culmination of many years of hard work by many talented people dedicated to the belief that security, continuity, and IT operations management processes can be improved, and operational resilience can be actively directed, controlled, and measured. These people have spent countless hours poring over codes of practice, interviewing senior personnel in organizations with high-performance resilience programs, applying and field testing the concepts in this book, and codifying the 26 most common process areas that compose a convergent view of operational resilience.

CERT-RMM is a major component of this book. Early models were created by Richard Caralli, working with members of the Financial Services Technology Consortium over a four-year period from 2004 through 2008. The model was significantly enhanced as additional model team members joined our efforts. The resulting model included in this book (CERT-RMM v1.1) is the work of the CERT-RMM Model Team, which includes Richard Caralli, David White, Julia Allen, Lisa Young, and Pamela Curtis.

CERT-RMM v1.1 was refined and recalibrated through benchmarking activities performed over a period of two years by security and continuity professionals at prominent financial institutions. The model team is forever indebted to the following people who participated in that effort (listed here with the companies at which they worked during the benchmarking effort):

- Ameriprise Financial: Barry Gorelick
- Capital Group: Michael Gifford and Bo Trowbridge
- Citi: Andrew McCruden, Patrick Keenan, Victor Zhu, and Joan Land

- Discover Financial Services: Rick Webb, Kent Anderson, Kevin Novak, and Ric Robinson
- JPMorgan Chase & Co.: Judith Zosh, Greg Pinchbeck, and Kathryn Wakeman
- Marshall & Ilsley Corporation: Gary Daniels and Matthew Meyer
- MasterCard Worldwide: Randall Till
- PNC Financial Services: Jeffery Gerlach and Louise Hritz
- U.S. Bank: Jeff Pinckard, Mike Rattigan, Michael Stickney, and Nancy Hofer
- Wachovia: Brian Clodfelter

In addition, we are grateful for the contributions of people from organizations that bravely performed early appraisal pilots using the model, including Johnny E. Davis, Kimberly A. Farmer, William Gill, Mark Hubbard, Walter Dove, Leonard Chertoff, Deb Singer, Deborah Williams, Bill Sabbagh, Jody Zeugner, Tim Thorpe, and the many other participants from the Environmental Protection Agency; and Nader Mehravari, Joan Weszka, Michael Freeman, Doug Stopper, Eric Jones, and many other talented people from Lockheed Martin Corporation.

Last, but certainly not least, we owe much of the momentum that created this model to Charles Wallen from American Express. In 2005, as the Executive Director of the Business Continuity Standing Committee for the Financial Services Technology Consortium, Charles came to the CERT Program at the Software Engineering Institute with a desire to create a resiliency maturity model based on work being performed at CERT. Five years later (which is only four years and 46 weeks longer than we hoped it would take!), we have a functional model.

We would also like to thank those who supported this effort at the Software Engineering Institute and CERT.

We thank Rich Pethia, Director–CERT Program, for his support, patience, encouragement, and direction during the development and piloting of the model. We have special thanks for William Wilson, Deputy Director–CERT Program, and especially Barbara Laswell, Director–CERT Enterprise Workforce Development Directorate, for their day-to-day direction and assistance in helping us build a community of believers and helping us navigate through all of the challenges inherent in a long, arduous effort. In particular, Barbara has been an internal champion from the beginning and an ardent source of encouragement in the most trying times of the development of this model.

A special thanks goes to all of those who contributed essays in Chapter 7. Your insight has been invaluable in helping us understand how the community can make use of this important work.

Finally, special thanks to our Addison-Wesley partners, especially Peter Gordon, for their guidance and assistance with the design, editing, and final production of this book.

From Richard Caralli

I owe the completion of this book to so many SEI and CERT people. Lisa Young worked tirelessly to do much of the basic research for this work and to create many interim deliverables. Her knowledge of security and continuity codes of practice is astonishing. No matter what request we made of her, she was always willing to jump in and help. David White single-handedly led the charge to make organizations aware of CERT-RMM. He devoted countless hours to getting the message out, no matter where that journey took him. It turned out in the process that he also had significant knowledge of the subject matter and taught us a few things! This book would not be possible without him. Julia Allen saved the day. When Lisa, David, and I were struggling with too many commitments, Julia seamlessly swooped in and single-handedly completed a significant portion of the model. I can never thank her enough for her contributions and her willingness to put her own important research aside and become a part of our team. And if you ever have the fortune to work with Julia, you also get the side benefits of knowing a genuinely kind, collaborative, and intelligent person who gives everything unconditionally. This also reminds me of my friend Pamela Curtis. Pamela has contributed tirelessly to the development effort of CERT-RMM and in making us all look good with her constant polishing and refinement of the model. To call her a technical editor does not adequately characterize the impact she has had on this book. Her quick comprehension of the subject matter redefined forever what we will expect technical editors to do. She has truly raised the bar.

From Julia Allen

I thank my two coauthors, Rich and David; Rich for his vision and leadership of CERT's operational resilience work over many years, particularly when there were many doubters of its value, and David for his commitment, insight, and fieldwork to validate the model. They have both been my mentors and teachers. I thank Lisa Young for leading our efforts in appraisal and assessment and for valuable lessons learned in applying CERT-RMM to meet customer needs. I benefited significantly from Pamela Curtis's steady hand, challenging comments, and unique ability to connect the dots across all CERT-RMM process areas. I greatly appreciate Barbara Laswell's recognition of the power in integrating CERT's enterprise security governance guidance with CERT-RMM, which was the catalyzing event for my joining the CERT-RMM development team. I will be forever grateful for the opportunity she offered me to contribute to this body of work, and for Rich's and the team's warm welcome. I would be remiss if I did not recognize and thank two SEI colleagues who helped form, shape, and influence my thinking regarding how to adapt process maturity concepts and practices for application to the operational and software security domains. Eileen Forrester and I worked on this over many years; she is one of the most capable thinkers in this space with whom I've had the good fortune to work. And Suzie Garcia, the queen of CMMI, codified process maturity and capability modeling concepts. I would like to thank Gene Kim, CTO of Tripwire, for articulating and advocating the numerous connections between information security, IT operations, audit, and risk management, and for introducing the SEI to some of the most experienced and competent leaders in this field, including all of the participants in our joint Best in Class Security and Operations Round Table, held in October 2003. I am incredibly blessed and fortunate to be able to contribute every day to a profession I love, in collaboration with smart, talented, passionate, and committed colleagues.

From David White

My contributions to this work and this book would not have been possible without the support, encouragement, and leadership of Rich Caralli and Bill Wilson. They were both champions for changes in my career trajectory that led to my involvement and success in this work; I am forever grateful. Rich's knowledge of the subject matter and vision for the model were ever present and provided the necessary guidance for me and the team to reach this point. Julia Allen, my friend and coauthor, was a very welcome addition to the team. I thank her for sharing her knowledge and for being a source of inspiration, a sounding board, and a really hard worker. I am thankful to Lisa Young for always being available when I needed to talk through an issue with the model, for sharing her encyclopedic knowledge of practice bodies, for partnering with me on the first appraisal, and for her constant friendship and support. Pamela Curtis has been exacting and thorough in helping us with language consistency, in finding and resolving loose ends, and in working hard to drive this model to completion; thank you, Pamela. Charles Wallen's vision and tireless advocacy for this work and its importance to the financial sector were critically important to our early outreach activities and to engaging the first users of the model. At the U.S. Environmental Protection Agency, Johnny Davis provided the leadership and vision that enabled our successful first RMM appraisal. The appraisal team was tireless and tenacious in producing sound and beneficial results; I thank my fellow appraisal team members Kimberly Farmer, Steve Masters, and Lisa Young. Lockheed Martin Corporation supported an RMM pilot to evaluate the model for its use. The pilot and its success were made possible by the leadership and vision of Nader Mehravari, the tenacity and support of Joan Weszka, the appraisal process knowledge and skills of Michael Freeman, the site knowledge and hard work of Eric Jones, and the exacting and thorough preparation by Doug Stopper. I also thank Nader and his team for sharing their brilliant insights about the model and its use in a large organization. There are many other people who could be named here; I am fortunate to have worked with many great people in pursuit of this work.

PART ONE

About the CERT Resilience Management Model

Organizations in every sector—industry, government, and academia—face increasingly complex business and operational environments. They are constantly bombarded with conditions and events that can introduce stress and uncertainty that may disrupt the effective operation of the organization.

Stress related to managing operational resilience—the ability of the organization to achieve its mission even under degraded circumstances—can come from many sources. For example:

- Technological advances are helping organizations to automate business processes and make them more effective at achieving their missions. But the cost to organizations is that the technology often introduces complexities, takes specialized support and resources, and creates an environment that is rife with vulnerabilities and risks.
- Organizations increasingly depend on partnerships to achieve their mission. External partners provide essential skills and functions, with the aim of increasing productivity and reducing costs. As a result, the organization must expose itself to new risk environments. By employing a chain of partners to execute a business process, the organization cedes control of mission assurance in exchange for cost savings.
- The increasing globalization of organizations and their supply chains poses a problem for management in that governance and oversight must cross organizational and geographical lines like never before. And it must be acknowledged that the emerging worldwide sociopolitical environment is forcing organizations to consider threats and risks that have previously not been on their radar screens. Recent well-publicized events have changed the view of what is feasible and has expanded the range of outcomes that an organization must attempt to prevent and from which it must be prepared to recover.

All of these new demands conspire to force organizations to rethink how they perform operational risk management and how they address the resilience of high-value business services and processes. The traditional, and typically compartmentalized, disciplines of security, business continuity, and information technology (IT) operations must be expanded to provide protection and continuity strategies for high-value services and supporting assets that are commensurate with these new operating complexities.

In addition, organizations lack a reliable means to answer the question, "How resilient am I?" They also lack the ability to assess and measure their capability for managing operational resilience ("Am I resilient enough?") as they have no credible yardstick against which to measure. Typically, capability is measured by the way that an organization has performed during an event or is described in vague terms that cannot be measured. For example, when organizations are asked to describe how well they are managing resilience, they typically characterize success in terms of what hasn't happened: "We haven't been attacked, so we must be doing everything right." Because there will always be new and emerging threats, knowing how well the organization performs today is necessary but not sufficient; it is more important to be able to predict how it will perform in the future when the risk environment changes.

CERT recognizes that organizations face challenges in managing operational resilience in complex environments. The solution to addressing these challenges must have several dimensions. First and foremost, it must consider that the management activities for security, business continuity, and IT operations—typical operational risk management activities—are converging toward a continuum of practices that are focused on managing operational resilience. Second, the solution must address the issues of measurement and metrics, providing a reliable and objective means for assessing capability and a basis for improving processes. And finally, the solution must help organizations improve deficient processes—to reliably close gaps that ultimately translate into weaknesses that diminish operational resilience and impact an organization's ability to achieve its strategic objectives.

As a process improvement model, the CERT Resilience Management Model seeks to allow organizations to use a process definition as a benchmark for identifying the current level of organizational capability, setting an appropriate and attainable desired target for performance, measuring the gap between current performance and targeted performance, and developing action plans to close the gap. By using the model's process definition as a foundation, the organization can obtain an objective characterization of performance not only against a base set of functional practices but also against practices that indicate successively increasing levels of capability.

Do You Need CERT-RMM?

The use of models for process improvement is common throughout the world. Models for improving manufacturing processes are typically the most recognizable, but models such as CMMI are widely adopted across a range of industries.

All organizations have some type of operational element—they may produce software or cars or deliver consulting services, but they all share the need to carry out functions that directly and indirectly support their mission on a daily basis. Regardless of what is being produced or what service is being delivered, managing operations that are critical for day-to-day and long-term success is what many people in organizations are charged to do. What makes this so challenging?

Do You Have These Common Problems?

Many organizations accept that with operations comes operational risk. They see it as an unpleasant by-product of doing business, and perhaps as something they can't do anything about. But according to Towers Perrin, operational risk has been identified as the most important category of risk facing executives today [van Opstal 2007].

For security and continuity professionals, operational risk is our playing field. Much of what we do on a daily basis is directly focused on avoiding or mitigating operational risk even though the tasks we perform might not appear at first glance to be risk management activities.

The way that security and continuity management has evolved in organizations has resulted in inefficiencies that have become commonly acceptable limitations on success. For example, do any of the following conditions exist in your organization?

- Security and continuity activities are compartmentalized and lack coordination toward common goals.
- Budgets for security and continuity activities are typically held by IT.
- There is no governance over the security and continuity activities.
- Risk appetite of higher-level management is not considered in security and continuity activities.
- Processes for security and continuity management are not defined and managed.
- Technology drives security and continuity management solutions rather than a layered approach of people, procedures, tools, and technologies.
- Work related to security and continuity management is not planned or tracked.
- Performance of staff during times of disruption depends on conditions and the heroic efforts of smart people, or the ability to repeat effective behaviors is questionable.
- The impact of a disruption on the organization is difficult to predict based on past performance.
- Many codes of practice are used, but the effectiveness of these practices is not measured, nor is redundancy in these practices identified and eliminated.
- Compliance activities take an inordinate amount of staff time and resources but do not advance the state of the organization's security and continuity practice.

The list can go on and on. However, all of these conditions indicate the lack of a systematic approach to managing operational risk that is typically characterized by silos, lack of coordination and collaboration, ad hoc processes, unknown and unpredictable outcomes, and heroics: working longer and harder, lowering expectations, throwing more resources at problems, cutting corners, and depending on the right people to be available at the right time. Unfortunately, disruption doesn't really adapt to our management shortcomings; instead, it exploits them.

How Does CERT-RMM Help You Solve These Problems and Benefit Your Organization?

While the intention of developing CERT-RMM was initially to produce a model in the likeness of CMMI that could be used for model-based process improvement, there is a broad range of uses for the model that address many of the challenges listed above.

CERT-RMM helps you manage your way through changing risk conditions by focusing on stabilizing operational resilience processes and meeting resilience objectives. It uses a process orientation as a way to "glue together" people, procedures and methods, and tools, equipment, and technology—all important elements in managing operational resilience. And CERT-RMM's focus on continuous process improvement supports an organizational reality: operational resilience is *never achieved*—it must be continually managed.

Whether you use CERT-RMM as a process improvement model or just as a starting point for renovating and rejuvenating your resilience program, you may find many side benefits:

- You can realize the benefits of a convergent view. When operational risk is managed in organizational silos, the benefits to the organization are suboptimal. Silos allow for different (and sometimes divergent) risk processes, risk definitions, and risk measurement criteria, all of which can dramatically reduce the organization's overall ability to identify and address operational risks. Convergence ensures that all operational risk management activities are coordinated, aligned with organizational drivers, and free from the artificial constraints that impact effectiveness (in other words, optimal).
- You can make your security and continuity practices work better. CERT-RMM doesn't replace your administrative, technical, or physical security and sustainment practices. Instead, it provides a framework that the organization can use to ensure that these practices are producing results, are efficient, and support operational resilience objectives.
- You can measure progress. Because CERT-RMM is a process improvement model, a new world of measurement capabilities is provided to security and continuity practitioners. Processes such as incident management can be measured directly to know when they are working, when they are failing, and what gaps should be closed. In addition, the process orientation of the model provides opportunities to measure performance so that an organization can determine that it is getting benefits from its investment in security and continuity activities.
- You can more confidently characterize your operational resilience management posture. In our complex world, it is no longer acceptable to characterize

operational resilience in terms of events and outcomes that haven't happened. An organization needs to be able to understand its capability for managing operational resilience so that it has some degree of predictability about how it will perform during times of stress. The capability levels in CERT-RMM give an organization a way to characterize their competency and their ability to sustain good behaviors in bad times.

- You can determine where to allocate your limited resources. Legacy budgeting processes simply aren't effective for addressing the allocation of resources to operational resilience activities. These processes tend to be tied to organizational structures (such as IT controlling the "security" budget) that artificially limit the ability to fund and account for all of the organization's activities that are involved in managing operational resilience. CERT-RMM provides not only a process for formalizing resilience budgeting and accounting but also a broad view of all of the operational resilience capabilities that need resources.

- You can convert from a compliance mind-set to an improvement mind-set. Compliance activities divert the organization's attention away from its goals and toward the act of complying. However, the ability to comply with various laws, regulations, and obligations should be an outcome of effective operational resilience management processes. In addition, the act of compliance can often give the organization a false sense of capability—many organizations are "in compliance" with a code of practice or an industry regulation yet have a significantly diminished ability to manage during stressful times. An improvement mind-set focuses on ensuring the work products of operational resilience management processes are being created through planned and executed work. These work products can typically be used to satisfy the range of compliance requests and concurrently improve the organization's ability to be operationally resilient.

CHAPTER 1

INTRODUCTION

The CERT Resilience Management Model (CERT-RMM) is the result of many years of research and development committed to helping organizations meet the challenge of managing operational risk and resilience in a complex world. It embodies the process management premise that "the quality of a system or product is highly influenced by the quality of the process used to develop and maintain it" by defining *quality* as the extent to which an organization controls its ability to operate in a mission-driven, complex risk environment [CMMI Product Team 2006].

CERT-RMM brings several innovative and advantageous concepts to the management of operational resilience:

- First, it seeks to holistically improve risk and resilience management through purposeful and practical convergence of the disciplines of security management, business continuity management, and aspects of IT operations management (the *convergence* advantage).
- Second, it elevates these disciplines to a process approach, which enables the application of process improvement innovations and provides a useful basis for metrics and measurement. It also provides a practical organizing and integrating framework for the vast array of practices in place in most organizations (the *process* advantage).
- Finally, it provides a foundation for process institutionalization and organizational process maturity—concepts that are important for sustaining any process but are absolutely *critical* for processes that operate in complex environments, typically during times of stress (the *maturity* advantage).

CERT-RMM v1.1 comprises 26 process areas that cover four areas of operational resilience management: Enterprise Management, Engineering, Operations, and Process Management. The practices contained in these process areas are codified from a management perspective; that is, the practices focus on the activities that an organization performs to actively *direct, control, and manage* operational resilience in an environment of uncertainty, complexity, and risk. For example, the model does not prescribe specifically how an organization should secure information; instead, it focuses on the equally important processes of identifying high-value information assets, making decisions about the levels needed to protect and sustain these assets, implementing strategies to achieve these levels, and maintaining these levels throughout the life cycle of the assets during stable times and, more important, during times of stress. In essence, the managerial focus supports the specific actions taken to secure information by making them more effective and more efficient.

1.1 The Influence of Process Improvement and Capability Maturity Models

Throughout its history, the Software Engineering Institute (SEI) has directed its research efforts toward helping organizations to develop and maintain quality products and services, primarily in the software and systems engineering and acquisition processes. Proven success in these disciplines has expanded opportunities to extend process improvement knowledge to other areas such as the quality of service delivery (as codified in the CMMI for Services model) and to cyber security and resilience management (CERT-RMM).

The SEI's research in product and service quality reinforces three critical dimensions on which organizations typically focus: people, procedures and methods, and tools and equipment [CMMI Product Team 2006]. However, processes link these dimensions together and provide a conduit for achieving the organization's mission and goals across all organizational levels. Figure 1.1 illustrates these three critical dimensions.

Traditionally, the disciplines concerned with managing operational risk have taken a technology-centric view of improvement. That is, of the three critical dimensions, organizations often look to technology—in the form of software-based tools and hardware—to fix security problems, to enable continuity, or even to improve IT operations and service delivery. Technology can be very effective in managing risk, but technology cannot always substitute for skilled people and resources, procedures and methods that define and connect tasks and activities, and processes to provide structure and stability toward the achievement of common objectives and goals. In our experience, organizations often ask for the one or two technological advances that will keep their data secure or improve the way they handle incidents, while failing to recognize that the lack of defined processes and process management diminishes their overall capability for managing operational resilience. Most organizations are already technology-savvy when it comes to security and continuity, but the way they *manage* these disciplines is immature. In fact, incidents such as security breaches often can be traced back to poorly designed and managed processes at the enterprise and operational levels, not technology failures. Consider the following: Your organization probably has numerous

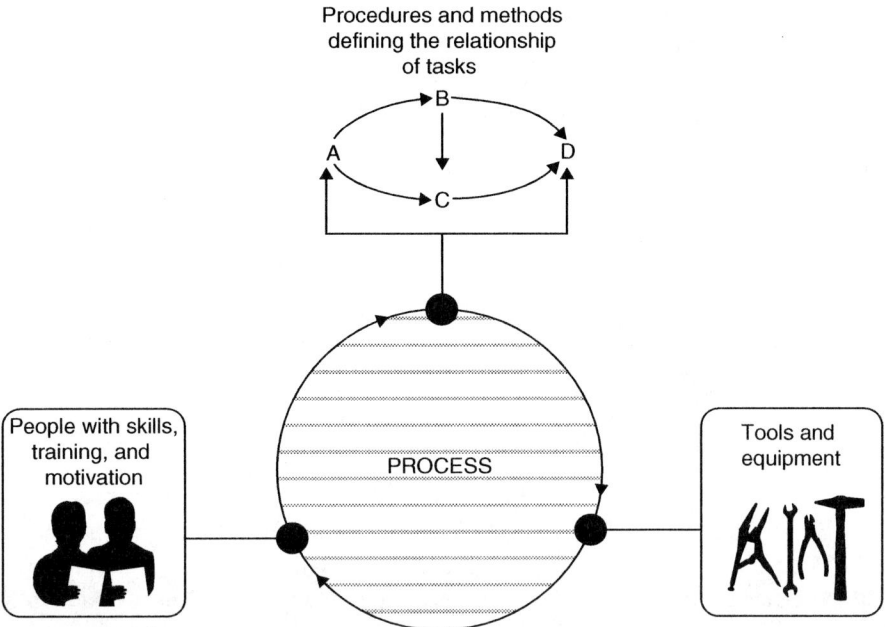

FIGURE 1.1
The Three Critical Dimensions

firewall devices deployed across its networks. But what kinds of traffic are these firewalls filtering? What rulesets are being used? Do these rulesets reflect management's resilience objectives and the needs for protecting and sustaining the assets with firewalls? Who sets and manages the rulesets? Under whose direction? All of these questions typify the need to augment technology with process so that the technology supports and enforces strategic objectives.

In addition to being technology-focused, many organizations are practice-focused. They look for a representative set of practices to solve their unique operational resilience management challenges and end up with a complex array of practices sourced from many different bodies of knowledge. The effectiveness of these practices is measured by whether they are used or "sanctioned" by an industry or satisfy a compliance requirement *instead of* by how effective they are in helping the organization reduce exposure or improve predictability in managing impact. The practices are not the problem; organizations go wrong in assuming that practices *alone* will bring about a sustainable capability for managing resilience in a complex environment.

Further damage is done by practice-based assessments or evaluations. Simply verifying the existence of a practice sourced from a body of knowledge does not provide for an adequate characterization of the organization's ability to *sustain* that practice over the long term, particularly when the risk environment changes or when disruption occurs. This can be done only by examining the degree to which the organization embeds the practice in its culture, is able and committed to performing the practice, can control the practice and ensure that the practice is effective through measurement and analysis, and can prove the practice is performed according to established procedures and processes. In short, practices are made better by the degree to which they have been institutionalized through *processes*.

1.2 The Evolution of CERT-RMM

The CERT Resilience Management Model is the result of an evolutionary development path that incorporates concepts from other CERT tools, techniques, methods, and activities.

In 1999, CERT officially released the Operationally Critical Threat, Asset, and Vulnerability Evaluation (OCTAVE) method for information security risk management. OCTAVE provided a new way to look at information security risk from an operational perspective and asserted that business people are in the best position to identify and analyze security risk. This effectively repositioned IT's role in security risk assessment and placed the responsibility closer to the operations activity in the organization [Alberts 1999].

In October 2003, a group of 20 IT and security professionals from financial, IT, and security services, defense organizations, and the SEI met at the SEI to begin to build an executive-level community of practice for IT operations and security. The desired outcome for this Best in Class Security and Operations Roundtable (BIC-SORT) was to better capture and articulate the relevant bodies of knowledge that enable and accelerate IT operational and security process improvement. The bodies of knowledge identified included IT and information security governance, audit, risk management, IT operations, security, project management, and process management (including benchmarking), as depicted in Figure 1.2.

In Figure 1.2, the upper four capabilities (white text) include processes that provide oversight and top-level management. Governance and audit serve as enablers and accelerators. Risk management informs decisions and choices. Strategy serves as the explicit link to business drivers to ensure that value is being delivered. The lower four capabilities (black text) include processes that provide detailed management and execution in accordance with the policies, procedures, and guidelines established by higher-level management. We observed that these capabilities were all connected in high-performing IT operations and security organizations.

Workshop topics and results included defining what it means to be best in class, areas of pain and promise (potential solutions), how to use improvement frameworks

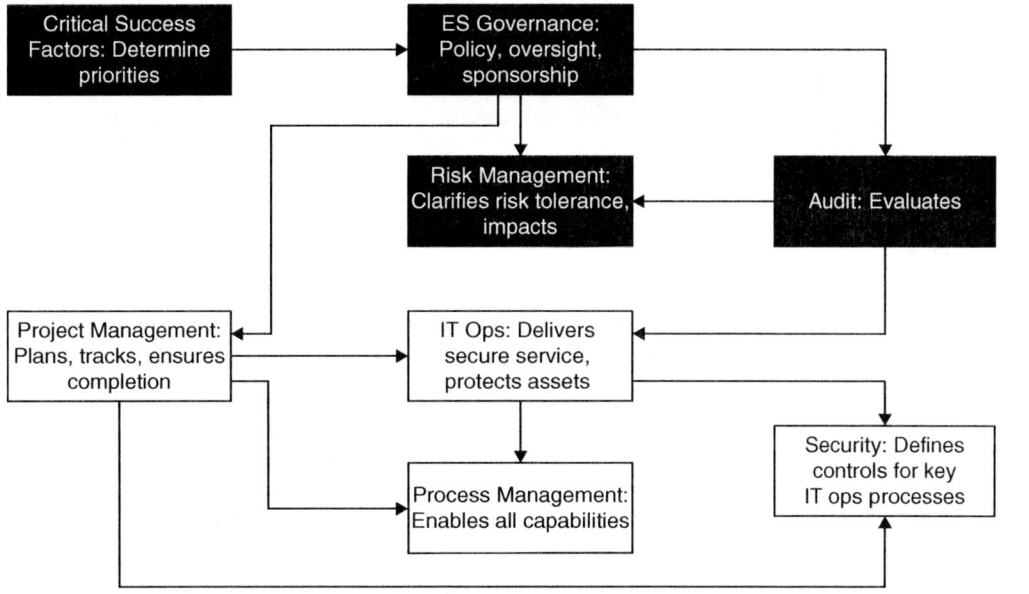

FIGURE 1.2
Bodies of Knowledge Related to Security Process Improvement

and models in this domain, the applicability of Six Sigma, and emerging frameworks for enterprise security management (precursors of CERT-RMM) [Allen 2004].

In December 2004, CERT released a technical note entitled *Managing for Enterprise Security* that described security as a process reliant on many organizational capabilities. In essence, the security challenge was characterized as a business problem owned by everyone in the organization, not just IT [Caralli 2004]. This technical note also introduced operational resilience as the objective of security activities and began to describe the convergence between security management, business continuity management, and IT operations management as essential for managing operational risk.

In March 2005, CERT hosted a meeting with representatives of the Financial Services Technology Consortium (FSTC).[1] At the time of this meeting, FSTC's Business Continuity Standing Committee was actively organizing a project to explore the development of a reference model to measure and manage operational resilience capability. Although our approaches to operational resilience had different starting points (security versus business continuity), our efforts were clearly focused on solving the same problem: How can an organization predictably and systematically control operational resilience through activities such as security and business continuity?

---

1. FSTC has since been incorporated into the Financial Services Roundtable (www.fsround.org).

In April 2006, CERT introduced the concept of a process improvement model for operational resilience in the technical report *Sustaining Operational Resiliency: A Process Improvement Approach to Security Management* [Caralli 2006]. This technical report defined fundamental resilience and process improvement concepts and detailed candidate focus areas (called "capability areas") that could be included in an eventual model. This document was the foundation for developing the first instantiation of the model.

In May 2007, as a result of work with FSTC, CERT published an initial framework for managing operational resilience in the technical report *Introducing the CERT Resiliency Engineering Framework: Improving the Security and Sustainability Processes* [Caralli 2007]. In this document, the initial outline for a process improvement model for managing operational resilience was published.

In March 2008, a preview version of a process improvement model for managing operational resilience was released by CERT under the title *CERT Resiliency Engineering Framework, v0.95R* [REF Team 2008a]. This model included an articulation of 21 "capability areas" that described high-level processes and practices for managing operational resilience and, more significantly, provided an initial set of elaborated generic goals and practices that defined capability levels for each capability area.

In early 2009, the name of the model was changed to the CERT Resilience Management Model to reflect the managerial nature of the processes and to properly position the "engineering" aspects of the model. Common CMMI-related taxonomy was applied (including the use of the term *process areas*), and generic goals and practices were expanded with more specific elaborations in each process area. CERT began releasing CERT-RMM process areas individually in 2009, leading up to the "official" release of v1.0 of the model in a technical report published in 2010. The model continues to be available by process area at www.cert.org/resilience.

The publication of this book marks the official release of CERT-RMM v1.1. Version 1.1 includes minor changes to process areas resulting from field use and piloting of the model. In addition, version 1.1 introduces the concept of the *operational resilience management system,* which broadly defines the organization's collective capability and mechanism for managing operational resilience. More about the operational resilience management system can be found in Section 2.2.

CERT-RMM

CERT-RMM draws upon and is influenced by many bodies of knowledge and models. Figure 1.3 illustrates these relationships. (See Tables 1.1 and 1.2 for details about the connections between CERT-RMM and CMMI models.)

At the descriptive level of the model, the process areas in CERT-RMM have been either developed specifically for the model or sourced from existing CMMI models and modified to be used in the context of operational resilience management. CERT-RMM also draws upon concepts and codes of practice from other security,

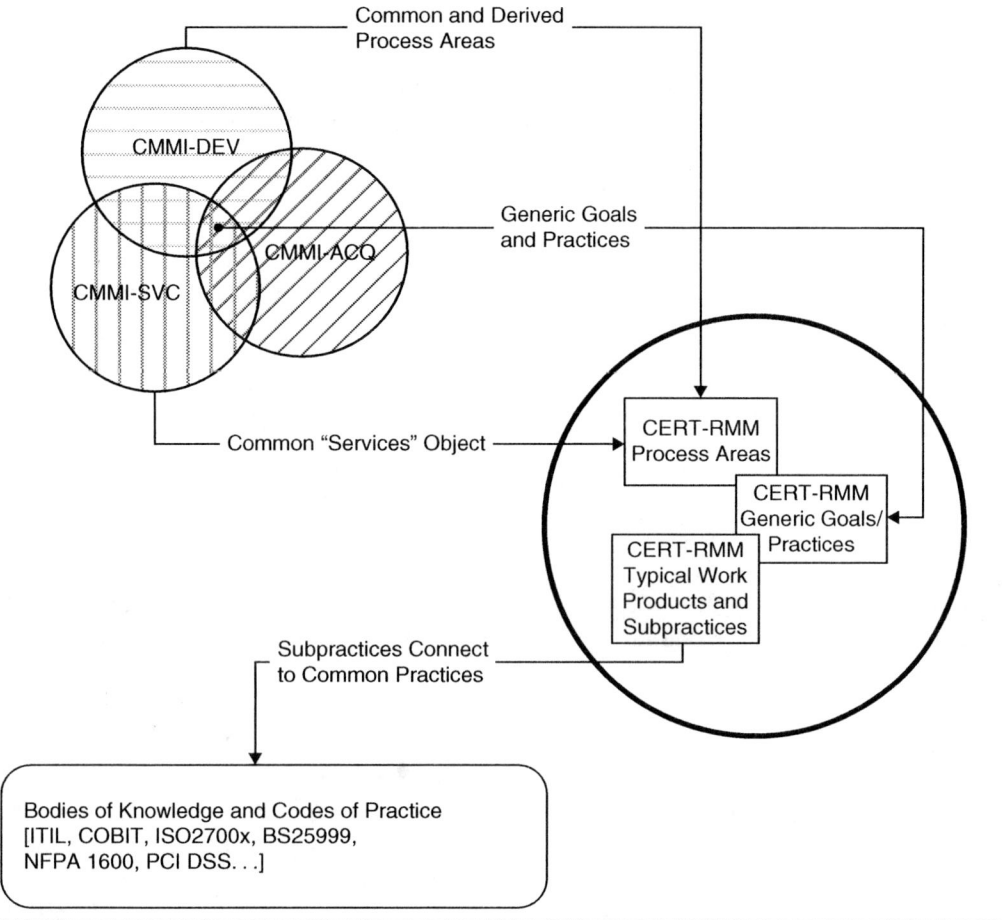

FIGURE 1.3
CERT-RMM Influences

business continuity, and IT operations models, particularly at the typical work products and subpractices level. This allows users of these codes of practice to incorporate model-based process improvement without significantly altering their installed base of practices. The *CERT Resiliency Engineering Framework: Code of Practice Crosswalk, Preview Version, v0.95R* [REF Team 2008b] details the relationships between common codes of practice and the specific practices in the CERT-RMM process areas. The Crosswalk is periodically updated to incorporate new and updated codes of practice as necessary. The Crosswalk can be found at www.cert.org/resilience.

Familiarity with common codes of practice or CMMI models is not required to comprehend or use CERT-RMM. However, familiarity with these practices and models will aid in understanding and adoption.

As a descriptive model, CERT-RMM focuses at the process description level but doesn't necessarily address how an organization would achieve the intent and purpose of the description through deployed practices. However, the subpractices contained in each CERT-RMM process area describe actions that an organization might take to implement a process, and these subpractices can be directly linked to one or more tactical practices used by the organization. Thus, the range of material in each CERT-RMM process area spans from highly descriptive processes to more prescriptive subpractices.

In terms of scope, CERT-RMM covers the activities required to establish, deliver, and manage operational resilience activities in order to ensure the resilience of services. A resilient service is one that can meet its mission whenever necessary, even under degraded circumstances. Services are broadly defined in CERT-RMM. At a simple level, a service is a helpful activity that brings about some intended result. People and technology can perform services; for example, people can deliver mail, and so can an email application. A service can also produce a tangible product.

From an organizational perspective, services can provide internal benefits (such as paying employees) or have an external focus (such as delivering newspapers). Any service in the organization that is of value to meeting the organization's mission should be made resilient.

Services rely on assets to achieve their missions. In CERT-RMM, assets are limited to people, information, technology, and facilities. A service that produces a product may also rely on raw materials, but these assets are outside of the immediate scope of CERT-RMM. However, the use of CERT-RMM in a production environment is not precluded, since people, information, technology, and facilities are a critical part of delivering a product, and their operational resilience can be managed through the practices in CERT-RMM.

CERT-RMM does not cover the activities required to establish, deliver, and manage services. In other words, CERT-RMM does not address the development of a service from requirements or the establishment of a service management system. These activities are covered in the CMMI for Services model (CMMI-SVC) [CMMI Product Team 2009]. However, to the extent that the "management" of the service requires a strong resilience consideration, CERT-RMM can be used with CMMI-SVC to extend the definition of high-quality service delivery to include resilience as an attribute of quality.

CERT-RMM contains practices that cover enterprise management, resilience engineering, operations management, process management, and other supporting processes for ensuring active management of operational resilience. The "enterprise" orientation of CERT-RMM does not mean that it is an enterprise-focused model or that it must be adopted at an enterprise level; on the contrary, CERT-RMM is focused on the operations level of the organization, where services are typically executed. Enterprise aspects of CERT-RMM describe how horizontal functions of the organization, such as managing people, training, financial resource management, and risk management, affect operations. For example, if an organization is generally poor at risk management, the effects typically manifest at an operational level in poor risk identification, prioritization, and mitigation, misalignment with risk appetite and tolerances, and diminished service resilience.

CERT-RMM was developed to be scalable across various industries, regardless of their size. Every organization has an operational component and executes services that require a degree of operational resilience commensurate with achieving the mission. Although CERT-RMM was constructed in the financial services industry, it is already being piloted and used in other industrial sectors and government organizations, both large and small.

Finally, understanding the process improvement focus of CERT-RMM can be tricky. An example from software engineering is a useful place to start. In the CMMI for Development model (CMMI-DEV), the focus of improvement is software engineering activities performed by a "project" [CMMI Product Team 2006]. In CERT-RMM, the focus of improvement is operational resilience management activities *to achieve service resilience* as performed by an "organizational unit." This concept can become quite recursive (but no less effective) if the "organizational unit" happens to be a unit of the organization that has primary responsibility for operational resilience management "services," such as the information security department or a business continuity team. In this context, the operational resilience management activities are also the services of the organizational unit.

1.3 CERT-RMM and CMMI Models

CMMI v1.2 includes three integrated models: CMMI for Development, CMMI for Acquisition, and the newly released CMMI for Services. *The CMMI Framework* provides a common structure for CMMI models, training, and appraisal components. CMMI for Development and CMMI for Acquisition are early life-cycle models in that they address software and system processes through the implementation phase but do not specifically address these assets in operation. The CMMI for Services model addresses not only the development of services and a service management system but also the operational aspects of service delivery.

CERT-RMM is primarily an operations-focused model, but it reaches back into the development phase of the life cycle for assets such as software and systems to ensure consideration of early life-cycle quality requirements for protecting and sustaining these assets once they become operational. Like CMMI for Services, CERT-RMM also explicitly addresses developmental aspects of services and assets by promoting a requirements-driven, engineering-based approach to developing and implementing resilience strategies that become part of the "DNA" of these assets in an operational environment.

Because of the broad nature of CERT-RMM, emphasis on using CMMI model structural elements was prioritized over explicit consideration of integration with existing CMMI models. That is, while CERT-RMM could be seen as defining an "operations" constellation in CMMI, this was not an early objective of CERT-RMM research and development. Instead, the architects and developers of CERT-RMM focused on the core processes for managing operational resilience, integrating CMMI model elements to the extent possible. Thus, because the model structures are similar, CMMI users will be able to easily navigate CERT-RMM.

Table 1.1 provides a summary of the process area connections between CERT-RMM and the CMMI models. Table 1.2 summarizes other CMMI model and CERT-RMM similarities. Future versions of CERT-RMM will attempt to smooth out significant differences in the models and incorporate more CMMI elements where necessary.

TABLE 1.1 Process Areas in CERT-RMM and CMMI Models

CMMI Models Process Areas	Equivalent CERT-RMM Process Areas
CAM—Capacity and Availability Management *(CMMI-SVC only)*	**TM—Technology Management** CERT-RMM addresses capacity management from the perspective of technology assets. It does not address the capacity of services. Availability management is a central theme of CERT-RMM, significantly expanded from CMMI-SVC. Service availability is addressed in CERT-RMM by managing the availability requirement for people, information, technology, and facilities. Thus, the process areas that drive availability management include • **RRD—Resilience Requirements Development** (where availability requirements are established) • **RRM—Resilience Requirements Management** (where the life cycle of availability requirements is managed) • **EC—Environmental Control** (where the availability requirements for facilities are implemented and managed) • **KIM—Knowledge and Information Management** (where the availability requirements for information are implemented and managed) • **PM—People Management** (where the availability requirements for people are implemented and managed) • **TM—Technology Management** (where the availability requirements for software, systems, and other technology assets are implemented and managed)

CMMI Models Process Areas	Equivalent CERT-RMM Process Areas
IRP—Incident Resolution and Prevention *(CMMI-SVC only)*	**IMC—Incident Management and Control** In CERT-RMM, IMC expands IRP to address a broader incident management system and incident life cycle at the asset level. Workarounds in IRP are expanded in CERT-RMM to address incident response practices.
MA—Measurement and Analysis	**MA—Measurement and Analysis** is carried over intact from CMMI. In CERT-RMM, MA is directly connected to MON—Monitoring, which explicitly addresses data collection that can be used for MA activities.
OPD—Organizational Process Definition	**OPD—Organizational Process Definition** is carried over from CMMI, but development-life-cycle–related activities and examples are deemphasized or eliminated.
OPF—Organizational Process Focus	**OPF—Organizational Process Focus** is carried over intact from CMMI.
OT—Organizational Training	**OTA—Organizational Training and Awareness** OT is expanded to include awareness activities in OTA.
REQM—Requirements Management	**RRM—Resilience Requirements Management** Basic elements of REQM are included in RRM, but the focus is on managing the resilience requirements for assets and services, regardless of where they are in their development cycle.
RD—Requirements Development	**RRD—Resilience Requirements Development** Basic elements of RD are included in RRM, but practices differ substantially.
RSKM—Risk Management	**RISK—Risk Management** Basic elements of RSKM are reflected in RISK, but the focus is on operational risk management activities and the enterprise risk management capabilities of the organization.
SAM—Supplier Agreement Management	**EXD—External Dependencies Management** In CERT-RMM, SAM is expanded to address all external dependencies, not only suppliers. EXD practices differ substantially.
SCON—Service Continuity *(CMMI-SVC only)*	**SC—Service Continuity** In CERT-RMM, SC is positioned as an operational risk management activity that addresses what is required to sustain assets and services balanced with preventive controls and strategies (as defined in CTRL).
TS—Technical Solution	**RTSE—Resilient Technical Solution Engineering** RTSE uses TS as the basis for conveying the consideration of resilience attributes as part of the technical solution.

TABLE 1.2 Other Connections Between CERT-RMM and the CMMI Models

Element	Connection
Generic goals and practices	The generic goals and practices have been adapted mostly intact from CMMI. Slight modifications have been made as follows: • The numbering scheme used in CERT-RMM uses GG.GP notation. For example, GG1.GP2 is generic goal 1, generic practice 2. • Generic practice 2.1 in CMMI focuses on policy, but in CERT-RMM it is expanded to address governance, with policy as an element. • Generic practice 2.6 in CMMI is "Manage Configurations," but in CERT-RMM it is clarified to explicitly focus on "work product" configurations to avoid confusion with traditional configuration management activities as defined in IT operations.
Continuous representation	CERT-RMM adopts the continuous representation concept from CMMI intact.
Capability levels	CERT-RMM defines four capability levels up to capability level 3—"defined." Definitions of capability levels in CMMI are carried over for CERT-RMM.
Appraisal process	The CERT-RMM capability appraisal process uses many of the elements of the SCAMPI process. The "project" concept in CMMI is implemented in CERT-RMM as an "organizational unit." CERT-RMM capability appraisals have constructs inherited from SCAMPI. See Section 6.4.1 for the use of SCAMPI in CERT-RMM capability appraisals.

1.4 Why CERT-RMM Is Not a *Capability Maturity* Model

The development of maturity models in the security, continuity, IT operations, and resilience space is increasing dramatically. This is not surprising, since models like CMMI have proven their ability to transform the way that organizations and industries work. Unfortunately, not all maturity models contain the rigor of models like CMMI, nor do they accurately deploy many of the maturity model constructs used successfully by CMMI. It is important to have some basic knowledge about the construction of maturity models in order to understand what differentiates CERT-RMM and why the differences ultimately matter.

In its simplest form, a maturity model is an organized way to convey a path of experience, wisdom, perfection, or acculturation. The subject of a maturity model can be an object or things, ways of doing something, characteristics of something, practices, or processes. For example, a simple maturity model could define a path of successively improved tools for doing math: using fingers, using an abacus, using an adding machine, using a slide rule, using a computer, or using a hand-held calculator. Thus, a hand-held calculator may be viewed as a more mature tool than a slide rule.

A capability maturity model (in the likeness of CMMI) is a much more complex instrument, with several distinguishing features. One of these features is that the maturity dimension in the model is a characterization of the maturity of *processes*. Thus, what is conveyed in a capability maturity model is the degree to which processes are institutionalized *and* the degree to which the organization demonstrates process maturity.

As you will learn in Chapter 5, these concepts correlate to the description of the "levels" in CMMI. For example, at the "defined" level, the characteristics of a defined process (governed, staffed with trained personnel, measured, etc.) are applied to a software or systems engineering process. Likewise for the "managed" level, where the characteristics of a managed process are applied to software or systems engineering processes. Unfortunately, many so-called maturity models that claim to be based on CMMI attempt to use CMMI maturity level descriptions yet do not have a *process* orientation.

Another feature of CMMI—as implied by its name—is that there are really two maturity dimensions in the model. The *capability dimension* describes the degree to which a process has been institutionalized. Institutionalized processes are more likely to be retained during times of stress. They apply to an individual process area, such as incident management and control. On the other hand, the *maturity dimension* is described in maturity levels, which define levels of organizational maturity that are achieved through raising the capability of a *set of process areas* in a manner prescribed by the model.

From the start, the focus in developing CERT-RMM was to describe operational resilience management from a process perspective, which would allow for the application of process improvement tools and techniques and provide a foundational platform for better and more sophisticated measurement methodologies and techniques. The ultimate goal in CERT-RMM is to ensure that operational resilience processes produce intended results (such as improved ability to manage incidents or an accurate asset inventory), and as the processes are improved, so are the results and the benefits to the organization. Because CERT-RMM is a process-focused model at its core, it was perfectly suited for the application of CMMI's capability dimension. Thus, the model contained in this book constitutes a maturity model that has a capability dimension. However, this is not the same as a *capability maturity* model, since CERT-RMM does not yet provide an *organizational* expression of maturity. Describing organizational maturity for managing operational resilience by defining a prescriptive path through the model (i.e., by providing an order by which process areas should be addressed) requires additional study and research, and all indications from early model use, benchmarking, and piloting are that a capability maturity model for operational resilience management founded on CERT-RMM is achievable in the future.

CHAPTER 2

UNDERSTANDING KEY CONCEPTS IN CERT-RMM

Several key terms and concepts are noteworthy because they form the foundation for CERT-RMM. Although all are defined in the glossary, each employs words with multiple possible meanings and interpretations to those with different backgrounds. So they merit some additional discussion to ensure that CERT-RMM content that uses and builds on these concepts is correctly interpreted.

2.1 Foundational Concepts

2.1.1 Disruption and Stress

The objective of many maturity models is to improve the processes associated with building, developing, or acquiring the target object of the model, such as the development and acquisition of a particular product or service or the enhancement of workforce competencies and skills. CERT-RMM differs in that its focus is on improving how organizations behave and respond in advance of and during times of stress and disruption. So, for example, the objective of CMMI-SVC is to deliver high-quality services. The objective of CERT-RMM is to ensure that high-quality services are resilient in the face of stress and disruption.[1]

Organizations are constantly bombarded with events and conditions that can cause stress and may disrupt their effective operation. Controlling organizational behavior and response during times of disruption and stress is a primary focus of operational resilience management—the ability to adapt to operational risks, including realized risks.

Stress related to managing operational risk, and thus operational resilience, can come from many sources, including

---

1. CMMI-SVC achieves its objectives by focusing on the improvement of the service management and delivery process, with services as the object of improvement. CERT-RMM achieves its objectives by focusing on the improvement of the operational resilience management process, with services as the beneficiary of improvement.

- pervasive use of technology
- operational complexity
- increased reliance on intangible assets, such as digital information and software
- global economy and economic pressures
- open borders
- geopolitical and cultural shifts
- regulatory and legal constraints
- a view of security as an IT problem, not an organization-wide concern

The explosion of computing power and cheap storage means that *technology* is in everyone's hands. Technology is a critical enabler of most of the organization's important products, services, and processes. It is constantly changing and provides increasing opportunities for operational risk, organizational stress (including stress to an organization's supply chain), and disruption.

More and changing technology often means more *complexity*. While the automation of manual and mechanical processes through the application of technology makes these processes more productive, it also makes them more complex. Implementation of new technologies can introduce new risks that are not identified until they are realized. And technological advances, while providing demonstrable opportunities for improvements in effectiveness and efficiency, often increase the likelihood that something will go wrong.

The number and extent of *intangible and virtual assets*, such as digital information, software, and supply chain products and services, are rapidly increasing [Caralli 2006, p. 40]. Intangibility may increase the likelihood and impact of potential risks. Intangible assets are more challenging to identify, locate, and therefore protect, and protection levels are difficult to sustain without concerted effort. This quality of digital assets forces organizations to pay more attention to the convergence of cyber and physical security issues because the controls to protect and sustain these must work together.

Trading in a *global economy* provides less insulation from global risks and, correspondingly, less control. Economic disruptions and downturns often result in increased cyber attacks and increased risk to global supply chain products, services, and partners. People often change their behavior during uncertain economic times, so the potential for insider threats and attacks may also increase.

Participation in the global economy brings a requirement for more *open borders* to compete and thrive. Open borders can introduce additional stress when organizational core competencies are outsourced to realize cost savings. Outsourcing can often cause such core competencies to diminish or disappear altogether, which makes it difficult to competently manage outsourced partners. Open borders extend the risk environment to arenas, partners, and countries that are often unknown and untested. In addition, transferring functions to outsourcing partners often means the transfer of risk management even though the primary organization continues to be the owner and responsible entity for ensuring that the risks associated with outsourced products and services are sufficiently mitigated.

Having supply chain partners in other countries can introduce additional stress and potential disruption when navigating *cultural* norms and conducting business in non-native languages. It also can cause an organization to be affected by *political instability* such as governments at risk (and thus unable to fulfill their agreements) and economically linked worker protests. Organizations should be cognizant of any region that may harbor terrorists with antinational sentiments. In addition, too much presence in a country can result in outsourcing backlash and financial services backlash directed toward the primary organization attempting to conduct business in the region.

All business leaders are well aware of the increasing requirements and constraints introduced by the growing number of *laws and regulations* with which they are expected to comply. Assessing for and ensuring compliance can be costly, not only in labor resources but also in opportunity costs. Many organizations, in an attempt to be fully compliant, adopt a prescriptive, checklist-like approach to assessing compliance and thus a prescriptive view of the risks that may result from non-compliance. This prohibits them from fully articulating their risk exposure and likely overinvesting in controls for compliance that may not be necessary.

Historically, and often still today, *security is viewed as a technology problem* and thus is relegated to the IT department. As a result, the budgets for managing operational risk for information technologies often reside with IT, not in the business units that are most likely to be impacted when operational risks are realized. Most organizations address risk management, security (both physical and cyber), business continuity, disaster recovery, and IT operations as siloed, compartmentalized functions with little to no integration and communication even though they share many of the same issues, solutions, and core competencies. When an incident or disruption occurs, the response is generally localized and discrete, not orchestrated across all affected lines of business and organizational units. This condition calls for harmonization and convergence, which is addressed next.

2.1.2 Convergence

Convergence is a fundamental concept for managing operational resilience. For CERT-RMM purposes, it is defined as the harmonization of operational risk management activities that have similar objectives and outcomes.[2] These activities include

---

[2] These activities are bound by their operational risk focus. However, collectively they do not represent the full range of activities that define operational risk management.

- security planning and management
- business continuity and disaster recovery management
- IT operations and service delivery management

Other support activities are typically included, such as financial management, communications, human resource management, and organizational training and awareness. This concept is depicted in Figure 2.1.

Many organizations are now beginning to realize that security, business continuity, and IT operations management are complementary and collaborative functions that have the same goal: to improve and sustain operational resilience. They share this goal because each function is focused on managing operational risk. This convergent view is often substantiated by popular codes of practice in each domain. For example, security practices now explicitly reference and include business continuity and IT operations management practices as an acknowledgment that security practices alone do not address both the conditions and consequences of risk. Thus the degree or level to which convergence has been achieved directly affects the level of operational resilience for the organization. Correspondingly, the level of operational resilience affects the ability of the organization to meet its mission.

The business case for convergence ultimately comes down to economics. When organizational functions and activities share many of the same objectives, issues, solutions, and core competencies, it makes good business sense to tackle them using a common, collaborative approach. Security planning

FIGURE 2.1
Convergence of Operational Risk Management Activities

and management, business continuity and disaster recovery management, and IT operations and service delivery management are bound by the same operational risk drivers. A convergent approach allows for better alignment between risk-based activities and organizational risk tolerances and appetite. In other words, such activities are likely to have risks in common with similar thresholds that can be managed and mitigated using similar, if not identical, approaches.

Redundant activities can be eliminated along with their associated costs. Staff resources can be more effectively deployed and optimized. Convergence enforces a focus on organizational and service missions. It facilitates a process that is owned by line of business and organizational unit managers and consistently implemented across the organization. A common, collaborative approach greatly influences how operational risk and operational resilience management work is planned, executed, and managed to the end objective of greater effectiveness, efficiency, and reduced risk exposure.

If this is such an obvious win, what gets in the way? These activities and functions (and the people who perform them) have a long history of operating independently. Organizational structures and traditional funding models tend to solidify this separation. Numerous codes of practice for each discipline exist, reinforcing their separateness. Compliance drives their use, rather than performance. Misuse sustains an entrenched and isolated view of who should be doing what. Risk drivers that apply to all of these activities are unclear, poorly defined, and not communicated. The same can be said for enterprise and strategic objectives and critical success factors that are intended to drive all of these activities. Governance and visible sponsorship for converged activities is rarely present; this is also the case for developing a process orientation and process definition for converged activities.

2.1.3 Managing Operational Resilience

The demands and stress factors described above conspire to force organizations to rethink how they perform some aspects of operational risk management and how they address the resilience of high-value business processes and services. Security, business continuity, and IT operations constitute a large segment of operational risk management activities for almost all organizations.

Operational risk is defined as the potential impact on assets and their related services that could result from inadequate or failed internal processes, failures of systems or technology, the deliberate or inadvertent actions of people, or external events. To more effectively manage and mitigate operational risk requires that an organization focus its attention on operational resilience. Operational resilience addresses the organization's ability to adapt to risk that affects its core operational capacities. It is an emergent property of effective and efficient operational risk management [Caralli 2006].

Operational resilience management is the direction and coordination of activities to achieve resilience objectives that align with the organization's strategic objectives and critical success factors.

The operational resilience management system is the mechanism through which operational resilience management is performed. An operational resilience management system includes the plan, program, processes, procedures, practices, and people that are necessary to manage operational resilience. As with all systems, the operational resilience management system is composed of independent yet interrelated elements that are unified in their focus on achieving a common goal. Because operational resilience is highly dependent on cultural change and commitment, the operational resilience management system virtually spans the organization, drawing from many organizational capabilities, people, and skills.

Simply put, the operational resilience management system has four broad objectives:

- Prevent the realization of operational risk to a high-value service (instantiated by a *protect* strategy).
- Sustain a high-value service if risk is realized (instantiated by a *sustain* strategy).
- Effectively address consequences to the organization if risk is realized, and return the organization to a "normal" operating state.
- Optimize the achievement of these objectives to maximize effectiveness at the lowest cost.

Requirements form the basis for managing operational resilience. Protection and sustainment strategies for an organizational service and associated assets are based on resilience requirements that reflect how the service and assets are used to support the organization's strategic objectives. When the organization fails to meet these requirements (either because of poor practices or as a result of an incident, disaster, or other disruptive event), the operational resilience of the service and assets is diminished, the service mission is at risk, and one or more of the organization's strategic objectives is not met. Thus, operational resilience depends on establishing requirements in order to build resilience into assets and services and to keep these assets and services productive in the accomplishment of strategic objectives.

Through extensive review of existing codes of practice in the areas of security, business continuity, and IT operations management, as well as from experience with helping organizations to adopt a convergent view, CERT developers have codified in CERT-RMM a process definition for resilience management processes. The process definition embodies a requirements-driven foundation and describes the range of processes that characterize the organizational capabilities necessary to actively direct, control, and manage operational resilience.

2.2 Elements of Operational Resilience Management

CERT-RMM defines several foundational concepts that provide useful levels of abstraction applied throughout the model. These concepts include

- services
- business processes
- assets
- resilience requirements
- strategies for protecting and sustaining assets and services
- life-cycle coverage

These concepts are key to understanding CERT-RMM's process-based approach to managing operational resilience. All are described in the sections that follow. Figure 2.2 depicts the relationships among services, business processes, and CERT-RMM assets.

2.2.1 Services

A service is the limited number of activities that the organization carries out in the performance of a duty or in the production of a product.[3] In the gas utilities industry, services include gas production, gas distribution, and gas transmission. In the financial services sector, services include retail/consumer banking, commercial banking, and loan processing. Services can be externally focused and customer-facing, such as the production of shrink-wrapped software or providing web services for conducting market surveys. Services can be internally focused, such as human resources transactions (hiring, performance reviews) and monthly financial reporting. Services typically align with a particular line of business or organizational unit but can cross units and organizational boundaries (such as in the case of a global supply chain to produce an automobile). While the focus of CERT-RMM is on processes for managing operational resilience, resilience of services is key for mission assurance. Thus, one of the foundational concepts in CERT-RMM is that improving operational resilience

---

3. In the CMMI for Services model, a service is defined as a product that is intangible and non-storable [CMMI Product Team 2009]. CMMI for Services focuses on the high-quality delivery of services. CERT-RMM extends this concept by focusing on resilience as an attribute of high-quality service delivery, which ultimately impacts organizational health and resilience. In CERT-RMM, services are used as an organizing principle; the resilience of these services is the focus of improving operational resilience management processes and the operational resilience management system.

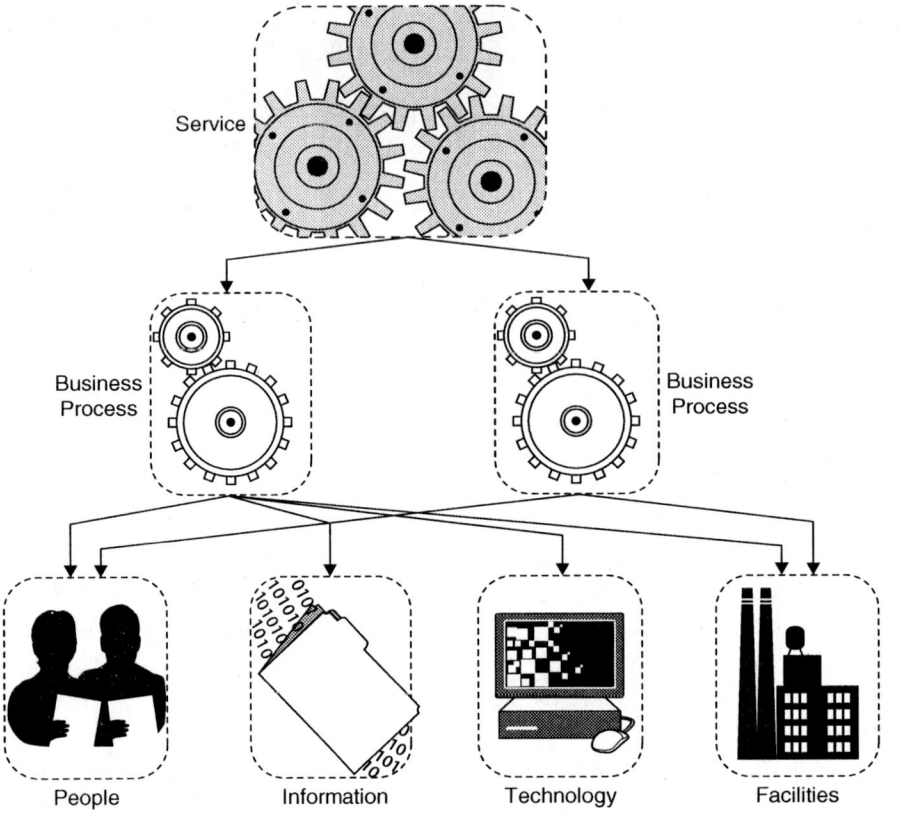

FIGURE 2.2
Relationships Among Services, Business Processes, and Assets

management processes has a significant, positive effect on service resilience. Figure 2.3 depicts the relationship between services and operational resilience management processes.

So what makes a service resilient? CERT-RMM identifies the following activities as contributing to service resilience:

- identification and mitigation of risks to the service and its supporting assets (see Section 2.2.3, "Assets")
- implementation of service continuity processes and plans
- management and deployment of people, including external partners
- management of IT operations
- identification and deployment of effective controls for information and technology assets
- management of the operational environment where services are performed

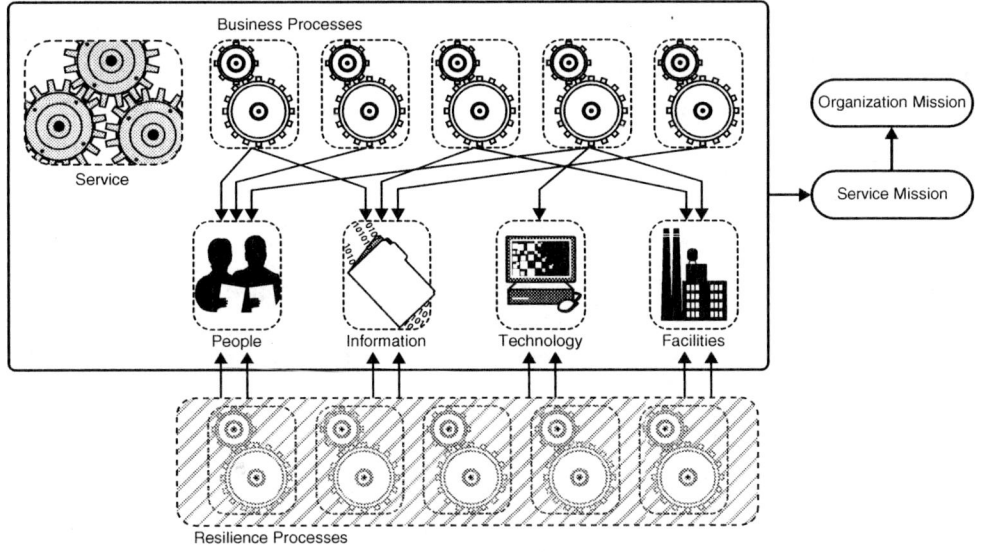

FIGURE 2.3
Relationship Between Services and Operational Resilience Management Processes

A key aspect of services is the concept of *high-value* services, those that are critical to the success of the organization's mission. The high-value services of the organization are the focus of the organization's operational resilience management activities. These services directly support the achievement of strategic objectives and therefore must be protected and sustained to the extent necessary to minimize disruption. Failure to keep these services viable and productive may result in significant inability to meet strategic objectives and, in some cases, the organization's mission. To appropriately define the scope of the organization's operational resilience management system, the high-value services of the organization must be identified, prioritized, and communicated as a common target for success. High-value services serve as the focus of attention throughout CERT-RMM as the means by which to establish priorities for managing risk and improving processes, given that it is not possible (nor does it make good business sense) to mitigate all risks and improve all processes. High-value services are fueled by organizational assets such as people, information, technology, and facilities.

2.2.2 Business Processes

A business process is a series of discrete activities or tasks that contribute to the fulfillment of a service mission. Think of a business process as the next level of decomposition for a service, and a service as the aggregation of all of the business processes necessary for service mission success. A single business process may support multiple services. Like services, business processes can traverse the organization and cross organizational lines. In addition, business processes are often performed outside of the boundaries of the organization. Each business process mission must enable the service mission it supports. In CERT-RMM, any discussion of services can be understood to refer to all the component business processes of the services as well.

2.2.3 Assets

An asset is something of value to the organization. Services and business processes are "fueled" by assets—the raw materials that services need to operate.[4] A service cannot accomplish its mission unless there are

- people to operate and monitor the services
- information and data to feed the process and to be produced by the service
- technology to automate and support the service
- facilities in which to perform the service

Success at achieving the organization's mission relies on critical dependencies between organizational goals and objectives, services, and associated high-value assets. Operational resilience starts at the asset level. To ensure operational resilience at the service level, related assets must be protected from threats and risks that could disable them. Assets must also be sustainable (able to be recovered and restored to a defined operating condition or state) during times of disruption and stress. The optimal mix of protect and sustain strategies depends on performing trade-off analysis that considers the value of the asset and the cost of deploying and maintaining the strategy.

As shown in Figure 2.4, failure of one or more assets (due to disruptive events, realized risk, or other issues) has a cascading impact on the mission of related business processes, services, and the organization as a whole. Failure can impede mission assurance of associated services and can translate into failure to achieve organizational goals and objectives. Thus, ensuring the operational resilience of high-value assets is paramount to organizational success.

The first step in establishing the operational resilience of assets is to identify and define the assets. Because assets derive their value and importance through their association with services, the organization must first determine which services are high-value. This provides structure and guidance for developing an inventory of high-value assets for which resilience requirements will have to be established and

---

4. In CERT-RMM, we take a "cyber" approach to resilience. That is, we specifically exclude considerations of other tangible, raw materials that are important to the delivery of some services and most manufacturing processes. This is not to say that physical materials cannot be considered in CERT-RMM, but explicit processes and practices for this are not included in the core model.

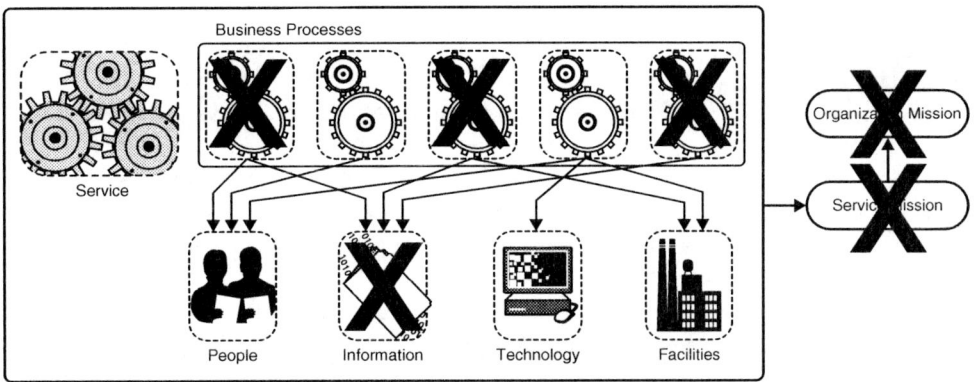

FIGURE 2.4
Impact of Disrupted Asset on Service Mission

satisfied. Inventorying these assets is also essential to ensuring that changes are made in resilience requirements as operational and environmental changes occur.

Each type of asset for a specific service must be identified and inventoried. The following are descriptions of the four asset types used in CERT-RMM:

- **People** are those individuals who are vital to the expected operation and performance of the service. They execute the process and monitor it to ensure that it is achieving its mission, and they make corrections to the process when necessary to bring it back on track. People may be internal or external to the organization.
- **Information** is any information or data, in paper or electronic form, that is vital to the intended operation of the service. Information may also be the output or by-product of the execution of a service. Information can be as small as a bit or a byte, a record or a file, or as large as a database. Because of confidentiality and privacy concerns, information must also be categorized as to its organizational sensitivity. Categorization provides another level of important description to an information asset that may affect its protection and continuity strategies. Examples of information include Social Security numbers, a vendor database, intellectual property, and institutional knowledge.
- **Technology** describes any technology component or asset that supports or automates a service and facilitates its ability to accomplish its mission. Technology has many layers, some of which are specific to a service (such as an application system) and others that are shared by the organization (such as the enterprise-wide network infrastructure) to support more than one service. Organizations must describe technology assets in terms that facilitate development and satisfaction of resilience requirements. In some organizations, this may be at the application system level; in others, it might be more granular, such as at the server or personal computer level. CERT-RMM characterizes technology assets as software, systems,

or hardware. Technology assets can also include firmware and other assets, including physical interconnections between these assets, such as cabling.

- **Facilities** are any physical plant assets that the organization relies upon to execute a service. Facilities are the places where services are executed and can be owned and controlled by the organization or by external business partners (referred to as *external entities* in the model). Facilities are often shared such that more than one service is executed in and dependent upon them. For example, a substantial number of services are executed inside of a headquarters office building. Facilities provide the physical space for the actions of people, the use and storage of information, and the operations of technology components. Thus, resilience planning for facilities must integrate tightly with planning for the other assets. Examples of facilities include office buildings, data centers, and other real estate where services are performed.

As shown in Figure 2.5, relationships among assets have implications for resilience. Information is the most "embedded" type of asset; its resilience is linked to the technologies in which it is developed, processed, stored, and transmitted as well as the facilities within which the technology physically resides.

High-value assets have *owners* and *custodians*. Asset owners are the persons or organizational units, internal or external to the organization, that have primary responsibility for the viability, productivity, and resilience of the asset. For example, an information asset such as customer data may be owned by the customer relations department or the customer relationship manager. It is the

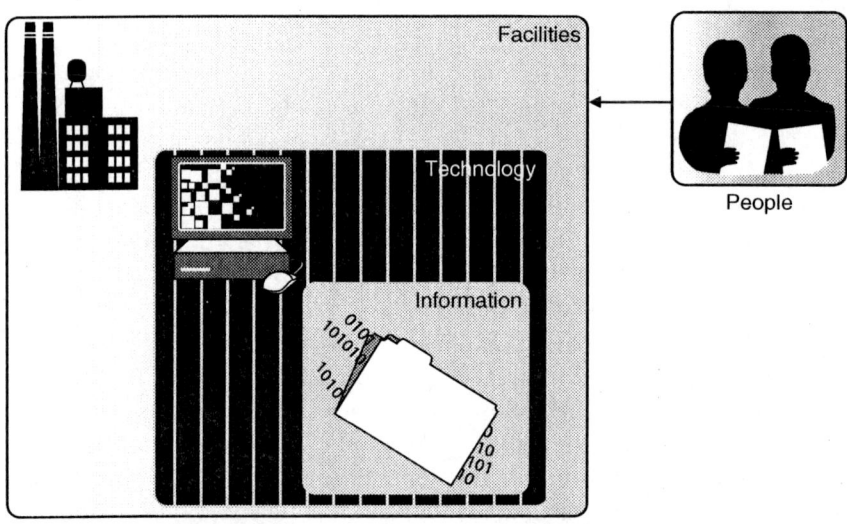

FIGURE 2.5
Putting Assets in Context

owner's responsibility to ensure that the appropriate levels of confidentiality, integrity, and availability requirements are defined and satisfied to keep the asset productive and viable for use in services.

Asset custodians are persons or organizational units, internal or external to the organization, that agree to and are responsible for implementing and managing controls to satisfy the resilience requirements of high-value assets while they are in their care. For example, the customer data in the preceding example may be stored on a server that is maintained by the IT department. In essence, the IT department takes custodial control of the customer data asset when the asset is in its domain. The IT department must commit to taking actions commensurate with satisfying the requirements for protection and continuity of the asset by its owners. However, in all cases, owners are responsible for ensuring the proper protection and continuity of their assets, regardless of the actions (or inactions) of custodians.

2.2.4 Resilience Requirements

An operational resilience requirement is a constraint that the organization places on the productive capability of a high-value asset to ensure that it remains viable and sustainable when charged into production to support a high-value service. In practice, operational resilience requirements are a derivation of the traditionally described security objectives of confidentiality, integrity, and availability. Well known as descriptive properties of information assets, these objectives are also extensible to other types of assets—people, technology, and facilities—with which operational resilience management is concerned. For example, in the case of information, if the integrity requirement is compromised, the information may not be usable in the form intended, thus impacting associated business processes and services. Correspondingly, unintended changes made to the information (compromise of integrity) may cause the business process or service to produce unintended results.

Resilience requirements provide the foundation for how assets are protected from threats and made sustainable so that they can perform as intended in support of services. Resilience requirements become a part of an asset's DNA (just like its definition, owner, and value) which transcends departmental and organizational boundaries because the requirements stay with the asset regardless of where it is deployed or operated.

Resilience requirements are an important element of the operational resilience management system. To develop complete resilience requirements, the organization considers not just specific asset-level requirements but organizational drivers (strategic goals and objectives and critical success factors), risk appetite, and risk tolerances. As shown in Figure 2.6, organizational drivers provide the rationale for investing in resilience activities, and risk appetite and tolerances

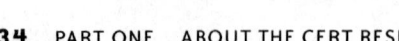

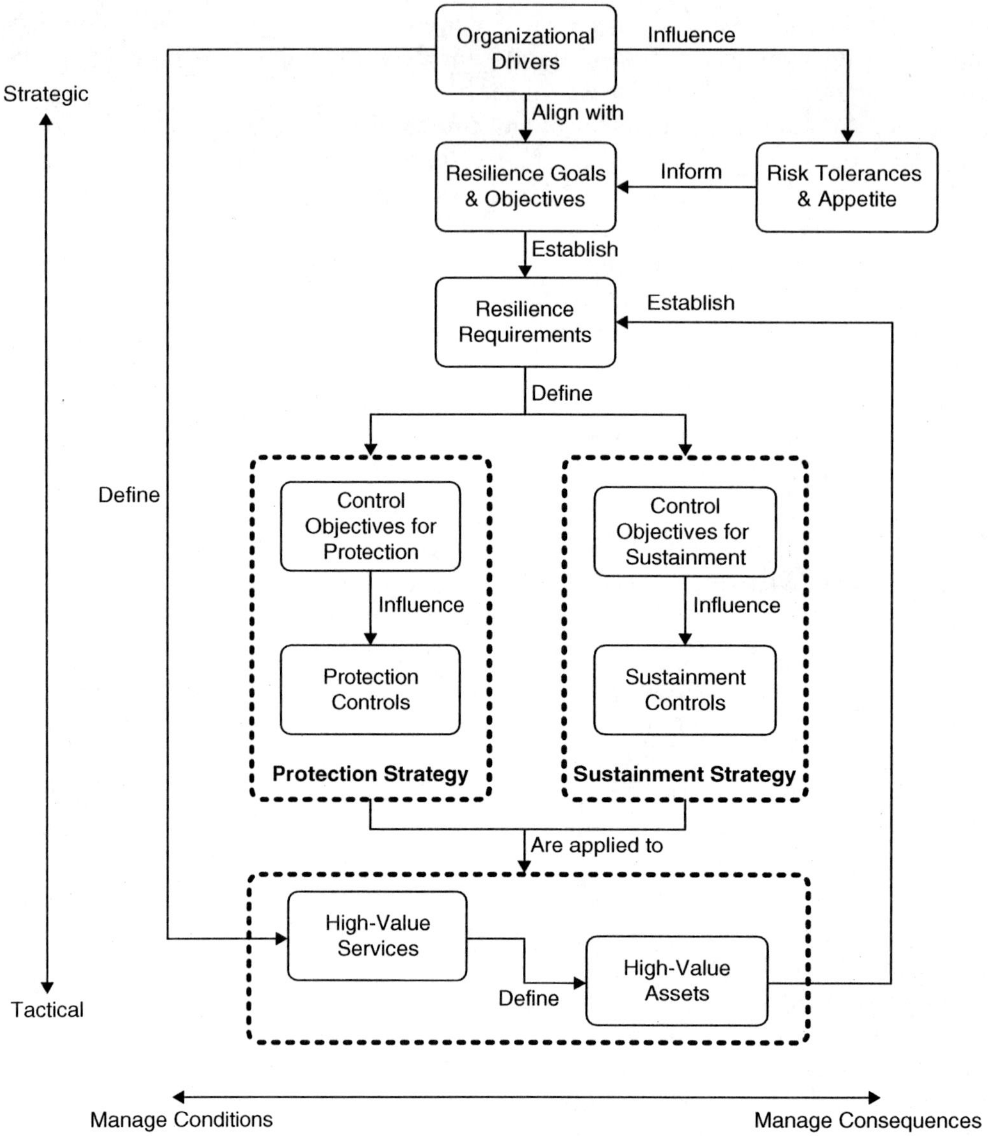

FIGURE 2.6
Driving Operational Resilience Through Requirements

provide parameters for prioritizing risk mitigation actions. Organizational drivers are also important because they enable the identification of the organization's high-value services. These are the services that are critical in achieving the organization's mission and that should therefore be the focus of the organization's operational resilience management activities and resources.

Resilience requirements form the basis for protection and sustainment strategies. These strategies determine the type and level of controls needed to ensure the operational resilience of high-value services and their associated assets (i.e., controls that protect services and assets from disruption as much as possible and that sustain services and assets in the event of disruption). Conversely, controls must satisfy the requirements from which they derive. Aligning control objectives with resilience requirements can help the organization to avoid deploying an extensive number of overlapping and redundant controls.

The importance of requirements to the operational resilience management system cannot be overstated. Resilience requirements embody the strategic objectives, risk appetite, critical success factors, and operational constraints of the organization. They represent the alignment factor that ties practice-level activities performed in security and business continuity to what must be accomplished at the service and asset level in order to move the organization toward mission success.

2.2.5 Strategies for Protecting and Sustaining Assets

As discussed in the preceding section, protection and sustainment strategies are used to identify, develop, implement, and manage controls commensurate with an asset's resilience requirements. As the name implies, protection strategies are protective. They address how to minimize risks to the asset resulting from exposure to threats and vulnerabilities. Sustainment strategies are focused on asset and service continuity. Such strategies define how to keep the asset operational when under stress and how to keep associated services operable when the asset is not available. Each asset needs an optimized mix of protection and sustainment strategies.

Protection strategies translate into activities designed to minimize an asset's exposure to sources of disruption and to the exploitation of vulnerabilities. As shown in Figure 2.7, these strategies manage the conditions of risk by reducing threat and asset exposure. Such activities typically fall into the "security" function

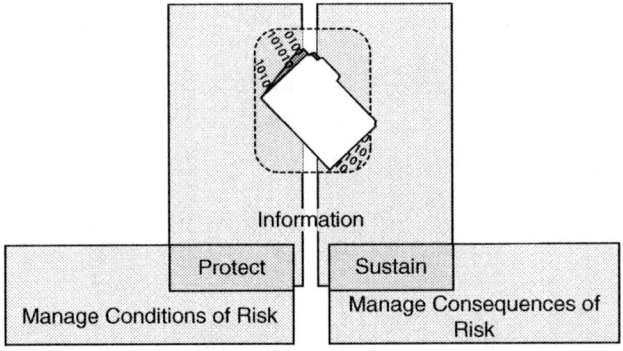

FIGURE 2.7
Optimizing Information Asset Resilience

but may also be embedded in IT operations processes. Activities that implement protection strategies often appear as processes, procedures, policies, and controls.

Sustainment strategies translate into activities designed to keep assets operating as close to normal as possible when faced with disruptive, stressful events. These strategies aid in managing the consequences of risk by making consequences less likely and allowing the organization to respond more effectively to address consequences when an event occurs. Such activities typically fall into the "business continuity" function. Activities that implement sustainment strategies often also appear as processes, procedures, policies, plans, and controls.

The optimization of protection and sustainment strategies and activities that minimize risk to assets and services while making efficient use of limited resources defines the management challenge of operational resilience.

2.2.6 Life-Cycle Coverage

Each of the assets covered in CERT-RMM has a life cycle. From a generic perspective, the majority of operational resilience management processes in CERT-RMM focus on the deployment and operation life-cycle phases, as shown in Figure 2.8.

However, some practices in CERT-RMM cover earlier life-cycle phases to ensure that operational resilience is considered during asset design and development, which can fortify an asset's defense against vulnerabilities and disruption in the operations phase. For example, the practices in Resilience Requirements Development and Resilience Requirements Management can be considered early life-cycle activities (in the plan, design, develop, and acquire phases) that address the development and management of resilience requirements early in the life of an asset.

Depending on the asset, the life-cycle treatment in CERT-RMM can appear to be inconsistent; however, model architects were purposeful in determining which early life-cycle activities to include in the model for maximum effectiveness in meeting operational resilience objectives.

The following briefly describes CERT-RMM life-cycle coverage for each asset type and for services.

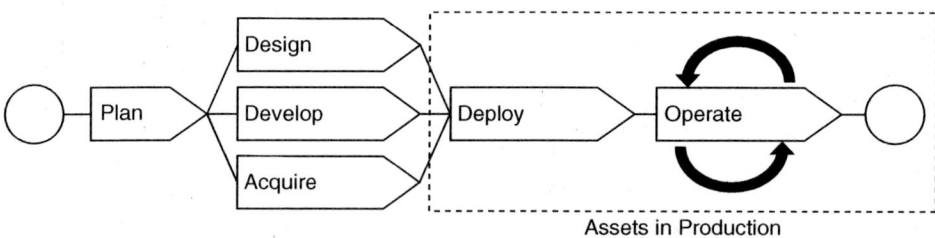

FIGURE 2.8
Generic Asset Life Cycle

People Life Cycle

People are hired, trained, and deployed in services. The activities of hiring and training staff, as well as determining their fitness for duty or purpose, are considered early life-cycle activities. Thus, some of the practices included in CERT-RMM address the hiring, training, and development of people. CERT-RMM also addresses the late life-cycle activity of decommissioning people deployed to services, which might include transfer, voluntary separation, or termination.

Information Life Cycle

Information is created or developed, used by people and services, and then disposed of at the end of its useful life. CERT-RMM practices address the early life-cycle activities related to the development and management of information resilience requirements, the development and implementation of respective controls to meet the requirements, the secure and sustainable use of the information, and the secure disposition of the information. Thus, CERT-RMM covers the entire information life cycle.

Technology Life Cycle

Technology is most closely defined by traditional life-cycle descriptions. Software, systems, and hardware are planned, designed, developed or acquired, implemented, and operated. For the most part, CERT-RMM focuses on the operations phase of the life cycle for technology assets. However, process areas such as Controls Management address the early consideration of controls that have to be designed into software and systems. And the Resilient Technical Solution Engineering process area provides a useful process definition for managing the consideration and inclusion of resilience quality attributes in software and systems throughout their development life cycle. Correspondingly, the External Dependencies Management process area includes these same considerations when software and systems are being acquired.

Figure 2.9 depicts the reach back into earlier life-cycle phases for these categories of technology assets.

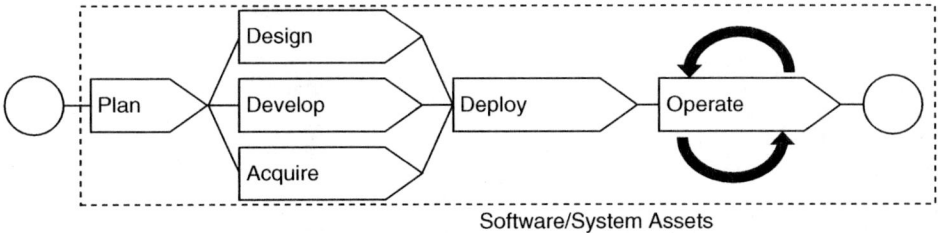

FIGURE 2.9
Software/System Asset Life Cycle

Facilities Life Cycle

Facilities are planned, designed, developed or acquired, constructed, operated, and then retired at the end of their useful life. CERT-RMM practices address early life-cycle activities of developing and managing resilience requirements for facilities; for developing, implementing, and managing physical facilities controls; for maintaining the vital physical and electronic systems of the facility; and for the closure or disposition of the facility.

Services Life Cycle

For services, operational resilience management processes primarily focus on the deployment and operations phases of a service's life cycle[5] as shown in Figure 2.10.

At a high level in CERT-RMM, services are identified, prioritized, and communicated as the basis for organizational success. Service profiles and attributes are kept up-to-date in an accessible service repository. Assets (as defined above) associated with or used by each service are identified and kept current as are interdependencies between services and business processes.

From a model perspective, the processes defined in CERT-RMM mostly act on the service while it is in operation to ensure that it can meet its mission consistently over time. However, some early life-cycle activities for services are included in CERT-RMM. For example, the resilience requirements for services are defined and managed in Resilience Requirements Definition and Resilience Requirements Management, respectively. Through the lens of associated assets, the resilience attributes for the service are identified in these processes and carried out through other processes such as Controls Management and Service Continuity. When controls and service continuity plans are established, these

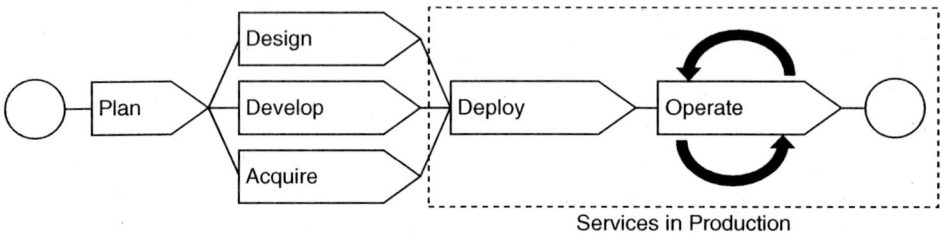

FIGURE 2.10
Services Life Cycle

---

5. The early life-cycle activities for services (design, development, and implementation) are covered in the CMMI for Services model. CERT-RMM addresses services in operation as they support the achievement of organizational goals and objectives.

processes can be considered early life cycle; conversely, when controls and service continuity plans are implemented and managed, these processes are considered to be in the operations phase of the life cycle for services.

In addition, changing conditions that affect services in the operations phase are reflected in changes to controls and service continuity plans. These conditions include

- changes in a service's or asset's resilience requirements
- identification of new vulnerabilities, threats, and risks
- asset changes, such as staff changes, changes to information assets and technology, and relocation of facilities
- changes in a service's or asset's protective controls
- changes in the plan's stakeholders, including external entities and public agencies
- organizational changes, including staff and geographic changes
- changes in lines of business, industry, and product or services mix
- significant technical infrastructure changes
- changes in relationships with external entities such as vendors and business partners
- changes in or additions to regulatory or legal obligations
- results of service continuity plan execution
- results of service continuity plan testing

Other CERT-RMM Life Cycles

Other life cycles are also addressed in CERT-RMM. For example, the incident life cycle is the focus of the Incident Management and Control process area. In addition, service continuity as defined in the Service Continuity process area defines a life cycle for creating a service continuity program and planning, developing, testing, and executing service continuity plans.

2.3 Adapting CERT-RMM Terminology and Concepts

Organizations adopting CERT-RMM may decide to replace some of the terminology used in these key concepts with whatever is comfortable, familiar, and useful to them. However, users of CERT-RMM are strongly encouraged to interpret and apply the foundational concepts (disruption and stress, convergence, operational resilience) and the elements of operational resilience (services, business processes, assets, and resilience requirements, strategies to protect and sustain, and life-cycle coverage) to gain the benefits of managing and improving operational resilience using the model.

CHAPTER 3

MODEL COMPONENTS

This chapter introduces the CERT-RMM process areas and their categories and describes the process area components and their categories. You will need to fully understand this information to make use of the process areas contained in Part Three. It may be helpful to skim a few process areas before you read this section to become familiar with their general construction and layout.

3.1 The Process Areas and Their Categories

As in CMMI models, a process area in CERT-RMM is "a cluster of related practices in an area that, when implemented collectively, satisfy a set of goals considered important for making improvement in that area" [CMMI Product Team 2009, p. 10]. CERT-RMM has 26 process areas (PAs) that are organized into high-level operational resilience categories: Engineering, Enterprise Management, Operations, and Process Management. Table 3.1 shows the 26 CERT-RMM process areas by category.

TABLE 3.1 Process Areas by Category

Category	Process Area
Engineering	Asset Definition and Management
Engineering	Controls Management
Engineering	Resilience Requirements Development
Engineering	Resilience Requirements Management
Engineering	Resilient Technical Solution Engineering
Engineering	Service Continuity
Enterprise Management	Communications
Enterprise Management	Compliance
Enterprise Management	Enterprise Focus

Continues

TABLE 3.1 Process Areas by Category *(Continued)*

Category	Process Area
Enterprise Management	Financial Resource Management
Enterprise Management	Human Resource Management
Enterprise Management	Organizational Training and Awareness
Enterprise Management	Risk Management
Operations	Access Management
Operations	Environmental Control
Operations	External Dependencies Management
Operations	Identity Management
Operations	Incident Management and Control
Operations	Knowledge and Information Management
Operations	People Management
Operations	Technology Management
Operations	Vulnerability Analysis and Resolution
Process Management	Measurement and Analysis
Process Management	Monitoring
Process Management	Organizational Process Definition
Process Management	Organizational Process Focus

Categories are further elaborated and described in Section 4.1.

3.1.1 Process Area Icons

The process area categories are reinforced visually in the model by process area icons. The process area icons show the process area tags (explained below and in Section 3.4) and the symbol of the process area's operational resilience management area. Figure 3.1 shows an example of a process area icon from each operational resilience management area.

3.2 Process Area Component Categories

CERT-RMM process areas contain three categories of components: Required, Expected, and Informative. These categories aid in establishing process improvement objectives and in adapting the model to an organization's unique circumstances.[1]

Table 3.2 lists the model components in each category.

---

1. Much of the nomenclature used in CERT-RMM is derived from CMMI. Thus, if you are already familiar with CMMI models, you should notice no differences in the way that these components are defined or used.

Service Continuity Process Area
Engineering category

Communications Process Area
Enterprise Management category

Environmental Control Process Area
Operations category

Monitoring Process Area
Process Management category

FIGURE 3.1
Examples of Process Area Icons

TABLE 3.2 CERT-RMM Components by Category

Required	Expected	Informative
Specific goal statements	Specific practice statements	Purpose statements
Generic goal statements	Generic practice statements	Introductory notes
		Related process areas section
		Summary of specific goals and practices
		Goal and practice titles
		Typical work products
		Subpractices
		Notes
		Example blocks
		Generic practice elaborations
		References
		Amplifications

3.2.1 Required Components

Required components describe what an organization must achieve to satisfy a process area. There are two required components in CERT-RMM: *specific goal statements* and *generic goal statements*. Goal satisfaction is used in CERT-RMM–based capability appraisals to determine capability levels (see Part Two, Section 6.4). Satisfaction of a goal means that it is visibly and verifiably implemented in the organization's processes.

Note that it is the goal *statements* that are required components, not the goal titles. The goal title of specific goal 1 in Asset Definition and Management is "Establish Organizational Assets"; the goal title of generic goal 1 is "Achieve Specific Goals."

3.2.2 Expected Components

Expected components describe the practices that an organization will typically implement to achieve required components. *Specific practice statements* and *generic practice statements* are both expected components in CERT-RMM. To satisfy goals, the specific and generic practices are expected to be present in the planned and implemented processes of the organization unless acceptable alternatives are present.

Again, note that it is the practice *statements* that are expected components, not the practice titles.

3.2.3 Informative Components

Informative components provide guidance and suggestions about how to achieve the required and expected components. The informative components in CERT-RMM are listed in Table 3.2.

For example, "Identify high-value services" is a subpractice in Asset Definition and Management specific goal 2, specific practice 1, and "List of high-value services and associated assets" is a typical work product.

3.3 Process Area Component Descriptions

3.3.1 Purpose Statements

Purpose statements summarize the content of the process area and collectively represent the goals of the process area. For example, for the Service Continuity process area, "The purpose of Service Continuity is to ensure the continuity of essential operations of services and related assets if a disruption occurs as a result of an incident, disaster, or other disruptive event."

3.3.2 Introductory Notes

The introductory notes provide explanatory matter on the contents of the process area. They are designed to explain the scope of the process area and how developing competency in that area is important to achieving and sustaining resilience. Unique conditions and terminology are included in the introductory notes, as well as a summary of the goals of the process area.

3.3.3 Related Process Areas Section

The related process areas section lists references to other process areas and reflects the high-level relationships among capabilities. This information is useful in deciding which other capabilities are complementary and should be considered by the organization when improving capability.

The following are two examples of relationships from the Service Continuity process area:

> *The consideration of consequences as a foundational element for developing a service continuity plan is addressed in the Risk Management process area.*

> *The identification of vital records and databases for service continuity is addressed in the Knowledge and Information Management process area.*

3.3.4 Summary of Specific Goals and Practices

The summary of specific goals and practices is a table that lists the tag and title of all of the specific goals in the process area and the tag and title of the specific practices of each specific goal.

3.3.5 Specific Goals and Practices

The specific goals of each process area state at a high level the unique capabilities that characterize the process and are required for improving the process. They describe *what* to do to achieve the capabilities. Specific goals are decomposed into specific practices, which are considered to be the base practices that reflect the process area's body of knowledge. Specific practices are expected components of the process area that, when achieved, should promote accomplishment of the associated goal. They begin to articulate *how* to achieve process capabilities. Specific practices provide suggested ways to meet their associated goals, but in implementation they may differ from organization to organization.

Figure 3.2 shows a specific goal from the Asset Definition and Management process area with its required component, the specific goal statement.

ADM:SG1 Establish Organizational Assets

> *Organizational assets (people, information, technology, and facilities) are identified and the authority and responsibility for these assets are established.*

FIGURE 3.2
A Specific Goal and Specific Goal Statement

Figure 3.3 shows a specific practice from the Asset Definition and Management process area with its expected component, the specific practice statement.

3.3.6 Generic Goals and Practices

Generic goals are called "generic" because the same goal statement applies to multiple process areas. A generic goal describes the capabilities that must be present to institutionalize the processes that implement a process area. A generic goal is a required model component and is used in appraisals to determine whether a process area is satisfied.

Figure 3.4 shows a generic goal from the Asset Definition and Management process area with its required component, the generic goal statement.

Generic practices are called "generic" because the same practice applies to multiple process areas. A generic practice is the description of an activity that is considered important in achieving the associated generic goal. (See Part Two, Chapter 5, for a more detailed description of generic goals and practices.)

Figure 3.5 shows a generic practice from the Asset Definition and Management process area with its expected component, the generic practice statement.

3.3.7 Typical Work Products

Typical work products describe the artifacts typically produced by a specific practice. As informative elements, these artifacts are not set in stone; rather, they are suggested from experience, and an organization may have similar or additional artifacts.

ADM:SG2.SP2 Analyze Asset-Service Dependencies

> *Instances where assets support more than one service are identified and analyzed.*

FIGURE 3.3
A Specific Practice and Specific Practice Statement

ADM:GG2 Institutionalize a Managed Process

> *Asset definition and management is institutionalized as a managed process.*

FIGURE 3.4
A Generic Goal and Generic Goal Statement

ADM:GG2.GP1 Establish Process Governance

> *Establish and maintain governance over the planning and performance of the asset definition and management process.*

FIGURE 3.5
A Generic Practice and Generic Practice Statement

Typical process artifacts are useful as model elements because they provide a baseline from which measurement of the performance of the practice can be gauged.

3.3.8 Subpractices, Notes, Example Blocks, Generic Practice Elaborations, References, and Amplifications

Subpractices are informative elements associated with each specific practice and relevant to typical work products. Subpractices are a transition point for process-area–specific practices because the focus changes at this point from *what* must be done to *how*. While not prescriptive or detailed, subpractices can help organizations determine how they can satisfy the specific practices and achieve the goals of the process area. Each organization will have its own subpractices that it has either organically developed or has acquired from a code of practice.

Subpractices can include notes and example blocks. Notes provide expanded and explanatory detail for subpractices where necessary. Examples provide relevant and real-world illustrations and depictions that support understanding of the subpractices.

Generic practice and subpractice elaborations provide guidance about how the generic practice should be applied uniquely to the process area. For example, in every process area, subpractice 1 of generic goal 2, generic practice 3 ("Provide Resources"), is "Staff the process." In the Incident Management and Control process area, the subpractice elaboration lists examples of staff required to perform the incident management and control process, such as staff responsible for triaging events.

References are pointers to related, additional, or more detailed information in other process areas or other components within the same process area. The *CERT Resiliency Engineering Framework: Code of Practice Crosswalk, Preview Version, v0.95R* [REF Team 2008b] contains subpractice references to common codes of practice that aid in effectively adopting CERT-RMM regardless of what practices an organization has already invested in and implemented.

Amplifications explain or describe a unique aspect of a practice. They are used in Asset Definition and Management to describe the differences between asset types. Otherwise, they are infrequently used in the current version of the model. Future versions of the model will use amplifications to describe how a particular process area is addressed for a specific asset type, such as software, systems, or facilities.

Figure 3.6 illustrates the structure of the major model components and indicates whether all or part of each component is required, expected, or informative.

3.4 Numbering Scheme

Process areas in CERT-RMM are tagged with a two- to four-letter tag. The tags for all the process areas are shown in Table 3.3.

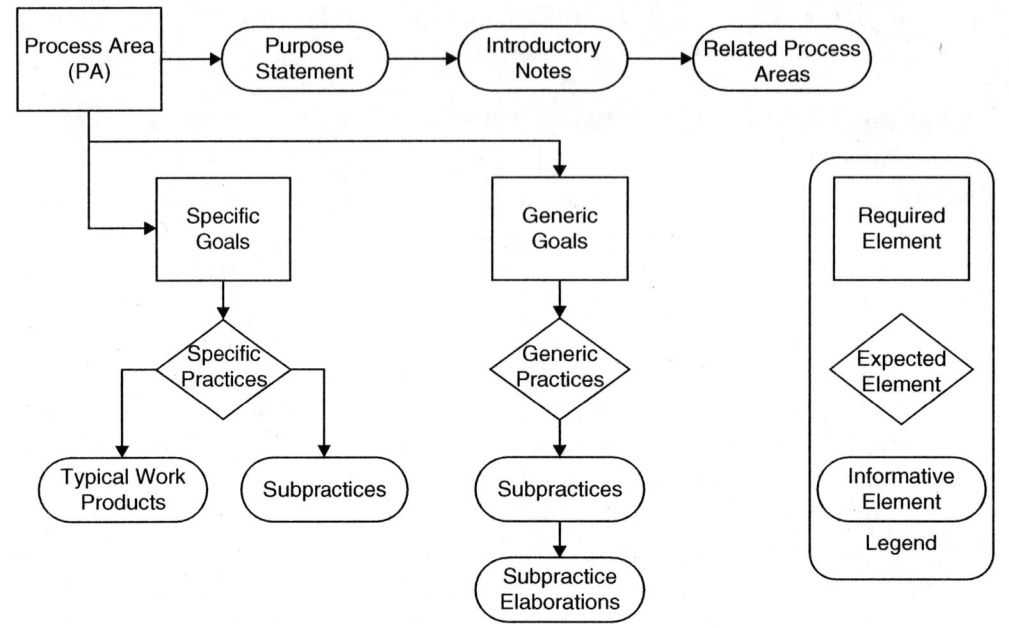

FIGURE 3.6
Summary of Major Model Components

TABLE 3.3 Process Area Tags

Process Area	Tag
Asset Definition and Management	ADM
Access Management	AM
Communications	COMM
Compliance	COMP
Controls Management	CTRL
Environmental Control	EC
Enterprise Focus	EF
External Dependencies Management	EXD
Financial Resource Management	FRM
Human Resource Management	HRM
Identity Management	ID
Incident Management and Control	IMC
Knowledge and Information Management	KIM
Measurement and Analysis	MA
Monitoring	MON

Process Area	Tag
Organizational Process Definition	OPD
Organizational Process Focus	OPF
Organizational Training and Awareness	OTA
People Management	PM
Risk Management	RISK
Resilience Requirements Development	RRD
Resilience Requirements Management	RRM
Resilient Technical Solution Engineering	RTSE
Service Continuity	SC
Technology Management	TM
Vulnerability Analysis and Resolution	VAR

Specific and generic goals are tagged and numbered as follows: SG refers to a specific goal; GG refers to a generic goal. These are appended to the CERT-RMM process area tags and numbered. For example, "ADM:SG1" is specific goal 1 in the Asset Definition and Management process area, and "ADM:GG3" is generic goal 3 in the Asset Definition and Management process area.

Specific and generic practices are tagged and numbered as follows: SP refers to a specific practice; GP refers to a generic practice. These are appended to the CERT-RMM process area tags and the specific goal and generic goal tags, respectively, and are numbered. For example, "ADM:SG1.SP1" is specific practice 1 in specific goal 1 in ADM, and "ADM:GG2.GP3" is generic practice 3 in generic goal 2 in ADM.

Typical work products are numbered sequentially beginning with "1" within each specific practice. Subpractices are numbered sequentially beginning with "1" in each specific or generic practice. Subpractices are referenced in text with their specific or generic practice tag. For example, "ADM:SG2.SP1 subpractice 1" is subpractice 1 in specific practice 1 in specific goal 2 in ADM, and "ADM:GG2.GP3 subpractice 2" is subpractice 2 in generic practice 3 in generic goal 2 in ADM.

3.5 Typographical and Structural Conventions

Typographical and structural conventions have been used in the model to distinguish model components and make them easier to recognize. Also, references to other process areas or process area components are always styled in italic in CERT-RMM.

These conventions can be seen in Figure 3.7, which shows extracts of process area pages with model components identified.

COMMUNICATIONS
Enterprise

Purpose

The purpose of Communications is to develop, deploy, and manage internal and external communications to support resilience activities and processes.

Introductory Notes

Communication is a basic organizational activity and competency. From a resilience perspective, communication is an essential function, tying together disparate parts of the organization that collectively have a vested interest in protecting high-value assets and services and sustaining assets and services during and after a disruptive event.

Internally, communication processes are embedded in operational resilience management processes such as incident management, governance, and compliance, and support the development and execution of plans for sustaining the required level of resilience; externally, communication processes provide much needed information to relevant stakeholders on the capability of the organization to protect and sustain assets and services, handle disruptions, and preserve customer confidence in unsettled and stressful times. Most importantly, communications are a critical success factor in ensuring the successful execution of service continuity plans and decision making, particularly during a crisis or disaster.

VAR:SG2 Identify and Analyze Vulnerabilities

A process for identifying and analyzing vulnerabilities is established and maintained.

The identification and analysis of vulnerabilities are essential elements of managing vulnerabilities *before* they are exploited. Information learned through the identification of vulnerabilities is contextualized using enterprise risk information.

VAR:SG2.SP1 Identify Sources of Vulnerability Information

The sources of vulnerability information are identified.

Information about potential vulnerabilities is available from a wide variety of organizational and external sources. External or public sources typically provide information that is focused on common technologies that are used by a wide range of organizations. Internal sources typically provide information about vulnerabilities that are unique to the organization and range across all types of assets, including people, information, and facilities. Internal sources of vulnerability information are often generated by other operational resilience management processes such as incident management and monitoring, or through IT service delivery and operations processes such as the service desk and problem management. These sources may provide information about vulnerabilities that the organization has observed or that have been exploited, resulting in disruption to the organization.

FIGURE 3.7
Format of Model Components *(Continues)*

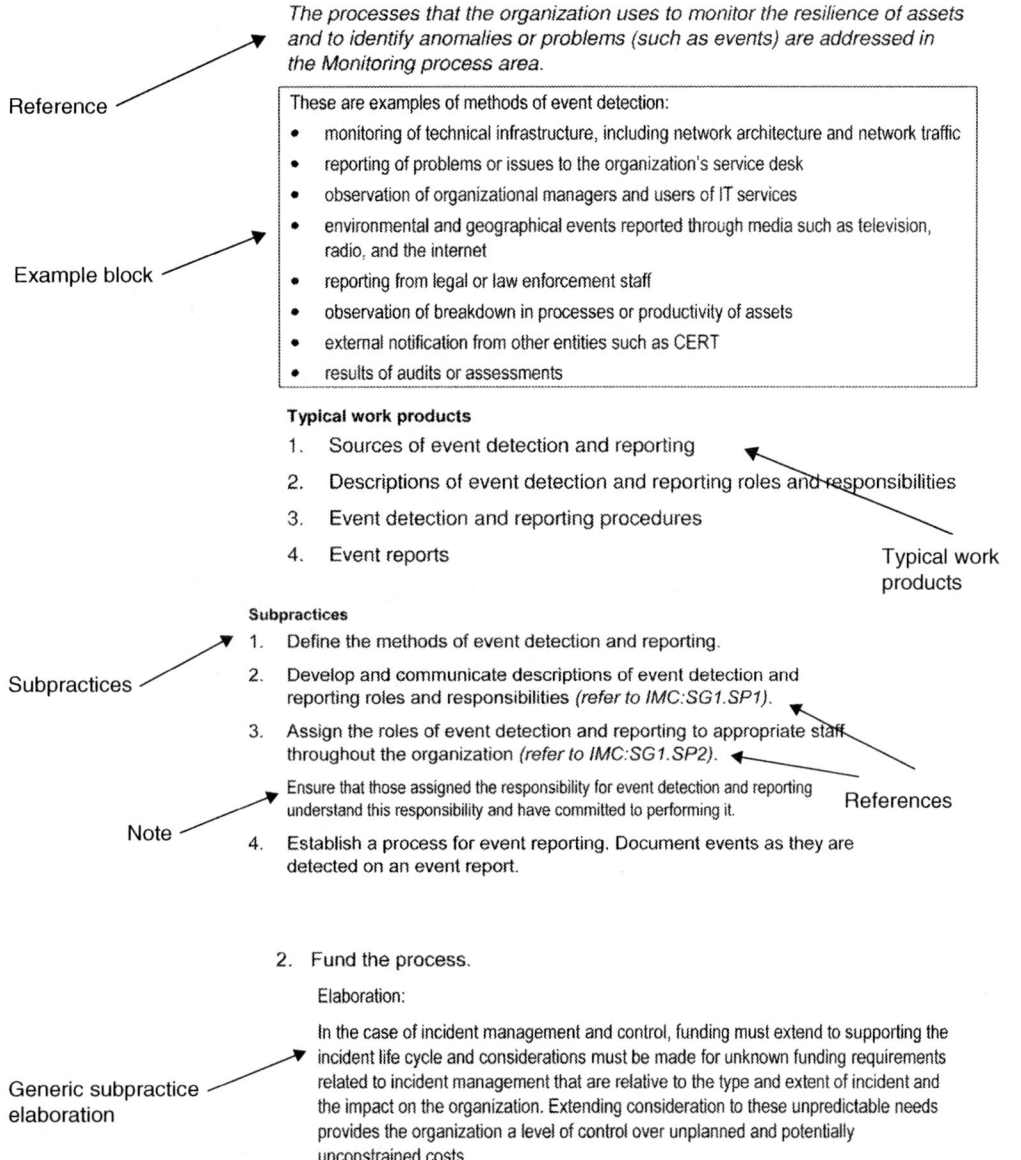

FIGURE 3.7
Format of Model Components *(Continued)*

CHAPTER 4

MODEL RELATIONSHIPS

Successful process improvement efforts align with and help to accomplish business and strategic objectives. Otherwise, there is no reason for the organization to invest in improving processes. Business and strategic objectives may reflect the organization's critical success factors (to improve sales volume) or compliance regulations (to meet stricter information privacy rules) or even address a continuing issue or challenge for the organization (to prevent further data breaches). These objectives should drive how you use model-based process improvement methods, techniques, and tools, including CERT-RMM.

CERT-RMM in its entirety looks ominous at first glance. One reason for this is that operational resilience management encompasses many disciplines and practices. Another reason is that CERT-RMM provides extensive elaborative material to help you make practical use of the model. Once you understand the relationships in the model—and you are able to connect these with your own operational resilience management processes—the CERT-RMM processes that are most relevant to you will be fairly easy to identify and adopt.

There are two types of relationships that are useful to understand as you become familiar with the model. The *model view* helps you to understand the model from an architectural perspective. The way that process areas are grouped provides perspective on the area of operational resilience management that those process areas are intended to support. The *objective view* helps you see the model through relationships that support a particular objective and what you want to accomplish. For example, if your objective is to improve the management of vulnerabilities to high-value information assets, the objective view links together the process areas that would satisfy this objective. Because CERT-RMM allows you to develop an approach to improvement that addresses specific objectives, understanding each of these types of relationships can also be important in helping you develop meaningful targeted improvement roadmaps, as discussed in Section 6.3.

Understanding the key relationships that exist among CERT-RMM process areas aids your adoption and application of the model. For this reason, each process area references other process areas and details the nature of the relationships between them. These references can be found in the "Related Process Areas" section of each process area in Part Three.

In this section, we describe the model view and provide two visual examples of how CERT-RMM process areas relate to each other to accomplish a common objective. As the model continues to be used and adopted, additional objectives and relationships will be developed and described.

4.1 The Model View

The model view simply arranges the process areas by process category. Process areas in each category share common characteristics that form the foundational architecture of the model.

4.1.1 Enterprise Management

The enterprise is an important concept in managing operational resilience. At the enterprise level, the organization establishes and carries out many activities that set the tone for operational resilience, such as governance, risk management, and financial responsibility.

The process areas in the Enterprise Management category represent functions and activities that are essential to broadly supporting the operational resilience management system. This does not mean that these processes are or have to be functionally positioned at an enterprise level. Instead, they represent organization-wide competencies that affect the operational resilience of organizational units. For example, the practices in the Risk Management process area may be performed by an organizational unit, but their effectiveness may be limited by the overall risk management capability of the organization.

The process areas that represent the Enterprise Management category are

- Communications [COMM]
- Compliance Management [COMP]
- Enterprise Focus [EF]
- Financial Resource Management [FRM]
- Human Resource Management [HRM]
- Organizational Training and Awareness [OTA]
- Risk Management [RISK]

Figure 4.1 depicts the relationships that drive resilience activities at the enterprise level.

Chapter 4 Model Relationships 55

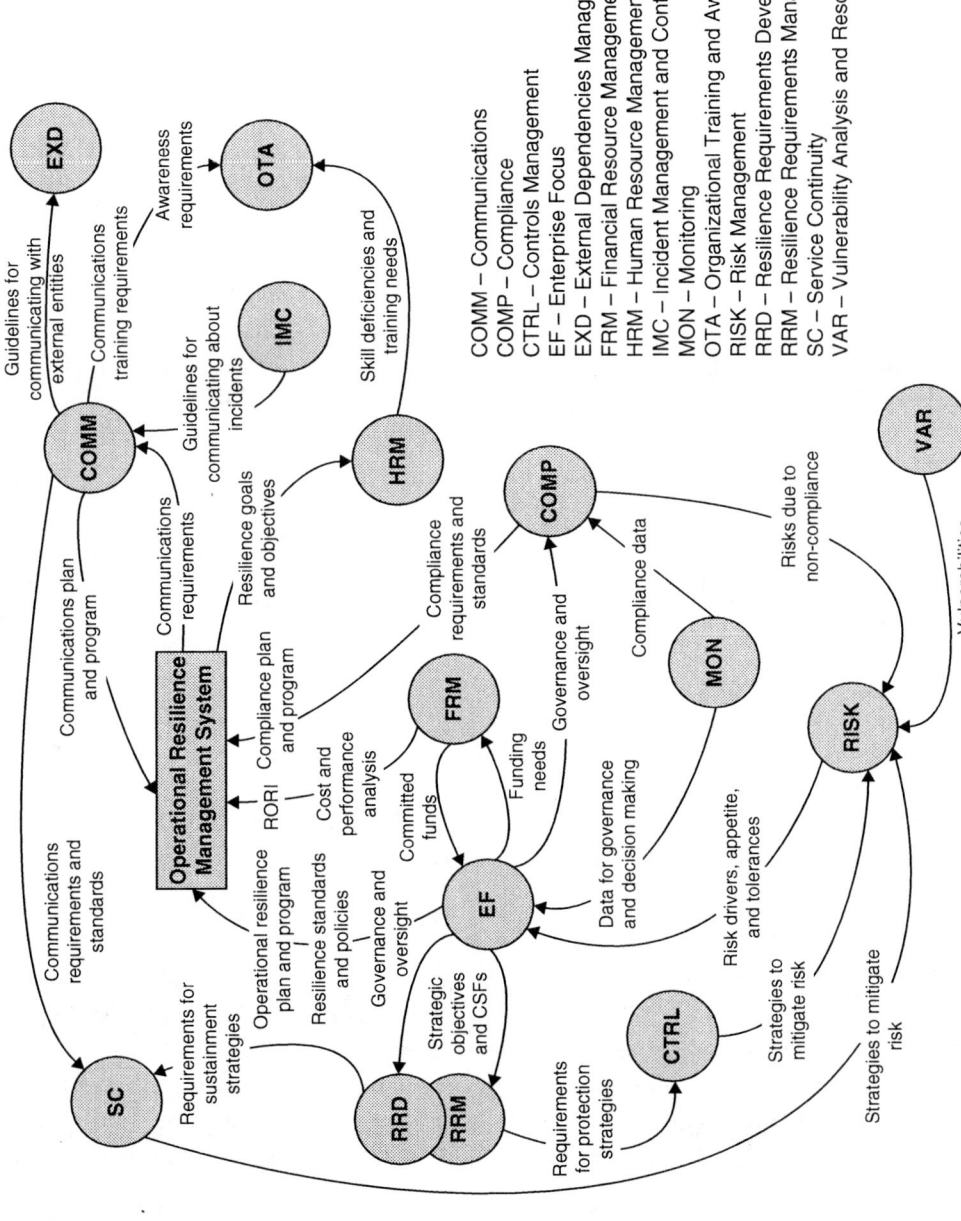

FIGURE 4.1
Relationships That Drive Resilience Activities at the Enterprise Level

4.1.2 Engineering

Aspects of operational resilience management are requirements-driven. Thus, the process areas in the Engineering category represent those that are focused on establishing and implementing resilience for organizational assets, business processes, and services through a requirements-driven process. These processes establish the basic building blocks for resilience and create the foundation to protect and sustain assets and, by reference, the business processes and services that those assets support.

Engineering process areas fall into three broad categories:

- *Requirements Management* addresses the development and management of the security (protect) and resilience (sustain) objectives for assets and services.
- *Asset Management* establishes the important people, information, technology, and facilities assets across the enterprise.
- *Establishing and Managing Resilience* addresses the selection, implementation, and management of preventive controls and the development and implementation of service continuity and impact management plans and programs. It also addresses early life-cycle consideration of resilience quality attributes for software and systems.

The Engineering process areas include:

Requirements Management
- Resilience Requirements Development [RRD]
- Resilience Requirements Management [RRM]

Asset Management
- Asset Definition and Management [ADM]

Establishing and Managing Resilience
- Controls Management [CTRL]
- Resilient Technical Solution Engineering [RTSE]
- Service Continuity [SC]

4.1.3 Operations

The Operations process areas represent the core activities for managing the operational resilience of assets and services in the operations life-cycle phase. These process areas are focused on sustaining an adequate level of operational resilience as prescribed by the organization's strategic drivers, critical success factors, and risk appetite. These process areas represent core security, business continuity, and

IT operations and service delivery management activities and focus specifically on the resilience of people, information, technology, and facilities assets.

Operations process areas fall into three broad categories:

- *Supplier Management* addresses the management of external dependencies and the potential impact on the organization's operational resilience.
- *Threat, Vulnerability, and Incident Management* addresses the organization's continuous cycle of identifying and managing threats, vulnerabilities, and incidents to minimize organizational disruption.
- *Asset Resilience Management* addresses the asset-level activities that the organization performs to manage operational resilience of people, information, technology, and facilities to ensure that business processes and services are sustained.

The Operations process areas are:

Supplier Management
- External Dependency Management [EXD]

Threat and Incident Management
- Access Management [AM]
- Identity Management [ID]
- Incident Management and Control [IMC]
- Vulnerability Analysis and Resolution [VAR]

Asset Resilience Management
- Environmental Control [EC]
- Knowledge and Information Management [KIM]
- People Management [PM]
- Technology Management [TM]

Figure 4.2 depicts the relationships that drive threat and incident management.

4.1.4 Process Management

Process Management processes represent those that are focused on measuring, managing, and improving operational resilience management processes. These process areas represent the extension of process improvement concepts to operational resilience management and, in turn, to the disciplines of security and business continuity. Process areas in this category are intended to catalyze the organization's view of resilience as a repeatable, predictable, manageable,

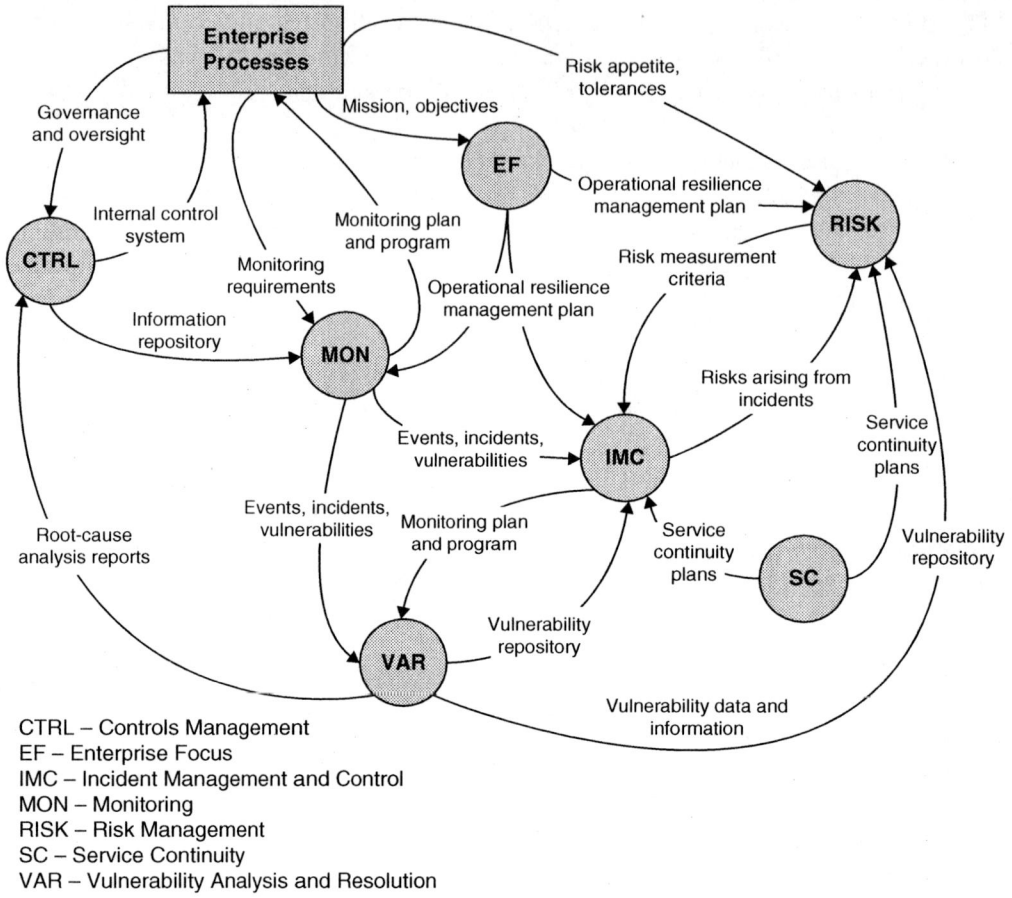

FIGURE 4.2
Relationships That Drive Threat and Incident Management

and improvable process over which it has a significant level of active and direct control.

Process Management process areas can be divided into two broad categories:

- *Data Collection and Logging* addresses the organization's competencies for identifying, collecting, logging, and distributing information needed to ensure that operational resilience management processes are performed consistently and within acceptable tolerances.
- *Process Management* addresses the activities the organization performs to improve and optimize operational resilience management processes and to make these processes consistent throughout the organization.

Process Management process areas are:

Data Collection and Logging
- Monitoring [MON]

Process Management
- Organizational Process Definition [OPD]
- Organizational Process Focus [OPF]
- Measurement and Analysis [MA]

4.2 Objective Views for Assets

Objective views in CERT-RMM can address a number of useful perspectives, such as

- how operational resilience management is planned and executed
- the specific processes that drive asset-based resilience, such as relationships that drive information resilience
- how people are addressed in operational resilience management
- the development and deployment of protection strategies and controls
- the service continuity planning process

With a large model, the number of possible objective views could be significant and would be beyond the scope of this book. A basic set of objective views can address the operational resilience management of the assets that are the focus of the model. The following describes these views and provides four figures that graphically depict model objectives.

4.2.1 People

Figure 4.3 shows the CERT-RMM process areas that participate in managing the operational resilience of people. They establish people as an important asset in service delivery and ensure that people meet job requirements and standards, have appropriate skills, are appropriately trained, and have access to other assets as needed to do their jobs.

4.2.2 Information

Figure 4.4 shows the CERT-RMM process areas that drive the operational resilience management of information. Information is established as a key element in service delivery. Requirements for protecting and sustaining information are established and used by processes such as risk management, controls management, and service continuity planning.

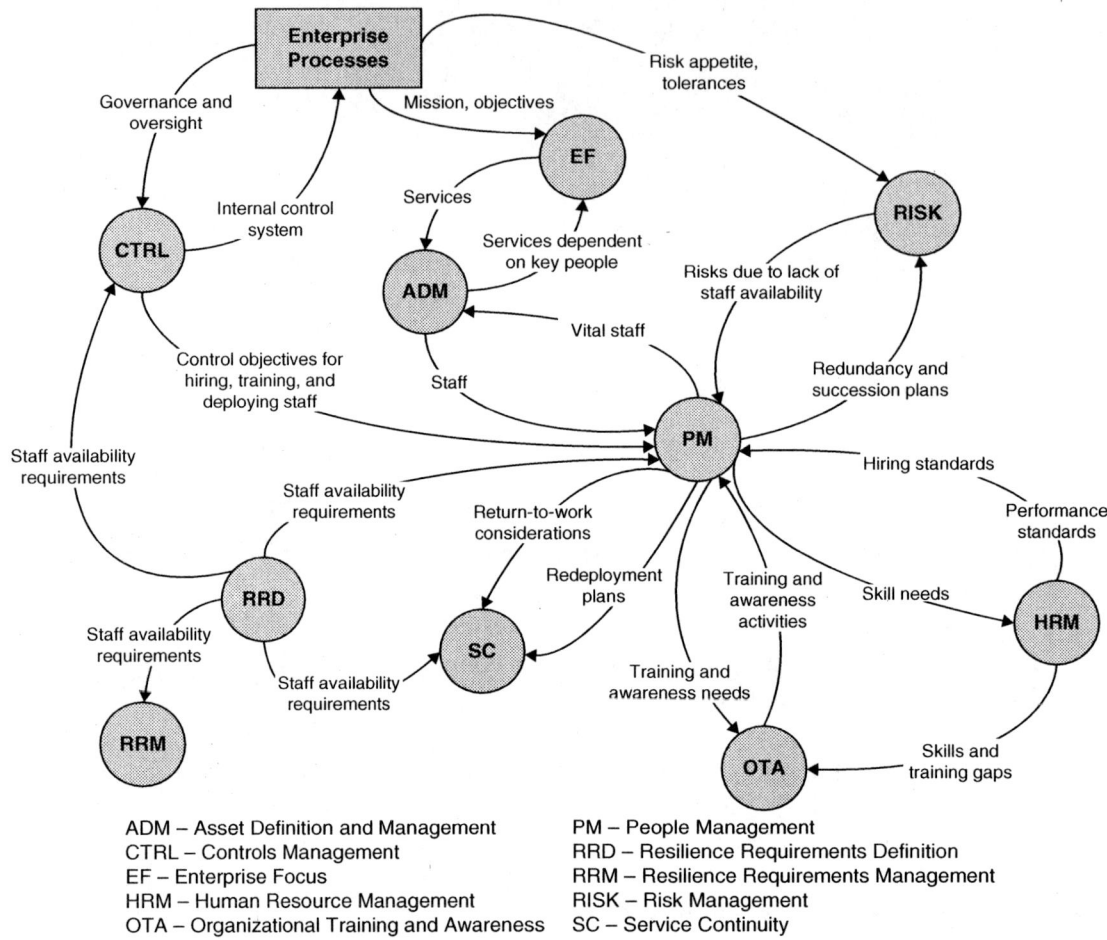

FIGURE 4.3
Relationships That Drive the Resilience of People

4.2.3 Technology

Figure 4.5 shows the CERT-RMM process areas that drive the operational resilience management of technology. These relationships address the specific complexities of software and system resilience, as well as the resilience of architectures where the technology assets reside, development and acquisition processes, and processes such as configuration management and capacity planning and management.

4.2.4 Facilities

Figure 4.6 shows the CERT-RMM process areas that drive the operational resilience management of facilities. As with information and technology assets,

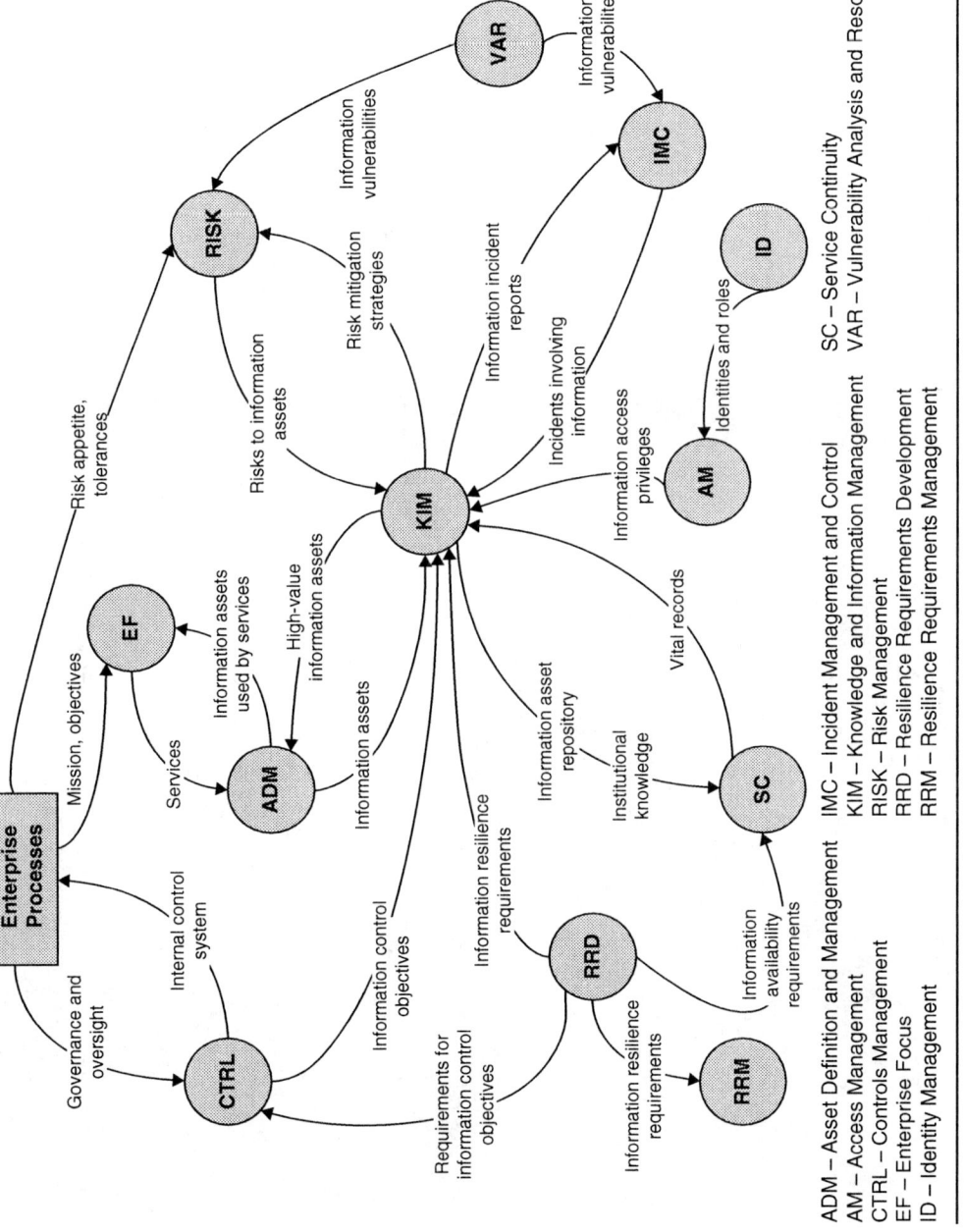

FIGURE 4.4
Relationships That Drive Information Resilience

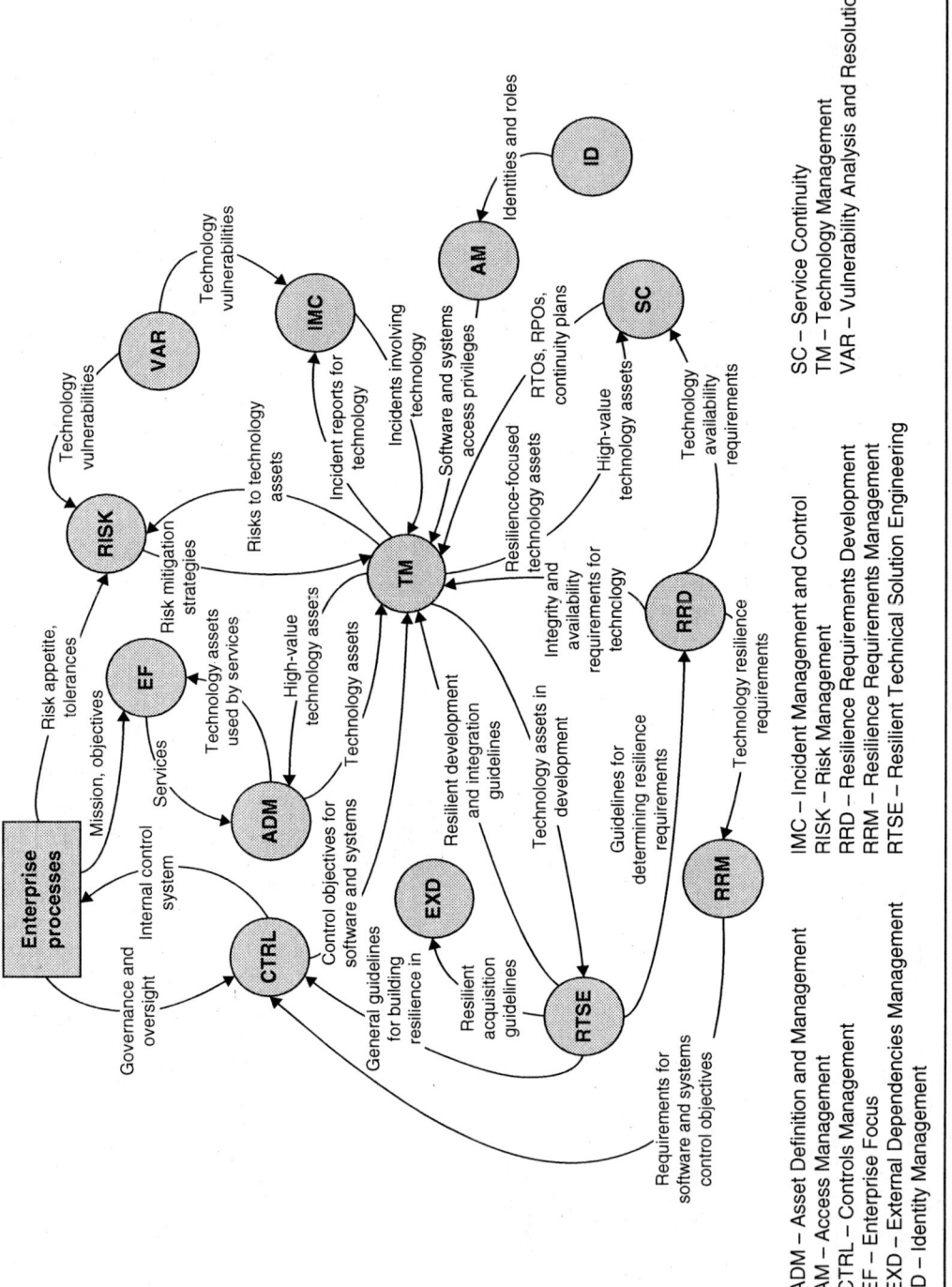

FIGURE 4.5
Relationships That Drive Technology Resilience

Chapter 4 Model Relationships **63**

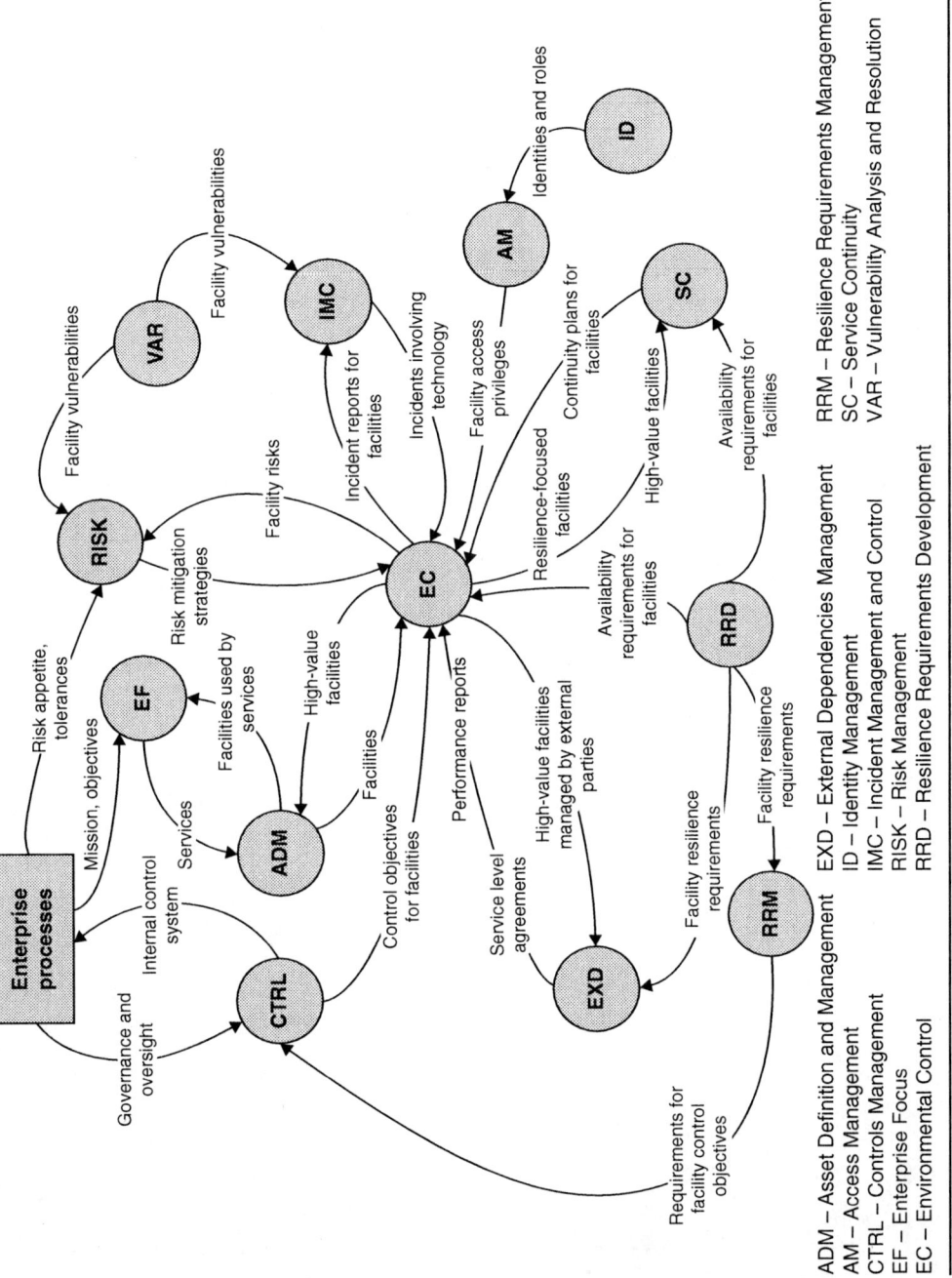

FIGURE 4.6
Relationships That Drive Facility Resilience

ADM – Asset Definition and Management
AM – Access Management
CTRL – Controls Management
EF – Enterprise Focus
EC – Environmental Control

EXD – External Dependencies Management
ID – Identity Management
IMC – Incident Management and Control
RISK – Risk Management
RRD – Resilience Requirements Development

RRM – Resilience Requirements Management
SC – Service Continuity
VAR – Vulnerability Analysis and Resolution

relationships that drive the resilience of facilities have special considerations such as protecting facilities from disruption, ensuring that facilities are sustained, managing the environmental conditions of facilities, determining the dependencies of facilities on their geographical region, and planning for the retirement of a facility. Because facilities are often owned and managed by an external entity, consideration must also be given to how external entities implement and manage the resilience of facilities under the organization's direction.

PART TWO

Process Institutionalization and Improvement

The concept of using a maturity model to improve operational resilience may not at first glance appear to provide significant advantages over the simple implementation of a code of practice. Codes of practice, after all, typically represent a cumulative view of how an industry faces a challenge such as information security and can be of great benefit to all organizations that share this challenge. For some organizations, using practices alone will bring about improvement—improvement in the way that passwords and user IDs are managed, how incidents are handled, or how continuity plans are developed and tested. But lasting improvement depends on the organization's ability to develop and inculcate a culture around managing operational resilience—that the operational resilience of the organization is everyone's job and responsibility. Security and continuity training and awareness alone do not create such a culture or provide it with the foundation it needs to flourish, particularly during times of stress.

At its core, a maturity model is about improving the organization's capacity and competency for producing high-quality results, no matter the circumstances. When such an approach is taken, the practices performed by the organization are embedded within a culture of improvement so that the performance of these practices is measured and improved and the capability is sustained. This is critical in managing operational risk because not all risks can be identified and responses to realized risk cannot always be planned.

A maturity model with a capability dimension provides a platform for measuring process institutionalization—the degree to which a process is embedded in the culture. Measuring the level of institutionalization of operational resilience management processes tells the organization something about how likely it is to retain these processes in changing risk environments.

In Part Two of this book, we discuss the capability dimension of CERT-RMM and the impact it can have on transforming the organization's performance. We also provide guidance on how to use the model to begin an improvement effort or to get a "health check" on how your organization is managing operational resilience today.

CHAPTER 5

INSTITUTIONALIZING OPERATIONAL RESILIENCE MANAGEMENT PROCESSES

5.1 Overview

This chapter describes the process institutionalization aspects of CERT-RMM. It describes the "continuous representation" of CERT-RMM, the resultant capability levels, and the associated generic goals and generic practices of CERT-RMM, which have been sourced intact from CMMI. These model components directly address process institutionalization.

The capability dimension of CERT-RMM sets it apart from other models in the operational resilience space because this dimension determines the degree to which

- a process (or a practice) has been ingrained in the way work is defined, executed, and managed
- there is commitment and consistency to performing the process

Higher degrees of process institutionalization often equate to more stable processes that produce consistent results over time. Highly institutionalized operational resilience management processes should help the organization to improve service resilience not only because the process is stable but also because institutionalized processes are more likely to be retained during times of stress. Because the operational resilience of an organization is fundamentally tied to how well it performs during times of stress, the capability dimension of CERT-RMM is foundationally important to any organization that wants to improve its operational resilience.

5.2 Understanding Capability Levels

CERT-RMM is not a prescriptive model; that is, there is no guidance provided to adopt the model in any sequential or prescriptive path. Process improvement is unique to each organization; thus, CERT-RMM provides the basic structure to allow organizations to chart their own specific improvement path using the model as the basis.

The ability to incrementally improve processes in an individual process area (or a group of process areas) is embedded in the model's *continuous representation*.[1] The improvement path in a continuous representation is defined by *capability levels*. Levels characterize improvement from an ill-defined state to a state where processes are characterized and used consistently across organizational units. This concept is an important enabler of the principle of convergence, particularly in large, distributed organizations.

To reach a particular level, an organization must satisfy all of the appropriate goals of the process area (or a set of process areas), as well as the generic goals that apply to the specific capability level. The structure of the continuous representation for CERT-RMM is provided in Figure 5.1.

Because there is no staged representation in CERT-RMM, technically the concept of organizational maturity for managing operational resilience processes doesn't exist. However, it could be argued that an organization that reaches higher capability levels in each process area is exhibiting a higher degree of organizational maturity.

The capability dimension of CERT-RMM is also used for process improvement appraisal activities. Appraisal activities are described in Section 6.4.

CERT-RMM currently defines four capability levels, designated by the numbers 0 through 3, as shown in Table 5.1.

A capability level for a process area is achieved when all of the generic goals are satisfied up to that level. By design, capability level 2 is defined by generic goal 2 and capability level 3 is defined by generic goal 3. Thus, the generic goals and practices at each level define the meaning of the capability levels. Because capability is cumulative, reaching capability level 3 means that the organization is also performing the goals and practices at capability levels 1 and 2. (See Section 5.4 for more information about generic goals and practices.)

---

1. In CERT-RMM, there is no staged representation as in CMMI models. The staged representation uses *maturity levels*, which define levels of organizational maturity. In addition, the levels in a staged representation correlate to a collection of process areas that are prescribed or "staged" at each level. This concept does not exist in CERT-RMM because all improvement activities are undertaken in an individual process area or a collection of process areas that are chosen by the organization to satisfy its unique process improvement objectives.

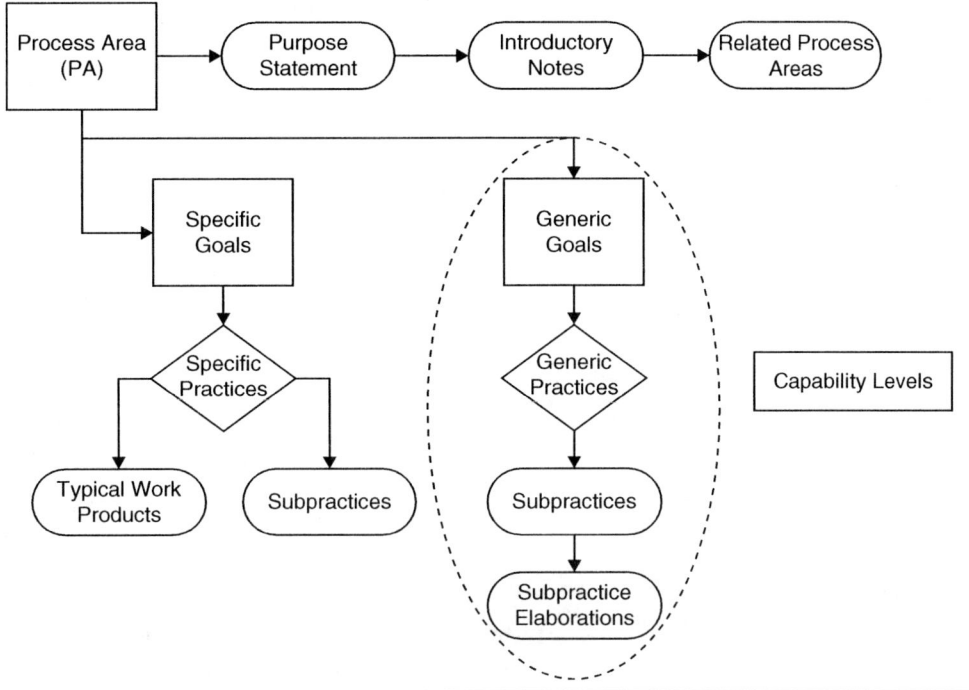

FIGURE 5.1
Structure of the CERT-RMM Continuous Representation

TABLE 5.1 Capability Levels in CERT-RMM

Capability Level Number	Capability Level
0	Incomplete
1	Performed
2	Managed
3	Defined

5.3 Connecting Capability Levels to Process Institutionalization

Capability levels describe the degree to which a process has been institutionalized. Likewise, the degree to which a process is institutionalized is defined by the generic goals and practices. Table 5.2 links capability levels to the progression of processes and generic goals.

The progression of capability levels and the degree of process institutionalization are characterized in the following descriptions.

TABLE 5.2 Capability Levels Related to Goals and Process Progression

Capability Level Number	Generic Goal Number	Capability Level	Progression of Processes
0	N/A	Incomplete	No process or partially performed process
1	GG1	Performed	Performed process
2	GG2	Managed	Managed process
3	GG3	Defined	Defined process

5.3.1 Capability Level 0: Incomplete

An incomplete process is a process that either is not performed or is partially performed. One or more of the specific goals of the process area are not satisfied. No generic goals exist for this level since there is no reason to institutionalize a partially performed process [CMMI Product Team 2006].

5.3.2 Capability Level 1: Performed

Capability level 1 characterizes a *performed* process. A performed process is a process that satisfies *all* of the specific goals of the process area.[2] It supports and enables the work needed to perform operational resilience practices as defined by the specific goals.

Although achieving capability level 1 results in important improvements, those improvements can be lost over time if they are not institutionalized. The application of institutionalization through the generic goals at levels 2 and 3 helps to ensure that improvements are maintained [CMMI Product Team 2006].

When organizations perform a compliance review against a code of practice, they are in essence evaluating whether a process is performed. However, because operational resilience management processes are critically important during times of stress, simply verifying that a process is performed does not provide any indication or predictability about how the organization will perform in the future. In CERT-RMM, two additional and important levels of capability can be evaluated—managed and defined—which provide a better indicator of an organization's ability to predict performance.

5.3.3 Capability Level 2: Managed

A capability level 2 process is characterized as a *managed* process. Because capability levels are cumulative, a managed process is a *performed* process that has the

---

2. In CERT-RMM, as in CMMI models, all of the specific goals of a process area must be satisfied to state that the process is being performed or that the organization is performing the process at capability level 1.

basic infrastructure in place to support the process. At capability level 2, the process

- is planned and executed in accordance with policy
- employs skilled people who have adequate resources to produce controlled outputs
- involves relevant stakeholders
- is monitored, controlled, and reviewed
- is evaluated for adherence to the organization's process description

A critical distinction between a performed and a managed process is that a managed process is planned and the performance of the process is managed against the plan. Corrective actions are taken when the actual results and performance deviate significantly from the plan. A managed process achieves the objectives of the plan and is institutionalized for consistent performance [CMMI Product Team 2006].

The process discipline reflected by capability level 2 helps to ensure that existing practices are retained during times of stress [CMMI Product Team 2006]. From an operational resilience management perspective, it is at capability level 2 where the organization can begin to answer some vital questions about its viability in a complex, risk-evolving environment, such as these:

- Are we able to achieve consistent results from our processes today and tomorrow, and are we committed to doing so?
- Can we repeat our current successes consistently over time?
- Can we achieve the same results from our processes during times of stress and when we don't have access to our best employees and other resources?
- Can we obtain consistent results from our processes across organizational units and lines of business?

Organizations operating at capability level 2 should begin to know with some degree of certainty that they can achieve and sustain operational resilience goals regardless of changes in risk environments or when faced with new and emerging threats. Thus, instead of shifting its planning and practices for security and business continuity to address the next new and sensational threat, the organization stays on course and defines and refines its processes to address *whatever* risk comes its way. This indicates that the organization has invested in and nurtured its capabilities for sustaining these practices through sponsorship, ability and commitment, institutionalization, and measurement.

5.3.4 Capability Level 3: Defined

A capability level 3 process is characterized as a defined process. A defined process is a *managed* process (capability level 2) that is tailored from the organization's set of standard processes according to the organization's tailoring guidelines. The process also contributes work products, measures, and other process improvement information as organizational process assets for use by all organizational units [CMMI Product Team 2006].

What does this ultimately mean to the organization? One of the principal challenges for effective operational resilience management is the ability to get all parts of the organization to coalesce around common goals and objectives. When different parts of the organization operate with different goals, assumptions, and practices, it is difficult if not impossible to ensure that the organization's collective goals and objectives can be reached. This is particularly true with crosscutting concerns such as operational risk management. If the organization's risk assumptions are not reflected consistently in security, continuity, and IT operations activities, the organization's risk management process will be less than effective and perhaps significantly detrimental to overall operational resilience.

At capability level 3, alignment begins to occur because the standards, process descriptions, and procedures used for operational resilience management at the organizational unit level are tailored from the organization's standard set of operational resilience management processes. At capability level 2, each organizational unit may be improving the degree to which processes are institutionalized for that unit, but the organization is not necessarily reaping improvement benefits as a whole. At capability level 3, this begins to occur because there is more consistency across units, and improvements made by each organizational unit can be accessed and used by the organization through an organization-level improvement infrastructure.

Another critical distinction at capability level 3 is that processes are typically described more rigorously than at capability level 2. A defined process clearly states the purpose, inputs, entry criteria, activities, roles, measures, verification steps, outputs, and exit criteria. At capability level 3, processes are managed more proactively using an understanding of the interrelationships of the process activities and details [CMMI Product Team 2006].

5.3.5 Other Capability Levels

If your organization uses the CMMI models, you are likely to be familiar with two other capability levels—capability level 4 (quantitatively managed) and capability level 5 (optimized). Both levels address the use of statistical and other quantitative techniques to control and improve processes. Beginning at capability level 4, process quality and performance are understood in statistical terms, and at capability level 5, common causes of process variation are understood and used for improving the range of process performance.

In CERT-RMM, it is unclear at this point whether these capability levels exist for operational resilience management or, more specifically, whether they have meaning. In other words, should an organization strive for some level of quantitatively managed operational resilience processes, and if so, what benefits would this bring to the organization? Thus, these additional levels are not defined in the model.

5.4 CERT-RMM Generic Goals and Practices

Generic goals and practices are common to all process areas. They are the roadmap for helping the organization raise its performance of each process area to the next capability level. The degree of process institutionalization is embodied in the generic goals and practices and expressed in the names of the generic goals, except for goal 1, "Achieve Specific Goals," which refers to the achievement of all of the specific goals and the performance of all of the specific practices of a process area.

The generic goals and practices used in CERT-RMM have been sourced from CMMI models. Thus, if you are a current user of CMMI models, you will be able to use the same process institutionalization features of CMMI in your CERT-RMM process improvement effort. However, there are a few differences, mostly in wording:

- Generic practice 2.1 in CMMI models is "Establish an Organizational Policy," while in CERT-RMM, the corresponding practice is "Establish Process Governance." In CERT-RMM, policy is an artifact of effective governance, which is required for all processes to reach capability level 2.
- In CMMI, generic practice 2.3, "Provide Resources," is similar between the models, but CERT-RMM expands the definition of "resources" to include financial resources.
- Generic practice 2.6 in CMMI is "Manage Configurations," but in CERT-RMM, it is retitled as "Manage Work Product Configurations" to avoid confusion with traditional configuration management activities as defined in IT operations.
- CERT-RMM includes subpractices in its articulation of generic goals and practices, which were eliminated in current versions of CMMI models.

Remember, only the generic goals for capability levels 1, 2, and 3 from CMMI are included in CERT-RMM. The CERT-RMM Generic Goals and Practices are included in Appendix A.

5.4.1 CERT-RMM Elaborated Generic Goals and Practices

Since generic goals and practices apply to each process area, naturally there is variation in how each generic goal and practice affects the core subject matter of a process area. For example, generic practice 2.1, which calls for governance over the process, will differ widely depending on whether the process deals with incident management or organizational training and awareness. Thus, in each process area, the CERT-RMM model includes customized examples of the generic goals and practices. These customized examples are called *elaborations,* and therefore each process area has a unique set of elaborated generic goals and practices associated with it.

Elaborated generic goals and practices are included with each process area, beginning in Part Three of this book.

5.5 Applying Generic Practices

Applying the generic practices in CERT-RMM is mostly straightforward but can be confusing. It is easiest to start with a simple example.

When you are achieving the specific goals of the Asset Definition and Management process area, you are formally identifying, documenting, and managing the assets that the organization depends on to ensure that high-value services meet their missions. Consider generic practice GG2.GP2, "Establish and maintain the plan for performing the process." In this context, generic practice GG2.GP2 reminds you that you need to *plan* the activities related to identifying, documenting, and managing assets throughout their life cycle. Thus, the application of this generic practice improves the institutionalization of the Asset Definition and Management process area by instilling a planning discipline.

In some cases, the application of a generic practice to the specific goals in a process area will seem recursive. For example, consider the application of generic practice GG2.GP2 to a process area that already includes a specific goal directed at planning. In the Incident Management and Control process area, planning for incident management is a major aspect of the process. The application of generic practice GG2.GP2 in this case reminds you that you must *plan* the activities involved in creating the plan for managing incidents.

5.6 Process Areas That Support Generic Practices

While generic goals and generic practices are the model components that directly address process institutionalization, some process areas also address institutionalization by supporting the implementation of the generic practices. Thus, implementing the specific practices in some process areas may also help with the implementation of a generic practice.

Table 5.3 shows the relationship between CERT-RMM process areas and generic practices.

TABLE 5.3 CERT-RMM Generic Practices Supported by Process Areas

Generic Practice	Related Process Area	How the Process Area Helps to Implement the Generic Practice
GG2.GP1 Establish Process Governance	Enterprise Focus	Enterprise Focus addresses the governance aspect of managing operational resilience. Mastery of the Enterprise Focus process area can help to achieve GG2.GP1 in other process areas.
GG2.GP3 Provide Resources	Human Resource Management Financial Resource Management	Human Resource Management ensures that resources have the proper skill sets and their performance is consistent over time. Financial Resource Management addresses the provision of other resources to the process, such as financial capital.
GG2.GP5 Train People	Organizational Training and Awareness	Organizational Training and Awareness ensures that resources are properly trained.
GG2.GP8 Monitor and Control the Process	Monitoring Measurement and Analysis	Monitoring provides the structure and process for identifying and collecting relevant information for controlling processes. Measurement and Analysis provides general guidance about measuring, analyzing, and recording information that can be used in establishing measures for monitoring actual performance of the process [CMMI Product Team 2006].
GG2.GP10 Review Status with Higher-Level Managers	Enterprise Focus	As part of the governance process, Enterprise Focus requires oversight of the resilience process, including identifying corrective actions.
GG3.GP1 Establish a Defined Process	Organizational Process Definition	Organizational Process Definition establishes the organizational process assets necessary to implement the generic practice [CMMI Product Team 2006].
GG3.GP2 Collect Improvement Information	Organizational Process Definition Organizational Process Focus	Organizational Process Definition establishes the organizational process assets. Organizational Process Focus addresses the incorporation of experiences into the organizational process assets [CMMI Product Team 2006].

CHAPTER 6

USING CERT-RMM

There are many effective and appropriate ways for an organization to use CERT-RMM to guide, inform, or otherwise support improvements to its operational resilience management activities. For those familiar with process improvement, CERT-RMM can be used as the body of knowledge that supports model-based process improvement activities for operational resilience management processes. However, not all organizations embrace the term *process improvement* and instead are simply looking for a way to evaluate their performance or organize their practices. All of these uses of CERT-RMM are legitimate.

In this chapter, we briefly explore the ways in which an organization could use CERT-RMM and provide a broader understanding of the concepts that help an organization determine how to make use of CERT-RMM to meet its unique needs. Section 6.1 provides selected examples of how the model can be effectively used by an organization. One such example is to use CERT-RMM to support model-based process improvement, a process that is more fully described in Section 6.2. Section 6.3 details a number of decisions around the scope of a CERT-RMM-based improvement effort, such as the organizational scope (which business units are involved), the model scope (which process areas are included), and the capability level targets (selecting "performed," "managed," or "defined" as the target for each process area). Using the model as a basis for diagnosis can be accomplished in a variety of ways, ranging from a formal appraisal to an informal review, as described in Section 6.4. Gaps that may be revealed through diagnostic methods should be analyzed in consideration of the improvement objectives to make sure that closing the gaps would be of value to the organization. Part of planning improvements to existing practices or planning the implementation of new practices is to determine where in the organization the practices will be performed or instantiated. Gap analysis and implementation planning are discussed in Section 6.5.

6.1 Examples of CERT-RMM Uses

This section provides several examples of how CERT-RMM can be used. This is not a complete list, but it provides insight into how CERT-RMM can be applied to a broad set of challenges and objectives. The examples given describe using CERT-RMM to

- support the achievement of strategic and operational objectives
- evaluate, guide, and compare the implementation of resilience activities
- organize and structure the use of many codes of practice
- catalyze model-based process improvement

6.1.1 Supporting Strategic and Operational Objectives

CERT-RMM can be used as a source of guidance and information to support the achievement of specific objectives related to security, business continuity, IT operations, or managing operational risk in general. Organizational objectives that are directly or indirectly tied to resilience management activities can be strong drivers for CERT-RMM-based improvements.

Such objectives may be high-level and strategic. For example, consider an organization that sells various products both online and in its brick-and-mortar stores. The organization has established a strategic objective to increase the relative percentage of online sales by 25% over three years. Operational risk has been identified as a key constraint to the strategy—publicity associated with security breaches and downtime associated with business continuity failures could severely impede the achievement of the strategic objective. This organization can use CERT-RMM to guide the convergence and improvement of its security and business continuity processes to control and manage operational risks that could undermine achievement of this strategic objective.

Such objectives could also be more tactical. For example, consider an organization that recently suffered financial losses when information systems were offline following a security incident. Prior to the incident, warning signs were clear but had not been recognized. During the incident, confusion and ad hoc procedures resulted in longer downtime. The organization now understands that both its monitoring activities and its incident management activities have to be improved to avoid such losses in the future. CERT-RMM can be used to determine the degree of improvement necessary, guide these improvements, and measure the extent to which the improvements are institutionalized.

6.1.2 A Basis for Evaluation, Guidance, and Comparison

CERT-RMM is the codification of an extensive body of knowledge. It includes

- security practices and security management experience from CERT and other reputable organizations and thought leaders that have been developed based on years of work with public- and private-sector organizations on security improvement
- business continuity and disaster recovery expertise from numerous financial industry organizations whose survival is critically dependent on the maturity of these capabilities
- converged security, business continuity, and IT operations practices from numerous practice bodies and standards

Many professionals with responsibilities for their organization's operational resilience activities will find the model to be a useful basis to support the design, review, and comparison of such activities. Such guidance can be particularly useful when converging existing practices or when implementing new activities.

For example, consider an organization that has recently experienced an increase in access problems: employees with appropriate credentials have been unable to access certain systems and facilities. The team that has been assembled to diagnose the problem and propose improvements can use the Access Management (AM) and Identity Management (ID) process areas as reference sources for evaluating the current practices. If deficiencies are discovered, the model can be used as a source of guidance for improving practices or implementing new practices to address the issue.

Organizations and groups will also find the model to be a useful basis for characterizing, comparing, and learning from one another's practices. Diagnostic activities as described in Section 6.4.1 can be used as a basis for formal or informal comparisons among organizations of their respective implementation and institutionalization of resilience activities. Formal benchmarking can be a valuable activity for industry groups to evaluate their collective resilience posture or for the components of a large enterprise to ensure that the overall enterprise is similarly prepared. Informal comparisons can also provide insights and support information sharing among a group of organizations.

6.1.3 An Organizing Structure for Deployed Practices

Many organizations have implemented practices from best-practice bodies or standards related to security, business continuity, and IT operations. Sometimes, such organizations discover that these practices

- might not be providing the benefit that the organization expected
- may be performed less consistently than when first implemented
- might have eroded in their effectiveness because the organization has changed or the operational risk environment for the organization has changed

CERT-RMM can be used to guide the implementation of a process superstructure that will serve to refresh, institutionalize, integrate, streamline, and give purpose to the practices that have already been implemented. The concept of a "superstructure" is not meant to imply an additional layer of activities, though that might be appropriate in some organizations and in some circumstances. An effective and efficient process superstructure can be implemented by following the guidance in the model for converging the various operational risk management practices to ensure that they are based on common and consistent risk assumptions and that they are being performed to support organizational objectives.

The model can also be used to support the institutionalization of existing practices to ensure that they are reliably and consistently performed, especially during times of stress, and without dependence on specific people or operating parameters that may not be present during a time of stress.

6.1.4 Model-Based Process Improvement

By far, organizations will find CERT-RMM most beneficial for process improvement. The unique aspects of CERT-RMM—the process focus and the capability dimension—were developed to help organizations evolve to a more enlightened treatment of managing operational resilience and sustaining capabilities over the long run. Regardless of the scope of improvement—a single aspect of operational resilience such as incident management or a comprehensive and broad view that incorporates all 26 process areas—CERT-RMM was built to enable an organization to easily begin a process improvement approach.

6.2 Focusing CERT-RMM on Model-Based Process Improvement

Most process improvement efforts can be structured to answer some variation of the following four questions:

- How do I decide what to do and in what order?
- How do I do it?
- How do I know if what I did worked?
- How do I decide what to do next?

These four questions can be directly mapped to the Plan, Do, Check, Act (PDCA) cycle, which was based on W. Edwards Deming's Shewhart cycle [Deming 2000, Imai 1986]. Effective methods for improvement and management of change typically use some variation of this approach. This section starts with identifying the impetus or stimulus for change and making the business case to initiate a process improvement program. It then describes an effective process for initiating any organizational change. Specific considerations for CERT-RMM–based process improvement are described in Section 6.3.

6.2.1 Making the Business Case

In today's business climate, organizations are constantly dealing with the demand to do more with less. The resources required to run the business, let alone to invest in new initiatives, are always at a premium—time, money, staff expertise, information, technology, and facilities, not to mention energy and attention span. All investment decisions are about doing what is best for the organization (and its stakeholders). However, what is best is sometimes hard to define, hard to quantify, and even harder to defend when the demand for investment dollars exceeds the supply.

Business leaders are increasingly aware of the need to invest in operational resilience—to better prepare for and recover from disruptive events, to protect and sustain high-value services and supporting assets (information, technology, facilities, and people) that are essential to meet business objectives, and to satisfy compliance requirements. So how do we ensure that investments in operational resilience will increase our confidence that services will continue to meet their mission, even during times of stress and disruption? And by so doing, how are we able to justify such investments to senior managers?

Making the business case for operational resilience, and specifically for investing in the adoption of CERT-RMM processes, is accomplished by articulating the business need and showing how CERT-RMM meets it—in a tangible and measurable way over a reasonable period of time for an affordable cost with a positive return. A well-articulated business need is the driver and stimulus for change. In the context of operational risk, it is often the answer to the question, Where does it hurt the most, or what high-impact, high-loss event(s) would put us out of business? A key step in this process is to identify the senior manager who most cares about the answers to these questions and to make sure he or she is on board as the visible champion and sponsor of the CERT-RMM improvement program.

In addition, those making the case for operational resilience must be able to demonstrate that investments are subject to the same decision criteria as other business investments, so that they can be prioritized, evaluated, and traded off in a similar fashion. Again, this ties back to business mission, strategic objectives, and critical success factors, which are the basis for determining the high-value services that support the accomplishment of strategic objectives (refer to the Enterprise Focus process area). Protecting and sustaining high-value services is the name of the game.

Once the business need is agreed to and a decision is made to take action to meet it, what is needed next is a process for ensuring that the need is met.

6.2.2 A Process Improvement Process

In large part, process improvement is about managing change, whether intentional or unintentional (including change caused by a disruptive event). The SEI has adapted Deming's PDCA approach into a method for technology adoption and software process improvement called IDEAL. The IDEAL model is an organizational improvement model that serves as a roadmap for initiating, planning, and implementing improvement actions [McFeeley 1996]. It is named for the five phases it describes: initiating, diagnosing, establishing, acting, and learning, as shown in Figure 6.1.

The catalyst that causes an organization to execute IDEAL is described above: identifying a business need, making the case for meeting it, and using it as the impetus or stimulus for change. This can include an objective to be met (such as those noted in Section 6.1.1), unanticipated events or circumstances, a new compliance requirement, or a problem to be solved, such as a poor organizational response to a disruptive event or a security breach.

Critical groundwork is completed during the initiating phase. The business reasons for undertaking the improvement effort are clearly articulated. The effort's contributions to business goals and objectives are identified. The support of managers who will serve as visible sponsors and champions for the effort is

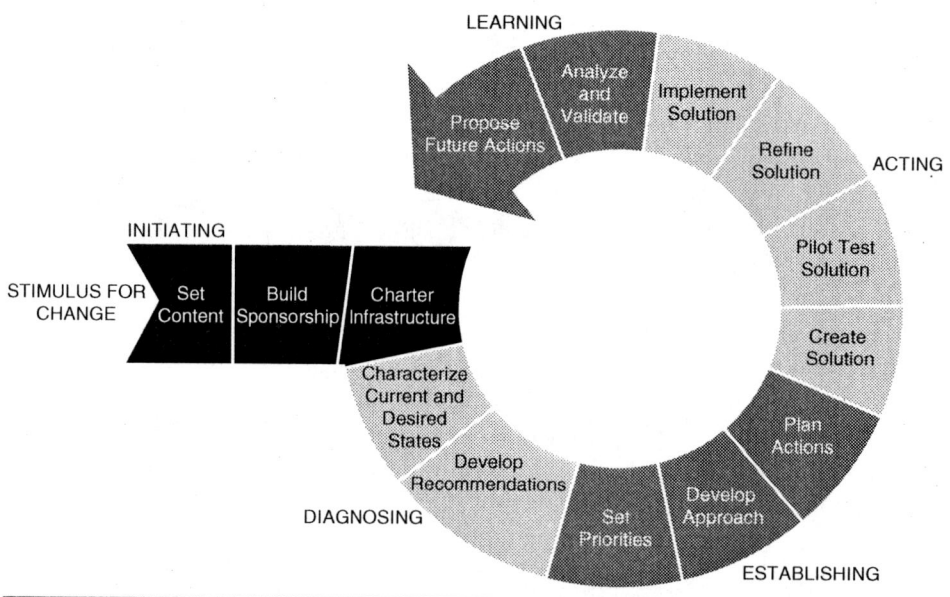

FIGURE 6.1
The IDEAL Model for Process Improvement

secured, and resources are allocated on an order-of-magnitude basis. Finally, an infrastructure for managing implementation details is put in place.

The diagnosing phase builds upon the initiating phase to develop a more complete understanding of the improvement effort. During the diagnosing phase, two characterizations of the organization are developed: the current state of the organization and the desired future state. These organizational states are used to develop an approach for improving business practice. The CERT-RMM capability appraisal is focused on the diagnosing phase of IDEAL. (See Section 6.4.1 for more details on the appraisal process.)

The purpose of the establishing phase is to develop a detailed work plan. Priorities are set that reflect the recommendations made during the diagnosing phase as well as the organization's broader operations and the constraints of its operating environment. Specific actions, milestones, deliverables, and responsibilities are incorporated into an action plan.

The activities of the acting phase help an organization implement the work that has been conceptualized and planned in the previous three phases. These activities will typically consume more calendar time and more resources than all of the other phases combined.

The learning phase completes the improvement cycle. One of the goals of the IDEAL model is to continuously improve the ability to implement change. In the learning phase, the entire IDEAL experience is reviewed to determine what was accomplished, whether the effort accomplished the intended goals, and how the organization can implement change more effectively and/or efficiently in the future. Records are kept throughout the IDEAL cycle with this phase in mind. These include CERT-RMM work products such as changes to resilience requirements, updates to service continuity plans, and incident reports.

As with any process improvement activity, some phases and activities such as those described for IDEAL are generic—they can be interpreted and applied with minimal customization based on the specific improvement initiative. Correspondingly, there are phases and activities that will require interpretation and tailoring when considering CERT-RMM in its entirety or when the focus of improvement is on specific process areas such as Incident Management and Control or Service Continuity. The remainder of this chapter describes some unique considerations or applications of the IDEAL model when using it as the basis for improving operational resilience management processes as defined in CERT-RMM.

6.3 Setting and Communicating Objectives Using CERT-RMM

A key element of any improvement effort is to establish and communicate clear improvement objectives. In addition to the stimulus for change or business objectives for change described in Section 6.1.1, objectives for a CERT-RMM–based improvement effort should include a clear delineation of scope. Scoping an improvement effort includes two key parts: the *organizational scope* and the *model scope*. The organizational scope is simply the part of the organization or an activity of the organization that is the focus of the improvement effort. Section 6.3.1 describes the elements and terminology of organizational scoping. The model scope is the designation of which parts of CERT-RMM will be used to guide the improvement effort. Section 6.3.2 provides information about how to establish a model scope and describes both coarse-grained and fine-grained scoping options that are available in CERT-RMM.

Most improvement efforts will include capability level targets for selected CERT-RMM process areas. Establishing such targets is an effective and efficient way to communicate the extent of process institutionalization that is desired for the organization. Section 6.3.3 provides information about establishing and communicating capability level targets.

When scoping an improvement effort or establishing capability level targets for an improvement effort, it is important to consider the following:

- **Organizational or strategic objectives**—Both the organizational scope and the model scope should be set in the context of the organizational or strategic objectives that are driving the change. Some parts of the organization might be more or less appropriate for inclusion in the scope based on such objectives. The parts of the model that are included in the model scope should be closely aligned to the overall objectives. Remember that the organizational or strategic objectives can be diverse—they can be as simple as improving sales or as complex as preventing further data breaches or denials of service.
- **Timing**—The scoping and objectives for an improvement effort may change over the course of time as a result of planned or unplanned changes to the organization or its operating environment. It may also be appropriate to establish a time-phased approach for both scope and objectives to ensure that the improvement effort is able to generate visible results quickly enough to be sustained (in other words, consider tackling low-hanging fruit to generate some quick wins to build momentum and support).
- **Regulatory mandates or industry initiatives**—Sometimes the driver for change comes from outside the organization in the form of a new regulatory mandate or industry initiative. In these cases, both the organizational scope and the model scope may be determined by the external driver. A phased approach that expands the organization and model scope over time may be appropriate to ensure that the approach for dealing with an external driver is consistent with and supports business objectives (versus being a compliance checklist exercise).
- **Sponsorship**—Scoping should always be established with a careful consideration of sponsorship. The organizational scope should generally be aligned to the

organizational reach or influence of the sponsor, and the model scope should generally be aligned to the responsibilities of the sponsor. It may also be appropriate to consider a phased approach to sponsorship in which successive layers of sponsorship are identified and secured as the scope of the effort increases over time.

For any improvement effort or CERT-RMM deployment, it may be appropriate or necessary to iterate the selection of organizational scope, model scope, and capability level targets in order to optimize them to the objectives and sponsorship for the improvement.

6.3.1 Organizational Scope

The organizational scope is the part of the organization that is the focus of the CERT-RMM deployment. In broad terms, the organizational scope should be bounded so that there are clear lines drawn for what is included in the improvement activities. This section presents some language and conventions that can be used to establish and describe the organizational scope.

The simplest scheme for organizational scoping is to focus on an explicit part of the organization. However, an organization may choose to bound the improvement effort around a specific system (such as the payroll system), a network, or a specific service, or according to another convention that is consistent with the improvement objectives. For example, an organization that had a data breach of a classified system might bound the improvement effort around that system. Thus, the effort would focus on the services provided by the system (which must meet their mission consistently) and the assets related to the system. The effort might also include the organizational units that have responsibility for managing the system and ensuring its resilience.

CERT-RMM has a strong enterprise undertone. This is because effective operational resilience management requires capabilities that often have enterprise-wide significance, such as risk management. However, the enterprise nature of CERT-RMM should not be interpreted to mean that it must be adopted or applied at an enterprise level. On the contrary, CERT-RMM can be most effective when applied to a well-defined organizational scope and where enterprise influences can be measured.

The following terms can be used to describe the organizational scope and will be used in Section 6.5 to describe planning issues associated with CERT-RMM deployment:

- **Organizational unit**—a distinct subset of an organization or enterprise. Typically, the organizational unit is a segment or layer of the organizational structure that may be clearly designated by drawing a box around part of the organization chart.

- **Organizational subunit**—any sub-element of an organizational unit. An organizational subunit is fully contained within the organizational unit.
- **Organizational superunit**—any part of an organization that is at a higher level than the organizational unit.

The organizational scope is established by clearly identifying one or more organizational units that will be the focus of the improvement.

Figure 6.2 shows the typical relationships among organizational unit, organizational subunit, and organizational superunit on a generic organization chart. In this example, the organizational unit is defined as a specific segment of the organization as shown on the organization chart with multiple subunits. In this example, the term *organizational superunit* can be used to refer to element 1 on the organization chart, as shown; it can also be used to refer to the entire organization.

For some improvement objectives, it may be optimal to designate an organizational unit that comprises all of the parts of the organization that are directly involved in the delivery of a specific service or that are responsible for a specific system. On an organization chart, such an organizational unit would be indicated by selecting the various elements of the organization that are responsible for the service, as shown in Figure 6.3. In this case, the term *organizational subunit* is less meaningful but could still be used to refer to elements such as 1.1.2 or 1.3.3.1. The term *organizational superunit* can be used to refer to element 1 or to the entire organization.

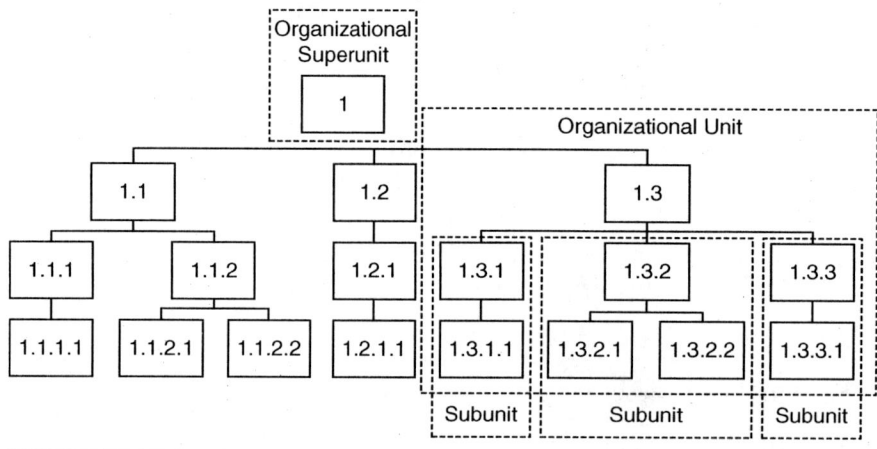

FIGURE 6.2
Organizational Unit, Subunit, and Superunit on an Organization Chart

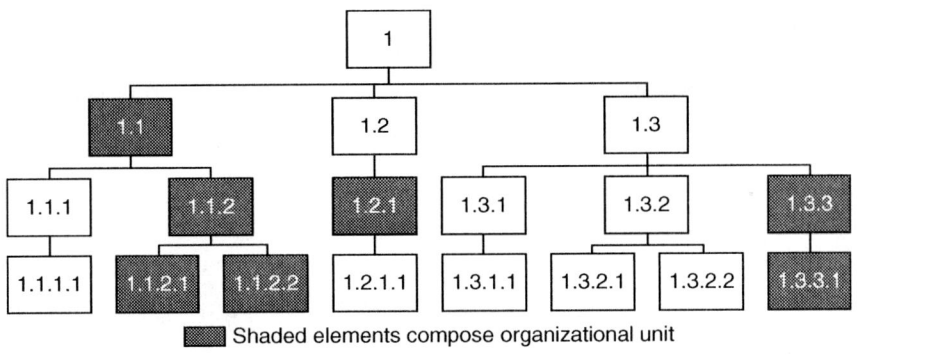

FIGURE 6.3
Alternate Organizational Unit Designation on an Organization Chart

6.3.2 Model Scope

The model scope represents the parts of CERT-RMM that will be used to guide the improvement effort. In other words, the model scope specifies which parts of the model will be deployed in the organizational units that compose the organizational scope.

The model scope is determined by selecting specific CERT-RMM process areas. Process areas should be chosen based on the objectives and business case for the improvement effort and in consideration of the other factors described above such as timing, regulatory mandates, and sponsorship.

For example, the organization described in the first example in Section 6.1.1 might choose the following process areas as its initial model scope to help manage operational risk in support of its online sales growth objective:

- Service Continuity (SC)—to ensure that business continuity practices are adequate to sustain the operation of its online sales infrastructure
- Knowledge and Information Management (KIM)—to improve the protection of customer information
- Risk Management (RISK)—to establish common guidelines for risk tolerance and procedures to evaluate and mitigate identified risks in a consistent manner
- Communications (COMM)—to institute procedures and guidelines for communications that will support the organization's objective to preserve customer confidence even during times of stress

Similarly, the organization described in Section 6.1.1 as having suffered financial losses due to a security incident might choose the following process areas as its model scope to facilitate improvements to its incident management process and to implement more effective monitoring capabilities:

- Incident Management and Control (IMC)—to ensure that appropriate practices are institutionalized to support incident response
- Monitoring (MON)—to consistently instrument and monitor its operational environment so that potential threats can be identified early

Both example organizations might choose additional process areas in later phases of an improvement effort or might identify additional needs resulting from implementing improvements in these initial process areas.

There are no firm rules about the minimum or maximum number of process areas that should be selected to include in the model scope. Care should be taken to select as many process areas as needed to achieve the objectives, but few enough that progress can be demonstrated in a reasonable time frame for the sponsor and key stakeholders. If the objectives require a large number of process areas, then a time-phased approach should be considered.

6.3.2.1 Targeted Improvement Roadmaps

Targeted improvement roadmap (TIR) is a term that is used to designate a specific collection of CERT-RMM process areas that serve a particular improvement objective. An organization could declare a TIR to represent its unique objectives for managing operational resilience, or it might use a TIR that was designed by another organization or group. Industry groups might establish TIRs to represent their specific operational resilience concerns or to address an industry initiative or new regulatory mandate. Also, an organization could establish TIRs for specific tiers of suppliers or external dependencies and use the TIRs to support the evaluation, selection, and monitoring of those entities. Appendix B contains several example TIRs.

In some cases, it may be appropriate to establish a finer-grained model scope than can be set by choosing entire process areas. CERT-RMM provides for several fine-grained scoping options that can be used in such cases, as described below.

6.3.2.2 Practice-Level Scope

Practice-level scope enables the model scope to be limited to selected specific and generic practices within a process area. This option does not have to be applied to all process areas when establishing the model scope, but it may be appropriate for one or more process areas to address specific improvement needs or concerns. This scoping option may be useful in the early phases of an improvement effort, in response to very narrow improvement objectives, or to be consistent with the span of influence of the improvement sponsor.

For example, suppose that an organization's improvement objective is focused narrowly on information technology disaster recovery activities. From the Knowledge and Information Management (KIM) process area, the organization might choose to include only specific practices KIM:SG5.SP3, Verify Validity of Information, and KIM:SG6.SP1, Perform Information Duplication and Retention, because it is concerned about its information backup practices and about ensuring the validity of information assets that will be used during disaster recovery operations.

6.3.2.3 Asset Scope

Because CERT-RMM addresses four asset types—people, information, technology, and facilities—the scope of the improvement effort could be focused on one or more process areas that could be tailored to focus on one or more asset types. For example, if the Asset Definition and Management process area is chosen, the scope of application of this process area could be limited to the "information" asset. Some process areas are already bound by an asset scope. These include Human Resource Management and People Management (people), Knowledge and Information Management (information), Technology Management (software, systems, and hardware), and Environmental Control (facilities). This option may be useful based on certain improvement objectives, a phased improvement strategy, or to tailor the model scope to best fit the span of influence of the improvement sponsor.

For example, an organization may limit the asset scope for phase 1 of a multi-phased improvement project to information and technology assets only. This is consistent with the span of influence of the improvement sponsor and with the immediate organizational objective related to improving information security. If the model scope for the improvement project includes the Asset Definition and Management (ADM) process area, for phase 1 of the effort, ADM will be applied to information and technology assets only.

6.3.2.4 Resilience Scope

CERT-RMM addresses the convergence of three broad categories of operational resilience management activities: security, business continuity, and IT operations. Resilience scope is an option that limits one or more process areas to a subset of these resilience activities. This scoping option is useful in organizations where convergence of these activities is not yet occurring or where convergence is an organizational objective.

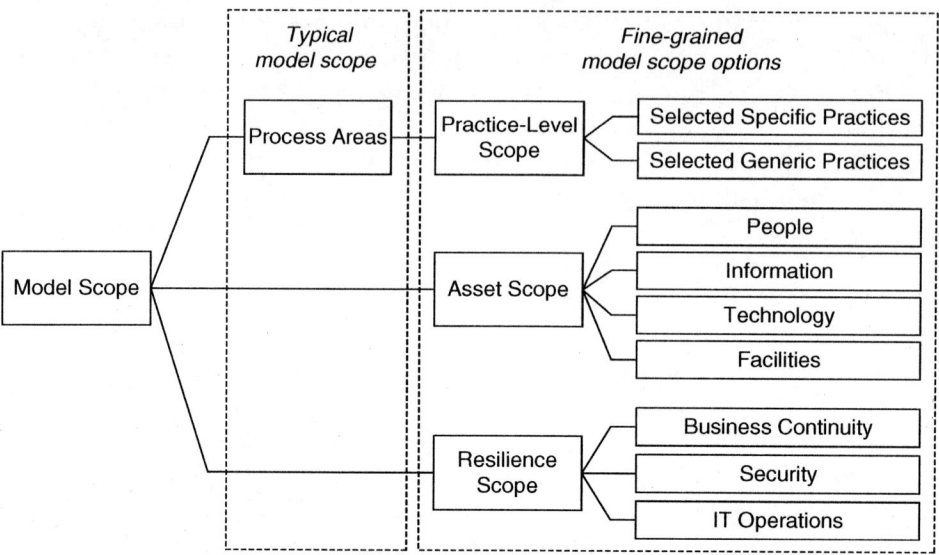

FIGURE 6.4
Model Scope Options

For example, an organization in which business continuity, security, and IT operations activities are still compartmentalized may initiate an improvement effort that is sponsored by the information security manager. The organization can use the resilience scope option to limit the interpretation of selected process areas so that they apply to security activities only. If the model scope includes the Compliance (COMP) process area, for example, it would be interpreted to apply exclusively to *security-related* compliance obligations.

Figure 6.4 shows the relationship of the four model scope options.

6.3.3 Capability Level Targets

Capability levels are used in the model to describe the achievement of the generic goals in a process area and are a measure of the extent to which a process area has been institutionalized (performed, managed, defined) by the organization (refer to Section 5.2). Establishing capability level targets is an important element in all CERT-RMM-based improvement efforts.

When establishing capability level targets, the organization should consider the importance of the generic practices relative to the organization's risk tolerance, threat environment, size, improvement time frame, and improvement objectives. It may be valuable to review the generic goals and generic practices and envision what the implementation of those practices and the achievement of those goals would look like for the organization during normal operations and during times of stress. Capability level targets should be established for each process area and need not be the same. Capability level 1 (performed) may be completely appropriate for a process area, even if capability level 3 (defined) is the established target for another process area in the model scope. The capability level descriptions in Section 5.3 are valuable reference material for the selection of capability level targets.

6.3.3.1 Targeted Improvement Profile

Capability level targets can be efficiently communicated in a targeted improvement profile (TIP), which is typically represented as a bar chart showing the capability level target for each process area in the model scope. Figure 6.5 provides an example of a TIP for five process areas. Figure 6.6 provides another TIP example in which fine-grained scoping options have been selected for several of the process areas. A targeted improvement profile may be integrated with a targeted improvement roadmap. In this case, the TIR may include not only the process areas selected for a specific objective, but also the TIP, which describes the capability levels that must be achieved in each process area.

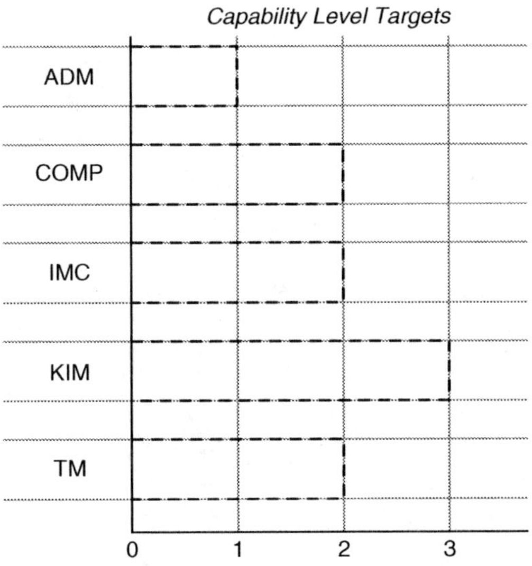

FIGURE 6.5
CERT-RMM Targeted Improvement Profile

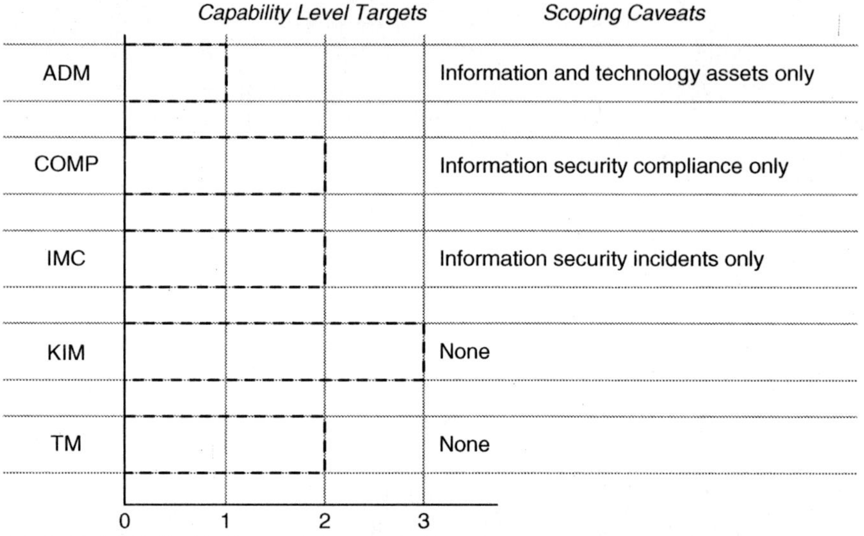

FIGURE 6.6
CERT-RMM Targeted Improvement Profile with Scope Caveats

The next section describes diagnostic methods that can be used to evaluate an organization to determine whether the capability level targets are being achieved.

6.4 Diagnosing Based on CERT-RMM

Diagnosing based on CERT-RMM is the process by which the model is used as a basis to evaluate the organization's current resilience practices. Diagnosing can be performed formally or informally, as described in the following sections.

6.4.1 Formal Diagnosis Using the CERT-RMM Capability Appraisal Method

Formal diagnosis based on CERT-RMM is performed using the CERT-RMM Capability Appraisal Method (CAM). The CERT-RMM CAM is based on the Standard CMMI Appraisal Method for Process Improvement (SCAMPI), which has been used effectively by the CMMI community for many years [SCAMPI Upgrade Team 2006]. Similar to SCAMPI, three classes of CERT-RMM capability appraisals are available—A, B, and C—all of which are compliant with the Appraisal Requirements for CMMI (ARC) v1.2.

The class A appraisal is the most rigorous and the only one of the three methods that provides official capability level ratings. The class B appraisal has more tailoring options than class A and results in the characterization of implemented practices in the organization according to a three-point scale. Class C is even more

TABLE 6.1 Classes of Formal CERT-RMM Capability Appraisals

Characteristic	Class A	Class B	Class C
Depth of investigation	High	Medium	Low
Objective evidence requirements	High	Medium	Low
Results provided	Capability level ratings and goal satisfaction ratings	Characterization of practice implementations on a three-point scale	Characterization of planned or intended practices on a flexible scale
Appraisal team size	4 or more	2 or more	1 or more
Allowed tailoring	Low	Medium	High
Resource requirements	High	Medium	Low

tailorable and can be used to evaluate planned approaches to practice implementation. Some distinctions among the three methods are provided in Table 6.1.[1]

An organization might choose a class A appraisal because it desires a rigorous examination of implemented practices that produces a rating to acknowledge or memorialize its starting point or results for an improvement project. Class A appraisals are also useful when two or more organizations are to be compared, which might be useful to evaluate different parts of a large enterprise, for example.

At the other end of the spectrum, class C appraisals are fairly lightweight and can be flexibly used to evaluate planned implementations of practices or for a less rigorous examination of implemented practices. Large organizations might choose class C appraisals to evaluate the intent of organizational policies and guidelines relative to the model. This can be an effective and efficient way to evaluate whether the resilience policies and guidelines in a large enterprise would, if followed, produce the practices that are expected in the model.

Scoping an appraisal is an important activity in planning the appraisal. The same considerations for scoping an improvement project (as described in Section 6.3.1) are used in scoping an appraisal activity. The scope of an appraisal is typically the same as the scope of the improvement effort. However, it is not required that the scope of the appraisal or other diagnostic process match the scope of the overall improvement effort. In some cases, it may be efficient to diagnose at the organizational subunit level.

Capability level ratings from class A appraisals can be shown as an overlay on the TIP diagram to clearly indicate gaps between the desired and current states,

---

1. For more on appraisal classes, see www.sei.cmu.edu/cmmi/tools/appraisals/classes.cfm.

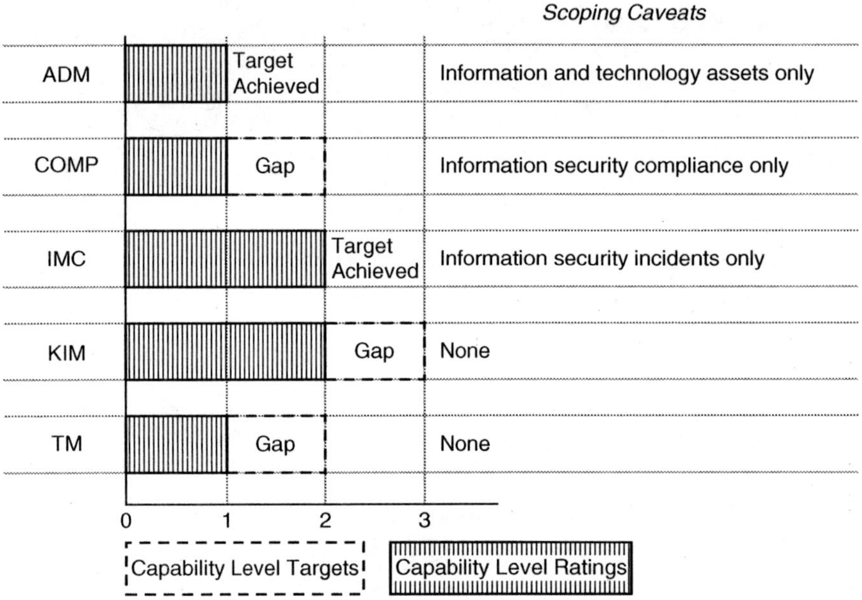

FIGURE 6.7
Capability Level Ratings Overlaid on Targeted Improvement Profile

as shown in Figure 6.7. Section 6.5 provides information about analyzing and using the gaps that are identified through diagnostic activities as input to planning improvements for an organization.

Appraisal results can be an important diagnostic input to inform the starting point or results of an improvement effort. Informal diagnoses can also be useful, as described in the following section.

6.4.2 Informal Diagnosis

Informal diagnosis based on CERT-RMM includes any methods, other than the formal appraisals described above, that are used to compare the organization's practices to the guidance in CERT-RMM. Examples of informal diagnosis methods include

- meetings or tabletop exercises in which the people who are responsible for the practices in a given process area come together, review the model guidance, and discuss the extent to which the organization's practices achieve the model intent
- reviews or analyses, supported by written reports, performed by a single person or a small group to compare the organization's practices to the model guidance
- informal collection and review of evidence that demonstrates whether the organization is performing the model practices

In all cases, the outcomes of such diagnoses are informal findings related to the organization's performance as compared to the model guidance. Such activities can be useful to guide informal process improvement activities or to provide information for scoping or setting capability level targets for a more formal process improvement project. Informal reviews can also be useful when the model is being used as a basis for evaluation as described in Section 6.1.2.

Both formal and informal diagnostic activities provide valuable input for planning an improvement activity. Additional considerations for planning improvement activities are described in the next section.

6.5 Planning CERT-RMM–Based Improvements

When planning a CERT-RMM deployment, analyzing gaps and determining where various practices should be optimally implemented in the organization are key activities. CERT-RMM–specific considerations related to those activities are addressed in this section.

6.5.1 Analyzing Gaps

Diagnostic activities typically reveal gaps between current and desired performance. Such gaps are necessary input to planning improvements for an organization. However, before plans are established to close any gaps that are revealed, it is important to reconsider the identified gaps in light of the overall improvement objectives. The following questions may be useful in analyzing and prioritizing the gaps in support of the improvement planning process:

- Will closing a gap support the improvement objective?
- Is the cost of closing a gap justifiable in light of the improvement objective?
- Which of the identified gaps are most important to close first?
- Can the gap be closed in one improvement iteration, or should a phased approach be deployed?

If it is determined that one or more of the identified gaps are acceptable and will not be closed, it may be appropriate to revisit and revise the objectives for the improvement activity. This iterative approach is valuable to ensure that the organization is spending improvement resources in the most productive manner. For example, if the organization chose to focus improvement efforts on a recent data breach, analyzing gaps can help the organization to prioritize improvement activities to maximize outcome at the lowest cost.

6.5.2 Planning Practice Instantiation

Part of planning improvements to existing practices or planning the implementation of new practices is to determine where in the organization the practices will be performed or instantiated. The terms *organizational unit*, *superunit*, and *subunit* (see Section 6.3.1) can be valuable in describing where a particular practice is to be performed in relation to the organizational scope for the improvement campaign.

Most organizations will find that different practices within a single CERT-RMM process area may be optimally performed at different levels in the organization. For example, in the Service Continuity (SC) process area, a large organization might choose to implement specific practice SC:SG1.SP2, Establish Standards and Guidelines for Service Continuity, at a very high level in the organization so that consistent standards and guidelines are established and deployed across the organization. The same organization might choose to implement specific practice SC:SG3.SP2, Develop and Document Service Continuity Plans, at a much lower level in the organization.

If the immediate or long-term improvement objective for a given process area is to achieve capability level 3, planning should include the determination of where the organizational process assets will reside. (This can be done using OPD:SG1.SP3, Establish the Organization's Measurement Repository, and GG3, Institutionalize a Defined Process.) If the long-term plan includes a larger organizational scope than the immediate plan, then the optimal location for the organizational process assets might be different from what would be indicated by the immediate plan. Strategic consideration should be given to this issue to avoid unnecessary rework in future improvement phases. For example, Figure 6.8 shows two alternative locations for the organizational process assets in an organization. If the organization never plans to deploy CERT-RMM beyond the organizational unit shown in the figure, then either location for the organizational process assets will suffice. Suppose, however, that the organization ultimately plans to deploy CERT-RMM to the units designated by 1.1 and 1.2; in this case, the organizational process assets should be located at the highest level in the organization.

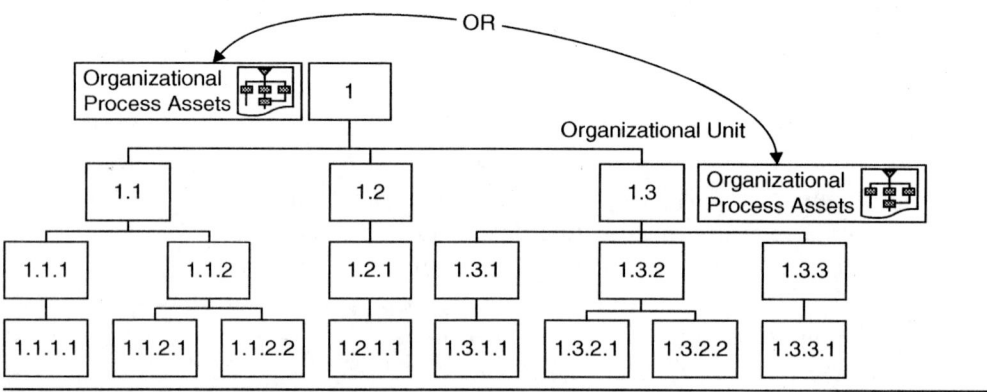

FIGURE 6.8
Alternate Locations for Organizational Process Assets

CERT-RMM is agile and flexible enough to support a wide range of improvement activities in an organization. The key to any successful improvement effort is to understand the objectives and to design the improvement activity to accomplish those objectives. Fine-grained scoping options are available in CERT-RMM to enable an organization to optimize the organization and model scope for an improvement. Formal and informal methods for diagnosis and comparison are available to use the model as a basis for evaluation and gap identification.

CHAPTER 7

CERT-RMM PERSPECTIVES

This chapter consists of short essays written by invited contributing authors. The essays discuss how CERT-RMM can be applied for different purposes and, in one case, how CERT-RMM's "tires" were kicked to see how it could be used to help improve an existing program.

Unfortunately, there are a lot of stories that cannot be told in this chapter. This is because when organizations use CERT-RMM for benchmarking, appraisal, or improvement purposes, their experiences often tell a story that can expose their weaknesses or conversely make them a target. For example, an organization that reports a low level of capability in incident management as a result of using the model may be exposing a significant weakness in its security posture; an organization performing at a high level of capability in this area may be inviting unwanted "tests" of its resilience.

For this reason, the authors have decided not to develop and publish case studies on CERT-RMM adoption or use. While this denies potential users informative material to help their adoption process, it is also indicative of the level of valuable information attained by users of the model for helping them improve and reinforce their security, continuity, and IT operations management processes.

Using CERT-RMM in the Utility Sector

By Darren Highfill and James Stevens

Author comments: Darren Highfill is a security architect for the electric utility industry focused on emergent technologies and new problem domains. Darren is the chair of the SG-Security Working Group within the UCA International Users Group[1] and serves as the

Continues

---

1. The UCA International Users Group is a not-for-profit corporation consisting of utility user and supplier companies that is dedicated to promoting the integration and interoperability of electric/gas/water utility systems through the use of international standards-based technology.

technical lead for the Advanced Security Acceleration Project for the Smart Grid (ASAP-SG). James Stevens is a senior member of the Technical Staff at the Software Engineering Institute (SEI) and has been working in the SEI's CERT Program for over 15 years. James is currently the technical lead for the SEI's Smart Grid Maturity Model project, an implementation model used by utilities to support strategic planning and goal setting for grid modernization. James and Darren have been working together on the ASAP-SG Architectural Team for the past year developing security guidelines for smart grid systems. Here, they look at some of the notable challenges currently facing the electric power sector and discuss how a model like CERT-RMM might help address some of these issues.

Reliability and Resilience

Every industry has its own vocabulary, and the electric power industry is no different. These unique vocabularies facilitate communication between industry members but can sometimes act as roadblocks when translating ideas between groups outside of a particular industry. The usage of the words *reliability* and *resilience* in the electric power industry present a potential roadblock for that sector in embracing a model for improving operational resilience such as CERT-RMM. The term *reliability* has a strong definition reinforced by regulatory structure. The term *resilience*, on the other hand, is not one that has significant resonance in this domain, although the generic concept is gaining some traction.

Effective transition of CERT-RMM to the stakeholders in this domain requires an understanding of the relationship between the concepts of reliability and resilience. This requires determining whether the concepts of reliability and resilience are equivalent and, if not, defining the relationship between them. Perhaps the best place to start is to look at how the terms are defined by their stakeholders. The North American Electric Reliability Corporation[2] (NERC) defines reliability in terms of adequacy and security:

- *adequacy*—the ability of the bulk power system to supply the aggregate electrical demand and energy requirements of customers at all times, taking into account scheduled and reasonably expected unscheduled outages of system elements
- *security*—the ability of the bulk power system to withstand sudden disturbances such as electric short circuits or unanticipated loss of system elements from credible contingencies

CERT-RMM defines resilience as "the emergent property of an organization that can continue to carry out its mission after disruption that does not exceed its operational limit."[3]

---

2. NERC is an international, independent, self-regulatory, not-for-profit organization whose mission is to ensure the reliability of the bulk power system in North America.
3. Adapted from a WordNet definition of *resilience* at http://wordnetweb.princeton.edu/perl/webwn?s=resilience.

The definitions contain significant conceptual overlap; both require the protection and sustainment of a mission in the face of disruption. The definition of reliability perhaps goes slightly beyond the concept of resilience as defined by CERT-RMM, identifying the capacity for the system to provide electrical power based on demand. There is certainly enough conceptual overlap between the definitions that we do not think there would be much argument with the idea that a resilient system is more reliable than a system that is not resilient, nor with the idea that a system cannot be reliable unless it is resilient. It is probably not correct, however, to say that a resilient system is a reliable system, in the terms used by the power industry.

Resilience, however, is fundamental to reliability. This leads us to the conclusion that resilient operations are a necessity for the reliable operation of the electrical infrastructure. The bulk electric system will not be reliable if all of its supporting operations are not resilient. The focus of CERT-RMM, of course, is on understanding and improving operational resilience, and therefore it is potentially an important tool for a utility looking to ensure reliability of operations.

Regulation and Peer Pressure

The electric grid is a fundamental enabler of our nation's economy and is recognized as an element of the nation's critical infrastructure. Increasingly, our nation's and the world's electric infrastructure is becoming reliant upon distributed intelligence and communications capabilities as the grid continues to grow smarter. With these dependencies comes recognition of the need to protect the electrical infrastructure from not only physical but also cyber attack.

The United States faces a number of structural challenges to ensuring the adequate protection of its electrical infrastructure. One of the more significant challenges is that no single organization controls the operation of the electrical grid. The sector is made up of a number of public and private organizations, all of which must coordinate with the others to ensure the successful delivery of electric power to the customer. While the power system has been engineered to be reliable with outage events that are few and far between, the system is only as reliable as its weakest links. The failure in any one organization under the right circumstances can lead quickly to much larger impacts, as the blackout of August 2003 so kindly reminded us.

On January 17, 2008, the Federal Energy Regulatory Commission (FERC) took a number of steps that it hoped would increase the level of the cyber security and therefore the reliability in the Bulk Electric System (BES).[4] FERC

---

4. The Bulk Electric System is generally considered to be the generation and transmission of electricity over high-voltage transmission lines.

mandated compliance with eight Critical Infrastructure Protection (CIP) Reliability Standards developed by NERC. The fines for non-compliance with these standards can exceed over $1 million a day.

While most agree that the NERC CIP standards are a step in the right direction, significant debate continues as to whether standards alone are sufficient for ensuring the reliability of the grid. Requiring adherence to a standard can certainly raise the bar of practice within the sector, but ultimately all that can be measured is an organization's adherence to the standard. It also often shifts an organization's focus from managing its cyber security risks to managing compliance and the associated documentation. This focus can lead to a misapplication of limited organizational resources. Moreover, organizations may find themselves investing in technologies and other resources that help them maintain compliance instead of focusing on things that will help them manage their cyber security risks. This misdirection of resources can also incentivize organizations to take steps to avoid compliance requirements. Such behavior has already been seen with the NERC CIP standards, as some utilities have gone so far as to declare they have no critical cyber assets.

Mandatory standards are often necessary to raise the bar of a community, but caution is in order to avoid a "set it and forget it" mentality, which in many cases may be even more dangerous. Furthermore, the issues of compliance and the level of effort required to support audit are receiving increasing criticism.[5]

Utilities like nothing better than to simultaneously impress rate payers, utility commissions, shareholders, and regulators. Establishment of a common set of metrics for the electric utility industry would provide a means to do just that while also demonstrating satisfaction of the key criteria for NERC. CERT-RMM provides a metrics-driven method through which the electric utility community can view adequacy and reliability. For example, consider a simple subset of CERT-RMM process areas that address how an organization manages operational risk. These process areas might include

- Risk Management (RISK), to determine how operational risks are being identified, analyzed, and mitigated, and how the risk process is being managed
- Controls Management (CTRL), to determine how operational controls to protect and sustain infrastructure are being identified, implemented, managed, and continuously monitored
- Service Continuity (SC), to determine how service continuity is planned, tested, implemented, and improved as the infrastructure changes and the risk environment changes

---

5. "SANS Founder Slams 'Terribly Damaging' US Cyber Security Law," www.computerweekly.com/Articles/2010/03/25/240719/Sans-founder-slams-39terribly-damaging39-US-cyber-security.htm.

Not only can determining the degree to which organizations that share the common bond of providing reliable electric service have matured their processes in these areas inform us about the strength of the reliability and resilience of the electric system, but individual operators would be able to do compensatory planning for interconnections with organizations that do not exhibit high levels of capability in these core processes. In other words, the "metric" can inform an organization about which organizations are the weaker links, enabling them to plan for addressing these weaknesses when necessary. In the end, the electric generation and transmission system benefits as a whole when all organizations raise their capabilities.

At the end of the day, what we all care about is that utilities are capable of managing their cyber security risks. Instead of providing a list of proscriptive controls with which a utility must comply ("one size fits all"), utilities would have the opportunity to demonstrate cyber security risk management capabilities. Use of CERT-RMM metrics would allow organizations to expend their energies on productive security measures and potentially obviate the need to spend so much effort on compliance and auditing.

Grid Modernization and Transformation

The energy delivery infrastructure in the United States and in much of the rest of the world is at the beginning of a significant modernization effort that will transform it from an aging analog technology base to a "smart grid" in which there is pervasive use of digital technology. This will enable features such as demand-side management, distributed generation, real-time pricing, and many others. As the infrastructure becomes increasingly dependent upon digital technologies for monitoring and control, requirements must likewise increase to ensure the resilient operations of the digital technology infrastructure.

A lot of work has been done to address the security, IT operations, and continuity issues for the digital technologies (technology assets, in CERT-RMM–speak) that are being deployed in the name of grid modernization, and it is recognized that much work remains to be done. In fact, both authors of this essay are involved in a number of efforts to help ensure the security and sustainability of technologies that will implement the smart grid. That being said, the ability of an organization to ensure the security and sustainability of these systems over time and with a reliable degree of predictability, particularly during times of stress, has not received sufficient attention at the community level, in the authors' opinion.

CERT-RMM was built to help organizations improve their capability for managing operational resilience and therefore reliability. It provides a unique platform for an organization to identify, understand, and improve the organizational processes that support its operational resilience. By using CERT-RMM's guidance for measuring current competencies across the entire scope of their resilience processes (security, IT operations, and business continuity), electric service organizations can understand their current state and identify a baseline for future evaluations. They can also use this guidance to set improvement targets and to establish plans for closing any gaps it identifies.

Grid modernization presents a unique opportunity for the electricity delivery infrastructure to embrace models such as CERT-RMM. Fully instantiating a process improvement model typically runs into organizational barriers that include issues such as the inability of the current organizational structure to support the necessary changes and the lack of funding resources. However, grid modernization is bringing significant changes to the organizational structures traditionally found in the utility space. We are seeing this today as organizations adapt and evolve to embrace and manage the new opportunities being created. The inclusion of process improvement efforts for resilient operations at the start of a project reduces the barriers to entry. The ability of the effort to be seen as an organizational investment and not as a costly commitment provides an opportunity to leverage support from senior managers. Smart grid projects are likely to lead to significant organizational change and will require support from senior managers. If the organization includes process improvement from the outset, senior managers' support can ideally be leveraged as the organization changes.

Grid Modernization

The transformation to a smart grid will require changes not only to the structure of the electric power grid and to operational processes within electric utilities but also to the relationships between and among the electricity providers, consumers, and regulators. This grid modernization provides us with an excellent opportunity to examine, enhance, and perhaps enrich all of these relationships.

Addressing Resilience as a Key Aspect of Software Assurance Throughout the Software Life Cycle

By Julia Allen and Michele Moss

Author comments: Julia Allen is a senior researcher in the CERT Program at the Software Engineering Institute (SEI), a unit of Carnegie Mellon University in Pittsburgh, Pennsylvania. Allen's areas of interest include enterprise security governance, operational resilience, and software security and assurance. Julia is the author of The CERT Guide to System and Network Security Practices *(Addison-Wesley, 2001), the* CERT Podcast Series *Security for Business Leaders, and the CERT governance portal. She is a coauthor of* Software Security Engineering: A Guide for Project Managers *(Addison-Wesley, 2008) and a contributing author to the CERT Resilience Management Model. Michele Moss, an industry-recognized thought leader in the integration and benchmarking of assurance practices, led the development of the Assurance Process Reference Model for CMMI. She is the cochair of the DHS Software Assurance Working Group on Processes and Practices and a member of the U.S. Technical Advisory Group for ISO/IEC JTC1/SC7. As part of Booz Allen Hamilton's security governance service area, she leads the Software Assurance Governance Capability and has responsibility for continuously improving the integration of mission and information assurance into IT processes and practices.*

Software assurance is defined as "the level of confidence that software is free from vulnerabilities, either intentionally designed into the software or accidentally inserted at any time during its life cycle, and that the software functions in the intended manner" [CNSS 2009].

In CERT's work to develop a Master of Software Assurance curriculum, this definition is extended as follows:

Application of technologies and processes to achieve a required level of confidence that software systems and services function in the intended manner, are free from accidental or intentional vulnerabilities, provide security capabilities appropriate to the threat environment, and recover from intrusions and failures [Mead 2010].

Operational resilience is defined as "the organization's ability to adapt to changing operational risk environments," and *operational resilience management* is defined as "the process by which an organization designs, develops, implements, and manages the protection and sustainment of high-value services, related business processes, and associated assets such as people, information, technology, and facilities" [Caralli 2010].

Managing operational resilience is the focus of CERT-RMM. In comparing the definitions and intent, the connections and overlaps between software assurance and resilience become obvious when developing, acquiring, and operating software applications and software systems, two of the high-value technology assets addressed in CERT-RMM. Software cannot meet assurance requirements (security, safety, and reliability) if it is not resilient in the face of stress and disruption, including attack. Resilient software functions in the intended manner in the face of adversity, resists threats, provides features that support critical services when disrupted (sometimes in degraded mode), recovers from intrusions and failures, and is able to be restored to its pre-disruption state[6] in a reasonable period of time.[7] These are all quality attributes of assured and secure software.

---

6. In business continuity parlance, this is referred to as the "recovery point objective."
7. And this is referred to as the "recovery time objective."

Resilient software and systems do not become survivable and resistant to threat (that is, assured) without an organizational commitment to address resilience as part of assurance throughout development, acquisition, and operations life-cycle phases. These assets must be specifically designed, developed, and acquired with consideration of the types of threats they will face, the operating conditions and changing risk environment in which they will operate, and the priority and sustainment needs of the services they support. Typical software and system development and acquisition life cycles understandably focus on identifying and satisfying functional requirements; that is, most of the effort goes into defining what the software or system must do to fulfill its use case, purpose, objectives, and, ultimately, its mission. However, quality attributes such as security, sustainability, availability, performance, and reliability can in the long run be equally important to the usability and longevity of software and system assets and require considerable resources to address in the operations phase if they are not considered early in the development and acquisition life cycles.

Unfortunately, requirements for quality attributes such as assurance and resilience can be harder to define, design, and implement, and in many cases they require significant business impact and cost analysis up front to ensure that they are worth investing in. This leads to a tendency to ignore these requirements early in the development and acquisition life cycles and to bolt on solutions to address them in later life-cycle phases, when they are more costly, less effective, and typically harder to manage and sustain in an operational mode. The failure to consider quality attributes is a primary reason why software and systems in operation are subject to high levels of operational risk resulting from failed technology and processes. In essence, ignoring quality attributes creates additional security, continuity, and other related operational risks that must be managed in the operations phase of the life cycle, typically at higher cost, lower efficacy, and potentially increased consequences to the organization. In some cases, these problems may be so significant as to shorten the expected life of the software and systems, diminish the organization's confidence in their ability to perform, and result in cumulatively lower than expected return on investment.

As an element of software assurance, developing and acquiring resilient software and systems requires a dedicated process that encompasses the asset's life cycle. As described in CERT-RMM's Resilient Technical Solution Engineering (RTSE) process area, the process is as follows:

- Establish a plan for addressing resilience as part of the organization's (or supplier's) regular development life cycle and integrate the plan into the organization's corresponding development process. Plan development and execution include identifying and mitigating risks to the success of the project.
- Identify practice-based guidelines, such as threat analysis and modeling, that apply to all phases, as well as those that apply to a specific life-cycle phase.

- Elicit, identify, develop, and validate assurance and resilience requirements (using methods for representing attacker and defender perspectives, for example). Such processes, methods, and tools are performed alongside similar processes for functional requirements.
- Use architectures as the basis for design that reflect a resilience and assurance focus, including security, sustainment, and operations controls.
- Develop assured and resilient software and systems through processes that include secure coding of software, software defect detection and removal, and the development of resilience and assurance controls based on design specifications.
- Test assurance and resilience controls for software and systems and refer issues back to the design and development cycle for resolution.
- Conduct reviews throughout the development life cycle to ensure that resilience (as one aspect of assurance) is kept in the forefront and given adequate attention and consideration.
- Perform system-specific continuity planning and integrate related service continuity plans to ensure that software, systems, hardware, networks, telecommunications, and other technical assets that depend on one another are sustainable.
- Perform a post-implementation review of deployed systems to ensure that resilience (as well as assurance) requirements are being satisfied as intended.
- Monitor software and systems in operation to determine if there is variability that could indicate the effects of threats or vulnerabilities and to ensure that controls are functioning properly.
- Implement configuration management and change control processes to ensure that software and systems are kept up-to-date to address newly discovered vulnerabilities and weaknesses (particularly in vendor-acquired products and components) and to prevent the intentional or inadvertent introduction of malicious code and other exploitable vulnerabilities.

In addition to RTSE, there are a number of goals and practices in other CERT-RMM process areas that organizations should consider when developing and acquiring software and systems that need to meet assurance and resilience requirements. These are as follows:

- Resilience requirements for software and system technology assets in operation, including those that may influence quality attribute requirements in the development process, are developed and managed in the Resilience Requirements Development (RRD) and Resilience Requirements Management (RRM) process areas, respectively.
- Identifying and adding newly developed and acquired software and system assets to the organization's asset inventory are addressed in the Asset Definition and Management (ADM) process area.

- The management of resilience for technology assets as a whole, particularly for deployed, operational assets, is addressed in the Technology Management (TM) process area. This includes, for example, asset fail-over, backup, recovery, and restoration.
- Acquiring software and systems from external entities and ensuring that such assets meet their resilience requirements throughout the asset life cycle are addressed in the External Dependencies Management (EXD) process area. That said, RTSE-specific goals and practices should be used to aid in evaluating and selecting external entities that are developing software and systems (EXD:SG3.SP3), formalizing relationships with such external entities (EXD:SG3.SP4), and managing an external entity's performance when developing software and systems (EXD:SG4).
- Monitoring for events, incidents, and vulnerabilities that may affect software and systems in operation is addressed in the Monitoring (MON) process area.
- Service continuity plans are identified and created in the Service Continuity (SC) process area. These plans may be inclusive of software and systems that support the services for which planning is performed.

In terms of other model connections, RTSE is strongly influenced by two SEI Capability Maturity Model Integration (CMMI) process areas [CMMI Product Team 2006]:

- Requirements Development (RD), the purpose of which is to produce and analyze customer requirements and software and system product and product component requirements.
- Technical Solution (TS), the purpose of which is to design, develop, and implement solutions to software and system requirements. (Solutions, designs, and implementations encompass software and system products, product components, and product-related life-cycle processes, either singly or in combination as appropriate.)

RTSE is also strongly influenced by CERT's ongoing research in software assurance and the work of other leaders in the software assurance and software security communities. There is a growing number of reputable sources to consider when identifying and selecting candidate guidelines for the development and acquisition of resilient software and systems across the life cycle, particularly for software security and assurance, such as

- Building Security In Maturity Model (BSIMM2) v2.0; http://bsimm2.com/
- Open Web Applications Security Project (OWASP) Software Assurance Maturity Model (SAMM) v1.0; www.owasp.org/index.php/Category:Software_Assurance_Maturity_Model

- Microsoft's Security Development Lifecycle, Version 4.1; www.microsoft.com/security/sdl/
- Department of Homeland Security Assurance for CMMI Process Reference Model; https://buildsecurityin.us-cert.gov/swa/procwg.html

The Department of Homeland Security Assurance for CMMI Process Reference Model (PRM) is the result of synthesizing a variety of existing software security life cycles, practices, and research into a set of practices for assurance that can be embedded within a diverse set of existing development approaches and processes. The practices identify recommended activities (the "what") for enhancing a product or service that relies on software and systems. Organizations can use the model for a self-assessment or to aid in developing specifications for external entities that may be providing a technology solution.

Organizations using CERT-RMM can use the Assurance for CMMI PRM as a framework for enhancing their resilience technology solutions. Through a simple gap analysis, a project or organization can identify and prioritize areas of risk in the engineering of resilient technical solutions that PRM practices can help mitigate.

There are a variety of ways (the "how") organizations can implement the assurance practices identified in the Assurance for CMMI PRM. The Building Security In Maturity Model (BSIMM2) v2.0, Open Web Applications Security Project (OWASP) Software Assurance Maturity Model (SAMM) v1.0, and Microsoft's Security Development Lifecycle, Version 4.1, are examples of how the practices can be implemented.

For example, an organization with a weakness associated with the Assurance for CMMI practice "Establish and maintain the strategic assurance training needs of the organization" could consider using detailed implementation approaches in supporting codes of practice, such as

- the Microsoft SDL training guidelines on basic concepts, common baseline, and custom training
- OpenSAMM practices for technical security awareness training, role-specific guidance, and comprehensive security training and certifications
- BSIMM2 training-related practices for creating the software security satellite, making customized, role-based training available on demand, and providing recognition for skills and career path progression

Similarly, an organization implementing secure coding practices may identify an improvement opportunity associated with the Assurance for CMMI practice "Identify deviations from assurance coding standards." Detailed practices on maturing the use of static analysis tools during coding are provided in

- the Microsoft SDL practices for basic code scanning tools, use of static analysis tools, and in-house security tool customization

- OpenSAMM practices for creating review checklists from known security requirements, using automated code analysis tools, and customizing code analysis for application-specific concerns
- BSIMM2 practices for providing easily accessible security standards and (compliance-driven) requirements, enforcing standards through mandatory automated code review and centralized reporting, and building an automated code review factory with tailored rules

Organizations are continuing to gain a better understanding of techniques that successfully mitigate resilience risks related to the increased use of technology solutions (software and systems) to support organizational missions. As specific practices are identified to solve emerging challenges, the CERT-RMM RTSE process area and the Assurance for CMMI PRM can provide a framework for connecting the resilience management and technology development practices of an organization.[8]

Raising the Bar on Business Resilience

By Nader Mehravari, PhD

Author comments: Dr. Nader Mehravari has over 28 years of experience with a variety of national and international projects and contracts, dealing with modern information technologies ranging from the underlying networking and computing infrastructure to end-user and enterprise-wide applications. He has been with Lockheed Martin Corporation since 1992. Currently, he is the director of the Corporate Business Resiliency Strategic Initiative where he is to define and implement a modern integrated approach to disaster recovery, business continuity, pandemic planning, and crisis management for the Lockheed Martin Corporation. Before joining LM, he was a distinguished member of Technical Staff at AT&T Bell Laboratories, where he was involved with the life-cycle activities associated with the implementation of networking, switching, transmission, and telecommunications systems and services for AT&T and its customers from 1982 to 1992. He holds a number of patents; has authored more than 50 refereed conference and journal articles; and has given numerous lectures, presentations, tutorials, and courses. He is a senior member of IEEE and has served on a number of its committees and conference boards. He received his MS and PhD in electrical engineering from Cornell University in 1980 and 1982, respectively, and his BS in electrical engineering from the George Washington University in 1978.

---

8. RTSE assumes that the organization has one or more existing, defined processes for software and system development into which resilience controls and activities can be integrated. If this is not the case, the organization should not attempt to implement the goals and practices identified in RTSE or in other CERT-RMM process areas that are involved in developing software and system technical solutions.

Introduction

As part of our journey toward improving Lockheed Martin Corporation's resilience to disruptive events, small or large, natural or man-made, intentional or accidental, we have been in search of innovative techniques that we could add to our existing proven collection of tools in our "toolbox." This journey has led us to examine a variety of new and not-so-new methods from such domains as disaster recovery, business continuity, crisis management, and related preparedness planning arenas. One such tool that we discovered, studied, tested, and have since added to our resilience toolbox is the CERT Resilience Management Model (CERT-RMM). This is a short description of our successful encounter with CERT-RMM.

Our Definition of Business Resilience

Enterprises, large or small, public or private, civilian or federal, continue to invest in a variety of preparedness planning activities, including IT disaster recovery, business continuity, pandemic planning, crisis management, and emergency management. Prior to encountering CERT-RMM, we had determined that one of the changes that we had to institutionalize across the enterprise was to approach all preparedness activities in an integrated fashion, as opposed to independent pursuits. We refer to this integrated approach to all these aspects of preparedness as "business resilience."

We define business resilience management (BRM) as the practice of planning, developing, executing, and governing activities to ensure that an enterprise

- identifies and mitigates operational risks that can lead to business disruptions before they occur
- prepares for and responds to disruptive events (natural or man-made, accidental or intentional) in a manner that demonstrates command and control of incident response
- recovers and restores mission-critical business operations following a disaster within acceptable time frames

For us, BRM comprises such components as business continuity, IT disaster recovery, crisis management, emergency management, and pandemic planning.

Disruptive events may include fire, flood, earthquakes, severe weather, power outages, IT failures, data corruption, strikes or other labor actions, terrorist attacks, civil unrest, and chemical, biological, and nuclear hazards. Incidents requiring crisis management may include employee kidnappings, workplace violence, minor weather events, and business crises (for example, a product failure or the loss of a key customer, trading partner, or service provider).

The Need for a Management/Maturity Model

Given Lockheed Martin's long history of process orientation and its extensive experience with CMMI, it was a natural step for us to identify the need for a management model that could be used to guide our journey in raising the bar on business resilience.

Operational management or maturity models are structured collections of elements that describe certain aspects of maturity within an organization. The principle behind maturity models is that an organization develops and adopts new processes and practices from which it learns, optimizes, and moves to the next level. The concept was proven with the inception of CMM and CMMI, created by Carnegie Mellon University's Software Engineering Institute originally for government contractors to help evaluate and improve processes related to software engineering.

For our business resilience proposes, a maturity model would serve several purposes:

- To assess current level of competencies—A maturity model would serve as a common "ruler" across the enterprise to gauge the current posture of individual business entities and/or the enterprise as a whole through such techniques as self-assessment, assessment by an internal appraiser, assessment by an independent third party, and audits.
- To guide future direction and investments—A maturity model would facilitate business-centered objective setting by encouraging such questions as: Where do we want to be? and How good do we need to get? It would assist in determining the investment required to reach the next and/or desired state. This is a critical step, since it is not necessary for all organizations to reach the highest levels of maturity.
- To measure progress toward the desired goal—A maturity model would act as a program management instrument to ensure that investments are turning into improved capabilities.
- To ensure that plans and processes evolve to stay at the desired level—Once the desired level is reached, a maturity model facilitates implementation of necessary operation and maintenance activities to ensure that the organization stays at the desired level.

Selecting a Model

Following an environmental scan of the relevant fields and industries, we identified several existing maturity models that could potentially be applicable to or had been specifically designed for business resilience applications. Following our well-established and implemented systems engineering practices, we then performed a detailed trade study in which we performed a comparative analysis of the candidate models.

Our trade study considered such criteria as

- applicability to Lockheed Martin's business model
- completeness and comprehensiveness of the framework
- expandability beyond its current scope

- ease of customization
- integrated approach to components of business resilience
- applicability to other operations processes than business resilience
- openness of the framework
- consistency with national and/or international standards
- availability of a variety of assessment methodologies
- availability of full documentation
- availability of training material
- addressing the complete range of assets
- addressing governance and management structures
- familiarity of the model to other management/maturity models being used for other purposes
- usage by other industries of interest

Our analysis identified CERT-RMM as the most promising model for use within our enterprise. These are some of the characteristics that set CERT-RMM apart from others:

- It promotes the convergence of information security, business continuity, and IT operations activities as a means to actively direct, control, and manage operational resilience and risk.
- It comprehensively models an enterprise from the perspective of the interrelationships among its mission, services and products, business processes, and assets, capturing the needs of large enterprises like ours.
- It has a strong risk management approach where operational risks resulting in asset disruption are well captured.
- It considers risks associated with the protection of assets (through information security techniques) and risks associated with the sustainment of assets (through disaster recovery, business continuity, pandemic planning, and crisis management techniques).
- It treats resilience activities (e.g., disaster recovery, business continuity, pandemic planning, and crisis management planning) as yet another class of business processes intended to manage operational risks.
- It focuses on measuring and institutionalizing resilience processes.

Its developers captured best practices from the financial industry, which is known for its high-quality and effective resilience practices.

Kicking the Tires

As a large, distributed, complex, and process-matured enterprise, it is critical for Lockheed Martin to ensure that any potential new process-oriented management model is truly applicable to our business entities. In order to do so, we performed a trial during which we applied a subset of CERT-RMM process areas to disaster recovery operational processes and command media at one of our business entities.

The overall goal of the pilot was to evaluate the applicability and utility of CERT-RMM for use at Lockheed Martin with the specific goal of answering such questions as these:

- Does CERT-RMM align well with Lockheed Martin's business model and operational practices?
- How can lessons learned from use of CERT-RMM in an organization that has attained CMMI Maturity Level 5 be understood?
- Would the use of CERT-RMM benefit attainment and maintenance of business continuity and disaster recovery readiness posture?
- What appraisal methods are efficient and economical enough for use along with CERT-RMM?
- Would a SCAMPI C appraisal using CERT-RMM be useful for evaluating business continuity and disaster recovery readiness?
- How well can CERT-RMM identify disaster recovery planning implementation gaps?

As part of the preparation for the pilot, we conducted a week-long CERT-RMM training, which was delivered by members of the CERT-RMM development team at CERT. This provided an opportunity to both train the business resilience subject matter experts and the pilot appraisal team about CERT-RMM.

At the time of our pilot, CERT-RMM did not define or specify an accompanying assessment methodology, but it had the flexibility that it could be deployed along with a variety of assessment methodologies. For the subject pilot, the traditional CMM SCAMPI C assessment methodology was used.

The pilot was very successful in the sense that it clearly demonstrated that the model and the appraisal process were successful in revealing insights about both the disaster recovery practices at the piloted business unit as well as the applicable local and corporate command media.

Going Forward

We have identified a variety of ways in which CERT-RMM will have a role in our journey toward the goal of raising the bar on Lockheed Martin's resilience to disruptive events and continually reducing the associated operational risks to our employees, our customers, and our assets. In particular, we envision CERT-RMM

- contributing to our common business resilience taxonomy and nomenclature
- serving as a contributing reference model for our integrated business resilience framework

- serving as a maturity model to gauge the preparedness posture of individual business entities and/or the enterprise as a whole in the areas of disaster recovery and business continuity
- serving as a mechanism to reveal insights about existing policies and guidelines
- serving as a guiding tool in the developing of new command media
- serving as a means to communicate key harmonization and convergence across business resilience and information security

In summary, we have found that CERT-RMM is a comprehensive and flexible framework that, in conjunction with project management methodologies, could provide an efficient and economical way to assist in improving the principles and practices associated with the protection of an enterprise.

Measuring Operational Resilience Using CERT-RMM

By Julia Allen and Noopur Davis

Author comments: Noopur Davis is a visiting scientist at the Software Engineering Institute, Carnegie Mellon University, where she works on the Resilience Management Model (RMM). She is also a principal of Davis Systems, a firm that provides software process management consulting and training services. She has been involved in the software field for over 25 years as a developer, manager of multinational distributed software teams, and consultant. She has trained, launched, and coached dozens of software teams at organizations such as Intuit, Microsoft, Adobe, Hewlett Packard, and United Defense. Prior to Davis Systems, she was a senior member of Technical Staff at the SEI, director of Engineering at Intergraph Corporation, and senior systems analyst at Chrysler Corporation.

How might business leaders go about answering these two key questions:

- How resilient is my organization?
- Have our processes made us more resilient?

And to inform these, answering this question:

- What should be measured to determine if performance objectives for operational resilience are being achieved?

Consistent, timely, and accurate measurements are important feedback for managing any activity, including operational resilience. When conducting measurement and analysis (as defined in the Measurement and Analysis process area), the organization establishes the objectives for measurement (i.e., what it intends to accomplish) and determines the measures that are useful for managing operational resilience as well as for providing meaningful data to manage key processes such as governance, compliance, monitoring, and improvement.

The first step in defining a meaningful measurement program is to determine the required or desired level of operational resilience for the organization. The "organization" may be the enterprise, any line of business or organizational unit of the enterprise, or a supply chain or other form of business relationship that includes external entities. CERT-RMM provides a process-based structure of goals and practices at four levels of capability (incomplete, performed, managed, and defined) and a companion appraisal method. Defining the required or desired level of capability establishes the baseline against which operational resilience can be measured. Ideally, the required level for each process area is established during strategic and operational planning as well as when planning for continuity of operations, not as an afterthought during times of stress and service disruption. The required level should be no less than, and no more than, that which is required to meet business mission objectives.

An effective measurement and analysis process includes the following activities and objectives:

- specifying the objectives of measurement and analysis such that they are aligned with identified information needs and objectives
- specifying the measures, analysis techniques, and mechanisms for data collection, data storage, reporting, and feedback
- implementing the collection, storage, analysis, and reporting of the data
- providing objective results that can be used in making informed decisions, and taking appropriate corrective actions

Integrating measurement and analysis into the operational resilience management system supports

- planning, estimating, and executing operational resilience management activities
- tracking the performance of operational resilience management activities against established plans and objectives, including resilience requirements
- identifying and resolving issues in the operational resilience management processes
- providing a basis for incorporating measurement into additional operational resilience management processes in the future

Example metrics for answering the questions posed above appear in CERT-RMM v1.1 (refer to generic goal 2, generic practice 8, in each process area). They include key process metrics and performance indicators that can be used, in whole or in part, to demonstrate that the required level of operational resilience has been achieved for a given process area. Examples of metrics for 5 of the 26 process areas are included in Table 7.1.

TABLE 7.1 Examples of Metrics in Selected CERT-RMM Process Areas

Process Area	Example Metrics
Knowledge and Information Management	• percentage of information assets that do not have stated owners or custodians • frequency and timeliness of information asset backups; frequency of backup restoration testing • percentage of information assets for which encryption is required and not yet implemented
Technology Management	• percentage of technology assets (software, hardware, systems) for which the cost of compromise (loss, damage, disclosure, disruption of access) has been quantified • percentage of technology assets for which some form of risk assessment has been performed as required by policy • number of unauthorized changes to technology assets during a stated time interval
Service Continuity	• percentage of service continuity plans tested (and number of times tested by time period) • percentage of service continuity plans that failed one or more test objectives • percentage of high-value services and supporting assets that do not have service continuity plans • percentage of unmet recovery time objectives and recovery point objectives
Vulnerability Analysis and Resolution	• percentage of high-value assets that have been monitored, assessed, and audited for vulnerabilities within a stated time interval • percentage of vulnerabilities that have been satisfactorily remediated, by time interval
Resilience Requirements Definition	• percentage of services and assets for which resilience requirements have been defined and documented (or conversely, for which requirements are not stated or are incomplete) • elapsed time between identification of new assets and the development of resilience requirements for those assets

As the model is used by more organizations, it will be increasingly possible to identify, define, deploy, pilot test, and measure effective security and resilience metrics, as well as collect measurement experiences in support of benchmarking. These metrics may be performance- or process-based. We will be working with collaborators and customers to determine what metrics are most useful for determining process effectiveness, to develop metrics templates and structured definitions, and to update the model to reflect results. Automated approaches for collecting and reporting metrics will be essential for long-term use and success.

PART THREE

CERT-RMM Process Areas

In Part Three, we present the CERT-RMM process areas. Each process area includes the purpose statement, introductory notes, related process areas, and the summary of specific goals and practices. At the specific goals and practices level, extensive supporting information is provided to explain the purpose and intent of the goals and practices, and to introduce and describe underlying concepts. Each process area also includes elaborated generic goals and practices. These elaborations give you suggestions for how to implement the generic goals and practices relative to the subject matter of the process area. These elaborations represent the knowledge and experience of the core model project team, as well as the practical knowledge gained from working with high-functioning organizations.

To facilitate the evolution and calibration of the model, the CERT website will always contain the most current versions of the process areas, as well as new process areas. Please visit this space often to obtain the most up-to-date information about the model.

ASSET DEFINITION AND MANAGEMENT
Engineering

Purpose

The purpose of Asset Definition and Management is to identify, document, and manage organizational assets during their life cycle to ensure sustained productivity to support organizational services.

Introductory Notes

Mission success for an organization relies on the success of each service in achieving its mission. In turn, mission assurance for services depends on the availability, productivity, and ultimately the resilience of high-value assets that the service relies upon—people to perform and monitor the service, information to fuel the service, technology to support the automation of the service, and facilities in which to operate the service. Whenever any high-value asset is affected by disruptive events (by the realization of operational risk), the assurance of the mission is less certain and predictable. An organization must be able to identify its high-value assets, document them, and establish their value in order to develop strategies for protecting and sustaining assets commensurate with their value to services.

The Asset Definition and Management process area seeks to establish organizational assets as the focus of the operational resilience management system. High-value organizational assets are identified and profiled (establishing ownership, a common definition, and value), and the relationship between the assets and the organizational services they support is established. The organization also defines and manages the process for keeping the asset inventory current and ensures that changes to the inventory do not result in gaps in strategies for protecting and sustaining assets.

The Asset Definition and Management process area is a higher-order competency that establishes the inventory of high-value organizational assets of all types. The resilience aspects of these assets (and their related services) are addressed in asset-specific process areas as noted in "Related Process Areas" below.

The Asset Definition and Management process area has three specific goals: to inventory assets, associate the assets with services, and manage the assets. To meet these goals, the organization must engage in the following practices:

- Establish a means to identify and document assets.
- Establish ownership and custodianship for the assets.
- Link assets to the services they support.
- Establish resilience requirements (including those for protecting and sustaining) for assets and associated services. (*This is addressed in the Resilience Requirements Definition and Resilience Requirements Management process areas.*)
- Provide change management processes for assets as they change and as the inventory of assets changes.
- Establish risk management processes to identify, analyze, and mitigate risks to high-value assets. (*This is addressed in the Risk Management process area.*)
- Establish continuity processes to develop, test, and implement service continuity and restoration plans for high-value assets. (*This is addressed in the Service Continuity process area.*)
- Monitor the extent to which high-value assets are adequately protected and sustained, and develop and implement adjustments as necessary. (*This is addressed in the Monitoring process area.*)

Related Process Areas

The identification, documentation, analysis, and management of asset-level resilience requirements are addressed in the Resilience Requirements Development and Resilience Requirements Management process areas.

The identification, assessment, and mitigation of risks to high-value assets are addressed in the Risk Management process area.

The development, implementation, and management of strategies for protecting people are addressed in the People Management process area.

The development, implementation, and management of strategies for protecting information assets are addressed in the Knowledge and Information Management process area.

The development, implementation, and management of strategies for protecting technology assets are addressed in the Technology Management process area.

The development, implementation, and management of strategies for protecting facility assets are addressed in the Environmental Control process area.

The development and implementation of service continuity plans for high-value assets and their related services are performed in the Service Continuity process area. Service continuity plans describe strategies for sustaining high-value assets and services.

The identification and prioritization of high-value organizational services are performed in the Enterprise Focus process area.

Summary of Specific Goals and Practices

ADM:SG1 Establish Organizational Assets
    ADM:SG1.SP1   Inventory Assets
    ADM:SG1.SP2   Establish a Common Understanding
    ADM:SG1.SP3   Establish Ownership and Custodianship
ADM:SG2 Establish the Relationship Between Assets and Services
    ADM:SG2.SP1   Associate Assets with Services
    ADM:SG2.SP2   Analyze Asset-Service Dependencies
ADM:SG3 Manage Assets
    ADM:SG3.SP1   Identify Change Criteria
    ADM:SG3.SP2   Maintain Changes to Assets and Inventory

Specific Practices by Goal

ADM:SG1 ESTABLISH ORGANIZATIONAL ASSETS

Organizational assets (people, information, technology, and facilities) are identified and the authority and responsibility for these assets are established.

The assets of the organization must be identified, prioritized, documented, and inventoried.

The highest-level concept in the operational resilience management system is a service. Services are defined as the limited number of activities that the organization carries out in the performance of a duty or in the production of a product. Services are the prime resource that the organization uses to accomplish its mission. Each service has a mission that must be accomplished in order to support the organization's strategic objectives. Failure to accomplish the mission of a service is a potentially serious impediment to accomplishing the organization's mission.

An important aspect of services is that they are "fueled" by assets—the raw materials that services need to operate.

> A service cannot accomplish its mission unless there are
> - **people** to operate and monitor the service
> - **information** and data to feed the process and to be produced by the service
> - **technology** to automate and support the service
> - **facilities** in which to perform the service

These assets may or may not be directly owned by the organization. For example, outsourcing of call center functions may mean that the organization does not control the people, information, technology, or facilities that enable the service;

however, the organization retains responsibility for the ownership and resilience of the assets. In order to properly determine resilience requirements (and to implement appropriate strategies for protecting and sustaining assets), the organization must define these assets from a service perspective and establish ownership and responsibility for their resilience.

ADM:SG1.SP1 INVENTORY ASSETS

Organizational assets are identified and inventoried.

Success at achieving the organization's mission relies upon critical dependencies between organizational goals and objectives, services, and associated high-value assets. Lack of performance of these assets (due to disruptive events, realized risk, or other issues) impedes mission assurance of associated services and can translate into failure to achieve organizational goals and objectives. Thus, ensuring the operational resilience of high-value assets is paramount to organizational success.

The first step in establishing the operational resilience of assets is to identify and define the assets. Because assets derive their value and importance through their association with services, the organization must first identify and establish which services are of high value. This provides structure and guidance for developing an inventory of high-value assets for which resilience requirements have to be established and satisfied. Inventorying these assets is also essential to ensuring that changes are made in resilience requirements as operational and environmental changes occur.

Establishing criteria for determining the value of services and associated assets is performed in the Risk Management process area. Identifying and prioritizing high-value organizational services are performed in the Enterprise Focus process area.

Each type of asset for a specific service must be identified and inventoried. The following are descriptions of the four asset types.

> **People** are those who are vital to the expected operation and performance of the service. They execute the process and monitor it to ensure that it is achieving its mission, and make corrections to the process when necessary to bring it back on track. People may be internal or external to the organization.

> **Information** is any information or data, on any media, including paper or electronic form, that is vital to the intended operation of the service. Information may also be the output or by-product of the execution of a service. Information can be as small as a bit or a byte, a record or a file, or as large as a database. (The organization must determine how granularly to define information with respect to its purpose in a service.) Because of confidentiality and privacy concerns, information must also be categorized as to its organizational sensitivity. Categorization provides another level of important description to an information asset that may affect strategies to protect and sustain it. Examples of information include Social Security numbers, a vendor database, intellectual property, and institutional knowledge.

> **Technology** describes any technology component or asset that supports or automates a service and facilitates its ability to accomplish its mission. Technology has many layers, some that are specific to a service (such as an application system) and others that are shared by the organization (such as the enterprise-wide network infrastructure) to support more than one service. Organizations must describe technology assets in terms that facilitate development and satisfaction of resilience requirements. In some organizations, this may be at the application system level; in others, it might be more granular, such as at the server or personal computer level. Examples of technology assets include software, hardware, and firmware, including physical interconnections between these assets such as cabling.

> **Facilities** are any physical plant assets that the organization relies upon to execute a service. Facilities are the places where services are executed and can be owned and controlled by the organization or by external business partners. Facilities are also often shared such that more than one service is executed in and dependent upon them. (For example, a headquarters office building has a substantial number of services being executed inside of it.) Facilities provide the physical space for the actions of people, the use and storage of information, and the operations of technology components. Thus, resilience planning for facilities must integrate tightly with planning for the other assets. Examples of facilities include office buildings, data centers, and other real estate where services are performed.

Organizations may use many practical methods to inventory these assets. Human resources databases identify and describe the roles of vital staff. Fixed asset catalogs often describe all levels of technology components. Facilities and real estate databases have information about high-value physical plant assets. However, bear in mind that internal databases may not cover people, technology, and facilities that are not under the direct control of the organization. In contrast to people, technology, and facilities, less tangible assets such as information and intellectual property may not be identified and regularly inventoried because they are often difficult to describe and bound. For example, a staff member may have information that is critical to the effective operation of a service that has not been documented or is not known to other staff members. This must be resolved in order to properly define security and continuity requirements for these assets.

Typical work products

1. Asset inventory (of all high-value assets of each type)
2. Asset database

Subpractices

1. Identify and inventory vital staff.
2. Identify and inventory high-value information assets.

3. Identify and inventory high-value technology components.
4. Identify and inventory high-value facilities.
5. Develop and maintain an asset database that establishes a common source for all high-value assets.

ADM:SG1.SP2 ESTABLISH A COMMON UNDERSTANDING

A common and consistent definition of assets is established and communicated.

Proper description of organizational assets is essential to ensuring a common understanding of these assets between owners and custodians. *(The difference between owners and custodians is explained in ADM:SG1.SP3.)* A consistent description aids in developing resilience requirements and ensuring satisfaction of these requirements. It defines the boundaries and extent of the asset, which is useful for defining ownership and responsibility for the resilience of the asset. In addition, an asset's description can be easily communicated within and outside of the organization to facilitate communication of resilience requirements to internal constituencies and external business partners.

At a minimum, all high-value assets (as identified in ADM:SG1.SP1) should be defined to the extent possible. Differences in the level of description are expected from asset to asset, and an organization must decide how much information is useful in facilitating requirements definition and satisfaction. The description of the asset should detail why it is considered to be of high value to the organization. There are some common elements that should be collected, at a minimum, for each asset.

> These are examples of information that should be collected and documented for assets:
> - asset type (people, information, technology, or facilities)
> - categorization of asset by sensitivity (generally for information assets only)
> - asset location (typically where the custodian is managing the asset)
> - asset owners and custodians (particularly where this is external to the organization)
> - the format or form of the asset (particularly for information assets that might exist on paper and electronically)
> - location where backups or duplicates of this asset exist (particularly for information assets)
> - the services that are dependent on the asset *(See ADM:SG2.)*
> - the value of the asset in either qualitative or quantitative terms

An organization may also choose to document the asset's resilience requirements as part of the asset profile so that there is a common source for communicating and updating these requirements and so that their association with an asset is established. In addition, strategies to protect and sustain an asset may be documented as part of the asset profile. *(Resilience requirements for assets are developed and documented in the Resilience Requirements Development process area.)*

There are additional considerations for describing each type of asset.

> **People**
>
> In describing people, be sure to describe a role where possible, rather than the actual persons who perform the role. If a particular person or persons in the organization are vital to the successful operation of a service because of their detailed knowledge and experience, this should be noted in the description of the asset. This may affect the resilience requirements of the asset when defined.

> **Information Assets**
>
> Because information is an intangible asset, it must be accurately described. Some organizations find media conventions such as record, file, and database to be natural limiters of the description of an information asset. Information asset descriptions should also address the level of sensitivity of the asset based on the organization's categorization scheme. This will aid in ensuring that confidentiality and privacy sensitivities are considered in the development and satisfaction of resilience requirements.

> **Technology and Facilities Assets**
>
> Organizations often view technology components and facilities as shared enterprise assets. This should be considered when defining these assets and when developing resilience requirements. In addition, because technology and facilities are tangible assets, the current value of the asset should be included in the definition. This will provide additional data on the value of the asset to the organization and serve as a guide for comparing value versus cost of activities to protect and sustain assets.

Typical work products

1. Asset profiles (for all high-value assets of each type)
2. Updated asset database (including asset profiles)

Subpractices

1. Create an asset profile for each high-value asset (or similar work product) and document a common description.

    Be sure to address the entire range of information that should be collected for each type of asset, including at a minimum the owner and the custodian(s) of the asset. Also, include the resilience requirements of the asset as established or acquired by the organization. *(Refer to the Resilience Requirements Development process area for more information.)*

2. Describe and document the "acceptable use" of the asset. Ensure alignment between acceptable uses and resilience requirements.

3. Categorize information assets as to their level of sensitivity.
4. Update the asset database with asset profile information.
   All information relevant to the asset (collected from the asset profile) should be contained with the asset in its entry in the asset database.

ADM:SG1.SP3 Establish Ownership and Custodianship

The ownership and custodianship of assets are established.

High-value assets have owners and custodians. Asset owners are the persons or organizational units, internal or external to the organization, that have primary responsibility for the viability, productivity, and resilience of the asset. For example, an information asset such as customer data may be owned by the "customer relations department" or the "customer relationship manager." It is the owner's responsibility to ensure that the appropriate levels of confidentiality, integrity, and availability requirements are defined and satisfied to keep the asset productive and viable for use in services.

Asset custodians are persons or organizational units, internal or external to the organization, that are responsible for implementing and managing controls to satisfy the resilience requirements of high-value assets while they are in their care. For example, the customer data in the above example may be stored on a server that is maintained by the IT department. In essence, the IT department takes custodial control of the customer data asset when the asset is in its domain. The IT department must commit to taking actions commensurate with satisfying the owner's requirements to protect and sustain the asset. However, in all cases, owners are responsible for ensuring that their assets are properly protected and sustained, regardless of the actions (or inactions) of custodians.

In practice, custodianship brings many challenges for asset owners in ensuring that the resilience requirements of their assets are being satisfied. In some cases, custodians of assets must resolve conflicting requirements obtained from more than one asset owner. This can occur in cases where a server contains more than one information asset from different owners with unique and sometimes competing requirements. In addition, custodianship may occur outside of organizational boundaries, as is commonly seen in outsourcing arrangements. In such a case, asset owners must clearly communicate the resilience requirements of their assets to external custodians and must expend additional effort in monitoring the satisfaction of those requirements.

The owner of each high-value asset is established in order to define responsibility and accountability for the asset's resilience and its contributions to services. Accordingly, owners are responsible for developing and validating the resilience requirements for high-value assets that they own. They are also responsible for the implementation of proper controls to meet resilience requirements, even if they assign this responsibility to a custodian of the asset.

The identification, documentation, analysis, and management of asset-level resilience requirements are addressed in the Resilience Requirements Development and Resilience Requirements Management process areas.

> Ownership of assets typically varies depending on the asset type.
> - **People** are part of the organizational unit or line of business where their job responsibilities and accountabilities are managed. This organizational unit or line of business is considered the "owner" of these resources in that it has authority and accountability for their work assignments and their training, deployment, and performance.
> - **Information assets** are generally owned by a person, organizational unit, or line of business where the asset originates (i.e., where the service is owned which the asset supports) or where responsibility for the asset's confidentiality, integrity, and availability has been established.
> - **Technology and facilities assets** tend to be shared by the enterprise, and therefore it may be difficult to establish a single owner.
> - **Technology assets** are most often owned by IT but could be owned by an organizational unit or line of business that manages its technology support structure separately from IT or the enterprise.
> - **Facilities** may be owned by a central group (such as facilities management) or may be owned by an organizational unit or line of business.

In some cases, the organization may group a set of assets together into a service and identify an owner of the service. This aggregation often is more practical when there are many assets in an organization and protection and sustainment strategies at the asset level would not be practical.

The organization should also, to the extent possible, identify relevant custodians for each high-value asset. Custodians take custodial care of assets under the direction of owners and are usually responsible for satisfying the asset's resilience requirements on an operational basis. Identifying the custodians of high-value assets also helps to identify the operational environment of the assets where risks may emerge and where continuity plans would have to be implemented.

Typical work products

1. Owner identification
2. Custodian identification
3. Updated asset profiles (including owner and custodian)
4. Updated asset database (including owner and custodian)

Subpractices

1. Document and describe the owner of each asset on the asset profile (or similar work product).
2. Group assets that are collectively needed to perform a specific service, and identify service owners, if necessary.

3. Document and describe the physical location of the asset and the custodian of the asset.
4. Update asset profiles to establish and document the asset's association to a service. If the asset is connected to more than one service, be sure this is noted as part of the asset profile.
5. Update the asset database with asset-to-service association information. All information relevant to the asset (collected from the asset profile) should be contained with the asset in its entry in the asset database.

ADM:SG2 ESTABLISH THE RELATIONSHIP BETWEEN ASSETS AND SERVICES

The relationship between assets and the services they support is established and examined.

The relationship between assets and the services they support must be understood in order to effectively develop, implement, and manage resilience strategies that support the accomplishment of the service's mission. Associating assets to services helps the organization to determine where critical dependencies exist, to validate resilience requirements, and to develop and implement commensurate resilience strategies.

ADM:SG2.SP1 ASSOCIATE ASSETS WITH SERVICES

Assets are associated with the service or services they support.

To provide a service-focused review of operational resilience, the assets collected in the development of the asset inventory must be associated with the services they support. This helps the organization view resilience from a service perspective and to identify critical dependencies that are essential to determining effective strategies for protecting and sustaining assets.

Establishing criteria for determining the relative value of services and associated assets is performed in the Risk Management process area. Identifying and prioritizing high-value organizational services are performed in the Enterprise Focus process area.

Typical work products

1. List of high-value services and associated assets
2. Updated asset profiles (including service information)
3. Updated asset database (including service information)

Subpractices

1. Identify high-value services.
    A list of high-value services is created in the Enterprise Focus process area. Assets can be associated with services in this practice, but it is best to have a validated list of services to which assets are associated. *(Refer to the Enterprise Focus process area for more information.)*

2. Assign assets in the asset database to one or more services.
3. Update the asset profile to reflect the service association.
4. Update the asset database to reflect the service association.

ADM:SG2.SP2 ANALYZE ASSET-SERVICE DEPENDENCIES

Instances where assets support more than one service are identified and analyzed.

Because services traverse the organization, and because there are shared assets and resources that many services depend upon, it is important to identify these dependencies to ensure that they are addressed during the development of resilience requirements and in the development of strategies to protect and sustain assets and their related services.

When dependencies result in a shared environment for an asset, consideration must be given to the effects that this situation will have on the satisfaction of resilience requirements at the service level. For example, if resilience requirements are set for a facility and more than one service is performed in that facility, the requirements for protecting and sustaining the facility must be sufficient to meet the needs of both services that share the facility. By identifying these potential conflicts early, an organization can actively mitigate them (by revising requirements or other actions) before they become an exposure that affects the operational resilience of the affected services.

Typical work products

1. List of potential conflicts due to asset dependencies
2. Mitigation actions and resolutions

Subpractices

1. Identify asset dependencies and potential conflicts.
2. Develop mitigation plans to reduce the effects of dependencies that could affect the operational resilience of associated services.
3. Implement actions to reduce or eliminate conflict.
    This practice may require the organization to revisit existing resilience requirements and revise them where necessary. It may also necessitate changes in current strategies for protecting and sustaining existing assets. (Refer to the Resilience Requirements Management process area for more information about managing change to resilience requirements. Refer to the Controls Management and the Service Continuity process areas for managing changes to strategies for protecting and sustaining services and their supporting assets.)

ADM:SG3 MANAGE ASSETS

The life cycle of assets is managed.

Changes to high-value assets may require commensurate changes in resilience requirements and the strategies that organizations deploy to ensure that these assets are adequately protected and sustained. In fact, managing changes to the operational environment (i.e., through keeping accurate inventories of assets and services and their requirements) is an essential activity for managing and controlling operational resilience. The organization must actively monitor for changes that significantly alter assets, identify new assets, or call for the retirement of assets for which there is no longer a need or whose relative value has been reduced. The objective of this goal is to ensure that the organization's scope for operational resilience management remains known and controllable.

ADM:SG3.SP1 IDENTIFY CHANGE CRITERIA

The criteria that would indicate changes in an asset or its association with a service are established and maintained.

(This practice is complementary to specific practice RRM:SG1.SP3 in Resilience Requirements Management.)

In order to identify changes to high-value assets that could affect their productivity and resilience, the organization must have a set of criteria that are consistently applied. These criteria must cover all assets—people, technology, information, and facilities. Changes in assets must be translated to changes in resilience requirements—either the requirements are altered or rewritten, or in the case where the asset is eliminated (for example, when vital staff leave the organization), the requirements are retired.

These are examples of triggers that can affect high-value assets:
- changes in organizational structure and staff—termination or transfer of staff between organizational units or changes in roles and responsibilities
- changes in technology infrastructure and configuration
- real estate transactions that add, alter, or change existing facilities
- creation or alteration of information
- changes in services affecting the assets on which they rely
- contracts that the organization enters into that would identify new assets
- acquisition of assets such as technology or facilities

Owners of high-value assets must have knowledge of these criteria and be able to apply them in order to identify changes that must be managed.

Typical work products

1. Asset inventory baseline
2. Asset change criteria

Subpractices

1. Establish an asset inventory baseline from which changes will be managed.
2. Develop and document criteria for establishing when a change in asset inventory must be considered.
    Ensure that these criteria are commensurate with the organization's risk tolerances.

ADM:SG3.SP2 MAINTAIN CHANGES TO ASSETS AND INVENTORY

Changes to assets are managed as conditions dictate.

(This practice is complementary to specific practice RRM:SG1.SP3 in Resilience Requirements Management.)

Organizational and operational conditions are continually changing. These changes result in daily changes to the high-value assets that help the organization's services achieve their missions. For example, the following are common organizational events that would affect high-value assets:

- staff changes, including the addition of new staff members (either internally or externally), the transfer of existing staff members from one organizational unit to another, and the termination of staff members
- changes to information such as the creation, alteration, or deletion of paper and electronic records, files, and databases
- technology refresh, such as the addition of new technical components, changes to existing technical components, and the elimination or retirement of existing technology
- facilities changes, such as the addition of new facilities (whether owned by the organization or an external business partner), alteration of existing facilities, and the retirement of a facility

Besides the addition of new assets, this practice also addresses changes to the description or composition of an asset. For example, if an asset takes an additional form (such as when a paper asset is imaged or an electronic asset is printed), this must be documented as part of the asset description to ensure that current protection and sustainment strategies align properly and provide coverage across a range of asset media. Assets may also change ownership, custodianship, location, or value—all of which must be updated to ensure a current asset profile and inventory.

In addition, whenever assets are eliminated (for example, a server is retired or vital staff members leave the organization), owners of those assets must ensure that their resilience requirements are either eliminated (if possible) or are transferred and updated to the assets that replace them. Doing this is especially critical when assets are shared between services and have common resilience requirements.

Typical work products

1. Asset change documentation
2. Asset inventory status
3. Updated asset and service resilience requirements
4. Updated asset and service protection strategies and controls
5. Updated strategies and continuity plans for sustaining assets and services

Subpractices

1. Document the asset changes by updating asset profiles and the asset database.
2. Maintain a requirement change history with the rationale for performing the changes.
3. Evaluate the impact of asset changes on existing resilience requirements and activities and commitments for protecting and sustaining assets.
   Update asset resilience requirements, asset protection strategies, and plans for sustaining assets as necessary.
4. Establish communication channels to ensure custodians are aware of changes in assets.
   Update service level agreements (SLAs) with custodians if necessary to reflect commitment to changes.

Elaborated Generic Practices by Goal

Refer to the Generic Goals and Practices document in Appendix A for general guidance that applies to all process areas. This section provides elaborations relative to the application of the Generic Goals and Practices to the Asset Definition and Management process area.

ADM:GG1 ACHIEVE SPECIFIC GOALS

The operational resilience management system supports and enables achievement of the specific goals of the Asset Definition and Management process area by transforming identifiable input work products to produce identifiable output work products.

ADM:GG1.GP1 PERFORM SPECIFIC PRACTICES

Perform the specific practices of the Asset Definition and Management process area to develop work products and provide services to achieve the specific goals of the process area.

Elaboration:

Specific practices ADM:SG1.SP1 through ADM:SG3.SP2 are performed to achieve the goals of the asset definition and management process.

ADM:GG2 INSTITUTIONALIZE A MANAGED PROCESS

Asset definition and management is institutionalized as a managed process.

ADM:GG2.GP1 ESTABLISH PROCESS GOVERNANCE

Establish and maintain governance over the planning and performance of the asset definition and management process.

Refer to the Enterprise Focus process area for more information about providing sponsorship and oversight to the asset definition and management process.

Subpractices

1. Establish governance over process activities.

   Elaboration:

   > Governance over the asset definition and management process may be exhibited by
   > - developing and publicizing higher-level managers' objectives and requirements
   > - sponsoring policies, procedures, standards, and guidelines, including the documentation of assets and for establishing asset ownership and custodianship
   > - making higher-level managers aware of applicable compliance obligations related to the process, and regularly reporting on the organization's satisfaction of these obligations to higher-level managers
   > - sponsoring and funding process activities
   > - aligning asset inventory, asset ownership, and asset-service relationship activities with identified resilience needs and objectives and stakeholder needs and requirements
   > - sponsoring the development, documentation, and management of asset inventories
   > - verifying that the process supports strategic resilience objectives and is focused on the assets and services that are of the highest relative value in meeting strategic objectives
   > - regular reporting from organizational units to higher-level managers on process activities and results
   > - creating dedicated higher-level management feedback loops on decisions about the process and recommendations for improving the process
   > - providing input on identifying, assessing, and managing operational risks to assets, including guidance for resolving asset inventory inconsistencies and other anomalies
   > - conducting regular internal and external audits and related reporting to audit committees on process effectiveness
   > - creating formal programs to measure the effectiveness of process activities, and reporting these measurements to higher-level managers

2. Develop and publish organizational policy for the process.

   Elaboration:

   > The asset definition and management policy should address
   > - responsibility, authority, and ownership for performing process activities, including collecting and documenting asset inventory information
   > - procedures, standards, and guidelines for
   >   - documenting asset descriptions and relevant information
   >   - describing and identifying asset owners
   >   - describing and identifying asset custodians
   > - the development of criteria to provide guidance on asset inventory updating, reconciliation, and change control
   > - the association of assets to core organizational services, and the prioritization of assets in the inventory
   > - methods for measuring adherence to policy, exceptions granted, and policy violations

ADM:GG2.GP2 PLAN THE PROCESS

Establish and maintain the plan for performing the asset definition and management process.

Elaboration:

The plan for performing the asset definition and management process is created to ensure that an accurate inventory of assets is developed and maintained and can form a foundation for managing operational resilience. Developing and maintaining an asset inventory may be challenging because most organizations have a significant number of assets. Thus, the plan must address how the inventory will be taken and maintained at various levels of the organization. For practicality, most organizations may take inventory at an organizational unit level and have a method or tool to aggregate the inventory at an enterprise level.

Subpractices

1. Define and document the plan for performing the process.

   Elaboration:

   Special consideration in the plan may have to be given to the organization's approach for taking an initial inventory of assets (developing the asset inventory baseline) and for maintaining the asset inventory. The plan should address who is responsible for creating and maintaining the inventory and how ownership and custodianship are determined (or assigned). The plan should also include provisions for how the inventory is to be reconciled and how inventory duplication is resolved.

2. Define and document the process description.
3. Review the plan with relevant stakeholders and get their agreement.
4. Revise the plan as necessary.

ADM:GG2.GP3 PROVIDE RESOURCES

Provide adequate resources for performing the asset definition and management process, developing the work products, and providing the services of the process.

Subpractices

1. Staff the process.

   Elaboration:

   The diversity of asset types (people, information, technology, facilities) requires that staff members assigned to the asset definition and management process have appropriate knowledge of the assets being inventoried and the services with which they are associated.

   > These are examples of staff required to perform the asset definition and management process:
   > - staff responsible for
   >   - identifying high-value assets (e.g., people, information, technology, and facilities) and the services with which they are associated
   >   - developing and maintaining the asset inventory, including asset profiles and the asset database
   >   - identifying asset dependencies, potential conflicts, and mitigation plans to reduce the effects of dependencies that could affect the operational resilience of associated services
   >   - managing changes to assets, changes to the asset inventory, and associated changes to requirements, controls, strategies, and plans (This includes communicating changes to affected stakeholders, including asset custodians.)
   >   - developing process plans and programs and ensuring they are aligned with stakeholder requirements and needs
   >   - managing external entities that have contractual obligations for asset definition and management activities
   > - owners and custodians of high-value assets that support the accomplishment of operational resilience management objectives
   > - internal and external auditors responsible for reporting to appropriate committees on process effectiveness

   Refer to the Organizational Training and Awareness process area for information about training staff for resilience roles and responsibilities.

Refer to the Human Resource Management process area for information about acquiring staff to fulfill roles and responsibilities.

2. Fund the process.

   Elaboration:

   Considerations for funding the asset definition and management process should extend beyond the initial development of the asset inventory to the maintenance of the inventory. Initial costs may be higher if the organization does not have a formal or usable asset baseline to serve as a foundation.

   Refer to the Financial Resource Management process area for information about budgeting for, funding, and accounting for asset definition and management.

3. Provide necessary tools, techniques, and methods to perform the process.

   Elaboration:

   Developing and maintaining the asset inventory may require tools, techniques, and methods that allow for asset documentation and profiling, reporting, and updating on a regular basis. The need for these tools may be greater if the asset inventory is developed across many organizational units and must be aggregated at the enterprise level. Tools should provide for proper and secure change control over the asset database and should limit access to the asset baseline. The asset inventory database should be searchable and expandable to include additional information such as documentation of associated services and the asset's resilience requirements.

   > These are examples of tools, techniques, and methods to support the asset definition and management process:
   > - methods for identifying high-value assets
   > - methods, techniques, and tools for creating asset profiles and baselines
   > - methods and tools for aggregating local asset inventories into an enterprise inventory
   > - asset inventory database management system
   > - methods, techniques, and tools for asset inventory change management and control

ADM:GG2.GP4 ASSIGN RESPONSIBILITY

Assign responsibility and authority for performing the asset definition and management process, developing the work products, and providing the services of the process.

Elaboration:

Specific practice ADM:SG1.SP2 describes the use of human resources databases to identify roles of vital staff to aid in determining high-value people assets and calls for describing roles rather than actual persons who perform the role. Specific practice ADM:SG3.SP1 discusses the effects of changes in roles. These descriptions of roles specific to the definition and management of high-value people assets should not be confused with assigning the roles, responsibilities, and authorities necessary to perform the asset definition and management process.

Refer to the Human Resource Management process area for more information about establishing resilience as a job responsibility, developing resilience performance goals and objectives, and measuring and assessing performance against these goals and objectives.

Subpractices

1. Assign responsibility and authority for performing the process.

   Elaboration:

   Responsibility and authority for creating the asset inventory baseline may differ from responsibility and authority for maintaining the asset inventory and performing change control processes.

2. Assign responsibility and authority for performing the specific tasks of the process.

   Elaboration:

   > Responsibility and authority for performing asset definition and management tasks can be formalized by
   > - defining roles and responsibilities in the process plan
   > - including process tasks and responsibility for these tasks in specific job descriptions
   > - developing policy requiring organizational unit managers, line of business managers, project managers, and asset and service owners and custodians to participate in and derive benefit from the process for assets and services under their ownership or custodianship
   > - including process tasks in staff performance management goals and objectives with requisite measurement of progress against these goals
   > - developing and implementing contractual instruments (including service level agreements) with external entities to establish responsibility and authority for performing process tasks on outsourced functions
   > - including process tasks in measuring performance of external entities against contractual instruments

   Refer to the External Dependencies Management process area for additional details about managing relationships with external entities.

3. Confirm that people assigned with responsibility and authority understand it and are willing and able to accept it.

ADM:GG2.GP5 TRAIN PEOPLE

Train the people performing or supporting the asset definition and management process as needed.

Refer to the Organizational Training and Awareness process area for more information about training the people performing or supporting the process.

Refer to the Human Resource Management process area for more information about creating an inventory of skill sets, establishing a skill set baseline, identifying required skill sets, and measuring and addressing skill deficiencies.

Subpractices

1. Identify process skill needs.

   Elaboration:

   > These are examples of skills required in the asset definition and management process:
   > - knowledge of the tools, techniques, and methods necessary to identify and inventory high-value assets, including those necessary to perform the process using the selected methods, techniques, and tools identified in ADM:GG2.GP3 subpractice 3
   > - knowledge unique to each type of asset that is required to identify and inventory each type
   > - knowledge necessary to work effectively with asset owners and custodians
   > - knowledge necessary to elicit and prioritize stakeholder requirements and needs and interpret them to develop effective requirements, plans, and programs for the process

2. Identify process skill gaps based on available resources and their current skill levels.
3. Identify training opportunities to address skill gaps.

   Elaboration:

   > These are examples of training topics:
   > - profiling, defining, and documenting high-value assets, including any unique considerations by asset type
   > - managing and controlling changes to asset inventories, asset profiles, and asset databases
   > - supporting asset owners and custodians in understanding the process and their roles and responsibilities with respect to its activities
   > - working with external entities that have responsibility for process activities
   > - using process methods, tools, and techniques, including those identified in ADM:GG2:GP3 subpractice 3

4. Provide training and review the training needs as necessary.

ADM:GG2.GP6 MANAGE WORK PRODUCT CONFIGURATIONS

Place designated work products of the asset definition and management process under appropriate levels of control.

Elaboration:

ADM:SG3.SP2 specifically addresses the change control process over assets and the asset inventory. However, other work products of the asset definition and management process must also be managed and controlled.

The tools, techniques, and methods used to capture and maintain the asset inventory should be employed to perform consistent and structured version control over the inventory to ensure that information is current, accurate, and "official." The tools, techniques, and methods can also be used to securely store the asset inventory, to provide access control over inquiry, modification, and deletion, and to track version changes and updates.

> These are examples of asset definition and management work products placed under control:
> - asset inventory
> - asset database
> - asset profiles
> - asset owners and custodians
> - association of assets to high-value services
> - asset dependencies, dependency conflicts, mitigation actions, and resolutions
> - asset inventory change control system or method
> - asset inventory change criteria
> - process plan
> - policies and procedures
> - contracts with external entities

ADM:GG2.GP7 IDENTIFY AND INVOLVE RELEVANT STAKEHOLDERS

Identify and involve the relevant stakeholders of the asset definition and management process as planned.

Elaboration:

Several ADM-specific practices address the involvement of owners and custodians as key stakeholders in the asset definition and management process. For example, ADM:SG1.SP3 calls for establishing ownership and custodianship for all high-value assets and making sure owners and custodians understand their responsibilities, as well as their relationship with one another. ADM:SG3.SP1 requires that asset owners have knowledge of asset change criteria, including possible changes in asset ownership and custodianship.

Subpractices

1. Identify process stakeholders and their appropriate involvement.

   Elaboration:

   > These are examples of stakeholders of the asset definition and management process:
   > - asset owners and custodians
   > - service owners
   > - organizational unit and line of business managers responsible for high-value assets and the services they support
   > - staff responsible for establishing, implementing, and maintaining an internal control system for assets
   > - external entities responsible for managing high-value assets
   > - human resources (for people assets)
   > - information technology staff (for technology assets)
   > - staff responsible for physical security (for facility assets)
   > - internal and external auditors

   > Stakeholders are involved in various tasks in the asset definition and management process, such as
   > - planning for the process
   > - creating an asset inventory baseline
   > - creating asset profiles
   > - associating assets with services and analyzing asset-service dependencies
   > - managing changes to assets and to the asset inventory
   > - reviewing and appraising the effectiveness of process activities
   > - resolving issues in the process

2. Communicate the list of stakeholders to planners and those responsible for process performance.
3. Involve relevant stakeholders in the process as planned.

ADM:GG2.GP8 MONITOR AND CONTROL THE PROCESS

Monitor and control the asset definition and management process against the plan for performing the process and take appropriate corrective action.

Refer to the Monitoring process area for more information about the collection, organization, and distribution of data that may be useful for monitoring and controlling processes.

Refer to the Measurement and Analysis process area for more information about establishing process metrics and measurement.

Refer to the Enterprise Focus process area for more information about providing process information to managers, identifying issues, and determining appropriate corrective actions.

Subpractices

1. Measure actual performance against the plan for performing the process.
2. Review accomplishments and results of the process against the plan for performing the process.

   Elaboration:

   > These are examples of metrics for the asset definition and management process:
   > - percentage of organizational assets that have been inventoried, by asset type
   > - number or level of discrepancies between the current inventory and the documented inventory
   > - number of changes made to the asset inventory during a stated period
   > - number of assets that do not have an assigned owner or custodian (if applicable)
   > - number of assets with incomplete asset profiles or other incomplete information
   > - number of asset-service dependency conflicts with unimplemented or incomplete mitigation plans
   > - number of high-value asset risks referred to the risk management process; number of risks where corrective action is still pending (by risk rank)
   > - level of adherence to process policies; number of policy violations; number of policy exceptions requested and number approved
   > - number of process activities that are on track per plan
   > - rate of change of resource needs to support the process
   > - rate of change of costs to support the process

3. Review activities, status, and results of the process with the immediate level of managers responsible for the process and identify issues.

   Elaboration:

   > Periodic reviews of the asset definition and management process are needed to ensure that
   > - newly acquired assets are included in the inventory
   > - assets that have been modified are reflected accurately in the inventory
   > - assets that have been retired are removed from the inventory
   > - asset-service mapping is accurate and current
   > - ownership and custodianship over assets are established and documented
   > - change control processes are operating appropriately to minimize discrepancies between the organization's asset base and the asset inventory
   > - access to the asset inventory is being limited to only authorized staff

> - status reports are provided to appropriate stakeholders in a timely manner
> - asset and service dependency issues are referred to the risk management process when necessary
> - actions requiring management involvement are elevated in a timely manner
> - the performance of process activities is being monitored and regularly reported
> - key measures are within acceptable ranges as demonstrated in governance dashboards or scorecards and financial reports
> - administrative, technical, and physical controls are operating as intended
> - controls are meeting the stated intent of the resilience requirements
> - actions resulting from internal and external audits are being closed in a timely manner

4. Identify and evaluate the effects of significant deviations from the plan for performing the process.

   Elaboration:

   Discrepancies result when assets are acquired, modified, or retired but not reflected accurately in the asset inventory. Assets form the foundation for operational resilience management because they are the target of strategies required to protect and sustain services. To the extent that the asset definition and management process results in inventory discrepancies, the organization's overall ability to manage operational resilience is impeded.

5. Identify problems in the plan for performing and executing the process.
6. Take corrective action when requirements and objectives are not being satisfied, when issues are identified, or when progress differs significantly from the plan for performing the process.
7. Track corrective action to closure.

ADM:GG2.GP9 Objectively Evaluate Adherence

Objectively evaluate adherence of the asset definition and management process against its process description, standards, and procedures, and address non-compliance.

   Elaboration:

> These are examples of activities to be reviewed:
> - identifying assets and services
> - associating assets and services
> - identifying asset-service dependencies
> - developing asset profiles
> - documenting asset descriptions
> - identifying asset change criteria
> - making changes to the asset inventory

Asset Definition and Management **145**

> - the alignment of stakeholder requirements with process plans
> - assignment of responsibility, accountability, and authority for process activities
> - determination of the adequacy of process reports and reviews in informing decision makers regarding the performance of operational resilience management activities and the need to take corrective action, if any
> - verification of process controls
> - use of process work products for improving strategies to protect and sustain assets and services

> These are examples of work products to be reviewed:
> - asset profiles
> - asset inventory database
> - asset-service relationship matrix
> - asset inventory change control logs
> - process plan and policies
> - dependency issues that have been referred to the risk management process
> - process methods, techniques, and tools
> - contracts with external entities
> - metrics for the process *(Refer to ADM:GG2.GP8 subpractice 2.)*

ADM:GG2.GP10 REVIEW STATUS WITH HIGHER-LEVEL MANAGERS

Review the activities, status, and results of the asset definition and management process with higher-level managers and resolve issues.

Refer to the Enterprise Focus process area for more information about providing sponsorship and oversight to the operational resilience management system.

ADM:GG3 INSTITUTIONALIZE A DEFINED PROCESS

Asset definition and management is institutionalized as a defined process.

ADM:GG3.GP1 ESTABLISH A DEFINED PROCESS

Establish and maintain the description of a defined asset definition and management process.

Establishing and tailoring process assets, including standard processes, are addressed in the Organizational Process Definition process area.

Establishing process needs and objectives and selecting, improving, and deploying process assets, including standard processes, are addressed in the Organizational Process Focus process area.

Subpractices

1. Select from the organization's set of standard processes those processes that cover the asset definition and management process and best meet the needs of the organizational unit or line of business.
2. Establish the defined process by tailoring the selected processes according to the organization's tailoring guidelines.
3. Ensure that the organization's process objectives are appropriately addressed in the defined process, and ensure that process governance extends to the tailored processes.
4. Document the defined process and the records of the tailoring.
5. Revise the description of the defined process as necessary.

ADM:GG3.GP2 COLLECT IMPROVEMENT INFORMATION

Collect asset definition and management work products, measures, measurement results, and improvement information derived from planning and performing the process to support future use and improvement of the organization's processes and process assets.

Elaboration:

> These are examples of improvement work products and information:
> - asset inventory
> - conflicts arising from asset-service relationships
> - metrics and measurements of the viability of the process *(Refer to ADM:GG2.GP8 subpractice 2.)*
> - changes and trends in operating conditions, risk conditions, and the risk environment that affect process results
> - lessons learned in post-event review of incidents and disruptions in continuity
> - process lessons learned that can be applied to improve operational resilience management performance, such as poorly documented or profiled assets and difficulties in assigning and executing asset ownership and custodianship responsibilities
> - the level to which the asset inventory, asset profiles, and the asset database reflect the current status of all assets
> - reports on the effectiveness and weaknesses of controls, including issues related to change control on the asset inventory
> - asset-service dependency mitigation plans that are not executed and the risks associated with them
> - resilience requirements that are not being satisfied or are being exceeded

Establishing the measurement repository and process asset library is addressed in the Organizational Process Definition process area. Updating the measurement repository and process asset library as part of process improvement and deployment is addressed in the Organizational Process Focus process area.

Subpractices

1. Store process and work product measures in the organization's measurement repository.
2. Submit documentation for inclusion in the organization's process asset library.
3. Document lessons learned from the process for inclusion in the organization's process asset library.
4. Propose improvements to the organizational process assets.

ACCESS MANAGEMENT
Operations

Purpose

The purpose of Access Management is to ensure that access granted to organizational assets is commensurate with their business and resilience requirements.

Introductory Notes

In order to support services, assets such as information, technology, and facilities must be made available (accessible) for use. This requires that persons (employees and contractors), objects (such as systems), and entities (such as business partners) have sufficient (but not excessive) levels of access to these assets.

Effective access management requires balancing organizational needs against the appropriate level of controls based on an asset's resilience requirements and business objectives. Insufficient access may translate into higher levels of asset protection but may impede the organization's ability to use the assets to their productive capacity. On the other hand, excessive levels of access (due to inadequate levels of control) expose assets to potential unauthorized or inadvertent misuse, which may diminish their productive capacity. Finding the right level of access for persons, objects, and entities so that they can perform their job responsibilities while satisfying the protection needs for the asset is a process that involves business owners, organizational units, and the owners and custodians of assets. In essence, these parties must come to agreement on what level of protection is sufficient given the need to meet objectives. Access management encompasses the processes that the organization uses to address this balancing act.

Access privileges and restrictions are the mechanisms for linking persons, objects, and entities (and their organizational roles) to the assets they need to perform their responsibilities. Access privileges and restrictions are operationalized (i.e., made operational or implemented) through logical and physical *access controls*, which may be administrative, technical, or physical in nature and can be discretionary (i.e., at the will of the asset owner) or mandatory (constrained by policies, regulations, and laws).

Access controls differ significantly from access privileges and restrictions. In the purest sense, an access control is the administrative, technical, or physical mechanism that provides a gate at which identities must present proper credentials to pass. Some examples of access controls are access and security policies, access control lists in application systems and databases, and key card and key pad readers for facilities. Access controls are established relative to the resilience requirements for an asset and service they protect—they are the mechanism that enforces the resilience requirements of confidentiality, integrity, and availability. When an identity presents an access request to an access control, and the identity has the necessary credentials required by the control (i.e., is authenticated and authorized to have the level of access requested), access is provided.

Access controls are a key element of the protection provided to an asset and form a substantial portion of the organization's protection strategy for assets and services. Because the operational environment is constantly changing, it is difficult for an organization to keep access controls current and reflective of actual business and resilience requirements. The Access Management process area establishes processes to ensure that access to organizational assets remains consistent with the business and resilience requirements of those assets even as the organization's operating environment changes. At a summary level, this includes activities to

- involve owners of assets in the process of establishing and maintaining access privileges
- manage changes to access privileges as the identities, user roles, business requirements, and resilience requirements change
- monitor and analyze relationships between identities, roles, and current access privileges to ensure alignment with business and resilience requirements
- adjust access privileges when they are not aligned with business and resilience requirements
- ensure that the access privileges granted to a user by the system of access controls reflect the privileges assigned by the asset owner

Clearly, access management is strongly tied to identity management. In identity management, persons, objects, and entities are established as identities that may require some level of access to organizational assets. However, access privileges and restrictions are tied to identities by the roles that are attributed to the identities. Thus, as identities change, or as their roles change, there is a cascading effect on access privileges that must be managed. For example:

- New identities may be established that must be provided access privileges.
- The access privileges of existing identities may have to be changed as the job responsibilities associated with the identity change.

- The access privileges of existing identities may have to be eliminated or deprovisioned as job responsibilities expire (either through new assignments or voluntary or involuntary termination).

The selection of the appropriate access controls to enforce those rights for a given asset is outside of the scope of this process area. These activities are performed in the operations process area associated with each type of asset (e.g., Knowledge and Information Management for information assets). *(Overall management of the organization's internal control system is addressed in the Controls Management process area.)*

Related Process Areas

The creation, maintenance, and deprovisioning of identities and their associated attributes are addressed in the Identity Management process area.

The selection and implementation of appropriate access controls for assets are addressed in the Knowledge and Information Management process area (for information), the Technology Management process area (for technology assets), and the Environmental Control process area (for facilities).

The analysis and mitigation of risks related to inappropriate or excessive levels of access privileges are addressed in the Risk Management process area.

Summary of Specific Goals and Practices

AM:SG1 Manage and Control Access
    AM:SG1.SP1   Enable Access
    AM:SG1.SP2   Manage Changes to Access Privileges
    AM:SG1.SP3   Periodically Review and Maintain Access Privileges
    AM:SG1.SP4   Correct Inconsistencies

Specific Practices by Goal

AM:SG1 MANAGE AND CONTROL ACCESS

Access granted to organizational assets is managed and controlled.

Access privileges describe and define a level of access to an organizational asset—information, technology, or facilities—commensurate with an identity's job responsibilities and the business and resilience requirements of the asset. In other words, access privileges define what assets identities can access and what they can do when they access these assets. Access privileges must be closely managed in order to prevent vulnerabilities that could lead to unauthorized and inadvertent misuse of organizational assets.

To manage and control access privileges, the organization must establish processes for approving and assigning these privileges, managing changes to them, and monitoring and analyzing the current access environment to ensure that it is in alignment with business and resilience requirements and does not result in additional risk to organizational assets.

AM:SG1.SP1 ENABLE ACCESS

Appropriate access to organizational assets is informed by resilience requirements and owner approval.

Access privileges and restrictions describe the level and extent of access provided to identities. Access privileges should be commensurate with the various roles represented by an identity but concurrently must be congruent with the resilience requirements of the assets to which the privileges are granted.

Access privileges are assigned and approved by asset owners based on the role of the person, object, or entity that is requesting access. Asset owners are the persons or organizational units, internal or external to the organization, that have primary responsibility for the viability, productivity, and resilience of a high-value organizational asset. It is the owner's responsibility to ensure that requirements for protecting and sustaining assets are defined for assets under the owner's control. In part, these requirements are satisfied by defining and assigning access privileges that are commensurate with the requirements. Therefore, the asset owner is responsible for granting and revoking access privileges to an identity based on the identity's role *and* the asset's resilience requirements. To be successful, asset owners must be aware of identities that need access to their assets and must evaluate the need with respect to business and resilience requirements before granting approval.

The organization must have processes in place to support the access request and approval process. This process begins with the registration of an identity *(as detailed in the Identity Management process area)* and then proceeds with assigning access privileges. In some cases, these activities may occur simultaneously. When assigning access privileges, the organization should have processes in place to allow

- the owners or sponsors of identities to request access (type and extent) from owners of organizational assets
- asset owners to determine the appropriate type and extent of access based on the identity's role
- asset owners to approve and grant access privileges

Access privileges are usually focused on three common types of assets: information, technology, and facilities.

- Information assets may be physical (such as paper files) or electronic (databases). The types of access privileges assigned for information assets typically include inquire, modify or change, and delete.
- Technology assets span the physical and electronic realm and cover a significantly diverse set of organizational assets.
  Access to technology assets can be physical but also logical (by allowing a person, object, or entity to log on to a server or network). Logical and physical access may allow a person to modify or change a hardware or software configuration or permit removal or destruction of a technology asset.

> These are examples of technology assets:
> - all types of software, such as application systems and operating systems, including any remote software that is not contained in an organization-controlled facility but is used or accessed by the organization's users
> - all types of hardware, such as personal computers, servers, network components, telecommunications components, and peripheral devices such as routers and disk storage devices, including any remote hardware that is not contained in an organization-controlled facility but is used or accessed by the organization's users
> - networks and other shared communication devices, including fax machines

- Facilities are buildings and other physical plant. Access privileges for physical assets generally provide or prevent entry to the facility and may limit the time period for which entry is permitted. Access privileges for facilities may be combined with access privileges for information and technology assets. This would be operationalized by allowing entry to the places where these assets are located or stored.

It should also be noted that not all access privileges are equal. In some cases, privileges are special or universal, providing trusted levels of access that are not generally provided unless the person, object, or entity is in a trusted or privileged position. Examples of such privileges include the ability to change the access control list on a file folder in a file sharing system and the possession of system administration privileges. As with general access rights, identities that request special privileges must have the approval of the owner of the assets that could be affected by the special rights.

The granting of access privileges should not be confused with the implementation of access controls. For example, an identity may be provided an appropriate and approved level of access to an organizational asset (such as permission to alter medical records), but the controls implemented over the asset may be insufficient to accommodate the privilege (such as access controls for "read" access only).

Typical work products

1. Access requests
2. Access approval

3. Access control policy
4. Access rights and responsibilities
5. Access acknowledgment

Subpractices

1. Establish access management policies and procedures.

    The organization should establish policies and procedures for requesting, approving, and providing access to persons, objects, and entities. The access management policy should establish the responsibilities of requestors, asset owners, and asset custodians (who typically are called upon to implement access requests). The policy should cover all affected assets—information, technology, and facilities—and address clear guidelines for access requests that originate externally to the organization (i.e., from contractors or business partners). The policy should also cover the type and extent of access that will be provided to objects such as systems and processes.

    The types of documentation required to fulfill the access management policy should be described and exhibited in the policy.

    The access management policy should be communicated to all who need to know and their responsibilities should be clearly detailed in the policy. The policy should also describe disciplinary measures for violations of the policy.

2. Complete and submit access requests.

    Access requests should be sponsored by an appropriate person in the organization (i.e., a supervisor or manager) and should be directly submitted to and approved by the owner of the assets (or the agents of the owner) to which access is being requested.

    Access requests should include proper justification for the request and should be approved by the sponsor of the request.

3. Approve access requests.

    Access should be granted in accordance with the justification for the request and the resilience requirements that have been established for the asset. Asset owners are responsible for reviewing the request, justification, and resilience requirements to decide whether to approve or deny access. The access provided should be commensurate with and not exceed the requestor's job responsibilities. If possible, the approval for the access should be limited to a specific time period (one week, one month, one year), to prevent the privilege from extending beyond the requestor's need. Limiting the term of the approval also provides the asset owner a chance to review privileges when they come up for renewal and to make changes if necessary.

    If the custodian of the asset is different from the owner, the owner should communicate in writing the approval for the request as well as any modifications of the request that the owner deems appropriate given the review of the request. Access requests should not be forwarded to custodians for implementation unless they have been approved by asset owners.

If an asset owner decides to extend access rights that exceed stated resilience requirements or extend beyond the need established by the requestor's job responsibilities, the owner should document this decision and identify any potential risk that may occur as a result. Risks should be addressed through the organization's formal risk management process.

4. Provide users (access holders) with a written statement of their access rights and responsibilities.

    Users should be required to acknowledge (in writing) that they understand their access privileges and will not exploit these privileges or any privileges that they have not been assigned.

5. Implement access requests.

    Access requests should be provided to custodians or others in the organization who are authorized to implement access privileges.

    Custodians should be part of the approval process and should sign the access request when the privilege has been implemented.

AM:SG1.SP2 MANAGE CHANGES TO ACCESS PRIVILEGES

Changes to access privileges are managed as assets, roles, and resilience requirements change.

The continual evolution of the operational environment and the identity community (persons, objects, and entities) requires constant changes to be made to access privileges to organizational assets. There are many different scenarios that may result in legitimate changes to access privileges, such as

- changes in job responsibilities and roles, such as when employees are promoted, take other positions in the organization, or leave the organization
- changes to outsourcing arrangements or the roles of external contractors
- changes to internal and external systems and processes that access organizational assets
- changes in the identity community (i.e., addition or deletion of identity, changes to the identity's roles) *(Changes to the identity community are addressed in ID:SG2.SP1 in the Identity Management process area.)*
- changes to the assets to which access privileges are provided and/or changes to the resilience requirements of the assets (which could cascade through all access privileges)
- periodic review and maintenance of access privileges (as described in AM:SG2.SP3)

In order to get a handle on this ever-changing environment, the organization must establish criteria to determine when a change in the operational environment would trigger a change in access privileges.

Owners of organizational assets have a role in the change management of access privileges. Owners are responsible for initiating and approving changes as required *before* corresponding access controls are modified to accommodate the changes. This may involve communication between asset owners and asset custodians who are responsible for implementing and maintaining those access controls. Owners are also responsible for following up to ensure that access privileges have been granted only to the approved limit.

There may also be planned changes to access privileges that must be considered. Planned changes may occur when normal operations are suspended due to a disaster or crisis. When this occurs, users may need additional privileges to perform roles that are not in their usual job responsibilities. These planned changes should be considered and approved in advance so that they can be implemented quickly when necessary. The organization should also have processes for returning user access to normal operations when the need for special privileges has been terminated.

Note: This practice is typically tied to or affected directly by changes in identities or identity profiles. Thus, the organization should consider performing this practice in conjunction with ID:SG2.SP1 in the Identity Management process area.

Typical work products

1. Documented change management processes for access control systems
2. Access privileges change criteria
3. Authorization for change in access privileges

Subpractices

1. Establish an enterprise-wide change management process for access privileges.
   In many organizations, the human resources and legal departments can be effective clearinghouses for changes to access privileges. Human resources departments are often the first to be notified of a change in an employee's job responsibilities or the addition of new employees. These actions often translate into direct changes in access privileges. Legal departments, on the other hand, often have access to contract information that provides external entities and agencies with access privileges and may be informed of changes in these relationships that would warrant access privilege changes.
2. Establish organizational criteria that may signify changes in access privileges.
   Change criteria can help the organization to determine the types of changes that must be monitored in an attempt to identify inconsistencies between identities and the privileges that have been assigned to them.

   Examples of change criteria that can be useful for this purpose can be found in ID:SG2.SP1 subpractice 1 in the Identity Management process area.
3. Manage changes to access privileges.
   Typically, the activities related to altering access privileges fall to custodians who implement controls commensurate with resilience requirements. Asset owners

must stay informed about changes in access privileges related to the assets under their ownership and care and should notify custodians to make changes commensurately. Custodians should not make changes to access privileges for any reason without authorization and approval from asset owners.

Changes that are detected through human resources and legal processes should also be referred to asset owners for review and approval before any actions are taken by custodians.

AM:SG1.SP3 PERIODICALLY REVIEW AND MAINTAIN ACCESS PRIVILEGES

Periodic review is performed to identify excessive or inappropriate levels of access privileges.

Constant change in the operational environment creates the potential that at any time the current level of access provided to persons, objects, and entities (as reflected in access privileges) may not match the current level of need based on business and resilience requirements. In other words, the privileges provided to identities are out of synch with what they *should be* allowed to do. This provides a fertile ground where vulnerabilities to organizational assets can breed and be exploited.

Typically, this misalignment is a by-product of staff members switching jobs or roles—they often retain the privileges they had in the former role and are provided new privileges to support their new role. When this happens, the former privileges may continue to be used (perhaps for unauthorized purposes) and could result in fraud, collusion, or other exposures. In addition, over time, access privileges that are not terminated when the need for those privileges expires provide entry points from which internal and external actors can exploit organizational assets. These types of vulnerabilities are controllable by the organization if it implements proper change control processes for access privileges.

Periodic review of access rights is the primary responsibility of the owners of organizational assets. They must ensure that the requirements they have set for their assets are being implemented through proper assignment of access privileges and implementation of corresponding access controls. Owners are also responsible for taking action whenever access rights do not correspond with legitimate identity needs and existing resilience requirements. This requires that they have frequent conversations with asset custodians to ensure that access controls are accordingly modified if necessary.

During periodic review, there are two particular problems that owners of assets should be attuned to:

- The first is misalignment between existing access privileges and the resilience requirements established for the assets. In this case, access privileges that have been provisioned to identities violate the resilience requirements that owners have set for the assets.

- The second is misalignment between existing access privileges and the roles and job responsibilities of the identities that possess the privileges. In this case, there is no violation of the resilience requirements, but privileges that are more extensive than necessary have been provisioned to identities that do not require this level of access.

The organization must determine the appropriate time intervals for reviewing access privileges based on the potential vulnerabilities and risks that may result from misalignment.

Typical work products

1. Guidelines and timetables for access privilege review
2. List of excessive or inappropriate access privileges
3. Documentation of actions proposed and taken

Subpractices

1. Establish regular review cycle and process.

    The mismanagement of access privileges is a major source of potential risks and vulnerabilities to the organization. Because assets and the identity community that needs access to the assets are pervasive across the organization, and in some cases extend beyond the organization, the ability to ensure that only authorized identities have appropriate privileges is an ongoing challenge. The organization must establish responsibility for regular review of access privileges and a process for correcting inconsistencies.

    The review cycle should consider the potential risks of excessive privileges as input to the time interval for performing regular review. Where access privileges provide special rights (such as "superusers"), the review cycle may have to be more frequent.

2. Perform periodic review of access privileges by asset.

    Periodic review of access rights is the responsibility of the owners of organizational assets. Reviews should be performed in accordance with the time intervals determined in AM:SG1.SP3 subpractice 1. Failure to perform these reviews on a regular basis should subject asset owners to disciplinary measures.

    In addition to identifying inconsistencies and misalignment, periodic review should also be performed to reaffirm the current need for access privileges.

3. Identify inconsistencies or misalignment in access privileges.

    Asset owners should document any inconsistencies or misalignment in access privileges. Owners should identify privileges that are
    - excessive
    - out of alignment with the identity's role or job responsibility
    - assigned but never approved by the asset owner
    - in violation of the asset's resilience requirements

Owners should also identify identities that may have been provisioned with access privileges but are no longer considered as valid identities.

A disposition for each inconsistency or misalignment should be documented, as well as the actions that have to be taken to correct these issues.

AM:SG1.SP4 CORRECT INCONSISTENCIES

Excessive or inappropriate levels of access privileges are corrected.

Excessive or inappropriate levels of access privileges must be corrected in a timely manner to avoid exposing the organization to additional risk. The longer that these privileges are allowed, the greater the potential that they will be exploited by unauthorized or inadvertent actions.

As a result of periodic review, asset owners may authorize custodians to take one or more of these actions:

- Change, disable, or deprovision access privileges to better reflect the identity's role and job responsibilities.
- Disable or deprovision certain privileges to preserve resilience requirements.
- Deprovision an identity that is no longer valid. *(This action is addressed in ID:SG2.SP3 in the Identity Management process area.)*
- Take no action, but identify and characterize resulting risks and develop an appropriate mitigation strategy.

These corrections apply to the privileges extended to any identity that exists outside of the organization's direct control, such as business partners and suppliers.

Typical work products

1. Written authorization for changes
2. Justification for not taking corrective action
3. Access privileges to be deprovisioned
4. Risk statements
5. Correction status

Subpractices

1. Develop corrective actions to address excessive or inappropriate levels of access privileges.
    Corrective actions must be initiated by asset owners and should involve asset custodians to determine the best course of action for the organization.
2. Correct access privileges as required.
    Generally, review of access privileges will result in disabling or deprovisioning privileges. (Disabling privileges typically occurs when the need for the privilege is

temporarily unjustified but may be justifiable in the future.) In a few cases, the asset owner may request a change to an access privilege instead, such as reducing the current level or extent of privileges.

Typically, the activities related to changing, disabling, or deprovisioning access privileges fall to custodians who implement controls commensurate with resilience requirements. Asset owners should notify custodians to make changes as described in their documentation of issues and corrective action. Custodians should not make changes to access privileges for any reason without written authorization and approval from asset owners.

Changes that are detected through human resources and legal processes should also be referred to asset owners for review and approval before any actions are taken by custodians. This should also be performed for access privileges that must be deprovisioned due to the deprovisioning of an identity.

Identities that have been found to be no longer valid should be deprovisioned. (*Deprovisioning of identities is addressed in ID:SG2.SP3 in the Identity Management process area.*)

3. Document disposition for excessive or inappropriate levels of access privileges that will not result in changes or deprovisioning.

    In some cases, asset owners may decide to take no action. In such a case, the asset owner should document the justification for taking no action and identify resulting risks. (*See AM:SG1.SP4 subpractice 4.*)

4. Identify risks related to excessive or inappropriate levels of access privileges.

    Risks related to allowing excessive or unjustified levels of access privileges must be analyzed and mitigated so that they do not affect the organization's operational resilience. Asset owners who permit access privileges that do not align with resilience requirements or are excessive considering the identity's job responsibilities and role should document and address risks according to the organization's risk management process. At a minimum, asset owners should be required to document a risk profile and statement regarding the access privileges.

    Risks are addressed and managed in the Risk Management process area.

5. Update status on corrective actions.

    The organization should perform status checks for all actions related to excessive or inappropriate levels of access privileges to ensure that a proper disposition is provided for each.

Elaborated Generic Practices by Goal

Refer to the Generic Goals and Practices document in Appendix A for general guidance that applies to all process areas. This section provides elaborations relative to the application of the Generic Goals and Practices to the Access Management process area.

AM:GG1 ACHIEVE SPECIFIC GOALS

The operational resilience management system supports and enables achievement of the specific goals of the Access Management process area by transforming identifiable input work products to produce identifiable output work products.

AM:GG1.GP1 PERFORM SPECIFIC PRACTICES

Perform the specific practices of the Access Management process area to develop work products and provide services to achieve the specific goals of the process area.

Elaboration:

Specific practices AM:SG1.SP1 through AM:SG1.SP4 are performed to achieve the goals of the access management process.

AM:GG2 INSTITUTIONALIZE A MANAGED PROCESS

Access management is institutionalized as a managed process.

AM:GG2.GP1 ESTABLISH PROCESS GOVERNANCE

Establish and maintain governance over the planning and performance of the access management process.

Refer to the Enterprise Focus process area for more information about providing sponsorship and oversight to the access management process.

Subpractices

1. Establish governance over process activities.

    Elaboration:

    > Governance over the access management process may be exhibited by
    > - developing and publicizing higher-level managers' objectives and requirements for the process
    > - sponsoring process policies, procedures, standards, and guidelines, including those for requesting and approving access privileges
    > - providing guidance for resolving access inconsistencies and repeated violations of access policy
    > - making higher-level managers aware of applicable compliance obligations related to the process, and regularly reporting on the organization's satisfaction of these obligations to higher-level managers

- sponsoring and funding process activities
- verifying that the process supports strategic resilience objectives and is focused on the assets and services that are of the highest relative value in meeting strategic objectives
- regular reporting from organizational units to higher-level managers on process activities and results
- creating dedicated higher-level management feedback loops on decisions about the process and recommendations for improving the process
- providing input on identifying, assessing, and managing operational risks to assets, including those related to inappropriate or excessive levels of access privileges
- conducting regular internal and external audits and related reporting to audit committees on process effectiveness
- creating formal programs to measure the effectiveness of process activities, and reporting these measurements to higher-level managers

2. Develop and publish organizational policy for the process.

   Elaboration:

   The access management policy should address
   - responsibility, authority, and ownership for performing process activities, including requesting, approving, and providing access to persons, objects, and entities
   - the responsibilities of requestors, asset owners, and asset custodians
   - all affected assets—information, technology, and facilities
   - access requests that originate from outside of the organization
   - procedures, standards, and guidelines for
     - approving and provisioning access privileges
     - approving and provisioning special access privileges that provide trusted levels of access
     - providing change management over access privileges
     - identifying and addressing inconsistencies between approved and granted privileges
     - enforcing disciplinary actions for violations of the access policy
   - requirements for periodically reconciling access privileges and identifying inappropriate access
   - methods for measuring adherence to policy, exceptions granted, and policy violations

   Refer to AM:SG1.SP1 subpractice 1 for a description of policies and procedures for access management.

AM:GG2.GP2 Plan the Process

Establish and maintain the plan for performing the access management process.

> *Elaboration:*
>
> For practical purposes, access management is likely to be a highly decentralized activity that is specific to the type of asset (information, technology, or facilities) being accessed. For this reason, the organization may have a plan that covers the general management of access to organizational assets but also specific plans that address the special considerations unique to each type of asset.
>
> Of importance in AM:GG2.GP2 is that the organization understands what plans have to be developed and that these plans are created accordingly. The plan (or plans) should be directly influenced by the organization's resilience requirements and should focus on how the organization can manage access privileges and access controls relative to its unique blend of assets and the extent of access requests and identities.
>
> *Subpractices*
>
> 1. Define and document the plan for performing the process.
>
>   *Elaboration:*
>
>   In the case where plans are developed specific to an asset type (information, technology, or facilities) or access type (logical or physical), these plans should be coordinated and should reflect the organization's overall plan for access management.
>
> 2. Define and document the process description.
> 3. Review the plan with relevant stakeholders and get their agreement.
> 4. Revise the plan as necessary.

AM:GG2.GP3 Provide Resources

Provide adequate resources for performing the access management process, developing the work products, and providing the services of the process.

> *Subpractices*
>
> 1. Staff the process.
>
>   *Elaboration:*
>
>   Staffing the access management process will likely cross many organizational lines. Access management involves organizational unit staff (such as asset owners) as well as information technology staff (such as those who implement and manage access controls for information and technology assets as directed by asset owners).

Access management may also involve physical security staff such as security guards and those who implement and manage physical access controls for facilities. Information technology staff may also be involved in physical access management where systems and technology are used to implement physical access controls.

> These are examples of staff required to perform the access management process:
> - staff responsible for submitting access requests, such as supervisors, managers, and identity owners
> - asset owners responsible for reviewing and approving access requests, ensuring that access privileges and controls are commensurate with job roles and responsibilities and are not inappropriate or excessive
> - asset custodians responsible for implementing access requests and controls as direct by asset owners
> - users who have been granted access privileges
> - staff responsible for managing changes to access privileges, including human resources and legal departments
> - asset owners responsible for conducting regular reviews of access privileges by asset, identifying inconsistencies, and correcting or justifying these
> - staff responsible for developing process plans and programs and ensuring they are aligned with stakeholder requirements and needs
> - staff responsible for managing external entities that have contractual obligations for process activities
> - owners and custodians of high-value assets that support the accomplishment of operational resilience management objectives
> - internal and external auditors responsible for reporting to appropriate committees on process effectiveness

Refer to the Organizational Training and Awareness process area for information about training staff for resilience roles and responsibilities.

Refer to the Human Resource Management process area for information about acquiring staff to fulfill roles and responsibilities.

2. Fund the process.

   Refer to the Financial Resource Management process area for information about budgeting for, funding, and accounting for access management.

3. Provide necessary tools, techniques, and methods to perform the process.

   Elaboration:

   Tools, techniques, and methods will likely involve those that help the organization implement and manage the creation and approval of access requests and the change management of access privileges.

For AM:GG2.GP3 subpractice 3, tools, techniques, and methods do not include those necessary to implement and manage administrative (policy), technical, and physical access controls.

> These are examples of tools, techniques, and methods to support the access management process:
> - access request and approval management systems and methods
> - tools and techniques that aid in associating roles, responsibilities, identities, and access privileges, by asset owner and by asset type
> - access privilege database systems
> - tools and techniques that assist in reviewing access privileges by asset, by asset type, by asset owner, and by user
> - access privilege change management tools and methods
> - tools and techniques that assist in managing the list of excessive or inappropriate access privileges and tracking resolution actions to closure

Refer to the Knowledge and Information Management, Technology Management, and Environmental Control process areas for practices related to implementing and managing controls for information, technology, and facilities assets, respectively.

AM:GG2.GP4 ASSIGN RESPONSIBILITY

Assign responsibility and authority for performing the access management process, developing the work products, and providing the services of the process.

Refer to the Human Resource Management process area for more information about establishing resilience as a job responsibility, developing resilience performance goals and objectives, and measuring and assessing performance against these goals and objectives.

Subpractices

1. Assign responsibility and authority for performing the process.

   Elaboration:

   Responsibility for performing and managing the access management process may be distributed across the organization and may involve both organizational units and information technology. Responsibility may be delineated between access approval and authorization processes and the implementation and management of access controls. Organizational unit managers (and, specifically, asset owners) are typically responsible for the approval and authorization processes, while information technology and physical security staff are responsible for the implementation and management of access controls. Change management for access privileges is typically a shared responsibility among organizational units, information technology, and physical security because they must coordinate activities to ensure that privileges are approved for only authorized staff.

AM:GG2.GP4 subpractice 1 does not specifically cover responsibility for the development and implementation of access controls for information, technology, or facilities. AM:GG2.GP4 subpractice 1 is limited to responsibility for the approval of access privileges and the management of changes to access privileges.

> Refer to the Knowledge and Information Management, Technology Management, and Environmental Control process areas for information about developing and implementing access controls for information, technology, and facilities assets, respectively.

2. Assign responsibility and authority for performing the specific tasks of the process.

   Elaboration:

   > Responsibility and authority for performing access management tasks can be formalized by
   > - defining roles and responsibilities in the process plan
   > - including process tasks and responsibility for those tasks in specific job descriptions
   > - developing policy requiring organizational unit managers, line of business managers, project managers, and asset and service owners and custodians to participate in and derive benefit from the process for assets and services under their ownership or custodianship
   > - developing policy requiring asset custodians (including information technology staff) to perform process activities relative to organizational unit and asset owner instructions
   > - acknowledgment of access policy by users and other identities that request access (to affirm their responsibilities in the process)
   > - including process tasks in staff performance management goals and objectives with requisite measurement of progress against those goals
   > - developing and implementing contractual instruments (including service level agreements) with external entities to establish responsibility and authority for performing process tasks on outsourced functions
   > - including process tasks in measuring performance of external entities against contractual instruments

   > Refer to the External Dependencies Management process area for additional details about managing relationships with external entities.

3. Confirm that people assigned with responsibility and authority understand it and are willing and able to accept it.

AM:GG2.GP5 TRAIN PEOPLE

Train the people performing or supporting the access management process as needed.

Refer to the Organizational Training and Awareness process area for more information about training the people performing or supporting the process.

Refer to the Human Resource Management process area for more information about inventorying skill sets, establishing a skill set baseline, identifying required skill sets, and measuring and addressing skill deficiencies.

Subpractices

1. Identify process skill needs.

   Elaboration:

   Skill needs relative to AM:GG2.GP5 subpractice 1 do not include the implementation and management of access controls, which may require extensive skill levels. These skill needs are addressed in the process areas relative to each of the asset types as specified in AM:GG2.GP4 subpractice 1.

   > These are examples of skills required in the access management process:
   > - knowledge of the tools, techniques, and methods necessary to manage access privileges, including those necessary to perform the process using the selected methods, techniques, and tools identified in AM:GG2.GP3 subpractice 3
   > - knowledge unique to each type of asset that is required to establish and maintain privileges for each type
   > - knowledge necessary to work effectively with asset owners and custodians
   > - knowledge necessary to elicit and prioritize stakeholder requirements and needs and interpret them to develop effective requirements, plans, and programs for the process

2. Identify process skill gaps based on available resources and their current skill levels.
3. Identify training opportunities to address skill gaps.

   Elaboration:

   > These are examples of training topics:
   > - understanding service desk procedures for handling access requests
   > - documenting, processing, routing, reviewing, and approving access requests
   > - ensuring access privileges are properly associated with roles, rights, responsibilities, and identities
   > - managing and controlling changes to access privileges and supporting databases
   > - deprovisioning access privileges
   > - supporting asset owners and custodians in understanding the process and their roles and responsibilities with respect to its activities

4. Provide training and review the training needs as necessary.

AM:GG2.GP6 MANAGE WORK PRODUCT CONFIGURATIONS

Place designated work products of the access management process under appropriate levels of control.

Elaboration:

AM:SG1.SP2 addresses the change control process over access privileges. However, other work products of the access management process (such as access requests and access policy acknowledgments) must also be managed and controlled.

Tools, techniques, and methods should be employed to support the initiation, approval, and acceptance of access requests and corresponding access privileges. Access privileges are operationalized using access control mechanisms. For example, an access privilege allowing modification of information may be represented by an entry in a file's access control list. Thus, managing work products such as access privileges may necessarily involve management of the access controls themselves, even though access controls are not within the scope of AM:GG2.GP6.

These are examples of access management work products placed under control:
- access control policy and acknowledgments from users that they understand and will abide by the policy
- access requests and approvals
- access rights and responsibilities
- change management processes for access control systems
- access privilege change criteria and authorizations for change
- access privilege database
- list of excessive or inappropriate access privileges
- list of access privileges to be deprovisioned
- process plan
- policies and procedures
- contracts with external entities

AM:GG2.GP7 IDENTIFY AND INVOLVE RELEVANT STAKEHOLDERS

Identify and involve the relevant stakeholders of the access management process as planned.

Elaboration:

Several AM-specific practices address the involvement of asset owners and custodians as key stakeholders in the access management process. For example,

AM:SG1.SP1 describes the role of asset owners in assigning, approving, and revoking access privileges and the role of asset custodians in implementing access requests. AM:SG1.SP2 and AM:SG1.SP3 provide guidance on the role of asset owners in initiating, reviewing, and approving changes to access privileges and the role of asset custodians in maintaining access controls.

Subpractices

1. Identify process stakeholders and their appropriate involvement.

   Elaboration:

   Stakeholders of the plan include organizational staff who request, grant, or support the provision of access privileges to organizational assets.

   > These are examples of stakeholders of the access management process:
   > - asset owners and custodians
   > - service owners
   > - organizational unit and line of business managers responsible for assets
   > - owners and sponsors of identities requiring access
   > - staff responsible for developing, implementing, and managing an internal control system for assets
   > - external entities responsible for making access requests and managing access to assets
   > - human resources and legal departments as advisors on changes to access privileges
   > - internal and external auditors

   > Stakeholders are involved in various tasks in the access management process, such as
   > - planning for the process
   > - reviewing, initiating, approving, and revoking access requests and privileges
   > - translating access requests/privileges to access controls
   > - reconciling access privileges with roles, responsibilities, and identities
   > - identifying and correcting inappropriate levels of access privileges
   > - reviewing and appraising the effectiveness of process activities
   > - resolving issues in the process

2. Identify these stakeholders to planners and those responsible for process performance.
3. Involve relevant stakeholders in the process as planned.

AM:GG2.GP8 Monitor and Control the Process

Monitor and control the access management process against the plan for performing the process and take appropriate corrective action.

Refer to the Monitoring process area for more information about the collection, organization, and distribution of data that may be useful for monitoring and controlling processes.

Refer to the Measurement and Analysis process area for more information about establishing process metrics and measurement.

Refer to the Enterprise Focus process area for more information about providing process information to managers, identifying issues, and determining appropriate corrective actions.

Subpractices

1. Measure actual performance against the plan for performing the process.
2. Review accomplishments and results of the process against the plan for performing the process.

   Elaboration:

   > These are examples of metrics for the access management process:
   > - percentage of access requests that adhere to the process policy
   > - percentage of access requests approved (based on policy)
   > - percentage of access requests denied (based on policy)
   > - percentage of policy acknowledgment forms that have been fully executed
   > - number of duplicate access requests
   > - percentage of unapproved access requests that result in allowing access privileges
   > - percentage of access requests that are inappropriate given the requestor's role or job responsibilities
   > - percentage of access privileges incorrectly approved based on user's role or job responsibilities
   > - rate of requests to change current access privileges
   > - percentage of unapproved changes to access privileges
   > - the mean and median time frames between a change in access privileges requiring deprovisioning and the actual deprovisioning
   > - number of risks related to inappropriate or excessive levels of access privileges that have been referred to the risk management process; number of such risks where corrective action is still pending (by risk rank)
   > - level of adherence to process policies; number of policy violations; number of policy exceptions requested and number approved
   > - number of process activities that are on track per plan
   > - rate of change of resource needs to support the process
   > - rate of change of costs to support the process

3. Review activities, status, and results of the process with the immediate level of managers responsible for the process and identify issues.

   Elaboration:

   > Periodic reviews of the access management process are needed to ensure that
   > - policies are in place for managing access privileges
   > - ownership and custodianship over assets and access privileges for assets are established and documented access requests are submitted and approved according to policy
   > - change control processes are operating appropriately to ensure changes to access privileges are made and documented in a timely manner
   > - access privileges are periodically reconciled with roles, responsibilities, and identities
   > - access privilege inconsistencies are identified and corrected in a timely manner
   > - access privileges are deprovisioned when they are no longer valid or necessary
   > - status reports are provided to appropriate stakeholders in a timely manner
   > - unresolved issues surrounding inappropriate or excessive access privileges are referred to the risk management process when necessary
   > - actions requiring management involvement are elevated in a timely manner
   > - the performance of process activities is being monitored and regularly reported
   > - key measures are within acceptable ranges as demonstrated in governance dashboards or scorecards and financial reports
   > - administrative, technical, and physical controls are operating as intended
   > - internal controls are meeting the stated intent of the resilience requirements
   > - actions resulting from internal and external audits are being closed in a timely manner

4. Identify and evaluate the effects of significant deviations from the plan for performing the process.

   Elaboration:

   Deviations from the access management plan may occur when access requestors and asset owners fail to follow organizational policies regarding access request and approval. Significant deviations typically occur when changes in the operational environment and user community are not reflected in the current level of access privileges permitted. These deviations may permit unauthorized or inadvertent access to assets that can affect operational resilience.

5. Identify problems in the plan for performing and executing the process.
6. Take corrective action when requirements and objectives are not being satisfied, when issues are identified, or when progress differs significantly from the plan for performing the process.
7. Track corrective action to closure.

AM:GG2.GP9 OBJECTIVELY EVALUATE ADHERENCE

Objectively evaluate adherence of the access management process against its process description, standards, and procedures, and address non-compliance.

Elaboration:

These are examples of activities to be reviewed:
- access request and approval process
- making changes to existing access privileges
- the alignment of stakeholder requirements with process plans
- assignment of responsibility, accountability, and authority for process activities
- determining the adequacy of process reports and reviews in informing decision makers regarding the performance of operational resilience management activities and the need to take corrective action, if any
- verification of process controls, including identifying and correcting excessive or inappropriate levels of access
- use of process work products for improving strategies to protect and sustain assets and services

These are examples of work products to be reviewed:
- access control policy and policy exceptions and waivers
- access privilege requests
- access privilege database
- access privilege change criteria
- action plans (for addressing inconsistencies)
- process plan and policies
- access privilege issues that have been referred to the risk management process
- process methods, techniques, and tools
- metrics for the process *(Refer to AM:GG2.GP8 subpractice 2.)*
- contracts with external entities

AM:GG2.GP10 REVIEW STATUS WITH HIGHER-LEVEL MANAGERS

Review the activities, status, and results of the access management process with higher-level managers and resolve issues.

Refer to the Enterprise Focus process area for more information about providing sponsorship and oversight to the operational resilience management system.

AM:GG3 INSTITUTIONALIZE A DEFINED PROCESS

Access management is institutionalized as a defined process.

AM:GG3.GP1 ESTABLISH A DEFINED PROCESS

Establish and maintain the description of a defined access management process.

Establishing and tailoring process assets, including standard processes, are addressed in the Organizational Process Definition process area.

Establishing process needs and objectives and selecting, improving, and deploying process assets, including standard processes, are addressed in the Organizational Process Focus process area.

Subpractices

1. Select from the organization's set of standard processes those processes that cover the access management process and best meet the needs of the organizational unit or line of business.
2. Establish the defined process by tailoring the selected processes according to the organization's tailoring guidelines.
3. Ensure that the organization's process objectives are appropriately addressed in the defined process, and ensure that process governance extends to the tailored processes.
4. Document the defined process and the records of the tailoring.
5. Revise the description of the defined process as necessary.

AM:GG3.GP2 COLLECT IMPROVEMENT INFORMATION

Collect access management work products, measures, measurement results, and improvement information derived from planning and performing the process to support future use and improvement of the organization's processes and process assets.

Elaboration:

> These are examples of improvement work products and information:
> - access requests
> - approval of access requests
> - issues related to change control on access privileges
> - inconsistencies in levels of access privileges
> - exceptions and waivers permitted to process policies

> - metrics and measurements of the viability of the process *(Refer to AM:GG2.GP8 subpractice 2.)*
> - changes and trends in operating conditions, risk conditions, and the risk environment that affect process results
> - lessons learned in post-event review of incidents and disruptions in continuity
> - process lessons learned that can be applied to improve operational resilience management performance, such as excessive or inappropriate access privileges and difficulties in assigning and executing asset ownership and custodianship responsibilities
> - the level to which the status of the asset privileges by asset type, asset owner, or other meaningful categorization schemes is current
> - reports on the effectiveness and weaknesses of controls
> - asset privilege corrective action plans that are not executed and the risks associated with them
> - resilience requirements that are not being satisfied or are being exceeded

Establishing the measurement repository and process asset library is addressed in the Organizational Process Definition process area. Updating the measurement repository and process asset library as part of process improvement and deployment is addressed in the Organizational Process Focus process area.

Subpractices

1. Store process and work product measures in the organization's measurement repository.
2. Submit documentation for inclusion in the organization's process asset library.
3. Document lessons learned from the process for inclusion in the organization's process asset library.
4. Propose improvements to the organizational process assets.

COMMUNICATIONS
Enterprise

Purpose

The purpose of Communications is to develop, deploy, and manage internal and external communications to support resilience activities and processes.

Introductory Notes

Communication is a basic organizational activity and competency. From a resilience perspective, communication is an essential function, tying together disparate parts of the organization that collectively have a vested interest in protecting high-value assets and services and sustaining assets and services during and after a disruptive event.

Internally, communications processes are embedded in operational resilience management processes such as incident management, governance, and compliance, and support the development and execution of plans for sustaining the required level of resilience; externally, communications processes provide much-needed information to relevant stakeholders on the capability of the organization to protect and sustain assets and services, handle disruptions, and preserve customer confidence in unsettled and stressful times. Most important, communications are a critical success factor in ensuring the successful execution of service continuity plans and decision making, particularly during a crisis or disaster.

The Communications process area seeks to capture the communications activities that support and enable effective management of operational resilience. This requires foundational processes for basic and ongoing communications needs as well as more flexible ones for supporting the communications demands of managing events and executing service continuity plans. In the Communications process area, the organization establishes communications requirements that reflect the needs of stakeholders that are important to managing operational resilience. Communications guidelines and standards are developed to ensure the consistency and accuracy of messages and communications methods across all resilience processes. The communications infrastructure is established and managed to ensure effective and continuous communications flow when needed.

The organization also regularly assesses its communications abilities, particularly after an event, incident, or crisis, to revise communications requirements and to make improvements in the type and media of communications and the communications infrastructure.

The Communications process area focuses on communications processes that directly support the management of operational resilience. These processes are likely to be part of a larger (and in some cases, enterprise-wide) communications process in the organization. Thus, the Communications process area is not considered a substitute for this larger process.

Related Process Areas

The definition of the resilience program and the development of program objectives are established in the Enterprise Focus process area.

The data and information that the organization needs to provide governance and control over the operational resilience management system are established in the Monitoring process area and used in the Enterprise Focus process area.

The guidelines and standards for communicating about events, incidents, and crises are addressed in the Incident Management and Control process area.

The guidelines and standards for communicating with external entities to coordinate management of events are addressed in the External Dependencies Management process area.

Specific communications activities relevant to service continuity plans are developed and implemented in the Service Continuity process area.

Awareness communications relative to operational resilience management are addressed in the Organizational Training and Awareness process area.

Summary of Specific Goals and Practices

COMM:SG1 Prepare for Resilience Communications
    COMM:SG1.SP1   Identify Relevant Stakeholders
    COMM:SG1.SP2   Identify Communications Requirements
    COMM:SG1.SP3   Establish Communications Guidelines and Standards
COMM:SG2 Prepare for Communications Management
    COMM:SG2.SP1   Establish a Resilience Communications Plan
    COMM:SG2.SP2   Establish a Resilience Communications Program
    COMM:SG2.SP3   Identify and Assign Plan Staff
COMM:SG3 Deliver Resilience Communications
    COMM:SG3.SP1   Identify Communications Methods and Channels
    COMM:SG3.SP2   Establish and Maintain Communications Infrastructure
COMM:SG4 Improve Communications
    COMM:SG4.SP1   Assess Communications Effectiveness
    COMM:SG4.SP2   Improve Communications

Specific Practices by Goal

COMM:SG1 PREPARE FOR RESILIENCE COMMUNICATIONS

The requirements, guidelines, and standards for resilience communications are established.

An organization may have many diverse communications needs related to managing operational resilience. For example, effective oral and written communications support the organization's ability to provide

- awareness about resilience plans, processes, and activities
- information about events, incidents, and disruptions that the organization is addressing
- support to the successful execution of service continuity plans
- emergency and on-demand information to first responders and public service providers
- proactive information to external stakeholders (vendors, suppliers, and business partners) on the status of the organization's resilience program and effectiveness in meeting goals
- regular communications to regulators, lawmakers, and other constituencies that have a vested interest in the organization's resilience

Resilience communications are typically part of a larger enterprise or organizational communications strategy. To ensure that these communications activities are consistent with the organization's larger communications processes, and to address the range of communications needs required to support resilience processes, the organization establishes communications standards and guidelines that provide structure and context for resilience communications.

The essential elements for communications—the audience (stakeholders), the requirements (based on security and business continuity needs), and the standards by which communications are delivered—are established in this goal.

COMM:SG1.SP1 IDENTIFY RELEVANT STAKEHOLDERS

Internal and external stakeholders to which the organization must communicate relative to resilience activities are identified.

Organizations have many types of stakeholders that require communications related to managing operational resilience. These stakeholders may be very diverse depending on the type of communications needs they have, the frequency of the communications (whether discrete or continuous, circumstantial, or ongoing), and the level of communications necessary (notifications, press releases, crisis communications, etc.). Understanding the level and extent of stakeholders helps the organization to effectively develop and satisfy communications requirements.

Communications stakeholders are both internal and external to the organization. Internal stakeholders are identified to ensure ongoing communication about the organization's resilience activities, promote resilience awareness, and ensure that staff can effectively communicate and collaborate during disruptive events. Likewise, external stakeholders may need information about the organization's level of resilience, or they may have to be able to effectively communicate with the organization during times of crisis. These external organizations may even have a stated role in the communications plans or the service continuity of the organization. In addition, some regulatory and legal entities may require ongoing communications as evidence that an organization has taken appropriate actions to prepare for specific threats such as natural disasters and terrorism. Thus, the list of external stakeholders is developed to ensure proactive communications and message delivery regarding the organization's preparedness and capabilities for managing resilience.

Because there are many stakeholders that require information, the organization must identify the relevant stakeholders and distribute information about communications plans to them as necessary.

Typical work products

1. List of stakeholders that need to receive communications
2. Classes or roles of stakeholders
3. List of appropriate internal and external stakeholders
4. Stakeholder involvement plan

Subpractices

1. Identify relevant stakeholders that may have a vested interest or vital role in communications about resilience.

    When determining which stakeholders to include in the list, consider
    - rationale for stakeholder involvement
    - roles and responsibilities of the relevant stakeholders
    - relationships between stakeholders
    - relative importance of the stakeholder to the success of the program
    - resources (e.g., training, materials, time, and funding) needed to ensure stakeholder interaction

> These are examples of stakeholders that may need to receive communications:
> - members of the incident handling and management team (if the organization has established such a team) or internal staff who have incident handling and management job responsibilities
> - shareholders
> - asset owners and service owners
> - information technology staff
> - middle and higher-level managers

- business continuity staff (if they will be required to enact continuity or restoration plans as a result of an incident)
- human resources departments, particularly if safety is an issue
- communications and public relations staff
- staff involved in governance and oversight functions
- support functions such as legal and audit
- legal and law enforcement staff as required
- external media outlets, including newspaper, television, radio, and internet
- customers, business partners, and upstream suppliers
- local, state, and federal emergency management
- local utilities such as power, gas, telecommunications, and water, if affected
- regulatory and governing agencies

Stakeholders and their communications needs may be defined as a part of other operational resilience management processes. For example, the communications needs of staff involved in the incident management process may be defined by that process. These communications requirements should be considered independently of the processes and practices in the Communications process area because they have a specialized purpose and involve specific stakeholders.

2. Establish a plan that describes the involvement of all communications stakeholders. The plan identifies all internal and external stakeholders, including their roles and classes, as well as the types, frequencies, and levels of communication they are to receive in specified circumstances.

Refer to the Incident Management and Control process area for the identification and communications requirements of stakeholders relative to the incident management process.

Refer to the Service Continuity process area for the identification and communications requirements of stakeholders relative to the development and execution of service continuity plans.

Refer to the Monitoring process area for the identification of stakeholders that may have communications needs relative to monitoring and control processes. These stakeholders, as identified in MON:SG1.SP2, may overlap or be a subset of those that need specific and general resilience communications.

COMM:SG1.SP2 IDENTIFY COMMUNICATIONS REQUIREMENTS

The types and extent of communications needed by the organization to support stakeholders are identified.

The foundation for communications requirements is the needs of stakeholders. The variety of communications types and duration is directly related to the diversity of the stakeholder community. For example, an internal communication might be about general awareness or about a specific event or incident. External communications might be public relations messages, critical communications during a crisis, or the execution of a service continuity plan.

In addition to stakeholders, communications requirements may also be derived directly from the needs of other operational resilience management processes. For example, the ways in which the organization must distribute information collected in the monitoring process may create requirements that must be met by the communications process. Moreover, many operational resilience management processes have communications processes embedded in their practices; this occurs in the process areas Incident Management and Control, Service Continuity, and Enterprise Focus (particularly in the governance cycle). These processes may directly provide requirements that must be considered in the larger, enterprise-focused communications process.

The organization must establish communications requirements as the foundation for the development and execution of a communications plan to support operational resilience management processes. Requirements help the organization to determine the scope of the communications process, plan, and program and to ensure the development of appropriate and cost-effective delivery mechanisms and infrastructure to support communications needs. Requirements determine whether communications methods are

- oral or written, or both
- provided on a one-time basis, at regular intervals, on an ongoing basis, or on demand
- provided on media that are disposable or able to be archived
- provided on more than one media type (paper, electronic, etc.)

> These are examples of communications requirements:
> - providing awareness messages and training to staff
> - expressing resilience status to vendors, business partners, and other external agencies
> - providing information to news media on the organization's resilience efforts or efforts to contain an incident or event (before, during, or after the event)
> - communication among staff collaborating on managing incidents and events
> - crisis communications between the organization and first responders and other emergency and public service staff
> - communication between the organization and its environmental and public infrastructure partners
> - spontaneous communications between staff performing their roles in executing a service continuity plan

Communications requirements also provide the foundation for the development and implementation of an infrastructure (people, processes, and technology) to support all types of resilience communication.

Service continuity plans and the organization's incident management process (and other similar processes) may have very specific communications requirements. Thus, these requirements may be developed outside of the organization's communications process to ensure accuracy and adequate coverage.

Typical work products

1. Communications requirements by stakeholder and process

Subpractices

1. Analyze the resilience program to identify the types and extent of communications that are necessary to satisfy resilience program objectives.
2. Document the communications needs of stakeholders.
   Because managing operational resilience is a broad, enterprise-wide activity, communications activities may need to cover diverse topics and may require focused messages to particular stakeholders. Communications needs must be purposefully aimed at distributing the appropriate message to each stakeholder group.
3. Establish communications requirements for operational resilience management processes.
   Communications requirements must be established by stakeholder and documented. Essential information about each requirement must be collected so that the requirements can be analyzed and prioritized.
4. Analyze and prioritize communications requirements.
   Through analysis of communications requirements, the organization should seek to determine
   - the scope of the requirement
   - the potential infrastructure required to support the requirement
   - the resources (human, capital, or expense) needed to support the requirement
   - alternatives for meeting the requirement
   - requirements that cannot be met, and the potential risk to the organization that results
   - duplicative requirements or requirements that can be met through consolidated processes
5. Revise the communications needs of the organization as changes to the resilience program and strategy are made.

COMM:SG1.SP3 ESTABLISH COMMUNICATIONS GUIDELINES AND STANDARDS

The enterprise guidelines and standards for satisfying communications needs are established and maintained.

The effectiveness of communications is dependent on message clarity, the use of appropriate message media, the accuracy and consistency of the message, and the ability to confirm receipt of the communication. The inability to ensure high-quality and effective communications may result in a dilution of the message or in misunderstanding, misinterpretation, or confusion.

To ensure message consistency, accuracy, and completeness, as well as fitness for the intended purpose and stakeholder audience, the organization should establish communications guidelines and standards. These guidelines and standards should reflect the organization's operational resilience management objectives and be implemented at a level that sufficiently ensures their use in all communications processes. All staff involved in the communications process should be bound by adherence to the guidelines and standards, and the guidelines and standards should be extensible to vendors and business partners who may handle specific and unique communications activities for the organization.

Guidelines and standards are typically organization-specific and may reflect the organization's culture, industry and peer group, and environmental and geographical location.

Even though the requirements for communications may be specifically developed in other processes, such as the development of service continuity plans or in the incident management process, these requirements should be implemented under the auspices of the communications standards and guidelines that are established in COMM:SG1.SP3.

Typical work products

1. Resilience communications guidelines and standards

Subpractices

1. Develop resilience communications guidelines and standards.

> Communications guidelines and standards may address
> - alignment with and reflection of organizational strategy, policies, and governance processes
> - appropriateness of various types of media and message content for different types of communications requirements
> - approval levels and processes for approving message content and delivery
> - determination of who is authorized to create messages and deliver them in the organization
> - requirements for crisis communications between the organization and first responders and other emergency and public service staff
> - communications between the organization and its environmental and public infrastructure partners
> - specific guidelines for communicating with regulators, law enforcement, or other governmental or legal entities
> - specific guidelines for vendors and business partners when communicating on behalf of the organization
> - specific guidelines for vendors and business partners who perform communications processes on behalf of the organization

> - a taxonomy for industry-specific terms and a glossary
> - templates for standardized types of communications and media interaction
> - documentation requirements for use of trademarks and other identity guidelines
> - quality assurance processes and practices to perform fact-checking and to ensure consistency and accuracy
> - technical guidelines and standards for communications during crisis situations and for interaction with public service providers and first responders

COMM:SG2 PREPARE FOR COMMUNICATIONS MANAGEMENT

The process for developing, deploying, and managing resilience communications is established.

Resilience communications, especially communications about serious incidents or crises, cannot be effectively managed by reaction. The organization must plan its approach to communications, align this plan with strategic objectives, and provide sponsorship and oversight to the plan.

Managing communications requires the organization to establish a communications plan that addresses the unique and specific needs that arise from the processes involved in managing operational resilience. The communications plan is carried out through a communications program that is staffed with resources that are properly trained and authorized to develop, implement, and manage communications processes and specifically meet the needs of resilience communications.

In many organizations, the practices in COMM:SG2 may be a subset of the organization's overall communications capability. Therefore, these practices may be satisfied by existing processes that are expanded to specifically include and address the requirements established in COMM:SG1.SP2. However, it may be necessary for an organization to establish plans and programs for resilience communications where existing communications competencies are not adequate. This must be considered in the development of a communications plan *(in COMM:SG2.SP1)* and a corresponding communications program *(COMM:SG2.SP2)*.

COMM:SG2.SP1 ESTABLISH A RESILIENCE COMMUNICATIONS PLAN

Planning for the resilience communications process is performed.

The resilience communications plan details how the organization will meet the requirements of stakeholders and other operational resilience management processes *(as established in COMM:SG1.SP2)*. The plan should specifically detail how the requirements will be met and should provide for the establishment of a resilience communications program as a conduit for implementing the plan. The plan may be a subset of the organization's enterprise communications plan.

Specifically, the plan must address the development, delivery, and maintenance of communications and related materials to provide the organizational message to each class of stakeholder. The plan should address near-term development and delivery and should be adjusted with some regularity in response to new or changing needs and from the assessment of the effectiveness of communications activities.

The plan may establish the communications requirements, guidelines, and standards to be upheld by other operational resilience management processes. For example, the plan may address how provisions for communications during crisis management or disruptive events have to be handled in service continuity plans.

Communications needs are temporal and may change as a result of changes in technology, policy, strategy, and risks being managed. A routine process to maintain and update messages, content, intent, methods, and channels is a necessary part of communications planning.

Typical work products

1. Resilience communications plan
2. Documented requests for commitment to the plan
3. Documented commitments to the plan

Subpractices

1. Develop and implement a resilience communications plan.

    The resilience communications plan may be a subset of the organization's enterprise communications plan with specific references to meeting the requirements of resilience communications.

    The resilience communications plan should address the following, at a minimum:
    - the strategy and objectives for resilience communications
    - the structure of the resilience communications program to carry out the plan (See COMM:SG2.SP2.)
    - the identification of stakeholders with which communications are required
    - the types of media and channels by which communications will be handled
    - the various message types and level of communications appropriate to various stakeholders (For example, incident communications may be vastly different for incident responders than for those who simply need to know.)
    - the frequency and timing of communications
    - special controls over communications (i.e., encryption or secured communications) that are appropriate for some stakeholders
    - the roles and responsibilities necessary to carry out the plan (See COMM:SG2.SP3.)
    - applicable training needs and requirements (particularly for specialized types of communications)

- resources that will be required to meet the plan provisions
- internal and external resources that are involved in supporting the communications process
- relevant costs and budgets associated with communications activities

   Specific types of planning may be necessary for communications processes that are embedded in other operational resilience management processes such as incident management and service continuity planning. In these cases, the resilience communications plan should, at a minimum, reference the planning activities in these other processes and should ensure that this planning follows the structure and guidelines of the Communications process area.

2. Establish commitments to the communications plan.

   The resilience communications plan may be a subset of the organization's enterprise communications plan with specific references to meeting the requirements of resilience communications.

3. Revise the plan and commitments as necessary.

COMM:SG2.SP2 ESTABLISH A RESILIENCE COMMUNICATIONS PROGRAM

A program for executing the resilience communications management plan is established and maintained.

A resilience communications program details the specific activities that the organization will perform to satisfy the communications plan and, in turn, to meet resilience communication requirements. The program addresses fundamental tasks such as

- identifying relevant stakeholders of the communications process
- collecting communications requirements
- analyzing and prioritizing requirements
- establishing and enforcing communications guidelines and standards
- establishing methods, procedures, and processes to develop, implement, and manage communications processes and to develop and distribute timely and effective communications
- establishing and maintaining an appropriate infrastructure to support the attainment of communications requirements
- managing external service providers who may have a role in supporting or carrying out communications requirements

   The program details the roles and responsibilities that the plan relies upon for execution and establishes the communications flow and infrastructure that support the communications plan. Because resilience communications span the organization and needs can be diverse, the program must detail how the organization can meet these challenges in the most efficient and effective manner.

Typical work products

1. Program scope and objectives
2. Project plans for program activities

Subpractices

1. Establish a resilience communications program.

    The program for resilience communications should address how the organization will carry out the communications plan, meet the needs of stakeholders, and ensure effective communications. It should include provisions for how the organization will
    - identify and prioritize stakeholders
    - collect communications requirements from stakeholders
    - analyze and prioritize requirements
    - set the scope of the communications program
    - establish and enforce standards and guidelines
    - enforce consistency across all communications activities related to resilience, whether or not they occur in other operational resilience management processes
    - identify appropriate communications methods and channels
    - plan for and implement an infrastructure to support communications
    - manage external service providers who support communications activities on behalf of the organization

COMM:SG2.SP3 IDENTIFY AND ASSIGN PLAN STAFF

Staff are assigned authority and accountability for carrying out the communications plan and program.

The diverse and expansive nature of communications requirements for supporting operational resilience management processes requires knowledgeable, skilled, and experienced staff to be successful.

- Communications plan and program resources may fall into one or more of the following categories:
- internal communications and awareness
- public relations and external communications and outreach
- notification and escalation communications (related to managing incidents, communicating about risks or vulnerabilities, etc.)
- coordination-focused communications

Internal communications and public relations activities are informational types of communication. They present informative messages about the organization's activities related to resilience and can even encompass such communications as testimony on congressional panels, conference presentations, and communication with regulators for compliance purposes. Notification and escalation communications represent communications processes that are embedded into other operational resilience management processes that require a free flow of information to achieve process goals. Coordination communications tend to be oral, spontaneous, and event- or response-driven and focus on coordinating the activities of a service continuity plan or the response component of an incident.

Resources must be available in the organization to staff or support all of these types of communications as needed. Internal communications and public relations activities tend to be carried out by communications professionals—staff who have specific training and skills in communications and who work primarily in communications roles in the organization. Notification, escalation, and coordination communications may be carried out by anyone in the organization who is in a primary or supporting resilience role. Thus, staff on an incident response team may be involved in a communications role because of the nature of their work. These types of communications are typically supported by a communications infrastructure and knowledgeable staff who support the infrastructure or are trained in effective communications during times of stress and disruption.

Regardless of the communications type, the organization must provide training (sometimes specialized) to staff who support and enable communications processes. This may begin with a skills inventory and gap analysis so that effective training programs can be identified and used. For staff involved in communications roles during the execution of service continuity plans, communications training may be extensive and may involve frequent exercises and tests to ensure effectiveness.

Communications resources may be internal or external to the organization. Thus, where the organization does not have direct control over communications resources, it must attempt to ensure that proper training is provided to carry out plan and program requirements.

Specific skills training for resilience staff is addressed in the Organizational Training and Awareness process area.

Skill inventories and gap analysis are addressed in the Human Resource Management process area.

Cross-training and training for succession planning are addressed in the Human Resource Management process area.

Managing relationships with external entities is addressed in the External Dependencies Management process area.

Typical work products

1. Job descriptions for roles and responsibilities in the plan
2. List of available and skilled resources
3. List of skill and resource gaps

4. Mitigation plans to address skill and resource gaps
5. Updated communications plan with resources assigned

Subpractices

1. Develop detailed job descriptions for each role and responsibility detailed in the communications plan.
   Because some communications processes are embedded in other operational resilience management processes, these job descriptions may not be communications-specific and could be part of a larger resource commitment or assignment.
2. Establish a list of candidate and skilled resources to fill each role and responsibility in the communications plan.
   Remember that these roles and responsibilities may already exist as part of the organization's enterprise communications capabilities.

   Skills and resource gaps for each role and responsibility should be identified and resolved.
3. Assign resources to communications process roles and responsibilities.
4. Ensure that organizational training is provided to communications staff with respect to the specific resilience communications roles they perform.
   This is especially important for communications roles in other operational resilience management processes, such as incident management and in the execution of service continuity plans.

COMM:SG3 DELIVER RESILIENCE COMMUNICATIONS

The activities necessary to deliver communications for resilience activities on an operational and event-driven basis are established.

Resilience communications must be delivered on an as-needed basis, according to the organization's requirements. Because resilience communications can be diverse, the organization may need to develop and implement a broad array of processes, practices, technology, and infrastructure to support those requirements. The organization should consider and identify various communications methods and channels (as appropriate to support requirements) and develop and implement an infrastructure (physical and technical) to support those methods and channels. Through these actions, the organization seeks to deliver timely, relevant, consistent, high-quality, and purposeful communications proactively or during an event, incident, or crisis.

COMM:SG3.SP1 IDENTIFY COMMUNICATIONS METHODS AND CHANNELS

Communications methods and channels relative to stakeholder and organizational needs are identified and established.

Effective communication requires a sender and a receiver. Depending on the goals, objectives, and target audiences outlined in the communications plan and program, the methods and channels used to deliver communications may vary. The methods and channels that the organization chooses must be able to support and enable communications requirements as stated in the communications plan and program.

Communications methods and channels may be formal or informal, oral or written, peer-to-peer, peer-to-subordinate, or peer-to-superior. Messages can also be delivered non-verbally through actions and gestures. Communications methods and channels can include

- policy statements
- procedures manuals and company handbooks
- specific press releases and wires
- company hotlines, such as those that allow for reporting of ethics violations
- email messages and text messaging
- intranet and internet sites and webcasts
- newsletters, posters, and flyers, as well as bulletin boards and other gathering spots
- newspapers, magazines, and other print media
- television, radio, podcasts, videocasts, and other public media
- presentations, tutorials, and symposia
- emergency broadcast systems and methods
- closed communications channels such as two-way radio, CB radio, and satellite phone
- secured communications channels (to provide for classified conversations) such as STUs (secure telephone units)

Methods and tools for communicating with staff, customers, end users, service provider staff, and other stakeholders during the course of service delivery are also part of the enterprise-wide communications strategy and execution. These methods and tools have to be regularly reviewed, tailored, and possibly supplemented to meet ongoing communications requirements.

Typical work products

1. Documented communications methods and channels (by stakeholder class or requirement)
2. Tools, techniques, and methods for communication

Subpractices

1. Inventory communications methods and channels that currently exist in the organization.

2. Identify the appropriate communications methods and channels (media and message) for each type of stakeholder.

    Ensure that the methods and channels will enable the organization to meet the requirements of the communications plan and program and the stakeholders' requirements.

    Ensure that the organization is capable of performing the methods and channels identified and that there is sufficient infrastructure to support these methods and channels.

3. Identify communications methods and channels that do not currently exist in the organization.
4. Identify tools, techniques, and methods required to use the identified methods and channels.

COMM:SG3.SP2 Establish and Maintain Communications Infrastructure

An infrastructure appropriate to meet the organization's resilience communications needs is established and managed.

Communications methods and channels are typically supported and enabled by a communications infrastructure. This infrastructure may be as simple as a manual process for developing and distributing a newsletter or as complex as the development and implementation of a wireless network to support voice and data communications during a crisis. From a generic standpoint, the organization's communications infrastructure must support

- communications requirements from stakeholders
- the specific requirements and scope of the communications plan and program
- the communications methods and channels that the organization chooses to use

Because it is likely that communications methods and channels extend beyond the organization's direct span of control, the communications infrastructure may be developed, implemented, managed, and owned by an external business partner. The organization must seek to ensure that this infrastructure meets its requirements and is reliable for delivering the specific types of communications for which it has been contracted.

Important considerations for an appropriate communications infrastructure include

- the nature and extent of the message
- the immediacy of the message (whether on-demand, spontaneous, etc.)
- whether the message to be delivered over the infrastructure is sensitive, confidential, or classified

- how messages will be stored and protected, if necessary
- the scope of end users of the message (i.e., how extensive is the audience)
- whether the communication is to be one-way or interactive

Specialized infrastructure may be required to meet the communications demands of processes such as incident management and to carry out specific activities in service continuity plans. In these cases, the organization may develop and implement infrastructure that directly and uniquely supports these activities outside of that which is required for general communications.

Typical work products

1. Infrastructure requirements
2. Infrastructure architecture, map, or diagram for communications flows
3. Communications tools, techniques, and methods

Subpractices

1. Identify and inventory existing communications infrastructure and capabilities that may be able to meet plan and program objectives and communications requirements.

   Many communications requirements may be substantially met by existing capabilities and infrastructure as part of the organization's larger communications process. Inventorying existing capabilities and infrastructure may help the organization to accurately determine additional infrastructure needs and reduce the overall cost of providing communications services.

2. Identify infrastructure needs to support communications requirements, methods, and channels.

   In order to successfully develop infrastructure to support communications requirements, the organization may need to decompose these requirements into functional requirements. Functional requirements represent the people, processes, and technologies that are needed to meet the communications requirements. Without knowing these requirements, the organization may find it difficult to accurately identify infrastructure needs.

   If the organization cannot meet infrastructure needs (or contract with business partners to meet them), the organization may not be able to meet communications requirements. The organization should identify any requirements that cannot be met and determine if this poses any additional risk to the organization.

3. Implement and manage communications infrastructure.

COMM:SG4 IMPROVE COMMUNICATIONS

Resilience communications are reviewed to identify and implement improvements in the communications process.

The importance of communications processes to supporting the management of operational resilience requires that the organization continually assess its effectiveness in meeting communications requirements and make improvements where necessary. This is especially true given the dynamic nature of the operational and risk environment, emerging threats, and changes in technology and the geographical environment for facilities.

Some communications processes are fairly static—that is, they are foundational activities that are not typically affected by change. For example, the organization may have structured processes for addressing the print and television media that are valid no matter what the current operating conditions are. Other communications processes must continually evolve. For example, crisis communications processes evolve as the organization is put to the test and as lessons are learned and shared. To some extent, every incident or crisis situation may pose new and emerging challenges that the organization has not previously encountered and that will cause a review of communications requirements, plans and programs, methods and channels, and infrastructure.

Learning from communications processes is focused on improving the organization's ability to proactively meet its communications requirements rather than to resort to ad hoc methods and processes that may in fact harm the organization, particularly during an event, incident, or crisis. While all situations cannot be planned for, the organization can establish foundational competencies and improve these capabilities with what is learned from communications efforts—particularly those performed during times of stress. Eventually, this should result in a shift to planning and away from reacting.

Improving resilience communications requires the organization to formally assess the effectiveness of its communications processes and to develop and implement improvements in these processes on an ongoing basis.

COMM:SG4.SP1 Assess Communications Effectiveness

The effectiveness of resilience communications plans and programs is assessed and corrective actions are identified.

Communications activities must be reviewed regularly to ensure that they continue to meet the needs of stakeholders and support operational resilience management processes.

Day-to-day communications, such as staff communications and press releases, are generally vetted before they are released to help prevent miscommunication and misinterpretation. Event, incident, and crisis communications, on the other hand, may not exhibit problems until execution. The organization may not be able to foresee all of the potential circumstances that could diminish effectiveness and ultimately impact the success of incident management and service continuity processes.

Assessing communications effectiveness should aim to answer basic questions such as these:

- Did the communication meet the purpose?
- Was the message clear, concise, unambiguous, and timely?
- Were all stakeholders that have a need to know included in the distribution of the information?
- Did the communications infrastructure support the process as intended?
- Were communications methods and channels effective for the purpose?
- Were spontaneous communications inhibited by technical glitches, lack of training of staff, or other obstacles?

Event, incident, and crisis communications may require additional levels of observation and examination to identify issues, concerns, obstacles, and errors. In some cases, these types of communications can be tested when service continuity plans are exercised or when incident drills are performed. These activities provide information that could improve communications competencies before they result in impacting the organization's effectiveness. However, the organization should specifically plan for collecting effectiveness information during event, incident, and crisis communications so that real-time issues can be brought to light post-activity.

> These are examples of methods that can be used to evaluate the effectiveness of communications activities:
> - questionnaires or surveys designed to measure people's awareness of specific topics
> - behavioral measures to objectively evaluate shifts in the population's behavior after a communications awareness activity (For example, the strength of passwords could be evaluated before and after a password-awareness activity.)
> - external entity observations, evaluations, and benchmarking activities
> - interviews with those who reported events or incidents and those who are involved in investigation
> - interviews of specific knowledge experts who have a detailed understanding of the area affected
> - formal post-incident and post-plan execution reviews of communications effectiveness *(See IMC:SG5.SP1, IMC:SG5.SP3, and SC:SG6.SP2.)*
> - consultation with law enforcement personnel
> - consultation with legal and audit personnel
> - consultation with product vendors and software or hardware suppliers (if their products are involved)
> - consultation with emergency management personnel and other public service providers

Typical work products

1. Communications analysis report
2. Recommendations for plan or program improvements
3. Recommendations for improvements to event, incident, and crisis management communications processes

Subpractices

1. Establish and implement a formal communications review activity.

    For event, incident, and crisis communications, this review should be performed during service continuity plan exercises and drills of the incident management process. In addition, communications issues that arise during an event, incident, or crisis should be uncovered in post-incident or post-event reviews.

    The evaluation of service continuity plan exercises is performed in SC:SG5.SP3 and the post-execution review of service continuity plans is performed in SC:SG6.SP2 in the Service Continuity process area.

2. Prepare an analysis report on the effectiveness of communications activities.

    For post-incident review, this process may include the communications issues identified in a post-incident analysis report (*as described in IMC:SG5.SP1*). For a post-plan execution review, this process may include areas of improvement for service continuity plans (*as described in SC:SG6.SP2*).

3. Compare outcomes of communications processes with plan objectives and expectations.
4. Document suggested improvements to the communications plan and program based on the evaluation of the effectiveness of awareness activities.

COMM:SG4.SP2 IMPROVE COMMUNICATIONS

Lessons learned in managing resilience communications are used to improve communications plans and programs.

The importance of communications to the operational resilience management system requires that the organization make a sizeable investment in human and capital resources. Thus, communications processes must be effective and efficient, preserve the organization's investment, and prevent the organization from being impacted as a result of poorly designed and implemented communications.

Lessons learned from regular review of communications processes, and in particular during event, incident, and crisis communications, can strengthen resilience communications and help to improve the organization's overall communications competency. These lessons learned can serve as a benchmark for continuous improvement of communications processes.

Typical work products

1. Service continuity plans
2. Resilience policy
3. Updated communications plan and program
4. Training needs and requirements
5. Communications process improvements list

Subpractices

1. Review results of communications assessment activities and effectiveness analysis reports.
2. Review communications processes, plans, and programs and update for any perceived deficiencies or omissions.

    This process may require the organization to revisit the effectiveness of meeting communications requirements and to perform analysis of requirements to determine why they are not being met.

    In addition, the organization may need to revisit and revise resilience policies and strategies, training needs and requirements, and the communications processes that are embedded in other operational resilience management processes. Specifically, service continuity plans may have to be updated to improve communications effectiveness.
3. Revise the communications methods, channels, and supporting work products as necessary.

Elaborated Generic Practices by Goal

Refer to the Generic Goals and Practices document in Appendix A for general guidance that applies to all process areas. This section provides elaborations relative to the application of the Generic Goals and Practices to the Communications process area.

COMM:GG1 ACHIEVE SPECIFIC GOALS

The operational resilience management system supports and enables achievement of the specific goals of the Communications process area by transforming identifiable input work products to produce identifiable output work products.

COMM:GG1.GP1 PERFORM SPECIFIC PRACTICES

Perform the specific practices of the Communications process area to develop work products and provide services to achieve the specific goals of the process area.

Elaboration:

Specific practices COMM:SG1.SP1 through COMM:SG4.SP2 are performed to achieve the goals of the communications process.

COMM:GG2 INSTITUTIONALIZE A MANAGED PROCESS

Communications is institutionalized as a managed process.

COMM:GG2.GP1 ESTABLISH PROCESS GOVERNANCE

Establish and maintain governance over the planning and performance of the communications process.

Refer to the Enterprise Focus process area for more information about providing sponsorship and oversight to the communications process.

Subpractices

1. Establish governance over process activities.

    Elaboration:

    > Governance over the communications process may be exhibited by
    > - developing and publicizing higher-level managers' objectives and requirements for the process
    > - sponsoring process policies, procedures, standards, and guidelines, including the standards and guidelines described in COMM:SG1.SP3
    > - making higher-level managers aware of applicable compliance obligations related to the process, and regularly reporting on the organization's satisfaction of these obligations to higher-level managers
    > - sponsoring and funding process activities
    > - aligning process requirements, plans, and programs with identified resilience needs and objectives and stakeholder needs and requirements
    > - sponsoring, supporting, and overseeing the communications plan and program as well as the process plan
    > - verifying that the process supports strategic resilience objectives and is focused on the assets and services that are of the highest relative value in meeting strategic objectives
    > - regular reporting from organizational units to higher-level managers on process activities and results
    > - creating dedicated higher-level management feedback loops on decisions about communications and recommendations for improving the process
    > - providing input on identifying, assessing, and managing operational risks to communications, including risks to plans, programs, methods, and channels
    > - conducting regular internal and external audits and related reporting to audit committees on process effectiveness
    > - establishing formal programs to measure the effectiveness of process activities, and reporting these measurements to higher-level managers

2. Develop and publish organizational policy for the process.

   Elaboration:

   > The communications policy should address
   > - responsibility, authority, and ownership for performing process activities, including identifying stakeholders and requirements and establishing standards and guidelines
   > - standards and guidelines as described in COMM:SG1.SP3, including
   >   - identifying and documenting communications requirements
   >   - identifying communications media types and message content for different types of requirements
   >   - identifying communications methods and channels
   >   - communicating with specific types of stakeholders based on their roles
   > - managing the communications plan and program as well as the process plan
   > - approving communications methods and channels by purpose and stakeholder
   > - communications infrastructure requirements
   > - methods for measuring adherence to policy, exceptions granted, and policy violations

COMM:GG2.GP2 PLAN THE PROCESS

Establish and maintain the plan for performing the communications process.

Elaboration:

COMM:SG2.SP1 requires the development of a plan for how the organization will carry out a program to support resilience communications. In COMM:GG2.GP2, the planning elements required in COMM:SG2.SP1 are formalized and structured, and performed in a managed way. The plan for the communications process should reflect the organization's stated preferences for general resilience communications, communications during events and incidents, communications to external stakeholders, public relations, and communications needs as required by other resilience processes. The plan should also address how the process will be actualized (through individual roles, dedicated teams, virtual teams, etc.).

Subpractices

1. Define and document the plan for performing the process.

   Elaboration:

   Foundational elements such as communications requirements, stakeholders, and communications standards and guidelines (which are essential to support communications processes) are addressed in COMM:SG1 and should be reflected in the plan as called for here.

2. Define and document the process description.

Elaboration:

Foundational elements such as communications requirements, stakeholders, and communications standards and guidelines (which are essential to support communications processes) are addressed in COMM:SG1. The process for developing, deploying, and managing resilience communications is described in COMM:SG2. Practices described in COMM:SG1 and COMM:SG2 should be reflected in the process description as called for here.

3. Review the plan with relevant stakeholders and get their agreement.
4. Revise the plan as necessary.

COMM:GG2.GP3 PROVIDE RESOURCES

Provide adequate resources for performing the communications process, developing the work products, and providing the services of the process.

Elaboration:

COMM:SG2.SP3 requires the assignment of resources to the communications plan and program. In COMM:GG2.GP3, resources are formally identified and assigned to plan elements.

Subpractices

1. Staff the process.

Elaboration:

This generic practice related to communications refers to staffing the communications process program, not the provision of communications resources in processes such as incident management and service continuity.

> These are examples of staff required to perform the communications process:
> - staff responsible for
>   - identifying relevant stakeholders, their roles, and the plan for their involvement
>   - identifying, analyzing, prioritizing, and maintaining communications requirements that satisfy resilience program objectives
>   - developing communications guidelines and standards
>   - developing and maintaining the communications plan and program, as well as the process plan
>   - identifying and assigning qualified staff to carry out the communications plan and program and addressing any skill and resource gaps
>   - identifying communications methods and channels, as well as the methods, techniques, and tools that support these

- defining communications infrastructure requirements and architecture, along with supporting methods, techniques, and tools to fulfill these requirements
- identifying and implementing improvements to the communications plan, program, and process plan, and making recommendations to improve event, incident, and crisis management communications processes
• internal and external auditors responsible for reporting to appropriate committees on process effectiveness

Refer to the Organizational Training and Awareness process area for information about training staff for resilience roles and responsibilities.

Refer to the Human Resource Management process area for information about acquiring staff to fulfill roles and responsibilities.

2. Fund the process.

   Refer to the Financial Resource Management process area for information about budgeting for, funding, and accounting for communications.

3. Provide necessary tools, techniques, and methods to perform the process.

Elaboration:

Resilience communications require the provision of significant levels of tools, techniques, and methods to support the broad range of communications requirements. In COMM:SG3.SP1 and COMM:SG3.SP2, the supporting structure for communications is established. In COMM:GG2.GP3 subpractice 3, the provision of this structure is formally tied to the communications plan and program, and the ability of the tools, techniques, and methods to support stated communications requirements is validated.

These are examples of tools, techniques, and methods to support the communications process:
• communications requirements management tools
• methods and techniques to support various types and levels of communications
• methods, techniques, and tools to support various types of stakeholders, communications channels, and media
• communications infrastructure, diagramming, and mapping tools
• survey tools for assessing communications effectiveness
• methods for training stakeholders on resilience communications

COMM:GG2.GP4 A*ssign* R*esponsibility*

Assign responsibility and authority for performing the communications process, developing the work products, and providing the services of the process.

Elaboration:

COMM:SG2.SP3 requires the assignment of staff responsibility, accountability, and authority for communications plan and program tasks. In COMM:GG2.GP4, commitments are formally identified to support resource allocations to plan elements.

Refer to the Human Resource Management process area for more information about establishing resilience as a job responsibility, developing resilience performance goals and objectives, and measuring and assessing performance against these goals and objectives.

Subpractices

1. Assign responsibility and authority for performing the process.

Elaboration:

Keep in mind that specialized communications needs may arise unexpectedly when an incident or crisis occurs, requiring virtual teams or responsibilities to be assigned quickly.

2. Assign responsibility and authority for performing the specific tasks of the process.

> Responsibility and authority for performing communications tasks can be formalized by
> - defining roles and responsibilities in the communications plan and program and in the process plan
> - including process tasks and responsibility for these tasks in specific job descriptions
> - developing policy requiring organizational unit managers, line of business managers, project managers, and asset and service owners and custodians to participate in and derive benefit from the process for assets and services under their ownership or custodianship
> - including process tasks in staff performance management goals and objectives, with requisite measurement of progress against these goals
> - developing and implementing contractual instruments (including service level agreements) with external entities to establish responsibility and authority for performing process tasks on outsourced functions
> - including process tasks in measuring performance of external entities against contractual instruments

Refer to the External Dependencies Management process area for additional details about managing relationships with external entities.

3. Confirm that people assigned with responsibility and authority understand it and are willing and able to accept it.

COMM:GG2.GP5 TRAIN PEOPLE

Train the people performing or supporting the communications process as needed.

Refer to the Organizational Training and Awareness process area for more information about training the people performing or supporting the process.

Refer to the Human Resource Management process area for more information about inventorying skill sets, establishing a skill set baseline, identifying required skill sets, and measuring and addressing skill deficiencies.

Subpractices

1. Identify process skill needs.

    Elaboration:

    > These are examples of skills required in the communications process:
    > - knowledge of the tools, techniques, and methods necessary to provide all levels and types of communication in support of stakeholders, channels, and media, including those necessary to perform the process using the selected methods, techniques, and tools identified in COMM:GG2.GP3 subpractice 3
    > - knowledge unique to each type of stakeholder, channel, and media that is required to meet communications requirements
    > - knowledge necessary to establish and maintain the communications infrastructure
    > - knowledge necessary to work effectively with stakeholders, including asset owners and custodians
    > - knowledge necessary to elicit and prioritize stakeholder requirements and needs and interpret them to develop effective communications requirements, plans, and programs as well as the process plan

2. Identify process skill gaps based on available resources and their current skill levels.
3. Identify training opportunities to address skill gaps.

    Elaboration:

    Certification training is an effective way to improve communications skills and attain competency. Training and certification in crisis communications or specialized public relations are available for staff who focus specifically on communications regarding incidents and other resilience issues.

    > These are examples of training topics:
    > - communications requirements identification
    > - communications media and channels
    > - communications types and levels
    > - development and implementation of communications infrastructure
    > - use of communications infrastructure
    > - working with stakeholders in a crisis situation
    > - identifying communications lessons learned

4. Provide training and review the training needs as necessary.

COMM:GG2.GP6 Manage Work Product Configurations

Place designated work products of the communications process under appropriate levels of control.

Elaboration:

COMM:SG4.SP2 specifically addresses the change control process over communications plans, programs, and processes. However, other work products of the communications process (such as the communications process plan and communications process policies) must also be managed and controlled.

Tools, techniques, and methods should be employed to perform consistent and structured version control over the communications infrastructure to ensure that all methods, channels, and media are the most current and "official." The tools, techniques, and methods can also be used to provide access control over inquiry, modification, and deletion and to track version changes and updates.

These are examples of communications work products placed under control:
- stakeholder lists, including classes and roles
- communications requirements
- communications plan and program
- communications standards and guidelines
- job descriptions that include communications roles and responsibilities
- communications infrastructure work products (requirements, tools, techniques, and methods)
- training needs and requirements
- process plan
- process improvements
- policies and procedures
- contracts with external entities

COMM:GG2.GP7 Identify and Involve Relevant Stakeholders

Identify and involve the relevant stakeholders of the communications process as planned.

Elaboration:

Stakeholders both provide and receive communications. Several COMM-specific practices address aspects of the involvement of stakeholders in the communications process. For example, COMM:SG1.SP1 calls for the identification of internal and external stakeholders that require information relative to resilience activities. COMM:SG1.SP2 captures the communications needs of stakeholders to serve as a source of communications process requirements. COMM:SG1.SP3 establishes guidelines and standards informed by stakeholder needs and requirements. COMM:SG2.SP2 and COMM:SG2.SP3 describe the development of communications plans and programs that meet stakeholder requirements. COMM:SG3.SP1 requires that communications methods and channels meet stakeholder needs.

COMM:GG2.GP7 generically covers the role of stakeholders across all aspects of the communications process: developing plans and programs, executing plans and programs, and receiving communications.

Subpractices

1. Identify process stakeholders and their appropriate involvement.

Elaboration:

In COMM:GG2.GP7 subpractice 1, stakeholders are limited to those that have direct responsibility for the development and execution of the communications plan and process. Stakeholders that require direct communications in order to enable or support a service continuity plan or to communicate an incident or a response fall outside of this activity.

COMM:SG1.SP1 subpractice 1 lists examples of stakeholders of the communications process.

> Stakeholders are involved in various tasks in the communications process, such as planning for the process
> - making decisions about communications
> - making commitments to communications plans, programs, and activities and to the process plan
> - communicating communications plans, programs, and activities
> - coordinating communications activities
> - reviewing and appraising the effectiveness of process activities
> - establishing requirements for the process
> - resolving issues in the process
> - receiving and responding to various types of communications

2. Communicate the list of stakeholders to planners and those responsible for process performance.
3. Involve relevant stakeholders in the process as planned.

COMM:GG2.GP8 MONITOR AND CONTROL THE PROCESS

Monitor and control the communications process against the plan for performing the process and take appropriate corrective action.

Refer to the Monitoring process area for more information about the collection, organization, and distribution of data that may be useful for monitoring and controlling processes.

Refer to the Measurement and Analysis process area for more information about establishing process metrics and measurement.

Refer to the Enterprise Focus process area for more information about providing process information to managers, identifying issues, and determining appropriate corrective actions.

Subpractices

1. Measure actual performance against the plan for performing the process.
2. Review accomplishments and results of the process against the plan for performing the process.

    Elaboration:

    > These are examples of metrics for the communications process:
    > - number of communications delivered by event type, stakeholder type, method and channel type (or other meaningful categorization) per unit of time
    > - percentage of communications media and channels operating within expected tolerances (e.g., press release must be issued within one hour of a significant event)
    > - percentage increase or decrease in length of time to commence communications by event type
    > - number and percentage of stakeholders that do not receive communications within expected tolerances, by stakeholder type and by event type
    > - number of communications methods and channels required to deliver same or similar messages
    > - percentage of uptime or availability of preferred communications methods, channels, and infrastructure
    > - number of recommendations for improvement referred to the event, incident, and crisis management communications processes
    > - number of process risks referred to the risk management process; number of risks where corrective action is still pending (by risk rank)
    > - level of adherence to process policies; number of policy violations; number of policy exceptions requested and number approved
    > - number of process activities that are on track per plan
    > - rate of change of resource needs to support the process
    > - rate of change of costs to support the process

3. Review activities, status, and results of the process with the immediate level of managers responsible for the process and identify issues.

    Elaboration:

    COMM:SG4.SP1 and COMM:SG4.SP2 call for assessing the effectiveness of resilience communications, identifying improvement actions, and revising plans, programs, methods, and channels to reflect such improvements. In COMM:GG2.GP8 subpractice 3, the review activities are formalized and performed consistently to ensure identification of issues and concerns that need attention and could affect the process in the future. Because communications may be planned or on-demand, formal reviews may be periodic or post-incident or -event.

> Periodic reviews of the communications process are needed to ensure that
> - the communications plan, program, and process plan are meeting the resilience needs of the organization
> - media and channels are meeting communications requirements
> - stakeholders are receiving timely, accurate, and complete messages when required
> - communications requirements are valid (continue to be valid)
> - communications infrastructure is adequately supporting requirements
> - communications are being revised and improved on a timely basis when problems or issues arise
> - event-driven or spontaneous communications adequately meet needs
> - training is adequate for meeting communications requirements
> - status reports are provided to appropriate stakeholders in a timely manner
> - process issues are referred to the risk management process when necessary
> - communications issues are referred to the event, incident, and crisis management communications processes when necessary
> - actions requiring management involvement are elevated in a timely manner
> - the performance of process activities is being monitored and regularly reported
> - key measures are within acceptable ranges as demonstrated in governance dashboards or scorecards and financial reports
> - administrative, technical, and physical controls are operating as intended
> - controls are meeting the stated intent of the resilience requirements
> - actions resulting from internal and external audits are being closed in a timely manner

4. Identify and evaluate the effects of significant deviations from the plan for performing the process.

   Elaboration:

   Because communications can be spontaneous, deviations from the plan for performing the process are to be expected. In addition, deviations from the communications plan may occur when organizational units fail to follow the enterprise-sponsored plan. These deviations may affect the operational resilience of the organizational unit's services but may also have a cascading effect on enterprise operational resilience objectives.

5. Identify problems in the plan for performing and executing the process.
6. Take corrective action when requirements and objectives are not being satisfied, when issues are identified, or when progress differs significantly from the plan for performing the process.
7. Track corrective action to closure.

COMM:GG2.GP9 OBJECTIVELY EVALUATE ADHERENCE

Objectively evaluate adherence of the communications process against its process description, standards, and procedures, and address non-compliance.

Elaboration:

> These are examples of activities to be reviewed:
> - identification of communications requirements
> - development of communications guidelines, standards, and plans as well as the process plan
> - alignment of stakeholder requirements with process plans and programs
> - assignment of responsibility, accountability, and authority for process activities
> - development of communications infrastructure requirements and diagrams
> - delivery of communications messages (if possible, particularly during an event)
> - determining the adequacy of communications reports and reviews in informing decision makers regarding the performance of operational resilience management activities and the need to take corrective action, if any
> - verification of communications controls
> - use of communications work products for improving strategies for protecting and sustaining assets and services

> These are examples of work products to be reviewed:
> - communications requirements
> - communications plans
> - communications infrastructure requirements and diagrams
> - established communications media and channels
> - examples of written, delivered communications
> - communications logs and analysis reports
> - process plans, programs, and policies
> - issues that have been referred to the risk management process
> - process methods, techniques, and tools
> - metrics for the process *(Refer to COMM:GG2.GP8 subpractice 2.)*
> - contracts with external entities

COMM:GG2.GP10 REVIEW STATUS WITH HIGHER-LEVEL MANAGERS

Review the activities, status, and results of the communications process with higher-level managers and resolve issues.

Refer to the Enterprise Focus process area for more information about providing sponsorship and oversight to the operational resilience management system.

COMM:GG3 INSTITUTIONALIZE A DEFINED PROCESS

Communications is institutionalized as a defined process.

COMM:GG3.GP1 ESTABLISH A DEFINED PROCESS

Establish and maintain the description of a defined communications process.

Establishing and tailoring process assets, including standard processes, are addressed in the Organizational Process Definition process area.

Establishing process needs and objectives and selecting, improving, and deploying process assets, including standard processes, are addressed in the Organizational Process Focus process area.

Subpractices

1. Select from the organization's set of standard processes those processes that cover the communications process and best meet the needs of the organizational unit or line of business.
2. Establish the defined process by tailoring the selected processes according to the organization's tailoring guidelines.
3. Ensure that the organization's process objectives are appropriately addressed in the defined process, and ensure that process governance extends to the tailored processes.
4. Document the defined process and the records of the tailoring.
5. Revise the description of the defined process as necessary.

COMM:GG3.GP2 COLLECT IMPROVEMENT INFORMATION

Collect communications work products, measures, measurement results, and improvement information derived from planning and performing the process to support future use and improvement of the organization's processes and process assets.

Elaboration:

COMM:SG4.SP1 and COMM:SG4.SP2 call for assessing the effectiveness of resilience communications, identifying improvement actions, and revising plans, programs, methods, and channels to reflect such improvements. In COMM:GG3.GP2, all improvement information is collected and documented in support of establishing and maintaining a defined process for communications.

> These are examples of improvement work products and information:
> - direct feedback from process stakeholders
> - analysis reports
> - issues related to effectiveness of chosen methods and channels
> - infrastructure downtime reports
> - metrics and measurements of the viability of the process *(Refer to COMM:GG2.GP8 subpractice 2.)*
> - changes and trends in operating conditions, risk conditions, and the risk environment that affect results
> - lessons learned in post-event review of incidents and disruptions in continuity
> - lessons learned that can be applied to improve operational resilience management performance, such as poorly exercised methods and channels and insufficient and untimely stakeholder notification and involvement
> - the degree to which methods, channels, and infrastructure are current
> - reports on the effectiveness and weaknesses of controls
> - resilience requirements that are not being satisfied or are being exceeded

Establishing the measurement repository and process asset library is addressed in the Organizational Process Definition process area. Updating the measurement repository and process asset library as part of process improvement and deployment is addressed in the Organizational Process Focus process area.

Subpractices

1. Store process and work product measures in the organization's measurement repository.
2. Submit documentation for inclusion in the organization's process asset library.
3. Document lessons learned from the process for inclusion in the organization's process asset library.
4. Propose improvements to the organizational process assets.

COMPLIANCE
Enterprise

Purpose

The purpose of Compliance is to ensure awareness of and compliance with an established set of relevant internal and external guidelines, standards, practices, policies, regulations, and legislation, and other obligations (such as contracts and service level agreements) related to managing operational resilience.

Introductory Notes

Regulations, standards, and guidelines are developed and issued by a variety of governmental, regulatory, and industry bodies. Their purpose is to enforce (and reinforce) acceptable levels of behavior to ensure that organizations and the services they provide to citizens and customers remain viable and sustainable. In particular, the evolving importance of security and resilience has resulted in a new wave of regulatory bodies and regulations that seek not only to ensure organizational survivability but the survivability of entire industries and to limit undesirable events that have the potential to affect the socioeconomic structure of the global economy.

"Compliance" characterizes the activities that the organization performs to identify the internal and external guidelines, standards, practices, policies, regulations, and legislation to which it is subject and to comply with these obligations in an orderly, systematic, efficient, timely, and accurate manner. Compliance management addresses the policies and practices in the organization that support the satisfaction of compliance obligations as an enterprise-wide activity that involves more than just legal and administrative activities.

Organizations typically focus their efforts on compliance with externally directed obligations, but compliance processes also often address compliance with internally generated standards and policies such as the organization's information security policy and internal control system. In addition, compliance is not only important for reinforcing appropriate behaviors; it is also a primary tool in governing the security and resilience activities in the organization and ensuring they are effectively meeting their goals and objectives.

The Compliance process area addresses the organization's ability to establish a compliance plan and program, to identify relevant regulations, standards, and guidelines (to which it must comply), and to develop and implement the proper procedures and activities to ensure compliance in a timely and accurate manner. Compliance management requires the organization to understand its obligations and to collect relevant data in a manner that supports and enables the satisfaction of obligations in a way that meets the organization's requirements but does not divert focus from its core service delivery.

Related Process Areas

A primary component of the compliance process—governance and oversight—is addressed in the Enterprise Focus process area.

Addressing the risks of non-compliance and the risks related to weaknesses identified in the compliance process is performed in the Risk Management process area.

The monitor process, which may provide information about the effectiveness of internal controls for compliance purposes, is addressed in the Monitoring process area.

Summary of Specific Goals and Practices

COMP:SG1 Prepare for Compliance Management
    COMP:SG1.SP1   Establish a Compliance Plan
    COMP:SG1.SP2   Establish a Compliance Program
    COMP:SG1.SP3   Establish Compliance Guidelines and Standards
COMP:SG2 Establish Compliance Obligations
    COMP:SG2.SP1   Identify Compliance Obligations
    COMP:SG2.SP2   Analyze Obligations
    COMP:SG2.SP3   Establish Ownership for Meeting Obligations
COMP:SG3 Demonstrate Satisfaction of Compliance Obligations
    COMP:SG3.SP1   Collect and Validate Compliance Data
    COMP:SG3.SP2   Demonstrate the Extent of Compliance Obligation Satisfaction
    COMP:SG3.SP3   Remediate Areas of Non-Compliance
COMP:SG4 Monitor Compliance Activities
    COMP:SG4.SP1   Evaluate Compliance Activities

Specific Practices by Goal

COMP:SG1 Prepare for Compliance Management

The organizational environment and processes for identifying, satisfying, and monitoring compliance obligations are established.

Many organizations and industries (both public and private) are highly regulated by government, their industry, or other agencies. In addition, as part of their governance structure, most organizations have their own internal regulations in the form of policies and procedures, as well as commitments to quality programs. Compliance with all of these obligations (many of which overlap) requires significant organizational resources and commitment. It can be a complex and time-consuming activity that results in duplication of effort and diverts resources away from meeting the organization's strategic objectives.

To be effective and efficient, compliance must be integrated with an organization's operational processes. Thus, regardless of the origins of compliance obligations, the organization is collecting, documenting, analyzing, coordinating, and reporting the data it needs for compliance as a natural outcome of operating its services. From a governance perspective, higher-level managers must be able to be confident that compliance obligations have been satisfied and, where they have not, that the organization has good reason to be non-compliant based on a thorough examination of risk.

To achieve this, the organization must establish a foundation for managing compliance as an organization-wide process that emanates from its operational commitments. This helps the organization avoid "fire-drill" compliance activities that pull resources from operational activities to collect data and fulfill obligations, and keeps the organization from realizing fines and penalties that could result from lack of compliance.

To establish a foundation for managing compliance, the organization must create a compliance plan and program and establish compliance standards and guidelines for consistency and repeatability.

COMP:SG1.SP1 ESTABLISH A COMPLIANCE PLAN

A strategic plan for managing compliance to obligations is established.

The strategic plan for addressing compliance helps the organization to make organization-focused decisions about the most effective and efficient approach for meeting compliance obligations and for managing the activities required to meet these obligations. The plan is developed to minimize duplication of effort, facilitate compliance with diverse bodies of regulation, and provide maximum assurance that obligations will be met in a timely manner.

The plan establishes the basis for the development and implementation of the organization's compliance program, which directs the compliance activities from an enterprise view and seeks to meet the broad compliance objectives of the plan.

Typical work products

1. Plan for compliance management
2. Documented requests for commitment to the plan
3. Resource commitments to the plan

Subpractices

1. Develop a strategic plan for managing compliance.
   A plan for compliance management should address at a minimum
   - the organization's stated approach to compliance management
   - objectives for the organization's compliance program
   - the roles and responsibilities for carrying out the compliance plan
   - resources that will be required to meet the objectives of the plan
   - applicable training needs and requirements
   - relevant costs and budgets associated with carrying out the plan
2. Establish sponsorship and resource commitments for the compliance plan.
3. Revise the plan and commitments on a cycle commensurate with the organization's strategic planning process.

COMP:SG1.SP2 ESTABLISH A COMPLIANCE PROGRAM

A program is established to carry out the activities and practices of the compliance plan.

The organization's compliance program is established to carry out the compliance plan. The program establishes the tasks, functions, and activities that are performed to ensure that compliance is managed as envisioned in the plan.

In the compliance program, the organization states the structure and processes it will use to meet the compliance objectives (as stated in the compliance plan) and outlines the roles and responsibilities of staff throughout the organization for their contributions to compliance activities. In many cases, the compliance program includes the definition and installation of a "compliance office" that assumes the responsibility for compliance activities, but this may vary widely across organizations and industries.

Another important element of the compliance program is the formal connection to the organization's governance and oversight functions. In the area of resilience management, the compliance program seeks to relay information about lack of compliance to the governance function so that appropriate organizational actions can be commenced. Some organizations seek to formalize this role by the establishment of a higher-level compliance officer position.

The compliance program may call for centralized management or may be decentralized into organizational units and lines of business. The decision on how to structure the compliance program is made by the organization depending on its organizational structure, the extensiveness of its compliance obligations, and other factors (such as technical infrastructure).

Typical work products

1. Compliance program charter
2. Compliance program management plan

3. Compliance program objectives
4. Compliance organizational structure

Subpractices

1. Establish a compliance program.

    The compliance program is responsible for ensuring that the objectives of the compliance plan are achieved. Program management includes staffing the program, assigning accountability and responsibility to plan activities, tasks, and projects, and measuring performance. Much of what is included in the Compliance process area is expected to be carried out through the direction of the organization's compliance program.

    The compliance program should address
    - a compliance program charter that addresses the objectives of the compliance plan
    - the establishment of a compliance office or similar construct
    - the structure of the compliance program
    - the roles and responsibilities for carrying out the compliance program, including the establishment of the compliance officer role if warranted
    - procedures for identifying compliance obligations
    - procedures for data collection, analysis, and reporting
    - compliance standards and guidelines
    - reporting mechanisms to receive complaints
    - procedures for response to improper activities
    - monitoring, auditing, and other evaluation techniques to identify problem areas
    - investigation procedures
    - enforcement process to take appropriate corrective action for violations of compliance obligations
    - remediation procedures
    - the selection and use of tools for data collection and analysis
    - the selection and use of tools for reducing redundancy in duplicative obligations

2. Assign resources to the compliance program.

    Resources are required to perform the activities of the compliance program. Staffing for the compliance program, depending on its size and complexity, may be virtual (i.e., spread throughout the organization) or dedicated (program-specific staff). Depending on complexity, compliance program activities may have to be pushed out into the organization, and the organization may have to implement automated means (i.e., software-based tools and programs) to collect data, analyze overlap of obligations, and coordinate activities across many organizational units and lines of business.

3. Provide funding for the compliance program.

    Funding the organization's operational resilience management system and related activities, tasks, and projects is addressed in the Financial Resource Management process area.

4. Provide sponsorship and oversight to the compliance program.
   As an increasingly critical organizational entity, the compliance program must be viewed as the responsibility of all staff and managed so that compliance objectives are met consistently. Sponsorship provides the support for the importance of the program, and oversight ensures that compliance issues are identified and addressed on a timely basis. This may be the role of the compliance officer if that position is established.

COMP:SG1.SP3 Establish Compliance Guidelines and Standards

The guidelines and standards for satisfying compliance obligations are established and communicated.

Guidelines and standards for compliance activities ensure consistent levels of data collection, formatting, analysis, reporting, quality, and performance management. They also provide a foundation from which a common understanding of compliance can be communicated as a means for improving efficiency and effectiveness in meeting compliance obligations satisfactorily. Guidelines and standards also facilitate an enterprise view of compliance and an ability to manage compliance activities in alignment with strategic objectives.

In addition, guidelines and standards for compliance provide a basis for performing compliance activities that must be coordinated with suppliers and vendors.

Typical work products

1. Compliance guidelines and standards

Subpractices

1. Develop and communicate compliance guidelines and standards.
   Guidelines and standards for compliance management are typically organization-specific. However, guidelines and standards may address areas such as
   - formats and methods for collecting and coordinating data
   - formats for preparing and submitting compliance reports
   - remediation standards—documentation, approvals, reporting, follow-up, etc.
   - tool evaluation, acquisition, installation, and use
   - data retention, storage, and access control
   - requirements for identification and documentation of risks related to non-compliance
   - requirements and formats for inclusion of compliance requirements in external entity contracts

COMP:SG2 ESTABLISH COMPLIANCE OBLIGATIONS

The organization's compliance obligations are identified, documented, and communicated.

The foundation of efficient and effective compliance management is an understanding of the organization's compliance obligations. Otherwise, the organization cannot effectively design a compliance plan and program that specifically address its unique needs and support the organization's timely satisfaction of these obligations. An inventory of compliance obligations ensures that all staff who are responsible for compliance activities are aware of the range of organizational obligations. This also avoids the potential for surprise obligations that the organization has not planned for or has not considered in its compliance plans and program.

COMP:SG2.SP1 IDENTIFY COMPLIANCE OBLIGATIONS

Compliance obligations are identified and documented.

Compliance obligations for the organization come from several sources:

- federal, state, and local governments
- foreign governments and trade associations
- industry associations and groups
- external codes of practice
- internal policies, procedures, and guidelines
- quality and process improvement certifications
- contracts and agreements with external entities such as suppliers and vendors

Compliance obligations from these (and other organization-defined) sources form the basis for the extent and scope of the activities the organization must perform to satisfy these obligations. Identification of compliance obligations not only gives the organization a starting point for improving the compliance process, but it also provides a basis for analyzing the overlap of compliance obligations, which ultimately helps the organization to streamline and simplify compliance activities.

An inventory of compliance obligations also provides a baseline from which new obligations can be identified and integrated into the organization's compliance processes. This helps the organization to avoid surprises that may render the compliance process ineffective and force the organization to resort to ad hoc practices as it must become familiar with and satisfy new obligations.

> These are examples of compliance obligations:
> - the organization's internal policies and procedures, including the information security policy, policy on sexual harassment, ethics policy, and other human resources and workforce directives
> - internal agreements, including non-disclosure agreements, confidentiality agreements, and non-compete agreements
> - industry-specific obligations, such as
>   - Gramm-Leach-Bliley Act (GLBA)
>   - European Union Data Protection Directive (EUDPD)
>   - FERC regulations
>   - Payment Card Industry Data Security Standard (PCI DSS)
>   - Family Educational Rights and Privacy Act (FERPA)
>   - Basel Accords
>   - Patriot Act
> - general obligations affecting many organizations, such as the Sarbanes-Oxley Act (SOX) and the Health Insurance Portability and Accountability Act (HIPAA)
> - compliance obligations related to retaining certifications, such as ISO 9000, CMMI, and ITIL
> - contracts and agreements with external entities such as suppliers

Typical work products

1. Sources of compliance obligations
2. Inventory of compliance obligations

Subpractices

1. Interview service owners, auditors, and legal staff to identify compliance obligations.
2. Identify compliance obligations that the organization may have to satisfy because of its external entity affiliations.

    By virtue of its association with external entities, the organization may inherit obligations as part of its contractual relationship. These obligations must be identified so that the organization places them in its scope for compliance management and so that it does not incur fines and penalties as a result of non-compliance.

3. Identify internal policies and procedures that should be included in the inventory of compliance obligations.

    Internal compliance obligations can represent the policies, procedures, standards, and guidelines that the organization establishes to promote acceptable behaviors, ethics, and practices. These obligations can be as important to the organization as those that are levied by outside agencies and thus should be included in the compliance management process.

4. Identify sources of potential new compliance obligations.

> Sources of information for potential compliance obligations include
> - compliance journals and mailing lists
> - trade associations
> - professional associations such as ISACA, ISSA, DRII, ITIL user groups, IIA, and RMA
> - industry trade shows
> - internal departments such as audit, legal, and risk management

5. Develop an inventory of compliance obligations.
    This inventory serves as the basis for the organization's compliance management program. The obligations should be identified and documented. Information about each obligation such as the following should be captured:
    - source of the obligation (internal department, vendor contract, internal policies and procedures)
    - requirements of the obligation (the specifics regarding what needs to be complied with)
    - obligation categorization (data privacy and security, risk, etc.)
    - organizational unit or line of business that owns the obligation
    - time parameters for satisfying the obligation (e.g., due dates and requirements for recertification of results)
    - standards and guidelines for compliance (e.g., how the organization must report data)
    - known information about fines and penalties that may be levied for non-reporting or for lack of compliance

COMP:SG2.SP2 ANALYZE OBLIGATIONS

Compliance obligations are analyzed and organized to facilitate satisfaction.

Detailed analysis is needed to help the organization to avoid duplication in its efforts to satisfy diverse obligations that have similar requirements. For example, a governmental agency and an industry body may both require categorization and protection of a certain type of data (such as health care records), and because of the similarity of the requirements, the organization could satisfy both obligations through fewer, less redundant activities.

The organization can perform analysis on compliance obligations in many ways. As a simple activity, the organization can use affinity analysis, in which similar obligations are mapped into categories based on the nature, type, and extent of their requirements. Regardless of the technique used, the objective is to group the requirements of compliance obligations in a way that makes efficient use of the organization's compliance processes, especially data collection and analysis, which can be time-consuming and tedious.

Typical work products

1. Analysis results
2. Mapping or categorization of similar compliance obligations
3. List of conflicting obligations

Subpractices

1. Establish a technique for performing analysis on compliance obligations.
   The technique should allow the organization to establish categories of obligations and requirements (such as privacy and data security) and use these categories to map obligations from their sources. The organization should be able to integrate the categories with its compliance data collection and analysis processes.
2. Analyze compliance obligations and document results.
   These results form the foundation for the organization's compliance activities. They also allow the organization to prioritize obligations for satisfaction.
3. Identify conflicting obligations.
   In some cases, analysis will reveal compliance obligations and requirements that conflict. By identifying these requirements early, the organization can perform additional review and analysis to determine the most effective strategy for satisfaction.

COMP:SG2.SP3 ESTABLISH OWNERSHIP FOR MEETING OBLIGATIONS

The responsibility for satisfying compliance obligations is established.

Establishing ownership for satisfying compliance obligations is a way to ensure that these obligations are known, accepted, and planned for. When ownership is established, compliance activities may be integrated into the day-to-day operational activities of owners because they are aware of their responsibilities and can address them in the course of normal business. In addition, owners can ensure that the compliance obligations for which they are responsible are also reflected in the resilience requirements for the high-value assets and services under their control. Reflecting compliance obligations in resilience requirements ensures that they are considered in controls that the organization implements and manages for protecting and sustaining assets and services. In this way, the organization "embeds" compliance controls into services and may even provide for streamlined testing and reporting on these controls as part of satisfying compliance obligations.

Typically, ownership may be defined in the organization's compliance plan and program (as established in COMP:SG1.SP1 and COMP:SG1.SP2) and it may be included in the documentation of compliance obligations (as established in COMP:SG2.SP1). However, additional resources throughout the organization may have to be identified and assigned to compliance activities and tasks.

Typical work products

1. Designated compliance roles
2. Updated inventory of compliance obligations
3. List of unassigned compliance obligations

Subpractices

1. Establish the owner for each compliance obligation.
   Ownership may be assigned either to a specific compliance obligation or to a category of obligations (as defined through analysis). The owner of the obligation must confirm acceptance of the obligation and the responsibility for satisfaction. Including these tasks in job responsibilities and performance management activities may further enforce this responsibility.
2. Establish training requirements for compliance roles, if necessary.
3. Identify compliance obligations that have not been assigned or accepted.
   Compliance obligations that have not been assigned pose a risk to the organization that the obligations will not be satisfied, possibly resulting in fines, legal penalties, or even damage to reputation.

COMP:SG3 DEMONSTRATE SATISFACTION OF COMPLIANCE OBLIGATIONS

The organization demonstrates that its compliance obligations are being satisfied.

Demonstrating that compliance obligations are satisfied is a process that begins with data collection and includes activities for data validation, formatting, and reporting (disclosure). The organization collects the data necessary to "prove" that it is meeting compliance obligations, formats this data according to the requirements of the obligation, and reports it to satisfy the obligation. However, for the organization, this is not the end of the compliance process. In some cases, the organization may not be able to comply and may have to commence remediation processes that will ensure it complies within an acceptable time frame.

COMP:SG3.SP1 COLLECT AND VALIDATE COMPLIANCE DATA

Data required to satisfy compliance obligations is collected and validated.

Data collection and validation are often the most time-consuming tasks in meeting compliance obligations. The effectiveness of data collection significantly affects the organization's ability to demonstrate that it meets obligations in a timely and high-quality manner. Challenges in data collection can include inconsistency, poor quality, lack of ability to verify, lack of integrity, and lack of repeatability of data collection processes.

In many cases, data collection is not as simple as data accumulation. For example, control testing may have to be done in order to verify compliance, after which data on compliance is accumulated, formatted, and reported.

When designing data collection processes, the organization must thoroughly understand its compliance obligations so that the antecedent processes (such as control testing) can be incorporated and addressed.

Data collection also extends to storage and retrieval processes. The data collected for compliance purposes can be organizationally sensitive, and the resulting compliance reports (including cases of non-compliance) may be harmful to the organization. As part of data collection and validation, the organization must consider storage and retrieval processes that are commensurate with the level of sensitivity of the data being collected and reported.

Because compliance is a cyclical activity, the organization should implement an appropriate infrastructure to support repeatability of compliance activities. As related to data, this infrastructure should allow for ease of data accumulation, inquiry, analysis, and reporting, as well as provide for the implementation and management of access controls to ensure appropriate handling of compliance data.

Typical work products

1. List of key controls and process control points
2. Data collection strategy (by obligation)
3. Data quality criteria
4. Compliance knowledgebase
5. Policies for appropriate handling of compliance data

Subpractices

1. Develop strategies for data collection and validation.

    These strategies should be commensurate with the compliance obligations and the structure of the organization and must take into consideration that data collection may be pushed out to lower levels of the organization. In addition, the strategy should address issues related to data collection, storage, and retrieval infrastructure to facilitate these processes.

2. Establish compliance knowledgebase or information repository.

    A common accessible repository for compliance data provides a mechanism to ensure that all staff involved in compliance processes have access to data that is accurate, complete, and timely. It also allows the organization to enforce access control policies for appropriate handling of compliance data.

    The repository may include documentation of the compliance obligations and their owners and due dates, the results of compliance and substantive testing of controls, compliance targets and metrics, compliance reports, non-compliance reports, remediation plans, and tracking data to provide status on satisfying compliance obligations.

The data in the information repository may be arranged by category of compliance obligation or by other categories such as key control points.

3. Implement processes for data validation and integrity checking.

    Data that is accumulated and collected in the information repository is not necessarily ready for analysis or disposition. The organization must develop processes for data validation and integrity checking to ensure that compliance data is accurate, complete, and timely. The processes should establish data quality criteria and track the quality of compliance documentation.

Fundamental qualities of data include
- accuracy
- integrity
- standards
- consistency
- completeness
- timeliness
- accessibility or availability
- usability
- auditability

COMP:SG3.SP2 DEMONSTRATE THE EXTENT OF COMPLIANCE OBLIGATION SATISFACTION

The extent to which compliance obligations are satisfied is demonstrated through compliance activities.

Demonstrating that compliance obligations are satisfied, or that remediation actions are required, goes beyond simply preparing and submitting compliance reports. The organization must address non-compliance issues (such as identifying associated risk and relevant costs) by establishing activities that interface with the organization's governance process and determine areas that may need remediation to meet compliance obligations.

The organization must also gather data related to the efficiency and effectiveness of the compliance process in order to identify areas that must be improved.

Typical work products

1. Minimum requirements for compliance
2. List of compliance stakeholders
3. Compliance reports
4. Required remediation actions
5. Compliance knowledgebase

Subpractices

1. Establish minimum requirements for compliance.

    The organization should specify the minimum requirements for an adequate level of compliance using the guidelines and standards identified in COMP:SG1.SP3 subpractice 1.

2. Determine the stakeholders of the compliance reports and data.

    The stakeholders that will be the recipients of compliance information should be identified, as well as those that will have to be notified of non-compliance.

    One of the primary stakeholders for compliance data is the organization's governance and oversight processes.

3. Prepare and submit compliance reports as necessary.

    If the organization has to disclose that it is not in compliance, it should have processes to address the potential resulting fallout. This may require public relations campaigns, notification of risk and financial managers, and other actions. The organization may also need to notify its customers or vendors, business partners, and suppliers.

    Situations of non-compliance or the need for remediation as a result of non-compliance should also be referred to the organization's governance process.

    Public relations and other communications processes are addressed in the Communications process area.

    Governance and oversight processes are addressed in the Enterprise Focus process area.

4. Track progress against compliance obligations and identify obligations that may not be met on time.

    Obligations that will not be met should be reported to appropriate stakeholders on a timely basis. These instances may pose additional risk to the organization.

5. Identify risks and potential costs of non-compliance.

    In some cases the organization may consider not complying with certain obligations. In these cases, the organization should determine and thoroughly analyze the risks associated with non-compliance in advance of a decision not to comply and report these risks to appropriate stakeholders.

    > These are examples of risks of non-compliance:
    > - significant fines
    > - potential imprisonment
    > - damage to the organization's reputation
    > - loss of trust from customers or suppliers
    > - legal action or lawsuits

    The identification of risks should also include risks related to weaknesses that resulted in the inability to satisfy compliance obligations.

    There may also be costs to the organization associated with non-compliance. These costs should be itemized and presented to appropriate stakeholders in advance of a decision not to comply.

> These are examples of costs of non-compliance:
> - productivity loss
> - reputation damage and resulting loss in sales or revenue
> - forensic investigation fees
> - costs of notifying victims in the event of a privacy or security breach
> - remediation costs
> - fines and penalties
> - legal costs associated with non-compliance, and lawsuits resulting from non-compliance

These risks and costs may also have to be reported through the organization's governance process to obtain input from oversight committees.

If the organization decides that non-compliance is the best course of action, the decision should be documented, along with a detailed description of the risks associated with non-compliance and the organization's plan to address those risks. The decision should also be appropriately approved by management and reviewed in the organization's governance process.

All risks should be referred to the organization's formal risk management process as outlined in the Risk Management process area.

6. Identify areas that may need remediation for compliance purposes.
   One of the objectives of the compliance process is to identify areas where the organization is not performing as expected, whether measured against external regulations and laws or internally generated policies and procedures. As a result of going through the compliance process, the organization may learn of areas that need attention, particularly if they are keeping the organization from complying. These areas may require the creation of detailed remediation plans and strategies so that compliance can be achieved.

   Activities related to the development and tracking of remediation plans are addressed in COMP:SG3.SP3.

7. Gather performance data on the achievement of compliance obligations.
   Actual data regarding compliance (date of submission of compliance reports, effort expended on compliance activities, etc.) should be recorded in the compliance knowledgebase for use in improving compliance processes.

COMP:SG3.SP3 Remediate Areas of Non-Compliance

Remediation of areas of non-compliance is performed to ensure satisfaction of compliance obligations.

Areas of non-compliance are deficiencies in practices, processes, and procedures that not only affect the organization's ability to satisfy compliance obligations but may indicate serious weaknesses in the organization's internal control system and governance structure. As part of the organization's formal risk management process, these areas must be identified, analyzed, and addressed (typically through remediation plans) to ensure satisfaction of compliance obligations and to improve the organization's operational resilience by addressing weaknesses that can result in disruptions.

Typical work products

1. List of risks related to areas of remediation
2. Required remediation actions
3. Remediation plans and strategies

Subpractices

1. Identify areas of suggested remediation.

    Areas of remediation are foremost those areas in which the organization is unable to satisfy a compliance obligation. For example, if the organization is required to protect health care records and finds that the proper access controls are not in place to meet this requirement, an area of remediation is created. An area of remediation is typically also an area of weakness that may pose risk to the organization and may result in unwanted consequences (lawsuits, legal fines and penalties, loss of reputation). In the example, the risk would be related to lack of satisfaction of the confidentiality requirement.

    Areas of remediation may be reported directly by staff or others associated with the organization. This reporting may occur through ethics hotlines or other anonymous methods or on employees' yearly code of ethics reports.

2. Analyze areas of suggested remediation and develop detailed remediation plans.

    Analysis includes determining the activities that must be performed to bring the organization into compliance, as well as to identify associated operational risks and develop dispositions for them.

    Remediation plans should address
    - the actions the organization must take to satisfy obligations
    - changes to the internal control system
    - assignment of responsibility and authority to perform the work
    - relevant time considerations (i.e., deadlines)
    - relevant costs associated with the actions
    - documentation of any decisions related to non-compliance and risk

3. Assign resources to perform remediation.

    Assign accountability and responsibility to carry out remediation plans.

4. Track remediation activities to completion.

5. Assess remediation activities to determine if satisfaction of compliance obligations has been performed.

    The organization should verify that remediation activities result in satisfaction of compliance obligations. If they don't, the organization should develop additional actions to remedy any gaps.

6. Update satisfaction of compliance obligations (as a result of remediation), if appropriate.
   In addition to communication with stakeholders and submission of compliance reports, this may include notification of oversight committees and the governance process that appropriate actions have been taken.

COMP:SG4 MONITOR COMPLIANCE ACTIVITIES

The organization's satisfaction of compliance obligations is monitored and adjusted as necessary.

Continuous improvement in the compliance process reduces the type and extent of resources that the organization must devote to compliance-related activities. Because there is often a trade-off between compliance activities and those that contribute directly to accomplishing the organization's mission, the ability to make the compliance process more efficient results in less disruption to services and reduces the extent to which the organization is drawn off course to meet its compliance obligations.

COMP:SG4.SP1 EVALUATE COMPLIANCE ACTIVITIES

Satisfaction of the organization's compliance obligations is independently monitored and improved.

Objective and independent evaluation of the organization's compliance process is a means for obtaining critical information about the efficiency and effectiveness of the organization's compliance activities. In addition, and perhaps more important, it is a means for the organization to evaluate the effectiveness of the internal control system in meeting compliance obligations. Internal controls are often expensive to implement and operate in production. Reducing the number and extent of internal controls while maintaining the ability to meet compliance obligations is a way that improvement in the compliance process can translate to direct cost savings and efficiency for the organization.

The organization can employ a number of assessment methods with increasing levels of efficacy. Objective and independent evaluations are most desirable, but the organization may also want to implement a self-assessment capability to allow improvement at the lowest levels of the organization. Audits, as commissioned through the governance and oversight processes, are typically the most objective and independent measure of the organization's compliance processes and satisfaction of compliance obligations; however, evidence from these activities can be damaging to the organization, particularly if the audits are performed by external auditors or agencies.

In some cases, the organization may invest in monitoring processes that collect and accumulate data at the control level. This can be an efficient way of not only providing data for satisfying compliance obligations but also facilitating the evaluation process by providing a more continuous examination of the efficacy of the controls.

The ongoing compliance process can be costly and time-consuming to an organization. The extent to which the organization learns to make these processes more efficient and repeatable significantly affects their overall impact on the organization's resources.

There are many areas that can be improved in the compliance process, such as

- data collection, accumulation, and analysis
- consolidation and coordination of obligations (collect data once, comply many times)
- standards and guidelines for compliance
- improvements in the organization's internal control system (which would improve ability to comply in the future)

Typical work products

1. Evaluation methods
2. Evaluation reports

Subpractices

1. Establish and maintain clearly stated criteria for evaluations.
    Criteria for evaluations should address
    - what will be evaluated
    - when or how often a process will be evaluated
    - how the evaluation will be conducted
    - who must be involved in the evaluation
2. Evaluate compliance processes for adherence to compliance standards and guidelines and for meeting compliance obligations using the stated criteria.
3. Identify deficiencies and areas for improvement, particularly where the satisfaction of compliance obligations has been impaired.
    The deficiencies identified can be related to the efficacy of the compliance process or the efficacy of internal controls in meeting the objectives of the compliance obligations.
4. Identify and apply lessons learned that could improve the organization's compliance process.
    This practice may result in the reduction and/or elimination of overlapping and redundant controls, identification of areas where compliance activities can be automated, and overall improvements in the organization's approach to compliance. Cost data may be collected in the evaluation process that the organization can use to determine if it is complying with obligations at the lowest possible cost.

Elaborated Generic Practices by Goal

Refer to the Generic Goals and Practices document in Appendix A for general guidance that applies to all process areas. This section provides elaborations relative to the application of the Generic Goals and Practices to the Compliance process area.

COMP:GG1 ACHIEVE SPECIFIC GOALS

The operational resilience management system supports and enables achievement of the specific goals of the Compliance process area by transforming identifiable input work products to produce identifiable output work products.

COMP:GG1.GP1 PERFORM SPECIFIC PRACTICES

Perform the specific practices of the Compliance process area to develop work products and provide services to achieve the specific goals of the process area.

Elaboration:

Specific practices COMP:SG1.SP1 through COMP:SG4.SP1 are performed to achieve the goals of the compliance process.

COMP:GG2 INSTITUTIONALIZE A MANAGED PROCESS

Compliance is institutionalized as a managed process.

COMP:GG2.GP1 ESTABLISH PROCESS GOVERNANCE

Establish and maintain governance over the planning and performance of the compliance process.

Refer to the Enterprise Focus process area for more information about providing sponsorship and oversight to the compliance process.

Subpractices

1. Establish governance over process activities.

    Elaboration:

    > Governance over the compliance process may be exhibited by
    > - developing and publicizing higher-level managers' objectives and charter for the process
    > - establishing a higher-level compliance officer position to provide direct oversight of the process and to interface with higher-level managers
    > - sponsoring process policies, procedures, standards, and guidelines, including submitting compliance reports and remediating areas of non-compliance
    > - sponsoring and providing oversight over the organization's compliance plan and program
    > - regular reporting from organizational units to higher-level managers on process activities and results

- making higher-level managers aware of applicable compliance obligations, and regularly reporting on the organization's satisfaction of these obligations to higher-level managers
- sponsoring and funding process activities
- aligning compliance obligations and the controls that satisfy these with identified resilience needs and objectives and stakeholder needs and requirements
- verifying that the process supports strategic resilience objectives and is focused on the assets and services that are of the highest relative value in meeting strategic objectives
- creating dedicated higher-level management feedback loops on decisions about compliance and recommendations for improving the process
- providing inputs on identifying, assessing, and managing risks due to non-compliance
- conducting regular internal and external audits and related reporting to audit committees on compliance issues, failures to meet compliance obligations, and process effectiveness
- creating formal programs to measure the effectiveness and efficiency of process activities, and reporting these measurements to higher-level managers

2. Develop and publish organizational policy for the process.

Elaboration:

The compliance management policy should address
- responsibility, authority, and ownership for performing process activities, including the identification of all compliance obligations and the remediation action for areas that are non-compliant
- procedures, standards, and guidelines for
  - collecting and formatting data
  - data sufficiency and validation
  - approvals and approval processes
  - preparing and submitting compliance reports
  - tool evaluation and acquisition
  - remediation for non-compliance
  - data retention and access control
- the identification and analysis of compliance obligations
- appropriate handling of compliance data
- monitoring the status of compliance obligations
- methods for measuring adherence to policy, exceptions granted, and policy violations

COMP:GG2.GP2 PLAN THE PROCESS

Establish and maintain the plan for performing the compliance process.

Elaboration:

Specific practice COMP:SG1.SP1 requires a plan for managing compliance obligations for operational resilience. Establishing a compliance charter and program based on the plan is called for in specific practice COMP:SG1.SP2.

Subpractices

1. Define and document the plan for performing the process.
2. Define and document the process description.
3. Review the plan with relevant stakeholders and get their agreement.
4. Revise the plan as necessary.

COMP:GG2.GP3 PROVIDE RESOURCES

Provide adequate resources for performing the compliance process, developing the work products, and providing the services of the process.

Elaboration:

Specific practices COMP:SG1.SP1 and COMP:SG1.SP2 require the assignment of resources to the compliance plan and program.

Subpractices

1. Staff the process.

Elaboration:

Because compliance is an activity that is typically shared across the organization and is often an extension of job responsibilities, the assignment of human resources to carrying out the compliance plan and program may be virtual and temporal. However, the organization may have resources dedicated to specific types of compliance activities (such as compliance with Sarbanes-Oxley requirements) or who are assigned to manage the overall compliance program and plan (such as a compliance officer); in these cases, compliance activities may compose the majority of their job responsibilities.

> These are examples of staff required to perform the compliance process:
> - staff responsible for
>   - developing the compliance plan and program and the process plan and ensuring they are aligned with stakeholder requirements and needs
>   - carrying out and meeting the objectives of the compliance plan and process plan

- defining compliance standards, guidelines, and procedures, including the identification of compliance obligations and data collection, analysis, and reporting approaches for these obligations
- implementing compliance standards, guidelines, and procedures, including implementing automated means to collect, analyze, validate, and report compliance data
- coordinating process activities across organizational units and lines of business
- remediating obligations that are in non-compliance, including obligation owners
- managing external entities that have contractual obligations for process activities
  - owners responsible for satisfying compliance obligations
  - a compliance officer responsible for all compliance activities, if one is called for in the plan
  - owners and custodians of high-value services and assets that support the accomplishment of operational resilience and compliance objectives
  - internal and external auditors responsible for reporting to appropriate committees on the satisfaction of compliance obligations and process effectiveness

Refer to the Organizational Training and Awareness process area for information about training staff for resilience roles and responsibilities.

Refer to the Human Resource Management process area for information about acquiring staff to fulfill roles and responsibilities.

2. Fund the process.

   Considerations for funding the compliance process should extend beyond the initial development of the compliance knowledgebase or information repository to the maintenance of the knowledgebase. Initial costs may be higher if the organization does not have a formal or usable baseline of identified compliance obligations to serve as a foundation.

   Refer to the Financial Resource Management process area for information about budgeting for, funding, and accounting for compliance.

3. Provide necessary tools, techniques, and methods to perform the process.

   Elaboration:

   These are examples of tools, techniques, and methods to support the compliance management process:
   - evaluation methods for tools acquired to support process activities
   - compliance database management system, knowledgebase, or information repository
   - techniques and tools for developing and maintaining traceability between the sources of compliance obligations and compliance plans, programs, and obligation owners (This includes establishing categories of obligations and requirements.)

- methods, techniques, and tools for coordinating process activities across organizational units and lines of business
- tools for enforcing compliance reporting formats and for compliance reporting
- methods, techniques, and tools for compliance evaluation and self-assessment
- methods, techniques, and tools for collecting, analyzing, validating, and managing compliance data
- tools for reducing redundancy in duplicative obligations
- monitoring, auditing, and other evaluation techniques to identify problem areas
- methods and tools for managing changes to compliance data
- methods and tools for compliance data retention, storage, and access control
- methods such as ethics hotlines and other anonymous methods for staff who are concerned about areas of potential non-compliance

COMP:GG2.GP4 ASSIGN RESPONSIBILITY

Assign responsibility and authority for performing the compliance process, developing the work products, and providing the services of the process.

Elaboration:

Specific practices COMP:SG1.SP1 and COMP:SG1.SP2 require the assignment of roles and responsibilities for carrying out the compliance plan and program. Ownership of compliance obligations is specifically assigned in COMP:SG2.SP3 so that the responsibility and authority for meeting all relevant compliance obligations are established.

Refer to the Human Resource Management process area for more information about establishing resilience as a job responsibility, developing resilience performance goals and objectives, and measuring and assessing performance against these goals and objectives.

Subpractices

1. Assign responsibility and authority for performing the process.

    Elaboration:

    From an enterprise perspective, the organization may establish a compliance group or a compliance process group led by a compliance officer to take responsibility for coordinating the overall compliance process. This group may also formally interface with higher-level managers for the purposes of reporting on organizational progress against compliance obligations and process goals as part of the governance process.

    However, on a tactical level, meeting compliance obligations typically involves organizational unit staff and those who have been established as the owners of compliance obligations.

2. Assign responsibility and authority for performing the specific tasks of the process.

   Elaboration:

   > Responsibility and authority for performing compliance tasks can be formalized by
   > - defining roles and responsibilities in the process plan
   > - including process tasks and responsibility for these tasks in specific job descriptions
   > - identifying compliance obligation ownership in job descriptions
   > - assigning staff to compliance program management activities
   > - developing policy requiring organizational unit managers, line of business managers, project managers, and asset and service owners and custodians to participate in and derive benefit from the process for assets and services under their ownership or custodianship
   > - including process tasks in staff performance management goals and objectives with requisite measurement of progress against these goals
   > - developing and implementing contractual instruments (including service level agreements) with external entities to establish responsibility and authority for performing process tasks on outsourced functions
   > - including process tasks in measuring performance of external entities against contractual instruments

3. Confirm that people assigned with responsibility and authority understand it and are willing and able to accept it.

COMP:GG2.GP5 TRAIN PEOPLE

Train the people performing or supporting the compliance process as needed.

Refer to the Organizational Training and Awareness process area for more information about training the people performing or supporting the process.

Refer to the Human Resource Management process area for more information about inventorying skill sets, establishing a skill set baseline, identifying required skill sets, and measuring and addressing skill deficiencies.

Subpractices

1. Identify process skill needs.

   Elaboration:

   > These are examples of skills required in the compliance process:
   > - knowledge of the tools, techniques, and methods necessary to identify, analyze, and report on the fulfillment of compliance obligations, including those necessary to perform the process using the selected methods, techniques, and tools identified in COMP:GG2.GP3 subpractice 3

> - knowledge unique to each source of compliance obligations
> - knowledge necessary to successfully remediate areas of non-compliance
> - knowledge necessary to work effectively with asset and service owners and custodians
> - oral and written communications skills to prepare compliance reports and defend these reports if required with regulatory bodies
> - knowledge necessary to elicit and prioritize stakeholder requirements and needs and interpret them to develop effective compliance obligations, plans, and programs

2. Identify process skill gaps based on available resources and their current skill levels.

   Elaboration:

   Because staff involved in the compliance process may perform these activities on an ad hoc basis as part of their job responsibilities, it cannot be assumed that they possess the necessary skills for collecting data, organizing and analyzing it, and preparing reports.

3. Identify training opportunities to address skill gaps.

   Elaboration:

   Certification and training are effective ways to improve compliance skills and attain competency. Education in specialized standards or regulations that necessitate compliance activities is useful, as is generalized training in procedures designed to audit compliance activities. Certification is often available for standards bodies and codes of practice, which requires participants to demonstrate understanding of the related body of knowledge.

> These are examples of training topics:
> - data collection, analysis, and validation
> - data mapping and affinity analysis techniques
> - compliance reporting
> - key compliance controls
> - compliance evaluation methods
> - specific training on compliance sources, obligations, guidelines, and standards
> - managing and controlling changes to the compliance obligation inventory, knowledgebase, and information repository
> - supporting asset and service owners and custodians in understanding the process and their roles and responsibilities with respect to its activities
> - working with external entities that have responsibility for process activities
> - using methods, tools, and techniques, including those identified in COMP:GG2:GP3 subpractice 3

4. Provide training and review the training needs as necessary.

COMP:GG2.GP6 MANAGE WORK PRODUCT CONFIGURATIONS

Place designated work products of the compliance process under appropriate levels of control.

Elaboration:

Work products of the compliance process (such as the compliance process plan and compliance process policies) must be managed and controlled. The organization may also include work products such as compliance reports that may require strict version control to ensure that only the "approved" version is remitted to compliance bodies and regulators.

Tools, techniques, and methods used to capture and maintain the compliance obligations inventory, knowledgebase, and information repository should be employed to perform consistent and structured version control over these work products to ensure that the information is current, accurate, and "official." The tools, techniques, and methods can also be used to securely store these work products, to provide access control over inquiry, modification, and deletion, and to track version changes and updates.

> These are examples of compliance work products placed under control:
> - plans, program plans, program charters, process plan, procedures, and policies
> - guidelines and standards
> - obligations, including sources of obligations
> - obligation inventory, mapping, and categorization
> - obligation roles and owners
> - data, including collection strategy and quality criteria
> - knowledgebase or information repository
> - evaluation criteria, methods, and reports
> - list of stakeholders
> - remediation risks
> - required remediation actions, plans, and strategies
> - contracts with external entities

COMP:GG2.GP7 IDENTIFY AND INVOLVE RELEVANT STAKEHOLDERS

Identify and involve the relevant stakeholders of the compliance process as planned.

Elaboration:

Many COMP-specific practices address the involvement of stakeholders in the compliance process. For example, specific practice COMP:SG2.SP3 addresses the identification of stakeholders as owners responsible for compliance obligations. Specific practice COMP:SG3.SP2 identifies stakeholders that will receive compliance reports and data, including areas of non-compliance and the risks associated with them.

Subpractices

1. Identify process stakeholders and their appropriate involvement.

   Elaboration:

   Stakeholders of the plan for the compliance process include those that own compliance obligations (are responsible for identifying and meeting compliance obligations), oversee the compliance process, and are involved in any aspect of compliance (data collection, reporting, etc.).

   The constituents that establish compliance obligations (i.e., governing bodies or industry organizations that issue regulations, laws, etc.) may also be considered stakeholders of the organization's plan for the compliance process because they are recipients of compliance information and ultimately decide whether compliance obligations have been met.

   > These are examples of stakeholders of the compliance process:
   > - regulators, governing bodies, and agencies that establish sources of compliance obligations
   > - asset owners and custodians
   > - service owners
   > - organizational unit and line of business managers responsible for high-value assets and the services they support
   > - staff responsible for developing, implementing, and managing an internal control system for assets and services
   > - higher-level managers responsible for the organization's governance and oversight processes including oversight committees
   > - staff responsible for participating in decisions to not comply with certain obligations
   > - external entities responsible for managing high-value assets
   > - staff involved in self-assessment
   > - internal and external auditors

   > Stakeholders are involved in various tasks in the compliance process, such as
   > - planning for the process
   > - making decisions about the process
   > - making commitments to compliance plans and activities and to the process plan
   > - communicating compliance plans and activities
   > - coordinating process activities

- satisfying compliance obligations
- reviewing and appraising the effectiveness of process activities
- establishing requirements for the process
- resolving issues in the process, including participating in decisions regarding non-compliance and evaluating the costs and risks associated with such decisions

2. Communicate the list of stakeholders to planners and those responsible for process performance.
3. Involve relevant stakeholders in the process as planned.

COMP:GG2.GP8 MONITOR AND CONTROL THE PROCESS

Monitor and control the compliance process against the plan for performing the process and take appropriate corrective action.

Refer to the Monitoring process area for more information about the collection, organization, and distribution of data that may be useful for monitoring and controlling processes.

Refer to the Measurement and Analysis process area for more information about establishing process metrics and measurement.

Refer to the Enterprise Focus process area for more information about providing process information to managers, identifying issues, and determining appropriate corrective actions.

Subpractices

1. Measure actual performance against the plan for performing the process.
2. Review accomplishments and results of the process against the plan for performing the process.

These are examples of metrics for the compliance process:
- percentage of compliance obligations met by deadline or in advance of deadline
- percentage of compliance obligations not met by deadline
- time expended to gather, organize, analyze, and report data for each compliance obligation
- percentage of compliance obligations that are not being met
- number of compliance exceptions arising from the process
- number of compliance exceptions escalated to higher-level managers for review
- percentage of redundant data elements being stored for different compliance obligations
- percentage of compliance reports that meet or do not meet standards and guidelines
- number of manual versus automated data collection activities
- timeliness of completing the scheduled process activities

- number and type of controls in place (required) for compliance
- reduction in number and type of controls necessary for compliance obligations
- number of compliance remediation risks referred to the risk management process; number of risks where corrective action is still pending (by risk rank)
- level of adherence to process policies; number of policy violations; number of policy exceptions requested and number approved
- number of process activities that are on track per plan
- rate of change of resource needs to support the process
- rate of change of costs to support the process

3. Review activities, status, and results of the process with the immediate level of managers responsible for the process and identify issues.

    Elaboration:

    Periodic reviews of the compliance process are needed to ensure that
    - relevant obligations have been identified and communicated
    - data has been collected, analyzed, and validated
    - data residing in obligation inventories, knowledgebases, and information repositories is subject to change management and has been properly validated
    - obligations have been satisfied
    - areas of non-compliance have been identified and remediated or referred to decision makers for disposition
    - risks related to non-compliance have been identified, properly referred, and addressed

4. Identify and evaluate the effects of significant deviations from the plan for performing the process.

    Elaboration:

    Deviations from the compliance plan may occur because compliance obligations vary widely, and thus the satisfaction of these obligations may require process deviations. The organization must determine if the deviations are appropriate given the compliance obligations and whether the deviation will result in an impact on operational resilience. Deviations that occur due to differences between the enterprise view of compliance and the activities performed at the organizational unit level may be less significant to the overall process but should be reviewed to ensure that the intent of the enterprise process is preserved.

5. Identify problems in the plan for performing and executing the process.
6. Take corrective action when requirements and objectives are not being satisfied, when issues are identified, or when progress differs significantly from the plan for performing the process.
7. Track corrective action to closure.

COMP:GG2.GP9 OBJECTIVELY EVALUATE ADHERENCE

Objectively evaluate adherence of the compliance process against its process description, standards, and procedures, and address non-compliance.

Elaboration:

These are examples of activities to be reviewed:
- identifying and documenting compliance obligations
- collecting, analyzing, and validating compliance data
- satisfying compliance obligations
- identifying areas of non-compliance
- identifying risks related to non-compliance
- the alignment of stakeholder requirements with process plans and programs
- assignment of responsibility, accountability, and authority for process activities
- determination of the adequacy of compliance reports and reviews in informing decision makers regarding the performance of operational resilience management activities and the need to take corrective action, if any
- verification of compliance controls
- use of compliance process work products for improving strategies for protecting and sustaining assets and services

These are examples of work products to be reviewed:
- process plans, programs, charters, and policies
- obligations and their status
- remediation and non-compliance issues that have been referred to the risk management process
- compliance reports
- compliance methods, techniques, and tools
- metrics for the process *(Refer to COMP:GG2.GP8 subpractice 2.)*
- contracts with external entities

COMP:GG2.GP10 REVIEW STATUS WITH HIGHER-LEVEL MANAGERS

Review the activities, status, and results of the compliance process with higher-level managers and resolve issues.

Refer to the Enterprise Focus process area for more information about providing sponsorship and oversight to the operational resilience management system.

COMP:GG3 INSTITUTIONALIZE A DEFINED PROCESS

Compliance is institutionalized as a defined process.

COMP:GG3.GP1 ESTABLISH A DEFINED PROCESS

Establish and maintain the description of a defined compliance process.

Establishing and tailoring process assets, including standard processes, are addressed in the Organizational Process Definition process area.

Establishing process needs and objectives and selecting, improving, and deploying process assets, including standard processes, are addressed in the Organizational Process Focus process area.

Subpractices

1. Select from the organization's set of standard processes those processes that cover the compliance process and best meet the needs of the organizational unit or line of business.
2. Establish the defined process by tailoring the selected processes according to the organization's tailoring guidelines.
3. Ensure that the organization's process objectives are appropriately addressed in the defined process, and ensure that process governance extends to the tailored processes.
4. Document the defined process and the records of the tailoring.
5. Revise the description of the defined process as necessary.

COMP:GG3.GP2 COLLECT IMPROVEMENT INFORMATION

Collect compliance work products, measures, measurement results, and improvement information derived from planning and performing the process to support future use and improvement of the organization's processes and process assets.

Elaboration:

> These are examples of improvement work products and information:
> - compliance knowledgebase or information repository
> - satisfied compliance obligations and compliance reports
> - lessons learned from data collection, analysis, and validation
> - lessons learned from satisfying compliance obligations
> - metrics and measurements of the viability of the process *(Refer to COMP:GG2.GP8 subpractice 2.)*

> - changes and trends in operating conditions, risk conditions, and the risk environment that affect process results
> - lessons learned in post-event review of incidents and disruptions in continuity
> - compliance lessons learned that can be applied to improve operational resilience management performance, such as remediation actions and risks and decisions to not comply with specific obligations
> - the current status of compliance obligations, including the inventory
> - reports on the effectiveness and weaknesses of controls
> - resilience requirements that are not being satisfied or are being exceeded

Establishing the measurement repository and process asset library is addressed in the Organizational Process Definition process area. Updating the measurement repository and process asset library as part of process improvement and deployment is addressed in the Organizational Process Focus process area.

Subpractices

1. Store process and work product measures in the organization's measurement repository.
2. Submit documentation for inclusion in the organization's process asset library.
3. Document lessons learned from the process for inclusion in the organization's process asset library.
4. Propose improvements to the organizational process assets.

CONTROLS MANAGEMENT
Engineering

Purpose

The purpose of Controls Management is to establish, monitor, analyze, and manage an internal control system that ensures the effectiveness and efficiency of operations through assuring mission success of high-value services and the assets that support them.

Introductory Notes

Internal control is a governance process used by the organization to ensure effective and efficient achievement of organizational objectives and to provide reasonable assurance of success. The internal control process is pervasive throughout the organizational structure from higher-level managers to staff and is reflected in all levels of operations—in many cases, down to the transaction level.

The organization's high-level managers have the responsibility to set the tone for internal control so that the objectives of the organization are reflected in all operational activities. In this way, the organization ensures success by building in success criteria at all operational levels.

The internal control process is typically reflected in the organization's *internal control system*. By definition, the internal control system is the aggregation of the activities an organization undertakes to ensure success. While this is primarily operational in implementation, there are other broad objectives of the internal control system, including promoting ethical behavior, preventing and detecting fraud, ensuring compliance with laws and regulations, and providing more predictability in the overall performance of the organization. At the operational level, the internal control system is the aggregation of the policies, procedures, methods, technologies, and tools that provide assurance that management directives are carried out. For example, an organization may find it vital to its profitability that all intellectual property be kept confidential and only provided to staff with a justifiable need to know. Thus, a policy may be drafted that provides guidance on the effective handling and distribution of this information.

The policy is a means for implementing management's directives and minimizing impact on organizational success and achievement.

Internal control in a broad sense is focused on ensuring that the financial condition of an organization is accurately reflected in its financial and accounting records. However, at an operational level, internal control relates to implementing policies, procedures, methods, technologies, and tools that support service mission assurance. Typically this involves the development of high-level control objectives that align with service mission assurance requirements and strategies to protect and sustain services that satisfy these requirements. Control objectives are then translated into appropriate policies, procedures, methods, technologies, and tools—referred to as operational controls—that are needed to meet each objective. From an operational resilience management perspective, these operational controls are critical to protecting assets, sustaining assets, and preventing disruption to assets as they are deployed in the execution of a service. That said, effective controls management for operational resilience means identifying the most cost-effective strategies for protecting and sustaining assets and services. The organization should seek the optimum mix in contrast to, for example, deploying an extensive number of overlapping and redundant controls in reaction to new compliance requirements.

In the Controls Management process area, the organization establishes control objectives that reflect the organization's objectives and mission and defines the target for the development of enterprise- and operational-level controls. Enterprise controls are developed to address organization-wide directives that universally affect all operational layers. Operational controls are developed, implemented, monitored, analyzed, and managed at the services level to ensure services meet their mission and, specifically, that assets related to services are protected from disruption. These controls may be administrative, technical, or physical in nature and typically are implemented in layers to reinforce strategies to protect and sustain assets and to meet control objectives. Enterprise and operational controls are analyzed and validated to ensure that they meet control objectives as implemented; gaps in effectiveness are identified on a periodic basis and addressed so that control objectives are attained on a consistent basis. It should be noted that the internal control environment in an organization is vast; however, in Controls Management the focus is on controls that relate directly to the deployment of people and the use of information, technology, and facilities in executing services. Depending on the organization, this may include administrative controls, such as separation of duties, or more specific controls, such as the implementation of a physical access control system at a facility. In other words, the subset of operational controls used by the organization to ensure operational resilience is specific to the high-value services that the organization relies on to carry out its mission. Thus, this subset is likely only a small part of the organization's overall internal control system.

The Controls Management and Service Continuity process areas establish the range of controls necessary to ensure that services achieve their missions even when disrupted. Controls Management focuses on controls that support protection and sustainment strategies—those that help to prevent services and assets from exposure to vulnerabilities and threats and those that help services and assets respond and recover when disrupted. However, all threat conditions cannot be known or anticipated. Service Continuity also focuses on sustaining services and assets under degraded conditions and in returning them to a normal operating state when possible. Service Continuity is also important because controls that have been implemented may not always meet control objectives or may not be operating effectively. In these cases, until control remediation actions can occur, the service continuity process sustains services and their supporting assets in the near term.

Related Process Areas

Strategic goals, objectives, critical success factors, and governance for the operational resilience management system, as well as the identification of high-value services, are addressed in the Enterprise Focus process area.

Identification, analysis, and mitigation strategies for operational risks are addressed in the Risk Management process area.

Ensuring compliance with identified obligations related to managing operational resilience, including those satisfied by the internal control system, is addressed in the Compliance process area.

The relationship between assets and services is established in the Asset Definition and Management process area.

The identification and implementation of controls for information assets are performed in the Knowledge and Information Management process area.

The identification and implementation of controls for facilities are performed in the Environmental Control process area.

The identification and implementation of controls for technology assets are performed in the Technology Management process area.

Controls related to establishing and managing the contributions and availability of people are identified and implemented in the People Management process area.

The development of service continuity plans as a control for protecting and sustaining services and assets is addressed in the Service Continuity process area.

Monitoring the internal control system for the operational resilience management system is addressed in the Monitoring process area.

Supporting information needs for managing the internal control system in support of operational resilience is addressed in the Measurement and Analysis process area.

Summary of Specific Goals and Practices

CTRL:SG1 Establish Control Objectives
    CTRL:SG1.SP1 Define Control Objectives
CTRL:SG2 Establish Controls
    CTRL:SG2.SP1 Define Controls
CTRL:SG3 Analyze Controls
    CTRL:SG3.SP1 Analyze Controls
CTRL:SG4 Assess Control Effectiveness
    CTRL:SG4.SP1 Assess Controls

Specific Practices by Goal

CTRL:SG1 ESTABLISH CONTROL OBJECTIVES

Organizational objectives to be achieved through the selection and implementation of controls are established.

A control objective is a performance target for a control or an internal control system. The organization uses control objectives as a means for selecting, analyzing, and managing an appropriate level of controls to achieve the organization's strategic objectives. Control objectives broadly reflect management's directives at an enterprise, line of business, or organizational unit level.

Control objectives can be developed for various organizational processes and systems. For example, a set of financial control objectives can be established to ensure that accounting and financial transactions are accurate, timely, valid, and documented. Conversely, control objectives can be established for information technology processes to ensure that systems and software meet their objectives with reasonable assurance, in an efficient and effective manner, and with a high degree of fraud prevention.

Control objectives can also be established with varying degrees of specificity. For example, a control objective may be established at the enterprise level that requires separation of duties between staff who enter invoices into a payment system and staff who approve payment of invoices. Conversely, a control objective may be established for an application system to ensure that a vendor is not paid twice for the same invoice.

CTRL:SG1.SP1 DEFINE CONTROL OBJECTIVES

Control objectives are established as the basis for the selection, implementation, and management of the organization's internal control system.

Control objectives are broad-based targets for the effective and efficient performance of controls. Establishing control objectives is an activity that guides the organization's ability to link controls to management directives.

For operational resilience management, control objectives are defined relative to the organization's strategic objectives, risk appetite and environment, and the resilience requirements of high-value assets and services. The control objectives are driven by strategies for protecting and sustaining service-related assets to ensure that their exposure to vulnerabilities and threats is managed. Based on the control objectives and the larger protection and sustainment strategies, specific controls are selected, analyzed, and managed to ensure that control objectives are satisfied.

Typical work products

1. Management directives and guidelines for selecting control objectives
2. Control objectives
3. Criteria for prioritizing control objectives
4. List of prioritized control objectives

Subpractices

1. Identify management directives and organizational guidelines upon which to base the definition of control objectives. (*Refer to EF:SG1.SP1 for more information.*)

    Sources of management directives and guidelines may include the following:
    - strategic objectives and statements of risk appetite, tolerance, and thresholds
    - internal policies, procedures, standards, and guidelines that the organization establishes to promote acceptable behaviors, ethics, and practices
    - line of business and organizational unit business objectives and operating plans supported by interviews with organizational unit and line of business managers
    - resilience requirements for services and supporting assets supported by interviews with service owners, business process owners, and asset owners and custodians
    - relationships, contracts, service level agreements, and obligations with external entities (*Refer to the External Dependencies Management process area for additional information about managing relationships with external entities.*)
    - legal and regulatory compliance obligations supported by interviews with auditors and legal staff
    - ethics and integrity codes of practice and statements

2. Define and document control objectives that result from management directives and guidelines.

    Affinity analysis of directives and guidelines may be useful in identifying categories of control objectives.

    These are examples of control objectives:
    - Prevent unauthorized use of purchase orders.
    - Ensure adequate supplies of materials.
    - Establish an enterprise architecture for information technology.
    - Develop and communicate policies regarding standards of ethical behavior.

- Identify and assess risks that may cause material misstatements of financial records.
- Educate and train staff.
- Manage external entity relationships.
- Establish a compliance program.

3. Prioritize control objectives.

   The intent of prioritization is to determine the control objectives that most need attention because of their potential to affect operational resilience.

   Assigning a relative priority to each control objective or category aids in determining the level of resources to apply when defining, analyzing, assessing, and addressing gaps in controls (refer to CTRL:SG2, CTRL:SG3, and CTRL:SG4).

   Management directives and guidelines can be used to establish criteria for prioritizing control objectives.

CTRL:SG2 ESTABLISH CONTROLS

Controls that support control objectives and strategies for protecting and sustaining high-value services and assets are established.

A control is a policy, procedure, method, technology, or tool that satisfies a stated control objective. For operational resilience management, the focus is limited to the subset of controls that reduce exposure to threats and vulnerabilities that can affect the productive capacity of people, information, technology, and facilities as they are deployed in services, as well as those that help services and assets respond and recover when disrupted.

Controls can be broad or specific. Enterprise-level controls typically apply universally to all operational processes. An example of such a control is to perform required background checks on all prospective employees before they are hired. Operational-level controls are more specific. The implementation of an access control system on a data center is an operational-level control.

All controls can be categorized as one of three types:

- Administrative controls (often called "management" controls) ensure alignment to management's intentions and include such actions as governance, setting policy, monitoring, auditing, enforcing separation of duties, and developing and implementing service continuity plans. Enterprise-level controls are typically administrative in nature because other than stating management's intention, they have little ability to *prevent* unwanted activities or disruptions. Administrative controls can be used to implement resilience requirements for confidentiality, integrity, and availability, although generally they have to be coupled with technical and physical controls to be effective.
- Technical controls are operational controls that are implemented through technological means. They include electronic access controls, firewalls, encryption, and

intrusion detection systems. Operational controls are often technical because they exist in automated processes, manifested in software, systems, hardware, networks, and telecommunications infrastructure. Technical controls are effective for implementing all types of resilience requirements.

- Physical controls are operational controls that provide physical barriers to access. Physical controls can apply to people (in a safety sense), technology, and other tangible assets such as facilities. These controls typically include picture IDs, card readers and locks on file room doors, and other physical security methods. Physical controls are most effective for implementing integrity and availability requirements but can also be used to ensure confidentiality.

Controls can also be categorized by where and when they are implemented in the execution of a service to ensure the effective and efficient operation of that service (as well as protecting and sustaining its supporting assets). Controls can be preventive, detective, compensating, or correcting. Preventive controls attempt to deter or prevent undesirable events from occurring. Preventive controls are typically technical or physical in nature, but some administrative controls can also be used in a preventive way. Detective controls, on the other hand, attempt to detect undesirable acts. They provide evidence that a loss has occurred but do not prevent a loss from occurring. Compensating controls may provide a level of redundancy that helps to further reduce the risk that undesirable events could affect a service. Correcting controls support detective controls by helping to "fix" a problem that has been detected.

A layering of all types of controls is essential to an effective internal control system. From an operational resilience standpoint, preventive controls are essential because they are proactive and contribute to protection of assets. However, detective controls play a critical role in providing evidence that the preventive controls are (or are not) functioning adequately.

The most effective mix of controls depends on the management directives and guidelines that have to be satisfied and the overall cost to the organization. Controls are often expensive to implement and to manage long term, particularly preventive controls, so the organization must strike an optimal balance between the satisfaction of directives and the cost of controls.

These are examples of preventive controls:
- separation of duties
- two-person rules to limit risk of fraud or error by one person
- proper authorization and approval of transactions
- physical safeguards and electronic access control for assets
- supervision and monitoring of ongoing operational activity
- adequate documentation
- use of passwords

> These are examples of detective controls:
> - audits
> - reviews
> - variance analyses
> - physical inventory
> - retention of documentation, logs, and records to substantiate transactions
> - periodic and regular operational reviews

CTRL:SG2.SP1 DEFINE CONTROLS

Controls that protect services and assets from disruption are identified and established.

Administrative, technical, and physical controls are established to meet operational resilience management control objectives. Controls can be at the enterprise level or at the service and asset level.

Enterprise-level controls derive from enterprise-level control objectives. At a strategic level, they establish the boundaries, parameters, checks, and balances that the organization imposes on all organizational units and lines of business to ensure objectives are achieved. This includes any external control requirements that the organization inherits from its market sector affiliations and competitive environment. An example of this type of requirement is laws and regulations—they broadly affect the sector in which an organization operates and must be met by all organizational units. Ensuring the confidentiality of health-related information is an example of an enterprise-level control objective; the use of encryption for sensitive patient information is an example of an enterprise-level control.

Enterprise-level controls may also be derived from the results of risk identification activities such as security assessments and business impact analysis.

Table CTRL.1 provides one example of the relationships among an enterprise control objective, a risk, and controls to meet the objective and mitigate the risk.

TABLE CTRL.1

Enterprise Control Objective	Risk	Enterprise Controls
The person who requisitions the purchase of goods or services should not be the person who approves the purchase.	Fraud, mistake, or error by one person	End-to-end responsibility for any series of financially related transactions to be distributed among two or more staff members or departments
		Periodic rotation of job duties between staff members or departments

With respect to service-level controls, high-value services are identified, prioritized, and communicated in the Enterprise Focus process area *(refer to EF:SG1.SP3)*. Assuring service mission success is the focus for defining service-level controls that meet their corresponding control objectives.

Table CTRL.2 provides one example of the relationships among a service-level control objective, a risk, and controls to meet the objective and mitigate the risk.

TABLE CTRL.2

Service-Level Control Objective	*Risk*	*Service Controls*
Access to the network and any network-connected system (e.g., file and print services, application servers, database servers) is controlled to prevent access by unauthorized entities.	Users may have inappropriate or unauthorized access to the network and network-connected systems and services.	System owner grants network access to staff based on approved access request forms. Periodically, IT managers verify the current network/system access list with system owners to ensure network/system access is appropriate and accurate. Administrative access, enabling the administrator to grant network/system access, is restricted to IT managers.

In large part, service-level controls derive from the aggregation of all supporting asset-level controls. Using the example above, access controls on the network asset, network-connected system assets, application server assets, and database server assets are the access controls for the service they support. In addition, controls such as the service continuity plans developed in the Service Continuity process area serve as essential controls for sustaining services.

With respect to asset-level controls, the relationship between assets and services is established in the Asset Definition and Management process area *(ADM:SG2)*. Controls for protecting and sustaining high-value assets that support high-value services are also required for service mission assurance.

Asset-level controls are identified and implemented in the following process areas:

- information assets: Knowledge and Information Management process area *(See KIM:SG2.SP2.)*
- facilities: Environmental Control process area *(See EC:SG2.SP2.)*
- technology assets: Technology Management process area *(See TM:SG2.SP2.)*
- people: People Management process area *(See all SGs and SPs.)*

Service-level and asset-level controls that are identified in other CERT-RMM process areas are established in this specific practice as the basis for satisfying control objectives.

Typical work products

1. Enterprise-level controls (including responsible entity)
2. Service- and asset-level controls (including responsible entity)
3. Traceability matrix of control objectives and controls

Subpractices

1. Establish enterprise-level controls to satisfy control objectives.
   These can be a combination of controls that already exist, controls that have to be updated, and new controls that have to be implemented.
2. Confirm or assign responsibility for implementing enterprise-level controls.
   Confirmation is required for existing and updated controls. Assignment is required for new controls. This responsibility is typically assumed by organizational unit and line of business managers or their designees and is accomplished through operating plans and directives and guidelines at this level.

   Enterprise-level controls may also be implemented through service- and asset-level controls as described in subpractices 3, 4, and 5.
3. Establish service- and asset-level controls to satisfy control objectives.
   These can be a combination of controls that already exist, controls that have to be updated, and new controls that have to be implemented.
4. Confirm or assign responsibility for implementing service- and asset-level controls.
   Confirmation is required for existing and updated controls. Assignment is required for new controls. This responsibility is typically assumed by service and asset owners and asset custodians and is accomplished in the service and asset process areas referenced above.
5. Develop a bidirectional traceability matrix that maps control objectives and enterprise-, service-, and asset-level controls.
   Service- and asset-level controls that are identified in other CERT-RMM process areas are mapped to control objectives in this specific practice. Each control objective has one or more controls that are intended to satisfy it.

   Refer to CTRL:SG3 and CTRL:SG4 for the treatment of control objectives that are not adequately addressed by existing, updated, and new controls.

CTRL:SG3 ANALYZE CONTROLS

Controls are analyzed to ensure they satisfy control objectives.

Existing controls must be analyzed to determine that they meet resilience requirements and can achieve stated control objectives. In addition, proposed new controls must be analyzed to ensure that they harmonize with and enhance the internal control system in a cost-effective manner.

Analysis of controls includes the activities that the organization performs to

- ensure a proper mix and layering of controls to meet a stated control objective or a series of objectives
- identify control gaps
- identify updates to existing controls and identify proposed new controls and other methods to address control gaps
- identify risks that could arise as a result of remaining gaps even when controls are operating effectively *(Refer to CTRL:SG4 and the Risk Management process area.)*
- identify costly control redundancy and conflicting controls and eliminate them where possible

CTRL:SG3 establishes a baseline analysis of the extent to which existing controls and proposed new controls cover and achieve control objectives for the resilience of services and supporting assets. CTRL:SG4 uses this established baseline as the foundation for periodically assessing the extent to which controls continue to achieve control objectives and the extent to which control objectives continue to meet resilience requirements.

Refer to the Risk Management process area for further details about identifying, analyzing, and mitigating risks to services and assets arising from inadequate controls.

CTRL:SG3.SP1 ANALYZE CONTROLS

Controls are analyzed to determine their ability to achieve control objectives.

Analysis of controls is focused on ensuring that controls (both existing and proposed) meet one or more control objectives and, by extension, resilience requirements. Analysis also ensures that all service-level control objectives are adequately satisfied by one or more service-level controls and asset-level controls for assets that support the service. Analysis may range from a subjective review of the control's ability to meet the control objective to the development and execution of tests that demonstrate the control's capability. The organization must determine the level of analysis necessary in each case; however, the importance of the control in supporting operational resilience should determine the extent of analysis required and which analysis techniques are deployed.

Controls analysis should also help the organization to identify

- any gaps where the control does not fully meet one or more control objectives
- any gaps where an enterprise-level control objective that addresses the resilience of services and supporting assets is not adequately satisfied by one or more controls

- any gaps where a service control objective is not adequately satisfied by one or more service- or asset-level controls

In these cases, the organization must either redesign and update existing controls or identify proposed new controls (including "helper" controls such as compensating controls). Analysis is repeated to ensure the control objective is satisfied by updated and proposed controls.

The analysis process should facilitate the identification of risks that arise when a control cannot fully satisfy control objectives. Such risks are referred to the risk management process, where they can either be mitigated in other ways, or the organization may have to choose to accept and manage the risk over time. Accepting the risk of a gap in controls may be the disposition when the control objective's priority does not warrant further investment in updated or new controls.

Finally, controls analysis should be used to determine how any proposed new control fits with the current internal control system and whether the proposed control is redundant or conflicts with any existing control. Often, control layering is confused with control redundancy. Control layering is a purposeful design and implementation of controls that collectively meet one or more control objectives. However, control redundancy results when more than one type of control is used to meet the same control objective but is unnecessary. Because controls can be costly, the identification and treatment of redundant and conflicting controls must be performed during the analysis process.

Typical work products

1. Analysis results
2. Control objectives that are satisfied by controls
3. Updated traceability matrix of control objectives and the controls that satisfy them
4. Control gaps
5. Updates to existing controls
6. Proposed new controls
7. Risks related to unsatisfied control objectives
8. Risks related to redundant and conflicting controls

Subpractices

1. Analyze existing controls against control objectives.

    Affinity analysis of control objectives may be useful in identifying categories of controls needed to satisfy these. Conversely, affinity analysis of controls may be useful in determining the extent to which they cover control objectives.

    Conducting surveys and interviews with the owners of enterprise-level controls, owners of service-level controls, and owners and custodians of asset-level controls may aid the analysis process. The assessment practices described in CTRL:SG4.SP1 may also aid in the analysis process.

2. Identify gaps where an existing control does not fully meet one or more control objectives.
3. Identify gaps where enterprise control objectives for the resilience of services and assets and service control objectives are not adequately satisfied by existing controls.

    For example, the organization may have
    - resource (human and financial) limitations or constraints
    - lack of adequate infrastructure or supporting processes and technology
    - insufficient funding for risk mitigation
    - an inability to determine benefits that outweigh the investment in controls to satisfy a compliance obligation

4. Identify updates to existing controls and proposed new controls to address gaps. This includes identifying gaps where the control objective's priority *(refer to CTRL:SG1.SP1 subpractice 3)* does not warrant further investment in updated or new controls. *(Such gaps are addressed in subpractice 6.)*
5. Identify redundant and conflicting controls and make changes to address them. This includes identifying conflicts between enterprise-level controls, service-level controls, and asset-level controls *(refer to CTRL:SG2.SP1)*.

    Additional updates to existing controls and proposed new (perhaps combined) controls are identified to resolve these issues.
6. Identify risks that may result from unsatisfied control objectives as well as redundant and conflicting controls.

    Risks resulting from unsatisfied control objectives and redundant and conflicting controls should be documented and referred to the risk management process for analysis and resolution.

CTRL:SG4 ASSESS CONTROL EFFECTIVENESS

The ability of the internal control system to satisfy resilience requirements is assessed.

Enterprise- and service-level control objectives and associated controls are objectively assessed to ensure that they support the required resilience of services and their associated assets. A review of the alignment between the organization's resilience requirements and the internal control system is performed to determine if control objectives are missing or inadequately covered. Risks associated with unsatisfied control objectives are also considered *(refer to CTRL:SG3.SP1)*.

Assessing the internal control system is an ongoing activity that allows the organization to measure the effectiveness of controls across resilience activities. For example, through monitoring and ongoing measurement and analysis, the organization can determine whether controls are satisfying control objectives, strategies for protecting and sustaining services and assets, and resilience requirements. These activities can also ascertain if controls for resilience activities are effective and producing the intended results. Monitoring and measurement are two ways that the organization collects necessary data (and invokes a vital feedback loop) to know how well controls are performing in support of the operational resilience management system.

Weaknesses in the internal control system may be identified by a variety of means, including control self-assessments, business impact analyses, internal audits, external audits, and assessments against an established standard (*in addition, refer to the Compliance process area*).

Some key questions to ask (in concert with practices in the Risk Management and Compliance process areas) include these:

- Has the organization identified control gaps resulting in risks that are not cost-effective to control?
- Is the justification to accept a gap in the internal control system commensurate with the risk appetite, risk tolerance, and value of the services and assets that remain unprotected?
- Are there areas of non-compliance that can be addressed in a cost-effective manner by updating existing controls or adding new controls?

CTRL:SG3 establishes a baseline analysis of the extent to which existing controls and proposed new controls cover and achieve control objectives for the resilience of services and supporting assets. CTRL:SG4 uses this established baseline as the foundation for periodically assessing the extent to which controls continue to achieve control objectives and the extent to which control objectives continue to meet resilience requirements. Thus, CTRL:SG4 captures the continuous monitoring, review, and improvement activities that are essential to ensure that controls remain effective.

Refer to the Compliance process area for further details about ensuring that compliance obligations are fulfilled, including those that rely on the internal control system.

Refer to the Risk Management process area for further details about identifying, analyzing, and mitigating risks to services and assets arising from inadequate controls.

Refer to the Monitoring process area for further details about collecting, recording, and distributing information about the internal control system for the operational resilience management system.

Refer to the Measurement and Analysis process area for further details about supporting management information needs for managing the internal control system in support of operational resilience.

CTRL:SG4.SP1 ASSESS CONTROLS

Controls are assessed for effectiveness in meeting control objectives and satisfying resilience requirements.

Performing periodic assessment of the internal control system is necessary to ensure that controls continue to meet control objectives, that control objectives continue to implement strategies for protecting and sustaining services (and their supporting assets), and that resilience requirements are satisfied. Conversely, assessment of the internal control system identifies areas where controls are ineffective and inefficient along with determining whether controls have to be modified to reflect changing business and risk conditions. Control assessment provides opportunities to save costs by eliminating redundant controls and resolving control conflicts.

One of the objectives of the assessment process is to identify areas where the internal control system is not performing as expected, when measured against relevant internal and external guidelines, standards, practices, policies, regulations, legislation, and other obligations such as contracts and service level agreements related to managing operational resilience *(refer also to the Compliance process area)*. As a result of conducting the assessment process, the organization may learn of areas that need attention, particularly if they are keeping the organization from meeting business objectives or compliance obligations. These areas may require the creation of detailed remediation plans and strategies to ensure that control objectives are sufficiently achieved by controls.

Typical work products

1. Assessment scope
2. Assessment results
3. Problem areas
4. Updates to existing controls
5. Proposed new controls
6. Remediation plans
7. Updates to service continuity plans
8. Risks related to unresolved problems

Subpractices

1. Select the scope for the assessment.
   Typically, this will be one or more high-value services and the high-value assets that support them. The scope of an assessment should also periodically include enterprise-level control objectives and controls for operational resilience *(refer to CTRL:SG2.SP1)*.

2. Perform the assessment.

    Various assessment techniques can be used ranging from informal self-assessments to more structured formal assessments against established standards. Affinity analysis, interviews, and surveys *(refer to CTRL:SG3.SP1)* may provide useful insight. In addition, results from business impact analyses *(refer to the Service Continuity process area)*, risk assessments *(refer to the Risk Management process area)*, and internal audits and external audits *(refer to the Compliance process area)* can contribute.

3. Identify problem areas.

    Problem areas arise where controls are ineffective or inefficient or provide insufficient coverage of control objectives, and where controls are redundant and conflicting.

    While controls may be effective and efficient in support of a specific control objective, this may not be the case when controls span control objectives.

4. Identify updates to existing controls and proposed new controls to address problem areas.

    Organizations can realize efficiencies of scale by requiring specific controls for a given type of asset. For example, standardizing desktop and laptop system configurations or deploying access control systems across a range of technology assets that support multiple high value services can reduce the cost of controls.

    Straightforward changes can be addressed by service and asset owners and the line of business and organizational unit managers to whom they report. For more complex changes that require broader organizational planning and coordination, a remediation plan may be required.

    Remediation plans should address
    - the actions the organization must take to ensure that controls satisfy control objectives effectively and efficiently
    - changes to the internal control system
    - assignment of responsibility and authority to perform the work
    - schedule and costs to perform the work
    - documentation of risk mitigation strategies and residual risks

    The actions called for in remediation plans must be tracked to closure. Plans are updated as required.

    Any changes to existing controls and the addition of any new controls may result in the need for a reassessment.

5. Identify updates to service continuity plans that may result from changes to the internal control system.

    Refer to the Service Continuity process area.

6. Identify risks that may result from unresolved problems.

    Risks resulting from unresolved problems in the internal control system should be documented and referred to the risk management process for analysis and resolution.

    Unresolved problems that result in new mitigation strategies and residual risks that have to be managed should be periodically included in the scope for reassessment of the originally selected services and assets.

Elaborated Generic Practices by Goal

Refer to the Generic Goals and Practices document in Appendix A for general guidance that applies to all process areas. This section provides elaborations relative to the application of the Generic Goals and Practices to the Controls Management process area.

CTRL:GG1 ACHIEVE SPECIFIC GOALS

The operational resilience management system supports and enables achievement of the specific goals of the Controls Management process area by transforming identifiable input work products to produce identifiable output work products.

CTRL:GG1.GP1 PERFORM SPECIFIC PRACTICES

Perform the specific practices of the Controls Management process area to develop work products and provide services to achieve the specific goals of the process area.

Elaboration:

Specific practices CTRL:SG1.SP1 through CTRL:SG4.SP1 are performed to achieve the goals of the controls management process.

CTRL:GG2 INSTITUTIONALIZE A MANAGED PROCESS

Controls management is institutionalized as a managed process.

CTRL:GG2.GP1 ESTABLISH PROCESS GOVERNANCE

Establish and maintain governance over the planning and performance of the controls management process.

Refer to the Enterprise Focus process area for more information about providing sponsorship and oversight to the controls management process.

Subpractices

1. Establish governance over process activities.

   Elaboration:

   > Governance over the controls management process may be exhibited by
   > - developing and publicizing higher-level managers' objectives and charter for establishing and managing the internal control system
   > - establishing a higher-level position, such as a chief compliance officer, to provide direct oversight of the process and to interface with higher-level managers
   > - sponsoring and providing oversight of process policies, procedures, standards, and guidelines, including management directives and guidelines that serve as the basis for selecting control objectives
   > - sponsoring and providing oversight over the organization's internal control system, remediation plans, and process plan
   > - regular reporting from organizational units to higher-level managers on process activities and results
   > - making higher-level managers aware of applicable compliance obligations related to the internal control system, and regularly reporting on the organization's satisfaction of these obligations to higher-level managers
   > - sponsoring and funding process activities
   > - aligning control objectives with identified resilience needs and objectives and stakeholder needs and requirements
   > - verifying that the process supports strategic resilience objectives and is focused on the assets and services that are of the highest relative value in meeting strategic objectives
   > - creating dedicated higher-level management feedback loops on decisions about the internal control system and recommendations for improving the process
   > - providing inputs on identifying, assessing, and managing risks due to missing, ineffective, inefficient, redundant, and conflicting controls
   > - conducting regular internal and external audits and related reporting to audit committees on process effectiveness
   > - creating formal programs to measure the effectiveness and efficiency of process activities, and reporting these measurements to higher-level managers

2. Develop and publish organizational policy for the process.

   Elaboration:

   > The controls management policy should address
   > - responsibility, authority, and ownership for performing process activities
   > - procedures, standards, and guidelines for
   >   - defining and selecting control objectives
   >   - prioritizing control objectives
   >   - evaluating and acquiring tools for monitoring the performance of controls
   >   - analyzing and assessing controls
   >   - identifying gaps in controls and approaches for addressing them
   >   - identifying redundant and conflicting controls
   >   - identifying risks associated with problems in the internal control system
   > - periodically assessing the internal control system
   > - methods for measuring adherence to policy, exceptions granted, and policy violations

CTRL:GG2.GP2 PLAN THE PROCESS

Establish and maintain the plan for performing the controls management process.

Elaboration:

The plan for the controls management process should be directly influenced by the management directives and guidelines and resilience requirements that serve as the basis for defining control objectives.

The plan for the controls management process should not be confused with remediation plans for changes to the internal control system that require broad organizational planning and coordination as described in CTRL:SG4.SP1. The plan for the controls management process details how the organization will perform controls management, including the development of remediation plans.

Subpractices

1. Define and document the plan for performing the process.
2. Define and document the process description.
3. Review the plan with relevant stakeholders and get their agreement.
4. Revise the plan as necessary.

CTRL:GG2.GP3 PROVIDE RESOURCES

Provide adequate resources for performing the controls management process, developing the work products, and providing the services of the process.

Subpractices

1. Staff the process.

> These are examples of staff required to perform the controls management process; such people may include organizational unit managers, line of business managers, project managers, and asset and service owners and custodians:
> - staff responsible for
>   - developing the process plan and ensuring it is aligned with stakeholder requirements and needs
>   - defining process standards, guidelines, and procedures
>   - implementing process standards, guidelines, and procedures, including implementing automated means to collect, analyze, validate, and report on the status and effectiveness of controls
>   - coordinating process activities across organizational units and lines of business
>   - analyzing and assessing controls
>   - addressing issues and problem areas in controls resulting from analysis and assessment, including developing and executing remediation plans
>   - managing external entities that have contractual obligations for process activities
> - owners of enterprise-level controls that affect the resilience of services and assets
> - service owners and asset owners and custodians responsible for implementing controls
> - a compliance officer who assumes responsibility for all process activities as they affect the organization's ability to meet compliance obligations
> - owners and custodians of high-value services and assets that support the accomplishment of operational resilience and process objectives
> - internal and external auditors responsible for reporting to appropriate committees on the satisfaction of control objectives and process effectiveness

Refer to the Organizational Training and Awareness process area for information about training staff for resilience roles and responsibilities.

Refer to the Human Resource Management process area for information about acquiring staff to fulfill roles and responsibilities.

2. Fund the process.
    Refer to the Financial Resource Management process area for information about budgeting for, funding, and accounting for controls management.
3. Provide necessary tools, techniques, and methods to perform the process.

Elaboration:

> These are examples of tools, techniques, and methods to support the controls management process:
> - affinity analysis methods for categorizing control objectives and analyzing controls
> - methods for prioritizing control objectives
> - techniques and tools for developing and maintaining traceability between control objectives and controls
> - methods for conducting surveys and interviews
> - methods and techniques for identifying and addressing gaps in controls as well as conflicting and redundant controls
> - methods, techniques, and tools for control analysis and assessment
> - methods, techniques, and tools for coordinating process activities across organizational units and lines of business
> - methods, techniques, and tools for collecting, analyzing, validating, and managing information about the internal control system
> - monitoring, auditing, and other assessment techniques to identify problem areas
> - methods and tools for managing changes to controls

CTRL:GG2.GP4 ASSIGN RESPONSIBILITY

Assign responsibility and authority for performing the controls management process, developing the work products, and providing the services of the process.

Elaboration:

As identified in specific practice CTRL:SG2.SP1, responsibility for enterprise-level controls is typically assumed by organizational unit and line of business managers or their designees; responsibility for service- and asset-level controls is typically assumed by service and asset owners and custodians.

Refer to the Human Resource Management process area for more information about establishing resilience as a job responsibility, developing resilience performance goals and objectives, and measuring and assessing performance against these goals and objectives.

Subpractices

1. Assign responsibility and authority for performing the process.

Elaboration:

From an enterprise perspective, the organization may assign responsibility to a compliance group or a compliance process group led by a compliance officer to take responsibility for coordinating the overall controls management process as it relates to the fulfillment of compliance obligations. This group may also formally interface with higher-level managers for the purposes of reporting on the internal control system and the satisfaction of process goals as part of the governance process *(refer to CTRL:GG2.GP1).*

2. Assign responsibility and authority for performing the specific tasks of the process.

   Elaboration:

   > Responsibility and authority for performing controls management tasks can be formalized by
   > - defining roles and responsibilities in the process plan
   > - including process tasks and responsibility for these tasks in specific job descriptions
   > - identifying ownership of specific control objectives and controls in job descriptions
   > - assigning staff to monitor and measure the internal control system
   > - developing policy requiring organizational unit managers, line of business managers, project managers, and asset and service owners and custodians to participate in and derive benefit from the process for assets and services under their ownership or custodianship
   > - including process tasks in staff performance management goals and objectives with requisite measurement of progress against these goals
   > - developing and implementing contractual instruments (including service level agreements) with external entities to establish responsibility and authority for performing process tasks on outsourced functions
   > - including process tasks in measuring performance of external entities against contractual instruments

3. Confirm that people assigned with responsibility and authority understand it and are willing and able to accept it.

CTRL:GG2.GP5 TRAIN PEOPLE

Train the people performing or supporting the controls management process as needed.

Refer to the Organizational Training and Awareness process area for more information about training the people performing or supporting the process.

Refer to the Human Resource Management process area for more information about inventorying skill sets, establishing a skill set baseline, identifying required skill sets, and measuring and addressing skill deficiencies.

Subpractices

1. Identify process skill needs.

   Elaboration:

   > These are examples of skills required in the controls management process:
   > - knowledge of the tools, techniques, and methods necessary to analyze, assess, and manage the internal control system, including those necessary to perform the process using the selected methods, techniques, and tools identified in CTRL:GG2.GP3 subpractice 3
   > - knowledge unique to each control objective
   > - knowledge necessary to successfully remediate control gaps, problem areas, redundancies, and conflicts
   > - knowledge necessary to work effectively with asset and service owners and custodians
   > - oral and written communication skills to prepare reports on the effectiveness of the internal control system and defend these reports if required
   > - knowledge necessary to elicit and prioritize stakeholder requirements and needs and interpret them to develop effective control objectives and controls

2. Identify process skill gaps based on available resources and their current skill levels.

3. Identify training opportunities to address skill gaps.

   Elaboration:

   > These are examples of training topics:
   > - affinity analysis techniques
   > - control analysis and assessment methods
   > - survey and interview techniques
   > - specific training on management directives and guidelines
   > - managing and controlling changes to controls
   > - supporting asset and service owners and custodians in understanding the process and their roles and responsibilities with respect to its activities
   > - working with external entities that have responsibility for process activities
   > - using process methods, tools, and techniques, including those identified in CTRL:GG2:GP3 subpractice 3

4. Provide training and review the training needs as necessary.

CTRL:GG2.GP6 MANAGE WORK PRODUCT CONFIGURATIONS

Place designated work products of the controls management process under appropriate levels of control.

Elaboration:

> These are examples of controls management work products placed under control:
> - management directives and guidelines
> - control objectives and their priorities
> - enterprise-, service-, and asset-level controls
> - traceability matrix of control objectives and controls, including responsible staff
> - analysis and assessment results, including control gaps
> - updates to existing controls
> - proposed new controls
> - redundant and conflicting controls
> - risks related to unsatisfied control objectives
> - risks related to redundant and conflicting controls
> - remediation plans
> - updates to service continuity plans
> - process plan
> - policies and procedures
> - contracts with external entities

CTRL:GG2.GP7 IDENTIFY AND INVOLVE RELEVANT STAKEHOLDERS

Identify and involve the relevant stakeholders of the controls management process as planned.

Subpractices

1. Identify process stakeholders and their appropriate involvement.

   Elaboration:

   Stakeholders of the controls management process include those that are responsible for control objectives and controls, oversee the controls management process, and are involved in any aspect of ensuring the effectiveness of the internal control system and managing risks resulting from unresolved problems.

   Stakeholders of the compliance process are also stakeholders of the controls management process for controls that directly support compliance process activities and the fulfillment of compliance obligations.

These are examples of stakeholders of the controls management process:
- stakeholders of the compliance process for compliance obligations that are satisfied by controls
- organizational unit and line of business managers responsible for high-value assets and the services they support
- service owners
- asset owners and custodians
- staff responsible for developing, implementing, and managing an internal control system for assets and services
- higher-level managers responsible for the organization's governance and oversight processes for the internal control system
- staff responsible for participating in decisions to not resolve control problem areas, including gaps in controls and ineffective, inefficient, missing, redundant, and conflicting controls
- external entities responsible for managing high-value services and assets and the controls associated with them
- staff involved in self-assessment
- internal and external auditors

Stakeholders are involved in various tasks in the controls management process, such as
- planning for the process
- making decisions about the process
- making commitments to the process plan and activities
- communicating the process plan and activities
- coordinating process activities
- satisfying compliance obligations that rely on controls
- reviewing and appraising the effectiveness of process activities
- establishing requirements for the process
- resolving issues and risks identified in the process

2. Communicate the list of stakeholders to planners and those responsible for process performance.
3. Involve relevant stakeholders in the process as planned.

CTRL:GG2.GP8 *Monitor and Control the Process*

Monitor and control the controls management process against the plan for performing the process and take appropriate corrective action.

Refer to the Monitoring process area for more information about the collection, organization, and distribution of data that may be useful for monitoring and controlling processes.

Refer to the Measurement and Analysis process area for more information about establishing process metrics and measurement.

Refer to the Enterprise Focus process area for more information about providing process information to managers, identifying issues, and determining appropriate corrective actions.

Subpractices

1. Measure actual performance against the plan for performing the process.
2. Review accomplishments and results of the process against the plan for performing the process.

These are examples of metrics for the controls management process:
- number of controls and number of controls by category
- percentage of control objectives that are fully satisfied by existing controls
- percentage of controls that span multiple control objectives
- percentage of controls that require updates; percentage of control objectives that are affected by updated controls
- percentage of proposed new controls; percentage of control objectives that are affected by proposed new controls
- percentage of redundant controls; percentage of control objectives that are affected by redundant controls
- percentage of conflicting controls; percentage of control objectives that are affected by conflicting controls
- time and resources expended to conduct an analysis of controls (establish the baseline)
- time and resources expended to conduct an assessment of controls (periodic)
- number of problem areas resulting from the assessment of controls
- number of problem areas escalated to higher-level managers for review
- percentage of control objectives requiring remediation plans
- percentage of controls that have been fully automated
- timeliness of resolving control gaps (implementation of control updates and proposed new controls; resolution of redundant and conflicting controls)
- reduction in number of controls
- number of process risks referred to the risk management process; number of risks where corrective action is still pending (by risk rank)
- level of adherence to process policies; number of policy violations; number of policy exceptions requested and number approved
- number of process activities that are on track per plan
- rate of change of resource needs to support the process
- rate of change of costs to support the process

3. Review activities, status, and results of the process with the immediate level of managers responsible for the process and identify issues.

Elaboration:

Reviews of the controls management process may result from periodic assessment or post-event audits that seek to identify problems that must be corrected. Elevating the results of these assessments and audits to managers provides an opportunity to correct controls management process deficiencies and to make managers aware of variations in the process that not only have localized impact but may also affect the organization's resilience as a whole.

> Periodic reviews of the controls management process are needed to ensure that
> - control objectives are satisfied and continue to be satisfied across time and in the face of changing business and risk conditions
> - control problem areas have been identified and remediated
> - risks related to control problem areas have been identified, properly referred, and addressed
> - actions requiring management involvement are elevated in a timely manner
> - the performance of process activities is being monitored and regularly reported
> - key measures are within acceptable ranges as demonstrated in governance dashboards or scorecards and financial reports
> - actions requiring management involvement are elevated in a timely manner
> - actions resulting from internal and external audits are being closed in a timely manner

4. Identify and evaluate the effects of significant deviations from the plan for performing the process.
5. Identify problems in the plan for performing and executing the process.
6. Take corrective action when requirements and objectives are not being satisfied, when issues are identified, or when progress differs significantly from the plan for performing the process.
7. Track corrective action to closure.

CTRL:GG2.GP9 OBJECTIVELY EVALUATE ADHERENCE

Objectively evaluate adherence of the controls management process against its process description, standards, and procedures, and address non-compliance.

Elaboration:

> These are examples of activities to be reviewed:
> - establishing management directives and guidelines that serve as the basis for defining control objectives
> - identifying and documenting control objectives
> - satisfying control objectives
> - identifying problem areas in controls (gaps, updates, need for new controls, remediation of redundant and conflicting controls)
> - identifying risks and remediation plans arising from problem areas in controls
> - the alignment of stakeholder requirements with the process plan
> - assignment of responsibility, accountability, and authority for process activities
> - determination of the adequacy of process reports and reviews in informing decision makers regarding the performance of operational resilience management activities and the need to take corrective action, if any
> - use of process work products for improving strategies for protecting and sustaining assets and services

> These are examples of work products to be reviewed:
> - management directives and guidelines
> - control objectives and their priorities
> - assessment results
> - risks resulting from problem areas in controls that have been referred to the risk management process
> - remediation plans
> - process plan and policies
> - process methods, techniques, and tools
> - metrics for the process (*Refer to CTRL:GG2.GP8 subpractice 2.*)
> - contracts with external entities

CTRL:GG2.GP10 REVIEW STATUS WITH HIGHER-LEVEL MANAGERS

Review the activities, status, and results of the controls management process with higher-level managers and resolve issues.

Refer to the Enterprise Focus process area for more information about providing sponsorship and oversight to the operational resilience management system.

CTRL:GG3 INSTITUTIONALIZE A DEFINED PROCESS

Controls management is institutionalized as a defined process.

CTRL:GG3.GP1 ESTABLISH A DEFINED PROCESS

Establish and maintain the description of a defined controls management process.

Establishing and tailoring process assets, including standard processes, are addressed in the Organizational Process Definition process area.

Establishing process needs and objectives and selecting, improving, and deploying process assets, including standard processes, are addressed in the Organizational Process Focus process area.

Subpractices

1. Select from the organization's set of standard processes those processes that cover the controls management process and best meet the needs of the organizational unit or line of business.
2. Establish the defined process by tailoring the selected processes according to the organization's tailoring guidelines.
3. Ensure that the organization's process objectives are appropriately addressed in the defined process, and ensure that process governance extends to the tailored processes.
4. Document the defined process and the records of the tailoring.
5. Revise the description of the defined process as necessary.

CTRL:GG3.GP2 COLLECT IMPROVEMENT INFORMATION

Collect controls management work products, measures, measurement results, and improvement information derived from planning and performing the process to support future use and improvement of the organization's processes and process assets.

Elaboration:

These are examples of improvement work products and information:
- metrics and measurements of the viability of the process (*Refer to CTRL:GG2.GP8 subpractice 2.*)
- changes and trends in operating conditions, risk conditions, and the risk environment that affect process results
- lessons learned from control analyses and assessments
- lessons learned from satisfying control objectives
- lessons learned in post-event review of continuity exercises, incidents, and disruptions in continuity
- lessons learned that can be applied to improve operational resilience management performance and controls, such as remediation plans and risks resulting from control problem areas
- resilience requirements that are not being satisfied or are being exceeded

Establishing the measurement repository and process asset library is addressed in the Organizational Process Definition process area. Updating the measurement repository and process asset library as part of process improvement and deployment is addressed in the Organizational Process Focus process area.

Subpractices

1. Store process and work product measures in the organization's measurement repository.
2. Submit documentation for inclusion in the organization's process asset library.
3. Document lessons learned from the process for inclusion in the organization's process asset library.
4. Propose improvements to the organizational process assets.

ENVIRONMENTAL CONTROL
Operations

Purpose

The purpose of Environmental Control is to establish and manage an appropriate level of physical, environmental, and geographical controls to support the resilient operations of services in organizational facilities.

Introductory Notes

Facilities are a subset of the physical plant assets of the organization that are relied upon to execute a service. They are hubs of activity where many of the organization's services intersect, such as office buildings and warehouses. Facilities can be owned by the organization but just as often are leased from an external provider, and they may even encompass workers' homes and other locations where high-value services are physically executed.

People, information, and technology assets "live" within a physical facility—they provide the physical space for the actions of people (people work in offices), the use and storage of information (such as in file rooms and on servers), and the operation of technology components (such as in data centers and server farms). Because of its nature as an activity hub, when a facility is disrupted, there is often a widespread cascading effect on the operability of these other assets, impacting mission assurance of associated services and possibly translating to a failure to achieve organizational goals and objectives.

As a complicating factor, organizations frequently execute their services in facilities that they do not own or control. These arrangements sometimes also mean that the organization's assets are co-located with the assets of other organizations. This presents challenges not only for facilities management but for ensuring the operational resilience of services that depend on these facilities to meet their missions.

The Environmental Control process area addresses the importance of facilities in the operational resilience of services as well as the unique issues that facility assets inherit because of their geographical location and the environment in which they operate. In this process area, facility assets are prioritized according to their value in supporting high-value organizational services. Physical, technical, and administrative controls that sustain the operational viability of facility assets are selected, implemented, and managed, and the effectiveness of these controls is monitored. In addition, facility risks are identified and mitigated in an attempt to prevent disruption where possible. Because a facility is intricately tied to the geographical location in which it operates, the unique dependencies of the facility on its adjacent environment are identified and actively managed.

Related Process Areas

The establishment and management of resilience requirements for facility assets are performed in the Resilience Requirements Development and Resilience Requirements Management process areas.

The identification, definition, and management of facility assets are addressed in the Asset Definition and Management process area.

The risk management cycle for facility assets is addressed in the Risk Management process area.

The management of the internal control system that ensures the protection of facility assets is addressed in the Controls Management process area.

The selection, implementation, and management of access controls for facility assets are performed in the Access Management process area.

The development of service continuity plans for facilities is performed in the Service Continuity process area.

The establishment and management of relationships with external entities to ensure the resilience of services that are executed in facilities they own and operate are addressed in the External Dependencies Management process area.

Summary of Specific Goals and Practices

EC:SG1 Establish and Prioritize Facility Assets
    EC:SG1.SP1 Prioritize Facility Assets
    EC:SG1.SP2 Establish Resilience-Focused Facility Assets
EC:SG2 Protect Facility Assets
    EC:SG2.SP1 Assign Resilience Requirements to Facility Assets
    EC:SG2.SP2 Establish and Implement Controls
EC:SG3 Manage Facility Asset Risk
    EC:SG3.SP1 Identify and Assess Facility Asset Risk
    EC:SG3.SP2 Mitigate Facility Risks
EC:SG4 Control Operational Environment
    EC:SG4.SP1 Perform Facility Sustainability Planning
    EC:SG4.SP2 Maintain Environmental Conditions
    EC:SG4.SP3 Manage Dependencies on Public Services
    EC:SG4.SP4 Manage Dependencies on Public Infrastructure
    EC:SG4.SP5 Plan for Facility Retirement

Specific Practices by Goal

EC:SG1 ESTABLISH AND PRIORITIZE FACILITY ASSETS

Facility assets are prioritized to ensure resilience of high-value services that they support.

In this goal, the organization establishes the subset of facility assets (from its facility asset inventory) on which it must focus operational resilience activities because of their importance to the sustained operation of essential services.

In many cases, all facility assets may be considered of high value to the organization. However, from a risk and resilience perspective, these assets must be prioritized. Prioritization establishes the facility assets that are of most value to the organization (based on their support for high-value services) and for which protective controls and sustainability measures are required. Failure to prioritize facility assets may lead to inadequate operational resilience of high-value assets and excessive levels of operational resilience for non-high-value assets.

EC:SG1.SP1 PRIORITIZE FACILITY ASSETS

Facility assets are prioritized relative to their importance in supporting the delivery of high-value services.

The prioritization of facility assets must be performed in order to ensure that the organization properly directs its operational resilience resources to the assets that most directly contribute to the services supporting the organization's mission. These assets require the organization's direct attention because their interruption or disruption has the potential to cause significant organizational consequences.

Facility asset prioritization is performed relative to related services—that is, facility assets associated with high-value services are those that must be most highly prioritized for operational resilience activities. However, the organization can use other criteria to establish high-priority facility assets, such as the following:

- the use of the facility asset in the general management and control of the organization (corporate headquarters, primary data centers, etc.)
- facility assets that are important to supporting more than one service
- the value of the asset in directly supporting the organization's achievement of critical success factors and strategic objectives
- the organization's tolerance for "pain"—the degree to which it can suffer a loss or destruction of the facility asset and continue to meet its mission

Typically, the organization selects a subset of facility assets from its asset inventory; however, it is feasible that the organization may compile a list of high-value facility assets based on risk or other factors. However, failure to select assets from the organization's asset inventory poses additional risk that some high-value facility assets may never have been inventoried. (*The identification, definition, management, and control of organizational assets are addressed in the Asset Definition and Management process area.*)

Typical work products

1. List of high-value facility assets

Subpractices

1. Compile a list of high-value facility assets from the organization's asset inventory. Facilities assets that are essential to the successful operation of organizational services should be included on the list of facility assets. (*An inventory of high-value facilities is established in practice ADM:SG1.SP1 in the Asset Definition and Management process area.*) This list may suffice for this subpractice or may be expanded if necessary.

> These are examples of high-value facilities:
> - office buildings (such as the headquarters building or a branch office)
> - manufacturing facilities (such as manufacturing plants)
> - data centers and other processing centers (such as call centers, payment processing locations)
> - physical plants (such as telecommunications hubs)
> - other physical structures where significant people, information, or technology assets exist (such as off-site data storage centers and SCADA operation centers)

2. Prioritize facility assets.

   The prioritization of facility assets is necessary so that the organization can ensure it focuses protection and sustainability activities on facilities that have the most potential for impacting the organization if they are disrupted or destroyed.

   Unlike other organizational assets, facilities tend to be "hubs" of services; that is, many services tend to be performed in or supported by a single facility. An example of this would be a data center where many application systems (and their associated hardware, software, and network components) support a number of organizational services. Because the loss of a facility can have widespread cascading effects on a number of services, the organization should consider this strongly when prioritizing facility assets. One means for supporting this criterion is to review the mapping between services and facility assets. (*The association of services to facility assets is performed in practice ADM:SG2.SP1 in the Asset Definition and Management process area.*) This information may also be gathered as the result of a business impact analysis activity at the organizational unit level.

3. Periodically validate and update the list of high-value facility assets based on operational and organizational environment changes.

EC:SG1.SP2 ESTABLISH RESILIENCE-FOCUSED FACILITY ASSETS

Facility assets that specifically support the organization's service continuity plans are identified and established.

Some facility assets are specifically designated to support the organization's ability to execute service continuity plans. They provide physical locations where people can work temporarily, information can be stored and retrieved when needed, and technology components such as systems, hardware, and software can be operated. In many cases, resilience-focused assets may be owned by the organization (i.e., the organization may have a secondary data center) or may be contracted for and provided by an external provider (such as the use of a shared data center to recover systems and networks).

A resilience-focused asset may also serve as a primary facility that has been designated as a recovery site during an incident. For example, an organization may have two geographically dispersed data centers where day-to-day processing occurs; however, when an incident affects one of the data centers, the other is capable of being used to support operations of the other for a specified time period. When this occurs, primary facilities also are designated as resilience facilities, increasing the need for protection and sustainability.

Typical work products

1. List of resilience-focused facility assets

Subpractices

1. Compile a list of resilience-focused facility assets from the organization's asset inventory.
   These facility assets should include those that would be required for the successful execution of service continuity plans and service restoration plans.
2. Periodically reconcile the list of resilience-focused facilities to the organization's service continuity plans and resilience-focused strategies.

EC:SG2 PROTECT FACILITY ASSETS

Administrative, technical, and physical controls for facility assets are identified, implemented, monitored, and managed.

Facility assets are one of the most tangible and visible assets of the organization. They provide a physical presence to the organization and are the intersection point for people, processes, and technologies that fuel organizational services. Thus, the availability of facilities is important to the viability of organizational services—an organization has only to close an office building for one day to realize that many job functions go unperformed during such a disruption, no matter the cause.

Facility assets present unique challenges for managing operational resilience. Facility assets are often leased from external business partners, and therefore the organization may not have direct control or influence over their protection or sustainability. Facility assets also often take non-traditional forms. For example, in a distributed workforce employees may work at home, whereby their home location becomes an extension of the organization's physical plant.

Facility assets are also uniquely connected to their immediate environment in that their operational resilience is often dependent on the resilience of public services (police, fire, ambulance, and first responders) and infrastructure (electricity, gas, water, telecommunications). Because organizations have very little if any control over the immediate environment, managing operational resilience for facilities may require extensive considerations of redundancy, co-location, geographical dispersion, etc.

Protecting facility assets from vulnerabilities, threats, and risks requires that the organization develop appropriate resilience requirements for these assets and follow through with the development, implementation, and management of an appropriate level of administrative, technical, and physical controls to manage the conditions that could cause disruption of these assets. The organization selects and designs controls based on the facility asset's resilience requirements and the conditions that require availability of the facilities. The effectiveness of these controls is monitored on a regular basis to ensure that they meet the facility asset's resilience requirements.

The establishment and management of relationships with external entities to ensure the resilience of services that are executed in facilities they own and operate are addressed in the External Dependencies Management process area.

EC:SG2.SP1 Assign Resilience Requirements to Facility Assets

Resilience requirements that have been defined are assigned to facility assets.

Resilience requirements form the basis for the actions that the organization takes to protect and sustain facility assets. These requirements are established commensurate with the value of an asset to services that it supports. The resilience requirements for facility assets must be assigned to the assets so that the appropriate type and level of protective controls can be designed, implemented, and monitored to meet the requirements.

Resilience requirements for facility assets are developed in the Resilience Requirements Development process area. However, facility asset resilience requirements may not be formally defined or they may be assumed to be the responsibility of the facility asset owner (if the organization is not the owner). The assignment of these requirements is necessary as a foundational step for controls management.

Typical work products

1. Facility asset resilience requirements

Subpractices

1. Assign resilience requirements to facility assets.
   Resilience requirements for a facility asset are likely to be concentrated on the availability of the facility. The requirements must take into consideration the shared use of the facility both within the organization (as more than one service is likely to be performed in the facility) as well as outside of the organization (as a leased facility may be shared with other organizations that have differing resilience requirements).
2. Document the requirements (if they are currently not documented) and include them in the asset definition.

EC:SG2.SP2 ESTABLISH AND IMPLEMENT CONTROLS

Administrative, technical, and physical controls that are required to meet the established resilience requirements are identified and implemented.

The organization must implement an internal control system that protects the continued operation of facility assets commensurate with their role in supporting organizational services. Controls are the methods, policies, and procedures that the organization uses to provide an acceptable level of protection over high-value assets such as facilities. They typically fall into three categories: administrative (or managerial), technical, and physical, the latter of which is most typically associated with facilities.

- Administrative controls (often called "management" controls) ensure alignment to management's intentions and include such work products as governance, policy, training and awareness, pre-employment screening, and the development and implementation of service continuity plans. Administrative controls for facilities include policies on who can enter facilities, when, and under what conditions or criteria.
- Technical controls are the technical manifestation of protection methods for facility assets. Most prominently, they include access controls such as card-controlled entry gates and appropriate lighting or fencing, but they can also include such hardware artifacts as encryption.
- Physical controls manage the physical access to facility assets. These controls typically include artifacts such as picture IDs, locks on file room doors, and other physical barrier methods. By far, physical controls are the most pervasive type of protective controls applied to facilities and are often associated with security activities.

Operational resilience for facilities involves a thorough consideration of several types of controls. These include not only access controls but controls that address the viability and operability of a facility in its geographical location and immediate environment. Because facilities lack sufficient portability (in contrast with information assets and some technology assets), controls that prevent a facility from being impacted by vulnerabilities and threats in its immediate environment must be considered and implemented.

Typical work products

1. Facility asset administrative controls
2. Facility asset technical controls
3. Facility asset physical controls
4. List of required controls over the design, leasing, co-location, or construction of facility assets

Subpractices

1. Establish and implement administrative controls for facility assets.

> Administrative controls for protecting facility assets include
> - policies and standards for providing access to facilities
> - standards for facility site selection, construction, and management (addressing issues of co-location, geographical dispersion, proximity, etc.)
> - availability of adequate utility and communications providers
> - relevant health and safety regulations and standards
> - hiring procedures, particularly where they apply to physical security staff such as security guards
> - evacuation procedures
> - fire suppression and handling procedures
> - procedures for handling events such as hardware failure, bomb threats, and loss of electrical power, water, or other utilities
> - resilience training and awareness
> - logging, monitoring, and auditing controls to detect and report unauthorized access and use of facilities *(See the Monitoring process area.)*
> - development, testing, and implementation of service continuity plans, including facility asset substitution or restoration *(See the Service Continuity process area.)*

2. Establish and implement technical controls for facility assets.

> Technical controls include such controls as
> - access controls, such as
>   - electronic key pads, card readers, and other electronic authenticators
>   - "mantraps"

> - biometric authenticators
> - access logging and monitoring systems
> - application systems for managing and controlling physical access
> - environmental monitoring and control systems (particularly for data centers)
> - inventory tracking and monitoring (via RFID or other technology)
> - systems for monitoring viability of public services such as electricity, gas, water, and telecommunications
> - direct connection alarm systems that report to public authorities

3. Establish and implement physical controls for facility assets.

> Physical controls for protecting facility assets include such controls as
> - physical barrier controls around a facility, including barriers and gates
> - physical security buffers
> - external doors suitably protected with control mechanisms such as bars, alarms, and locks
> - staffed reception areas or other means to control physical access
> - clean desk and clean screen policies
> - physical access controls on file rooms and work areas
> - intruder detection systems to cover all doors, windows, unoccupied areas, etc., including motion detectors and visual monitoring and recording
> - facility controls that notify staff when non-employees are on the premises

4. Establish and specify controls over the design, construction, or leasing of facility assets.

    A specific subset of controls should be considered during the design, construction, or leasing of facility assets. These controls are typically technical or physical in nature and are focused on sustaining the operability and viability of facilities, thus contributing to a facility's operational resilience.

> When designing, constructing, or acquiring a facility, the following controls should be considered:
> - secured facility site—buildings should be unobtrusive and give minimum indication of their purpose, with no obvious signage
> - geographical location—proximity to climatic, geological, and hydrological events
> - environmental conditions—dust, vibration, noise, electrical supply interference, communications interference, electromagnetic radiation
> - availability of support utilities—water, sewage, electricity, heating/ventilation, air conditioning
> - business factors—educated and skilled workforce, tax incentives, insurance costs
> - walls—fire rating, load, floor-to-ceiling barrier, reinforcement for use in secured areas
> - partitions—considerations similar to those for walls, plus the requirement of extension above dropped ceilings and below raised floors

> - doors—fire rating, directional opening, resistance to being forced open, intrusion detection alarms, type of locks
> - windows—characteristics of window material, intrusion detection mechanism, placement of windows
> - ceiling—fire rating, load, waterproof (especially in shared tenant facilities), drop ceiling
> - floor—fire rating, load, raised floor, electrical grounding, non-conductive material
> - heating, ventilation, air conditioning (HVAC)—power source, protected intake vents to prevent tampering, emergency power off, air pressure, specialized chilling and cooling for technical equipment
> - power supplies—backup or redundant power supply, clean power supply, circuit breakers, access to power distribution panels, emergency power off
> - liquid and gas lines—accessible shutoff valve, positive flow, leakage sensor, placement of liquid and gas lines
> - fire detection and suppression—fire or smoke detector and alarm, gas discharge system, placement of detectors and sprinkler heads
> - emergency lighting—essential power supply and battery for emergency lighting
> - moisture—water or liquid detection and alarm
> - cables and cableways—routing, protection from fire, moisture, and unauthorized access

5. Monitor the effectiveness of administrative, technical, and physical controls, and identify deficiencies that must be resolved.

EC:SG3 MANAGE FACILITY ASSET RISK

Operational and environmental risks to facility assets are identified and managed.

The management of risk for facility assets is the specific application of risk management tools, techniques, and methods to the facility assets whether or not they are owned by the organization. Facility assets are more prone to certain types of operational risk, particularly external conditions such as failures of public infrastructure and natural disasters. In addition, because facility assets are often not in the direct control of the organization (because they are leased or shared), the organization may be exposed to additional risks that would generally be detectable and controllable if the organization owned and maintained them. As hubs of activities and services, facility assets are subject to risks that can result in widespread and cascading consequences to the organization.

EC:SG3.SP1 IDENTIFY AND ASSESS FACILITY ASSET RISK

Risks to facility assets are periodically identified and assessed.

Operational risks that can affect facility assets must be identified and mitigated in order to actively manage the resilience of these assets and, more important, the resilience of services to which these assets are associated. Special attention should be given to operational risks such as natural disasters and environmental conditions to which facilities are typically prone.

The identification of facility asset risks forms a baseline from which a continuous risk management process can be established and managed.

The subpractices included in this practice are generically addressed in goals RISK:SG3 and RISK:SG4 in the Risk Management process area.

Typical work products

1. Facility asset risk statements, with impact valuation
2. List of facility asset risks, with categorization and prioritization

Subpractices

1. Determine the scope of risk assessment for facility assets.
    Determining which facility assets to include in regular risk management activities depends on many factors, including the value of the asset to the organization, its resilience requirements, and the ownership and control of the facility.
2. Identify risks to facility assets.
    Identification of risk for facilities requires an examination of the types of threats, vulnerabilities, events, or incidents to which the facility may be subjected. The types of events or incidents that could occur at a given facility may be based on the history of previous events at that site or a similar site, events that may be common to the type of service, or natural disasters particular to certain geography. Operational risks should be identified in this context so that mitigation actions are more focused and directed. Types of facility asset threats, vulnerabilities, events, and incidents to consider may include
    - non-criminal events such as human-made and natural disasters
    - crime-related events such as theft, trespassing, and sabotage
    - the demographic/social/political climate in which the facility is located
    - geographical proximity to other high-value organizational facilities
    - people, including those who might have detailed knowledge about the facility asset
3. Analyze risks to facility assets.
4. Categorize and prioritize risks to facility assets.
5. Assign a risk disposition to each facility asset risk.
6. Monitor the risk and the risk strategy on a regular basis to ensure that the risk does not pose additional threat to the organization.
7. Develop a strategy for the risks that the organization decides to mitigate.

EC:SG3.SP2 MITIGATE FACILITY RISKS

Risk mitigation strategies for facility assets are developed and implemented.

The mitigation of facility asset risk involves the development of strategies that seek to minimize the risk to an acceptable level. This includes reducing the likelihood of risks to facility assets, minimizing exposure to these risks, developing service continuity plans to keep the asset viable during times of disruption or to provide a suitable substitute facility, and developing recovery and restoration plans to address the consequences of realized risk. In the case of facility assets, restoration may be a more extensive consideration—for example, restoration may mean that a new facility must be constructed or acquired, therefore recovery operations in a temporary or leased facility may be needed for a longer period of time. This temporary arrangement can also bring additional risk to the organization that must be addressed until restoration has been accomplished.

Risk mitigation for facility assets requires the development and implementation of risk mitigation plans (which may include the development of new or revision of existing facility asset controls) and the monitoring of these plans for effectiveness.

The subpractices included in this practice are generically addressed in goal RISK:SG5 in the Risk Management process area.

Typical work products

1. Facility asset risk mitigation plans
2. List of those responsible for addressing and tracking risks
3. Status on facility asset risk mitigation plans

Subpractices

1. Develop and implement risk mitigation strategies for all risks that have a "mitigation" or "control" disposition.
2. Validate the risk mitigation plans by comparing them to existing protection and sustainability strategies.
3. Identify the person or group responsible for each risk mitigation plan and ensure that they have the authority to act and the proper level of skills and training to implement and monitor the plan.
4. Address residual risk.
   Service continuity plans that involve the use of temporary or leased facilities while restoration can be completed for a facility may result in residual risk. This risk should be characterized and addressed in the risk management cycle if necessary.
5. Implement the risk mitigation plans and provide a method to monitor the effectiveness of these plans.
6. Monitor risk status.
7. Collect performance measures on the risk management process.

EC:SG4 CONTROL OPERATIONAL ENVIRONMENT

The operational environment of the facility is controlled to ensure its availability.

The *availability* of a facility—the most important challenge for the operational resilience of facilities—is dependent on several factors. First, the facility must provide access to people (both inside and outside of the organization) who need to use it to perform their job responsibilities *and* prevent access from those who do not have a legitimate need. Second, the facility must be operationally viable—it must be structurally sound, fit for purpose, and connected to vital services such as electricity, water, and telecommunications. Finally, availability of a facility is tied to its geographical location. Any event that affects the surrounding environment of the facility can impede access (and egress to some extent).

Certain operational risks, such as the following, can significantly affect the availability of a facility in supporting high-value services:

- Electronic or physical access systems can be compromised, allowing unauthorized access that may affect the availability of the facility (particularly if it is destroyed in some way) or preventing access by authorized individuals.
- Geographical events specific to the facility can occur, including hurricanes, tornadoes, winter storms, and other natural events.
- Sociopolitical events can prevent people and business partners from accessing the facility because of dangerous conditions or because of perceived danger (such as when a bomb threat is issued).
- The systems and the structures of the facility can fail, thereby rendering the facility unusable for a period of time.
- The public infrastructure that the facility depends upon can fail, thereby causing the facility to be unusable for a period of time.
- Business partners (who own or manage facilities that the organization leases or shares with other organizations) may fail to ensure the availability of their facilities, thereby posing cascading risks to the organization.

Unfortunately, facilities cannot be easily duplicated or replicated, so ensuring their availability (or more important, preserving their ability to support high-value services) is problematic. In addition, because facilities are high-cost assets, strategies for ensuring their availability are often more difficult and costly than those that are focused on information assets, technology, and in some cases, people.

To effectively control the operational environment for facilities, the organization must perform several activities. Foremost, the organization must plan for facility sustainability to ensure the continued operation of the facility (or the ability to replicate and sustain the continued operation of the facility). In addition, the organization must address the environmental conditions of the facility (to ensure that it remains viable) and consider the challenges presented by the facility's geographical environment, including its access to public and private services and infrastructure.

EC:SG4.SP1 PERFORM FACILITY SUSTAINABILITY PLANNING

The availability of high-value facilities is ensured through sustainability planning.

Because facilities operate as hubs for services, planning for the continued operation of a facility—or in many cases, the replication of functionality at a redundant or backup facility—is a critical activity in ensuring operational resilience.

An organization has several options when performing sustainability planning for facilities. The most costly option is to construct or acquire a redundant facility that would back up an existing facility in a seamless way if disrupted. This is not always a valid option because of cost and co-location, proximity, and geographical dispersion issues. Less costly options may involve the alternate use of other organization-owned facilities (if possible) or the use of shared space (either leased space or shared services). Options that include the use of externally owned facilities bring additional risks that must be considered. Finally, instead of full facility redundancy, the organization may consider only those elements that must be made redundant (such as providing an organization-controlled source of power or telecommunications) that would render a facility usable for an acceptable specific period of time.

Facility sustainability planning is typically performed as part of developing service continuity plans for services or may be instantiated in continuity plans specifically focused on high-value facilities regardless of their use. The actions that the organization needs to take to ensure that services can be executed when facilities are disrupted are included in service continuity plans. In addition to providing facility redundancy and backup, additional issues such as "return to work" considerations may be addressed and included in facility continuity plans.

The development and management of service continuity plans are addressed in the Service Continuity process area. This practice may not be able to be completed unless considerations of the practices in the Service Continuity process area have been made.

Considerations for "return to work" issues are addressed in the People Management process area.

Typical work products

1. Results of business impact analysis
2. Service continuity plans (specifically addressing facility sustainability)

Subpractices

1. Perform business impact analysis.

   Business impact analysis can help the organization to identify high-value facilities for which service continuity plans must be developed and implemented. This analysis may concentrate on reviewing the business impact of loss of services due to the loss of a facility or specifically focus on the facility itself and its associated services and the impact of their loss on the organization.

2. Develop service continuity plans that address facility availability.
    Depending on the organization's focus, service continuity plans can be specifically developed for high-value facilities (which would affect associated services) or may be developed from a services viewpoint (which addresses facilities as an associated asset).

EC:SG4.SP2 MAINTAIN ENVIRONMENTAL CONDITIONS

Environmental conditions of facility assets are maintained.

The environmental condition of a facility is important for keeping it viable and operational. Failure to monitor and correct conditions may affect the availability of the facility to support the services that are convergent there. These are examples of systems that can affect environmental conditions:

- HVAC systems must be fully operational to ensure the comfort of workers as well as to keep technical equipment from overheating and failing.
- Fire suppression systems must be active to prevent fire damage and to ensure staff safety.
- Dust and air control systems must provide purified air required for production processes, particularly if "clean room" conditions are necessary.
- Power conditioning systems must condition power to ensure consistent delivery and the avoidance of "spikes."
- Security systems must be able to monitor the facility and provide authenticated access to authorized staff.
- Water systems must provide potable water for drinking purposes and other water for supporting production processes (such as for chillers for equipment and for air conditioning).

Maintaining environmental conditions includes the performance of regular maintenance activities. The criteria used to establish guidelines for maintenance are relative to the value of the related services supported by the assets that are located in the facility. The organization may use other criteria to establish guidelines for maintenance, such as

- corrective maintenance (i.e., correcting and repairing problems that degrade the operational capability of the facility services)
- preventive maintenance (i.e., preventing potential facility problems from occurring through preplanned activities)
- adaptive maintenance (i.e., adapting the facility to a different operating environment)
- perfective maintenance (i.e., developing or acquiring an additional or improved operational capability of the facility)

Typical work products

1. List of facility control equipment
2. Equipment service intervals and specifications
3. List of maintenance staff authorized to carry out repairs and service
4. Documented maintenance records
5. Maintenance change requests
6. Updated service continuity plans

Subpractices

1. Identify control systems that require regular maintenance in support of sustainability.
2. Document equipment suppliers' recommended service intervals and specifications.
3. Document a list of maintenance staff authorized to carry out repairs and service.
   Maintenance staff should be subject to the organization's standards for authorizing and providing access. *(The management of access controls is addressed in the Access Management process area.)*
4. Document all suspected or actual faults and all preventive, corrective, and other types of maintenance.
   Maintenance records should be retained for all facility control equipment and stored appropriately with access only to authorized individuals. Risks related to control systems and their maintenance may need additional analysis and resolution.

   These activities may result in additions or revisions to existing service continuity plans or may require separate plans to be developed. Actions that are required for service continuity planning should be identified and executed as part of this activity.
5. Implement maintenance and test maintenance changes in a non-operational environment when appropriate.
6. Establish appropriate controls over sensitive or confidential information when maintenance is performed.
   Maintenance activities can result in often-undetected vulnerabilities to information assets. All controls over information assets should be reaffirmed before maintenance is performed, and information access and modification logs should be checked after maintenance is performed.

   Appropriate controls over information assets are addressed in the Knowledge and Information Management process area.
7. Communicate maintenance changes to appropriate entities.
8. Implement maintenance according to change request procedures.
9. Document and communicate results of maintenance.

EC:SG4.SP3 MANAGE DEPENDENCIES ON PUBLIC SERVICES

Dependencies on public services for facility assets are identified and managed.

Because they are geographically static, facilities rely on public services that are in operation in the immediate environment in which the facilities exist. These public services may be vital to a facility's continued operation during a disruption and, by default, to the services that are performed in the facility. Thus, a thorough consideration of these services must be given for service continuity planning and incorporated into requisite service continuity plans.

Public services generally include services that are specific to the geographical region of the facility and are financed by public funds. (In some cases, depending on the organization and its size, these services may have been privatized and therefore may be financed by and under the direct control of the organization.) Public services include

- fire response and rescue services
- local and, in some cases, federal law enforcement (police, National Guard, FBI, etc.)
- emergency management services, including paramedics and first responders
- other services, such as animal control

Identifying and managing dependencies on public services may be performed as part of the organization's service continuity planning process or in the development of specific service continuity plans. (*The development and management of service continuity plans are addressed in the Service Continuity process area.*)

Typical work products

1. Results of business impact analysis (documenting public service dependencies for facilities)
2. List of public service providers on which facilities are dependent
3. Key contacts list
4. Updated service continuity plans

Subpractices

1. Identify and document public services on which facilities rely.
   Typically, this activity results from business impact analysis. However, it can be included as part of service continuity planning or facility asset definition, depending on the organization. A resulting list of public services for each facility should be documented and made available for inclusion in service continuity plans as appropriate.
2. Develop a key contacts list for organizational services that can be included as part of service continuity plans.

EC:SG4.SP4 M*anage* D*ependencies on* P*ublic* I*nfrastructure*

Dependencies on public infrastructure for facility assets are identified and managed.

Facility assets are a primary point where an organization intersects physically with its geographical environment. Facilities are vitally dependent on public infrastructure and services to operate and to remain viable. These services include

- telecommunications and telephone services
- electricity, natural gas, and other energy sources
- water and sewer services
- trash collection and disposal, and other support services

These dependencies must be carefully evaluated for several reasons. First, the organization must be prepared to address the loss of these services, which can affect organizational services that are supported by a facility. Second, the organization may need to consider the resilience of public services when developing service continuity plans for a facility—the inability to retain telecommunications, power, or water services may adversely impact the organization's ability to execute the facility's service continuity plan. Consideration of these public services may also cause the organization to make decisions about capital improvements (such as implementing backup power systems) that would be necessary to ensure a minimal level of operational resilience for the facility.

Typical work products

1. Results of business impact analysis (documenting public infrastructure dependencies for facilities)
2. List of public infrastructure providers on which facilities are dependent
3. Key contacts list
4. Updated service continuity plans

Subpractices

1. Identify and document internal infrastructure dependencies that the organization relies upon to provide services.

    Remember that these dependencies may be internal as well as external, particularly when the organization has control over certain aspects of facility infrastructure such as power or telecommunications that it provides for its own operations.

    Typically, this activity results from business impact analysis. However, it can be included as part of service continuity planning or facility asset definition, depending on the organization. A resulting list of public infrastructure providers for each facility should be documented and made available for inclusion in service continuity plans as appropriate.

2. Identify and document external resources that the organization relies upon to provide services.
3. Develop a key contacts list for public infrastructure services that can be included as part of the service continuity plans.
4. Update service continuity plans as appropriate.
    This practice may result in updates to existing service continuity plans or in the development of actions and activities that seek to provide an acceptable minimum level of redundancy in certain public infrastructure services.

EC:SG4.SP5 PLAN FOR FACILITY RETIREMENT

The retirement of a facility is planned for to minimize operational impact.

The retirement of a facility can have widespread and unintended effects on the resilience of organizational services. If it is not appropriately planned and executed, temporary or permanent disruptions in operations can result. This is particularly true for facilities because they serve as a convergence point for many organizational services. Thus, the organization must carefully plan and execute the retirement of a facility (and the cut-over to a new facility, if planned) so that disruption can be minimized and any potential impacts can be identified in advance and appropriately mitigated. In some cases, this may require the organization to develop special-purpose service continuity plans (or enhance existing plans) to address the unique issues that may result from retirement.

Typical work products

1. Facility retirement standards and guidelines
2. Service continuity plans (specific to retirement)
3. List of business partners and vendors that facilitate service delivery and will be affected by facility retirement
4. Key contacts list

Subpractices

1. Develop a plan for facility retirement.
    This practice applies not only to facilities that the organization owns but also to the retirement of a service contract for an outside facility that the organization leases or shares with another organization.

    As part of the plan, the organization should identify and document the services that will be affected by the facility retirement and include the stakeholders of these services in the planning process.
2. Develop and implement service continuity plans to support the retirement of the facility asset.
    These plans are developed to ensure that potential problems that arise in the retirement of the facility do not affect the operational resilience of services that rely on

the facility. These plans may be temporary or sufficiently generic that they can be used whenever facilities are retired.
3. Archive facility work products.
   This may include any facility training manuals, service continuity plans, maintenance records, and other documents that may have to be referenced by the organization in the future.
4. Retire the facility by executing the retirement plan.
   This includes monitoring the retirement for any potential problems and executing service continuity plans where necessary.

Elaborated Generic Practices by Goal

Refer to the Generic Goals and Practices document in Appendix A for general guidance that applies to all process areas. This section provides elaborations relative to the application of the Generic Goals and Practices to the Environmental Control process area.

EC:GG1 ACHIEVE SPECIFIC GOALS

The operational resilience management system supports and enables achievement of the specific goals of the Environmental Control process area by transforming identifiable input work products to produce identifiable output work products.

EC:GG1.GP1 PERFORM SPECIFIC PRACTICES

Perform the specific practices of the Environmental Control process area to develop work products and provide services to achieve the specific goals of the process area.

Elaboration:

Specific practices EC:SG1.SP1 through EC:SG4.SP5 are performed to achieve the goals of the environmental control process.

EC:GG2 INSTITUTIONALIZE A MANAGED PROCESS

Environmental control is institutionalized as a managed process.

EC:GG2.GP1 ESTABLISH PROCESS GOVERNANCE

Establish and maintain governance over the planning and performance of the environmental control process.

Refer to the Enterprise Focus process area for more information about providing sponsorship and oversight to the environmental control process.

Subpractices

1. Establish governance over process activities.

    Elaboration:

    > Governance over the environmental control process may be exhibited by
    > - establishing a higher-level management position responsible for the resilience of the organization's facility assets
    > - developing and publicizing higher-level managers' objectives and requirements for the process
    > - providing oversight over the development, acquisition, implementation, and management of high-value facility assets
    > - sponsoring process policies, procedures, standards, and guidelines, including the documentation of facility assets and establishing asset ownership and custodianship
    > - providing oversight over the establishment, implementation, and maintenance of the organization's internal control system for facility assets
    > - making higher-level managers aware of applicable compliance obligations related to environmental control, and regularly reporting on the organization's satisfaction of these obligations to higher-level managers
    > - sponsoring and funding process activities
    > - providing guidance for prioritizing facility assets relative to the organization's high-priority strategic objectives
    > - providing guidance on identifying, assessing, and managing operational risks related to facilities, including guidance for ensuring facility asset availability during disruptive events
    > - regular reporting from facility asset owners to higher-level managers on facility controls and process activities and results
    > - creating dedicated higher-level management feedback loops on decisions about the process and recommendations for improving the process
    > - conducting regular internal and external audits and related reporting to audit committees on facilities controls and the effectiveness of the process
    > - creating formal programs to measure the effectiveness of process activities, and reporting these measurements to higher-level managers

2. Develop and publish organizational policy for the process.

    Elaboration:

    > The environmental control policy should address
    > - responsibility, authority, and ownership for performing process activities, including establishing and implementing administrative, technical, and physical controls to meet resilience requirements

> - access to facilities, such as who can enter, when, and under what conditions or criteria
> - clean desk and clean screen policies
> - procedures, standards, and guidelines for
>   - facility site selection, construction, and management (addressing issues of co-location, geographical dispersion, proximity, etc.)
>   - facility retirement
>   - documenting facility asset descriptions and relevant information
>   - describing facility owners and custodians
>   - managing dependencies on public services and public infrastructure, including establishing agreements or credentialing with public-private service providers
>   - developing and documenting resilience requirements for facility assets
>   - establishing, implementing, and maintaining an internal control system for facilities *(Refer to EC:SG2.SP2.)*
>   - maintaining environmental conditions for facilities
>   - managing facility operational risk
>   - establishing facility service continuity plans and procedures
>   - retiring facilities at the end of their useful life
>   - health and safety
>   - evacuation
>   - fire suppression and handling
>   - disruptive event handling such as hardware failure, bomb threats, and loss of electrical power, water, or other utilities
> - the association of facility assets to core organizational services, and the prioritization of assets for service continuity
> - methods for measuring adherence to policy, exceptions granted, and policy violations

EC:GG2.GP2 PLAN THE PROCESS

Establish and maintain the plan for performing the environmental control process.

Elaboration:

The plan for performing the environmental control process is created to ensure that facility assets remain available and viable to support organizational services. The plan must address the resilience requirements of the facility assets, dependencies of services on these facility assets, and consideration of multiple asset owners and custodians at various levels of the organization. In addition, because facilities have a strong geographical connection, the plan must extend to external stakeholders that can enable or adversely affect facility resilience.

Subpractices

1. Define and document the plan for performing the process.

   Elaboration:

   Special consideration in the plan may have to be given to the establishment, implementation, and maintenance of an internal control system for facility assets, as well as facility sustainability planning. These activities address the protection and sustainability of the facility asset commensurate with its resilience requirements.

2. Define and document the process description.
3. Review the plan with relevant stakeholders and get their agreement.
4. Revise the plan as necessary.

EC:GG2.GP3 PROVIDE RESOURCES

Provide adequate resources for performing the environmental control process, developing the work products, and providing the services of the process.

Elaboration:

The diversity of activities required to protect and sustain all types of facility assets requires an extensive level of organizational resources and skills and a significant number of external resources (for example, as described in EC:SG4.SP3 for public services and in EC:SG4:SP4 for public infrastructure). In addition, these activities require a major commitment of financial resources (both expense and capital) from the organization.

Subpractices

1. Staff the process.

   Elaboration:

   > These are examples of staff required to perform the environmental control process:
   > - staff responsible for
   >   - identifying high-value facility assets and the services with which they are associated
   >   - establishing and maintaining physical security (such as security guards)
   >   - managing changes to facility asset requirements, controls, strategies, and plans (This includes communicating changes to affected stakeholders, including asset owners and custodians.)
   >   - developing process plans and supporting the development of facility service continuity plans and ensuring they are aligned with stakeholder requirements and needs

> - managing external entities that have contractual obligations for managing facility assets
> - information, application, and technical security staff
> - business continuity and disaster recovery staff
> - IT operations and service delivery staff
> - facilities management staff
> - technicians who implement and maintain physical security access and surveillance systems
> - staff involved in facilities risk management, including insurance and risk indemnification staff
> - staff involved in maintaining the physical plant (such as HVAC contractors)
> - staff involved in providing public services and public infrastructure to facilities
> - contractors responsible for the construction of facilities
> - owners and custodians of facility assets (to identify and enforce resilience requirements and support the accomplishment of operational resilience management objectives)
> - internal and external auditors responsible for reporting to appropriate committees on process effectiveness

Refer to the Organizational Training and Awareness process area for information about training staff for resilience roles and responsibilities.

Refer to the Human Resource Management process area for information about acquiring staff to fulfill roles and responsibilities.

2. Fund the process.

   Elaboration:

   At a minimum, funding must be available to support the establishment, implementation, and maintenance of an internal control system for facilities, as well as the development, implementation, testing, and execution of service continuity plans for facilities. In some cases, capital funding may be required for projects that enhance or support the protection and sustainability of facilities, which may result in developing additional facilities or establishing contracts with external entities to provide or support facilities when needed.

   Refer to the Financial Resource Management process area for information about budgeting for, funding, and accounting for environmental control. Refer to the External Dependencies Management process area for information about establishing and managing relationships with external entities.

3. Provide necessary tools, techniques, and methods to perform the process.

Elaboration:

Because of the extensive level of controls that have to be implemented and managed, necessary tools, techniques, and methods will be diverse. An example of a necessary tool for managing the environmental control process for facilities is a physical access system (such as a card reader, biometric device, or proximity reader).

In addition, developing and maintaining the facility inventory may require tools, techniques, and methods that allow for asset documentation and profiling, reporting, and updating on a regular basis. The need for these tools may be greater if the asset inventory is developed across many organizational units and must be aggregated at the enterprise level. The facility asset inventory database should be searchable and expandable to include additional information such as documentation of associated services and the asset's resilience requirements.

These are examples of tools, techniques, and methods for managing facility assets:
- methods for identifying and prioritizing high-value assets
- techniques and tools for documenting and profiling assets
- methods and techniques for assigning resilience requirements to facility assets and determining the extent to which facility assets satisfy these requirements
- methods, techniques, and tools for controlling physical access to facility assets, such as controlled entry gates, lighting, fencing, motion detectors, picture IDs, locks, and card readers
- logging, monitoring, and auditing tools to detect and report unauthorized access and use of facilities *(Refer to the Monitoring process area.)*
- environmental monitoring and control systems
- facility inventory tracking and monitoring systems (via RFID or other technology)
- systems for monitoring the viability of public services, such as electricity, gas, water, and telecommunications
- direct connection alarm systems that report to public authorities
- methods, techniques, and tools for identifying, assessing, and mitigating risks to facility assets *(Refer also to the Risk Management process area.)*
- tools for managing the maintenance of environmental conditions, such as equipment service intervals, staff authorized to carry out repairs and service, suspected and actual faults, and maintenance change requests
- tools for managing public service and infrastructure provider and key contacts lists
- methods and tools for aggregating local asset inventories into an enterprise inventory
- asset inventory database management system
- methods, techniques, and tools for asset change management and control

EC:GG2.GP4 Assign Responsibility

Assign responsibility and authority for performing the environmental control process, developing the work products, and providing the services of the process.

Elaboration:

Of paramount importance in assigning responsibility for the environmental control process is the establishment of facility owners and custodians, which is described in ADM:SG1.SP3. Owners are responsible for establishing facility resilience requirements, ensuring these requirements are met by custodians, and identifying and remediating gaps where requirements are not being met. Owners may also be responsible for establishing, implementing, and maintaining an internal control system commensurate with meeting facility resilience requirements if this activity is not performed by a custodian.

Refer to the Human Resource Management process area for more information about establishing resilience as a job responsibility, developing resilience performance goals and objectives, and measuring and assessing performance against these goals and objectives.

Refer to the Asset Definition and Management process area for more information about establishing ownership and custodianship of facility assets.

Subpractices

1. Assign responsibility and authority for performing the process.

Elaboration:

Responsibility and authority may extend to not only staff inside the organization, but to those with whom the organization has a contractual (custodial) agreement for managing facilities (including implementation and management of controls and facility sustainability).

2. Assign responsibility and authority for performing the specific tasks of the process.

Elaboration:

> Responsibility and authority for performing environmental control tasks can be formalized by
> - defining roles and responsibilities in the process plan
> - including process tasks and responsibility for these tasks in specific job descriptions
> - developing policy requiring organizational unit managers, line of business managers, project managers, and asset and service owners and custodians to participate in and derive benefit from the process for facility assets under their ownership or custodianship

> - developing and implementing contractual instruments (including service level agreements) with external entities to establish responsibility and authority for performing process tasks on outsourced functions
> - including process activities in staff performance management goals and objectives with requisite measurement of progress against these goals
> - including process tasks in measuring performance of external entities against contractual instruments

3. Confirm that people assigned with responsibility and authority understand it and are willing and able to accept it.

EC:GG2.GP5 TRAIN PEOPLE

Train the people performing or supporting the environmental control process as needed.

Refer to the Organizational Training and Awareness process area for more information about training the people performing or supporting the process.

Refer to the Human Resource Management process area for more information about creating an inventory of skill sets, establishing a skill set baseline, identifying required skill sets, and measuring and addressing skill deficiencies.

Subpractices

1. Identify process skill needs.

   Elaboration:

   > These are examples of skills required in the environmental control process:
   > - knowledge necessary to establish, implement, and maintain an internal control system for facilities as described in EC:SG2.SP2
   > - ability to implement and manage physical constructs and systems for facilities such as HVAC systems, fire suppression, and utilities
   > - knowledge necessary to identify, assess, and mitigate facility operational risk to ensure risk is minimized to an acceptable level *(Refer to the Risk Management process area.)*
   > - knowledge of the tools, techniques, and methods necessary to manage facility assets, including those necessary to perform the process using the selected methods, techniques, and tools identified in EC:GG2.GP3 subpractice 3
   > - knowledge necessary to work effectively with asset owners and custodians and public service and public infrastructure providers, including strong communication skills
   > - knowledge necessary to elicit and prioritize stakeholder requirements and needs and interpret them to develop effective process requirements and plans

2. Identify process skill gaps based on available resources and their current skill levels.
3. Identify training opportunities to address skill gaps.

Elaboration:

Training may be particularly useful and necessary for asset owners who may not have the requisite skills for ensuring the protection and sustainability of facilities. Training may also be necessary for practitioners (such as security practitioners and maintenance contractors) who do not have specific experience in managing controls for facilities or in ensuring their sustainability.

> These are examples of training topics:
> - ensuring the protection and sustainability of facilities, particularly for asset owners and custodians
> - for security practitioners and maintenance contractors, specific training in managing controls for facilities to ensure their sustainability, particularly when dealing with a disruptive event
> - dealing effectively with public service and public infrastructure providers
> - supporting asset owners and custodians in understanding the process and their roles and responsibilities with respect to its activities
> - working with external entities that have responsibility for process activities
> - using process methods, tools, and techniques, including those identified in EC:GG2:GP3 subpractice 3

4. Provide training and review the training needs as necessary.

EC:GG2.GP6 Manage Work Product Configurations

Place designated work products of the environmental control process under appropriate levels of control.

Elaboration:

All work products related to facility administrative, technical, and physical controls (such as configurations, logs, policies, standards, records, etc.) should be placed under control.

In addition to the specific work products included throughout the environmental control process, additional work products such as facility control documentation, control logs and exception reports (including physical security system logs), fire inspection reports, surveillance tapes or recordings, facility visitor logs, and facility asset retirement records may be placed under control.

> These are examples of environmental control work products placed under control:
> - facility asset inventory
> - facility asset resilience requirements
> - facility asset controls (administrative, technical, physical, and those with respect to design, leasing, co-location, and construction) and supporting documentation
> - facility asset owners and custodians
> - facility asset risk statements (categorized, prioritized, with impact valuation) and mitigation plans
> - service continuity plans that address facility sustainability
> - facility equipment service levels, specifications, and authorized maintenance staff
> - maintenance records, including change requests
> - key contacts lists for public service and public infrastructure providers
> - facility dependencies on public services and public infrastructure
> - facility retirement standards, practices, and records
> - process plan
> - policies and procedures
> - contracts with external entities

EC:GG2.GP7 IDENTIFY AND INVOLVE RELEVANT STAKEHOLDERS

Identify and involve the relevant stakeholders of the environmental control process as planned.

Elaboration:

The primary stakeholders for the environmental control process are facility asset owners and custodians. In addition, EC:SG4.SP5 calls for involving stakeholders in planning for facility retirement.

Subpractices

1. Identify process stakeholders and their appropriate involvement.

Elaboration:

Because of the significant connection between facilities and their geographic environment, a substantial number of stakeholders are likely to be external to the organization.

> These are examples of stakeholders of the environmental control process:
> - owners and custodians of facility assets, including external entities responsible for managing facility assets
> - staff responsible for managing operational risks to facilities
> - staff responsible for the physical security of facility assets

- staff responsible for establishing, implementing, and maintaining an internal control system for facilities
- staff required to develop, test, implement, and execute service continuity plans for facilities
- staff involved in the retirement of facilities, including all affected service providers
- external entities such as public service providers, public infrastructure providers, and contractors that provide essential facility services such as those related to maintaining environmental conditions
- staff in other organizational support functions, such as accounting and general services administration (particularly as related to facility inventory valuation and retirement)

Stakeholders are involved in various tasks in the environmental control process, such as
- planning for the process, including facility retirement
- creating a facility asset baseline
- creating facility profiles
- associating facility assets with services and analyzing asset-service dependencies
- assigning resilience requirements to facilities
- establishing, implementing, and managing facility controls
- developing service continuity plans
- managing facility risks
- controlling facility operational environments
- maintaining facilities and facility equipment
- managing facility external dependencies
- reviewing and appraising the effectiveness of process activities
- resolving issues in the process

2. Communicate the list of stakeholders to planners and those responsible for process performance.
3. Involve relevant stakeholders in the process as planned.

EC:GG2.GP8 Monitor and Control the Process

Monitor and control the environmental control process against the plan for performing the process and take appropriate corrective action.

Refer to the Monitoring process area for more information about the collection, organization, and distribution of data that may be useful for monitoring and controlling processes.

Refer to the Measurement and Analysis process area for more information about establishing process metrics and measurement.

Refer to the Enterprise Focus process area for more information about providing process information to managers, identifying issues, and determining appropriate corrective actions.

Subpractices

1. Measure actual performance against the plan for performing the process.
2. Review accomplishments and results of the process against the plan for performing the process.

> These are examples of metrics for the environmental control process:
> - percentage of organizational facility assets that have been inventoried
> - level of discrepancies between actual inventory and stated inventory
> - number of changes made to the facility asset inventory during a stated period
> - number of facility assets that do not have stated owners or custodians
> - number of facility assets with incomplete asset profiles or other incomplete information (particularly the lack of stated resilience requirements)
> - availability statistics for public infrastructure providers (such as percentage downtime for power suppliers)
> - level of adherence to external entity service level agreements and agreed maintenance levels
> - number of manual versus automated data collection activities
> - timeliness of completing scheduled facility maintenance activities
> - actual level of maintenance versus scheduled or expected
> - number of scheduled maintenance activities missed
> - number of physical access controls that have been circumvented; number of attempted or successful intrusions to facilities
> - downtime statistics for physical access systems such as card readers
> - downtime statistics for physical access monitoring such as surveillance cameras
> - downtime statistics for support systems such as HVAC and fire suppression
> - number of risks to facility assets referred to the risk management process; number of risks where corrective action is still pending (by risk rank)
> - level of adherence to process policies including clean desk and screen policies; number of policy exceptions requested and number approved
> - number of policy violations including violations of access control policies for facilities and visitor policies
> - number of process activities that are on track per plan
> - rate of change of resource needs to support the process
> - rate of change of costs to support the process

3. Review activities, status, and results of the process with the immediate level of managers responsible for the process and identify issues.

Elaboration:

> Periodic reviews of the environmental control process are needed to ensure that
> - the facility asset inventory is accurate and complete
> - newly acquired facility assets are included in the inventory
> - changes to facility assets (additions, maintenance actions, retirements) are accurately reflected in the inventory
> - the facility asset-service mapping is accurate and current
> - ownership and custodianship over facility assets are established and documented
> - access to the facility asset inventory is being limited to only authorized staff
> - access to facility assets is limited to authorized staff
> - status reports are provided to appropriate stakeholders in a timely manner
> - facility asset-service dependency issues are referred to the risk management process when necessary
> - actions requiring management involvement are elevated in a timely manner
> - the performance of process activities is being monitored and regularly reported
> - key measures are within acceptable ranges as demonstrated in governance dashboards or scorecards and financial reports
> - administrative, technical, and physical controls are operating as intended
> - controls are meeting the stated intent of the resilience requirements
> - actions resulting from internal and external audits are being closed in a timely manner

4. Identify and evaluate the effects of significant deviations from the plan for performing the process.

Elaboration:

Discrepancies result when facility assets are acquired, modified, or retired but not reflected accurately in the facility asset inventory. Assets form the foundation for operational resilience management because they are the target of strategies to protect and sustain them. To the extent that the environmental control process results in inventory discrepancies, the organization's overall ability to manage operational resilience is impeded.

5. Identify problems in the plan for performing and executing the process.
6. Take corrective action when requirements and objectives are not being satisfied, when issues are identified, or when progress differs significantly from the plan for performing the process.

Elaboration:

For facility assets, corrective action may require the revision of existing administrative, technical, and physical controls, development and implementation of new controls, or a change in the type of controls (preventive, detective, corrective, compensating, etc.).

7. Track corrective action to closure.

EC:GG2.GP9 OBJECTIVELY EVALUATE ADHERENCE

Objectively evaluate adherence of the environmental control process against its process description, standards, and procedures, and address non-compliance.

Elaboration:

These are examples of activities to be reviewed:
- identifying and prioritizing facility assets
- identifying facility resilience requirements
- establishing and implementing facility controls
- identifying and managing facility risks
- developing service continuity plans for facilities
- maintaining facility environmental conditions
- identifying and managing facility dependencies
- retiring facilities
- the alignment of stakeholder requirements with process plans
- assignment of responsibility, accountability, and authority for process activities
- determination of the adequacy of process reports and reviews in informing decision makers regarding the performance of operational resilience management activities and the need to take corrective action, if any
- verification of internal controls
- use of process work products for improving strategies for protecting and sustaining assets and services

These are examples of work products to be reviewed:
- facility asset inventory
- facility internal controls documentation
- facility risk statements
- facility risk mitigation plans
- service continuity plans
- facility maintenance records and change logs
- business impact analysis results
- key provider and contact lists
- facility retirement standards
- process plan and policies
- dependency issues that have been referred to the risk management process
- process methods, techniques, and tools
- metrics for the process *(Refer to EC:GG2.GP8 subpractice 2.)*
- contracts with external entities

EC:GG2.GP10 Review Status with Higher-Level Managers

Review the activities, status, and results of the environmental control process with higher-level managers and resolve issues.

Refer to the Enterprise Focus process area for more information about providing sponsorship and oversight to the operational resilience management system.

EC:GG3 Institutionalize a Defined Process

Environmental control is institutionalized as a defined process.

EC:GG3.GP1 Establish a Defined Process

Establish and maintain the description of a defined environmental control process.

Establishing and tailoring process assets, including standard processes, are addressed in the Organizational Process Definition process area.

Establishing process needs and objectives and selecting, improving, and deploying process assets, including standard processes, are addressed in the Organizational Process Focus process area.

Subpractices

1. Select from the organization's set of standard processes those processes that cover the environmental control process and best meet the needs of the organizational unit or line of business.
2. Establish the defined process by tailoring the selected processes according to the organization's tailoring guidelines.
3. Ensure that the organization's process objectives are appropriately addressed in the defined process, and ensure that process governance extends to the tailored processes.
4. Document the defined process and the records of the tailoring.
5. Revise the description of the defined process as necessary.

EC:GG3.GP2 Collect Improvement Information

Collect environmental control work products, measures, measurement results, and improvement information derived from planning and performing the process to support future use and improvement of the organization's processes and process assets.

Elaboration:

> These are examples of improvement work products and information:
> - facility asset inventory
> - inventory inconsistencies and issues
> - reports on the effectiveness and weaknesses of controls
> - improvements based on risk identification and mitigation
> - effectiveness of service continuity plans in execution
> - lessons learned in post-event review of incidents and disruptions in facility continuity
> - maintenance issues and concerns for facility infrastructure and physical plant
> - conflicts and risks arising from dependencies on external entities
> - lessons learned in retiring facilities from active use
> - metrics and measurements of the viability of the process *(Refer to EC:GG2.GP8 subpractice 2.)*
> - changes and trends in operating conditions, risk conditions, and the risk environment that affect process results
> - lessons learned about the process that can be applied to improve operational resilience management performance, such as poorly documented or profiled assets and difficulties in assigning and executing asset ownership and custodianship responsibilities
> - the level to which the facility asset inventory, asset profiles, and the asset database reflect the current status of all assets
> - asset-service dependency mitigation plans that are not executed and the risks associated with them
> - resilience requirements that are not being satisfied or are being exceeded

Establishing the measurement repository and process asset library is addressed in the Organizational Process Definition process area. Updating the measurement repository and process asset library as part of process improvement and deployment is addressed in the Organizational Process Focus process area.

Subpractices

1. Store process and work product measures in the organization's measurement repository.
2. Submit documentation for inclusion in the organization's process asset library.
3. Document lessons learned from the process for inclusion in the organization's process asset library.
4. Propose improvements to the organizational process assets.

ENTERPRISE FOCUS
Enterprise

Purpose

The purpose of Enterprise Focus is to establish sponsorship, strategic planning, and governance over the operational resilience management system.

Introductory Notes

Managing operational resilience requires a vast array of skills and competencies. These skills and competencies traverse the organization and must converge to achieve and sustain a desired level of operational resilience.

Because resilience is an enterprise concern, the focus and direction for the operational resilience management system must come from the top: leadership to set direction and ethical standards, sponsorship to provide support and resources, and governance to ensure that the process is achieving its goals as expected. In addition, managing operational resilience must be aligned with and supportive of the achievement of the organization's strategic objectives. Focusing on these objectives provides the rationale for investing in resilience activities—because they enable the organization to achieve its mission.

The Enterprise Focus process area seeks to ensure that the enterprise owns the operational resilience management system and provides the necessary level of leadership and governance over the process. The strategic objectives of the organization are explicitly defined as the alignment factor for resilience plans, programs, and activities. Higher-level managers provide sponsorship to ensure resilience activities are properly and adequately funded and to promote and nurture a resilience-aware culture throughout the organization. Finally, the organization's governance activities are expanded to focus directly on resilience—program objectives are set, standards for acceptable and ethical behavior are established, and the process is monitored to ensure it is achieving its goals. Higher-level managers also provide input and recommendations when the operational resilience management system is not performing within established standards.

Enterprise Focus establishes the "critical few" for the organization—the high-value services that must be resilient to ensure mission achievement. This sets the focus for all operational risk-based activities in the organization. Through an enterprise focus, the direction and target for operational resilience management are established, operational risk management activities are coordinated, and actions are taken that enable the organization to perform adequately in achieving its targets.

Related Process Areas

Organizational risk drivers, risk appetite, and risk tolerance are established in the Risk Management process area.

The establishment of plans and programs to ensure service continuity is addressed in the Service Continuity process area.

The relationship between services and assets is addressed in Asset Definition and Management.

The management of compliance activities is addressed in the Compliance process area.

The development and achievement of resilience goals and objectives for staff are addressed in the Human Resource Management process area.

Providing awareness training for staff, both internal and external to the organization, is addressed in the Organizational Training and Awareness process area.

The Monitoring process area outlines processes for identifying, gathering, and communicating relevant data for decision-making processes.

The establishment of resilience funding needs and the allocation of funds are addressed in the Financial Resource Management process area.

Summary of Specific Goals and Practices

EF:SG1 Establish Strategic Objectives
    EF:SG1.SP1   Establish Strategic Objectives
    EF:SG1.SP2   Establish Critical Success Factors
    EF:SG1.SP3   Establish Organizational Services

EF:SG2 Plan for Operational Resilience
    EF:SG2.SP1   Establish an Operational Resilience Management Plan
    EF:SG2.SP2   Establish an Operational Resilience Management Program

EF:SG3 Establish Sponsorship
    EF:SG3.SP1   Commit Funding for Operational Resilience Management
    EF:SG3.SP2   Promote a Resilience-Aware Culture
    EF:SG3.SP3   Sponsor Resilience Standards and Policies

EF:SG4 Provide Resilience Oversight
    EF:SG4.SP1   Establish Resilience as a Governance Focus Area
    EF:SG4.SP2   Perform Resilience Oversight
    EF:SG4.SP3   Establish Corrective Actions

Specific Practices by Goal

EF:SG1 ESTABLISH STRATEGIC OBJECTIVES

The strategic objectives of the organization are established as the foundation for the operational resilience management system.

The strategic objectives of the organization are derived from the organization's strategic planning process, which typically addresses a future time span of two to five years. The strategic objectives of the organization form the basis for operational resilience targets and activities and must be clearly documented and communicated at the organizational unit and line of business levels.

The organization's strategic objectives may be expressed in various forms. They may be articulated as organizational goals and objectives that form the basis for the performance of managers and staff. They may also be expressed in terms of critical success factors (CSFs), which complement goals and objectives by detailing the areas in which organizational performance is critical to meeting these goals and objectives.

Strategic objectives are important for the operational resilience management system because they provide a target that must be attained by services. Resilience activities must meet strategic objectives by protecting and sustaining assets and services to the extent necessary to attain these objectives. Failure to keep assets and services resilient may significantly impair the organization's ability to meet strategic objectives.

As a target for operational resilience management, the organization must clearly articulate its strategic objectives, describe its critical success factors, and identify the services that it performs that are of high value in meeting these objectives and satisfying these factors. Through these activities, the goals for operational resilience management are made clear, tangible, and achievable.

EF:SG1.SP1 ESTABLISH STRATEGIC OBJECTIVES

Strategic objectives are identified and established as the basis for resilience activities.

Strategic objectives are the performance targets that the organization sets to accomplish its mission, vision, values, and purpose. They are decomposed into an organizational roadmap for performance so that all staff members are moving in the same direction.

Effective operational resilience ensures that the organization can reach its strategic objectives. The management of operational resilience must be specifically focused on enabling the achievement of strategic objectives and addressing a range of potential disruptions that can interrupt their achievement.

Strategic objectives range from general to specific. General objectives include mission, vision, and values, while specific objectives are goal-oriented and outline the targets the organization is attempting to reach (such as opening 100 stores in China or improving revenue by 14% in the next year). Strategic objectives emanate from the organization's strategic planning process. (*Resilience planning as part of the organization's overall strategic planning process is addressed in EF:SG2.SP1.*)

From a resilience management perspective, the identification, comprehension, and communication of the organization's strategic objectives provide essential and necessary guidance and direction for the operational resilience management system.

Typical work products

1. Organizational strategic objectives
2. Organizational mission, vision, values, and purpose statement

Subpractices

1. Identify the organization's mission, vision, values, and purpose.
   This information should be readily available in company literature such as staff handbooks and annual reports. Because some organizations are very large, this information may exist at each organizational unit or line of business level, rather than at an enterprise level.
2. Identify the organization's strategic objectives.
   These objectives should be readily available in the organization's strategic plan (which may be composed at an enterprise or organizational unit or line of business level). These objectives are also typically the basis for the performance goals for staff and business partners and may be found as part of performance management activities.

EF:SG1.SP2 ESTABLISH CRITICAL SUCCESS FACTORS

The critical success factors of the organization are identified and established.

Critical success factors are the limited number of areas in which the organization must consistently and effectively perform to succeed in meeting its strategic objectives. Critical success factors reflect management's implicit focus. They are areas that should receive constant and careful attention from managers. When critical success factors are identified, defined, and communicated, they represent a powerful set of criteria against which an organization can validate or align its activities, including those being performed to manage operational resilience.

Critical success factors have sources and dimensions. Sources represent the places where critical success factors originate. Because organizations are multidimensional, critical success factors can originate at every layer of management. In addition, because organizations typically have open borders, critical success factors can also be derived through industry affiliation or operating climate. In general, critical success factors have five sources:

- the industry in which the organization operates (e.g., financial services)
- the competitive environment or peer relationship of the organization (e.g., top 20 banks in the United States)
- the organization's operating environment (e.g., geographical location, current sociopolitical climate)
- temporal issues (e.g., weather, increase in terrorist activity)
- management's view of the organization (e.g., current priorities, budget climate)

In addition to sources, critical success factors have dimensions. Critical success factors can be internal or external (representing the extent to which the organization has span of control) or monitoring or adapting (keeping the status quo versus growing and evolving the organization). Dimensions are important because they represent the depth and breadth of critical success factors.

In essence, critical success factors establish a set of performance indicators that the operational resilience management system must contribute to achieving and form an important alignment factor between the policy-making level and the operational level of the organization.

Typical work products

1. Critical success factors of the organization
2. Critical success factors performance indicators

Subpractices

1. Collect data to support the development of critical success factors.
    Data may be collected through document review (the organization's charter, strategic plan and objectives, etc.) and interviews of key organizational managers.
2. Consolidate and analyze critical success factor data.
    Data can be developed into activity statements and developed into summary themes through affinity grouping.
3. Derive the critical success factors for the organization.
    Critical success factors can be developed for many layers of the organization. Typically, the organization has a set of enterprise-level critical success factors that influence organizational unit or line of business critical success factors, which in turn are reflected in manager- and staff-level critical success factors. Depending on the level at which an organization manages operational resilience, critical success factors may have to be developed at one or more of these levels.

    The critical success factors should represent a range of sources and dimensions.

4. Perform affinity analysis between strategic objectives and critical success factors. Affinity analysis documents the direct relationship between the achievement of a critical success factor and the accomplishment of a strategic objective.
5. Identify the key performance indicators to measure accomplishment of each critical success factor.
6. Monitor the accomplishment of critical success factors and take corrective action as necessary.

EF:SG1.SP3 ESTABLISH ORGANIZATIONAL SERVICES

The high-value services that support the accomplishment of strategic objectives are established.

The high-value services of the organization are the focus of the organization's operational resilience management activities. These services directly support the achievement of strategic objectives and therefore must be protected and sustained to the extent necessary to minimize disruption. Failure to keep these services viable and productive may result in significant inability to meet strategic objectives and, in some cases, the organization's mission.

In order to appropriately scope the organization's operational resilience management system and corresponding operational resilience management activities, the high-value services of the organization must be identified, prioritized, and communicated as a common target for success.

High-value services are fueled by organizational assets such as people, information, technology, and facilities. (*The link between high-value services and their supporting assets is established in the Asset Definition and Management process area.*)

Typical work products

1. Service profiles
2. Service repository
3. Service affinity analysis
4. Prioritized list of high-value services

Subpractices

1. Inventory organizational services and develop service repository.

    The organization should have at its disposal an inventory of standard services that represents the activities that the organization performs to achieve its mission. The inventory of services should include service profiles that describe the services in sufficient detail to capture the activities, tasks, and expected outcomes of the services and the assets that are of high value to the services. The service profile should also detail the business processes that cumulatively compose the service. A service repository should be created that is accessible by all who need to understand the organization's standard services.

> Sources of information about services include
> - strategic planning work products
> - business plans
> - industry, market, and competitive analyses
> - customer requests
> - contracts and other customer-focused documents
> - business process inventories and business process reengineering documentation
> - standard work process documentation and repositories

2. Document service attributes in a service profile.

    Service attributes help to describe services using a common language and taxonomy.

    Service attributes to consider in developing service profiles include
    - inputs to the service
    - outputs from the service
    - assets associated with or used by the service (*This activity is formally performed in ADM:SG2.SP1 in the Asset Definition and Management process area.*)
    - the owners and stakeholders of the service
    - related services and business processes
    - expected service levels

    > Service-level information may include
    > - provider and user responsibilities
    > - availability of the service
    > - service hours and exceptions
    > - anticipated service volume
    > - response times for service requests, incidents, and problems
    > - performance or quality targets
    > - key metrics to monitor
    > - reporting and escalation procedures
    > - consequences of failure
    > - variations available (such as "gold" service)

    - service-focused resilience requirements (*This activity is formally performed in RRD:SG2.SP2 in the Resilience Requirements Development process area.*)

3. Perform affinity analysis between organizational services and objective measures such as strategic objectives and critical success factors.

    Affinity analysis compares the organization's standard services to the objective measures used by the organization to determine and validate the value of the services. Affinity analysis using the organization's strategic objectives and critical success factors is a means to help the organization prioritize services and to identify high-value services that must be made resilient.

4. Define high-value services from the organization's standard services repository.

   Organizationally high-value services are those that must meet their resilience requirements consistently in order to ensure that the organization can accomplish its strategic objectives and mission. These services are the focus of the resilience activities performed in the organization.

5. Revise the organization's service profiles and service repository and service levels as necessary.

   The organization must revise service profiles and the service repository as necessary to ensure that they reflect the most current information about services, particularly high-value services. Otherwise, the organization's resilience activities may be misdirected.

EF:SG2 PLAN FOR OPERATIONAL RESILIENCE

Planning for the operational resilience management system is performed.

Managing operational resilience enables the achievement of strategic objectives and critical success factors and therefore must be specifically acknowledged and addressed at the highest levels of the organization, particularly in strategic planning performed at the enterprise level. Failing to consider operational resilience as a constraint in the development of the organization's strategic plan can result in an underappreciation of the activities, tasks, and practices that must be performed to ensure that potential barriers to achieving business objectives are identified and addressed. Proper consideration of operational resilience and its role in supporting strategic objectives *(as described in EF:SG1.SP1)* is achieved by establishing a plan and a program for the operational resilience management system.

EF:SG2.SP1 ESTABLISH AN OPERATIONAL RESILIENCE MANAGEMENT PLAN

A plan for managing operational resilience is established as the basis for the operational resilience management program.

The organization must develop and implement a plan for managing operational resilience that is based on meeting strategic objectives and critical success factors and that considers the organization's risk tolerances and appetite. The operational resilience management plan is a part of the organization's strategic business plan that specifically addresses the actions, activities, and tasks that must be performed to reach resilience goals. The resilience plan becomes the foundation for the performance of the operational resilience management system in the organization.

Strategic business planning typically includes standard elements that describe the intentions of the organization and the means for achieving the intentions. In general, strategic plans include

- a description of the organization's vision, purpose, and values
- the organization's mission statement
- an articulation of the organization's critical success factors (*See EF:SG1.SP2.*)
- short- and long-term strategic objectives with corresponding actions, activities, and tasks to reach them
- a schedule for achieving the strategic objectives over the period of the plan (typically two to three years)

The strategic business plan sets forth the direction for the organization in the near and long term. The strategic objectives stated in the plan form the basis for the goals and objectives of everyone in the organization—from C-level executives to middle managers to staff. The actions of all staff must be commensurate with the strategic objectives in order for the organization to succeed in reaching business goals.

In much the same way, the organization must plan for success in managing operational resilience. Not only are the goals for operational resilience important, they are also critical for the organization to meet its strategic objectives. Thus, the organization must develop a resilience plan alongside its strategic business plan to detail the actions that must be taken to minimize disruptions that could draw the organization off course in achieving its strategic objectives.

Typical work products

1. Operational resilience management plan
2. Operational resilience management plan commitments

Subpractices

1. Develop the operational resilience management plan.
    The resilience plan should be developed in conjunction with the development of the organization's strategic business plan. The elements of the resilience plan should focus on the development of operational resilience objectives that are to be achieved by performing resilience activities throughout the organization and that correspond to the achievement of strategic objectives. The resilience plan should address
    - the organization's philosophy on resilience management
    - the structure of the resilience program for managing the resilience plan (*Establishing the resilience program is addressed in EF:SG2.SP2.*)
    - the strategic resilience objectives
    - coverage of the essential activities as described in the operational resilience management program
    - linkages to the organization's plan for service continuity (*Planning for service continuity is addressed in the Service Continuity process area.*)
    - roles and responsibilities for carrying out the strategic resilience objectives
    - resources that will be required to meet the resilience objectives

- applicable training needs and requirements
- relevant costs or budgets associated with meeting the resilience objectives

2. Establish commitments to the plan.
3. Revise the plan and commitments on a cycle commensurate with the organization's strategic business planning process.

EF:SG2.SP2 ESTABLISH AN OPERATIONAL RESILIENCE MANAGEMENT PROGRAM

A program is established to carry out the activities and practices of the operational resilience management plan.

The organization sets resilience program goals based on the resilience plan objectives and related program activities, tasks, and practices. The resilience program oversees and "owns" the operational resilience management system and the achievement of resilience objectives. This practice includes establishing a formal resilience program, staffing the program, assigning accountability and responsibility, providing oversight, and measuring performance.

Typical work products

1. Operational resilience program charter
2. Operational resilience program management plan

Subpractices

1. Establish the operational resilience management program.

    The operational resilience management program is typically responsible for ensuring that the strategic resilience objectives as documented in the operational resilience plan are achieved. Program management includes staffing the program, assigning accountability and responsibility to plan activities, tasks, and projects, and measuring performance. The operational resilience management program should draft a charter that describes its functions, scope, and objectives.

2. Fund the operational resilience management program.

    Funding the organization's operational resilience management program and related activities, tasks, and projects is addressed in the Financial Resource Management process area.

3. Assign resources to the operational resilience management program.

    Remember that some staff members will have explicit resilience-focused roles and responsibilities, while others will contribute to resilience processes through the execution of their job responsibilities. Typically, the operational resilience management program will be operated by staff whose job responsibilities are resilience-focused. The organization should confirm that staff involved in carrying out the operational resilience management program have the requisite skills and training. (*Training for resilience-focused roles is addressed in the Human Resource Management process area.*)

4. Provide oversight to the operational resilience management program.
    The organization must oversee the activities of the operational resilience management program to ensure that strategic resilience objectives are being met consistently. Corrective actions must be identified and implemented when course correction is necessary. *(Governance over the operational resilience management program and process is addressed in EF:SG4.)*
5. Gather performance data on the achievement of strategic resilience objectives.

EF:SG3 ESTABLISH SPONSORSHIP

Visible sponsorship of higher-level managers for the operational resilience management system is established.

Sponsorship by higher-level managers is a key factor in the success of the operational resilience management system. Sponsorship means that higher-level managers take an active interest in the success of the operational resilience management system through actions such as including resilience in strategic planning, adequately funding resilience activities, communicating the importance of resilience, and providing oversight. Sponsorship also means that higher-level managers are willing to invest in resilience activities and be measured on their success.

Visible sponsorship of the operational resilience management program can take many forms, such as

- approval and support for achieving strategic resilience objectives
- commitment to allocate the necessary resources (financial and human) for meeting the objectives
- visible, continued support for the resilience program (through inclusion on meeting agendas and the establishment of a resilience committee on the organization's board or leadership council)
- active encouragement of staff participation through support of goal setting and performance management for resilience
- establishing guiding principles, direction, and expectations for the organization through supporting resilience policies, guidelines, and standards
- delegation of responsibility and authority for accomplishing program objectives
- agreement to provide oversight and decisions on corrective activity

Through sponsorship, higher-level managers set the tone for the organization—in essence, they represent to the organization that resilience is important and is everyone's job rather than an exercise driven by external compliance or industry and regulatory obligations.

EF:SG3.SP1 Commit Funding for Operational Resilience Management

A commitment by higher-level managers to fund resilience activities is established.

Budgeting is a process of allocating funds to organizational activities that support and promote strategic objectives. When resilience is considered a strategic competency, funding for resilience activities must be included as part of the organization's capital and expense funding needs rather than as an afterthought that is indirectly funded through IT activities or as needed when disruptive events occur.

Sponsorship of the operational resilience management system is made actionable by higher-level managers' commitments to funding the resilience program and the accompanying activities and tasks. This requires that they commit to

- supporting the business case for operational resilience management
- including resilience needs in the funding of strategic objectives
- ensuring that resilience needs are adequately funded
- releasing funds as necessary to support the attainment of strategic resilience objectives

Sponsoring a financial commitment to resilience is different from allocating and budgeting the funds for resilience activities. (*The establishment of resilience funding needs and the allocation of funds are addressed in the Financial Resource Management process area.*)

Typical work products

1. Business case for resilience

Subpractices

1. Develop the business case for the operational resilience management program and process.

    Sponsorship of the investment in the operational resilience management system must be based on a sound business case. The investment in resilience must bring about tangible, measurable, and demonstrable value to the organization. The business case for resilience should
    - justify the investment through itemization of tangible benefits and results
    - articulate the strategic outcomes that would result from investments in resilience activities
    - articulate the potential risks and costs associated with not investing in resilience activities
    - establish that the funding necessary for resilience is appropriate and adequate
    - provide sufficient information to allow comparative evaluations of alternative actions
    - establish the accountability and commitments for the achievement of the benefits and strategic outcomes

2. Establish operational resilience management program and process funding as a regular part of the organization's strategic plan budgeting (capital and expense) exercise.
3. Approve allocation of funding to operational resilience management program and process activities.

EF:SG3.SP2 PROMOTE A RESILIENCE-AWARE CULTURE

A resilience-aware culture is promoted through goal setting and achievement.

The success of enterprise-wide programs or initiatives often depends on the organization's ability to get all stakeholders (internal and external) moving in the same direction toward a common goal and for the common good. Evolving from a narrow security- or business-continuity-focused view to an operational resilience view requires significant changes in organizational structure, approach, and activities. Visible sponsorship by higher-level managers is a key factor in catalyzing this type of organizational change.

Higher-level managers promote a resilience-aware culture by their actions. These actions can be very broad but are typically focused on giving staff members a reason to "invest" their time and part of their job responsibilities in operational resilience management. These are some of the activities that higher-level managers can perform to promote a resilience-aware culture:

- Communicate and promote the importance of resilience at all opportunities.
- Communicate the need for change based on the impact on achieving strategic objectives, and quell resistance efforts.
- Build a sponsorship alliance of higher-level and middle managers to promote and sustain the message.
- Sponsor the development, implementation, and enforcement of resilience policies, standards, and guidelines. (See EF:SG3.SP3.)
- Sponsor the organizational training and awareness program. *(This is addressed in the Organizational Training and Awareness process area.)*
- Sponsor resilience awards and recognition programs for staff who make significant contributions to sustaining the organization's operational resilience.
- Set performance goals and objectives that focus on resilience and be willing to be measured on them.
- Keep resilience on the organizational performance scorecard of all staff.
- Provide opportunities for staff members to speak freely about resilience issues, concerns, and impediments.
- Sponsor inclusion of resilience concepts in job descriptions and in the hiring of new staff or the promotion of existing staff.
- Sponsor inclusion of resilience concepts in contracts with suppliers and business partners.

The development and achievement of resilience goals and objectives for staff are addressed in the Human Resource Management process area.

Providing awareness training for staff, both internal and external to the organization, is addressed in the Organizational Training and Awareness process area.

Typical work products

1. Resilience performance goals and objectives
2. Rewards and recognition programs

Subpractices

1. Establish a plan for visible promotion of a resilience-aware culture with appropriate success metrics.
   The plan should address the specific activities that higher-level managers perform to support and promote a resilience-aware culture.
2. Establish performance management of higher-level managers for resilience.
   Higher-level managers should have explicit resilience goals that are reflected in the goals of middle managers and staff. Performance management activities should measure higher-level managers on their ability to promote and communicate the importance of resilience programs and activities.
3. Establish rewards and recognition programs to support resilience acculturation.
4. Measure to the extent possible the level of acculturation of resilience awareness that is the direct result of sponsorship.

EF:SG3.SP3 SPONSOR RESILIENCE STANDARDS AND POLICIES

The development, implementation, enforcement, and management of resilience standards and policies are sponsored.

Policies establish an acceptable range of behaviors that managers intend to enforce and reinforce as a means to ensure accomplishment of common goals. Policies are unenforceable and lack effectiveness unless they are sponsored by higher-level managers and higher-level managers express their intention to hold stakeholders to compliance with the policies.

Polices are an expression of higher-level managers' level of commitment to the operational resilience management system. Lack of policy sponsorship typically renders policies less effective as an administrative control because stakeholders may assume that the policies are not being enforced or that they are simply meant to be used as a guideline rather than a requirement.

The existence of policies, standards, and guidelines to support the operational resilience management system is considered to be a pervasive indicator of process maturity across all operational resilience management process areas. Policies are an important component of institutionalizing a managed process. *(Appropriate goals and practices related to policy development and implementation to support the operational resilience management system are generically described in GG2:GP1.)*

Typical work products

1. Policy statements from higher-level managers

Subpractices

1. Establish policy statements reflecting higher-level managers' commitment to managing resilience.

EF:SG4 PROVIDE RESILIENCE OVERSIGHT

Governance over the operational resilience management system is established and performed.

Governance is a process of providing strategic direction for the organization while ensuring that it meets its obligations, appropriately manages risk, and efficiently uses financial and human resources. From a resilience perspective, the concept of governance is extended to provide oversight over the operational resilience management system and to ensure that the process supports and sustains strategic objectives. Governance also typically includes the concepts of sponsorship (setting the managerial tone), compliance (ensuring that the organization is meeting its compliance obligations), and alignment (ensuring that processes such as those for operational resilience management align with strategic objectives).

The activities involved in governance are often confused with management activities. Governance is focused on providing oversight to the operational resilience management system, not performing or managing process tasks to completion. For example, the process of overseeing the identification, definition, and inventorying of high-value assets is a governance task, while performing these tasks is part of operational resilience process management. Effective resilience process governance means that senior leadership (which typically includes boards of directors and higher-level managers) provides sponsorship and oversight to the process and provides direction and guidance on course correction when deemed necessary.

The inclusion of operational resilience as a focus area of the organization's broader governance activities is necessary to ensure that the operational resilience management system is viable, meets its goals and objectives, aligns with the organization's strategic objectives, and is performed to comply with all applicable laws and regulations. Failure to provide governance over the operational resilience management system may result in a lack of awareness of operational resilience issues and problems that may result in consequences to the organization.

Effective governance over the operational resilience management system requires the establishment of resilience as a governance focus area, processes for providing oversight and review, and a means for identifying, documenting, communicating, implementing, and monitoring corrective actions.

EF:SG4.SP1 ESTABLISH RESILIENCE AS A GOVERNANCE FOCUS AREA

Governance activities are extended to the operational resilience management system and accomplishment of the process goals.

Governance is a demonstration of the attention and sponsorship of management to the operational resilience management system. Higher-level managers understand their responsibility for governing the operational resilience management system as exhibited by their sponsorship of related processes, procedures, policies, standards, and guidelines.

Most organizations have defined governance processes. Typically, they extend to areas such as strategic planning, financial management, human resources, and audit. Increasingly, governance processes include areas such as business continuity and security—which extend to operational resilience and risk management. Governance also extends to improving and sustaining a resilience-aware culture.

Effective governance is necessary to reinforce desirable behaviors and to catalyze organizational change, particularly when there are significant barriers to organizational effectiveness. Because resilience is generally a new focus area in many organizations, a change in an organization's existing governance structure may be warranted to ensure adequate coverage of resilience and to encourage significant behavioral changes throughout the organization. In some cases, the resilience needs of the organization will compete with compliance obligations and the accomplishment of strategic objectives. Extending governance to the operational resilience management system provides an opportunity for higher-level managers to resolve this conflict to the overall benefit of the organization.

Typical work products

1. Operational resilience management system governance framework
2. Committee charters for resilience governance
3. Code of conduct (addressing resilience issues)

Subpractices

1. Establish a governance framework for the operational resilience management system.
    The governance framework for operational resilience management specifies the structure for extending the governance activity to the operational resilience management system. The framework may address a wide range of resilience topics and needs, such as

- the development of resilience committees
- the specific inclusion of resilience topics on existing governance committees
- the extension of resilience governance activities beyond the board of directors and higher-level managers to organizational unit and line of business managers and other levels of the organizational structure
- the recasting of committee charters to include resilience responsibilities
- the establishment of a structure for monitoring and managing performance, including clear measures for success (*This is addressed in EF:SG4.SP2.*)
- the identification and inclusion of appropriate stakeholders in the resilience governance process
- the procedures, policies, standards, guidelines, and regulations around which governance for the operational resilience management system will be based
- an operational-resilience–focused code of ethics

2. Assign roles and responsibilities for governance over the operational resilience management system.

    Governance must have ownership and accountability to be effective. Typically, an organization will have a board of directors or similar construct that will own the governance process and from which the governance activity will emanate. Board members or their equivalent will have specific roles in committees that extend to resilience. Extending governance to resilience activities may require the organization to extend roles and responsibilities to other higher-level or middle managers deep into the organization.

3. Identify the procedures, policies, standards, guidelines, and regulations that will form the basis for resilience governance activities.

EF:SG4.SP2 PERFORM RESILIENCE OVERSIGHT

Oversight is performed over the operational resilience management system for adherence to established procedures, policies, standards, guidelines, and regulations.

The governance function has responsibility to ensure that the organization's internal control system (whether financial, security, etc.) is implemented and functioning properly. A formal operational resilience management oversight committee or governance function is established with consistent and regular processes and procedures to "govern" the operational resilience management system.

The oversight function validates the operational resilience management system for adherence to established procedures, policies, standards, guidelines, and regulations. Exceptions to these foundational elements are addressed through a standard and consistent process, and corrective action feedback is provided to ensure alignment.

Even without a specific focus on resilience, governance is concerned with the continued effective operation of the organization toward its strategic objectives. To do this, governance requires the establishment of a benchmark from which it can measure performance. This includes the development or expansion of common tools such as an organizational dashboard or scorecard that includes not only typical information such as key metrics (key performance indicators, key risk indicators, and key control indicators), but also resilience-specific information (such as the ability to meet resilience requirements for high-value assets and services) to establish that the organization is on course.

Finally, auditing and monitoring are critical processes that extend to the timely oversight of the operational resilience management system. Auditing and monitoring the operational resilience management system on a regular basis enable the organization to identify and correct processes that are not meeting key metrics.

Governance activities include the responsibility for ensuring proper compliance with relevant resilience regulations and laws. (*The processes for compliance with these regulations and laws are addressed in the Compliance process area.*)

Governance relies upon timely and accurate data for decision making. (*The Monitoring process area outlines processes for identifying, gathering, and communicating relevant data for decision-making processes.*)

Typical work products

1. Governance dashboard or scorecard
2. Performance criteria (key indicators and metrics)
3. List of governance stakeholders
4. Data monitoring and collection methods
5. Audit plans and reports

Subpractices

1. Identify key governance stakeholders.

    Key governance stakeholders include those staff, internal and external, who are responsible for providing oversight over the operational resilience management system and developing and implementing corrective actions for poor performance.

2. Establish a governance dashboard or scorecard for measuring and managing operational resilience management system performance.

    A resilience dashboard or scorecard is a means to provide general information about the state of resilience in the organization and the effectiveness of the organization's operational resilience management activities. The dashboard or scorecard is populated from data that is monitored for and collected throughout the organization for the purposes of governance. Key indicators are established and monitored to determine performance. These key indicators incorporate the organization's tolerances and thresholds as well as standards and policies that provide a foundation for measurement and determination of process variation that is detrimental to the organization.

> Key indicators and metrics include
> - **key performance indicators** (KPI) that highlight performance against strategic objectives
> - **key risk indicators** (KRI) that provide risk thresholds that, when crossed, indicate levels of risk that may exceed the organization's risk tolerance or appetite
> - **key control indicators** (KCI) that provide information about the effectiveness of the internal control system, including administrative controls, process controls, and controls on information technology and related assets

3. Monitor and collect data for measuring key indicators and metrics and report on these indicators to key stakeholders.
4. Review audit reports on a regular basis for indicators of problems.
5. Establish a process for handling exceptions to the organization's acceptable behaviors.
    Not all decisions will be clear-cut, and there will be conflicting priorities. The governance framework must provide for processes to resolve these conflicts and to result in decisions that are in the best overall interest of the organization. Exceptions to existing procedures, policies, standards, guidelines, and regulations may become an acceptable operating construct.
6. Establish reporting procedures to communicate results of measurement against indicators to governance stakeholders.
7. Provide reports on performance to governance stakeholders.

EF:SG4.SP3 E*stablish* C*orrective* A*ctions*

Corrective actions are identified to address performance issues.

The establishment of key metrics provides the organization with a means to identify performance issues and gaps that can result in an inability to achieve strategic objectives. Governance over the operational resilience management system relies upon the ability to identify these performance gaps in a timely and complete manner so that corrective actions can be taken before the organization's operational capacity is affected.

The governance function is responsible for interpreting the data collected for measurement of key metrics. Gaps in performance are analyzed and, if necessary, are escalated so that corrective actions can be developed and implemented.

Typical work products

1. Corrective action plans

Subpractices

1. Identify and analyze (measurements of) key indicators that do not meet established metrics.
2. Develop corrective actions to close perceived gaps.
3. Identify persons or groups responsible for implementing and managing corrective actions.
   Ensure that persons or groups accountable for implementing and managing corrective actions have the requisite skills and training.
4. Report on the success of the corrective actions to key stakeholders.
   If the corrective actions are not initially successful, additional corrective actions may have to be developed and implemented in order to provide continuing oversight.
5. Perform root-cause analysis to determine underlying causes of process variation for continuous improvement.

Elaborated Generic Practices by Goal

Refer to the Generic Goals and Practices document in Appendix A for general guidance that applies to all process areas. This section provides elaborations relative to the application of the Generic Goals and Practices to the Enterprise Focus process area.

EF:GG1 ACHIEVE SPECIFIC GOALS

The operational resilience management system supports and enables achievement of the specific goals of the Enterprise Focus process area by transforming identifiable input work products to produce identifiable output work products.

EF:GG1.GP1 PERFORM SPECIFIC PRACTICES

Perform the specific practices of the Enterprise Focus process area to develop work products and provide services to achieve the specific goals of the process area.

Elaboration:
Practices EF:SG1.SP1 through EF:SG4.SP3 are performed to achieve the goals of the enterprise focus process.

EF:GG2 INSTITUTIONALIZE A MANAGED PROCESS

Enterprise focus is institutionalized as a managed process.

EF:GG2.GP1 ESTABLISH PROCESS GOVERNANCE

Establish and maintain governance over the planning and performance of the enterprise focus process.

Elaboration:

The Enterprise Focus process area is responsible for governing the operational resilience management system, which includes providing governance over all process area processes and practices described in the CERT Resilience Management Model. *(The practices contained in EF:SG4, Provide Resilience Oversight, describe how this is accomplished.)*

Process governance described here in EF:GG2.GP1 specifically addresses governance of the enterprise focus process. Governance of governance can be confusing and appear somewhat recursive on initial reading.

Subpractices

1. Establish governance over process activities.

Elaboration:

> Governance over the enterprise focus process may be exhibited by
> - developing and publicizing higher-level managers' objectives for the process
> - establishing a higher-level officer position and steering committee to provide direct oversight of the process and to interface with higher-level managers
> - chartering the formation of an operational resilience process group or similar construct to serve as the change agent for ensuring successful execution of operational resilience management system plans for all or selected process areas
> - sponsoring process policies, procedures, standards, and guidelines
> - sponsoring and providing oversight of the organization's operational resilience program, plans, and strategies
> - sponsoring and funding process activities
> - regular reporting from organizational units to higher-level managers on process activities and results
> - creating dedicated higher-level management feedback loops on decisions about the process and recommendations for improving the process
> - conducting regular internal and external audits and related reporting to audit committees on process effectiveness
> - creating formal programs to measure the effectiveness of process activities, and reporting these measurements to higher-level managers

2. Develop and publish organizational policy for the process.

   Elaboration:

   > The enterprise focus policy should address
   > - sponsorship for the process, including statements reflecting higher-level managers' commitment to managing resilience
   > - establishment of strategic objectives, plans, and critical success factors of the organization as the foundation for the process
   > - the requirements for a strategic resilience plan and an operational resilience management program
   > - responsibility, authority, and ownership (roles and responsibilities[1]) for performing process activities
   > - proper compliance with relevant resilience-focused regulations and laws
   > - procedures, standards, and guidelines for
   >   - conducting acceptable and ethical behavior, including a code of conduct and code of ethics
   >   - identifying the high-value services that must be resilient to ensure mission achievement and the accomplishment of strategic objectives
   >   - managing and monitoring performance, including clear measures for success
   > - management and periodic monitoring of the status of all operational resilience management risks, which can be adjusted when needed, including capturing the potential risks and costs associated with not investing in resilience activities
   > - methods for measuring adherence to policy and codes, exceptions granted, and policy and code violations

EF:GG2.GP2 PLAN THE PROCESS

Establish and maintain the plan for performing the enterprise focus process.

Subpractices

1. Define and document the plan for performing the process.
2. Define and document the process description.
3. Review the plan with relevant stakeholders and get their agreement.
4. Revise the plan as necessary.

EF:GG2.GP3 PROVIDE RESOURCES

Provide adequate resources for performing the enterprise focus process, developing the work products, and providing the services of the process.

---

1. Roles may include the chief risk officer, chief compliance officer, chief security and/or chief information security officer, chief privacy officer, chief information officer, chief financial officer, general counsel, business unit executives and leaders, vice president of human resources/relations, vice president of public relations, etc.

Subpractices

1. Staff the process.

> These are examples of staff required to perform the enterprise focus process:
> - board members and higher-level and other managers responsible for the governance of operational resilience management and ensuring that the operational resilience management system aligns with, supports, and sustains strategic objectives
> - board members and higher-level and other managers responsible for ensuring that the organization meets its resilience compliance obligations
> - board members and higher-level and other managers responsible for establishing policies and codes of ethics and conduct, and ensuring that they are enforced
> - security, business continuity, and IT operations officers, directors, and managers
> - team members of the operational resilience process group
> - owners and custodians of high-value services that support the accomplishment of strategic objectives
> - internal and external auditors responsible for reporting to appropriate committees on process effectiveness

Refer to the Organizational Training and Awareness process area for information about training staff for resilience roles and responsibilities.

Refer to the Human Resource Management process area for information about acquiring staff to fulfill roles and responsibilities.

2. Fund the process.

   Refer to the Financial Resource Management process area for information about budgeting for, funding, and accounting for the enterprise focus process.

3. Provide necessary tools, techniques, and methods to perform the process.

   Elaboration:

   > These are examples of tools, techniques, and methods to support the enterprise focus process:
   > - methods for data collection and monitoring to ensure timely and accurate data for decision making
   > - methods, techniques, and tools for making the business case for resilience and for assisting in making security governance investment decisions
   > - methods and techniques for identifying key performance indicators, key risk indicators, and key control indicators (key metrics)
   > - tools such as organizational dashboards or scorecards that present key metrics (including resilience-specific information) to measure and manage operational resilience process performance
   > - methods and techniques for deriving critical success factors and performing affinity analysis between these and the organization's strategic objectives

- methods, techniques, and tools for developing an inventory of standard services, service profiles, and a service repository
- methods and techniques for defining organizationally high-value services
- methods for promoting and nurturing a resilience-aware culture *(Refer to the Organizational Training and Awareness process area for more information about training and awareness activities.)*
- templates for committee charters
- techniques and tools for performing root-cause analysis to examine process variations for improvement

EF:GG2.GP4 ASSIGN RESPONSIBILITY

Assign responsibility and authority for performing the enterprise focus process, developing the work products, and providing the services of the process.

Elaboration:

The resilience strategic plan described in EF:SG2.SP1 addresses roles and responsibilities for carrying out strategic resilience objectives. EF:SG2.SP2 assigns accountability and responsibility for operational resilience management program activities, tasks, projects, and performance. EF:SG4.SP1 describes the responsibility of higher-level managers for governing the operational resilience management system and the reflection of this in committee charters. EF:SG4.SP2 specifies governance responsibilities for ensuring proper compliance with relevant resilience regulations and laws and the role of key stakeholders in providing oversight.

Refer to the Human Resource Management process area for more information about establishing resilience as a job responsibility, developing resilience performance goals and objectives, and measuring and assessing performance against these goals and objectives.

Subpractices

1. Assign responsibility and authority for performing the process.
2. Assign responsibility and authority for performing the specific tasks of the process.

Elaboration:

Responsibility and authority for performing enterprise focus process tasks can be formalized by
- chartering documents for board committees, executive steering committees, and operational resilience process groups (or equivalent)
- defining the roles and responsibilities in the operational resilience management strategic plan, program, and committee charters
- developing policy specifying roles and responsibilities of board members and higher-level managers for process activities
- including process tasks and responsibility for these tasks in specific job descriptions
- including process tasks in staff performance management goals and objectives with the requisite measurement of progress against these goals

3. Confirm that people assigned with responsibility and authority understand it and are willing and able to accept it.

EF:GG2.GP5 TRAIN PEOPLE

Train the people performing or supporting the enterprise focus process as needed.

Refer to the Organizational Training and Awareness process area for more information about training the staff performing or supporting the process.

Refer to the Human Resource Management process area for more information about creating an inventory of skill sets, establishing a skill set baseline, identifying required skill sets, and measuring and addressing skill set deficiencies.

Subpractices

1. Identify process skill needs.

   Elaboration:

   > These are examples of skills required in the enterprise focus process:
   > - developing, disseminating, and enforcing policy
   > - establishing and managing an operational resilience process group or similar construct
   > - knowledge necessary to perform the process using selected methods, techniques, and tools identified in EF:GG2.GP3 subpractice 3
   > - knowledge necessary to collect, coordinate, and elevate process-specific operational risks to the risk management process
   > - knowledge necessary to implement, manage, and monitor corrective action plans
   > - strong communication skills for building and sustaining a resilience-aware culture

2. Identify process skill gaps based on available resources and their current skill levels.
3. Identify training opportunities to address skill gaps.

   Elaboration:

   > These are examples of training topics:
   > - roles and responsibilities of boards members, steering committees, and similar organizational officers and entities
   > - deriving critical success factors and performing affinity analysis
   > - interpreting and using decision dashboards and scorecards
   > - selecting and using key performance indicators, key risk indicators, and key control indicators for measuring performance
   > - using process methods, tools, and techniques, including those identified in EF:GG2.GP3 subpractice 3
   > - obtaining familiarity with relevant codes of practice such as COSO or regulations such as Gramm-Leach-Bliley

4. Provide training and review the training needs as necessary.

EF:GG2.GP6 *MANAGE WORK PRODUCT CONFIGURATIONS*

Place designated work products of the enterprise focus process under appropriate levels of control.

Elaboration:

> These are examples of enterprise focus work products placed under control:
> - organizational strategic objectives and critical success factors
> - service profiles, service repository, and the prioritized list of high-value services
> - strategic resilience plan and resilience program charter and management plan
> - business case for resilience
> - resilience performance goals and objectives
> - policy statements from board members and higher-level managers
> - operational resilience management system governance framework and committee charters
> - governance dashboards and scorecards
> - key indicators and metrics (KPIs, KRIs, KCIs)
> - governance stakeholder list
> - audit plans and reports
> - corrective action plans
> - process plan
> - policies and procedures
> - contracts with external entities

EF:GG2.GP7 *IDENTIFY AND INVOLVE RELEVANT STAKEHOLDERS*

Identify and involve the relevant stakeholders of the enterprise focus process as planned.

Elaboration:

Several EF-specific practices address the involvement of stakeholders in the enterprise focus process. For example, EF:SG1.SP3 calls for identifying and documenting stakeholders of services in the service profile. EF:SG3.SP2 describes the importance of involving all stakeholders in promoting a resilience-aware culture. EF:SG4.SP1 and EF:SG4.SP2 require that stakeholders be identified and included in the operational resilience governance process. EF:SG4.SP3 requires that key stakeholders receive reports on the success of corrective actions.

Subpractices

1. Identify process stakeholders and their appropriate involvement.

Elaboration:

> These are examples of stakeholders of the enterprise focus process:
> - higher-level managers responsible for promoting a resilience-aware culture by their actions
> - those responsible for sponsoring and enforcing all resilience policies, procedures, standards, and guidelines
> - staff involved in providing oversight for the creation, review, and sustainment of the operational resilience management plan, program, and processes
> - staff involved in providing oversight for the development and implementation of corrective actions for poor performance and the results of such actions
> - those responsible for reviewing and ensuring action is taken based on key indicator and metrics reports
> - owners and custodians of high-value services that support the accomplishment of strategic objectives

> Stakeholders are involved in various tasks in the enterprise focus process, such as
> - planning for the process, including the strategic operational resilience management plan and resilience program management plan
> - making decisions that impact the process
> - making commitments to process plans and activities
> - communicating process plans and activities, including building and sustaining a resilience-aware culture
> - managing operational risks to the process
> - identifying organizational services, particularly high-value services
> - managing and monitoring the performance of the operational resilience management system
> - overseeing the operational resilience management system, as well as developing and implementing corrective action plans when dictated by poor performance
> - resolving issues in the process

2. Communicate the list of stakeholders to planners and those responsible for process performance.
3. Involve relevant stakeholders in the process as planned.

EF:GG2.GP8 MONITOR AND CONTROL THE PROCESS

Monitor and control the enterprise focus process against the plan for performing the process and take appropriate corrective action.

Refer to the Monitoring process area for more information about the collection, organization, and distribution of data that may be useful for monitoring and controlling processes.

Refer to the Measurement and Analysis process area for more information about establishing process metrics and measurement.

Subpractices

1. Measure actual performance against the plan for performing the process.
2. Review accomplishments and results of the process against the plan for performing the process.

Elaboration:

> These are examples of metrics for the enterprise focus process:
> - percentage of critical success factors that are on track according to plan per their key performance indicators
> - percentage of organizational services for which a complete service profile has been documented in the service repository
> - percentage of services considered to be high-value
> - percentage of service profiles and service levels that have been reviewed within their review time frame
> - percentage of strategic resilience plan commitments and objectives that are on track according to plan
> - percentage of operational resilience management program and process activities for which adequate funds have been allocated
> - percentage of staff demonstrating resilience awareness commensurate with job description
> - percentage of committee charters that include resilience responsibilities
> - percentage of key metrics (KPIs, KRIs, KCIs) that are within acceptable ranges
> - percentage of key metrics that are outside of acceptable ranges and for which a corrective action plan exists
> - percentage of high-value assets for which a comprehensive strategy and internal control system have been implemented to mitigate risks as necessary and to maintain these risks within acceptable thresholds
> - percentage of key external resilience requirements (laws, regulations, standards, etc.) for which the organization has been deemed by objective audit to be in compliance
> - percentage of key operational resilience management roles for which responsibilities, accountabilities, and authority are assigned and required skills identified, including key governance stakeholders.
> - percentage of board meetings and/or designated committee meetings for which operational resilience management is on the agenda
> - percentage of incidents that caused damage, compromise, or loss beyond established thresholds to the organization's assets and stakeholders
> - dollar amount of estimated damage or loss resulting from all incidents

- percentage of external entity relationships for which resilience requirements have been implemented in the agreements with these entities
- percentage of organizational units with an established service continuity plan
- percentage of required internal and external audits completed and reviewed by the board or other designated oversight body
- percentage of audit findings that have been resolved
- level of capability achieved in other operational resilience management process areas
- level of adherence to operational resilience management policies
- level of adherence to process policies; number of policy violations; number of policy exceptions requested and number approved
- number of policy violations for policies related to other operational resilience management process areas
- number of enterprise-level and process risks referred to the risk management process; number of risks where corrective action is still pending (by risk rank)
- number of process activities that are on track per plan
- rate of change of resource needs to support the process
- rate of change of costs to support the process

3. Review activities, status, and results of the process with the immediate level of managers responsible for the process and identify issues.

   Elaboration:

   Periodic reviews of the enterprise focus process are needed to ensure that
   - operational resilience management is considered a key strategic concern and indicator
   - strategic operational resilience management activities are on track and key metrics are within acceptable ranges as demonstrated in governance dashboards or scorecards
   - operational resilience management policies are effective
   - issues, concerns, and risks in the operational resilience management system are being given a proper level of oversight
   - administrative, technical, and physical controls are operating as intended
   - controls are meeting the stated intent of the resilience requirements
   - actions resulting from internal and external audits are being closed in a timely manner

4. Identify and evaluate the effects of significant deviations from the plan for performing the process.
5. Identify problems in the plan for performing and executing the process.

6. Take corrective action when requirements and objectives are not being satisfied, when issues are identified, or when progress differs significantly from the plan for performing the process.

Elaboration:

EF:SG4.SP3 specifically describes practices for developing corrective action plans when performance issues exist with key indicators and metrics (KPIs, KRIs, KCIs). In these cases, root-cause analysis is performed to identify improvements to the enterprise focus process.

7. Track corrective action to closure.

EF:GG2.GP9 OBJECTIVELY EVALUATE ADHERENCE

Objectively evaluate adherence of the enterprise focus process against its process description, standards, and procedures, and address non-compliance.

Elaboration:

These are examples of activities to be reviewed:
- identification of the organization's strategic objectives and critical success factors (because they serve as the source of operational resilience requirements)
- development of service profiles, service attributes, service levels, and service resilience requirements
- selection process for high-value services
- development and revision cycles for operational resilience management plans to ensure that changes are commensurate with the organization's strategic business planning process
- sponsorship of higher-level managers for the operational resilience management program to establish that the program is enacted and that regular actions occur that build and sustain a resilience-aware culture
- development and ongoing updating of the business case for resilience
- enactment of the governance framework for operational resilience management and the assignment of clear roles and responsibilities for governance over the operational resilience management system
- regular reporting of process performance to designated stakeholders
- tracking of corrective action plans and internal and external audit findings to closure

These are examples of work products to be reviewed:
- organizational strategic objectives and critical success factors
- service profiles, service repository, and the prioritized list of high-value services
- strategic resilience plan and resilience program charter and management plan
- business case for resilience

- resilience performance goals and objectives
- policy statements from higher-level managers
- operational resilience management system governance framework and committee charters
- governance dashboards and scorecards
- key indicators and metrics (KPIs, KRIs, KCIs)
- governance stakeholder list
- audit plans and reports
- corrective action plans
- contracts with external entities

EF:GG2.GP10 REVIEW STATUS WITH HIGHER-LEVEL MANAGERS

Review the activities, status, and results of the enterprise focus process with higher-level managers and resolve issues.

Elaboration:

Status reporting on the enterprise focus process is likely part of the formal governance structure or may be performed through other organizational reporting requirements (such as through the chief risk officer or the chief resilience officer to an immediate superior). Audits of the process may be escalated to higher-level managers and board members through the organization's audit committee of the board of directors or similar construct.

EF:GG3 INSTITUTIONALIZE A DEFINED PROCESS

Enterprise focus is institutionalized as a defined process.

EF:GG3.GP1 ESTABLISH A DEFINED PROCESS

Establish and maintain the description of a defined enterprise focus process.

Establishing and tailoring process assets, including standard processes, are addressed in the Organizational Process Definition process area.

Establishing process needs and objectives and selecting, improving, and deploying process assets, including standard processes, are addressed in the Organizational Process Focus process area.

Subpractices

1. Select from the organization's set of standard processes those processes that cover the enterprise focus process and best meet the needs of the organizational unit or line of business.

2. Establish the defined process by tailoring the selected processes according to the organization's tailoring guidelines.
3. Ensure that the organization's process objectives are appropriately addressed in the defined process, and ensure that process oversight extends to the tailored processes.
4. Document the defined process and the records of the tailoring.
5. Revise the description of the defined process as necessary.

EF:GG3.GP2 COLLECT IMPROVEMENT INFORMATION

Collect enterprise focus work products, measures, measurement results, and improvement information derived from planning and performing the process to support future use and improvement of the organization's processes and process assets.

Elaboration:

> These are examples of improvement work products and information:
> - policy violations
> - service profiles and repositories
> - repository inconsistencies and issues
> - reports on the effectiveness and weaknesses of controls
> - improvements based on key indicators and metrics corrective action plans
> - effectiveness of operational resilience management plans in execution
> - lessons learned in post-event review of incidents and disruptions in continuity
> - maintenance issues and concerns for assets and services
> - conflicts and risks arising from dependencies on external entities
> - resilience requirements that are not being satisfied or are being exceeded
> - lessons learned in executing operational resilience management plans, in observing sponsorship actions of higher-level managers, and in building a resilience-aware culture
> - metrics and measurements of the viability of the process (*Refer to EF:GG2.GP8 subpractice 2.*)
> - changes and trends in operating conditions, risk conditions, and the risk environment that affect operational resilience
> - relevant internal and external audit reports and resolutions

Establishing the measurement repository and process asset library is addressed in the Organizational Process Definition process area. Updating the measurement repository and process asset library as part of process improvement and deployment is addressed in the Organizational Process Focus process area.

Subpractices

1. Store process and work product measures in the organization's measurement repository.
2. Submit documentation for inclusion in the organization's process asset library.
3. Document lessons learned from the process for inclusion in the organization's process asset library.
4. Propose improvements to the organizational process assets.

EXTERNAL DEPENDENCIES MANAGEMENT
Operations

Purpose

The purpose of External Dependencies Management is to establish and manage an appropriate level of controls to ensure the resilience of services and assets that are dependent on the actions of external entities.

Introductory Notes

Outsourcing services, development, production, and even asset management have become normal and routine operational elements for many organizations because they often provide the ability to engage specialist skills and equipment at a cost savings over internal equivalents. Increasingly, organizations are also exposing technology systems, information, and other high-value assets to customers to enable the seamless and efficient flow of business processes. The External Dependencies Management process area addresses the identification of risks associated with the actions of external entities, the formalization of the relationship with such entities, and the ongoing management of those dependencies and relationships, all in a manner to ensure that appropriate resilience measures are in place to protect and sustain the organization's services and assets that are dependent upon such actions and entities.

For the purpose of this process area, the term *organization* is used to refer to the entity—the enterprise or a part of the enterprise such as an organizational unit or department—that is using the process area. An external dependency exists when an entity that is external to the organization has access to, control of, ownership in, possession of, responsibility for (including development, operations, maintenance, or support), or other defined obligations related to one or more assets or services of the organization. Such entities may be contractors or customers, but they may also be other units or groups within the enterprise. In this process area, all such entities are referred to as "external entities."

The success of the organization in accomplishing its overall mission depends on its ability to sustain mission assurance of services in a consistent and efficient manner. Some services are fully executed inside of organizational boundaries, giving the organization more direct control over mission assurance. However, in many cases, the organization does not control all of the activities in a service that contribute to meeting the service mission; instead, these activities may be performed by external entities.

Dependence on external entities may increase risk levels for organizations in managing the end-to-end resilience of their services. When the execution of a service extends outside of the organization's direct control, there is less ability to directly affect or predict mission assurance, in part because mission assurance is dependent on the resilience of the external entity. From an asset perspective—people, information, technology, and facilities—this can be problematic. In its role in support of a service, an external entity may

- use its own assets—If the external entity fails to protect and sustain these assets, the service and its outcome may be compromised.
- access the assets of the organization (which likely includes the ability to control or modify those assets)—The external entity's actions could affect the resilience of the assets and thereby compromise the service.
- possess and use the assets of the organization (which includes the responsibility for custodial care of those assets)—If the external entity fails to meet the resilience requirements of the assets (as specified by the organization), there is a potential impact on the service mission.
- develop, deliver, commission, or install a new or revised asset for the organization.
- provide supporting services that aid in protecting and sustaining an organization's asset.

Consider also that an external entity may not have a direct role in executing a specific service. In a support role (for example, storing information in an off-site storage facility), an external entity may also fail to adequately protect and sustain the asset such that it will not be available for use in a service when needed.

Regardless of the degree of external dependence, the organization retains responsibility for service mission assurance. The organization is responsible for setting the resilience requirements for services and related assets, communicating them to and requiring them of external entities, and monitoring to ensure external entities are meeting them. The evaluation and selection of external entities based on their abilities to sustain resilience are important first steps in ensuring service resilience.

External dependencies also arise when the organization outsources asset design or development activities—including facility development or software or system development. *(Refer to the Resilient Technical Solutions Engineering process area for more information about developing systems and software in a manner that supports the organization's resilience requirements and program.)* Additional external dependencies arise when the organization is reliant on services that are part of the environment in which it operates, such as energy, telecommunications, and emergency response providers. All such external dependencies can significantly affect an organization's ability to achieve its service missions.

The External Dependencies Management process area comprises four goals: to identify and prioritize external dependencies, to manage risks associated with external dependencies, to formalize binding relationships with external entities, and to monitor and manage external entity performance against all contractual specifications, including those for operational resilience.

Related Process Areas

The establishment and management of resilience requirements for the organization's assets, including those provided or controlled by external entities, are performed in the Resilience Requirements Development and the Resilience Requirements Management process areas.

The risk management cycle for external dependencies is addressed in the Risk Management process area.

The development, validation, testing, and improvement of plans to sustain service continuity for both the organization and external entities are addressed in the Service Continuity process area.

The availability of people to support the continued operation of services, including both employees of the organization and people provided by external entities, is addressed in the People Management process area.

Controls to manage the performance of people in support of the resilient operation of services, including both employees of the organization and people provided by external entities, are addressed in the Human Resource Management process area.

The identification, definition, management, and control of the organization's assets, including those provided or controlled by external entities, are addressed in the Asset Definition and Management process area.

The resilience of technology assets, including those in the control of the organization and those developed, provided, managed, or controlled by external entities, is addressed in the Technology Management process area.

The resilience of information assets, including those in the control of the organization and those provided, controlled, or accessed by external entities, is addressed in the Knowledge and Information Management process area.

The resilience of facility assets and control of the physical environment, including facilities in the full control of the organization and those provided or managed by external entities, are addressed in the Environmental Control process area.

The development of software and system assets that meet the organization's resilience requirements is addressed in the Resilient Technical Solution Engineering process area.

Summary of Specific Goals and Practices

EXD:SG1 Identify and Prioritize External Dependencies
    EXD:SG1.SP1   Identify External Dependencies
    EXD:SG1.SP2   Prioritize External Dependencies
EXD:SG2 Manage Risks Due to External Dependencies
    EXD:SG2.SP1   Identify and Assess Risks Due to External Dependencies
    EXD:SG2.SP2   Mitigate Risks Due to External Dependencies
EXD:SG3 Establish Formal Relationships
    EXD:SG3.SP1   Establish Enterprise Specifications for External Dependencies
    EXD:SG3.SP2   Establish Resilience Specifications for External Dependencies
    EXD:SG3.SP3   Evaluate and Select External Entities
    EXD:SG3.SP4   Formalize Relationships
EXD:SG4 Manage External Entity Performance
    EXD:SG4.SP1   Monitor External Entity Performance
    EXD:SG4.SP2   Correct External Entity Performance

Specific Practices by Goal

EXD:SG1 IDENTIFY AND PRIORITIZE EXTERNAL DEPENDENCIES

External dependencies are identified and prioritized to ensure the resilience of the high-value services that they support.

In this goal, the organization identifies, characterizes, and prioritizes its external dependencies. The prioritization of external dependencies establishes one or more subsets on which the organization must focus its operational resilience activities due to the external dependencies' importance to the sustained operation of high-value services.

Prioritization of external dependencies is a risk management activity. The organization establishes the dependencies that are of most value to the services they support and that require controls to protect and sustain them. Failure to prioritize external dependencies may lead to inadequate operational resilience of high-value services and assets and excessive levels of operational resilience for services and assets that are not high-value.

EXD:SG1.SP1 IDENTIFY EXTERNAL DEPENDENCIES

A list of external dependencies is established and maintained.

Organizations have many types of external dependencies. Any asset or service that is subject to the actions of an external entity is the source of an external dependency. It is important for the organization to identify and characterize all such external dependencies so that they can be understood, formalized, monitored, and managed as part of the organization's comprehensive risk management process.

The most common type of external dependency occurs when the organization outsources certain activities of a service (or the entire service) to an external entity. Another example would be outsourcing the development of a technology asset, such as a software application, or an information asset, such as a custom database.

A less common type of external dependency occurs when the organization provides its customers with access to or use of high-value organizational assets. This is becoming more and more common in certain types of enterprises, particularly in cases where technology interfaces are provided to key customers for the seamless integration of services between the two organizations. (For example, the organization may process certain transactions on behalf of the customer through a tightly coupled technological interface that provides the customer with access to certain organizational assets.)

The organization may use any number of techniques to establish a catalog or detailed list of external dependencies. The organization's list of services should be examined to discover services that may be subject to external dependencies, in whole or in part. The organization's inventory of assets should also be examined to discover assets that are in the control of external entities or are in other ways subject to external dependencies. The organization may find value and efficiency in establishing close service links or overlap to facilitate information sharing between the external dependencies list, the services listing, and the asset inventory. (*Services are addressed in the Enterprise Focus process area; assets are addressed in the Asset Definition and Management process area.*)

The organization's customer database and supplier database may also be valuable sources of insight when establishing the catalog of external dependencies. The organization's set of current supplier and vendor contracts and related service level agreements (SLAs) are additional sources.

The purpose of the catalog of external dependencies is to support the identification and prioritization of external dependencies and the management of risks associated with selected dependencies.

The organization's external dependencies will change over time as a result of changes to relationships with essential suppliers and customers, changes in services, the life cycle of assets, and many other reasons. Once the list of external dependencies is established, it is important that it be maintained. A process for updating the list on a regular basis should be established.

Typical work products

1. List of external dependencies and entities
2. Documented process for updating the list of external dependencies and entities

Subpractices

1. Establish a process for creating and maintaining the list of external dependencies and entities.
2. Establish a set of information that is collected and stored to define each external dependency and the responsible external entity.

    The data that is collected, stored, and routinely updated as part of defining an external dependency and its corresponding external entity is used to help prioritize the external dependency and identify risks associated with the external dependency. The data fields should therefore be set in consideration of the criteria, thresholds, and process for prioritizing external dependencies (*see EXD:SG1.SP2*) and in consideration of the risk identification process for external dependencies (*see EXD:SG2.SP1*).

These are examples of information to collect, store, and update to define an external dependency:
- a description of the external dependency, including
  - the organizational services that rely on the external dependency
  - the organizational assets that rely on the external dependency
  - the criticality and priority of the external dependency based on its importance to high-value services and assets
- the organizational owner of the external dependency
- the name of the external entity that is responsible for the external dependency
- key points of contact at the external entity
- the organizational owner of the external entity relationship (i.e., the department and/or person in the organization who is responsible for the relationship with the external entity)
- compliance and other obligations that apply to the external dependency, the external entity, or the relationship with the external entity

---

These are examples of information to collect, store, and update to define an external entity responsible for an external dependency:
- the name of the external entity
- the names of the external dependencies for which the external entity is responsible
- the products, services, assets, or other inputs (external dependencies) that may be supplied by the external entity, which may include
  - general support services, such as producing the organization's payroll or staffing customer call centers
  - services that directly affect resilience processes such as security operations or IT service delivery and operations management
  - resilience-specific services such as backup and recovery of data, provision of backup facilities for operations and processing, and provision of support technology

> - environmental services such as power, telecommunications, fire and police support, emergency medical services, and emergency management services
> - technology and information assets, such as application software and databases
> - key points of contact at the external entity
> - the organizational owner of the external entity relationship (i.e., the department and/or person in the organization who is responsible for the relationship with the external entity)
> - the external entity's legal entity type (corporation, government entity, etc.)
> - the nature of the relationship with the external entity (customer, supplier, public service, or other)
> - type, status, and duration of contracts or other agreements in place with the external entity
> - the monetary value or other parameter used to describe the value of the relationship with the external entity
> - the organizational assets that are owned, developed, controlled, used, operated, or otherwise influenced by the external entity
> - the financial status of the external entity
> - the status of any pending disputes or litigation with the external entity

3. Review the organization's asset inventory to ensure that any external entities that possess, develop, control, operate, or otherwise influence high-value assets are identified as external dependencies.
4. Review the organization's list of services to identify services that are subject to external dependencies; add any such dependencies to the list of external dependencies.
5. Review supplier and customer databases to identify additional external dependencies.
6. Review current contracts and SLAs to identify additional external dependencies.
7. Update the external dependency list on a regular basis.

    The frequency and timing of such updates should be adjusted as a function of the organization's risk tolerance to the external dependencies. It may be prudent to update different external dependencies at different frequencies based on the risks and characterization details of external dependencies and the relevant external entities. It may be appropriate to increase the update frequency during times of increased risk to the organization or when an external entity is undergoing change or is at risk. Contract award, renewal, or termination should trigger appropriate updates to the external dependency list, as should changes in points of contact or other material changes in the relationship.

    Understanding the risks identified in EXD:SG2.SP1 may assist in setting and revising the update frequency.

EXD:SG1.SP2 PRIORITIZE EXTERNAL DEPENDENCIES

External dependencies are prioritized relative to their importance in supporting the delivery of high-value services.

The prioritization of external dependencies must be performed to ensure that the organization properly directs its operational resilience resources to the external dependencies that most directly impact and contribute to services that support the organization's mission. These external dependencies require the organization's direct attention because their disruption has the potential to cause the most significant organizational consequences.

External dependency prioritization is performed relative to services—that is, external dependencies associated with high-value services are those that must be given the highest priority for operational resilience activities.

However, the organization can use other criteria to establish high-priority external dependencies, such as

- actions of the external entity in the support, maintenance, or custodial care of high-value organizational assets
- the extent to which the organization would rely on the actions of the external entity during off-normal operations, crises, or other times of operational stress
- actions of the external entity in supporting the organization's resilience process
- an external dependency resulting from external entity access to highly sensitive or classified information or to the organization's trade secrets or proprietary information such as intellectual property (*Categorization of information assets is addressed in KIM:SG1.SP2, and intellectual property management is addressed in KIM:SG4.SP2.*)
- external dependencies that are of high value to more than one service
- actions of the external entity in developing, providing, or commissioning new assets for the organization
- the organization's tolerance for "pain"—the degree to which it can suffer degraded performance of the external dependency and continue to meet its mission

Several tiers or classes of prioritization may be appropriate depending on the complexity of the organization's operations and variations in the nature of the external dependencies. It is important that consistent and meaningful criteria be developed for prioritizing the external dependencies and that the criteria be uniformly applied to the full set of external dependencies. The prioritization and criteria should be reviewed and updated on a regular basis to ensure that the prioritization scheme and the list of prioritized external dependencies are appropriate for the organization's risk environment and tolerance.

Typical work products

1. Criteria for prioritizing external dependencies
2. Prioritized list of external dependencies
3. Results of external dependency affinity analyses

Subpractices

1. Establish prioritization criteria and scheme for external dependencies.
    Prioritization criteria should express and distinguish the importance of external dependencies in the continued operation of the organization. The prioritization scheme should be developed in consideration of the various types of external dependencies and external entities on which the organization relies. Thresholds should be considered to distinguish one or more tiers of external dependencies so that appropriate controls can be applied to the various sets of external dependencies to protect and sustain the organization's operations.
2. Apply the prioritization criteria to the list of external dependencies to produce a prioritized list.
    Depending on the prioritization scheme developed by the organization, the result might be several lists, tiers, or sets of external dependencies.

    Be sure that external dependencies that are required for the successful execution of security activities, service continuity plans, and service restoration plans are prioritized appropriately.
3. Periodically validate and update the prioritization criteria and scheme based on changes to the operational environment.
4. Periodically update the prioritized list of external dependencies based on changes in the prioritization criteria and scheme, the operating environment, or the list of external dependencies.
5. Perform affinity analyses to inform dependency prioritization and risk identification.
    Affinity analyses should be performed to identify situations such as
    - the reliance of more than one high-value asset or service on a single external dependency or entity
    - external entities that are dependent on others to meet their agreements with the organization and thus may create chains of external dependencies that are very difficult to manage or control

EXD:SG2 MANAGE RISKS DUE TO EXTERNAL DEPENDENCIES

Risks due to external dependencies are identified and managed.

The management of risk due to external dependencies is the specific application of risk management tools, techniques, and methods to these high-value relationships of the organization. Most organizations have many external dependencies, all of which can be the source of additional risks. Risks from external dependencies can result in consequences due to the impact on assets or services that may be in the control of, supplied by, operated by, or otherwise affected by external entities.

Managing risks due to external dependencies involves understanding the nature of each essential external dependency and the specifics of how the organization may be affected by the realization of such risks.

EXD:SG2.SP1 IDENTIFY AND ASSESS RISKS DUE TO EXTERNAL DEPENDENCIES

Risks associated with external dependencies are periodically identified and assessed.

Risks due to external dependencies must be identified and assessed so that they can be effectively managed to maintain the resilience of the organization's high-value services.

The identification of risks due to external dependencies forms a baseline from which a continuous risk management process can be established and managed.

The subpractices included in this practice are generically addressed in RISK:SG3 and RISK:SG4 in the Risk Management process area.

Typical work products

1. External dependency risk statements, with impact valuation
2. List of external dependency risks, with categorization and prioritization

Subpractices

1. Determine the scope of risk assessment for external dependencies.

    Determining which external dependencies to include in regular risk assessment activities depends on many factors, including the impact on the organization of any disruption in a high-value service that could result due to the realization of such risks.

2. Identify risks due to external dependencies.

    Identification of risks due to external dependencies requires an understanding of the actions of the associated external entity in the operation, support, or resilience of the organization's services. External entities will be responsible for varying dependencies in the support of the organization's operations. The information gathered in the identification and characterization of the external dependencies in support of EXD:SG1.SP1 may be useful in identifying such risks.

> Issues to consider when identifying risks associated with a specific external dependency that relies on a specific external entity include
> - the financial condition of the external entity
> - risks to the availability of the external entity's vital staff
> - reliance by the external entity on subcontractors
> - risks to assets owned, developed, and operated by the external entity that are used in providing the necessary service to the organization

> - scalability of the external entity to meet demand surges or growth in operations as may be required
> - the ability of the external entity to protect and sustain its operations, particularly in times of disruption and stress, including service continuity plans, protective and detective controls, and other key risk management elements
> - level of resilience experience or maturity of the external entity, including demonstrated strengths or weaknesses
> - risks due to the location of the external entity, which may include specific environmental risks due to geography or operating risks associated with local public services
> - unique regulatory and compliance risks associated with the external dependency or the external entity, especially as may be compounded by differing local laws (This may be particularly relevant if the external entity is based in another country.)
> - reliance on communications infrastructure or other high-value technology assets that enable smooth conduct of operations between the organization and the external entity

Risk statements should be developed for each identified risk. *(RISK:SG3.SP1 and RISK:SG3.SP2 provide additional information about identifying risks and developing risk statements.)*

3. Analyze risks due to external dependencies.

    The analysis of risks should include an evaluation of the potential impact of the risk on the organization.

> Topics to consider when analyzing risks associated with a dependency on a specific external entity include
> - the value of assets or services that are accessed, modified, provided, developed, or controlled by the external entity
> - operational throughput that relies on the performance of the external entity (for example, the number of customers or the transaction volume that would be impacted by the realization of the risk)
> - legal liabilities that might accrue to the organization as a result of the risk
> - risks that could arise if the organization has not developed contingency plans or service continuity plans to minimize the impact of any disruptions to the external entity's operations on which the organization relies
> - alternative sources for whatever assets or services the external entity provides that could be or already are established
> - historical key performance measures of the external entity

4. Categorize and prioritize risks due to external dependencies.

    RISK:SG4.SP2 provides additional information about risk categorization and prioritization.

5. Assign a risk disposition to each identified risk.

    RISK:SG4.SP3 provides additional information about risk disposition.

EXD:SG2.SP2 Mitigate Risks Due to External Dependencies

Risk mitigation strategies for external dependencies are developed and implemented.

The mitigation of risk due to external dependencies involves the development of strategies that seek to minimize the risk to an acceptable level. This includes reducing the likelihood of risks, minimizing exposure to them, developing service continuity plans, and developing recovery and restoration plans to address the consequences of realized risk.

Risk mitigation for external dependencies requires the development of risk mitigation plans (which may include the development of new controls or the revision of existing controls that apply to external dependencies and external entities) and the implementation and monitoring of these plans for effectiveness.

The subpractices included in this practice are generically addressed in RISK:SG5 in the Risk Management process area.

Typical work products

1. External dependency risk mitigation plans
2. List of those responsible for addressing and tracking risks
3. Status reports on external dependency risk mitigation plans

Subpractices

1. Develop risk mitigation strategies and plans for all risks due to external dependencies that have a "mitigation" or "control" disposition.
2. Validate the risk mitigation plans by comparing them to existing strategies for protecting and sustaining external dependencies.
3. Identify the person or group responsible for each risk mitigation plan and ensure that the person or group has the authority to act and the proper level of skills and training to implement and monitor the plan.
4. Monitor and manage residual risk.
5. Implement the risk mitigation plans and provide a method for monitoring their effectiveness.
6. Monitor risk status on a regular basis to ensure that the risk, its mitigation strategy, and its risk mitigation plan do not pose additional threat to the organization.

EXD:SG3 Establish Formal Relationships

Relationships with external entities are formally established and maintained.

Requirements in the form of contractual specifications provide the basis for formal agreements that are established to define and govern the relationships between the organization and the actions of external entities. Enterprise-level requirements are established and included in any such agreement with an external entity. Specifications (including those for satisfying resilience requirements) are established that are unique to a particular external dependency. Ideally, external entities are selected from a qualified set of candidates based on their demonstrable ability to achieve the specifications established by the organization; any specifications that cannot be met are identified and managed as risks by the organization. The entire relationship between the organization and the external entity is established, defined, and bound by a formal agreement that includes all contractual specifications. The agreement is updated throughout the life cycle of the relationship with the external entity as needed.

EXD:SG3.SP1 ESTABLISH ENTERPRISE SPECIFICATIONS FOR EXTERNAL DEPENDENCIES

Enterprise specifications that apply in general to external entities are established and maintained.

The organization has a set of values and behaviors that it follows when carrying out its operations. These values and behaviors may be derived to support the organization's strategy or designed to create or reinforce the organization's public image. They may also be a reflection of the organization's market sector or the function of regulations or other constraints with which the organization must comply. Regardless of the source, the organization's values and behaviors should be reflected in high-level organizational policies that govern the behavior of staff and external entities whenever they are representing or performing services for the organization.

From a resilience perspective, such policies, standards, and guidelines are essential controls that aid in protecting and sustaining the organization's operation. For example, the organization may have a policy that requires certain minimum due diligence prior to allowing staff members to access certain information assets.

When external entities support the execution of the organization's services, they become an extension of the organization and should be subject to the same or similar policies, standards, and guidelines as the organization's staff. These enterprise-level policies, standards, and guidelines must be translated to a set of enterprise-level specifications and reflected in agreements with each external entity to ensure a seamless implementation of the organization's resilience strategy.

The enterprise specifications for external dependencies should consider the prioritization criteria and scheme for external dependencies (*see EXD:SG1.SP2*). It may be appropriate for certain or all enterprise specifications to apply to all external entities. Alternatively, it may be appropriate for different sets of enterprise specifications to apply to different tiers or sets of prioritized external dependencies and the relevant external entities.

The organization's enterprise resilience requirements should be reflected in the enterprise specifications for external dependencies. (*Enterprise resilience requirements are addressed in the Resilience Requirements Development process area.*)

> These are examples of enterprise specifications for external entities:
> - compliance with regulations or legal statutes that affect the organization
> - agreement related to the treatment of the organization's intellectual property
> - adherence to certain staff and human resources policies
> - policies regarding the security of certain information or technology assets, including the use of resilience guidelines in the development of software and system assets *(Refer to the Resilient Technical Solution Engineering process area.)*
> - physical access policies for organization-owned or -managed facilities
> - adherence to special agreement provisions such as non-disclosure statements
> - requirements for contract flow-down provisions or pre-approval of subcontractors
> - insurance and indemnification requirements related to the handling of certain assets
> - indemnification and defense requirements associated with legal or contract violations
> - security clearance requirements for facilities or staff
> - policies on ethics, behavior, non-discrimination, and harassment
> - procedural requirements related to staff turnover
> - policies on performance monitoring and reporting
> - minimum requirements for financial attributes of the organization and related reporting

Typical work products

1. List of enterprise specifications that apply to external dependencies and entities
2. Agreement templates that reflect enterprise specifications

Subpractices

1. Establish a list of enterprise-level specifications that apply to external dependencies and entities.
2. Include specifications to adhere to relevant policies, standards, and guidelines (particularly those that support or affect the resilience of the organization or its operations) in the list of enterprise specifications for external dependencies and entities.
3. Include relevant compliance and regulatory requirements in the list of enterprise specifications for external dependencies and entities.
4. Include the enterprise specifications for external dependencies and entities in contract and agreement templates as appropriate.
5. Review and update the enterprise specifications for external dependencies and entities on a regular basis.
6. Ensure that changes are initiated to agreements with external entities when the enterprise specifications change.

EXD:SG3.SP2 ESTABLISH RESILIENCE SPECIFICATIONS FOR EXTERNAL DEPENDENCIES

Resilience specifications that apply to specific external dependencies and entities are established and maintained.

External dependencies occur as a result of an external entity's access to, control of, ownership in, development of, possession of, responsibility for (including operations, maintenance, or support), or other defined obligations related to one or more high-value assets or services of the organization. The organization's high-value assets and services all have specific resilience requirements that must be established as specifications for any associated external dependency and responsible entity.

For each external dependency, the organization should establish a detailed set of specifications that the external entity must meet in order to support and extend the resilience of the organization's operations. It is important that these specifications be thorough, detailed, definitive, adequate for use as criteria when selecting external entities, suitable as language in agreements with external entities, and appropriate for use as a basis for monitoring the performance of the external entity.

The specifications for a specific external dependency and entity include, as appropriate, required characteristics of the external entity (e.g., financial condition and experience), required behaviors of the external entity (e.g., security and training practices), and performance parameters that must be exhibited by the external entity (e.g., recovery time after an incident and response time to service calls).

When developing specifications for external dependencies, the organization should

- consider the type of organizational assets or services impacted by the external dependency and their importance to the organization's mission and operations
- understand the extent to which the external entity takes custodial control of the organization's assets, and any resilience requirements of those assets that must be satisfied
- consult internal and external stakeholders responsible for the associated assets and services
- be aware of other assets or services that may rely upon the same external dependency and entity (as would be indicated by the affinity analysis in EXD:SG1.SP2)
- review the resilience requirements established in the Resilience Requirements Development process area for the assets or services in question
- review and select appropriate resilience guidelines established in the Resilient Technical Solution Engineering process area for the development of all software and system assets
- include the enterprise-level specifications (as identified in EXD:SG3.SP1)

The resilience specifications for an external dependency must clearly cover the resilience requirements of the assets or services that rely on the external entity. They should also include key features and capabilities of the external entity.

Typical work products

1. Documented resilience specifications
2. Service level agreements

Subpractices

1. For each external dependency, establish a list of resilience specifications that apply to the responsible external entity.

    The process for determining and documenting the resilience specifications that apply to an external dependency and entity will vary based on the action of the entity in relation to the organization's operations and the priority of the external dependency (as determined in EXD:SG1.SP2).

    At a minimum, the resilience specifications should include a clear and definitive statement of the external entity's services, support, products, assets, or staff on which the organization relies.

2. Include specific characteristics of the external entity that are required.

    Specifications for characteristics are often expressed as minimum acceptable characteristics.

Required external entity characteristics might include
- industry experience
- management experience
- technology and systems architecture
- process controls
- financial condition
- reputation, including references
- degree of reliance on other external entities
- legal, regulatory, and compliance history
- ability to meet future needs
- CERT-RMM capability ratings

---

3. Include resilience requirements for assets that will be developed, provided, or maintained by external entities.
4. Include required behaviors, standards of performance, and service levels that are required of the external entity.

    Specifications that describe required behaviors and performance parameters are often documented as SLAs that are included in requests for proposals (RFPs) *(see EXD:SG3.SP3)*. It is valuable to develop the SLA before entering into a relationship with an external entity so that the SLA can be used as part of the evaluation process to select an external entity. Ultimately, the SLA should be incorporated into the formal contractual agreement with an external entity *(see EXD:SG3.SP4)*.

From a resilience perspective, the SLA should include the performance specifications for security, business continuity, and IT operations that are necessary to support the resilience of the associated asset or service (the external dependency). For example, if the external entity is performing payroll operations for the organization, the SLA may require that the external entity keep all payroll data confidential and destroy the data within a specific number of days of its use. SLAs often specify deadlines or time parameters for availability, support, and/or recovery activities (such as a requirement for X% availability over a Y-month period).

Consider the following topics when establishing required behaviors and standards of performance for external dependencies and entities:
- availability, including hours of operation and minimum uptime measures
- performance, including throughput, latency, response time, and other measures of operational performance
- change management, including minimum time frames for notifications, testing requirements, and patch management procedures
- quality of service, including response time, dispute and escalation procedures, service desk support, and problem tracking
- security, including incident management procedures and performance, vulnerability and penetration management, logical and physical access controls, identity management, and security standards compliance
- business continuity, including requirements for business continuity plan development, testing protocols and frequency, recovery time in the event of an incident, and prioritization of services or assets for recovery in the event of an incident. (This may also include recovery time objectives [RTOs] and recovery point objectives [RPOs] for specific technology assets [*see TM:SG5.SP1*].)
- asset segregation and marking
- physical and/or logical separation of technology and/or information assets
- monitoring and reporting requirements, including measurements and reporting criteria, required audits, rights to audit, audit protocols, reports on external dependencies, asset status reports, and dashboards
- communications and coordination, particularly in the event of security or business continuity incidents

---

5. Periodically review and update resilience specifications for external dependencies and entities as conditions warrant.

EXD:SG3.SP3 EVALUATE AND SELECT EXTERNAL ENTITIES

External entities are selected based on an evaluation of their ability to meet the specifications for external dependencies.

External entities should be selected according to an organized and thorough process and according to explicit specifications and selection criteria. The selection process and criteria should be designed to ensure that the selected entity can fully meet the organization's specifications as established in EXD:SG3.SP1 and EXD:SG3.SP2.

From a resilience perspective, the selection process for external entities is often an extension of or supplement to the organization's standard procurement processes. Resilience specifications may simply serve as additional requirements for consideration and evaluation as part of the standard procurement process. In all cases, due diligence should be performed on candidate external entities to evaluate their ability to meet the resilience specifications that have been established for the actions they hope to perform for the organization.

In some cases, external entities cannot be selected from a pool of candidates; they may be inherited in the course of an acquisition or merger, or they may be the only provider of a high-value service on which the organization depends (this is often the case for public services). In cases in which external entities cannot be selected, the due diligence process for selection should still be performed to identify any specifications that are not met by the external entity. It may be appropriate to alter the specifications by changing the actions or nature of the dependence on the external entity to resolve the unmet specifications. In cases where the specifications cannot be changed, any unmet specifications should be treated as risks under EXD:SG2.

Typical work products

1. Requests for proposals or other types of external entity solicitation documents that include specifications in cases in which proposals and bids are being sought by the organization
2. External entity selection criteria
3. Evaluation of each external entity proposal against the selection criteria
4. Selection decision and supporting rationale

Subpractices

1. Establish a selection process for external entities that includes consideration of applicable specifications.
2. Establish external entity selection criteria.
   The criteria should include measures and thresholds of the candidate external entity's ability to meet the resilience specifications established in EXD:SG3.SP1 and EXD:SG3.SP2.

> These are examples of factors that should be considered for the development of criteria for external entity selection:
> - organizational mission, vision, values, goals, objectives, purpose, and critical success factors
> - the risk tolerance of both the organization and the external entity
> - the type of external entity relationship and whether the relationship supports a high-value service or is an essential part of the service
> - the nature of the service—whether the external entity will take custodial control of the organization's high-value assets or use its own in providing the service
> - the nature of the asset—the extent to which the asset (such as software or information) supports a high-value service or is an essential element of accomplishing the service
> - the ability of the external entity to participate in monitoring, testing, and verification activities
> - if the external entity is likely to have multiple customers, the ability of the external entity to provide service during periods of concurrent usage

3. Include the resilience specifications for external entities in RFPs, other solicitations of interest, and other documents or processes that are designed to identify and/or qualify candidate external entities.
4. Evaluate external entities based on their abilities to meet the resilience specifications and in accordance with the established selection criteria.
5. Perform due diligence on candidate external entities.

    The due diligence process should be designed to verify that the candidate can meet the organization's specifications. If the external entity is engaged with a high-value service or asset in support of the organization's mission, it may be appropriate to test the controls that are in use by the candidate to protect and sustain its services and assets as part of the due diligence process.

    The due diligence may be performed iteratively as part of a staged procurement process with multiple down-select stages, or the due diligence may be performed completely on each qualified candidate to help understand and reveal differences among the candidates.

    The due diligence process and results should be documented. The resulting documents should be adequately protected in accordance with the organization's policies and in compliance with any non-disclosure or other agreements in place with the candidate.

6. Select external entities and document the selection and decision rationale.
7. If any resilience specifications are unmet by the selected external entity, revise the selection criteria to adjust the specifications or treat the unmet specifications as identified risks in EXD:SG2.SP1.

EXD:SG3.SP4 FORMALIZE RELATIONSHIPS

Formal agreements with external entities are established and maintained.

Formal agreements should be established with external entities. The agreement content may take different forms depending on the

- type of relationship between the organization and the external entity
- type of products or services (external dependencies) being provided by the external entity (particularly if the services are for sustaining security and resilience rather than general services)
- level of integration of the external entity with the service (i.e., the extent to which the organization relies on the external entity to meet the service mission)
- degree to which the external entity takes custodial control of the organization's asset(s) in order to provide necessary products and services

Types of agreements may include contracts, memoranda of agreement, purchase orders, and licensing agreements. In some cases, agreements such as mutual-aid agreements may spell out what services a public authority provides for the organization during normal operations and during crises. In cases in which the external entity and the organization are part of the same legal entity or share a common parent legal entity, the organization or the parent entity may have special procedures for establishing and enforcing agreements. Agreements are often composed from multiple sections or multiple documents, each of which describes some aspect of the arrangement and agreement. In all cases, the agreement, regardless of form, should

- be enforceable by the organization
- include detailed and complete specifications that must be met by the external entity (See EXD:SG3.SP1 and EXD:SG3.SP2.)
- include any required performance standards or work products from the organization
- be changed to reflect changes in specifications over the life of the relationship

Typical work products

1. Agreements with external entities

Subpractices

1. Select an agreement type that best fits the performance standards required by the organization and that is enforceable if problems arise.

2. Properly document the agreement terms, conditions, specifications, and other provisions.

All agreement provisions should be documented in the agreement in language that is unambiguous.

The agreement should not contain any general exceptions for achieving the resilience specifications unless they are carefully considered and negotiated. It may, however, contain scenarios of types of unforeseen events for which the external entity is not expected to prepare. Any exceptions granted to resilience specifications or scenarios for which the external entity is not required to prepare should be treated as risks under EXD:SG2.

All agreements should establish and enable procedures for monitoring the performance of external entities and inspecting the services or products they deliver to the organization.

These are examples of elements and dependencies that should be addressed in the agreement (sourced in part from *Outsourcing Technology Services IT Examination Handbook* [FFIEC 2004]):

- work to be performed, services to be provided, or products to be delivered—Clearly describe the responsibilities of the external entity, including required activities, services, deliverables, and time frames.
- all relevant enterprise-level specifications *(See EXD:SG3.SP1.)*
- external entity resilience specifications *(see EXD:SG3.SP2)*, including
  - performance standards—Clearly and measurably define minimum service requirements and remedies for failing to achieve them. These are commonly expressed as SLAs, which are incorporated and made part of the agreement.
  - security, confidentiality, and privacy—The agreement should define obligations of the external entity to protect the organization's assets. The external entity should be prohibited from using such assets except as necessary for the performance of the agreement and should be required to protect against unauthorized use or disclosure. Define disclosure obligations for security breaches and disclosures. The agreement should include any regulatory, legal, or compliance obligations.
  - business resumption and contingency plans—Address the external entity's responsibility for backup and record protection, including equipment, program, and data files, and maintenance and testing of service continuity plans. Include a requirement for any specific recovery time frames and require copies of plans.
  - staff performance or prescreening—Address any requirements related to external entity staff, including any performance or licensing requirements, prescreening requirements, or other qualifications. If any external entity staff members are considered to be vital to the successful performance of the external entity, provisions should be included to address the availability of the vital staff, including notification requirements in the event that they become unavailable.
- controls—Include provisions that address external entity internal controls, compliance with regulations, record keeping, records access, notification and approval rights for material changes in external entity legal structure or form, financial health and reporting, and insurance.

- change procedures—Include procedures for changing any of the agreement provisions by mutual agreement.
- audit—Address audit requirements and provisions for independent audit and review, including audit report requirements and any required periodic reviews.
- reporting—Include frequency and type of reports required.
- subcontracting provisions—The external entity's rights and ability to subcontract its obligations under the agreement to others should be included.
- cost—Fully describe all costs associated with the agreement (base, recurring, special, etc.), including provisions and circumstances for changing cost agreements.
- dispute resolution—Consider including specific provisions for escalation and dispute resolution procedures. Include responsibilities for continued operation and delivery during dispute periods.
- termination—Consider events that would warrant or allow termination by either the organization or the external entity and include time frames for notification and expenses for termination.
- regulatory compliance—Ensure that the external entity will comply with applicable regulations and provide access to regulatory agencies as necessary.
- escrow provisions—If the external entity is providing services based on proprietary or single-source software or other single-source assets, consider including an escrow agreement that would allow the organization to secure the software or single-source assets during extraordinary events.
- external entity assets—If the external entity will be using assets that are supplied by entities external to itself, the agreement should include provisions, as appropriate, for the repair or replacement of the assets, insurance provisions for the assets, conditions under which the assets may be withdrawn by the external entity, and provisions to replace the assets as needed.
- legal topics such as ownership and license, indemnification, liability, assignment of the agreement to others, and jurisdiction including considerations for foreign-based providers.

3. Ensure that the organization and the external entity agree to all agreement provisions and specifications before executing the agreement.

   Negotiation may be required to reach agreement with the external entity on all of the agreement provisions. Any specifications that are waived as a result of negotiations should be treated as risks under EXD:SG2. Once negotiations are complete and the organization and the external entity agree to all of the agreement provisions, the agreement should be executed by representatives from both organizations.

4. Update the agreement as required throughout the duration of the agreement according to provisions established in the agreement.

EXD:SG4 MANAGE EXTERNAL ENTITY PERFORMANCE

The performance of external entities is managed.

The organization must manage external entities by monitoring performance against specifications and taking corrective actions as appropriate.

EXD:SG4.SP1 MONITOR EXTERNAL ENTITY PERFORMANCE

The performance of external entities is monitored against the specifications.

The performance of external entities against the agreement terms and specifications—particularly those focused on the resilience of the organization's assets and services—must be periodically monitored. This includes all external dependencies for which the entity is responsible. The organization uses the specifications and formal agreements established in EXD:SG3 as the basis and criteria for monitoring the external entity. Any deviations from the established specifications must be analyzed to understand the potential impact on the organization.

To ensure that performance monitoring is performed on a timely and consistent basis, the organization should establish procedures that determine the frequency, protocol, and responsibility for monitoring a particular external entity. (Responsibility is typically assigned to the organizational owner of the relationship.) These procedures should be consistent with the terms of the agreement with the external entity *(see EXD:SG3.SP4)*. It may be appropriate to adjust the monitoring frequency in response to changes in the risk environment, changes to external dependencies, or changes in the external entity.

When the external entity is responsible for producing or delivering assets to the organization, the monitoring process should include inspection of the assets to ensure that they meet all stated specifications, including asset resilience requirements.

Typical work products

1. Reports on external entities
2. Relationship management databases showing current performance monitoring information
3. Inspection reports on external entity deliverables

Subpractices

1. Establish procedures and responsibility for monitoring external entity performance and inspecting any external entity deliverables.
   Procedures should be consistent with the agreement between the organization and the external entity and should be based on verifying that the external entity is achieving the specifications as defined in the agreement. All agreement specifications should be considered for monitoring; it may be appropriate to prioritize

monitoring and inspection activities based on a risk analysis of the specifications (which includes all external dependencies). Monitoring and inspection procedures should address the external entity's required characteristics, required behaviors, and required performance parameters.

These are examples of appropriate periodic monitoring activities:
- reviews of the financial condition, viability, and risks of the external entity
- audits of the external entity's controls and control environment both for the entity and for external dependencies for which the entity is responsible
- testing the external entity's service continuity plans independently or in an integrated manner
- information security risk assessments, vulnerability scans, penetration tests, log reviews, and access control inspections
- review of compliance activities and records
- audits of performance specifications
- evaluations of changes in staff and review of staff prescreening activities
- inspection of deliverables against any or all specifications
- review of insurance coverage
- evaluation of any subcontractor usage

---

2. Meet periodically with external entity representatives to review the result of monitoring activities, the specifications in the agreement, and any changes in either the organization or the external entity that might impact performance under the agreement.
3. Evaluate any deviations in the performance of the external entity from the established specifications to determine the risk to the organization's operation and to inform the selection of corrective actions.

EXD:SG4.SP2 CORRECT EXTERNAL ENTITY PERFORMANCE

Corrective actions are implemented to support external entity performance as necessary.

Implementing corrective actions is a necessary part of managing external entity performance. The objective of any corrective action is to minimize the disruption to the organization's operation or the risk of any such disruption based on external dependencies. The range of corrective actions should be established in the agreement with the external entity, and an evaluation of alternatives should be completed prior to implementing corrective actions.

In cases in which the external entity is developing or otherwise providing an asset or assets to the organization, the appropriate corrective action may be to reject the delivery of the assets.

Corrective actions should be documented in accordance with specifications in the agreement and used to inform and improve ongoing monitoring of the external entity.

Typical work products

1. Corrective action reports or documentation
2. Correspondence with an external entity documenting corrective actions

Subpractices

1. Evaluate alternative corrective actions to select the optimal corrective action.

   The agreement should be reviewed to identify appropriate and allowable corrective actions for consideration. The various alternatives should be evaluated based on their likelihood to succeed in correcting the situation and mitigating any associated risks.

   It may be valuable and appropriate to include the external entity in the discussion and consideration of alternatives, especially if both the organization and the external entity desire to continue the relationship.

2. Communicate with the external entity to review selected corrective actions. Communication provisions in the agreement should be followed to formalize the communication.
3. Implement selected corrective actions.
4. Monitor as appropriate to ensure that issues are remedied in a timely manner.
5. Update the agreement with the external entity as required.

Elaborated Generic Practices by Goal

Refer to the Generic Goals and Practices document in Appendix A for general guidance that applies to all process areas. This section provides elaborations relative to the application of the Generic Goals and Practices to the External Dependencies Management process area.

EXD:GG1 ACHIEVE SPECIFIC GOALS

The operational resilience management system supports and enables achievement of the specific goals of the External Dependencies Management process area by transforming identifiable input work products to produce identifiable output work products.

EXD:GG1.GP1 PERFORM SPECIFIC PRACTICES

Perform the specific practices of the External Dependencies Management process area to develop work products and provide services to achieve the specific goals of the process area.

Elaboration:

Specific practices EXD:SG1.SP1 through EXD:SG4.SP2 are performed to achieve the goals of the external dependencies management process.

EXD:GG2 INSTITUTIONALIZE A MANAGED PROCESS

External dependencies management is institutionalized as a managed process.

EXD:GG2.GP1 ESTABLISH PROCESS GOVERNANCE

Establish and maintain governance over the planning and performance of the external dependencies management process.

Refer to the Enterprise Focus process area for more information about providing sponsorship and oversight to the external dependencies management process area.

Subpractices

1. Establish governance over process activities.

   Elaboration:

   > Governance over the external dependencies management process may be exhibited by
   > - extending the role of the chief acquisition or procurement officer (or equivalent) to include ensuring that all RFPs and agreements with external entities reflect resilience specifications
   > - developing and publicizing higher-level managers' objectives and requirements for managing the process
   > - providing oversight of external entity access to, control of, ownership in, possession of, responsibility for (including development, operations, maintenance, or support), or other defined obligations related to one or more assets or services of the organization
   > - sponsoring and providing oversight of policy, procedures, standards, and guidelines for evaluating, selecting, and managing relationships with external entities, including the management of the process
   > - providing oversight of the process for establishing formal agreements with external entities, including contracts and SLAs
   > - making higher-level managers aware of applicable compliance obligations related to external dependencies, and regularly reporting on the organization's satisfaction of these obligations to higher-level managers
   > - oversight over the establishment, implementation, and maintenance of an appropriate level of controls to ensure the resilience of services and assets that rely upon the actions of external entities
   > - sponsoring and funding process activities
   > - providing guidance for prioritizing external dependencies relative to the organization's high-priority strategic objectives
   > - providing guidance on identifying, assessing, and managing operational risks related to external dependencies

- providing guidance for resolving violations of enterprise and resilience specifications by external entities
- verifying that the process supports strategic resilience objectives and is focused on the assets and services that are of the highest relative value in meeting strategic objectives
- regular reporting from organizational units to higher-level managers on process activities and results
- creating dedicated higher-level management feedback loops on decisions about external dependencies and recommendations for improving the process
- conducting regular internal and external audits and related reporting to appropriate committees on the effectiveness of the process
- creating formal programs to measure the effectiveness of process activities, and reporting these measurements to higher-level managers

2. Develop and publish organizational policy for the process.

   Elaboration:

   The external dependencies management policy should address
   - responsibility, authority, and ownership for performing process activities
   - procedures, standards, and guidelines for
     - identifying and prioritizing external dependencies
     - associating external dependencies with services and assets
     - managing operational risks resulting from external dependencies
     - evaluating and selecting external entities
     - formalizing and enforcing agreements with external entities, including changing any provisions by mutual agreement
     - developing and documenting enterprise and resilience specifications for external entities, including organizational policies to which external entities are expected to adhere
     - standards of performance and service levels *(Refer to EXD:SG3.SP2 subpractice 4.)*
     - establishing service continuity plans and procedures for external entities
     - monitoring the performance of external entities, including inspecting the services or products they deliver (Such procedures specify frequency, protocol, and responsibility for monitoring and inspection.)
     - terminating relationships with external entities as specified in formal agreements
     - issue escalation and dispute resolution
   - requesting, approving, providing, and terminating access for external entities *(Refer to the Access Management process area for more information about granting access [rights and privileges] to organizational assets. Refer to the Identity Management process area for more information about creating and maintaining identities for persons, objects, and entities.)*
   - methods for measuring adherence to policy, exceptions granted, and policy violations

EXD:GG2.GP2 PLAN THE PROCESS

Establish and maintain the plan for performing the external dependencies management process.

Elaboration:

A plan for performing the external dependencies management process is developed to ensure that the organization can satisfy its operational resilience requirements when an external entity has access to, control of, ownership in, possession of, responsibility for (including development, operations, maintenance, or support), or other defined obligations related to one or more assets or services of the organization. The plan must address the enterprise and resilience specifications for the service being performed or the product being provided (i.e., the external dependency) by the external entity. In addition, because external entities can be located in many geographical locations, the plan must address those external entities and stakeholders that can enable or adversely affect operational resilience.

The plan for the external dependencies management process should not be confused with service continuity (recovery, restoration) plans for assets and services that are under the control of external entities. The plan for the external dependencies management process details how the organization will manage external dependencies and relationships with external entities, including the development of service continuity plans where such entities are involved. (*The generic practices for service continuity planning are described in SC:SG1 through SC:SG4 in the Service Continuity process area.*)

Subpractices

1. Define and document the plan for performing the process.
2. Define and document the process description.
3. Review the plan with relevant stakeholders and get their agreement.
4. Revise the plan as necessary.

EXD:GG2.GP3 PROVIDE RESOURCES

Provide adequate resources for performing the external dependencies management process, developing the work products, and providing the services of the process.

Elaboration:

A wide range of organizational resources and skills is required to oversee and manage external entity access to, control of, ownership in, possession of, responsibility for (including development, operations, maintenance, or support), or other defined obligations related to one or more assets or services of the organization. This includes the diversity of activities required to identify, prioritize, evaluate, select, formalize agreements with, and manage a wide range of relationships with external entities. In addition, these activities may require a major commitment of financial resources (both expense and capital) from the organization.

Subpractices

1. Staff the process.

    Elaboration:

    > These are examples of staff required to perform the external dependencies management process:
    > - staff responsible for
    >   - identifying and prioritizing existing external dependencies and keeping this information up-to-date based on changing business conditions
    >   - service continuity as it involves external dependencies and entities
    >   - preparing RFPs, including applicable SLAs
    >   - evaluating proposals and selecting external entities
    >   - establishing formal agreements with external entities
    >   - monitoring the performance of external entities to ensure they are meeting their agreements and specifications, and taking corrective action when appropriate
    >   - inspecting deliverables
    > - staff involved in identifying, assessing, and mitigating risks that may arise due to external dependencies and when engaging external entities
    > - facilities management staff for physical assets that are under the control of external entities
    > - asset and service owners and custodians (to identify and enforce resilience specifications that must be satisfied by external dependencies and entities)

    Refer to the Organizational Training and Awareness process area for information about training staff for resilience roles and responsibilities.

    Refer to the Human Resource Management process area for information about acquiring staff to fulfill roles and responsibilities.

2. Fund the process.

    Refer to the Financial Resource Management process area for information about budgeting for, funding, and accounting for external dependencies.

3. Provide necessary tools, techniques, and methods to perform the process.

Elaboration:

> These are examples of tools, techniques, and methods to support the external dependencies management process:
> - methods, techniques, and tools for identifying and prioritizing the list of external dependencies and keeping it up-to-date
> - methods, techniques, and tools for identifying and managing risks due to external dependencies, including tracking open risks to closure and monitoring the effectiveness of risk mitigation plans
> - templates for RFPs, SLAs, and formal agreements
> - proposal evaluation checklists
> - methods, techniques, and tools for monitoring and reporting the performance of external entities
> - methods, techniques, and tools for inspecting deliverables
> - relationship management databases

EXD:GG2.GP4 ASSIGN RESPONSIBILITY

Assign responsibility and authority for performing the external dependencies management process, developing the work products, and providing the services of the process.

Elaboration:

Those responsible for services and assets are involved in identifying and prioritizing external dependencies and establishing resilience specifications that external entities must fulfill. Formal agreements identify external entity actions, including ensuring continuity of operations during times of stress. EXD:SG1.SP1 calls for identifying the organizational owner of each relationship with an external entity; EXD:SG4.SP1 calls for monitoring the performance of external entities against their specifications. Similarly, EXD:SG2.SP2 requires the identification of those responsible for addressing, tracking, and mitigating risks that arise from external dependencies and relationships with external entities.

In EXD:GG2.GP4, responsibilities are assigned to activities of the external dependencies management process.

Refer to the Human Resource Management process area for more information about establishing resilience as a job responsibility, developing resilience performance goals and objectives, and measuring and assessing performance against these goals and objectives.

Subpractices

1. Assign responsibility and authority for performing the process.

Elaboration:

The organization must ensure that responsibility and authority extend to all external entities and to any entities with which the external entity has contracted to provide services or products in support of the external entity's formal agreement with the organization.

2. Assign responsibility and authority for performing the specific tasks of the process.

Elaboration:

> Responsibility and authority for performing external dependencies management tasks can be formalized by
> - defining roles and responsibilities in the process plan
> - including process tasks and responsibility for these tasks in specific job descriptions
> - developing policy requiring organizational unit managers, line of business managers, project managers, and asset and service owners and custodians to participate in the process for services and assets under their ownership or custodianship
> - developing and implementing agreements, including contracts, SLAs, memoranda of agreement, purchase orders, and licensing agreements
> - including process tasks in staff performance management goals and objectives, with requisite measurement of progress against these goals

3. Confirm that people assigned with responsibility and authority understand it and are willing and able to accept it.

EXD:GG2.GP5 TRAIN PEOPLE

Train the people performing or supporting the external dependencies management process as needed.

Refer to the Organizational Training and Awareness process area for more information about training the people performing or supporting the process.

Refer to the Human Resource Management process area for more information about inventorying skill sets, establishing a skill set baseline, identifying required skill sets, and measuring and addressing skill deficiencies.

Subpractices

1. Identify process skill needs.

Elaboration:

> These are examples of skills required in the external dependencies management process:
> - identifying and prioritizing external dependencies
> - affinity analyses
> - elicitation of resilience specifications to be reflected in RFPs and agreements with external entities
> - evaluating and selecting external entities
> - negotiating agreements with external entities
> - prioritizing external entities based on the priority of the external dependencies for which the entity is responsible
> - knowledge of tools, techniques, and methods that can be used to identify, analyze, mitigate, and monitor operational risks resulting from external dependencies and from relationships with external entities
> - managing relationships with external entities
> - monitoring the performance of external entities, including the inspection of deliverables and knowing when corrective actions are called for

2. Identify process skill gaps based on available resources and their current skill levels.
3. Identify training opportunities to address skill gaps.

   Elaboration:

   > These are examples of training topics:
   > - contract negotiation
   > - prioritizing external dependencies based on established criteria
   > - developing resilience specifications for external entities
   > - cross-training to ensure adequate knowledge and coverage for all external dependencies
   > - terminating agreements with external entities
   > - supporting service owners and asset owners and custodians in understanding the process and their related roles and responsibilities
   > - using process methods, tools, and techniques, including those identified in EXD:GG2:GP3 subpractice 3

4. Provide training and review the training needs as necessary.

EXD:GG2.GP6 MANAGE WORK PRODUCT CONFIGURATIONS

Place designated work products of the external dependencies management process under appropriate levels of control.

Elaboration:

> These are examples of external dependencies work products placed under control:
> - list of external dependencies, with priorities
> - criteria for prioritizing external dependencies
> - affinity analyses results to inform dependency prioritization and risk identification
> - information that defines external dependencies, stored as a maintainable information repository or database
> - risk statements with impact valuation
> - list of external dependency risks with categorization and prioritization, risk disposition, mitigation plans, and current status
> - agreement templates, including enterprise specifications that apply to external entities
> - external dependencies and resilience specifications that apply to each external entity
> - RFPs, including applicable SLAs
> - criteria for selecting external entities
> - proposal evaluation results and decision rationale
> - agreements with external entities, including contracts, memoranda of agreement, purchase orders, and licensing agreements
> - performance-monitoring reports
> - relationship management databases
> - inspection reports on deliverables
> - corrective-action reports
> - process plan
> - policies and procedures

EXD:GG2.GP7 IDENTIFY AND INVOLVE RELEVANT STAKEHOLDERS

Identify and involve the relevant stakeholders of the external dependencies management process as planned.

Subpractices

1. Identify process stakeholders and their appropriate involvement.

Elaboration:

Because external entities may reside in a wide range of physical locations and provide and support numerous processes, services, and assets, a substantial number of stakeholders are likely to be external to the organization.

These are examples of stakeholders of the external dependencies management process:
- internal and external owners and custodians of organizational assets
- internal and external service owners
- organizational unit and line of business managers responsible for high-value assets and the services they support
- staff responsible for managing operational risks arising from external dependencies and relationships with external entities
- staff responsible for establishing, implementing, and maintaining an internal control system for organizational assets where an external dependency and an external entity are involved
- staff required to develop, test, implement, and execute service continuity plans that involve external dependencies and external entities
- acquisition and procurement staff
- internal and external auditors

Stakeholders are involved in various tasks in the external dependencies management process, such as
- planning for evaluating, selecting, and managing relationships with external entities
- creating and maintaining a prioritized inventory of all external dependencies
- establishing and periodically reviewing prioritization criteria
- analyzing services and assets to determine their dependencies on external entities
- identifying resilience specifications for external entities
- ensuring that service continuity plans reflect all external dependencies as well as the actions of external entities
- managing operational risks that arise from external dependencies and relationships with external entities
- monitoring the performance of external entities
- renegotiating and terminating relationships with external entities
- reviewing and appraising the effectiveness of process activities
- resolving issues in the process

---

2. Communicate the list of stakeholders to planners and those responsible for process performance.
3. Involve relevant stakeholders in the process as planned.

EXD:GG2.GP8 MONITOR AND CONTROL THE PROCESS

Monitor and control the external dependencies management process against the plan for performing the process and take appropriate corrective action.

Refer to the Monitoring process area for more information about the collection, organization, and distribution of data that may be useful for monitoring and controlling processes.

Refer to the Measurement and Analysis process area for more information about establishing process metrics and measurement.

Refer to the Enterprise Focus process area for more information about providing process information to managers, identifying issues, and determining appropriate corrective actions.

Subpractices

1. Measure actual performance against the plan for performing the process.
2. Review accomplishments and results of the process against the plan for performing the process.

   Elaboration:

   > These are examples of metrics for the external dependencies management process:
   > - number and percentage of external entities in a variety of categories, such as
   >   - by external dependency
   >   - by business process, by service, by asset or product
   >   - by type of service or product provided *(Refer to EXD:SG1.SP1 subpractice 2.)*
   >   - by prioritized tier (based on prioritization criteria)
   >   - by agreement type (formal contract with and without SLA, memorandum of agreement, purchase order, licensing agreement, and other, including no type of agreement)
   >   - by number or type of agreement changes
   >   - by status (RFP, source selection, awarded, contract initiated, performing as expected, out of compliance, in dispute or litigation, terminated, renewed, etc.)
   >   - by monetary value
   >   - by geographic region
   >   - by operational throughput that relies upon the external entity (for example, number of customers, transaction volume)
   >   - by number of entities external to itself upon which the external entity relies to meet its agreements with the organization
   >   - by CERT-RMM capability rating
   > - percentage of external dependencies without designated organizational owners
   > - percentage of external entities without designated organizational owners
   > - percentage of external entities whose financial status is at risk
   > - percentage of external entities that have undergone some form of assessment, risk assessment, and audit as required by policy

- percentage of external entities that
  - play a key role in fulfilling service continuity plans during disruptive events
  - have tested their service continuity plans, including their participation in the organization's service continuity plans per agreement
  - failed to perform as expected during a disruptive event
- percentage of external entities whose deliverables have failed to pass inspection
- percentage of external entities with corrective actions that have not been remedied in the designated time period
- number of external dependency risks referred to the risk management process; number of risks where corrective action is still pending (by risk rank)
- level of adherence to process policies; number of policy violations; number of policy exceptions requested and number approved
- number of process activities that are on track per plan
- rate of change of resource needs to support the process
- rate of change of costs to support the process

3. Review activities, status, and results of the process with the immediate level of managers responsible for the process and identify issues.

Elaboration:

Reviews will likely verify the accuracy and completeness of the list of external dependencies and their current status.

Periodic reviews of the external dependencies management process are needed to ensure that
- criteria for selecting and evaluating external entities reflect current business objectives and priorities
- new external dependencies are included and prioritized in an information repository or database, and terminated dependencies are removed
- agreements with external entities include stated resilience specifications
- the mapping of external dependencies to services and assets (and vice versa) is accurate and current
- ownership of external dependencies and external entities is established and documented
- the relationship management database captures the performance of all external entities
- poor or failed performance, disputes, and areas of non-compliance are addressed in a timely manner
- status reports are provided to appropriate stakeholders in a timely manner
- process issues are referred to the risk management process when necessary
- actions requiring management involvement are elevated in a timely manner

> - the performance of process activities is being monitored and regularly reported
> - key measures are within acceptable ranges as demonstrated in governance dashboards or scorecards and financial reports
> - actions resulting from internal and external audits are being closed in a timely manner

4. Identify and evaluate the effects of significant deviations from the plan for performing the process.
5. Identify problems in the plan for performing and executing the process.
6. Take corrective action when requirements and objectives are not being satisfied, when issues are identified, or when progress differs significantly from the plan for performing the process.

Elaboration:

Corrective action may require the revision of existing formal agreements.

7. Track corrective action to closure.

EXD:GG2.GP9 OBJECTIVELY EVALUATE ADHERENCE

Objectively evaluate adherence of the external dependencies management process against its process description, standards, and procedures, and address non-compliance.

Elaboration:

> These are examples of activities to be reviewed:
> - identifying and prioritizing external dependencies
> - specifying resilience specifications in agreements with external entities
> - identifying and managing risks due to engaging with external entities
> - evaluating and selecting external entities
> - formalizing relationships with external entities
> - reflecting the involvement of external entities in organizational service continuity plans and ensuring that external entities have service continuity plans for their own operations that are periodically tested
> - monitoring the performance of external entities and taking corrective action as required
> - identifying and managing changes to agreements with external entities
> - aligning stakeholder requirements with process plans
> - assigning responsibility, accountability, and authority for process activities
> - determining the adequacy of external dependencies reports and reviews in informing decision makers regarding the performance of operational resilience management activities and the need to take corrective action, if any

> These are examples of work products to be reviewed:
> - prioritized list of external dependencies with their current status
> - risk statements related to external dependencies and external entities
> - risk mitigation plans
> - service continuity plans for external entities, including vital staff
> - agreements with external entities
> - process plan and policies
> - process issues that have been referred to the risk management process
> - process methods, techniques, and tools
> - metrics for the process *(Refer to EXD:GG2.GP8 subpractice 2.)*

EXD:GG2.GP10 REVIEW STATUS WITH HIGHER-LEVEL MANAGERS

Review the activities, status, and results of the external dependencies management process with higher-level managers and resolve issues.

Elaboration:

Status reporting on the external dependencies management process may be part of the formal governance structure or be performed through other organizational reporting requirements (such as through the chief acquisition or procurement officer level or equivalent). Audits of the process may be escalated to higher-level managers through the organization's audit committee of the board of directors or similar construct in private or non-profit organizations.

Refer to the Enterprise Focus process area for more information about providing sponsorship and oversight to the operational resilience management system.

EXD:GG3 INSTITUTIONALIZE A DEFINED PROCESS

External dependencies management is institutionalized as a defined process.

EXD:GG3.GP1 ESTABLISH A DEFINED PROCESS

Establish and maintain the description of a defined external dependencies management process.

Elaboration:

Managing external dependencies, including relationships with the external entities responsible for them, is typically carried out at the organizational unit or line of business level (where ownership of the relevant service or asset resides) and may have to be geographically focused (due to the location of specific external entities). However, to achieve consistent results in managing these relationships, the activities at the organizational unit or line of business level must be derived from an enterprise definition of the external dependencies management process. Agreements (including resilience specifications), dependency priorities, and performance monitoring may be inconsistent across organizational units, particularly when a specific external entity supports multiple units or multiple external entities support a specific service or asset. Inconsistencies in managing relationships with external entities across the enterprise can impede operational resilience.

Establishing and tailoring process assets, including standard processes, are addressed in the Organizational Process Definition process area.

Establishing process needs and objectives and selecting, improving, and deploying process assets, including standard processes, are addressed in the Organizational Process Focus process area.

Subpractices

1. Select from the organization's set of standard processes those processes that cover the external dependencies management process and best meet the needs of the organizational unit or line of business.
2. Establish the defined process by tailoring the selected processes according to the organization's tailoring guidelines.
3. Ensure that the organization's process objectives are appropriately addressed in the defined process, and ensure that process governance extends to the tailored processes.
4. Document the defined process and the records of the tailoring.
5. Revise the description of the defined process as necessary.

EXD:GG3.GP2 COLLECT IMPROVEMENT INFORMATION

Collect external dependencies work products, measures, measurement results, and improvement information derived from planning and performing the process to support the future use and improvement of the organization's processes and process assets.

Elaboration:

> These are examples of improvement work products and information:
> - prioritized list of active external dependencies and their current status
> - inconsistencies and issues with external dependencies
> - improvements based on risk identification and mitigation
> - effectiveness of executed service continuity plans that rely upon external dependencies and entities

> - metrics and measurements of the viability of the process *(Refer to EXD:GG2.GP8 subpractice 2.)*
> - changes and trends in operating conditions, risk conditions, and the risk environment that affect external dependencies and relationships with external entities
> - lessons learned in post-event review of external entity incidents and disruptions in continuity
> - conflicts and risks arising from external dependencies and reliance on external entities
> - lessons learned in managing the life cycle of an engagement with an external entity
> - resilience specifications that are not being satisfied or are being exceeded

Establishing the measurement repository and process asset library is addressed in the Organizational Process Definition process area. Updating the measurement repository and process asset library as part of process improvement and deployment is addressed in the Organizational Process Focus process area.

Subpractices

1. Store process and work product measures in the organization's measurement repository.
2. Submit documentation for inclusion in the organization's process asset library.
3. Document lessons learned from the process for inclusion in the organization's process asset library.
4. Propose improvements to the organizational process assets.

FINANCIAL RESOURCE MANAGEMENT
Enterprise

Purpose

The purpose of Financial Resource Management is to request, receive, manage, and apply financial resources to support resilience objectives and requirements.

Introductory Notes

Every activity that an organization performs requires a commitment of financial resources. This is particularly true for managing operational resilience—activities like security and business continuity are resource-intensive, and the cost of these activities continues to increase as new threats emerge, technology becomes more pervasive and complex, and the organization shifts its asset base from tangible assets to intangible assets such as information. As the building blocks of organizational services, assets require increasingly sophisticated protection strategies and continuity plans. This requires the organization to make a financial commitment to asset development, implementation, and long-term operation and support.

Besides ensuring proper funding considerations for resilience activities, effective consideration of financial resources is also an organizational necessity for managing these activities. The cost of strategies to protect and sustain assets and services must be optimized to the value of the potential loss of the productivity of assets and services. In addition, understanding the true cost of protecting and sustaining these assets and services is paramount for effectively managing their resilience. Without relevant information about the costs of protecting and sustaining assets, the organization cannot know when costs are misaligned with asset value and contribution.

Financial Resource Management is focused on improving the organization's ability to apply financial resources to fund resilience activities while helping the organization to actively manage the cost and return on investment of these activities. The organization establishes a plan for defining financial resources and needs and assigning these resources to resilience activities. Budgets are established, funding gaps are identified, and costs are tracked and documented. Through effective financial management, the organization establishes its ability to measure return on resilience investments through calculating "risk versus reward" and by identifying cost recovery opportunities. In short, financial resource management provides for the possibility that resilience activities can become investments that the organization uses to move its strategic objectives forward and that can be recouped through improved value to stakeholders and customers.

Related Process Areas

Visible and active sponsorship and support for funding resilience activities are addressed in the Enterprise Focus process area.

The processes for identifying, analyzing, and mitigating risks that result from underfunding or lack of funding for resilience requirements are addressed in the Risk Management process area.

Summary of Specific Goals and Practices

FRM:SG1 Establish Financial Commitment
    FRM:SG1.SP1   Commit Funding for Operational Resilience Management
    FRM:SG1.SP2   Establish Structure to Support Financial Management

FRM:SG2 Perform Financial Planning
    FRM:SG2.SP1   Define Funding Needs
    FRM:SG2.SP2   Establish Resilience Budgets
    FRM:SG2.SP3   Resolve Funding Gaps

FRM:SG3 Fund Resilience Activities
    FRM:SG3.SP1   Fund Resilience Activities

FRM:SG4 Account for Resilience Activities
    FRM:SG4.SP1   Track and Document Costs
    FRM:SG4.SP2   Perform Cost and Performance Analysis

FRM:SG5 Optimize Resilience Expenditures and Investments
    FRM:SG5.SP1   Optimize Resilience Expenditures
    FRM:SG5.SP2   Determine Return on Resilience Investments
    FRM:SG5.SP3   Identify Cost Recovery Opportunities

Specific Practices by Goal

FRM:SG1 ESTABLISH FINANCIAL COMMITMENT

A commitment to funding resilience activities is established.

Establishing a commitment to funding the organization's operational resilience management system is a key factor in its success. Typically, funding for resilience activities is indirect, drawn as required from other budgets in areas such as information technology and security rather than allocated based on resilience needs and requirements. This leads to an ineffective and inefficient allocation of financial resources for managing operational resilience, which ultimately affects the organization's ability to successfully achieve resilience objectives.

Dedicated funding for operational resilience management requires active and visible sponsorship from higher-level managers. The budgeting and funding activity for resilience should coexist with activities used to develop funding for strategic objectives and operational plans. A structure to enforce and reinforce financial planning, budgeting, and resource allocation must be developed and implemented to ensure ongoing support for the operational resilience management system and to avoid funding these activities in an ad hoc, event-driven, or funds-available manner. The organization's commitment to funding operational resilience management should also extend to identifying the resources in the organization who are responsible for developing and funding resilience budgets and for managing the costs of resilience activities against these budgets.

FRM:SG1.SP1 COMMIT FUNDING FOR OPERATIONAL RESILIENCE MANAGEMENT

A commitment by higher-level managers to fund resilience activities is established.

(This practice is repeated from the Enterprise Focus process area and enhanced for emphasis. It assumes that there is visible and active support and sponsorship for the operational resilience management system by higher-level managers in the organization.)

Budgeting is a process of allocating funds to organizational activities that support and promote strategic objectives. When resilience is considered a strategic competency, funding for resilience activities must be included as part of the organization's capital and expense funding needs rather than as an afterthought that is indirectly funded through IT activities or as needed when disruptive events occur.

Sponsorship of the operational resilience management system is made actionable by higher-level managers' commitments to funding the resilience program and the accompanying activities and tasks. This requires that they commit to

- supporting the business case for operational resilience management
- including resilience needs in the funding of strategic objectives
- ensuring that resilience needs are adequately funded
- releasing funds as necessary to support the attainment of strategic resilience objectives

Typical work products

1. Business case for resilience
2. Documented strategy for funding resilience activities

Subpractices

1. Develop the business case for the operational resilience management program and process.
   Sponsorship of the investment in the operational resilience management system must be based on a sound business case. The investment in resilience must bring about tangible, measurable, and demonstrable value to the organization. The business case for resilience should

- justify the investment through itemization of tangible benefits and results
- articulate the strategic outcomes that would result from investments in resilience activities
- articulate the potential risks and costs associated with not investing in resilience activities
- establish that the funding necessary for resilience is appropriate and adequate
- provide sufficient information to allow comparative evaluations of alternative actions
- establish the accountability and commitments for the achievement of the benefits and strategic outcomes

2. Establish operational resilience management program and process funding as a regular part of the organization's strategic plan budgeting (capital and expense) exercise.

   The development of budgets to support the operational resilience management system is addressed in FRM:SG2.SP2.

3. Define the sources of funds that will be used to fund the operational resilience management program and process activities.

   As part of their sponsorship of the operational resilience management system, higher-level managers must identify the sources of funds that will be used. Higher-level managers may allocate a portion of existing operating budgets to resilience, create a pool of resources at the enterprise level for allocation, or develop dedicated funding streams (such as an add-on charge to customer services or products) to fund the resilience activities of the organization.

4. Approve allocation of funding to operational resilience management program and process activities.

   The allocation of funding for operational resilience management activities is addressed in FRM:SG3.SP1.

FRM:SG1.SP2 Establish Structure to Support Financial Management

The structure that supports the assignment and management of financial resources to resilience activities is established.

Organizations typically have a standardized budgeting and accounting structure that ensures consistency, accuracy, and reliability of financial data for financial management. The structure helps the organization to develop budgets, allocate funds to capital projects or to support operational processes, and to account for the use of funds against budgets—in essence, to control organizational finances.

Because the operational resilience management system is often cost-intensive, the organization must have a structure and process that extend to managing the financial aspects of resilience, including providing a means for

- budgeting for resilience activities
- allocating and delivering funds to resilience activities (whether these activities are scheduled or are performed during an emergency or event)

- accounting for and tracking the costs of providing resilience services
- identifying and understanding cost variances in providing resilience services
- providing financial governance over the operational resilience management system
- determining the cost-benefit ratio of resilience decisions and performing other analytical activities related to resilience
- forecasting future operational-resilience-management-related costs and investments
- committing resources to authority and accountability for managing the financial aspects of operational resilience management
- communicating the financial process and structure for operational resilience management to all in the organization with a need to know

Addressing the financial aspects of operational resilience management separately from other operating expenses and capital outlays ensures that the cost (and potential revenue) related to operational resilience is visible and can be actively managed as are other organizational expenses and capital improvements. In turn, this allows the organization to take actions to control costs, shift financial resources as necessary, and explain variations in costs related to events or other disruptions—in other words, to provide resilience at the lowest possible cost and highest possible return to the organization. In addition, implementing a structure that supports specific funding for managing operational resilience ensures that it is considered as a separate item, distinct from pools of funding supplied to less specific activities such as security, business continuity planning, and IT operations management.

Typical work products

1. Resilience accounting policies, procedures, and acceptable practices
2. Resilience chart of accounts
3. Tools and techniques for financial management

Subpractices

1. Establish resilience accounting policies and procedures.
    Resilience accounting policies and procedures establish the ways in which the organization expects resilience costs and investments to be documented, budgeted, funded, tracked, and accounted for. These policies and procedures should establish the financial management structure necessary for resilience accounting and should specifically address
    - expansion of the organization's chart of accounts to include resilience accounts
    - establishment of related charge strings and budgets for resilience activities and projects (which would roll up into the chart of accounts)
    - funding policies and procedures to fund resilience activities
    - policies and procedures for funding off-cycle or emergency funding requests related to resilience activities (to avoid overspending and lack of accountability)
    - resilience financial reporting requirements (both internally and externally)

2. Establish resilience accounts, cost strings, and budgeting processes.
3. Establish tools and techniques for resilience financial management.

> These are examples of tools and techniques that may be used to support financial management of resilience:
> - policies and procedures for generally accepted budgeting and accounting practices for operational resilience management
> - cost and accounting tracking systems
> - effort reporting systems
> - action item tracking systems
> - project management and scheduling programs
> - analytical programs or methods that provide for cost-benefit analysis or "what-if" analyses

4. Assign responsibility and accountability for resilience budgeting, funding, and accounting activities.

   Accountability for achieving the benefits, controlling the costs, managing the risks, and coordinating the activities and interdependencies of multiple projects should be clearly and unambiguously assigned and monitored. In order to assign financial responsibility, the organization specifically identifies and documents those staff who are authorized to make financial commitments to resilience management activities.

FRM:SG2 PERFORM FINANCIAL PLANNING

Planning for funding resilience management activities is performed.

Resilience activities tend to be funded in one or more of the following ways:

- as part of an organizational unit or line of business budget (typically for building and executing service continuity plans)
- as part of other support department budgets (typically IT, IT security, or IT operations, or possibly as part of the organization's risk management budget)
- when emergencies, events, or other disruptions arise (ad hoc, without specific budget or spending controls)

While these funding methodologies may be effective in the short term, the increasing importance of actively managing resilience demands that the organization be able to understand its resilience financial obligations, determine how to fund these obligations, and identify cost savings and optimization opportunities where possible to continually improve the efficiency of applying financial resources to what is traditionally thought of as a cost center.

Funding resilience competes with projects, activities, and initiatives that the organization may have in its sights to meet strategic objectives, improve revenue, and improve return to stakeholders. Because of this, specific consideration of and planning for resilience financial obligations give the organization control over these obligations so that they can not only be cost-effective but become investments in meeting these competing goals.

To perform financial planning for operational resilience management, the organization must specifically define its financial obligations, establish resilience budgets, and resolve funding gaps and conflicts that arise from competing objectives.

FRM:SG2.SP1 DEFINE FUNDING NEEDS

The financial obligations for managing the operational resilience management system are established.

The activities necessary for protecting and sustaining organizational assets and services are often cost-intensive and result in vaguely discernible returns to the organization. In some cases, they are simply a cost of operations—to keep services productive toward their mission and assets deployed to support services as necessary.

Unfortunately, the cost of resilience activities, particularly when viewed at the asset or service level, is often addressed through discretionary funds—those that have not been earmarked for any particular purpose. Thus, the funding of these activities is inconsistent, prone to reaction-based allocation, and not typically based on requirements. Meeting resilience requirements requires a certain level of non-discretionary, specifically allocated funding that provides for the people, processes, and technology necessary to meet the requirements. In other words, funding needs for managing resilience should be specifically identified and funds must be considered, allocated, and earmarked based on need.

To make effective optimization and trade-off decisions, the organization must confront the true cost of the requirements it has set to manage resilience. Viewing resilience costs from a requirements perspective provides a more accurate picture of the true cost of managing operational resilience, laying the groundwork for cost reduction and reallocation based on need rather than discretionary and arbitrary decisions.

Typical work products

1. Historical resilience accounting data
2. Resilience funding requirements (by asset or service, or both)
3. Estimation rationale and calculations for funding

Subpractices

1. Collect historical data that will be used as the basis for developing funding requirements.
    Historical data includes the cost, effort, and schedule data from previously executed projects, activities, and tasks.

2. Determine and document resilience funding requirements.
    Determining resilience funding requirements is not a trivial task. It takes a thorough examination of many factors at the asset, service, and enterprise levels. The following should be considered when determining resilience funding requirements:
    - the costs associated with developing, implementing, monitoring, and maintaining protective controls for assets and services
    - the costs associated with developing, testing, implementing, and maintaining service continuity plans
    - direct and indirect labor costs associated with resilience tasks and activities
    - allocated costs from the enterprise for shared services such as network security, physical security controls on buildings and facilities, and other allocated IT and facilities security services
    - associated overhead costs levied by the enterprise
    - costs for performing risk assessments and business impact analyses, and developing and implementing corrective actions
    - costs for tools, methodologies, and software licenses to support resilience activities
    - costs for labor, including direct labor, training, skills development, etc.
    - costs for external assistance (consulting and labor)
    - special projects that must be funded to improve or sustain resilience
    - costs related to potential operational environment changes that may occur in the future that would affect the budget
    - allowances for emergency funding or future-looking needs
    - actual costs of resilience services and activities in past performance periods
3. Validate funding assumptions through detailed analysis of resilience requirements.
    Funding assumptions must support the satisfaction of resilience requirements. Thus, they must be compared to these requirements for validation.

FRM:SG2.SP2 ESTABLISH RESILIENCE BUDGETS

Capital and expense budgets for resilience management are established.

Budgeting is an activity that emanates from strategic planning. The organization develops budgets to ensure that funding is available and allocated to support its strategic objectives. In much the same way, resilience objectives (which support strategic objectives) must be specifically funded.

As part of the organization's regular budgeting process, resilience budgets should be developed based on funding assumptions. In practice, this typically refers to organizational unit level budgeting of specific resilience accounts and/or the expansion of existing account budgets to allow for allocated costs from the enterprise.

The organization may also have to establish enterprise-level budgets that provide resilience services that are allocated across the organization and may have to specifically fund enterprise-level resilience program activities that support the operational resilience management system that traverses the organization.

Typical work products

1. Resilience line-item budgets (at organizational unit or line of business level)
2. Resilience line-item budgets (at enterprise level)
3. Project budgets for resilience projects
4. Resilience program budget

Subpractices

1. Determine the budget available for the resilience program.
2. Establish a budgeting method and process for resilience.
   There are a number of budgeting methods that may be in use in a typical organization. These methods should be employed when developing resilience budgets as well. Budgeting methods include activity-based costing, zero-based budgeting, and incremental budgeting.
3. Develop the operational-level resilience budgets.
   The budget should be based on the funding requirements as considered in FRM:SG2.SP1.
4. Develop the enterprise-level resilience budgets.
   These budgets are typically owned by departments such as information technology, IT security, risk management, legal, audit, or other enterprise departments that are responsible for aspects of security, business continuity, and IT operations management.
5. Assign authority and accountability for developing and managing the budgets.
   To ensure that budgets are used as a primary financial control in the deployment and execution of resilience activities and tasks, clear responsibility and authority for developing and managing resilience budgets must be assigned.
6. Review budgets on a regular basis and update as necessary.
7. Tie performance measures to the resilience budgets.
   Tying performance measures to resilience budgets ensures adequate financial performance and commitment to meeting resilience requirements.

FRM:SG2.SP3 RESOLVE FUNDING GAPS

Identify and resolve gaps in funding for resilience management and mitigate associated risks.

Identifying and resolving funding gaps for managing operational resilience are a process check that ensures that essential activities necessary for meeting resilience requirements are funded adequately. The failure to include essential activities and fund them appropriately potentially exposes the organization to additional risk.

The organization actively compares resilience budgets to the cost of activities necessary to support operational resilience, identifies potential gaps, and attempts to resolve these gaps by taking mitigating actions such as increasing budgets, reprioritizing activities, or developing other options.

Risks that result due to funding gaps may have to be resolved and mitigated. In addition, these risks may have to be escalated to oversight or governance personnel to ensure that they are aware that essential resilience functions are not being covered. Governance may result in corrective actions such as reallocation of funds, reprioritization of activities, or other actions to mitigate resulting risks.

Risks that result from underfunding of resilience requirements may have to be considered in the Risk Management process area. Escalating operational risk issues to higher-level managers for consideration and corrective action is addressed in the Enterprise Focus process area.

Typical work products

1. Documented resilience funding gaps
2. Resolution decisions for funding gaps

Subpractices

1. Perform gap analysis between resilience funding needs and established budgets.
2. Identify budget shortfalls.
3. Identify risks related to budget shortfalls.
   Risks identified as related to budget shortfalls should be referred to the organization's risk management process for inclusion in the continuous risk management cycle. *(The processes for identifying, analyzing, and mitigating risk are included in the Risk Management process area.)*
4. Develop and document decisions to resolve potential issues, concerns, and risks that result from funding gaps.

FRM:SG3 FUND RESILIENCE ACTIVITIES

The organization's essential activities for managing and sustaining operational resilience are funded.

The organization must have processes in place to ensure that access to funds for managing and sustaining operational resilience is provided. Typically, this occurs through normal funding mechanisms, but due to the nature of managing operational resilience, additional provisions may have to be made to ensure that off-cycle requests are handled in a timely manner.

FRM:SG3.SP1 FUND RESILIENCE ACTIVITIES

Access to funds for resilience management activities is provided.

Establishing and sustaining resilience requires the organization to have a structure and process for allocating and distributing funding for procuring the necessary goods and services to support resilience and the development, implementation, and management of strategies to both protect and sustain services and supporting assets. Access to resilience-directed funding is typically made through the organization's regular mechanisms for funding activities, expenses, and capital purchases, but special circumstances often arise when managing operational resilience that require off-cycle budget requests that must be met in a timely manner.

Funds requests are generally handled through funding mechanisms that are common to most organizations:

- Expense requests provide access to funds for approved expenses related to providing resilience services (such as travel).
- Purchase requests provide access to funds for approved expense-related and capital purchases (such as hardware and software or office supplies).
- Labor related to providing resilience services is generally funded through time and effort reporting.
- Overhead associated with shared costs of providing resilience services is generally funded through overhead allocation.

Off-budget or off-cycle requests for funds to provide resilience services can be a control weakness for many organizations because they typically occur during times of stress, and the usual mechanisms for funding are abandoned. Thus, the organization must have generally accepted processes and procedures for these types of funding requests so that they can be controlled to the extent possible.

Typical work products

1. Policies and procedures for funds access and application
2. Budget commitment request
3. Off-budget funding justification

Subpractices

1. Develop policies and procedures for accessing budgeted resilience funds.
    Policies and procedures should include provisions for
    - funding justifications
    - reviewing justifications and approving funding requests
    - emergency funding requests
    - reviewing and validating labor and allocation charges to resilience budgets (that are not part of a request process)

    Resilience projects (such as the development, design, and implementation of resilience requirements in a system or software development project) should be funded directly through project funding mechanisms.
2. Develop a process for addressing off-cycle or off-budget funds requests and approvals.
    This process should include a proper approval structure that allows for expedient provision of funds but does not impair the time-dependent nature of the requests.

FRM:SG4 ACCOUNT FOR RESILIENCE ACTIVITIES

Accounting for the financial commitment to resilience activities is performed and used for process improvement.

Gathering data on the cost of managing and supporting operational resilience is an essential activity for establishing financial management and responsibility and for performing cost-benefit analysis on the impact and value of these services. Without financial data, no conclusions can be drawn as to whether the investment in managing operational resilience is worth the organization's commitment. The organization establishes accounting processes that accumulate data on the expenditures and costs associated with providing services to manage and support the operational resilience of services and associated assets.

Accounting for resilience activities requires the organization to track and document related costs and to analyze these costs to ensure they are in line with expectations, to identify variances, and to determine the true cost of providing resilience services.

FRM:SG4.SP1 TRACK AND DOCUMENT COSTS

The costs associated with resilience management are tracked and documented.

In order to consider the true cost of providing resilience services to the organization, and the potential return on investment that results, the organization must have established and consistent procedures for tracking and documenting the various costs associated with managing operational resilience. This information is a fundamental element in accounting for resilience activities and is an essential input to controlling and managing costs. Without this information, organizational managers cannot provide an adequate level of resilience at the lowest possible cost to the organization.

Typical work products

1. Financial reports (on resilience costs)
2. Documentation of variances between budgeted and actual expenditures
3. Resilience cost accumulation and categorization scheme
4. Resilience budget projections

Subpractices

1. Develop and implement a means for collecting and tracking costs.
   There are several levels of cost accumulation and tracking that an organization must consider:
   - organizational level, including enterprise, organizational unit, line of business, or department
   - organizational unit, including asset, service, or project

- expenditure type, including labor, overhead, software, hardware, facilities management, etc.
2. Collect financial data on the costs related to providing resilience services.
    The organization's accounting system should be able to produce financial data to a level of granularity that allows the organization to track resilience costs for assets or services, or any other unit that the organization chooses. Financial data should be supplied regularly to authorized staff (such as department managers who are responsible for controlling resilience costs).
3. Calculate variances between budgeted costs and actual costs.
    Budget variances may be identified by any of the levels that the organization establishes for cost accumulation (as suggested in subpractice 1). The variances should be calculated at the levels that are most helpful for the organization to manage resilience costs.
4. Identify and document major budget variances.
5. Analyze budgets on a regular basis to determine potential period shortfalls or unspent items.
6. Revise budgets based on actual data if necessary.

FRM:SG4.SP2 PERFORM COST AND PERFORMANCE ANALYSIS

Cost and performance analysis for funded resilience management activities is performed.

Cost accounting and analysis for resilience activities provides the organization a tool for determining effectiveness and efficiency, to manage costs within budgets, to determine return on resilience investment, and to accurately project budgets and costs for resilience in the future.

Typical work products

1. Variance analysis reports
2. Recommendations and explanations for reducing variance
3. Determination of true cost of resilience (COR)

Subpractices

1. Perform analysis on budget variances and document explanations for the variances.
    The organization should attempt to determine if the variance is meaningful and whether it should be reduced or eliminated. The organization should particularly attempt to determine if the variance is the result of necessary increases in expenditure to maintain operational resilience.
2. Develop plans for reducing or eliminating variances.
3. Calculate the true cost of providing resilience services (COR).
    Based on cost accumulation and tracking, the organization should attempt to determine the true cost of providing resilience services so that this information can be used in optimization and return on investment calculations. The COR should be calculated at the level appropriate for making financial decisions about resilience (such as at the asset or service level).

4. Report financial exceptions.

    Financial exceptions may be indicators of issues and concerns in the operational resilience management system that must be escalated to oversight managers and committees. The organization should determine which types of financial exceptions should be reported and have a mechanism in place to report these exceptions on an as-needed basis.

FRM:SG5 OPTIMIZE RESILIENCE EXPENDITURES AND INVESTMENTS

The return to the organization for investment in resilience activities is measured and assessed.

The organization ultimately "invests" in operational resilience as a means for ensuring that its strategic objectives can be met. Foremost, the investment in resilience should optimize strategies to protect and sustain assets and services at the lowest possible cost to the organization. However, because resilience is typically a cost-driven activity, an organization may also seek to determine if its investment in resilience services and activities actually brings a return (by paying for itself through improved service uptime, quality, and reliability).

Optimizing resilience expenditures and investments requires the organization to examine the optimization of costs for providing resilience services, determining a "return on resilience investment," and seeking out ways to continually reduce overall costs while providing and supporting an acceptable level of resilience services.

FRM:SG5.SP1 OPTIMIZE RESILIENCE EXPENDITURES

The costs to implement and manage strategies to protect and sustain services and assets are optimized against the benefits.

The costs of attaining and sustaining an adequate level of operational resilience for an asset or service must be optimized against the value of the asset or service to the organization in order to rationalize and maximize the organization's investment in resilience.

Overspending on resilience services potentially redirects limited resources away from assets and services that need them; underspending results in high-value assets and services that are not adequately protected and likely cannot be sustained when disrupted.

In addition, optimization helps the organization to determine the right mix of strategies. For example, the development of a service continuity plan may be a lower-cost option than implementing a protective control while still adequately satisfying the asset's or service's resilience requirements.

> These are examples of types of data that must be considered to perform optimization calculations and determination:
> - value data, such as the value of the asset or service (often expressed in terms of the revenue at risk or other cost due to the productive loss of the asset or service over a specified period of time)
> - cost data, which may be expressed in terms of
>   - the cost of implementing and maintaining an adequate internal control system for the asset or service
>   - the cost of developing, testing, and implementing service continuity plans for the asset or service
>   - other accumulated costs that support these activities (labor, overhead, etc.)

Typical work products

1. Optimization calculations by asset, service, or other unit
2. Plan for re-optimizing resilience costs and services

Subpractices

1. Establish the scope of optimization calculations and examination.

    The organization must determine which of the assets and services should be candidates for consideration of optimization review and calculation. The assets and services prioritized as high-value are a foundational starting point for determining the scope of this activity.

2. Perform optimization calculations on high-value assets and/or services.

    This process relies upon accurate and timely cost accumulation and reporting and an accurate determination of the value of the assets or services under examination. Optimization calculations should be expressed in monetary values, but other acceptable values to the organization can be considered when necessary (such as productive hours or product output).

3. Identify opportunities for optimization.

    Optimization is a balancing act that requires consideration of many aspects of managing operational resilience, including
    - the current cost of protective controls and their effectiveness
    - the costs related to developing, testing, and maintaining service continuity plans
    - the value of the asset or service to the organization
    - risk assumptions regarding how much risk the organization would be willing to accept based on the current and future optimized mix of strategies for protecting and sustaining services and assets

4. Revise strategies to provide optimal operational resilience.

    Organizations may choose to take no action after analyzing their current balance of strategies for protecting and sustaining services and assets or may choose to develop a revised mix of these strategies that balances cost with the value of the assets and services. When optimization is not performed, the organization should document the rationale for taking no action and ensure that appropriate stakeholders in the organization are notified of this decision.

FRM:SG5.SP2 DETERMINE RETURN ON RESILIENCE INVESTMENTS

A return on resilience investments is calculated where possible.

Resilience activities are typically viewed by the organization as cost-intensive rather than an investment in the organization's ability to move toward the achievement of strategic objectives. In much the same way that information technology was once seen as a burden to the organization but is now viewed as a strategic enabler, the resources used in supporting resilience activities must be transformed into an organizational asset that improves stakeholder value and organizational growth.

To the extent possible, it is to the organization's advantage to quantify the true return that the organization realizes on the investment it makes in resilience. To do this, the organization must establish and collect objective and quantifiable variables that it wants to include in the calculation of return on investment, including quantifiable benefits, earnings, and avoided costs that result from the investment.

Calculating the return on resilience investment not only provides a way to justify resilience costs but provides direct support for the contributions that managing operational resilience makes toward achieving strategic objectives.

Typical work products

1. Established variables for determining return on resilience investment (RORI)
2. Calculated RORI for select resilience investments

Subpractices

1. Establish and collect objective and quantifiable variables to include in the RORI calculation.

> These are examples of variables to include in the RORI calculation:
> - relevant investment costs, including
>   - costs of protection strategies
>   - costs of service continuity strategies
>   - other labor, overhead, and materials costs related to the service or asset for which RORI is being calculated
> - relevant benefits of the investment that can be quantified, including
>   - revenue improvements
>   - quantifiable improvements in productivity and output
>   - reductions in labor and overhead costs
>   - costs that have been avoided

2. Establish the scope of the calculation.
    The scope of the calculation must be determined by the organization. Scope includes
    - the time period being measured (one month, a year, a production period)
    - the services and/or assets for which RORI is being calculated
    - the targeted RORI that will be used to establish whether the calculated RORI is acceptable
3. Perform the RORI calculation.
    Example of a simple RORI calculation:
    $$\text{RORI} = \frac{\text{Benefits derived from investment in resilience}}{\text{Relevant costs of resilience}}$$
4. Analyze results of the RORI calculation.
    Compare the results of the RORI calculation based on the targeted results and analyze the difference. If the RORI is negative, the organization must consider strategies to improve the RORI.
5. Develop and implement strategies to improve RORI.
    This may involve an analysis of cost optimization (*as described in FRM:SG5.SP1*) and a determination of cost reduction strategies that will result in a projected RORI that is acceptable to the organization.

FRM:SG5.SP3 IDENTIFY COST RECOVERY OPPORTUNITIES

Opportunities for the organization to recover costs and investments in resilience management activities are identified.

Resilience activities are a cost of doing business. Organizational units must budget for resilience activities and include these costs in the production of products or the delivery of services. Allocation of these costs helps organizational units to budget for resilience activities.

Resilience investments are capitalized where possible so that their costs can be amortized, reducing impact on the bottom line. Moving resilience costs to a capital investment where possible boosts the value of services and assets and provides an amortizable asset to the organization in lieu of an expense that has direct impact on the organization's bottom line.

Improved operational resilience benefits everyone connected to the organization, including customers. Recovery of resilience costs means that the organization shares the burden for this activity with partners or others that have an active interest in the organization's operational resilience instead of assuming these costs as an expense.

Typical work products

1. Resilience cost charge-backs
2. Standard costs for services and products (which include resilience costs)

Subpractices

1. Determine areas where resilience costs can be assigned to and included in the production costs for services and products.
    Consider that resilience costs may be included in projects (software or system development, the construction of a facility, etc.) as well as in standard services and products.
2. Determine the appropriate level of resilience cost charge-backs.
    The level of resilience costs that are appropriate to include in standard costs is determined and validated.
3. Include resilience costs in the determination of standard costs for services and products.

Elaborated Generic Practices by Goal

Refer to the Generic Goals and Practices document in Appendix A for general guidance that applies to all process areas. This section provides elaborations relative to the application of the Generic Goals and Practices to the Financial Resource Management process area.

FRM:GG1 ACHIEVE SPECIFIC GOALS

The operational resilience management system supports and enables achievement of the specific goals of the Financial Resource Management process area by transforming identifiable input work products to produce identifiable output work products.

FRM:GG1.GP1 PERFORM SPECIFIC PRACTICES

Perform the specific practices of the Financial Resource Management process area to develop work products and provide services to achieve the specific goals of the process area.

Elaboration:

Specific practices FRM:SG1.SP1 through FRM:SG5.SP3 are performed to achieve the goals of the financial resource management process.

FRM:GG2 INSTITUTIONALIZE A MANAGED PROCESS

Financial resource management is institutionalized as a managed process.

FRM:GG2.GP1 ESTABLISH PROCESS GOVERNANCE

Establish and maintain governance over the planning and performance of the financial resource management process.

Refer to the Enterprise Focus process area for more information about providing sponsorship and oversight to the financial resource management process.

Subpractices

1. Establish governance over process activities.

    Elaboration:

    FRM:SG1.SP2 calls for putting a process and structure in place for financial governance over the entire operational resilience management system. FRM:SG2.SP3 describes the role of governance in assessing the risks and taking appropriate action when essential resilience functions are not adequately funded.

    > Governance over the financial resource management process may be exhibited by
    > - developing and publicizing higher-level managers' objectives for funding resilience obligations and activities
    > - establishing a higher-level position and steering committee to provide direct oversight of the process and to interface with higher-level managers
    > - sponsoring process policies, procedures, standards, and guidelines
    > - sponsoring and providing oversight of the organization's process program, plans, and strategies
    > - sponsoring and funding process activities
    > - aligning the funding of resilience obligations with identified resilience needs and objectives and stakeholder needs and requirements
    > - regular reporting from organizational units to higher-level managers on funding resilience activities and results based on funds expended
    > - making higher-level managers aware of applicable compliance obligations with respect to financial obligations, and regularly reporting on the organization's satisfaction of these obligations to higher-level managers
    > - creating dedicated higher-level management feedback loops on decisions about the process and recommendations for improving the process
    > - providing input on identifying, assessing, and managing operational risks due to resilience funding gaps or budget shortfalls
    > - conducting regular internal and external audits and related reporting to audit committees on the effectiveness of funding resilience obligations and activities
    > - creating formal programs to measure the effectiveness of process activities, and reporting these measurements to higher-level managers

2. Develop and publish organizational policy for the process.

    Elaboration:

    > The financial resource management policy should address
    > - responsibility, authority, and ownership for performing process activities
    > - resilience budgeting, funding, accounting, and accessing and applying funds
    > - procedures, standards, and guidelines for
    >   - conducting resilience accounting, including budgets, off-cycle and emergency funding, and financial reporting

- allocating resources
- preparing, reviewing, and approving funding justifications
- requesting emergency funding
- reviewing and validating labor and allocation charges
- determining COR and RORI *(Refer to FRM:SG4.SP2 and FRM:SG5.SP2.)*
• regularly reviewing and tracking the status of all operational resilience management budgets and expenditures, and adjusting as necessary, including regularly calculating and reviewing COR and RORI to ensure that these are within agreed-to thresholds
• methods for measuring adherence to policy, exceptions granted, and policy violations

FRM:GG2.GP2 PLAN THE PROCESS

Establish and maintain the plan for performing the financial resource management process.

Elaboration:

The plan for the financial resource management process should not be confused with goal FRM:SG2, in which resilience funding requirements and line-item and program and project budgets are established.

Subpractices

1. Define and document the plan for performing the process.
2. Define and document the process description.
3. Review the plan with relevant stakeholders and get their agreement.
4. Revise the plan as necessary.

FRM:GG2.GP3 PROVIDE RESOURCES

Provide adequate resources for performing the financial resource management process, developing the work products, and providing the services of the process.

Subpractices

1. Staff the process.

   Elaboration:

   These are examples of staff required to perform the financial resource management process:
   • staff responsible for building the business case for resilience
   • higher-level and other managers responsible for determining, committing, allocating, budgeting, applying, and controlling funds for the operational resilience management system
   • higher-level and other managers responsible for ensuring that the organization meets its resilience-relevant financial obligations

- higher-level and other managers responsible for establishing process policies and ensuring they are enforced
- security, business continuity, and IT operations officers, directors, and managers with operational resilience management roles and responsibilities that require financial resources
- line and business unit managers and project managers with operational resilience management roles and responsibilities that require financial resources
- owners and custodians of high-value services and assets that support the accomplishment of operational resilience management objectives
- staff responsible for financial accounting and reporting of operational resilience management activities, including COR and RORI
- staff responsible for managing external entities to ensure such entities meet their resilience financial obligations
- internal and external auditors responsible for reporting to appropriate committees on process effectiveness and the adequacy of financial resources to fund resilience obligations

Refer to the Organizational Training and Awareness process area for information about training staff for resilience roles and responsibilities.

Refer to the Human Resource Management process area for information about acquiring staff to fulfill roles and responsibilities.

2. Fund the process.

Elaboration:

This generic practice applies to funding financial resource management process activities. This practice is separate and distinct from funding all of the other operational resilience management process areas.

Refer to the Financial Resource Management process area for information about budgeting for, funding, and accounting for the operational resilience management system.

3. Provide necessary tools, techniques, and methods to perform the process.

Elaboration:

Many of these tools, techniques, and methods should be available as applied to other aspects of organizational financial resource management. The intent here is to apply these to managing operational resilience.

These are examples of tools, techniques, and methods to support the financial resource management process:
- methods, techniques, and tools that support developing the business case for resilience, such as cost-benefit and "what-if" analyses, as well as collecting historical resilience accounting data
- methods and tools for determining budgets for resilience activities, such as activity-based costing, zero-based budgeting, and incremental budgeting

- tools and techniques for financial management, such as cost and accounting tracking systems and effort reporting systems
- methods for performing funding gap analysis between funding needs and established budgets
- scheme for resilience cost accumulation and categorization, such as by organizational level, organizational unit, asset, service, project, or expenditure type (labor, overhead, asset category, etc.)
- chart of accounts specific to resilience activities
- tools for performing variance analysis
- methods, techniques, and tools for determining COR and RORI
- tools for performing optimization calculations by asset, by service, or another categorization approach

FRM:GG2.GP4 Assign Responsibility

Assign responsibility and authority for performing the financial resource management process, developing the work products, and providing the services of the process.

Elaboration:

FRM:SG1.SP2 and FRM:SG2.SP2 call for assigning responsibility and authority for resilience budgeting, funding, and accounting activities. FRM:SG2.SP2 states that operational resilience management budgets may be owned by various departments, and FRM:SG4.SP1 requires budget owners to be responsible for controlling resilience costs. These activities apply universally to the operational resilience management system.

Refer to the Human Resource Management process area for more information about establishing resilience as a job responsibility, developing resilience performance goals and objectives, and measuring and assessing performance against these goals and objectives.

Subpractices

1. Assign responsibility and authority for performing the process.
2. Assign responsibility and authority for performing the specific tasks of the process.

Elaboration:

Responsibility and authority for performing financial resource management tasks can be formalized by
- defining roles and responsibilities in the process plan to include roles responsible for addressing and tracking financial risk
- including process tasks and responsibility for these tasks in specific job descriptions, particularly those of staff who own high-value organizational assets and services

> - developing and implementing contractual instruments (including service level agreements) with external entities to ensure such entities meet their resilience financial obligations for outsourced functions
> - developing policy requiring organizational unit managers, line of business managers, project managers, and asset and service owners to participate in and derive benefit from the process for budgets, assets, and services under their ownership or custodianship
> - including process tasks in staff performance management goals and objectives with requisite measurement of progress against these goals

Refer to the External Dependencies Management process area for additional details about managing relationships with external entities.

3. Confirm that people assigned with responsibility and authority understand it and are willing and able to accept it.

FRM:GG2.GP5 TRAIN PEOPLE

Train the people performing or supporting the financial resource management process as needed.

Refer to the Organizational Training and Awareness process area for more information about training the people performing or supporting the process.

Refer to the Human Resource Management process area for more information about creating an inventory of skill sets, establishing a skill set baseline, identifying required skill sets, and measuring and addressing skill set deficiencies.

Subpractices

1. Identify process skill needs.

    Elaboration:

    > These are examples of skills required in the financial resource management process:
    > - knowledge of tools, techniques, and methods that can be used for budgeting, funding, accounting, accessing, applying, and reporting on resilience budgets and funding, including those necessary to perform the process using the selected methods, techniques, and tools identified in FRM:GG2.GP3 subpractice 3
    > - knowledge necessary to develop operational resilience management business cases, determine COR, and calculate RORI
    > - strong communication skills for conveying the operational resilience management and process strategy, funding sources, budget allocations, and financial status to higher-level managers and key stakeholders so as to obtain their commitment
    > - knowledge necessary to elicit and prioritize stakeholder requirements and needs and interpret them to develop effective process requirements, funding justifications, and budgets

2. Identify process skill gaps based on available resources and their current skill levels.
3. Identify training opportunities to address skill gaps.

   Elaboration:

   > These are examples of training topics:
   > - process concepts and activities (e.g., cost accounting, variance analysis, budgeting, optimization)
   > - cost-benefit and return on investment analyses
   > - developing process strategy and structure
   > - establishing and managing a continuous process
   > - using process methods, tools, and techniques, including those identified in FRM:GG2.GP3 subpractice 3

4. Provide training and review the training needs as necessary.

FRM:GG2.GP6 Manage Work Product Configurations

Place designated work products of the financial resource management process under appropriate levels of control.

   Elaboration:

   > These are examples of financial resource management work products placed under control:
   > - business case for resilience
   > - funding strategy and requirements for resilience activities
   > - resilience accounting policies and procedures
   > - financial management tools and techniques
   > - resilience budgets and budget projections, including those for the overall resilience program as well as line-item budgets at the enterprise and organizational unit or line of business level and project budgets
   > - funding gaps and decisions about addressing them
   > - funding justifications
   > - resilience financial reports, including variance analysis
   > - resilience cost accumulation and categorization scheme
   > - current and historical calculations for COR and RORI
   > - resilience cost charge-backs
   > - process plan
   > - contracts with external entities

FRM:GG2.GP7 Identify and Involve Relevant Stakeholders

Identify and involve the relevant stakeholders of the financial resource management process as planned.

Elaboration:

FRM:SG5.SP1 requires that stakeholders be notified when the organization decides not to revise strategies that protect and sustain services and assets for optimal operational resilience.

Subpractices

1. Identify process stakeholders and their appropriate involvement.

   Elaboration:

   > These are examples of stakeholders of the financial resource management process:
   > - managers and staff
   >   - contributing to and reviewing resilience funding requirements and funding assumptions
   >   - contributing to and reviewing the business case for the operational resilience management program and process
   >   - whose existing operating budgets may be allocated to fund operational resilience management activities (such as line and business unit managers, project managers, IT security, IT operations, and those responsible for services and products that may incur an add-on charge)
   >   - contributing to funding gap analysis and assessing risks to budget shortfalls
   >   - contributing to optimization and return on investment calculations
   >   - involved in the review and adjustment of strategies to protect and sustain services and assets
   > - owners of identified assets and services
   >   - for which operational resilience management budgets and resources are accessed, allocated, and applied
   >   - who help determine asset and service values and the cost of controls to aid in optimization and return on investment decisions
   > - custodians of identified assets and services (who may need to participate in funding planning)

   > Stakeholders are involved in various tasks in the financial resource management process, such as
   > - planning for the process
   > - making decisions about the process
   > - making commitments to process plans and activities
   > - communicating process plans and activities
   > - coordinating process activities
   > - identifying budget sources and ownership for operational resilience management activities

> - reviewing and appraising the effectiveness of process activities, including analysis of variances as well as COR and RORI calculations
> - establishing requirements for the process
> - resolving issues in the process
> - identifying stakeholders associated with each line of business, program, asset, and service budget that contributes to operational resilience management activities
> - identifying stakeholders that have to be notified when optimization is not performed and when optimization actions are not taken (Such notification includes supporting rationale.)

2. Communicate the list of stakeholders to planners and those responsible for process performance.
3. Involve relevant stakeholders in the process as planned.

FRM:GG2.GP8 MONITOR AND CONTROL THE PROCESS

Monitor and control the financial resource management process against the plan for performing the process and take appropriate corrective action.

Refer to the Monitoring process area for more information about the collection, organization, and distribution of data that may be useful for monitoring and controlling processes.

Refer to the Measurement and Analysis process area for more information about establishing process metrics and measurement.

Refer to the Enterprise Focus process area for more information about providing process information to managers, identifying issues, and determining appropriate corrective actions.

Subpractices

1. Measure actual performance against the plan for performing the process.
2. Review accomplishments and results of the process against the plan for performing the process.

   Elaboration:

   > These are examples of metrics for the financial resource management process:
   > - financial cost data that is used as the basis for developing resilience funding requirements
   > - COR and RORI calculations, both current and historical for trend analysis purposes
   > - percentage of resilience activities with required budgets assigned, allocated, and applied, organized by line of business unit, project, asset, and service or other meaningful categorization scheme
   > - percentage of resilience activities without required budget allocations for which gap and risk analysis has been performed

- percentage of resilience activities subject to off-cycle or off-budget funding requests
- percentage of resilience activities tracking to planned budgets
- percentage of resilience activities with budget variances outside of established thresholds and for which resolution plans have been developed to reduce or eliminate these variances
- percentage of financial exceptions by reporting period
- percentage of high-value assets and services for which optimization calculations have been performed
- percentage of optimization opportunities where no action has been taken
- number of financial resource risks referred to the risk management process; number of risks where corrective action is still pending (by risk rank)
- level of adherence to process policies; number of policy violations; number of policy exceptions requested and number approved
- number of process activities that are on track per plan
- rate of change of resource needs to support the process
- rate of change of costs to support the process

3. Review activities, status, and results of the process with the immediate level of managers responsible for the process and identify issues.

Elaboration:

Periodic reviews of the financial resource management process are needed to ensure that
- resilience activities are being budgeted, accounted for, and controlled
- strategic operational resilience management activities and budgets are on track
- key financial metrics are within acceptable ranges as demonstrated in governance dashboards or scorecards and financial reports
- administrative, technical, and physical controls are operating as intended
- controls are meeting the stated intent of the resilience requirements
- financial reports are provided to appropriate stakeholders in a timely manner
- actions resulting from internal and external audits are being closed in a timely manner

4. Identify and evaluate the effects of significant deviations from the plan for performing the process.
5. Identify problems in the plan for performing and executing the process.
6. Take corrective action when requirements and objectives are not being satisfied, when issues are identified, or when progress differs significantly from the plan for performing the process.
7. Track corrective action to closure.

FRM:GG2.GP9 OBJECTIVELY EVALUATE ADHERENCE

Objectively evaluate adherence of the financial resource management process against its process description, standards, and procedures, and address non-compliance.

Elaboration:

These are examples of activities to be reviewed:
- the identification, commitment, allocation, and tracking of budgets for operational resilience management system activities
- the assignment of responsibility, accountability, and authority for budgeting, funding, and accounting of operational resilience management system activities
- the determination of the adequacy of operational resilience management financial reviews, including funding gap analysis and budget variance analysis
- the identification of risks resulting from budget shortfalls
- the review of off-budget and off-cycle funding requests and approvals
- the definition of any financial exceptions
- action and inaction on operational resilience management optimization calculations
- use of risk-based and financial information for improving strategies for protecting and sustaining services and assets
- the alignment of stakeholder requirements with process plans
- assignment of responsibility, accountability, and authority for process activities
- determination of the adequacy of process reports and reviews in informing decision makers regarding the performance of operational resilience management activities and the need to take corrective action, if any

These are examples of work products to be reviewed:
- process plan and policies
- business case for resilience
- funding strategy and requirements for resilience activities
- financial management tools and techniques
- resilience budgets and budget projections, including those for the overall resilience program as well as line-item budgets at the enterprise and organizational unit or line of business level and project budgets
- funding gaps and decisions for addressing them
- funding justifications
- resilience financial reports, including variance analysis
- resilience cost accumulation and categorization scheme
- current and historical calculations for COR and RORI
- resilience cost charge-backs
- metrics for the process *(Refer to FRM:GG2.GP8 subpractice 2.)*
- contracts with external entities

FRM:GG2.GP10 REVIEW STATUS WITH HIGHER-LEVEL MANAGERS

Review the activities, status, and results of the financial resource management process with higher-level managers and resolve issues.

Elaboration:

Status reporting on the financial resource management process is likely part of the formal governance structure or may be performed through other organizational reporting requirements (such as through the chief financial officer or the chief resilience officer to an immediate superior). Audits of the process may be escalated to higher-level managers and board directors through the organization's audit committee of the board of directors or similar construct.

Refer to the Enterprise Focus process area for more information about providing sponsorship and oversight to the operational resilience management system.

FRM:GG3 INSTITUTIONALIZE A DEFINED PROCESS

Financial resource management is institutionalized as a defined process.

FRM:GG3.GP1 ESTABLISH A DEFINED PROCESS

Establish and maintain the description of a defined financial resource management process.

Establishing and tailoring process assets, including standard processes, are addressed in the Organizational Process Definition process area.

Establishing process needs and objectives and selecting, improving, and deploying process assets, including standard processes, are addressed in the Organizational Process Focus process area.

Subpractices

1. Select from the organization's set of standard processes those processes that cover the financial resource management process and best meet the needs of the organizational unit or line of business.
2. Establish the defined process by tailoring the selected processes according to the organization's tailoring guidelines.
3. Ensure that the organization's process objectives are appropriately addressed in the defined process, and ensure that process oversight extends to the tailored processes.
4. Document the defined process and the records of the tailoring.
5. Revise the description of the defined process as necessary.

FRM:GG3.GP2 COLLECT IMPROVEMENT INFORMATION

Collect financial resource management work products, measures, measurement results, and improvement information derived from planning and performing the process to support future use and improvement of the organization's processes and process assets.

Elaboration:

> These are examples of improvement work products and information:
> - issues with the budgeting, commitment, allocation, tracking, variance analysis, gap analysis, off-cycle budget allocation, and optimization processes
> - reports on financial exception
> - optimization calculations and action or inaction with respect to these
> - metrics and measurements of the viability of the process *(Refer to FRM:GG2.GP8 subpractice 2.)*
> - changes and trends in operating conditions, risk conditions, and the risk environment that affect operational resilience management budget allocations and expenditures
> - lessons learned in post-event review of incidents and disruptions in continuity
> - process lessons learned that can be applied to improve controls and inform future budgeting activities
> - reports on the effectiveness and weaknesses of controls
> - resilience requirements that are not being satisfied or that are being exceeded

Establishing the measurement repository and process asset library is addressed in the Organizational Process Definition process area. Updating the measurement repository and process asset library as part of process improvement and deployment is addressed in the Organizational Process Focus process area.

Subpractices

1. Store process and work product measures in the organization's measurement repository.
2. Submit documentation for inclusion in the organization's process asset library.
3. Document lessons learned from the process for inclusion in the organization's process asset library.
4. Propose improvements to the organizational process assets.

HUMAN RESOURCE MANAGEMENT
Enterprise

Purpose

The purpose of Human Resource Management is to manage the employment life cycle and performance of staff in a manner that contributes to the organization's ability to manage operational resilience.

Introductory Notes

The way that an organization hires, manages, and terminates staff can have a significant effect on the organization's operational resilience. The Human Resource Management process area seeks to address the management of staff in a way that minimizes operational risk and contributes to the organization's ability to manage operational resilience.

In Human Resource Management, the organization consciously approaches the acquisition of staff as an activity that can improve operational resilience by ensuring the acquisition of necessary skill sets and the avoidance of introducing operational risk that results from poor hiring decisions. Staff are acquired with a view toward their contributions to meeting the organization's mission with an understanding and acceptance of their role in sustaining operational resilience. This helps staff to begin acculturation to the organization's philosophy on operational resilience as they become part of the organization.

The management of staff performance is a means by which the organization can enforce (and reinforce) its philosophy of operational resilience. In Human Resource Management, the organization reinforces the connection between staff and operational resilience by using the performance management program as a way to acculturate staff to their resilience roles and responsibilities. Job descriptions include these roles and responsibilities, which are enforced by the organization by their inclusion in annual goal setting. The organization specifically establishes acceptable performance behaviors and measures compliance with these behaviors on a regular basis as part of the performance management cycle. As a result, the organization inculcates a resilience-aware and -ready culture that is essential for supporting the resilience process and the organizational mission.

Human Resource Management also seeks to ensure that the organization's human resources do not pose additional operational risk to the organization when their employment is voluntarily or involuntarily severed. Changes in employment can have significant effects on operational resilience by potentially disrupting the contributions of staff to the productive capacity of services. In addition, because staff typically have other organizational assets in their possession, when they vacate their positions the repossession of these assets by the organization may be critical to operational resilience, particularly if sensitive information assets or technology assets are not returned. Finally, involuntary separations may be disruptive—they can affect services and the morale and motivation of remaining staff. Thus, the organization must act in a way that minimizes the impact of involuntary terminations and limits unpredictable effects on productive capacity.

The Human Resource Management competency covers the employment life cycle—hiring, performance management, and termination. It has four specific goals addressing the identification of skill requirements, the acquisition of appropriate staff, the management of staff performance in supporting operational resilience, and the termination of staff in a manner that minimizes organizational impact.

As people are a ubiquitous resource in an organization, there are many aspects of human resources that affect operational resilience. *People Management is focused on the availability of people to the services that they support. The management of people through their employment life cycle and the effect on operational resilience are addressed in the Human Resource Management competency. Finally, promoting awareness of the organization's efforts and providing training to resilience staff for their roles in managing operational resilience are addressed in the Organizational Training and Awareness competency.*

Related Process Areas

The training of staff to meet resilience requirements, needs, and gaps is established and managed in the Organizational Training and Awareness process area.

Determining funding needs for providing human resources to the operational resilience management system is addressed in the Financial Resource Management process area.

The management of operational risks through their life cycle is addressed in the Risk Management process area.

The specific activities involved in cross-training and succession planning as a means for improving and sustaining resilience are addressed in the People Management process area.

The management of intellectual property and knowledge as high-value organizational information assets is addressed in the Knowledge and Information Management process area.

Managing access to organizational assets on a recurring basis is addressed in the Access Management process area.

Summary of Specific Goals and Practices

HRM:SG1 Establish Resource Needs
    HRM:SG1.SP1   Establish Baseline Competencies
    HRM:SG1.SP2   Inventory Skills and Identify Gaps
    HRM:SG1.SP3   Address Skill Deficiencies

HRM:SG2 Manage Staff Acquisition
    HRM:SG2.SP1   Verify Suitability of Candidate Staff
    HRM:SG2.SP2   Establish Terms and Conditions of Employment

HRM:SG3 Manage Staff Performance
    HRM:SG3.SP1   Establish Resilience as a Job Responsibility
    HRM:SG3.SP2   Establish Resilience Performance Goals and Objectives
    HRM:SG3.SP3   Measure and Assess Performance
    HRM:SG3.SP4   Establish Disciplinary Process

HRM:SG4 Manage Changes to Employment Status
    HRM:SG4.SP1   Manage Impact of Position Changes
    HRM:SG4.SP2   Manage Access to Assets
    HRM:SG4.SP3   Manage Involuntary Terminations

Specific Practices by Goal

HRM:SG1 ESTABLISH RESOURCE NEEDS

The resource needs to staff the activities and tasks of the organization's resilience program and plan are identified and satisfied.

Skilled people are absolutely essential to successfully managing operational resilience and meeting the objectives of the organization's resilience program. This is particularly true for staff who are actively engaged in all aspects of resilience work—performing security duties, supporting business continuity activities, and managing IT operations—because these skill sets are typically in short supply.

In order to determine what skills the organization must possess to meet its resilience needs, baseline competencies must be established relative to the resilience program and plan to ensure the entire range of necessary skills is identified. Against this baseline, the organization must determine what skills it currently possesses in its pool of available human resources and identify skill gaps that not only can affect its ability to manage operational resilience but can pose additional risk to the organization in meeting its strategic objectives.

In establishing resource needs, the organization determines its baseline competencies, takes an inventory of its current skill sets (based on available resources), identifies gaps and related risks, and develops and implements a strategy for closing these gaps and reducing risk to an acceptable level.

The specific practices in this goal are intended for application to positions that have resilience as their primary responsibility. However, these practices can apply universally to all positions in the organization, particularly vital positions.

HRM:SG1.SP1 ESTABLISH BASELINE COMPETENCIES

The staffing and skill needs relative to the operational resilience management system are established.

The baseline competencies represent the staffing and skill set needs relative to carrying out the organization's resilience program and plan. These staffing and skill set needs may be concentrated in resilience staff (i.e., with staff members whose traditional positions are in the fields of security or business continuity) and may also be found in positions in the operational and business units of the organization where resilience tasks are often performed.

Baseline competencies can be gathered through detailed examination of the organization's resilience program and plan, as well as through review of job descriptions that the organization has developed for resilience positions. In the event that the organization has not developed job descriptions, gathering baseline competencies may be more difficult and may require an inventory of resilience positions from which a foundation for developing more extensive baselines can be created. The baseline competencies should be based on what the organization needs, not what it currently has in terms of staff and skills. By determining what the organization needs, the appropriate target for a sufficient level of staffing and skills is established.

An organization may want to expand this activity to include vital positions in the organization. In this way, the organization establishes a baseline for the skills necessary to meet organizational goals and strategic objectives. If gaps in these skills exist, the risk that strategic objectives will not be achieved is increased and the operational resilience of associated services is impacted.

Because skilled labor is a significant component of the costs of providing resilience services, the establishment of baseline competencies can aid the organization in determining and validating funding needs for the operational resilience management system. *(Determining funding needs is performed in FRM:SG2.SP1 in the Financial Resource Management competency.)*

Typical work products

1. Baseline competencies
2. Job descriptions

Subpractices

1. Establish and document baseline competencies necessary to meet the needs of the organization's operational resilience management system.
   Baseline competencies may be as detailed as the organization needs to describe its required skill sets. This may involve many layers of information, including
   - role (security administrator, network administrator, CIO, etc.)
   - position (CIO, senior security analyst, network engineer, etc.)
   - skills (Java programming, Oracle DBA, etc.)

- certifications (CISSP, MSCE, etc.)
- aptitudes and job requirements (able to work long hours, travel, or be on call)

2. Create or update job descriptions to reflect base competencies.

   Baseline competencies should be reflected in job descriptions to ensure that the needs of the organization are translated into skilled positions. In some cases, existing job descriptions may be a means for collecting baseline competencies, but there may be cases where job descriptions do not exist even though there are documented skill needs for the operational resilience management program.

HRM:SG1.SP2 INVENTORY SKILLS AND IDENTIFY GAPS

The current skill set for operational resilience management is inventoried and gaps in necessary skills are identified.

A skills inventory is a means for identifying and documenting the current skill set of the organization's human resources. It provides a snapshot of the organization's current capabilities and can be used to diagnose resource shortages and gaps based on the organization's needs as represented in the baseline competencies.

A skills inventory is not a job inventory; it does not represent the positions that the organization currently has deployed on its organization chart. Instead, a skills inventory captures the skills and aptitudes of the current pool of human resources regardless of their job position or roles and responsibilities. The skills inventory provides a collective view of the organization's capabilities, which in some cases may be more extensive than the positions currently employed by the organization. For example, there may be staff members who speak more than one language but are not using that skill in their current positions.

Taking a skills inventory gives the organization a true picture of its current competencies from which critical analysis and review of needs can be performed. It may also reveal that staff members have skills that are needed by the organization that were not previously known.

Typically, a skills inventory is self-reported—that is, skills are reported by staff to the organization—which means that the organization may have to do some validation of these skill sets.

The skills inventory is compared to the organization's baseline competencies in an attempt to identify skills that the organization does not possess. The resulting skill gap provides insight into the skill needs of the organization. These skills may be keeping the organization from performing adequately in managing operational resilience and may result in additional risk to the organization. When the skills inventory is expanded beyond resilience positions, skill gaps may indicate areas of risk that result in potentially diminished operational resilience.

Typical work products

1. Skills inventory
2. Identified skill gaps

Subpractices

1. Develop a skills inventory, particularly relative to resilience skills.

    The skills inventory should contain at a minimum relevant skills, certifications, and aptitudes that staff members currently possess. The organization should concentrate on resilience skills; however, if the organization intends to use the inventory for other process improvement purposes, it may expand the inventory to other skills for vital positions.

    The skills inventory is typically taken by survey. However, this requires that the organization structure the survey in a way that will yield specific skills information. For example, rather than asking whether staff members have skills in programming languages, the organization may want to ask if they have skills in Java or other specific languages that are relevant. In addition, the organization may need to validate the skills survey. Certifications may be one way to validate that the staff member possesses the skills, as well as aptitude testing.

2. Compare baseline competencies to the current skills inventory.
3. Identify skill gaps and deficiencies.

    Skill gaps and deficiencies expose the areas where the organization does not have the expertise, aptitude, skill, or experience to meet current needs. These gaps can result in risks to the organization in that significant resilience activities may not be performed appropriately or may not be performed at all.

4. Develop processes to keep the skills inventory current and for performing regular comparison to baseline competencies.

    As operational complexity changes, so do the organization's needs and the skill sets available to meet these needs. Keeping the skills inventory current allows the organization to perform frequent comparisons so that gaps can be identified before they result in risk to the organization.

HRM:SG1.SP3 ADDRESS SKILL DEFICIENCIES

Gaps in skills necessary to meet operational resilience management needs are addressed.

Deficiencies in skills may impede the organization's ability to adequately manage operational resilience. These deficiencies pose risk to the organization that must be addressed.

Addressing these deficiencies comes at a cost to the organization. However, through identification, the organization has an opportunity to perform analysis on these gaps (i.e., determining the risk versus reward of closing the gaps based on the relative cost) and make sound decisions about how to address them. An organization can address skill deficiencies in a number of ways:

- Existing staff may be trained to acquire new skills.
- New staff may be hired to acquire the necessary skills.

- The skills may be acquired by outsourcing the work that requires them.
- Jobs may be restructured to take advantage of newly identified skills that were not previously known by the organization.

Skill gaps may require the organization to recast existing positions and create new positions with higher-level skill requirements. These positions may have to be "priced," and in some cases, existing staff members may have to be promoted (based upon proper training) into these jobs.

If the skill deficiencies pose risks to the organization, these risks should be referred to the organization's risk management process for analysis and resolution, particularly if the organization does not intend to address the existing gaps.

The management of operational risks through their life cycle is addressed in the Risk Management process area.

Training may be required to fill gaps in skills. (Processes for providing training to resilience staff are addressed in the Organizational Training and Awareness process area.)

Typical work products

1. Strategy for obtaining needed skills
2. Training plans
3. Job requisitions
4. Outsourcing agreements
5. Identification of related risks that must be addressed

Subpractices

1. Develop a strategy for addressing skill gaps.

    The organization should develop a strategy for addressing skill gaps based on the comparison process. The strategy should seek to fill the skill gaps at the lowest possible cost to the organization. Each skill gap should have a documented disposition for how the organization intends to obtain the necessary skills or a determination that the organization does not intend to address the skill gap.

    For those gaps that the organization consciously does not intend to close, resultant risks should be identified and referred to the risk management process.

2. Update job descriptions to incorporate missing skills as necessary.

    Job descriptions should be updated if missing skills have been identified and should be included as part of existing positions. This will provide a basis from which job restructuring can be performed and may result in new or updated job descriptions.

3. Develop job requisitions for unfilled positions.

    For positions that must be hired to acquire skills, the organization should develop appropriate job descriptions and document job requisitions as necessary.

    For skills that can be acquired through outsourcing, the organization should develop proposals that document the skill requirements.

4. Develop training plans for skills that can be obtained by existing staff.
   The development of training plans is addressed in the Organizational Training and Awareness process area.
5. Refer resulting risks to the risk management process for disposition.

HRM:SG2 MANAGE STAFF ACQUISITION

The acquisition of staff to meet operational needs is performed with consideration of the organization's resilience objectives.

The processes that the organization uses to acquire staff can result in exposing the organization to additional operational risk. The organization must verify that candidate staff have the appropriate skills, credentials, and background to ensure that their employment will not adversely affect operational capacity and resilience. In addition, the organization must institute contractual instruments that protect the organization's interests before, during, and after staff are employed by the organization. Proactively, these actions reduce the potential that staff acquisition will result in additional operational risks and provide a foundation from which newly acquired staff can support and contribute to the organization's efforts to manage operational resilience.

The specific practices in this goal apply universally to all staff who are acquired for positions in the organization. However, for positions that directly support the organization's resilience program and objectives, these practices may be expanded to include specific requirements for credentials and employment agreements. These practices may also apply to staff who are acquired through outsourcing arrangements.

HRM:SG2.SP1 VERIFY SUITABILITY OF CANDIDATE STAFF

Candidate staff are evaluated for suitability against position requirements and risks.

Verifying the suitability of candidate staff prior to their employment is a vital risk management activity. Whenever new staff members join an organization, they potentially present risk—they may fail to meet critical requirements for the position, resulting in poor operational performance, or they may pose unacceptable risk based on their prior experience, behavior, or other criteria. Candidates who pose unacceptable risk or who fail to meet certain criteria should be hired with caution and an explicit consideration of potential risks to operational resilience.

Pre-employment verification actions may include interviewing, performing reference checks, or other forms of screening. The actions taken to verify the suitability of candidate staff must be completed consistently, ethically, with an appropriate level of rigor, in accordance with applicable laws or regulations, and in proportion to the risk associated with the position. Data collected on candidate staff should be handled with an appropriate level of confidentiality.

Typical work products

1. Documented verification procedures and guidelines
2. Documented screening criteria
3. Verification data

Subpractices

1. Establish baseline verification criteria that apply to all positions in the organization.

    Baseline verification criteria are developed that apply to all positions in the organization. For very large organizations, there may be multiple baselines, each of which would apply to a large specific segment of the population.

    The baseline verification criteria should reflect the general resilience obligations expected of all staff members in the organization. In addition, the verification criteria must be set in compliance with all applicable privacy, employment, and other laws and regulations, organizational policies, and collective bargaining agreements.

    > Baseline verification criteria should include
    > - confirmation of identity
    > - character references, both professional and personal
    > - accuracy of résumé or curriculum vitae, including employment history, academic achievements, and professional qualifications
    > - credit checks
    > - criminal and/or court record checks
    > - specific regulatory screening requirements, such as pre-employment drug testing
    >
    > Baseline verification criteria should be documented, included in job descriptions, and maintained in accordance with the organization's human resources policies and practices.

2. Establish job-specific verification criteria that apply to vital positions.

    Baseline requirements are supplemented with additional verification requirements for particular positions and vital staff. For example, the baseline requirements may be more extensive for positions that directly affect the organization's operational resilience (such as security positions and business continuity staff).

    For vital positions, additional attention should be given to ensure that specific requirements (including any additional resilience obligations) are appropriate to the circumstances of the position and that they are sufficient, given the risks associated with the position.

    > Specific verification criteria should include
    > - security clearances or other federal credentials
    > - specific certifications or accreditations required by the position (such as CISSP, CBCP, CISA, and CPA)
    > - certain physical requirements
    > - citizenship requirements (which may preclude employment in some positions)
    > - legal requirements

The additional verification criteria should be documented, included in job descriptions, and maintained in accordance with the organization's human resources policies and practices.

3. Establish verification program and procedures.

    A program is established and managed for performing the background verification checks on employment candidates. The program should include the design and documentation of procedures and the allocation and authorization of staff to perform the verification screening.

> Verification procedures should address
> - how and when verification checks are to be carried out
> - storage of the data collected during the procedures
> - handling of notifications of screening results, both within the organization and to the candidate
> - whether the candidate should be informed of the screening beforehand
> - compliance with any applicable rules, regulations, organizational policies, laws, collective bargaining agreements, or other requirements
> - variations of the verification process for contract, temporary, or other external entity staff

    Staff who are responsible for the verification procedures should be identified and given the necessary tools, resources, training, and authority to carry out the verification process.

4. Review and revise verification criteria and program as required.

    The verification criteria, program, and procedures should be reviewed and revised on a regular basis or as required to address changes in the resilience requirements for staff.

HRM:SG2.SP2 ESTABLISH TERMS AND CONDITIONS OF EMPLOYMENT

Employment agreements appropriate for the position and role are developed and executed.

Many positions in the organization require extraordinary levels of responsibility and trust. While these positions are needed by the organization to meet its strategic objectives, they can also expose the organization to risk, particularly when the staff who occupy these positions leave the organization. For this reason, the organization should establish baseline terms and conditions for all positions and document these terms and conditions in job descriptions.

Situations under which specific terms and conditions should be considered include positions that

- require high levels of trust and authority
- require confidential handling of knowledge and experience (trade secrets and intellectual property) gained during tenure with the organization

- provide access to information that could result in consequences to the organization if disclosed, including information that could result in direct impact on the life, safety, and health of staff and customers
- require privileged access to organizational facilities or organizational systems, networks, and other technical infrastructure components

Terms and conditions must often be enforced through employment agreements or similar constructs, executed before the candidate begins employment. Typically, these agreements include confidentiality and non-disclosure agreements and non-compete agreements, but the organization may have various other constructs at its disposal, so long as enforcement would survive legal challenges.

The management of intellectual property and knowledge as a high-value organizational information asset is addressed in the Knowledge and Information Management process area.

Typical work products

1. Job descriptions
2. Criteria for terms and conditions of employment
3. (Signed) employment agreements

Subpractices

1. Establish baseline terms and conditions of employment that apply to all positions in the organization.

    Baseline terms and conditions of employment are established that apply to all positions in the organization. For very large organizations, there may be multiple baselines, each of which would apply to a large specific segment of the population.

    The baseline terms and conditions of employment should reflect the resilience obligations of the position. In addition, the terms and conditions must be set in compliance with all applicable laws and regulations, organizational policies, and collective bargaining agreements.

> These are areas to consider when establishing the terms and conditions of employment:
> - the level of confidentiality and sensitivity of information that the candidate will require in a specific position
> - the organization's resilience policies and the organization's right to amend such policies
> - the organization's obligation for handling the staff member's personal information
> - any legal requirements with which staff are required to comply
> - the organization's policies on copyrights, trademarks, patents, and other intellectual property ownership issues

> - any obligations to report risks or threats
> - codes of ethics or codes of conduct that are required
> - conflict of interest or conflict of influence requirements, including notification and disclosure procedures and requirements
> - responsibilities that extend beyond the organization's premises or outside of normal working hours
> - agreements to changes in duties as a result of or during events
> - rights, actions, and procedures that will be followed in the event that the staff member fails to comply with the terms and conditions of employment

Baseline terms and conditions of employment should be documented, associated with job descriptions, and maintained in accordance with the organization's human resources policies and practices.

2. Ensure that terms and conditions are clearly documented in job descriptions.
3. Execute agreements as necessary to enforce employment terms and conditions.

In conjunction with an offer for employment, candidate staff should be made aware of all terms and conditions of employment in writing. As part of the offer acceptance, candidate staff should be required to execute agreements to indicate their acknowledgment of and agreement to all terms and conditions of employment.

It is appropriate and necessary for certain terms and conditions, such as non-disclosure requirements, to continue for a defined period of time after employment ends.

HRM:SG3 MANAGE STAFF PERFORMANCE

The performance of staff to support the organization's resilience program is managed.

The active management of staff helps to ensure their availability, productivity, and contribution to high-value services throughout their employment life cycle. By actively managing staff for resilience, the organization maintains staff awareness of and focus on resilience roles and responsibilities, equips them with the resources, skills, and abilities to perform resilience functions, and reduces the risk of human actions (erroneous and otherwise) that may cause harm to the organization's resilience.

A primary component of effective performance management is to maintain a continual dialogue between manager and staff member about work performance. Incorporating resilience roles, responsibilities, and functions into the dialogue is an effective way to emphasize the individual's contributions to managing and sustaining the organization's operational resilience. Performance appraisals that emphasize resilience objectives provide a regular checkpoint to document performance against these objectives and to gather data for improvement if necessary.

In this goal, it is assumed that the organization has an established performance management process (or practices) into which resilience measures and controls can be inserted. To establish resilience as a performance management target, the organization must first establish resilience as a job responsibility, establish resilience goals and objectives, measure performance against these objectives, and implement processes to correct behavior when necessary.

HRM:SG3.SP1 ESTABLISH RESILIENCE AS A JOB RESPONSIBILITY

Resilience obligations for staff are communicated, agreed to, and documented as conditions of employment.

Resilience obligations should be clearly documented in job descriptions so that staff members know their responsibilities and can plan their performance accordingly. The definition of resilience obligations in the job description establishes the foundation for performance management and measurement of the staff member's commitment to helping the organization sustain operational resilience.

When hiring staff, it is also important that resilience obligations be documented as part of the terms and conditions of employment. When employment is offered to a candidate, it should be offered subject to the candidate's understanding of resilience obligations and other terms and conditions of employment. The organization and the candidate should execute contractual agreements to signify agreement and commitment to the terms and conditions of employment.

Typical work products

1. Job descriptions

Subpractices

1. Insert resilience obligations into job descriptions.
    All job descriptions in the organization, particularly those with vital roles, should clearly state the candidate's or staff member's resilience roles, responsibilities, and job tasks.
2. Ensure that job descriptions and resilience requirements are communicated to candidate staff prior to employment.
    Candidate staff should be provided with written job descriptions that document the resilience requirements and obligations for the position.

HRM:SG3.SP2 ESTABLISH RESILIENCE PERFORMANCE GOALS AND OBJECTIVES

Goals and objectives for supporting the organization's resilience program are established as part of the performance management process.

Goals and objectives are a key administrative control for managing the resilience contributions of the organization's staff. Goals and objectives provide time-sensitive focal points and a solid framework for managing the resilience roles, responsibilities, and functions of staff. Additionally, they reinforce the expectation that staff will behave in compliance with organizational resilience policies and avoid actions, activities, and behaviors that expose the organization to risk.

To effectively use goals and objectives to support resilience, the organization should ensure that goals and objectives are established and reviewed on a regular basis, are maintained and updated in writing, and include behavioral and functional targets for resilience. Communicating about and developing resilience goals and objectives in collaboration with staff provide a strong cultural reinforcement of the importance of the organization's resilience posture and practices.

From a practical standpoint, resilience goals and objectives may specifically include security goals, business continuity goals, information (or other asset) protection goals, and other objectives related to appropriate behaviors and activities in support of the organization's resilience posture and program.

The resilience goals and objectives addressed in this specific practice are intended to be applied generally to all relevant staff members in the organization. However, for staff whose job responsibilities are directly focused on managing operational resilience (such as security managers and business continuity planners), a more specific and extensive set of resilience goals and objectives would be developed for performance management purposes.

Typical work products

1. Resilience goals and objectives

Subpractices

1. Review resilience obligations, roles, and responsibilities of the position as the basis for establishing resilience goals and objectives.

   Managers should review the resilience obligations for the position when establishing goals and objectives for a specific person. The relevant resilience requirements of the services and assets under the manager's and the staff member's control should also be established as a basis for direct goals and objectives related to resilience.

   This review provides an opportunity for updating the resilience obligations in job descriptions.

2. Formalize and establish resilience goals and objectives in writing.

   Resilience goals and objectives are established in writing on a regular basis as part of the organization's performance management process. These goals and objectives should align with
   - the organization's philosophy on operational resilience
   - the objectives of the organization's resilience plan and program
   - the relevant resilience requirements in the staff member's organizational unit or line of business (for assets and services under the staff member's ownership and control)
   - the resilience obligations as documented in the staff member's job description

Resilience goals and objectives should be specific, measurable, relevant, and timely.

> Resilience goals and objectives may include specific targets, behaviors, or measures that contribute to the organization's ability to manage operational resilience, such as
> - development, implementation, and enforcement of resilience requirements for assets and services under the staff member's control
> - compliance with organizational security policies
> - adherence to IT best practices or guidelines
> - awareness of resilience issues and demonstration of appropriate resilience behaviors
> - appropriate handling of sensitive information
> - work practices associated with accessing information, technology, and facilities
> - maintaining good password hygiene
> - maintenance of necessary skills and qualifications
> - providing resilience leadership
> - demonstrating readiness for resilience events or incidents

3. Ensure that the staff members understand resilience goals and objectives.

HRM:SG3.SP3 MEASURE AND ASSESS PERFORMANCE

Performance against goals and objectives is measured, achievements are acknowledged, and corrective actions are identified and communicated.

Measuring performance and providing feedback against established resilience goals and objectives and the organization's resilience policies are important mechanisms for encouraging acceptable behaviors. Performance metrics should be collected throughout a staff member's tenure, and feedback should be provided to the staff member on a regular basis.

Communication about performance should be a regular part of the dialogue between staff members and their managers and should be the focus of regular, documented performance appraisals. Including resilience topics in such dialogues is a means to promote awareness of and encourage resilience contributions.

Data collection and communications about staff members' performance should be performed in compliance with organizational policies, applicable regulations, and applicable collective bargaining agreements.

Typical work products

1. Performance evaluations
2. Recommendations for improvement
3. Revised resilience goals and objectives

Subpractices

1. Measure performance against resilience goals and objectives.

   Data should be collected throughout the goals and objectives period on the performance of staff against resilience goals and objectives. Additionally, any violations of the organization's resilience policies, as well as any exemplary resilience behaviors or accomplishments, should be noted.

2. Conduct performance evaluations.

   Performance feedback should be part of the routine dialogue between managers and staff. Formal performance evaluations should be conducted according to the organization's standard practices and schedule. The evaluations should include feedback on the achievement of resilience goals and objectives, any violations of the organization's resilience policies, any behaviors or actions that expose the organization to risk, and any exemplary behaviors or achievements related to resilience.

   Performance evaluations should be documented in writing.

3. Acknowledge performance achievements as appropriate.

   Private and public acknowledgment of resilience performance achievements can have a powerful effect on creating and reinforcing a culture of resilience.

4. Identify improvement opportunities and take corrective actions as necessary.

   Performance feedback conversations and the performance review in particular are opportunities to design and implement improvement plans or to take corrective actions for staff members as appropriate. Improvement plans are appropriate to address deficiencies in performance as well as to facilitate learning so that additional resilience roles and responsibilities can be assigned.

   Corrective actions should be taken whenever staff members violate policies or otherwise behave in a manner that creates risk for the organization.

5. Revise goals and objectives as needed.

   Goals and objectives should be revised as a routine part of the performance conversation and in consideration of the organization's operational environment.

HRM:SG3.SP4 ESTABLISH DISCIPLINARY PROCESS

A disciplinary process is established for staff who violate resilience policies.

A disciplinary process is an essential administrative control for enforcing organizational resilience policies. Awareness of the disciplinary process provides staff an additional incentive to comply with the organization's resilience policies and ensures fair and appropriate treatment in the event that wrongdoing is suspected. From the organization's perspective, a formalized disciplinary process provides a preplanned response to suspected resilience infractions that is designed to address all relevant concerns while protecting the organization to the fullest extent possible on all fronts.

The disciplinary process should be formalized and documented. It should ensure fair treatment of staff in compliance with all applicable regulations and agreements, protect the organization's interests, and include a range of acceptable responses that correspond to the seriousness of the infraction.

Investigation of resilience or security breaches is a critical first step of the formalized disciplinary process.

Typical work products

1. Investigation reports
2. Relevant documentation of disciplinary action

Subpractices

1. Establish an investigation process.
   An investigation process should be established to collect and review information (or evidence) whenever a staff member is suspected (or known) to have committed a breach of resilience policies or practices or to have otherwise performed in a manner that creates risk for the organization.
2. Establish a disciplinary process.
   Most organizations have disciplinary processes that address violations of the organization's policies and procedures. However, because violations of resilience policies can result in additional risk to the organization, it is imperative that the disciplinary process specifically address resilience infractions.

   The disciplinary process should provide for graduated response depending on the severity of the infraction as well as the staff member's role in the organization, tenure and level of training, and whether previous offenses have been documented. The process should comply with all relevant legal and regulatory bodies and should make provisions for coordination with public authorities, depending on the severity of the infraction. *(Some infractions may have to be managed through the organization's incident management processes, as described in the Incident Management and Control process area.)*
3. Revise the disciplinary process as needed.
   Revisions to the disciplinary process may be needed in response to changes in organizational policy, regulatory or compliance obligations, collective bargaining agreements, or contracts. It may also be appropriate to revise the process to incorporate lessons learned from experience in executing the process.

HRM:SG4 MANAGE CHANGES TO EMPLOYMENT STATUS

Changes in the employment status of staff members in the organization are managed.

There are specific risks that the organization must address relating to changes in the employment status of staff members. For example, when staff *voluntarily* terminate their employment (either to leave the organization or to change positions within the organization), the organization must be able to cover their roles and responsibilities, manage their access to high-value organizational assets, and manage the impact of their departure on the operational environment, including the effects on remaining staff.

When staff leave the organization *involuntarily*, additional risks are presented. In addition to covering the vacated roles and responsibilities, the organization must manage the termination in a way that minimizes operational impact and retains the organization's assets in their intended form and function to the extent possible (information, technology, or facilities are not destroyed, etc.). Assets in the possession of the terminated staff member, particularly information and technology assets, must be collected as well so that the potential effect on services that rely on those assets is minimized.

To manage the effects of employment changes on the organization's operational resilience, the organization must manage the impact of position changes, manage possession of organizational assets, and address the unique challenges and threats posed by involuntary separation and termination.

HRM:SG4.SP1 MANAGE IMPACT OF POSITION CHANGES

Administrative controls are established to sustain functions, obligations, and vital roles upon position changes or terminations.

When a staff member vacates a job (either through job change or voluntary or involuntary termination), one of the primary concerns for the organization is to sustain any resilience functions, obligations, or roles for which the person was responsible. This can be accomplished through reassignment of functions and roles to others and through reinforcement of obligations that persist beyond the period of employment.

Reassignment of resilience roles and functions to others should take place as soon as possible upon termination (or in advance of termination where possible) to ensure sustained coverage for the organization. Whenever possible, resilience roles and functions for the position being vacated should be reviewed with the person leaving to ensure that all such roles and functions are identified for reassignment.

Certain resilience obligations, such as confidentiality of information, trade secrets, and intellectual property, will persist beyond the period of employment for a defined length of time. Any such obligations should have been established upon hiring. When a position is vacated, it is prudent to review the obligations to ensure renewed or continued awareness on the part of the departing staff member.

Typical work products

1. Exit interview notes
2. Plan for sustaining roles and responsibilities
3. Executed confidentiality agreements
4. Executed non-compete agreements

Subpractices

1. Establish and execute an exit interview process.

    An exit interview process should be established. Exit interviews should be held with all persons who voluntarily leave a position, whether they are separating from the organization or taking another position within the organization.

    > Topics addressed in the exit interview should include
    > - any specific resilience roles and functions that are or have been performed by the departing person (This information is useful to confirm the job description and to enable the reassignment of the roles and functions.)
    > - review of any obligations that persist beyond the period of employment (or period in the position), such as confidentiality provisions
    > - inventory of organizational assets in the possession of the departing person and coordination of their return *(see PM:SG3.SP2)*, including badges, data, and mobile devices
    > - elicitation and review of knowledge held by the departing person that may be vital to the organization and that may not be documented or otherwise available to the organization *(The management of knowledge is addressed in the Knowledge and Information Management process area.)*

2. Develop a plan for reassignment of roles and responsibilities.

    To the extent possible, the organization should have developed a plan for the reassignment of roles and responsibilities for vital positions and staff in advance of voluntary or involuntary separation. This plan may include various strategies such as job sharing, outsourcing, cross-training, and succession planning, depending on the importance of the job position and role in the organization. The plan should be able to be executed in advance of a voluntary separation to ensure a smooth transition with minimal impact on resilience or immediately upon involuntary separation. For staff whose roles and responsibilities are directly focused on resilience activities, particularly those who have "superuser" or other privileged or trusted status, these plans are absolutely essential.

    The specific activities involved in cross-training and succession planning as a means for improving and sustaining resilience are addressed in the People Management process area.

3. Reassign resilience roles and functions upon a staff member's departure from a position.
4. Review and confirm understanding of confidentiality agreements and obtain assurances for compliance.

    For staff in roles that require ongoing considerations of confidentiality and non-compete clauses that extend beyond their current employment, the organization must establish that separated staff understand their responsibilities and agree to be bound by them. Departing staff members should be reminded of their agreements and the terms of the agreements should be reiterated to ensure understanding. The organization should also clearly explain the potential consequences of violating these agreements.

HRM:SG4.SP2 MANAGE ACCESS TO ASSETS

Access to and possession of organizational assets relative to position changes is managed.

When staff members vacate their positions, they are typically in possession of important organizational assets—information (usually in the form of organizational procedures, policies and manuals, trade secrets, customer data, and intellectual property) and technology (cell phones, PDAs, personal computers, etc.). These assets can be tangible (such as paper reports) or intangible (such as access to the customer information database). In addition, staff possess organizational credentials—ID cards, access cards, parking passes, etc.—that provide them access to these organizational assets, including facilities where they once worked. Access to these assets, including credentials, must be managed in order to limit potential effects on the organization when staff members vacate their positions. This is particularly true when a staff member's separation is involuntary.

For staff who are in resilience positions or who have privileged or trusted access to assets, managing access to and possession of these assets is extremely important for preventing potential disruptions or effects on operational resilience.

The processes for managing access to organizational assets on a day-to-day basis are addressed in the Access Management process area.

Typical work products

1. Asset inventory checklist
2. Asset inventory sign-off
3. Request for changes to access privileges
4. Verification of access changes

Subpractices

1. Secure the return of all organizational assets, property, and information upon a staff member's departure.

    Procedures should be put in place to ensure that all of the organizational assets, property, and information in the possession of a staff member are returned when the staff member leaves the organization. For staff members who voluntarily separate from the organization, this process should be performed in advance of their separation date. For involuntarily separations, this process should be performed without advance notice immediately upon separation.

> These are examples of organizational assets that should be returned upon departure:
> - software
> - identification badges and access cards
> - computing and communications devices and hardware (including personal computers, PDAs, cell phones, mobile email devices, pagers, and job-specific tools and equipment such as meter-reading devices)
> - corporate documents (such as policy and procedures manuals, customer lists, and other proprietary documents)
> - notes and documents that contain organizational information (trade secrets, intellectual property, customer contracts)
> - tools and other equipment
> - credit cards
> - electronic media
> - information, in any form (paper, electronic), including intellectual property

In cases where staff members use their own computing equipment or media or are allowed to purchase corporate equipment in their possession, procedures should be in place to retrieve organizational information and/or software from such equipment and to securely erase corporate information or software from any such media.

In many organizations the return of assets is coordinated as part of the exit review process *(see HRM:SG4.SP1)*.

2. Inventory all organizational assets, property, and information in possession of staff upon position changes, and make necessary adjustments.
3. Discontinue all access to organizational assets upon termination or position changes.

   Access rights to all organizational assets, including facilities, technology, and information, should be discontinued upon termination. *(Access privileges and controls are addressed in the Access Management process area.)*

HRM:SG4.SP3 *Manage Involuntary Terminations*

Administrative controls and procedures are established to manage the effects of involuntary terminations.

Certain terminations are involuntary—typically related to job performance or a violation of company policy, rules, or regulations. Special controls and procedures must be established to address and manage the potential impacts on the organization in these cases.

When terminations are involuntary, staff may exhibit a range of behaviors from introspection to aggressiveness. In many cases, there is increased risk of impact on the organization, either directly and immediately (such as causing damage to organizational assets) or after termination (such as causing reputation damage or by exposing confidential information). To the extent possible, the organization must act to minimize impact through proactive actions that occur before termination and through resilience practices that allow the organization to swiftly address issues and ensure affected services are sustained.

Typical work products

1. Criteria for involuntary terminations
2. Procedures for managing involuntary terminations

Subpractices

1. Establish criteria for determining potential risks related to involuntary terminations.

    Because the effects of involuntary terminations can be unpredictable, criteria should be established for advance consideration of possible effects. This helps the organization to predetermine the type and extent of response necessary during the termination process and the immediate aftereffects.

> These are examples of criteria that should be considered with involuntary terminations:
> - Employee (or consultant) is disgruntled or is considered to be psychologically unstable.
> - Employee (or consultant) has committed serious violations of organizational policies or is under suspicion for such violations.
> - Employee (or consultant) has been charged with or convicted of a felony offense under the law.
> - Employee (or consultant) has exhibited violent behaviors or tendencies.

1. Establish procedures for managing involuntary terminations.

    Procedures should be established for managing involuntary terminations. Ideally, these procedures should be implemented in advance of termination activities so that the impact of the termination and the potential effects are minimized.

> These are examples of procedures that may be appropriate in involuntary terminations:
> - cessation of access privileges prior to or precisely concurrent with announcing an involuntary termination
> - escort from the organization's premises
> - coordination with public law enforcement authorities
> - identification, isolation, and review of systems or information that may have been compromised by the employee

Elaborated Generic Practices by Goal

Refer to the Generic Goals and Practices document in Appendix A for general guidance that applies to all process areas. This section provides elaborations relative to the application of the Generic Goals and Practices to the Human Resource Management process area.

HRM:GG1 ACHIEVE SPECIFIC GOALS

The operational resilience management system supports and enables achievement of the specific goals of the Human Resource Management process area by transforming identifiable input work products to produce identifiable output work products.

HRM:GG1.GP1 PERFORM SPECIFIC PRACTICES

Perform the specific practices of the Human Resource Management process area to develop work products and provide services to achieve the specific goals of the process area.

Elaboration:

Specific practices HRM:SG1.SP1 through HRM:SG4.SP3 are performed to achieve the goals of the human resource management process.

HRM:GG2 INSTITUTIONALIZE A MANAGED PROCESS

Human resource management is institutionalized as a managed process.

HRM:GG2.GP1 ESTABLISH PROCESS GOVERNANCE

Establish and maintain governance over the planning and performance of the human resource management process.

Refer to the Enterprise Focus process area for more information about providing sponsorship and oversight to the human resource management process.

Subpractices

1. Establish governance over process activities.

   Elaboration:

   > Governance over the human resource management process may be exhibited by
   > - developing and publicizing higher-level managers' objectives and requirements for the process
   > - establishing a higher-level position, such as the director of human resources or the equivalent, responsible for the resilience of the organization's human resources

- establishing oversight over the verification, acquisition, management, and termination of human resources, including terms and conditions of employment, confidentiality agreements, and the plan for sustaining and reassigning roles and responsibilities for vital positions
- establishing acceptable performance behaviors to build a resilience-aware and -ready culture, and establishing measures that demonstrate compliance with these behaviors
- sponsoring and providing oversight of policy, procedures, standards, and guidelines for the acceptable performance of human resources, the disciplinary process for non-compliance with policy, and establishing personal ownership and responsibility for resilience
- providing oversight over the establishment, implementation, and maintenance of the organization's internal control system for human resources
- making higher-level managers aware of applicable laws, compliance obligations, collective bargaining agreements, and contracts related to human resources, and regularly reporting on the organization's satisfaction of these obligations to higher-level managers
- sponsoring and funding process activities
- providing guidance for identifying skill requirements and suitability of candidates to meet resilience objectives, including the identification of vital positions
- regular reporting from organizational units to higher-level managers on process activities and results
- creating dedicated higher-level management feedback loops on decisions about the process and recommendations for improving the process
- providing input on identifying, assessing, and managing operational risks related to human resources, particularly when managing changes to employment status (e.g., investigation, disciplinary action, layoff, and termination)
- conducting regular internal and external audits and related reporting to appropriate committees on human resource controls and the effectiveness of the process
- creating formal programs to measure the effectiveness of process activities, and reporting these measurements to higher-level managers

2. Develop and publish organizational policy for the process.

   Elaboration:

   The human resource management policy should address
   - responsibility, authority, and ownership for performing process activities
   - acceptable performance of human resources with respect to operational resilience management, including establishing personal ownership and responsibility for resilience
   - disciplinary action and termination
   - procedures, standards, and guidelines for
     – describing and identifying baseline competencies for resilience staff

> - documenting descriptions, resilience roles, and skills needed for roles
> - criteria for screening and determining suitability of candidates for sensitive positions
> - terms and conditions of employment
> - managing operational risks resulting from human resources
> - sustaining and reassigning vital roles and responsibilities
> - managing the impact of changes to employment status
> - establishing, implementing, and maintaining an internal control system for human resources
>
> - methods for measuring adherence to policy, exceptions granted, policy violations, and for the investigation and discipline process for non-compliance with policy

HRM:GG2.GP2 PLAN THE PROCESS

Establish and maintain the plan for performing the human resource management process.

Elaboration:

A plan for performing the human resource management process is created to ensure that qualified staff are hired and that they perform in a manner that contributes to the organization's ability to manage operational resilience. The plan must address the resilience requirements of human resources, the dependencies of services on such resources, and the roles that people fulfill at various levels of the organization. In addition, because human resources are the engine behind many services in the organization, the plan must extend to external conditions that can enable or adversely affect the resilience of people.

The plan for the human resource management process should not be confused with the organization's resilience program and plan as described in HRM:SG1.SP1, training plans as described in HRM:SG1.SP3, improvement plans as described in HRM:SG3.SP3, and plans for sustaining and reassigning roles and responsibilities as described in HRM:SG4.SP1. The plan for the human resource management process details how the organization will perform human resource management, including the development of strategies and plans for managing people.

Subpractices

1. Define and document the plan for performing the process.

   Elaboration:

   Special consideration in the plan may have to be given to skill development and planning for sustaining and reassigning various roles. These activities address protecting and sustaining human resources to support operational resilience.

Special consideration in the plan may have to be given to the establishment, implementation, and maintenance of an internal control system for human resources.
2. Define and document the process description.
3. Review the plan with relevant stakeholders and get their agreement.
4. Revise the plan as necessary.

HRM:GG2.GP3 *Provide Resources*

Provide adequate resources for performing the human resource management process, developing the work products, and providing the services of the process.

Elaboration:

The diversity of activities required to protect and sustain people requires an extensive level of organizational resources and skills and a significant number of external resources. In addition, these activities require a major commitment of financial resources (both expense and capital) from the organization.

Subpractices

1. Staff the process.

    Elaboration:

    > These are examples of staff required to perform the human resource management process:
    > - staff responsible for
    >   - information, application, and technical security
    >   - business continuity and disaster recovery
    >   - workforce development and benefits administration
    >   - ensuring the success of the performance management process
    >   - training and skill development
    >   - career development counseling
    >   - managing external entities that have contractual obligations for human resource management activities
    > - staff involved in operational risk management, including those involved with insurance and risk indemnification
    > - staff involved in organizational change management
    > - internal and external auditors responsible for reporting to appropriate committees on process effectiveness

    Refer to the Organizational Training and Awareness process area for information about training staff for resilience roles and responsibilities.

2. Fund the process.
   Refer to the Financial Resource Management process area for information about budgeting for, funding, and accounting for human resource management.
3. Provide necessary tools, techniques, and methods to perform the process.

   Elaboration:

   > These are examples of tools, techniques, and methods to support the human resource management process:
   > - a performance management system that supports establishing performance goals and objectives and evaluating performance against them
   > - job description templates that reflect standard resilience obligations, roles and responsibilities, required skills, and specific job requirements (e.g., certifications)
   > - methods, techniques, and tools for identifying, documenting, maintaining, and validating the resilience skills of current human resources as a skills inventory
   > - tools for performing skill gap analysis (between baseline competencies and current skill sets)
   > - training plan templates for specific roles and responsibilities
   > - methods, techniques, and tools necessary to perform background verification checks
   > - methods, techniques, and tools to capture, securely store, and ensure authorized access to sensitive verification data
   > - templates for employment agreements, terms and conditions, confidentiality agreements, and non-compete agreements
   > - templates for asset inventory checklist capture and sign-off
   > - disciplinary process checklists
   > - exit interview, termination, and layoff checklists

HRM:GG2.GP4 Assign Responsibility

Assign responsibility and authority for performing the human resource management process, developing the work products, and providing the services of the process.

Elaboration:

Of paramount importance in assigning responsibility for the human resource management process is establishing job responsibilities and assigned roles for all operational resilience management system activities. Staff are responsible for establishing resilience requirements for all assets and services, ensuring these requirements are met by asset/service owners and custodians, and identifying and remediating gaps where requirements are not being met. Staff also have the responsibility to develop resilience-specific performance goals and objectives and to measure and assess performance against these goals and objectives.

Subpractices

1. Assign responsibility and authority for performing the process.

   Elaboration:

   Responsibility and authority may extend not only to staff inside the organization but to those with whom the organization has a contractual (custodial) agreement for managing human resources (by contracting staff or supplementing staff through outsourcing).

2. Assign responsibility and authority for performing the specific tasks of the process.

   Elaboration:

   > Responsibility and authority for performing human resource management tasks can be formalized by
   > - defining roles and responsibilities in the process plan to include roles responsible for workforce development, performance management, and background verification
   > - including process tasks and responsibility for these tasks in specific job descriptions
   > - developing policy requiring
   >   - organizational unit managers, line of business managers, project managers, and asset and service owners and custodians to participate in and derive benefit from the process for assets and services under their ownership or custodianship
   >   - staff to take personal responsibility for acquiring the necessary skill sets to fulfill their job description and roles in sustaining operational resilience
   >   - compliance with resilience directives
   > - including process tasks in staff performance management goals and objectives, with requisite measurement of progress against these goals
   > - developing and implementing contractual instruments (including service level agreements) with external entities to establish responsibility and authority for performing process tasks on outsourced functions
   > - including process tasks in measuring performance of external entities against contractual instruments

   Refer to the External Dependencies Management process area for additional details about managing relationships with external entities.

3. Confirm that people assigned with responsibility and authority understand it and are willing and able to accept it.

HRM:GG2.GP5 TRAIN PEOPLE

Train the people performing or supporting the human resource management process as needed.

Elaboration:

The basis for determining training needs for operational resilience management derives from having a comprehensive inventory of current skill sets, establishing a skill set baseline, identifying required skill sets, and measuring and addressing skill set deficiencies.

Refer to the Organizational Training and Awareness process area for more information about training the people performing or supporting the process.

Subpractices

1. Identify process skill needs.

   Elaboration:

   These are examples of skills required in the human resource management process:
   - knowledge of tools, techniques, and methods necessary to perform process tasks, including those identified in HRM:GG2.GP3 subpractice 3
   - knowledge necessary to elicit baseline competencies from the organization's resilience program and plan as well as from resilience job descriptions
   - knowledge necessary to develop, populate, and maintain a skills inventory
   - knowledge necessary to compare baseline competencies with current skills and identify and prioritize key skill gaps and deficiencies requiring action
   - knowledge necessary to identify operational risks emerging from the process that should be referred to the risk management process for disposition
   - knowledge necessary to establish and conduct verification programs and procedures in support of candidate screening
   - knowledge necessary to establish the appropriate terms and conditions of employment that reflect the resilience obligations of the job as well as applicable laws and regulations
   - knowledge necessary to evaluate staff performance against resilience goals and objectives, identify improvements, and take corrective actions
   - knowledge necessary to investigate resilience and security breaches and take necessary disciplinary action
   - knowledge necessary to manage sustaining and reassigning resilience roles and responsibilities regardless of cause or initiating event

2. Identify process skill gaps based on available resources and their current skill levels.
3. Identify training opportunities to address skill gaps.

Elaboration:

> These are examples of training topics:
> - skill deficiencies of existing staff *(The development of training plans is addressed in the Organizational Training and Awareness process area.)*
> - general awareness training on the importance of operational resilience in ensuring that all categories of assets (people, information, technology, and facilities) are protected and sustained
> - training for human resources practitioners (such as placement specialists, compensation analysts, and benefits managers) who do not have specific experience in resilience job roles or skills
> - working with external entities that have responsibility for process activities
> - using process methods, tools, and techniques, including those identified in HRM:GG2.GP3 subpractice 3

4. Provide training and review the training needs as necessary.

HRM:GG2.GP6 MANAGE WORK PRODUCT CONFIGURATIONS

Place designated work products of the human resource management process under appropriate levels of control.

Elaboration:

All work products related to human resources documents, such as personal information about pre-employment verification data and performance evaluations, should be placed under control, with appropriate levels of access privileges.

> These are examples of human resource management work products placed under control:
> - baseline competencies
> - job descriptions
> - skills inventory, including skill gaps and deficiencies
> - training plans
> - job requisitions
> - outsourcing agreements
> - verification procedures and guidelines
> - screening criteria
> - employment agreements, including terms and conditions of employment
> - resilience goals and objectives
> - performance evaluations

- disciplinary process investigation reports and supporting documentation
- confidentiality and non-compete agreements
- notes from exit interviews
- signed-off versions of asset inventories for all terminated staff
- process plan
- policies and procedures
- contracts with external entities

HRM:GG2.GP7 IDENTIFY AND INVOLVE RELEVANT STAKEHOLDERS

Identify and involve the relevant stakeholders of the human resource management process as planned.

Subpractices

1. Identify process stakeholders and their appropriate involvement.

   Elaboration:

   These are examples of stakeholders of the human resource management process:
   - staff involved in identifying resilience baseline competencies and skills
   - owners and custodians of information, technology, and facility assets to which people need access
   - staff responsible for
     - managing operational risks that involve people
     - establishing, implementing, and maintaining an internal control system for human resources
     - developing, testing, implementing, and executing service continuity plans involving people
     - developing, implementing, or managing organizational training, skill development, and knowledge transfer
   - external entities such as employment recruiters, temporary placement agencies, and contractors that provide human resources services
   - staff in other organizational support functions such as payroll or general services administration
   - human resources staff
   - legal counsel
   - public authorities such as law enforcement that may have to be involved in disciplinary actions
   - internal and external auditors

> Stakeholders are involved in various tasks in the human resource management process, such as
> - planning for human resource recruiting and placement
> - planning for compensation, benefits, and skills analysis
> - establishing baseline competencies required to meet resilience requirements
> - creating human resource job role profiles and skills inventory
> - associating human resources with services and analyzing service dependencies
> - establishing, implementing, and managing human resource access controls
> - developing service continuity and succession plans for job roles
> - managing operational risks from people
> - assessing the adequacy of internal controls and separation of duties
> - training and development of people
> - managing external dependencies on people
> - overseeing industrial relations, collective bargaining, and grievance procedures for human resources
> - providing feedback to the organization on resilience job roles and skills
> - reviewing and appraising the effectiveness of process activities
> - resolving issues in the process

2. Communicate the list of stakeholders to planners and those responsible for process performance.
3. Involve relevant stakeholders in the process as planned.

HRM:GG2.GP8 MONITOR AND CONTROL THE PROCESS

Monitor and control the human resource management process against the plan for performing the process and take appropriate corrective action.

Elaboration:

Refer to the Monitoring process area for more information about the collection, organization, and distribution of data that may be useful for monitoring and controlling processes.

Refer to the Measurement and Analysis process area for more information about establishing process metrics and measurement.

Refer to the Enterprise Focus process area for more information about providing process information to managers, identifying issues, and determining appropriate corrective actions.

Subpractices

1. Measure actual performance against the plan for performing the process.
2. Review accomplishments and results of the process against the plan for performing the process.

Elaboration:

> These are examples of metrics for the human resource management process:
> - percentage of human resources who have job descriptions
> - percentage of job descriptions for which resilience goals and objectives are included
> - number and percentage of skill deficiencies for vital staff
> - cost, schedule, and effort required to address skill gaps
> - percentage of human resources that have met the pre-employment verification criteria
> - number of jobs for which skills are defined
> - schedule for collecting and reviewing measures of policy compliance
> - number of resilience awareness and training courses delivered versus number of planned courses
> - number of changes made to the human resources skills inventory during a stated period
> - number and type of performance reviews performed
> - statistics for staff availability to conduct service continuity planned tests
> - timeliness of completing scheduled human resource performance review activities
> - percentage of confidentiality and non-compete agreements executed for people in sensitive positions
> - number of infractions referred to the incident management process
> - number of infractions requiring coordination with public authorities
> - number of skill gap and other process risks referred to the risk management process; number of risks where corrective action is still pending (by risk rank)
> - level of adherence to process policies including clean desk and screen policies; number of policy violations including access control policies; number of policy exceptions requested and number approved
> - number of violations of resilience policies subject to disciplinary action
> - number of process activities that are on track per plan
> - rate of change of resource needs to support the process
> - rate of change of costs to support the process

3. Review activities, status, and results of the process with the immediate level of managers responsible for the process and identify issues.

   Elaboration:

   > Periodic reviews of the human resource management process are needed to ensure that
   > - recruiting and hiring reflect the identified skill gaps that have to be filled
   > - changes to human resources are accurately communicated, implemented, and documented. (This is particularly critical when dealing with terminations and layoffs.)

> - resilience roles are included in job descriptions
> - actions requiring management involvement are elevated in a timely manner
> - the performance of process activities is being monitored and regularly reported
> - key measures are within acceptable ranges as demonstrated in governance dashboards or scorecards and financial reports
> - administrative, technical, and physical controls are operating as intended
> - controls are meeting the stated intent of the resilience requirements
> - actions resulting from internal and external audits are being closed in a timely manner

4. Identify and evaluate the effects of significant deviations from the plan for performing the process.
5. Identify problems in the plan for performing and executing the process.
6. Take corrective action when requirements and objectives are not being satisfied, when issues are identified, or when progress differs significantly from the plan for performing the process.
7. Track corrective action to closure.

HRM:GG2.GP9 OBJECTIVELY EVALUATE ADHERENCE

Objectively evaluate adherence of the human resource management process against its process description, standards, and procedures, and address non-compliance.

Elaboration:

> These are examples of activities to be reviewed:
> - assignment of responsibility, accountability, and authority for process activities
> - determination of the adequacy of process reports and reviews in informing decision makers regarding the performance of operational resilience management activities and the need to take corrective action, if any
> - validation of the organization's hiring, background check, and other vetting processes for new and continuing employees as well as external entities
> - verification of the internal control system for human resources

> These are examples of work products to be reviewed:
> - process plan and policies
> - disciplinary process reports, particularly for repeat offenders
> - layoff and involuntary termination reports
> - metrics for the process *(Refer to HRM:GG2.GP8 subpractice 2.)*
> - contracts with external entities

HRM:GG2.GP10 REVIEW STATUS WITH HIGHER-LEVEL MANAGERS

Review the activities, status, and results of the human resource management process with higher-level managers and resolve issues.

Refer to the Enterprise Focus process area for more information about providing sponsorship and oversight to the operational resilience management system.

HRM:GG3 INSTITUTIONALIZE A DEFINED PROCESS

Human resource management is institutionalized as a defined process.

HRM:GG3.GP1 ESTABLISH A DEFINED PROCESS

Establish and maintain the description of a defined human resource management process.

Establishing and tailoring process assets, including standard processes, are addressed in the Organizational Process Definition process area.

Establishing process needs and objectives and selecting, improving, and deploying process assets, including standard processes, are addressed in the Organizational Process Focus process area.

Subpractices

1. Select from the organization's set of standard processes those processes that cover the human resource management process and best meet the needs of the organizational unit or line of business.
2. Establish the defined process by tailoring the selected processes according to the organization's tailoring guidelines.
3. Ensure that the organization's process objectives are appropriately addressed in the defined process, and ensure that process governance extends to the tailored processes.
4. Document the defined process and the records of the tailoring.
5. Revise the description of the defined process as necessary.

HRM:GG3.GP2 COLLECT IMPROVEMENT INFORMATION

Collect human resource management work products, measures, measurement results, and improvement information derived from planning and performing the process to support future use and improvement of the organization's processes and process assets.

Elaboration:

> These are examples of improvement work products and information:
> - the status of human resources with respect to skill currency, skill gaps, and skill deficiencies
> - metrics and measurements of the viability of the process *(Refer to HRM:GG2.GP8 subpractice 2.)*
> - changes and trends in operating conditions, risk conditions, and the risk environment that affect process results
> - lessons learned in post-event review of incidents and disruptions in continuity
> - process lessons learned that can be applied to improve operational resilience management performance
> - reports on the effectiveness and weaknesses of controls
> - process action plans and strategies that are not being satisfied and the risks associated with these
> - the disposition of process risks that have been referred to the risk management process
> - resilience requirements that are not being satisfied or are being exceeded

Establishing the measurement repository and process asset library is addressed in the Organizational Process Definition process area. Updating the measurement repository and process asset library as part of process improvement and deployment is addressed in the Organizational Process Focus process area.

Subpractices

1. Store process and work product measures in the organization's measurement repository.
2. Submit documentation for inclusion in the organization's process asset library.
3. Document lessons learned from the process for inclusion in the organization's process asset library.
4. Propose improvements to the organizational process assets.

IDENTITY MANAGEMENT
Operations

Purpose

The purpose of Identity Management is to create, maintain, and deactivate identities that may need some level of trusted access to organizational assets and to manage their associated attributes.

Introductory Notes

Identity management is a process that addresses the life cycle of identities for objects and entities (systems, devices, or other processes) and for persons who need some level of trusted access to organizational assets (information; systems, servers, and networks; and facilities).

In identity management, identities for persons, objects, and entities are created so that they are made known to the organization and can be managed throughout their useful life. In the case of persons, these identities typically represent users of information, systems, and facilities who have unique identifying names (such as a user ID) and for whom information is known about their job roles and responsibilities in the organization. The creation of an identity is a means for profiling the person, object, or entity such that the identity retains a particular set of specific information (often referred to as the identity's DNA) as it traverses the organization and is provided different levels of trusted access to diverse organizational assets. This concept may even extend beyond the organization's borders. For example, a particular person, object, or entity may have more than one identity across different organizations that can be accumulated into a single identity (through a process called "federation").

The importance of establishing identities and understanding their DNA is so that they can be assigned access to organizational assets (through a process called "provisioning") and so that this access can be managed as the operational environment changes. This is tremendously important to managing operational resilience in that unauthorized or unintended access to organizational assets may result in unwanted outcomes, such as

- disclosure of information (resulting in violations of privacy and confidentiality requirements)
- unauthorized use of systems and servers (to carry out fraudulent activities)
- unauthorized entry to secured facilities (which could affect the life, safety, and health of staff and customers)
- destruction or loss of vital information and systems that the organization relies upon day-to-day to carry out its strategic objectives

Because the operating environment is complex and the persons, objects, and entities that need access to organizational assets are ever-changing, the organization must actively manage the population of identities to ensure that it is valid. This is a challenging task that requires coordination and cooperation between the areas of the organization where identities are created and managed (for example, in the IT department) and other departments such as human resources (where changes to the community of users are detected) and legal (where new business partners and vendors may have contractual agreements that require access to or ownership of assets).

Roles and responsibilities are linked to an organizational identity; that is, what a person or object has responsibility for in the organization (the person or object's role) determines the type and extent of access that is provided. Some roles are trusted—extraordinary access to organizational access is provided as a necessity for performing a distinct (and sometimes unique) job function. The role is associated with specific access privileges and restrictions that are imposed on the identity when access is provisioned.

Identities must be deprovisioned—that is, when the person, object, or entity ceases to exist in the organization, the identity is eliminated and by reference all of its access privileges and restrictions are eliminated as well. The failure to deprovision an identity can result in significant operational risk to an organization because it may provide an identity to which an unauthorized (and perhaps unknown) person, object, or entity can associate. If this occurs and requisite access privileges have not been terminated, the identity can be stolen and provided by default with all of the existing privileges.

Identity management is often seen as a technical construct. This is because many of the processes for managing identities are operationalized as software packages and focus on electronic access to intangible assets such as information or to technical assets such as software, systems, hardware, and networks. However, in a broad sense, identity management is about establishing the existence of a person, object, or entity in the organization to which one or more access privileges can be assigned. These privileges can be electronic or physical (such as when providing access privileges to technology and facility assets). In some cases, identities may be established without any access privileges being provided.

To properly manage organizational identities, the organization must have processes to establish identities, deprovision identities, and manage changes that occur in the population of identities based on changes in the operating environment. Identities must be described in sufficient detail so that their attributes, including their roles and responsibilities, are clear and can be used as the basis for determining the appropriateness of assigning access privileges and restrictions.

Identity management and the management of access privileges are tightly coupled but distinct activities. An identity must exist to describe a particular role or responsibility in the organization. Access privileges are provided to the identity by virtue of its role. While connected, each of these activities represents a distinct aspect of access control and management that must be mastered to ensure that only authorized staff have access to organizational assets based on their need.

Related Process Areas

Access control and management are addressed in the Access Management process area.

Risks related to inconsistencies between identities and the persons, objects, and entities they represent are addressed in the Risk Management process area.

Summary of Specific Goals and Practices

ID:SG1 Establish Identities
    ID:SG1.SP1   Create Identities
    ID:SG1.SP2   Establish Identity Community
    ID:SG1.SP3   Assign Roles to Identities
ID:SG2 Manage Identities
    ID:SG2.SP1   Monitor and Manage Identity Changes
    ID:SG2.SP2   Periodically Review and Maintain Identities
    ID:SG2.SP3   Correct Inconsistencies
    ID:SG2.SP4   Deprovision Identities

Specific Practices by Goal

ID:SG1 ESTABLISH IDENTITIES

Identities are created to represent persons, objects, and entities that require access to organizational assets.

An identity documents the existence of a person, object, or entity that requires access to organizational assets such as information, technology, and facilities to fulfill its role in executing services. An identity most often represents a person (often referred to as a "user") but can be as diverse as a software application or system or other technology (such as a fax machine or process control device) that requires access to organizational information or systems. Persons, objects, and entities are usually internal to the organization (i.e., employed or controlled directly by the organization) but may be external (provided access to organizational assets in order to provide support services).

Managing the identities in an organization requires that the persons, objects, and entities be identified, profiled, and registered (through an identity profile) and that the organization establish a baseline identity community from which to perform identity-related activities.

ID:SG1.SP1 CREATE IDENTITIES

Persons, objects, and entities that require access to organizational assets are registered and profiled.

To become part of the organizational "community," identities must be registered and profiled. In essence, registration makes an identity "known" to the organization as a person, object, or entity that may require access to organizational assets and that may have to be authenticated and authorized to use access privileges.

The creation or registration of identities involves identifying the person, object, or entity and documenting detailed information about its role and position in the organization (or in an external organization, if applicable). The information that defines an identity is typically referred to as the identity's "DNA" because it is retained by the identity regardless of where it exists inside of or external to the organization. From an organizational perspective, the process of registration may occur when a new employee is hired by the organization and the person's role and job responsibilities are defined based on business requirements. However, it could also occur when an existing employee has a change in job responsibilities that would require registration as an authorized user of organizational assets. Because the organizational environment is constantly changing, registration is an ongoing organizational activity that requires continuous processes.

Registration is performed for persons, objects, and entities that are internal and external to the organization. Thus, a vendor, agency, or business partner may be registered as an identity by the organization, as could a system or process from an external organization.

The typical vehicle for documenting the organization's identities is the identity profile. The profile contains all of the relevant information necessary to describe the unique attributes, roles, and responsibilities of the associated person, object, or entity. The identity profile is generally initiated and approved by an organizational unit or line of business to which the person belongs and where decisions about use of organizational assets can be made. In the case of objects and entities such as systems and processes, the organizational unit or line of business that "owns" the relationship essentially sponsors the identity creation and registration with the owner of the systems and processes that have to be registered.

Once established, an identity is the basis for assigning roles and access privileges in the organization. *(The association of privileges to identities and the ongoing management of privileges are addressed in the Access Management process area.)*

Typical work products

1. Justification for creation of identity
2. Identity profile

Subpractices

1. Establish an identity profile for persons, objects, and entities.

    Typically, the catalyst for the creation of an identity profile is a documented need for access to one or more organizational assets. The need may be established in advance of creating the profile (i.e., before a new employee begins employment) or concurrently with an access request to use an organizational asset. Not all persons, objects, and entities known to the organization will have an identity profile.

    An identity should have a sponsor—an organizational entity or person who is requesting the creation of the identity and agreeing to own the identity profile. The creation of an identity should be based on need and should be justified and authorized by the sponsor.

    The identity profile is the physical instantiation of an identity. The profile should include information such as
    - the name of the sponsor of the profile (This person has responsibility for approving subsequent actions to the profile.)
    - the person, object, or entity's name, location, department, and direct supervisor
    - other HR information (address, phone, etc.) if appropriate
    - a unique identifier for the identity (such as a user ID)
    - the identity's job responsibilities and position in the organizational structure
    - the "roles" associated with the identity (See ID:SG1.SP3.)
    - additional identity information such as "organization" if the identity is external to the organization
    - any account groups that the identity may belong to (for example, accounts payable or engineering)
    - the owner of an object or entity (if the identity profile is for an object or entity such as a system or business process)
    - profile expiration or termination (if pre-established)
    - special credentials of the person, object, or entity that would be needed to determine authorization and/or authentication for access to an organizational asset
    - special restrictions on the person, object, or entity (such as work visa information)

ID:SG1.SP2 ESTABLISH IDENTITY COMMUNITY

The identity community is established and documented.

The identity community can be defined as the collection of the organization's identity profiles. The identity community defines the baseline population of persons, objects, and entities—internal and external to the organization—that could be or are authorized to access and use organizational assets such as information, technology, and facilities commensurate with their job responsibilities and roles. (In some cases, however, an identity may be established but have no access privileges associated with it.) Establishing the identity community is a foundational activity for protecting organization assets, managing changes to identities, and managing access privileges *(as described in the Access Management process area).*

The organization must implement processes to collect and organize identities in a manner that defines and bounds the community of persons, objects, and entities. These processes establish a

- single, consistent source of information about identities and their range of influence and access
- baseline from which changes to identities can be monitored, identified, and managed
- scope for access control monitoring and analysis to identify unnecessary identities as well as to review access privileges and bring them into alignment with business and resilience requirements
- basis for the federation of identities (the process of aggregating the identity of a person, object, or entity across organizational units, organizations, systems, or other domains where it has multiple identities)

The degree to which the identity community is reflective of the current level of access provided to organizational assets is important in controlling access and ensuring that it does not result in additional vulnerabilities to high-value assets.

Typical work products

1. Identity repository

Subpractices

1. Create and maintain an identity repository.
2. Deposit identity profiles as they are created into the identity repository.
3. Establish access controls to ensure protection of identity information.
   Information contained on identity profiles can be considered sensitive and may have to be protected for privacy concerns under certain regulations and laws. In some cases, information such as Social Security number, date of birth, work visa information, and level of clearance may be included in the profile. This information,

if subjected to unauthorized access, may not only subject the organization to potential fines and legal penalties but also expose the owner of the identity to possible identity theft.

ID:SG1.SP3 ASSIGN ROLES TO IDENTITIES

Organizational roles are established and associated with identities.

Roles define a particular function that is associated with an identity. People, in particular, typically have many different roles in the organization that align with their job responsibilities. For example, a person may concurrently

- serve as the administrator over a payroll system
- be an authorized user of organizational facilities such as the data center or the call center
- be a reviewer of medical records or staff files
- be authorized to approve the payment of expenses

Roles are different from job responsibilities. Job responsibilities define what the person (or in some cases, object or entity) is bound to accomplish as a condition of employment. Roles describe the various positions that must be taken to carry out the job responsibilities. In some cases, roles are generic (commonly seen across all persons, objects, and entities), but others are trusted and specific (attributable only to a limited number of persons, objects, and entities). An identity will typically have more than one role assigned to it based on job responsibilities and the expected behaviors of the identity.

From a practical standpoint, roles are more easily defined for objects and entities such as systems and processes. For example, the role of a system may be to acquire information from another system on a nightly basis to facilitate reconciliation. When applied to people, roles become more extensive because staff members typically perform many different roles in carrying out their job responsibilities.

The establishment of roles is important because they establish the foundation for the assignment and association of access privileges to organizational assets. Particularly with people, access privileges are assigned to roles in an identity to avoid blanket assignments of access to assets based on criteria such as level and pay grade. (For example, a higher-level manager who has responsibility for the department that manages the payroll system may have no justifiable reason to inquire on a staff member's payroll records.)

Roles must be developed and assigned to identities based on the knowledge and experience of business owners and the owners of organizational assets. For example, if a role calls for access to confidential medical records, there must be a justifiable business purpose for the access and the owner of the medical records must sponsor the creation of and approve the role for the particular identity. In operation, because roles are usually tied to access requests, roles may not be assigned to identities until access has been requested. In addition, because roles have varying degrees of trust and responsibility, a single identity may possess many roles that exhibit the entire range of trust and responsibility.

Typical work products

1. Identity roles
2. Authorization for assignment of roles
3. Justification for assignment of roles
4. Updated identity profile

Subpractices

1. Develop, authorize, and justify roles.
    Line of business and organizational unit managers, asset owners, and human resources staff should be involved in the process of developing and assigning roles, including providing approval for the creation of a role and the association of the role with an identity. In some cases, the role created will be identical to a role established in an application system or other technology (such as a physical access control system), and in other cases, the role will be more descriptive of the identity's position and job responsibilities.

    The roles developed should be authorized and justified by the sponsors of the identities.
2. Assign roles to identities.
    Roles may be established at the time of creation of the identity profile or after it has been created.

ID:SG2 MANAGE IDENTITIES

Identities are managed to ensure they reflect the current environment of associated persons, objects, and entities.

Identities that have been registered represent the pool of persons, objects, and entities that can have access to high-value organizational assets. Unfortunately, these persons, objects, and entities are not a static group—changes in employment, business partnerships and relationships, and services bring about changes to the organization's pool of identities that must be managed on a daily basis.

The organization must be able to monitor for changes and ensure that identity profiles accurately represent the current pool of persons, objects, and entities in the organization. When misalignment occurs, the organization is potentially at risk because identities exist without corresponding persons, objects, or entities associated with them, possibly resulting in unauthorized or unintended access to organizational assets. When identities do not have associated objects, the organization must act to deprovision these identities to reduce potential effects on operational resilience.

ID:SG2.SP1 MONITOR AND MANAGE IDENTITY CHANGES

Changes to identities are monitored for and managed.

The pool of identities in an organization is dynamic—considering people alone, employees are hired, reassigned, transferred, and terminated on nearly a daily basis. The dynamic nature of the pool of identities is dictated by the almost constant change in an organization's business requirements and objectives as it adjusts to changing operational demands and risk environments. Changes in the environment must be accurately reflected in the inventory of identity profiles in a timely manner. Otherwise, the inventory will not reflect the current authorized level of access to organizational assets and cannot be relied upon as the baseline for managing protection of these assets.

Effective change management of the identity community requires organizational processes for monitoring the environment and identifying the addition and deletion of identities. Changes to identities—typically to the attributes and the roles—must also be monitored and managed. The organization must establish the criteria that indicate changes in the identity community and apply these criteria consistently throughout the enterprise.

This activity must also expand outside of the organization's boundaries to external suppliers and other business partners that have been provisioned an identity by the organization and have been extended access rights to the organization's assets. Thus, the environment that must be monitored for changes can be vast and requires significant attention to reflect the actual and current pool of identities that are authorized to access and affect organizational assets. In addition, the identity profiles of current users should be updated accordingly.

Typical work products

1. Identity change criteria

Subpractices

1. Establish organizational criteria that may signify changes in the identity community. Change criteria can help the organization to determine the types of changes that must be monitored in an attempt to identify inconsistencies between identities and associated persons, objects, and entities.

> These are examples of conditions that signal a change in the identity community:
> - the addition of new employees (through notification by human resources or other hiring and benefits organizations)
> - changes in user responsibilities due to
>   - transfers to different organizational units or departments
>   - promotion or demotion
>   - changes in job descriptions

> - changes in organizational structures
> - changes in structure of services
> - merger with or acquisition of other organizations
> - termination of job responsibilities or employment
> - addition, changes to, or deletion of supplier agreements and relationships (which may involve persons or systems and processes that have registered identities)
> - addition, changes to, or termination of other business partnerships

2. Monitor for and manage changes to the identity community.

    Because changes occur constantly, inconsistency between the identity community and associated persons, objects, and entities can occur regularly. The organization should have processes to monitor for and manage changes so that inconsistencies are kept to a manageable minimum and do not pose risk to the organization. The termination of need for an identity in the organization is the most typical case that causes misalignment. As employees leave the organization, this is often not reflected in the active community of identities in a timely manner. In addition, as changes are made to systems and process control devices by business partners, the need for an organizational identity may expire but not be immediately known by the organization. These situations must be identified and monitored (as should those characterized in the organization's change criteria) so that timely identification of inconsistencies can occur.

    One means that the organization can use to proactively manage these issues is to place time restrictions on identities so that they expire automatically, particularly if they are tied through technical means to access rights on systems, facilities, and information assets.

ID:SG2.SP2 PERIODICALLY REVIEW AND MAINTAIN IDENTITIES

Periodic review is performed to identify identities that are invalid.

Periodic review of identities is a detective and compensating control that can help the organization to keep the identity community viable and accurate. The periodic review should be performed by the organization with the intent of identifying identities that are no longer valid, are duplicated, or that have changed in some way but have not been detected by the organization's change management process *(as described in ID:SG2.SP1)*.

Allowing identities that are invalid or duplicated can have dire organizational consequences, particularly if these identities have access privileges associated with them. This can result in unauthorized

- use and modification of information
- use of systems and technology
- entry to and use of facilities

In addition to identifying invalid or duplicated identities, identity review may also uncover identities with invalid roles or responsibilities to which access privileges have been provisioned. These issues must also be uncovered during regular review and corrected in a timely manner.

Typical work products

1. Guidelines and timetables for identity review
2. List of inaccurate identity profiles
3. List of vacant or invalid identity profiles
4. List of redundant identity profiles
5. Documentation of actions proposed and actions taken

Subpractices

1. Establish a regular review cycle and process.

    Because of the potential risks of invalid or duplicate identities, the organization should establish a periodic review process to ensure alignment. The review cycle should consider the potential risks of unassigned identities as input to the time interval for performing this review. If excessive levels of invalid or duplicate identities are being detected on review, the review cycle should be appropriately adjusted.

2. Perform review of the identity community.

    Inconsistencies between the identity community and active persons, objects, and entities may allow unauthorized access to organizational assets. These inconsistencies must be identified on a regular and timely basis so that actions can be taken to limit potential misuse. The types of inconsistencies that may be identified include identity profiles that
    - do not reflect the current status, attributes, and roles of the associated person, object, or entity
    - are not associated with a valid or current person, object, or entity
    - are duplicative (more than one identity profile associated with a single person, object, or entity)
    - are being shared by more than one person, object, or entity

3. Identify inconsistencies in the identity community.

    Inconsistencies should be documented, as well as the actions that should be taken to eliminate or mitigate them.

ID:SG2.SP3 CORRECT INCONSISTENCIES

Inconsistencies between the identity community and the persons, objects, and entities they represent are corrected.

Inconsistencies between the identity community and the active, authorized community of associated persons, objects, and entities must be corrected in a timely manner to prevent vulnerabilities and risks that result from potential unauthorized use. While the potential for misuse is primarily concentrated on access privileges, the identity profile is the basis for this access and can be an effective first point of action. (This is particularly true in organizations where the identity profile is used to control all access rights.)

Correcting inconsistencies typically requires the organization to take one or more actions:

- Create new identity profiles. (In some cases, new identity profiles must be created when one or more persons have been sharing a single identity profile. This must be authorized, however, by relevant line of business and organizational unit managers, asset owners, and human resources staff.)
- Make changes to the existing identity profile (to account for changing aptitudes or roles).
- Eliminate or deprovision duplicate identity profiles.
- Deprovision identity profiles that do not represent an active person, object, or entity.
- Federate duplicated identity.

This correction process also importantly extends to any persons, objects, or entities outside of the organization such as suppliers and business partners.

Correcting inconsistencies may also require the involvement of business owners and sponsors of identity profiles. For example, the deprovisioning of an identity should be acknowledged and approved by business owners, as should any changes to an active identity profile. Deprovisioning of identity profiles is addressed in ID:SG2.SP4.

Typical work products

1. Written authorization for changes
2. Justification for forgoing corrective action
3. Correction status

Subpractices

1. Develop corrective actions to address inconsistencies in identity profiles.
   This may require detailed involvement of business units and owners who sponsored the creation of identity profiles.
2. Correct identity profiles as required.
   Corrections should be made only on the authorization and written acknowledgment of business units and owners of identity profiles.
3. Document disposition for inconsistencies that will not result in changes or corrections.

In some cases, the organization may determine that changes are not required or warranted. This may pose additional risk to the organization that may have to be addressed through acceptance or mitigation. These risks should be referred to the organization's risk management process and should be fully acknowledged by business units, owners, or other sponsors of created identities. The decision to not correct inconsistencies should be documented and approved.

The management of risks is addressed in the Risk Management process area.

4. Update status of corrective actions.

    The organization should perform status checks on all inconsistencies identified and ensure that a proper disposition—even if no action is taken—is provided for each.

ID:SG2.SP4 DEPROVISION IDENTITIES

Identities for which need has expired or has been eliminated are deprovisioned.

Deprovisioning is a process of deactivating or eliminating an identity (i.e., discarding or destroying the identity profile) as well as all of the privileges and restrictions associated with the identity. If the associated persons, objects, or entities no longer exist, then the identity should be deprovisioned.

Deprovisioning may occur as a result of the regular process of hiring and terminating staff. Human resources departments often feed hiring and termination information to those who are responsible for maintaining the organization's identity repositories as a catalyst for timely and effective creation and deprovisioning of identities. However, deprovisioning may be the result of corrective actions taken to remedy inconsistencies in the identity community. The organization must have processes for regular deprovisioning, particularly with respect to staff.

The elimination or deactivation of an identity also has implications for access privileges. The primary reason for deprovisioning is to prevent unauthorized or accidental access to organizational assets. Thus, when this process is not automated, the act of deprovisioning an identity may require an extensive identification and elimination of associated access privileges. (*The deprovisioning of access privileges associated with an identity's roles is addressed in the Access Management process area.*)

As with all identity management activities, business owners and units should be involved in the deprovisioning process.

Typical work products

1. Written authorization for deprovisioning
2. Deprovisioned identity profiles
3. Updated identity repository

Subpractices

1. Obtain written approval from line of business and organizational unit managers, asset owners, and human resources staff for deprovisioning identities.

    Line of business and organizational unit managers, asset owners, and human resources staff may recommend whether the identity should be simply deactivated (indicating that it may be used in the future) or eliminated (destroying the identity and requiring re-creation if the need arises in the future).

2. Identify and trace access privileges associated with the identity's roles.

    The deprovisioning of the identity profile should ensure that all relevant access privileges are eliminated as well. Depending on how the organization manages identity profiles, this may be a simple or extensive activity.

3. Deprovision identities as required.

Elaborated Generic Practices by Goal

Refer to the Generic Goals and Practices document in Appendix A for general guidance that applies to all process areas. This section provides elaborations relative to the application of the Generic Goals and Practices to the Identity Management process area.

ID:GG1 ACHIEVE SPECIFIC GOALS

The operational resilience management system supports and enables achievement of the specific goals of the Identity Management process area by transforming identifiable input work products to produce identifiable output work products.

ID:GG1.GP1 PERFORM SPECIFIC PRACTICES

Perform the specific practices of the Identity Management process area to develop work products and provide services to achieve the specific goals of the process area.

Elaboration:

Specific practices ID:SG1.SP1 through ID:SG2.SP4 are performed to achieve the goals of the identity management process.

ID:GG2 INSTITUTIONALIZE A MANAGED PROCESS

Identity management is institutionalized as a managed process.

ID:GG2.GP1 ESTABLISH PROCESS GOVERNANCE

Establish and maintain governance over the planning and performance of the identity management process.

Refer to the Enterprise Focus process area for more information about providing sponsorship and oversight to the identity management process.

Subpractices

1. Establish governance over process activities.

   Elaboration:

   > Governance over the identity management process may be exhibited by
   > - developing and publicizing higher-level managers' objectives and requirements for the process
   > - sponsoring policies, procedures, standards, and guidelines for the process
   > - making higher-level managers aware of applicable compliance obligations related to the process, and regularly reporting on the organization's satisfaction of these obligations to higher-level managers
   > - sponsoring and funding process activities
   > - verifying that the process supports strategic resilience objectives
   > - regular reporting from organizational units to higher-level managers on process activities and results
   > - creating dedicated higher-level management feedback loops on decisions about the process and recommendations for prioritizing process requirements and improving the process
   > - providing input on identifying, assessing, and managing operational risks related to the process, including guidance for resolving identity inconsistencies and other anomalies
   > - conducting regular internal and external audits and related reporting to audit committees on process effectiveness
   > - creating formal programs to measure the effectiveness of process activities, and reporting these measurements to higher-level managers

2. Develop and publish organizational policy for the process.

   Elaboration:

   > The identity management policy should address
   > - responsibility, authority, and ownership for performing process activities, including line of business and organizational unit managers, asset owners, and human resources staff approval of roles and associated identities
   > - procedures, standards, and guidelines for
   >   - approving and provisioning identity profiles
   >   - approving and provisioning identity profiles that provide trusted levels of access (including special credentials)
   >   - approving and provisioning identity profiles that exclude levels of access (including special restrictions)
   >   - assigning roles to identities

> - assigning access privileges to roles
> - managing changes to identity profiles
> - identifying and correcting inconsistencies between identity profiles and the persons, objects, and entities they represent
> - deprovisioning identities
> - methods for measuring adherence to policy, exceptions granted, and policy violations

ID:GG2.GP2 PLAN THE PROCESS

Establish and maintain the plan for performing the identity management process.

Elaboration:

For practical purposes, identity management may be a highly centralized activity that relies on a set of designated administrators who have the requisite authority to provide identity management of guest accounts and group management in their geography or for a set of specific assets. For this reason, the organization may have a plan that covers the general management of identity profiles and also specific plans that address the special considerations unique to each type of identity or asset. Identity management may also be tightly coupled with the access management processes, tools, techniques, and methods.

Subpractices

1. Define and document the plan for performing the process.

   Elaboration:

   In the case where plans are developed specific to asset type (i.e., information, technology, or facilities) or access type (i.e., logical or physical), these plans should be coordinated and should be reflective of the organization's overall plan for identity management.

2. Define and document the process description.
3. Review the plan with relevant stakeholders and get their agreement.
4. Revise the plan as necessary.

ID:GG2.GP3 PROVIDE RESOURCES

Provide adequate resources for performing the identity management process, developing the work products, and providing the services of the process.

Subpractices

1. Staff the process.

Elaboration:

> These are examples of staff required to perform the identity management process:
> - staff responsible for
>   - establishing, registering, and profiling identities for persons, objects, and internal and external entities, possibly including organizational unit and line of business managers, asset owners, and human resources
>   - creating and maintaining an identity repository
>   - authorizing, justifying, and assigning roles to identities
>   - ensuring that identity information is appropriately protected to meet privacy and security requirements
>   - reviewing, monitoring, and managing changes to identities, including deprovisioning
> - physical security staff responsible for issuing and monitoring the use of identity badges or other types of physical identity tokens
> - information technology staff responsible for implementing identity controls using systems and other technologies
> - internal and external auditors responsible for reporting to appropriate committees on process effectiveness

Refer to the Organizational Training and Awareness process area for information about training staff for resilience roles and responsibilities.

Refer to the Human Resource Management process area for information about acquiring staff to fulfill roles and responsibilities.

2. Fund the process.

   Refer to the Financial Resource Management process area for information about budgeting for, funding, and accounting for identity management.

3. Provide necessary tools, techniques, and methods to perform the process.

   Elaboration:

   Tools, techniques, and methods will likely involve those that help the organization to implement and manage the life cycle of identities for persons, objects, and entities that need some level of trusted access to organizational assets.

   ID:GG2.GP3 subpractice 3 tools, techniques, and methods do not include those necessary to implement and manage administrative (policy), technical, or physical access controls. *(Refer to the Access Management process area for more information about this aspect.)*

   > These are examples of tools, techniques, and methods to support the identity management process:
   > - tools, techniques, and methods for
   >   - creating identity profiles and an identity repository
   >   - associating specific access privileges and restrictions with a given role

> - aggregating multiple identities of a person, object, or entity (federation)
> - managing changes to identities
> - reviewing identities and correcting inconsistencies between stored identities and the people, objects, and entities they represent
> - deprovisioning identities
> - methods for developing role definitions and authorizing and justifying the assignment of roles to identities
> - tools for tracking corrective actions to resolve identity inconsistencies to closure

Refer to the Knowledge and Information Management, Technology Management, and Environmental Control process areas for practices related to implementing and managing controls for information, technology, and facilities assets respectively.

ID:GG2.GP4 ASSIGN RESPONSIBILITY

Assign responsibility and authority for performing the identity management process, developing the work products, and providing the services of the process.

Refer to the Human Resource Management process area for more information about establishing resilience as a job responsibility, developing resilience performance goals and objectives, and measuring and assessing performance against these goals and objectives.

Subpractices

1. Assign responsibility and authority for performing the process.

   Elaboration:

   Responsibility for performing and managing the identity management process may be distributed across the organization and involve both organizational units and information technology. Identities can be internal or external to the organization. The creation and registration of identities may be triggered by the hiring of new staff, a change of responsibility for existing staff, or the addition of a new business partner or vendor that needs access to assets. Line of business and organizational unit managers (and specifically asset owners) are typically responsible for the authorization, justification, and approval processes that make up the identity profile, while information technology and physical security staff are responsible for mapping the role to the requisite privileges and access to assets. Change management for identities is typically a shared responsibility among organizational units, information technology, and physical security because they must coordinate activities to ensure that privileges are granted to only credentialed entities.

   ID:GG2.GP4 subpractice 1 does not specifically cover responsibility for the development and implementation of access controls for information, technology, or facilities. ID:GG2.GP4 subpractice 1 is limited to responsibility for creating, registering, and deprovisioning identities and managing changes to identities.

Refer to the Knowledge and Information Management, Technology Management, and Environmental Control process areas for information about developing and implementing access controls for information, technology, and facilities assets respectively.

2. Assign responsibility and authority for performing the specific tasks of the process.

   Elaboration:

   > Responsibility and authority for performing identity management tasks can be formalized by
   > - defining roles and responsibilities in the process plan
   > - including process tasks and responsibility for these tasks in specific job descriptions
   > - developing policy requiring line of business managers, project managers, asset owners, and human resources staff to participate in the justification, authorization, and approval of identities and associated roles for assets under their ownership
   > - developing policies requiring information technology and physical security staff to perform process tasks relative to manager and asset owner instructions
   > - including process tasks in staff performance management goals and objectives, with requisite measurement of progress against these goals
   > - developing and implementing contractual instruments (including service level agreements) with external entities to establish responsibility and authority for performing process tasks on outsourced functions
   > - including process tasks in measuring performance of external entities against contractual instruments

   Refer to the External Dependencies Management process area for additional details about managing relationships with external entities.

3. Confirm that people assigned with responsibility and authority understand it and are willing and able to accept it.

ID:GG2.GP5 TRAIN PEOPLE

Train the people performing or supporting the identity management process as needed.

Refer to the Organizational Training and Awareness process area for more information about training the people performing or supporting the process.

Refer to the Human Resource Management process area for more information about creating a skill set inventory, establishing a skill set baseline, identifying required skill sets, and measuring and addressing skill deficiencies.

Subpractices

1. Identify process skill needs.

Elaboration:

> These are examples of skills required in the identity management process:
> - knowledge of tools, techniques, and methods used to manage and maintain identities, including those necessary to perform the process using the selected methods, techniques, and tools identified in ID:GG2.GP3 subpractice 3
> - knowledge necessary to elicit and prioritize stakeholder requirements and needs and interpret them to develop effective requirements for the process
> - knowledge necessary to analyze and prioritize process requirements
> - knowledge necessary to associate identities with roles and assign appropriate access privileges based on these
> - knowledge necessary to manage identities in a manner appropriate for accessing each type of organizational asset (i.e., information; systems, servers, and networks; and facilities) by each type of identity (persons, objects, and entities)

2. Identify process skill gaps based on available resources and their current skill levels.
3. Identify training opportunities to address skill gaps.

Elaboration:

> These are examples of training topics:
> - eliciting and capturing stakeholder identity management requirements
> - creating and registering identities, including federated identities
> - credentialing identities
> - assigning roles and access privileges to identities
> - managing changes to identities
> - deprovisioning identities
> - using controls to protect and secure identity profiles and repositories
> - working with external entities to establish their identities in accordance with policy
> - using process methods, tools, and techniques

4. Provide training and review the training needs as necessary.

ID:GG2.GP6 MANAGE WORK PRODUCT CONFIGURATIONS

Place designated work products of the identity management process under appropriate levels of control.

Elaboration:

Tools, techniques, and methods should be employed to support the creation, provisioning, change management, and deprovisioning of identities and corresponding roles as a baseline from which changes to identities can be monitored and managed. These tools may also be used as a basis for federation of identities.

Identity Management

> These are examples of identity management work products placed under control:
> - lists of internal and external stakeholders and a plan for their involvement
> - identity profiles
> - identity repositories
> - identity roles and associated access privileges
> - identity change criteria
> - lists of identity profiles that are inaccurate or inconsistent, including required change management action
> - deprovisioned identities
> - process plan
> - policies and procedures
> - contracts with external entities

ID:GG2.GP7 IDENTIFY AND INVOLVE RELEVANT STAKEHOLDERS

Identify and involve the relevant stakeholders of the identity management process as planned.

Subpractices

1. Identify process stakeholders and their appropriate involvement.

    Elaboration:

    > These are examples of stakeholders of the identity management process:
    > - staff associated with each process requirement, object, profile, and asset
    > - organizational unit and line of business managers who typically initiate and approve establishing and updating identities
    > - business owners and owners of organizational assets, to ensure that roles and access privileges are appropriately assigned to identities and regularly reviewed and updated
    > - new and existing staff who require a current identity profile
    > - terminated staff whose identities are deprovisioned
    > - human resources
    > - legal counsel and staff
    > - chief privacy officer or equivalent to ensure sensitive identity information is adequately protected
    > - business partners, vendors, and outsourcers that require an identity to gain access
    > - staff responsible for reviewing identities and updating identities
    > - staff associated with each external entity that has an active identity
    > - staff associated with the deprovisioning of identities
    > - internal and external auditors

> Stakeholders are involved in various tasks in the identity management process, such as
> - establishing requirements for the process
> - planning for the process
> - making decisions about process scope and activities
> - vetting and reviewing identity profiles, roles associated with profiles, and access privileges associated with roles
> - reviewing and appraising the effectiveness of process activities
> - resolving issues in the process and with identity inconsistencies, including reconciling and approving changes to identities
> - federating identities
> - deprovisioning identities

2. Communicate the list of stakeholders to planners and those responsible for process performance.
3. Involve relevant stakeholders in the process as planned.

ID:GG2.GP8 M*onitor and* C*ontrol the* P*rocess*

Monitor and control the identity management process against the plan for performing the process and take appropriate corrective action.

Elaboration:

Refer to the Monitoring process area for more information about the collection, organization, and distribution of data that may be useful for monitoring and controlling processes.

Refer to the Measurement and Analysis process area for more information about establishing process metrics and measurement.

Refer to the Enterprise Focus process area for more information about providing process information to managers, identifying issues, and determining appropriate corrective actions.

Subpractices

1. Measure actual performance against the plan for performing the process.
2. Review accomplishments and results of the process against the plan for performing the process.

Elaboration:

> These are examples of metrics for the identity management process:
> - elapsed time between identity request and granting of identity credentials
> - percentage of identity profiles that accurately represent the current pool of persons, objects, and entities in the organization

- percentage of identity requests approved (based on policy)
- percentage of identity requests denied (based on policy)
- percentage of identity requests approved that, on further investigation, should have been denied based on, for example, a mismatch with designated roles
- percentage of identities where roles have been authorized and justified by identity owners
- number of identities belonging to external entities
- number of duplicate identity requests
- rate of change requests to current identity profiles
- number and percentage of inaccurate identity profiles, vacant or invalid identity profiles, and redundant identity profiles
- number of deprovisioned identities
- number of incidents involving the identity repository; number successfully resolved; number awaiting resolution
- number of identity-related risks referred to the risk management process; number of risks where corrective action is still pending (by risk rank)
- level of adherence to process policies; number of policy violations; number of policy exceptions requested and number approved
- number of process activities that are on track per plan
- rate of change of resource needs to support the process
- rate of change of costs to support the process

3. Review activities, status, and results of the process with the immediate level of managers responsible for the process and identify issues.

   Elaboration:

   Periodic reviews of the identity management process are needed to ensure that
   - policies are in place to guide the process for managing identity profiles
   - identity requests are submitted and approved according to policy
   - changes to identities are made in a timely manner and documented
   - identity profiles are periodically reconciled
   - identity inconsistencies are identified and corrected in a timely manner
   - identities are deprovisioned in a timely manner
   - key measures are within acceptable ranges as demonstrated in governance dashboards or scorecards and financial reports
   - administrative, technical, and physical controls are operating as intended
   - actions resulting from internal and external audits are being closed in a timely manner

4. Identify and evaluate the effects of significant deviations from the plan for performing the process.

Elaboration:

Discrepancies result when identities are created, changed, federated, or deprovisioned, but not accurately reflected in the identity community, identity profiles, or the identity repository. Authorized access to assets and the services they support is based on accurate, up-to-date identities. To the extent that the identity management process results in an inaccurate definition of the identity community or population, the organization's overall ability to manage operational resilience is impeded.

5. Identify problems in the plan for performing and executing the process.
6. Take corrective action when requirements and objectives are not being satisfied, when issues are identified, or when progress differs significantly from the plan for performing the process.
7. Track corrective action to closure.

ID:GG2.GP9 OBJECTIVELY EVALUATE ADHERENCE

Objectively evaluate adherence of the identity management process against its process description, standards, and procedures, and address non-compliance.

Elaboration:

> These are examples of activities to be reviewed:
> - developing identity profiles
> - identifying identity change criteria
> - making changes to identity profiles and to the identity repository
> - resolution of identity inconsistencies
> - timeliness of identity deprovisioning
> - the alignment of stakeholder requirements and needs with the process plan
> - assignment of responsibility, accountability, and authority for process activities
> - determination of the adequacy of process reports and reviews in informing decision makers regarding the performance of operational resilience management activities and the need to take corrective action, if any
> - verification of identity management data confidentiality, integrity, and availability controls
> - use of process data to improve strategies for protecting and sustaining assets

> These are examples of work products to be reviewed:
> - identity profiles
> - identity repository
> - identity change control logs
> - deprovisioned identities
> - process plan and policies

- process scope and requirements
- process methods, techniques, and tools *(Refer to ID:GG2.GP3 subpractice 3.)*
- metrics for the process *(Refer to ID:GG2.GP9 subpractice 2.)*
- contracts with external entities

ID:GG2.GP10 REVIEW STATUS WITH HIGHER-LEVEL MANAGERS

Review the activities, status, and results of the identity management process with higher-level managers and resolve issues.

Refer to the Enterprise Focus process area for more information about providing sponsorship and oversight to the operational resilience management system.

ID:GG3 INSTITUTIONALIZE A DEFINED PROCESS

Identity management is institutionalized as a defined process.

ID:GG3.GP1 ESTABLISH A DEFINED PROCESS

Establish and maintain the description of a defined identity management process.

Establishing and tailoring process assets, including standard processes, are addressed in the Organizational Process Definition process area.

Establishing process needs and objectives and selecting, improving, and deploying process assets, including standard processes, are addressed in the Organizational Process Focus process area.

Subpractices

1. Select from the organization's set of standard processes those processes that cover the identity management process and that best meet the needs of the organizational unit or line of business.
2. Establish the defined process by tailoring the selected processes according to the organization's tailoring guidelines.
3. Ensure that the organization's process objectives are appropriately addressed in the defined process, and that process governance extends to the tailored processes.
4. Document the defined process and the records of the tailoring.
5. Revise the description of the defined process as necessary.

ID:GG3.GP2 COLLECT IMPROVEMENT INFORMATION

Collect identity management work products, measures, measurement results, and improvement information derived from planning and performing the process to support future use and improvement of the organization's processes and process assets.

Elaboration:

> These are examples of improvement work products and information:
> - the current status of identity profiles
> - the status of confidentiality, integrity, and availability for identity profiles and repositories, as determined by the results of integrity and security tests
> - metrics and measurements of the viability of the process *(Refer to ID:GG2.GP8 subpractice 2.)*
> - changes and trends in operating conditions, risk conditions, and the risk environment that affect process results
> - lessons learned in post-event review of incidents and disruptions in continuity
> - process lessons learned that can be applied to improve operational resilience management performance, such as poorly documented or inconsistent identities
> - reports on the effectiveness and weaknesses of controls
> - process requirements that are not being satisfied and the risks associated with them
> - resilience requirements that are not being satisfied or are being exceeded

Establishing the measurement repository and process asset library is addressed in the Organizational Process Definition process area. Updating the measurement repository and process asset library as part of process improvement and deployment is addressed in the Organizational Process Focus process area.

Subpractices

1. Store process and work product measures in the organization's measurement repository.
2. Submit documentation for inclusion in the organization's process asset library.
3. Document lessons learned from the process for inclusion in the organization's process asset library.
4. Propose improvements to the organizational process assets.

INCIDENT MANAGEMENT AND CONTROL
Operations

Purpose

The purpose of Incident Management and Control is to establish processes to identify and analyze events, detect incidents, and determine an appropriate organizational response.

Introductory Notes

Throughout an organization's operational environment, disruptions occur on a regular basis. They may occur as the result of intentional actions against the organization, such as a denial-of-service attack or the proliferation of a computer virus, or because of actions over which the organization has no control, such as a flood or earthquake. Disruptive events can be innocuous and go unnoticed by the organization or, at the other extreme, they can significantly impact operational capacities that affect the organization's ability to carry out its goals and objectives.

To manage operational resilience, an organization must become adept at preventing disruptions whenever possible and ensuring continuity of operations when a disruption occurs. However, because not all disruptions can be prevented, the organization must have the capability to identify events that can affect its operations and to respond appropriately. This requires the organization to have processes to recognize potential disruptions, analyze them, and determine how (or if) and when to respond.

The Incident Management and Control process area focuses the organization's attention on the life cycle of an incident—from event detection to analysis to response. The organization establishes the incident management plan and program and assigns appropriate resources. Event detection and reporting capabilities are established, and the organization sets criteria to establish when events become incidents that demand its attention. Events are triaged and analyzed, and incidents are validated. Supporting activities such as communication, logging and tracking events and incidents, and preserving event and incident evidence are defined and established. Most important, the organization performs post-incident review to determine what can be learned from incident management and applied to improve strategies for protecting and sustaining services and assets, as well as improvements in the incident management process and life cycle.

Incident management begins with event identification, triage, and analysis. An event can be one or more minor occurrences that affect organizational assets and have the potential to disrupt operations. An event may not require a formal response from the organization—it may be an isolated issue or problem that is immediately or imminently fixable and does not pose organizational harm. For example, a user may report opening an email attachment and then the user's workstation does not operate properly. This "event" may be an isolated problem or an operator error that requires attention but may not require an organizational response.

Other events (or series of events) require the organization to take notice. Upon triage and analysis, these events may be declared as "incidents" by the organization. An incident is an event (or series of events) of higher magnitude that significantly affects organizational assets and associated services and requires the organization to respond in some way to prevent or limit organizational impact. For example, several customers may independently report that they are unable to place orders via the internet (events). The problem is deemed to be caused by a denial-of-service attack that is being targeted against the web portal (incident). In this case, the organization must be able to recognize, analyze, and manage the incident successfully. When an organization is dealing with an incident whose impact on the organization is rapidly escalating or immediate, the incident is deemed a "crisis." A crisis requires immediate organizational action because the effect of the incident is already being felt by the organization and must be limited or contained.

Incidents affect the productivity of the organization's assets and, in turn, associated services. Because assets span physical and electronic forms, incidents can be either cyber or physical in nature, depending on the target of the incident. Incidents that affect the people and facilities assets are typically physical in nature. In the case of information and technology assets, incidents can be cyber (such as unauthorized access to electronic information or to technology components) or physical (such as unauthorized access to paper or other media on which information assets are stored or to technology assets that are physically accessible).

Operational resilience is predicated on the organization's ability to identify disruptive events, prevent them where possible, and respond to them when the organization is impacted. The extent to which the organization performs event management must be commensurate with the desired level of operational resilience that it needs to achieve its mission.

Incident management is a broad organizational function. It includes many types of activities that traverse the enterprise and require varying skill sets. To provide effective coverage of these activities, the Incident Management and Control process area has five goals that address

- incident planning and assignment of resources
- event and incident identification and reporting

- event analysis
- incident response and recovery
- incident learning and knowledge management

Related Process Areas

Developing, testing, and implementing service continuity plans are addressed in the Service Continuity process area.

Reporting incidents according to applicable laws, rules, and regulations is addressed in the Compliance process area.

The processes for identifying and detecting events that could become incidents are addressed in the Monitoring process area.

Managing risks to organizational assets that arise from incidents is addressed in the Risk Management process area.

Summary of Specific Goals and Practices

IMC:SG1 Establish the Incident Management and Control Process
    IMC:SG1.SP1   Plan for Incident Management
    IMC:SG1.SP2   Assign Staff to the Incident Management Plan
IMC:SG2 Detect Events
    IMC:SG2.SP1   Detect and Report Events
    IMC:SG2.SP2   Log and Track Events
    IMC:SG2.SP3   Collect, Document, and Preserve Event Evidence
    IMC:SG2.SP4   Analyze and Triage Events
IMC:SG3 Declare Incidents
    IMC:SG3.SP1   Define and Maintain Incident Declaration Criteria
    IMC:SG3.SP2   Analyze Incidents
IMC:SG4 Respond to and Recover from Incidents
    IMC:SG4.SP1   Escalate Incidents
    IMC:SG4.SP2   Develop Incident Response
    IMC:SG4.SP3   Communicate Incidents
    IMC:SG4.SP4   Close Incidents
IMC:SG5 Establish Incident Learning
    IMC:SG5.SP1   Perform Post-Incident Review
    IMC:SG5.SP2   Integrate with the Problem Management Process
    IMC:SG5.SP3   Translate Experience to Strategy

Specific Practices by Goal

IMC:SG1 ESTABLISH THE INCIDENT MANAGEMENT AND CONTROL PROCESS

The organizational process for identifying, analyzing, responding to, and learning from incidents is established.

Incident management is a risk management activity that is foundational to managing the security and resilience of an organization's high-value assets and services.

The organization must establish processes for identifying, analyzing, responding to, and learning from incidents to prevent the consequences of unanticipated risks and to manage these consequences when realized. The incident management process is also a source of knowledge that can be used by the organization to continually improve continuity plans and practices and strategies for protecting and sustaining services and assets.

The establishment of incident management and control processes begins with the planning for incident management and the identification and assignment of resources to carry out the plans.

IMC:SG1.SP1 PLAN FOR INCIDENT MANAGEMENT

Planning is performed for developing and implementing the organization's incident management and control process.

Because each organization is unique, it must develop an incident management plan and process that fit its organizational and strategic drivers, business objectives, critical success factors, and general risk environment. These factors should determine the organization's baseline philosophy regarding identification, analysis, and response to incidents and should be reflected in the organization's plan for carrying out these activities. Specifically, the organization must plan for how it will

- identify events and incidents (e.g., through a service desk or problem management reporting activity, or through monitoring)
- analyze these events and incidents and determine an appropriate response
- respond to incidents (e.g., a local response or a coordinated enterprise response)
- structure and staff the plan (by assigning individuals or groups to specific roles or by creating a specialized incident response team such as a computer security incident response team [CSIRT] or similar group)

The organization should develop and document its plan for incident management and outline the specific objectives of the plan. The plan should reflect the organization's philosophy of incident management and response. The objectives of the plan should be translated into specific actions and assigned to individuals or groups to be performed when necessary.

Typical work products

1. Incident management plan
2. Documented requests for commitments to the plan
3. Documented commitments to the plan

Subpractices

1. Establish the incident management plan content.
   The incident management plan should address at a minimum
   - the organization's philosophy on incident management
   - the structure of the incident management process
   - the requirements and objectives of the incident management process relative to managing operational resilience
   - a description of how the organization will identify incidents, analyze them, and respond to them
   - the roles and responsibilities necessary to carry out the plan
   - applicable training needs and requirements
   - resources that will be required to meet the objectives of the plan (*See IMC:SG1.SP2.*)
   - relevant costs and budgets associated with incident management activities
2. Establish commitments to the plan.
   Documented commitments by those responsible for implementing and supporting the plan (particularly the commitment of higher-level managers) are essential for plan effectiveness.
3. Revise the plan and commitments as necessary.

IMC:SG1.SP2 ASSIGN STAFF TO THE INCIDENT MANAGEMENT PLAN

Staff are identified and assigned to the incident management plan.

The incident management plan must be staffed to ensure the plan's objectives can be carried out when necessary. The organization must identify the staff necessary to achieve the plan's objectives and ensure that staff are assigned and aware of their roles and responsibilities with respect to satisfying these objectives. Staff should be provided sufficient autonomy and authority to carry out their duties as required by the plan. The organization must determine the types of training needed for those involved in the incident management process and provide training that is commensurate with incident management responsibilities and accountabilities.

Typical work products

1. Job descriptions for roles and responsibilities in the plan
2. List of available and skilled staff
3. List of skill gaps and gaps in the availability of staff
4. Mitigation plans to address skill and staff gaps
5. Updated incident management plan (with staff assignments)

Subpractices

1. Develop detailed job descriptions for each role and responsibility detailed in the incident management plan.

2. Establish a list of candidate and skilled staff to fill each role and responsibility in the incident management plan.
   Skill or staff gaps for each role and responsibility should be identified and resolved.
3. Assign staff to incident management roles and responsibilities.
4. Ensure that training is provided to staff respective to their incident management job responsibilities.
   The training of staff who are vital to the management of operational resilience is covered in the Organizational Training and Awareness process area.

IMC:SG2 DETECT EVENTS

A process for detecting, reporting, triaging, and analyzing events is established and maintained.

Incidents originate as organizational events. The organization must be able to monitor and identify events as they occur, as well as to determine when an event or a series of events constitutes an incident that requires a coordinated and planned response. Failure to properly identify events in a timely manner can shift the organization's resilience management burden from prevention to reactive management of organizational impact, which is much more costly.

In order to apply incident management processes, the organization must have a foundational structure for event detection, reporting, logging, and tracking, and for collecting and storing event evidence. Because incidents originate as one or more events, foundational processes related to event detection and reporting also support incident reporting, logging, and tracking.

IMC:SG2.SP1 DETECT AND REPORT EVENTS

Events are detected and reported.

The monitoring, identification, and reporting of events are the foundation for incident identification and commence the incident life cycle. Events potentially affect the productivity of organizational assets and, in turn, associated services. These events must be captured and analyzed so that the organization can determine whether an event will become (or has become) an incident that requires organizational action. The extent to which an organization can identify events improves its ability to manage and control incidents and their potential effects.

At a minimum, the organization should identify the most effective methods for event detection and provide a process for reporting events so that they can be triaged, analyzed, and addressed. Staff should be assigned to the task of monitoring various organizational processes (both technical and non-technical) to identify and report events. Typically the organization's service desk is often the front line for collecting event data and for commencing the incident management process.

The processes that the organization uses to monitor the resilience of assets and to identify anomalies or problems (such as events) are addressed in the Monitoring process area.

> These are examples of methods of event detection:
> - monitoring of technical infrastructure, including network architecture and network traffic
> - reporting of problems or issues to the organization's service desk
> - observation of organizational managers and users of IT services
> - environmental and geographical events reported through media such as television, radio, and the internet
> - reporting from legal or law enforcement staff
> - observation of a breakdown in processes or productivity of assets
> - external notification from other entities such as CERT
> - results of audits or assessments

Typical work products

1. Sources of event detection and reporting
2. Descriptions of event detection and reporting roles and responsibilities
3. Event detection and reporting procedures
4. Event reports

Subpractices

1. Define the methods of event detection and reporting.
2. Develop and communicate descriptions of event detection and reporting roles and responsibilities (*refer to IMC:SG1.SP1*).
3. Assign the roles of event detection and reporting to appropriate staff throughout the organization (*refer to IMC:SG1.SP2*).
   Ensure that those assigned the responsibility for event detection and reporting understand this responsibility and have committed to performing it.
4. Establish a process for event reporting. Document events as they are detected on an event report.
5. Submit event reports to appropriate incident management staff per the organization's event reporting process.
6. Provide proper training and awareness for managers and users of technology assets (systems, networks, etc.) to identify anomalies and report them to the service desk or other authorized source for investigation and resolution.

IMC:SG2.SP2 Log and Track Events

Events are logged and tracked from inception to disposition.

The organization should have a formal process for logging events as they are identified and for tracking them through the incident life cycle. Logging and tracking ensure that the event is properly progressing through the incident life cycle and, most important, is closed when an appropriate response and post-incident review have been completed. Logging and tracking facilitate event triage and analysis activities, provide the ability to quickly obtain a status of the event and the organization's disposition, provide the basis for conversion from event to incident declaration, and may be useful in post-incident review processes when trending and root-cause analysis are performed. Logging and tracking may also support forensic activities and in some cases may be required by law enforcement. In essence, logging and tracking create an incident knowledgebase of both events and incidents to which the organization has been subjected. *(Refer to IMC:SG5 for post-incident review practices.)*

The organization must decide the degree to which the logging and tracking process is formalized. Logging and tracking should allow for the possibility that some events will go on to be declared as incidents, and as a result, additional information will be collected as the incident proceeds through incident handling and response activities. Basic information about events (and incidents) should include

- a unique organization-derived identifier (such as an event or incident number)
- a brief description of the event (type of event)
- an event category (based on categories predefined by the organization such as "denial of service," "virus intrusion," or "physical access violation")
- the organizational assets, services, and organizational units that are affected by the event (including the seriousness of the organizational consequences)
- a brief description of how the event was identified and reported, and by whom, and other relevant details as necessary (application system, network segment, operating system, etc.)
- if the event was determined to be an incident *(refer to IMC:SG2.SP4 and IMC:SG3)*, the individuals or teams to whom the incident was assigned for containment, analysis, and response (typically referred to as the "incident owner")
- costs associated with the event or incident
- relevant dates (such as when the event or incident was detected or occurred, when the event or incident was closed, and, if applicable, when the post-incident review was performed)
- the actions taken in response to the event or incident

Typical work products

1. Logged event reports
2. Incident management knowledgebase
3. Event and incident status reports

Subpractices

1. Develop and implement an incident management knowledgebase that allows for the entry of event reports (and the tracking of declared incidents) through all phases of their life cycle.
    Guidelines and standards for the consistent documentation of events should be developed and communicated to all who are involved in the reporting and logging processes.
2. Enter event reports into the incident management knowledgebase as they are received.
    Refer to IMC:SG2.SP4 and IMC:SG3 for a description of events that are determined to be incidents.
3. Establish and distribute standard reports that provide status information about events as they move through the life cycle.
    The status of events should be checked regularly to ensure that they are moving through the organization's established incident management process and are not stalled or awaiting activity. Events that need additional attention should be identified and resolved.

IMC:SG2.SP3 COLLECT, DOCUMENT, AND PRESERVE EVENT EVIDENCE

The process for collecting, documenting, and preserving event evidence is established and managed.

An event may become an organizational incident that has the potential to be a violation of local, state, or federal rules, laws, and regulations. This is often not known early in the investigation of an event, so the organization must be vigilant in ensuring that all event and incident evidence is handled properly in case an eventual legal issue, civil or criminal, is raised.

To properly collect, document, and preserve evidence, the organization must have processes for these activities, and the processes must be known to all staff who are involved in any aspect of the incident life cycle. Staff must be trained in proper identification and handling of evidence, ensuring that the integrity of the evidence is not altered. Because it is unpredictable whether an event or incident will result in legal action, an organization must also consider early involvement of legal and possibly law enforcement staff in the incident identification and analysis process to avoid problems with evidence retention, destruction, and tampering.

Typical work products

1. List of relevant rules, laws, regulations, and policies regarding incident forensics
2. Event/incident evidence documentation and preservation guidelines

Subpractices

1. Identify relevant rules, laws, regulations, and policies for which incident evidence may be required.

    Because there may be compliance issues related to the collection and preservation of incident data, this practice must be considered in the context of the organization's compliance program. (*This is addressed in the Compliance process area.*)

2. Develop and communicate consistent guidelines and standards for the collection, documentation, and preservation of evidence for events/incidents.

3. Document events and related evidence information in the incident management knowledgebase where practical (*see IMC:SG2.SP2*).

    Rules, laws, regulations, and policies may require specific documentation for forensic purposes. These specific requirements must be included in the organization's logging and tracking process as described in IMC:SG2.SP2. Some information about events may be confidential or sensitive, so the organization must be careful to appropriately limit access to event information to only those who need to know about it.

IMC:SG2.SP4 ANALYZE AND TRIAGE EVENTS

Events are analyzed and triaged to support event resolution and incident declaration.

The triage of event reports is an analysis activity that helps the organization to gather additional information for event resolution and to assist in incident declaration, handling, and response. Triage consists of categorizing, correlating, prioritizing, and analyzing events. Through triage, the organization determines the type and extent of an event (e.g., physical versus technical), whether the event correlates to other events (to determine if they are symptomatic of a larger issue, problem, or incident), and in what order events should be addressed or assigned for incident declaration, handling, and response. Triage also helps the organization to determine if the event needs to be escalated to other organizational or external staff (outside of the incident management staff) for additional analysis and resolution.

Some events will never proceed to incident declaration; the organization determines these events to be inconsequential. For events that the organization deems as low priority or of low impact or consequence, the triage process results in closure of the event and no further actions are performed.

Events that exit the triage process warranting additional attention may be referred to additional analysis processes for resolution or declared as an incident and subsequently referred to incident response processes for resolution. These events may be declared as incidents during triage, through further event analysis, through the application of incident declaration criteria, or during the development of response strategies, depending on the organization's incident criteria, the nature and timing of the event(s), and the consequences of the event that the organization is currently experiencing or that is imminent. *(Incident declaration and analysis are addressed in IMC:SG3.)*

Typical work products

1. Updated event reports (categorized and prioritized; disposition)
2. Updated incident knowledgebase
3. Open events status report

Subpractices

1. Assign a category to events from the organization's standard category definitions.
2. Perform correlation analysis on event reports to determine if there is affinity between two or more events.
3. Prioritize events.
   Events may be prioritized based on event knowledge, the results of categorization and correlation analysis, incident declaration criteria *(refer to IMC:SG3.SP1)*, and experience with past declared incidents.
4. Assign a disposition to events as available.
   Possible dispositions for event reports include
   - closed
   - referred for further analysis
   - referred to organizational unit or line of business for disposition
   - declared as incident and referred to incident handling and response process
5. Escalate events to the appropriate stakeholders if they require additional analysis.
6. Update the incident knowledgebase with information gathered in the triage process and the event disposition.
   Events that have been declared as incidents as a result of the triage process should be appropriately designated in the incident knowledgebase.
7. Assign events that have not been assigned a "closed" status for further analysis and resolution.
8. Periodically review the incident knowledgebase for events that have not been closed or for which there is no disposition.
   Events that have not been closed or that do not have a disposition should be reprioritized and analyzed for resolution.

IMC:SG3 DECLARE INCIDENTS

Incidents are declared and analyzed to support response planning.

Incident declaration defines the point at which the organization has established that an incident has occurred, is occurring, or is imminent and will have to be handled and responded to.

Transition from event detection to incident declaration can be immediate, particularly when it is clear to the organization that there are significant effects on organizational assets and associated services and a response is required to limit these effects and their impact. Thus, the extended time from event detection to incident declaration may be immediate, requiring little additional review and analysis. In other cases, incident declaration requires more thoughtful analysis; thus, the organization may need to use predefined criteria developed from experience to help guide incident declaration.

Once an incident has been declared, the organization must perform additional analysis to develop and implement an appropriate action plan for handling and response. This action plan may represent a routine activity (such as asking users to stop opening email messages containing greeting card announcements) or a specifically designed response that is unique to the incident and requires significant levels of organizational coordination and logistical support.

The development of the organization's response to an incident is addressed in IMC:SG4.

IMC:SG3.SP1 DEFINE AND MAINTAIN INCIDENT DECLARATION CRITERIA

Criteria for declaring incidents are defined and maintained.

Each organization has many unique factors that must be considered in determining when to declare an incident. Through experience, an organization may have a baseline set of events that define standard incidents, such as a virus outbreak, unauthorized access to a user account, or a denial-of-service attack. However, in reality, incident declaration may occur on an event-by-event basis.

To guide the organization in determining when to declare an incident (particularly if incident declaration is not immediately apparent), the organization must define incident declaration criteria.

These are examples of criteria that guide an organization's determination of an incident:
- Is the event common to the organization? Has it occurred before? Did past occurrences of the event result in an incident declaration?
- Is the event isolated (i.e., only one user has reported it) or are there multiple occurrences of the same event being reported across the enterprise (through the service desk or similar construct)?
- Is the impact of the event imminent or immediate? Is the organization already suffering some effects from the event? Is there a crisis that has been precipitated by the event?
- Does the event affect core business drivers such as a high-value service that produces revenue?
- Does the event constitute a violation of organizational policy or constitute fraud or theft?
- Is the life or safety of staff or external entities at risk?

> - Are the integrity and operability of a facility at risk?
> - Are the integrity and operability of a high-value service or system at risk?
> - Are there other organizational impacts that are imminent or already being incurred, such as damage to the organization's reputation?
> - Is there a potential legal infraction or possible future legal (civil or criminal) concerns?

Typical work products

1. Incident declaration criteria

Subpractices

1. Establish incident declaration criteria for use in guiding when to declare an incident.
2. Distribute incident declaration criteria to all sources and relevant staff who may need to declare an incident.
3. Update incident declaration criteria as required based on experience in past declarations.

IMC:SG3.SP2 ANALYZE INCIDENTS

Incidents are analyzed to support the development of an appropriate incident response.

Incident analysis is primarily focused on helping the organization to determine an appropriate response to a declared incident by examining its underlying causes and actions and the effects of the underlying event(s) that have already been detected by the organization. Analysis is performed to further understand the incident, to develop and implement action to contain its impact, and to recover from any resulting damage. Incident analysis may be informed by the correlation and prioritization activities performed in event triage.

Incident analysis requires skills from across the organization. Depending on the nature of the incident, analysis may involve asset owners, information technology staff, physical security staff, auditors, and legal staff, as well as external stakeholders such as vendors and suppliers, law enforcement staff, and vulnerability clearinghouses. Incident analysis may involve staff to whom the incident has been escalated or assigned (including the incident owner). (*Incident escalation is addressed in IMC:SG4.SP1.*)

Incident analysis should be focused on properly defining the underlying problem, condition, or issue and in helping the organization to prepare the most appropriate and timely response to the incident. It should also help the organization to determine whether the incident has legal ramifications. Analysis activities must feed the organization's evidence collection process in case of future legal actions (*see IMC:SG2.SP3*) as well as the post-incident review processes (*see IMC:SG5*) for process improvement.

> These are examples of activities that may be performed to analyze incidents:
> - interviews with those who reported the underlying event(s), as well as those who are involved in its investigation
> - interviews of specific knowledge experts who have a detailed understanding of the area affected
> - interviews of asset owners for assets (such as information) that have been affected by the incident
> - review of relevant logs and audit trails of network and physical activity
> - consultation of vulnerability and incident databases such as the US-CERT Vulnerability Notes Database and the MITRE Corporation's Common Vulnerabilities and Exposures list
> - consultation with law enforcement staff
> - consultation with legal and audit staff
> - consultation with product vendors and software/hardware suppliers (if their products are involved)
> - consultation with emergency management staff (if the incident is a safety concern)

Typical work products

1. Incident analysis report
2. Reports from analysis tools and techniques
3. Updated incident knowledgebase

Subpractices

1. Establish and communicate a standardized and consistent incident analysis approach and structure.
2. Identify relevant analysis tools, techniques, and activities that the organization will use to analyze incidents and develop appropriate responses.
   Provide appropriate levels of training for incident management staff on analysis tools and techniques.
3. Analyze open event reports and previously declared incidents.
   Open event reports may correlate to the incident under analysis and provide additional information that is useful in developing an appropriate response. Reviewing documentation on previously declared incidents may inform the development of a response action plan, particularly if significant organizational (and external) coordination is required.
4. Document analysis on an incident analysis report.
   Ensure that analysis is appropriately documented on the incident analysis report and in the incident knowledgebase and made available for use in evidence collection, response development, and post-incident review.

IMC:SG4 RESPOND TO AND RECOVER FROM INCIDENTS

The process for responding to and recovering from incidents is established.

The nature of a declared incident is that the organization has already incurred some effect, however limited, that requires the organization to act. Responding to and recovering from an incident often requires two primary actions from the organization:

- immediate limitation or containment of the scope and impact of the incident
- the development and implementation of an appropriate response to stop the ongoing or future effect of the incident, repairing any remaining damage, and restoring organizational assets and services to the state in which they existed prior to the disruption

Responding and recovering may also require a carefully coordinated and executed collaboration between organizational units and external entities (such as emergency providers) and a plan for handling incident logistics, particularly if the incident is significant or catastrophic. The logistics of these coordinating activities can often be planned in advance; however, execution may occur on demand or spontaneously.

In addition, to avoid reputation damage, the organization must also craft and implement a communications process that facilitates collaboration and logistical execution and keeps stakeholders aware of the incident's evolution and resolution. *(Refer to the Communications process area for more information about developing, deploying, and managing internal and external communications in support of a declared incident.)*

IMC:SG4.SP1 ESCALATE INCIDENTS

Incidents are escalated to the appropriate stakeholders for input and resolution.

Incidents that the organization has declared and that require an organizational response must be escalated to those stakeholders that can implement, manage, and bring to closure an appropriate and timely solution. These stakeholders are typically internal to the organization (such as a standing incident response team or an incident-specific team) but could be external in the form of contractors or other suppliers. *(Refer to the External Dependencies Management process area for information about managing relationships with external entities.)* The organization must establish processes to ensure that incidents are referred to the appropriate stakeholders because failure to do so will impede the organization's response and may increase the level to which the organization is impacted.

Because communication is a vital tool in incident escalation, the organization's incident communications plan must be developed, implemented, and tested in order to support effective escalation *(see IMC:SG4.SP3)*. *(Communications activities in support of operational resilience, including when dealing with an incident, are described in the Communications process area.)*

Typical work products

1. Incident escalation procedures
2. Escalation criteria

Subpractices

1. Develop incident escalation criteria.
   These criteria should provide guidance on when escalation is appropriate and necessary, and the level of escalation required.
2. Develop incident escalation procedures.
   Incident escalation procedures should consider the type and extent of the incident and the appropriate stakeholders.
3. Communicate incident escalation criteria and procedures to those who have responsibility for identifying and escalating incidents.
   Ensure that stakeholders such as the service desk are included in the escalation process.
4. Escalate incidents to appropriate stakeholders for resolution.

IMC:SG4.SP2 DEVELOP INCIDENT RESPONSE

A response to a declared incident is developed and implemented to prevent or limit organizational impact.

Responding to an organizational incident is often dependent on proper advance planning by the organization in establishing, defining, and staffing an incident management capability. In addition, the organization typically has service continuity plans that can be executed in parallel if an incident has resulted in drastically affected operations. *(Developing, testing, and implementing service continuity plans are addressed in the Service Continuity process area.)*

Responding to an incident describes the actions the organization takes to prevent or contain the impact of an incident on the organization while it is occurring or shortly after it has occurred. The range, scope, and breadth of the organizational response will vary widely depending on the nature of the incident. Incident response may be as simple as notifying users to avoid opening a specific type of email message or as complicated as having to implement service continuity plans that require relocation of services and operations to an off-site provider. The broad range of potential incidents requires the organization to have a broad range of capability in incident response.

The organization's response to an incident must be founded on a well-structured incident response capability and plan *(as developed in IMC:SG1.SP1)*. Depending on the organization, the actions related to incident response can include

- containing damage (i.e., by taking hardware or systems offline or by locking down a facility)
- collecting evidence (including logs and audit trails)
- interviewing relevant staff (those who are involved in reporting or analyzing the incident and those who are affected by it)
- communicating to stakeholders, including asset owners and incident owners
- developing and implementing corrective actions and controls
- implementing continuity and restoration plans or other emergency actions *(See the Service Continuity process area for more information about continuity planning and response.)*

The organization must consider the best response structure for its unique organizational structure and context. For some organizations, it makes sense to establish one or more permanent teams that are responsible for repeatable capabilities to respond to a broad range of incidents, supplementing the response with subject matter experts where necessary. In other cases, an organization may establish a virtual "team" of individuals who may be quickly called upon to perform specific duties to respond to an incident. In addition, the organization may have standardized responses for certain types of incidents (such as denial-of-service attacks) that have been developed through lessons learned. Some of these responses might be reflected in standard service continuity plans that the organization has already developed.

In responding to any incident, the organization must consider who is responsible for coordinating the overall response and ensure that those who must be involved in the response have been notified. Responders must update the incident knowledgebase to detail and document the steps taken to contain and repair incident damage so that future incidents can use this information in root-cause analysis and problem diagnosis. *(See IMC:SG2.SP4 and IMC:SG3.SP2 for more details.)* In addition, the organization must ensure that actions taken to contain or repair incident damage are performed in a way that ensures no additional vulnerabilities are introduced or that the effect on day-to-day operations is limited.

Typical work products

1. Incident response strategy and plan
2. Service continuity plans
3. Restoration plans
4. Updated incident knowledgebase

Subpractices

1. Develop an incident response strategy and plan to limit incident effects and to repair incident damage.

The incident response strategy and plan should address at a minimum
- the essential activities (administrative, technical, and physical) that are required to contain or limit damage and provide service continuity
- existing continuity of operations and restoration plans in the organization's plan inventory
- the resources and skills required to perform the incident response strategy and plan
- coordination activities with other internal staff and external agencies that must be performed to implement the strategy
- the levels of authority and access needed by responders to carry out the strategy and plan
- objectives for measuring when the strategy and plan are successful
- the estimated cost of implementing the strategy and plan
- the essential activities necessary to restore services to normal operation (recovery), the resources involved in these activities, and their estimated cost
- legal and regulatory obligations that must be met by the strategy
- standardized responses for certain types of incidents

2. Identify staff who are responsible for coordinating incident response (across all potential types of incidents) and ensure they have the authority and responsibility to act.
3. Update the incident knowledgebase with information about the incident response strategy and plan.

IMC:SG4.SP3 Communicate Incidents

A plan for the communication of incidents to relevant stakeholders and a process for managing ongoing incident communications are established.

Miscommunications or inaccurate information about organizational incidents can have dire effects that far exceed the potential damage caused by an incident itself. As a result, the organization must proactively manage communications when incidents are detected and throughout their life cycle. This requires the organization to develop and implement a communications plan that can be readily implemented to manage communications to internal and external stakeholders on a regular basis and as needed. This plan should provide relevant information to these entities and control or limit the degree to which misinformation and conjecture can develop. It must also consider the needs of a wide range of stakeholders that have a vested interest in obtaining information about organizational incidents in a controlled and regular manner.

The basic structure of the plan may be static, but the plan should be flexible to address a broad range of incident types, stakeholders, and corresponding communications needs. In addition, the organization should consider developing partnerships with external stakeholders so that a coordinated communications strategy can be developed and implemented when incidents affect the organization's external operational environment as well.

> These are examples of stakeholders that may have to be included in an incident communication plan:
> - members of the incident handling and management team (if the organization has established such a team), or internal staff who have incident handling and management job responsibilities
> - shareholders
> - asset owners (if their asset is the target of the incident) and service owners
> - information technology staff (if the target of the incident is the organization's technical architecture and infrastructure)
> - middle and higher-level managers
> - business continuity staff (if they will be required to enact continuity or restoration plans as a result of the incident)
> - human resources departments, particularly if safety is an issue
> - communications and public relations staff
> - support functions such as legal, audit, and human resources
> - legal and law enforcement staff (including federal agencies), if the incident may have legal ramifications
> - external media outlets, including newspaper, television, radio, and internet
> - affected customers or upstream suppliers
> - local, state, and federal emergency management staff
> - local utilities (power, gas, telecommunications, water, etc.), if affected
> - regulatory and governing agencies

Typical work products

1. List of incident stakeholders, communications protocols, and channels
2. Incident communications plan
3. Incident status reports (from incident knowledgebase)

Subpractices

1. Identify relevant stakeholders that may have a vested interest or vital role in communications about an organizational incident.
2. Identify the appropriate communications protocols and channels (media and message) for each type of stakeholder.
3. Develop and implement an organizational incident management communications plan.
   The incident communications plan should address at a minimum
   - the stakeholders with which communications about incidents are required
   - the types of media by which communications will be handled
   - the various message types and level of communications appropriate to various stakeholders (For example, incident communications may be vastly different for incident responders than for those who may simply need to know.)

- special controls over communications (i.e., encryption or secured communications) that are appropriate for some stakeholders
- the roles and responsibilities necessary to carry out the plan
- the frequency and timing of communications
- internal and external resources that are involved in supporting the communications process

4. Identify and obtain commitment from staff who are required to carry out the incident communications plan.
   Ensure that these staff members have the appropriate level of training and skills necessary to execute and support the plan.
5. Identify and train staff responsible for incident communication and provide general guidelines for incident response and other staff for appropriate communication of incident information.

IMC:SG4.SP4 CLOSE INCIDENTS

Incidents are closed after relevant actions have been taken by the organization.

(Closure of an incident can be performed only after post-incident review practices have been completed. Practices in IMC:SG5 must be completed before IMC:SG4.SP4 can be accomplished.)

Incident closure refers to the retirement of an incident that has been responded to (i.e., there are no further actions required and the organization is satisfied with the result) and for which the organization has performed a formal post-incident review *(see IMC:SG5)*. The organization must have a process for formal closure of incidents (including the practices in IMC:SG5) which results in formally logging a status of "closed" in the incident knowledgebase.

A "closed" status indicates to all relevant stakeholders that no further actions are required or outstanding for the incident. It also provides notification to those affected by the incident that it has been addressed and that they should not be subject to continuing effects.

Typical work products

1. Criteria for incident closure
2. Updated incident knowledgebase

Subpractices

1. Establish criteria for incident closure.
   The criteria for incident closure will vary by organization but will generally occur after post-incident review has occurred. However, some organizations may establish concrete closure rules.
2. Define and assign the responsibility for incident closure.
   Typically, this action will be the responsibility of the incident owner or incident manager. Only authorized staff should be permitted to close an incident.

3. Update the incident knowledgebase to indicate that an incident has been closed.
4. Track incidents that have been open for an extended period of time without closure and resolve.

> Incidents that appear to be open for an extended period of time may not have followed the organization's incident management process or may not have been formally closed. The status of incidents in the incident database should be reviewed regularly to determine if open incidents should be closed or need additional action.

IMC:SG5 ESTABLISH INCIDENT LEARNING

Lessons learned from identifying, analyzing, and responding to incidents are translated into actions to improve strategies for protecting and sustaining services and assets.

One of the most important aspects of incident management and control is the ability to understand why an incident occurred and what can be done by the organization to prevent it in the future. From a risk management standpoint, using incident lessons learned to improve controls and protection strategies and to optimize these strategies with continuity planning and response effectively shifts the organization's attention from a response mode to a preventive mode.

Incident learning involves a post-incident review by relevant stakeholders, an active link to the organization's problem management process, and a formal translation of lessons learned to improve strategies for protecting and sustaining services and assets.

The practices of this goal should be considered as part of the closure activity as described in IMC:SG4.SP4.

IMC:SG5.SP1 PERFORM POST-INCIDENT REVIEW

Post-incident review is performed to determine underlying causes.

Post-incident review is a formal part of the incident closure process. The organization conducts a formal examination of the causes of the incident and the ways in which the organization responded to it, as well as the administrative, technical, and physical control weaknesses that may have allowed the incident to occur.

To be effective, post-incident review requires the input of all relevant stakeholders in the incident management process. This includes those who

- reported the incident
- detected the incident
- triaged and analyzed the incident
- responded to the incident
- were affected by the incident
- had the incident communicated to them

Post-incident review should include a significant root-cause analysis process. The organization should employ commonly available techniques (such as cause-and-effect diagrams) to perform root-cause analysis as a means of potentially preventing future incidents of similar type and impact. (*Root-cause analysis is also useful for linking to the organization's problem management process, as detailed in IMC:SG5.SP2.*) Considerations of other processes that may have caused or aided the incident should be given, particularly as they may exist in processes such as change management and configuration management.

Typical work products

1. Criteria for incident closure
2. Post-incident analysis report
3. Recommendations for control improvement
4. Recommendations for improvements to incident management process
5. Updated incident knowledgebase

Subpractices

1. Establish and implement a formal post-incident response activity and require it as part of closing an incident.
2. Assign responsibility for post-incident review activities to appropriate staff and ensure they are properly trained.
3. Identify root-cause analysis tools and techniques and ensure all staff who participate in analysis are trained in their use.
   These tools and techniques may include cause-and-effect diagrams, interrelationship diagrams, causal factor tree analysis, etc.
4. Prepare a post-incident analysis report.
   This report should detail the organization's recommendations for improvement in administrative, technical, and physical controls, as well as improvements to the incident management process.
5. Document the results of post-incident root-cause analysis in the incident knowledgebase so that this information is available for use in other processes such as problem management.

IMC:SG5.SP2 INTEGRATE WITH THE PROBLEM MANAGEMENT PROCESS

A link between incident handling and the organization's problem management process is established.

Problem management is the process that an organization uses to identify recurring problems, examine root causes, and develop solutions for these problems to prevent future, similar incidents. There is a strong link between incident management and control and problem management in that incident management is often the process where symptoms of a larger problem are first presented. The organization's problem management process and system (which are beyond the scope of CERT-RMM) need information from post-incident review to be effective; likewise, incident management may rely on information from problem management to diagnose and respond to incidents, particularly if no action has been taken to resolve identified problems or root causes. Formal linkages between problem management and incident management strengthen the organization's overall ability to prevent incidents and minimize costly and reactive response activities.

Typical work products

1. Problem report

Subpractices

1. Establish a problem management system to ensure that all operational events that are not part of standard operation (incidents, problems, and errors) are recorded, analyzed, and resolved in a timely manner.
2. Document problem reports that arise from incident management and deliver these reports to the problem management process.
    The organization's incident knowledgebase can serve as a central repository that links the incident management and problem management processes so that duplicative effort in documenting issues and problems can be avoided.
3. Periodically review problem reports and their status to determine their impact on future incident detection and analysis.
4. Update the incident knowledgebase with information gathered in the problem management process.

IMC:SG5.SP3 TRANSLATE EXPERIENCE TO STRATEGY

The lessons learned from incident management are analyzed and translated into service and asset protection and continuity strategies.

The costs associated with incident detection and response are an investment for the organization only to the extent that what is learned in these processes can be used by the organization to make it more efficient and effective in dealing with future events and in enhancing its approach to resilience. Lessons learned in incident management should serve as a benchmark for determining the validity and effectiveness of the organization's current strategies for protecting and sustaining assets. In addition, lessons learned should provide valuable information for continuous improvement of the incident management process.

> These are examples of areas that have to be addressed after an incident:
> - Update protection strategies and controls to protect assets and services from future incidents of similar type and nature.
> - Update policies to reflect lessons learned.
> - Update training for employees regarding the incident.
> - Revise continuity plans and strategies to protect and sustain services and assets.
> - Review and revise life-cycle processes.
> - Review and revise asset-level resilience requirements, if necessary.
> - Revise incident criteria.
> - Develop standardized responses to common incidents.
> - Improve incident management processes.

Typical work products

1. Controls strategy
2. Service continuity plans
3. Resilience policy
4. Training needs and requirements
5. Incident management process improvements list
6. Service and asset resilience requirements
7. Updated incident knowledgebase

Subpractices

1. Review incident knowledgebase information and update the following areas accordingly:
    - protection strategies and controls for assets involved in the incident
    - continuity plans and strategies for sustaining assets involved in the incident
    - information security and other organizational policies that need to reflect new standards, procedures, and guidelines based on what is learned in the incident handling
    - training for staff on information security, business continuity, and IT operations
2. Review incident management and control processes and update them for any perceived deficiencies or omissions.
3. Update resilience requirements for assets and services based on what is learned in the incident management process.
4. Quantify and monitor the types, volumes, and costs of incidents.

Elaborated Generic Practices by Goal

Refer to the Generic Goals and Practices document in Appendix A for general guidance that applies to all process areas. This section provides elaborations relative to the application of the Generic Goals and Practices to the Incident Management and Control process area.

IMC:GG1 ACHIEVE SPECIFIC GOALS

The operational resilience management system supports and enables achievement of the specific goals of the Incident Management and Control process area by transforming identifiable input work products to produce identifiable output work products.

IMC:GG1.GP1 PERFORM SPECIFIC PRACTICES

Perform the specific practices of the Incident Management and Control process area to develop work products and provide services to achieve the specific goals of the process area.

Elaboration:

Specific practices IMC:SG1.SP1 through IMC:SG5.SP3 are performed to achieve the goals of the incident management and control process.

IMC:GG2 INSTITUTIONALIZE A MANAGED PROCESS

Incident management and control is institutionalized as a managed process.

IMC:GG2.GP1 ESTABLISH PROCESS GOVERNANCE

Establish and maintain governance over the planning and performance of the incident management and control process.

Refer to the Enterprise Focus process area for more information about providing sponsorship and oversight to the incident management and control process.

Subpractices

1. Establish governance over process activities.

   Elaboration:

   > Governance over the incident management and control process may be exhibited by
   > - developing and publicizing higher-level managers' objectives and requirements for the process
   > - sponsoring process policies, procedures, standards, and guidelines and the roles of staff in the process
   > - making higher-level managers aware of applicable compliance obligations related to the process, and regularly reporting on the organization's satisfaction of these obligations to higher-level managers
   > - sponsoring and funding process activities
   > - providing input to the organization's designated process for identifying, analyzing, and responding to events and incidents and the chosen means for implementing and managing the process (i.e., dedicated team, virtual team, etc.)

- regular reporting from organizational units to higher-level managers on events and incidents that may affect the organization's ability to achieve its goals
- verifying that the process supports strategic resilience objectives and is focused on the assets and services that are of the highest relative value in meeting strategic objectives
- creating dedicated higher-level management feedback loops and oversight on incident management and recommendations for improving the process
- providing input on identifying, assessing, and managing operational risks resulting from incidents
- conducting regular internal and external audits and related reporting to audit committees on process effectiveness
- providing visible, continued support for the process through board-level activities such as inclusion on meeting agendas or committees
- creating formal programs to measure the effectiveness of process activities, and reporting these measurements to higher-level managers

2. Develop and publish organizational policy for the process.

Elaboration:

The incident management and control policy should address
- responsibility, authority, and ownership for performing process activities
- procedures, standards, and guidelines for
  - detecting, logging, reporting, and tracking events
  - collecting and preserving evidence
  - triaging events
  - analyzing events
  - declaring an incident from one or more events
  - responding to incidents, including escalation procedures and developing incident response
  - recovering from incidents
  - communicating incidents
- post-incident review, problem resolution, and closure
- methods for measuring adherence to policy, exceptions granted, and policy violations

IMC:GG2.GP2 PLAN THE PROCESS

Establish and maintain the plan for performing the incident management and control process.

Elaboration:

Specific practice IMC:SG1.SP1 requires the development of a plan for how the organization will carry out incident management and control. In generic practice

IMC:GG2.GP2 as related to incident management, the planning elements required in IMC:SG1.SP1 are formalized and structured and are performed in a managed way. The plan for the incident management and control process should reflect the organization's stated philosophy of incident management and the preferred means for handling incidents (i.e., through a dedicated or permanent team, a virtual team, etc.).

Subpractices

1. Define and document the plan for performing the process.
2. Define and document the process description.
3. Review the plan with relevant stakeholders and get their commitment.
4. Revise the plan as necessary.

IMC:GG2.GP3 PROVIDE RESOURCES

Provide adequate resources for performing the incident management and control process, developing the work products, and providing the services of the process.

Elaboration:

Specific practice IMC:SG1.SP2 requires the formal assignment of resources to the incident management and control process plan.

Subpractices

1. Staff the process.

    Elaboration:

    > These are examples of staff required to perform the incident management and control process:
    > - staff responsible for
    >   - identifying, detecting, logging, reporting, and tracking events
    >   - collecting and preserving evidence for events and incidents
    >   - triaging events
    >   - analyzing events and incidents, including declaring an incident from one or more events
    >   - developing and executing plans for responding to incidents, including escalation
    >   - recovering from incidents
    >   - communicating incidents
    >   - performing post-incident reviews, resolving problems, and closing incidents
    >   - developing incident management plans and ensuring they are aligned with stakeholder requirements and needs
    >   - managing external entities that have contractual obligations for process activities

> - owners and custodians of high-value assets that support the accomplishment of operational resilience management objectives
> - internal and external auditors responsible for reporting to appropriate committees on process effectiveness

Refer to the Organizational Training and Awareness process area for information about training staff for resilience roles and responsibilities.

Refer to the Human Resource Management process area for information about acquiring staff to fulfill roles and responsibilities.

2. Fund the process.

Elaboration:

In the case of incident management and control, funding must extend to supporting the incident life cycle and consideration must be given to unknown funding requirements related to incident management that are relative to the type and extent of incident and the impact on the organization. Extending consideration to these unpredictable needs provides the organization a level of control over unplanned and potentially unconstrained costs.

Refer to the Financial Resource Management process area for information about budgeting for, funding, and accounting for incident management and control.

3. Provide necessary tools, techniques, and methods to perform the process.

Elaboration:

> These are examples of tools, techniques, and methods to support the incident management and control process:
> - methods, techniques, and tools for
>   - event identification, detection *(refer to IMC:SG2)*, and reporting
>   - analyzing events and incidents, including determining when one or more events should be declared an incident
>   - collecting, documenting, and preserving evidence for events and incidents
>   - recovering from events
> - methods and tools for event and incident logging and tracking
> - methods for triaging events
> - root-cause analysis techniques and tools, such as cause-and-effect diagrams, interrelationship diagrams, and causal factor tree analysis
> - incident databases and knowledgebases, including predetermined response and recovery actions for specific types of incidents
> - methods and techniques for responding to events
> - communications methods for reporting and escalating incidents
> - methods for conducting post-incident reviews and ensuring lessons learned are reflected in process activities

IMC:GG2.GP4 ASSIGN RESPONSIBILITY

Assign responsibility and authority for performing the incident management and control process, developing the work products, and providing the services of the process.

Elaboration:

Specific practice IMG:SG1.SP1 indicates that the incident management plan should define the roles and responsibilities necessary to carry out the plan, as well as document commitments from those responsible. Specific practice IMC:SG1.SP2 requires the assignment of staff to the incident management plan, as well as the identification of skill and staff gaps for each area of responsibility. Generic practice IMC:GG2.GP4 requires the assignment of responsibility for the activities in the incident management life cycle, including the identification of events and incidents, analysis of incidents, and incident response.

Refer to the Human Resource Management process area for more information about establishing resilience as a job responsibility, developing resilience performance goals and objectives, and measuring and assessing performance against these goals and objectives.

Subpractices

1. Assign responsibility and authority for performing the process.

   Elaboration:

   Incident management and control activities may be temporal (i.e., involved with response to a specific incident) or permanent (involved with support activities that are not related to any specific incident).

   To assign responsibility and authority for performing the incident management and control process, organizations may establish dedicated incident management teams that address the majority of incident handling and management activities or assign staff to virtual teams that come together when required. Other structures may also be implemented, such as decentralized dedicated teams, which would require varying levels of responsibility and authority to be assigned.

2. Assign responsibility and authority for performing the specific tasks of the process.

   Elaboration:

   > Responsibility and authority for performing incident management and control tasks can be formalized by
   > - defining roles and responsibilities in the process plan
   > - assigning staff to dedicated or virtual incident handling and management teams as a primary job responsibility

- including process tasks and responsibility for these tasks in specific job descriptions
- including process tasks in staff performance management goals and objectives with requisite measurement of progress against these goals
- developing policy requiring organizational unit managers, line of business managers, project managers, and asset and service owners and custodians to participate in and derive benefit from the process for assets and services under their ownership or custodianship
- developing and implementing contractual instruments (including service level agreements) with external entities to establish responsibility and authority for performing process tasks on outsourced functions, assets, and services
- including process tasks in measuring performance of external entities against contractual instruments

Refer to the External Dependencies Management process area for additional details about managing relationships with external entities.

3. Confirm that people assigned with responsibility and authority understand it and are willing and able to accept it.

IMC:GG2.GP5 TRAIN PEOPLE

Train the people performing or supporting the incident management and control process as needed.

Refer to the Organizational Training and Awareness process area for more information about training the people performing or supporting the process.

Refer to the Human Resource Management process area for more information about inventorying skill sets, establishing a skill set baseline, identifying required skill sets, and measuring and addressing skill deficiencies.

Subpractices

1. Identify process skill needs.

   Elaboration:

   These are examples of skills required in the incident management and control process:
   - event detection, reporting, and tracking, including service desk activities
   - documenting and logging event reports
   - collecting and preserving evidence
   - technical analysis of events and incidents, including triage
   - declaring incidents
   - escalating and communicating incidents
   - understanding and applying laws, rules, and regulations

> - performing incident response, including damage containment
> - creating, managing, and deploying incident response teams
> - developing and implementing administrative, technical, and physical controls
> - performing root-cause analysis and post-incident review
> - using tools, techniques, and methods necessary to handle incidents throughout their life cycle, including those necessary to perform the process using the selected methods, techniques, and tools identified in IMC:GG2.GP3 subpractice 3
> - knowledge unique to each type of asset or service that may be the target of an incident
> - working effectively and collaborating with asset owners and custodians
> - eliciting and prioritizing stakeholder requirements and needs and interpreting them to develop effective incident management plans and plans for handling specific types of incidents

2. Identify process skill gaps based on available resources and their current skill levels.
3. Identify training opportunities to address skill gaps.

Elaboration:

Training can be obtained for all aspects of incident handling and for forming and managing formal incident teams. In addition, certification programs are available to certify incident handlers and for developing and participating on incident management teams.

> These are examples of training topics:
> - event and incident detection
> - event and incident logging
> - incident containment and evidence preservation
> - incident forensics tools and techniques
> - event and incident analysis
> - event triaging
> - incident declaration
> - escalation procedures
> - incident response
> - incident response teams
> - incident communications, including general communications skill development
> - post-incident review
> - supporting asset owners and custodians in understanding the process and their roles and responsibilities with respect to its activities
> - working with external entities that have responsibility for process activities
> - using process methods, tools, and techniques, including those identified in IMC:GG2:GP3 subpractice 3

4. Provide training and review the training needs as necessary.

IMC:GG2.GP6 MANAGE WORK PRODUCT CONFIGURATIONS

Place designated work products of the incident management and control process under appropriate levels of control.

Elaboration:

Generic practice IMC:GG2.GP6 generically covers the recommended updating of the incident knowledgebase as described in several IMC-specific practices, as well as other work products of the incident management and control process.

The tools, techniques, and methods used to populate and maintain the incident knowledgebase should be employed to perform consistent and structured version control over the knowledgebase to ensure that incident information is current, accurate, and "official." The tools, techniques, and methods can also be used to securely store the knowledgebase, provide access control over inquiry, modification, and deletion, and to track version changes and updates.

These are examples of incident management and control work products placed under control:
- event reports, including sources of event detection and reporting
- incident management plans and the process plan
- incident response strategy and plan
- event and incident status reports
- incident communications plan
- list of incident stakeholders
- incident management policies, procedures, standards, and guidelines
- incident knowledgebase
- event and incident evidence
- incident declaration criteria
- incident escalation procedures and criteria
- post-incident analysis reports
- list of incident management process improvements
- contracts with external entities

IMC:GG2.GP7 IDENTIFY AND INVOLVE RELEVANT STAKEHOLDERS

Identify and involve the relevant stakeholders of the incident management and control process as planned.

Elaboration:

Stakeholders of the incident management and control process may extend across the organization and externally to business partners and vendors. The identification of these stakeholders in generic practice IMC:GG2.GP7 is in addition to the identification of stakeholders of the incident communications process described in IMC:SG4.SP3, although it is recognized that these may be the same or similar.

Subpractices

1. Identify process stakeholders and their appropriate involvement.

   Elaboration:

   > These are examples of stakeholders of the incident management and control process:
   > - incident owners
   > - asset owners and custodians
   > - service owners
   > - organizational unit and line of business managers responsible for high-value assets and the services they support
   > - staff who serve key roles in incident communications activities, such as public relations
   > - staff who provide input to and resolution of incidents as they are escalated
   > - staff responsible for developing, implementing, and managing an internal control system for assets
   > - external entities involved in process activities and responsible for managing high-value assets
   > - human resources
   > - information technology staff
   > - service desk staff
   > - staff responsible for physical security
   > - legal and law enforcement staff, including federal agencies
   > - internal and external auditors
   > - regulatory and governing agencies

   > Stakeholders are involved in various tasks in the incident management and control process, such as
   > - detecting events and incidents
   > - planning for incident handling, management, and response
   > - making commitments to process plans and activities
   > - collecting, documenting, and preserving event and incident evidence
   > - analyzing events and incidents
   > - declaring incidents
   > - responding to incidents, including participating on incident response teams
   > - communicating events and incidents and the status of incidents as they move through the incident life cycle

> - escalating incidents
> - coordinating process activities
> - reviewing and appraising the effectiveness of process activities
> - performing post-incident review and improvement processes

2. Communicate the list of stakeholders to planners and those responsible for process performance.
3. Involve relevant stakeholders in the process as planned.

IMC:GG2.GP8 MONITOR AND CONTROL THE PROCESS

Monitor and control the incident management and control process against the plan for performing the process and take appropriate corrective action.

Refer to the Monitoring process area for more information about the collection, organization, and distribution of data that may be useful for monitoring and controlling processes.

Refer to the Measurement and Analysis process area for more information about establishing process metrics and measurement.

Refer to the Enterprise Focus process area for more information about providing process information to managers, identifying issues, and determining appropriate corrective actions.

Subpractices

1. Measure actual performance against the plan for performing the process.
2. Review accomplishments and results of the process against the plan for performing the process.

   Elaboration:

   > These are examples of metrics for the incident management and control process:
   > - percentage of operational time that high-value services and assets were unavailable (as seen by users and customers) due to incidents
   > - percentage of incidents that exploited existing vulnerabilities with known solutions, patches, or workarounds
   > - number and percentage of events or incidents handled in a specific period
   > - number and percentage of events or incidents that are contained in a specific period
   > - percentage of incidents that require escalation
   > - percentage of incidents that require involvement of law enforcement
   > - number of events or incidents that have been logged but not closed

- average time between event detection and related incident declaration, response, or closure
- percentage increase in the volume of events and incidents in a specific period
- extent of consequences to the organization due to incidents by incident type (also referred to as "magnitude")
- percentage increase in the elapsed time of the incident life cycle by incident type
- number and percentage of recurrence of specified events or incidents
- percentage increase in resource needs (training, skill building, additional human resources) to support incident management
- number of post-incident review activities that result in control changes or improvements to the process
- number of incidents referred to the risk management process; number of risks where corrective action is still pending (by risk rank)
- level of adherence to process policies; number of policy violations; number of policy exceptions requested and number approved
- number of process activities that are on track per plan
- rate of change of resource needs to support the process
- rate of change of costs to support the process

3. Review activities, status, and results of the process with the immediate level of managers responsible for the process and identify issues.

Elaboration:

Incident learning processes as described in IMC:SG5 are intended to provide a standard and consistent post-incident review and examination. However, reviews of the incident management and control process may result from periodic audits or examinations, particularly if metrics indicate a rise in incidents of specific types or with increasing impact, or an extension of time required to resolve incidents.

If the incident management and control process is decentralized (i.e., spread across organizational units), post-incident reviews may provide management insight into variations between the organizational units that could impact the organization's overall incident management capability.

Periodic reviews of the incident management and control process are needed to ensure that
- the process is known and accessible
- events and incidents are identified, reported, and addressed on a timely basis
- events and incidents are logged and closed
- proper forensic procedures are used to collect and preserve evidence
- events are properly triaged and analyzed for root causes
- incidents are properly declared

> - incidents are properly escalated to designated stakeholders
> - incident response capabilities are commensurate with the priority of an incident
> - incidents are communicated appropriately to stakeholders at a level commensurate with their involvement
> - event and incident status reports are provided to appropriate stakeholders in a timely manner
> - post-incident reviews are performed to improve the process
> - actions requiring management involvement are elevated in a timely manner
> - the performance of process activities is being monitored and regularly reported
> - key measures are within acceptable ranges as demonstrated in governance dashboards or scorecards and financial reports
> - administrative, technical, and physical controls are operating as intended
> - controls are meeting the stated intent of the resilience requirements
> - actions resulting from internal and external audits are being closed in a timely manner

4. Identify and evaluate the effects of significant deviations from the plan for performing the process.
5. Identify problems in the plan for performing and executing the process.
6. Take corrective action when requirements and objectives are not being satisfied, when issues are identified, or when progress differs significantly from the plan for performing the process.
7. Track corrective action to closure.

IMC:GG2.GP9 OBJECTIVELY EVALUATE ADHERENCE

Objectively evaluate adherence of the incident management and control process against its process description, standards, and procedures, and address non-compliance.

Elaboration:

> These are examples of activities to be reviewed:
> - identifying and detecting events and incidents, including service desk procedures
> - logging, tracking, and reporting events and incidents
> - establishing incident validation criteria
> - collecting, documenting, and preserving evidence
> - triaging events
> - analyzing events and incidents
> - declaring incidents

- escalating incidents
- communicating incidents
- responding to incidents
- recovering from incidents so as to minimize disruption and impact
- closing incidents (and addressing incidents that have not been closed)
- performing post-incident reviews
- the alignment of stakeholder requirements with process plans
- assignment of responsibility, accountability, and authority for process activities
- determination of the adequacy of process reports and reviews in informing decision makers regarding the performance of operational resilience management activities and the need to take corrective action, if any
- use of process work products for improving strategies for protecting and sustaining assets and services

---

These are examples of work products to be reviewed:
- incident management plans
- event and incident service desk reports and documentation
- incident management policies, procedures, standards, and guidelines
- incident knowledgebase
- evidence collection and preservation guidelines, as well as documentation on past collection activities
- event and incident analysis reports
- incident declaration criteria
- incident escalation criteria and procedures
- incident response documentation (of past response actions)
- incident communications plan and status reports
- post-incident review reports
- issues that have been referred to the risk management process
- process methods, techniques, and tools
- metrics for the process *(Refer to IMC:GG2.GP8 subpractice 2.)*
- contracts with external entities

IMC:GG2.GP10 REVIEW STATUS WITH HIGHER-LEVEL MANAGERS

Review the activities, status, and results of the incident management and control process with higher-level managers and resolve issues.

Refer to the Enterprise Focus process area for more information about providing sponsorship and oversight to the operational resilience management system.

IMC:GG3 INSTITUTIONALIZE A DEFINED PROCESS

Incident management and control is institutionalized as a defined process.

IMC:GG3.GP1 ESTABLISH A DEFINED PROCESS

Establish and maintain the description of a defined incident management and control process.

Elaboration:

Incident management and control may be performed in either a centralized or decentralized manner. The way in which the organization institutionalizes the incident management and control process varies based on the size of the organization, the diversity of operational environments, and other factors. This may lead to a range of implementation methods, including the use of a dedicated centralized team, dedicated virtual teams, decentralized dedicated teams, or other combinations.

Establishing and tailoring process assets, including standard processes, are addressed in the Organizational Process Definition process area.

Establishing process needs and objectives and selecting, improving, and deploying process assets, including standard processes, are addressed in the Organizational Process Focus process area.

Subpractices

1. Select from the organization's set of standard processes those processes that cover the incident management and control process and best meet the needs of the organizational unit or line of business.
2. Establish the defined process by tailoring the selected processes according to the organization's tailoring guidelines.
3. Ensure that the organization's process objectives are appropriately addressed in the defined process, and ensure that process governance extends to the tailored processes.
4. Document the defined process and the records of the tailoring.
5. Revise the description of the defined process as necessary.

IMC:GG3.GP2 COLLECT IMPROVEMENT INFORMATION

Collect incident management and control work products, measures, measurement results, and improvement information derived from planning and performing the process to support future use and improvement of the organization's processes and process assets.

Elaboration:

Specific goal IMC:SG5 and its specific practices describe capturing lessons learned in post-incident review and translating these into improvements to incident management and control process activities. Such improvement directly supports the improvement of service continuity and strategies to protect and sustain assets and services.

> These are examples of improvement work products and information:
> - service desk reports or similar documentation of reported events
> - incident reports from the incident knowledgebase and the level to which the knowledgebase reflects the current status of all incidents
> - issues related to collecting, documenting, and preserving evidence
> - issues related to deploying forensic tools and techniques
> - lessons learned in triaging and analyzing events and in analyzing incidents
> - communications issues
> - issues related to declaring incidents
> - incident response successes and failures
> - issues related to closing incidents
> - lessons learned in post-incident review
> - problem reports and corresponding actions
> - changes to asset and service resilience requirements resulting from post-incident review
> - metrics and measurements of the viability of the process *(Refer to IMC:GG2.GP8 subpractice 2.)*
> - changes and trends in operating conditions, risk conditions, and the risk environment that affect process results
> - recommendations for control improvements
> - recommended updates to service continuity plans

Establishing the measurement repository and process asset library is addressed in the Organizational Process Definition process area. Updating the measurement repository and process asset library as part of process improvement and deployment is addressed in the Organizational Process Focus process area.

Subpractices

1. Store process and work product measures in the organization's measurement repository.
2. Submit documentation for inclusion in the organization's process asset library.
3. Document lessons learned from the process for inclusion in the organization's process asset library.
4. Propose improvements to the organizational process assets.

KNOWLEDGE AND INFORMATION MANAGEMENT
Operations

Purpose

The purpose of Knowledge and Information Management is to establish and manage an appropriate level of controls to support the confidentiality, integrity, and availability of the organization's information, vital records, and intellectual property.

Introductory Notes

The importance of information as an organizational asset continues to grow. The focus of organizations has increasingly turned to intangible assets such that the ratio of tangible assets to intangible assets continues to decrease. This supports the assertion that information is one of the most—if not the most—high-value organizational assets. It is the raw material that is used by and created in services. The protection of this intellectual and enterprise capital—to ensure that it is available in the form intended for use in services—is the focus of the Knowledge and Information Management process area.

An information asset can be described as information or data that is of value to the organization, including such diverse information as patient records, intellectual property, vital business records and contracts, and customer information. The unique aspect of information assets is that they can exist in physical form (on paper, CDs, or other media) or electronic form (files, databases, on personal computers). The Knowledge and Information Management process area addresses the importance of information assets in the operational resilience of services, as well as unique attributes specific to information assets such as those described in Table KIM.1.

TABLE KIM.1 Attributes of Information Assets

Attribute	Description
Confidentiality	For an information asset, the quality of being accessible only to authorized people, processes, and devices
Integrity	For an information asset, the quality of being in the condition intended by the owner and so continuing to be useful for the purposes intended by the owner
Availability	For an information asset, the quality of being accessible to authorized users (people, processes, or devices) whenever it is needed
Privacy	The assurance that information about an individual is disclosed only to people, processes, and devices authorized by that individual or permitted under privacy laws and regulations
Sensitivity	A measure of the degree to which an information asset must be protected based on the consequences of its unauthorized access, modification, or disclosure

In this process area, information assets are prioritized according to their value in supporting high-value organizational services. Physical, technical, and administrative controls that keep information assets viable and sustainable are selected, implemented, and managed, and the effectiveness of these controls is monitored. In addition, information asset risks are identified and mitigated in an attempt to prevent disruption when possible. Information is categorized as to its organizational sensitivity, and consideration is given to the backup and storage of important information and vital records in case of loss or destruction, or to support the execution of service continuity plans.

Knowledge management is also performed in this process area: the requirement to identify and document the organizational and intellectual knowledge of staff that is important to the effective operation of the organization's services. This information asset is often not documented, has poorly developed security requirements, and lacks adequate protection. It is also often one of the most high-value information assets in the organization.

Related Process Areas

The establishment and management of resilience requirements for information assets are performed in the Resilience Requirements Development and Resilience Requirements Management process areas.

The identification, definition, inventorying, management, and control of information assets are addressed in the Asset Definition and Management process area.

The risk management cycle for information assets is addressed in the Risk Management process area.

The management of the internal control system that ensures the protection of information assets is addressed in the Controls Management process area.

The selection, implementation, and management of access controls for information assets are performed in the Access Management process area.

Summary of Specific Goals and Practices

KIM:SG1 Establish and Prioritize Information Assets
    KIM:SG1.SP1   Prioritize Information Assets
    KIM:SG1.SP2   Categorize Information Assets
KIM:SG2 Protect Information Assets
    KIM:SG2.SP1   Assign Resilience Requirements to Information Assets
    KIM:SG2.SP2   Establish and Implement Controls
KIM:SG3 Manage Information Asset Risk
    KIM:SG3.SP1   Identify and Assess Information Asset Risk
    KIM:SG3.SP2   Mitigate Information Asset Risk
KIM:SG4 Manage Information Asset Confidentiality and Privacy
    KIM:SG4.SP1   Encrypt High-Value Information
    KIM:SG4.SP2   Control Access to Information Assets
    KIM:SG4.SP3   Control Information Asset Disposition
KIM:SG5 Manage Information Asset Integrity
    KIM:SG5.SP1   Control Modification of Information Assets
    KIM:SG5.SP2   Manage Information Asset Configuration
    KIM:SG5.SP3   Verify Validity of Information
KIM:SG6 Manage Information Asset Availability
    KIM:SG6.SP1   Perform Information Duplication and Retention
    KIM:SG6.SP2   Manage Organizational Knowledge

Specific Practices by Goal

KIM:SG1 ESTABLISH AND PRIORITIZE INFORMATION ASSETS

Information assets are prioritized to ensure the resilience of high-value services in which they are used.

In this goal, the organization establishes the subset of information assets (from its information asset inventory) on which it must focus operational resilience activities because of their importance to the sustained operation of essential services.

    Prioritization of information assets is a risk management activity. It establishes the information assets that are of most value to the organization and for which measures to protect and sustain them are required. Failure to prioritize information assets may lead to inadequate operational resilience of high-value assets and excessive levels of operational resilience for non-high-value assets.

Information assets may also be of high priority to the organization because of their sensitivity. The unique nature of these information assets may require a higher level of resilience controls.

KIM:SG1.SP1 PRIORITIZE INFORMATION ASSETS

Information assets are prioritized relative to their importance in supporting the delivery of high-value services.

The prioritization of information assets must be performed in order to ensure that the organization properly directs its operational resilience resources to the assets that most directly impact and contribute to services that support the organization's mission. These assets require the organization's direct attention because their disruption has the potential to cause the most significant organizational consequences.

Information asset prioritization is performed relative to services—that is, information assets associated with high-value services are those that must be most highly prioritized for operational resilience activities.

> However, the organization can use other criteria to establish high-priority information assets, such as
> - the use of the asset in the general management and control of the organization (contracts, articles of incorporation, etc.)
> - highly sensitive or classified information *(Categorization of information assets is addressed in KIM:SG1.SP2.)*
> - information that represents the organization's trade secrets or proprietary information such as intellectual property *(Intellectual property management is addressed in KIM:SG4.SP2.)*
> - information assets that are of high value to more than one service
> - value of the asset in directly supporting the organization's achievement of critical success factors and strategic objectives
> - the organization's tolerance for "pain"—the degree to which it can suffer a loss or destruction of the information asset and continue to meet its mission

Typically, the organization selects a subset of information assets from its asset inventory; however, the organization could compile a list of high-value information assets based on risk or other factors. However, failure to select assets from the organization's asset inventory poses additional risk that some high-value information assets may never have been inventoried. *(The identification, definition, management, and control of information assets are addressed in the Asset Definition and Management process area.)*

Typical work products

1. List of high-value information assets

Subpractices

1. Compile a list of high-value information assets from the organization's information asset inventory.

    These assets should include those that would be required for the successful execution of service continuity plans and service restoration plans. Assets that are generally important to the successful operation of the organization (vital records, contracts, etc.) should also be included in the organization's list. The list of high-value information assets should be the focus of operational risk and resilience activities.

2. Periodically validate and update the list of high-value information assets based on operational and organizational environment changes.

KIM:SG1.SP2 CATEGORIZE INFORMATION ASSETS

Information assets that support high-value services are categorized as to their organizational sensitivity.

The categorization of information assets is a key consideration in the development of adequate resilience requirements and in the implementation of strategies to protect and sustain them.

An information sensitivity categorization scheme and the corresponding information handling processes and procedures provide a way for the organization to put its mark on information assets relative to their risk tolerances and to allow for an appropriate level of corresponding handling, protection, and resilience. Failure to provide an information sensitivity categorization scheme allows for organizational staff to determine sensitivity using their own guidelines and judgment, which may vary widely. A consistently applied sensitivity categorization scheme also ensures consistent handling of information assets across the organization and with external entities.

Sensitivity categorization is a characteristic of an information asset that should be documented as part of the information asset inventory. (*See ADM:SG1.SP2 in the Asset Definition and Management process area.*)

Typical work products

1. Information asset sensitivity categorization scheme
2. Information asset sensitivity categorization
3. Information asset handling procedures and guidelines

Subpractices

1. Develop an information asset sensitivity categorization scheme.

    The sensitivity categorization scheme is unique to the organization and should cover all categories of information assets. The categorization levels should be appropriately defined and communicated and integrated with information asset handling and labeling procedures.

> These are examples of information asset sensitivity categorization levels:
> - unclassified, which typically includes
>   - public or non-sensitive (information that is approved for public use)
>   - restricted or internal use only (memos, project plans, audit reports)
>   - confidential or proprietary (organizational intellectual property, product designs, customer information, employee records)
> - classified, which may include levels such as
>   - secret
>   - top secret

2. Assign responsibility for the assignment of sensitivity categorization levels to information assets.

    All staff who handle information assets (including those who are external to the organization) should be trained in the organization's sensitivity categorization scheme and be authorized to assign a categorization level. Training should also be provided for proper handling of each category of information asset.

3. Assign sensitivity categorization levels to information assets.

    This practice typically occurs when the information asset is defined. The categorization level should be kept as part of the definition of the information asset in the asset inventory.

4. Establish policies for proper handling of information assets according to the sensitivity categorization scheme.

5. Establish policies and procedures for proper labeling for each category of information asset.

KIM:SG2 PROTECT INFORMATION ASSETS

Administrative, technical, and physical controls for information assets are identified, implemented, monitored, and managed.

Information assets are typically some of the most vulnerable assets of the organization. Information assets come in many different forms, are often under-appreciated, and may be highly intangible (such as the knowledge of staff). Information assets are also subject to the entire range of resilience requirements—information must often be limited to those with proper authorization (confidentiality), must be reliable and usable in the form intended (integrity), and must be made available when needed to support vital services (availability).

Protecting information assets from vulnerabilities, threats, and risks requires that the organization develop appropriate resilience requirements for these assets and follow through with the development, implementation, and management of an appropriate level of administrative, technical, and physical controls to manage the conditions that could cause disruption of these assets.

The organization selects and designs controls based on the information asset's resilience requirements and the range of media on which the information asset resides (paper, electronic files, etc.). The effectiveness of these controls is monitored on a regular basis to ensure that they meet the information asset's resilience requirements.

KIM:SG2.SP1 Assign Resilience Requirements to Information Assets

Resilience requirements that have been defined are assigned to information assets.

Resilience requirements form the basis for the actions that the organization takes to protect and sustain information assets. These requirements are established commensurate with the value of the asset to services that it supports. The resilience requirements for information assets must be assigned to the assets so that the appropriate type and level of protective controls can be designed, implemented, and monitored to meet the requirements.

Resilience requirements for information assets are developed in the Resilience Requirements Development process area. However, information asset resilience requirements may not be formally defined or they may be assumed based on the acquisition of information assets. These requirements may be under management but not formally associated with information assets. Thus, the assignment of these requirements is necessary as a foundational step for controls management.

Typical work products

1. Information asset resilience requirements

Subpractices

1. Assign resilience requirements to high-value information assets.
2. Document the requirements (if they are currently not documented) and include them in the asset definition.

KIM:SG2.SP2 Establish and Implement Controls

Administrative, technical, and physical controls that are required to meet the established resilience requirements are identified and implemented.

The organization must implement an internal control system that protects and sustains the essential operation of information assets commensurate with their role in supporting essential organizational services. Controls are essentially the methods, policies, and procedures that the organization uses to protect and sustain high-value assets at an acceptable level. They typically fall into three categories: administrative (or managerial), technical, and physical. This is necessary particularly for information assets because they come in so many different forms and are pervasive across the organization.

- Administrative controls (often called "management" controls) ensure alignment to management's intentions and include such artifacts as governance, policy, monitoring, auditing, separation of duties, and the development and implementation of service continuity plans.
- Technical controls are the technical manifestation of protection methods for information assets. Most prominently, they include electronic access controls, but they can also include such hardware devices as firewalls. By far, technical controls are the most pervasive type of protective controls and are often associated with security activities.
- Physical controls prevent the physical access to and modification of information assets. These controls typically include devices such as card readers on file room doors and other physical barrier methods.

Typical work products

1. Information asset administrative controls
2. Information asset technical controls
3. Information asset physical controls

Subpractices

1. Establish and implement administrative controls for information assets.

> Administrative controls for protecting information assets include
> - information security policies that govern the behavior of users, including
>   - policies for the proper sensitivity categorization of information assets
>   - policies for the proper disposition of information assets
>   - policies for the proper backup and archiving of information assets
>   - policies for the removal of information assets from the workplace
> - training to ensure proper information asset definition and handling *(See the Organizational Training and Awareness process area.)*
> - logging, monitoring, and auditing controls to detect and report unauthorized access and use *(See the Monitoring process area.)*
> - governance over the proper use and distribution of information, and the protection of information assets *(See the Enterprise Focus process area.)*
> - development, testing, and implementation of service continuity plans, including information asset recovery and restoration *(See the Service Continuity process area.)*

2. Establish and implement technical controls for information assets.

> Technical controls include such controls as
> - access controls for systems, databases, files, and other electronic forms of information, including user and privilege management and access management (via passwords, etc.)
> - automated backup, retention, and recovery of information assets
> - modification controls that prevent unauthorized modification and that log and report modification actions by authorized individuals

3. Establish and implement physical controls for information assets.

> Physical controls for protecting information assets include such controls as
> - clean desk and clean screen policies
> - physical access controls on file rooms and work areas where paper and technical information assets are stored
> - facility controls that notify staff when non-employees are on the premises

4. Monitor the effectiveness of administrative, technical, and physical controls, and identify deficiencies that must be resolved.

KIM:SG3 MANAGE INFORMATION ASSET RISK

Operational risks to information assets are identified and managed.

The management of risk for information assets is the specific application of risk management tools, techniques, and methods to the information assets of the organization. Because of their pervasiveness across the organization, and the various forms in which they can be found, there are many opportunities for information assets to be threatened and for risk to be realized by the organization. Risks to information assets can result in consequences to the organization, including the disruption of high-value services due to the lack of information integrity and availability.

Managing information asset risks involves determining the places where information assets "live"—where they are stored, transported, or processed—typically called "containers." It is at these points where vulnerabilities and threats to information assets arise and where mitigation controls must be implemented to protect the assets from disruption or misuse. These containers include technology, physical constructs, and even people who have knowledge or information that can be disclosed or made unavailable when needed for high-value services.

KIM:SG3.SP1 IDENTIFY AND ASSESS INFORMATION ASSET RISK

Risks to information assets are periodically identified and assessed.

Operational risks that can affect information assets must be identified and mitigated in order to actively manage the resilience of these assets and, more important, the resilience of services with which these assets are associated.

The identification of information asset risks forms a baseline from which a continuous risk management process can be established and managed.

The subpractices included in this practice are generically addressed in goals RISK:SG3 and RISK:SG4 in the Risk Management process area.

Typical work products

1. Information asset risk statements, with impact valuation
2. List of information asset risks, with categorization and prioritization

Subpractices

1. Determine the scope of risk assessment for information assets.
   Determining which information assets to include in regular risk management activities depends on many factors, including the value of the asset to the organization and its resilience requirements.

2. Identify risks to information assets.
   Identification of risk for information assets requires an examination of where these assets are stored, transported, and processed. These places could be internal or external to the organization. Operational risks should be identified in this context so that mitigation actions are more focused and directed. Typical information asset containers include
   - technical containers, such as information systems or hardware such as servers, network segments, or personal computers
   - physical containers, such as paper, file rooms, storage spaces, or other media such as CDs, disks, flash drives
   - people, including those who might have detailed knowledge about the information asset

3. Analyze risks to information assets.

4. Categorize and prioritize risks to information assets.

5. Assign a risk disposition to each information asset risk.

6. Monitor the risk and the risk strategy on a regular basis to ensure that the risk does not pose additional threat to the organization.

7. Develop a strategy for those risks that the organization decides to mitigate.

KIM:SG3.SP2 MITIGATE INFORMATION ASSET RISK

Risk mitigation strategies for information assets are developed and implemented.

The mitigation of information asset risk involves the development of strategies that seek to minimize the risk to an acceptable level. This includes reducing the likelihood of risks to information assets, minimizing exposure to these risks, developing service continuity plans to keep the information assets viable during times of disruption, and developing recovery and restoration plans to address the consequences of realized risk.

Risk mitigation for information assets requires the development of risk mitigation plans (which may include the development of new or revision of existing information asset controls) and to implement and monitor these plans for effectiveness.

The subpractices included in this practice are generically addressed in goal RISK:SG5 in the Risk Management process area.

Typical work products

1. Information asset risk mitigation plans
2. List of those responsible for addressing and tracking risks
3. Status on information asset risk mitigation plans

Subpractices

1. Develop and implement risk mitigation strategies for all risks that have a "mitigation" or "control" disposition.
2. Validate the risk mitigation plans by comparing them to existing strategies for protecting and sustaining information assets.
3. Identify the person or group responsible for each risk mitigation plan and ensure that they have the authority to act and the proper level of skills and training to implement and monitor the plan.
4. Address residual risk.
5. Implement the risk mitigation plans and provide a method to monitor the effectiveness of these plans.
6. Monitor risk status.
7. Collect performance measures on the risk management process.

KIM:SG4 MANAGE INFORMATION ASSET CONFIDENTIALITY AND PRIVACY

The confidentiality and privacy considerations of information assets are managed.

Confidentiality and privacy are fundamental resilience requirements for information assets. These requirements are unique to information assets because the inadvertent or intentional disclosure of information to unauthorized staff can result in significant consequences to the organization, including reputation damage, harmful effects to customers and stakeholders (such as identity theft), and legal and financial penalties.

Typically, breaches of the confidentiality and privacy requirements do not directly result in disruption of associated services. Instead, because of the nature of the consequences of the breach, the disruption typically occurs at the enterprise or organizational level, and this in turn has a negative impact on one or more operational services. Thus, while the damage is referential, there is still an impact on operations that must be managed.

The development, implementation, and management of appropriate controls can limit potential breaches of confidentiality and privacy and minimize impact on operational services. These controls include encryption of data and information, controlling access to these assets, and controlling how these assets are disposed of after their useful life.

General controls relative to preserving the confidentiality and privacy of information assets may be included as part of practice KIM:SG2.SP2. However, the specific practices contained in KIM:SG4.SP1 through KIM:SG4.SP3 are targeted baseline controls that must be implemented to manage the confidentiality and privacy aspects of information assets that affect operational resilience.

KIM:SG4.SP1 ENCRYPT HIGH-VALUE INFORMATION

Cryptographic controls are applied to information assets to ensure confidentiality and prevent accidental disclosure.

Encryption provides an additional layer of control over information assets by ensuring that they are accessible only by those who have the appropriate "keys" to decipher them. In addition to access controls, encryption provides another layer of protection because the information that is accessible is useless to anyone who does not hold the privilege of having the keys necessary to read it.

Encryption is an especially important control for information assets that are frequently transmitted electronically via networks, for media that are mobile (such as disks), and for public or private communications segments.

Encryption is typically applied to electronic forms of information assets, such as files, databases, and other media. However, paper-based information may also be encrypted (using codes) so that it is rendered meaningless to those who do not have the means to manually decipher it.

Typical work products

1. Policy and guidelines for encryption application
2. Encryption methodologies and technologies

3. Cryptographic key management policies and procedures
4. Encrypted information assets

Subpractices

1. Establish an organizational policy and program addressing the proper use of encryption and cryptographic means for protecting information assets.
    Encryption policies should relate to the use of cryptographic technologies that are appropriate or required for each level of information asset sensitivity categorization.
2. Establish a list of acceptable cryptographic technologies preferred by the organization.
    The use of cryptographic technologies requires organizational processes for managing the assignment, use, storage, disposal, and protection of cryptographic keys (such as public and private keys). There must be physical protection controls in place for the cryptographic infrastructure (servers, networks, etc.) so that the encryption process is not compromised, thereby reducing the effectiveness of encryption technologies.
3. Encrypt information assets based on policy and information asset sensitivity categorization.

KIM:SG4.SP2 CONTROL ACCESS TO INFORMATION ASSETS

Access controls are developed and implemented to limit access to information assets.

Controlling access to information assets is a front-line defense for ensuring that these assets are provided only to authorized staff. Access controls can be electronic (i.e., implemented and enforced through user IDs, passwords, and application system or technical infrastructure access control methodologies) or physical (placing files in rooms with card readers, putting files in locked desk drawers, implementing clean desk and clean screen policies). The organization must decide upon the right mix of controls to address the various forms of information assets and any special considerations of the assets.

Typical work products

1. List of information assets requiring access control
2. Documented access controls for information assets

Subpractices

1. Identify the information assets to which access must be controlled.
    Information assets to which access must be controlled are identified through analysis of their resilience requirements for confidentiality. Based on these requirements, the organization should prioritize information assets and determine the appropriate levels of access controls to satisfy resilience requirements. (*The selection, implementation, and management of access controls are performed in the Access Management process area.*)

In addition, information assets that have special confidentiality and privacy considerations required by rules, laws, and regulations must be prioritized for access controls. (*Managing compliance with these rules, laws, and regulations is addressed in the Compliance process area.*)

Laws and regulations concerning confidentiality and privacy include
- Family Educational Rights and Privacy Act (FERPA)
- Health Insurance Portability and Accountability Act (HIPAA)
- Gramm-Leach-Bliley Act (GLBA)
- Fair Credit Reporting Act (FCRA)
- Children's Online Privacy Protection Act (COPPA)

---

2. Develop and implement access controls to satisfy confidentiality- and privacy-related resilience requirements.

These controls must consider and address
- various forms in which the information asset exists (paper, electronic files, CDs, microfiche, etc.)
- places where the asset lives (on staff members' desks, in fax machines, in file rooms, on servers, across networks, on portable media, etc.)
- rules, laws, and regulations to which the asset is subject
- the information asset's resilience requirements (which presumably would consider how the asset is used and its value to the organization)
- use of the information by staff external to the organization or not under the organization's direct control
- the information asset's sensitivity categorization

---

3. Manage access controls on an ongoing basis to ensure continued satisfaction of confidentiality- and privacy-related resilience requirements.

KIM:SG4.SP3 CONTROL INFORMATION ASSET DISPOSITION

The means for disposing of information assets is controlled.

The controlled disposition of information assets is necessary to ensure that they are not disclosed to unauthorized staff. As an information asset is retired from service, it must be disposed of in a manner commensurate with its resilience requirements and sensitivity categorization, and in accordance with any applicable rules, laws, and regulations.

Proper disposition of information assets is highly dependent on the type of asset, its form, its sensitivity categorization, and other factors such as whether the disposition must be logged or tracked. The organization must develop specific guidelines to address a range of disposition issues and address them through provision of proper disposition methods such as the use of shredders or incineration.

Typical work products

1. Information asset disposition guidelines

Subpractices

1. Develop and implement guidelines for the appropriate disposition of information assets.
2. Communicate these guidelines to all staff who are responsible for the resilience of information assets.

KIM:SG5 MANAGE INFORMATION ASSET INTEGRITY

The integrity of information assets to support high-value services is managed.

To be usable for the purposes intended in supporting high-value services, information assets must possess certain qualities of integrity. They must be

- complete and intact (possessing all of their intended characteristics)
- accurate and valid (being in form and content precisely and exactly as intended)
- authorized and official (approved for use as intended)

Information integrity provides a level of reliability that is required for the continued support of high-value services. When this integrity is violated—through unauthorized, inappropriate, or even unintentional modification of an information asset—the usability of the information asset is reduced because of real or perceived devaluation of its reliability. The consequences of improper or unauthorized modification of an information asset are vast—service delivery may be affected, operational and organizational decisions may be impeded, and the organization may suffer reputation damage, fines, legal penalties, or even the loss of life of staff, customers, or business partners as a result.

Managing information asset integrity involves controlling modification to these assets, performing configuration management, and periodically verifying the continued validity of the assets.

KIM:SG5.SP1 CONTROL MODIFICATION OF INFORMATION ASSETS

The modification of information assets is controlled.

Controlled modification of information assets by authorized staff ensures the continued integrity of these assets for their intended purposes. A simple way of controlling modification is to control access to these information assets—either electronically (via controlling access to networks, servers, application systems, and databases and files) or physically (by limiting access to file rooms, work areas, and facilities).

In addition to access controls, information assets can be protected from unauthorized modification by limiting the ways in which the information assets can be accessed. For example, information assets are typically modified through authorization-controlled gateways such as network and server directories or through the access control mechanisms of information systems. However, information assets are often directly modified—through direct access to a file or database or by altering information written on a paper file. By limiting the types and number of access points, the organization can also control how information assets are modified.

For effectiveness, the organization must thoroughly consider which staff are authorized to make modifications to information assets (based on the unique integrity requirements of each information asset) and implement electronic and physical controls to meet these requirements. However, because access controls are not infallible, the organization must also be able to deploy detective controls that allow for logging of information asset modification and periodic review of these logs for anomalies.

The subpractices included in this practice are generically addressed in the Access Management process area.

Typical work products

1. Information asset access control lists
2. List of staff members authorized to modify information assets
3. Information asset modification logs
4. Audit reports

Subpractices

1. Establish organizationally acceptable tools, techniques, and methods for modifying information assets.
2. Identify and document staff who are authorized to modify information assets, relative to the assets' integrity requirements.
   This information may be specifically included as part of the information assets' resilience requirements.
3. Implement tools, techniques, and methods to monitor and log modification activity on high-value information assets.
4. Perform periodic audits of information asset modification logs and identify and address anomalies.
   This activity may require the organization to restore information assets to an earlier version to reverse any unauthorized modification or alteration that is detected on audit logs. (*See KIM:SG5.SP2 for configuration control practices.*)

KIM:SG5.SP2 MANAGE INFORMATION ASSET CONFIGURATION

Information asset baselines are created and changes are managed.

Establishing an information asset baseline provides a foundation for managing the integrity of assets as they change over their life cycle. Configuration management of information assets establishes additional controls over the assets so that they are always in a form that is available and authorized for use. In this way, concerns about the validity and reliability of information assets are reduced.

Most information assets are expected to change over time—the normal course of operations will result in the creation of new information (which is essentially a modification of existing information), changes to existing information, and elimination or replacement of old or unusable information. Establishing point-in-time captures of information assets (configuration items) ensures that these assets can be restored to an acceptable form when necessary—after a disruption, when an unauthorized modification has occurred, or under any circumstances where integrity is suspect. In fact, for some assets, an organization may want to freeze a baseline information asset configuration, thus permitting no modifications or alterations to the assets over their life cycle.

Poor information asset configuration control affects the potential resilience of an information asset and the services that it supports. It also may impede the ability to execute service continuity plans that depend upon ready access to accurate and complete information.

Typical work products

1. Information asset baseline configuration
2. Configuration management policies and procedures
3. Configuration control logs and reports

Subpractices

1. Establish an information asset baseline to serve as the foundation for information asset change control.
    Remember that technical assets such as software programs can also be considered as information assets. These assets must also be included in information asset configuration management.
2. Develop and implement configuration control policies, procedures, and techniques.
3. Review configuration control logs and identify anomalies.

KIM:SG5.SP3 VERIFY VALIDITY OF INFORMATION

Controls are implemented to sustain the validity and reliability of information assets.

The information processing cycle—data is processed into information—is continuous. An information asset consumed in the operation of a service may exit the service as an altered asset or an entirely new asset. The alteration of information assets through the processing cycle must be controlled to ensure that the resulting information assets remain complete, accurate, and reliable. This alteration can be due to direct manipulation (such as from unauthorized access) or other operational risks (such as the loss of power during processing that results in a corrupted file or database).

There are several means by which an organization can manage potential operational risks that can affect the validity of information assets. For example:

- the use of processing "completeness" controls (which ensure that a service or a system receives complete information as expected)
- implementation of preventive controls that check for duplication of information or enforce syntax and format on information (such as acceptable formats for dates, "xx/xx/xxxx," and telephone numbers, "xxx-xxx-xxxx")
- validation of processing output, such as selecting records for recalculation or review

Typical work products

1. Information asset accuracy and completeness controls
2. Information asset validation procedures
3. Audit logs and reports

Subpractices

1. Establish requirements for the inclusion of data validation controls in services and related systems.
   The inclusion of data validation controls ensures that information assets retain their integrity when charged into the production cycles of processes and systems.
2. Perform regular review of information asset output from processes.
   Validation of service and system output ensures that changes to information assets are valid, that the information assets are complete and accurate, and that the assets can continue to be used without concerns about reliability.
3. Periodically verify (through monitoring and auditing) that changes are valid and authorized.
   Regularly audit and validate that information has the level of integrity required.

KIM:SG6 MANAGE INFORMATION ASSET AVAILABILITY

The availability of information assets to support high-value services is managed.

The availability of an information asset is paramount to supporting high-value services. Information may be accurate and complete, but if a service cannot use it or it isn't available on demand or in a timely matter, the service may not be able to meet its mission.

A significantly broad range of operational risks can affect the availability of information assets for use in supporting high-value services, such as

- the accidental or intentional alteration or modification of an information asset (which renders the information unavailable due to its resulting lack of quality and reliability)
- the destruction or loss of information due to a natural disaster such as a flood
- failure of a system disk drive or file sharing software
- failures of personal computers
- loss of paper files, CDs, and flash drives

Fortunately, information assets are often able to be cost-effectively duplicated and stored. Through proper configuration management and strong information asset retention and backup processes, organizations may find that the availability of information is controllable, even in light of a range of potential operational risks. However, this is less true of information assets that have not been formally recorded or are not easily duplicated, such as institutional knowledge that is retained by knowledgeable staff. This information must be claimed by the organization to ensure availability.

KIM:SG6.SP1 PERFORM INFORMATION DUPLICATION AND RETENTION

High-value information assets are backed up and retained to support services when needed.

The duplication and retention of information assets are primary controls for ensuring information asset availability. These controls must be applied not only to information assets that are critical to supporting high-value services but also to the restoration of these services when disrupted.

In addition to performing backup and retention of information assets that support services, the organization needs to address the retention and protection of its vital records—charters, articles of incorporation, customer contracts, employee records, etc. These information assets may not directly support a particular service, but they are critical to the overall continued viability of the organization and must be accessible particularly during disruptive events.

Typical work products

1. Information asset backup and retention procedures
2. Information asset repositories

Subpractices

1. Develop information asset backup and retention procedures.
   Information asset backup and retention procedures should include

   - standards for the frequency of backup and storage (which may be established and connected to the organization's configuration management of information assets) and the retention period for each information asset
   - the types and forms of information asset retention (paper, CDs, tapes, etc.)
   - the identification of organization-authorized storage locations and methods, as well as guidelines for appropriate proximity of these storage locations
   - procedures for accessing stored copies of information assets
   - standards for the protection and environmental control of information assets in storage (particularly if the assets are stored in locations not owned by the organization)
   - standards for the testing of the validity of the information assets to be used in restorative activities
   - periodic revision of the guidelines as operational conditions change

   The application of these guidelines should be based on the value of the asset and its availability requirements during an emergency, which may be indicated by a service continuity plan.

2. Back up and store information assets as prescribed and according to their availability requirements.

3. Periodically test the organization's backup and storage procedures and guidelines to ensure continued validity as operational conditions change.
   Stored information assets should be periodically tested to ensure that they are complete, accurate, and current and can be used for restorative purposes when necessary.

KIM:SG6.SP2 MANAGE ORGANIZATIONAL KNOWLEDGE

The organizational and intellectual knowledge of staff is identified and documented.

The intellectual property of the organization is often tangible—that is, it can be viewed in annual reports, research documents, strategies and plans, or other physical forms. However, the organization also possesses institutional information that is less visible because it represents the knowledge of skilled, experienced people in the organization. Much of this institutional knowledge is often not documented but is vitally important to normal operations, especially in a disruptive situation. Unfortunately, the existence and tangibility of this knowledge are frequently established only during times of stress when people are needed to perform heroic actions to restore normal operating conditions.

The availability of institutional knowledge is directly tied to the availability of the people who possess it. Thus, when institutional knowledge is not captured and documented, the availability of this type of information asset is subject to the availability constraints of people. Because staff may be personally affected during an emergency situation, their knowledge may not be attainable unless archived.

The issues of institutional knowledge also extend beyond the organization's borders—external entities may have specialized knowledge that the organization needs during times of stress that may not be available. To the extent possible, this knowledge should also be retained by the organization, even though the activities related to this knowledge have been outsourced to external vendors.

Typical work products

1. List of vital staff and related institutional knowledge
2. Documented information assets related to institutional knowledge
3. Information asset repository

Subpractices

1. Identify vital staff who may have institutional knowledge.
2. Identify information assets that may be in intangible forms.
3. Document information assets as necessary.
4. Develop and implement procedures for regular identification, capture, and revision of institutional knowledge.
   Cross-training is a form of institutional knowledge transfer. Cross-training should be considered for all vital staff as a part of identifying and documenting institutional knowledge. (*Training is addressed in the Organizational Training and Awareness process area.*)

Elaborated Generic Practices by Goal

Refer to the Generic Goals and Practices document in Appendix A for general guidance that applies to all process areas. This section provides elaborations relative to the application of the Generic Goals and Practices to the Knowledge and Information Management process area.

KIM:GG1 ACHIEVE SPECIFIC GOALS

The operational resilience management system supports and enables achievement of the specific goals of the Knowledge and Information Management process area by transforming identifiable input work products to produce identifiable output work products.

KIM:GG1.GP1 PERFORM SPECIFIC PRACTICES

Perform the specific practices of the Knowledge and Information Management process area to develop work products and provide services to achieve the specific goals of the process area.

Elaboration:

Specific practices KIM:SG1.SP1 through KIM:SG6.SP2 are performed to achieve the specific goals of the knowledge and information management process.

KIM:GG2 INSTITUTIONALIZE A MANAGED PROCESS

Knowledge and information management is institutionalized as a managed process.

KIM:GG2.GP1 ESTABLISH PROCESS GOVERNANCE

Establish and maintain governance over the planning and performance of the knowledge and information management process.

Refer to the Enterprise Focus process area for more information about providing sponsorship and oversight to the knowledge and information management process.

Subpractices

1. Establish governance over process activities.

   Elaboration:

   > Governance over the knowledge and information management process may be exhibited by
   > - establishing a higher-level position, often the chief information officer or chief knowledge officer, responsible for the resilience of the organization's information assets and institutional knowledge
   > - developing and publicizing higher-level managers' objectives and requirements for the process
   > - oversight over the management of the confidentiality, integrity, availability, and privacy of information assets
   > - sponsoring and providing oversight of policy, procedures, standards, and guidelines for the documentation of information assets and for establishing asset ownership and custodianship
   > - making higher-level managers aware of applicable compliance obligations related to the process, and regularly reporting on the organization's satisfaction of these obligations to higher-level managers
   > - oversight over the establishment, implementation, and maintenance of the organization's internal control system for the systems that store, transmit, and process information assets
   > - sponsoring and funding process activities
   > - providing guidance for prioritizing information assets and institutional knowledge relative to the organization's high-priority strategic objectives
   > - providing guidance on information asset sensitivity categorization and handling procedures

- providing guidance on identifying, assessing, and managing operational risks related to information assets
- providing guidance for resolving violations of information asset confidentiality, integrity, availability, and privacy
- verifying that the process supports strategic resilience objectives and is focused on the assets and services that are of the highest relative value in meeting strategic objectives
- regular reporting from organizational units to higher-level managers on process activities and results
- creating dedicated higher-level management feedback loops on decisions about the process and recommendations for improving the process
- conducting regular internal and external audits and related reporting to appropriate committees on controls and the effectiveness of the process
- creating formal programs to measure the effectiveness of process activities, and reporting these measurements to higher-level managers

2. Develop and publish organizational policy for the process.

Elaboration:

The knowledge and information management policy should address
- responsibility, authority, and ownership for performing process activities
- procedures, standards, and guidelines for
  - documenting and maintaining information asset descriptions and relevant information about asset-service relationships
  - describing and identifying information asset owners and custodians
  - categorizing information assets based on sensitivity and other defined business criteria
  - developing and documenting resilience requirements for information assets
  - establishing, implementing, and maintaining an internal control system for information assets, including access control and configuration management
  - managing information asset operational risk
  - establishing service continuity plans and procedures for information assets, including backup, retention, restoration, and archiving
  - proper disposition of information assets at the end of their useful life
  - removing information assets from the workplace
  - clean desk and clean screen policies
  - applying encryption as a control for information asset confidentiality and privacy, as well as cryptographic key management
- the association of information assets to core organizational services, and the prioritization of assets and institutional knowledge required for service continuity
- requesting, approving, and providing access to information assets to persons, objects, and entities, including type and extent of access as well as requests

> that originate externally to the organization *(Refer to the Access Management process area for more information about granting access [rights and privileges] to information assets. Refer to the Identity Management process area for more information about creating and maintaining identities for persons, objects, and entities.)*
> - methods for measuring adherence to policy, exceptions granted, and policy violations

KIM:GG2.GP2 PLAN THE PROCESS

Establish and maintain the plan for performing the knowledge and information management process.

Elaboration:

A plan for performing the knowledge and information management process is created to preserve the confidentiality, integrity, and privacy of information assets and to ensure that information assets and institutional knowledge remain available and viable to support organizational services. The plan must address the resilience requirements of the information assets, dependencies of services on these assets, and consideration of multiple asset owners and custodians at various levels of the organization. In addition, because information is often an intangible asset that can be stored, processed, and transmitted anywhere, the plan must extend to external stakeholders that can enable or adversely affect information asset resilience.

Subpractices

1. Define and document the plan for performing the process.

   Elaboration:

   Special consideration in the plan may have to be given to establishing, implementing, and maintaining an internal control system for information assets, as well as duplication and retention of high-value information assets. These activities address protecting and sustaining information assets and preserve collective institutional knowledge commensurate with asset resilience requirements.

2. Define and document the process description.
3. Review the plan with relevant stakeholders and get their agreement.
4. Revise the plan as necessary.

KIM:GG2.GP3 PROVIDE RESOURCES

Provide adequate resources for performing the knowledge and information management process, developing the work products, and providing the services of the process.

Elaboration:

The diversity of activities required to protect and sustain information assets requires an extensive level of organizational resources and skills and a significant number of external resources. In addition, these activities require a major commitment of financial resources (both expense and capital) from the organization.

Subpractices

1. Staff the process.

Elaboration:

> These are examples of staff required to perform the knowledge and information management process:
> - information, application, and technical security staff, including those who establish, implement, or maintain information asset internal controls
> - staff responsible for controlling modifications to information assets and verifying their continued validity and reliability
> - staff involved in managing and protecting the assignment, use, storage, disposal, and protection of cryptographic keys
> - business continuity and disaster recovery staff
> - IT operations and service delivery staff
> - privacy, security, confidentiality officer or equivalent
> - staff responsible for establishing and maintaining physical security over areas where information assets are stored or processed (such as security guards)
> - staff involved in operational risk management of information assets, including insurance and risk indemnification staff
> - staff responsible for developing service continuity and risk mitigation plans and ensuring they are aligned with stakeholder requirements and needs
> - external entities responsible for creating, storing, processing, transmitting, duplicating, retaining, and disposing of information assets
> - staff responsible for managing external entities that have contractual obligations for process activities
> - owners and custodians of high-value information assets (to identify and enforce resilience requirements and support the accomplishment of operational resilience management objectives)
> - internal and external auditors responsible for reporting to appropriate committees on process effectiveness

Refer to the Organizational Training and Awareness process area for information about training staff for resilience roles and responsibilities.

Refer to the Human Resource Management process area for information about acquiring staff to fulfill roles and responsibilities.

2. Fund the process.

   Refer to the Financial Resource Management process area for information about budgeting for, funding, and accounting for knowledge and information management.

3. Provide necessary tools, techniques, and methods to perform the process.

   Elaboration:

   > These are examples of tools, techniques, and methods to support the knowledge and information management process:
   > - methods, techniques, and tools for managing risks to information assets, including tracking open risks to closure and monitoring the effectiveness of information asset risk mitigation plans
   > - methods, techniques, and tools for describing and categorizing information assets and maintaining the asset inventory that contains this information
   > - methods, techniques, and tools for maintaining information assets, including asset configuration management and monitoring and logging of modification activities
   > - methods for establishing, implementing, and maintaining the internal control system for information assets
   > - methods, techniques, and tools for encryption and key management
   > - methods for the proper disposition and disposal of information assets
   > - methods, techniques, and tools for information asset backup, retention, recovering, and archiving
   > - database systems for information asset inventories and knowledge management

KIM:GG2.GP4 ASSIGN RESPONSIBILITY

Assign responsibility and authority for performing the knowledge and information management process, developing the work products, and providing the services of the process.

Elaboration:

Of paramount importance in assigning responsibility for the knowledge and information management process is the establishment of information asset owners and custodians *(described in ADM:SG1.SP3)*. Owners are responsible for establishing information asset resilience requirements, ensuring these requirements are met by custodians, and identifying and remediating gaps where requirements are not being met. Owners may also be responsible for establishing, implementing, and maintaining an internal control system commensurate with meeting privacy, confidentiality, integrity, and availability requirements if this activity is not performed by a custodian.

Refer to the Human Resource Management process area for more information about establishing resilience as a job responsibility, developing resilience-related performance goals and objectives, and measuring and assessing performance against these goals and objectives.

Refer to the Asset Definition and Management process area for more information about establishing ownership and custodianship of information assets.

Subpractices

1. Assign responsibility and authority for performing the process.

    Elaboration:

    Responsibility and authority may extend not only to staff inside the organization but to those with whom the organization has a contractual (custodial) agreement for managing information assets (including implementation and management of controls and sustaining services that use the information assets).

2. Assign responsibility and authority for performing the specific tasks of the process.

    Elaboration:

    > Responsibility and authority for performing knowledge and information management tasks can be formalized by
    > - defining roles and responsibilities in the process plan
    > - including process tasks and responsibility for these tasks in specific job descriptions
    > - developing policy requiring organizational unit managers, line of business managers, project managers, and asset and service owners and custodians to participate in and derive benefit from the process for assets and services under their ownership or custodianship
    > - developing and implementing contractual instruments (as well as service level agreements) with external entities to establish responsibility and authority for creating, storing, processing, transmitting, duplicating, retaining, and disposing of information assets, where applicable
    > - including process tasks in staff performance management goals and objectives, with requisite measurement of progress against these goals
    > - including process tasks in measuring performance of external entities against service level agreements

    Refer to the External Dependencies Management process area for additional details about managing relationships with external entities.

3. Confirm that people assigned with responsibility and authority understand it and are willing and able to accept it.

KIM:GG2.GP5 TRAIN PEOPLE

Train the people performing or supporting the knowledge and information management process as needed.

Refer to the Organizational Training and Awareness process area for more information about training the people performing or supporting the process.

Refer to the Human Resource Management process area for more information about inventorying skill sets, establishing a skill set baseline, identifying required skill sets, and measuring and addressing skill deficiencies.

Subpractices

1. Identify process skill needs.

   Elaboration:

   > These are examples of skills required in the knowledge and information management process:
   > - prioritization and sensitivity categorization of information assets
   > - methods for eliciting, developing, and documenting information resilience requirements
   > - knowledge of tools, techniques, and methods that can be used to identify, analyze, mitigate, and monitor operational risks to information assets
   > - establishing, implementing, and maintaining the internal control system for information assets
   > - capturing institutional information that represents the knowledge of skilled, experienced people in the organization
   > - protecting and sustaining information assets to meet their resilience requirements and their confidentiality, integrity, availability, and privacy requirements

2. Identify process skill gaps based on available resources and their current skill levels.
3. Identify training opportunities to address skill gaps.

   Elaboration:

   > These are examples of training topics:
   > - information asset risk management concepts and activities (e.g., risk identification, evaluation, monitoring, and mitigation)
   > - information asset definition, sensitivity categorization, prioritization, and handling
   > - information asset resilience requirements development
   > - establishing, implementing, and maintaining internal controls for protecting and sustaining information assets

- cross-training to support institutional knowledge transfer
- proper techniques for information asset disposal
- information asset configuration and change management
- supporting information asset owners and custodians in understanding the process and their roles and responsibilities with respect to its activities
- working with external entities that have responsibility for knowledge information and management activities
- using process methods, tools, and techniques, including those identified in KIM:GG2:GP3 subpractice 3

4. Provide training and review the training needs as necessary.

KIM:GG2.GP6 MANAGE WORK PRODUCT CONFIGURATIONS

Place designated work products of the knowledge and information management process under appropriate levels of control.

Elaboration:

KIM:SG1.SP1 and KIM:SG1.SP2 specifically address use of and updates to the information asset inventory, including the designation of information assets as high-value, information asset sensitivity categorization, and handling.

These are examples of information asset work products placed under control:
- inventory, sensitivity categorization scheme, and sensitivity categories
- information asset resilience requirements (confidentiality, integrity, availability, and privacy)
- administrative, technical, and physical controls
- list of operational risks by asset and asset sensitivity category with prioritization, risk disposition, mitigation plans, and current status
- risk statements with impact valuation
- encryption and key management methods, techniques, and technologies
- encrypted information assets
- access control lists
- disposition guidelines
- baseline configurations and configuration control logs and reports
- information asset and institutional knowledge repositories
- backup media
- process plan
- policies and procedures
- contracts with external entities

KIM:GG2.GP7 IDENTIFY AND INVOLVE RELEVANT STAKEHOLDERS

Identify and involve the relevant stakeholders of the knowledge and information management process as planned.

Subpractices

1. Identify process stakeholders and their appropriate involvement.

   Elaboration:

   Because of the significant connection between information assets and the technology, facility, and people assets that store, transmit, and process the information, many of the stakeholders are likely to be external to the organization.

   > These are examples of stakeholders of the knowledge and information management process:
   > - owners and custodians of information assets
   > - owners and custodians of technology and facility assets that are used in storing, transmitting, and processing information assets
   > - service owners
   > - organizational unit and line of business managers responsible for high-value information assets and the services they support
   > - staff responsible for managing operational risks to information assets
   > - staff responsible for establishing, implementing, and maintaining an internal control system for information assets, including those responsible for access control, configuration management, and encryption
   > - staff required to develop, test, implement, and execute duplication and retention plans for information assets
   > - external entities that are involved in creating, storing, processing, transmitting, duplicating, retaining, and disposing of information assets
   > - staff in other organizational support functions, such as accounting or general services administration (particularly as related to information asset valuation and disposition)
   > - internal and external auditors

   > Stakeholders are involved in various tasks in the knowledge and information management process, such as
   > - planning for the process
   > - creating an information asset repository
   > - creating information asset descriptions, including asset sensitivity categorization and handling

- associating information assets with services and analyzing service dependencies
- developing information asset resilience requirements
- assigning resilience requirements to the systems that store, transmit, and process information assets
- establishing, implementing, and managing information asset controls
- developing service continuity plans (duplication, retention, restoration, archival) for information assets
- managing operational risks to information assets
- controlling the operational environment in which information assets "live"
- managing information asset external dependencies for assets that are created, stored, processed, transmitted, duplicated, retained, and disposed of by external entities
- managing relationships with external entities that provide information asset services
- reviewing and appraising the effectiveness of process activities
- resolving issues in the process

2. Communicate the list of stakeholders to planners and those responsible for process performance.
3. Involve relevant stakeholders in the process as planned.

KIM:GG2.GP8 MONITOR AND CONTROL THE PROCESS

Monitor and control the knowledge and information management process against the plan for performing the process and take appropriate corrective action.

Refer to the Monitoring process area for more information about the collection, organization, and distribution of data that may be useful for monitoring and controlling processes.

Refer to the Measurement and Analysis process area for more information about establishing process metrics and measurement.

Refer to the Enterprise Focus process area for more information about providing process information to managers, identifying issues, and determining appropriate corrective actions.

Subpractices

1. Measure actual performance against the plan for performing the process.
2. Review accomplishments and results of the process against the plan for performing the process.

Elaboration:

> These are examples of metrics for the knowledge and information management process:
> - percentage of information assets that have been inventoried
> - level of discrepancies between actual inventory and stated inventory
> - number of changes made to the information asset inventory during a stated period
> - number of information assets that do not have stated owners or custodians
> - number of information assets with incomplete descriptions or other incomplete information (particularly the lack of stated resilience requirements)
> - percentage of high-value information assets for which some form of risk assessment has been performed as required by policy
> - percentage of high-value information assets for which the cost of compromise (loss, unauthorized access, disclosure, disruption in access) has been quantified
> - level of adherence to external entity service level agreements and agreed maintenance levels for information assets subject to external entity services
> - number of manual versus automated data collection activities
> - number of physical or logical access controls that have been circumvented; number of attempted or successful intrusions into technology assets or facility assets where information assets "live"
> - number of information assets for which encryption is required and is yet to be implemented
> - frequency and timeliness of information asset backups
> - frequency of information asset backup restoration testing
> - frequency with which the monitoring logs are validated and placed under configuration control
> - number of policy violations related to confidentiality and privacy of information assets
> - number of information asset and process risks referred to the risk management process; number of risks where corrective action is still pending (by risk rank)
> - level of adherence to information asset and process policies; number of policy violations including those related to the confidentiality, privacy, and access control of information assets; number of policy exceptions requested and number approved
> - number of process activities that are on track per plan
> - rate of change of resource needs to support the process
> - rate of change of costs to support the process

3. Review activities, status, and results of the process with the immediate level of managers responsible for the process and identify issues.

Elaboration:

Reviews will likely verify the accuracy and completeness of the information asset inventory.

> Periodic reviews of the knowledge and information management process are needed to ensure that
> - newly acquired information assets are included in the inventory and retired assets are deleted from the inventory
> - information assets have stated resilience requirements
> - information assets that have been modified are reflected accurately in the inventory
> - information asset-service mapping is accurate and current
> - ownership and custodianship over information assets are established and documented
> - administrative, technical, and physical controls are operating as intended
> - controls are meeting the stated intent of the resilience requirements
> - institutional knowledge is being identified, collected, and stored
> - status reports are provided to appropriate stakeholders in a timely manner
> - information asset issues are referred to the risk management process when necessary
> - actions requiring management involvement are elevated in a timely manner
> - the performance of process activities is being monitored and regularly reported
> - key measures are within acceptable ranges as demonstrated in governance dashboards or scorecards and financial reports
> - actions resulting from internal and external audits are being closed in a timely manner

4. Identify and evaluate the effects of significant deviations from the plan for performing the process.
5. Identify problems in the plan for performing and executing the process.
6. Take corrective action when requirements and objectives are not being satisfied, when issues are identified, or when progress differs significantly from the plan for performing the process.

Elaboration:

For information assets, corrective action may require the revision of existing administrative, technical, and physical controls, development and implementation of new controls, or a change in the type of controls (i.e., preventive, detective, corrective, compensating, etc.). Because of the tightly coupled nature of information and the systems that store, transmit, and process information, corrective action may also involve technology and facility asset controls.

7. Track corrective action to closure.

KIM:GG2.GP9 O*BJECTIVELY* E*VALUATE* A*DHERENCE*

Objectively evaluate adherence of the knowledge and information management process against its process description, standards, and procedures, and address non-compliance.

Elaboration:

These are examples of activities to be reviewed:
- identifying and prioritizing information assets
- identifying information asset resilience requirements
- establishing and implementing information asset controls
- identifying and managing information asset risks
- developing service continuity plans for information assets (backup, retention, restoration, archival) and the technology and facility assets where information assets are stored, processed, and transmitted
- identifying and managing information asset dependencies
- identifying and managing changes to information assets
- properly disposing of information assets at the end of their useful life
- aligning stakeholder requirements with process plans
- assigning responsibility, accountability, and authority for process activities
- determining the adequacy of process reports and reviews in informing decision makers regarding the performance of operational resilience management activities and the need to take corrective action, if any
- verifying information controls
- using process work products for improving strategies for protecting and sustaining information assets

These are examples of work products to be reviewed:
- information asset inventory
- information asset internal controls documentation
- information asset resilience requirements documentation
- information asset risk statements
- information asset risk mitigation plans
- service continuity plans for information assets and the technology and facility assets where information assets are stored, processed, and transmitted
- information asset maintenance records and change logs
- business impact analysis results for information assets
- lists of key providers and contacts for information assets
- retirement standards for information assets
- process plan and policies
- information asset issues that have been referred to the risk management process
- process methods, techniques, and tools
- metrics for the process *(Refer to KIM:GG2.GP8 subpractice 2.)*
- contracts with external entities

KIM:GG2.GP10 Review Status with Higher-Level Managers

Review the activities, status, and results of the knowledge and information management process with higher-level managers and resolve issues.

Elaboration:

Status reporting on the knowledge and information management process may be part of the formal governance structure or may be performed through other organizational reporting requirements (such as through the chief risk officer or the chief resilience officer level). Audits of the process—particularly the validation of the organization's information asset inventory and internal control system at points in time—may be escalated to higher-level managers through the organization's audit committee of the board of directors or similar construct in private or non-profit organizations.

Refer to the Enterprise Focus process area for more information about providing sponsorship and oversight to the operational resilience management system.

KIM:GG3 Institutionalize a Defined Process

Knowledge and information management is institutionalized as a defined process.

KIM:GG3.GP1 Establish a Defined Process

Establish and maintain the description of a defined knowledge and information management process.

Elaboration:

Knowledge and information management tends to be tightly coupled with the systems that store, transmit, and process the information. Due to this coupling, knowledge and information management is typically carried out at the organizational unit or line of business level for convenience and accuracy and may have to be geographically focused (because of the location of specific information, technology, and facility assets). However, to achieve consistent results in creating and managing information assets, the activities at the organizational unit or line of business level must be derived from an enterprise definition of the knowledge and information management process. The information asset inventory may be inconsistent across organizational units, particularly when assets have shared ownership across organizational lines, but the defined process remains consistent. The level of completeness and accuracy of information asset descriptions across organizational units may affect asset management at the enterprise level and impede operational resilience.

In addition, a variable mix of administrative, technical, and physical controls may be used across the organization to meet the resilience requirements for information assets, but the process is consistent with the enterprise definition.

Establishing and tailoring process assets, including standard processes, are addressed in the Organizational Process Definition process area.

Establishing process needs and objectives and selecting, improving, and deploying process assets, including standard processes, are addressed in the Organizational Process Focus process area.

Subpractices

1. Select from the organization's set of standard processes those processes that cover the knowledge and information management process and best meet the needs of the organizational unit or line of business.
2. Establish the defined process by tailoring the selected processes according to the organization's tailoring guidelines.
3. Ensure that the organization's process objectives are appropriately addressed in the defined process, and ensure that process governance extends to the tailored processes.
4. Document the defined process and the records of the tailoring.
5. Revise the description of the defined process as necessary.

KIM:GG3.GP2 COLLECT IMPROVEMENT INFORMATION

Collect knowledge and information management work products, measures, measurement results, and improvement information derived from planning and performing the process to support future use and improvement of the organization's processes and process assets.

Elaboration:

> These are examples of improvement work products and information:
> - information asset inventories
> - inventory inconsistencies and issues
> - reports on the effectiveness and weaknesses of controls
> - improvements based on risk identification and mitigation
> - effectiveness of information asset service continuity plans (and supporting technology and facility asset service continuity plans) in execution
> - metrics and measurements of the viability of the process *(Refer to KIM:GG2.GP8 subpractice 2.)*
> - changes and trends in operating conditions, risk conditions, and the risk environment that affect process results
> - lessons learned in post-event review of information asset incidents and disruptions in continuity (including confidentiality, integrity, availability, and privacy)
> - maintenance issues and concerns for information assets
> - conflicts and risks arising from dependencies on external entities
> - lessons learned in backing up, retaining, restoring, archiving, updating, and disposing of information assets
> - resilience requirements that are not being satisfied for information assets or are being exceeded

Establishing the measurement repository and process asset library is addressed in the Organizational Process Definition process area. Updating the measurement repository and process asset library as part of process improvement and deployment is addressed in the Organizational Process Focus process area.

Subpractices

1. Store process and work product measures in the organization's measurement repository.
2. Submit documentation for inclusion in the organization's process asset library.
3. Document lessons learned from the process for inclusion in the organization's process asset library.
4. Propose improvements to the organizational process assets.

MEASUREMENT AND ANALYSIS
Process

Purpose

The purpose of Measurement and Analysis is to develop and sustain a measurement capability that is used to support management information needs for managing the operational resilience management system.

Introductory Notes

Consistent, timely, and accurate measurements are important feedback for managing any activity. Measurement and Analysis represents a means for applying metrics, measurement, and analysis to the resilience equation. This process area represents the organization's application of measurement as a foundational activity to provide data and analysis results that can be effectively used to inform and improve the management of the resilience process.

In the Measurement and Analysis process area, the organization establishes the objectives for measurement (i.e., what it intends to accomplish) and determines the measures that would be useful to managing the operational resilience management system as well as to providing meaningful data to higher-level managers for the processes of governance, compliance, monitoring, and improvement. The organization collects relevant data, analyzes this data, and provides reports to managers and other stakeholders to support decision making.

In a generic sense, the measurement and analysis process includes the following activities and objectives:

- specifying the objectives of measurement and analysis such that they are aligned with identified information needs and objectives
- specifying the measures, analysis techniques, and mechanisms for data collection, data storage, reporting, and feedback
- implementing the collection, storage, analysis, and reporting of the data
- providing objective results that can be used in making informed decisions, and taking appropriate corrective actions

Integrating measurement and analysis into the operational resilience management system supports

- planning, estimating, and executing operational resilience management activities
- tracking the performance of operational resilience management activities against established plans and objectives, including resilience requirements
- identifying and resolving issues in operational resilience management processes
- providing a basis for incorporating measurement into additional operational resilience management processes in the future

Measurement and analysis activities are often most effective when focused at the organizational unit or line of business level. Since operational resilience management is an enterprise-wide concern, however, it's important for the enterprise to have mechanisms in place to make use of that local data at the enterprise level, particularly as the enterprise matures. Repositories for measurement data at the organizational unit or line of business level will be useful for local optimization, but as data is shared across organizational units for the overall improvement benefit of the enterprise, measurement repositories may also be needed at the enterprise level.

Related Process Areas

Measurement and analysis needs are informed by the organization's governance activities, which are addressed in the Enterprise Focus process area.

Some of the data specified for Measurement and Analysis may be gathered and distributed through processes described in the Monitoring process area.

Measurements may be necessary as evidence of compliance; compliance requirements are addressed in the Compliance process area.

Summary of Specific Goals and Practices

MA:SG1 Align Measurement and Analysis Activities
    MA:SG1.SP1   Establish Measurement Objectives
    MA:SG1.SP2   Specify Measures
    MA:SG1.SP3   Specify Data Collection and Storage Procedures
    MA:SG1.SP4   Specify Analysis Procedures
MA:SG2 Provide Measurement Results
    MA:SG2.SP1   Collect Measurement Data
    MA:SG2.SP2   Analyze Measurement Data
    MA:SG2.SP3   Store Data and Results
    MA:SG2.SP4   Communicate Results

Specific Practices by Goal

MA:SG1 ALIGN MEASUREMENT AND ANALYSIS ACTIVITIES

Measurement objectives and activities are aligned with identified information needs and objectives.

Measurement activities should provide needed information to the organization's resilience management process and program. Failure to design the measurement and analysis activities in consideration of the organization's needs may lead to inconsistent, incomplete, or inaccurate data collection, inappropriate use or disclosure of measurement data, or inefficient use of measurement resources.

The specific practices covered under this goal may be addressed concurrently or in any order:

- When establishing measurement objectives, experts often think ahead about necessary criteria for specifying measures and analysis procedures. They also think concurrently about the constraints imposed by data collection and storage procedures.
- It often is important to specify the essential analyses that will be conducted before attending to details of measurement specification, data collection, or storage.

MA:SG1.SP1 ESTABLISH MEASUREMENT OBJECTIVES

Measurement objectives are established and maintained based on information needs and objectives.

Measurement objectives document the purposes for which measurement and analysis are done and specify the kinds of actions that may be taken based on the results of data analyses.

The sources for measurement objectives may be management, technical, asset, or process implementation needs.

The measurement objectives may be constrained by existing processes, available resources, or other measurement considerations. Judgments may have to be made about whether the value of the results will be commensurate with the resources devoted to doing the work.

Modifications to identified information needs and objectives may, in turn, be indicated as a consequence of the process and results of measurement and analysis.

Sources of information needs and objectives may be identified at the organizational unit level or at the enterprise level and may include the following:

- monitoring of operational resilience management system performance
- documented management objectives and resilience strategies

- requirements for protecting and sustaining high-value organizational assets and associated services
- risk conditions currently under management consideration
- process improvement objectives and process performance targets
- contractual, legal, and compliance obligations
- supply chain monitoring, including the resilience program status both upstream and downstream
- industry benchmarks
- interviews with managers and other stakeholders that have special information needs

> These are examples of measurement objectives:
> - Reduce the total number of controls under management.
> - Maintain or improve supplier-customer relationships.
> - Improve availability or uptime statistics.
> - Complete the development (or update) of service continuity plans for the organization.
> - Complete risk analyses on all high-value assets and services.
> - Regularly test controls and plans to protect and sustain services and assets.
> - Improve awareness survey results.
> - Improve compliance with regulations, laws, and policies at the lowest cost.
> - Provide resilience awareness training to all new employees within three months of hire.
> - Complete the implementation or rollout of certain administrative, technical, and physical controls.
> - Achieve and improve recovery time objective(s) and/or recovery point objective(s) (RTO and RPO).
> - Reduce exposure to known threats and vulnerabilities.
> - Improve risk identification.
> - Reduce the cost of resilience services and strategies for protecting and sustaining assets.
> - Improve the effectiveness and efficiency of measurement and analysis.
> - Minimize the total number of access controls under management.
> - Achieve internal service level agreements or monitor supplier achievement of external service level agreements.

The development and management of resilience requirements are addressed in the Resilience Requirements Definition and Resilience Requirements Management process areas, respectively. These requirements should be considered in the development of measurement objectives.

(Measurement objectives may overlap with monitoring requirements in that monitoring requirements typically represent information needs that are useful for process control and management. Practice MON:SG1.SP3 focuses on the development of monitoring requirements and should be considered as a source of information for the development of measurement objectives.)

Typical work products

1. Measurement objectives

Subpractices

1. Document information needs and objectives.

   Information needs and objectives are documented to allow traceability to subsequent measurement and analysis activities. *(Refer to MON:SG1.SP3 for information about establishing monitoring requirements that may overlap with measurement information needs and goals.)*

2. Prioritize information needs and objectives.

   It may be neither possible nor desirable to subject all initially identified information needs to measurement and analysis. Priorities may also have to be set within the limits of available resources. *(Refer to MON:SG1.SP4 for information about the prioritization of monitoring requirements.)*

3. Document, review, and update measurement objectives.

   It is important to carefully consider the purposes and intended uses of measurement and analysis.

   The measurement objectives are documented, reviewed by managers and other relevant stakeholders, and updated as necessary. Doing so enables traceability to subsequent measurement and analysis activities and helps ensure that the analyses will properly address identified information needs and objectives.

   It is important that users of measurement and analysis results be involved in setting measurement objectives and deciding on plans of action. It may also be appropriate to involve those who provide the measurement data. *(Refer to MON:SG1.SP2 for information about the establishment of monitoring stakeholders and their inclusion in the monitoring process. These stakeholders may also provide information to, or receive information from, the measurement and analysis process.)*

4. Provide feedback for refining and clarifying information needs and objectives as necessary.

   Identified information needs and objectives may have to be refined and clarified as a result of setting measurement objectives. Initial descriptions of information needs may be unclear or ambiguous. Conflicts may arise between existing needs and objectives. Precise targets on an already existing measure may be unrealistic.

5. Maintain traceability of the measurement objectives to the identified information needs and objectives.

   There must always be a good explanation for why a measurement is being analyzed.

   Of course, the measurement objectives may also change to reflect evolving information needs and objectives.

MA:SG1.SP2 SPECIFY MEASURES

The measures necessary to meet measurement objectives are established.

Measurement objectives are refined into precise, quantifiable measures.

Measures may be either "base" or "derived." Data for base measures is obtained by direct measurement. Data for derived measures comes from other data, typically by combining two or more base measures.

These are examples of base measures:
- number of high-value assets by category (people, information, technology, facilities)
- number of risk analyses conducted during a certain period of time
- number of vulnerabilities identified in a specific time range
- total number of controls under management
- number of service continuity plans updated within the past 12 months
- total number of incidents declared in the past quarter

These are examples of derived measures:
- percentage of high-value technology assets for which a risk analysis was conducted in the previous 12 months
- percentage of staff who have undergone resilience policy training in the previous 12 months
- percentage of vulnerabilities identified in the past month that have been analyzed and resolved
- trends (growth or decline) in incidents declared
- trends in time elapsed from incident declaration to closure
- percentage of unmet test objectives for exercising service continuity plans
- percentage of vital staff (or resilience staff) who have participated in service continuity plan exercises in the past year

---

Derived measures typically are expressed as ratios, composite indices, or other aggregate summary measures. They are often more quantitatively reliable and meaningfully interpretable than the base measures used to generate them.

Typical work products

1. Specifications of base and derived measures

Subpractices

1. Identify candidate measures based on documented measurement objectives.

    The measurement objectives are refined into specific measures. The identified candidate measures are categorized and specified by name and unit of measure.

2. Identify existing measures that already address the measurement objectives.
    Specifications for measures may already exist, perhaps established for other purposes earlier or elsewhere in the organization.
3. Specify operational definitions for the measures.
    Operational definitions are stated in precise and unambiguous terms. They address two important criteria:
    - Communication—What has been measured, how was it measured, what are the units of measure, and what has been included or excluded?
    - Repeatability—Can the measurement be repeated, given the same definition, to get the same results?
4. Prioritize, review, and update measures.
    Proposed specifications of the measures are reviewed for their appropriateness with potential end users and other relevant stakeholders. Priorities are set or changed, and specifications of the measures are updated as necessary.

MA:SG1.SP3 SPECIFY DATA COLLECTION AND STORAGE PROCEDURES

The techniques for collecting and storing measurement data are specified.

Explicit specification of collection methods helps ensure that the right data is collected properly. It may also aid in further clarifying information needs and measurement objectives.

Proper attention to storage and retrieval procedures helps ensure that data is available and accessible for future use and that the information is adequately protected and sustained according to applicable resilience requirements.

(Monitoring activities, particularly for the collection, storage, and distribution of data, may overlap significantly with MA:SG1.SP3. Specifically, MON:SG2.SP1, Establish and Maintain Monitoring Infrastructure, MON:SG2.SP3, Collect and Record Information, and MON:SG2.SP4, Distribute Information, may all be useful for achieving MA:SG1.SP3 if the information being monitored for and collected is related directly to measurement and analysis activities.)

Typical work products

1. Data collection and storage procedures
2. Data collection tools

Subpractices

1. Identify existing sources of data that is generated from current processes or transactions.
    Existing sources of data may already have been identified when specifying the measures. Appropriate collection mechanisms may exist whether or not pertinent data has already been collected.

2. Identify measures for which data is needed but is not currently available.
3. Specify how to collect and store the data for each required measure.
   Explicit specifications are made for how, where, and when the data will be collected. Procedures for collecting valid data are specified. The data is stored in an accessible manner for analysis, and it is determined whether it will be saved for possible re-analysis or documentation purposes.

> Questions to be considered typically include the following:
> - Have the frequency of collection and the points in the process where measurements will be made been determined?
> - Has the timeline that is required to move measurement results from the points of collection to repositories, other databases, or end users been established?
> - Who is responsible for obtaining the data?
> - Who is responsible for data storage, retrieval, and security?
> - Have necessary supporting tools been developed or acquired?
> - What are the resilience requirements for the data?

Practice MON:SG2.SP2 establishes information collection standards and parameters that may be useful for collecting measurement and analysis data. If measurement and analysis data is collected through a monitoring process, the collection specifications should be included in the standards and parameters.

4. Create data collection mechanisms and process guidance.
   Data collection and storage mechanisms are well integrated with other normal work processes. Data collection mechanisms may include manual or automated forms and templates. Clear, concise guidance on correct procedures is available to those responsible for doing the work. Training is provided as necessary to clarify the processes necessary for collection of complete and accurate data and to minimize the burden on those who must provide and record the data.
5. Support automatic collection of the data where appropriate and feasible.
   Automated support can aid in collecting more complete and accurate data.

> These are examples of such automated support:
> - asset counts from inventory management systems
> - employee population from human resources management systems
> - automated tracking of system availability statistics
> - automatic counts and statistics from event or incident tracking systems
> - statistics from automated patch and configuration management tools

However, some data cannot be collected without human intervention (e.g., customer satisfaction or other human judgments), and setting up the necessary infrastructure for other automation may be costly.

Practice MON:SG1.SP2 addresses the essential infrastructure necessary to meet data collection, storage, and distribution standards for monitoring purposes. This infrastructure and the related infrastructure requirements may overlap those of the measurement and analysis process.

6. Prioritize, review, and update data collection and storage procedures.

    Proposed procedures are reviewed for their appropriateness and feasibility with those who are responsible for providing, collecting, and storing the data. They also may have useful insights about how to improve existing processes or may be able to suggest other useful measures or analyses. (*See MON:SG2.SP2 for related activities.*)

7. Update measures and measurement objectives as necessary.

    Priorities may have to be reset based on the following:
    - the importance of the measures
    - the amount of effort required to obtain the data

    Considerations include whether new forms, tools, or training would be required to obtain the data.

MA:SG1.SP4 SPECIFY ANALYSIS PROCEDURES

The techniques for analysis and reporting are specified.

Specifying the analysis procedures in advance ensures that appropriate analyses will be conducted and reported to address the documented measurement objectives (and thereby the information needs and objectives on which they are based). This approach also provides a check that the necessary data will in fact be collected.

For operational resilience management purposes, analysis methods and techniques are likely to be extensive and cover a wide range of disciplines.

Typical work products

1. Analysis specifications and procedures
2. Data analysis tools

Subpractices

1. Specify and prioritize the analyses that will be conducted and the reports that will be prepared.

    Early attention should be paid to the analyses that will be conducted and to the manner in which the results will be reported. These should meet the following criteria:
    - The analyses explicitly address the documented measurement objectives.
    - Presentation of the results is clearly understandable by the audiences to whom the results are addressed.

    Priorities may have to be set within available resources.

2. Select appropriate data analysis methods and tools.

> Issues to be considered typically include the following:
> - choice of visual display and other presentation techniques (e.g., pie charts, bar charts, histograms, radar charts, line graphs, scatter plots, or tables)
> - choice of appropriate descriptive statistics (e.g., arithmetic mean, median, or mode)
> - decisions about statistical sampling criteria when it is impossible or unnecessary to examine every data element
> - decisions about how to handle analysis in the presence of missing data elements
> - selection of appropriate analysis tools

> Descriptive statistics are typically used in data analysis to do the following:
> - examine distributions on the specified measures (e.g., central tendency, extent of variation, or data points exhibiting unusual variation)
> - examine the interrelationships among the specified measures (e.g., comparisons of incident types and frequency across organizational units or lines of business)
> - display changes over time

3. Specify administrative procedures for analyzing the data and communicating the results.

> Issues to be considered typically include the following:
> - identifying the persons and groups responsible for analyzing the data and presenting the results
> - determining the timeline to analyze the data and present the results
> - determining the venues for communicating the results (e.g., progress reports, transmittal memos, written reports, or staff meetings)

4. Review and update the proposed content and format of the specified analyses and reports.

   All of the proposed content and format are subject to review and revision, including analytic methods and tools, administrative procedures, and priorities. The relevant stakeholders consulted should include intended end users, sponsors, data analysts, and data providers.

5. Update measures and measurement objectives as necessary.

   Just as measurement needs drive data analysis, clarification of analysis criteria can affect measurement. Specifications for some measures may be refined further based on the specifications established for data analysis procedures. Other measures may prove to be unnecessary, or a need for additional measures may be recognized.

   The exercise of specifying how measures will be analyzed and reported may also suggest the need for refining the measurement objectives themselves.

6. Specify criteria for evaluating the utility of the analysis results and for evaluating the conduct of the measurement and analysis activities.

Criteria for evaluating the utility of the analysis might address the extent to which the following apply:
- The results are (1) provided on a timely basis, (2) understandable, and (3) used for decision making.
- The work does not cost more to perform than is justified by the benefits that it provides.

Criteria for evaluating the conduct of the measurement and analysis might include the extent to which the following apply:
- The amount of missing data or the number of flagged inconsistencies is beyond specified thresholds.
- There is selection bias in sampling (e.g., only satisfied end users are surveyed to evaluate end-user satisfaction, or only unsuccessful projects are evaluated to determine overall productivity).
- The measurement data are repeatable (e.g., statistically reliable).
- Statistical assumptions have been satisfied (e.g., about the distribution of data or about appropriate measurement scales).

MA:SG2 PROVIDE MEASUREMENT RESULTS

Measurement results, which address identified information needs and objectives, are provided.

The primary reason for performing measurement and analysis is to address identified information needs and objectives. Measurement results based on objective evidence can help to monitor performance, achieve resilience plan obligations, fulfill compliance obligations, make informed management and technical decisions, and enable corrective actions to be taken.

MA:SG2.SP1 COLLECT MEASUREMENT DATA

Measurement data is collected consistent with measurement objectives.

The data necessary for analysis is obtained and checked for completeness and integrity.

Practice MON:SG2.SP3 specifically addresses the collection of monitoring data that may also include measurement data for the purposes of measurement and analysis.

Typical work products

1. Base and derived measurement data sets
2. Results of data integrity tests

Subpractices

1. Obtain the data for base measures.

   Data is collected as necessary for previously used as well as for newly specified base measures.

   Data that was collected earlier may no longer be available for reuse in existing databases, paper records, or formal repositories.

2. Generate the data for derived measures.

   Values are newly calculated for all derived measures.

3. Perform data integrity checks as close to the source of the data as possible.

   All measurements are subject to error in specifying or recording data. It is always better to identify such errors and to identify sources of missing data early in the measurement and analysis cycle.

   Checks can include scans for missing data, out-of-bounds data values, and unusual patterns and correlation across measures. It is particularly important to do the following:
   - Test and correct for inconsistency of categorizations made by human judgment (i.e., to determine how frequently people make differing categorization decisions based on the same information, otherwise known as "inter-coder reliability").
   - Empirically examine the relationships among the measures that are used to calculate additional derived measures. Doing so can ensure that important distinctions are not overlooked and that the derived measures convey their intended meanings (otherwise known as "criterion validity").

   Controls over information that are relevant to measurement and analysis are addressed in KIM:SG5.SP3 in the Knowledge and Information Management process area.

MA:SG2.SP2 ANALYZE MEASUREMENT DATA

Measurement data is analyzed against measurement objectives.

The measurement data is analyzed as planned, additional analyses are conducted as necessary, results are reviewed with relevant stakeholders, and necessary revisions for future analyses are noted.

Typical work products

1. Analysis results and draft reports

Subpractices

1. Conduct initial analyses, interpret the results, and draw preliminary conclusions.

   The results of data analyses are rarely self-evident. Criteria for interpreting the results and drawing conclusions should be stated explicitly.

2. Conduct additional measurement and analysis as necessary, and prepare results for presentation.

The results of planned analyses may suggest (or require) additional, unanticipated analyses. In addition, they may identify needs to refine existing measures, to calculate additional derived measures, or even to collect data for additional base measures to properly complete the planned analysis. Similarly, preparing the initial results for presentation may identify the need for additional, unanticipated analyses.

3. Review the initial results with relevant stakeholders.

    It may be appropriate to review initial interpretations of the results and the way in which they are presented before distributing and communicating them more widely.

    Reviewing the initial results before their release may prevent needless misunderstandings and lead to improvements in the data analysis and presentation.

    Relevant stakeholders with whom reviews may be conducted include asset owners and custodians, resilience staff, vital management personnel, and data providers.

4. Refine criteria for future analyses.

    Valuable lessons that can improve future efforts are often learned from conducting data analyses and preparing results. Similarly, ways to improve measurement specifications and data collection procedures may become apparent, as may ideas for refining identified information needs and objectives.

MA:SG2.SP3 STORE DATA AND RESULTS

Measurement data, analyses, and results are stored.

Storing measurement-related information enables the timely and cost-effective future use of historical data and results. The information also is needed to provide sufficient context for interpretation of the data, measurement criteria, and analysis results.

Information stored typically includes the following:

- measurement plans
- specifications of measures
- sets of data that have been collected
- analysis reports and presentations

The stored information contains or references the information needed to understand and interpret the measures and to assess them for reasonableness and applicability (e.g., measurement specifications used in different business units when comparing across business units).

Data sets for derived measures typically can be recalculated and need not be stored. However, it may be appropriate to store summaries based on derived measures (e.g., charts, tables of results, or report prose).

Interim analysis results need not be stored separately if they can be efficiently reconstructed.

The organization should determine whether to store data in a centralized manner at the enterprise level, in a decentralized manner at the organizational unit level, or some combination.

Measurement and analysis data may constitute an organizational asset that requires controls to ensure confidentiality, integrity, and availability. *(Controls over information assets are addressed in the Knowledge and Information Management process area.)*

Typical work products

1. Stored data inventory

Subpractices

1. Review the data to ensure its completeness, integrity, accuracy, and currency.
2. Store the data according to the data storage procedures.
3. Make the stored contents available for use only by appropriate groups and staff.
4. Prevent the stored information from being used inappropriately.
   Ways to prevent inappropriate use of the data and related information include controlling access to data and educating people on the appropriate use of information.

These are examples of inappropriate use:
- disclosure of information that was provided in confidence
- faulty interpretations based on incomplete, out-of-context, or otherwise misleading information
- measures used to improperly evaluate the performance of people
- impugning the integrity of specific individuals

Specific controls over the confidentiality, integrity, and availability of measurement information are specified in goal KIM:SG4 in the Knowledge and Information Management process area.

MA:SG2.SP4 COMMUNICATE RESULTS

The results of measurement and analysis activities are communicated to relevant stakeholders.

The results of the measurement and analysis process are communicated to relevant stakeholders in a timely and usable fashion to support decision making and assist in taking corrective action.

Relevant stakeholders include risk managers and higher-level managers, relevant resilience staff, asset owners and custodians, data analysts, and data providers.

Typical work products

1. Delivered reports and related analysis results
2. Contextual information or guidance to aid in the interpretation of analysis results

Subpractices

1. Keep relevant stakeholders apprised of measurement results on a timely basis.
   Measurement results are communicated in time to be used for their intended purposes. Reports are unlikely to be used if they are distributed with little effort to follow up with those who need to know the results.

   To the extent possible and as part of the normal way they do business, users of measurement results are kept personally involved in setting objectives and deciding on plans of action for measurement and analysis. The users are regularly kept apprised of progress and interim results.

2. Assist relevant stakeholders in understanding the results.
   Results are reported in a clear and concise manner appropriate to the methodological sophistication of the relevant stakeholders. They are understandable, easily interpretable, and clearly tied to identified information needs and objectives.

   The data is often not self-evident to practitioners who are not measurement experts. Measurement choices should be explicitly clear about the following:
   - how and why the base and derived measures were specified
   - how the data was obtained
   - how to interpret the results based on the data analysis methods that were used
   - how the results address information needs

These are examples of actions to assist in the understanding of results:
- discussing the results with the relevant stakeholders
- providing a transmittal memo that provides background and explanation
- briefing users on the results
- providing training on the appropriate use and understanding of measurement results

---

Elaborated Generic Practices by Goal

Refer to the Generic Goals and Practices document in Appendix A for general guidance that applies to all process areas. This section provides elaborations relative to the application of the Generic Goals and Practices to the Measurement and Analysis process area.

MA:GG1 ACHIEVE SPECIFIC GOALS

The operational resilience management system supports and enables achievement of the specific goals of the Measurement and Analysis process area by transforming identifiable input work products to produce identifiable output work products.

MA:GG1.GP1 PERFORM SPECIFIC PRACTICES

Perform the specific practices of the Measurement and Analysis process area to develop work products and provide services to achieve the specific goals of the process area.

Elaboration:

Specific practices MA:SG1.SP1 through MA:SG2.SP4 are performed to achieve the goals of the measurement and analysis process.

MA:GG2 INSTITUTIONALIZE A MANAGED PROCESS

Measurement and analysis is institutionalized as a managed process.

MA:GG2.GP1 ESTABLISH PROCESS GOVERNANCE

Establish and maintain governance over the planning and performance of the measurement and analysis process.

Refer to the Enterprise Focus process area for more information about providing sponsorship and oversight to the measurement and analysis process.

Subpractices

1. Establish governance over process activities.

   Elaboration:

   > Governance over the measurement and analysis process may be exhibited by
   > - developing and publicizing higher-level managers' objectives for the process
   > - sponsoring process policies, procedures, standards, and guidelines
   > - sponsoring and funding process activities
   > - aligning measurement data collection and analysis with identified resilience needs and objectives and stakeholder needs and requirements
   > - verifying that the process supports strategic resilience objectives
   > - regular reporting from organizational units to higher-level managers on process activities and results
   > - creating dedicated higher-level management feedback loops on decisions about the process and recommendations for improving the process
   > - providing input on identifying, assessing, and managing operational risks to high-value services and assets
   > - conducting regular internal and external audits and related reporting to audit committees on process effectiveness
   > - creating formal programs to measure the effectiveness of process activities, and reporting these measurements to higher-level managers

2. Develop and publish organizational policy for the process.

   Elaboration:

   > The measurement and analysis policy should address
   > - responsibility, authority, and ownership for performing process activities
   > - procedures, standards, and guidelines for
   >   - specifying measures based on measurement objectives
   >   - analyses of measurement data
   >   - collection of measurement data
   >   - storage of measurement data
   >   - reporting of measurement data
   >   - establishing measurement repositories
   > - methods for measuring adherence to policy, exceptions granted, and policy violations

MA:GG2.GP2 PLAN THE PROCESS

Establish and maintain the plan for performing the measurement and analysis process.

Elaboration:

The plan for the measurement and analysis process should not be confused with measurement plans for collecting, analyzing, storing, and communicating specific measurement data as described in specific goal MA:SG2. The plan for the measurement and analysis process details how the organization will perform measurement and analysis, including the development of specific measurement plans.

Subpractices

1. Define and document the plan for performing the process.
2. Define and document the process description.
3. Review the plan with relevant stakeholders and get their agreement.
4. Revise the plan as necessary.

MA:GG2.GP3 PROVIDE RESOURCES

Provide adequate resources for performing the measurement and analysis process, developing the work products, and providing the services of the process.

Subpractices

1. Staff the process.

Elaboration:

Staff assigned to the measurement and analysis process must have appropriate knowledge of the related processes being measured and the objectivity to perform measurement and analysis activities without concern for personal detriment and without the expectation of personal benefit.

> These are examples of staff required to perform the measurement and analysis process:
> - staff responsible for
>   - specifying process objectives and ensuring they are aligned with information needs and objectives
>   - specifying measures, analysis techniques, and mechanisms for data collection, storage, reporting, and feedback
>   - data collection, storage, analysis, and reporting
>   - providing results to inform decision making and developing plans of action
>   - developing measurement plans and programs and ensuring they are aligned with stakeholder requirements and needs
>   - managing external entities that have contractual obligations for measurement and analysis activities
> - owners and custodians of high-value services and assets that support the accomplishment of operational resilience management objectives
> - internal and external auditors responsible for reporting to appropriate committees on process effectiveness and the adequacy of measures to accurately track the performance of operational resilience management processes

Refer to the Organizational Training and Awareness process area for information about training staff for resilience roles and responsibilities.

Refer to the Human Resource Management process area for information about acquiring staff to fulfill roles and responsibilities.

2. Fund the process.

   Refer to the Financial Resource Management process area for information about budgeting for, funding, and accounting for measurement and analysis.

3. Provide necessary tools, techniques, and methods to perform the process.

Elaboration:

Many of these tools, techniques, and methods should be available as applied to other aspects of organizational measurement and analysis. The intent here is to apply these to operational resilience management.

> These are examples of tools, techniques, and methods to support the measurement and analysis process:
> - statistical software tools
> - data collection, storage, and analysis methods, techniques, and tools, including those necessary to ensure data integrity and security

- tools to assist in calculating derived measures from base measures
- data reporting methods, techniques, and tools, including techniques for visual display and presentation of data
- techniques to assist in interpreting results based on the data analysis methods that were used
- methods, techniques, and tools for developing and managing measurement inventories, databases, and repositories
- tools for developing and maintaining traceability between information needs and measurement objectives

MA:GG2.GP4 ASSIGN RESPONSIBILITY

Assign responsibility and authority for performing the measurement and analysis process, developing the work products, and providing the services of the process.

Elaboration:

Specific practice MA:SG1.SP3 calls for determining responsibilities for data collection, storage, retrieval, and security. Specific practice MA:SG1.SP4 calls for identifying those responsible for data analysis and presentation.

Refer to the Human Resource Management process area for more information about establishing resilience as a job responsibility, developing resilience performance goals and objectives, and measuring and assessing performance against these goals and objectives.

Subpractices

1. Assign responsibility and authority for performing the process.
2. Assign responsibility and authority for performing the specific tasks of the process.

Elaboration:

Responsibility and authority for performing measurement and analysis tasks can be formalized by
- defining roles and responsibilities in the process plan to include roles responsible for providing, collecting, analyzing, storing, retrieving, reporting, and ensuring the integrity and security of measurement data
- including process tasks and responsibility for these tasks in specific job descriptions
- developing policy requiring organizational unit managers, line of business managers, project managers, and asset and service owners and custodians to participate in and derive benefit from the process for assets and services under their ownership or custodianship

> - including process tasks in staff performance management goals and objectives with requisite measurement of progress against these goals
> - developing and implementing contractual instruments (including service level agreements) with external entities to establish responsibility and authority for performing process tasks on outsourced functions
> - including process tasks in measuring performance of external entities against contractual instruments

Refer to the External Dependencies Management process area for additional details about managing relationships with external entities.

3. Confirm that people assigned with responsibility and authority understand it and are willing and able to accept it.

MA:GG2.GP5 TRAIN PEOPLE

Train the people performing or supporting the measurement and analysis process as needed.

Refer to the Organizational Training and Awareness process area for more information about training the people performing or supporting the process.

Refer to the Human Resource Management process area for more information about inventorying skill sets, establishing a skill set baseline, identifying required skill sets, and measuring and addressing skill deficiencies.

Subpractices

1. Identify process skill needs.

    Elaboration:

    > These are examples of skills required in the measurement and analysis process:
    > - knowledge of tools, techniques, and methods used to collect, analyze, store, retrieve, report, and ensure the integrity and security of measurement data, including those necessary to perform the process using the selected methods, techniques, and tools identified in MA:GG2.GP3 subpractice 3
    > - knowledge unique to each type of service and asset that is required to effectively perform process activities
    > - knowledge necessary to elicit and prioritize information needs and objectives and interpret them to develop effective measurement objectives
    > - knowledge necessary to identify measurement specifications that reflect measurement objectives
    > - knowledge necessary to interpret measurement data and represent it in reports in ways that are meaningful and appropriate for managers and stakeholders

2. Identify process skill gaps based on available resources and their current skill levels.
3. Identify training opportunities to address skill gaps.

   Elaboration:

   > These are examples of training topics:
   > - statistical or other analysis techniques
   > - data collection, analysis, and reporting techniques
   > - data storage techniques
   > - development of resilience measurements that reflect information needs and objectives
   > - supporting service and asset owners and custodians in understanding the process and their roles and responsibilities with respect to its activities
   > - using process methods, tools, and techniques, including those identified in MA:GG2.GP3 subpractice 3

4. Provide training and review the training needs as necessary.

MA:GG2.GP6 MANAGE WORK PRODUCT CONFIGURATIONS

Place designated work products of the measurement and analysis process under appropriate levels of control.

Elaboration:

> These are examples of measurement and analysis work products placed under control:
> - measurement objectives
> - measurement specifications
> - data collection and storage procedures and tools
> - data analysis specifications, procedures, and tools
> - measurement data sets
> - analysis results, reports, and presentations
> - data inventories, repositories, and databases
> - process plan
> - policies and procedures
> - contracts with external entities

MA:GG2.GP7 IDENTIFY AND INVOLVE RELEVANT STAKEHOLDERS

Identify and involve the relevant stakeholders of the measurement and analysis process as planned.

Elaboration:

Several MA-specific practices address the involvement of stakeholders in the measurement and analysis process. For example, MA:SG1.SP1 calls for involving relevant stakeholders in the formulation of measurement objectives, and MA:SG1.SP2 calls for involving them in the prioritization and review of measurement specifications.

Subpractices

1. Identify process stakeholders and their appropriate involvement.

   Elaboration:

   > These are examples of stakeholders of the measurement and analysis process:
   > - service owners and asset owners and custodians
   > - staff involved in specifying and prioritizing information needs
   > - staff involved in establishing measurement objectives, measures, procedures, and techniques
   > - staff involved in prioritizing, reviewing, and updating specifications of measures
   > - end users, sponsors, data analysts, and data providers involved in reviewing and updating proposed content and format of specified analyses and reports
   > - staff involved in assessing and interpreting measurement data and deciding on plans of action (Early reviewers of analysis results may include asset owners and custodians, resilience staff, vital management personnel, and data providers. Decision makers include risk managers and higher-level managers, relevant resilience staff, asset owners and custodians, data analysts, and data providers.)
   > - users of measurement results, including organizational unit and line of business managers
   > - staff involved in providing meaningful feedback to those responsible for providing the raw data on which measurement analysis and results depend
   > - external entities responsible for managing high-value services, assets, and outsourced functions
   > - internal and external auditors

   > Stakeholders are involved in various tasks in the measurement and analysis process, such as
   > - establishing requirements for the process
   > - planning for the process
   > - establishing measurement objectives and plans
   > - making decisions about process activities
   > - assessing measurement data, results, and reports
   > - providing feedback to those responsible for providing the raw data on which the analysis results depend
   > - reviewing and appraising the effectiveness of process activities
   > - resolving issues in the process

2. Communicate the list of stakeholders to planners and those responsible for process performance.
3. Involve relevant stakeholders in the process as planned.

MA:GG2.GP8 MONITOR AND CONTROL THE PROCESS

Monitor and control the measurement and analysis process against the plan for performing the process and take appropriate corrective action.

Elaboration:

While this practice is self-referencing, practices in the Measurement and Analysis process area provide more information about measuring and analyzing operational resilience management processes that can also be applied to the measurement and analysis process.

Refer to the Monitoring process area for more information about the collection, organization, and distribution of data that may be useful for monitoring and controlling processes.

Refer to the Enterprise Focus process area for more information about providing process information to managers, identifying issues, and determining appropriate corrective actions.

Subpractices

1. Measure actual performance against the plan for performing the process.
2. Review accomplishments and results of the process against the plan for performing the process.

Elaboration:

> These are examples of metrics for the measurement and analysis process:
> - total number of measurement objectives; total number of base and derived measures; ratio of number of base and derived measures for each measurement objective; ratio means and medians
> - percentage of operational resilience management system performance indicators or targets for which measurement data is collected, analyzed, and reported
> - percentage of organizational units, projects, and activities using operational resilience management measures to assess the performance of operational resilience management processes
> - percentage of measurement objectives achieved (against defined targets, if relevant)
> - schedule for collection, analysis, and review of measurement data
> - number of process risks referred to the risk management process; number of risks where corrective action is still pending (by risk rank)
> - level of adherence to process policies; number of policy violations; number of policy exceptions requested and number approved
> - number of process activities that are on track per plan
> - rate of change of resource needs to support the process
> - rate of change of costs to support the process

3. Review activities, status, and results of the process with the immediate level of managers responsible for the process and identify issues.

   Elaboration:

   > Periodic reviews of the measurement and analysis process are needed to ensure that
   > - the performance of resilience activities is being measured and regularly reported
   > - strategic operational resilience management activities are on track according to plan
   > - actions requiring management involvement are elevated in a timely manner
   > - the performance of process activities is being monitored and regularly reported
   > - key measures are within acceptable ranges as demonstrated in governance dashboards or scorecards and financial reports
   > - administrative, technical, and physical controls are operating as intended
   > - controls are meeting the stated intent of the resilience requirements
   > - actions resulting from internal and external audits are being closed in a timely manner

4. Identify and evaluate the effects of significant deviations from the plan for performing the process.
5. Identify problems in the plan for performing the process and in the execution of the process.
6. Take corrective action when requirements and objectives are not being satisfied, when issues are identified, or when progress differs significantly from the plan for performing the process.
7. Track corrective action to closure.

MA:GG2.GP9 OBJECTIVELY EVALUATE ADHERENCE

Objectively evaluate adherence of the measurement and analysis process against its process description, standards, and procedures, and address non-compliance.

Elaboration:

> These are examples of activities to be reviewed:
> - the alignment of information needs and objectives with measurement objectives; the alignment of measurement objectives with measurement specifications
> - the alignment of stakeholder requirements with process plans
> - assignment of responsibility, accountability, and authority for resilience process activities
> - assignment of responsibility, accountability, and authority for measurement and analysis activities

- determining the adequacy of measurement reports and reviews in informing decision makers regarding the performance of operational resilience management activities and the need to take corrective action, if any
- verification of measurement data integrity and security controls
- use of measurement data for improving strategies to protect and sustain assets and services

These are examples of work products to be reviewed:
- process plan and policies
- measurement objectives
- specifications for base and derived measures
- data collection, analysis, and storage methods, techniques, and tools
- analysis results, reports, and presentations, including variance from required performance indicators and targets and trends in base and derived measures
- metrics for the process *(Refer to MA:GG2.GP9 subpractice 2.)*

MA:GG2.GP10 REVIEW STATUS WITH HIGHER-LEVEL MANAGERS

Review the activities, status, and results of the measurement and analysis process with higher-level managers and resolve issues.

Refer to the Enterprise Focus process area for more information about providing sponsorship and oversight to the operational resilience management system.

MA:GG3 INSTITUTIONALIZE A DEFINED PROCESS

Measurement and analysis is institutionalized as a defined process.

MA:GG3.GP1 ESTABLISH A DEFINED PROCESS

Establish and maintain the description of a defined measurement and analysis process.

Establishing and tailoring process assets, including standard processes, are addressed in the Organizational Process Definition process area.

Establishing process needs and objectives and selecting, improving, and deploying process assets, including standard processes, are addressed in the Organizational Process Focus process area.

Subpractices

1. Select from the organization's set of standard processes those processes that cover the measurement and analysis process and best meet the needs of the organizational unit or line of business.

2. Establish the defined process by tailoring the selected processes according to the organization's tailoring guidelines.
3. Ensure that the organization's process objectives are appropriately addressed in the defined process, and ensure that process governance extends to the tailored processes.
4. Document the defined process and the records of the tailoring.
5. Revise the description of the defined process as necessary.

MA:GG3.GP2 COLLECT IMPROVEMENT INFORMATION

Collect measurement and analysis work products and improvement information derived from planning and performing the process to support future use and improvement of the organization's processes and process assets.

Elaboration:

> These are examples of improvement work products and information:
> - the degree to which measurement data is current
> - the integrity and security status of measurement data based on integrity and security tests
> - data analysis reports and presentations
> - changes and trends in operating conditions, risk conditions, and the risk environment that affect measurement results
> - lessons learned in post-event review of incidents and disruptions in continuity
> - process lessons learned that can be applied to improve operational resilience management performance
> - reports on the effectiveness and weaknesses of controls
> - process requirements that are not being satisfied and the risks associated with them
> - resilience requirements that are not being satisfied or are being exceeded

Establishing the measurement repository and process asset library is addressed in the Organizational Process Definition process area. Updating the measurement repository and process asset library as part of process improvement and deployment is addressed in the Organizational Process Focus process area.

Subpractices

1. Store process and work product measures in the organization's measurement repository.
2. Submit documentation for inclusion in the organization's process asset library.
3. Document lessons learned from the process for inclusion in the organization's process asset library.
4. Propose improvements to the organizational process assets.

MONITORING
Process

Purpose

The purpose of Monitoring is to collect, record, and distribute information about the operational resilience management system to the organization on a timely basis.

Introductory Notes

Monitoring is an enterprise-wide activity that the organization uses to "take the pulse" of its day-to-day operations and, in particular, its operational resilience management processes. Monitoring provides the information that the organization needs to determine whether it is being subjected to threats and vulnerabilities that require action to prevent organizational impact. Monitoring also provides valuable information about operating conditions that could indicate a need for active organizational involvement.

Many operational resilience management processes implicitly require monitoring capacities in order to achieve higher-maturity goals. For example, monitoring provides data about changes in the user environment that can result in necessary changes in access privileges. Effective monitoring also informs the organization when new vulnerabilities emerge (either inside or outside of the organization) or when events or incidents require the organization's attention. This information may require the organization to change its strategy, improve control selection, implementation, and management, or improve the details of its service continuity plans. In addition, the organization's compliance process—which is by nature data-intensive—benefits from monitoring activities by receiving up-to-date information that can be important to compliance activities. In essence, monitoring is a core capability that the organization must master in order to improve and sustain a level of adequate resilience.

Monitoring is also a data collection activity that allows the organization to measure process effectiveness across resilience capabilities. For example, through monitoring, the organization can determine whether its resilience goals are being met. It can also ascertain whether its security activities are effective and producing the intended results. Monitoring is one way that the organization collects necessary data (and invokes a vital feedback loop) to know how well it is performing in managing the operational resilience management system.

The Monitoring process area focuses on the activities the organization performs to collect, record, and distribute relevant data to the organization for the purposes of managing resilience and providing data for measuring process effectiveness. To do this, the organization must establish the stakeholders of the monitoring process (i.e., those that have a need for timely information about resilience activities) and determine their requirements and needs. The organization must also determine its monitoring requirements for managing both operational resilience and the operational resilience management system and ensure that resources have been assigned to meet these requirements. Data collection, recording, and distribution take organizational resources. Thus, the organization must consider and implement an infrastructure that supports and enables its monitoring needs and capabilities. Finally, the organization must collect, organize, record, and make available the necessary information in a manner that is timely and accurate and that ensures data confidentiality, integrity, and availability.

Related Process Areas

The Monitoring process area provides essential data necessary to manage several operational resilience management processes. These processes include Incident Management and Control, Vulnerability Assessment and Resolution, Risk Management, and others. From a process improvement perspective, all operational resilience management process areas may rely upon data collected and distributed through monitoring practices as described in this process area.

Summary of Specific Goals and Practices

MON:SG1 Establish and Maintain a Monitoring Program
    MON:SG1.SP1   Establish a Monitoring Program
    MON:SG1.SP2   Identify Stakeholders
    MON:SG1.SP3   Establish Monitoring Requirements
    MON:SG1.SP4   Analyze and Prioritize Monitoring Requirements
MON:SG2 Perform Monitoring
    MON:SG2.SP1   Establish and Maintain Monitoring Infrastructure
    MON:SG2.SP2   Establish Collection Standards and Guidelines
    MON:SG2.SP3   Collect and Record Information
    MON:SG2.SP4   Distribute Information

Specific Practices by Goal

MON:SG1 ESTABLISH AND MAINTAIN A MONITORING PROGRAM

A program for identifying, recording, collecting, and reporting important resilience information is established and maintained.

Monitoring is not simply a process of accumulating data; instead, it is a process of data collection and distribution with the purpose of providing timely, accurate, complete, and useful information about the current state of operational processes, any potential threats or vulnerabilities, and information about the effectiveness of the organization's operational resilience management activities.

Monitoring encompasses a wide array of organizational activities that serve many different uses and purposes.

> For example, monitoring is performed to collect data on
> - the secure and accurate functioning of systems and networks
> - key performance indicators that demonstrate achievement of strategic objectives and resilience goals
> - the actions of persons, objects, and entities when they access and use organizational assets
> - vulnerabilities, threats, and risks to organizational assets
> - events and incidents that can disrupt organizational assets and services
> - the physical movement of persons and objects through organizational facilities and physical plant
> - the status of compliance with regulations, laws, and guidelines
> - the efficiency of services to meet their goals
> - the effectiveness of the organization's internal control system
> - activities, issues, and concerns that may require the involvement of organizational oversight or governance
> - changes in the organization's risk environment that would warrant changes in operational risk and resilience management strategies
> - process efficiency in meeting resilience goals and continually improving

Effective monitoring at an enterprise level is a significant challenge that requires careful planning and program management. Requirements for data collection and distribution must be thoughtfully established by those who need accurate and timely information to manage their processes (commonly referred to as "stakeholders") and to improve them. The extent to which the organization must establish monitoring as an enterprise-level capability depends on the requirements of stakeholders. In many cases, data can be collected efficiently and distributed to many stakeholders, all of which may have vastly different needs for it.

Of note is that not all monitoring activities may be under the direct control of the organization. For example, if the organization has outsourced security operations, many of the monitoring processes relevant to managing operational resilience will probably be performed by the outsourcer and, in some cases, by one of its subcontractors. It is extremely important for the organization to identify where these monitoring processes are being performed and ensure that monitoring requirements (including the accuracy, validity, and timeliness of data) are being met.

To address monitoring as an organizational competency, the organization must establish a monitoring program and plan and identify stakeholders and their requirements as a foundation for an efficient and effective data collection, organization, and distribution process.

MON:SG1.SP1 ESTABLISH A MONITORING PROGRAM

A program for identifying, collecting, and distributing monitoring information is established and maintained.

The monitoring program establishes the organization's approach to developing, deploying, coordinating, managing, and improving monitoring-related activities (such as data collection and distribution) in order to meet monitoring requirements established by organizational stakeholders. Because monitoring requirements can be vast in scope and breadth, the organization must determine how it can meet these requirements in the most efficient and effective manner.

> The monitoring program is responsible for ensuring that the organization performs several fundamental monitoring tasks, including
> - identifying relevant stakeholders of the monitoring process
> - collecting monitoring requirements
> - analyzing and prioritizing requirements based on strategic objectives and business needs
> - establishing methods, procedures, and processes to collect and distribute data to meet the monitoring requirements
> - establishing and managing an appropriate infrastructure to support data collection and distribution
> - establishing and enforcing data collection guidelines and standards
> - coordinating and managing external entities that have contractual commitments for monitoring processes
> - providing guidance on the protection and storage of monitoring data

The organization's monitoring program must take into consideration the scope and breadth of the activities necessary to meet these goals, including the human resources necessary to fulfill requirements, the funding required for monitoring processes, and any training or skills improvement activities that will be needed to meet requirements.

Typical work products

1. Monitoring plan and program
2. Documented scope of the monitoring program
3. Documented commitments to the plan and program

Subpractices

1. Establish the plan and scope for a resilience monitoring program.

    The plan and program for monitoring should address how the organization will
    - identify relevant stakeholders of the monitoring program
    - collect monitoring requirements
    - analyze and prioritize monitoring requirements
    - collect and distribute data to meet the requirements
    - establish and enforce collection and distribution guidelines and standards
    - coordinate and manage monitoring activities performed by external entities
    - store and protect monitoring data
    - resource, fund, and perform monitoring activities

    The plan and program for monitoring should also provide guidance on the types of assets and services that should specifically be included in monitoring activities (i.e., to provide direction on developing monitoring requirements).

2. Establish commitments to the plan.

    Documented commitments by those responsible for implementing and supporting the plan are essential for program effectiveness.

3. Revise the plan and commitments as necessary.

MON:SG1.SP2 IDENTIFY STAKEHOLDERS

The organizational and external entities that rely upon information collected from the monitoring process are identified.

Stakeholders of the organization's monitoring processes are those internal and external people, entities, or agencies that require information about the operational resilience management processes for which they have responsibility and for which they must achieve resilience goals, objectives, and obligations.

Stakeholders are essential to the monitoring process because their requirements shape and form the monitoring activities that the organization performs. The scope of monitoring is in part devised through the needs of stakeholders of the process, and the tangible processes the organization puts in place to perform monitoring are designed around these needs.

Stakeholders range from high-level personnel such as the CEO and CIO to operations-level staff such as system administrators and security guards.

These are examples of types of stakeholders that may need information from the monitoring process:
- boards of directors and governors
- higher-level managers (CXO)
- information technology staff, including
    - system administrators and managers
    - application managers

> - network managers and technicians
> - telecommunications staff
> - security administrators
> - CSIRT teams
> - external entities, such as business partners and vendors
> - security guards, police, or other public agencies
> - external agencies, such as regulatory bodies
> - internal and external auditors

The organization must effectively identify stakeholders of the monitoring process and determine their needs and requirements. The identification process may be difficult but can be enabled by reviewing the organization's operational resilience management processes and commencing conversations with stakeholders of these processes. For external stakeholders, the organization may begin with a review of significant contracts with external entities or may have conversations with outsourcers.

The establishment of monitoring requirements is addressed in practice MON:SG1.SP3.

Typical work products

1. List of internal and external stakeholders
2. Stakeholder involvement plan

Subpractices

1. Identify stakeholders of the monitoring process.
   The list should include internal and external stakeholders and should be seeded by examining operational resilience management processes and their organizational owners.
2. Develop and document a stakeholder involvement plan.
   To facilitate the organization's enterprise-level monitoring processes, information about the stakeholders and their specific justification for inclusion in the process should be documented.

> These are examples of the type of information that should be collected:
> - rationale for stakeholders' involvement (the processes they own)
> - roles and responsibilities of the relevant stakeholders
> - relationships between stakeholders
> - resources (e.g., training, materials, time, and funding) needed to ensure stakeholder interaction

MON:SG1.SP3 ESTABLISH MONITORING REQUIREMENTS

The requirements for monitoring operational resilience management processes are established.

The scope of the monitoring activity determines how extensive the organization's processes must be and may be a deciding factor in how the organization develops and implements appropriate infrastructure to meet the requirements of stakeholders. The scope is a direct reflection of the needs and requirements of stakeholders.

The requirements of stakeholders must clearly establish the information and data that they need on a regular basis to manage, measure, direct, control, and improve processes for which they have responsibility.

Requirements must consider
- the type and extent of data necessary
- the granularity of data necessary (e.g., by asset, by business process, by service)
- the sources of the data
- who is authorized to distribute, receive, and use the data
- the format(s) of the data (e.g., on paper, electronically, by cell phone, on monitors)
- the distribution frequency of the data and the data refresh (i.e., discretely, such as on a weekly basis, or continuous)
- how the data will be distributed (i.e., remotely, locally)
- the retention of the data (i.e., where it will be stored, by whom, and how it will be protected)
- special needs related to reading, communicating, or understanding the data (systems or special coding books to allow log reading, specialized training, etc.)
- disposition of the data once used

Clearly, these requirements will vary widely by stakeholder and will require extensive consideration and planning to satisfy. In addition, while these requirements form the basis for the organization's program and plan for monitoring, they also establish the requirements for infrastructure that must be implemented and managed to meet the requirements as stated. In some cases, the organization may decide to outsource some of these requirements instead of making permanent investments in infrastructure. (*Infrastructure considerations are addressed in MON:SG2.SP1.*)

The organization must systematically collect, document, analyze, and prioritize the monitoring requirements from stakeholders. However, the organization may also need to decompose these general requirements into functional requirements that relate to resources and infrastructure. For example, if a system administrator needs to have a daily log of the activity of users with special privileges, this log must be able to be produced (by a system or special program) and delivered to the system administrator or the administrator's designees. Thus, the monitoring requirement will have to be translated into other requirements (such as the ability for the operating system to produce the report needed) to be satisfied.

Typical work products

1. Monitoring requirements by stakeholder or process
2. Functional requirements
3. Parameters for requirements refresh and change control

Subpractices

1. Establish monitoring requirements for the operational resilience management processes.

    Monitoring requirements must be established by stakeholder and documented. Essential information about each requirement must be collected so that the requirements can be analyzed and prioritized.

These are examples of monitoring requirements:
- audit logs that display the use of trusted user IDs and identities and the actions taken
- activity logging for the use of application systems
- control reports that identify violations of or transactions that fail preventive or detective controls
- logs of changes to access controls
- logs of entry to and exit from facilities
- incidents, faults, and alarms
- maintenance requirements for hardware
- network traffic monitoring
- firewall alerts and notifications
- "whistle-blower" reports of unethical or unacceptable behavior of employees or contractors
- service desk reports

---

2. Identify the level and type of monitoring activities required to meet monitoring requirements.

    Monitoring requirements may have to be decomposed to functional requirements in order to determine their feasibility. Functional requirements describe at a detailed level what must be performed to meet the monitoring requirement. At a minimum, functional requirements must specify format, frequency, and source but should also detail infrastructure requirements (if so dependent). If the monitoring requirements will have to be met through a sourcing contract (i.e., via an outsourcer), functional requirements will have to be more extensive so that they can be reflected in requests for proposals (RFPs) and contract terms.

> Examples of functional requirements for a monitoring requirement to "identify violations of preventive and detective controls in a vendor payment system" might include
> - development of a capability to log and store control violations in the vendor payment application
> - real-time, online delivery of alerts to selected managers and supervisors
> - development and distribution of paper-based control reports on a daily basis

3. Establish parameters for requirements refresh and review.
   Because monitoring activities can be labor-, time-, and cost-intensive, monitoring requirements must be reviewed and validated on a regular basis. This allows the organization to avoid monitoring activities that are not purposeful and to direct resources to activities that are next on the priority list.

MON:SG1.SP4 ANALYZE AND PRIORITIZE MONITORING REQUIREMENTS

Monitoring requirements are analyzed and prioritized to ensure they can be satisfied.

Once requirements have been established for monitoring processes, the organization must determine if the requirements can be satisfied. Satisfaction of the requirements may result in infrastructure and resource needs that the organization does not currently possess and require expenditures for outsourcing or other arrangements to obtain.

> Through analysis of monitoring requirements, the organization seeks to determine
> - the scope of the requirement (what it covers)
> - the potential infrastructure needs to support the requirement
> - the resources (human, capital, or expense) needed to support the requirement
> - alternatives for meeting the requirement
> - requirements that cannot be met, and the potential risk that results
> - duplicative requirements or requirements that can be met through efficient data collection (i.e., collect data once, meet many requirements)

The analysis of monitoring requirements is dependent upon a thorough review of functional requirements. Functional requirements express the potential demands on the organization needed to meet monitoring requirements. If functional requirements cannot be met for any reason (including cost or lack of human resources), alternatives will have to be identified and analyzed (such as outsourcing), or a decision must be made to forgo satisfaction of the requirement.

Because not all monitoring requirements will be able to be met, the organization may need to look at its operational resilience management processes and prioritize requirements so that high-priority needs (such as the detection of events or incidents) are given precedence. Process areas such as Access Management, Vulnerability Analysis and Resolution, Incident Management and Control, Identity Management, and Environmental Control may have significant monitoring needs just to keep them operational and functional.

When the organization cannot meet a requirement, it typically indicates that the information needed to keep operational resilience management processes operating or to improve these processes is not available. In some cases, this may pose additional risk to the organization because events, incidents, vulnerabilities, and threats may go unnoticed or undetected. For example, if the organization is unable to produce a daily log of users who have special privileges and the actions that these users take, there is a potential that unauthorized or inadvertent actions may take place without the organization's knowledge. Thus, not only is the monitoring requirement unfulfilled, but the organization takes on additional risk by not being able to operate a corresponding detective control. This risk must be identified, characterized, and addressed through the organization's risk management process.

Typical work products

1. Prioritized requirements
2. Requirements gaps (or requirements that cannot be met)
3. Alternatives for meeting requirements
4. Risks related to unsatisfied requirements
5. Accepted requirements

Subpractices

1. Analyze monitoring requirements.
    Analysis should address resource and infrastructure needs. Functional requirements should be a primary consideration in analysis because these requirements may become significant constraints in providing monitoring services.
2. Assign priority to monitoring requirements.
    Not all monitoring requirements may be satisfied due to resource constraints. In addition, some requirements may be of higher priority because they support strategies to protect and sustain higher-priority assets and services. Thus, the organization should attempt to prioritize monitoring requirements so that qualitative decisions can be made regarding which requirements must be satisfied versus those that may be left unsatisfied.

    Requirements on which the organization has put a high priority and which it intends to satisfy should be considered accepted requirements, and appropriate processes should be provided to meet these requirements.
3. Identify monitoring requirements that may not be able to be satisfied.
    Some monitoring requirements may not be able to be satisfied.

> For example, the organization may have
> - resource (human and financial) limitations or constraints
> - lack of adequate infrastructure or supporting processes or technology
> - insufficient funding for outsourcing requirements
> - an inability to determine clear benefits from the investment in satisfying a monitoring requirement

The organization should clearly document those requirements that cannot be satisfied, communicate this decision to stakeholders (and attempt to negotiate the requirements, if appropriate), and determine any potential consequences that may result.

4. Identify risks that result from unsatisfied requirements.

In some cases, the inability to satisfy a monitoring requirement may pose additional operational risk to the organization. This is particularly true when monitoring processes are a fundamental part of other operational resilience management processes such as incident management or vulnerability management. In these cases, the inability to satisfy a monitoring requirement should be documented, and any resulting risk should be referred to the organization's risk management process for analysis and resolution.

The risk management cycle is addressed in the Risk Management process area.

MON:SG2 PERFORM MONITORING

The monitoring process is performed throughout the enterprise.

Monitoring activities are typically thought of as technology-driven and therefore as part of the domain of information technology. In reality, monitoring activities are often performed throughout the organization, take many forms (from service desk calls to automated monitoring of networks and systems), and involve many different people and their skills.

Effective monitoring requires people, processes, and technology that have to be deployed and managed to meet monitoring requirements and provide timely and accurate information to other operational resilience management processes. This requires the establishment of appropriate infrastructure to support the process, collection standards and processes to ensure consistency and accuracy of information, the active collection of data, and the distribution of data to relevant stakeholders.

Depending on resources, the criticality of the monitoring processes, and the objectives for gathering and distributing monitoring data, the organization may perform monitoring processes, establish infrastructure, and distribute information through internal activities or source some or all of these processes to outsourcers. In some cases, monitoring may be included as part of the outsourcing of an organizational service. Thus, monitoring practices can be performed either in-house or by external entities.

MON:SG2.SP1 ESTABLISH AND MAINTAIN MONITORING INFRASTRUCTURE

A monitoring infrastructure commensurate with meeting monitoring requirements is established and maintained.

Monitoring is a data-collection-intensive activity that is often dependent on support services and technologies to meet requirements. While typically a technology-driven activity, many monitoring processes are manual and people-intensive in nature. Relative to the types of monitoring that the organization requires, an appropriate infrastructure must be established and supported to ensure consistent, accurate, and timely satisfaction of requirements. This infrastructure can encompass people, processes, and technology and will likely make use of the organization's existing installed base of technology and manual processes. However, in some cases, the supporting infrastructure may extend beyond the organization's borders to outsourcers and other external entities that help the organization to meet requirements.

> Supporting infrastructure may extend beyond the organization's borders where
> - the organization does not have a core competency in collecting and distributing required information
> - collecting and distributing information are not cost-effective for the organization
> - an existing relationship with an external entity can be expanded to meet monitoring requirements

Important considerations for an appropriate supporting infrastructure include the protection and timeliness of data collected and distributed. Monitoring data can expose the organization's weaknesses and therefore must be protected from unauthorized, inappropriate access where it is stored or collected, and in transmission to users and stakeholders. In addition, the timeliness of the collected data is paramount to providing an appropriate response to events, incidents, and threats and other actions the organization may take for improving operational resilience management processes.

In addition to meeting timeliness and protection requirements, the infrastructure should also ensure that the provisions of the organization's monitoring plan and program can be accomplished.

When the infrastructure is not under the direct control of the organization, special contractual arrangements and provisions should be enacted to ensure that protection and timeliness requirements can be met and that corresponding monitoring requirements can be satisfied.

Typical work products

1. Infrastructure requirements
2. Infrastructure map or diagram
3. Data collection tools, techniques, methods, and procedures

Subpractices

1. Identify and inventory existing monitoring infrastructure and capabilities that may address the program objectives and monitoring requirements.

    Monitoring requirements may be able to be met substantially by existing infrastructure and manual processes. Examining existing infrastructure and inventorying existing monitoring capabilities provide the organization an ability to accurately determine additional infrastructure needs and to prepare for meeting them.

2. Identify infrastructure needs to support accepted requirements.

    Infrastructure needs may range from manual processes to automated, highly technical processes and are predicated on monitoring requirements that have been accepted by the organization.

    Based on requirements and existing capabilities, infrastructure requirements have to be articulated and addressed. This process can be aided by examination of the functional requirements that have been developed as a result of analysis of monitoring requirements (as performed in practice MON:SG1.SP3).

    Infrastructure needs that cannot be met by the organization (whether technical or manual) may result in the inability to meet monitoring requirements. In this case, the monitoring requirements that cannot be met, and any resulting risk to the organization, should be characterized and addressed by the organization. *(See subpractice 3 in MON:SG1.SP4.)*

3. Implement and manage monitoring infrastructure.

    An appropriate infrastructure for supporting monitoring requirements must be implemented and managed to ensure consistent and accurate collection and distribution of data.

MON:SG2.SP2 ESTABLISH COLLECTION STANDARDS AND GUIDELINES

The standards and parameters for collecting information and managing data are established.

Because monitoring is fundamentally a data collection activity, the organization should implement standards and parameters that ensure enterprise-wide quality assurance for the monitoring process. These standards and parameters should address data accuracy, completeness, and timeliness and should apply across the organization to ensure consistency and repeatability.

Standards and parameters should also address appropriate measures to store monitoring data, to make it available as needed, and to protect it from unacceptable exposure or use. In addition, relevant historical data may be captured as part of the monitoring process that can also provide a foundation for forensic discovery and analysis. This evidence must be appropriately preserved. *(Practices for the appropriate handling of forensic data are specifically addressed in practice IMC:SG2.SP3 in the Incident Management and Control process area.)*

Collection of extraneous or irrelevant information may not instill confidence in stakeholders that the monitoring program is operating as planned or is meeting the objectives of the program or monitoring requirements. Thus, standards and parameters should also address the filtering and validation of data to ensure it exhibits high levels of integrity.

When collected and stored, monitoring data creates an organizational asset that must be appropriately managed. *(The activities for managing knowledge and information assets are addressed in the Knowledge and Information Management process area.)*

Typical work products

1. Standards and parameters for collection of data
2. Standards and parameters for storage of data
3. Monitoring operating procedures

Subpractices

1. Develop and maintain standards and parameters for collection of monitoring data.

> These are examples of standards and parameters for data collection:
> - defining what needs to be collected based on the monitoring requirements
> - the acceptable media for the repository (electronic, paper, etc.)
> - acceptable formats for data
> - validation procedures to ensure data integrity
> - collection time periods, including whether the data collection is discrete or continuous
> - retention period for monitoring data
> - federal, state, or local laws and regulations that may affect how data is collected and stored

2. Develop and maintain standards and parameters for the handling and storage of monitoring data collected.

> These are examples of standards and parameters for storage of data collected:
> - categorizing the information *(See KIM:SG1.SP2.)*
> - storage and handling procedures for the specific media type (paper or electronic)
> - protection and security standards for monitoring data (by category)
> - retention periods
> - proper procedures for disposal of monitoring data

3. Review, refine, and develop monitoring operating procedures.

   Detailed processes, standard operating procedures, or work instructions may be created during monitoring infrastructure implementation, but they will have to be regularly reviewed, tailored, and possibly supplemented to meet ongoing monitoring needs.

MON:SG2.SP3 COLLECT AND RECORD INFORMATION

Information relevant to the operational resilience management system is collected and recorded.

The basic organizational activities involved in monitoring are data collection and recording. Data collection may be a discrete (i.e., periodic) or continuous activity, depending on the stakeholders' requirements for immediacy, availability, and usability.

Data collection is dependent on having appropriate media to meet the requirements of stakeholders. These requirements may be infrastructure-related (i.e., involve storage arrays, etc.).

Collection media may include
- electronic logs, data files, databases, or information repositories
- paper reports or other physical media such as CDs
- alarms and notifications that warn when a threshold has been reached or exceeded
- real-time surveillance devices, such as video

In a broad sense, monitoring is an activity of not only data collection but also usage of this data to protect and sustain organizational assets and services and to monitor and improve operational resilience management processes. However, the Monitoring process area addresses only the establishment of monitoring requirements and the collection and distribution of relevant monitoring data. It does not address the usage of this data to manage operational resilience or to improve operational resilience processes. The usage of monitoring data is considered to be included as a part of all relevant operational resilience management process areas where appropriate and is not replicated in this process area.

Typical work products

1. Collection methods and procedures
2. Collection media or information repository

Subpractices

1. Develop collection methods and procedures.

   Collection methods and procedures must ensure the organization's ability to meet monitoring requirements (particularly high-priority requirements) with the available infrastructure and capacity.

2. Assign resources to monitoring processes.
    Ensure that monitoring support staff have received appropriate training to perform the necessary monitoring activities.

> These are examples of training:
> - operating, monitoring, and configuring monitoring systems components
> - supporting stakeholders in understanding and interpreting monitoring data
> - securing data collected from monitoring system components

3. Monitor, collect, and record data.
4. Establish and maintain policies for proper handling, labeling, and categorization of data collected during monitoring activities.

> These are examples of items to include in policies:
> - protection against tampering or unauthorized access
> - alterations to the type of data being collected
> - log files being edited, deleted, or altered
> - storage capacity of collection mechanisms to avoid the file media capacity being exceeded, resulting in overwriting or failing to collect relevant data
> - information categorization, labeling, and handling instructions
> - requirements for encryption, secure storage, and secure transport or distribution of information

Data categorization is addressed in the Knowledge and Information Management process area.

MON:SG2.SP4 Distribute Information

Collected and recorded information is distributed to appropriate stakeholders.

The continuous and effective management of operational resilience is highly dependent on information collected in the monitoring process.

> This information is useful for
> - identifying, preventing, and responding to disruptive events
> - determining the effectiveness of strategies to protect and sustain assets and services
> - determining the effectiveness of operational resilience management processes
> - improving operational resilience management processes when necessary

To meet these objectives, monitoring information must be available for use when needed by stakeholders. Thus, the organization must establish viable distribution methods and channels to move collected information to stakeholders as requested in a reliable and consistent manner.

The frequency of distribution of monitoring information is dependent upon the monitoring requirements established by stakeholders. Considering how the monitoring information will be used, stakeholders may require distribution of this information on a discrete basis (i.e., at points in time on a regular basis) or continuously (on demand, highly available). For example, a once-daily report of users who have exercised special privileges may be sufficient for a system security administrator; in contrast, immediate alarms and notifications of potential denial-of-service attacks may be necessary to adequately protect the organization from impact.

The variety and extensiveness of distribution requirements may affect infrastructure capabilities and capacities. Thus, distribution requirements must be included when considering an adequate infrastructure for supporting monitoring processes. *(Considerations of monitoring infrastructure are addressed in practice MON:SG2.SP1.)*

Distribution of monitoring information may also vary significantly depending on whether the monitoring processes are internal or external. External processes may have to be contractually arranged to meet the distribution demands of stakeholders, so their distribution requirements must be clearly identified in contracts and service level agreements.

Typical work products

1. Distribution plans, procedures, and processes
2. Distribution media and methods
3. Distribution channels

Subpractices

1. Identify media and methods of distribution based on requirements.

    Based on requirements for data distribution, the organization should identify the types of media and methods of distribution that will have to be supported to deliver to stakeholders.

    In the case of external collection and distribution of data, the media and methods will have to be included in contractual arrangements and service level agreements.

    Collection media (as described in practice MON:SG2.SP3) may be the same as media used to distribute information. In other words, if data is collected directly to CD it may also be distributed on CD.

    Because monitoring information is a high-value organizational information asset, the protection considerations of this asset must be identified. Appropriate controls may have to be designed and implemented to protect monitoring data from unauthorized use and access. *(Considerations of strategies to protect and sustain information assets are addressed in the Knowledge and Information Management process area.)*

2. Develop and document plans, processes, and procedures for distribution of information to internal and external stakeholders.
   These plans, processes, and procedures should also take into consideration distribution of monitoring information from external sources.
3. Develop infrastructure to meet distribution requirements.
   Monitoring infrastructure is addressed in MON:SG2.SP1.
4. Distribute monitoring information according to requirements.

Elaborated Generic Practices by Goal

Refer to the Generic Goals and Practices document in Appendix A for general guidance that applies to all process areas. This section provides elaborations relative to the application of the Generic Goals and Practices to the Monitoring process area.

MON:GG1 ACHIEVE SPECIFIC GOALS

The operational resilience management system supports and enables achievement of the specific goals of the Monitoring process area by transforming identifiable input work products to produce identifiable output work products.

MON:GG1.GP1 PERFORM SPECIFIC PRACTICES

Perform the specific practices of the Monitoring process area to develop work products and provide services to achieve the specific goals of the process area.

Elaboration:

Specific practices MON:SG1.SP1 through MON:SG2.SP4 are performed to achieve the goals of the monitoring process.

MON:GG2 INSTITUTIONALIZE A MANAGED PROCESS

Monitoring is institutionalized as a managed process.

MON:GG2.GP1 ESTABLISH PROCESS GOVERNANCE

Establish and maintain governance over the planning and performance of the monitoring process.

Refer to the Enterprise Focus process area for more information about providing sponsorship and oversight to the monitoring process.

Subpractices

1. Establish governance over process activities.

Elaboration:

> Governance over the monitoring process may be exhibited by
> - developing and publicizing higher-level managers' objectives and requirements for the process
> - sponsoring process policies, procedures, standards, and guidelines
> - making higher-level managers aware of applicable compliance obligations related to the process, and regularly reporting on the organization's satisfaction of these obligations to higher-level managers
> - sponsoring and funding process activities
> - aligning data collection and distribution activities with identified resilience needs and objectives and stakeholder needs and requirements
> - verifying that the process supports strategic resilience objectives
> - regular reporting from organizational units to higher-level managers on process activities and results
> - creating dedicated higher-level management feedback loops on decisions about the process and recommendations for prioritizing process requirements and improving the process
> - conducting regular internal and external audits and related reporting to audit committees on process effectiveness
> - creating formal programs to measure the effectiveness of process activities, and reporting these measurements to higher-level managers

2. Develop and publish organizational policy for the process.

Elaboration:

> The monitoring policy should address
> - responsibility, authority, and ownership for performing process activities
> - information categorization, labeling, and handling
> - protection against tampering and unauthorized access
> - encryption, secure storage, and secure transport and distribution of information
> - procedures, standards, and guidelines for
>   - altering data based on the type of data, including editing, deleting, and altering log files
>   - storage capacity of collection mechanisms and actions to take if capacity is exceeded by type of media
>   - collection of data
>   - recording and storage of data, including collection media (electronic logs, data files, databases, and information repositories)
>   - distribution of data, including distribution media, methods, and channels
>   - service level agreement terms and conditions for external entities involved in process activities
> - methods for measuring adherence to policy, exceptions granted, and policy violations

MON:GG2.GP2 PLAN THE PROCESS

Establish and maintain the plan for performing the monitoring process.

> Elaboration:
>
> The plan for the monitoring process should not be confused with the monitoring plan and program for identifying, collecting, and distributing specific monitoring data as described in specific practice MON:SG1.SP1. The plan for the monitoring process details how the organization will perform monitoring, including the development of specific monitoring plans and programs.

> *Subpractices*
>
> 1. Define and document the plan for performing the process.
> 2. Define and document the process description.
> 3. Review the plan with relevant stakeholders and get their agreement.
> 4. Revise the plan as necessary.

MON:GG2.GP3 PROVIDE RESOURCES

Provide adequate resources for performing the monitoring process, developing the work products, and providing the services of the process.

> *Subpractices*
>
> 1. Staff the process.
>
>   Elaboration:
>
>   Staff assigned to the monitoring process must have appropriate knowledge of the related processes being monitored and the objectivity to perform monitoring activities without concern for personal detriment and without the expectation of personal benefit.
>
>   > These are examples of staff required to perform the monitoring process:
>   > - staff responsible for
>   >   - collecting, analyzing, and prioritizing process requirements based on strategic objectives, business needs, and stakeholder requirements and needs
>   >   - developing process plans and programs and ensuring they are aligned with stakeholder requirements and needs
>   >   - establishing an appropriate infrastructure for data collection, recording, and distribution
>   >   - data collection, recording, distribution, and storage
>   >   - data protection and security, so as to ensure data confidentiality, integrity, and availability
>   >   - managing external entities that have contractual obligations for process activities

> - owners and custodians of high-value services and assets that support the accomplishment of operational resilience management objectives
> - internal and external auditors responsible for reporting to appropriate committees on process effectiveness and the adequacy of collected data to accurately track the performance of operational resilience management processes

Refer to the Organizational Training and Awareness process area for information about training staff for resilience roles and responsibilities.

Refer to the Human Resource Management process area for information about acquiring staff to fulfill roles and responsibilities.

2. Fund the process.

   Elaboration:

   Refer to the Financial Resource Management process area for information about budgeting for, funding, and accounting for monitoring.

3. Provide necessary tools, techniques, and methods to perform the process.

   Elaboration:

   Many of these tools, techniques, and methods should be available as applied to other aspects of organizational monitoring. The intent here is to apply these to operational resilience management.

> These are examples of tools, techniques, and methods to support the monitoring process:
> - data collection methods, techniques, and tools, including those necessary to manage collection media
> - data recording and storage methods, techniques, and tools
> - data protection and security methods, techniques, and tools, including those necessary to ensure data confidentiality, integrity, and availability
> - data distribution methods, techniques, and tools
> - methods, techniques, and tools for developing and managing collection media
> - tools for developing and maintaining traceability between stakeholder requirements and process requirements, plans, and programs

MON:GG2.GP4 ASSIGN RESPONSIBILITY

Assign responsibility and authority for performing the monitoring process, developing the work products, and providing the services of the process.

Elaboration:

Specific practice MON:SG1.SP1 calls for documenting commitments by those responsible for implementing the monitoring plan and program. Specific practice MON:SG1.SP2 calls for documenting the roles and responsibilities of relevant stakeholders.

Refer to the Human Resource Management process area for more information about establishing resilience as a job responsibility, developing resilience performance goals and objectives, and measuring and assessing performance against these goals and objectives.

Subpractices

1. Assign responsibility and authority for performing the process.
2. Assign responsibility and authority for performing the specific tasks of the process.

   Elaboration:

   > Responsibility and authority for performing monitoring tasks can be formalized by
   > - defining roles and responsibilities in the process plan, including roles responsible for collecting, recording, distributing, and ensuring the confidentiality, integrity, and availability of monitoring data
   > - including process tasks and responsibility for these tasks in specific job descriptions
   > - developing policy requiring organizational unit managers, line of business managers, project managers, and asset and service owners and custodians to participate in and derive benefit from the process for assets and services under their ownership or custodianship
   > - including process activities in staff performance management goals and objectives, with requisite measurement of progress against these goals
   > - developing and implementing contractual instruments (including service level agreements) with external entities to establish responsibility and authority for performing process tasks on outsourced functions
   > - including process tasks in measuring performance of external entities against contractual instruments

   Refer to the External Dependencies Management process area for additional details about managing relationships with external entities.

3. Confirm that people assigned with responsibility and authority understand it and are willing and able to accept it.

MON:GG2.GP5 TRAIN PEOPLE

Train the people performing or supporting the monitoring process as needed.

Refer to the Organizational Training and Awareness process area for more information about training the people performing or supporting the process.

Refer to the Human Resource Management process area for more information about inventorying skill sets, establishing a skill set baseline, identifying required skill sets, and measuring and addressing skill deficiencies.

Subpractices

1. Identify process skill needs.

    Elaboration:

    > These are examples of skills required in the monitoring process:
    > - knowledge of tools, techniques, and methods used to collect, record, distribute, and ensure the confidentiality, integrity, and availability of monitoring data, including those necessary to perform the process using the selected methods, techniques, and tools identified in MON:GG2.GP3 subpractice 3
    > - knowledge unique to each type of service, asset, and operational resilience management process area that is required to effectively perform process activities
    > - knowledge necessary to elicit and prioritize stakeholder requirements and needs and interpret them to develop effective process requirements, plans, and programs
    > - knowledge necessary to analyze and prioritize process requirements
    > - knowledge necessary to interpret monitoring data and represent it in ways that are meaningful and appropriate for managers and stakeholders

2. Identify process skill gaps based on available resources and their current skill levels.
3. Identify training opportunities to address skill gaps.

    Elaboration:

    > These are examples of training topics:
    > - operating, monitoring, and configuring monitoring system components
    > - supporting stakeholders in understanding and interpreting monitoring data
    > - data collection, recording, distribution, and storage techniques and tools
    > - securing data collected from monitoring system components to ensure data confidentiality, integrity, and availability
    > - supporting service and asset owners and custodians in understanding the process and their roles and responsibilities with respect to its activities
    > - working with external entities that have responsibility for process activities
    > - using process methods, tools, and techniques, including those identified in MON:GG2.GP3 subpractice 3

4. Provide training and review the training needs as necessary.

MON:GG2.GP6 MANAGE WORK PRODUCT CONFIGURATIONS

Place designated work products of the monitoring process under appropriate levels of control.

Elaboration:

> These are examples of monitoring work products placed under control:
> - process requirements, plans, and programs, including commitments to the plans and programs
> - list of internal and external stakeholders and a plan for their involvement
> - prioritized process requirements, accepted requirements, and risks resulting from unsatisfied requirements
> - infrastructure requirements
> - data collection and storage standards and parameters
> - data collection, handling, and storage methods, procedures, techniques, and tools
> - data distribution plans, procedures, processes, media, methods, and tools
> - collection media, including electronic logs, data files, databases, and information repositories
> - process plan
> - policies and procedures
> - contracts with external entities

MON:GG2.GP7 IDENTIFY AND INVOLVE RELEVANT STAKEHOLDERS

Identify and involve the relevant stakeholders of the monitoring process as planned.

Elaboration:

Several MON-specific practices address the involvement of stakeholders in the monitoring process. For example, MON:SG1.SP2 calls for identifying stakeholders that require information about operational resilience management processes for which they are responsible; MON:SG1.SP3 establishes monitoring requirements based on stakeholder requirements and needs.

Subpractices

1. Identify process stakeholders and their appropriate involvement.

   Elaboration:

   > These are examples of stakeholders of the monitoring process *(refer to MON:SG1.SP2)*:
   > - boards of directors and governors
   > - higher-level and other managers
   > - service owners and asset owners and custodians
   > - information technology staff, such as system administrators and CSIRT teams
   > - external entities such as business partners, vendors, and outsourcers

- police and security guards
- public agencies
- regulatory bodies
- internal and external auditors
- owners of operational resilience management processes
- staff identified as being associated with each process requirement, program, and distribution channel
- staff identified as being associated with each external entity that is collecting and distributing monitoring data

Stakeholders are involved in various tasks in the monitoring process, such as
- establishing requirements for the process
- planning for the process
- establishing process plans and programs
- making decisions about process scope and activities
- assessing collected data
- providing feedback to those responsible for providing the monitoring data on which the analysis results depend
- reviewing and appraising the effectiveness of process activities
- resolving issues in the process

2. Communicate the list of stakeholders to planners and those responsible for process performance.
3. Involve relevant stakeholders in the process as planned.

MON:GG2.GP8 MONITOR AND CONTROL THE PROCESS

Monitor and control the monitoring process against the plan for performing the process and take appropriate corrective action.

Elaboration:

While this practice is self-referencing, practices in the Monitoring process area provide more information about collecting and recording data relevant to operational resilience management processes that can also be applied to the monitoring process.

Refer to the Measurement and Analysis process area for more information about establishing process metrics and measurement.

Refer to the Enterprise Focus process area for more information about providing process information to managers, identifying issues, and determining appropriate corrective actions.

Subpractices

1. Measure actual performance against the plan for performing the process.
2. Review accomplishments and results of the process against the plan for performing the process.

   Elaboration:

   > These are examples of metrics for the monitoring process:
   > - percentage of operational resilience management system performance indicators or targets for which monitoring data is collected, recorded, and distributed
   > - percentage of organizational units, projects, and activities using monitoring data to assess the performance of operational resilience management processes
   > - percentage of accepted monitoring requirements (accepted requirements divided by total requirements)
   > - number of requirements gaps (total requirements minus accepted requirements)
   > - number of risks resulting from unsatisfied monitoring requirements, designated as high, medium, low, or some other organizational risk ranking method
   > - number of such risks (as well as process risks) referred to the risk management process; number of risks where corrective action is still pending (by risk rank)
   > - schedule for collecting, recording, and distributing monitoring data, including elapsed time from high-value data collection to data distribution to key stakeholders
   > - number of new and changed monitoring requirements over time
   > - level of adherence to process policies; number of policy violations; number of policy exceptions requested and number approved
   > - number of process activities that are on track per plan
   > - rate of change of resource needs to support the process
   > - rate of change of costs to support the process

3. Review activities, status, and results of the process with the immediate level of managers responsible for the process and identify issues.

   Elaboration:

   > Periodic reviews of the monitoring process are needed to ensure that
   > - the performance of resilience activities is being monitored and regularly reported
   > - strategic operational resilience management activities are on track according to plan
   > - actions requiring management involvement are elevated in a timely manner
   > - the performance of process activities is being monitored and regularly reported
   > - key measures are within acceptable ranges as demonstrated in governance dashboards or scorecards and financial reports
   > - administrative, technical, and physical controls are operating as intended
   > - controls are meeting the stated intent of the resilience requirements
   > - actions resulting from internal and external audits are being closed in a timely manner

4. Identify and evaluate the effects of significant deviations from the plan for performing the process.
5. Identify problems in the plan for performing and executing the process.
6. Take corrective action when requirements and objectives are not being satisfied, when issues are identified, or when progress differs significantly from the plan for performing the process.
7. Track corrective action to closure.

MON:GG2.GP9 OBJECTIVELY EVALUATE ADHERENCE

Objectively evaluate adherence of the monitoring process against its process description, standards, and procedures, and address non-compliance.

Elaboration:

> These are examples of activities to be reviewed:
> - the alignment of stakeholder requirements and needs with the process scope, requirements, plans, programs, and process plans
> - assignment of responsibility, accountability, and authority for resilience process activities
> - assignment of responsibility, accountability, and authority for monitoring process activities
> - determining the adequacy of process reports and reviews in informing decision makers regarding the performance of operational resilience management activities and the need to take corrective action, if any
> - verification of monitoring data confidentiality, integrity, and availability controls
> - use of monitoring data for improving strategies to protect and sustain assets and services

> These are examples of work products to be reviewed:
> - process plan and policies
> - process scope, requirements, plans, and programs
> - data collection, recording, and distribution methods, techniques, and tools
> - metrics for the process *(Refer to MON:GG2.GP9 subpractice 2.)*
> - contracts with external entities

MON:GG2.GP10 REVIEW STATUS WITH HIGHER-LEVEL MANAGERS

Review the activities, status, and results of the monitoring process with higher-level managers and resolve issues.

Refer to the Enterprise Focus process area for more information about providing sponsorship and oversight to the operational resilience management system.

MON:GG3 INSTITUTIONALIZE A DEFINED PROCESS

Monitoring is institutionalized as a defined process.

MON:GG3.GP1 ESTABLISH A DEFINED PROCESS

Establish and maintain the description of a defined monitoring process.

Establishing and tailoring process assets, including standard processes, are addressed in the Organizational Process Definition process area.

Establishing process needs and objectives and selecting, improving, and deploying process assets, including standard processes, are addressed in the Organizational Process Focus process area.

Subpractices

1. Select from the organization's set of standard processes those processes that cover the monitoring process and best meet the needs of the organizational unit or line of business.
2. Establish the defined process by tailoring the selected processes according to the organization's tailoring guidelines.
3. Ensure that the organization's process objectives are appropriately addressed in the defined process, and ensure that process governance extends to the tailored processes.
4. Document the defined process and the records of the tailoring.
5. Revise the description of the defined process as necessary.

MON:GG3.GP2 COLLECT IMPROVEMENT INFORMATION

Collect monitoring work products, measures, measurement results, and improvement information derived from planning and performing the process to support future use and improvement of the organization's processes and process assets.

Elaboration:

> These are examples of improvement work products and information:
> - the degree to which monitoring data is current
> - the confidentiality, integrity, and availability status of monitoring data based on integrity and security tests
> - metrics and measurements of the viability of the process *(Refer to MON:GG2.GP8 subpractice 2.)*
> - changes and trends in operating conditions, risk conditions, and the risk environment that affect process results
> - lessons learned in post-event review of incidents and disruptions in continuity

> - process lessons learned that can be applied to improve operational resilience management performance
> - reports on the effectiveness and weaknesses of controls
> - process requirements that are not being satisfied and the risks associated with them
> - resilience requirements that are not being satisfied or are being exceeded

Establishing the measurement repository and process asset library is addressed in the Organizational Process Definition process area. Updating the measurement repository and process asset library as part of process improvement and deployment is addressed in the Organizational Process Focus process area.

Subpractices

1. Store process and work product measures in the organization's measurement repository.
2. Submit documentation for inclusion in the organization's process asset library.
3. Document lessons learned from the process for inclusion in the organization's process asset library.
4. Propose improvements to the organizational process assets.

ORGANIZATIONAL PROCESS DEFINITION
Process

Purpose

The purpose of Organizational Process Definition is to establish and maintain a usable set of organizational process assets and work environment standards for operational resilience.

Introductory Notes

Organizational process assets enable consistent resilience management process performance across the organization and provide a basis for cumulative, long-term benefits to the organization.

The organization's process asset library is a collection of items maintained by the organization for use by the people and organizational units of the organization. This collection of items includes descriptions of processes and process elements, descriptions of life-cycle models, process tailoring guidelines, process-related documentation, and data. The organization's process asset library supports organizational learning and process improvement by allowing the sharing of best practices and lessons learned across the organization.

The organization's set of standard processes is tailored by organizational units to create their defined processes. The other organizational process assets are used to support tailoring and the implementation of the defined processes. The work environment standards are used to guide creation of organizational unit work environments.

A standard process is composed of other processes (i.e., subprocesses) or process elements. A process element is the fundamental (i.e., atomic) unit of process definition and describes the activities and tasks to consistently perform work. Process architecture provides rules for connecting the process elements of a standard process. The organization's set of standard processes may include multiple process architectures.

> The organizational process assets may be organized in many ways, depending on the implementation of the Organizational Process Definition process area. Examples include the following:
> - The organization's set of standard processes may be stored in the organization's process asset library, or they may be stored separately.
> - A single repository may contain both the measurements and the process-related documentation, or they may be stored separately.

Related Process Areas

Refer to the Organizational Process Focus process area for more information about organizational-process–related matters.

Summary of Specific Goals and Practices

OPD:SG1 Establish Organizational Process Assets
    OPD:SG1.SP1   Establish Standard Processes
    OPD:SG1.SP2   Establish Tailoring Criteria and Guidelines
    OPD:SG1.SP3   Establish the Organization's Measurement Repository
    OPD:SG1.SP4   Establish the Organization's Process Asset Library
    OPD:SG1.SP5   Establish Work Environment Standards
    OPD:SG1.SP6   Establish Rules and Guidelines for Integrated Teams

Specific Practices by Goal

OPD:SG1 ESTABLISH ORGANIZATIONAL PROCESS ASSETS

A set of organizational process assets is established and maintained.

OPD:SG1.SP1 ESTABLISH STANDARD PROCESSES

The organization's set of standard processes is established and maintained.

Standard processes may be defined at multiple levels in an enterprise and they may be related in a hierarchical manner. For example, an enterprise may have a set of standard processes that is tailored by individual organizational units (e.g., a division or site) in the enterprise to establish its set of standard processes. The set of standard processes may also be tailored for each of the organization's lines of business or product lines. Thus "the organization's set of standard processes" can refer to the standard processes established at the organization level and standard processes that may be established at lower levels, although some organizations may have only a single level of standard processes.

Multiple standard processes may be required to address the needs of different levels of organizational units or disciplines (for example, security versus business continuity). The organization's set of standard processes contains process elements that may be interconnected according to one or more process architectures that describe the relationships among these process elements.

The organization's set of standard processes typically includes technical, management, administrative, and support processes.

The organization's set of standard processes should collectively cover all processes needed by the organization and its organizational units.

Typical Work Products

1. Organization's set of standard processes

Subpractices

1. Decompose each standard process into constituent process elements to the level of detail needed to understand and describe the process.

    Each process element covers a bounded and closely related set of activities. The descriptions of the process elements may be templates to be filled in, fragments to be completed, abstractions to be refined, or complete descriptions to be tailored or used unmodified. These elements are described in sufficient detail such that the process, when fully defined, can be consistently performed by appropriately trained and skilled people.

> These are examples of process elements:
> - templates for creating plans and policies
> - descriptions of work product design methodology
> - templates for documenting incidents
> - templates for conducting management reviews

2. Specify the critical attributes of each process element.

> These are examples of critical attributes:
> - process roles
> - applicable procedures, standards, and guidelines
> - applicable methods, tools, techniques, and resources
> - process performance objectives
> - entry criteria
> - inputs
> - product and process measures to be collected and used
> - verification points (e.g., peer reviews)
> - outputs
> - interfaces
> - exit criteria

3. Specify the relationships of the process elements.

> These are examples of relationships:
> - ordering of the process elements
> - interfaces among the process elements
> - interfaces with external processes
> - interdependencies among the process elements

> The rules for describing the relationships among process elements are referred to as "process architecture." The process architecture provides essential requirements and guidelines. The detailed specifications of these relationships are covered in the descriptions of the defined processes that are tailored from the organization's set of standard processes.

4. Ensure that the organization's set of standard processes adheres to applicable process policies, standards, and models.

   Adherence to applicable process policies, standards, and models is typically demonstrated by developing a mapping from the organization's set of standard processes to the relevant process policies, standards, and models. In addition, this mapping will be a useful input to future appraisals.

5. Ensure that the organization's set of standard processes satisfies the process needs and objectives of the organization.

   Refer to the Organizational Process Focus process area for more information about establishing and maintaining the organization's process needs and objectives.

6. Ensure that there is appropriate integration among the processes that are included in the organization's set of standard processes.
7. Document the organization's set of standard processes.
8. Conduct peer reviews on the organization's set of standard processes.
9. Revise the organization's set of standard processes as necessary.

OPD:SG1.SP2 ESTABLISH TAILORING CRITERIA AND GUIDELINES

Tailoring criteria and guidelines for the organization's set of standard processes are established and maintained.

The tailoring criteria and guidelines describe the following:

- how the organization's set of standard processes and organizational process assets are used to create the defined processes
- mandatory requirements that must be satisfied by the defined processes (e.g., the subset of the organizational process assets that are essential for any defined process)

- options that can be exercised and criteria for selecting among the options
- procedures that must be followed in performing and documenting process tailoring

> These are examples of reasons for tailoring:
> - adapting the process for a new organizational unit, line of business, or other work environment
> - customizing the process for a specific asset type or discipline (such as security)
> - elaborating the process description so that the resulting defined process can be performed

Flexibility in tailoring and defining processes is balanced with ensuring appropriate consistency in the processes across the organization. Flexibility is needed to address contextual variables such as the domain, technical difficulty of the work, and experience of the people implementing the process. Consistency across the organization is needed so that organizational standards, objectives, and strategies are appropriately addressed and process data and lessons learned can be shared.

Tailoring criteria and guidelines may allow for using a standard process "as is," with no tailoring.

Typical work products

1. Tailoring guidelines for the organization's set of standard processes
2. Process documentation standards
3. Standard process requirements waivers

Subpractices

1. Specify the selection criteria and procedures for tailoring the organization's set of standard processes.

> These are examples of criteria and procedures:
> - criteria for selecting process elements from the organization's set of standard processes
> - procedures for tailoring the selected process elements to accommodate specific process characteristics and needs

> These are examples of tailoring actions:
> - modifying process elements
> - replacing process elements
> - reordering process elements

2. Specify the standards for documenting the defined processes.
3. Specify the procedures for submitting and obtaining approval of waivers from the requirements of the organization's set of standard processes.
4. Document the tailoring guidelines for the organization's set of standard processes.
5. Conduct peer reviews on the tailoring guidelines.
6. Revise the tailoring guidelines as necessary.

OPD:SG1.SP3 ESTABLISH THE ORGANIZATION'S MEASUREMENT REPOSITORY

The organization's measurement repository is established and maintained.

The repository contains both product and process measures that are related to the organization's set of standard processes. It also contains or refers to the information needed to understand and interpret the measures and assess them for reasonableness and applicability. For example, the definitions of the measures are used to compare similar measures from different processes.

Typical work products

1. Definition of the common set of product and process measures for the organization's set of standard processes
2. Design of the organization's measurement repository
3. Organization's measurement repository (that is, the repository structure and support environment)
4. Organization's measurement data
5. Procedures for storing, updating, and retrieving measures

Subpractices

1. Determine the organization's needs for storing, retrieving, and analyzing measurements.
2. Define a common set of process and product measures for the organization's set of standard processes.

    The measures in the common set are selected based on the organization's set of standard processes. They are selected for their ability to provide visibility into process performance to support expected business objectives. The common set of measures may vary for different standard processes.

    Operational definitions for the measures specify the procedures for collecting valid data and the point in the process where the data will be collected.

> These are examples of classes of commonly used measures:
> - estimates of work product size (e.g., pages)
> - estimates of effort and cost (e.g., person hours)
> - actual measures of size, effort, and cost

> - quality measures (e.g., number of incidents reported)
> - peer review coverage
> - test coverage
> - reliability measures (e.g., mean time to failure)

Refer to the Measurement and Analysis process area for more information about defining measures.

3. Design and implement the measurement repository.
4. Specify the procedures for storing, updating, and retrieving measures.
5. Conduct peer reviews on the definitions of the common set of measures and the procedures for storing and retrieving measures.
6. Enter the specified measures into the repository.

    Refer to the Measurement and Analysis process area for more information about collecting and analyzing data.
7. Make the contents of the measurement repository available for use by the organization and organizational units as appropriate.
8. Revise the measurement repository, common set of measures, and procedures as the organization's needs change.

> These are examples of when the common set of measures may have to be revised:
> - New processes are added.
> - Processes are revised and new measures are needed.
> - Finer granularity of data is required.
> - Greater visibility into the process is required.
> - Measures are retired.

OPD:SG1.SP4 ESTABLISH THE ORGANIZATION'S PROCESS ASSET LIBRARY

The organization's process asset library is established and maintained.

> These are examples of items to be stored in the organization's process asset library:
> - organizational policies
> - defined process descriptions
> - procedures (e.g., estimating procedure)
> - development plans
> - acquisition plans
> - quality assurance plans
> - training materials
> - process work products (e.g., checklists and templates)
> - lessons-learned reports

Typical work products

1. Design of the organization's process asset library
2. Organization's process asset library
3. Selected items to be included in the organization's process asset library
4. Catalog of items in the organization's process asset library
5. Procedures for storing and retrieving library items

Subpractices

1. Design and implement the organization's process asset library, including the library structure and support environment.
2. Specify the criteria for including items in the library.
   The items are selected based primarily on their relationship to the organization's set of standard processes.
3. Specify the procedures for storing and retrieving items.
4. Enter the selected items into the library and catalog them for easy reference and retrieval.
5. Make the items available for use by organizational units.
6. Periodically review the use of each item and use the results to maintain the library contents.
7. Revise the organization's process asset library as necessary.

> These are examples of when the library may have to be revised:
> - New items are added.
> - Items are retired.
> - Current versions of items are changed.

OPD:SG1.SP5 ESTABLISH WORK ENVIRONMENT STANDARDS

Work environment standards are established and maintained.

Work environment standards allow the organization to benefit from common tools, training, and maintenance, as well as cost savings from volume purchases. Work environment standards address the needs of all stakeholders and consider productivity, cost, availability, security, and workplace health, safety, and ergonomic factors. Work environment standards can include guidelines for tailoring and/or the use of waivers that allow adaptation of the organizational unit's work environment to meet specific needs.

Organizational Process Definition

> These are examples of work environment standards:
> - procedures for operation, safety, and security of the work environment
> - standard workstation hardware and software
> - standard application software and tailoring guidelines for it
> - standard production and calibration equipment
> - process for requesting and approving tailoring or waivers
> - procedures for the operation, safety, and security of the environment in which the IT, security, or continuity professional must work
> - procedures for working with external visitors or entities in the work environment
> - procedures for working in a classified environment

Typical work products

1. Work environment standards

Subpractices

1. Evaluate commercially available work environment standards appropriate for the organization.
2. Adopt existing work environment standards and develop new ones to fill gaps based on the organization's process needs and objectives.

OPD:SG1.SP6 ESTABLISH RULES AND GUIDELINES FOR INTEGRATED TEAMS

Organizational rules and guidelines for the structure, formation, and operation of integrated teams are established and maintained.

When executing work that crosses organizational lines, particularly work that represents convergent disciplines such as operational risk management, service continuity, and incident response, integrated teams must be structured, formed, and operated effectively.

Operating rules and guidelines for integrated teams define and control how teams are created and how they interact to accomplish objectives. Members of integrated teams must understand the standards for work and participate according to those standards.

Structuring integrated teams involves defining the number of teams, the type of each team, and how each team relates to the others in the structure. Forming integrated teams involves chartering each team, assigning team members and team leaders, and providing resources to each team to accomplish work.

Typical work products

1. Rules and guidelines for structuring and forming integrated teams

Subpractices

1. Establish and maintain empowerment mechanisms to enable timely decision making.

    In a successful teaming environment, clear channels of responsibility and authority must be established. Issues can arise at any level of the organization when integrated teams assume too much or too little authority and when it is unclear who is responsible for making decisions. Documenting and deploying organizational guidelines that clearly define the empowerment of integrated teams can prevent these issues.

2. Establish rules and guidelines for structuring and forming integrated teams.

> Organizational process assets can help the organizational unit to structure and implement integrated teams. Such assets may include the following:
> - team structure guidelines
> - team formation guidelines
> - team authority and responsibility guidelines
> - guidelines for establishing lines of communication, authority, and escalation
> - team leader selection criteria

3. Define the expectations, rules, and guidelines that guide how integrated teams work collectively.

> These rules and guidelines establish organizational practices for consistency across integrated teams and can include the following:
> - how interfaces among integrated teams are established and maintained
> - how assignments are accepted and transferred
> - how resources and inputs are accessed
> - how work gets done
> - who checks, reviews, and approves work
> - how work is approved
> - how work is delivered and communicated
> - who reports to whom
> - what the reporting requirements (e.g., cost, schedule, performance status), measures, and methods are
> - which progress reporting measures and methods are used

4. Maintain the rules and guidelines for structuring and forming integrated teams.
5. Establish and maintain organizational guidelines to help team members balance their team and home organization responsibilities.

    A "home organization" is the organizational unit to which team members are assigned when they are not on an integrated team. A home organization may be called a "functional organization," "home base," "home office," or "direct organization."

Elaborated Generic Practices by Goal

Refer to the Generic Goals and Practices document in Appendix A for general guidance that applies to all process areas. This section provides elaborations relative to the application of the Generic Goals and Practices to the Organizational Process Definition process area.

OPD:GG1 ACHIEVE SPECIFIC GOALS

The operational resilience management system supports and enables achievement of the specific goals of the Organizational Process Definition process area by transforming identifiable input work products to produce identifiable output work products.

OPD:GG1.GP1 PERFORM SPECIFIC PRACTICES

Perform the specific practices of the Organizational Process Definition process area to develop work products and provide services to achieve the specific goals of the process area.

Elaboration:

Specific practices OPD:SG1.SP1 through OPD:SG1.SP6 are performed to achieve the goals of the organizational process definition process.

OPD:GG2 INSTITUTIONALIZE A MANAGED PROCESS

Organizational process definition is institutionalized as a managed process.

OPD:GG2.GP1 ESTABLISH PROCESS GOVERNANCE

Establish and maintain governance over the planning and performance of the organizational process definition process.

Refer to the Enterprise Focus process area for more information about providing sponsorship and oversight to the organizational process definition process.

Subpractices

1. Establish governance over process activities.

    Elaboration:

    > Governance over the organizational process definition process may be exhibited by
    > - establishing an operational resilience process group (ORPG) to facilitate the development and maintenance of standard processes and process assets
    > - developing and publicizing higher-level managers' objectives and requirements for the process

- sponsoring and funding process activities
- sponsoring and providing oversight of policy, procedures, standards, and guidelines for process definition activities and for organizational use of these activities and work products
- guiding and supporting the enforcement of standard processes and process assets
- providing input on standard process definitions
- making higher-level managers aware of applicable compliance obligations related to organization process definition, and regularly reporting on the organization's satisfaction of these obligations to higher-level managers
- verifying that the process supports strategic resilience objectives and is focused on the assets and services that are of the highest relative value in meeting strategic objectives
- regular reporting from organizational units to higher-level managers on operational process definition activities and results, and the use and tailoring of standard processes
- creating dedicated higher-level management feedback loops on decisions about the process and recommendations for improving the process
- conducting regular internal and external audits and related reporting to audit committees on process effectiveness
- creating formal programs to measure the effectiveness of process activities, and reporting these measurements to higher-level managers

2. Develop and publish organizational policy for the process.

   Elaboration:

   The organizational process definition policy should address
   - responsibility, authority, and ownership for performing operational process definition activities, including process selection and tailoring
   - the definition and use of standard processes for managing operational resilience
   - procedures, standards, and guidelines for
     - selecting and tailoring standard processes in accordance with criteria and guidelines
     - contributing to, using, storing, updating, and retrieving measures from the measurement repository
     - contributing to, using, storing, and retrieving items from the process asset library
     - the work environment *(Refer to OPD:SG1.SP5 for examples.)*
     - the structure, formation, and operation of integrated teams
     - obtaining waivers to the use of standard processes and work environment standards
   - methods for measuring adherence to policy, exceptions granted, and policy violations

OPD:GG2.GP2 PLAN THE PROCESS

Establish and maintain the plan for performing the organizational process definition process.

Elaboration:

The plan for performing the organizational process definition process can be part of (or referenced by) the organization's process improvement plan.

Subpractices

1. Define and document the plan for performing the process.

   Elaboration:

   Special consideration in the plan may have to be given to how the organization incorporates organizational process definition activities for staff who are not under direct control, including external entities such as contractors, service providers, suppliers, and other business partners.

2. Define and document the process description.
3. Review the plan with relevant stakeholders and get their agreement.
4. Revise the plan as necessary.

OPD:GG2.GP3 PROVIDE RESOURCES

Provide adequate resources for performing the organizational process definition process, developing the work products, and providing the services of the process.

Subpractices

1. Staff the process.

   Elaboration:

   A process group typically manages the organizational process definition activities. This group typically is staffed by a core of professionals whose primary responsibility is coordinating organizational process improvement.

   > These are examples of staff required to perform the organizational process definition process:
   > - operational resilience process group members
   > - process owners
   > - subject matter experts, including staff knowledgeable about each operational resilience management process area and how to reflect process requirements in standard process definitions and process measures

- subject matter experts in project management, configuration management, quality assurance, and relevant engineering disciplines such as security and business continuity
- staff responsible for developing standard process definitions and work environment standards and ensuring they are aligned with stakeholder requirements and needs
- external entities involved in developing and using standard process definitions
- staff responsible for managing external entities that have contractual obligations to use the work products of the organizational process development process
- internal and external auditors responsible for reporting to appropriate committees on process effectiveness

Refer to the Human Resource Management process area for information about acquiring staff for resilience roles and responsibilities.

2. Fund the process.

   Refer to the Financial Resource Management process area for information about budgeting for, funding, and accounting for organizational process definition activities.

3. Provide necessary tools, techniques, and methods to perform the process.

Elaboration:

These are examples of tools, techniques, and methods to support the organizational process definition process:
- database and repository management systems
- process modeling tools
- web page builders and browsers
- templates and other tools in support of documenting process element descriptions and standard process definitions
- templates for documenting process and product measures
- peer review checklists
- templates for integrated team charters

OPD:GG2.GP4 ASSIGN RESPONSIBILITY

Assign responsibility and authority for performing the organizational process definition process, developing the work products, and providing the services of the process.

Refer to the Human Resource Management process area for more information about establishing resilience as a job responsibility, developing resilience performance goals and objectives, and measuring and assessing performance against these goals and objectives.

Organizational Process Definition 621

Subpractices

1. Assign responsibility and authority for performing the process.

   Elaboration:

   Responsibility and authority may extend not only to staff inside the organization but to external entities with which the organization has a contractual agreement for using standard process definitions, standard process and product measures, and work environment standards.

2. Assign responsibility and authority for performing the specific tasks of the process.

   Elaboration:

   > Responsibility and authority for performing organizational process definition tasks can be formalized by
   > - defining roles and responsibilities in the process plan
   > - including process tasks and responsibility for these tasks in specific job descriptions
   > - developing policy requiring organizational unit managers, line of business managers, project managers, and asset and service owners to participate in and derive benefit from operational resilience management processes, services, and assets under their ownership or custodianship
   > - developing policy requiring the use and tailoring, if needed, of standard process definition and work environment standards
   > - including process tasks in staff performance management goals and objectives, with requisite measurement of progress against these goals
   > - developing and implementing contractual instruments (as well as service level agreements) with external entities to use and tailor standard processes and work environment standards, where applicable
   > - including process work products in measuring performance of external entities against service level agreements

   Refer to the External Dependencies Management process area for additional details about managing relationships with external entities.

3. Confirm that people assigned with responsibility and authority understand it and are willing and able to accept it.

OPD:GG2.GP5 TRAIN PEOPLE

Train the people performing or supporting the organizational process definition process as needed.

Refer to the Human Resource Management process area for more information about inventorying skill sets, establishing a skill set baseline, identifying required skill sets, and measuring and addressing skill deficiencies.

Subpractices

1. Identify process skill needs.

   Elaboration:

   > These are examples of skills required in the organizational process definition process:
   > - process modeling and definition
   > - database management
   > - process and product measurement
   > - knowledge unique to each operational resilience management process area, and assets and services that are the focus of these processes
   > - expertise in relevant engineering disciplines such as security and business continuity
   > - communication
   > - team building
   > - knowledge of the tools, techniques, and methods necessary to develop and maintain process work products, including those necessary to perform the process using the selected methods, techniques, and tools identified in OPD:GG2.GP3 subpractice 3
   > - knowledge necessary to elicit and prioritize stakeholder requirements and needs and interpret them to develop effective standard process definitions, measures, and work environment standards

2. Identify process skill gaps based on available resources and their current skill levels.
3. Identify training opportunities to address skill gaps.

   Elaboration:

   > These are examples of training topics:
   > - process improvement reference models
   > - planning, managing, and monitoring processes
   > - process modeling and definition
   > - developing a tailorable standard process
   > - developing work environment standards
   > - ergonomics

> - supporting resilience staff in understanding the organizational process development process and their roles and responsibilities with respect to its activities
> - working with external entities that have responsibility for using organizational process development work products
> - using organizational process development methods, tools, and techniques, including those identified in OPD:GG2:GP3 subpractice 3

OPD:GG2.GP6 MANAGE WORK PRODUCT CONFIGURATIONS

Place designated work products of the organizational process definition process under appropriate levels of control.

Elaboration:

Specific practice OPD SG1.SP1 calls for documenting all standard process definitions. OPD:SG1.SP2 requires the documentation of tailoring guidelines for standard processes. This generic practice covers all organizational process definition work products that are to be placed under control.

> These are examples of organizational process definition work products placed under control:
> - organization's set of standard processes
> - process asset library
> - tailoring guidelines for the organization's set of standard processes
> - process documentation standards
> - requirements waivers
> - templates, checklists, and other process elements
> - definitions of the common set of product and process measures
> - organization's measurement repository and data
> - work environment standards
> - empowerment rules and guidelines for people and integrated teams
> - organizational process documentation for issue resolution
> - process plan
> - policies and procedures
> - contracts with external entities

OPD:GG2.GP7 IDENTIFY AND INVOLVE RELEVANT STAKEHOLDERS

Identify and involve the relevant stakeholders of the organizational process definition process as planned.

Subpractices

1. Identify process stakeholders and their appropriate involvement.

Elaboration:

> These are examples of stakeholders of the organizational process definition process:
> - business process and operational resilience process owners
> - asset owners and custodians
> - service owners
> - organizational unit and line of business managers responsible for high-value services and assets
> - project managers and others responsible for standing up integrated teams
> - external entities responsible for managing high-value assets and services and for using standard process definitions
> - internal and external auditors

> Stakeholders are involved in various tasks in the organizational process definition process, such as
> - reviewing the organization's set of standard processes
> - resolving issues with the tailoring guidelines
> - assessing the definitions of the common set of process and product measures
> - reviewing the work environment standards
> - establishing and maintaining organizational rules and guidelines for the structuring and forming of integrated teams
> - establishing and maintaining integrated team empowerment mechanisms
> - planning for the process
> - making decisions about the process
> - making commitments to process plans and activities
> - reviewing and appraising the effectiveness of process activities
> - establishing requirements for the process
> - resolving issues in the process

2. Communicate the list of stakeholders to planners and those responsible for process performance.
3. Involve relevant stakeholders in the process as planned.

OPD:GG2.GP8 MONITOR AND CONTROL THE PROCESS

Monitor and control the organizational process definition process against the plan for performing the process and take appropriate corrective action.

Refer to the Monitoring process area for more information about the collection, organization, and distribution of data that may be useful for monitoring and controlling processes.

Refer to the Measurement and Analysis process area for more information about establishing process metrics and measurement.

Refer to the Enterprise Focus process area for more information about providing process information to managers, identifying issues, and determining appropriate corrective actions.

Subpractices

1. Measure actual performance against the plan for performing the process.
2. Review accomplishments and results of the process against the plan for performing the process.

   Elaboration:

   > These are examples of metrics for the organizational process definition process:
   > - percentage of organizational units (including projects) using the process architectures and process elements of the organization's set of standard processes
   > - percentage of standard processes that have been tailored, by organizational unit
   > - number of unapproved changes to the process asset library
   > - number of waivers by standard process
   > - number of waivers by work environment standard
   > - defect density of each process element of the organization's set of standard processes
   > - percentage of product and process measures residing in the measurement repository that are used in status reports
   > - number of worker's compensation claims due to ergonomic problems
   > - schedule for development of a process or process change
   > - number of process risks referred to the risk management process; number of risks where corrective action is still pending (by risk rank)
   > - level of adherence to process policies; number of policy violations; number of policy exceptions requested and number approved
   > - number of process activities that are on track per plan
   > - rate of change of resource needs to support the process
   > - rate of change of costs to support the process

3. Review activities, status, and results of the process with the immediate level of managers responsible for the process and identify issues.

   Elaboration:

   > Periodic reviews of the organizational process definition process are needed to ensure that
   > - standard processes are in active use by all organizational units
   > - skills necessary to develop and tailor organizational process definitions are available or obtainable

> - the effectiveness of standard organizational processes and tailoring guidelines is regularly monitored, reported, evaluated, and improved
> - the waiver process is not abused
> - the performance of process activities is being monitored and regularly reported
> - process issues are referred to the risk management process when necessary
> - actions requiring management involvement are elevated in a timely manner
> - key measures are within acceptable ranges as demonstrated in governance dashboards or scorecards and financial reports
> - actions resulting from internal and external audits are being closed in a timely manner

4. Identify and evaluate the effects of significant deviations from the plan for performing the process.
5. Identify problems in the plan for performing and executing the process.
6. Take corrective action when requirements and objectives are not being satisfied, when issues are identified, or when progress differs significantly from the plan for performing the process.
7. Track corrective action to closure.

OPD:GG2.GP9 *Objectively Evaluate Adherence*

Objectively evaluate adherence of the organizational process definition process against its process description, standards, and procedures, and address non-compliance.

Elaboration:

> These are examples of activities to be reviewed:
> - establishment of organizational process assets and ensuring they are maintained
> - establishment of tailoring guidelines and criteria
> - ensuring that the set of standard processes satisfies the organization's process needs and objectives
> - definition of a common set of process and product measures that provide visibility into process performance
> - establishment of work environment standards and ensuring they are adopted and maintained
> - determination of rules and guidelines for the degree of empowerment provided to people and integrated teams
> - the alignment of stakeholder requirements with organizational process definition process plans
> - assignment of responsibility, accountability, and authority for process activities

- determination of the adequacy of process reports and reviews in informing decision makers regarding the performance of operational resilience management activities and the need to take corrective action, if any
- use of process work products for improving strategies to protect and sustain assets and services

These are examples of work products to be reviewed:
- organization's set of standard processes and process documentation
- tailoring guidelines for the organization's set of standard processes
- templates, checklists, and other process elements
- organization's measurement data
- work environment standards
- empowerment rules and guidelines for people and integrated teams
- process plan and policies
- issues that have been referred to the risk management process
- process methods, techniques, and tools
- contracts with external entities
- metrics for the process *(Refer to OPD:GG2.GP8 subpractice 2.)*

OPD:GG2.GP10 REVIEW STATUS WITH HIGHER-LEVEL MANAGERS

Review the activities, status, and results of the organizational process definition process with higher-level managers and resolve issues.

Refer to the Enterprise Focus process area for more information about providing sponsorship and oversight to the operational resilience management system.

OPD:GG3 INSTITUTIONALIZE A DEFINED PROCESS

Organizational process definition is institutionalized as a defined process.

OPD:GG3.GP1 ESTABLISH A DEFINED PROCESS

Establish and maintain the description of a defined organizational process definition process.

Elaboration:

Organizational process definition is itself a defined process. The subpractices that normally appear in this practice are not included due to their metalevel and recursive nature (selecting from the organization's set of standard processes, tailoring standard processes, meeting organizational process objectives, documenting the tailored process, and revising as necessary). *(Refer to the Generic Goals and Practices document in Appendix A for further guidance.)*

OPD:GG3.GP2 COLLECT IMPROVEMENT INFORMATION

Collect organizational process definition work products, measures, measurement results, and improvement information derived from planning and performing the process to support the future use and improvement of the organization's processes and process assets.

Elaboration:

> These are examples of improvement work products and information:
> - submission of lessons learned to the organization's process asset library
> - submission of measurement data to the organization's measurement repository
> - status of the change requests submitted to modify the organization's standard process
> - record of non-standard tailoring requests and waivers
> - status of performance review input from integrated teams
> - changes and trends in operating conditions, risk conditions, and the risk environment that affect process activities
> - lessons learned in post-event review of incidents and disruptions in continuity that have to be reflected in process assets
> - resilience requirements that are not being satisfied or are being exceeded

Subpractices

1. Store process and work product measures in the organization's measurement repository. *(Refer to OPD:SG1.SP3 for further details.)*
2. Submit documentation for inclusion in the organization's process asset library. *(Refer to OPD:SG1.SP4 for further details.)*
3. Document lessons learned from the process for inclusion in the organization's process asset library.
4. Propose improvements to the organizational process assets.

ORGANIZATIONAL PROCESS FOCUS
Process

Purpose

The purpose of Organizational Process Focus is to plan, implement, and deploy organizational process improvements based on a thorough understanding of current strengths and weaknesses of the organization's operational resilience processes and process assets.

Introductory Notes

The organization's processes include all operational resilience processes used by the organization and its organizational units. Candidate improvements to the organization's processes and process assets are obtained from various sources, including the measurement of processes, lessons learned in implementing processes, results of process appraisals, results of post-event or incident handling, results of customer satisfaction evaluation, results of benchmarking against other organizations' processes, and recommendations from other improvement initiatives in the organization.

Process improvement occurs in the context of the organization's needs and is used to address the organization's objectives. The organization encourages participation in process improvement activities by those who perform the process. The responsibility for facilitating and managing the organization's process improvement activities, including coordinating the participation of others, is typically assigned to an operational resilience process group. The organization provides the long-term commitment and resources required to sponsor this group and to ensure the effective and timely deployment of improvements.

Careful planning is required to ensure that process improvement efforts across the organization are adequately managed and implemented. Results of the organization's process improvement planning are documented in a process improvement plan.

The "organization's process improvement plan" addresses appraisal planning, process action planning, pilot planning, and deployment planning. Appraisal plans describe the appraisal timeline and schedule, the scope of the appraisal, resources required to perform the appraisal, the reference model against which the appraisal will be performed, and logistics for the appraisal.

Process action plans usually result from appraisals and document how improvements targeting weaknesses uncovered by an appraisal will be implemented. Sometimes the improvement described in the process action plan should be tested on a small group before deploying it across the organization. In these cases, a pilot plan is generated.

When the improvement is to be deployed, a deployment plan is created. This plan describes when and how the improvement will be deployed across the organization.

Organizational process assets are used to describe, implement, and improve the organization's processes.

Related Process Areas

Refer to the Organizational Process Definition process area for more information about establishing organizational process assets, including standard processes.

Summary of Specific Goals and Practices

OPF:SG1 Determine Process Improvement Opportunities
    OPF:SG1.SP1   Establish Organizational Process Needs
    OPF:SG1.SP2   Appraise the Organization's Processes
    OPF:SG1.SP3   Identify the Organization's Process Improvements
OPF:SG2 Plan and Implement Process Actions
    OPF:SG2.SP1   Establish Process Action Plans
    OPF:SG2.SP2   Implement Process Action Plans
OPF:SG3 Deploy Organizational Process Assets and Incorporate Experiences
    OPF:SG3.SP1   Deploy Organizational Process Assets
    OPF:SG3.SP2   Deploy Standard Processes
    OPF:SG3.SP3   Monitor the Implementation
    OPF:SG3.SP4   Incorporate Experiences into Organizational Process Assets

Specific Practices by Goal

OPF:SG1 DETERMINE PROCESS IMPROVEMENT OPPORTUNITIES

Strengths, weaknesses, and improvement opportunities for the organization's processes are identified periodically and as needed.

Strengths, weaknesses, and improvement opportunities may be determined relative to a process standard or model. Process improvements should be selected to address the organization's needs.

OPF:SG1.SP1 ESTABLISH ORGANIZATIONAL PROCESS NEEDS

The descriptions of process needs and objectives for the organization are established and maintained.

The organization's processes operate in a business context that must be understood. The organization's business objectives, needs, and constraints determine the needs and objectives of the organization's processes. Typically, issues related to customer satisfaction, finance, technology, quality, human resources, marketing, service continuity, and resilience are important process considerations.

Organizational process needs may be strongly influenced by the organization's strategic objectives, critical success factors, and other factors. *(Refer to the Enterprise Focus process area for information about establishing these factors as aligning principles for process management and improvement.)*

The organization's process needs and objectives cover aspects that include the following:

- characteristics of processes
- process performance objectives, such as impact avoidance and reduction of recovery time objectives
- process effectiveness

Typical work products

1. Organization's process needs and objectives

Subpractices

1. Identify policies, standards, and business objectives that are applicable to the organization's processes.
    Refer to the Enterprise Focus process area for more information about establishing these work products.
2. Examine relevant process standards and models for best practices.
3. Determine the organization's process performance objectives.
    Process performance objectives may be expressed in quantitative or qualitative terms. Refer to the Measurement and Analysis process area for more information about establishing measurement objectives.

> Examples of process performance objective topics include the following:
> - business case for resilience
> - customer satisfaction
> - vulnerability and incident rates
> - realized risk, impact, and risk reduction and mitigation
> - productivity
> - compliance with regulations

4. Define essential characteristics of the organization's processes.
   Essential characteristics of the organization's processes are determined based on the following:
   - processes currently being used in the organization
   - standards imposed by the organization
   - standards commonly imposed by the organization's market sector
   - standards commonly imposed by customers of the organization

> These are examples of process characteristics:
> - level of detail
> - process notation
> - granularity of process elements

5. Document the organization's process needs and objectives.
6. Revise the organization's process needs and objectives as needed.

OPF:SG1.SP2 APPRAISE THE ORGANIZATION'S PROCESSES

The organization's processes are appraised periodically and as needed to maintain an understanding of their strengths and weaknesses.

Process appraisals may be performed for the following reasons:

- to identify processes to be improved
- to confirm progress and make the benefits of process improvement visible
- to satisfy the needs of a customer-supplier relationship
- to motivate and facilitate buy-in

The buy-in gained during a process appraisal can be eroded significantly if it is not followed by an appraisal-based action plan.

Typical work products

1. Organization's process appraisal plans
2. Appraisal findings that address strengths and weaknesses of the organization's processes
3. Improvement recommendations for the organization's processes

Subpractices

1. Obtain sponsorship of the process appraisal from higher-level managers.
   Higher-level managers' sponsorship includes the commitment to have the organization's managers and staff participate in the process appraisal and to provide resources and funding to analyze and communicate findings of the appraisal.
2. Define the scope of the process appraisal.

Process appraisals may be performed on the entire organization or may be performed on a smaller part of an organization such as an organizational unit or line of business.

Process appraisals may also be scoped to specific types of assets (such as information, software, systems, hardware, or facilities) or from the vantage point of a specific discipline (such as security, continuity, or IT operations).

The scope of the process appraisal addresses the following:
- definition of the organization (e.g., sites, organizational units) to be covered by the appraisal
- definition of the assets and disciplines to be covered by the appraisal
- identification of the support functions that will represent the organization in the appraisal
- processes to be appraised

3. Determine the method and criteria to be used for the process appraisal.

   Process appraisals can occur in many forms. They should address the needs and objectives of the organization, which may change over time. For example, the appraisal may be based on a process model, such as the CERT Resilience Management Model, or on a national or international standard, such as ISO 27001. Appraisals may also be based on a benchmark comparison with other organizations in which practices that may contribute to improved performance are identified. The characteristics of the appraisal method may vary, including time and effort, makeup of the appraisal team, and the method and depth of investigation.

4. Plan, schedule, and prepare for the process appraisal.
5. Conduct the process appraisal.
6. Document the appraisal's activities and deliver the findings.

OPF:SG1.SP3 *IDENTIFY THE ORGANIZATION'S PROCESS IMPROVEMENTS*

Improvements to the organization's processes and process assets are identified.

Typical work products

1. Analysis of candidate process improvements
2. Identification of improvements for the organization's processes

Subpractices

1. Determine candidate process improvements.

   > Candidate process improvements are typically determined by doing the following:
   > - measuring processes and analyzing measurement results
   > - reviewing processes for effectiveness and suitability
   > - assessing customer satisfaction
   > - reviewing lessons learned from tailoring the organization's set of standard processes
   > - reviewing lessons learned from implementing processes

> - reviewing process improvement proposals submitted by the organization's managers, staff, and other relevant stakeholders
> - soliciting inputs on process improvements from higher-level managers and other leaders in the organization
> - examining results of process appraisals and other process-related reviews
> - reviewing results of other organizational improvement initiatives

2. Prioritize candidate process improvements.
   Criteria for prioritization may include
   - estimated cost and effort to implement the process improvements
   - expected improvement against the organization's improvement objectives and priorities
   - potential barriers to the process improvements, and strategies for overcoming these barriers

> These are examples of techniques to help determine and prioritize possible improvements to be implemented:
> - a cost-benefit analysis that compares the estimated cost and effort to implement the process improvements and their associated benefits
> - a gap analysis that compares current conditions in the organization with optimal conditions
> - force-field analysis of potential improvements to identify potential barriers and strategies for overcoming those barriers
> - cause-and-effect analyses to provide information about the potential effects of different improvements, which can then be compared

3. Identify and document the process improvements to be implemented.
4. Revise the list of planned process improvements to keep it current.

OPF:SG2 PLAN AND IMPLEMENT PROCESS ACTIONS

Process actions that address improvements to the organization's processes and process assets are planned and implemented.

The successful implementation of improvements requires participation in process action planning and implementation by process owners, those performing the process, and support organizations.

OPF:SG2.SP1 ESTABLISH PROCESS ACTION PLANS

Process action plans to address improvements to the organization's processes and process assets are established and maintained.

> Establishing and maintaining process action plans typically involve the following roles:
> - management steering committees that set strategies and oversee process improvement activities
> - process groups that facilitate and manage process improvement activities
> - process action teams that define and implement process actions
> - process owners who manage deployment
> - practitioners who perform the process

This stakeholder involvement helps to obtain buy-in on process improvements and increases the likelihood of effective deployment.

Process action plans are detailed implementation plans. These plans differ from the organization's process improvement plan by targeting improvements that are defined to address weaknesses and that are usually identified by appraisals.

Typical work products

1. Organization's approved process action plans

Subpractices

1. Identify strategies, approaches, and actions to address identified process improvements.

    New, unproven, and major changes are piloted before they are deployed.

2. Establish process action teams to implement actions.

    The teams and staff performing the process improvement actions are called "process action teams." Process action teams typically include process owners and those who perform the process.

3. Document process action plans.

> Process action plans typically cover the following:
> - the process improvement infrastructure
> - process improvement objectives
> - process improvements to be addressed
> - procedures for planning and tracking process actions
> - strategies for piloting and implementing process actions
> - responsibility and authority for implementing process actions
> - resources, schedules, and assignments for implementing process actions
> - methods for determining the effectiveness of process actions
> - risks associated with process action plans

4. Review and negotiate process action plans with relevant stakeholders.
5. Review process action plans as necessary.

OPF:SG2.SP2 IMPLEMENT PROCESS ACTION PLANS

Process action plans are implemented.

Typical work products

1. Commitments among process action teams
2. Status and results of implementing process action plans
3. Plans for pilots

Subpractices

1. Make process action plans readily available to relevant stakeholders.
2. Negotiate and document commitments among process action teams and revise their process action plans as necessary.
3. Track progress and commitments against process action plans.
4. Conduct joint reviews with process action teams and relevant stakeholders to monitor the progress and results of process actions.
5. Plan pilots needed to test selected process improvements.
6. Review the activities and work products of process action teams.
7. Identify, document, and track to closure issues encountered when implementing process action plans.
8. Ensure that results of implementing process action plans satisfy the organization's process improvement objectives.

OPF:SG3 DEPLOY ORGANIZATIONAL PROCESS ASSETS AND INCORPORATE EXPERIENCES

Organizational process assets are deployed across the organization and process-related experiences are incorporated into organizational process assets.

The specific practices under this specific goal describe ongoing activities. New opportunities to benefit from organizational process assets and changes to them may arise. Deployment of standard processes and other organizational process assets must be continually supported in the organization.

OPF:SG3.SP1 DEPLOY ORGANIZATIONAL PROCESS ASSETS

Organizational process assets are deployed across the organization.

Deploying organizational process assets or changes to them should be performed in an orderly manner. Some organizational process assets or changes to them may not be appropriate for use in some parts of the organization (e.g., because of stakeholder requirements or the current life-cycle phase being implemented). It is therefore important that those who are or will be executing the process, as well as other supporting functions (e.g., training, quality assurance), be involved in deployment as necessary.

Refer to the Organizational Process Definition process area for more information about the deployment of organizational process assets, including the support of the organization's process asset library.

Typical work products

1. Plans for deploying organizational process assets and changes to them across the organization
2. Training materials for deploying organizational process assets and changes to them
3. Documentation of changes to organizational process assets
4. Support materials for deploying organizational process assets and changes to them

Subpractices

1. Deploy organizational process assets across the organization.

> These are typical activities performed as a part of the deployment of process assets:
> - identifying organizational process assets that should be adopted by those who perform the process
> - determining how organizational process assets are made available (e.g., via a website)
> - identifying how changes to organizational process assets are communicated
> - identifying resources (e.g., methods, tools) needed to support the use of organizational process assets
> - planning the deployment
> - assisting those who use organizational process assets
> - ensuring that training is available for those who use organizational process assets

Refer to the Organizational Training and Awareness process area for more information about establishing an organizational training capability.

2. Document changes to organizational process assets.
    Documenting changes to organizational process assets serves two main purposes:
    - to enable the communication and review of changes
    - to understand the relationship of changes in the organizational process assets to changes in process performance and results
3. Deploy changes that were made to organizational process assets across the organization.

> These are typical activities performed as a part of deploying changes:
> - determining which changes are appropriate for those who perform the process
> - planning the deployment
> - arranging for the support needed for the successful deployment of changes

4. Provide guidance and consultation on the use of organizational process assets.

OPF:SG3.SP2 DEPLOY STANDARD PROCESSES

The organization's set of standard processes are deployed to organizational units (including projects at their start-up) and changes are deployed to them as appropriate.

It is important that organizational units use proven and effective processes to perform critical activities (e.g., planning, identifying requirements, and obtaining resources).

Organizational units should also periodically update their defined processes to incorporate the latest changes made to the organization's set of standard processes when it benefits them. This periodic update helps to ensure that all organizational unit activities derive the full benefit of what other units have learned.

Refer to the Organizational Process Definition process area for more information about standard processes and tailoring guidelines.

Typical work products

1. The organization's list of organizational units and the status of process deployment for each (e.g., existing and planned projects and newly acquired organizational units)
2. Guidelines for deploying the organization's set of standard processes for new organizational units
3. Records of tailoring and implementing the organization's set of standard processes

Subpractices

1. Identify organizational units in the organization that are starting up or recently acquired.
2. Identify existing organizational units that would benefit from implementing the organization's current set of standard processes.
3. Establish plans to implement the organization's current set of standard processes in the identified organizational units.
4. Assist organizational units in tailoring the organization's set of standard processes to meet their needs.
   Refer to each resilience management process area for more information about establishing an organizational unit's defined processes.
5. Maintain records of tailoring and implementing processes for the identified organizational units.
6. Ensure that the defined processes resulting from process tailoring are incorporated into plans for process-compliance audits.
   Process-compliance audits are objective evaluations of organizational unit activities against the unit's defined processes.
7. As the organization's set of standard processes is updated, identify which organizational units should implement the changes.

OPF:SG3.SP3 MONITOR THE IMPLEMENTATION

The organization's set of standard processes and use of process assets are monitored.

By monitoring implementation, the organization ensures that the organization's set of standard processes and other process assets are appropriately deployed to an organizational unit or line of business. Monitoring implementation helps the organization to develop an understanding of the organizational process assets being used and where they are used in the organization. Monitoring also helps to establish a broader context for interpreting and using process and product measures, lessons learned, and improvement information obtained from organizational units.

Refer to the Monitoring process area for more information about gathering and distributing process improvement information.

Typical work products

1. Results of monitoring process implementation
2. Status and results of process-compliance audits
3. Results of reviewing selected process work products created as part of process tailoring and implementation

Subpractices

1. Monitor use of the organization's process assets (including standard processes) and changes to them.
2. Review selected process assets.
   Reviewing selected process assets ensures that the organization and all organizational units are making appropriate use of the organization's set of standard processes.
3. Review results of process-compliance audits to determine how well the organization's set of standard processes has been deployed.
4. Identify, document, and track to closure issues related to implementing the organization's set of standard processes.

OPF:SG3.SP4 INCORPORATE EXPERIENCES INTO ORGANIZATIONAL PROCESS ASSETS

Process-related work products, measures, and improvement information derived from planning and performing the process are incorporated into organizational process assets.

Typical work products

1. Process improvement proposals
2. Process lessons learned
3. Measurements of organizational process assets
4. Improvement recommendations for organizational process assets

5. Records of the organization's process improvement activities
6. Information about the use of organizational process assets and improvements to them

Subpractices

1. Conduct periodic reviews of the effectiveness and suitability of the organization's set of standard processes and related organizational process assets relative to the organization's strategic objectives.
2. Obtain feedback about the use of organizational process assets.
3. Derive lessons learned from defining, piloting, implementing, and deploying organizational process assets.
4. Make lessons learned available to staff as appropriate.
   Actions may be necessary to ensure that lessons learned are used appropriately.

These are examples of the inappropriate use of lessons learned:
- evaluating the performance of staff
- judging process performance or results

These are examples of ways to prevent the inappropriate use of lessons learned:
- controlling access to lessons learned
- educating staff about the appropriate use of lessons learned

---

5. Analyze measurement data obtained from the use of the organization's common set of measures.

   Refer to the Measurement and Analysis process area for more information about analyzing measurement data.

   Refer to the Organizational Process Definition process area for more information about establishing the organization's measurement repository.

6. Appraise processes, methods, and tools in use in the organization and develop recommendations for improving organizational process assets.

This appraisal typically includes the following:
- determining which processes, methods, and tools are of potential use to other parts of the organization
- appraising the quality and effectiveness of organizational process assets
- identifying candidate improvements to organizational process assets
- determining compliance with the organization's set of standard processes and tailoring guidelines

---

7. Make the best of the organization's processes, methods, and tools available to staff as appropriate.

8. Manage process improvement proposals.
    Process improvement proposals can address both process and technology improvements.

> The activities for managing process improvement proposals typically include the following:
> - soliciting process improvement proposals
> - collecting process improvement proposals
> - reviewing process improvement proposals
> - selecting the process improvement proposals to be implemented
> - tracking the implementation of process improvement proposals

   Process improvement proposals are documented as process change requests or problem reports as appropriate.
   Some process improvement proposals may be incorporated into the organization's process action plans.
9. Establish and maintain records of the organization's process improvement activities.

Elaborated Generic Practices by Goal

Refer to the Generic Goals and Practices document in Appendix A for general guidance that applies to all process areas. This section provides elaborations relative to the application of the Generic Goals and Practices to the Organizational Process Focus process area.

OPF:GG1 ACHIEVE SPECIFIC GOALS

The operational resilience management system supports and enables achievement of the specific goals of the Organizational Process Focus process area by transforming identifiable input work products to produce identifiable output work products.

OPF:GG1.GP1 PERFORM SPECIFIC PRACTICES

Perform the specific practices of the Organizational Process Focus process area to develop work products and provide services to achieve the specific goals of the process area.

   Elaboration:

   Specific practices OPF:SG1.SP1 through OPF:SG3.SP4 are performed to achieve the goals of the organizational process focus process.

OPF:GG2 INSTITUTIONALIZE A MANAGED PROCESS

Organizational process focus is institutionalized as a managed process.

OPF:GG2.GP1 ESTABLISH PROCESS GOVERNANCE

Establish and maintain governance over the planning and performance of the organizational process focus process.

Refer to the Enterprise Focus process area for more information about providing sponsorship and oversight to the organizational process focus process.

Subpractices

1. Establish governance over process activities.

   Elaboration:

   > Governance over the organizational process focus process may be exhibited by
   > - establishing an operational resilience process group (ORPG) to facilitate the appraisal and improvement of standard processes and process assets
   > - developing and publicizing higher-level managers' objectives, requirements, and needs for processes and process improvement
   > - sponsoring and funding process activities
   > - sponsoring and providing oversight of policy, procedures, standards, and guidelines for process activities and for organizational use of these activities and work products
   > - guiding and supporting the appraisal and enforcement of improved processes and process assets
   > - sponsoring process appraisals
   > - providing input on process improvements
   > - making higher-level managers aware of applicable compliance obligations related to operational resilience process improvement, and regularly reporting on the organization's satisfaction of these obligations to higher-level managers
   > - verifying that the process supports strategic resilience objectives and is focused on the assets and services that are of the highest relative value in meeting strategic objectives
   > - regular reporting from organizational units to higher-level managers on operational process focus activities and results, appraisal results, and the use of improved processes
   > - creating dedicated higher-level management feedback loops on decisions about the process and recommendations for improving the process
   > - conducting regular internal and external audits and related reporting to audit committees on process effectiveness
   > - creating formal programs to measure the effectiveness of process activities, and reporting these measurements to higher-level managers

2. Develop and publish organizational policy for the process.

   Elaboration:

   > The organizational process focus policy should address
   > - responsibility, authority, and ownership for performing operational process focus activities, including process appraisal, improvement action planning, and process deployment

> - the improvement and deployment of standard processes and supporting assets for managing operational resilience
> - procedures, standards, and guidelines for
>   - establishing process needs and objectives
>   - process appraisal
>   - identifying and prioritizing process improvements
>   - process performance
>   - developing process improvement action plans and tracking process actions
>   - process deployment, including training and changes to process assets
> - methods for measuring adherence to policy, exceptions granted, and policy violations

OPF:GG2.GP2 PLAN THE PROCESS

Establish and maintain the plan for performing the organizational process focus process.

Elaboration:

The plan for performing the organizational process focus process, which is often called "the process improvement plan," differs from the process action plans described in OPF:SG2.SP1 and OPF:SG2.SP2. The plan called for in this generic practice addresses the comprehensive planning for all of the specific practices in this process area, from the establishment of organizational process needs all the way through to the incorporation of process-related experiences into the organizational process assets.

Subpractices

1. Define and document the plan for performing the process.

   Elaboration:

   Special consideration in the plan may have to be given to how the organization incorporates organizational process focus activities for staff who are not under direct control, including external entities such as contractors, service providers, suppliers, and other business partners.

2. Define and document the process description.
3. Review the plan with relevant stakeholders and get their agreement.
4. Revise the plan as necessary.

OPF:GG2.GP3 PROVIDE RESOURCES

Provide adequate resources for performing the organizational process focus process, developing the work products, and providing the services of the process.

Subpractices

1. Staff the process.

   Elaboration:

   A process group typically manages the organizational process focus activities. This group typically is staffed by a core of professionals whose primary responsibility is coordinating organizational process improvement.

   > These are examples of staff required to perform the organizational process focus process:
   > - operational resilience process group members
   > - process owners
   > - subject matter experts, including staff knowledgeable about each operational resilience management process area and how to interpret process needs and objectives
   > - subject matter experts in project management, configuration management, quality assurance, and relevant engineering disciplines such as security and business continuity
   > - process appraisal team members (potentially members of the ORPG)
   > - process action planning team members (potentially members of the ORPG)
   > - staff responsible for deploying standard processes and process assets and ensuring they are aligned with stakeholder requirements and needs
   > - staff responsible for monitoring process performance to ensure effective implementation
   > - external entities involved in using process assets and reporting experiences and improvements
   > - staff responsible for managing external entities that have contractual obligations to use the work products of the process
   > - internal and external auditors responsible for reporting to appropriate committees on process effectiveness

   Refer to the Human Resource Management process area for information about acquiring staff for resilience roles and responsibilities.

2. Fund the process.

   Refer to the Financial Resource Management process area for information about budgeting for, funding, and accounting for organizational process focus activities.

3. Provide necessary tools, techniques, and methods to perform the process.

   Elaboration:

   > These are examples of tools, techniques, and methods to support the organizational process focus process:
   > - techniques for determining and prioritizing process improvements, such as cost-benefit analyses *(Refer to OPF:SG1.SP3.)*

- process appraisal methods, techniques, and tools, such as checklists and data management systems
- methods for determining the effectiveness of process improvement actions
- methods for eliciting process needs and objectives
- action planning techniques and tools
- process improvement tools
- database management systems for capturing process use experiences, lessons learned, and suggested improvements
- web page builders and browsers
- process asset library *(Refer to the Organizational Process Definition process area.)*
- process measurement repository *(Refer to the Organizational Process Definition process area.)*

OPF:GG2.GP4 ASSIGN RESPONSIBILITY

Assign responsibility and authority for performing the organizational process focus process, developing the work products, and providing the services of the process.

Refer to the Human Resource Management process area for more information about establishing resilience as a job responsibility, developing resilience performance goals and objectives, and measuring and assessing performance against these goals and objectives.

Subpractices

1. Assign responsibility and authority for performing the process.

   Elaboration:

   Two groups are typically established and assigned responsibility for process improvement: (1) a management steering committee for process improvement to provide sponsorship by higher-level managers, and (2) a process group to facilitate and manage the process improvement activities.

   Responsibility and authority may extend not only to staff inside the organization but to external entities with which the organization has a contractual agreement for improving and implementing standard processes and process assets.

2. Assign responsibility and authority for performing the specific tasks of the process.

   Elaboration:

   Responsibility and authority for performing organizational process focus tasks can be formalized by
   - defining roles and responsibilities in the process plan
   - including process tasks and responsibility for these tasks in specific job descriptions

- developing policy requiring organizational unit managers, line of business managers, project managers, and asset and service owners to participate in and derive benefit from the operational resilience management processes, services, and assets under their ownership or custodianship
- developing policy requiring the improvement and deployment of standard processes and process assets
- including organizational process definition focus tasks in staff performance management goals and objectives, with requisite measurement of progress against these goals
- developing and implementing contractual instruments (as well as service level agreements) with external entities to improve and implement standard processes and process assets, where applicable
- including process work products in measuring performance of external entities against service level agreements

Refer to the External Dependencies Management process area for additional details about managing relationships with external entities.

3. Confirm that people assigned with responsibility and authority understand it and are willing and able to accept it.

OPF:GG2.GP5 TRAIN PEOPLE

Train the people performing or supporting the organizational process focus process as needed.

Refer to the Human Resource Management process area for more information about inventorying skill sets, establishing a skill set baseline, identifying required skill sets, and measuring and addressing skill deficiencies.

Subpractices

1. Identify process skill needs.

   Elaboration:

   These are examples of skills required in the organizational process focus process:
   - process appraisal
   - process action planning
   - database management
   - process measurement for the purpose of process improvement
   - knowledge unique to each operational resilience management process area, and assets and services that are the focus of these process areas
   - expertise in relevant engineering disciplines such as security and business continuity
   - communication

- team building
- action planning
- experience reporting and the development of case studies
- knowledge of the tools, techniques, and methods necessary to improve and deploy standard processes and process assets, including those necessary to perform the process using the selected methods, techniques, and tools identified in OPF:GG2.GP3 subpractice 3
- knowledge necessary to elicit and prioritize stakeholder requirements and needs and interpret them to identify process needs and objectives

2. Identify process skill gaps based on available resources and their current skill levels.
3. Identify training opportunities to address skill gaps.

Elaboration:

These are examples of training topics:
- process improvement reference models, such as the CERT Resilience Management Model
- improving, deploying, and monitoring processes
- process modeling
- planning and managing process improvement, including appraisal and action planning
- facilitation
- change management
- supporting resilience staff in understanding the process and their roles and responsibilities with respect to its activities
- working with external entities that have responsibility for using process work products
- using process methods, tools, and techniques, including those identified in OPD:GG2:GP3 subpractice 3

OPF:GG2.GP6 MANAGE WORK PRODUCT CONFIGURATIONS

Place designated work products of the organizational process focus process under appropriate levels of control.

Elaboration:

Specific practice OPF:SG1.SP1 calls for documenting process needs and objectives. OPF:SG1.SP2 requires that process appraisal plans, findings, and improvement recommendations be captured. OPF:SG2.SP1 requires the documentation of process improvement action plans; OPF:SG3.SP1, changes to process assets resulting from action plans. This generic practice covers all organizational process focus work products that are to be placed under control.

These are examples of organizational process focus work products placed under control:
- process needs and objectives
- appraisal plans, findings, and improvement recommendations
- process improvement proposals
- organization's approved process action plans and status and results of implementation, including lessons learned
- pilot plans
- training materials for deploying organizational process assets
- plans and guidelines for deploying the organization's set of standard processes for current, new, and acquired organizational units
- changes to process assets
- process-compliance audit results
- process asset measures

OPF:GG2.GP7 *Identify and Involve Relevant Stakeholders*

Identify and involve the relevant stakeholders of the organizational process focus process as planned.

Subpractices

1. Identify process stakeholders and their appropriate involvement.

   Elaboration:

   These are examples of stakeholders of the organizational process focus process:
   - business process and operational resilience process owners
   - asset owners and custodians
   - service owners
   - organizational unit, line of business, and project managers responsible for ensuring that standard process definitions and process assets are deployed and improved
   - external entities responsible for deploying standard process definitions and process assets
   - those responsible for reviewing and tracking progress and commitments against process action plans
   - internal and external auditors

   Stakeholders are involved in various tasks in the organizational process focus process, such as
   - coordinating and collaborating on process improvement activities with process owners, those who are or will be performing the process, and support organizations (e.g., training staff and external entities)

> - establishing process needs and objectives
> - appraising processes
> - implementing process action plans
> - coordinating and collaborating on the execution of pilots to test selected improvements
> - deploying process assets and changes to process assets
> - communicating the plans, status, activities, and results related to planning, implementing, and deploying process improvements

2. Communicate the list of stakeholders to planners and those responsible for process performance.
3. Involve relevant stakeholders in the process as planned.

OPF:GG2.GP8 MONITOR AND CONTROL THE PROCESS

Monitor and control the organizational process focus process against the plan for performing the process and take appropriate corrective action.

Refer to the Monitoring process area for more information about the collection, organization, and distribution of data that may be useful for monitoring and controlling processes.

Refer to the Measurement and Analysis process area for more information about establishing process metrics and measurement.

Refer to the Enterprise Focus process area for more information about providing process information to managers, identifying issues, and determining appropriate corrective actions.

Subpractices

1. Measure actual performance against the plan for performing the process.
2. Review accomplishments and results of the process against the plan for performing the process.

   Elaboration:

   > These are examples of metrics for the organizational process focus process:
   > - number and percentage of process improvement proposals submitted, accepted, implemented, and rejected
   > - percentage of improvements resulting from appraisals
   > - percentage of improvements resulting from experience reports and lessons learned
   > - CERT Resilience Management Model capability levels
   > - schedule for deployment of an organizational process asset (including status against schedule, i.e., met or exceeded and by how much)
   > - percentage of organizational units using the organization's current set of standard processes (or tailored versions of same)

> - issue trends associated with implementing the organization's set of standard processes (i.e., number of issues identified and number closed)
> - number of process risks referred to the risk management process; number of risks where corrective action is still pending (by risk rank)
> - level of adherence to process policies; number of policy violations; number of policy exceptions requested and number approved
> - number of process activities that are on track per plan
> - rate of change of resource needs to support the process
> - rate of change of costs to support the process

3. Review activities, status, and results of the process with the immediate level of managers responsible for the process and identify issues.

Elaboration:

> Periodic reviews of the organizational process focus process are needed to ensure that
> - standard processes and process assets are in active use by all organizational units
> - process improvement proposals are reviewed and acted upon in a timely manner
> - changes and improvements to standard processes and process assets are deployed in a timely manner by all organizational units
> - skills necessary to conduct process appraisals, perform action planning, and deploy process assets are available or obtainable
> - the effectiveness and suitability of process assets are regularly monitored, reported, evaluated, and improved
> - the performance of process activities is being monitored and regularly reported, including the capture of lessons learned
> - results from process-compliance audits are reviewed and acted upon in a timely manner
> - process issues are referred to the risk management process when necessary
> - actions requiring management involvement are elevated in a timely manner
> - key measures are within acceptable ranges as demonstrated in governance dashboards or scorecards and financial reports
> - actions resulting from internal and external audits are being closed in a timely manner

4. Identify and evaluate the effects of significant deviations from the plan for performing the process.
5. Identify problems in the plan for performing and executing the process.
6. Take corrective action when requirements and objectives are not being satisfied, when issues are identified, or when progress differs significantly from the plan for performing the process.
7. Track corrective action to closure.

OPF:GG2.GP9 OBJECTIVELY EVALUATE ADHERENCE

Objectively evaluate adherence of the organizational process focus process against its process description, standards, and procedures, and address non-compliance.

Elaboration:

These are examples of activities to be reviewed:
- appraisal planning and conduct
- process improvement action planning
- determining and prioritizing process improvement opportunities
- planning and coordinating process improvement activities
- deploying the organization's set of standard processes and process assets
- process-compliance audits

These are examples of work products to be reviewed:
- process needs and objectives
- appraisal plans
- process improvement proposals and plans
- process action plans
- process deployment plans
- process-compliance audit results
- process asset measures
- experiences and lessons learned in using process assets

OPF:GG2.GP10 REVIEW STATUS WITH HIGHER-LEVEL MANAGERS

Review the activities, status, and results of the organizational process focus process with higher-level managers and resolve issues.

Refer to the Enterprise Focus process area for more information about providing sponsorship and oversight to the operational resilience management system.

Elaboration:

These reviews are typically in the form of a briefing presented to the management steering committee by the process group and the process action teams.

These are examples of presentation topics:
- status of improvements being developed by process action teams
- results of pilots
- results of deployments
- schedule status for achieving significant milestones (e.g., readiness for an appraisal, or progress toward achieving a targeted organizational maturity level or capability level profile)

OPF:GG3 INSTITUTIONALIZE A DEFINED PROCESS

Organizational process focus is institutionalized as a defined process.

OPF:GG3.GP1 ESTABLISH A DEFINED PROCESS

Establish and maintain the description of a defined organizational process focus process.

Elaboration:

Organizational process focus is itself a defined process. The subpractices that normally appear here are not included due to their metalevel and recursive nature (appraising processes, improving and deploying processes, and monitoring process performance). (Refer to the Generic Goals and Practices document in Appendix A for further guidance.)

OPF:GG3.GP2 COLLECT IMPROVEMENT INFORMATION

Collect organizational process focus work products, measures, measurement results, and improvement information derived from planning and performing the process to support the future use and improvement of the organization's processes and process assets.

Elaboration:

> These are examples of improvement work products and information:
> - criteria used for prioritizing candidate process improvements
> - appraisal findings that address strengths and weaknesses of the organization's processes
> - status of improvement activities against the schedule
> - records of tailoring the organization's set of standard processes and their implementation in organizational units
> - changes and trends in operating conditions, risk conditions, and the risk environment that affect process activities
> - lessons learned in post-event review of incidents and disruptions in continuity that have to be reflected in process assets
> - resilience requirements that are not being satisfied or are being exceeded

Subpractices

1. Store process and work product measures in the organization's measurement repository. (Refer to OPD:SG1.SP3 for further details.)
2. Submit documentation for inclusion in the organization's process asset library. (Refer to OPD:SG1.SP4 for further details.)
3. Document lessons learned from the process for inclusion in the organization's process asset library. (Refer to OPF:SG3.SP4 for further details.)
4. Propose improvements to the organizational process assets as described in the specific goals and practices of the Organizational Process Focus process area.

ORGANIZATIONAL TRAINING AND AWARENESS
Enterprise

Purpose

The purpose of Organizational Training and Awareness is to promote awareness in and develop skills and knowledge of people in support of their roles in attaining and sustaining operational resilience.

Introductory Notes

Organizational Training and Awareness is an enterprise process area that seeks to ensure that the organization's staff are aware of resilience needs and concerns and that they behave in a manner consistent with the organization's operational resilience requirements and goals. This requires that they be made aware of the organization's resilience plans and programs and that they understand their role in these plans and programs. Staff must also be provided specialized training on a regular basis that establishes resilience as an organizational competency and encourages improvement in skill sets relative to their specific or general roles in managing operational resilience.

Organizational Training and Awareness focuses exclusively on skills, knowledge, and cognizance for resilience activities, not generalized training across the organization. However, these resilience training and awareness activities should integrate with and be supported by the organization's overall training and awareness program and plan. Specifically, training refers to imparting the necessary skills and knowledge to people for performing their roles and responsibilities in support of the organization's operational resilience management system. Awareness is aimed at focusing the attention of staff throughout the organization on resilience issues, concerns, policies, plans, and practices and increasing their cognizance of and acculturation to resilience. Training imparts skills and knowledge to enable staff to perform a specific resilience function; awareness activities create cognizance to bring about desired behaviors in support of the resilience process and to support a risk-aware culture in the organization.

An organizational training and awareness program is a comprehensive capability that typically includes the following activities:

- identifying the training and awareness needs of the organization
- sourcing training and awareness materials
- providing training and implementing awareness activities, using a variety of methods
- establishing and maintaining records of training and awareness activities
- evaluating the effectiveness of the training and awareness program
- revising the program to improve effectiveness and in response to changes in training and awareness needs

The Organizational Training and Awareness process area has four specific goals. The Establish Awareness Program goal addresses the creation, planning, and organization of an awareness program. Conduct Awareness Activities puts awareness plans into action throughout the enterprise and evaluates their effectiveness. The Establish Training Capability goal addresses the creation, planning, and organization of a training capability. Conduct Training addresses the delivery and evaluation of training activities.

Organizational Training and Awareness is a complementary process area to the Human Resource Management and People Management process areas. Organizational Training and Awareness focuses on general awareness, skill building, and ongoing training. Human Resource Management is focused on managing the employment life cycle and performance of an employee in support of operational resilience. People Management identifies key staff and manages their availability to the services they support, ensuring the resilience of the "people" asset.

Related Process Areas

Managing the resilience of the people in the organization is performed in the People Management process area.

Managing the employment life cycle and performance of an employee in support of operational resilience is addressed in the Human Resource Management process area.

Awareness activities for external entities such as business partners and vendors are addressed in the External Dependencies Management process area.

Awareness communications are addressed in the Communications process area.

Tracking awareness activities for compliance purposes is addressed in the Compliance process area.

Guidance about tracking awareness activities for governance functions is addressed in the Enterprise Focus process area.

Summary of Specific Goals and Practices

OTA:SG1 Establish Awareness Program
    OTA:SG1.SP1   Establish Awareness Needs
    OTA:SG1.SP2   Establish Awareness Plan
    OTA:SG1.SP3   Establish Awareness Delivery Capability
OTA:SG2 Conduct Awareness Activities
    OTA:SG2.SP1   Perform Awareness Activities
    OTA:SG2.SP2   Establish Awareness Records
    OTA:SG2.SP3   Assess Awareness Program Effectiveness
OTA:SG3 Establish Training Capability
    OTA:SG3.SP1   Establish Training Needs
    OTA:SG3.SP2   Establish Training Plan
    OTA:SG3.SP3   Establish Training Capability
OTA:SG4 Conduct Training
    OTA:SG4.SP1   Deliver Training
    OTA:SG4.SP2   Establish Training Records
    OTA:SG4.SP3   Assess Training Effectiveness

Specific Practices by Goal

OTA:SG1 ESTABLISH AWARENESS PROGRAM

An awareness program that supports the organization's resilience program is established.

An awareness program is a means by which the organization can highlight important behaviors and begin the process of acculturating staff and external entities to important organizational goals, objectives, and critical success factors. Awareness differs significantly from skill-based training. Awareness focuses on communicating a message to gather support for an organizational imperative; skill-based training is aimed at imparting knowledge to staff that is necessary to perform a role or fulfill a responsibility. Awareness of resilience makes staff more cognizant of their role in supporting the organization's operational resilience management system and in ensuring adequate operational resilience for high-value services and assets.

To establish an effective awareness program, an organization must identify awareness needs and establish a plan and capability to meet those needs. Adjustments to the plan and the program are made over the course of time to address changes in needs and to make overall improvements.

OTA:SG1.SP1 ESTABLISH AWARENESS NEEDS

The awareness needs of the organization are established and maintained.

Awareness needs reflect the message that is to be communicated regarding resilience to all entities, internal and external, that have a vested interest in the resilience activities of the organization (referred to as "staff"). These may be derived from the organization's resilience strategic plans, policies, or other goal and objectives. Awareness needs are derived by determining the set of resilience topics, plans, issues, or policies of which various sets of the organization's population have to be kept aware. For many organizations, the awareness needs may be consistent across the organization's entire population; for others, different parts of the organization may have different awareness needs. If high-value business processes are outsourced, there may be awareness needs that span one or more external entities. All of these populations should be identified and their awareness needs documented.

Awareness needs are temporal and may change as a result of changes in technology, policy, strategy, and risks being managed. A routine process to maintain and update awareness needs should be put in place.

> Sources of awareness needs include
> - resilience requirements that specify how assets and services have to be protected and sustained
> - organizational policies that attempt to enforce and reinforce acceptable behaviors or implement necessary controls across the enterprise, such as keeping payroll data confidential
> - vulnerabilities under watch or that are being actively managed, such as email and internet viruses
> - laws and regulations to which the organization is subject because of its industry, geographical location, or type of business, such as
>   - confidentiality and privacy regulations
>   - other federal, state, and local laws that restrict disclosure of information or modification of information
> - service continuity and communications plans that are of importance to staff in being prepared to act in the event of an incident or disaster
> - event reporting procedures that include instructions for when and to whom to report an event or incident

Typical work products

1. Stated objectives for awareness
2. List of staff members requiring awareness
3. Awareness needs for each staff group

Subpractices

1. Analyze the organization's operational resilience program to identify the types and extent of awareness efforts that are necessary to satisfy resilience program objectives.

Because managing operational resilience requires acculturation of both internal and external entities (staff), the types and extent of awareness efforts may have to be extensive and rigorous. The objectives of awareness efforts must be clearly stated and must help the organization achieve staff acculturation to the organization's philosophy of managing operational resilience.

2. Document the awareness needs of the organization by staff group.
   Because managing operational resilience is a broad, enterprise-wide activity, awareness presentations may need to cover a broad range of topics and may require focused messages for particular staff groups. Awareness presentations must be purposefully aimed at communicating the appropriate message to each group.
3. Determine the resources necessary to meet the awareness needs.
4. Revise the awareness needs of the organization as changes to the resilience program and strategy are made.

OTA:SG1.SP2 ESTABLISH AWARENESS PLAN

A plan for developing, implementing, and maintaining an awareness program is established and maintained.

The awareness plan details how the organization intends to carry out consistent and repeatable awareness efforts for each staff group. The plan must address the development, delivery, and maintenance of awareness presentations and materials to meet the awareness needs identified for each staff group. The plan should address near-term development and delivery and should be periodically adjusted based on new or changing needs and feedback from assessing the effectiveness of awareness activities.

Typical work products

1. Awareness plan
2. Documented commitments to the plan

Subpractices

1. Establish awareness plan content.
   Awareness plans typically include the following:
   - awareness needs and objectives
   - topics for awareness presentations and materials
   - identification of various staff groups and descriptions of how needs and topics vary by audience
   - schedules based on calendar-based and event-based awareness needs (An example of a calendar-based awareness need is "provide annual refresh training on login procedures and guidelines for choosing and managing secure passwords." An example of an event-based awareness need is "provide security and business continuity initiation briefing to new employees within ten days of starting work.")

- methods to distribute awareness presentations and materials
- requirements and quality standards for awareness presentations and materials, which may include identity guidelines for use of organizational trademarks
- identification of awareness program roles and responsibilities
- resource requirements

2. Establish commitments to the plan.
   Documented commitments by those responsible for implementing and supporting the plan are essential for the plan to be effective.
3. Determine resources necessary to carry out the plan.
4. Revise the plan and commitments as necessary.

OTA:SG1.SP3 Establish Awareness Delivery Capability

A capability for consistent and repeatable delivery of awareness artifacts is established and maintained.

The organization must be able to deliver awareness artifacts on a repeatable basis and ensure that the message communicated about operational resilience is consistent.

Establishing a capability for implementing the awareness plan requires the selection of appropriate awareness approaches, sourcing or developing awareness materials, obtaining appropriate awareness facilitators or instructors (if needed), delivering internal communications about awareness activities, and revising the awareness capability as needed.

Awareness activities for external entities such as business partners and vendors are addressed in the External Dependencies Management process area.

Typical work products

1. Awareness approaches by staff group
2. Awareness materials and supporting work products

Subpractices

1. Select the appropriate approaches to satisfy specific organizational awareness needs based on staff group.
   Many factors influence the selection of appropriate awareness approaches for the various segments of the organization's population. Typically, these include audience-specific roles, knowledge and daily behaviors, differences in work environment, budget, and consideration of organizational and work group culture. The selection of an approach should be based primarily on the best and most efficient means to create and support awareness for a given population, in light of any constraints.

> These are examples of awareness approaches:
> - distributing artifacts and workplace tools containing awareness messages (mouse pads, notepads, pens, mugs, hand tools, etc.)
> - poster campaigns
> - signage
> - screen savers
> - newsletters—paper-based or electronic
> - email messages, letters, and memos from higher-level managers
> - messages, reminders, and news items posted to internal web portals, electronic message boards, and physical bulletin boards
> - agenda items and supporting materials to be covered in organization-wide or team-based meetings
> - on-demand electronic briefings delivered via DVD or streaming network media
> - trainer-facilitated sessions delivered live or delivered remotely via teleconference, videoconference, or streaming network media
> - lunch seminars
> - acknowledgment or awards programs

2. Determine whether to develop the awareness materials internally, acquire them externally, or some combination.

> Criteria to consider when considering whether to develop awareness materials internally or to obtain the materials externally include
> - cost versus benefit
> - schedule and availability
> - availability of in-house expertise
> - availability and suitability of materials from qualified external entities

3. Develop or obtain awareness materials.

    These materials may contain sensitive information about incidents and other security events that can be used to raise general awareness about managing operational resilience. The organization should make provisions for adequately protecting this information from external entities that may be involved in awareness activities, either as providers or as participants.

    Guidelines for establishing and maintaining relationships with external entities that serve as sources of awareness materials are addressed in the External Dependencies Management process area.

4. Develop or obtain qualified instructors or facilitators as needed.

    If instructor- or facilitator-led sessions are among the awareness activities that have been selected, qualified instructors or facilitators are required. To ensure that the instructors or facilitators have the necessary skills and knowledge to deliver the awareness materials, criteria can be established for evaluating candidates.

For internal candidates, it may be necessary to provide specific training. For external resources, it is important to work with the provider to understand which of their staff will perform the work. This can be a factor in selecting or continuing to work with a specific provider.

5. Deliver internal communications about planned awareness activities.

    It may be appropriate to deliver communications about planned awareness activities. For example, if people are expected to attend events, communications about the schedule of the events are necessary. For some activities, it may be appropriate to inform higher-level and other managers about the awareness plans and ask them to support and reinforce the plans by calling attention to the awareness activities in their regular communications or meetings with staff.

    Awareness communications are addressed in the Communications process area.

6. Revise the awareness materials and supporting artifacts as necessary.

> Situations in which awareness materials will have to be revised include
> - changes in existing awareness needs and requirements—for example, as a result of the implementation of a new procedure or technology
> - emergence of new awareness needs and requirements—for example, a new risk or vulnerability for which awareness is a suitable or necessary control
> - assessment of effectiveness of awareness presentations suggesting that awareness materials have to be changed
> - training refresh—for example, changing an awareness poster from time to time in order to be noticed by the intended audience

OTA:SG2 CONDUCT AWARENESS ACTIVITIES

Awareness activities that support the organization's resilience program are performed.

The organization must perform awareness activities in order to carry out awareness plans and to fulfill the objectives of the awareness program. To ensure that awareness activities are being performed as prescribed, awareness activity records are established to track participation in awareness activities, and the effectiveness of the awareness activities is assessed.

OTA:SG2.SP1 PERFORM AWARENESS ACTIVITIES

Awareness activities are performed according to the awareness plan.

Awareness activities implement the awareness approaches that the organization has considered and developed to meet the specific staff needs. These activities can take many forms, as noted in the subpractices in OTA:SG1.SP3. Primarily, awareness activities will take the form of formal awareness presentations, but they could be supplemented by more continuous activities such as newsletters, email messages, or posters and other signage.

Awareness activities must meet the broad needs of staff members, and the logistics of performing these activities must be planned. The activities must be scheduled, advertised (if necessary), and resourced.

Typical work products

1. Awareness activity materials
2. Awareness activity schedules
3. Awareness activity logistics
4. List of staff responsible for each awareness activity

Subpractices

1. Determine the mix and frequency of awareness activities.
2. Plan and schedule awareness activities, including regular awareness presentations.
3. Perform logistics planning for each scheduled awareness activity.
4. Assign resources to each scheduled awareness activity.
5. Perform awareness activities according to the schedule and the plan.
   Awareness materials are distributed to the target populations according to the schedule and the approaches established in the plan.
6. Track the delivery of awareness activities against the plan and schedule.

OTA:SG2.SP2 ESTABLISH AWARENESS RECORDS

Records of awareness activities performed are established and maintained.

Awareness activity records enable the organization to verify that awareness activities have been conducted according to plan. They provide evidence that staff and external entities have attended required activities appropriate for their job responsibility and role in the organization.

Records may also be necessary for compliance purposes to prove that the organization provides awareness presentations and requires staff and external entities to attend.

Recording awareness activities also facilitates evaluating activity effectiveness, particularly awareness presentations, through instruments such as evaluations and suggestion boxes.

The tracking of awareness activities for compliance purposes is addressed in the Compliance process area.

Guidance about tracking awareness activities for governance functions is addressed in the Enterprise Focus process area.

Typical work products

1. Awareness activity records
2. Awareness activity waivers

Subpractices

1. Keep records of all awareness activities conducted throughout the organization.

> These are examples of information that may be appropriate to record about awareness activities (not all of these would apply to every type of awareness activity):
> - a description of the specific awareness activity, when it occurred, and its duration
> - the population reached by an awareness activity
> - measures of participation, including specific records of attendance for awareness events
> - feedback received from participants

   If the awareness activity is required for certain staff groups or individual staff members, the organization should keep records for each attendee indicating whether or not the attendee completed the activity successfully.

   For staff who have been exempted from awareness activities for any reason, the organization should keep records documenting the rationale for the waiver, and the staff member's manager (or similarly appropriate person) should approve the waiver.

2. Make awareness activity records available to appropriate people or processes. Awareness activity records may be important in considering promotions or job assignments and thus should be made available to those who must make these types of decisions on a regular basis.

OTA:SG2.SP3 ASSESS AWARENESS PROGRAM EFFECTIVENESS

The effectiveness of the awareness program is assessed and corrective actions are identified.

A process should be implemented to evaluate the effectiveness of the awareness program by assessing how well program activities meet the awareness needs of the organization and staff.

Typically, assessing awareness program effectiveness occurs in the form of evaluations of awareness activities, but it may be a more challenging task for informal methods of awareness such as posters or regular communications.

> These are examples of methods that can be used to evaluate the effectiveness of awareness activities:
> - questionnaires or surveys designed to measure people's awareness of specific topics
> - focus groups to elicit the awareness of a group of people after an awareness activity has occurred and to gather recommendations for awareness activity improvements
> - selective interviews to inquire about awareness and any changes in behavior that may have occurred as a result of awareness activities

- behavioral measures to objectively evaluate shifts in the population's behavior after an awareness activity—for example, evaluating the strength of passwords before and after a password-awareness activity
- observations, evaluations, and benchmarking activities conducted by external entities

Typical work products

1. Evaluations of the awareness program and its activities
2. Awareness methods surveys
3. Focus group or interview results
4. Assessment results from staff (internal and external)

Subpractices

1. Assess staff awareness level based on the staff members' respective job responsibilities and roles.

    The purpose of this assessment is to determine whether awareness is sufficient to support the organization's resilience posture and program.

    For external entities that are being assessed, this should be included as part of the regular review of their contracts and performance.

2. Provide a mechanism for evaluating the effectiveness of each awareness activity with respect to the objectives for that activity.

    For awareness presentations, this mechanism should include evaluations of the material and the presenters.

3. Document suggested improvements to the awareness plan and program based on the evaluation of the effectiveness of the awareness activities.

OTA:SG3 ESTABLISH TRAINING CAPABILITY

Training capabilities that support the operational resilience management system are established and maintained.

Training capability is established to provide focused and specific training to people who have roles and responsibilities that are focused on the operational resilience management system. The organization identifies the training needed to impart to people the necessary skills and knowledge to perform their roles and meet their responsibilities. A training plan is developed to guide the delivery of the training. Training materials and other resources are lined up to support the training plan.

Identifying staff with resilience roles and responsibilities, managing their performance, and conducting skills and knowledge gap analyses are addressed in the Human Resource Management process area.

OTA:SG3.SP1 ESTABLISH TRAINING NEEDS

The training needs of the organization are established and maintained.

Resilience training needs reflect the skills and competencies required at a tactical level to carry out the activities required for managing operational resilience. These activities cover a broad range of disciplines, including security activities, business continuity, IT operations, and service delivery. As a result, the training needs for resilience staff tend to be vast and must seek not only to include these disciplines but to address the convergence of these disciplines toward the goal of actively managing resilience.

Training needs are established by identifying people in the organization with resilience roles and responsibilities and analyzing gaps in their knowledge and skills that have to be addressed in order for them to succeed in their resilience roles. Training needs should also be informed by the organization's resilience plan and strategy. *(Refer to the Enterprise Focus process area.)*

Some staff may have resilience roles only during times of stress or when the organization is responding to a disruption. It is important in the needs analysis process to account for these or any other secondary roles that people may have that are key to the resilience process but occur on a more discrete rather than continuous basis.

These are examples of sources of resilience training needs:
- the organization's resilience process and strategy
- the roles and responsibilities of staff in the traditional security, business continuity, and IT operations and service delivery domains
- the roles and responsibilities of staff involved in the operational resilience process management process (as described by the process areas in the CERT Resilience Management Model)
- the organization's vulnerability management process, which may highlight certain skills and knowledge that are required for the successful management of vulnerabilities
- the organization's human resource management process, which may identify training needs based on gap analysis of skills and knowledge, cross-training, and succession planning
- the process of service continuity, which may identify certain training needs associated with service continuity planning
- the organization's compliance management process, which may identify explicit training requirements based on legislation and other compliance obligations
- the organization's incident management process, which may identify training needs based on specific plans and practices for identifying and responding to incidents
- analyses of any assets that are accessed by or are in the possession of external entities and of business processes or services that are dependent on external entities, which may identify training needs for external entities

Skill inventories and gap analyses are explicitly addressed in the Human Resource Management process area.

Cross-training and training for succession planning are also addressed in the People Management process area and are key inputs for the training needs established in Organizational Training and Awareness.

Typical work products

1. Training needs

Subpractices

1. Collect information about skill gaps, cross-training, and succession planning by reviewing the job responsibilities of staff involved in resilience processes, as well as current performance levels.
   Input to this process may be derived from the processes in the Human Resource Management and People Management process areas.
2. Analyze the organization's resilience requirements, goals, and objectives to determine future training needs.
3. Determine the roles and skills necessary to perform the standard processes that constitute the operational resilience management system.
4. Document the resilience training needs of the organization.
   The training needs should focus not only on the skills and knowledge needed to perform particular roles in the supporting disciplines of security, business continuity, and IT operations and service delivery, but also on the convergence aspects of these disciplines toward operational resilience management. The training needs should also adequately cover the capabilities represented by the operational resilience management system.
5. Document the training necessary to perform the roles in the organization's set of standard operational resilience management processes.
6. Revise the resilience training needs of the organization as necessary.

OTA:SG3.SP2 ESTABLISH TRAINING PLAN

A plan for developing, implementing, and maintaining a resilience training program is established and maintained.

A tactical training plan is created to plan the development, delivery, and maintenance of training materials to meet the organization's resilience training needs. The plan should address near-term development and delivery and should be periodically adjusted in response to new or changing needs and to the assessment of effectiveness of training activities.

Typical work products

1. Resilience training plan
2. Documented commitments to the training plan

Subpractices

1. Establish resilience training plan content.
    Training plans typically include the following:
    - training needs
    - training topics
    - schedules based on training activities and their dependencies
    - methods used for training
    - requirements and quality standards for training materials
    - training tasks, roles, and responsibilities
    - required resources, including tools, facilities, environments, staffing, and skills and knowledge
2. Establish commitments to the resilience training plan.
    Because resilience training can cover a broad range of topics, documented commitments by those responsible for implementing and supporting the plan are essential for the plan to be effective.
3. Revise the plan and commitments as necessary.

OTA:SG3.SP3 ESTABLISH TRAINING CAPABILITY

A capability for delivering training to resilience staff is established and maintained.

The organization must be capable of providing resilience training across a broad range of topics and to a vast audience of resilience staff. The training must cover the topic areas of security, business continuity, and IT operations and service delivery, as well as the supporting process areas established by the operational resilience management system, including compliance management, financial resource management, and relationships with external entities, to name a few.

Capabilities for implementing the training plan must be established and maintained, including the selection of appropriate training approaches, sourcing or developing training materials, obtaining appropriate instructors, announcing the training schedule, and revising the awareness capability as needed.

If training needs have been identified for people who are not part of the organization—for example, external entities such as outsourcer, vendor, or supplier staff—then this practice should also be extensible to establish and maintain the capability to train those people as well.

Guidelines on incorporating training requirements into external entity agreements or for making organizational training assets available for use by external entities are included in the External Dependencies Management process area.

Typical work products

1. Resilience training materials and supporting work products

Subpractices

1. Select the appropriate approaches to satisfy specific organizational training needs and competencies.

    Many factors may affect the selection of training approaches, such as audience-specific knowledge, costs and schedule, and work environment. Selection of an approach requires consideration of the means to provide skills and knowledge in the most effective way possible given the constraints.

    > These are examples of training approaches:
    > - classroom training
    > - computer-aided instruction
    > - guided self-study
    > - formal apprenticeship and mentoring programs
    > - facilitated videos
    > - chalk talks
    > - brown-bag lunch seminars
    > - structured on-the-job training

2. Determine whether to develop training materials internally or acquire them externally.

    > Criteria to consider when deciding whether to develop training materials internally or to obtain the materials externally include
    > - cost-benefit analysis
    > - schedule and availability
    > - availability of in-house expertise
    > - availability and suitability of materials from external entities

3. Develop or obtain training materials.

    (*Refer to the External Dependencies Management process area for guidelines on establishing and maintaining relationships with external sources of training materials.*) Depending on the specific content, some customized materials may contain sensitive or proprietary information, in which case suitable provisions should be included in the external entity agreement.

4. Develop or obtain qualified instructors.

    To ensure that internally provided training instructors have the necessary knowledge and training skills, criteria can be defined to identify, develop, and qualify them. In the case of externally provided training, the organization's training staff can investigate how the training provider determines which instructors will deliver the training. This can also be a factor in selecting or continuing to use a specific training provider.

5. Describe the training in the organization's training curriculum.

> These are examples of the information provided in the training descriptions for each course:
> - topics covered in the training
> - intended audience
> - prerequisites and preparation for participating
> - training objectives
> - length of the training
> - lesson plans
> - completion criteria for the course
> - criteria for granting training waivers

6. Revise the training materials and supporting work products as necessary.

> These are examples of situations in which the training materials and supporting work products may have to be revised:
> - Training needs change (e.g., when new technology associated with the training topic is available).
> - An evaluation of the training identifies the need for change (e.g., evaluations of training effectiveness surveys, training program performance assessments, or instructor evaluation forms).

OTA:SG4 CONDUCT TRAINING

Training necessary for staff to perform their roles effectively is provided.

The organization must perform resilience training to ensure that staff are appropriately skilled in their roles to support the operational resilience management system. Training must be delivered according to the training plans developed and must address the vast range of needs represented in the operational resilience management system. Training records are established for the purpose of tracking training activities, and the effectiveness of the training activities is evaluated.

OTA:SG4.SP1 DELIVER RESILIENCE TRAINING

Training is delivered according to the training plan.

Resilience training is provided by the organization (or its training provider as appropriate) to fulfill the resilience training needs and training plan. The appropriate mix of training is determined based on the needs, and the staff selected to participate in the training are determined based on their current skill level.

Training delivery for the operational resilience management system is not a trivial task. The broad range of skills necessary to address and adequately perform the competencies required to manage operational resilience requires extensive training. In addition, the intensity of the training may range from informal activities to hands-on, skill-based training.

Typical work products

1. Delivered training courses
2. Training schedule

Subpractices

1. Select the staff who will receive the training necessary to perform their roles effectively.

    Training is intended to impart knowledge and skills to people performing various roles within the organization. Some people already possess the knowledge and skills required to perform well in their designated roles. Training can be waived for these people, but care should be taken that training waivers are not abused.

2. Schedule the training, including any resources, as necessary (e.g., facilities and instructors).

    Training should be planned and scheduled. Training is provided that has a direct bearing on the expectations of work performance. Therefore, optimal training occurs in a timely manner with regard to imminent job performance expectations. These expectations often include the following:
    - training in the use of specialized tools
    - training in procedures that are new to the individual who will perform them

3. Conduct the training.

    Experienced instructors should perform training. When possible, training is conducted in settings that closely resemble actual performance conditions and includes activities to simulate actual work situations. This approach includes integration of tools, methods, and procedures for competency development. Training is tied to work responsibilities so that on-the-job activities or other outside experiences will reinforce the training within a reasonable time after the training.

4. Track the delivery of training against the plan.

OTA:SG4.SP2 ESTABLISH TRAINING RECORDS

Records of delivered training are established and maintained.

Training records enable the organization to verify that training activities have been conducted according to plan. Training records may also be required to prove that a compliance obligation has been met or to support the retention of credentials or certification. Such records also facilitate the evaluation of training effectiveness.

Since this practice is related to the organization's resilience training, the training records may be a subset of the full organizational training records.

Refer to the Compliance process area for information about tracking training activities for compliance purposes.

Typical work products

1. Training records
2. Training waivers

Subpractices

1. Keep records of all staff (including external entities) indicating whether or not they successfully completed each training course or other approved training activity.
2. Keep records of all staff who have been waived from specific training.
    The rationale for granting a waiver should be documented, and both the manager responsible and the manager of the excepted individual should approve the waiver for organizational training.
3. Keep records of all staff who successfully complete their designated required training.
4. Make training records available to the appropriate people or processes.
    Training records may be important in considering promotions or job assignments and thus should be made available to those who must make these types of decisions on a regular basis.

OTA:SG4.SP3 ASSESS TRAINING EFFECTIVENESS

The effectiveness of the training program is assessed and corrective actions are identified.

A process should exist to determine the effectiveness of training for meeting the training needs of staff involved in the operational resilience management system.

These are examples of methods used to assess training effectiveness:
- testing in the training context
- post-training surveys of training participants
- surveys of managers' satisfaction with post-training effects
- assessment mechanisms embedded in training materials

Typical work products

1. Training effectiveness surveys
2. Instructor evaluation forms
3. Examination results or results from assessment mechanisms

Subpractices

1. Provide a mechanism for assessing the effectiveness of each training course with respect to established organizational, project, or individual learning (or performance) objectives.
2. Collect other data that can be used to evaluate training effectiveness.
   Data can be gathered through surveys or other mechanisms from course participants or from their managers to determine the impact of the training on course participants' ability to perform their resilience roles and responsibilities.
3. Document suggested improvements to the training plan based on the evaluation of the effectiveness of training activities.

Elaborated Generic Practices by Goal

Refer to the Generic Goals and Practices document in Appendix A for general guidance that applies to all process areas. This section provides elaborations relative to the application of the Generic Goals and Practices to the Organizational Training and Awareness process area.

OTA:GG1 ACHIEVE SPECIFIC GOALS

The operational resilience management system supports and enables achievement of the specific goals of the Organizational Training and Awareness process area by transforming identifiable input work products to produce identifiable output work products.

OTA:GG1.GP1 PERFORM SPECIFIC PRACTICES

Perform the specific practices of the Organizational Training and Awareness process area to develop work products and provide services to achieve the specific goals of the process area.

Elaboration:

Specific practices OTA:SG1.SP1 through OTA:SG4.SP3 are performed to achieve the goals of the organizational training and awareness process.

OTA:GG2 INSTITUTIONALIZE A MANAGED PROCESS

Organizational training and awareness is institutionalized as a managed process.

OTA:GG2.GP1 ESTABLISH PROCESS GOVERNANCE

Establish and maintain governance over the planning and performance of the organizational training and awareness process.

Refer to the Enterprise Focus process area for more information about providing sponsorship and oversight to the organizational training and awareness process.

Subpractices

1. Establish governance over process activities.

   Elaboration:

   > Governance over the organizational training and awareness process may be exhibited by
   > - establishing a higher-level position, often the director of human resources, responsible for resilience awareness, training, and staff skill and knowledge development (This role may be assisted by the operational resilience process group [ORPG].)
   > - developing and publicizing higher-level managers' objectives and requirements for resilience training and awareness
   > - sponsoring and guiding the development of training and awareness plans that meet the organization's needs for managing operational resilience
   > - sponsoring the development and implementation of training and awareness programs
   > - sponsoring and funding process activities
   > - sponsoring and providing oversight of policy, procedures, standards, and guidelines for training and awareness activities and programs and for organizational use of these activities and programs
   > - guiding and supporting the enforcement of training and awareness requirements
   > - providing input on content for training and awareness programs, courses, and plans relative to organizational strategic objectives, risk appetite and tolerance, and current organizational health and condition
   > - making higher level-managers aware of applicable compliance obligations related to resilience training and awareness, and regularly reporting on the organization's satisfaction of these obligations to higher-level managers
   > - verifying that the process supports strategic resilience objectives and is focused on the assets and services that are of the highest relative value in meeting strategic objectives
   > - regular reporting from organizational units to higher-level managers on training and awareness activities and results
   > - creating dedicated higher-level management feedback loops on decisions about the process and recommendations for improving the process
   > - conducting regular internal and external audits and related reporting to audit committees on process effectiveness
   > - creating formal programs to measure the effectiveness of process activities, and reporting these measurements to higher-level managers

2. Develop and publish organizational policy for the process.

   Elaboration:

   > The organizational training and awareness policy should address
   > - identifying resilience training and awareness needs
   > - responsibility, authority, and ownership for performing resilience training and awareness process activities, including programs and courses
   > - developing resilience training and awareness plans
   > - required participation in process activities as a condition of ongoing employment as related to resilience roles and responsibilities
   > - procedures, standards, and guidelines for
   >   - developing training and awareness attendance requirements
   >   - creating, delivering, and maintaining training materials
   >   - creating, managing, and maintaining training records
   >   - assessing the effectiveness of training and awareness programs
   > - methods for measuring adherence to policy, exceptions granted, and policy violations

OTA:GG2.GP2 PLAN THE PROCESS

Establish and maintain the plan for performing the organizational training and awareness process.

Elaboration:

Specific practices OTA:SG1.SP2 and OTA:SG3.SP2 require the development of plans for how the organization will carry out organizational resilience awareness and training, respectively. In generic practice OTA:GG2.GP2, the planning elements required in specific practices OTA:SG1.SP2 and OTA:SG3.SP2 are formalized and structured and performed in a managed way. These are separate and distinct from the organizational training and awareness process plan.

Subpractices

1. Define and document the plan for performing the process.

   Elaboration:

   Special consideration in the plan may have to be given to training and awareness for skill development, sustaining skill competencies, and reassignment planning for various roles. These activities aid in protecting and sustaining people to support operational resilience.

Special consideration in the plan may also have to be given to how the organization incorporates training and awareness activities for resources that are not under its direct control, including external entities such as contractors, outsourcing partners, training suppliers, and other business partners.
2. Define and document the process description.
3. Review the plan with relevant stakeholders and get their agreement.
4. Revise the plan as necessary.

OTA:GG2.GP3 Provide Resources

Provide adequate resources for performing the organizational training and awareness process, developing the work products, and providing the services of the process.

Elaboration:

Specific practices OTA:SG1.SP2 and OTA:SG3.SP2 require the assignment of resources to the organizational resilience awareness and training plans, respectively. In generic practice OTA:GG2.GP3, resources are formally identified and assigned to plan elements. These are separate and distinct from the resources required to execute the organizational training and awareness process plan.

The diversity of activities required to ensure adequate, up-to-date training and awareness of resilience staff requires an extensive level of organizational resources and skills and may require a significant number of external resources. In addition, these activities may require a major commitment of financial resources (both expense and capital) from the organization.

Subpractices

1. Staff the process.

   Elaboration:

   This generic goal related to organizational training and awareness refers to staffing the organizational training and awareness process plan, not the individual organizational training and awareness plans. Assigning resources to organizational training and awareness plans is included in specific practices OTA:SG1.SP2 and OTA:SG3.SP2.

   > These are examples of staff required to perform the organizational training and awareness process:
   > - subject matter experts, including staff knowledgeable of each operational resilience management process area and how to reflect process requirements in awareness and training materials
   > - curriculum designers
   > - instructional designers

- instructors
- training administrators
- human resources staff
- staff responsible for developing training and awareness plans and programs and ensuring they are aligned with stakeholder requirements and needs
- external entities involved in creating, delivering, and maintaining training and awareness materials
- staff responsible for managing external entities that have contractual obligations for resilience training and awareness activities
- internal and external auditors responsible for reporting to appropriate committees on process effectiveness

Refer to the Human Resource Management process area for information about acquiring staff for resilience roles and responsibilities.

2. Fund the process.

   Refer to the Financial Resource Management process area for information about budgeting for, funding, and accounting for organizational training and awareness.

3. Provide necessary tools, techniques, and methods to perform the process.

Elaboration:

These are examples of tools, techniques, and methods to support the organizational training and awareness process:
- methods and tools for building and distributing awareness messages, including pens, mugs, posters, signage, screen savers, newsletters, etc. (as described in OTA:SG1.SP3 subpractice 1)
- instruments for analyzing training needs
- training workstations and other hardware needs
- instructional design tools
- packages for developing presentation materials
- tools, methods, and procedures that closely resemble actual performance conditions and simulate actual work situations
- methods for delivering awareness and training materials, from user on-demand training to classroom-based training
- tools for tracking awareness and training course attendance and successful and unsuccessful completion by designated staff
- methods for evaluating the effectiveness of awareness activities, including surveys, focus groups, interviews, etc. (as described in OTA:SG2.SP3)
- methods for evaluating the effectiveness of training activities, including testing, assessment mechanisms, etc. (as described in OTA:SG4.SP3)
- tools used to capture and securely store training records and ensure such records are accessed only by authorized staff

OTA:GG2.GP4 ASSIGN RESPONSIBILITY

Assign responsibility and authority for performing the organizational training and awareness process, developing the work products, and providing the services of the process.

Elaboration:

Specific practices OTA:SG1.SP2 and OTA:SG3.SP2 require the assignment of responsibility to the organizational awareness and training plans. In generic practice OTA:GG2.GP4, commitments are formally identified to support resource allocations to plan elements. These are separate and distinct from the assignment of responsibilities for the organizational training and awareness process plan.

Refer to the Human Resource Management process area for more information about establishing resilience as a job responsibility, developing resilience performance goals and objectives, and measuring and assessing performance against these goals and objectives.

Subpractices

1. Assign responsibility and authority for performing the process.

Elaboration:

Responsibility and authority may extend not only to staff inside the organization but to those external entities with which the organization has a contractual agreement for creating, delivering, and maintaining awareness and training materials.

2. Assign responsibility and authority for performing the specific tasks of the process.

Elaboration:

> Responsibility and authority for performing organizational training and awareness tasks can be formalized by
> - defining roles and responsibilities in the process plan
> - including process tasks and responsibility for these tasks in specific job descriptions
> - developing policy requiring organizational unit managers, line of business managers, project managers, and asset and service owners to participate in and derive benefit from the process for services and assets under their ownership or custodianship
> - developing policy requiring participation in process activities as a condition of ongoing employment
> - including process tasks in staff performance management goals and objectives, with requisite measurement of progress against these goals
> - developing and implementing contractual instruments (as well as service level agreements) with external entities to establish responsibility and authority for creating, delivering, and maintaining awareness and training materials, where applicable
> - including process tasks in measuring performance of external entities against service level agreements

Refer to the External Dependencies Management process area for additional details about managing relationships with external entities.

3. Confirm that people assigned with responsibility and authority understand it and are willing and able to accept it.

OTA:GG2.GP5 TRAIN PEOPLE

Train the people performing or supporting the organizational training and awareness process as needed.

Elaboration:

Specific practices OTA:SG1.SP1 and OTA:SG3.SP1 call for establishing awareness needs and training needs for resilience awareness and training plans and programs, respectively.

Refer to the External Dependencies Management process area for more information about awareness training for external entities such as business partners, suppliers, and vendors.

Refer to the Human Resource Management process area for more information about inventorying skill sets, establishing a skill set baseline, identifying required skill sets, and measuring and addressing skill deficiencies.

Subpractices

1. Identify process skill needs.

   Elaboration:

   These skill needs are related to delivering the organizational training and awareness process, not the development and delivery of subject matter information related to security, business continuity, IT operations management, or the management of operational resilience. The identification of skill needs for subject matter areas is included in the subpractices for generic practice GG2.GP5 in each of the individual process areas.

   > These are examples of skills required in the organizational training and awareness process:
   > - curriculum and instructional design
   > - course delivery
   > - course and instructor evaluation
   > - measuring the effectiveness of awareness and training materials
   > - structuring and conducting participant surveys and interviews
   > - knowledge of the tools, techniques, and methods necessary to create, deliver, and maintain training and awareness work products, including those necessary to perform the process using the selected methods, techniques, and tools identified in OTA:GG2.GP3 subpractice 3

> - knowledge unique to each operational resilience management process area and assets and services that are the focus of these processes
> - knowledge necessary to elicit and prioritize stakeholder requirements and needs and interpret them to develop effective process requirements, plans, and programs

2. Identify process skill gaps based on available resources and their current skill levels.
3. Identify training opportunities to address skill gaps.

Elaboration:

> These are examples of training topics:
> - knowledge and skills needs analysis
> - instructional design
> - instructional techniques
> - refresher training on subject matter
> - supporting resilience staff in understanding the process and their roles and responsibilities with respect to its activities
> - working with external entities that have responsibility for resilience training and awareness activities
> - using process methods, tools, and techniques, including those identified in OTA:GG2:GP3 subpractice 3

4. Provide training and review the training needs as necessary.

OTA:GG2.GP6 MANAGE WORK PRODUCT CONFIGURATIONS

Place designated work products of the organizational training and awareness process under appropriate levels of control.

Refer to the Compliance process area for information about tracking of awareness activities for compliance purposes.

Elaboration:

Specific practices OTA:SG2.SP2 and OTA:SG4.SP2 address the record keeping and documentation process over organizational training and awareness activities.

> These are examples of organizational training and awareness work products placed under control:
> - awareness and training needs
> - awareness and training plans and programs
> - awareness and training records and waivers

> - awareness and training materials and supporting work products
> - instructor evaluation forms
> - awareness and training effectiveness surveys
> - survey and interview results
> - awareness and training examinations and assessment results
> - policies and procedures
> - contracts with external entities

OTA:GG2.GP7 *IDENTIFY AND INVOLVE RELEVANT STAKEHOLDERS*

Identify and involve the relevant stakeholders of the organizational training and awareness process as planned.

Elaboration:

Many OTA-specific practices address the involvement of stakeholders in the organizational training and awareness process. For example, specific practice OTA:SG1.SP1 calls for identifying staff groups and their particular awareness needs. Specific practice OTA:SG1.SP2 ensures these needs are carried out in the awareness training plan.

Subpractices

1. Identify process stakeholders and their appropriate involvement.

   Elaboration:

   > These are examples of stakeholders of the organizational training and awareness process:
   > - staff who are required to determine the degree to which their constituencies understand the organization's resilience goals, objectives, standards, policies, and processes, including
   >   - asset owners and custodians
   >   - service owners
   >   - business process owners
   >   - organizational unit and line of business managers responsible for high-value services and assets
   > - external entities responsible for managing high-value assets and services
   > - human resources (for ensuring the resilience of people assets)
   > - information technology staff (for ensuring the resilience of technology assets)
   > - staff responsible for physical security (for ensuring the resilience of facility assets)
   > - internal and external auditors

> Stakeholders are involved in various tasks in the organizational training and awareness process, such as
> - planning for the process
> - making decisions about the process
> - making commitments to process plans and activities
> - communicating process plans and activities
> - coordinating process activities
> - reviewing and appraising the effectiveness of process activities
> - establishing requirements for the process
> - resolving issues in the process

2. Communicate the list of stakeholders to planners and those responsible for process performance.
3. Involve relevant stakeholders in the process as planned.

OTA:GG2.GP8 Monitor and Control the Process

Monitor and control the organizational training and awareness process against the plan for performing the process and take appropriate corrective action.

Refer to the Monitoring process area for more information about the collection, organization, and distribution of data that may be useful for monitoring and controlling processes.

Refer to the Measurement and Analysis process area for more information about establishing process metrics and measurement.

Refer to the Enterprise Focus process area for more information about providing process information to managers, identifying issues, and determining appropriate corrective actions.

Subpractices

1. Measure actual performance against the plan for performing the process.
2. Review accomplishments and results of the process against the plan for performing the process.

   Elaboration:

   > These are examples of metrics for the organizational training and awareness process:
   > - number of training courses and awareness sessions delivered (e.g., planned versus actual)
   > - percentage of new users (internal and external) who have satisfactorily completed awareness training before being granted network access
   > - percentage of users (internal and external) who have satisfactorily completed periodic awareness refresher training as required by policy

- number of staff members trained (planned versus actual); percentage of staff trained versus expected
- percentage of external staff trained (versus expected or contracted)
- percentage of favorable post-training evaluation ratings, including instructor ratings
- percentage of favorable training program quality survey ratings
- schedule of delivery of training and awareness sessions (actual frequency versus planned frequency)
- percentage of passing scores (by participants) on training examinations
- percentage of passing scores (by participants) on awareness examinations
- percentage of staff waived from training or awareness activities
- number of training and awareness risks referred to the risk management process; number of risks where corrective action is still pending (by risk rank)
- level of adherence to process policies; number of policy violations; number of policy exceptions requested and number approved
- number of process activities that are on track per plan
- rate of change of resource needs to support the process
- rate of change of costs to support the process

3. Review activities, status, and results of the process with the immediate level of managers responsible for the process and identify issues.

   Elaboration:

   Periodic reviews of the organizational training and awareness process are needed to ensure that
   - training and awareness plans and programs are developed and implemented
   - training and awareness needs have been identified and are being satisfied
   - training and awareness activities are conducted as scheduled
   - all staff regularly attend training and awareness events as required by their roles and responsibilities
   - the waiver process is not abused
   - training and awareness activities are recorded
   - skills necessary to develop and deliver training and awareness programs are available or obtainable
   - the performance and effectiveness of training and awareness programs are regularly monitored, reported, evaluated, and improved
   - training and awareness materials are regularly reviewed and updated as required
   - training and awareness issues are referred to the risk management process when necessary
   - actions requiring management involvement are elevated in a timely manner
   - key measures are within acceptable ranges as demonstrated in governance dashboards or scorecards and financial reports
   - actions resulting from internal and external audits are being closed in a timely manner

4. Identify and evaluate the effects of significant deviations from the plan for performing the process.

Elaboration:

Deviations from the organizational training and awareness plan may occur when organizational units fail to follow the enterprise-sponsored process. These deviations may affect the operational resilience of the organizational unit's services but may also have a cascading effect on enterprise operational resilience objectives.

5. Identify problems in the plan for performing and executing the process.
6. Take corrective action when requirements and objectives are not being satisfied, when issues are identified, or when progress differs significantly from the plan for performing the process.
7. Track corrective action to closure.

OTA:GG2.GP9 OBJECTIVELY EVALUATE ADHERENCE

Objectively evaluate adherence of the organizational training and awareness process against its process description, standards, and procedures, and address non-compliance.

Elaboration:

These are examples of activities to be reviewed:
- the identification of training and awareness needs and the development of plans and programs to meet these needs
- regular offering of and attendance at training and awareness activities
- the alignment of stakeholder requirements with process plans and programs
- assignment of responsibility, accountability, and authority for process activities
- determination of the adequacy of process reports and reviews in informing decision makers regarding the performance of operational resilience management activities and the need to take corrective action, if any
- use of process work products for improving strategies to protect and sustain assets and services

These are examples of work products to be reviewed:
- tactical plans for training and awareness
- awareness and training materials and supporting work products
- awareness and training records, including waivers
- instructor, awareness session, and training evaluation forms
- surveys
- process plan and policies
- issues that have been referred to the risk management process

- process methods, techniques, and tools
- contracts with external entities
- metrics for the process (Refer to OTA:GG2.GP8 subpractice 2.)

OTA:GG2.GP10 REVIEW STATUS WITH HIGHER-LEVEL MANAGERS

Review the activities, status, and results of the organizational training and awareness process with higher-level managers and resolve issues.

Refer to the Enterprise Focus process area for more information about providing sponsorship and oversight to the operational resilience management system.

OTA:GG3 INSTITUTIONALIZE A DEFINED PROCESS

Organizational training and awareness is institutionalized as a defined process.

OTA:GG3.GP1 ESTABLISH A DEFINED PROCESS

Establish and maintain the description of a defined organizational training and awareness process.

Establishing and tailoring process assets, including standard processes, are addressed in the Organizational Process Definition process area.

Establishing process needs and objectives and selecting, improving, and deploying process assets, including standard processes, are addressed in the Organizational Process Focus process area.

Subpractices

1. Select from the organization's set of standard processes those processes that cover the organizational training and awareness process and best meet the needs of the organizational unit or line of business.

    Elaboration:

    Each organizational unit will perform organizational training and awareness in a slightly different manner depending on operational concerns, identified needs and skill gaps, availability of supporting infrastructure, and requirements.

2. Establish the defined process by tailoring the selected processes according to the organization's tailoring guidelines.
3. Ensure that the organization's process objectives are appropriately addressed in the defined process, and ensure that process governance extends to the tailored processes.
4. Document the defined process and the records of the tailoring.
5. Revise the description of the defined process as necessary.

OTA:GG3.GP2 COLLECT IMPROVEMENT INFORMATION

Collect organizational training and awareness work products, measures, measurement results, and improvement information derived from planning and performing the process to support future use and improvement of the organization's processes and process assets.

Elaboration:

> These are examples of improvement work products and information:
> - results of training effectiveness surveys
> - training program performance assessment results
> - course evaluations
> - training records
> - training requirements from a stakeholder group
> - proper and improper use of awareness and training waivers
> - reports on the weaknesses of controls that can be addressed in training and awareness activities
> - changes and trends in operating conditions, risk conditions, and the risk environment that affect process offerings
> - lessons learned in post-event review of incidents and disruptions in continuity, including lack of staff preparedness to fulfill roles and responsibilities
> - resilience requirements that are not being satisfied or are being exceeded

Establishing the measurement repository and process asset library is addressed in the Organizational Process Definition process area. Updating the measurement repository and process asset library as part of process improvement and deployment is addressed in the Organizational Process Focus process area.

Subpractices

1. Store process and work product measures in the organization's measurement repository.
2. Submit documentation for inclusion in the organization's process asset library.
3. Document lessons learned from the process for inclusion in the organization's process asset library.
4. Propose improvements to the organizational process assets.

PEOPLE MANAGEMENT
Operations

Purpose

The purpose of People Management is to establish and manage the contributions and availability of people to support the resilient operation of organizational services.

Introductory Notes

People are an essential asset in the organization's ability to produce products and deliver services in the pursuit of strategic objectives. Without people and their skills, knowledge, information, and other valuable traits, many business processes could not operate effectively and the mission of organizational services would be in jeopardy.

The People Management process area focuses specifically on the "people" asset and their role in supporting the operation of business processes and services. Unlike information, technology, and facilities, the primary resilience requirement for people is availability—the availability of people to perform their roles and responsibilities in supporting organizational services as intended and when necessary. Events that disrupt the contributions of people affect the successful outcome of business processes and services and may impede the organization's mission. Even in highly automated operating environments where people have diminished roles, the unavailability of people may render services unable to meet their missions.

To properly manage people and their contributions to services, the organization must address several key aspects of resilience. It must

- identify the vital people in the organization, based on their roles and responsibilities
- identify and manage risks that would interrupt or disrupt the contributions of people or make people unavailable to perform their roles and responsibilities
- manage the processes that ensure continued availability of people or that provide for appropriate substitutions and replacements when necessary
- manage the availability of people during and after disruptive events and other times of stress

While there is an assumption that people who support organizational services are typically employed directly by the organization, there are many cases where they are acquired through outsourcing and supplier relationships or may be otherwise external to the organization. These external staff are included in the scope of the People Management process area because their availability could affect the successful operation of business processes and services. Therefore, the "staff" referred to in this process area can be understood to include both internal and external people. In addition, the availability of people also extends to staff who are deployed in vital resilience roles in disciplines such as security, business continuity and disaster recovery, first response, and IT operations management.

The People Management process area considers the effects on the organization due to interruptions and disruptions that affect the performance and availability of people. Thus, considerations such as cross-training of staff and succession planning are included to ensure a steady stream of effective staff for vital job roles and responsibilities. In addition, the impact of staff turnover, particularly in vital roles in high-value services, is also considered and addressed. When disruptions occur, People Management focuses the organization on preparing staff to accept and perform new roles, however temporary, until a return to business as usual can be accomplished. This can be a challenge because of physiological and physical constraints that the organization may have to identify and address before staff can effectively be re-introduced to a post-event workplace environment. All of these potential issues must be acknowledged and addressed by the organization in order to ensure sustained productivity of people throughout the enterprise.

As people are a ubiquitous resource in an organization, there are many aspects of people that affect operational resilience. People Management is focused on the availability of people to the services that they support. *The management of people through their employment life cycle and the effect on operational resilience are addressed in the Human Resource Management process area. Finally, promoting awareness of the organization's efforts and providing training to resilience staff for their roles in managing operational resilience are addressed in the Organizational Training and Awareness process area.*

Related Process Areas

The establishment and management of resilience requirements for people are performed in the Resilience Requirements Definition and Resilience Requirements Management process areas.

The identification of people and their support for services is addressed in the Asset Definition and Management process area.

The risk management cycle for people is addressed in the Risk Management process area.

The management of the internal control system that ensures people are adequately protected is addressed in the Controls Management process area.

The role of people in sustaining high-value organizational services and business processes is addressed in the Service Continuity process area.

The management of the human resources life cycle (from hiring to termination) is addressed in the Human Resource Management process area.

The awareness and acculturation of staff to the organization's philosophy and approach to managing operational resilience are addressed in the Organizational Training and Awareness process area.

Summary of Specific Goals and Practices

PM:SG1 Establish Vital Staff
    PM:SG1.SP1   Identify Vital Staff
PM:SG2 Manage Risks Associated with Staff Availability
    PM:SG2.SP1   Identify and Assess Staff Risk
    PM:SG2.SP2   Mitigate Staff Risk
PM:SG3 Manage the Availability of Staff
    PM:SG3.SP1   Establish Redundancy for Vital Staff
    PM:SG3.SP2   Perform Succession Planning
    PM:SG3.SP3   Prepare for Redeployment
    PM:SG3.SP4   Plan to Support Staff During Disruptive Events
    PM:SG3.SP5   Plan for Return-to-Work Considerations

Specific Practices by Goal

PM:SG1 ESTABLISH VITAL STAFF

The vital staff of the organization are identified and prioritized.

In this goal, the organization establishes the vital staff who must be resilient due to their roles in supporting effective operation of business processes and services. While all staff in an organization must be resilient to some degree, a select group of staff are absolutely essential to the sustained operation of the organization, particularly under stressful conditions.

Prioritization of staff is a risk management activity. It establishes the staff who are of significant value to the organization and for whom additional protective controls and measures to sustain them are required. Failure to prioritize may jeopardize the organization's ability to withstand disruptive events and recover to normal operating conditions.

People may also be categorized as vital because of the level of access they have to other organizational assets.

PM:SG1.SP1 IDENTIFY VITAL STAFF

The vital staff from a resilience perspective are identified and characterized.

The identification and characterization of vital staff must be performed to ensure that the organization properly considers them in the development and deployment of its strategies to protect and sustain them.

In most cases, people are identified as vital because of the role, function, or responsibility they have. However, certain people may be identified as vital because they are of high value to the organization for other reasons. The criteria that distinguish vital staff will vary by organization but should include people who

- perform roles that are vital to the continued operation of high-value services
- perform vital resilience functions such as security and disaster recovery
- are assigned executive authority for decision making and management control over the organization
- have access to, control of, or protection responsibility for valuable or sensitive organizational assets
- are valuable due to their knowledge, experience, or organizational or community reputation

It is likely that the different groups of vital staff will require varying levels of special consideration based on the potential effects they have, either directly or indirectly, on the organization's operational resilience and its ability to manage it.

Typically, the organization selects a subset of vital staff from its staff inventory; however, it is feasible that the organization may compile a list of vital staff based on risk or other factors. (*The identification, definition, management, and control of people as an organizational asset are addressed in the Asset Definition and Management process area.*)

When identifying vital staff, wherever possible, it is important to describe the role, function, or responsibility or other reason that supports their designation as vital. In addition, vital staff are often identified and described in service continuity plans and other strategies; thus, the staff identified in this practice may have to be reconciled against those plans on a periodic basis. (*Service continuity plans are addressed in the Service Continuity process area.*)

Typical work products

1. List (or lists) of vital staff

Subpractices

1. Identify vital service-support staff.

    Service-support staff include people who have vital roles in the continued effective operation of the organization's services. The extent to which the organization can tolerate an interruption to the availability of these staff members should be considered when compiling this list.

    (An inventory of high-value staff is established in ADM:SG1.SP1 in the Asset Definition and Management process area.) This list may suffice for this subpractice or may be expanded if necessary.

    > Examples of service-support staff include those who
    > - operate or run significant business processes (which may not be operable without them)
    > - have knowledge, information, or intellectual property needed to operate business processes
    > - have a skill set that is unique or in limited supply in the organization
    > - perform a role that can only be performed by people (i.e., cannot be automated or requires significant interpretation and reasoning)

2. Identify vital resilience staff.

    Resilience staff includes people who primarily perform vital resilience functions in the organization, including security, disaster recovery, and incident response. The extent to which the organization can tolerate an interruption to the availability of these staff should be considered when compiling this list.

    > Examples of resilience staff include those who
    > - perform security functions such as network security monitoring, access control, or security administration
    > - perform business impact analysis and develop service continuity plans
    > - manage high-value IT systems and applications
    > - manage high-value IT infrastructure
    > - manage access to, backup of, and restoration of high-value information assets
    > - manage physical security (protection and access) of high-value areas and facilities

3. Identify vital managers.

    To remain viable, particularly in times of stress, an organization must sustain its ability for executive decision making and control. This list of vital managers should include higher-level managers who are crucial to the command and control of the organization and their alternates. Alternates should be individuals who have the responsibility and authority for decision making and control in the event that vital managers are unavailable.

The extent to which the organization can tolerate an interruption to the availability of executive authority should be considered when compiling this list. Additionally, there may be regulatory requirements related to executive control that have to be considered and can be satisfied through the compilation of this list.

> These are examples of vital managers:
> - chief executive/financial/operating officers
> - chief risk officer
> - chief technology officer or chief information officer
> - chief information security officer
> - higher-level managers in organizational units and lines of business
> - vital higher-level roles in legal, human resources, communications/public relations, and operations
> - acceptable alternates to these positions

4. Identify staff who have access to, control of, or protection responsibility for highly valuable or highly sensitive organizational assets.

    This list of vital staff should include people who have trusted or special access to valuable or sensitive organizational assets. Such access is appropriate and necessary for people with certain roles in the organization and could be essential during a disruptive event.

> These are examples of trusted, privileged, or special roles:
> - technology staff with special and trusted access to software, hardware, systems, and networks (such as superusers)
> - production and operations supervisors (who can stop or start processes at will)
> - human resources staff with trusted access to confidential employee information
> - legal and audit staff with trusted access to sensitive organizational information and knowledge
> - physical security and protection staff who have trusted (and universal) access to facilities and buildings

5. Identify other vital staff.

    This list should include any other staff who may be vital to the organization's ability to achieve its strategic objectives or to sustain its operations under adverse conditions. Such staff might include people who are valuable because of what they know, whom they know, or other reasons. When compiling this list, the organization should consider the importance of these people not only to the viability of the organization but in whatever role they might play during disruptive events or other incidents that may draw the organization temporarily off course.

6. Reconcile the list of vital staff periodically to service continuity plans and other resilience strategies.

7. Periodically validate and update the list of vital staff based on changes in the operational and organizational environment.

PM:SG2 MANAGE RISKS ASSOCIATED WITH STAFF AVAILABILITY

Operational risks related to the availability of staff are identified and managed.

There are many types and categories of risk that are associated with people in the organization. On one hand, there are the risks related to the actions of people, such as when human error occurs or when staff members exploit organizational assets for their own gain. These risks involve people as a threat actor and result in a multitude of potential effects on the organization, such as disclosure of information, misappropriation of funds, and negative impact on the life, safety, and health of others.

On the other hand, there are risks associated with the interruption and interference of people in performing their job responsibilities. These risks to the availability of staff impact the organization by affecting the services that these staff members support and, in turn, the organization's ability to meet its mission. This can result in loss of revenue, increased labor costs, fines and legal penalties, and in some cases extreme effects such as loss of life.

Risk management for vital staff is focused on the identification of risks to the availability and productivity of these people. Managing risk related to vital staff involves the determination of the conditions under which their availability could be threatened, as well as the potential impact on the organization as a result.

PM:SG2.SP1 IDENTIFY AND ASSESS STAFF RISK

Risks to the availability of staff are periodically identified and assessed.

Operational risks that can affect staff must be identified and mitigated in order to actively manage the resilience of staff and, more important, the resilience of services that depend on the staff.

The identification of staff risks forms a baseline from which a continuous risk management process can be established and managed.

Typical risks that affect staff availability include natural disasters (that prevent vital staff from reporting to work), staff issues (such as poor performance or excessive absenteeism), inappropriate behaviors (such as failing to report to work to purposely affect the success of a business process or strategic objective), and other issues such as return-to-work considerations after a disruptive event that has psychological effects on staff.

Risks associated with the availability of staff also extend to their knowledge and experience. For example, the unavailability of a vital person who has extensive knowledge about a process or has information that is required by a process can impact the organization negatively by interfering with the availability of this knowledge and information for its intended purpose.

The subpractices included in this practice are generically addressed in RISK:SG3 and RISK:SG4 in the Risk Management process area.

Risks related to the actions that people take (as threat actors) are addressed in other process areas such as Knowledge and Information Management (for information asset risks), Technology Management (for technology-related risks), and Environmental Control (for facility-related risks).

Typical work products

1. Risk statements, with impact valuation
2. List of staff risks, with categorization and prioritization

Subpractices

1. Determine the scope of risk assessment for staff.
   Determining which staff to include in regular risk management activities depends on many factors. For most organizations, the scope will be limited to vital staff or a subset of vital staff.
2. Identify risks to the availability of staff.
3. Analyze risks to the availability of staff.
4. Categorize and prioritize staff risks.
5. Assign a risk disposition to each staff risk.
6. Monitor the risk and the risk strategy on a regular basis to ensure that the risk does not pose additional threat to the organization.
7. Develop a strategy for risks that the organization decides to mitigate.

PM:SG2.SP2 MITIGATE STAFF RISK

Mitigation strategies for the risks related to the availability of staff are developed and implemented.

The mitigation of staff risk involves the development of strategies that seek to minimize the risk to an acceptable level. This includes reducing the likelihood of risks to the availability of staff, minimizing exposure to such risks, developing plans to keep staff available during times of disruption, and developing recovery and restoration plans to address the consequences of realized risk. Risk mitigation also includes the implementation of controls to minimize the likelihood and impact of risks from staff. For example, training more than one person in vital roles may reduce the potential impact when one or more people cannot report to work because there is an acceptable backup.

Risk mitigation for staff requires the development of risk mitigation plans (which may include the development of new or revision of existing staff controls) and to implement and monitor these plans for effectiveness.

The subpractices included in this practice are generically addressed in RISK:SG5 in the Risk Management process area.

Typical work products

1. Staff risk mitigation plans
2. List of those responsible for addressing and tracking risks
3. Status on information asset risk mitigation plans

Subpractices

1. Develop and implement risk mitigation strategies for all risks that have a "mitigation" or "control" disposition.
2. Validate the risk mitigation plans by comparing them to existing strategies to protect and sustain staff availability.
3. Identify the person or group responsible for each risk mitigation plan and ensure that they have the authority to act and the proper level of skills and training to implement and monitor the plan.
4. Address residual risk.
5. Implement the risk mitigation plans and provide a method to monitor the effectiveness of these plans.
6. Monitor risk status.
7. Collect performance measures on the risk management process.

PM:SG3 MANAGE THE AVAILABILITY OF STAFF

The availability of staff to support high-value services is managed.

People provide direct support for the efficient and effective operation of organizational business processes and services. Thus, the availability of staff is critical to the resilience of these processes and services.

There are many potential events that can impair the availability of staff. For example, staff may be unavailable due to common causes such as illness or paid time off. Conversely, staff may also be unavailable on a broad scale due to natural disasters, civil unrest, or other catastrophic events.

In addition to their value to day-to-day operations, people are also a significant component of the organization's service continuity management program, and thus lack of availability can render service continuity plans and the organization's response to events ineffective. Developing and implementing plans to sustain staff availability during certain widespread or catastrophic events is a complex and challenging undertaking. When staff are facing issues of life and safety, loss or injury of family and friends, or considerable destruction of personal property, it is unlikely that they will be available or, if available, productive during or immediately following such an event.

Most of the actions that an organization can take to actively manage the availability of staff involve planning for staff redundancy and backup support for the roles that people play in the successful execution of business processes and services. This involves establishing redundancy for vital staff and performing succession planning to the extent possible to ensure a smooth transition when vital staff are unavailable. The organization must also address the availability of staff during times of stress; thus, they must consider how to redeploy staff when necessary to meet basic organizational needs, provide support for staff when they have been redeployed, and assist staff in transitioning back to their roles after a significant disruptive event.

PM:SG3.SP1 ESTABLISH REDUNDANCY FOR VITAL STAFF

Redundancy for vital staff is established to ensure continuity of services.

One of the most significant risks to an organization that can impact operational resilience is the loss of the skills and knowledge of staff. This risk can be increased when staff have institutional knowledge that has not been captured by the organization, documented, and communicated. Thus, a primary control for the organization to effectively (and proactively) ensure availability of vital staff is to establish redundancy through identifying, training, authorizing, and credentialing backup staff.

Strategies for providing redundancy for vital staff may extend beyond the organization's borders. For example, in some cases, staff inside the organization may not have the requisite foundation to be trained for another role in the organization. Thus, the organization may include in its redundancy strategy provisions for procuring staff with the right skills from outside of the organization, either from a temporary agency or from a provider of consulting services. In many cases, the ability to "purchase" skills is an effective strategy for providing redundancy that helps the organization to sustain operational resilience, even during times of stress.

It must be noted, however, that a key objective of redundancy is the transfer of institutional knowledge; therefore, simply providing a resource that can be trained may not be sufficient if the specific knowledge and experience of the person being replaced has not been captured and cannot be transferred. (*The processes for capturing institutional knowledge are addressed in the Knowledge and Information Management process area.*)

Typical work products

1. Strategic plan for providing redundancy for vital staff and services
2. List of designated backup staff for the organization's vital staff
3. Procedures for cross-training and credentialing
4. Procedures for outsourcing redundancy

Subpractices

1. **Determine which vital staff positions must have redundancy.**
   The organization must determine (from a risk and resilience perspective) which vital staff positions must be made redundant. This may involve extensive research and may be considered part of the organization's regular risk identification, assessment, and mitigation activities. The result of this practice should be the identification of the positions that are vital to the organization and that require redundancy strategies to ensure operational resilience.
2. **Identify backup staff for vital staff positions.**
   The identified staff should be documented and should consent to serving as a backup as part of their position responsibilities.
3. **Develop a strategic plan for providing staff redundancy.**
   The strategic plan for addressing staff redundancy should consider all relevant options for ensuring uninterrupted provision of support for organizational business processes and services. Options such as cross-training, job rotation, succession planning, and outsourcing should be thoroughly researched, and the most effective options (that would present the least risk to operational resilience) should be documented and considered. The strategies chosen may be specific to the job function that is being considered, so a mix of strategies may ultimately be needed.

   Keep in mind that the strategies for redundancy, particularly during disruptive events and times of stress, may be instantiated in the organization's service continuity plans. (*The development of service continuity plans is addressed in the Service Continuity process area.*)
4. **Provide training to redundant staff to perform necessary roles and responsibilities.**
   To be effective, the backup staff must have the skills and knowledge to perform the required functions and must be equipped with all necessary access privileges, credentials, authority, equipment, and supplies. Backup staff should be trained, briefed, and equipped to perform the necessary functions. Training should involve demonstration that the requisite skills can be applied as needed.

   It is also important to establish protocols for engaging the backup staff. For certain positions, it is appropriate for an "on-call" structure to be established to ensure the constant availability of the backup. It may also be important for other staff in the organization to be informed when a backup person is assuming the duties of a vital staff position so that it is clear who is responsible for the duties at any point in time.

PM:SG3.SP2 PERFORM SUCCESSION PLANNING

Vital management roles and responsibilities are supported through succession planning.

Succession planning is a form of redundancy focused on providing smooth transition for vital management roles in the organization. It is also a prudent activity that is often required by regulatory bodies and oversight agencies to ensure that an organization (particularly a publicly held company), its stakeholders, and its customers will not be adversely affected by the loss of one or more vital higher-level managers.

Succession planning is an extensive and systematic activity. It requires higher-level managers to look into the organization to identify potential successors and then mentor, train, and groom them to take roles in the future contingent upon vacancies that have not yet occurred. This requires an adept balance of human resources management, strategic planning, and skill building to create an effective succession chain.

Succession plans are typically focused on vital higher-level managers. However, depending on the organization, there may be other technical and administrative managers who are not easily replaced and for whom succession planning should be performed.

A named successor to a vital manager is distinct from a backup manager. The successor must have the full set of skills, knowledge, authority, access, and credentials to serve as a permanent replacement for a vital manager. Therefore, it may be efficient for the organization to have such successors serve in backup roles as well. To be effective and able to perform the necessary roles and functions, successor managers must be trained, authorized, and credentialed to perform the functions of vital managers on a permanent basis.

Typical work products

1. List of vital managers to include in succession planning
2. Succession strategy
3. Documented succession plans for vital managers
4. Training plan and records for successors

Subpractices

1. Identify vital positions that have to be included in succession planning.
   Succession planning begins with the identification of scope. This may require a risk-management–based activity that seeks to identify the potential impact of the loss of a vital organization resource for a period of time. The result of this practice is a list of vital managers for whom succession strategies and plans must be created and applied.
2. Develop strategies for creating a succession chain.
   The succession strategy must consider the positions that must be addressed as well as the pool of existing managers who can be considered in the succession chain. In some cases, the organization may decide that there are no internal candidates who can serve in the succession chain, which may lead to hiring new managers specifically for the purpose of grooming them for a future position.

   Strategies for succession planning must also consider the time element of replacement. In some cases, the grooming process may be conducted over several years, particularly when the organization has advance (but not necessarily public) knowledge that a vital position will be vacated in the future. In other cases, the time element may be short due to the loss of a manager as a result of illness, accident, or termination.

3. Establish detailed succession plans for vital management positions.

    The succession plan should align with the organization's strategy and include provisions for mentoring, training, and job rotation activities.

4. Mentor and train successors to perform necessary functions.

PM:SG3.SP3 PREPARE FOR REDEPLOYMENT

Plans are established and staff are prepared to redeploy to other roles during a disruptive event or in the execution of a service continuity plan.

During a disruptive event or during the execution of a service continuity plan, the focus of the organization turns to sustaining the operations of high-value services to the fullest extent possible while stabilizing the situation and conditions for eventual return to business as usual. During such times of stress, the availability of staff is paramount, although they may need to immediately shift to alternate roles to best serve the organization.

To facilitate these *temporary* changes in job functions, it is necessary to plan the redeployments in advance to the extent possible and to inform, train, and equip staff to perform alternate duties.

It may also be necessary for staff to report to alternate work sites or work from home during certain events. In those cases, staff should be made aware of the plans for alternate work sites, informed as to where they will receive instructions for reporting to such work sites, and provided with necessary access (logical access for working from home, or access to the alternate work site).

Typical work products

1. Documented strategies and plans for staff redeployment
2. Training plans for redeployment
3. Service continuity plans
4. Credentials for first responders

Subpractices

1. Establish plans for staff redeployment during disruptive events.

    This planning should be conducted in collaboration with the development of the organization's service continuity plans but should focus primarily on the availability of staff and their redeployment.

    Access, equipment, and supplies needed for the redeployment should be sourced as part of the planning process.

Additional actions may have to be taken by the organization to ensure the availability of the staff named in the redeployment plans. *(These considerations are addressed in PM:SG3.SP3.)*

The development of service continuity plans (which may contain information about staff availability and redeployment) is addressed in the Service Continuity process area.

2. Notify staff of the plans for their redeployment during disruptive events.
   Staff should be made aware of and indicate their understanding of the redeployment plans in advance of execution. Staff should also be made aware of how they will receive information and communications prior to an anticipated event or during an event. *(Communications issues are addressed in the Communications process area.)*
3. Provide appropriate training for staff in advance of redeployment.
   Training and skill building required for redeployment may be integrated with training provided for redundancy of vital positions (as outlined in PM:SG3.SP1).
4. Obtain and provide credentials for first responders.
   The availability of vital staff may be impeded if they do not have the credentials they need to perform their roles during a disruptive event. In many cases, it is likely that public (governmental) authorities will restrict access to a region around an event site. The restriction may continue for the duration of investigatory, safety restoration, or environmental cleanup activities. Access to the organization's facilities may be barred for the duration of the closure of the area. If the facility contains high-value assets that require human intervention, then the lack of access can have a serious operational impact.

   To plan for the availability of vital staff in such scenarios, the organization must coordinate in advance with governmental authorities to acquire and maintain credentials for first-responder staff.
5. Review and update plans for staff redeployment during disruptive events as needed.

PM:SG3.SP4 PLAN TO SUPPORT STAFF DURING DISRUPTIVE EVENTS

Plans are developed and implemented to ensure support is provided for staff as they are deployed during a disruptive event.

A key objective during a disruptive event is to ensure the availability of staff. Unfortunately, when disruptive events are significant in size, complexity, and impact, staff are generally focused on their own personal needs (as victims of the event) and are not particularly inclined to take on their job functions or redeployment roles. Thus, the organization must develop the means to provide for and support the basic needs of staff so that they can become available to support the organization's objectives during an event.

This is obviously a complex undertaking: the organization must be adept at bringing resources to bear while being supportive and empathetic to the physiological and psychological situations that staff are faced with—loss of property, injuries, basic sustenance needs, and even loss of life. The success of service continuity planning and plans is dependent upon how well the organization plans and addresses the basic physiological, psychological, and safety needs of staff in these situations—otherwise, service continuity plans will be ineffective because a basic component of these plans will not be available.

Typical work products

1. Support strategy
2. Prioritized areas of support
3. Documented plans to support staff during disruptive events
4. Service continuity plans

Subpractices

1. Establish a strategy for support considerations during disruptive events.

    As part of the organization's overall service continuity planning, considerations for supporting staff during disruptive events should be conducted.

    Event scenarios should be established as the basis for planning. The events should range from specific, local disruptions that impact the organization's work sites to far-reaching, general disruptions that impact the general locale or region around one or more work sites.

2. Identify areas of support that the organization must provide.

> Areas of support may include the following:
> - Financial—It may be necessary to provide emergency financial support to help staff care for themselves or their families.
> - Transportation—Assistance may be needed to transport people to primary or secondary work sites.
> - Accounting for all individuals—Plans should include provisions for accounting for all staff and their location and condition.
> - Payroll—The payroll system should remain in operation throughout the event. Depending on the scale of the event, it may be necessary to assist people with check cashing or other banking issues.
> - Crisis counseling and family support—Provisions should be made for supporting the emotional needs of staff and/or their families.
> - Notifications—Notifications of injuries or fatalities should be planned carefully and performed by higher-level managers where possible.
> - Communications—Provisions should be made for communicating with staff during the event.

3. Develop plans to support staff during disruptive events.

    The plans should consider the actions the organization has to take to provide support in each of the prioritized areas. This may require other resources to be procured or committed (such as the ability to run the payroll system or to obtain services from an outsourcer). As with all types of continuity plans, the organization should document the plan and the resources needed to fulfill the plan and should test the plan on a regular basis to ensure that it is working properly.

4. Assign resources to the plans to support staff during disruptive events.

    As with all types of continuity plans, resources must be available to enact and carry out the support activities that are provided to other staff who will be called upon to perform their job responsibilities or to be redeployed.

    Staff responsible for executing the plans may require additional training to obtain necessary skills and knowledge.

5. Review and update the plans to support staff during disruptive events as needed.

PM:SG3.SP5 PLAN FOR RETURN-TO-WORK CONSIDERATIONS

Plans are developed and implemented to address return-to-work issues for staff after a disruptive event.

The availability of staff to return to work after a disruptive event is paramount to recovery. Unfortunately, there may be psychological and physiological barriers to returning to work that may affect the availability of staff and their productivity. Proactive consideration of these issues will make transition back to the workplace less problematic and may avoid issues related to lack of availability of staff that can ultimately affect operational resilience.

The organization must develop strategies and plans to address transition issues that can occur as the result of significant and catastrophic events so that the effects of the events do not carry over into the organization's attempt to return to business as usual.

Typical work products

1. Documented transition strategies for return to business as usual
2. Contracts with external entities
3. Service continuity plans

Subpractices

1. Establish a strategy for transitioning staff back to the workplace.

    As part of the organization's overall service continuity planning (particularly recovery planning), staff issues that could impede a return to work should be addressed. This may require the organization to perform scenario planning and analysis to determine the types of transition issues that may arise from its unique geographical locations, industry, or workforce.

2. Identify and procure resources that will be needed to ensure effective transition. Resource issues may include the identification of external resources such as crisis counseling and support. It may be appropriate to place such resources under a retainer contract to ensure their availability during an event.
3. Review and revise the plans to address return-to-work considerations after a disruptive event as appropriate.

Elaborated Generic Practices by Goal

Refer to the Generic Goals and Practices document in Appendix A for general guidance that applies to all process areas. This section provides elaborations relative to the application of the Generic Goals and Practices to the People Management process area.

PM:GG1 ACHIEVE SPECIFIC GOALS

The operational resilience management system supports and enables achievement of the specific goals of the People Management process area by transforming identifiable input work products to produce identifiable output work products.

PM:GG1.GP1 PERFORM SPECIFIC PRACTICES

Perform the specific practices of the People Management process area to develop work products and provide services to achieve the specific goals of the process area.

Elaboration:

Specific practices PM:SG1.SP1 through PM:SG3.SP5 are performed to achieve the goals of the people management process.

PM:GG2 INSTITUTIONALIZE A MANAGED PROCESS

People management is institutionalized as a managed process.

PM:GG2.GP1 ESTABLISH PROCESS GOVERNANCE

Establish and maintain governance over the planning and performance of the people management process.

Refer to the Enterprise Focus process area for more information about providing sponsorship and oversight to the people management process.

Subpractices

1. Establish governance over process activities.

   Elaboration:

   > Governance over the people management process may be exhibited by
   > - developing and publicizing higher-level managers' objectives and requirements for the process
   > - establishing a higher-level position, such as the director of human resources or the equivalent, responsible for the resilience of the organization's people
   > - sponsoring and providing oversight of policy, procedures, standards, and guidelines for managing people
   > - providing oversight over the establishment, implementation, and maintenance of the organization's internal control system for managing people
   > - making higher-level managers aware of applicable compliance obligations related to people, and regularly reporting on the organization's satisfaction of these obligations to higher-level managers
   > - sponsoring and funding process activities
   > - providing guidance on identifying, assessing, and managing operational risks related to people, particularly risks associated with the availability of staff to support high-value services
   > - ensuring that vital staff are identified, characterized, and validated, and that the list of vital staff is regularly reviewed and updated
   > - verifying that the process supports strategic resilience objectives and is focused on staff responsible for assets and services that are of the highest relative value in meeting strategic objectives
   > - regular reporting from organizational units to higher-level managers on process activities and results
   > - creating dedicated higher-level management feedback loops on decisions about the process and recommendations for improving the process
   > - conducting regular internal and external audits, and related reporting to appropriate committees on people asset controls and the effectiveness of the process
   > - creating formal programs to measure the effectiveness of process activities, and reporting these measurements to higher-level managers

2. Develop and publish organizational policy for the process.

   > The people management policy should address
   > - responsibility, authority, and ownership for performing process activities
   > - the availability of vital people (managers, service-support and resilience staff, and others) to protect high-value assets and support high-value services during normal operations and during disruptive events

- procedures, standards, and guidelines for
  - the identification, characterization, and prioritization of vital staff
  - managing operational risks to the availability of people
  - sustaining and reassigning vital roles and responsibilities
  - managing the impact of changes to vital staff
  - establishing, implementing, and maintaining an internal control system for people management
  - cross-training and credentialing
  - providing redundancy for vital staff and services, including outsourcing redundancy
  - engaging backup and "on-call" staff
  - succession planning
  - redeploying and supporting staff during disruptive events *(Refer also to the Service Continuity process area.)*
- methods for measuring adherence to policy, exceptions granted, policy violations, and the investigation and discipline process for non-compliance with policy

PM:GG2.GP2 PLAN THE PROCESS

Establish and maintain the plan for performing the people management process.

Elaboration:

A plan for performing the people management process is created to ensure that qualified people are hired and perform in a manner that contributes to the organization's ability to manage operational resilience. The plan must address the resilience requirements of people, the dependencies of services on them, and the roles that people fulfill at various levels of the organization. In addition, because people are the engine behind many business processes in the organization, the plan must extend to external conditions that can enable or adversely affect the availability of people.

The plan for the people management process should not be confused with the organization's service continuity plans *(refer to the Service Continuity process area)*, staff risk mitigation plans (as described in PM:SG2.SP2), strategic plans for providing redundancy for vital staff and services (as described in PM:SG3.SP1), succession and training plans for vital managers (as described in PM:SG3.SP2), plans for staff redeployment (as described in PM:SG3.SP3), plans to support staff during disruptive events (as described in PM:SG3.SP4), and plans to address return-to-work considerations after a disruptive event (as described in PM:SG3.SP5). The plan for the people management process details how the organization will perform the people management process, including the development of strategies and plans for managing people.

Subpractices

1. Define and document the plan for performing the process.

   Elaboration:

   Special consideration in the plan may have to be given to ensure that vital staff are adequately trained for various roles during normal operations and during disruptive events *(refer to the Organizational Training and Awareness process area)*. These activities aid in ensuring that people are available and sustainable to support operational resilience.

   Special consideration in the plan may have to be given to the establishment, implementation, and maintenance of an internal control system for people assets.

2. Define and document the process description.
3. Review the plan with relevant stakeholders and get their agreement.
4. Revise the plan as necessary.

PM:GG2.GP3 PROVIDE RESOURCES

Provide adequate resources for performing the people management process, developing the work products, and providing the services of the process.

   Elaboration:

   All people management practices require that higher-level managers ensure that qualified people are available to meet operational resilience management objectives and requirements. In PM:GG2.GP3, resources are formally identified and assigned to people management process plan elements. The diversity of activities required to ensure the availability of people requires an extensive level of organizational resources and skills and a significant number of external resources. In addition, these activities require a major commitment of financial resources (both expense and capital) from the organization.

Subpractices

1. Staff the process.

   Elaboration:

   > These are examples of staff required to perform the people management process:
   > - staff responsible for
   >   - the identification, characterization, and prioritization of vital staff and managing the impact of changes to vital staff
   >   - business continuity and disaster recovery, including those responsible for redeploying and supporting people assets during disruptive events *(Refer also to the Service Continuity process area.)*

> - cross-training, skill development, and credentialing
> - sustaining and reassigning vital roles and responsibilities
> - succession planning
> - the availability and notification of backup and on-call staff
> - managing external entities that have contractual obligations for people management activities, including cases where staff redundancy has been accomplished via outsourcing
>
> - staff involved in identifying, assessing, and mitigating risks to the availability of people assets
> - external entities responsible for providing qualified staff who fulfill resilience roles and responsibilities
> - internal and external auditors responsible for reporting to appropriate committees on process effectiveness

Refer to the Organizational Training and Awareness process area for information about training staff for resilience roles and responsibilities.

Refer to the Human Resource Management process area for information about acquiring staff to fulfill roles and responsibilities.

2. Fund the process.

Elaboration:

Refer to the Financial Resource Management process area for information about budgeting for, funding, and accounting for people management.

3. Provide necessary tools, techniques, and methods to perform the process.

Elaboration:

> These are examples of tools, techniques, and methods to support the people management process:
> - criteria and checklists for the identification, characterization, and prioritization of vital staff based on their roles and responsibilities
> - traceability matrices or other techniques to reconcile lists of vital staff to service continuity plans
> - methods for performing risk impact valuation
> - methods, techniques, and tools for risk identification, risk analysis, risk categorization and prioritization, risk mitigation, and risk status tracking *(Refer also to the Risk Management process area.)*
> - traceability matrices or other techniques to map designated backup and redundant staff to vital staff
> - training plan templates for specific roles and responsibilities, including staff in backup and redundant roles

- training plan templates in support of succession planning for vital positions
- training plan templates for staff who have to be redeployed during disruptive events
- call-tree structures that are used to enact the communications protocol for backup staff
- checklists that specify criteria for the credentialing of first responders
- service continuity event scenarios
- methods, techniques, and tools for effective communication to all concerned staff and stakeholders during a disruptive event

PM:GG2.GP4 ASSIGN RESPONSIBILITY

Assign responsibility and authority for performing the people management process, developing the work products, and providing the services of the process.

Elaboration:

Of paramount importance in assigning responsibility for the people management process is identifying the vital, high-value people in the organization based on their roles and responsibilities for all operational resilience management processes, as described in ADM:SG1.SP1 and PM:SG1.SP1. Vital people are responsible for ensuring their availability during normal operations as well as during disruptive events. Such availability includes identifying backup and redundant staff to cover vital roles as required.

Refer to the Human Resource Management process area for more information about establishing resilience as a job responsibility, developing resilience performance goals and objectives, and measuring and assessing performance against these goals and objectives.

Refer to the Asset Definition and Management process area for more information about establishing ownership and custodianship of people assets.

Subpractices

1. Assign responsibility and authority for performing the process.

   Elaboration:

   Responsibility and authority may extend not only to staff inside the organization but to those with whom the organization has a contractual agreement for ensuring the availability of people (including outsourcing, contract staff, and preparing for backup, redundancy, and redeployment of people assets).

2. Assign responsibility and authority for performing the specific tasks of the process.

Elaboration:

> Responsibility and authority for performing people management tasks can be formalized by
> - defining roles and responsibilities in the process plan to include roles responsible for identifying vital staff and risks associated with their availability
> - including process tasks and responsibility for these tasks in specific job descriptions
> - developing policy requiring
>   - organizational unit managers, line of business managers, project managers, and asset and service owners and custodians to participate in and derive benefit from the process for assets and services under their ownership or custodianship that require people
>   - people to take personal responsibility for acquiring the necessary skill sets to fulfill their job description and roles in sustaining operational resilience
>   - people to take personal responsibility for ensuring their availability during normal operations, as well as during disruptive events
> - including process tasks in staff performance management goals and objectives, with requisite measurement of progress against these goals
> - developing and implementing contractual instruments (including service level agreements) with external entities to establish responsibility and authority for performing process tasks on outsourced functions
> - including process tasks in measuring performance of external entities against contractual instruments

Refer to the External Dependencies Management process area for additional details about managing relationships with external entities.

3. Confirm that people assigned with responsibility and authority understand it and are willing and able to accept it.

PM:GG2.GP5 TRAIN PEOPLE

Train the people performing or supporting the people management process as needed.

Elaboration:

The basis for determining training needs for operational resilience management derives from having a comprehensive list of vital people, risks to their availability, designated backups, and substitutions and replacements when necessary; ensuring service continuity and redeployment of staff during disruptive events; and being able to implement return-to-work plans after a disruptive event.

Refer to the Organizational Training and Awareness process area for more information about training the people performing or supporting the process.

Refer to the Human Resource Management process area for more information about inventorying skill sets, establishing a skill set baseline, identifying required skill sets, and measuring and addressing skill deficiencies.

Subpractices

1. Identify process skill needs.

   Elaboration:

   > These are examples of skills required in the people management process:
   > - knowledge of tools, techniques, and methods necessary to perform process tasks, including those identified in PM:GG2.GP3 subpractice 3
   > - knowledge necessary to identify vital staff from
   >   - the organization's resilience program and plan
   >   - the inventory of vital staff *(Refer to ADM:SG1.SP1.)*
   >   - compliance obligations
   >   - those called for in service continuity plans
   >   - those called for in resilience job descriptions
   > - knowledge necessary to ensure the availability and redeployment of resilience roles and responsibilities during normal operations and disruptive events, including the identification and readiness of appropriate backup staff, substitutions, and replacements when necessary
   > - knowledge necessary to identify operational risks emerging from the process, including those that should be referred to the risk management process for disposition
   > - knowledge necessary to develop and implement succession plans
   > - knowledge necessary to determine credentialing criteria for first responders
   > - knowledge necessary to evaluate staff availability against resilience goals and objectives, identify improvements, and take corrective actions

2. Identify process skill gaps based on available resources and their current skill levels.
3. Identify training opportunities to address skill gaps.

   Elaboration:

   > These are examples of training topics:
   > - training specifically targeted to owners and custodians of high-value assets and services to ensure they fully understand their roles and responsibilities for operational resilience *(Refer to the Organizational Training and Awareness process area.)*
   > - training specifically targeted to addressing deficiencies of existing staff who are designated as potential backups and replacements for vital staff *(The development of training plans is addressed in the Organizational Training and Awareness process area.)*

> - general awareness training on the role of service continuity in meeting operational resilience goals and objectives, including ensuring the availability of vital staff
> - exercising service continuity scenarios to ensure a high level of preparedness during disruptive events, particularly for vital staff and first responders
> - preparation for credentialing examinations
> - working with external entities that have responsibility for process activities
> - using process methods, tools, and techniques, including those identified in PM:GG2.GP3 subpractice 3

4. Provide training and review the training needs as necessary.

PM:GG2.GP6 MANAGE WORK PRODUCT CONFIGURATIONS

Place designated work products of the people management process under appropriate levels of control.

Elaboration:

All work products related to sensitive staff information, such as information about skill gaps and succession plans, should be placed under an appropriate level of control.

> These are examples of people management work products placed under control:
> - list(s) of vital staff, including designated backups, substitutions, and replacements
> - list of staff risks, including risk statement, impact valuation, categorization, and prioritization, as well as the identification of those responsible for addressing and tracking risks and risk status
> - staff risk mitigation plans
> - training plans
> - plan for providing redundancy for vital staff and high-value services
> - succession plans for vital staff
> - service continuity plans *(Refer also to the Service Continuity process area.)*
> - credentials for first responders
> - plans to support staff during disruptive events
> - transition strategies for return to business as usual after a disruptive event
> - process plan
> - policies and procedures
> - contracts with external entities

PM:GG2.GP7 *IDENTIFY AND INVOLVE RELEVANT STAKEHOLDERS*

Identify and involve the relevant stakeholders of the people management process as planned.

Subpractices

1. Identify process stakeholders and their appropriate involvement.

   Elaboration:

   > These are examples of stakeholders of the people management process:
   > - staff involved in identifying vital staff
   > - owners and custodians of information, technology, and facility assets to which people need access
   > - owners and custodians of high-value services that require the availability of vital staff
   > - staff responsible for managing operational risks, including risks to the availability of people assets
   > - staff responsible for establishing, implementing, and maintaining an internal control system for people assets
   > - staff responsible for developing, testing, implementing, and executing service continuity plans involving people
   > - staff responsible for developing, implementing, and managing organizational training, skill development, and knowledge transfer, particularly for vital staff
   > - staff involved in organizational change management
   > - external entities that are involved in providing redundant staff to ensure uninterrupted service
   > - staff involved in ensuring service continuity
   > - staff involved in succession planning
   > - human resources staff
   > - training staff
   > - public authorities, such as regulatory bodies and oversight agencies responsible for ensuring minimal adverse effects due to the loss of vital higher-level managers
   > - government authorities responsible for establishing criteria for and overseeing the credentialing of first responders
   > - internal and external auditors

   > Stakeholders are involved in various tasks in the people management process, such as
   > - identifying vital staff
   > - planning for the availability of staff
   > - associating staff with services and analyzing service dependencies
   > - developing service continuity and succession plans for job roles
   > - managing operational risks from people
   > - assessing the adequacy of internal controls
   > - training and development of vital staff, including those in designated backup and redundancy roles

- succession planning
- managing external dependencies on people
- overseeing credentialing of first responders
- providing feedback to the organization on resilience job roles and skills
- making commitments to process plans and activities
- reviewing and appraising the effectiveness of process activities
- resolving issues in the process
- interfacing with government and other public authorities

2. Communicate the list of stakeholders to planners and those responsible for process performance.
3. Involve relevant stakeholders in the process as planned.

PM:GG2.GP8 MONITOR AND CONTROL THE PROCESS

Monitor and control the people management process against the plan for performing the process and take appropriate corrective action.

Elaboration:

Refer to the Monitoring process area for more information about the collection, organization, and distribution of data that may be useful for monitoring and controlling processes.

Refer to the Measurement and Analysis process area for more information about establishing process metrics and measurement.

Refer to the Enterprise Focus process area for more information about providing process information to managers, identifying issues, and determining appropriate corrective actions.

Subpractices

1. Measure actual performance against the plan for performing the process.
2. Review accomplishments and results of the process against the plan for performing the process.

   Elaboration:

   These are examples of metrics for the people management process:
   - percentage of vital staff who do not have redundancy plans
   - percentage of vital managers who do not have succession plans
   - cost, schedule, and effort required to address training gaps for vital staff and those designated to serve as backups and replacements

- schedule for collecting and reviewing measures of policy compliance
- statistics for vital staff available (on hand) to conduct service continuity planned exercises and tests
- results from service continuity exercises and tests that reflect the availability (or not) of vital staff and their designees
- percentage of first responders who do not have appropriate credentials
- number of reports to public authorities regarding the loss of a vital higher-level manager
- number of people availability risks referred to the risk management process; number of risks where corrective action is still pending (by risk rank)
- level of adherence to process policies; number of policy violations; number of policy exceptions requested and number approved
- number of process activities that are on track per plan
- rate of change of resource needs to support the process
- rate of change of costs to support the process

3. Review activities, status, and results of the process with the immediate level of managers responsible for the process and identify issues.

Elaboration:

People management reviews are likely to concentrate on the availability of vital staff, including succession planning and coverage during disruptive events, as well as normal operations of high-value services and assets. An additional area of concentration is the internal control system for people assets.

Periodic reviews of the people management process are needed to ensure that
- vital staff are identified, characterized, and prioritized and backup, redundancy, and succession plans are in place
- staff affected by redeployment plans are informed, trained, and equipped to perform alternate duties
- the process has been exercised and tested in preparation for disruptive events and other service continuity activities
- actions requiring management involvement are elevated in a timely manner
- process issues are referred to the risk management process when necessary
- the performance of process activities is being monitored and regularly reported
- key measures are within acceptable ranges as demonstrated in governance dashboards or scorecards and financial reports
- administrative, technical, and physical controls are operating as intended
- controls are meeting the stated intent of the resilience requirements
- actions requiring management involvement are elevated in a timely manner
- actions resulting from internal and external audits are being closed in a timely manner

4. Identify and evaluate the effects of significant deviations from the plan for performing the process.
5. Identify problems in the plan for performing and executing the process.
6. Take corrective action when requirements and objectives are not being satisfied, when issues are identified, or when progress differs significantly from the plan for performing the process.

Elaboration:

For people assets, corrective action may require the revision of existing administrative, technical, and physical controls, development and implementation of new controls, or a change in the type of controls (preventive, detective, corrective, compensating, etc.).

7. Track corrective action to closure.

PM:GG2.GP9 OBJECTIVELY EVALUATE ADHERENCE

Objectively evaluate adherence of the people management process against its process description, standards, and procedures, and address non-compliance.

Elaboration:

These are examples of activities to be reviewed:
- assigning responsibility, accountability, and authority for people management process activities
- determining the adequacy of process reports and reviews in informing decision makers regarding the performance of operational resilience management activities and the need to take corrective action, if any
- validating the lists of vital staff based on changes in the operational and organizational environment
- validating people asset risk management plans as compared to existing strategies for protecting and sustaining people
- verifying the internal control system for people assets

These are examples of work products to be reviewed:
- process plan and policies
- list(s) of vital staff
- risks to the availability of people assets, in particular vital staff and risk mitigation plans, as well as issues that have been referred to the risk management process
- process methods, techniques, and tools
- contracts with external entities
- metrics for the process *(Refer to PM:GG2.GP9 subpractice 2.)*

PM:GG2.GP10 Review Status with Higher-Level Managers

Review the activities, status, and results of the people management process with higher-level managers and resolve issues.

Refer to the Enterprise Focus process area for more information about providing sponsorship and oversight to the operational resilience management system.

PM:GG3 Institutionalize a Defined Process

People management is institutionalized as a defined process.

PM:GG3.GP1 Establish a Defined Process

Establish and maintain the description of a defined people management process.

Establishing and tailoring process assets, including standard processes, are addressed in the Organizational Process Definition process area.

Establishing process needs and objectives and selecting, improving, and deploying process assets, including standard processes, are addressed in the Organizational Process Focus process area.

Subpractices

1. Select from the organization's set of standard processes those processes that cover the people management process and best meet the needs of the organizational unit or line of business.
2. Establish the defined process by tailoring the selected processes according to the organization's tailoring guidelines.
3. Ensure that the organization's process objectives are appropriately addressed in the defined process, and ensure that process governance extends to the tailored processes.
4. Document the defined process and the records of the tailoring.
5. Revise the description of the defined process as necessary.

PM:GG3.GP2 Collect Improvement Information

Collect people management work products, measures, measurement results, and improvement information derived from planning and performing the process to support future use and improvement of the organization's processes and process assets.

Elaboration:

> These are examples of improvement work products and information:
> - the availability status of vital people assets with respect to backup, substitution, replacement, redeployment, and succession planning
> - reports on the effectiveness and weaknesses of controls
> - process action plans and strategies that are not being satisfied and the risks associated with them
> - the disposition of process risks that have been referred to the risk management process
> - changes and trends in operating conditions, risk conditions, and the risk environment that affect people assets, as well as the results of the process
> - lessons learned in post-event review of continuity exercises, incidents, and disruptions in continuity, including lack of people available to fulfill roles and responsibilities
> - process lessons learned that can be applied to improve operational resilience management performance
> - resilience requirements that are not being satisfied or are being exceeded

Establishing the measurement repository and process asset library is addressed in the Organizational Process Definition process area. Updating the measurement repository and process asset library as part of process improvement and deployment is addressed in the Organizational Process Focus process area.

Subpractices

1. Store process and work product measures in the organization's measurement repository.
2. Submit documentation for inclusion in the organization's process asset library.
3. Document lessons learned from the process for inclusion in the organization's process asset library.
4. Propose improvements to the organizational process assets.

RISK MANAGEMENT
Enterprise

Purpose

The purpose of Risk Management is to identify, analyze, and mitigate risks to organizational assets that could adversely affect the operation and delivery of services.

Introductory Notes

Risk management is a basic and essential organizational capability. The organization must identify, analyze, and mitigate risk commensurate with its risk tolerances and appetite to ensure that it prevents potential disruptions that could interfere with its ability to meet its mission. At a tactical level, to accomplish this goal, the organization must control operational risk—the risk that results from operating services and associated assets on a day-to-day basis. Operational risk encompasses the potential impact that could result from

- failed internal processes
- inadvertent or deliberate actions of people
- problems with systems or technology
- external events

Managing operational risk significantly influences operational resilience. The risk of disruption to any asset potentially renders associated services unable to meet their mission, hence reducing operational resilience. The organization must identify this risk, analyze it, and determine the extent to which it could affect operations. Mitigating such risk requires a careful balance between strategies for protecting and sustaining assets and services while considering the cost of these strategies and the value of the assets and services to the organization.

The Risk Management process area establishes the organization's responsibility to develop and implement an operational risk management plan and program that comprehensively and cooperatively cover the high-value assets and services of the organization. The organization explicitly establishes its risk tolerances and appetite based on its strategic drivers, market position, competitive environment, financial position, and other factors. With this appetite as a guide, risks to the assets of the organization are periodically identified, analyzed, and categorized, and mitigation strategies are developed and implemented for those risks that the organization cannot afford to ignore. The impact of risk is considered and measured against the organization's risk evaluation criteria. Most important, the information gathered in risk assessment can be used to improve the effectiveness of strategies to protect and sustain assets and services.

All uses of "risk" in Risk Management refer to operational risk, specifically, risk to the operation and delivery of services. Other risk categories are beyond the scope of this process area.

Related Process Areas

The identification of vulnerabilities that may pose risk to the organization is performed in the Vulnerability Analysis and Resolution process area.

The development and implementation of control strategies to mitigate risk are performed in the Controls Management process area.

The development, testing, and implementation of service continuity plans to address the consequences of realized risk are performed in the Service Continuity process area.

Summary of Specific Goals and Practices

RISK:SG1 Prepare for Risk Management
    RISK:SG1.SP1   Determine Risk Sources and Categories
    RISK:SG1.SP2   Establish an Operational Risk Management Strategy

RISK:SG2 Establish Risk Parameters and Focus
    RISK:SG2.SP1   Define Risk Parameters
    RISK:SG2.SP2   Establish Risk Measurement Criteria

RISK:SG3 Identify Risk
    RISK:SG3.SP1   Identify Asset-Level Risks
    RISK:SG3.SP2   Identify Service-Level Risks

RISK:SG4 Analyze Risk
    RISK:SG4.SP1   Evaluate Risk
    RISK:SG4.SP2   Categorize and Prioritize Risk
    RISK:SG4.SP3   Assign Risk Disposition

RISK:SG5 Mitigate and Control Risk
    RISK:SG5.SP1   Develop Risk Mitigation Plans
    RISK:SG5.SP2   Implement Risk Strategies

RISK:SG6 Use Risk Information to Manage Resilience
    RISK:SG6.SP1   Review and Adjust Strategies to Protect Assets and Services
    RISK:SG6.SP2   Review and Adjust Strategies to Sustain Services

Specific Practices by Goal

RISK:SG1 PREPARE FOR RISK MANAGEMENT

Preparation for risk management is performed.

Preparation for operational risk management requires the organization to develop and maintain a strategy for identifying, analyzing, and mitigating operational risks. This strategy is documented in a risk management plan and addresses the activities that the organization performs enterprise-wide to carry out a continuous risk management program. This includes identifying the sources and types of operational risk and establishing a strategy that details the organization's approach, activities, and objectives for managing these risks as a fundamental operational resilience management process.

RISK:SG1.SP1 DETERMINE RISK SOURCES AND CATEGORIES

The sources of risk to assets and services are identified and the categories of risk that are relevant to the organization are determined.

Identifying risk sources helps the organization to determine and categorize the types of operational risk that are most likely to affect day-to-day operations and to seed an organization-specific risk taxonomy that can be used as a tool for managing risk on a continuous basis as operating conditions change and evolve. The sources of risk can be both internal and external to the organization.

Categorizing operational risks provides the organization a means by which to perform advanced analysis and mitigation activities that allow for similar types of risks to be effectively neutralized or contained by limited actions by the organization.

Typical work products

1. Operational risk sources list
2. Operational risk categories list
3. Operational risk taxonomy

Subpractices

1. Determine operational risk sources.
    Risk sources are the fundamental areas of risk that can affect organizational services and associated assets while they are in operation to meet the organization's mission. Risk sources represent common areas where risks may originate. Typical internal and external sources include
    - poorly designed and executed business processes and services
    - inadvertent actions of people, such as accidental disclosures or modifications of information

- intentional actions of people, such as insider threat and fraud
- failure of systems to perform as intended, or risks posed by the complexity and unpredictability of interconnected systems
- failures of technology, such as the unanticipated results of the execution of software and the failure of hardware components such as servers and telecommunications
- external events and forces, such as natural disasters, failures of public infrastructure, and failures in the organization's supply chain

Advance definition of specific risk sources for the organization provides a means for early identification of risk and can seed mitigation plans that can cover a broad array of operational risks before the organization realizes the consequences of these risks.

2. Determine operational risk categories.

    Risk categories provide a means for collecting and organizing risk for ease of analysis and mitigation. Typical operational risk categories align with the various sources of operational risk such as failed processes, actions of people, systems and technology, and external events but can be as granular as necessary for the organization to effectively manage risk. Operational risks may also align with the types of assets they are most likely to affect—risks to the availability of people, the confidentiality, integrity, and availability of information, etc.

3. Create an operational risk taxonomy.

    An organization-specific risk taxonomy is a way to collect and catalog common operational risks that the organization is subject to and must manage. The risk taxonomy is a means for communicating these risks and for developing organizational unit and line-of-business–specific mitigation actions if operational assets and services are affected by them.

RISK:SG1.SP2 ESTABLISH AN OPERATIONAL RISK MANAGEMENT STRATEGY

A strategy for managing operational risk relative to strategic objectives is established and maintained.

Because of the pervasive nature of operational risk, a comprehensive operational risk management strategy is needed to ensure proper consideration of risk and the effects on operational resilience. The strategy provides a common foundation for the performance of operational risk management activities (which are typically dispersed throughout the organization) and for the collection, coordination, and elevation of operational risk to the organization's enterprise risk management process.

Typical items addressed in an operational risk management strategy include

- the scope of operational risk management activities
- the methods to be used for operational risk identification, analysis, mitigation, monitoring, and communication
- the sources of operational risk
- how the sources of operational risk should be organized, categorized, compared, and consolidated

- parameters for measuring and taking action on operational risks
- risk mitigation techniques to be used, such as the development of layered administrative, technical, and physical controls and the development of service continuity plans
- definition of risk measures to monitor the status of the operational risks
- time intervals for risk monitoring and reassessment
- staff involved in operational risk management and the extent of their involvement in the activities noted above

The operational risk management strategy should be developed to facilitate the accumulation of operational risks as input to the organization's enterprise risk management strategy and program. The strategy should be documented and communicated to all relevant stakeholders, internal and external, that are responsible for any operational risk management activity.

Typical work products

1. Operational risk management strategy

Subpractices

1. Develop and document an operational risk management strategy that aligns with the organization's overall enterprise risk management strategy.
2. Communicate the operational risk management strategy to relevant stakeholders and obtain their commitment to the activities.

RISK:SG2 ESTABLISH RISK PARAMETERS AND FOCUS

Risk tolerances are identified and documented and the focus of risk management activities is established.

Risk parameters help the organization to establish a foundation for consistent risk consideration and measurement. Risk parameters reflect the organization's stated risk tolerances and appetite and ensure that there is consistent measurement of operational risk across the organization. They provide common and consistent criteria for comparing risks and for characterizing the severity of consequences to the organization if risk is realized. This facilitates the organization's process for prioritizing risk and for developing mitigation strategies.

RISK:SG2.SP1 DEFINE RISK PARAMETERS

The organization's risk parameters are defined.

Risk parameters provide the organization a means for consistent measurement of operational risk across the organization. The establishment of risk tolerance thresholds, in particular, reflects the organization's level of risk adversity by providing levels of acceptable risk in each operational risk category that the organization establishes. Risk parameters also establish the organization's philosophy on risk management—how risks will be controlled, who is authorized to accept risk on behalf of the organization, and how often and to what degree operational risk should be assessed.

Typical work products

1. Operational risk thresholds
2. Risk management requirements

Subpractices

1. Define risk thresholds for each risk category.
   Risk thresholds are a management tool to determine when risk is in control or has exceeded acceptable organizational limits. They must be set for each category of operational risk that the organization establishes as a means for measuring and managing risk. For example, a risk threshold for virus intrusions may be whenever more than 200 users are affected; this would indicate that management needs to act to prevent operational disruption.
2. Establish risk management parameters.

RISK:SG2.SP2 ESTABLISH RISK MEASUREMENT CRITERIA

Criteria for measuring the organizational impact of realized risk are established.

A specific type of risk parameter that requires the organization's attention is risk measurement criteria. Risk measurement criteria are objective criteria that the organization uses for evaluating, categorizing, and prioritizing operational risks. Without these criteria, the organization would have a difficult time consistently gauging the potential effect that an operational risk could have on one or more important impact areas for the organization.

Typical work products

1. Organizational impact areas
2. Risk measurement criteria

Subpractices

1. Define organizational impact areas.
   Organizational impact areas identify the categories where realized risk may have meaningful and disruptive consequences. These areas typify what is important to the organization and to the accomplishment of its mission.

> These are examples of organizational impact areas:
> - reputation and customer confidence
> - financial health and stability
> - staff productivity
> - safety and health of staff and customers
> - fines and legal penalties
> - compliance with regulations

2. Prioritize impact areas for the organization.

    The prioritization of impact areas allows the organization to determine the relative importance of these areas to allow them to be used for risk prioritization and mitigation.

3. Define and document risk measurement and evaluation criteria.

    Risk measurement and evaluation criteria provide the bounds on the severity of consequences to the organization across the organizationally defined impact areas. The consistent application of these criteria across all operational risks ensures that risks are prioritized according to organizational importance (even if they are specific to an organizational unit or line of business) and are mitigated accordingly. The range of criteria can be either qualitative (high, medium, low) or quantitative (based on levels of loss, fines, number of customers lost, etc.).

4. Define and document risk likelihood.

    While risk probability may be difficult to establish for operational risks, the organization should establish parameters for risk probability that are used to further guide risk prioritization and mitigation. These parameters can be qualitative (high, medium, or low) or quantitative (based on experience where available).

RISK:SG3 IDENTIFY RISK

Operational risks are identified.

The level and extent of operational risks to which the organization is subjected directly affect the organization's operational resilience. A key activity in managing and controlling operational resilience is the identification of operational risk and the mitigation of this risk before the organization is subjected to the consequences of realized risk.

RISK:SG3.SP1 IDENTIFY ASSET-LEVEL RISKS

Operational risks that affect assets that support services are identified.

Operational risks that can affect assets such as people, information, technology, and facilities must be identified and mitigated in order to actively manage the operational resilience of these assets and, more important, the services to which these assets are connected.

Risk identification is a foundational risk management activity. It requires the organization to identify and assess the types and extent of threats, vulnerabilities, and disruptive events that can pose risk to the operational capacity of assets and services. It is not an attempt to identify all operational risks, but only those that have meaning in the context of the categories of risk and the risk parameters established by the organization. Identified risks form a baseline from which a continuous risk management process can be established and managed.

There are many techniques that can be used to identify risk, such as

- using questionnaires and surveys
- interviewing vital managers and subject matter experts
- review of process controls
- using tools, techniques, and methodologies, such as information security risk assessments
- performing internal audits and performance reviews
- performing business impact analysis
- performing scenario planning and analysis
- using risk taxonomies for similar organizations and industries
- using lessons-learned databases, such as the incident knowledgebase
- reviewing vulnerability catalogs, such as the US-CERT Vulnerability Notes Database and MITRE's Common Vulnerabilities and Exposures (CVE) project

The identification of vulnerabilities that may pose risk to the organization is performed in the Vulnerability Analysis and Resolution process area. The activities performed in this process area can be used as a source for seeding a list of operational risks.

Typical work products

1. Organizational risk identification toolkit
2. List of operational risks, by asset category

Subpractices

1. Identify the tools, techniques, and methods that the organization can use to identify operational risks to organizational assets.
    Ensure that these tools, techniques, and methods are accessible to staff and that appropriate training is available.
2. Identify the operational risks (at the asset level) that can negatively impact high-value organizational services.

3. Develop risk statements.
    Develop risk statements that clearly articulate the context, conditions, and consequences of the risk.

> Risk statements should include information about
> - the asset affected (people, information, technology, or facilities)
> - a weakness or vulnerability of the asset that could be exploited
> - actors who would exploit the weakness
> - the means that an actor would use
> - the motive of the actor
> - the undesired outcome
> - resilience requirements that would be affected by the risk
> - the likelihood (if known) of the risk being realized
> - the consequences to the organization of the undesired outcome
> - the severity of the consequences (as measured by applying risk measurement criteria)

Consequences resulting from realized risk should be described relative to the impact areas that the organization defined as part of defining risk measurement criteria. (For example, consequences should be articulated in terms of how the organization's reputation is affected, or if any fines and legal penalties result.)

4. Identify the relevant stakeholders associated with each documented risk.

RISK:SG3.SP2 IDENTIFY SERVICE-LEVEL RISKS

Operational risks that potentially affect services as a result of asset risk are identified.

The disruption of asset productivity due to operational risk affects the ability of associated services to meet their mission. Thus, risks associated with organizational assets must be examined in the context of these services to determine if there is a potential impact on mission assurance, which in turn could affect the organization's ability to meet its mission. Examining risk in the context of services provides the organization additional information that must be considered when prioritizing risks for disposition and mitigation.

The identification of high-value services is performed in the Enterprise Focus process area. The association of services to their associated assets is performed in the Asset Definition and Management process area. Relevant practices in these process areas must be performed before operational risks can be examined in a service context.

Typical work products

1. Updated risk statements, with service context and consequences
2. List of operational risks, by service

Subpractices

1. Identify the services that are associated with each asset-specific risk statement. Update the risk statement to reflect associated services.
2. Determine the effect on the service that could result from the realization of risk at the asset level.
3. Update risk statement information to reflect service-specific consequences and the severity of the consequences due to realized risk.

RISK:SG4 ANALYZE RISK

Risks are analyzed to determine priority and importance.

Risk analysis is performed by the organization to determine the relative importance of each identified operational risk and is used to facilitate the organization's risk disposition and mitigation activities. Risk analysis helps the organization to place identified risks in the context of the organization's risk drivers (tolerances, appetite, and measurement criteria), which further facilitates mitigation planning.

RISK:SG4.SP1 EVALUATE RISK

Risks are evaluated against risk tolerances and criteria, and the potential impact of risk is characterized.

To determine the extent of the operational risk, the consequences of the risk must be evaluated using the organization's risk measurement criteria. Not all risks are the same for all organizations; what might be a major concern for one organization might be minor for another for many reasons, such as financial solvency, market position, cash reserves, and industry. Using the organization's risk measurement criteria for valuation ensures that the risks that are most important to the organization's unique operating circumstances are prioritized higher than those that do not directly impact organizational drivers.

Typical work products

1. Updated risk statements with impact valuation

Subpractices

1. Evaluate the identified risks using the defined risk parameters and risk measurement criteria.
    Each risk is evaluated and assigned values in accordance with the defined risk parameters and risk measurement criteria. (These include likelihood, consequence, consequence severity, and thresholds.) The organization may weight the valuation of the risks by adjusting for the priority of impact areas (reputation, finance, etc.) that it established as part of the risk measurement criteria. This will ensure that impact areas of most importance to the organization will influence more strongly

which risks are prioritized higher for mitigation. The organization can further influence the prioritization by applying a probability factor, if known.

2. Assign a valuation to each risk statement.
The valuation can be qualitative (high, medium, or low) or can be a quantitative relative risk score that combines likelihood, impact area weighting, and consequence value. The valuation assigned to the risk statement will be used as a factor in deciding what to do with the risk.

RISK:SG4.SP2 CATEGORIZE AND PRIORITIZE RISK

Risks are categorized and prioritized relative to risk parameters, and risks that have to be mitigated are identified.

Categorizing operational risks can aid significantly in helping the organization to prioritize these risks for disposition and mitigation. This allows the organization to view risks according to their source, taxonomy, or other commonality, which may provide insight into disposition strategies at an aggregate level. It can also facilitate further analysis and effectively streamline the risk mitigation process, resulting in more effective mitigation strategies that cover a range of potential risks.

Typical work products

1. List of risks, with categorization and prioritization

Subpractices

1. Categorize and group risks according to the defined risk categories.
Risks are categorized into defined risk categories or other forms of categorization. This may result in merging similar risk statements or eliminating risk statements. Related risks are identified and grouped for efficient handling, and the cause-and-effect relationship between related risks is identified.

2. Prioritize risks for disposition and mitigation.
A relative priority is determined for each risk statement (or merged risk statements) based on the assigned risk valuation. The intent of prioritization is to determine the risks that most need attention because of their potential to affect operational resilience.

RISK:SG4.SP3 ASSIGN RISK DISPOSITION

The disposition of each identified risk is documented and approved.

An important part of risk management is to determine a strategy for each identified risk and to implement actions to carry out the strategy. Strategy development begins with assigning a risk disposition to each risk, that is, a statement of the organization's intention for addressing the risk.

Risk dispositions can vary widely across organizations but typically include

- risk avoidance—altering operations to avoid the risk while still providing the essential service
- risk acceptance—acknowledgment of the risk but consciously not taking any action (in essence, accepting the potential consequences of the risk)
- risk monitoring—performing further research and deferring action on the risk until the need to address the risk is apparent
- risk transfer—assigning the risk to a willing and able entity
- risk control and mitigation—taking active steps to minimize the risk

Because risk can rarely be eliminated, the organization must actively seek to monitor the disposition of known risks to ensure that risk conditions do not warrant changes in the assigned disposition.

Typical work products

1. List of risks, with risk dispositions
2. List of risks prioritized for mitigation

Subpractices

1. Assign a risk disposition to each risk statement based on risk valuation and prioritization.

    A risk disposition is assigned to each risk statement or group of statements. The organization must establish a range of acceptable and consistent risk dispositions and their definitions.

    > Possible risk dispositions include
    > - avoid
    > - accept
    > - monitor
    > - research or defer
    > - transfer
    > - mitigate or control

    Risks that are to be accepted must be approved by a sufficient level of organizational management that accepts responsibility and authority for the potential impact on operational resilience that could result. For risks that are to be transferred, there must be a clear and willing organization or person able to accept the risk. Risks that are to be researched or deferred must be carefully examined to ensure that delaying mitigation will not result in the realization of the risk or effects on operational resilience.

2. Obtain approval for the proposed disposition of each risk, particularly risks that are not going to be mitigated.

3. Develop a strategy to carry out the proposed risk disposition.
4. Monitor the risk and the risk strategy on a regular basis to ensure that the risk does not pose additional threat to the organization.
    Continuous risk management requires that the organization periodically review identified risks to ensure that they have been minimized or that changes in the risk environment do not warrant changes in the risk disposition.
5. Develop a strategy for risks that the organization decides to mitigate.
    The development of risk mitigation plans is performed in RISK:SG5.

RISK:SG5 MITIGATE AND CONTROL RISK

Risks to assets and services are mitigated and controlled to prevent disruption of operational resilience.

Risk mitigation involves the development of strategies that seek to minimize the risk to an acceptable level. This includes actions to

- reduce the likelihood (probability) of the vulnerability or threat and resulting risk
- minimize exposure to the vulnerability or threat from which the risk arises
- develop service continuity plans that would keep an asset or service in production if affected by realized risk
- develop recovery and restoration plans to address the consequences of realized risk

An organization may mitigate risks through any combination of these actions depending on the affected assets and services, their value to the organization, and the cost of the mitigation strategies versus the value of the assets and services. Mitigation may also involve revisiting resilience requirements, improving controls, and improving strategies to sustain assets and services.

Risk mitigation requires the organization to perform two distinct actions: (1) develop risk mitigation plans and (2) implement and monitor these plans for effectiveness.

The development of protection strategies through the selection and implementation of controls is performed in the Controls Management process area. The development and implementation of service continuity plans are performed in the Service Continuity process area.

RISK:SG5.SP1 DEVELOP RISK MITIGATION PLANS

Risk mitigation plans are developed.

When the consequences of risk exceed the organization's risk thresholds and are determined to be unacceptable, the organization must act to mitigate risk to the extent possible.

Risk mitigation requires the development of risk mitigation plans that may include a wide range of activities. In some cases, risk mitigation will simply require adjustments to current strategies for protecting and sustaining assets and services. In other cases, the organization will find itself designing and implementing new controls and developing and implementing new service continuity plans. The result of risk assessment can be very costly risk mitigation plans and activities, so the organization must consider these costs in the plan development. In addition, because not all risk can be mitigated, the organization must be able to address residual risk—the risk that remains and is accepted by the organization after mitigation plans are implemented. This risk must be analyzed and determined to be acceptable before the risk mitigation plan is in place.

Typical work products

1. Risk mitigation plans
2. List of those responsible for addressing and tracking risk

Subpractices

1. Develop risk mitigation plans for all risks that have a "mitigation" or "control" disposition.

    Developing risk mitigation plans is an extensive activity that will vary by organization. There are some common elements of risk mitigation plans that should be considered for all plans:
    - how the threat or vulnerability will be reduced
    - the actions that will prevent or limit an actor from exploiting a threat or vulnerability
    - the controls that will have to be implemented or updated to reduce exposure, including an articulation of administrative, physical, and technical controls
    - the service continuity plans that would be used to reduce the impact of consequences should risk be realized
    - the staff who are responsible for implementing and monitoring the mitigation plan
    - the cost of the plan, and a cost-benefit analysis that demonstrates the value of the plan commensurate with the value of the related assets and services or avoidance of consequences
    - the implementation specifics of the plan (when, where, how)
    - the residual risk that would not be addressed by the plan

2. Validate the risk mitigation plans by comparing them to existing strategies to protect and sustain assets and services.

    The risk mitigation plans should be validated against the current controls in place to protect assets and services and the service continuity plans available to manage the consequences of risk. Any gaps should be reflected in the plan. *(Improving controls and strategies to sustain services as a result of risk management activities is addressed in RISK:SG6.)*

3. Identify the person or group responsible for each risk mitigation plan and ensure they have the authority to act and the proper level of skills and training to implement and monitor the plan.

4. Address residual risk.

   Residual risk must be specifically accepted, deferred, or transferred. Otherwise, it must be considered as a risk that must be mitigated, requiring reconsideration of the risk mitigation plan.

RISK:SG5.SP2 IMPLEMENT RISK STRATEGIES

Risk strategies and mitigation plans are implemented and monitored.

Effective management and control of risk require the organization to monitor risk and the status of risk strategies. Because the operational environment is constantly changing, risks identified and addressed may have to be revisited, and a new disposition and strategy may have to be developed.

The risk management strategy defines the intervals at which the status of risk strategies must be revisited. This may align with the organization's regular intervals of risk identification, or it may be an activity that is performed independently of risk identification.

The implementation of risk strategies requires the monitoring of risks according to their disposition and the implementation and monitoring of risk mitigation plans.

Typical work products

1. Risk mitigation plans
2. Updated list of risks, with current status

Subpractices

1. Monitor risk status.

   The disposition of risks that are not being mitigated must be periodically assessed and revised as necessary. Some risks may, under future circumstances, require the development of a mitigation plan.
2. Provide a method for tracking open risks to closure.
3. Implement the risk mitigation plans and provide a method to monitor the effectiveness of these plans.
4. Provide continued commitment of resources for each plan to allow successful execution of the risk management activities.
5. Collect performance measures on the risk management process.

RISK:SG6 USE RISK INFORMATION TO MANAGE RESILIENCE

Information gathered from identifying, analyzing, and mitigating risk is used to improve the operational resilience management system.

Because of the direct effect of risk management on operational resilience, continuous risk management processes can be a force in improving and sustaining operational resilience. What is learned in risk identification, assessment, and mitigation directly affects existing strategies for protecting and sustaining assets and services, which can benefit from the risk management process.

To use risk information to manage operational resilience, the organization must directly use risk information as input to validating the effectiveness of current protection and sustainment strategies and to improve these strategies based on an understanding of risk.

RISK:SG6.SP1 Review and Adjust Strategies to Protect Assets and Services

Controls implemented to protect assets and services from risk are evaluated and updated as required based on risk information.

The controls that an organization uses to protect assets and services from operational risk are typically based on resilience requirements. However, considerations of risk as identified in the risk management process can result in improvements and enhancements to the internal control system that cannot be envisioned through translation of resilience requirements into an internal control system. Thus, improving and sustaining the organization's operational resilience is also dependent upon using the lessons learned in risk management to improve controls by implementing missing controls and updating existing controls to consider new and emerging risks.

Typical work products

1. Controls list (of controls that have to be fixed, revised, or developed)
2. Control revision plan

Subpractices

1. Compare risk mitigation plans to existing internal control systems for affected assets and services.
   Comparing risk mitigation plans to existing internal control systems may help the organization to identify controls that are not working properly, controls that have to be updated or revised, and missing controls.
2. Revise existing controls or develop and implement additional controls that are necessary to mitigate risks.

RISK:SG6.SP2 Review and Adjust Strategies to Sustain Services

Service continuity plans are developed to ensure services are sustained and plans are evaluated and updated as required based on risk information.

Just as the controls structure can be improved to prevent risk realization, the organization's ability to sustain assets and services in light of realized risk can be improved through what is learned in the risk management cycle. This can result in the identification of inadequate plans, plans that have to be revised or updated, or missing plans. Validating plans through identified risks also provides another means to ensure plan effectiveness in covering a range of possible threats and operational risks.

Typical work products

1. Service continuity plan list (of plans that have to be fixed, revised, or developed)
2. Service continuity plan revision plan

Subpractices

1. Compare risk mitigation plans to existing service continuity plans for affected assets and services.
   Comparing risk mitigation plans to existing plans will identify plans that may be inadequate, in need of updating and revision, or missing.
2. Revise existing service continuity plans or develop and implement additional plans that are necessary to mitigate risks.

Elaborated Generic Practices by Goal

Refer to the Generic Goals and Practices document in Appendix A for general guidance that applies to all process areas. This section provides elaborations relative to the application of the Generic Goals and Practices to the Risk Management process area.

RISK:GG1 ACHIEVE SPECIFIC GOALS

The operational resilience management system supports and enables achievement of the goals of the Risk Management process area by transforming identifiable input work products to produce identifiable output work products.

RISK:GG1.GP1 PERFORM SPECIFIC PRACTICES

Perform the specific practices of the Risk Management process area to develop work products and provide services to achieve the specific goals of the process area.

> Elaboration:
>
> Specific practices RISK:SG1.SP1 through RISK:SG6.SP2 are performed to achieve the goals of the risk management process.

RISK:GG2 INSTITUTIONALIZE A MANAGED PROCESS

Risk management is institutionalized as a managed process.

RISK:GG2.GP1 ESTABLISH PROCESS GOVERNANCE

Establish and maintain governance over the planning and performance of the risk management process.

Refer to the Enterprise Focus process area for more information about providing sponsorship and oversight to the risk management process.

Subpractices

1. Establish governance over process activities.

   Elaboration:

   > Governance over the risk management processes may be exhibited by
   > - developing and publicizing higher-level managers' objectives and requirements for the process
   > - establishing a higher-level risk officer position to provide direct oversight of the process and to interface with higher-level managers
   > - sponsoring and providing oversight of process policies, procedures, standards, and guidelines, including establishing risk tolerances, thresholds, and evaluation criteria
   > - sponsoring and providing oversight of the organization's risk management program, plans, and strategies, including the process plan
   > - sponsoring and funding process activities
   > - ensuring that high-priority risks referred to the process from other operational resilience processes are addressed in a timely manner
   > - regular reporting from organizational units to higher-level managers on process activities and results
   > - implementing a risk management steering committee
   > - making higher-level managers aware of applicable compliance obligations related to managing risk, and regularly reporting on the organization's satisfaction of these obligations to higher-level managers
   > - verifying that the process supports strategic resilience objectives and is focused on assets and services that are of the highest relative value in meeting strategic objectives
   > - creating dedicated higher-level management feedback loops on decisions about the process and recommendations for improving the process
   > - conducting regular internal and external audits, and related reporting to appropriate committees on process effectiveness
   > - creating formal programs to measure the effectiveness of process activities, and reporting these measurements to higher-level managers

2. Develop and publish organizational policy for the process.

   Elaboration:

   > The risk management policy should address
   > - responsibility, authority, and ownership for performing process activities
   > - procedures, standards, and guidelines for
   >   - identifying risk sources and categories of risk
   >   - defining risk parameters (such as risk tolerance thresholds) and risk measurement criteria
   >   - assigning risk priorities based on risk valuation
   >   - assigning risk dispositions
   >   - developing risk mitigation plans
   > - periodically monitoring the status of all risks and adjusting as necessary
   > - methods for measuring adherence to policy, exceptions granted, and policy violations

RISK:GG2.GP2 PLAN THE PROCESS

Establish and maintain the plan for performing the risk management process.

Elaboration:

The plan for the risk management process should be directly influenced by the strategic and operational planning processes of the organization and reflect strategic objectives and initiatives where appropriate.

The plan for the risk management process should not be confused with a risk management plan or plans for mitigating risk as described in RISK:SG5.SP1. The plan for the risk management process details how the organization will perform risk management, including the development of risk management and mitigation plans.

Subpractices

1. Define and document the plan for performing the process.

   Elaboration:

   Special consideration in the plan may have to be given to the adequacy of the internal control system for information, technology, facility, and people assets and the services they support.

2. Define and document the process description.
3. Review the plan with relevant stakeholders and get their agreement.
4. Revise the plan as necessary.

RISK:GG2.GP3 PROVIDE RESOURCES

Provide adequate resources for performing the risk management process, developing the work products, and providing the services of the process.

Subpractices

1. Staff the process.

   Elaboration:

   It should be noted that this generic goal related to risk management refers to staffing the risk management process plan, not the individual risk management mitigation plans. *(Assigning resources to risk management mitigation plans is described in RISK:SG5.SP2.)*

   > These are examples of staff required to perform the risk management process. Such people may include organizational unit managers, line of business managers, project managers, and asset and service owners and custodians.
   > - the chief risk officer or equivalent
   > - a risk management steering council, group, or process group
   > - staff responsible for
   >   - identifying operational risk sources and categories
   >   - identifying and assessing operational risks, including risks identified by the process and other resilience management processes
   >   - business impact analysis
   >   - scenario planning and analysis
   >   - assigning risk disposition to risk statements based on risk valuation and prioritization
   >   - developing risk mitigation plans and implementing these plans, including accepting, deferring, or transferring residual risk
   >   - monitoring and tracking risks to closure
   >   - managing external entities that have contractual obligations for risk management activities
   > - higher-level managers responsible for defining risk parameters, including risk tolerance thresholds, authorization for levels of risk acceptance, organizational impact areas and priorities, and risk measurement criteria
   > - staff skilled in interview techniques and the use of questionnaires and surveys
   > - vital managers and subject matter experts
   > - external entities involved in process activities and in assessing risk on outsourced functions
   > - internal and external auditors responsible for reporting to appropriate committees on process effectiveness

Refer to the Organizational Training and Awareness process area for information about training staff for resilience roles and responsibilities.

Refer to the Human Resource Management process area for information about acquiring staff to fulfill roles and responsibilities.

2. Fund the process.

    Refer to the Financial Resource Management process area for information about budgeting for, funding, and accounting for risk management.

3. Provide necessary tools, techniques, and methods to perform the process.

    Elaboration:

    > These are examples of tools, techniques, and methods to support the risk management process:
    > - methods and tools for determining, documenting, and communicating risk sources, categories, parameters, and measurement criteria
    > - methods for operational risk identification, analysis, mitigation, monitoring, and communication with respect to identified assets and services *(Techniques for risk identification are described in RISK:SG3.SP1.)*
    > - techniques for risk assessment, including interview techniques, questionnaires, and surveys
    > - methods, techniques, and tools for business impact analysis
    > - tools for scenario planning and analysis
    > - tools for developing risk mitigation plans
    > - templates for documenting risk mitigation plans
    > - methods for tracking open risks to closure
    > - methods for keeping stakeholders apprised of the current status of open risks
    > - methods for monitoring the effectiveness of risk mitigation plans
    > - tools, techniques, and methods for version control of risk mitigation plans

RISK:GG2.GP4 ASSIGN RESPONSIBILITY

Assign responsibility and authority for performing the risk management process, developing the work products, and providing the services of the process.

Elaboration:

RISK:SG4.SP3 describes the level of management responsibility and authority required based on risk disposition but does not directly address responsibility and authority for carrying out the risk management process plan.

Refer to the Human Resource Management process area for more information about establishing resilience as a job responsibility, developing resilience performance goals and objectives, and measuring and assessing performance against these goals and objectives.

Subpractices

1. Assign responsibility and authority for performing the process.

   Elaboration:

   Organizations may establish a risk officer, a risk management group, or a risk management process group to take responsibility for the overall risk management process. This group may also formally interface with higher-level managers for the purposes of reporting on organizational progress against risk management process goals as part of the governance process.

2. Assign responsibility and authority for performing the specific tasks of the process.

   Elaboration:

   > Responsibility and authority for performing risk management tasks can be formalized by
   > - defining roles and responsibilities in the process plan to include roles responsible for addressing and tracking risk
   > - including process tasks and responsibility for these tasks in specific job descriptions, particularly for those staff who own high-value organizational assets
   > - developing policy requiring organizational unit managers, line of business managers, project managers, and asset and service owners and custodians to participate in and derive benefit from the process for assets and services under their ownership or custodianship
   > - including process activities in staff performance management goals and objectives, with requisite measurement of progress against these goals
   > - developing and implementing contractual instruments (including service level agreements) with external entities to establish responsibility and authority for performing process tasks on outsourced functions
   > - including process tasks in measuring performance of external entities against contractual instruments

   Refer to the External Dependencies Management process area for additional details about managing relationships with external entities.

3. Confirm that people assigned with responsibility and authority understand it and are willing and able to accept it.

RISK:GG2.GP5 TRAIN PEOPLE

Train the people performing or supporting the risk management process as needed.

Refer to the Organizational Training and Awareness process area for more information about training the people performing or supporting the process.

Refer to the Human Resource Management process area for more information about inventorying skill sets, establishing a skill set baseline, identifying required skill sets, and measuring and addressing skill deficiencies.

Subpractices

1. Identify process skill needs.

   Elaboration:

   > These are examples of skills required in the risk management process:
   > - knowledge of tools, techniques, and methods that can be used to identify, analyze, mitigate, and monitor operational risks to organizational assets and services, including those identified in RISK:GG2.GP3 subpractice 3
   > - knowledge necessary to develop, implement, and monitor risk mitigation plans
   > - knowledge necessary to collect, coordinate, and elevate operational risks to the organization's enterprise risk management process
   > - strong communication skills for conveying the operational risk management strategy, identified risks, and mitigation plans to higher-level managers and key stakeholders so as to obtain their commitment

2. Identify process skill gaps based on available resources and their current skill levels.
3. Identify training opportunities to address skill gaps.

   Elaboration:

   Certification training is an effective way to improve risk management skills and attain competency. While operational risk management certifications are not widespread, GIAC (Global Information Assurance Certification) does offer a Certified Project Manager Certification that includes risk management of IT projects and application development. The Information Systems Examination Board (ISEB) of the British Computer Society offers a Practitioner Certificate in Information Risk Management.

   > These are examples of training topics:
   > - risk management concepts and activities (e.g., risk identification, evaluation, monitoring, and mitigation)
   > - selection of protection strategies and measures for mitigating risk
   > - establishing risk tolerance, threshold, and evaluation criteria
   > - developing risk management strategy
   > - establishing and managing a continuous process
   > - using process tools and techniques
   > - working with external entities that have responsibility for process activities and for assessing risk on outsourced functions
   > - using process methods, tools, and techniques, including those identified in RISK:GG2.GP3 subpractice 3

4. Provide training and review the training needs as necessary.

RISK:GG2.GP6 MANAGE WORK PRODUCT CONFIGURATIONS

Place designated work products of the risk management process under appropriate levels of control.

Elaboration:

> These are examples of risk management work products placed under control:
> - operational risk source list, risk categories list, and taxonomy
> - operational risk management plan and strategy
> - operational risk parameters and measurement criteria
> - list of operational risks by asset category and service with prioritization, risk disposition, mitigations, and current status
> - risk statements with impact valuation
> - risk mitigation plans
> - process plan
> - policies and procedures
> - contracts with external entities

RISK:GG2.GP7 IDENTIFY AND INVOLVE RELEVANT STAKEHOLDERS

Identify and involve the relevant stakeholders of the risk management process as planned.

Elaboration:

Several RISK-specific practices address the involvement of stakeholders in the risk management process. For example, RISK:SG1.SP2 addresses the communication of the operational risk management strategy to relevant stakeholders. RISK:SG3.SP1 calls for identifying relevant stakeholders associated with each documented risk.

Subpractices

1. Identify process stakeholders and their appropriate involvement.

   Elaboration:

   > These are examples of stakeholders of the risk management process:
   > - organizational unit managers, line of business managers, project managers, and business process owners
   > - owners of identified assets and services (for which plans to manage risks must be developed)
   > - custodians of identified assets and services (who may need to execute or participate in plans)

- staff involved in identifying, analyzing, mitigating, and controlling risks to assets and services (such as information technology, human resources, legal, and compliance staff)
- staff involved in reviewing and adjusting strategies to protect and sustain assets and services
- the owner of any resilience management process who has referred risks to the process
- risk owners
- risk mitigation plan owners

Stakeholders are involved in various tasks in the risk management process, such as
- planning for the process
- making decisions about the process
- making commitments to process plans and activities
- communicating process plans and activities
- coordinating process activities
- developing process parameters
- identifying risk
- analyzing risk (particularly where technical expertise is required), including assessing the adequacy of the internal control system
- developing and implementing risk mitigation plans
- reviewing and appraising the effectiveness of process activities
- establishing requirements for the process
- resolving issues in the process

2. Communicate the list of stakeholders to planners and those responsible for process performance.
3. Involve relevant stakeholders in the process as planned.

RISK:GG2.GP8 MONITOR AND CONTROL THE PROCESS

Monitor and control the risk management process against the plan for performing the process and take appropriate corrective action.

Refer to the Monitoring process area for more information about the collection, organization, and distribution of data that may be useful for monitoring and controlling processes.

Refer to the Measurement and Analysis process area for more information about establishing process metrics and measurement.

Refer to the Enterprise Focus process area for more information about providing process information to managers, identifying issues, and determining appropriate corrective actions.

Subpractices

1. Measure actual performance against the plan for performing the process.
2. Review accomplishments and results of the process against the plan for performing the process.

Elaboration:

> These are examples of metrics for the risk management process:
> - percentage of identified assets and services for which some form of risk assessment has been performed and documented as required by policy
> - percentage of identified assets and services for which the impact or cost of compromise *(refer to RISK:SG2.SP2)* has been quantified
> - percentage of identified risks that do not have a defined risk disposition
> - percentage of identified risks that have a defined mitigation plan against which status is reported in accordance with policy
> - percentage of identified risks that have not been tracked to closure
> - change in volume of risks that have been identified over a selected period
> - percentage of previously identified risks that have converted to a risk disposition of "mitigate"
> - percentage of identified assets for which a mitigation plan has been implemented to mitigate risks as necessary and to maintain these risks within acceptable risk parameters and risk measurement criteria
> - percentage of identified services for which a mitigation plan has been implemented to mitigate risks as necessary and to maintain these risks within acceptable risk parameters and risk measurement criteria
> - percentage of security incidents that caused damage, compromise, or loss to identified assets or services beyond established risk parameters and risk measurement criteria
> - percentage of realized risks that have exceeded established risk thresholds
> - percentage of identified or realized risks that have been characterized as "high" impact according to the organization's risk evaluation criteria
> - level of adherence to process policies; number of policy violations; number of policy exceptions requested and number approved
> - number of process activities that are on track per plan
> - rate of change of resource needs to support the process
> - rate of change of costs to support the process

3. Review activities, status, and results of the process with the immediate level of managers responsible for the process and identify issues.

Elaboration:

Reviews of the risk management process may result from periodic examination or post-event audits that seek to identify problems that must be corrected.

Elevating the results of these examinations to managers provides an opportunity to correct risk management process deficiencies and to make managers aware of variations in the risk management process that not only have localized impact but may also affect the organization's resilience as a whole.

> Periodic reviews of the risk management process are needed to ensure that
> - actions requiring management involvement are elevated in a timely manner
> - the performance of process activities is being monitored and regularly reported
> - key measures are within acceptable ranges as demonstrated in governance dashboards or scorecards and financial reports
> - administrative, technical, and physical controls are operating as intended to protect assets and services from risk
> - actions requiring management involvement are elevated in a timely manner
> - actions resulting from internal and external audits are being closed in a timely manner
> - work products accurately reflect what is essential for managing operational risk to ensure mission success, or are corrected or modified if necessary

4. Identify and evaluate the effects of significant deviations from the plan for performing the process.

   Elaboration:

   Deviations from the risk management plan may occur because operational risks for assets and services vary widely, and thus the mitigation of these risks may require process deviations. The organization must determine if the deviations are appropriate given the risk parameters and whether the deviation will result in an impact on operational resilience.

   In addition, deviations from the risk management plan may occur when organizational units fail to follow the enterprise-sponsored process. These deviations may affect the operational resilience of the organizational unit's services but may also have a cascading effect on enterprise operational resilience objectives.

5. Identify problems in the plan for performing the process and in the execution of the process.
6. Take corrective action when requirements and objectives are not being satisfied, when issues are identified, or when progress differs significantly from the plan for performing the process.
7. Track corrective action to closure.

RISK:GG2.GP9 OBJECTIVELY EVALUATE ADHERENCE

Objectively evaluate adherence of the risk management process against its process description, standards, and procedures, and address non-compliance.

Elaboration:

> These are examples of activities to be reviewed:
> - risk planning, including establishing tolerances, thresholds, and other parameters
> - risk assessment, including risk identification, analysis, and prioritization
> - risk mitigation planning
> - risk monitoring
> - use of risk-based information for improving strategies for protecting and sustaining assets and services
> - assignment of responsibility, accountability, and authority for process activities
> - determining the adequacy of process reports and reviews in informing decision makers regarding the performance of operational resilience management activities and the need to take corrective action, if any

> These are examples of work products to be reviewed:
> - process plan and policies
> - risk management plans and risk mitigation plans
> - operational risk sources, risk categories, and risk taxonomy
> - operational risk management strategy
> - risk parameters, impact areas, and measurement criteria
> - operational risks by asset category and service
> - risk statements
> - risk dispositions and priorities
> - risk owners (those responsible for each risk with the authority to act)
> - list of controls necessary to mitigate risks
> - process methods, techniques, and tools
> - metrics for the process *(Refer to RISK:GG2.GP9 subpractice 2.)*
> - contracts with external entities

RISK:GG2.GP10 REVIEW STATUS WITH HIGHER-LEVEL MANAGERS

Review the activities, status, and results of the risk management process with higher-level managers and resolve issues.

Refer to the Enterprise Focus process area for more information about providing sponsorship and oversight to the operational resilience management system.

RISK:GG3 INSTITUTIONALIZE AS A DEFINED PROCESS

Risk management is institutionalized as a defined process.

RISK:GG3.GP1 Establish a Defined Process

Establish and maintain the description of a defined risk management process.

Establishing and tailoring process assets, including standard processes, are addressed in the Organizational Process Definition process area.

Establishing process needs and objectives and selecting, improving, and deploying process assets, including standard processes, are addressed in the Organizational Process Focus process area.

Subpractices

1. Select from the organization's set of standard processes those processes that cover the risk management process and best meet the needs of the organizational unit or line of business.
2. Establish the defined process by tailoring the selected processes according to the organization's tailoring guidelines.
3. Ensure that the organization's process objectives are appropriately addressed in the defined process, and ensure that process governance extends to the tailored processes.
4. Document the defined process and the records of the tailoring.
5. Revise the description of the defined process as necessary.

RISK:GG3.GP2 Collect Improvement Information

Collect risk management work products, measures, measurement results, and improvement information derived from planning and performing the process to support future use and improvement of the organization's processes and process assets.

Elaboration:

> These are examples of improvement work products and information:
> - metrics and measurements of the viability of the process *(Refer to RISK:GG2.GP8 subpractice 2.)*
> - changes and trends in operating conditions that affect risk sources and categories
> - changes in risk conditions and the risk environment that affect risk parameters, measurement criteria, or risk dispositions
> - lessons learned in post-event review of continuity exercises, incidents, and disruptions in continuity, particularly those that result in losses or compromises that exceed risk parameters and measurement criteria
> - process lessons learned that can be applied to improve operational resilience management performance and internal controls
> - issues with the risk identification, analysis, prioritization, overall assessment, mitigation, and monitoring processes
> - lessons learned from both successfully and unsuccessfully mitigating identified risks
> - risk mitigation plan costs and benefits for future return on investment analysis
> - resilience requirements that are not being satisfied or are being exceeded

Establishing the measurement repository and process asset library is addressed in the Organizational Process Definition process area. Updating the measurement repository and process asset library as part of process improvement and deployment is addressed in the Organizational Process Focus process area.

Subpractices

1. Store process and work product measures in the organization's measurement repository.
2. Submit documentation for inclusion in the organization's process asset library.
3. Document lessons learned from the process for inclusion in the organization's process asset library.
4. Propose improvements to the organizational process assets.

RESILIENCE REQUIREMENTS DEVELOPMENT
Engineering

Purpose

The purpose of Resilience Requirements Development is to identify, document, and analyze the operational resilience requirements for high-value services and related assets.

Introductory Notes

An operational resilience requirement is a constraint that the organization places on the productive capability of a high-value asset to ensure that it remains viable and can be sustained when charged into production to support a high-value service. In practice, operational resilience requirements are a derivation of the traditionally described security objectives of confidentiality, integrity, and availability. Well known as descriptive properties or quality attributes of information assets, these objectives are also extensible to other types of assets—people, technology, and facilities—with which operational resilience management is concerned.

Resilience requirements provide the foundation for protecting assets from threats and sustaining them to the extent practical and possible so that they can perform as intended in support of services. In essence, resilience requirements become a part of an asset's DNA (just like its definition, owner, and value) that transcends departmental and organizational boundaries because the requirements stay with the asset regardless of where it is deployed or operated.

Requirements drive engineering-based processes, such as operational resilience management. In operational resilience management, the Resilience Requirements Development process area requires the organization to establish resilience requirements at the enterprise, service, and asset levels. Resilience requirements also drive or influence operational resilience management process areas. For example, resilience requirements form the basis for developing controls and strategies for protecting assets (Controls Management) and for developing service continuity plans for services and assets (Service Continuity).

The importance of requirements to the operational resilience management system cannot be overstated. Resilience requirements embody the strategic objectives, risk appetite, critical success factors, and operational constraints of the organization. They represent the alignment factor that ties practice-level activities performed in security and business continuity to what must be accomplished at the service and asset level in order to move the organization toward fulfilling its mission.

Depending on the organization, three types of operational resilience requirements may be elicited: enterprise, service, and asset.

- **Enterprise**—Enterprise operational resilience requirements reflect enterprise-level needs, expectations, and constraints. These requirements affect nearly all aspects of an organization's operations. Laws and regulations are examples of this type of requirement because they broadly affect the business in which an organization operates and must be met by all organizational functions and activities. A specific example of an enterprise requirement is "all health-related information that is covered by HIPAA regulations must be kept confidential to health workers and patients."
- **Service**—Service requirements establish the resilience needs of a service in pursuit of its mission. But because the capability of a service to meet its mission is directly related to the resilience of the assets that support the service, service requirements must reflect and be congruent with the operational resilience requirements of supporting assets. Service requirements tend to concentrate on the service's availability and recoverability, but these quality attributes can be directly affected by failure to meet the confidentiality, integrity, and availability requirements of people, information, technology, and facilities.
- **Asset**—Asset-specific requirements are set by the owners of the asset and are intended to establish the needs for protecting and sustaining an asset with respect to its role in supporting mission assurance of a service. In practice, asset-specific resilience requirements generally reflect the security objectives of confidentiality and integrity and the continuity requirement of availability. It must be considered that assets also may have conflicting requirements, particularly when they are deployed in supporting more than one service (e.g., a network server may support more than service). This conflict must be resolved to ensure that all services that are dependent on the asset are provided the necessary level of resilience to meet their mission.

The applicability of a specific type of resilience requirement varies depending on the asset type, as shown in Table RRD.1.

TABLE RRD.1 Extension of Resilience Requirements to All Types of Resilience Assets

Resilience Requirement	Asset Type			
	People	Information	Technology	Facilities
Confidentiality	—	x	—	—
Integrity	—	x	x	x
Availability	x	x	x	x

There are many ways in which an organization can elicit resilience requirements. Strategic planning efforts may establish enterprise-level requirements, as would direct interviewing of vital organizational managers. Service-level requirements may be established by owners of the service (e.g., an organizational unit or a line of business). Asset-level requirements may be established through regular security risk assessment and business impact analysis activities and through directly interviewing the owners of the assets, who understand their importance to services and are responsible for their productivity and resilience.

All resilience requirements must be analyzed for conflicts and interdependencies and must be validated against and support the accomplishment of enterprise-level organizational drivers (goals, objectives, and critical success factors). Otherwise, the protection and continuity strategies developed and implemented for assets and services will not align with what the organization needs to accomplish in order to remain viable.

The development of resilience requirements typically includes the following activities:

- identifying organizational drivers and preparing these work products so that they can be used as the foundation for setting resilience requirements
- developing and communicating enterprise-level requirements
- developing and communicating service- and asset-level requirements
- regularly analyzing the requirements to ensure alignment with current organizational drivers, to identify conflicts between enterprise- and asset-level requirements, and to satisfy operational constraints
- validating the requirements against organizational drivers and operational constraints

The Resilience Requirements Development process area has three specific goals:

1. The Identify Enterprise Requirements goal addresses the development of enterprise-level requirements that potentially affect all services and assets.

2. The Develop Service Requirements goal addresses the development of service-level requirements through the identification of asset requirements and the assignment of enterprise requirements to services.
3. The Analyze and Validate Requirements goal addresses the analysis of service-level requirements to ensure that they support strategic drivers and the resolution of conflicting requirements.

The goals of the Resilience Requirements Development process area are supported and managed long term by achievement of the goals in the Resilience Requirements Management process area.

Related Process Areas

The identification of high-value assets and the assignment of resilience requirements to assets and services are performed in the Asset Definition and Management process area.

The identification of high-value services is performed in the Enterprise Focus process area.

The identification and prioritization of risks to high-value services and supporting assets is performed in the Risk Management process area.

Resilience requirements are managed in the Resilience Requirements Management process area.

Summary of Specific Goals and Practices

RRD:SG1 Identify Enterprise Requirements
    RRD:SG1.SP1   Establish Enterprise Resilience Requirements
RRD:SG2 Develop Service Requirements
    RRD:SG2.SP1   Establish Asset Resilience Requirements
    RRD:SG2.SP2   Assign Enterprise Resilience Requirements to Services
RRD:SG3 Analyze and Validate Requirements
    RRD:SG3.SP1   Establish a Definition of Required Functionality
    RRD:SG3.SP2   Analyze Resilience Requirements
    RRD:SG3.SP3   Validate Resilience Requirements

Specific Practices by Goal

RRD:SG1 IDENTIFY ENTERPRISE REQUIREMENTS

The organization's enterprise-level resilience requirements are identified and established.

Enterprise-level operational resilience requirements are derived from identified organizational needs. At a strategic level, they establish the requirements that the enterprise imposes on all functions and activities in the organization, as well as externally imposed requirements.

RRD:SG1.SP1 ESTABLISH ENTERPRISE RESILIENCE REQUIREMENTS

The resilience requirements of the enterprise are established.

Enterprise-level resilience requirements directly reflect strategic drivers and compliance obligations. They establish the requirements that the enterprise imposes on all its functions and activities. This includes any external requirements that the enterprise inherits from its core business affiliations and competitive environment. Regulatory requirements are a common example of external requirements.

Enterprise-level requirements may also be derived from the results of enterprise risk identification activities such as security risk assessments and business impact analyses.

Sources of enterprise requirements include
- strategic objectives that must be supported and promoted by all organizational functions
- laws and regulations to which the enterprise is subject because of its geographical location or type of business, for example:
  - confidentiality and privacy regulations such as those included in HIPAA or GLBA
  - local laws that restrict disclosure or modification of information, as well as security breach notification
- business affiliations that may impose standards and restrictions for the good of all organizations in the business, for example, availability regulations that may be imposed on all organizations whose operations are tightly connected, such as financial institutions and telecommunications service providers
- organizational policies that attempt to enforce and reinforce acceptable behaviors across the enterprise, such as keeping payroll data confidential
- agreements with external entities that may impose additional constraints on the enterprise

---

Compliance obligations that may result in or form the basis for enterprise requirements are identified and managed in the Compliance process area.

Strategic objectives and critical success factors that may result in or form the basis for enterprise requirements are identified and managed in the Enterprise Focus process area.

Typical work products

1. Enterprise requirements list (derived from strategic objectives, laws, regulations, and policies)

Subpractices

1. Identify the legal, statutory, regulatory, and contractual requirements that an organization and all of its external entities (such as business partners, contractors, and service providers) are required to satisfy.

2. Identify business-specific constraints.
3. Identify the principles, objectives, and business requirements for processing, storing, and transmitting information that an organization has developed to support its operations.
4. Identify organizational strategic objectives, critical success factors, policies, or other indicators of importance that could result in enterprise requirements.
5. Develop and communicate a list of enterprise requirements that affect all organizational units and lines of business.

RRD:SG2 DEVELOP SERVICE REQUIREMENTS

The resilience requirements for services are developed and established based on the service mission and the requirements of supporting assets.

The needs of the organization are satisfied by consistent and efficient performance of services. These services depend on the contributions and support of assets to meet their missions. Thus, the resilience of these assets is paramount to mission assurance.

> Assets for which resilience requirements are typically developed include
> - people (to control and monitor the services)
> - information assets (to be used as input to and output from the processes)
> - technology assets (on which the services are dependent to accomplish their missions)
> - facilities (in which the other assets are located in order to execute the services to completion)

Owners of services are typically the best sources for developing service-level resilience requirements. However, these requirements are essentially derived from a consideration of the requirements of associated assets. Thus, the assets associated with a service must first be identified, then the contribution of the assets to achieving the service's mission must be determined, and finally the specific requirements of the assets must be identified. The link between service requirements and the requirements of associated assets is explicit and iterative. Thus, this process requires service owners to work with asset owners (if they are different) to develop requirements that reflect the service's needs at the asset level.

RRD:SG2.SP1 ESTABLISH ASSET RESILIENCE REQUIREMENTS

The resilience requirements of assets as they relate to the services they support are established.

The needs of the organization and the protection and continuity requirements of services are translated into asset-level resilience requirements. In practical application, this requires three distinct activities:

- identification of high-value services (High-value services are those on which the success of the organization's mission is dependent.)
- identification and association of assets to organizationally high-value services (Mission assurance of services relies on the consistent and effective productivity of related assets—people, technology, information, and facilities. The needs of the service in meeting its mission guide the development of asset-level resilience requirements.)
- development of asset-level requirements based on the asset's deployment in, contributions to, and support of associated services

Because of the association between services and assets, the resilience requirements of a service are essentially represented by the collective resilience requirements of associated assets.

Typical work products

1. List of organizationally high-value services
2. Services map (that details relationships between a service, associated business processes, and associated assets)
3. List of asset-specific resilience requirements (for each asset associated with an organizationally high-value service)

Subpractices

1. Interview asset owners to determine specific asset-level requirements.
2. Perform information security risk assessment (*refer to the Risk Management process area*) and/or business impact analysis to identify risks that must be reflected in asset requirements.
3. Document confidentiality, integrity, and availability requirements for each service-related asset.

    The identification and prioritization of services that are vital for meeting the organization's mission are performed in the Enterprise Focus process area.

    The identification of assets and the association of these assets to the services that they support are performed in the Asset Definition and Management process area.

RRD:SG2.SP2 ASSIGN ENTERPRISE RESILIENCE REQUIREMENTS TO SERVICES

Enterprise requirements that affect services are assigned to the services.

The collective set of resilience requirements for a service is not complete until enterprise requirements have been assigned to the service and its associated assets. In some cases, this will cause conflict because an enterprise requirement may be more stringent than a requirement that has already been set for an asset based on its association with a service. For example, an information asset may have no confidentiality requirement based on how it is used in supporting a service, but because it is health-related information, it might be subject to confidentiality and privacy regulations that impose constraints. Thus, the association of enterprise requirements to service and asset requirements may alter these requirements.

Typical work products

1. List of enterprise requirements (that are relevant to a service)
2. List of revised asset-specific resilience requirements

Subpractices

1. Identify enterprise-level requirements that are applicable to each service and associated asset.
2. Assign enterprise-level requirements to services and associated assets.

RRD:SG3 ANALYZE AND VALIDATE REQUIREMENTS

The resilience requirements for services are analyzed and validated.

Requirements must be analyzed and validated to ensure that they are aimed at providing the level of resilience that assets need to fulfill their roles in support of a service. The requirements are analyzed by first establishing a baseline understanding of the necessary functionality of an asset and then by determining whether the requirements meet enterprise resilience requirements, standards, regulatory factors, contracts with external entities, etc. The requirements are also analyzed to determine whether there are additional organizational constraints that must be considered before requirements are established. Finally, asset-level requirements are given a careful examination to ensure that they adequately specify what is needed to protect and sustain an asset commensurate with the contribution of the asset to accomplishing a service mission. Conflicts that arise through analysis and validation are identified and addressed.

RRD:SG3.SP1 ESTABLISH A DEFINITION OF REQUIRED FUNCTIONALITY

A definition of the required functionality of assets in the context of the services they support is established and maintained.

The expected behaviors of assets as they are associated with services are established to provide a baseline against which asset-level resilience requirements can be analyzed and validated. This provides a foundation for establishing that the requirements are properly aligned with organizational drivers and that they will provide the appropriate level of resilience when translated into protective controls and service continuity plans.

The required functionality of an asset in the context of a service may be included as part of the asset's description as produced in the Asset Definition and Management process area.

Typical work products

1. Asset functionality description

Subpractices

1. Document the asset functionality description for each asset that is associated with one or more services.
   Because the asset may be associated with one or more services, include in the baseline documentation all of the services with which the asset is associated and the required level of asset functionality in *each* instance.

RRD:SG3.SP2 ANALYZE RESILIENCE REQUIREMENTS

The requirements of assets are analyzed to identify conflicts, interdependencies, and shared requirements.

The analysis of asset resilience requirements is performed for two basic reasons: to identify conflicts between the requirements and the required functionality of the asset based on its association with a service, and to identify conflicts that arise because the asset is vital to more than one service requiring differing levels of resilience. This often occurs with information, technology, and facility assets that are shared by more than one service, such as a vendor database, a network server, or a data center facility.

The analysis process is also intended to identify requirements that cannot be met or that are incongruent with the baseline functionality of the asset.

Typical work products

1. Requirements conflicts
2. Conflict mitigation action plans
3. Revised asset-level requirements

Subpractices

1. Analyze asset requirements against baseline asset functionality and identify conflicts. Make adjustments to requirements as necessary.
   Because the asset may be associated with one or more services, be sure to identify conflicts that arise as a result. Resolve each conflict by revising requirements to fit the functionality of the asset for all instances in which it supports a service.
2. Develop conflict mitigation action plans to resolve requirements deficiencies and conflicts that result from analysis and validation activities.
3. Analyze asset requirements against enterprise requirements that have been assigned to services. Revise asset requirements to reflect enterprise requirements where necessary.

RRD:SG3.SP3 VALIDATE RESILIENCE REQUIREMENTS

Asset-level resilience requirements are validated to ensure they adequately specify what is needed to protect and sustain an asset commensurate with its value.

Asset-level requirements are objectively validated (qualitatively) to ensure that they support the required functionality of assets and their associated services. Any risks to protecting and sustaining assets that are introduced by requirements are identified and addressed. A review of the alignment between requirements and the organization's strategic drivers is performed and any missing or inadequate requirements are identified, reassessed, updated, and analyzed.

Typical work products

1. Requirements gaps
2. Revised asset requirements

Subpractices

1. Perform affinity analysis between strategic drivers (such as critical success factors) and asset requirements.
2. Carefully analyze requirements to ensure that they adequately specify what is needed to protect and sustain an asset relative to its association with a service.
3. Identify requirements gaps.
4. Revise requirements as necessary.

Elaborated Generic Practices by Goal

Refer to the Generic Goals and Practices document in Appendix A for general guidance that applies to all process areas. This section provides elaborations relative to the application of the Generic Goals and Practices to the Resilience Requirements Development process area.

RRD:GG1 ACHIEVE SPECIFIC GOALS

The operational resilience management system supports and enables achievement of the specific goals of the Resilience Requirements Development process area by transforming identifiable input work products to produce identifiable output work products.

RRD:GG1.GP1 PERFORM SPECIFIC PRACTICES

Perform the specific practices of the Resilience Requirements Development process area to develop work products and provide services to achieve the specific goals of the process area.

Elaboration:

Specific practices RRD:SG1.SP1 through RRD:SG3.SP3 are performed to achieve the goals of the resilience requirements development process.

RRD:GG2 INSTITUTIONALIZE A MANAGED PROCESS

Resilience requirements development is institutionalized as a managed process.

RRD:GG2.GP1 ESTABLISH PROCESS GOVERNANCE

Establish and maintain governance over the planning and performance of the resilience requirements development process.

Refer to the Enterprise Focus process area for more information about providing sponsorship and oversight to the resilience requirements development process.

Subpractices

1. Establish governance over process activities.

   Elaboration:

   > Governance over the resilience requirements development process may be exhibited by
   > - developing and publicizing higher-level managers' objectives for the development of asset resilience requirements
   > - sponsoring and providing oversight of policy, procedures, standards, and guidelines for effective and sufficient resilience requirements development
   > - making higher-level managers aware of applicable compliance obligations related to developing resilience requirements, and regularly reporting on the organization's satisfaction of these obligations to higher-level managers
   > - sponsoring and funding the development and regular validation of resilience requirements
   > - providing guidance and assigning priorities to assets (relative to strategic objectives) that must satisfy resilience requirements
   > - sponsoring regular audits and reviews to validate requirements
   > - sponsoring regular audits and reviews to ensure requirements form the basis for activities to protect and sustain assets
   > - identifying gaps in requirements and sponsoring actions to close the gaps
   > - verifying that the process supports strategic resilience objectives and is focused on the assets and services that are of the highest relative value in meeting strategic objectives
   > - reporting regularly from organizational units to higher-level managers on process activities and results
   > - creating dedicated higher-level management feedback loops on decisions regarding the development of resilience requirements and recommendations for improving the process
   > - conducting regular internal and external audits and related reporting to appropriate committees on the effectiveness of the process
   > - creating formal programs to measure the effectiveness of process activities, and reporting these measurements to higher-level managers

2. Develop and publish organizational policy for the process.

   Elaboration:

   > The resilience requirements development policy should address
   > - responsibility, authority, and ownership for developing requirements (particularly for assets) and for all process activities
   > - responsibility and authority for determining the adequacy and completeness of requirements
   > - procedures, standards, and guidelines for
   >   - documenting requirements and relevant information
   >   - distributing requirements to relevant custodians (those who must implement the requirements relative to assets in their care or possession)
   > - validating requirements relative to strategies for protecting and sustaining assets commensurate with the value of the assets and the services with which they are associated
   > - methods for measuring adherence to policy, exceptions granted, and policy violations

RRD:GG2.GP2 PLAN THE PROCESS

Establish and maintain the plan for performing the resilience requirements development process.

Elaboration:

The plan for the process of resilience requirements development should enable large-scale (either at the enterprise or organizational unit level) development of resilience requirements by owners of organizational assets (particularly information, technology, and facilities assets). The plan should also allow for the distribution of these requirements to custodians who are responsible for implementing strategies to meet the requirements for protecting and sustaining assets in their care or possession. The plan must support both internal staff involved in the process (typically asset owners) as well as external entities (which may include custodians).

Subpractices

1. Define and document the plan for performing the process.

   Elaboration:

   The services to which assets are associated have to be considered to provide insight into the level and extent of resilience requirements necessary. Thus, the plan should take into consideration the plan for establishing and prioritizing organizational services and associating them with assets.

Refer to the Enterprise Focus process area for information about identifying organizational services and associating them with organizational assets.

2. Define and document the process description.
3. Review the plan with relevant stakeholders and get their agreement.
4. Revise the plan as necessary.

RRD:GG2.GP3 PROVIDE RESOURCES

Provide adequate resources for performing the resilience requirements development process, developing the work products, and providing the services of the process.

Subpractices

1. Staff the process.

   Elaboration:

   The diversity of asset types (people, information, technology, and facilities) requires that staff assigned to the resilience requirements development process have appropriate knowledge of all assets that need to fulfill resilience requirements and the services with which they are associated.

   > These are examples of staff required to perform the resilience requirements development process:
   > - staff responsible for identifying enterprise operational resilience requirements such as laws, regulations, and other compliance obligations
   > - service owners to identify service resilience needs such as availability and recoverability
   > - asset owners and custodians to identify needs for protecting and sustaining assets
   > - business continuity and disaster recovery staff
   > - IT operations and service delivery staff
   > - physical security staff
   > - staff skilled in eliciting requirements across domains, functions, assets, and services
   > - staff responsible for identifying the relationships between a service, associated business processes, and associated assets
   > - staff responsible for resolving requirements conflicts
   > - staff responsible for managing the process plan and for ensuring that the plan is aligned with stakeholder requirements and needs
   > - external entities responsible for protecting and sustaining assets
   > - staff responsible for managing external entities that have contractual obligations for meeting resilience requirements
   > - internal and external auditors responsible for reporting to appropriate committees on process effectiveness

Refer to the Organizational Training and Awareness process area for information about training staff for resilience roles and responsibilities.

Refer to the Human Resource Management process area for information about acquiring staff to fulfill roles and responsibilities.

2. Fund the process.
   Refer to the Financial Resource Management process area for information about budgeting for, funding, and accounting for resilience requirements development.
3. Provide necessary tools, techniques, and methods to perform the process.

   Elaboration:

   > These are examples of tools, techniques, and methods to support the resilience requirements development process:
   > - tools for scenario planning and analysis
   > - tools, techniques, and methods for
   >   - eliciting, documenting, and analyzing requirements
   >   - validating requirements, including affinity analysis
   >   - performing security risk assessments and business impact analysis
   > - tools for requirements tracking
   > - methods for requirements conflict mitigation and resolution

RRD:GG2.GP4 Assign Responsibility

Assign responsibility and authority for performing the resilience requirements development process, developing the work products, and providing the services of the process.

Refer to the Human Resource Management process area for more information about establishing resilience as a job responsibility, developing resilience performance goals and objectives, and measuring and assessing performance against these goals and objectives.

Subpractices

1. Assign responsibility and authority for performing the process.

   Elaboration:

   The primary staff involved in the resilience requirements development process are service owners and asset owners and custodians.

   Refer to the Enterprise Focus process area for information about identifying organizational services and associating them with organizational assets.

   Refer to the Asset Definition and Management process area for more information about establishing asset ownership and custodianship.

2. Assign responsibility and authority for performing the specific tasks of the process.

Elaboration:

> Responsibility and authority for performing resilience requirements development tasks can be formalized by
> - defining roles and responsibilities in the process plan
> - including process tasks and responsibility for these tasks in specific job descriptions
> - developing policy that requires organizational unit managers, line of business managers, project managers, and asset and service owners and custodians to participate in and derive benefit from the process for assets and services under their ownership
> - including process activities in staff performance management goals and objectives with requisite measurement of progress against these goals
> - including process activities in contracts and service level agreements with external entities
> - including process tasks in measuring the performance of external entities against contracts and service level agreements

Refer to the External Dependencies Management process area for additional details about managing relationships with external entities.

3. Confirm that people assigned with responsibility and authority understand it and are willing and able to accept it.

RRD:GG2.GP5 TRAIN PEOPLE

Train the people performing or supporting the resilience requirements development process as needed.

Elaboration:

Expertise in developing resilience requirements requires a strong understanding of each type of resilience requirement (confidentiality, integrity, and availability) as well as the ability to understand strategies (including the internal control system) for protecting and sustaining the various types of assets. Knowledge across multiple functional domains of physical and logical security, business continuity, logistics, and crisis response may also be required.

Refer to the Organizational Training and Awareness process area for more information about training the people performing or supporting the process.

Refer to the Human Resource Management process area for more information about inventorying skill sets, establishing a skill set baseline, identifying required skill sets, and measuring and addressing skill deficiencies.

Subpractices

1. Identify process skill needs.

Elaboration:

Resilience requirements must be developed through working knowledge of how an asset is deployed and how it contributes to ensuring the mission of organizational services. Asset owners must be skilled in analyzing the dependencies among assets, services, and organizational goals and mission and translating these dependencies into resilience requirements that ensure that the asset is protected from threats and sustained if threatened. Functional working knowledge of the types of resilience requirements and their impact on assets is essential.

> These are examples of skills required in the resilience requirements development process:
> - eliciting and developing enterprise resilience requirements
> - eliciting and developing service resilience requirements
> - eliciting and developing asset resilience requirements
> - documenting resilience requirements, including mapping them to their sources
> - identifying the relationships between a service, associated business processes, and associated assets
> - understanding tools, techniques, and methods that can be used to develop, analyze, and validate requirements
> - establishing, implementing, and maintaining the internal control system for assets
> - protecting and sustaining assets to meet their resilience requirements

2. Identify process skill gaps based on available resources and their current skill levels.
3. Identify training opportunities to address skill gaps.

Elaboration:

Information security risk assessment training can provide fundamental knowledge about resilience requirements such as confidentiality and integrity. An active knowledge of business impact analysis techniques can provide foundational knowledge about availability requirements.

Training may also be needed for staff to use requirements development tools, techniques, and methods (particularly those supported by software) to document and analyze requirements.

> These are examples of training topics:
> - resilience requirements (confidentiality, integrity, and availability and which types of requirements are applicable to each type of asset)
> - requirements elicitation and facilitation
> - requirements specification and documentation
> - requirements analysis and validation
> - requirements tracking

- requirements gap analysis
- requirements conflict mitigation and resolution
- establishing, implementing, and maintaining internal controls for protecting and sustaining assets
- supporting asset owners and custodians in understanding the process and their roles and responsibilities with respect to its activities
- working with external entities that have responsibility for process activities
- using process methods, tools, and techniques, including those identified in RRD:GG2:GP3 subpractice 3

4. Provide training and review the training needs as necessary.

RRD:GG2.GP6 MANAGE WORK PRODUCT CONFIGURATIONS

Place designated work products of the resilience requirements development process under appropriate levels of control.

Elaboration:

Changes in strategic objectives or assets (and the services with which they are associated) will necessitate changes in resilience requirements. Because resilience requirements are the basis for strategies to protect and sustain assets, changes to these requirements may in turn translate to changes in strategies, such as the type and extent of controls and changes to service continuity plans.

Changes to resilience requirements are managed in the Resilience Requirements Management process area.

These are examples of resilience requirements development work products placed under control:
- resilience requirements (enterprise, service, asset)
- services map (relationships between a service, associated business processes, and associated assets)
- asset functionality descriptions
- requirements gaps
- requirements conflicts and mitigation action plans
- process plan
- policies and procedures
- contracts with external entities

RRD:GG2.GP7 IDENTIFY AND INVOLVE RELEVANT STAKEHOLDERS

Identify and involve the relevant stakeholders of the resilience requirements development process as planned.

Subpractices

1. Identify process stakeholders and their appropriate involvement.

   Elaboration:

   > These are examples of stakeholders of the resilience requirements development process:
   > - owners and custodians of assets, including
   >   - human resources (for people assets)
   >   - information technology staff (for technology assets)
   >   - staff responsible for physical security (for facility assets)
   > - service and business process owners
   > - organizational unit and line of business managers responsible for assets and their associated services
   > - staff involved in business impact analysis and security risk assessment
   > - staff responsible for identifying and managing operational risks to assets and services
   > - staff responsible for establishing, implementing, and maintaining an internal control system for assets
   > - external entities that are involved in ensuring that assets under their control meet their resilience requirements
   > - internal and external auditors

   > Stakeholders are involved in various tasks in the resilience requirements development process, such as
   > - planning for the development of resilience requirements
   > - participating in the elicitation and identification of enterprise, service, and asset resilience requirements
   > - resolving issues with the understanding of the requirements
   > - resolving requirements gaps and conflicts
   > - communicating requirements to those with a need to know
   > - identifying requirements conflicts
   > - managing operational risks to assets
   > - managing relationships with external entities that support process activities
   > - reviewing and appraising the effectiveness of process activities
   > - resolving issues in the resilience process

2. Communicate the list of stakeholders to planners and those responsible for process performance.
3. Involve relevant stakeholders in the process as planned.

RRD:GG2.GP8 MONITOR AND CONTROL THE PROCESS

Monitor and control the resilience requirements development process against the plan for performing the process and take appropriate corrective action.

Refer to the Monitoring process area for more information about the collection, organization, and distribution of data that may be useful for monitoring and controlling processes.

Refer to the Measurement and Analysis process area for more information about establishing process metrics and measurement.

Refer to the Enterprise Focus process area for more information about providing process information to managers, identifying issues, and determining appropriate corrective actions.

Subpractices

1. Measure actual performance against the plan for performing the process.
2. Review accomplishments and results of the process against the plan for performing the process.

   Elaboration:

   > These are examples of metrics for the resilience requirements development process:
   > - number and percentage of services and assets for which requirements have been defined and documented
   > - number and percentage of services and assets for which there are no stated requirements or that have incomplete requirements
   > - number and percentage of asset owners participating in the development of requirements
   > - number and percentage of asset custodians who are aware of and accept responsibility for implementing requirements
   > - number and percentage of documented requirements that have not been implemented
   > - number and percentage of requirements that have not been analyzed or validated
   > - number of redundant requirements for a specific asset
   > - number of requirements that conflict for a specific asset
   > - number and percentage of conflicts with unimplemented or incomplete mitigation plans
   > - number of action items required to address gaps and overlapping requirements
   > - number of requirements risks referred to the risk management process; number of risks where corrective action is still pending (by risk rank)
   > - extent of time between identification of new assets and the development of requirements for these assets
   > - costs of documenting, developing, analyzing, validating, and tracking requirements

> - level of adherence to requirements development policies; number of policy violations; number of policy exceptions requested and number approved
> - number of process activities that are on track per plan
> - rate of change of resource needs to support the process
> - rate of change of costs to support the process

3. Review activities, status, and results of the process with the immediate level of managers responsible for the process and identify issues.

Elaboration:

The results of periodic reviews should be elevated to higher-level managers to ensure that strategies for protecting and sustaining assets are in alignment with the resilience requirements of these assets (i.e., able to satisfy the requirements) as well as with the organization's enterprise resilience requirements and strategic objectives.

> Periodic reviews of the resilience requirements development process are needed to ensure that
> - all high-value services and assets have defined resilience requirements, including newly acquired assets
> - the service-business process-asset mapping is accurate and current
> - asset owners are involved in the process of developing and validating requirements
> - requirements are being communicated to custodians through formal channels
> - status reports are provided to appropriate stakeholders in a timely manner
> - requirements issues are referred to the risk management process when necessary
> - actions requiring management involvement are elevated in a timely manner
> - the performance of process activities is being monitored and regularly reported
> - key measures are within acceptable ranges as demonstrated in governance dashboards or scorecards and financial reports
> - actions resulting from internal and external audits are being closed in a timely manner

4. Identify and evaluate the effects of significant deviations from the plan for performing the process.
5. Identify problems in the plan for performing and executing the process.
6. Take corrective action when requirements and objectives are not being satisfied, when issues are identified, or when progress differs significantly from the plan for performing the process.
7. Track corrective action to closure.

RRD:GG2.GP9 OBJECTIVELY EVALUATE ADHERENCE

Objectively evaluate adherence of the resilience requirements development process against its process description, standards, and procedures, and address non-compliance.

Elaboration:

Objective evaluation of the resilience requirements development process is intended to ensure that high-quality resilience requirements are being developed, analyzed, and validated for assets. Because these requirements form the basis for an "engineering" approach to operational resilience management, the process is foundational to all other engineering activities in the model. Inconsistent adherence to the process can result in a lack of requirements or poorly developed requirements, which can cause cascading effects on managing operational resilience that will be realized in other process areas.

These are examples of activities to be reviewed:
- establishing enterprise, asset, and service resilience requirements
- obtaining commitments to requirements by owners and custodians
- analyzing requirements and resolving conflicts
- identifying and resolving requirements gaps
- aligning stakeholder requirements with the process plan
- assigning responsibility, accountability, and authority for process activities
- determining the adequacy of process reports and reviews in informing decision makers regarding the performance of operational resilience management activities and the need to take corrective action, if any

---

These are examples of work products to be reviewed:
- business impact analysis and security risk assessment results
- enterprise, service, and asset resilience requirements
- services map
- commitment documents
- requirements baseline and database
- requirements traceability matrix
- corrective actions, including conflict mitigation plans
- process plan and policies
- issues that have been referred to the risk management process
- process methods, techniques, and tools
- metrics for the process *(Refer to RRD:GG2.GP8 subpractice 2.)*
- contracts with external entities

RRD:GG2.GP10 Review Status with Higher-Level Managers

Review the activities, status, and results of the resilience requirements development process with higher-level managers and resolve issues.

Elaboration:

Assets that do not have resilience requirements or have poorly developed requirements should be brought to the attention of higher-level managers as a symptom of potential process inadequacies. Audits of the process should be conducted regularly for a wide range of organizational assets to ensure that the process is functioning properly across organizational units and the enterprise.

Refer to the Enterprise Focus process area for more information about providing sponsorship and oversight to the operational resilience management system.

RRD:GG3 Institutionalize a Defined Process

Resilience requirements development is institutionalized as a defined process.

RRD:GG3.GP1 Establish a Defined Process

Establish and maintain the description of a defined resilience requirements development process.

Elaboration:

The definition, analysis, and validation of asset resilience requirements are best performed at a level commensurate with direct ownership of the asset. Thus, this process may often be carried out at the organizational unit level. However, to ensure consistency of requirements across organizational units, the process must be tailored from the organization's enterprise process definition.

Establishing and tailoring process assets, including standard processes, are addressed in the Organizational Process Definition process area.

Establishing process needs and objectives and selecting, improving, and deploying process assets, including standard processes, are addressed in the Organizational Process Focus process area.

Subpractices

1. Select from the organization's set of standard processes those processes that cover the resilience requirements development process and best meet the needs of the organizational unit or line of business.
2. Establish the defined process by tailoring the selected processes according to the organization's tailoring guidelines.

3. Ensure that the organization's process objectives are appropriately addressed in the defined process, and ensure that process governance extends to the tailored processes.
4. Document the defined process and the records of the tailoring.
5. Revise the description of the defined process as necessary.

RRD:GG3.GP2 COLLECT IMPROVEMENT INFORMATION

Collect resilience requirements development work products, measures, measurement results, and improvement information derived from planning and performing the process to support future use and improvement of the organization's processes and process assets.

Elaboration:

> These are examples of improvement work products and information:
> - information about the types and extent of requirements changes (from baseline) *(Refer to the Resilience Requirements Management process area for information about the handling of requirements changes.)*
> - requirements coverage (of all identified assets and services)
> - requirements conflicts
> - gaps in requirements
> - the ease of understanding and traceability of requirements
> - the level of asset owner and custodian commitment to the requirements
> - metrics and measurements of the viability of the process *(Refer to RRD:GG2.GP8 subpractice 2.)*
> - changes and trends in operating conditions, risk conditions, and the risk environment that affect resilience requirements and the process
> - lessons learned in post-event review of asset incidents and disruptions in continuity (including confidentiality, integrity, availability, and privacy)
> - conflicts and risks arising from dependencies on external entities
> - resilience requirements that are not being satisfied or are being exceeded

Establishing the measurement repository and process asset library is addressed in the Organizational Process Definition process area. Updating the measurement repository and process asset library as part of process improvement and deployment is addressed in the Organizational Process Focus process area.

Subpractices

1. Store process and work product measures in the organization's measurement repository.
2. Submit documentation for inclusion in the organization's process asset library.
3. Document lessons learned from the process for inclusion in the organization's process asset library.
4. Propose improvements to the organizational process assets.

RESILIENCE REQUIREMENTS MANAGEMENT
Engineering

Purpose

The purpose of Resilience Requirements Management is to manage the resilience requirements of high-value services and associated assets and to identify inconsistencies between these requirements and the activities that the organization performs to meet the requirements.

Introductory Notes

In conjunction with the Resilience Requirements Development process area, the Resilience Requirements Management process area seeks to define the life cycle of resilience requirements—from inception, development, or acquisition to application, monitoring and measurement, and change management. In reality, resilience requirements constantly evolve as the organization encounters changes in strategic direction, operational complexity, and new or evolving risk environments. Unfortunately, requirements often are not revisited to ensure alignment with strategies for protecting and sustaining services and assets, potentially affecting the resilience of these services and ultimately the organization's mission. Thus, the organization must implement and make a commitment to dedicated processes that aim to constantly monitor and adjust requirements as these triggers for change are encountered.

The Resilience Requirements Management process area aims to ensure that the requirements that are established in the Resilience Requirements Development process area (or are otherwise acquired) remain viable for each high-value asset associated with a high-value service until it is retired (either because the asset is retired or its relative value is reduced) or until it is changed due to one or more organizational triggers. In addition, Resilience Requirements Management defines the organization's responsibility for monitoring the effectiveness of requirements (for protecting service-related assets and ensuring their continuity) and for recognizing when changes to requirements are necessary. Finally, the evolution of requirements often necessitates that an organization revisit the goals and practices in the Resilience Requirements Development process area because organizational drivers must be reestablished, new or revised enterprise-level or asset-level requirements must be developed, or changes to requirements must be analyzed and revalidated. The iterative nature of the Resilience Requirements Development and Resilience Requirements Management process areas is necessary to ensure that asset-level resilience requirements satisfactorily reflect and support strategic drivers, and this in turn supports the level of operational resilience that the organization desires.

The Resilience Requirements Management process area has one specific goal—to manage resilience requirements. In practice, this requires that the organization obtain and promote an understanding of the requirements, ensure commitment to satisfying the requirements, manage changes to the requirements, establish traceability of the requirements, and identify inconsistencies between the requirements and the activities that the organization performs to satisfy them.

Related Process Areas

The identification, development, documentation, and analysis of resilience requirements are performed in the Resilience Requirements Development process area.

The responsibility for managing requirements at the asset level is established in the Asset Definition and Management process area.

Ensuring that requirements reflect the protection and continuity needs of the owners of the assets is performed in the Resilience Requirements Development process area.

Identifying and establishing the ownership of the assets and the corresponding responsibilities for establishing and validating resilience requirements are performed in the Asset Definition and Management process area.

The monitoring and control of the satisfaction of resilience requirements for high-value business processes, services, and associated assets are performed in the Monitoring process area.

Summary of Specific Goals and Practices

RRM:SG1 Manage Requirements
- RRM:SG1.SP1 Obtain an Understanding of Resilience Requirements
- RRM:SG1.SP2 Obtain Commitment to Resilience Requirements
- RRM:SG1.SP3 Manage Resilience Requirements Changes
- RRM:SG1.SP4 Maintain Traceability of Resilience Requirements
- RRM:SG1.SP5 Identify Inconsistencies Between Resilience Requirements and Activities Performed to Meet the Requirements

Specific Practices by Goal

RRM:SG1 MANAGE REQUIREMENTS

Resilience requirements are actively managed and inconsistencies between requirements and the activities necessary to satisfy them are identified.

The requirements defined and established in Resilience Requirements Development are managed over the life of the associated assets by

- identifying and managing changes to requirements (by establishing change triggers and criteria)
- establishing a shared view and understanding of requirements between owners and custodians
- maintaining the relationship between requirements and associated assets and services
- identifying inconsistencies between requirements and associated assets and services, and the activities performed to satisfy the requirements
- taking corrective action when requirements are not being satisfied

RRM:SG1.SP1 OBTAIN AN UNDERSTANDING OF RESILIENCE REQUIREMENTS

An understanding of resilience requirements is obtained from providers to ensure consistency and accuracy.

The identification and implementation of asset resilience requirements require cooperation between service owners, asset owners, and asset custodians. This cooperation must be based on a mutual and shared understanding of requirements.

Resilience requirements can come from many different sources, but asset owners have the ultimate responsibility for identifying, collecting, and establishing these requirements and for communicating these requirements to all those with a need to know (e.g., owners of an information asset such as medical records would be responsible for setting the confidentiality, integrity, and availability requirements for these records relative to the services they support). The requirements that asset owners develop are based on their implicit understanding of the relative value of the assets (as defined by the services to which they are associated) as well as the needs of the organization (as established in work products such as strategic drivers). They are also influenced by enterprise-level requirements and the results of risk assessments and business impact analyses.

Establishing ownership of the assets and the corresponding responsibilities for establishing and validating resilience requirements is performed in the Asset Definition and Management process area.

Asset custodians must ensure that they clearly and completely understand the requirements so that there is a shared vision of the need for protecting and sustaining assets. Custodians must ensure that they act only on the requirements from authorized providers (generally asset owners or their approved designees). Custodians must agree to the requirements and must identify any organizational constraints they may know of in satisfying the requirements so that the constraints can be communicated to owners for their consideration and approval. The agreement between owners and custodians on how assets are to be protected and sustained is crucial in managing operational resilience.

Typical work products

1. Criteria for evaluation and acceptance of requirements (by custodians)
2. Agreed-to set of asset requirements (between asset owners and asset custodians)

Subpractices

1. Establish objective criteria for the evaluation and acceptance of requirements.
2. Analyze requirements to ensure that the established evaluation and acceptance criteria are met.
3. Reach an understanding (between owners and custodians) on the requirements so that custodians can commit to them.

RRM:SG1.SP2 OBTAIN COMMITMENT TO RESILIENCE REQUIREMENTS

Commitments to resilience requirements are obtained from those who are responsible for satisfying the requirements.

The resilience requirements set by asset owners require two actions to ensure implementation: (1) they must be communicated to all custodians who need to know them, and (2) custodians must make a commitment to implement and manage the requirements. Because requirements represent a wide range of needs for protecting assets, custodians in turn may represent a wide range of organizational entities and activities, so this practice may be extensive.

Owners must commit to developing and monitoring the requirements, and custodians must commit to performing activities that are commensurate with protecting and sustaining assets. Owners must ensure that commitments have been obtained from custodians both internal and external to the organization to implement the requirements as provided and to manage to the requirements as they change and evolve.

Typical work products

1. Documented commitments to requirements and requirement changes (e.g., service level agreements)

Subpractices

1. Document and communicate requirements through service level agreements between asset owners and custodians.
2. Document the custodian's understanding of requirements and obtain sign-off.

RRM:SG1.SP3 *Manage Resilience Requirements Changes*

Changes to resilience requirements are managed as conditions dictate.

The conditions under which organizations operate are continually changing. As a result, the risk environment for services and associated assets continues to evolve as well. An organization must become very adept at recognizing changes in conditions that precipitate considerations for changes in asset resilience requirements.

Managing changes to requirements involves consideration of several distinct activities:

- identifying change triggers and criteria

> These are examples of triggers that might require changes in resilience requirements:
> - changes in the organization's mission, goals, objectives, or critical success factors
> - changes in organizational lines of business or geographical operations
> - changes in organizational structure, including staff changes
> - changes that result in outsourcing services and assets or in changing current external entity relationships
> - market and economic conditions
> - social or political conditions, or geographically induced constraints
> - identification of internal or external fraud or the realization of risk and impact to the organization
> - redeployment or association of assets to new or different services
> - identification of conditions that would result in exposure to new risks (via risk assessment processes)

- identifying associated assets that may be affected by these triggers
- assessing the impact of changes on asset requirements
- identifying and documenting changes to existing requirements (or identifying new requirements, if necessary)
- communicating changes to requirements to those who are responsible for their implementation (custodians)

Change management for resilience requirements is a continuous process and therefore requires that the organization effectively assign responsibility and accountability for it. The organization must independently monitor that the change management process is operational and that asset-level resilience requirements have been updated on a regular basis so that they remain in direct alignment with organizational drivers. In most cases, these responsibilities will fall to asset owners as part of their management of the assets over their life cycles.

Typical work products

1. Requirements baseline
2. Requirements status
3. Requirements database, including change history
4. Requirements change criteria
5. Requirements change requests

Subpractices

1. Establish a requirements baseline from which changes will be managed.
2. Develop and document criteria for establishing when a change in requirements must be considered.
    Ensure that these criteria are commensurate with the organization's risk tolerances.
3. Analyze results of security risk assessments and/or business impact analysis to identify changes to requirements that are related to risk mitigation.
4. Document the requirements changes.
5. Maintain a requirements change history with rationale for performing the changes.
6. Evaluate the impact of requirements changes on existing activities and commitments for protecting and sustaining assets and services.
7. Establish communications channels to ensure custodians are aware of changes in requirements.
    Update service level agreements with custodians if necessary to reflect commitment to changes.

RRM:SG1.SP4 MAINTAIN TRACEABILITY OF RESILIENCE REQUIREMENTS

Traceability between resilience requirements and the activities performed to satisfy the requirements is established.

The development, implementation, and monitoring of resilience requirements necessitate that they be traceable from originating source to assets, and vice versa. Often, there is not a simple one-to-one relationship between requirement and asset because, in practical application, requirements are usually translated and decomposed into lower-level and discipline-specific (i.e., security and business continuity) activities. This is further complicated by two additional realities:

- A single resilience requirement may be associated with one asset or, more realistically, more than one asset. For example, a service that must be available 24 hours per day, 7 days per week, will generate availability requirements for associated people, supporting application systems and technology components, information and data, and the facilities in which these assets are accessible and productive.
- Assets may have more than one set of resilience requirements coming from different organizational constraints and owners and the enterprise, often in direct conflict.

This specific practice ensures that the source of the requirements can be traced to all of the assets that are the subject of the requirements, which is particularly important when requirements or assets undergo changes. In addition, this specific practice requires that the organization be able to trace requirements from assets back to their sources so that responsibility and accountability for the requirements can be ascertained and that changes can be more effectively accomplished and conflicts effectively resolved.

Resolving requirements conflicts is addressed in the Resilience Requirements Development process area.

Typical work products

1. Requirements traceability matrix
2. Requirements tracking system

Subpractices

1. Document requirements and their source or origination as part of an asset profile or documentation.
   Revise the profile as requirements change to ensure it reflects current asset needs.

   The maintenance of asset profiles is addressed in the Asset Definition and Management process area.
2. Maintain requirements traceability.
   Ensure traceability is maintained from strategies to protect and sustain services and assets to resilience requirements intended to implement these strategies to activities performed to satisfy the requirements.
3. Generate a requirements traceability matrix.

RRM:SG1.SP5 IDENTIFY INCONSISTENCIES BETWEEN RESILIENCE REQUIREMENTS AND ACTIVITIES PERFORMED TO MEET THE REQUIREMENTS

Inconsistencies between resilience requirements and the activities performed to satisfy the requirements are identified and managed.

The monitoring and control of the satisfaction of resilience requirements for high-value services and associated assets are performed in the Monitoring process area.

Custodians make commitments to perform activities and implement controls that are consistent with resilience requirements and that ensure the satisfaction of those requirements. This specific practice aims to ensure that custodians are capable and prepared to meet the requirements to which they have made commitments (whether or not they are under the direct control of the organization).

Because assets may derive requirements from more than one source, it is possible that custodians in good faith commit to the requirements but in reality are constrained in satisfying them. Identifying these inconsistencies proactively can help the organization to resolve conflicts, to reroute work as necessary, or to negotiate with owners to make changes to requirements as needed.

Typical work products

1. Documentation of inconsistencies
2. Corrective actions

Subpractices

1. Review the planned or implemented activities for consistency with requirements. Identify any changes made to the requirements.
2. Document custodial constraints that may impede satisfaction of requirements and update requirements as necessary *(refer to RRM:SG1.SP3)*.
3. Identify changes that have to be made in activities (or planned activities) to ensure satisfaction of requirements as specified.
4. Initiate corrective actions to enforce alignment between requirements and activities.

Elaborated Generic Practices by Goal

Refer to the Generic Goals and Practices document in Appendix A for general guidance that applies to all process areas. This section provides elaborations relative to the application of the Generic Goals and Practices to the Resilience Requirements Management process area.

RRM:GG1 ACHIEVE SPECIFIC GOALS

The operational resilience management system supports and enables achievement of the goals of the Resilience Requirements Management process area by transforming identifiable input work products to produce identifiable work products.

RRM:GG1.GP1 PERFORM SPECIFIC PRACTICES

Perform the specific practices of the Resilience Requirements Management process area to develop work products and provide services to achieve the specific goals of the process area.

Elaboration:

Specific practices RRM:SG1.SP1 through RRM:SG1.SP5 are performed to achieve the goals of the resilience requirements management process.

RRM:GG2 INSTITUTIONALIZE A MANAGED PROCESS

Resilience requirements management is institutionalized as a managed process.

RRM:GG2.GP1 ESTABLISH PROCESS GOVERNANCE

Establish and maintain governance over the planning and performance of the resilience requirements management process.

Refer to the Enterprise Focus process area for more information about providing sponsorship and oversight to the resilience requirements management process.

Subpractices

1. Establish governance over process activities.

   Elaboration:

   > Governance over the resilience requirements management process may be exhibited by
   > - developing and publicizing higher-level managers' objectives for managing asset resilience requirements
   > - sponsoring and providing oversight of policy, procedures, standards, and guidelines for effective management of resilience requirements, including traceability and change control
   > - sponsoring regular audits and reviews to ensure alignment between requirements and resilience activities
   > - making higher-level managers aware of applicable compliance obligations related to managing resilience requirements, and regularly reporting on the organization's satisfaction of these obligations to higher-level managers
   > - sponsoring and funding the management of resilience requirements, including change control
   > - verifying that the process supports strategic resilience objectives and is focused on the assets and services that are of the highest relative value in meeting strategic objectives

> - reporting regularly from organizational units to higher-level managers on process activities and results
> - creating dedicated higher-level management feedback loops on decisions regarding the management of resilience requirements and recommendations for improving the process
> - conducting regular internal and external audits and related reporting to appropriate committees on the effectiveness of the process
> - creating formal programs to measure the effectiveness of process activities, and reporting these measurements to higher-level managers

2. Develop and publish organizational policy for the process.

   Elaboration:

   > The resilience requirements management policy should address
   > - responsibility, authority, and ownership for managing requirements (particularly for assets) and for all process activities
   > - responsibility and authority for identifying requirements inconsistencies and performing corrective actions
   > - procedures, standards, and guidelines for
   >   - documenting acquired requirements and relevant information
   >   - distributing requirements and requirements changes to the custodians who must implement the requirements relative to assets in their care or possession
   >   - documenting commitments in the form of service level agreements
   >   - regular updating of requirements, reconciliation, and change control
   >   - requirements tracking and traceability
   > - methods for measuring adherence to policy, exceptions granted, and policy violations

RRM:GG2.GP2 PLAN THE PROCESS

Establish and maintain the plan for performing the resilience requirements management process.

Elaboration:

The plan for the process of resilience requirements management should enable large-scale (at the enterprise or organizational unit level, whichever is appropriate) management of resilience requirements by owners of organizational assets (particularly information, technology, and facilities assets). The plan should also allow for the distribution of these requirements to custodians who are responsible for implementing strategies to meet the requirements for protecting and sustaining assets in their care or possession. The plan must support both internal staff involved in the process (typically asset owners) and external entities (which may include custodians). The plan must support managing requirements that are developed as part of the resilience requirements development process, as well as requirements acquired from other internal and external sources.

Subpractices

1. Define and document the plan for performing the process.

   Elaboration:

   Special consideration may be given to the means of collecting and organizing requirements from all identified sources so that they can be managed by this process.

2. Define and document the process description.
3. Review the plan with relevant stakeholders and get their agreement.
4. Revise the plan as necessary.

RRM:GG2.GP3 PROVIDE RESOURCES

Provide adequate resources for performing the resilience requirements management process, developing the work products, and providing the services of the process.

Subpractices

1. Staff the process.

   Elaboration:

   The diversity of asset types (people, information, technology, and facilities) requires that staff assigned to the resilience requirements management process have appropriate knowledge of all assets that need to fulfill resilience requirements and the services with which they are associated.

   > These are examples of staff required to perform the resilience requirements management process:
   > - asset owners and custodians
   > - business continuity and disaster recovery staff
   > - IT operations and service delivery staff
   > - physical security staff
   > - staff skilled in understanding requirements across domains, functions, assets, and services
   > - staff responsible for
   >   - reconciling requirements conflicts and inconsistencies
   >   - requirements change control
   >   - requirements tracking and traceability

> - the process plan, ensuring it is aligned with stakeholder requirements and needs
> - managing external entities that have contractual obligations for meeting resilience requirements
> - external entities responsible for protecting and sustaining assets
> - internal and external auditors responsible for reporting to appropriate committees on process effectiveness

Refer to the Organizational Training and Awareness process area for information about training staff for resilience roles and responsibilities.

Refer to the Human Resource Management process area for information about acquiring staff to fulfill roles and responsibilities.

2. Fund the process.

   Refer to the Financial Resource Management process area for information about budgeting for, funding, and accounting for resilience requirements management.

3. Provide necessary tools, techniques, and methods to perform the process.

   Elaboration:

   > These are examples of tools, techniques, and methods to support the resilience requirements management process:
   > - tools, techniques, and methods for
   >   - requirements elicitation
   >   - requirements documentation
   >   - requirements analysis
   >   - requirements change control
   > - requirements database, including change history
   > - requirements tracking system
   > - tools for requirements traceability
   > - methods for resolving inconsistencies between requirements and activities performed to meet requirements

RRM:GG2.GP4 Assign Responsibility

Assign responsibility and authority for performing the resilience requirements management process, developing the work products, and providing the services of the process.

Refer to the Human Resource Management process area for more information about establishing resilience as a job responsibility, developing resilience performance goals and objectives, and measuring and assessing performance against these goals and objectives.

Subpractices

1. Assign responsibility and authority for performing the process.

Elaboration:

The primary staff involved in the resilience requirements management process are service owners and asset owners and custodians.

Refer to the Enterprise Focus process area for information about identifying organizational services and associating them with organizational assets.

Refer to the Asset Definition and Management process area for information about establishing asset ownership and custodianship.

2. Assign responsibility and authority for performing the specific tasks of the process.

   Elaboration:

   > Responsibility and authority for performing resilience requirements management tasks can be formalized by
   > - defining roles and responsibilities in the process plan
   > - including process tasks and responsibility for these tasks in specific job descriptions
   > - developing policy requiring organizational unit managers, line of business managers, project managers, and asset and services owners and custodians to participate in and derive benefit from the process for assets and services under their ownership or custodianship
   > - including process activities in staff performance management goals and objectives, with requisite measurement of progress against these goals
   > - including process activities in contracts and service level agreements with external entities
   > - including process tasks in measuring the performance of external entities against contracts and service level agreements

   Refer to the External Dependencies Management process area for additional details about managing relationships with external entities.

3. Confirm that people assigned with responsibility and authority understand it and are willing and able to accept it.

RRM:GG2.GP5 TRAIN PEOPLE

Train the people performing or supporting the resilience requirements management process as needed.

Elaboration:

Expertise in managing resilience requirements requires a strong understanding of each type of resilience requirement (confidentiality, integrity, and availability) as well as the ability to understand strategies (including the internal control system) for protecting and sustaining the various types of assets. Knowledge across multiple functional domains of physical and logical security, business continuity, logistics, and crisis response may also be required.

Refer to the Organizational Training and Awareness process area for more information about training the people performing or supporting the process.

Refer to the Human Resource Management process area for more information about inventorying skill sets, establishing a skill set baseline, identifying required skill sets, and measuring and addressing skill deficiencies.

Subpractices

1. Identify process skill needs.

   Elaboration:

   Effective management of resilience requirements (including changes to requirements) must be informed by working knowledge of how an asset is deployed and how it contributes to assuring the mission of organizational services. Asset owners and custodians must be skilled in preserving the dependencies among assets, services, and organizational mission and goals that have been translated into resilience requirements. Functional working knowledge of the types of resilience requirements and their impact on assets is essential.

   > These are examples of skills required in the resilience requirements management process:
   > - ability to understand and define the desired outcomes of resilience requirements
   > - negotiation skills
   > - project management skills, including estimating time, costs, and resources to manage resilience requirements and changes to requirements
   > - ability to use tools, techniques, and methods for managing resilience requirements, including tracking, traceability, and change control
   > - requirements change management skills (at the enterprise, service, and asset levels)
   > - ability to maintain the relationships between a service, associated business processes, and associated assets
   > - ability to maintain the internal control system for assets
   > - ability to protect and sustain assets to meet their resilience requirements

2. Identify process skill gaps based on available resources and their current skill levels.
3. Identify training opportunities to address skill gaps.

Elaboration:

Information security risk assessment training can provide fundamental knowledge about resilience requirements such as confidentiality and integrity. An active knowledge of business impact analysis techniques can provide foundational knowledge about availability requirements.

Training may also be needed for staff to use requirements management tools, techniques, and methods, particularly for requirements tracking and change control, which may be performed through the use of specialized application systems and databases.

> These are examples of training topics:
> - resilience requirements (confidentiality, integrity, and availability, and which types of requirements are applicable to each type of asset)
> - requirements elicitation and facilitation
> - requirements management tools, including requirements tracking
> - configuration and change management practices
> - negotiation and conflict resolution
> - maintaining internal controls for protecting and sustaining assets
> - supporting asset owners and custodians in understanding the process and their roles and responsibilities with respect to its activities
> - working with external entities that have responsibility for process activities
> - using process methods, tools, and techniques, including those identified in RRM:GG2:GP3 subpractice 3

4. Provide training and review the training needs as necessary.

RRM:GG2.GP6 MANAGE WORK PRODUCT CONFIGURATIONS

Place designated work products of the resilience requirements management process under appropriate levels of control.

Elaboration:

Changes in strategic objectives or assets (and the services with which they are associated) will necessitate changes in resilience requirements. Because resilience requirements are the basis for strategies to protect and sustain assets and services, changes to these requirements may in turn translate to changes in strategies, including the type and extent of controls, changes to service continuity plans, etc.

RRM:SG1.SP3 specifically addresses the change control process over resilience requirements. RRM:GG2.GP6 generically covers all work products of the resilience requirements management process.

> These are examples of resilience requirements management work products placed under control:
> - resilience requirements
> - requirements baseline
> - requirements status
> - requirements database
> - requirements traceability matrix
> - requirements tracking system
> - service level agreements
> - documentation of inconsistencies and corrective actions
> - process plan
> - policies and procedures
> - contracts with external entities

RRM:GG2.GP7 IDENTIFY AND INVOLVE RELEVANT STAKEHOLDERS

Identify and involve the relevant stakeholders of the resilience requirements management process as planned.

Subpractices

1. Identify process stakeholders and their appropriate involvement.

   Elaboration:

   > These are examples of stakeholders of the resilience requirements management process:
   > - owners and custodians of assets, including
   >   - human resources staff (for people assets)
   >   - information technology staff (for technology assets)
   >   - staff responsible for physical security (for facility assets)
   > - service and business process owners
   > - organizational unit and line of business managers responsible for assets and their associated services
   > - staff involved in business impact analysis and security risk assessment
   > - staff responsible for identifying and managing operational risks to assets and services
   > - staff responsible for establishing, implementing, and maintaining an internal control system for assets
   > - external entities that are involved in ensuring that assets under their control meet their resilience requirements
   > - internal and external auditors

> Stakeholders are involved in various tasks in the resilience requirements management process, such as
> - planning for the management of resilience requirements
> - resolving issues with the understanding of the requirements
> - assessing the impact of requirements changes
> - communicating requirements changes to those with a need to know
> - identifying inconsistencies between requirements and the activities performed to meet the requirements
> - managing operational risks to assets
> - managing relationships with external entities that support process activities
> - reviewing and appraising the effectiveness of process activities
> - resolving issues in the process

2. Communicate the list of stakeholders to planners and those responsible for process performance.
3. Involve relevant stakeholders in the process as planned.

RRM:GG2.GP8 MONITOR AND CONTROL THE PROCESS

Monitor and control the resilience requirements management process against the plan for performing the process and take appropriate corrective action.

Refer to the Monitoring process area for more information about the collection, organization, and distribution of data that may be useful for monitoring and controlling processes.

Refer to the Measurement and Analysis process area for more information about establishing process metrics and measurement.

Refer to the Enterprise Focus process area for more information about providing process information to managers, identifying issues, and determining appropriate corrective actions.

Subpractices

1. Measure actual performance against the plan for performing the process.
2. Review accomplishments and results of the process against the plan for performing the process.

Elaboration:

> These are examples of metrics for the resilience requirements management process:
> - number and percentage of services and assets for which requirements have been defined and documented
> - number and percentage of services and assets for which there are no stated requirements or that have incomplete resilience requirements

- number and percentage of asset owners actively participating in managing changes to requirements for the assets under their control
- number and percentage of documented requirements that have not been implemented
- number and percentage of asset custodians who are aware of and accept responsibility for implementing requirements
- number and percentage of documented requirements that have not been committed to
- number and percentage of requirements changed
- number of requirements changes and frequency of changes in total and by asset or asset type
- number and percentage of requirements changes that are not subject to the organization's change control process
- number of unapproved requirements
- number of requirements that cannot be traced to a source
- schedule for analysis of proposed requirements changes
- number of requirements satisfied by existing controls
- number of inconsistencies detected between requirements and the activities in place to satisfy the requirements
- number of action items required to address gaps and overlapping requirements
- number of requirements risks referred to the risk management process; number of risks where corrective action is still pending (by risk rank)
- costs of documenting, analyzing, managing, and tracking requirements and changes to requirements
- level of adherence to requirements management policies; number of policy violations; number of policy exceptions requested and number approved
- number of process activities that are on track per plan
- rate of change of resource needs to support the process
- rate of change of costs to support the process

3. Review activities, status, and results of the process with the immediate level of management responsible for the process and identify issues.

Elaboration:

The results of periodic reviews should be elevated to higher-level managers to ensure that the strategies for protecting and sustaining assets continue to be in alignment with (1) their resilience requirements (that is, able to satisfy the requirements) as requirements change and (2) the organization's enterprise resilience requirements and strategic objectives.

> Periodic reviews of the resilience requirements management process are needed to ensure that
> - requirements are being gathered, organized, analyzed, and validated
> - all high-value services and assets have defined resilience requirements, including newly acquired assets
> - asset owners are involved in the process of validating and changing requirements
> - requirements changes are being communicated to custodians through formal channels
> - requirements are changed as conditions dictate
> - inconsistencies between requirements and requisite activities are being identified and addressed
> - status reports are provided to appropriate stakeholders in a timely manner
> - requirements issues are referred to the risk management process when necessary
> - actions requiring management involvement are elevated in a timely manner
> - the performance of process activities is being monitored and regularly reported
> - key measures are within acceptable ranges as demonstrated in governance dashboards or scorecards and financial reports
> - actions resulting from internal and external audits are being closed in a timely manner

4. Identify and evaluate the effects of significant deviations from the plan for performing the process.
5. Identify problems in the plan for performing and executing the process.
6. Take corrective action when requirements and objectives are not being satisfied, when issues are identified, or when progress differs significantly from the plan for performing the process.
7. Track corrective action to closure.

RRM:GG2.GP9 OBJECTIVELY EVALUATE ADHERENCE

Objectively evaluate adherence of the resilience requirements management process against its process description, standards, and procedures, and address non-compliance.

Elaboration:

Objective evaluation of the resilience requirements management process is intended to ensure that requirements are up-to-date and available as the basis for the organization's development, implementation, and management of strategies to protect and sustain assets and services. Therefore, objective evaluation should be focused on determining whether there is alignment between requirements and the activities being performed to meet the requirements, as well as ensuring that requirements changes are managed and controlled.

These are examples of activities to be reviewed:
- gathering and organizing resilience requirements
- obtaining commitments to requirements by owners and custodians
- maintaining changes to requirements
- maintaining traceability of requirements
- correcting inconsistencies between requirements and strategies for protecting and sustaining assets and services
- aligning stakeholder requirements with the process plan
- assigning responsibility, accountability, and authority for process activities
- determining the adequacy of process reports and reviews in informing decision makers regarding the performance of operational resilience management activities and any need to take corrective action

These are examples of work products to be reviewed:
- enterprise, service, and asset resilience requirements
- commitment documents
- change logs
- requirements baseline and database
- requirements traceability matrix
- documentation of inconsistencies and corrective actions
- process plan and policies
- issues that have been referred to the risk management process
- process methods, techniques, and tools
- metrics for the process *(Refer to RRM:GG2.GP8 subpractice 2.)*
- contracts with external entities

RRM:GG2.GP10 REVIEW STATUS WITH HIGHER-LEVEL MANAGERS

Review the activities, status, and results of the resilience requirements management process with higher-level managers and resolve issues.

Elaboration:

Assets that do not have resilience requirements, have poorly defined requirements, or have outdated requirements should be brought to the attention of higher-level managers as a symptom of potential process inadequacies. In addition, inconsistencies between requirements and strategies for protecting and sustaining assets and services should also be reported. Audits of the process should be conducted regularly to ensure that the process is functioning properly across organizational units and the enterprise.

Refer to the Enterprise Focus process area for more information about providing sponsorship and oversight to the operational resilience management system.

RRM:GG3 INSTITUTIONALIZE A DEFINED PROCESS

Resilience requirements management is institutionalized as a defined process.

RRM:GG3.GP1 ESTABLISH A DEFINED PROCESS

Establish and maintain the description of a defined resilience requirements management process.

Elaboration:

The identification, tracking, and management of resilience requirements may be best performed at a level commensurate with direct ownership of the asset. Thus, this process may be often carried out at the organizational unit level. However, to ensure consistency of requirements across organizational units, the process must be tailored from the organization's enterprise process definition.

Establishing and tailoring process assets, including standard processes, are addressed in the Organizational Process Definition process area.

Establishing process needs and objectives and selecting, improving, and deploying process assets, including standard processes, are addressed in the Organizational Process Focus process area.

Subpractices

1. Select from the organization's set of standard processes those processes that cover the resilience requirements management process and best meet the needs of the organizational unit or line of business.
2. Establish the defined process by tailoring the selected processes according to the organization's tailoring guidelines.
3. Ensure that the organization's process objectives are appropriately addressed in the defined process, and ensure that process governance extends to the tailored processes.
4. Document the defined process and the records of the tailoring.
5. Revise the description of the defined process as necessary.

RRM:GG3.GP2 COLLECT IMPROVEMENT INFORMATION

Collect resilience requirements management work products, measures, measurement results, and improvement information derived from planning and performing the process to support future use and improvement of the organization's processes and process assets.

Elaboration:

> These are examples of improvement work products and information:
> - information about the types and extent of requirements changes (from baseline)
> - inconsistencies arising between requirements and strategies for protecting and sustaining assets and services
> - the ease of understanding and traceability of requirements
> - the level of asset owner and custodian commitment to the requirements
> - metrics and measurements of the viability of the requirements management process *(Refer to RRM:GG2.GP8 subpractice 2.)*
> - changes and trends in operating conditions, risk conditions, and the risk environment that affect resilience requirements and the process
> - lessons learned in post-event review of asset incidents and disruptions in continuity (including confidentiality, integrity, availability, and privacy)
> - conflicts and risks arising from dependencies on external entities
> - resilience requirements that are not being satisfied or are being exceeded

Establishing the measurement repository and process asset library is addressed in the Organizational Process Definition process area. Updating the measurement repository and process asset library as part of process improvement and deployment is addressed in the Organizational Process Focus process area.

Subpractices

1. Store process and work product measures in the organization's measurement repository.
2. Submit documentation for inclusion in the organization's process asset library.
3. Document lessons learned from the process for inclusion in the organization's process asset library.
4. Propose improvements to the organizational process assets.

RESILIENT TECHNICAL SOLUTION ENGINEERING
Engineering

Purpose

The purpose of Resilient Technical Solution Engineering is to ensure that software and systems are developed to satisfy their resilience requirements.

Introductory Notes

Software and systems are pervasive organizational assets that automate services and support business processes to help organizations meet their missions. The importance of resilient technical solutions—software and systems that resist threats, function satisfactorily in the face of adversity, and continue to help services meet their missions during times of stress—cannot be overstated.

Resilient software and systems do not become survivable and resistant to threat without an organizational commitment to address resilience throughout the development process. These assets must be specifically designed and developed with consideration of the types of threats they will face, the operating conditions and changing risk environment in which they will operate, and the priority and needs to sustain the services they support. Typical software and system development life cycles understandably focus on identifying and satisfying functional requirements; that is, most of the effort goes into defining and designing what the software or system must do to fulfill its use case, purpose, objectives, and ultimately its mission. However, requirements for quality attributes, such as security, availability, performance, reliability, and the ability to sustain software and system assets, can in the long run be equally important to the usability and longevity of software and system assets and require considerable resources to address in the operations phase if they are not considered early in the development life cycle.

Unfortunately, quality attribute requirements can be harder to define, design, and implement and in many cases require significant business impact and cost analysis up front to ensure that they are worth investing in. This leads to a tendency to ignore these requirements early in the development life cycle and to bolt on solutions to address them later in the design and implementation phases, when they are more costly, less effective, and typically harder to manage and sustain in an operational mode. The failure to consider requirements for quality attributes is a primary reason why software and systems in operation are subject to high levels of operational risk resulting from failed technology and processes. This expands an already complex operational risk environment brought about by the integration of software and systems with other technology assets such as information, hardware, networks, and telecommunications. In essence, ignoring quality attributes creates additional security, continuity, and other related operational risks that must be managed in the operations phase of the life cycle, typically at higher cost, lower efficacy, and potentially increased consequences to the organization. In some cases, these problems may be so significant as to shorten the expected life of the software and systems, diminish their overall operational resilience, and result in cumulatively lower than expected return on investment.

The functional aspects of software and systems do not have meaning if they are not resistant to disruption or cannot be sustained under degraded conditions. High-quality software and systems cannot be produced and sustained without addressing these issues early in the development life cycle. The controls necessary to demonstrate that integrity and availability requirements are met must be identified as early as the needs determination phase. Controls can then be designed to fit the architecture and functionality of the software and systems in their expected operating environment and can be implemented and made operable to ensure that they achieve the desired effect. This process cannot be short-changed; it must be wholly integrated into the organization's development process and must be measured, managed, and improved in the same manner as highly effective and mature software and system development processes.

Developing or acquiring resilient technical solutions such as software and systems requires a dedicated process that encompasses the asset's life cycle. The process begins with establishing a plan for addressing resilience as part of the organization's regular development life cycle and the integration of the plan into the organization's corresponding development process. The identification, development, and validation of quality attribute requirements are performed alongside similar processes for functional requirements. Resilient software and systems are designed through the elicitation and identification of resilience requirements and the design of architectures that reflect a resilience focus, including security, operations controls, and the ability to sustain software and system assets. Resilient software and systems are developed through processes that include secure coding of software, software defect detection and removal, and the development of resilience controls based on design specifications. The resilience controls for software and systems are tested, and issues are referred back to the design and development cycle for resolution. Reviews are conducted throughout the development life cycle to ensure that resilience is kept in the forefront and given adequate attention and consideration. System-specific continuity planning is performed and integrated with service continuity planning to ensure that software, systems, hardware, networks, telecommunications, and other technical assets can be sustained. A post-implementation review of deployed systems is performed to ensure that resilience requirements are being satisfied as intended.

In operation, software and systems are monitored to determine if there is variability that could indicate the effects of threats or vulnerabilities and to ensure that controls are functioning properly. Configuration management and change control processes are implemented to ensure software and systems are kept up-to-date to address newly discovered vulnerabilities and weaknesses (particularly in vendor-acquired products and components) and to prevent the intentional or inadvertent introduction of malicious code or other exploitable vulnerabilities.

To effectively integrate resilience considerations, the organization must establish guidelines for developing resilient software and systems, develop a plan for selecting, tailoring, and integrating selected guidelines into existing development life cycles and processes for any given development project, and then execute the plan. Plan development and execution include identifying and mitigating risks to the success of the development project.

The Resilient Technical Solution Engineering process area is strongly influenced by two Capability Maturity Model Integration (CMMI) process areas [CMMI Product Team 2006]:

- Requirements Development, the purpose of which is to produce and analyze customer requirements and software and system product and product component requirements
- Technical Solution, the purpose of which is to design, develop, and implement solutions to software and system requirements (Solutions, designs, and implementations encompass software and system products, product components, and product-related life-cycle processes, either singly or in combination as appropriate.)

There are a growing number of reputable sources to consider when identifying and selecting candidate guidelines for the development of resilient software and systems across the life cycle, particularly for software security and assurance.

> These are examples of sources of guidelines:
> - Building Security In Maturity Model (BSIMM2) v2.0, http://bsimm2.com/
> - Open Web Applications Security Project (OWASP) Software Assurance Maturity Model (SAMM) v1.0, www.owasp.org/index.php/Category:Software_Assurance_Maturity_Model
> - Microsoft's Security Development Lifecycle, Version 4.1, www.microsoft.com/security/sdl/
> - Department of Homeland Security Assurance for CMMI Process Reference Model, https://buildsecurityin.us-cert.gov/swa/procwg.html

The Resilient Technical Solution Engineering process area assumes that the organization has one or more existing, defined processes for software and system development into which resilience controls and activities can be integrated. If this is not the case, the organization should not attempt to implement the goals and practices identified in this process area.

Note: This process area does not address the unique aspects of the resilience of embedded systems or the resilience of hardware that is part of a software-intensive system.

Related Process Areas

Resilience requirements for software and system technology assets in operation, including those that may influence quality attribute requirements in the development process, are developed and managed in the Resilience Requirements Development and Resilience Requirements Management process areas, respectively.

Identifying and adding newly developed and acquired software and system assets to the organization's asset inventory are addressed in the Asset Definition and Management process area.

The management of resilience for technology assets as a whole, particularly for deployed, operational assets, is addressed in the Technology Management process area. This includes, for example, asset fail-over, backup, recovery, and restoration.

Acquiring software and systems from external entities and ensuring that such assets meet their resilience requirements throughout the asset life cycle are addressed in the External Dependencies Management process area. That said, RTSE-specific goals and practices should be used to aid in evaluating and selecting external entities that are developing software and systems (EXD:SG3.SP3), formalizing relationships with such external entities (EXD:SG3.SP4), and managing an external entity's performance when developing software and systems (EXD:SG4).

Monitoring for events, incidents, and vulnerabilities that may affect software and systems in operation is addressed in the Monitoring process area.

Service continuity plans are identified and created in the Service Continuity process area. These plans may be inclusive of software and systems that support the services for which planning is performed.

Summary of Specific Goals and Practices

RTSE:SG1 Establish Guidelines for Resilient Technical Solution Development
    RTSE:SG1.SP1   Identify General Guidelines
    RTSE:SG1.SP2   Identify Requirements Guidelines
    RTSE:SG1.SP3   Identify Architecture and Design Guidelines
    RTSE:SG1.SP4   Identify Implementation Guidelines
    RTSE:SG1.SP5   Identify Assembly and Integration Guidelines
RTSE:SG2 Develop Resilient Technical Solution Development Plans
    RTSE:SG2.SP1   Select and Tailor Guidelines
    RTSE:SG2.SP2   Integrate Selected Guidelines with a Defined Software and System Development Process

RTSE:SG3 Execute the Plan
    RTSE:SG3.SP1   Monitor Execution of the Development Plan
    RTSE:SG3.SP2   Release Resilient Technical Solutions into Production

Specific Practices by Goal

RTSE:SG1 ESTABLISH GUIDELINES FOR RESILIENT TECHNICAL SOLUTION DEVELOPMENT

Guidelines are developed to ensure proper consideration of resilience activities and controls in all phases of the life cycle.

Resilient technical solution development requires the integration of security and business continuity considerations into the organization's software and system development life cycle, methodologies, and processes. During all phases of development, resilience requirements must be considered and correspondingly translated into requirements, design, and implementation actions.

Integrating resilience into the life cycle cannot be performed as a bolt-on activity; resilience development activities must be fully incorporated into the development process to ensure that

- resilience requirements that are relevant for the software or system are identified (*Refer also to the Resilience Requirements Development and the Resilience Requirements Management process areas.*)
- resilience requirements are analyzed and planned for in the development life cycle
- software and system designs and architectures include appropriate levels of controls and satisfy resilience requirements
- resilience requirements are addressed early in and throughout the life cycle and maintained over the useful life of the asset
- to the extent possible and practical, operational software and systems do not contain vulnerabilities and weaknesses that arise from poor or inadequate consideration of resilience in prior life-cycle phases
- software and systems can be effectively and efficiently maintained through monitoring, change control, and configuration management

Integration of resilience requirements into the life cycle may require the expansion of life-cycle phases and activities. For example, consideration of protective controls during development requires expanded requirements definition and analysis activities and the development of assurance cases to provide evidence that resilience requirements are met. In some cases, additional activities have to be added to phases such as the design of specific security architectures, the use of misuse/abuse cases and attack patterns to anticipate risks to continuity, and secure coding practices to reduce known vulnerabilities. Incorporation of these additional considerations must be part of the organization's software and system development plan; otherwise, there is risk that the additional considerations may be viewed as optional and, as a result, be underfunded or underresourced.

Guidelines are a means for documenting the organization's requirements for considering and institutionalizing resilience in development projects. Guidelines are an important tool for enforcing (and reinforcing) a resilience viewpoint in development projects because they provide a consistent foundation. This is particularly important because organizations often

- execute many different development projects with different development teams simultaneously
- deploy more than one life-cycle methodology, some of which may be proprietary and depend on the involvement of external entities
- assemble software and systems from existing or legacy assets, open-source assets, or commercial off-the-shelf (COTS) assets
- outsource development projects

Resilience guidelines ensure consistency across projects (and external entities) and provide for expected outcomes regardless of the project under development, methodology deployed, or entities involved.

Guidelines for the acquisition of resilient software and systems, comparable to those used for development performed within the organization, may be established in this process area. *(Their use in evaluating and selecting external entities, in developing contractual agreements with external entities, and in managing ongoing relationships is addressed in the External Dependencies Management process area.)*

RTSE:SG1.SP1 I*DENTIFY* G*ENERAL* G*UIDELINES*

General guidelines for building resilience into software and systems are identified.

General guidelines apply to all life-cycle phases. Practices and controls that implement general guidelines will differ by life-cycle phase, becoming more detailed and precise as development progresses.

General guidelines include such topics as understanding the operational production environment within which the software and system will be deployed, performing trade-off analyses that balance resilience needs and requirements against costs and benefits, identifying and analyzing resilience project risks throughout the life cycle, addressing issues relevant to continuity of operations for the service or services that the software and systems are intended to support, conducting threat analysis, and collecting and reporting appropriate measures of progress and satisfaction of life-cycle phase exit criteria, particularly with respect to resilience.

Guidelines that address software and system interoperability, including establishing standards, developing an interoperability management strategy, and analyzing risks related to the interoperability of software and systems, are addressed in the Technology Management process area, specifically TM:SG5.SP4.

Typical work products

1. General guidelines for resilient software and systems

Subpractices

1. Identify general guidelines for the development of resilient software and systems.

    Guidelines are project-specific but should address topics such as the following:
    - project management, including
      - defining project objectives for resilience
      - defining the scope of resilience for the software or system (levels of required resilience based on risk thresholds)
      - understanding the operating environment and defining the operating constraints for resilience for the environments in which software and systems will be deployed
      - identifying operational concepts and associated scenarios for resilience
      - balancing resilience needs against costs and benefits
      - defining criteria (with respect to resilience) for approval to proceed from one project life-cycle phase to the next
    - risk management, including
      - identifying and analyzing resilience project risks *(Refer to the Risk Management process area.)*
      - identifying and analyzing resilience software and system risks during all life-cycle phases
    - threat analysis, including modeling, assessment, attack models and patterns, and misuse/abuse cases
    - interconnectivity and interoperability *(Refer to TM:SG5.SP4.)*
    - control identification and prioritization, including
      - controls for protecting and sustaining the service or services that the software and systems are intended to support
      - controls for protecting and sustaining the software and systems
      - software supply chain resilience controls, such as chain of custody, least privilege access, separation of duties, tamper resistance (such as code signing) and evidence of tampering, persistent protection of high-value information, compliance management, and code inspection, testing, and verification *(Refer to the Controls Management process area.)*
    - quality assurance, including methods for validating and verifying desired or attained levels of software and system resilience, sometimes referred to as "assurance cases"
    - measurement *(Refer to the Measurement and Analysis process area.)*

- reviews and documentation necessary to demonstrate successful completion of each life-cycle phase
- training for software engineers and project managers *(Refer to the Organizational Training and Awareness process area.)*

RTSE:SG1.SP2 IDENTIFY REQUIREMENTS GUIDELINES

Guidelines for determining software and systems resilience requirements are identified.

Requirements are the basis for architecture and design. Resilience requirements must be defined early in the development life cycle so that the resulting software or system can be evaluated in terms of its ability to support service continuity and other operational resilience requirements.

Resilience requirements derive from analyzing the needs of service owners for each software or system associated with a high-value service, relevant stakeholders, the operational environment, and information security risk assessments and/or business impact analyses. Requirements need to reflect confidentiality, integrity, and availability requirements as well as those for accountability, non-repudiation, correctness, predictability, and reliability.

Resilience requirements are identified and refined throughout the phases of the software and system life cycle. Design decisions, subsequent corrective actions, and feedback during each phase of the life cycle are analyzed for impact on derived and allocated requirements.

During requirements engineering, an important perspective is that of the attacker. An attacker typically seeks defects and other conditions outside of normal operations that will allow for a successful intrusion. Thus, it is important for requirements engineers to think about the attacker's objectives and not just the software or system functional requirements.

Constructing threat models and operational usage scenarios for high-value services and assets can be useful in demonstrating satisfaction of resilience requirements. Scenarios and misuse/abuse cases can also aid in validating that the software or system responds correctly during times of stress and disruption.

Typical work products

1. Requirements guidelines for resilient software and systems

Subpractices

1. Identify requirements guidelines for the development of resilient software and systems. Guidelines are project-specific but should address topics such as the following:
    - resilience requirements elicitation (from service owners, stakeholders, and other entities dependent upon the software and system) *(Resilience requirements for software and systems in operation are defined and managed in the Resilience Requirements Management process area and the Resilience Requirements Definition process area, respectively. Requirements resulting from these two process areas that are relevant for developed and acquired software and system assets also have to be considered.)*

- risk analysis during requirements engineering (Risk analysis results inform requirements prioritization.)
- threat analysis during requirements engineering
- requirements trade-off analyses (service owner needs, stakeholder needs, operational environment considerations, etc.)
- assumptions, decisions, and rationales
- methods for representing defender and attacker perspectives (such as misuse/abuse cases and scenarios)
- access control *(Refer to the Access Management process area.)*
- identity management *(Refer to the Identity Management process area.)*
- data security, including the use of encryption and credentials management *(Refer to the Knowledge and Information Management process area.)*
- control identification and prioritization during requirements engineering *(Refer to the Controls Management process area.)*
- analysis of any open-source, COTS, and legacy software that will be part of the system, including specification of resilience requirements to be met by such software
- requirements specification reviews, including means for validating desired or attained levels of software and system resilience
- quality assurance during requirements engineering
- monitoring and audit (for example, of system logs, for intrusion prevention and detection) during requirements engineering *(Refer to the Monitoring process area.)*
- measurement during requirements engineering *(Refer to the Measurement and Analysis process area.)*
- training for software requirements engineers *(Refer to the Organizational Training and Awareness process area.)*

RTSE:SG1.SP3 IDENTIFY ARCHITECTURE AND DESIGN GUIDELINES

Guidelines for designing resilience into software and systems are identified.

Architecture and design may be the most important phases for the development of resilient software and systems. Effective architecture and design choices not only will produce a structure that is more resilient and resistant to disruption but will also help prescribe and guide better decision making and guideline selection during implementation and assembly and integration. Poor, ill-informed decisions made during architecture and design can lead to design flaws that can never be overcome in later development phases or in operations.

A resilient architecture and its supporting design satisfy specified resilience requirements, reflect the defined operational production environment, and anticipate how best to adapt to changing conditions. A resilient architecture accounts for issues of interconnectivity, interoperability, service continuity, scale, and complexity. The design contains minimal to no detectable weaknesses that could be exploited when translated into implemented software and systems. A resilient architecture ensures that high-value services are operational during times of stress and the software and systems that support them are able to recover and return to operation in a reasonable period of time after a disruptive event.

Architecture and design guidelines for developing resilient software and systems cover design concepts, architecture, component design, detailed design, and design review and assessment.

Typical work products

1. Architecture and design guidelines for resilient software and systems

Subpractices

1. Identify architecture and design guidelines for the development of resilient software and systems.

    Guidelines are project-specific but should address topics such as the following:
    - risk analysis during architecture and design
    - threat analysis during architecture and design
    - design assumptions, decisions, and rationales
    - methods for representing defender and attacker perspectives (such as use scenarios)
    - attack surface
    - secure design patterns at the architecture and design level
    - access control *(Refer to the Access Management process area.)*
    - identity management *(Refer to the Identity Management process area.)*
    - data security, including the use of encryption and credentials management
    - control identification and prioritization during architecture and design *(Refer to the Controls Management process area.)*
    - analysis of open-source, COTS, and legacy software, including verification of required functional and resilience behavior and absence of malicious content
    - service-oriented architectures, virtualization, and cloud computing (software as a service)
    - integration with existing architectures (interconnectivity and interoperability)
    - analysis for system complexity and scale, including end-to-end business process and service vulnerability analysis and failure analysis
    - inspections and architectural and design reviews, including validating desired or attained levels of software and system resilience
    - quality assurance during architecture and design
    - monitoring and audit (for example, of system logs, for intrusion prevention and detection) during architecture and design *(Refer to the Monitoring process area.)*
    - measurement during architecture and design *(Refer to the Measurement and Analysis process area.)*
    - training for software architects and designers *(Refer to the Organizational Training and Awareness process area.)*

RTSE:SG1.SP4 IDENTIFY IMPLEMENTATION GUIDELINES

Guidelines for implementing resilient software and systems are identified.

Implementation includes the life-cycle phases of software coding and software and system testing. The purpose of implementation is to ensure that all resilience requirements are met, as reflected in the software and system architecture and design. Resilient software and systems are predictable in execution during both normal operations and times of stress. They are as free from exploitable vulnerabilities as possible.

Coding guidelines for resilient software include, for example, the use of secure coding standards and static and dynamic code analysis tools to ensure that standards are met and that identifiable software vulnerabilities have been eliminated. Standards may address, for example, input and output validation, exception handling, and the use of logging and tracing for debugging and diagnosis.

Testing guidelines for resilient software and systems include a wide range of testing techniques such as white box, black box, fuzz, and penetration testing, all designed to demonstrate the satisfaction of resilience requirements. In addition, software and systems are tested to produce evidence that attained levels of software and system resilience are as expected (sometimes referred to as "assurance cases"). Testing guidelines include the identification of approaches and cases that will be used during final inspection and when software needs to undergo regression testing as the result of a change that is made after the software is released into production, such as a patch to address a software vulnerability.

Typical work products

1. Coding guidelines for resilient software
2. Testing guidelines for resilient software
3. Testing guidelines for resilient systems

Subpractices

1. Identify coding guidelines for the development of resilient software.
   Guidelines are project-specific but should address topics such as the following:
   - risk analysis during coding
   - threat analysis during coding
   - attack surface evaluation and mitigation
   - secure design patterns at the implementation level
   - secure coding standards (language-specific)
   - code checklists, reviews, inspections, and static and dynamic code analysis, including tools to support these, which can be used to verify
     - that resilience requirements are satisfied
     - that architecture and design guidelines were followed
     - the absence of banned functions
     - the absence of commonly known vulnerabilities
     - that desired or attained levels of software resilience are present
   - conducting more in-depth reviews for the highest-risk, highest-value code
   - control identification and prioritization during coding (*Refer to the Controls Management process area.*)
   - quality assurance during coding

- monitoring and audit during coding
- measurement during coding
- training for software developers

2. Identify testing guidelines for the development of resilient software.

   Guidelines are project-specific but should address topics such as the following:
   - risk analysis during software testing
   - threat analysis during software testing
   - attack surface reevaluation and mitigation
   - at the software level, methods for
     - resilience requirements functional testing
     - unit testing (commonly referred to as "white box testing"), including code coverage analysis
     - black box testing that focuses on the software's externally visible behavior
     - fuzz testing
     - penetration testing, including assessment by external entities (*Refer to the External Dependencies Management process area.*)
     - testing for specific vulnerabilities as well as vulnerability regression testing
     - application of threat and attack models
     - testing open-source, COTS, and legacy software, including verification of required functional and resilience behavior and absence of malicious content
     - inspection testing in support of approval to release
     - regression testing
   - automation of software test methods and tools to support automation
   - software testing reviews, which can be used to verify
     - that resilience requirements are satisfied
     - that architecture and design guidelines were followed
     - the absence of banned functions
     - the absence of commonly known vulnerabilities
     - that desired or attained levels of software resilience are present
   - code integrity and handling (including strong configuration management, verifiable chain of custody, anti-tampering, monitoring and analysis of event and audit logs, and code signing)
   - conducting more in-depth testing for the highest-risk, highest-value software
   - demonstrating compliance with interoperability standards (*Refer to TM:SG5.SP4.*)
   - testing controls during software testing (*Refer to the Controls Management process area.*)
   - quality assurance during software testing, including criteria for releasing tested software into production
   - monitoring and audit during software testing
   - measurement during software testing
   - training for software test engineers

3. Identify testing guidelines for the development of resilient systems.

   Guidelines are project-specific but should address topics such as the following:
   - risk analysis during system testing

- threat analysis during system testing
- attack surface reevaluation and mitigation
- at the system level, methods for
  - resilience requirements functional testing
  - black box testing that focuses on the system's externally visible behavior
  - fuzz testing
  - penetration testing
  - testing for specific vulnerabilities as well as vulnerability regression testing
  - application of threat and attack models
  - integration testing
  - testing open-source, COTS, and legacy software in a system environment, including verification of required functional and resilience behavior
  - testing for system complexity and scale, including end-to-end business process and service vulnerability analysis and failure analysis
  - inspection testing in support of approval to release
  - regression testing
- automation of system test methods and tools to support automation
- system testing reviews, which can be used to verify
  - that resilience requirements are satisfied
  - that architecture and design guidelines were followed
  - that desired or attained levels of system resilience are present
- conducting more in-depth testing in a system environment for the highest-risk, highest-value business processes, services, and software
- demonstrating compliance with interoperability standards *(Refer to TM:SG5.SP4.)*
- testing controls during system testing *(Refer to the Controls Management process area.)*
- quality assurance during system testing, including criteria for releasing a tested system into production
- monitoring and audit during system testing
- measurement during system testing
- training for system test engineers

RTSE:SG1.SP5 IDENTIFY ASSEMBLY AND INTEGRATION GUIDELINES

Guidelines for the assembly and integration of resilient software into resilient systems are identified.

During assembly and integration, the logical design assumptions for software and systems meet the physical, business, technical, organizational, and individual user realities of the operational production environment. Vulnerabilities (and their exploitation) can increase significantly based on assembly-integration design errors, architectural mismatches among software assets, insecure identity management and services, false assumptions about an asset's properties, an over-reliance on perimeter-based network security mechanisms, and the use of assets in environments not envisioned by the assets' designers.

Business pressures for increased efficiency and flexibility are moving applications toward "just-in-time" service creation and delivery (for example, through dynamic assembly in a web services environment) and are therefore stressing the limits of resilience even further. User privacy concerns regarding the use of their identifiable information for tracking and tracing may create constraints and conflict with resilience goals. During assembly and integration, the potential system-wide effects of the emergent behavior of large numbers of software components and services have to be addressed in the operational production environment.

The assembly and integration of software and system assets to the end objective of ensuring resilience are not robust, well-understood disciplines, so they are subject to organizational interpretation and tailoring.

Typical work products

1. Assembly and integration guidelines for resilient systems

Subpractices

1. Identify assembly and integration guidelines for resilient systems.
   Guidelines are project-specific but should address topics such as the following:
   - for legacy software, COTS, and open-source software, analysis of existing software and system artifacts such as requirements specifications, architectures, designs, threat environment, code, test results, monitoring results, and vulnerabilities
   - use of analysis technologies such as reverse engineering, function abstraction, correctness verification, flow analysis, statistical analysis, test design and evaluation, and assurance auditing
   - analyzing interfaces with untrusted systems for vulnerabilities
   - end-to-end analysis of cross-software, cross-system work flows that support high-value business processes and services
   - containment and recovery from failures (failure analysis) in the context of service continuity (*Refer to the Service Continuity process area.*)
   - demonstrating compliance with interoperability standards (*Refer to TM:SG5.SP4.*)
   - testing of controls during assembly and integration (*Refer to the Controls Management process area.*)
   - at the assembled system level, methods for
     - resilience requirements functional testing
     - black box testing that focuses on the system's externally visible behavior
     - fuzz testing
     - penetration testing
     - testing for specific vulnerabilities, as well as vulnerability regression testing
     - application of threat and attack models
     - integration testing
     - testing open-source, COTS, and legacy software in a system environment, including verification of required functional and resilience behavior

- testing for system complexity and scale, including end-to-end business process and service vulnerability analysis and failure analysis
- inspection testing in support of approval to release
- regression testing
• quality assurance, including criteria for releasing an assembled system into production
• measurement during system assembly and integration
• training for assembly and integration engineers

RTSE:SG2 DEVELOP RESILIENT TECHNICAL SOLUTION DEVELOPMENT PLANS

Plans for addressing resilience in the development life cycle are based on documented guidelines.

Planning for the incorporation of resilience into the development life cycle ensures that resilience activities and controls are included as a required part of the production of software and systems.

Planning involves first identifying which software and system technology assets warrant the integration of resilience activities into their development life cycles, and at what level. The plan describes the selection and incorporation of appropriate guidelines for addressing resilience in the life-cycle phases. These guidelines ensure consistency of resilience activities across projects and when using different life-cycle methodologies. The plan details how resilience activities will be incorporated and how they will be monitored and measured to ensure resilience requirements are appropriately considered in preliminary and detailed design, implementation, and assembly and integration. The plan also calls for interim reviews of resilience activities at all key milestones and decision points of the development life cycle.

The plan should be communicated to all staff involved in the development life cycle so that there is broad awareness of the organization's mandate to address resilience as a project, software, and system requirement. This should extend to external entities as well, particularly when projects have been outsourced or when proprietary life-cycle methodologies are being used by projects. (*Refer to the External Dependencies Management process area.*)

The identification, definition, management, and control of technology assets are addressed in the Asset Definition and Management process area. This includes the inventory of high-value technology assets, those that are essential to the successful operation of organizational services.

The prioritization of technology assets relative to their importance in supporting the delivery of key services is addressed in the Technology Management process area, specifically TM:SG1.SP1, Prioritize Technology Assets. While the Technology Management process assumes that technology assets already exist via, for example, the organization's asset inventory, TM:SG1.SP1 can be effectively used to prioritize software and system assets that are yet to be developed or require significant upgrades or assets that are to be acquired.

The management of technology asset risk and the maintenance of operational technology assets via monitoring, configuration management, and change control are described in the Technology Management process area.

RTSE:SG2.SP1 SELECT AND TAILOR GUIDELINES

Guidelines are determined for a specific software or system development project using selection criteria.

Organizations need to have well-established, business-driven criteria to determine which guidelines to incorporate into the development life cycle for a specific software or system technology asset.

Determining which guidelines to incorporate is based, in large part, on the relative value of the asset and its resilience requirements *(as defined in the Resilience Requirements Development process area).*

Once criteria are established, they are used to select and tailor resilience guidelines for each life-cycle phase for a defined software or system development project *(refer to RTSE:SG1).*

Typical work products

1. Selection criteria
2. Selected requirements guidelines
3. Selected architecture and design guidelines
4. Selected implementation guidelines
5. Selected assembly guidelines

Subpractices

1. Identify selection criteria for resilience guidelines.
    Selection criteria may include the following:
    - the value of services that the software or system is intended to support
    - the relative value of the software or system to services that it is intended to support
    - the extent to which the software or system addresses actions called for in service risk mitigation plans (along with the corresponding risk impacts and valuations)
    - the priority of resilience objectives and requirements that must be satisfied by the software or system
    - cost/benefit trade-off analyses, such as the relative importance of identifying software flaws early in the software development life cycle versus the cost to implement the guidelines
    - make versus buy trade-off analyses
    - the availability of adequately trained staff
    - staff training costs
2. Select and tailor guidelines for a specific software or system asset.

Prioritize guideline selection criteria based on discussion with key stakeholders, such as service owners. Determine which guidelines to include in the software or system development plan by applying the most important selection criteria for a specific software or system development project. Tailor guidelines as appropriate for the project.

RTSE:SG2.SP2 I*NTEGRATE* S*ELECTED* G*UIDELINES WITH A* D*EFINED* S*OFTWARE AND* S*YSTEM* D*EVELOPMENT* P*ROCESS*

Selected resilience guidelines are integrated with a defined software and system development process and a documented plan.

Many organizations use documented approaches such as process models to define, manage, and improve software and system development processes that may even extend beyond life-cycle methodologies. Such approaches help ensure high-quality products that satisfy their requirements. However, these approaches do not typically address or incorporate resilience considerations. As a result, resilience as a property or quality of software and systems is absent.

Methods and models for improving software and system development processes must be extended to include resilience as a foundational element in process definition and as an expected attribute of software and systems that are produced through this process. Failure to include resilience as part of the development process may result in software and system assets that are unable to resist, tolerate, and recover from adverse or disruptive events. Such failures will likely affect the ability of key services and business processes to fulfill their mission.

Similarly, the plan for a specific software or system development project must be enhanced and updated to reflect resilience requirements and guidelines in the following areas:

- development process definitions
- tasks, progress measures, milestones, deliverables, and the assignment of resources (staff, funding, capital equipment, etc.) to implement resilience guidelines
- new risks introduced by resilience guidelines and the elevation of currently identified risks to a higher priority
- stakeholder involvement
- commitment to the updated plan
- decision criteria and authority at key project milestones

This specific practice assumes that

- defined development processes exist and are in use for any software or system that is required to meet resilience requirements
- documented plans exist and are used to develop any software or system that is required to meet resilience requirements

Typical work products

1. Updated development process definitions
2. Updated development plan

Subpractices

1. Update process definitions.

   The defined development process that is being used as the basis for a specific software or system development project is updated to reflect selected resilience guidelines *(refer to RTSE:SG1).*

   Process definitions are periodically reviewed and updated to reflect new requirements, new understanding, and new guidelines throughout the development process.

2. Update the development plan.

   The documented plan that is being used to conduct a specific software or system development project is updated to reflect tasks, progress measures, milestones, deliverables, and the assignment of resources necessary to implement selected resilience guidelines *(refer to RTSE:SG1).* In addition, updates to the plan should reflect any new risks introduced by the integration of resilience guidelines, as well as stakeholder involvement and necessary commitments to execute the updated plan.

   Development plans are periodically reviewed and updated throughout the development process.

RTSE:SG3 EXECUTE THE PLAN

Progress against the plan for developing resilient software and systems is monitored throughout the development life cycle.

Progress against the development plan is monitored on an ongoing basis by the development team, and status against the plan is periodically measured and reported to key stakeholders at project milestones identified in the development plan. The purpose of monitoring, measurement, and review is to ensure that software and systems satisfy their resilience requirements.

Upon successful completion of the development plan, software and systems are formally reviewed to ensure they have met specified resilience requirements. The result of a successful formal review is organizational approval to release the asset into production.

RTSE:SG3.SP1 MONITOR EXECUTION OF THE DEVELOPMENT PLAN

Execution of the development plan is monitored to ensure that software and system resilience requirements are satisfied.

The organization uses the development plan as the basis and criteria for monitoring project performance in satisfying resilience requirements. Any deviations from the plan with respect to resilience must be analyzed to understand the potential impact on the project, the software, the system, and the organization.

The monitoring process must include requirements, design, implementation, and assembly and integration reviews at identified milestones to ensure that software and systems satisfy all stated resilience requirements at the level appropriate to the life-cycle phase. In the case where requirements cannot be satisfactorily demonstrated, development plans must be renegotiated with owners and stakeholders and updated. Any new and residual risks must be identified and managed *(refer to the Risk Management process area)*.

To ensure that monitoring progress against the plan is performed on a timely and consistent basis, the organization should establish procedures that specify the frequency, protocol, and responsibility for monitoring a specific project's progress and performance in satisfying resilience requirements. (Responsibility is typically assigned to the organizational owner of the software or system or the applicable service owner.) These procedures should be consistent with development plan tasks and activities. It may be appropriate to adjust the monitoring frequency in response to changes in the risk environment, changes to resilience requirements, and changes in project staff.

Typical work products

1. Project review procedures
2. Project measures, reports, and review results
3. Updated project plans
4. Updated resilience guidelines
5. Updated process definitions

Subpractices

1. Monitor project performance against the development plan to ensure that resilience requirements are satisfied.

    This may include, for example, collecting, analyzing, and reporting
    - the effectiveness of resilience guidelines in satisfying resilience requirements
    - status toward meeting planned milestones that demonstrate the satisfaction of resilience requirements
    - actual expenditures against budgeted expenditures for implementing resilience guidelines
    - identified risks and risk mitigation plans
    - impacts to service continuity plans for the software or system in development
    - impacts to controls for protecting and sustaining services, software, and systems
    - improvements to resilience guidelines and process definitions that address resilience

2. Update development project plans, resilience guidelines, and process definitions as appropriate.

   Updates may include normal, expected changes and improvements. Updates may also include the results of having to renegotiate resilience requirements, failure to meet milestone review criteria, failure to implement resilience guidelines, cost and schedule deviations beyond established thresholds, and reassignment of vital staff. All of these conditions should be identified and managed as project risks.

RTSE:SG3.SP2 RELEASE RESILIENT TECHNICAL SOLUTIONS INTO PRODUCTION

Software and systems that demonstrate satisfaction of resilience requirements are released into production.

Prior to releasing software or system assets into an operational production environment, these assets should undergo a formal inspection against documented criteria to ensure they have met specified resilience requirements.

The result of satisfying inspection criteria is approval to release software and system assets into production (sometimes referred to as "authority or authorization to operate").

Typical work products

1. Inspection criteria
2. Inspection procedures
3. Inspection results
4. Production-ready software and system assets

Subpractices

1. Establish inspection criteria.

   Inspection criteria should be sufficient to provide an acceptable level of assurance and confidence to release software and systems into operational production environments. Such criteria will likely include
   - documented evidence in support of selected assurance cases (*Refer to RTSE:SG1.SP1.*)
   - results of testing approaches and test cases used during implementation and assembly as called for in resilience guidelines reflected in development plans (*Refer to RTSE:SG1.SP2 and SP3.*)
   - demonstrated satisfaction of resilience requirements overall and in support of service continuity plans for services supported by the assets being inspected
   - the availability of complete and thorough asset documentation, including updated asset inventories (*Refer to the Asset Definition and Management process area.*)
   - demonstrating that controls for protecting and sustaining services, software, and systems are implemented and adequate

Some criteria or subcriteria may be selected based on the priority of the software or system such that higher-value assets are subjected to more stringent or more comprehensive inspection.

2. **Inspect software and systems to ensure they have satisfied inspection criteria.**
To ensure that asset inspections are performed in a predictable, repeatable manner, the organization should establish procedures that specify the protocol and responsibility for performing an asset inspection against established criteria. Inspection procedures should include documentation of inspection results, including any actions that have to be closed prior to release and the identification of new and residual risks that have to be managed *(refer to the Risk Management process area)*.

Responsibility for assembling a qualified inspection team and conducting inspections may be assigned to managers who have direct responsibility for the service or services that the asset will be supporting as well as the asset's performance in the operational production environment. Quality assurance and internal audit staff may also fill this role. Staff conducting inspections should be sufficiently knowledgeable and experienced to verify and validate the satisfaction of all established inspection criteria.

3. **Approve assets for release.**
Assets are approved for release into the operational production environment upon demonstrating that they have met all established inspection criteria. The approval process may allow for waivers of specific criteria based on high-level manager approvals.

Elaborated Generic Practices by Goal

Refer to the Generic Goals and Practices document in Appendix A for general guidance that applies to all process areas. This section provides elaborations relative to the application of the Generic Goals and Practices to the Resilient Technical Solution Engineering process area.

RTSE:GG1 ACHIEVE SPECIFIC GOALS

The operational resilience management system supports and enables achievement of the specific goals of the Resilient Technical Solution Engineering process area by transforming identifiable input work products to produce identifiable output work products.

RTSE:GG1.GP1 PERFORM SPECIFIC PRACTICES

Perform the specific practices of the Resilient Technical Solution Engineering process area to develop work products and provide services to achieve the specific goals of the process area.

Elaboration:

Specific practices RTSE:SG1.SP1 through RTSE:SG3.SP2 are performed to achieve the goals of the resilient technical solution engineering process.

RTSE:GG2 INSTITUTIONALIZE A MANAGED PROCESS

Resilient technical solution engineering is institutionalized as a managed process.

RTSE:GG2.GP1 ESTABLISH PROCESS GOVERNANCE

Establish and maintain governance over the planning and performance of the resilient technical solution engineering process.

Refer to the Enterprise Focus process area for more information about providing sponsorship and oversight to the resilient technical solution engineering process.

Subpractices

1. Establish governance over process activities.

    Elaboration:

    > Governance over the resilient technical solution engineering process may be exhibited by
    > - establishing a higher-level position, often the chief information officer, responsible for the resilience of the organization's software and system assets
    > - developing and publicizing higher-level managers' objectives and requirements for developing resilient software and systems
    > - oversight over the development, acquisition, operations, and management of high-value software and system assets
    > - sponsoring and providing oversight of policies, procedures, standards, and guidelines for the development of software and system assets and for establishing asset ownership and custodianship
    > - making higher-level managers aware of applicable compliance obligations related to the development of resilient software and systems, and regularly reporting on the organization's satisfaction of these obligations to higher-level managers
    > - oversight over the establishment, implementation, and maintenance of the organization's internal control system for software and system assets, including those for protection, continuity, and sustainment during the development life cycle
    > - sponsoring and funding process activities
    > - implementing a technology steering committee that includes software and systems under development
    > - providing guidance for prioritizing software and system assets relative to the organization's high-priority strategic objectives
    > - providing guidance on identifying, assessing, and managing operational risks related to software and system assets in development
    > - providing guidance for resolving gaps or shortfalls in the satisfaction of software and system resilience requirements during development
    > - verifying that the process supports strategic resilience objectives and is focused on the assets and services that are of the highest relative value in meeting strategic objectives

- regular reporting from organizational units with responsibility for development projects to higher-level managers on process activities and results
- creating dedicated higher-level management feedback loops on decisions about the process and recommendations for improving the process
- conducting regular internal and external audits and related reporting to appropriate committees on software and system asset controls and the effectiveness of the process
- creating formal programs to measure the effectiveness of process activities, and reporting these measurements to higher-level managers

2. Develop and publish organizational policy for the process.

Elaboration:

The resilient technical solution engineering policy should address
- responsibility, authority, and ownership for performing process activities
- integrating resilience guidelines with a defined software development process
- procedures, standards, and guidelines for
  - developing software and systems that meet their resilience requirements during all life-cycle phases
  - describing and identifying software and system owners and custodians
  - developing and documenting resilience requirements for software and system assets *(Refer to the Resilience Requirements Development process area.)*
  - establishing, implementing, and maintaining an internal control system for software and systems, and controls to sustain services and the systems and software on which they depend
  - maintaining environmental conditions for physical components of systems (hardware and infrastructure)
  - managing software and system asset risk, in development and in operations
  - establishing software and system asset service continuity plans and procedures
  - retiring software and system assets at the end of their useful life
  - architectural interoperability
  - project reviews
  - formal inspections prior to releasing software and system assets into production
- the association of software and system assets to core organizational services, and the prioritization of assets for service continuity
- requesting, approving, and providing access to software and system assets to persons, objects, and entities, including type and extent of access and requests that originate externally to the organization *(Refer to the Access Management process area for more information about granting access [rights and privileges] to software and system assets. Refer to the Identity Management process area for more information about creating and maintaining identities for persons, objects, and entities.)*
- methods for measuring adherence to policy, exceptions granted, and policy violations

RTSE:GG2.GP2 PLAN THE PROCESS

Establish and maintain the plan for performing the resilient technical solution engineering process.

Elaboration:

A plan for performing the resilient technical solution engineering process is created to ensure that resilience is considered in the development process for all software and systems. The plan must address the inclusion of resilience guidelines in the software and system development plans and development life-cycle process definitions, as well as consideration of multiple asset owners, custodians, and stakeholders at various levels of the organization. In addition, because software and system assets may be developed and deployed in more than one geographical location by more than one development organization, the plan must extend to external stakeholders that can enable or adversely affect software and system resilience during development.

The plan for the resilient technical solution engineering process should not be confused with software and system development plans *(refer to RTSE:SG2.SP2 and RTSE:SG3)*. The plan for the resilient technical solution engineering process details how the organization will ensure that software and system assets are developed to satisfy their resilience requirements, including updating software and system development plans and life-cycle process definitions to reflect resilience guidelines.

Subpractices

1. Define and document the plan for performing the process.

   Elaboration:

   Special consideration in the plan may have to be given to establishing, implementing, and maintaining an internal control system for software and system assets, including planning to ensure these assets are protected, sustained, and continue to operate as intended. These activities are determined commensurate with software and system resilience requirements and the extent to which they support high-value services.

2. Define and document the process description.
3. Review the plan with relevant stakeholders and get their agreement.
4. Revise the plan as necessary.

RTSE:GG2.GP3 PROVIDE RESOURCES

Provide adequate resources for performing the resilient technical solution engineering process, developing the work products, and providing the services of the process.

Subpractices

1. Staff the process.

   Elaboration:

   > These are examples of staff required to implement and support the resilient technical solution engineering process:
   > - staff responsible for
   >   - software and system security during development and acquisition
   >   - business continuity and disaster recovery for software and system assets
   >   - implementing and maintaining software and system asset security controls (such as software architects, designers, developers, and testers trained in resilience requirements and guidelines)
   >   - configuration management, change management, and release management of software and system assets
   >   - trade-off analyses in support of guideline selection and prioritization
   >   - software and system development processes
   >   - project reviews
   >   - quality assurance
   > - staff involved in identifying and managing risk for software and systems in development
   > - external entities responsible for developing, implementing, and maintaining software and system assets
   > - owners and custodians of software and system assets (to identify and enforce resilience requirements)

   Refer to the Organizational Training and Awareness process area for information about training staff for resilience roles and responsibilities.

   Refer to the Human Resource Management process area for information about acquiring staff to fulfill roles and responsibilities.

2. Fund the process.

   Elaboration:

   At a minimum, funding must be available to execute software and system development plans that incorporate selected resilience guidelines.

   Refer to the Financial Resource Management process area for information about budgeting for, funding, and accounting for the development of resilience software and system assets.

3. Provide necessary tools, techniques, and methods to perform the process.

   Elaboration:

   Keep in mind that many of the automated tools used to support the resilient technical solution engineering process are themselves software assets that have to be managed according to the process.

These are examples of tools, techniques, and methods to support the resilient technical solution engineering process:
- project management tools
- threat analysis methods, techniques, and tools
- methods for representing defender and attacker perspectives such as misuse/abuse cases
- quality assurance methods such as vulnerability analysis
- methods and techniques for conducting resilience guidelines trade-off analyses and prioritizing resilience guidelines
- tools, techniques, and methods for
    - supporting and automating the guidelines that have been selected for each development life-cycle phase (requirements, architecture and design, implementation, and assembly and integration)
    - identifying and managing risks to software and system assets by life-cycle phase, including tracking open risks to closure and monitoring the effectiveness of asset risk mitigation plans
    - maintaining software and system assets, including asset configuration management, change control, release management, and monitoring and logging of modification activities
    - ensuring software and system asset integrity during development, such as code signing
    - controlling access to software and system assets
    - analyzing open-source, COTS, and legacy software
    - measuring, reviewing, testing, monitoring, auditing, and inspecting software and systems at key milestones in their development life cycle
    - software and system asset backup, retention, and restoration throughout the development life cycle
    - managing software and system assets that are provided by external entities
- methods for establishing, implementing, and maintaining the internal control system for software and system assets throughout the development life cycle
- methods for the proper retirement and disposal of software and system assets

RTSE:GG2.GP4 ASSIGN RESPONSIBILITY

Assign responsibility and authority for performing the resilient technical solution engineering process, developing the work products, and providing the services of the process.

Elaboration:

Of paramount importance in assigning responsibility for the resilient technical solution engineering process is the establishment of software and system asset owners *(which is described in ADM:SG1.SP3).* Owners are responsible for establishing asset resilience requirements, ensuring these requirements are met throughout the development life cycle, and identifying and remediating gaps and risks where requirements are not being met. Owners may also be responsible for establishing, implementing, and maintaining an internal control system commensurate with meeting asset resilience requirements.

Refer to the Human Resource Management process area for more information about establishing resilience as a job responsibility, developing resilience performance goals and objectives, and measuring and assessing performance against these goals and objectives.

Refer to the Asset Definition and Management process area for more information about establishing ownership and custodianship of software and system assets.

Subpractices

1. Assign responsibility and authority for performing the process.

    Elaboration:

    Responsibility and authority may extend not only to staff inside the organization but to those with whom the organization has a contractual agreement for developing, implementing, and managing software and system assets (including implementation and management of controls and ensuring assets are sustained).

2. Assign responsibility and authority for performing the specific tasks of the process.

    Elaboration:

    > Responsibility and authority for performing resilient technical solution engineering tasks can be formalized by
    > - defining roles and responsibilities in the process plan and in software and system development plans
    > - including process tasks and responsibility for those tasks in specific job descriptions
    > - developing policy requiring organizational unit managers, line of business managers, project managers, and asset and service owners and custodians to participate in the process for assets under their ownership or custodianship
    > - including process tasks in staff performance management goals and objectives, with requisite measurement of progress against those goals
    > - developing and implementing contractual instruments (as well as service level agreements) with external entities to establish responsibility and authority for outsourced and acquired software and system assets
    > - including process tasks in measuring performance of external entities against service level agreements *(Refer to the External Dependencies Management process area for additional details about managing relationships with external entities.)*

3. Confirm that people assigned with responsibility and authority understand it and are willing and able to accept it.

RTSE:GG2.GP5 TRAIN PEOPLE

Train the people performing or supporting the resilient technical solution engineering process as needed.

Refer to the Organizational Training and Awareness process area for more information about training the people performing or supporting the process.

Refer to the Human Resource Management process area for more information about inventorying skill sets, establishing a skill set baseline, identifying required skill sets, and measuring and addressing skill deficiencies.

Subpractices

1. Identify process skill needs.

   Elaboration:

   > These are examples of skills required in the resilient technical solution engineering process:
   > - software and system requirements engineering, architecture and design, implementation, and assembly and integration
   > - developing and selecting resilience guidelines that are used throughout the development life cycle
   > - managing the development of software and systems
   > - conducting effective trade-off analyses to inform decision making
   > - knowledge of tools, techniques, and methods that can be used to identify, analyze, mitigate, and monitor operational risks to software and system assets during their development life cycle
   > - establishing, implementing, and maintaining the internal control system for software and system assets during their development life cycle
   > - protecting and sustaining software and system assets to meet their resilience requirements

2. Identify process skill gaps based on available resources and their current skill levels.

3. Identify training opportunities to address skill gaps.

   Elaboration:

   > These are examples of training topics:
   > - software and system asset risk management concepts and activities (e.g., risk identification, analysis, mitigation, and monitoring) during development
   > - software and system asset resilience requirements development

- establishing, implementing, and maintaining an internal control system for protecting and sustaining software and system assets
- cross-training to ensure adequate knowledge and coverage of all software and system assets that are part of a specific development project
- proper techniques for inspecting software and system assets, including approval to release them into production
- software and system asset configuration, change, and release management
- supporting software and system asset owners and custodians in understanding the process and their roles and responsibilities with respect to its activities
- working with external entities that have responsibility for process activities
- using process methods, tools, and techniques, including those identified in RTSE:GG2:GP3 subpractice 3

4. Provide training and review the training needs as necessary.

RTSE:GG2.GP6 MANAGE WORK PRODUCT CONFIGURATIONS

Place designated work products of the resilient technical solution engineering process under appropriate levels of control.

Elaboration:

These are examples of resilient technical solution engineering work products placed under control:
- guidelines for the development of resilient software and systems, including general, requirements, architecture and design, implementation (coding and testing), and assembly and integration
- resilience guideline selection criteria
- development process definitions, updated to reflect resilience guidelines
- development plans, updated to reflect resilience guidelines
- administrative, technical, and physical controls for software and systems
- new and residual risks associated with resilience requirements and guidelines
- project review procedures
- project measures, reports, and results of reviews
- inspection criteria, procedures, and results
- production-ready software and system assets
- modification logs and audit reports
- baseline configuration items and configuration control logs and reports
- configuration management, change management, and release management systems
- baseline archives and backup media
- release builds, testing procedures, and release-build test results

- updated service continuity plans
- process plan
- policies and procedures
- contracts with external entities

Refer to the Technology Management process area for more information about managing software and system assets during operations.

RTSE:GG2.GP7 IDENTIFY AND INVOLVE RELEVANT STAKEHOLDERS

Identify and involve the relevant stakeholders of the resilient technical solution engineering process as planned.

Subpractices

1. Identify process stakeholders and their appropriate involvement.

   Elaboration:

   Because software and system assets may reside in a wide range of physical locations and be developed and maintained by internal and external entities, a substantial number of stakeholders are likely to be external to the organization.

   These are examples of stakeholders of the resilient technical solution engineering process:
   - owners and custodians of software and system assets
   - service and business process owners
   - organizational unit and line of business managers responsible for high-value software and system assets and the services they support
   - staff responsible for managing development risks to software and system assets
   - staff responsible for establishing, implementing, and maintaining an internal control system for software and system assets, including those responsible for configuration, change, and release management
   - staff required to develop, test, implement, and execute service continuity plans for software and system assets
   - staff responsible for maintaining process definitions for software and system development
   - staff in other organizational support functions, such as accounting or general services administration (particularly as related to software and system inventory valuation and retirement)
   - staff responsible for reviewing and approving assets prior to their release into production, including internal and external auditors

> Stakeholders are involved in various tasks in the resilient technical solution engineering process, such as
> - planning for software and system development, including the selection and tailoring of resilience guidelines
> - adding new software and systems to the technology asset inventory
> - creating software and system asset profiles and asset risk and vulnerability profiles
> - associating software and system assets with services and analyzing service dependencies
> - assigning resilience requirements for software and system assets
> - establishing, implementing, and maintaining controls for software and system assets
> - developing service continuity plans for software and system assets
> - managing development risks to software and system assets
> - managing software and system configurations, changes, and releases
> - controlling the development environment in which software and system assets reside
> - managing software and system asset external dependencies for assets developed and maintained by external entities
> - managing relationships with external entities that develop software and system assets (or components thereof)
> - reviewing and appraising the effectiveness of process activities
> - resolving issues in the process

2. Communicate the list of stakeholders to planners and those responsible for process performance.
3. Involve relevant stakeholders in the process as planned.

RTSE:GG2.GP8 MONITOR AND CONTROL THE PROCESS

Monitor and control the resilient technical solution engineering process against the plan for performing the process and take appropriate corrective action.

Refer to the Monitoring process area for more information about the collection, organization, and distribution of data that may be useful for monitoring and controlling processes.

Refer to the Measurement and Analysis process area for more information about establishing process metrics and measurement.

Refer to the Enterprise Focus process area for more information about providing process information to managers, identifying issues, and determining appropriate corrective actions.

Subpractices

1. Measure actual performance against the plan for performing the process.
2. Review accomplishments and results of the process against the plan for performing the process.

Elaboration:

> These are examples of metrics for the resilient technical solution engineering process:
> - percentage of resilience requirements unsatisfied by a specific software or system asset (this presumes that criteria for satisfaction are well established, such as evidence associated with one or more assurance cases)
>   - by life-cycle phase
>   - where lack of satisfaction has been identified as a residual risk to be managed
> - life-cycle costs associated with each resilience guideline (time, staff resources, and funding, including training)
> - number of high-impact defects and vulnerabilities for a specific software or system asset
>   - by life-cycle phase
>   - where such defects and vulnerabilities have established mitigation plans or have been identified as residual risks to be managed
> - number of software assets and number of system assets that do not have stated owners or custodians
> - number of software assets and number of system assets with incomplete asset profiles or other incomplete information (particularly the lack of stated resilience requirements)
> - percentage of software assets and percentage of system assets for which some form of risk assessment has been performed as required by policy
>   - by life-cycle phase
> - number of software and system development risks referred to the risk management process; number of risks where corrective action is still pending (by risk rank)
> - percentage of software assets and percentage of system assets for which the cost of compromise (loss, damage, disclosure, disruption in access to) has been quantified
> - number of unauthorized changes to software and system assets during a stated period
> - number of software and number of system assets that fail inspection and are not approved for release into production
>   - first time (with causes)
>   - number of times (with causes)
>   - time and resources to remediate per failure
> - level of adherence to external entity contracts and service level agreements
> - level of adherence to software and system development policies; number of policy violations; number of policy exceptions requested and number approved
> - number of process activities that are on track per plan
> - rate of change of costs to support the process

3. Review activities, status, and results of the process with the immediate level of managers responsible for the process and identify issues.

   Elaboration:

   > Periodic reviews of the resilient technical solution engineering process are needed to ensure that
   > - software and system assets have stated resilience requirements
   > - software and system assets are being developed in accordance with selected resilience guidelines
   > - software and system assets are satisfying their resilience requirements appropriate to the life-cycle phase under review
   > - administrative, technical, and physical controls are implemented during development
   > - controls are meeting the stated intent of software and system resilience requirements
   > - software and system process definitions and development plans are updated as required
   > - newly developed and acquired software and system assets are included in the asset inventory
   > - asset-service mapping is accurate and current
   > - ownership and custodianship of software and system assets are established and documented
   > - status reports are provided to appropriate stakeholders in a timely manner
   > - software and system development issues are referred to the risk management process when necessary
   > - actions requiring management involvement are elevated in a timely manner
   > - the performance of process activities is being monitored and regularly reported
   > - key measures are within acceptable ranges as demonstrated in governance dashboards or scorecards and financial reports
   > - actions resulting from inspections and internal and external audits are being closed in a timely manner

4. Identify and evaluate the effects of significant deviations from the plan for performing the process.
5. Identify problems in the plan for performing and executing the process.
6. Take corrective action when requirements and objectives are not being satisfied, when issues are identified, or when progress differs significantly from the plan for performing the process.

   Elaboration:

   For software and system assets, corrective action may require the revision of existing resilience requirements *(refer to the Resilience Requirements Management process area)*. Corrective action may also require the revision of existing

administrative, technical, and physical controls, development and implementation of new controls, or a change in the type of controls (preventive, detective, corrective, compensating, etc.).
7. Track corrective action to closure.

RTSE:GG2.GP9 OBJECTIVELY EVALUATE ADHERENCE

Objectively evaluate adherence of the resilient technical solution engineering process against its process description, standards, and procedures, and address non-compliance.

Elaboration:

> These are examples of activities to be reviewed:
> - identifying and prioritizing software and system assets that are to be developed
> - identifying software and system asset resilience requirements
> - identifying, selecting, and implementing software and system asset resilience guidelines
> - establishing and implementing software and system asset controls
> - identifying and managing software and system asset risks
> - developing service continuity plans for newly developed software and system assets
> - identifying and managing software and system asset dependencies
> - identifying and managing changes to software and system assets
> - decisions to not release software and system assets into production
> - aligning stakeholder requirements with the process plan
> - assigning responsibility, accountability, and authority for process activities
> - determining the adequacy of process reports and reviews in informing decision makers regarding the performance of operational resilience management activities and the need to take corrective action, if any
> - verifying controls on software and system assets
> - using process work products for improving strategies for protecting and sustaining software and system assets

> These are examples of work products to be reviewed:
> - resilience guidelines and costs to implement them
> - project review results by life-cycle phase
> - software and system asset internal controls documentation
> - software and system asset risk statements and mitigation plans
> - service continuity plans for newly developed software and system assets
> - business impact analysis results for newly developed software and system assets
> - results of inspections for releasing software and system assets into production
> - contracts with external entities

> - process plan and policies
> - software and system development issues that have been referred to the risk management process
> - process methods, techniques, and tools
> - metrics for the process *(Refer to RTSE:GG2.GP8 subpractice 2.)*

RTSE:GG2.GP10 Review Status with Higher-Level Managers

Review the activities, status, and results of the resilient technical solution engineering process with higher-level managers and resolve issues.

Elaboration:

Status reporting on the resilient technical solution engineering process may be part of the formal governance structure or may be performed through other organizational reporting requirements (such as through the chief risk officer or the chief resilience officer level). Audits of the process, particularly the validation and verification of asset resilience requirements satisfaction and the internal control system at points in time, may be escalated to higher-level managers through the organization's audit committee of the board of directors or similar construct in private or non-profit organizations.

Refer to the Enterprise Focus process area for more information about providing sponsorship and oversight to the operational resilience management system.

RTSE:GG3 Institutionalize a Defined Process

Resilient technical solution engineering is institutionalized as a defined process.

RTSE:GG3.GP1 Establish a Defined Process

Establish and maintain the description of a defined resilient technical solution engineering process.

Elaboration:

Managing the development of resilient software and systems is typically carried out by a project at the organizational unit or line of business level for convenience and accuracy and may have to be geographically focused (because of the location of specific assets and the skilled staff to develop them). However, to achieve consistent results in developing software and system assets, the activities at the project level must be derived from an enterprise definition of the resilient technical solution engineering process. Resilience guidelines and the selected software development process may be inconsistent across projects, particularly when assets support multiple services and thus have shared ownership across organizational lines, but the defined process remains consistent. The development of software and system assets by multiple organizational units and lines of business may affect asset management at the enterprise level and impede operational resilience.

In addition, a variable mix of administrative, technical, and physical controls may be used across the organization to meet the resilience requirements for software and system assets, but the process is consistent with the enterprise definition.

Establishing and tailoring process assets, including standard processes, are addressed in the Organizational Process Definition process area.

Establishing process needs and objectives and selecting, improving, and deploying process assets, including standard processes, are addressed in the Organizational Process Focus process area.

Subpractices

1. Select from the organization's set of standard processes those processes that cover the resilient technical solution engineering process and best meet the needs of the organizational unit or line of business.
2. Establish the defined process by tailoring the selected processes according to the organization's tailoring guidelines.
3. Ensure that the organization's process objectives are appropriately addressed in the defined process, and ensure that process governance extends to the tailored processes.
4. Document the defined process and the records of the tailoring.
5. Revise the description of the defined process as necessary.

RTSE:GG3.GP2 COLLECT IMPROVEMENT INFORMATION

Collect resilient technical solution engineering work products, measures, measurement results, and improvement information derived from planning and performing the process to support future use and improvement of the organization's processes and process assets.

Elaboration:

> These are examples of improvement work products and information:
> - updates to software and system development process definitions
> - updates to resilience guidelines
> - updates to software and system development plans
> - resilience requirements that are not being satisfied by software and system assets or are being exceeded

- reports on the effectiveness and weaknesses of controls
- improvements based on risk identification and mitigation
- software and system test and inspection results
- metrics and measurements of the viability of the process *(Refer to RTSE:GG2.GP8 subpractice 2.)*
- changes and trends in operating conditions, risk conditions, and the risk environment that affect process results
- lessons learned in post-event review of software and system asset incidents and disruptions in continuity
- conflicts and risks arising from dependencies on external entities
- lessons learned in updating, replacing, and retiring software and system assets from active use

Establishing the measurement repository and process asset library is addressed in the Organizational Process Definition process area. Updating the measurement repository and process asset library as part of process improvement and deployment is addressed in the Organizational Process Focus process area.

Subpractices

1. Store process and work product measures in the organization's measurement repository.
2. Submit documentation for inclusion in the organization's process asset library.
3. Document lessons learned from the process for inclusion in the organization's process asset library.
4. Propose improvements to the organizational process assets.

SERVICE CONTINUITY
Engineering

Purpose

The purpose of Service Continuity is to ensure the continuity of essential operations of services and related assets if a disruption occurs as a result of an incident, disaster, or other disruptive event.

Introductory Notes

The continuity of an organization's service delivery is a paramount concern in the organization's operational resilience activities. The organization can invest considerable time and resources in attempting to prevent a range of potential disruptive events, but no organization can mitigate all risk. As a result, the organization must be prepared to deal with the consequences of a disruption to its operations at any time. Significant disruption can result in dire circumstances for the organization, even bankruptcy or termination.

Service Continuity describes the organizational processes responsible for developing, deploying, exercising, implementing, and managing plans for responding to and recovering from events and restoring operations to business as usual. This requires that the organization have a plan and program for service continuity, assign adequate and sufficient resources to the plan and program, and have the requisite infrastructure to carry out the plan and program. Based on risk appetite and tolerance, the organization must determine which service continuity plans it needs to establish, develop the plans, and exercise them on a regular and sufficient basis to ensure they remain viable as long as the service is vital to the organization.

The organization also must consider the range of service continuity activities. Business continuity or contingency plans are developed and implemented to sustain a high-value service, while recovery and restoration plans are focused on bringing services back to an acceptable level of business as usual. To ensure that all plans can be executed at will when called upon, the organization must also develop sufficient logistics and delivery capabilities.

Before the organization can develop, exercise, and position service continuity plans for implementation, several other organizational activities must occur. These include identification of

- the high-value services and associated assets for which service continuity plans must be developed (*This is addressed in the Enterprise Focus and Asset Definition and Management process areas.*)
- the potential hazards or risks to these high-value services and assets (*This is addressed in the Vulnerability Analysis and Resolution and Risk Management process areas.*)
- the consequences of these risks to the organization and its susceptibility to them (*This is addressed in the Risk Management process area.*)

In managing operational risk and resilience, the Service Continuity process area is complementary to Controls Management. Controls Management focuses on "condition management" to prevent risk, while Service Continuity directs the organization's attention to "consequence management" or planning for managing the consequences of risks that are realized. Together, these process areas provide a comprehensive, coordinated, optimized, and holistic approach to managing asset and service resilience.

Related Process Areas

The development, implementation, and management of an internal control system to prevent risks and disruptive events are addressed in the Controls Management process area.

The identification and management of incidents that may require the execution of a service continuity plan are addressed in the Incident Management and Control process area.

Providing training for staff involved in service continuity plan testing and execution is addressed in the Organizational Training and Awareness process area.

The identification and prioritization of the organization's high-value services as strategic planning activities are addressed in the Enterprise Focus process area.

The consideration of consequences as a foundational element for developing a service continuity plan is addressed in the Risk Management process area.

The association of assets to the high-value services they support is performed in the Asset Definition and Management process area.

The development, implementation, and management of strategies for technology asset availability and integrity are addressed in the Technology Management process area.

The identification of vital records and databases for service continuity is addressed in the Knowledge and Information Management process area.

The resilience considerations of the organization's reliance on public services and public infrastructure are addressed in the Environmental Control process area.

Summary of Specific Goals and Practices

SC:SG1 Prepare for Service Continuity
    SC:SG1.SP1   Plan for Service Continuity
    SC:SG1.SP2   Establish Standards and Guidelines for Service Continuity
SC:SG2 Identify and Prioritize High-Value Services
    SC:SG2.SP1   Identify the Organization's High-Value Services
    SC:SG2.SP2   Identify Internal and External Dependencies and Interdependencies
    SC:SG2.SP3   Identify Vital Organizational Records and Databases
SC:SG3 Develop Service Continuity Plans
    SC:SG3.SP1   Identify Plans to Be Developed
    SC:SG3.SP2   Develop and Document Service Continuity Plans
    SC:SG3.SP3   Assign Staff to Service Continuity Plans
    SC:SG3.SP4   Store and Secure Service Continuity Plans
    SC:SG3.SP5   Develop Service Continuity Plan Training
SC:SG4 Validate Service Continuity Plans
    SC:SG4.SP1   Validate Plans to Requirements and Standards
    SC:SG4.SP2   Identify and Resolve Plan Conflicts
SC:SG5 Exercise Service Continuity Plans
    SC:SG5.SP1   Develop Testing Program and Standards
    SC:SG5.SP2   Develop and Document Test Plans
    SC:SG5.SP3   Exercise Plans
    SC:SG5.SP4   Evaluate Plan Test Results
SC:SG6 Execute Service Continuity Plans
    SC:SG6.SP1   Execute Plans
    SC:SG6.SP2   Measure the Effectiveness of the Plans in Operation
SC:SG7 Maintain Service Continuity Plans
    SC:SG7.SP1   Establish Change Criteria
    SC:SG7.SP2   Maintain Changes to Plans

Specific Practices by Goal

SC:SG1 Prepare for Service Continuity

The organizational processes for sustainability planning and execution are established.

Service continuity management requires both planning and execution. Planning involves establishing how the organization is going to address service continuity so that it is a consistent and pervasive organizational competency focused on operational resilience management. This involves developing a service continuity plan, establishing a service continuity program, assigning resources, and establishing service continuity standards and guidelines to ensure consistency.

SC:SG1.SP1 PLAN FOR SERVICE CONTINUITY

Planning is performed for developing and implementing the organization's service continuity process.

Service continuity management is a fundamental organizational process that ensures that high-value organizational services—both internally and externally focused—are able to continue to achieve their missions when disruptions occur. Service continuity cannot be effectively managed by reaction—the organization must plan its approach to service continuity, align this plan with strategic objectives, provide sponsorship and oversight to the plan to ensure that it is accepted by the organization as a strategic function, and obtain organizational commitments to the plan to ensure that service stakeholders understand and accept their responsibilities for service continuity.

The organization should develop and document its plan for service continuity and outline the specific objectives of the plan. The plan should reflect the organization's philosophy on service continuity and be translatable into a program for service continuity that can be implemented and managed.

The development of a plan for service continuity should not be confused with the development of service continuity plans. Service continuity plans are service-specific plans for sustaining services and associated assets under degraded conditions. A plan for service continuity is an organizational construct from which a service continuity program is developed and implemented as part of an operational resilience management system.

Typical work products

1. Plan for managing service continuity
2. Documented requests for commitment to the plan
3. Documented commitments to the plan

Subpractices

1. Establish the plan for managing service continuity.
    The plan for managing service continuity should address at a minimum
    - the organization's philosophy on service continuity
    - the structure of the service continuity program and process
    - the requirements of the service continuity program relative to managing operational resilience
    - the means and activities involved in identifying and prioritizing services and assets for continuity

- the roles and responsibilities necessary to carry out the plan and the program
- applicable training needs and requirements
- resources that will be required to meet the objectives of the plan
- relevant costs and budgets associated with service continuity

2. Establish commitments to the plan.
   Documented commitments by those responsible for implementing and supporting the plan are essential for plan effectiveness.
3. Revise the plan and commitments as necessary.

SC:SG1.SP2 ESTABLISH STANDARDS AND GUIDELINES FOR SERVICE CONTINUITY

The guidelines and standards for service continuity are established and communicated.

Guidelines and standards for service continuity ensure consistent plan documentation, distribution, testing, and execution enterprise-wide. They ensure that common, important elements of service continuity are considered by all organizational units and provide standards for consistent documentation, testing, and handling of plans. Guidelines and standards also provide the organization an ability to view service continuity at an enterprise level and to manage this function to meet organizational goals.

Typical work products

1. Service continuity management guidelines and standards

Subpractices

1. Develop and communicate service continuity guidelines and standards.
   Guidelines and standards are organization-specific but may address areas such as the following:
   - plan ownership and responsibility
   - requirements for when a plan must be developed
   - documentation requirements for plans
   - the standard content of plans (i.e., what must be addressed at a minimum)
   - testing requirements for plans, including testing intervals and reporting of results
   - identification and involvement of stakeholders
   - plan distribution and communication
   - plan versioning, storage, archiving, and security
   - training standards for service continuity and plan execution

SC:SG2 IDENTIFY AND PRIORITIZE HIGH-VALUE SERVICES

The services that are required to meet the organization's mission are identified and prioritized.

The high-value services of the organization must be identified as a baseline for identifying the extent and types of service continuity plans to be developed and implemented. Failure to identify and prioritize these services may result in the development of service continuity plans that are unnecessary or ineffective and increases the operational resilience management costs for the organization.

Prior to building service continuity plans, the organization must prioritize services, analyze service dependencies and interdependencies, and identify associated information and knowledge that must be addressed in the plans.

SC:SG2.SP1 IDENTIFY THE ORGANIZATION'S HIGH-VALUE SERVICES

The high-value services of the organization and their associated assets are identified.

The identification and prioritization of the organization's high-value services as strategic planning activities are addressed in the Enterprise Focus process area. This practice is included here to emphasize the importance of prioritizing high-value services as a foundational activity in the identification and development of service continuity plans.

A fundamental risk management principle is to focus on activities to protect and sustain services and assets that most directly affect the organization's ability to achieve its mission. Identifying high-value services, their associated assets, and the activities that support these services must be performed before the organization attempts to develop service continuity plans.

The association of assets to the high-value services they support is performed in the Asset Definition and Management process area.

Typical work products

1. Prioritized list of high-value organizational services, activities, and associated assets
2. Results of security risk assessment and business impact analyses

Subpractices

1. Identify the organization's high-value services, associated assets, and activities.
2. Analyze and document the relative value of providing these services and the resulting impact on the organization if these services are interrupted.

    Consideration of the consequences of the loss of high-value organizational services is typically performed as part of a business impact analysis. In addition, the consequences of risks to high-value services are identified and analyzed in risk assessment activities. The organization must consider this information when prioritizing high-value services.

    The consideration of consequences as the result of risk is addressed in the Risk Management process area.

3. Prioritize and document the list of high-value services that must be provided if a disruption occurs.

    The identification and prioritization of the organization's high-value services as strategic planning activities are addressed in the Enterprise Focus process area.

SC:SG2.SP2 IDENTIFY INTERNAL AND EXTERNAL DEPENDENCIES AND INTERDEPENDENCIES

The internal and external relationships necessary to ensure service continuity are identified and analyzed.

The resilience considerations of the organization's reliance on public services and public infrastructure are addressed in the Environmental Control process area. The association of internal and external assets to the services they support is addressed in the Asset Definition and Management process area. Managing relationships with external entities is addressed in the External Dependencies Management process area. This practice is included here to emphasize the need to determine the layers of support on which services depend in order to develop effective and comprehensive service continuity plans.

Services depend on organizational assets, both internal and external, to ensure continuity of operations. They also rely on external entities such as public agencies and infrastructure such as public utilities and telecommunications. These dependencies and interdependencies must be identified in order to ensure a robust consideration of the range of planning that must be incorporated into the service continuity plans.

Typical work products

1. List of public service providers on which services depend (*Refer also to EC:SG4.SP3 and SP4.*)
2. List of external entities, including business partners and vendors that facilitate service delivery
3. Key contacts list

Subpractices

1. Identify and document internal infrastructure dependencies that the organization relies upon to provide services.
   This practice requires that the organization document the association between services and the internal and external assets—people, information, technology, and facilities—that support the services. (*This practice is formally performed in the Asset Definition and Management process area.*)
2. Identify and document external entities that the organization relies upon to provide services.
3. Develop a key contacts list for organizational services that can be included as part of the service continuity plans.

SC:SG2.SP3 IDENTIFY VITAL ORGANIZATIONAL RECORDS AND DATABASES

Vital information required for service continuity is identified.

The resilience of information is addressed in the Knowledge and Information Management process area. This practice is included here to emphasize the importance of information assets in the development of effective and comprehensive service continuity plans.

Vital records and databases constitute high-value information assets that are essential to the continued operation of services during and after a disruption. Thus, these assets must be considered in the development of service continuity plans. Because information in the form of vital records and databases tends to be distributed organization-wide, vital records and databases must be inventoried to ensure that they are properly included in the service continuity plans. *(Developing and maintaining a comprehensive asset inventory are addressed in the Asset Definition and Management process area.)*

Vital records are typically distinguished from other types of information. Vital records include those records that the organization relies upon to protect the legal and financial rights of the organization and of individuals directly affected by disruption. In contrast, files and databases are types of information that are most typically associated with the direct operation of a specific service. For example, the vendor database is a necessary component of paying invoices. Vital records may be more universal in that they can apply to many service continuity plans, while files and databases may be more applicable to specific services.

Typical work products

1. Vital records, such as
   - organizational orders of succession
   - delegations of authority
   - contracts and service level agreements with external entities, including vendors and business partners
   - organizational legal operating charters
   - personnel records
2. Directory of vital staff (people assets) with contact information, roles, and responsibilities
3. List of files and databases that support high-value service operation

Subpractices

1. Identify and document vital records and databases.
   This practice is formally performed in the Knowledge and Information Management process area.
2. Identify and document vital staff and their specific roles in relation to the services being provided.
   This practice is formally performed in the People Management process area.
3. Ensure that vital records and databases are protected, accessible, and usable if a disruption occurs.

This practice is formally performed in the Knowledge and Information Management process area.

SC:SG3 DEVELOP SERVICE CONTINUITY PLANS

Service continuity plans for high-value organizational services are developed.

Service continuity plans are a proactively established description of the actions an organization will take if a service disruption occurs. They are generally focused on managing the organizational consequences of service disruption based on a range of potential events that can cause disruption, such as incidents and disasters. Service continuity plan development is in essence a risk management and control activity that seeks to limit or control the consequences of realized risk. Thus, the genesis for a service continuity plan may be risk assessment and mitigation activities or lessons learned from past disruptions.

Service continuity plans can take many forms, and often a service continuity plan is the aggregation of more than one type of plan.

> These are examples of types of service continuity plans:
> - Business continuity plans focus on the continued provision of a service under degraded circumstances.
> - Recovery plans focus on limiting and containing damage as a result of the disruption and dealing with the consequences of the disruption.
> - Restoration plans focus on performing the actions necessary to bring a service back to its expected and normal level of operation and output (as was in place before the disruption).

Typically, continuity and recovery plans provide for immediate, response-driven activities, while restoration plans are longer-term activities that may extend for a considerable time after the immediate consequences of disruption have been experienced.

Service continuity plans are best developed when they are the result of a comprehensive and optimized consideration of the requirements for protecting and sustaining a service. In other words, as a foundation for operational resilience, the organization should develop service continuity plans as a part of implementing strategies for protecting and sustaining services and assets to meet resilience requirements.

Service continuity plans come at a cost to the organization. The development and maintenance of these plans are cost-intensive, as is the regular exercising of the plans to ensure they work as intended. Executing a service continuity plan is also costly to the organization. Thus, the cost of these plans must be evaluated and balanced with protective controls that have been implemented to prevent disruption and the value of the services and assets that would be disrupted.

The development of service continuity plans involves the identification of plans to be developed, the development of the plans, the assignment of resources to the plans, and the maintenance of the plans.

SC:SG3.SP1 Identify Plans to Be Developed

Required service continuity plans are identified.

The organization identifies the service continuity plans to be developed, tested, executed, and maintained. This can be done through several means:

- in the regular course of designing and implementing resilience requirements for services and assets
- as the result of security risk assessment and management activities (in the development of preventive controls and mitigation actions)
- as part of the business impact analysis process (a typically business-continuity–driven activity that seeks to identify the consequences of service disruption)
- as a result of legal, regulatory, compliance, and audit activities (where existing controls may not be deemed as effective across a range of potential disruptive events)
- in response to a major event or catastrophe (whether or not the organization was affected)

Typical work products

1. List of service continuity plans (to be developed)

Subpractices

1. Identify service continuity plans to be developed.

SC:SG3.SP2 Develop and Document Service Continuity Plans

The required service continuity plans are developed and documented.

Required service continuity plans are developed by the organization or its assigned representatives. Plans are typically developed by the service owner, but this varies by organization and might include significant involvement of IT staff if the service is highly automated or has one or more application systems associated with it.

The contents of the plan and the documentation requirements are established by the organization as part of the organization's service continuity standards and guidelines. This ensures consistency and enterprise-wide understandability and applicability.

The development of service continuity plans occurs as both a foundational and an ongoing activity. Plans are developed at the time of service development and implementation but also on an ongoing basis as new risks are encountered and the operational environment changes.

Typical work products

1. Service continuity plan templates
2. Service continuity plans (including relevant stakeholders)

Subpractices

1. Document the service continuity plans using available templates as appropriate.

    A service continuity plan typically includes the following information:
    - identification of authority for initiating and executing the plan (plan ownership)
    - identification of the communication mechanism to initiate execution of the plan

2. Document the key elements of the specific plan, including
    - alternative activities that would have to be performed (technical or manual)
    - alternative resources and locations that would support the organization's high-value services
    - identification of
        - vital staff roles and responsibilities
        - high-value technology assets necessary to support the plan
        - high-value information assets and vital records necessary to support the plan
        - high-value facilities assets necessary to support the plan
        - relevant stakeholders of the plan and method of communicating with them

        (See subpractice 3 below.)
    - documentation of
        - the recovery sequence for the service
        - the restoration sequence for the service
        - security- and access-related issues that are required to execute the plan
        - any special handling of information or technology that is required
        - the test plan for the service continuity plan (See SC:SG5.SP2.)
        - the service continuity training plan
    - coordination activities with other internal staff and external entities that must be performed to implement the strategy
    - the levels of authority and access needed by responders to carry out the strategy and plan
    - the cost of the plan and the activities necessary to carry out the plan
    - the logistics of the plan

    Documentation of the plan must be consistent with the standards and guidelines established by the organization to ensure plan consistency, accuracy, and ability to implement. (See SC:SG1.SP2.)

    Consider also that the service continuity plan may in reality require the development of one or more subplans (such as a restoration plan or a recovery plan).

3. Identify the stakeholders of specific service continuity plans.

    Service continuity plans may have many different stakeholders. In addition to those who must execute and participate in the plans, other organizational groups (both internal and external) may have a vested interest in understanding them. For example, plans may be provided to public emergency management staff, to suppliers and vendors, and to external entities to which the organization is a supplier. These organizations may even have a stated role in the plans. In addition, some regulatory and legal entities may require that the organization submit service continuity plans as evidence that they have taken appropriate actions to prepare for specific threats such as natural disasters or terrorism.

Because there are many stakeholders for service continuity plans, the organization must identify the relevant stakeholders and communicate the plans to these stakeholders as necessary.

These are examples of relevant stakeholders:
- higher-level managers
- service and asset owners
- vendors, suppliers, and business partners
- public entities such as emergency management, public utilities, public infrastructure, and local government
- regulatory and legal entities
- industry groups (for response coordination)

Communicate the service continuity plans to stakeholders and review and adjust them as necessary.

Ensure that compliance obligations that require communication and submission of service continuity plans are identified and satisfied. (*Meeting compliance obligations is addressed in the Compliance process area.*)

SC:SG3.SP3 Assign Staff to Service Continuity Plans

Staff members are assigned to the service continuity plans to ensure effective execution.

The activities documented in the service continuity plans must be assigned to responsible and skilled individuals in the event that the plans must be executed. These staff members may be internal to the organization or external (through outsourcing arrangements and service contracts). The organization must define the staff requirements that are required to meet the objectives of the plans, identify potential internal and external staff who will be needed to meet these requirements, and assign staff to activities in the plans.

When staff members do not have the necessary skill sets to meet the basic, minimum requirements of the plans, the organization must provide training and ascertain that the staff members are able to perform to the objectives stated in the plans as a result of this training. (*Training for service continuity plans is addressed in SC:SG3.SP5.*)

Typical work products

1. Service continuity plan staff requirements
2. List of potential staff members (to fulfill staff requirements)

3. Staff and task assignments (as documented in service continuity plans)
4. Staff commitments to service continuity plans

Subpractices

1. Identify staff requirements to satisfy the objectives of the service continuity plans.
2. Identify staff members, both internal and external, to satisfy the resource requirements.
3. Assign staff to the service continuity plans.
   Ensure that those who are assigned tasks in the plans are aware of their assignments, have the authority to act as prescribed in the plans, and are held accountable for their activities. Ensure that these staff members commit to performing their roles as described in the plans.

SC:SG3.SP4 STORE AND SECURE SERVICE CONTINUITY PLANS

Service continuity plans are stored and made accessible to those with a need to know.

The ability to execute service continuity plans during a disruption is related to their accessibility and viability. When service continuity plans that are developed but misplaced or are allowed to be changed at will, they are not usable by those who are responsible for executing them. Given that many service continuity plans are executed under emergency or crisis circumstances, the ability to know where the current version of the plans is stored is invaluable. To achieve this, the organization must take steps to ensure that the plans are archived, that the most current versions of the plans are available, that the plans are secured and free from intentional or unintentional modification, and that those who need to access the plans can readily retrieve them when necessary.

An inventory of service continuity plans can be established through the development and maintenance of a service continuity database. This allows the organization to secure access, provides a one-stop place to archive plans, and allows for plan version control. It also provides a means from which to perform plan maintenance and change control. *(Change control over service continuity plans is addressed in SC:SG7.)*

Typical work products

1. Service continuity plan inventory or database

Subpractices

1. Establish a service continuity plan inventory or database.
2. Store and protect the service continuity plans in the plan inventory or database.
   Ensure that the service continuity plans are properly protected but accessible on demand to those who have proper authorization.

3. Establish access controls to ensure that service continuity plans can be accessed only by authorized individuals.

SC:SG3.SP5 Develop Service Continuity Plan Training

Training in the service continuity plans is developed and administered.

Training is an effective means for ensuring that participants in service continuity plans understand their roles and are capable of carrying out these roles in times of disruption and emergency. It is a means for communicating the contents of the service continuity plans to stakeholders and for ensuring that those responsible for carrying out the plans are qualified. Effective training increases the organization's capability in executing the plans and for ensuring that the plans' objectives are met. Poor advance training in service continuity plans often is a major contributor to their failure, which is typically learned under undesirable and unstable organizational conditions.

Not all staff members who are assigned to plans may have the requisite skills to perform the tasks they have been assigned. Thus, the organization must determine any skill gaps and ensure that appropriate training is made available and completed before the service continuity plans are validated.

The provision of training for skill sets necessary to execute service continuity plans is addressed in the Organizational Training and Awareness process area.

Typical work products

1. List of skill needs and gaps
2. Training strategy
3. Training records
4. Service continuity plan training materials
5. Training feedback evaluations

Subpractices

1. Identify any specialized training needs based on skill gaps for the activities described in the plans.
2. Develop a strategy for conducting service continuity plan training.
   The strategy should address how the training is delivered and the means by which the competency of the resources involved is ascertained. The strategy should also note the frequency of training offerings and how participation in the training is documented.
3. Develop training materials and resources to conduct plan training on a regular and ongoing basis.
4. Train resources as necessary to fulfill their responsibilities in the plan.
5. Update service continuity plans, if necessary, as a result of feedback from training.

SC:SG4 VALIDATE SERVICE CONTINUITY PLANS

Service continuity plans are validated to ensure they satisfy requirements and standards and to resolve conflicts between plans.

Before plans can be executed, the organization must validate the plans to ensure that they meet the organization's standards and guidelines, that they enable the satisfaction of resilience requirements, and that plans do not cause resource conflicts or other potential bottlenecks.

The identification, documentation, and analysis of operational resilience requirements for services and associated assets are addressed in the Resilience Requirements Development process area.

The management of requirements for services and associated assets is addressed in the Resilience Requirements Management process area.

SC:SG4.SP1 VALIDATE PLANS TO REQUIREMENTS AND STANDARDS

Service continuity plans are examined to ensure they satisfy requirements and standards.

The service continuity plans are part of the organization's overall operational resilience management strategy for services and assets. In essence, the plans are one of many functional controls that the organization implements to ensure that services and assets are resilient to disruption and interruption. Thus, service continuity plans are a means for satisfying the resilience requirements of services and assets. As a result, service continuity plans must be objectively reviewed to ensure that they are sufficient given the resilience requirements of related services and assets.

In addition, to ensure plan consistency, accuracy, completeness, and effectiveness, service continuity plans are examined against the organization's standards and guidelines for plan development. This ensures consistent levels of documentation, the inclusion of required elements (such as stakeholders), and the ability of the plans to meet stated objectives. This also provides the organization an ability to review the logic of the plans and to make appropriate adjustments where inconsistencies or gaps are found.

Typical work products

1. Requirements gaps
2. Plan content issues and concerns
3. Plan updates and remediation actions

Subpractices

1. Review plans for consistency in achieving stated resilience requirements for services and associated assets.
2. Review plans for adherence to service continuity plan development standards and guidelines *(refer to SC:SG1.SP2)*.

3. Identify plan omissions, gaps, and issues, and develop appropriate plan updates and remediation actions.

   The plan walk-through can identify issues that pose risk to the organization because of poor coverage, inability of a plan's stated activities to meet objectives, poor documentation, etc. These issues must be identified and addressed as risks to meeting the related service or asset resilience requirements. As with all risks, proper risk disposition and mitigation actions should follow this practice.

   Managing risks to high-value services and assets is addressed in the Risk Management process area.

SC:SG4.SP2 IDENTIFY AND RESOLVE PLAN CONFLICTS

Conflicts between service continuity plans are identified and resolved.

Because of the sheer volume of service continuity plans and the operational interconnection of many services and assets, service continuity plans often overlap or place reliance on the same set of organizational resources. For example, an organization may have an off-site facility that is named in more than one plan as a backup site, but if more than one plan is executed simultaneously, the facility may not be able to satisfy requirements as prescribed in any single plan. More commonly, some people are often named in multiple service continuity plans that may have to be executed simultaneously. These types of conflicts must be identified and resolved.

Typical work products

1. Plan conflicts
2. Plan updates and remediation actions

Subpractices

1. Review plans to determine plan conflicts.
2. Determine the severity of plan conflicts and develop appropriate mitigation actions to reduce or eliminate the conflicts.

   Conflicts that would impede successful plan execution pose operational risks that must be mitigated by the organization. Remember that the conflict may affect more than one plan, and therefore mitigation actions may have to be performed on more than one plan.

   > These are examples of possible actions the organization can take to resolve conflicts:
   > - Revise or rewrite conflicting plans.
   > - Prioritize plans to make use of conflicting resources.
   > - Resolve conflicting resources by replacing them with other resources.
   > - Provide training for staff members who would be affected by plan conflicts.

3. Rewrite or revise plans as necessary.

SC:SG5 EXERCISE SERVICE CONTINUITY PLANS

Service continuity plans are tested to ensure they meet their stated objectives.

In addition to validation, service continuity plans must be tested (typically called "exercised") on a regular basis to ensure that they will achieve their stated objectives when executed as the result of a disruption. Testing provides information about the effectiveness of the plan in advance of its use and provides an opportunity to improve the plan based on the test results.

To perform plan exercises, the organization must develop a testing program and standards (to ensure consistent test objectives and results), document test plans, test the plans, and debrief the test results to identify potential improvements and revisions.

SC:SG5.SP1 DEVELOP TESTING PROGRAM AND STANDARDS

A program and standards for service continuity plan testing are established and implemented.

Having a test program and standards helps ensure regular and consistent testing of service continuity plans to ensure their viability during an event or emergency. Testing is conducted in a controlled and measured environment and is the only opportunity for the organization to know whether the plans it has developed will achieve the stated objectives and satisfy requirements.

The organization establishes the plan testing standards, structure, and reporting requirements. The testing program and standards are enforced for all plan owners and developers to ensure consistency, comparability, and ability to interpret results at the organizational level. In addition, a consistent schedule of plan testing is established based on factors such as risk, potential consequences to the organization, and other organizationally derived factors. A quality review capability is established to review the results of plan tests and to look for trends and other information that could be used in improving the general state of service continuity plans and the testing of plans.

Typical work products

1. Plan test program
2. Plan test standards
3. Plan test schedule

Subpractices

1. Develop a testing program and test standards to apply universally across all testing of service continuity plans.

> The test program and test standards should address the following, at a minimum:
> - the organization's strategy for conducting service continuity plan tests
> - the establishment of high-quality test objectives
> - the level of involvement and commitment of plan stakeholders in the testing of the plan
> - reporting of test results
> - quality assurance review of test results
> - guidelines for addressing testing issues and concerns
> - guidelines on frequency of testing

2. Establish schedules for ongoing testing and review of plans.

SC:SG5.SP2 DEVELOP AND DOCUMENT TEST PLANS

Service continuity test plans are developed and documented.

Service continuity test plans must be documented to ensure that all involved in a test understand the test objectives, their roles in the test, and the manner in which the test will be conducted. Those with the most specific knowledge of the service continuity plan should be involved in developing and documenting the test plan.

One of the most important parts of the test documentation is the establishment of test objectives—what the test should be able to prove or disprove. Documenting a test plan also involves detailing specific information about the test environment and stakeholders involved in the test.

Typical work products

1. Service continuity plan test plans

Subpractices

1. Develop and document service continuity plan tests.

> The elements to be contained in a service continuity test plan include
> - stakeholders involved in the testing exercise
> - roles of each of the stakeholders and what is expected of them
> - objectives of the test
> - specific test activities to be performed
> - infrastructure requirements—information, technology, and facilities—and other conditions necessary to perform the test
> - expected test results
> - how to document and record the results of the test for later review

2. Review service continuity test plans with stakeholders.

SC:SG5.SP3 EXERCISE PLANS

Service continuity plans are exercised on a regular basis and results are documented.

On a regular basis, service continuity plans are exercised (tested) according to their test plan. The test should establish the viability, accuracy, and completeness of the plan. It should also provide information about the organization's level of preparedness to address the specific area(s) included in the plan. The test is performed under conditions established by the organization and the results of the test are recorded and documented.

Typical work products

1. Documented results of plan testing

Subpractices

1. Prepare to conduct service continuity plan tests.
   Ensure that all staff involved in the testing understand their roles, are equipped and trained to participate in the test, and understand how to document results. Ensure that testing infrastructure has been obtained and established, that other conditions have been met, and that all stakeholders have been notified of the test.
2. Execute the service continuity plan test.
3. Document and record the results in accordance with the organization's testing standards.

SC:SG5.SP4 EVALUATE PLAN TEST RESULTS

Opportunities for improving service continuity plans are identified and implemented as a result of testing.

The objective for developing and executing service continuity plan tests is to ensure that the plans work as intended, but also to identify required improvements to the plans and the test plans.

The evaluation of test results involves comparing the documented test results against the established test objectives. Areas where objectives could not be met are recorded and strategies are developed to review and revise the plans. Improvements to the testing process and plans are also identified, documented, and incorporated into future tests.

Typical work products

1. Documented results of test result analysis
2. Notable discrepancies between expected and actual test results
3. List of improvements to service continuity plans
4. List of improvements to service continuity test plans

Subpractices

1. Compare actual test results with expected test results and test objectives.
2. Document areas of improvement for service continuity plans.

> These are examples of improvement areas that may arise from plan testing:
> - plan activities that do not achieve objectives as documented
> - actual test results that do not match expected test results when expected test results are deemed valid
> - required changes to infrastructure
> - plan logistics that may need revision
> - lack of appropriate or sufficient resources
> - training gaps for plan staff and stakeholders
> - plan conflicts (particularly if more than one plan is tested simultaneously)
> - actual costs of executing the plans versus expected costs

3. Document areas of improvement for testing service continuity plans.

SC:SG6 EXECUTE SERVICE CONTINUITY PLANS

Service continuity plans are executed and reviewed.

Service continuity plans may be executed for a variety of reasons. Plans may be implemented in response to a perceived or known threat, as the result of an incident, or as a means to address an immediate crisis. Organizations may also implement their service continuity plans for other, less urgent reasons such as during the cut-over from one application system to another, while an office location is being moved, or as part of an organizational merger or acquisition.

Whatever the catalyst for executing the plan, the organization must be able to determine when the plan must be executed and who is responsible for initiating action.

Service continuity plans may be executed in response to an incident. (*The management of incidents and the organization's response is addressed in the Incident Management and Control process area.*)

SC:SG6.SP1 EXECUTE PLANS

Service continuity plans are executed as required.

The service continuity plans are executed as organizational conditions require.

Typical work products

1. Organizational conditions for executing service continuity plans
2. Documented results of executed service continuity plans

Subpractices

1. Determine the conditions under which a service continuity plan must be executed. Ensure that the owners of service continuity plans understand these conditions and have the authority and responsibility to execute the plans if necessary.
2. Execute plans as required.

SC:SG6.SP2 MEASURE THE EFFECTIVENESS OF THE PLANS IN OPERATION

Post-execution review is performed to identify corrective actions.

The debriefing of the execution of service continuity plans is an invaluable means for identifying plan shortcomings and for improving the plans. Plan improvements are documented through this process and incorporated into future plan versions. In some cases, new plans are developed in addition to or as replacements for existing plans. Logistical considerations of the plans are reviewed and analyzed, and changes are recommended. Unforeseen circumstances that arise during the execution of the plans—due to either the incident or the execution of the plan activities—are documented and addressed.

Typical work products

1. List of improvements to service continuity plans
2. List of improvements to service continuity test plans

Subpractices

1. Compare documented service continuity plan results with plan objectives and expectations.
2. Document areas of improvement for service continuity plans.
    Examples of areas of improvement that may result from plan execution are similar to those included in practice SC:SG5.SP4.
3. Document areas of improvement for testing service continuity plans.

SC:SG7 MAINTAIN SERVICE CONTINUITY PLANS

Changes to service continuity plans are identified and managed.

The testing and execution of service continuity plans are two sources of potential changes. However, the dynamic operating environment, sources of new threats and risks, and changes in other organizational entities such as staff, geographical locations, and relationships with external entities can require changes to service continuity plans and their corresponding test plans.

Because changes to plans may occur frequently, the organization must establish baseline criteria for changes and manage changes to the plans through regular review, updating, and version control.

SC:SG7.SP1 Establish Change Criteria

Change criteria for service continuity plans are established.

Because of changing operational and organizational conditions, service continuity plans may have a short useful life. Identifying and understanding the types of organizational and operational triggers that may indicate a need to revisit and revise service continuity plans ensures that these plans remain viable.

Typical work products

1. Criteria for making changes to service continuity plans

Subpractices

1. Develop and document criteria for determining when changes to a service continuity plan should be considered.

> These are examples of criteria (i.e., conditions) that may result in changes to service continuity plans:
> - changes in a service's or asset's resilience requirements
> - identification of new vulnerabilities, threats, and risks
> - asset changes, such as staff changes, changes to information assets and technology, and relocation of facilities
> - changes in a service's or asset's protective controls
> - changes in the plan's stakeholders, including external entities and public agencies
> - organizational changes, including staff and geographic changes
> - changes in lines of business, industry, product or services mix
> - significant technical infrastructure changes
> - changes in relationships with external entities such as vendors and business partners
> - changes in or additions to regulatory or legal obligations
> - results of service continuity plan execution
> - results of service continuity plan testing

SC:SG7.SP2 Maintain Changes to Plans

Changes are made to service continuity plans as conditions dictate.

Changes to service continuity plans are made as conditions dictate based on the change criteria established by the organization in practice SC:SG7.SP1. The changes are made to existing service continuity plans (although new plans may result), and versions of existing plans are incremented according to the organization's versioning protocol and standards.

Typical work products

1. Baseline service continuity plans (established upon initial plan development)
2. Updated service continuity plans (incremented version)
3. Updated service continuity plan inventory/database

Subpractices

1. Identify and document changes to service continuity plans based on defined criteria and conditions.
2. Increment versions of service continuity plans in the plan inventory/database.
3. Communicate the updated plans to appropriate stakeholders as required.

Elaborated Generic Practices by Goal

Refer to the Generic Goals and Practices document in Appendix A for general guidance that applies to all process areas. This section provides elaborations relative to the application of the Generic Goals and Practices to the Service Continuity process area.

SC:GG1 ACHIEVE SPECIFIC GOALS

The operational resilience management system supports and enables achievement of the specific goals of the Service Continuity process area by transforming identifiable input work products to produce identifiable output work products.

SC:GG1.GP1 PERFORM SPECIFIC PRACTICES

Perform the specific practices of the Service Continuity process area to develop work products and provide services to achieve the specific goals of the process area.

Elaboration:

Specific practices SC:SG1.SP1 through SC:SG7.SP2 are performed to achieve the goals of the service continuity process.

SC:GG2 INSTITUTIONALIZE A MANAGED PROCESS

Service continuity is institutionalized as a managed process.

SC:GG2.GP1 ESTABLISH PROCESS GOVERNANCE

Establish and maintain governance over the planning and performance of the service continuity process.

Refer to the Enterprise Focus process area for more information about providing sponsorship and oversight to the service continuity process.

Subpractices

1. Establish governance over process activities.

   Elaboration:

   > Governance over the service continuity process may be exhibited by
   > - sponsorship and oversight to ensure that the process is accepted by the organization as a strategic function with documented commitments to the plan and the process
   > - developing and publicizing higher-level managers' objectives and requirements for the process
   > - sponsoring process policies, procedures, standards, and guidelines, including those for testing service continuity plans
   > - regular reporting from organizational units to higher-level managers on service continuity process activities and results
   > - implementing a service continuity steering committee with oversight for all service continuity plans and test plans
   > - making higher-level managers aware of applicable compliance obligations related to the process, and regularly reporting on the organization's satisfaction of these obligations to higher-level managers
   > - sponsoring and funding process activities, including the development, documentation, and testing of service continuity plans
   > - aligning service continuity plans with identified resilience requirements and objectives and stakeholder needs and requirements, including the process plan
   > - verifying that the process supports strategic resilience objectives and is focused on the assets and services that are of the highest relative value in meeting strategic objectives
   > - creating dedicated higher-level management feedback loops on decisions about the process and recommendations for improving the process
   > - providing input on identifying, assessing, and managing operational risks to services
   > - conducting regular internal and external audits and related reporting to audit committees on process effectiveness
   > - creating formal programs to measure the effectiveness of process activities, and reporting these measurements to higher-level managers

2. Develop and publish organizational policy for the process.

   Elaboration:

   > The service continuity policy should address
   > - responsibility, authority, and ownership for performing process activities
   > - procedures, standards, and guidelines for
   >   - plan ownership
   >   - plan documentation

> - plan content
> - testing of plans, including test objectives, reporting, and frequency
> - involvement of stakeholders
> - plan versioning, storage, archiving, and security
> - plan training
> - responsibility and authority for developing, testing, and implementing service continuity plans
> - communication of plans to stakeholders
> - responsibility for testing (exercising) plans on a regular basis and methods used to do so
> - making changes to plans
> - post-plan reviews and revisions
> - methods for measuring adherence to policy, exceptions granted, and policy violations

SC:GG2.GP2 PLAN THE PROCESS

Establish and maintain the plan for performing the service continuity process.

Elaboration:

SC:SG1.SP1 requires the development of a plan for how the organization will carry out service continuity planning and execution. A plan for service continuity is an organizational construct from which a service continuity program is developed and implemented. In generic practice SC:GG2.GP2, the planning elements required in SC:SG1.SP1 and the plan for the service continuity process are formalized and structured and performed in a managed way. The plan for the service continuity process should be directly influenced by the strategic planning process of the organization and reflect strategic initiatives where appropriate.

The plan for the service continuity process should not be confused with a plan (and program) for service continuity or service-specific continuity plans *(refer to SC:SG3)*. The plan for the service continuity process details how the organization will perform service continuity planning, including the development of service continuity plans. Service continuity plans are service-specific plans for sustaining services and associated assets under degraded conditions.

Subpractices

1. Define and document the plan for performing the process.
2. Define and document the process description.
3. Review the plan with relevant stakeholders and get their agreement.
4. Revise the plan as necessary.

SC:GG2.GP3 PROVIDE RESOURCES

Provide adequate resources for performing the service continuity process, developing the work products, and providing the services of the process.

Elaboration:

SC:SG1.SP1 requires the assignment of resources to the plan for the service continuity process. SC:SG3:SP3 calls for the assignment of resources to service-specific continuity plans. In SC:GG2.GP3, resources are formally identified and assigned to process plan elements.

Subpractices

1. Staff the process.

> These are examples of staff required to perform the service continuity process:
> - staff responsible for
>   - developing process standards and guidelines
>   - developing service continuity plans, programs, and the process plan, and ensuring they are aligned with stakeholder requirements and needs
>   - identifying high-value services and their associated assets
>   - developing and maintaining the list of files and databases (vital records) that support high-value service operation
>   - the service continuity plan inventory/database
>   - developing and conducting service continuity training
>   - validating service continuity plans against requirements and standards
>   - service continuity plan testing
>   - identifying internal and external dependency relationships necessary to ensure service continuity
>   - managing changes to the plan for service continuity and service-specific continuity plans (This includes communicating changes to affected stakeholders, including service owners.)
>   - managing external entities that have contractual obligations for process activities
> - service owners
> - internal and external auditors responsible for reporting to appropriate committees on process effectiveness

Refer to the Organizational Training and Awareness process area for information about training staff for resilience roles and responsibilities.

Refer to the Human Resource Management process area for information about acquiring staff to fulfill roles and responsibilities.

2. Fund the process.

    Refer to the Financial Resource Management process area for information about budgeting for, funding, and accounting for service continuity.

3. Provide necessary tools, techniques, and methods to perform the process.

   Elaboration:

   > These are examples of tools, techniques, and methods to support the service continuity process:
   > - methods for identifying and prioritizing high-value services
   > - methods for analyzing service dependencies and interdependencies
   > - templates for developing and documenting service continuity plans
   > - methods, techniques, and tools for performing consistent and structured version control and for managing changes to service continuity plans
   > - tools for archiving, storing, and securing service continuity plans
   > - tools for providing access control over service continuity plan inquiries, modifications, and deletions
   > - tools for managing the service continuity plan inventory/database, including controlling access and managing changes
   > - methods for communicating with stakeholders *(Refer to the Communications process area.)*
   > - methods for distributing up-to-date versions of service continuity plans to stakeholders
   > - methods for analyzing plan dependencies and resolving conflicts
   > - methods, techniques, and tools for testing plans and documenting results
   > - methods and tools for capturing and maintaining the list of files and databases that constitute vital records *(Refer to the Knowledge and Information Management process area.)*

SC:GG2.GP4 ASSIGN RESPONSIBILITY

Assign responsibility and authority for performing the service continuity process, developing the work products, and providing the services of the process.

Elaboration:

SC:SG1.SP1 requires that the plan for managing service continuity address the roles and responsibilities for carrying out the plan and the program. SC:SG1.SP2 establishes standards and guidelines, including plan ownership and responsibility. SC:SG6 calls for identifying who is responsible for initiating action in any service continuity plan. In generic practice SC:GG2.GP4, resources are formally identified and assigned to plan elements.

Refer to the Human Resource Management process area for more information about establishing resilience as a job responsibility, developing resilience performance goals and objectives, and measuring and assessing performance against these goals and objectives.

Subpractices

1. Assign responsibility and authority for performing the process.
2. Assign responsibility and authority for performing the specific tasks of the process.

    Elaboration:

    > Responsibility and authority for performing service continuity tasks can be formalized by
    > - defining roles and responsibilities in the process plan
    > - including process tasks and responsibility for these tasks in specific job descriptions
    > - developing policy requiring organizational unit managers, line of business managers, project managers, and service and asset owners to participate in and derive benefit from the process for services and assets under their ownership or custodianship
    > - including process activities in staff performance management goals and objectives, with requisite measurement of progress against these goals
    > - developing and implementing contractual instruments (including service level agreements) with external entities to establish responsibility and authority for performing process tasks on outsourced functions
    > - including process tasks in measuring performance of external entities against contractual instruments

    Refer to the External Dependencies Management process area for additional details about managing relationships with external entities.

3. Confirm that people assigned with responsibility and authority understand it and are willing and able to accept it.

SC:GG2.GP5 TRAIN PEOPLE

Train the people performing or supporting the service continuity process as needed.

Elaboration:

SC:SG3.SP5 describes the activities necessary to develop and conduct effective service continuity training that conveys the contents of plans to those responsible for their execution. This specific practice also calls for identifying and filling service continuity skill gaps and needs before service continuity plans are validated.

Refer to the Organizational Training and Awareness process area for more information about training the people performing or supporting the process.

Refer to the Human Resource Management process area for more information about inventorying skill sets, establishing a skill set baseline, identifying required skill sets, and measuring and addressing skill deficiencies.

Subpractices

1. Identify process skill needs.

   Elaboration:

   > These are examples of skills required in the service continuity process:
   > - knowledge necessary to elicit and prioritize stakeholder requirements and needs and interpret them to develop service continuity plans and programs, including the process plan
   > - knowledge required to develop service continuity plans
   > - communication skills for conveying the contents of service continuity plans to stakeholders
   > - knowledge unique to each type of service that is required to develop service-specific continuity plans
   > - knowledge necessary to work effectively with service and asset owners and custodians
   > - knowledge necessary to plan and conduct service continuity testing
   > - knowledge of the tools, techniques, and methods necessary to perform the process using the selected methods, techniques, and tools identified in SC:GG2.GP3 subpractice 3

2. Identify process skill gaps based on available resources and their current skill levels.
3. Identify training opportunities to address skill gaps.

   Elaboration:

   Certification training is an effective way to improve service continuity skills and attain competency. Certifications such as the Business Continuity Certified Planner, Certified Specialist, and Certified Expert and the Certified Business Continuity Professional are available for staff who focus specifically on continuity planning and execution.

   > These are examples of training topics:
   > - service continuity plan development
   > - service continuity plan testing and revision
   > - change control for service continuity plans
   > - communicating service continuity plans
   > - conducting post-execution reviews
   > - identifying and resolving plan conflicts
   > - including external entities in plan development and execution

4. Provide training and review the training needs as necessary.

SC:GG2.GP6 MANAGE WORK PRODUCT CONFIGURATIONS

Place designated work products of the service continuity process under appropriate levels of control.

Elaboration:

SC:SG7.SP2 addresses the change control process over service continuity plans, including establishing criteria for making changes to plans. However, other work products of the service continuity process (such as the service continuity process plan and service continuity process policies) must also be managed and controlled. Tools, techniques, and methods should be employed to perform consistent and structured version control over service continuity plans to ensure that all who must rely on a plan have the most current and "official" version. The tools, techniques, and methods can also be used to securely store the service continuity plans, to provide access control over inquiry, modification, and deletion, and to track version changes and updates.

These are examples of service continuity work products placed under control:
- process guidelines and standards
- the plan for the process
- service-specific continuity plans
- business impact analysis results
- prioritized list of high-value services and associated assets
- list of public service providers, business partners, vendors, and other external entities
- key contacts lists
- files and databases that support high-value service operation, such as orders of succession and delegations of authority
- service continuity plan inventory/database
- service continuity plan test plans, standards, and schedule
- testing results
- training strategy, materials, and records
- change criteria for service continuity plan changes
- results of live service continuity plan execution
- policies and procedures
- contracts with external entities

SC:GG2.GP7 IDENTIFY AND INVOLVE RELEVANT STAKEHOLDERS

Identify and involve the relevant stakeholders of the service continuity process as planned.

Elaboration:

Several SC-specific practices address the involvement of stakeholders in the service continuity process. For example, SC:SG1.SP1 describes obtaining commitments to the plan for service continuity from service stakeholders. SC:SG1.SP2 requires that standards and guidelines address the identification and involvement of stakeholders. SC:SG3.SP2 calls for stakeholder identification for communication and review of service-specific continuity plans. Generic practice SC:GG2.GP7 generically covers the role of stakeholders throughout the service continuity process.

Subpractices

1. Identify process stakeholders and their appropriate involvement.

   Elaboration:

   SC:SG3.SP2 requires that stakeholders for service-specific continuity plans be identified and that plans be communicated to them. Subpractice 3 provides a list of examples of relevant stakeholders.

   > These are examples of stakeholders of the service continuity process:
   > - owners of high-value services and supporting assets (for which plans must be developed)
   > - custodians of high-value services and supporting assets (who may need to execute or participate in plans)
   > - organizational unit and line of business managers responsible for high-value services and supporting assets
   > - staff involved in developing plans
   > - external entities on which service continuity plans are dependent, such as public emergency management staff and other public agencies, partners, and suppliers
   > - external entities responsible for managing high-value services
   > - external entities to which the organization is a supplier
   > - regulatory and legal entities to which the organization is required to submit service continuity plans
   > - staff involved in versioning, storing, archiving, and securing plans
   > - staff involved in testing plans
   > - internal and external auditors

   > Stakeholders are involved in various tasks in the service continuity process, such as
   > - planning for the process
   > - making decisions about the process
   > - making commitments to service continuity plans and activities as well as the process plan
   > - developing service continuity plans and the process plan
   > - communicating service continuity plans and activities and process plans and activities
   > - coordinating process activities
   > - participating in the test and execution of service continuity plans
   > - reviewing and appraising the effectiveness of process activities
   > - establishing requirements for the process
   > - resolving issues in the process

2. Communicate the list of stakeholders to planners and those responsible for process performance.
3. Involve relevant stakeholders in the process as planned.

SC:GG2.GP8 MONITOR AND CONTROL THE PROCESS

Monitor and control the service continuity process against the plan for performing the process and take appropriate corrective action.

Elaboration:

SC:SG5.SP4 requires that the results of service continuity plan testing be evaluated to determine if plans accomplished their objectives and met service continuity requirements, standards, and guidelines and produced test results as expected. SC:SG6.SP2 calls for post-execution review of service continuity plans that have been executed to ensure that plan objectives and expectations were met.

In generic practice SC:GG2.GP8, the service continuity process is formally monitored to ensure it is performing in accordance with the process plan.

Refer to the Monitoring process area for more information about the collection, organization, and distribution of data that may be useful for monitoring and controlling processes.

Refer to the Measurement and Analysis process area for more information about establishing process metrics and measurement.

Refer to the Enterprise Focus process area for more information about providing process information to managers, identifying issues, and determining appropriate corrective actions.

Subpractices

1. Measure actual performance against the plan for performing the process.
2. Review accomplishments and results of the process against the plan for performing the process.

Elaboration:

> These are examples of metrics for the service continuity process:
> - number and percentage of service continuity plans
>   - completed
>   - tested, and number of times tested by time period
>   - executed, and number of times executed by event on date
>   - that have never been executed
> - number of service continuity plans that have not yet been developed (percentage of high-value services and supporting assets that do not have service continuity plans)
> - percentage of plans
>   - without established owners
>   - that require changes

- with missing components (assigned owner, resources, etc.)
- that exhibit dependencies on other plans
- that exhibit one or more conflicts (such as a single point of failure)
- that have not been tested
- that have failed one or more test objectives
- that have failed in execution
- that have not been reviewed post-execution
- that have been changed without authorization, review, or testing
• frequency of changes to plans by service or service type
• percentage of plan test objectives (RTOs and RPOs) unmet
• number of plans without identified stakeholders
• percentage of staff who have not been trained on their roles and responsibilities as defined in service continuity plans
• number of process risks referred to the risk management process; number of risks where corrective action is still pending (by risk rank)
• level of adherence to process policies; number of policy violations; number of policy exceptions requested and number approved
• number of process activities that are on track per plan
• rate of change of resource needs to support the process
• rate of change of costs to support the process

3. Review activities, status, and results of the process with the immediate level of managers responsible for the process and identify issues.

Elaboration:

Periodic reviews of the service continuity process are needed to ensure that
- the process is a planned and coordinated activity
- process planning is driven by managing and mitigating organizational risk
- internal and external dependencies that affect the process and service continuity plans are identified and considered
- vital organizational records are identified
- all service continuity plans have assigned owners
- service continuity plans are developed, resourced, and validated for high-value services, including new services that are developed or acquired
- service continuity plans are tested when developed and periodically as dictated by business conditions and the need to manage risk
- changes to service continuity plans and the plan inventory/database are controlled
- access to service continuity plans is limited to authorized staff
- the effectiveness of service continuity plans is measured
- the process is improved based on testing and experience in executing plans
- status reports are provided to appropriate stakeholders in a timely manner

> - process issues are referred to the risk management process when necessary
> - actions requiring management involvement are elevated in a timely manner
> - the performance of process activities is being monitored and regularly reported
> - key measures are within acceptable ranges as demonstrated in governance dashboards or scorecards and financial reports
> - actions resulting from internal and external audits are being closed in a timely manner

4. Identify and evaluate the effects of significant deviations from the plan for performing the process.
5. Identify problems in the plan for performing and executing the process.
6. Take corrective action when requirements and objectives are not being satisfied, when issues are identified, or when progress differs significantly from the plan for performing the process.
7. Track corrective action to closure.

SC:GG2.GP9 OBJECTIVELY EVALUATE ADHERENCE

Objectively evaluate adherence of the service continuity process against its process description, standards, and procedures, and address non-compliance.

Elaboration:

> These are examples of activities to be reviewed:
> - developing a plan for the process
> - developing process guidelines and standards
> - performing risk-based activities such as business impact analysis
> - identifying service-specific continuity plans to be developed
> - identifying external dependencies
> - validating service continuity plans
> - developing and testing service continuity plans
> - making and managing changes to service continuity plans based on test results and as needs dictate
> - storing, securing, and enforcing authorized access to service continuity plans
> - performing post-event review of service continuity plans in execution
> - the alignment of stakeholder requirements with service continuity plans and process plans
> - assignment of responsibility, accountability, and authority for process activities
> - determination of the adequacy of process reports and reviews in informing decision makers regarding the performance of operational resilience management activities and the need to take corrective action, if any
> - use of process work products for improving strategies for protecting and sustaining services and assets

> These are examples of work products to be reviewed:
> - the plan for the process
> - process guidelines and standards
> - service-specific continuity plans
> - business impact analysis results
> - lists of public agencies and other external entities, including business partners and vendors
> - service continuity test plans
> - testing results
> - training records
> - change criteria for plan changes
> - service continuity plan change logs
> - process plan and policies
> - process issues that have been referred to the risk management process
> - process methods, techniques, and tools
> - metrics for the process *(Refer to SC:GG2.GP8 subpractice 2.)*
> - contracts with external entities

SC:GG2.GP10 REVIEW STATUS WITH HIGHER-LEVEL MANAGERS

Review the activities, status, and results of the service continuity process with higher-level managers and resolve issues.

Refer to the Enterprise Focus process area for more information about providing sponsorship and oversight to the operational resilience management system.

SC:GG3 INSTITUTIONALIZE A DEFINED PROCESS

Service continuity is institutionalized as a defined process.

SC:GG3.GP1 ESTABLISH A DEFINED PROCESS

Establish and maintain the description of a defined service continuity process.

Establishing and tailoring process assets, including standard processes, are addressed in the Organizational Process Definition process area.

Establishing process needs and objectives and selecting, improving, and deploying process assets, including standard processes, are addressed in the Organizational Process Focus process area.

Subpractices

1. Select from the organization's set of standard processes those processes that cover the service continuity process and best meet the needs of the organizational unit or line of business.

2. Establish the defined process by tailoring the selected processes according to the organization's tailoring guidelines.
3. Ensure that the organization's process objectives are appropriately addressed in the defined process, and ensure that process governance extends to the tailored processes.
4. Document the defined process and the records of the tailoring.
5. Revise the description of the defined process as necessary.

SC:GG3.GP2 COLLECT IMPROVEMENT INFORMATION

Collect service continuity work products, measures, measurement results, and improvement information derived from planning and performing the process to support future use and improvement of the organization's processes and process assets.

Elaboration:

SC:SG5.SP4 requires that the results of service continuity plan testing be evaluated to determine if plans accomplished their objectives, met service continuity requirements, standards, and guidelines, and produced test results as expected. SC:SG6.SP2 calls for post-execution review of service continuity plans that have been executed, to ensure that plan objectives and expectations were met. Both of these specific practices and their work products may provide useful improvement information.

> These are examples of improvement work products and information:
> - results of business impact analysis
> - issues related to service continuity plan development
> - issues related to involving stakeholders in the development and execution processes
> - issues related to committing to plan ownership and custodianship
> - service continuity plan test results
> - issues related to external entities
> - issues related to internal and external dependencies and interdependencies
> - conflicts arising from resource contention between service continuity plans
> - lessons learned from plan testing
> - lessons learned from plan execution
> - metrics and measurements of the viability of the process *(Refer to SC:GG2.GP8 subpractice 2.)*
> - changes and trends in operating conditions, risk conditions, and the risk environment that affect service continuity plans and process results
> - lessons learned in post-event review of incidents and disruptions in continuity
> - resilience requirements that are not being satisfied or are being exceeded

Establishing the measurement repository and process asset library is addressed in the Organizational Process Definition process area. Updating the measurement repository and process asset library as part of process improvement and deployment is addressed in the Organizational Process Focus process area.

Subpractices

1. Store process and work product measures in the organization's measurement repository.
2. Submit documentation for inclusion in the organization's process asset library.
3. Document lessons learned from the process for inclusion in the organization's process asset library.
4. Propose improvements to the organizational process assets.

TECHNOLOGY MANAGEMENT
Operations

Purpose

The purpose of Technology Management is to establish and manage an appropriate level of controls related to the integrity and availability of technology assets to support the resilient operations of organizational services.

Introductory Notes

Technology is a pervasive organizational asset. Few organizational services are untouched by some aspect of technology—hardware, software, systems, tools, and infrastructure (such as networks) that support services. Technology assets directly support the automation (and efficiency) of services and are often inextricably tied to information assets because they provide the platforms on which information is stored, transported, or processed. For some organizations, technology is a prominent driver in accomplishing the mission and is considered a strategic element. Technology tends to be pervasive across all functions of the organization and therefore can be a significant contributor to strategic and competitive success.

From a broad perspective, technology describes any technology component or asset that supports or automates a service and facilitates its ability to accomplish its mission. Examples of technology assets include software, hardware, and firmware, including physical interconnections between these assets such as cabling. Technology has many layers, some of which are specific to a service (such as an application system) and others of which are shared by the organization (such as the enterprise-wide network infrastructure) to support more than one service. Organizations must describe technology assets sufficiently to facilitate development and satisfaction of resilience requirements. In some organizations, this may be at the application system level; in others, it might be more granular, such as at the server or personal computer level.

The Technology Management process area addresses the importance of technology assets in the operational resilience of services, as well as unique issues specific to technology, such as integrity and availability management.

In this process area, technology assets are prioritized according to their value in supporting high-value organizational services. Physical, technical, and administrative controls that keep technology assets viable and sustainable are selected, implemented, and managed, and the effectiveness of these controls is monitored. In addition, technology asset risks are identified and mitigated in an attempt to prevent disruption where possible.

The integrity of technology assets is addressed through mastery of capabilities such as configuration, change, and release management. The availability of technology assets, critical for supporting the resilience of services, is established and managed by controlling the operational environment in which the assets operate, by performing regular maintenance on these assets, and by limiting the potential effects of interoperability issues. Because technology assets may extend outside of the physical and logical boundaries of the organization, the organization must address the interaction with external entities that provide technology assets or support for technology assets to the organization.

Related Process Areas

The establishment and management of resilience requirements for technology assets are performed in the Resilience Requirements Development and Resilience Requirements Management process areas.

The identification, definition, management, and control of technology assets are addressed in the Asset Definition and Management process area.

The risk management cycle for technology assets is addressed in the Risk Management process area.

The management of the internal control system that ensures the protection of technology assets is addressed in the Controls Management process area.

The selection, implementation, and management of access controls for technology assets are performed in the Access Management process area.

The development of service continuity plans for technology assets is performed in the Service Continuity process area.

The establishment and management of relationships with external entities to ensure the resilience of services that are executed in facilities they own and operate are addressed in the External Dependencies Management process area.

Summary of Specific Goals and Practices

TM:SG1 Establish and Prioritize Technology Assets
    TM:SG1.SP1   Prioritize Technology Assets
    TM:SG1.SP2   Establish Resilience-Focused Technology Assets

TM:SG2 Protect Technology Assets
    TM:SG2.SP1   Assign Resilience Requirements to Technology Assets
    TM:SG2.SP2   Establish and Implement Controls
TM:SG3 Manage Technology Asset Risk
    TM:SG3.SP1   Identify and Assess Technology Asset Risk
    TM:SG3.SP2   Mitigate Technology Risk
TM:SG4 Manage Technology Asset Integrity
    TM:SG4.SP1   Control Access to Technology Assets
    TM:SG4.SP2   Perform Configuration Management
    TM:SG4.SP3   Perform Change Control and Management
    TM:SG4.SP4   Perform Release Management
TM:SG5 Manage Technology Asset Availability
    TM:SG5.SP1   Perform Planning to Sustain Technology Assets
    TM:SG5.SP2   Manage Technology Asset Maintenance
    TM:SG5.SP3   Manage Technology Capacity
    TM:SG5.SP4   Manage Technology Interoperability

Specific Practices by Goal

TM:SG1 ESTABLISH AND PRIORITIZE TECHNOLOGY ASSETS

Technology assets are prioritized to ensure the resilience of the high-value services that they support.

In this goal, the organization establishes the subset of technology assets (from its technology asset inventory) on which it must focus operational resilience activities because of their importance to the sustained operation of essential services.

Prioritization of technology assets is a risk management activity. The organization establishes the technology assets that are of most value to providing business services and for which controls to protect and sustain them are required. Failure to prioritize technology assets may lead to inadequate operational resilience of high-value assets or excessive levels of operational resilience for non-high-value assets.

TM:SG1.SP1 PRIORITIZE TECHNOLOGY ASSETS

Technology assets are prioritized relative to their importance in supporting the delivery of high-value services.

The prioritization of technology assets must be performed in order to ensure that the organization properly directs its operational resilience resources to the assets that most directly impact and contribute to services that support the organization's mission. These assets require the organization's direct attention because their interruption or disruption has the potential to cause significant organizational consequences, particularly because the health and viability of information assets are typically tied directly to the resilience of technology assets.

Technology asset prioritization is performed relative to related services—that is, technology assets associated with high-value services are those that must be most highly prioritized for operational resilience activities. The organization may use other criteria to establish high-priority technology assets, such as

- the relationship between the technology and the value of the information assets stored, transported, or processed by the technology
- technology assets such as networks that are considered to be foundational and are vital to supporting more than one organizational service
- proprietary technology assets provided by suppliers (such as application systems or specific types of hardware) that would materially affect the organization if the supplier is unreachable or drops support
- the degree to which the technology assets are "redundant"—that is, easily replaceable or able to be replicated if lost or destroyed
- technology assets that automate resilience controls (such as physical access systems) that are critical to sustaining operational resilience
- resilience technology assets that are specifically designated to support the organization's ability to support service continuity plans

Typically, the organization selects a subset of technology assets from its asset inventory; however, the organization could compile a list of high-value assets based on risk or other factors. However, failure to select assets from the organization's asset inventory poses additional risk that some high-value technology assets may never have been inventoried. (*The identification, definition, management, and control of technology assets are addressed in the Asset Definition and Management process area.*)

Typical work products

1. List of high-value technology assets

Subpractices

1. Compile a list of high-value technology assets from the organization's technology asset inventory.

    Technology assets that are essential to the successful operation of organizational services should be included on the list of technology assets. (*An inventory of high-value assets is established in practice ADM:SG1.SP1 in the Asset Definition and Management process area.*) This list may suffice for this subpractice or may be expanded if necessary.

> Technology includes the entire infrastructure necessary to design, manufacture, operate, maintain, and repair technological assets. These are examples of high-value technology assets:
> - software
> - hardware
> - firmware
> - network infrastructure, including cables and other types of interconnections
> - automated systems and applications
> - tools
> - telecommunications and utility services

2. Prioritize technology assets.

    The prioritization of technology assets is necessary to ensure the organization focuses on activities to protect and sustain the technology that is essential to the successful operation of organizational services.

    It must be considered that many high-value organizational services may rely upon shared technology assets such as email applications, web servers, or network infrastructure. The disruption or failure of these types of technology assets can cause cascading effects on many organizational services; therefore, they should be of higher priority in addressing operational resilience.

3. Periodically validate and update the list of high-value technology assets based on operational and organizational environment changes.

TM:SG1.SP2 ESTABLISH RESILIENCE-FOCUSED TECHNOLOGY ASSETS

Technology assets that specifically support execution of service continuity and service restoration plans are identified and established.

Service continuity plans may rely heavily on technology assets for successful execution. These assets may be those that are in production or others that are designated for resilience purposes. For example, the organization may have spare servers or telecommunications bandwidth that can be called into service when primary technology assets fail or when service continuity plans require specific assets to execute recovery and restoration activities.

Resilience technology assets may be contracted for and provided by an external entity. For example, an organization may contract with an outside disaster recovery provider to provide access to servers and other technology assets to allow off-site recovery of application systems. In such arrangements, the technology assets involved are typically not owned by the organization, but they should still be included in the organization's list of resilience technology assets.

If the organization owns facilities that are specifically designated for backup and recovery, the technology assets that are contained in these facilities are typically not used in daily operations and are owned by the organization. These assets should also be included in the organization's list of resilience technology assets and protected accordingly.

The identification of resilience facilities that may in turn contain resilience technology assets is performed in the Environmental Control process area. There should be coordination between the facility and technology assets that are identified in this specific practice.

Typical work products

1. List of resilience technology assets.

Subpractices

1. Compile a list of resilience technology assets from the organization's asset inventory.

    These technology assets should include those that would be required for the successful execution of service continuity plans and service restoration plans.

2. Periodically reconcile the list of resilience technology assets to the organization's service continuity plans and resilience strategies.

    These technology assets should also be reconciled to the resilience facilities identified in practice EC:SG1.SP2 in the Environmental Control process area.

TM:SG2 Protect Technology Assets

Administrative, technical, and physical controls for technology assets are identified, implemented, monitored, and managed.

Technology assets are pervasive across the organization. An organization may have hundreds or thousands of services that are supported or automated by technology assets. As a complicating factor, many of these assets may not be owned by the organization because services often traverse organizational boundaries and are supported or operated by business partners and vendors. Thus, the organization may not have direct control or influence over the controls for protecting and sustaining these assets.

Because of their pervasiveness, a primary consideration for technology assets is availability. Keeping technology assets productive consumes a large amount of organizational effort because these assets are directly tied to mission success for services. In addition, the complexity of technology assets, particularly software and systems, means that the integrity of the assets is paramount. The integrity of technology assets is ensured by strong change and configuration processes and controls and the protection of technology assets from inappropriate or unauthorized access.

To protect technology assets from vulnerabilities, threats, and risks, the organization should

- develop appropriate resilience requirements for the assets
- develop, implement, and manage an appropriate level of administrative, technical, and physical controls to manage the conditions that could cause disruption of the assets
- select and design controls based on the assets' resilience requirements and the range of conditions that require integrity of the asset configuration and availability of the assets to perform their intended functions
- monitor the effectiveness of these controls on a regular basis to ensure that they meet the technology assets' resilience requirements

TM:SG2.SP1 ASSIGN RESILIENCE REQUIREMENTS TO TECHNOLOGY ASSETS

Resilience requirements that have been defined are assigned to technology assets.

Resilience requirements form the basis for the actions that the organization takes to protect and sustain technology assets. These requirements are established commensurate with the value of the assets to services that they support. The resilience requirements for technology assets must be assigned to the assets so that the appropriate type and level of protective controls can be designed, implemented, and monitored to meet the requirements.

With technology assets, there may be instances of conflicting requirements because many of these assets are shared by more than one service and may be related to information assets that have specific data categorization or confidentiality requirements. These situations of shared requirements must be analyzed and considered when assigning resilience requirements to technology assets, with the intention of providing a baseline requirement that is sufficient to encompass the most stringent requirements.

Resilience requirements for technology assets are developed in the Resilience Requirements Development process area. However, technology asset resilience requirements may not be formally defined or they may be assumed to be the responsibility of the technology asset owner (if the organization is not the owner). The assignment of these requirements is necessary as a foundational step for controls selection and management.

Typical work products

1. Technology asset resilience requirements

Subpractices

1. Assign resilience requirements to technology assets.

    Resilience requirements for technology assets must take into consideration the shared nature of the technology within the organization (since more than one service is likely to use common technology) and technology outside of the

organization (such as an external service provider or co-location of communications equipment, which may have different resilience requirements).
2. Document the requirements (if they are currently not documented) and include them in the asset definition.

TM:SG2.SP2 Establish and Implement Controls

Administrative, technical, and physical controls that are required to meet the established resilience requirements are identified and implemented.

The organization must implement an internal control system that protects the continued operation of technology assets commensurate with their role in supporting organizational services. Controls are essentially the methods, policies, and procedures that the organization uses to provide an acceptable level of protection over high-value technology assets. Controls typically fall into three categories: administrative (or managerial), technical, and physical. All of these controls are necessary for technology assets because they come in so many different forms and are pervasive across the organization.

- Administrative controls ensure alignment to higher-level managers' intentions and include such work products as governance, policy, monitoring, auditing, separation of duties, and the development and implementation of service continuity plans. Administrative controls provide guidance regarding who can access technology assets, make changes to their configuration, or establish timetables governing when they can be used and for what purpose.
- Technical controls are the technical manifestation of protection methods for technology assets. In essence, technology assets often act as technical controls, such as when a firewall is deployed to manage network traffic or when specialized software is used to manage access to information. The use of technical assets as protective controls is most often associated with security activities.
- Physical controls manage the physical access and modification of technology assets. These controls typically include separating software development environments from production environments, locking equipment room doors, and other physical barrier methods.

Operational resilience for technology assets involves a thorough consideration of a wide range of controls. These include not only physical and logical access controls but controls that address the integrity, availability, and operability of the technology in its environment and in environments out of the direct control of the organization. Regardless of location, resilience requirements are the responsibility of the technology asset owners and must be provided to the custodian of technology assets for implementation.

Typical work products

1. Technology asset administrative controls
2. Technology asset technical controls
3. Technology asset physical controls

Subpractices

1. Establish and implement administrative controls for technology assets.

   Administrative controls for technology assets include
   - policies that govern technology users' behavior with regard to information assets
   - standards on selection, interoperability, and integration of technology assets
   - standards for the configuration and change management of technology assets such as software or the baseline configuration footprint of hardware
   - policies for the proper disposition of technology assets
   - certification and accreditation of systems and applications
   - policies for the removal of technology assets from the workplace
   - staff hiring procedures, particularly with regard to access to confidential information or performance of maintenance on technology assets
   - training to ensure proper technology asset definition and handling *(See the Organizational Training and Awareness process area.)*
   - logging, monitoring, and auditing controls to detect and report unauthorized access and use of technology *(See the Monitoring process area.)*
   - governance over the proper use and distribution of technology and the protection of technology assets *(See the Enterprise Focus process area.)*
   - development, testing, and implementation of service continuity plans (including technology asset recovery and restoration and the assignment of technology assets to plans) *(See the Service Continuity process area.)*

2. Establish and implement technical controls for technology assets.

   Technical controls include such controls as
   - configuration and change management
   - software quality assurance
   - software escrow
   - file integrity auditing software
   - access control lists and related methodologies
   - automated backup, retention, and recovery of technology assets
   - modification controls that prevent unauthorized modification and that log and report modification actions by authorized individuals

3. Establish and implement physical controls for technology assets.

> Physical controls for protecting technology assets include such controls as
> - security guards, surveillance cameras, fences, locking equipment cabinets or rooms, and other physical security mechanisms
> - physical access controls on file rooms and work areas where paper and technology assets are stored
> - fire alarms and protection
> - water alarms and protection
> - electrical power conditioning
> - limited entry points to areas where technology is stored, transported, or processed

4. Establish and specify controls over the design, construction, and acquisition of technology assets.

    These controls ensure that the development and acquisition of software and systems or the development and acquisition of hardware are performed with consideration of the operational resilience of these assets. *(These activities and related practices are specifically addressed in the Resilient Technical Solution Engineering process area.)*

5. Monitor the effectiveness of administrative, technical, and physical controls, and identify deficiencies that must be resolved.

TM:SG3 Manage Technology Asset Risk

Operational risks to technology assets are identified and managed.

Risks to technology assets are managed by the application of risk management tools, techniques, and methods to those assets. Because of the pervasiveness of technology assets across the organization, their complex nature, and the various forms in which they can be found, there are many opportunities for technology assets to be threatened and for risk to be realized by the organization. Risks to technology assets can result in cascading consequences to the organization, including the disruption of high-value services due to the lack of technology usability and availability.

Technology assets are prone to specific types of operational risk, including the failure of systems and technology due to

- complexity due to poor design, failure to "build security in," poor requirements, and immature software and systems engineering processes
- poor configuration and change management, which increases exposure to vulnerabilities
- inadvertent and deliberate actions of people, particularly technology staff or external people such as hackers
- environmental conditions in places where technology assets are located

Because technology assets can often act as "containers" for information assets, risks to technology assets can also have a cascading effect on information assets. In addition, because technology assets "live" in facilities, risks to facilities must be examined to determine if they can affect technology assets.

The identification and mitigation of risks to information are addressed in the Knowledge and Information Management process area. The identification and mitigation of risks to facilities are addressed in the Environmental Control process area.

TM:SG3.SP1 IDENTIFY AND ASSESS TECHNOLOGY ASSET RISK

Risks to technology assets are identified and assessed.

Operational risks that can affect technology assets must be identified and mitigated in order to actively manage the resilience of these assets and, more important, the resilience of services to which these assets are associated.

The identification of technology asset risks forms a baseline from which a continuous risk management process can be established and managed.

The subpractices included in this practice are generically addressed in goals RISK:SG3 and RISK:SG4 in the Risk Management process area.

Typical work products

1. Technology asset risk statements, with impact valuation
2. List of technology asset risks, with categorization and prioritization

Subpractices

1. Determine the scope of risk assessment for technology assets.
   Determining which technology assets to include in regular risk management activities depends on many factors, including the value of the assets to the organization, their resilience requirements, and the ownership and control of the specific technology.
2. Identify risks to technology assets.
   Identification of risks to technology assets is broad in scope because of the many types of technology assets. For example, operational risks to software assets may differ significantly from those that threaten hardware assets or networks. The type of technology asset and the environment in which the asset is operating will form a baseline scope for the identification of risk.
   Typically, operational risks for technology assets include such broad areas as
   - unauthorized access to and destruction of technology assets (including physical destruction of the assets or the manipulation of hardware or software configurations, rendering the assets unusable)
   - exerting unwanted control over the assets (such as with hacking or denial of service) that makes the assets unusable or unstable
   - poor design of technology assets that results in weaknesses that can be exploited

- poor implementation or operational controls that reduce the reliability, availability, and ability to sustain the assets (including deficient change and configuration management processes)
- physical and environmental conditions such as humidity, or exposure to natural conditions such as flood
- inadvertent or accidental misuse related to poor administrative controls such as appropriate use policies
- inadvertent or deliberate actions of custodians (particularly external to the organization) who have been entrusted to protect technology assets

Operational risks should be identified in the context of type and physical location so that mitigation actions are more focused and directed.

3. Analyze risks to technology assets.
4. Categorize and prioritize risks to technology assets.
   This may require the organization to view each class of technology asset separately (i.e., risks to software, risks to systems, risks to hardware such as servers, etc.).
5. Assign a risk disposition to each technology asset risk.
6. Monitor the risk and the risk strategy on a regular basis to ensure that the risk does not pose additional threat to the organization.
7. Develop a strategy for the risks that the organization decides to mitigate.
   Mitigation of operational risks for technology assets will be specific to the technology asset type and where the asset is installed and operating.

TM:SG3.SP2 MITIGATE TECHNOLOGY RISK

Risk mitigation strategies for technology assets are developed and implemented.

The mitigation of technology asset risk involves the development of strategies that seek to minimize the risk to an acceptable level. This includes reducing the likelihood of risks to technology assets, minimizing exposure to these risks, developing service continuity plans to keep the assets viable during times of disruption, and developing recovery and restoration plans to address the consequences of realized risk.

Because technology assets span a wide range and are pervasive in the organization, risk mitigation strategies may have to be extensive and require significant analysis. For example, mitigating the risk that software will fail due to poor design and addressing the physical security of a server require vastly different strategies and implementation considerations.

Risk mitigation for technology assets requires the development of risk mitigation plans (which may include the development of new or revision of existing technology asset controls) and implementing and monitoring these plans for effectiveness.

The subpractices included in this practice are generically addressed in RISK:SG5 in the Risk Management process area.

Typical work products

1. Technology asset risk mitigation plans
2. List of those responsible for addressing and tracking risks
3. Status of technology asset risk mitigation plans

Subpractices

1. Develop and implement risk mitigation strategies for all risks that have a "mitigate" or "control" disposition.
   > Because there are many categories of technology assets, each of which may have a distinct risk profile, it may be helpful to perform affinity grouping on risks to be mitigated before strategies are developed. A simple categorization—segregating by software, hardware, or firmware—can be used, or a more granular convention may be applied.
2. Validate the risk mitigation plans by comparing them to existing strategies for protecting and sustaining technology assets.
3. Identify the person or group responsible for each risk mitigation plan and ensure that they have the authority to act and the proper level of skills and training to implement and monitor the plan.
4. Address residual risk.
5. Implement the risk mitigation plans and provide a method to monitor the effectiveness of these plans.
6. Monitor risk status.
7. Collect performance measures on the risk management process.

TM:SG4 MANAGE TECHNOLOGY ASSET INTEGRITY

The integrity of technology assets is managed.

The integrity of a technology asset is important to ensuring that the asset is usable for its intended purposes. Whenever technology asset integrity is compromised, the information assets stored, transported, or processed by the asset, as well as the services that depend on the asset, are also potentially compromised. This may be because of loss of functionality, reduced reliability, or impairment of availability when needed.

To be usable for the purposes intended in supporting high-value services, technology assets must possess certain qualities of integrity. They must be

- complete and intact (possessing all of their intended characteristics)
- accurate and valid (being in form and content precisely and exactly as intended)
- authorized and official (approved for use as intended)

The integrity of a technology asset must be considered in the context of the type of asset. Thus, the concept of integrity is applied differently, depending on the type of technology asset:

- For software assets, integrity is relative to the modification of the software itself. This includes unauthorized modification of software code, systems, applications, operating systems, tools, and other software-based technology assets.
- For hardware assets, integrity is relative to the modification of either the physical structure of the asset or the configuration parameters of the asset (which are typically considered to be "software" in nature). Modification of the physical structure may occur if cabling is rerouted or a hard drive is replaced. Modification of the configuration parameters may occur if parameters of the operating system are changed to allow use of unauthorized tools or utilities.

Managing technology asset integrity involves controlling access to technology assets, actively managing configuration items, and performing change and release management.

TM:SG4.SP1 CONTROL ACCESS TO TECHNOLOGY ASSETS

Access to technology assets is controlled.

Controlled access to technology assets by authorized staff ensures the continued integrity of these assets by limiting their unauthorized or inadvertent modification.

Access controls for technology assets may take electronic or physical forms. For example, controlling the access to utility programs may prevent changes to a technical asset's baseline configuration. On the other hand, ensuring that a server is placed behind a physically protected barrier or in a secure room is a physical access control that may prevent destruction of the server or the ability to manipulate configuration settings directly from a console. For software technology assets (and in some cases, firmware), access controls tend to be electronic; for hardware technology assets, access controls can be electronic or physical.

These are examples of actions that require modification access to technology assets:
- modifying or updating software code
- making changes to application system code or modules
- maintaining databases or similar file structures
- modifying the configuration of a server or other hardware
- installing vendor patches to software or firmware
- managing the rulesets of a firewall or similar security device
- modifying the physical configuration of a server or other technical device (such as replacing a hard drive or installing additional memory)

- making modifications to the configuration of physical security systems, including the reprovisioning or deprovisioning of physical access cards and card readers
- making modifications to physical security systems and devices, including cameras and alarm systems

For effectiveness, the organization must thoroughly consider which staff members are authorized to access technology assets and make modifications (based on the unique integrity requirements of each technology asset) and implement electronic and physical controls to meet these requirements. Special consideration must be given to the access needs of information technology staff, who typically have more extensive access to technology assets than they need to perform their job responsibilities. However, because access controls are not infallible, the organization must also be able to deploy detective controls that allow for logging of modification to technology assets and periodic review of these logs for anomalies.

Managing access is a complementary control to other integrity-focused controls for technology assets such as configuration management, change management, and release management. However, access controls are typically focused on authorizing access to technology assets, while other controls such as configuration management focus on ensuring that modification is systematic, controlled, and monitored.

Typical work products

1. Technology asset access control lists
2. List of staff members authorized to modify technology assets
3. Technology asset modification logs
4. Audit reports

Subpractices

1. Establish access management policies and procedures for requesting and approving access privileges to technology assets.

    The organization should establish policies and procedures for requesting, approving, and providing access to technology assets to persons, objects, and entities.

    The access management policy should establish the responsibilities of requestors, asset owners, and asset custodians (who typically are called upon to implement access requests). The policy should address clear guidelines for access requests that originate externally to the organization (i.e., from contractors or business partners). The policy should also cover the type and extent of access that will be provided to objects such as systems and processes.

    The types of documentation required to fulfill the access management policy should be described and exhibited in the policy.

The access management policy should be communicated to all with a need to know and their responsibilities should be clearly detailed in the policy. The policy should also offer disciplinary measures for violations of the policy.

2. Establish organizationally acceptable tools, techniques, and methods for controlling access to technology assets.

    Selection of the level of configuration control is typically based on objectives, risk, and/or resources. Control levels may vary in relation to the project life cycle, type of system under configuration management, and specific resilience requirements.

3. Identify and document staff who are authorized to modify technology assets relative to the assets' resilience requirements.

    For technology assets, there is additional concern regarding access for information technology or resilience staff. These staff members often are in positions of trust and need to access and make modifications to technology assets (particularly software) to perform their job responsibilities. However, there is often an incorrect assumption that technology and resilience staff need extensive levels of modification privileges, which can lead to additional risk. These staff members should be specifically identified and their access privileges scrutinized for alignment with their *current* job responsibilities.

4. Implement tools, techniques, and methods to monitor and log modification activity on high-value technology assets.

    Because of the range of technology assets, these tools, techniques, and methods may be very extensive and diverse. Examples are automated software change control applications and utilities, configuration management systems, and paper logs from physical security systems.

5. Perform periodic audits of technology asset modification logs and identify and address anomalies.

TM:SG4.SP2 PERFORM CONFIGURATION MANAGEMENT

The configuration of technology assets is managed.

Configuration management is a fundamental resilience activity. It supports the integrity of technology assets by ensuring that they can be restored to an acceptable form when necessary (perhaps after a disruption) and provides a level of control over changes that can potentially disrupt the assets' support of organizational services. When integrity is suspect for any reason, the resilience of technology assets and associated services may be affected.

Establishing a technology asset baseline (commonly called a "configuration item") provides a foundation for managing the integrity of an asset as it changes over its life cycle. Configuration management also establishes additional controls over the asset so that it is always in a form that is available and authorized for use. In some cases, an organization may want to freeze a baseline technology asset configuration, thus permitting no modifications or alterations to the asset over its life cycle.

Configuration management of technology assets is a primary resilience control—it is a means for reconciling the assets' technical and physical attributes with their resilience requirements over time. This may involve all phases of the technology's life cycle, including development phases as well as operations and maintenance, with which configuration control is most often associated. While configuration management for technology assets is focused on the assets themselves (the software, systems, hardware, etc.), it may also naturally extend to other technology work products, such as test scripts and plans, asset documentation, and configuration standards and policies.

Configuration management for technology assets is tightly coupled with change control and management. Change control and management is the process of controlling changes to configuration items, which are created and managed in configuration management. Because change control and management is a specialized activity, particularly for technical assets, it is often considered a separate function with its own practices, tools, techniques, and methods. (*Change control for technical assets is addressed in TM:SG4.SP3.*)

The level of control required over technology asset configuration items can range from informal to formal. The level is typically dependent on the type of technology asset, how it is used, where it is deployed, and ultimately the resilience requirements for the asset. Software assets (particularly software code) and application systems tend to require strict levels of configuration control because they are changed frequently and must retain their integrity to be useful for intended purposes. For this reason, configuration management is a foundational element in software and systems engineering practices.

Configuration management of technology assets involves a range of activities, including

- identifying the configuration of selected assets that compose the baselines at given points in time
- controlling changes to configuration items
- building or providing specifications to the configuration management system
- maintaining the integrity of baseline configurations
- auditing configurations over time to ensure that baselines are updated

Configuration management can be approached at an enterprise level or specifically for each technology asset. The organization must decide the most effective approach and should account for the fact that configuration management for different types of technology assets (i.e., software-based assets versus hardware-based assets) may differ significantly and require separate processes. The content of TM:SG4.SP2 is intended to be applied to all configuration management processes across the range of technology assets that the organization deploys.

Typical work products

1. Standards, policies, and guidelines for technology asset configuration management
2. Identified configuration items
3. Baseline configuration items
4. Configuration control logs and reports
5. Configuration management system, tools, techniques, and methods
6. Configuration audit reports
7. Action items

Subpractices

1. Establish requirements for technology standards, guidelines, and policies for configuration management.

    Selection of the level of configuration control is typically based on objectives, risk, and/or resources. Control levels may vary in relation to the project life cycle, type of system under configuration management, and specific resilience requirements.

    Configuration management should extend to all technology assets, whether developed and implemented in-house or acquired.

2. Establish a configuration management database or system.

    A configuration management system includes the storage media, the procedures, and the tools for accessing the configuration system. The configuration items of the technology assets are stored in the configuration management system (however, this may vary significantly depending on the type of technology asset).

3. Identify the technology assets (configuration items) in detail that will be placed under configuration management.

    A configuration item can be a specific technology asset (such as software code or an operating system) or a series of assets that are related and tied together in a logical baseline configuration item. The organization must plan how it intends to address configuration items for each technical asset type and instantiate guidelines that will ensure consistency of definition and creation of configuration items.

    Configuration items should have specific identifiers and should include important characteristics relevant to the type of technology asset (such as "programming language" for a software code asset).

> These are examples of configuration items that may be placed under configuration control:
> - software and application code
> - application systems (both in operations and in development)
> - operating systems
> - hardware parameters and configuration files
> - firewall rulesets
> - configuration files for routers and other network devices and network routing tables

- software and hardware tools and utilities
- policies, manuals, codebooks, and other documents related to technology assets
- maintenance records for hardware

4. Create baseline configuration items.
5. Track and control changes to configuration items.

    This process includes the establishment of configuration management records and the communication of the contents of these records to appropriate stakeholders.

    This subpractice is typically performed through a formal change control and management process. (See TM:SG4.SP3.)
6. Review configuration control logs and identify anomalies.

    Periodically verify (through monitoring and auditing) that changes to configurations are valid and authorized.
7. Perform configuration audits.

    Regularly audit the integrity of the configuration item baselines to ensure that they are complete and correct and that they continue to meet configuration management standards and procedures. Identify action items that are required to repair any anomalies.

TM:SG4.SP3 PERFORM CHANGE CONTROL AND MANAGEMENT

Changes to technology assets are managed.

An important component of configuration management is the ability to control and manage changes to technology assets, particularly to configuration items. Because of the nature of the operational environment, most technology assets are expected to change over time; the addition of new functionality, the repair of software bugs and security vulnerabilities, or the retirement or replacement of hardware components will alter the original configuration of an asset. Defining and communicating change procedures, including both routine and emergency changes, ensure that changes to technology assets will be handled in an efficient and controlled manner, consistent with organizational policy, standards, and guidelines, with minimum impact on the integrity, availability, and ultimately the resilience of the asset and the services it supports.

Change control and management defines an organizational process that introduces structure and rigor to making changes to technology assets and provides a means for tracking these changes so that problems can be detected and remedied. This provides an enhanced level of confidence in the integrity of the technology assets and their ability to perform their intended functions.

Typical work products

1. Technology asset baseline configuration
2. Change management policies and procedures

3. Change requests
4. Change management database or system
5. Revision history of configuration items
6. Baseline archives

Subpractices

1. Develop and implement change control policies, procedures, and techniques.
   Change requests address not only new or changed requirements but also maintenance and/or failures in the technology assets. Changes are evaluated to ensure that they are consistent with all technical and resilience requirements.
2. Initiate and record change requests in the change control database or system.
   A change management system includes the storage media, the procedures, and the tools for recording and accessing change requests.
3. Analyze the impact of changes proposed in the change requests.
   Change requests are analyzed to determine the impact that the change will have on the resilience requirements, budget, and schedule.

   Changes are also evaluated for their impact beyond immediate project or contract requirements. Changes to a technology used in multiple services can resolve an immediate issue while causing a problem in other applications.
4. Obtain agreement and approval for changes to baselines from relevant stakeholders.
5. Track the status of change requests to closure.
   Ensure that all change requests have a disposition and that changes that have not been closed are provided an updated status.
6. Control configuration items.
   Check in and check out configuration items from the configuration management database or system for incorporation of changes in a manner that maintains the correctness and integrity of the configuration items.

> These are examples of check-in and check-out steps:
> - confirming that the changes are authorized
> - updating the configuration management database
> - archiving the replaced baseline and retrieving the new baseline configuration

Effective control over configuration items requires proper authentication and access controls to ensure that only those staff members who are authorized are able to check out, make changes to, and check in configuration items. Access management and identity controls must be implemented and managed to ensure that the change process does not cause loss of integrity.

Access management and identity management are addressed in the Access Management and Identity Management process areas respectively.

Because the configuration item can be categorized as an information asset, additional controls over information may have to be implemented. (*These controls are addressed in the Knowledge and Information Management process area.*)

TM:SG4.SP4 PERFORM RELEASE MANAGEMENT

The iteration of technology assets placed into the production environment is managed.

Release management is closely tied to configuration management and change control. While change control addresses the life-cycle process for managing a change request, the result is often a new "release" of a technology asset. Thus, release management addresses the successive release of versions of technology assets into an operations and production environment.

Patch management is a type of release management. Patch management is an important resilience control because it accomplishes two objectives:

1. It ensures that an approved and tested version of a technology asset is placed into production (thereby reducing potential disruptions caused by technology errors).
2. It helps the organization to manage vulnerabilities (particularly in software and systems), which are typically addressed in successive versions of technology assets (thereby reducing exposure to known threats).

Release management requires a process of planning, building, testing, and deploying technology assets and the associated version control and storage of these assets. Release management is intended to be integrated into configuration management and change control processes so that the organization's ability to control the integrity of technology assets (in order to control operational resilience) is enhanced.

Poor release management can diminish operational resilience by exposing the organization to potential technology asset defects by allowing incorrect or inadequate versions of a technology into production, such as those that are

- older or obsolete
- defective or prone to errors
- subject to known vulnerabilities, threats, and malfunctions
- poorly designed and tested

Typical work products

1. Release management policy, guidelines, and standards
2. Release "builds"
3. Release testing procedures
4. Release build test results

Subpractices

1. Develop and implement guidelines for the appropriate planning and release of technology assets.
    Communicate these guidelines to all staff members who are responsible for the resilience of technology assets.

2. Plan technology asset releases.
3. Develop release builds.

    A release build is the version of the technology asset that is to be released into production. For example, for a software asset, this may be an updated version of an operating system that is being distributed to desktop computers to fix a security flaw. For a hardware asset, a release build may be a newly configured server that is going to be implemented to replace an obsolete server.

    Release builds may be created by the organization or may be acquired from a business partner or vendor.

4. Test release builds.

    To minimize operational impact, the organization must test the release build in a segregated test environment to identify issues, concerns, and problems that may cascade into other operational areas when the build is released. Once all operational issues have been defined and addressed (in some cases by "rebuilding" the build), the organization can proceed to move the release build into the production environment.

5. Move release builds into the organization's production environment.

    This process will differ significantly depending on the type of technology asset that is being released to production.

    This process may involve updating configuration item baselines, updating the status of a change request in the change control database or system, and scheduling the physical implementation of the release version into the production environment.

TM:SG5 MANAGE TECHNOLOGY ASSET AVAILABILITY

The availability of technology assets to support high-value services is managed.

The availability of a technology asset is paramount to supporting organizational services. Information that is stored, transported, or processed by technology assets may be accurate and complete, but if it is not available on demand or in a timely matter, the service may not be able to meet its mission.

There is a distinction between planned downtime and unplanned downtime. Planned downtime is usually the result of a user- or management-initiated event that has been subjected to the change management process. Unplanned downtime typically arises from events or incidents outside the control of the organization, such as power outages, security breaches, and disasters like flooding or hurricanes. Unplanned downtime is the effect of diminished operational resilience.

A significantly broad range of operational risks can affect the availability of technology assets for use in supporting high-value services, such as

- accidental or deliberate destruction of the asset
- exposure to natural disaster such as a flood

- operator errors
- software errors, defects, and bugs
- hardware malfunctions or design flaws
- interoperability errors (due to poor integration or interface design)

Many technology assets can be replicated by using spare or easily acquired assets, although cost is a consideration for some assets. Through proper change control and configuration management, organizations may find that the availability of technology assets is controllable, even in light of a range of potential operational risks. However, this is less true of technology assets that are outside of the control of the organization. Resilience requirements must be provided to suppliers to ensure technology asset availability.

To effectively control the operational environment for technology assets, the organization must perform several activities. Foremost, the organization must plan for sustaining technology assets to ensure the continued operation of services. In addition, the organization must address the maintenance of technology assets, the management of technology asset capacity to support current and future service needs, issues related to technology asset complexity and interoperability, and the impact of suppliers and vendors from which technology assets are procured.

TM:SG5.SP1 PERFORM PLANNING TO SUSTAIN TECHNOLOGY ASSETS

The availability and functionality of high-value technology assets are ensured through developing plans to sustain them.

Planning for sustaining technology assets can take many forms. The organization may have redundancy for the assets so that when one fails, it can easily and quickly substitute another. Or, in the case where this is cost-prohibitive, the organization may have arrangements with outside providers to provide equal or similar services under a shared arrangement. Either way, the organization must ensure that the functionality of technology assets in their support of organizational services can be met as required and specified.

Planning for sustaining technology assets can be integrated into the development of service continuity plans for services or instantiated in plans specifically focused on high-value technologies. How this planning is performed may depend on the organization's overall approach to service continuity planning, the types of technology assets the plan addresses, the services that the technology assets support, and the level of planning being performed (i.e., enterprise, organizational unit, IT, etc.). For example, the organization may choose to develop service continuity plans for application systems as a part of developing plans for high-value services that rely on these applications. However, this becomes more difficult if more than one service relies on a single application; when this situation of shared technology assets results, the organization may streamline its approach and develop continuity plans for the shared assets upon which related services can then develop their own specific but referenced plans.

With respect to technology assets, there is a wide range of service continuity plans that may have to be developed. These plans may be developed specifically by asset type, or they can be bundled with the development of service continuity plans for services. In some cases, because a technology asset is shared (such as a network), the organization may have a specific plan that covers the enterprise asset for all services. These are examples of the technology assets that may be addressed specifically:

- desktop computers and related hardware
- organizational application systems (related software code and specialized equipment)
- productivity software such as email systems and word processing systems
- networks (servers, routers, cabling, and other related equipment)
- telecommunications equipment and software (including telecommunications infrastructure, phone systems, satellite communications, and cellular communications)
- processing hardware, including mainframes, servers, and their related assets such as operating systems
- disk drives and storage hardware and software
- printers and fax machines (particularly those that are high-value)
- security-specific systems, applications, utilities, and tools
- specialized equipment such as card readers, cash registers and point-of-sale terminals, and other technology that supports services

The development and management of service continuity plans are addressed in the Service Continuity process area. This practice may not be able to be completed unless consideration of the practices in the Service Continuity process area has been made.

Typical work products

1. Results of business impact analysis or risk assessment
2. Availability metrics for technology and related services
3. Recovery time objectives (RTOs)
4. Recovery point objectives (RPOs)
5. Service continuity plans (specifically addressing activities to sustain technology assets)

Subpractices

1. Develop an approach for sustaining technology assets.

    Technology assets are pervasive and tend to be linked to services; thus, the organization must determine how it will approach planning to sustain these to ensure that all high-value assets are addressed. This may involve separating technology assets into those that are shared and those that are proprietary (i.e., to a specific organizational unit or to support a specific service). Performing business impact analysis at the organizational unit level may give the organization some understanding of shared versus proprietary technology assets, and this information can be used in determining the best approach.

2. Establish availability metrics for high-value technology assets.

    Availability metrics establish the planned and required "uptime" for a technology asset. They are typically established as part of the asset's resilience requirement for availability and may be developed with consideration of the services that the asset supports.

    While availability metrics are most useful for managing technology assets in operation, they also play a significant part in the development plans to sustain technology assets in that they establish a parameter or target that must be attained by technology assets under disruptive conditions. In other words, the availability metric must be met by an asset not only in day-to-day operations but sometimes also under diminished conditions brought on by a disruption or event. These metrics must be considered in planning to determine whether they can be met under diminished conditions and, if not, what additional steps the organization may need to take (i.e., implement manual procedures) to ensure that associated services are not affected.

    Resilience requirements that would include the availability requirement for technology assets are developed and managed respectively in the Resilience Requirements Development and the Resilience Requirements Management process areas.

3. Establish recovery time objectives for high-value technology assets.

    Recovery time objectives (RTOs) establish the period of acceptable downtime of a technology asset (and typically the associated service), after which the organization will suffer an unwanted consequence or impact. RTOs are typically developed at the service level but will be inherited by technology assets that support these services. RTOs must be included in service continuity plans to establish the tolerances within which the plan must be operable.

4. Establish recovery point objectives for high-value technology assets.

    Recovery point objectives (RPOs) establish the point to which a technology asset must be restored to allow recovery of the asset and associated services after a disruption. RPOs must be developed and considered in service continuity plans, particularly restoration plans.

5. Develop service continuity plans that address technology availability.

    Depending on the organization's focus, service continuity plans can be specifically developed for high-value technology (which would affect associated services) or may be developed from a services viewpoint (which addresses technology as an associated asset).

TM:SG5.SP2 MANAGE TECHNOLOGY ASSET MAINTENANCE

Operational maintenance is performed on technology assets.

Meeting the availability requirements of technology assets (particularly hardware) typically requires the performance of regular maintenance activities. While these activities are typically physical in nature (for example, cleaning disk drives to ensure they do not have a mechanical failure), some maintenance may be virtual or electronic, such as when software patches are applied to optimize code performance. *(See patch management in TM:SG4.SP4.)* The criteria used to establish guidelines for maintenance are performed relative to the value of the related services supported by the assets that are located in the facility.

Several types of maintenance may be required based on the type of technology asset. These types of maintenance include

- corrective maintenance (i.e., correcting and repairing problems that degrade the operational capability of the technology)
- preventive maintenance (i.e., preventing potential technology problems from occurring through preplanned activities)
- adaptive maintenance (i.e., adapting technology assets to a different operating environment)
- perfective maintenance (i.e., developing or acquiring an additional or improved operational capability from the technology)

While regular maintenance on technology assets is an important component of ensuring availability, these activities also often bring additional risk because of errors, inadvertent actions, or deliberate actions. All maintenance activities to technology assets should be controlled, monitored, and authorized.

Technology assets included in facilities may be included as part of a facility's regular maintenance schedule and process. Thus, in some organizations, facility maintenance may encompass technology asset maintenance, particularly in facilities such as data centers where technology is integral to the facility. In this case, the organization's facility and technology asset maintenance programs should be coordinated. *(Maintenance to facility assets is addressed in the Environmental Control process area.)*

Typical work products
1. List of technology assets requiring regular maintenance
2. Equipment service intervals and specifications
3. List of maintenance staff authorized to carry out repairs and service

4. Documented maintenance records
5. Maintenance change requests

Subpractices

1. Identify technology systems that require regular maintenance activities.
2. Document equipment suppliers' recommended service intervals and specifications.
3. Document a list of maintenance staff authorized to carry out repairs and service.
   Maintenance staff should be subject to the organization's standards for authorizing and providing access. *(The management of access controls is addressed in the Access Management process area.)*
4. Document all suspected or actual faults and all preventive, corrective, and other types of maintenance.
   Maintenance records should be retained for all technology assets and stored appropriately with access only to authorized individuals. Risks related to software systems and their maintenance may need additional analysis and resolution.

   These activities may result in additions or revisions to existing service continuity plans or may require separate plans to be developed. Actions that are required for service continuity planning should be identified and executed as part of this activity.
5. Implement maintenance and test maintenance changes in a non-operational environment when appropriate.
6. Establish appropriate controls over sensitive or confidential information when maintenance is performed.
   Maintenance activities can result in often-undetected vulnerabilities to information assets. All controls over information assets should be reaffirmed before maintenance is performed, and information access and modification logs should be checked after maintenance is performed.

   Appropriate controls over information assets are addressed in the Knowledge and Information Management process area.
7. Communicate maintenance changes to appropriate entities.
8. Implement maintenance according to change request procedures.
9. Document and communicate results of maintenance.

TM:SG5.SP3 MANAGE TECHNOLOGY CAPACITY

The operating capacity of technology assets is managed.

Capacity is a significant factor in meeting the availability requirements of technology assets and, in turn, of the services that rely on these assets. The operating capacity of technology assets must be managed commensurate with operational demands to support services; otherwise, these services will be affected by diminished operability and potentially fail to meet their missions.

Capacity planning and management involve measurement of current demand, tests for anticipated demand, and gathering usage trends over time to be able to predict expansion needs. Consideration of capacity to ensure technology availability and meet business objectives requires a proactive approach to managing demand and anticipating future needs.

Capacity planning often takes into account that demand is widely variable and that technology assets may need to meet a wide range of capacity needs in operation. This variation is typically due to changing organizational and operational conditions, many of which are out of the direct control of the organization. For example, the following are common organizational events that could affect the capacity of technology assets:

- staff changes that require changes to technology assets, such as the addition of new users (either internally or externally), the transfer of existing staff members from one organizational unit to another, or the termination of staff members
- changes to information such as the creation, alteration, or deletion of paper and electronic records, files, and databases that are stored, transported, or processed by technology
- new service demands, such as launching a new product line or service, that tax the transaction processing capability of systems and networks
- technology refresh, such as the addition of new technical components (particularly new application systems) or changes to existing technical components
- technology retirement
- security events, such as a denial-of-service attack, that could diminish operating capacity

Capacity planning and management require a strategic view to ensure consideration of the organization's strategic objectives and their impact on technology is addressed. A strategy for capacity management also requires the selection of measures and analytic techniques to support availability and capacity management objectives and the establishment and maintenance of technology asset baselines and models to understand current capacity, availability, and levels of service provision (i.e., describe what the normal capacity, availability, and service levels are). In addition to understanding the capacity and availability of the technology assets, forecasting is done for future capacity, availability, and service levels based on trends in service resource use, service system performance, and business process requirements.

Typical work products

1. Capacity management strategy
2. Capacity forecasts
3. Capacity statistics and performance metrics

Subpractices

1. Identify technology assets that require capacity management and planning.
2. Document technology asset use, performance, capacity, and availability needs.
   This practice may result in updated performance and availability metrics and changes to RTOs and RPOs for related services.
3. Forecast technology asset use, performance, capacity, and availability needs.
4. Develop a strategy to meet the demand for capacity based on the resilience requirements for the technology asset and the services it supports.
   In this case, the strategy may need to consider the organization's strategic objectives and how the accomplishment of these objectives affects capacity of current technology assets and future capacity needs.
5. Periodically validate and update the capacity management strategy for technology assets based on operational and organizational environment changes.

TM:SG5.SP4 MANAGE TECHNOLOGY INTEROPERABILITY

The interoperability of technology assets is managed.

Technology assets rarely operate in isolation in organizations; instead, they are typically dependent on the services of other technology assets to support an organizational service. As a simple example, consider a server that supports a web service—it must be connected to a network and user interfaces such as personal computers to provide the service. Thus, these technology assets must be connected and interoperable to meet a shared goal.

In reality, most organizations have significant levels of technology complexity and interconnection where virtually all technology assets have some connection between them, particularly with assets such as application systems. Concepts such as "systems of systems" acknowledge the need for formal coordination of technology components toward a desired organizational outcome. This required interoperability creates another fundamental challenge for the organization in managing operational resilience.

The failure to actively identify and address issues related to interoperability poses an additional level of operational risk to the organization that can result in disruption of organizational services. Unfortunately, issues related to interoperability are often unknown until an unwanted outcome (such as when software code fails or produces an unexpected result) is realized by the organization. Thus, the organization must seek to actively identify interoperability issues and proactively address them before they cause degraded performance or service failures.

Managing interoperability of technology assets requires the organization to develop and maintain a strategy for identifying, analyzing, and mitigating operational risks related to technology asset interoperability. Some of the actions the organization must take are development-related—accurately defining interfaces, providing standards for design and architecture, and performing extensive testing. Other actions are review-focused in that the organization must actively seek to identify interoperability issues that have not yet been uncovered or realized so that they can be neutralized before they pose danger, including issues related to single points of failure and operational bottlenecks.

Typical work products

1. Architecture interoperability standards
2. Enterprise architecture steering committee
3. Interoperability risk management strategy

Subpractices

1. Establish interoperability standards.

    Interoperability standards provide the organization a means to enforce architecture and design principles that seek to minimize the effects of complexity and technology interoperability. These standards seek to prevent operational risks that result from interoperability as well as to provide the organization a level of control over permissible connections and complexity in accordance with the organization's risk tolerance. Standards may address issues such as
    - design, development, and implementation of interoperability-friendly architectures
    - appropriate integration of systems (either designed in-house or acquired)
    - appropriate interface design
    - requirements for data sharing and integrity across technology platforms and architectures
    - means for analyzing connections and identifying problems
    - guidelines for establishing and managing systems of systems
    - methods for identifying and analyzing risks

2. Develop interoperability management strategy.

    The interoperability strategy determines how the organization is going to address issues of interoperability and the standards and guidelines for interoperability that will be used across the enterprise. The strategy should include provisions for regular assessment of technology platform architectures to determine potential failure points and should establish an enterprise architecture steering committee or similar construct to ensure that there is specific governance over interoperability issues.

3. Identify and analyze risks related to interoperability of technology assets.

    The identification of risks that emanate from interoperability issues and concerns should be integrated into the organization's enterprise operational risk management strategy. The identification and analysis of these risks should be focused on
    - identifying behavioral patterns such as
        - unexpected or incorrect process outputs
        - significant processing failures or performance issues
        - increased levels of "unplanned" system or asset downtime

- identifying and analyzing single points of failure caused by incompatible processes or "handshakes"
- identifying processing or communications bottlenecks resulting from interoperability "choke" points

Risks identified as related to interoperability issues should be managed through the organization's regular risk management process as defined in the Risk Management process area.

4. Monitor the interoperability strategy on a regular basis to ensure that it does not pose additional risks to the organization.

Elaborated Generic Practices by Goal

Refer to the Generic Goals and Practices document in Appendix A for general guidance that applies to all process areas. This section provides elaborations relative to the application of the Generic Goals and Practices to the Technology Management process area.

TM:GG1 ACHIEVE SPECIFIC GOALS

The operational resilience management system supports and enables achievement of the specific goals of the Technology Management process area by transforming identifiable input work products to produce identifiable output work products.

TM:GG1.GP1 PERFORM SPECIFIC PRACTICES

Perform the specific practices of the Technology Management process area to develop work products and provide services to achieve the specific goals of the process area.

Elaboration:

Specific practices TM:SG1.SP1 through TM:SG5.SP4 are performed to achieve the goals of the technology management process.

TM:GG2 INSTITUTIONALIZE A MANAGED PROCESS

Technology management is institutionalized as a managed process.

TM:GG2.GP1 ESTABLISH PROCESS GOVERNANCE

Establish and maintain governance over the planning and performance of the technology management process.

Refer to the Enterprise Focus process area for more information about providing sponsorship and oversight to the technology management process.

Subpractices

1. Establish governance over process activities.

    Elaboration:

    > Governance over the technology management process may be exhibited by
    > - establishing a higher-level position, often the chief information officer, responsible for the resilience of the organization's technology assets
    > - developing and publicizing higher-level managers' objectives and requirements for the process
    > - oversight over the development, acquisition, implementation, and management of high-value technology assets
    > - sponsoring and providing oversight of policy, procedures, standards, and guidelines for the documentation of technology assets and for establishing asset ownership and custodianship
    > - making higher-level managers aware of applicable compliance obligations related to the process, and regularly reporting on the organization's satisfaction of these obligations to higher-level managers
    > - oversight over the establishment, implementation, and maintenance of the organization's internal control system for technology assets
    > - sponsoring and funding process activities
    > - implementing a technology steering committee
    > - providing guidance for prioritizing technology assets relative to the organization's high-priority strategic objectives
    > - providing guidance on identifying, assessing, and managing operational risks related to technology assets
    > - providing guidance for resolving violations of technology asset integrity and availability requirements
    > - verifying that the process supports strategic resilience objectives and is focused on the assets and services that are of the highest relative value in meeting strategic objectives
    > - regular reporting from organizational units to higher-level managers on process activities and results
    > - creating dedicated higher-level management feedback loops on decisions about the process and recommendations for improving the process
    > - conducting regular internal and external audits and related reporting to appropriate committees on technology asset controls and the effectiveness of the process
    > - creating formal programs to measure the effectiveness of process activities, and reporting these measurements to higher-level managers

2. Develop and publish organizational policy for the process.

   Elaboration:

   > The technology management policy should address
   > - responsibility, authority, and ownership for performing process activities
   > - procedures, standards, and guidelines for
   >   - documenting and maintaining technology asset descriptions and relevant information
   >   - describing and identifying technology owners and custodians
   >   - developing and documenting resilience requirements for technology assets
   >   - establishing, implementing, and maintaining an internal control system for all technologies, including configuration, change, and release management
   >   - maintaining environmental conditions for physical technologies (hardware, infrastructure)
   >   - managing technology asset operational risk
   >   - establishing technology asset service continuity plans and procedures
   >   - retiring technology assets at the end of their useful life
   >   - architectural interoperability
   >   - removing technology assets from the workplace
   > - the association of technology assets to core organizational services, and the prioritization of assets for service continuity
   > - requesting, approving, and providing access to technology assets to persons, objects, and entities, including type and extent of access and requests that originate externally to the organization *(Refer to the Access Management process area for more information about granting access [rights and privileges] to technology assets. Refer to the Identity Management process area for more information about creating and maintaining identities for persons, objects, and entities.)*
   > - methods for measuring adherence to policy, exceptions granted, and policy violations

TM:GG2.GP2 PLAN THE PROCESS

Establish and maintain the plan for performing the technology management process.

Elaboration:

A plan for performing the technology management process is created to preserve the integrity of technology assets and to ensure that technology assets remain available and viable to support organizational services. The plan must address the resilience requirements of the technology assets, dependencies of services on these assets, and consideration of multiple asset owners and custodians at various levels of the organization. In addition, because technology assets may have a strong geographical connection, the plan must extend to external stakeholders that can enable or adversely affect technology resilience.

The plan for the technology management process should not be confused with service continuity plans for classes of or specific technology assets. The plan for the technology management process details how the organization will perform technology management, including the development of service continuity plans for technology assets. (*The generic practices for service continuity planning are described in SC:SG1 through SC:SG4 in the Service Continuity process area.*)

Subpractices

1. Define and document the plan for performing the process.

   Elaboration:

   Special consideration in the plan may have to be given to establishing, implementing, and maintaining an internal control system for technology assets and for sustaining technology assets. These activities address actions required to protect and sustain technology assets commensurate with their resilience requirements.

2. Define and document the process description.
3. Review the plan with relevant stakeholders and get their agreement.
4. Revise the plan as necessary.

TM:GG2.GP3 PROVIDE RESOURCES

Provide adequate resources for performing the technology management process, developing the work products, and providing the services of the process.

   Elaboration:

   The diversity of activities required to protect and sustain technology assets requires an extensive level of organizational resources and skills and a significant number of external resources. In addition, these activities require a major commitment of financial resources (both expense and capital) from the organization.

Subpractices

1. Staff the process.

   Elaboration:

   > These are examples of staff required to protect and sustain technology assets:
   > - staff responsible for
   >   - information, application, hardware, and technical security
   >   - business continuity and disaster recovery
   >   - IT operations and service delivery

> - implementing and maintaining technology asset security controls (such as security-trained network and system administrators)
> - configuration management, change management, and release management of technology assets
> - establishing and maintaining physical security (such as security guards)
> - implementing and maintaining physical security access and surveillance systems
> - staff involved in technology risk management, including insurance and risk indemnification staff
> - facilities management staff for physical technology assets (hardware, infrastructure)
> - contractors responsible for developing, implementing, and maintaining technology assets
> - owners and custodians of technology assets (to identify and enforce resilience requirements)

Refer to the Organizational Training and Awareness process area for information about training staff for resilience roles and responsibilities.

Refer to the Human Resource Management process area for information about acquiring staff to fulfill roles and responsibilities.

2. Fund the process.

   Elaboration:

   At a minimum, funding must be available to support the development, implementation, testing, and execution of service continuity plans for technology assets. In some cases, capital funding may be required for projects that enhance or support actions to protect and sustain technology assets, which may result in developing additional facilities (to protect tangible technical assets) or establishing outsourcing contracts to support facilities when needed.

   Refer to the Financial Resource Management process area for information about budgeting for, funding, and accounting for technology management.

3. Provide necessary tools, techniques, and methods to perform the process.

   Elaboration:

   Keep in mind that tools used to support the technology management process are themselves technology assets that have to be managed according to the process.

> These are examples of tools, techniques, and methods so support the technology management process:
> - methods and techniques for prioritizing technology assets
> - methods, techniques, and tools for managing risks to technology assets, including tracking open risks to closure and monitoring the effectiveness of technology asset risk mitigation plans

> - methods, techniques, and tools for creating and maintaining the technology asset inventory, including database systems
> - methods, techniques, and tools for maintaining technology assets, including asset configuration management, change control, release management, and monitoring and logging of modification activities
> - methods, techniques, and tools for controlling access to technology assets
> - methods for establishing, implementing, and maintaining the internal control system for technology assets
> - methods for the proper retirement and disposal of technology assets
> - methods, techniques, and tools for technology asset backup, retention, and restoration
> - methods, techniques, and tools for managing technology assets that are provided by external entities

TM:GG2.GP4 ASSIGN RESPONSIBILITY

Assign responsibility and authority for performing the technology management process, developing the work products, and providing the services of the process.

Elaboration:

Of paramount importance in assigning responsibility for the technology management process is the establishment of technology asset owners and custodians *(which is described in ADM:SG1.SP3)*. Owners are responsible for establishing technology asset resilience requirements, ensuring these requirements are met by custodians, and identifying and remediating gaps where requirements are not being met. Owners may also be responsible for establishing, implementing, and maintaining an internal control system commensurate with meeting technology asset resilience requirements if this activity is not performed by a custodian.

Refer to the Human Resource Management process area for more information about establishing resilience as a job responsibility, developing resilience performance goals and objectives, and measuring and assessing performance against these goals and objectives.

Refer to the Asset Definition and Management process area for more information about establishing ownership and custodianship of technology assets.

Subpractices

1. Assign responsibility and authority for performing the process.

   Elaboration:

   Responsibility and authority may extend not only to staff inside the organization but to those with whom the organization has a contractual (custodial) agreement for developing, implementing, and managing technology assets (including implementation and management of controls, including those to sustain technology assets).

2. Assign responsibility and authority for performing the specific tasks of the process.

Elaboration:

> Responsibility and authority for performing technology management tasks can be formalized by
> - defining roles and responsibilities in the process plan
> - including process tasks and responsibility for these tasks in specific job descriptions
> - developing policy requiring organizational unit managers, line of business managers, project managers, and asset and service owners and custodians to participate in the process for assets under their ownership or custodianship
> - developing and implementing contractual instruments (as well as service level agreements) with external entities to establish responsibility and authority for outsourced technology assets
> - including process tasks in staff performance management goals and objectives, with requisite measurement of progress against these goals
> - developing and implementing contractual instruments (as well as service level agreements) with external entities to establish responsibility and authority for technology assets, where applicable
> - including process tasks in measuring performance of external entities against service level agreements *(Refer to the External Dependencies Management process area for additional details about managing relationships with external entities.)*

3. Confirm that people assigned with responsibility and authority understand it and are willing and able to accept it.

TM:GG2.GP5 TRAIN PEOPLE

Train the people performing or supporting the technology management process as needed.

Refer to the Organizational Training and Awareness process area for more information about training the people performing or supporting the process.

Refer to the Human Resource Management process area for more information about inventorying skill sets, establishing a skill set baseline, identifying required skill sets, and measuring and addressing skill deficiencies.

Subpractices

1. Identify process skill needs.

   Elaboration:

   > These are examples of skills required in the technology management process:
   > - prioritization and categorization of technology assets
   > - knowledge of tools, techniques, and methods that can be used to identify, analyze, mitigate, and monitor operational risks to technology assets
   > - establishing, implementing, and maintaining the internal control system for technology assets
   > - protecting and sustaining technology assets to meet their integrity and availability requirements
   > - operating and maintaining all categories of technology assets (hardware, software, systems, infrastructure, and tools)

2. Identify process skill gaps based on available resources and their current skill levels.
3. Identify training opportunities to address skill gaps.

   Elaboration:

   > These are examples of training topics:
   > - technology asset risk management concepts and activities (e.g., risk identification, analysis, mitigation, and monitoring)
   > - technology asset definition, prioritization, and handling
   > - technology asset resilience requirements development
   > - establishing, implementing, and maintaining internal controls for protecting and sustaining technology assets
   > - cross-training to ensure adequate knowledge and coverage for all technology assets and their operation
   > - proper techniques for technology asset disposal
   > - technology asset configuration, change, and release management
   > - supporting technology asset owners and custodians in understanding the process and their roles and responsibilities with respect to its activities
   > - working with external entities that have responsibility for process activities
   > - using process methods, tools, and techniques, including those identified in TM:GG2:GP3 subpractice 3

4. Provide training and review the training needs as necessary.

TM:GG2.GP6 MANAGE WORK PRODUCT CONFIGURATIONS

Place designated work products of the technology management process under appropriate levels of control.

Elaboration:

All work products related to technology asset administrative, technical, and physical controls (configurations, change requests, logs, policies, standards, etc.) should be placed under control.

> These are examples of technology management work products placed under control:
> - inventory of high-value and resilience technology assets
> - integrity and availability requirements
> - administrative, technical, and physical controls
> - list of operational risks by asset and asset category with prioritization, risk disposition, mitigation plans, and current status
> - risk statements with impact valuation
> - access control lists
> - modification logs and audit reports
> - baseline configuration items and configuration control logs and reports
> - configuration management, change management, and release management systems
> - baseline archives and backup media
> - release builds, testing procedures, and release build test results
> - recovery time and recovery point objectives
> - service continuity plans
> - equipment service intervals and specifications
> - capacity forecasts, statistics, and performance metrics
> - process plan
> - policies and procedures
> - contracts with external entities

Refer to the Environmental Control process area for more information about managing physical technology assets (such as hardware and infrastructure) that reside in facilities.

TM:GG2.GP7 IDENTIFY AND INVOLVE RELEVANT STAKEHOLDERS

Identify and involve the relevant stakeholders of the technology management process as planned.

Subpractices

1. Identify process stakeholders and their appropriate involvement.

Elaboration:

Because technology assets may reside in a wide range of physical locations and be developed and maintained by internal and external entities, a substantial number of stakeholders are likely to be external to the organization.

> These are examples of stakeholders of the technology management process:
> - owners and custodians of technology assets
> - service owners
> - organizational unit and line of business managers responsible for high-value technology assets and the services they support
> - staff responsible for managing operational risks to technology assets
> - staff responsible for establishing, implementing, and maintaining an internal control system for technology assets, including those responsible for configuration, change, and release management
> - staff required to develop, test, implement, and execute service continuity plans for technology assets
> - external entities such as public service providers, public infrastructure providers, and contractors that provide essential facility services such as those related to maintaining environmental conditions for physical technology assets (hardware, infrastructure)
> - staff in other organizational support functions, such as accounting or general services administration (particularly as related to technology inventory valuation and retirement)
> - internal and external auditors

> Stakeholders are involved in various tasks in the technology management process, such as
> - planning for the process
> - creating a technology asset baseline
> - creating technology asset profiles and asset risk and vulnerability profiles
> - associating technology assets with services and analyzing service dependencies
> - assigning resilience requirements for technology assets
> - establishing, implementing, and managing technology asset controls
> - developing service continuity plans for technology assets
> - managing operational risks to technology assets
> - managing technology asset configurations, changes, and releases
> - controlling the operational environment in which technology assets reside
> - managing technology asset external dependencies for assets developed, operated, and maintained by external entities
> - managing relationships with external entities that provide technology asset services
> - reviewing and appraising the effectiveness of process activities
> - resolving issues in the process

2. Communicate the list of stakeholders to planners and those responsible for process performance.
3. Involve relevant stakeholders in the process as planned.

TM:GG2.GP8 MONITOR AND CONTROL THE PROCESS

Monitor and control the technology management process against the plan for performing the process and take appropriate corrective action.

Refer to the Monitoring process area for more information about the collection, organization, and distribution of data that may be useful for monitoring and controlling processes.

Refer to the Measurement and Analysis process area for more information about establishing process metrics and measurement.

Refer to the Enterprise Focus process area for more information about providing process information to managers, identifying issues, and determining appropriate corrective actions.

Subpractices

1. Measure actual performance against the plan for performing the process.
2. Review accomplishments and results of the process against the plan for performing the process.

Elaboration:

> These are examples of metrics for the technology management process:
> - percentage of technology assets that have been inventoried as scheduled
> - level of discrepancies between actual inventory and stated inventory
> - number of changes made to the technology asset inventory during a stated period
> - number of technology assets that do not have stated owners or custodians
> - number of technology assets with incomplete asset profiles or other incomplete information (particularly the lack of stated resilience requirements)
> - percentage of technology assets for which some form of risk assessment has been performed as required by policy
> - percentage of technology assets for which the cost of compromise (loss, damage, disclosure, disruption in access) has been quantified
> - number of violations of access control policies for technology assets
> - number of electronic access controls that are able to be circumvented; number of attempted or successful intrusions into digital technology assets
> - number of physical access controls that are able to be circumvented; number of attempted or successful intrusions into physical technology assets
> - percentage of technology assets for which approved configuration settings have been implemented as required by policy
> - percentage of technology assets with configurations that deviate from approved standards
> - timeliness of completing scheduled maintenance (technology asset configuration, change, and release management) activities

- actual level of maintenance versus scheduled or expected (including patch management)
- number of scheduled maintenance activities missed
- number of unauthorized changes to technology assets during a stated period
- number of technology asset risks referred to the risk management process; number of risks where corrective action is still pending (by risk rank)
- change success rate (percentage of changes to technology assets that succeed without causing an incident, service outage, or impairment)
- level of adherence to external entity service level agreements and agreed maintenance levels
- level of adherence to technology asset policies; number of policy violations; number of policy exceptions requested and number approved
- number of process activities that are on track per plan
- rate of change of resource needs to support the process
- rate of change of costs to support the process

3. Review activities, status, and results of the process with the immediate level of managers responsible for the process and identify issues.

Elaboration:

Reviews will likely verify the accuracy and completeness of the technology asset inventory.

Periodic reviews of the technology management process are needed to ensure that
- newly acquired technology assets are included in the inventory
- changes to technology assets (additions, modifications, and retirements) are accurately reflected in the inventory
- technology assets have stated resilience requirements
- asset-service mapping is accurate and current
- ownership and custodianship over technology assets are established and documented
- administrative, technical, and physical controls are operating as intended
- controls are meeting the stated intent of the resilience requirements
- status reports are provided to appropriate stakeholders in a timely manner
- technology asset issues are referred to the risk management process when necessary
- actions requiring management involvement are elevated in a timely manner
- the performance of process activities is being monitored and regularly reported
- key measures are within acceptable ranges as demonstrated in governance dashboards or scorecards and financial reports
- actions resulting from internal and external audits are being closed in a timely manner

4. Identify and evaluate the effects of significant deviations from the plan for performing the process.
5. Identify problems in the plan for performing and executing the process.
6. Take corrective action when requirements and objectives are not being satisfied, when issues are identified, or when progress differs significantly from the plan for performing the process.

Elaboration:

For technology assets, corrective action may require the revision of existing administrative, technical, and physical controls, development and implementation of new controls, or a change in the type of controls (preventive, detective, corrective, compensating, etc.).

7. Track corrective action to closure.

TM:GG2.GP9 OBJECTIVELY EVALUATE ADHERENCE

Objectively evaluate adherence of the technology management process against its process description, standards, and procedures, and address non-compliance.

Elaboration:

These are examples of activities to be reviewed:
- identifying and prioritizing technology assets
- identifying technology requirements
- establishing and implementing technology asset controls
- identifying and managing technology asset risks
- developing service continuity plans for technology assets
- identifying and managing technology asset dependencies
- identifying and managing changes to technology assets
- retiring technology assets
- aligning stakeholder requirements with technology management process plans
- assigning responsibility, accountability, and authority for technology management process activities
- determining the adequacy of technology management reports and reviews in informing decision makers regarding the performance of operational resilience management activities and the need to take corrective action, if any
- verifying technology management controls
- using technology management work products for improving technology asset protection and sustainment strategies

> These are examples of work products to be reviewed:
> - technology asset inventory
> - technology asset internal controls documentation
> - technology asset risk statements
> - technology asset risk mitigation plans
> - service continuity plans for technology assets
> - technology asset maintenance records and change logs
> - business impact analysis results for technology assets
> - lists of key providers and contacts for technology assets
> - technology asset retirement standards
> - contracts with external entities
> - technology management process plan and policies
> - technology asset issues that have been referred to the risk management process
> - technology management methods, techniques, and tools
> - metrics for the technology management process *(Refer to TM:GG2.GP8 subpractice 2.)*

TM:GG2.GP10 REVIEW STATUS WITH HIGHER-LEVEL MANAGERS

Review the activities, status, and results of the technology management process with higher-level managers and resolve issues.

Elaboration:

Status reporting on the technology management process may be part of the formal governance structure or may be performed through other organizational reporting requirements (such as through the chief risk officer or the chief resilience officer level). Audits of the process—particularly the validation of the organization's technology asset inventory and internal control system at points in time—may be escalated to higher-level managers through the organization's audit committee of the board of directors or similar construct in private or non-profit organizations.

Refer to the Enterprise Focus process area for more information about providing sponsorship and oversight to the operational resilience management system.

TM:GG3 INSTITUTIONALIZE A DEFINED PROCESS

Technology management is institutionalized as a defined process.

TM:GG3.GP1 ESTABLISH A DEFINED PROCESS

Establish and maintain the description of a defined technology management process.

Elaboration:

Technology management is typically carried out at the organizational unit or line of business level for convenience and accuracy and may have to be geographically focused (because of the location of specific technology assets). However, to achieve consistent results in creating and managing technology assets, the activities at the organizational unit or line of business level must be derived from an enterprise definition of the technology management process. The technology asset inventory may be inconsistent across organizational units, particularly when assets have shared ownership across organizational lines, but the defined process remains consistent. The level of completeness and accuracy of technology asset descriptions across organizational units may affect asset management at the enterprise level and impede operational resilience.

In addition, a variable mix of administrative, technical, and physical controls may be used across the organization to meet the resilience requirements for technology assets, but the process is consistent with the enterprise definition.

Establishing and tailoring process assets, including standard processes, are addressed in the Organizational Process Definition process area.

Establishing process needs and objectives and selecting, improving, and deploying process assets, including standard processes, are addressed in the Organizational Process Focus process area.

Subpractices

1. Select from the organization's set of standard processes those processes that cover the technology management process and best meet the needs of the organizational unit or line of business.
2. Establish the defined process by tailoring the selected processes according to the organization's tailoring guidelines.
3. Ensure that the organization's process objectives are appropriately addressed in the defined process, and ensure that process governance extends to the tailored processes.
4. Document the defined process and the records of the tailoring.
5. Revise the description of the defined process as necessary.

TM:GG3.GP2 COLLECT IMPROVEMENT INFORMATION

Collect technology management work products, measures, measurement results, and improvement information derived from planning and performing the process to support future use and improvement of the organization's processes and process assets.

Elaboration:

> These are examples of improvement work products and information:
> - technology asset inventories
> - inventory inconsistencies and issues
> - reports on the effectiveness and weaknesses of controls
> - improvements based on risk identification and mitigation
> - effectiveness of technology asset service continuity plans in execution
> - metrics and measurements of the viability of the technology management process *(Refer to TM:GG2.GP8 subpractice 2.)*
> - changes and trends in operating conditions, risk conditions, and the risk environment that affect technology management results
> - lessons learned in post-event review of technology asset incidents and disruptions in continuity
> - maintenance issues and concerns for technology assets
> - conflicts and risks arising from dependencies on external entities
> - lessons learned in updating, replacing, and retiring technology assets from active use
> - resilience requirements that are not being satisfied for technology assets or are being exceeded

Establishing the measurement repository and process asset library is addressed in the Organizational Process Definition process area. Updating the measurement repository and process asset library as part of process improvement and deployment is addressed in the Organizational Process Focus process area.

Subpractices

1. Store process and work product measures in the organization's measurement repository.
2. Submit documentation for inclusion in the organization's process asset library.
3. Document lessons learned from the process for inclusion in the organization's process asset library.
4. Propose improvements to the organizational process assets.

VULNERABILITY ANALYSIS AND RESOLUTION
Operations

Purpose

The purpose of Vulnerability Analysis and Resolution is to identify, analyze, and manage vulnerabilities in an organization's operating environment.

Introductory Notes

A vulnerability is the susceptibility of an asset and associated service to disruption. Examples of vulnerabilities are weaknesses in the physical or technical infrastructure of the organization and flaws in the character of an individual employee. All assets of the organization that are operationally deployed—people, information, technology, and facilities—are subject to some level and type of vulnerability.

Vulnerabilities can result in operational risks and must be identified and remediated to avoid disruptions to the organization's ability to meet its strategic objectives. Vulnerability Analysis and Resolution is complementary to Risk Management. It requires that an organization identify weaknesses to its assets and services and understand the potential impact to the organization when these weaknesses are exploited.

As organizations have grown more dependent on their technical infrastructures, there has been a corresponding increase in focus on identifying only technical vulnerabilities. However, operational risk emanates from weaknesses in the protection of *all* types of assets, and thus the vulnerability analysis and resolution activity must cover not only weaknesses in the technical infrastructure but also potential threats to the viability of people, information, and facilities.

The identification and remediation of technical vulnerabilities are means for mitigating operational risk, but they do not fully constitute the activities of risk management. Instead, Vulnerability Analysis and Resolution informs the organization of threats that must be analyzed in the risk management process to determine whether they pose tangible risk to the organization based on its unique risk drivers, appetite, and tolerance. In turn, the risk management process informs vulnerability analysis and resolution processes to focus attention on the assets and services that are most critical to meeting strategic objectives.

The Vulnerability Analysis and Resolution process area describes the organization's ability to establish a vulnerability management strategy and to efficiently and effectively assign enterprise-wide resources to implement that strategy. The organization identifies and analyzes vulnerabilities across the enterprise and communicates relevant information about these vulnerabilities to other organizational processes that require this information. Strategies are developed to reduce the organization's exposure to vulnerabilities. In this way, the organization is mitigating risk where the exploited vulnerability has the potential to impact the organization.

Vulnerability Analysis and Resolution provides the organization an important opportunity to improve processes that may introduce vulnerabilities into the operating environment. Vulnerabilities are logged and tracked, and root-cause analysis and trending are performed on them to determine if breakdowns in other organizational processes are resulting in exposure. This knowledge is translated into improved strategies for protecting and sustaining assets and services as well as improvements in the processes.

Vulnerabilities may result in events and incidents that the organization must manage. *(The Incident Management and Control process area addresses the processes for identifying, analyzing, handling, and responding to incidents.)*

Vulnerability identification and analysis activities provide information about potential risks to the organization. *(Risks are identified, analyzed, and mitigated in the Risk Management process area.)*

Related Process Areas

The risk management cycle for organizational services, processes, and assets is addressed in the Risk Management process area.

Monitoring for events, incidents, and vulnerabilities is addressed in the Monitoring process area.

Summary of Specific Goals and Practices

VAR:SG1 Prepare for Vulnerability Analysis and Resolution
    VAR:SG1.SP1   Establish Scope
    VAR:SG1.SP2   Establish a Vulnerability Analysis and Resolution Strategy
VAR:SG2 Identify and Analyze Vulnerabilities
    VAR:SG2.SP1   Identify Sources of Vulnerability Information
    VAR:SG2.SP2   Discover Vulnerabilities
    VAR:SG2.SP3   Analyze Vulnerabilities
VAR:SG3 Manage Exposure to Vulnerabilities
    VAR:SG3.SP1   Manage Exposure to Vulnerabilities
VAR:SG4 Identify Root Causes
    VAR:SG4.SP1   Perform Root-Cause Analysis

Specific Practices by Goal

VAR:SG1 *PREPARE FOR VULNERABILITY ANALYSIS AND RESOLUTION*

Preparation for vulnerability analysis and resolution activities is conducted.

Preparation is conducted by establishing and maintaining a strategy for identifying, analyzing, and addressing vulnerabilities in the operational environment. This is typically documented in a vulnerability management plan. The vulnerability management strategy addresses the specific actions and management approach used to apply and control the vulnerability management activities within the organization. This includes scoping the operational environment to be scanned for potential vulnerabilities, the development of criteria to categorize the vulnerabilities, and the parameters used to identify, analyze, and potentially address vulnerabilities.

The operating environment of an asset consists of the physical or logical locations where the asset is deployed and the set of controls (administrative, technical, and physical) that are applied to that asset at that location.

VAR:SG1.SP1 *ESTABLISH SCOPE*

The assets and operational environments that must be examined for vulnerabilities are identified.

An asset and the services it supports are vulnerable to disruption if there is a weakness that is not currently remediated by an administrative, technical, or physical control. The universe of potential vulnerabilities in an organization's operational environment is almost limitless. The organization must therefore focus its vulnerability analysis and resolution activities toward identifying the vulnerabilities to the organization's most high-value assets and services. Otherwise, the organization can expend significant human and financial resources identifying vulnerabilities that have limited potential for posing operational risk to the organization.

The scoping activity establishes the ranges of assets that will be the focus of the organization's vulnerability analysis and resolution activities. The scoping activity should be driven by the resilience requirements of the identified assets.

Typical work products

1. Documented scope of vulnerability analysis and resolution activities

Subpractices

1. Identify the assets that are the focus of vulnerability analysis and resolution activities.

The organization's high-value assets are identified in the Asset Definition and Management process area. Further prioritization is performed in other process areas for specific asset types: Human Resource Management (people), Knowledge and Information Management (information), Technology Management (technology), and Environmental Control (facilities).

High-value assets should form the basis for the scope of vulnerability analysis and resolution activities. Deciding upon a proper scope, however, may also require an understanding of associated services and their value to supporting the organization's strategic objectives.

2. Identify the operational environments where vulnerabilities may exist for each asset.

    This will vary depending upon the type of asset under examination:
    - For an information asset, the operational environment will depend on where the asset is physically contained (in a file room or on a server) and on the form of the asset (paper or electronic).
    - For a technology asset, the operational environment includes where the asset is located physically (e.g., at a data center, in a server farm) and to what other assets it is connected (e.g., to a network).
    - For a facilities asset, the operational environment includes the physical and geographical location of the asset and its proximity to other organizational assets.

    The organization must prioritize the operational environments on which to focus vulnerability analysis and resolution activities to the highest benefit to the organization.

3. Define the scope of vulnerability analysis and resolution activities.

VAR:SG1.SP2 ESTABLISH A VULNERABILITY ANALYSIS AND RESOLUTION STRATEGY

An operational vulnerability analysis and resolution strategy is established and maintained.

A comprehensive vulnerability management strategy addresses items such as

- the determination and documentation of the scope of vulnerability analysis and resolution
- a plan for performing vulnerability analysis and resolution
- resources and accountability for vulnerability identification and remediation
- approved methods and tools to be used for the identification, analysis, remediation, monitoring, and communication of vulnerabilities
- a process for organizing, categorizing, comparing, and consolidating vulnerabilities
- thresholds for remediation and resolution activities
- time intervals for vulnerability identification and monitoring activities

The vulnerability analysis and resolution strategy should be guided by the risk criteria and tolerances of the organization and is often documented in an organizational vulnerability analysis and resolution plan. This plan should support and be developed along with the organization's risk management plan. The strategy is reviewed with relevant stakeholders to promote commitment and understanding.

Typical work products

1. Vulnerability analysis and resolution strategy
2. Vulnerability analysis and resolution plan
3. List of appropriate tools, techniques, and methods for identifying vulnerabilities

Subpractices

1. Develop and document an operational vulnerability analysis and resolution strategy.

    The strategy for addressing vulnerability analysis and resolution should be documented in a plan that can be communicated to relevant stakeholders and implemented. The plan should address
    - the scope of vulnerability analysis and resolution activities
    - the essential activities that are required for vulnerability analysis and resolution
    - a plan for collecting the data necessary for vulnerability activities
    - tools, techniques, and methods that have been approved for identifying and analyzing vulnerabilities across a range of assets
    - a schedule for performing vulnerability activities
    - the roles and responsibilities necessary to carry out the plan
    - the skills and training required to perform the vulnerability analysis and resolution strategy and plan
    - the relative costs associated with the activities, particularly for the purchase and licensing of tools, techniques, and methods
    - relevant stakeholders of the vulnerability activities and their roles
    - objectives for measuring when the plan and strategy are successful

2. Communicate the operational vulnerability analysis and resolution strategy to relevant stakeholders and obtain their commitment to the activities described in the strategy.

    Several operational resilience management processes rely on the types of information that will result from the vulnerability analysis and resolution process. Processes such as risk management, incident management and control, and service continuity should be considered as areas where regular communications about vulnerability activities and actual vulnerabilities would be necessary.

3. Assign resources to specific vulnerability analysis and resolution roles and responsibilities.

4. Identify the tools, techniques, and methods that the organization will use to identify vulnerabilities to assets.

The organization should compile a list of approved and recommended tools, techniques, and methods that can be used for vulnerability activities. Pre-approving tools, techniques, and methods ensures consistency and cost effectiveness, as well as validity of results. This list should cover the entire range of assets and include both procedural and automated methods.

VAR:SG2 IDENTIFY AND ANALYZE VULNERABILITIES

A process for identifying and analyzing vulnerabilities is established and maintained.

The identification and analysis of vulnerabilities are essential elements of managing vulnerabilities *before* they are exploited. Information learned through the identification of vulnerabilities is contextualized using enterprise risk information.

VAR:SG2.SP1 IDENTIFY SOURCES OF VULNERABILITY INFORMATION

The sources of vulnerability information are identified.

Information about potential vulnerabilities is available from a wide variety of organizational and external sources. External or public sources typically provide information that is focused on common technologies that are used by a wide range of organizations. Internal sources typically provide information about vulnerabilities that are unique to the organization and range across all types of assets, including people, information, and facilities. Internal sources of vulnerability information are often generated by other operational resilience management processes such as incident management and monitoring, or through IT service delivery and operations processes such as the service desk and problem management. These sources may provide information about vulnerabilities that the organization has observed or that have been exploited, resulting in disruption to the organization.

These are examples of sources of vulnerability data:
- vendors of software, systems, and hardware technologies that provide warnings on vulnerabilities in their products
- common free catalogs, such as the US-CERT Vulnerability Notes Database and the MITRE Corporation's Common Vulnerabilities and Exposures list
- industry groups
- vulnerability newsgroups and mailing lists
- the results of executing automated tools, techniques, and methods
- internal processes such as service desk, problem management, incident management and control, and monitoring, where vulnerabilities may be detected

Vulnerability data collection is a continuous process. Expanding the sources of vulnerability information helps the organization improve its identification of vulnerabilities in a timely manner and extends the organization's awareness of an expanding range of vulnerability types. The organization must ensure that as new vulnerability information sources become available, they are incorporated into the organization's vulnerability repository and corresponding identification and analysis activities.

Typical work products

1. List of sources of vulnerability information

Subpractices

1. Identify sources of relevant vulnerability information.

    The sources of vulnerability information should fit the organization's vulnerability identification and analysis needs. The internal sources of vulnerability information supplied by other operational resilience management processes should be included in the list.

2. Review sources on a regular basis and update as necessary.

    New sources of vulnerability information are continually emerging. The organization must review these sources and add them to its source list to be sure to have access to the most current, accurate, and extensive information about vulnerabilities.

VAR:SG2.SP2 DISCOVER VULNERABILITIES

A process is established to actively discover vulnerabilities.

Vulnerabilities are discovered from active review and capture from the organization's standard list of sources of vulnerability information. There are many techniques that an enterprise can use to discover vulnerabilities. These include

- performing internal vulnerability audits or assessments (using tools, techniques, and methods)
- performing external-entity assessments
- reviewing the results of internal and external audits
- periodically reviewing vulnerability catalogs, such as the US-CERT Vulnerability Notes Database and the MITRE Corporation's Common Vulnerabilities and Exposures list
- subscribing to vendor notification services
- subscribing to vulnerability notification services (mailing lists)
- reviewing reports from industry groups
- reviewing vulnerability newsgroups

- using lessons-learned databases, such as the incident knowledgebase (*The incident knowledgebase is addressed in the Incident Management and Control process area.*)
- monitoring high-value organizational processes and infrastructure (*Monitoring for events, incidents, and vulnerabilities is addressed in the Monitoring process area.*)
- using reports of vulnerabilities from other processes, such as the organization's service desk or the problem management process

The organization establishes a vulnerability repository as the central source of vulnerability life-cycle information. As vulnerabilities are discovered, they are submitted to the organization's vulnerability repository by capturing the information in a format that is usable in the organization's vulnerability identification and analysis process. The repository is an essential construct that is vital to the efficiency and effectiveness of other operational resilience management processes. For example, accurate, complete, and timely information about vulnerabilities can assist in the examination of incidents and events, provide threat information to the risk management process for the identification of risks, and form the basis for root-cause analysis and trending for overall improvement of the operational resilience management system.

Vulnerability identification is a continuous activity. Some techniques for identifying vulnerability information are performed on a discrete basis, while others, such as monitoring, are more continuous. For discrete activities, the organization must decide the appropriate time intervals that it will use to repeat the identification activities to ensure that it has the most current and accurate information in its vulnerability repository.

Typical work products

1. Vulnerability data and information
2. Vulnerability repository

Subpractices

1. Discover vulnerabilities.
    Data collection should be coordinated to discover vulnerabilities and populate the vulnerability repository as efficiently as possible.

These are examples of source documents from which vulnerabilities are discovered:
- reports from assessment tools and methods
- audit reports
- vulnerability databases
- emails from mailing lists
- vulnerability reports (from vulnerability databases)

> - vendor notifications
> - newsgroup messages
> - incident knowledgebase
> - communications from monitoring processes
> - service desk or problem management reports

2. Provide training to staff to perform data collection and discover vulnerabilities.
   Individuals involved in the vulnerability discovery process should be skilled and trained in the use of appropriate tools, techniques, and methodologies. They should have access to the sources of vulnerabilities, including automated tools. Where automated tools are involved, the organization should ensure that training is provided on the appropriate and secure use of the tools.
3. Populate the vulnerability repository.
   Basic information that should be collected about vulnerabilities includes
   - a unique organizational identifier for internal reference
   - description of the vulnerability
   - date entered into the repository
   - references to the source of the vulnerability
   - the importance of the vulnerability to the organization (critical, moderate, etc.)
   - individuals or teams assigned to analyze and remediate the vulnerability
   - a log of remediation actions taken to reduce or eliminate the vulnerability

   The vulnerability repository is a source of risk to the organization if accessed by unauthorized individuals. The organization should apply access controls to the vulnerability repository to permit only authorized individuals to view, modify, or delete information.
4. Provide access to the vulnerability repository to appropriate process stakeholders.

VAR:SG2.SP3 ANALYZE VULNERABILITIES

Vulnerabilities are analyzed to determine whether they have to be reduced or eliminated.

The mere identification of a vulnerability is not sufficient for determining whether the organization should act to counter it. With the number of vulnerabilities growing exponentially (particularly for technology assets), no organization can (or would want to) address all of them. The organization must analyze vulnerabilities to determine which ones require additional attention.

Through vulnerability analysis, the organization seeks to understand the potential threat that the vulnerability represents. The structure of the vulnerability—what it can do, how it is exploited, the potential effects—must be carefully considered in the context of the potentially affected assets and services. Vulnerability analysis includes activities to

- understand the threat and exposure
- review trend information to determine whether the vulnerability has existed before and what actions were taken to reduce or eliminate it
- identify and understand underlying causes for exposure to the vulnerability
- prioritize and categorize vulnerabilities for appropriate action to reduce or eliminate them
- refer vulnerabilities to the organization's risk management process when more extensive consideration of the impact of the potential threat must be performed to determine an appropriate mitigation strategy

As a result of analysis, some vulnerabilities will be determined to be of no relevance to the organization (i.e., the organization is not exposed to them or the exposure is negligible). Other vulnerabilities will have to be addressed through a simple fix (such as a software patch or by turning off unnecessary services), and some will have to have a formal strategy developed. The organization should assign a course of action to each vulnerability.

Typical work products

1. Vulnerability prioritization guidelines
2. Vulnerability analysis
3. List of vulnerabilities prioritized for disposition
4. Updated vulnerability repository

Subpractices

1. Develop prioritization guidelines for vulnerabilities.
    Prioritization guidelines should help the organization to sort and prioritize vulnerabilities consistently according to their relevance to the organization. The relevance to the organization may be characterized either in qualitative terms (high, medium, or low) or quantitative terms (through a numerical scale). The prioritization will provide the organization a structured means for determining the appropriate categorization for resolution actions.
2. Analyze the structure and action of the vulnerability.
    This may require the vulnerability to be decomposed into other artifacts such as threat, threat actor, motive, and potential outcome. In addition, relationships between vulnerabilities may be identified that could indicate similar root causes or origins that must be considered in resolution actions.
3. Prioritize and categorize vulnerabilities for disposition.
    Based on the organization's prioritization guidelines and the results of vulnerability analysis, vulnerabilities must be categorized by disposition.

> These are examples of categories for vulnerability resolution:
> - Take no action; ignore.
> - Fix immediately (typically the case for vendor updates or changes).
> - Develop and implement vulnerability resolution strategy (typically the case when the resolution is more extensive than simple actions such as vendor updates).
> - Perform additional research and analysis.
> - Refer the vulnerability to the risk management process for formal risk consideration.

Vulnerabilities that are referred to the risk management process are typically those that cannot be resolved without more extensive decomposition and consideration of organizational consequences and impact.

4. Update the vulnerability repository with analysis and prioritization and categorization information.

VAR:SG3 MANAGE EXPOSURE TO VULNERABILITIES

Strategies are developed to manage exposure to identified vulnerabilities.

Vulnerability resolution is the action that the organization takes to reduce or eliminate exposure to a vulnerability. It is the result of vulnerability analysis and prioritization.

Vulnerability resolution can also be a type of risk management activity. The actions to eliminate or reduce exposure to a vulnerability can be an outcome of the organization's formal risk management process, which is typically much more extensive than vulnerability analysis and resolution because it includes formal consideration of the organization's risk tolerances and the context of organizational consequence and impact.

In some cases, vulnerability resolution is relatively simple. Technical vulnerabilities posted on common vulnerability databases often include information about patching software, systems, firmware, or networks to reduce or eliminate vulnerabilities. Other types of vulnerabilities, including safety concerns for people or physical threats to facilities, may take more analysis and strategy development to address.

Vulnerability resolution may also extend beyond exposure reduction or elimination. Often, operational workarounds are necessary to avoid exposure to vulnerabilities when reduction or elimination is not possible.

VAR:SG3.SP1 MANAGE EXPOSURE TO VULNERABILITIES

Strategies are developed and implemented to manage exposure to identified vulnerabilities.

The organization must develop and implement an appropriate resolution strategy for vulnerabilities to which the organization has determined that exposure must be reduced or eliminated. This strategy can include actions to

- minimize the organization's exposure to the vulnerability (by reducing the likelihood that the vulnerability will be exploited)
- eliminate the organization's exposure to the vulnerability (by eliminating the threat, the threat actor, and/or the motive)

Managing exposure to vulnerabilities will likely require a consideration of these actions and the ways that they can be realized through the development and implementation of appropriate strategies. Strategies may span a wide range of activities, including

- implementing software, systems, and firmware patches
- developing and implementing operational workarounds
- developing and implementing new protective controls, or updating existing controls
- developing and implementing new service continuity plans, or updating existing plans

The organization must also consider the need to integrate managing exposure to vulnerabilities with other related organizational processes such as change management, configuration management, product acquisition, and monitoring.

Strategies for managing exposure may also require a consideration of the impact of the action against the continuing operations of the organization. For example, to reduce exposure to a vulnerability, the organization may be required to turn off or eliminate certain operating system services that staff members may need to perform their job functions. The organization must either determine a workaround to the loss of this service or allow the service to continue operating with the implementation of detective controls (such as audit logging and tracking) to ensure that it is not (or has not been) exploited by threat actors. Thus the organization's strategy may include the development and documentation of the workaround or the types and extent of detective controls that will be implemented.

Once the organization has developed a vulnerability management strategy, it must be monitored to ensure effective implementation and the achievement of results as documented in the strategy.

Typical work products

1. Vulnerability management strategies
2. Updated vulnerability repository, with resolution status information
3. Vulnerability management strategy status reports

Subpractices

1. Develop a vulnerability management strategy for all vulnerabilities that require resolution.

    The organization may choose to address vulnerabilities that do not require extensive analysis without extensive strategy development. Typically, these vulnerabilities include those identified by software vendors or vulnerability databases for which a solution is readily available.

    For vulnerabilities that require further analysis and consideration, the organization should document a strategy for implementation. The strategy should address the actions that the organization will take to reduce or eliminate exposure or to provide an operational workaround if preferable. The strategy should detail the staff who are responsible for implementing and monitoring the strategy, the time period for performance, the cost of the strategy, and other relevant details.

    If the vulnerability strategy requires more extensive involvement of the risk management process, it should be replaced by the development of risk mitigation strategies. (*The development of these strategies is addressed in the Risk Management process area.*)

2. Ensure that relevant stakeholders are informed of resolution activities.
3. Update the vulnerability repository with information about the vulnerability management strategy.
4. Monitor the status of open vulnerabilities.
5. Analyze the effectiveness of vulnerability management strategies to ensure that objectives are achieved.

VAR:SG4 IDENTIFY ROOT CAUSES

The root causes of vulnerabilities are examined to improve vulnerability analysis and resolution and reduce organizational exposure.

Organizations should identify, analyze, and resolve vulnerabilities as they are detected, but it is also necessary to perform more intensive analyses to understand how vulnerabilities originate and are related to each other. This provides the organization a powerful tool in proactively preventing future exposures.

Learning from vulnerability analysis and resolution activities involves performing root-cause analysis and translating vulnerability knowledge into actionable means for improving operational resilience.

VAR:SG4.SP1 PERFORM ROOT-CAUSE ANALYSIS

A review of identified vulnerabilities is performed to determine and address underlying causes.

Root-cause analysis is a general approach for determining the underlying causes of events or problems as a means for addressing the symptoms of such events or problems as they manifest in organizational disruptions. Few vulnerabilities have organic causes (i.e., emerge on their own); instead, they are typically created by other actions or inactions such as poor software design, failure of organizational policies and processes, improper training, or operational complexity. Performing root-cause analysis allows the organization to look further into the reasons why exposures are occurring and to determine how to address these issues before they result in vulnerabilities that have to be analyzed and resolved.

A primary activity in root-cause analysis is to determine how to eliminate or reduce the underlying cause of exposures. Root-cause analysis may result in the development of strategies to address the root causes that are identified. As with developing strategies for managing vulnerabilities, this may include developing or improving controls as well as strategies for sustaining assets and services. It may also result in updating resilience training and awareness activities to ensure understanding of root causes and elimination of practices and processes that result in exposures. Overall, the identification and resolution of root causes can be used to improve the organization's operational resilience by ensuring that lessons learned are translated to knowledge.

Many tools and techniques for root-cause analysis exist. The organization must familiarize itself with these tools and techniques, select those that are most appropriate for use, and provide training to relevant staff in their use.

Typical work products

1. Root-cause analysis reports
2. Updated vulnerability repository, with root-cause analysis

Subpractices

1. Identify and select root-cause tools, techniques, and methods appropriate for use in analyzing the underlying causes of vulnerabilities.
2. Identify and analyze the root causes of vulnerabilities.
3. Develop and implement strategies to address root causes.
4. Monitor the effects of implementing strategies to address root causes.

Elaborated Generic Practices by Goal

Refer to the Generic Goals and Practices document in Appendix A for general guidance that applies to all process areas. This section provides elaborations relative to the application of the Generic Goals and Practices to the Vulnerability Analysis and Resolution process area.

VAR:GG1 ACHIEVE SPECIFIC GOALS

The operational resilience management system supports and enables achievement of the specific goals of the Vulnerability Analysis and Resolution process area by transforming identifiable input work products to produce identifiable output work products.

VAR:GG1.GP1 PERFORM SPECIFIC PRACTICES

Perform the specific practices of the Vulnerability Analysis and Resolution process area to develop work products and provide services to achieve the specific goals of the process area.

Elaboration:

Specific practices VAR:SG1.SP1 through VAR:SG4.SP1 are performed to achieve the goals of the vulnerability analysis and resolution process.

VAR:GG2 INSTITUTIONALIZE A MANAGED PROCESS

Vulnerability analysis and resolution is institutionalized as a managed process.

VAR:GG2.GP1 ESTABLISH PROCESS GOVERNANCE

Establish and maintain governance over the planning and performance of the vulnerability analysis and resolution process.

Refer to the Enterprise Focus process area for more information about providing sponsorship and oversight to the vulnerability analysis and resolution process.

Subpractices

1. Establish governance over process activities.

   Elaboration:

   > Governance over the vulnerability analysis and resolution process may be exhibited by
   > - developing and publicizing higher-level managers' objectives and requirements for the process
   > - sponsoring process policies, procedures, standards, and guidelines
   > - oversight over the establishment, implementation, and maintenance of the organization's internal control system for the process
   > - making higher-level managers aware of applicable compliance obligations related to the process, and regularly reporting on the organization's satisfaction of these obligations to higher-level managers
   > - sponsoring and funding process activities
   > - aligning vulnerability data collection and distribution activities with identified resilience needs and objectives and stakeholder needs and requirements
   > - verifying that the process supports strategic resilience objectives and is focused on the assets and services that are of the highest relative value in meeting strategic objectives
   > - regular reporting from organizational units to higher-level managers on vulnerability analysis and resolution activities and results

- creating dedicated higher-level management feedback loops on decisions about the process, and recommendations for prioritizing process requirements and improving the process
- providing input on identifying, assessing, and managing operational risks related to identified vulnerabilities for all asset types (people, information, technology, and facilities)
- providing access to legal or other appropriate counsel to provide guidance on potential liabilities resulting from identified vulnerabilities
- conducting regular internal and external audits and related reporting to audit committees on process effectiveness
- creating formal programs to measure the effectiveness of process activities, and reporting these measurements to higher-level managers

2. Develop and publish organizational policy for the process.

   Elaboration:

   The vulnerability analysis and resolution policy should address
   - responsibility, authority, and ownership for performing process activities
   - information categorization, labeling, and handling
   - protection against tampering or unauthorized access
   - encryption, secure storage, and secure transport and distribution of information
   - procedures, standards, and guidelines for
     - identifying the assets that are the focus of vulnerability analysis and resolution activities
     - storage capacity of collection mechanisms and actions to take if capacity is exceeded by type of media
     - collection of vulnerability data
     - recording and storage of vulnerability data, including collection media (electronic logs, data files, databases, and information repositories)
     - distribution of vulnerability data, including media, methods, and channels
     - service level agreement terms and conditions for external entities involved in process activities
   - methods for measuring adherence to policy, exceptions granted, and policy violations

VAR:GG2.GP2 PLAN THE PROCESS

Establish and maintain the plan for performing the vulnerability analysis and resolution process.

Elaboration:

The plan for the vulnerability analysis and resolution process should not be confused with the organizational vulnerability analysis and resolution strategy and plan for identifying and analyzing vulnerabilities as described in specific practice VAR:SG1.SP2. The plan for the vulnerability analysis and resolution process details how the organization will perform vulnerability analysis and resolution, including the development of strategies and plans for vulnerability analysis and resolution.

Subpractices

1. Define and document the plan for performing the process.

   Elaboration:

   Special consideration in the plan may have to be given to the range of assets, asset types, and asset values (and related services) that are the focus of the vulnerability analysis and resolution activities. These activities help determine the scope of the vulnerability analysis and resolution activities that have the greatest potential to pose operational risks to the organization's assets and services.

2. Define and document the process description.
3. Review the plan with relevant stakeholders and get their agreement.
4. Revise the plan as necessary.

VAR:GG2.GP3 PROVIDE RESOURCES

Provide adequate resources for performing the vulnerability analysis and resolution process, developing the work products, and providing the services of the process.

Elaboration:

The diversity of activities required to analyze and resolve vulnerabilities for all asset types requires an extensive level of organizational resources and skills and a significant number of external resources. In addition, these activities require a major commitment of financial resources (both expense and capital) from the organization.

Staff assigned to the vulnerability analysis and resolution process must have appropriate knowledge of the assets being examined and the objectivity to perform vulnerability analysis and resolution activities without concern for personal detriment and without the expectation of personal benefit.

Subpractices

1. Staff the process.

   Elaboration:

   > These are examples of staff required to perform the vulnerability analysis and resolution process:
   > - staff responsible for
   >   - collecting, analyzing, and prioritizing process requirements based on strategic objectives, business needs, and stakeholder requirements and needs

- developing vulnerability analysis and resolution plans and programs and ensuring they are aligned with stakeholder requirements and needs
- establishing an appropriate infrastructure for vulnerability data collection, recording, and distribution
- vulnerability data collection, recording, distribution, and storage (associated with both electronic and physical assets)
- vulnerability data protection and security (associated with both electronic and physical assets), so as to ensure data confidentiality, integrity, and availability
- managing external entities that have contractual obligations for vulnerability analysis and resolution activities

• owners and custodians of high-value services and assets that support the accomplishment of operational resilience management objectives
• internal and external auditors responsible for reporting to appropriate committees on process effectiveness and the adequacy of collected data to accurately track the performance of operational resilience management processes

Refer to the Organizational Training and Awareness process area for information about training staff for resilience roles and responsibilities.

Refer to the Human Resource Management process area for information about acquiring staff to fulfill roles and responsibilities.

2. Fund the process.

   Refer to the Financial Resource Management process area for information about budgeting for, funding, and accounting for vulnerability analysis and resolution.

3. Provide necessary tools, techniques, and methods to perform the process.

   Elaboration:

   These are examples of tools, techniques, and methods to support the vulnerability analysis and resolution process:
   • methods, techniques, and tools for the identification, analysis, remediation, monitoring, and communication of vulnerabilities for all asset types
   • vulnerability data recording and storage methods, techniques, and tools (associated with both electronic and physical assets), including developing, populating, and maintaining the vulnerability repository
   • vulnerability data protection and security methods, techniques, and tools, including those necessary to ensure data confidentiality, integrity, and availability (associated with both electronic and physical assets)
   • vulnerability data distribution methods, techniques, and tools
   • methods, techniques, and tools for developing and managing collection media
   • tools for developing and maintaining traceability between stakeholder requirements and process requirements, plans, and programs

VAR:GG2.GP4 Assign Responsibility

Assign responsibility and authority for performing the vulnerability analysis and resolution process, developing the work products, and providing the services of the process.

Elaboration:

Specific practice VAR:SG1.SP2 calls for documenting the roles and responsibilities necessary to carry out the vulnerability analysis and resolution plan, as well as the roles of relevant stakeholders.

Refer to the Human Resource Management process area for more information about establishing resilience as a job responsibility, developing resilience performance goals and objectives, and measuring and assessing performance against these goals and objectives.

Subpractices

1. Assign responsibility and authority for performing the process.
2. Assign responsibility and authority for performing the specific tasks of the process.

   Elaboration:

   > Responsibility and authority for performing vulnerability analysis and resolution tasks can be formalized by
   > - defining roles and responsibilities in the process plan to include roles responsible for collecting, recording, distributing, and ensuring the confidentiality, integrity, and availability of vulnerability data
   > - including process tasks and responsibility for these tasks in specific job descriptions
   > - setting policy requiring organizational unit managers, line of business managers, project managers, and asset and service owners and custodians to participate in and derive benefit from the process for assets and services under their ownership or custodianship
   > - including process tasks in staff performance management goals and objectives, with requisite measurement of progress against these goals
   > - developing and implementing contractual instruments (including service level agreements) with external entities to establish responsibility and authority for performing process tasks on outsourced functions
   > - including process tasks in measuring performance of external entities against contractual instruments

3. Confirm that people assigned with responsibility and authority understand it and are willing and able to accept it.

VAR:GG2.GP5 TRAIN PEOPLE

Train the people performing or supporting the vulnerability analysis and resolution process as needed.

Refer to the Organizational Training and Awareness process area for more information about training the people performing or supporting the process.

Refer to the Human Resource Management process area for more information about inventorying skill sets, establishing a skill set baseline, identifying required skill sets, and measuring and addressing skill deficiencies.

Subpractices

1. Identify process skill needs.

   Elaboration:

   > These are examples of skills required in the vulnerability analysis and resolution process:
   > - knowledge of tools, techniques, and methods used to identify, analyze, remediate, monitor, and communicate vulnerabilities for all asset types, including those necessary to perform the process using the selected methods, techniques, and tools identified in VAR:GG2.GP3 subpractice 3
   > - knowledge of tools, techniques, and methods necessary to ensure the confidentiality, integrity, and availability of vulnerability data
   > - knowledge necessary to elicit and prioritize stakeholder requirements and needs and interpret them to develop effective process requirements, plans, and programs
   > - knowledge necessary to analyze and prioritize process requirements
   > - knowledge necessary to interpret vulnerability data and represent it in ways that are meaningful and appropriate for managers and stakeholders

2. Identify process skill gaps based on available resources and their current skill levels.
3. Identify training opportunities to address skill gaps.

   Elaboration:

   > These are examples of training topics:
   > - operating, monitoring, and configuring tools, including the vulnerability repository
   > - supporting stakeholders in understanding and interpreting vulnerability data
   > - vulnerability data collection, recording, distribution, and storage techniques and tools
   > - securing data collected from system components to ensure data confidentiality, integrity, and availability
   > - working with external entities that have responsibility for process activities
   > - using process methods, tools, and techniques, including those identified in VAR:GG2.GP3 subpractice 3

4. Provide training and review the training needs as necessary.

VAR:GG2.GP6 *Manage Work Product Configurations*

Place designated work products of the vulnerability analysis and resolution process under appropriate levels of control.

Elaboration:

> These are examples of vulnerability analysis and resolution work products placed under control:
> - vulnerability data
> - process strategy and plans, including the scope of the plans and commitments to the plans
> - list of sources of vulnerability information
> - list of internal and external stakeholders and a plan for their involvement
> - vulnerability prioritization guidelines
> - prioritized process requirements, accepted requirements, and risks resulting from unsatisfied requirements
> - infrastructure requirements
> - vulnerability data collection and storage standards and parameters
> - vulnerability data identification, monitoring, collection, analysis, remediation, handling, and storage methods, procedures, techniques, and tools
> - vulnerability data distribution plans, procedures, processes, media, methods, and tools
> - collection media, including electronic logs, data files, databases, and repositories
> - vulnerability status reports, including resolution strategies
> - policies and procedures
> - contracts with external entities

VAR:GG2.GP7 *Identify and Involve Relevant Stakeholders*

Identify and involve the relevant stakeholders of the vulnerability analysis and resolution process as planned.

Elaboration:
Several VAR-specific practices address the involvement of stakeholders in the vulnerability analysis and resolution process. For example, VAR:SG1.SP2 calls for reviewing the vulnerability analysis and resolution strategy with stakeholders to promote understanding and gain commitment, VAR:SG2.SP2 calls for providing stakeholder access to the vulnerability repository, and VAR:SG3.SP1 requires that stakeholders be informed of vulnerability resolution activities.

Subpractices

1. Identify process stakeholders and their appropriate involvement.

   Elaboration:

   > These are examples of stakeholders of the vulnerability analysis and resolution process:
   > - higher-level managers responsible for establishing organizational risk criteria and tolerances
   > - staff responsible for the organization's risk management plan
   > - asset owners, custodians, and users
   > - staff responsible for managing operational risks to assets
   > - staff responsible for establishing, implementing, and maintaining an internal control system for assets
   > - staff responsible for developing, testing, implementing, and executing service continuity plans
   > - external entities responsible for managing high-value assets and providing essential services
   > - internet service providers
   > - human resources (for people assets)
   > - legal counsel
   > - information technology staff, such as system administrators and CSIRTs
   > - staff responsible for physical security (for facility assets)
   > - internal and external auditors
   > - owners of operational resilience management processes, including risk management, incident management and control, and service continuity

   > Stakeholders are involved in various tasks in the vulnerability analysis and resolution process, such as
   > - reviewing the process strategy and committing to the activities described in the strategy
   > - establishing that plans (including the process plan) reflect the strategy
   > - making decisions about process scope and activities
   > - establishing requirements for the process
   > - establishing vulnerability prioritization guidelines
   > - assessing collected vulnerability data, including the vulnerability repository
   > - providing feedback to those responsible for providing the vulnerability data on which the analysis results depend
   > - reviewing and appraising the effectiveness of process activities
   > - resolving issues in the process

2. Communicate the list of stakeholders to planners and those responsible for process performance.

3. Involve relevant stakeholders in the process as planned.

VAR:GG2.GP8 MONITOR AND CONTROL THE PROCESS

Monitor and control the vulnerability analysis and resolution process against the plan for performing the process and take appropriate corrective action.

Elaboration:

Refer to the Monitoring process area for more information about the collection, organization, and distribution of data that may be useful for monitoring and controlling processes.

Refer to the Measurement and Analysis process area for more information about establishing process metrics and measurement.

Refer to the Enterprise Focus process area for more information about providing process information to managers, identifying issues, and determining appropriate corrective actions.

Subpractices

1. Measure actual performance against the plan for performing the process.
2. Review accomplishments and results of the process against the plan for performing the process.

Elaboration:

> These are examples of metrics for the vulnerability analysis and resolution process:
> - for high-value information, technology, and facilities assets (including assets owned and managed by external entities as well as internally):
>   - number of high-value assets (by type) subject to process activities (This is determined by the resilience requirements associated with identified assets and assumes an up-to-date asset inventory *[refer to the Asset Definition and Management process area]*.)
>   - percentage of high-value assets that have been monitored for vulnerabilities within an agreed-upon time interval
>   - percentage of high-value assets that have been audited or assessed for vulnerabilities within an agreed-upon time interval
>   - number of reported vulnerabilities by asset type or category for which some form of resolution or remediation is called for (course of action, reduction, elimination)
>   - percentage of vulnerabilities that have been satisfactorily remediated (or conversely, percentage of open vulnerabilities) by time interval (days, weeks, months)
>   - number of reported vulnerabilities for which a vulnerability management strategy exists
>   - percentage of vulnerabilities with a vulnerability management strategy that is on track per plan
>   - number and percentage of vulnerabilities requiring a root-cause analysis
> - number of vulnerabilities referred to the risk management process; number of vulnerabilities where corrective action is still pending (by risk rank)

- number of vulnerabilities referred to the incident management and control process by time interval
- number of vulnerabilities referred to the service continuity process by time interval
- schedule for collecting, recording, and distributing vulnerability data, including elapsed time from high-value data collection to data distribution to key stakeholders
- percentage of organizational units, lines of business, projects, and activities using vulnerability data to assess the performance of operational resilience management processes
- number of risks resulting from unsatisfied process requirements, designated as high, medium, or low, or some other organizational risk ranking method
- number of scope changes to process activities by time interval
- number of process risks referred to the risk management process; number of risks where corrective action is still pending (by risk rank)
- level of adherence to process policies; number of policy violations; number of policy exceptions requested and number approved
- number of process activities that are on track per plan
- rate of change of resource needs to support the process
- rate of change of costs to support the process

3. Review activities, status, and results of the process with the immediate level of management responsible for the process and identify issues.

   Elaboration:

   Periodic reviews of the vulnerability analysis and resolution process are needed to ensure that
   - current sources of vulnerability data are in use
   - assets subject to the process are identified, documented, and included in the scope of process activities
   - assets that have been retired are removed from the scope of the process
   - vulnerability data is identified, collected, and stored in a timely manner
   - the vulnerability repository is established and maintained
   - access to the vulnerability repository is limited to authorized staff
   - vulnerability management status reports are provided to appropriate stakeholders in a timely manner
   - vulnerabilities are referred to the risk management process when necessary
   - actions requiring management involvement are elevated in a timely manner
   - the performance of process activities is being monitored and regularly reported
   - key measures are within acceptable ranges as demonstrated in governance dashboards or scorecards and financial reports
   - administrative, technical, and physical controls are operating as intended
   - controls are meeting the stated intent of the resilience requirements
   - actions resulting from internal and external audits are being closed in a timely manner

4. Identify and evaluate the effects of significant deviations from the plan for performing the process.

   Elaboration:

   Discrepancies in the vulnerability repository may result when assets are acquired, modified, or retired but not reflected accurately in the asset inventory. To the extent that Vulnerability Analysis and Resolution process area activities result in inventory discrepancies, the organization's overall ability to manage the operational resilience of high-value assets subject to vulnerability analysis and resolution is impeded.

5. Identify problems in the plan for performing and executing the process.
6. Take corrective action when requirements and objectives are not being satisfied, when issues are identified, or when progress differs significantly from the plan for performing the process.
7. Track corrective action to closure.

VAR:GG2.GP9 OBJECTIVELY EVALUATE ADHERENCE

Objectively evaluate adherence of the vulnerability analysis and resolution process against its process description, standards, and procedures, and address non-compliance.

Elaboration:

> These are examples of activities to be reviewed:
> - the alignment of stakeholder requirements and needs with the process scope, strategy, plans, and management strategies for specific vulnerabilities
> - assignment of responsibility, accountability, and authority for process activities
> - determining the adequacy of process reports and reviews in informing decision makers regarding the performance of operational resilience management activities and the need to take corrective action, if any
> - verification of data confidentiality, integrity, and availability controls
> - use of process data for improving strategies for protecting and sustaining assets and services

> These are examples of work products to be reviewed:
> - process plan and policies
> - process scope and strategy, as well as strategies for managing specific vulnerabilities
> - vulnerabilities that have been referred to the risk management process
> - vulnerability data identification, analysis, recording, storage, remediation, monitoring, communication, protection, and distribution methods, techniques, and tools
> - metrics for the process *(Refer to VAR:GG2.GP8 subpractice 2.)*
> - contracts with external entities

VAR:GG2.GP10 Review Status with Higher-Level Managers

Review the activities, status, and results of the vulnerability analysis and resolution process with higher-level managers and resolve issues.

Refer to the Enterprise Focus process area for more information about providing sponsorship and oversight to the operational resilience management system.

VAR:GG3 Institutionalize a Defined Process

Vulnerability analysis and resolution is institutionalized as a defined process.

VAR:GG3.GP1 Establish a Defined Process

Establish and maintain the description of a defined vulnerability analysis and resolution process.

Establishing and tailoring process assets, including standard processes, are addressed in the Organizational Process Definition process area.

Establishing process needs and objectives and selecting, improving, and deploying process assets, including standard processes, are addressed in the Organizational Process Focus process area.

Subpractices

1. Select from the organization's set of standard processes those processes that cover the vulnerability analysis and resolution process and best meet the needs of the organizational unit or line of business.
2. Establish the defined process by tailoring the selected processes according to the organization's tailoring guidelines.
3. Ensure that the organization's process objectives are appropriately addressed in the defined process, and ensure that process governance extends to the tailored processes.
4. Document the defined process and the records of the tailoring.
5. Revise the description of the defined process as necessary.

VAR:GG3.GP2 Collect Improvement Information

Collect vulnerability analysis and resolution work products, measures, measurement results, and improvement information derived from planning and performing the process to support future use and improvement of the organization's processes and process assets.

Elaboration:

> These are examples of improvement work products and information:
> - changes in operating conditions, risk conditions, and the risk environment that affect process results
> - metrics and measurements of the viability of the process *(Refer to VAR:GG2.GP8 subpractice 2.)*
> - lessons learned in post-event review of incidents and disruptions in continuity
> - lessons learned that can be applied to improve operational resilience management performance
> - the currency status of vulnerability data
> - the confidentiality, integrity, and availability status of vulnerability data based on integrity and security tests
> - reports on the effectiveness and weaknesses of controls
> - process action plans and strategies that are not being satisfied and the risks associated with them
> - resilience requirements that are not being satisfied or are being exceeded

Establishing the measurement repository and process asset library is addressed in the Organizational Process Definition process area. Updating the measurement repository and process asset library as part of process improvement and deployment is addressed in the Organizational Process Focus process area.

Subpractices

1. Store process and work product measures in the organization's measurement repository.
2. Submit documentation for inclusion in the organization's process asset library.
3. Document lessons learned from the process for inclusion in the organization's process asset library.
4. Propose improvements to the organizational process assets.

PART FOUR

The Appendices

APPENDIX A

GENERIC GOALS AND PRACTICES

This appendix describes the generic goals and practices that the organization deploys to attain successively improving degrees of process institutionalization and capability maturity for operational resilience management. These practices exhibit the organization's commitment and ability to perform operational resilience management processes, as well as its ability to measure performance and verify implementation.

GG1 ACHIEVE SPECIFIC GOALS

The operational resilience management system supports and enables achievement of the specific goals of the process area by transforming identifiable input work products to produce identifiable output work products.

GG1.GP1 PERFORM SPECIFIC PRACTICES

Perform the specific practices of the process area to develop work products and provide services to achieve the specific goals of the process area.

This practice requires the organization to perform the practices, produce the work products, and deliver the services that are contained in the process definition for a process area. The organization may perform these practices in an improvised or reactive manner, and there may not be any process definition to support the performance of the practices. The degree to which the performance of practices is formalized varies from organization to organization and may be inconsistent within an organization. The success of achieving the work products and delivering the service of the practices may be directly related to the staff involved in the process.

GG2 INSTITUTIONALIZE A MANAGED PROCESS

The process is institutionalized as a managed process.

GG2.GP1 ESTABLISH PROCESS GOVERNANCE

Establish and maintain governance over the planning and performance of the process.

This practice establishes the foundation for higher-level managers' responsibility for overseeing, directing, and guiding the operational resilience management system. Higher-level managers set expectations for managing operational resilience in this practice and communicate these expectations to those who are responsible as appropriate. Regular reviews of operational resilience activities are performed and reported to higher-level managers for interpretation. Higher-level managers make recommendations where gaps are perceived in process performance.

The behavioral expectations of higher-level managers are instantiated in organizational policies that address operational resilience management, as well as in expectations for planning and performing operational resilience processes.

Higher-level managers are also responsible for ensuring appropriate levels of compliance with legal, regulatory, contractual, and government obligations.

Refer to the Enterprise Focus process area for more information about providing sponsorship of and oversight to the operational resilience management system.

Subpractices

1. Establish governance over process activities.

   The organization's governance activity is expanded to include oversight over the activities and processes that the organization uses to manage operational resilience and to perform the process.

2. Develop and publish organizational policy for the process.

   Establish the organizational expectations for planning and performing the process, and communicate these expectations via policy. The policy should reflect higher-level managers' objectives for the process.

GG2.GP2 PLAN THE PROCESS

Establish and maintain the plan for performing the process.

In this practice, the organization determines what is needed to perform the process and to achieve the established objectives, to prepare a plan for performing the process, to prepare a process description, and to get agreement on the plan from relevant stakeholders. In some cases, this generic practice may be applied to a planning process in a particular process area; in that case, this generic practice sets an expectation that the planning process itself needs to be planned.

Establishing a plan includes documenting the plan and providing a process description, *as well as assigning ownership* of the plan with requisite authority to carry out the plan. Maintaining the plan includes changing it as necessary to reflect corrective actions, changes in requirements, or improvements.

The plan for the process should be directly influenced by the strategic and operational planning processes of the organization and reflect strategic objectives and initiatives where appropriate.

The plan for performing the process typically includes the following elements and activities:

- process description
- standards and requirements for the work products and services of the process
- specific objectives for the performance of the process
- dependencies among the activities, work products, and services of the process
- the assignment of resources (typically funding, people, and tools) needed to perform the process
- assignment of responsibility and authority
- training needed to perform and support the process
- work products to be controlled and the level of control to apply
- measurement requirements to provide insight into the performance of the process, its work products, and its services
- involvement of identified stakeholders
- activities for monitoring and controlling the process
- activities for objectively evaluating the process
- activities for management review of the process and the work products

Refer to the Enterprise Focus process area for more information about creating, resourcing, and implementing a strategic resilience plan and establishing a resilience program as part of an operational resilience management system.

Refer to individual process areas for specific guidance on creating, implementing, and managing plans, where relevant.

Subpractices

1. Define and document the plan for performing the process.

    This plan may be a stand-alone document, embedded in a more comprehensive document, or distributed across multiple documents. In the case of the plan being distributed across multiple documents, ensure that a coherent picture of who does what is preserved.

2. Define and document the process description.

    The process description, which includes relevant standards and procedures, may be included as part of the plan for performing the process or may be included in the plan by reference.

3. Review the plan with relevant stakeholders and get their agreement.

    Review the planned process to ensure that it satisfies policy (and the requirements for governance), plans, requirements, and standards to provide assurance to stakeholders.

4. Revise the plan as necessary.

GG2.GP3 Provide Resources

Provide adequate resources for performing the process, developing the work products, and providing the services of the process.

This practice focuses on providing the resources necessary to perform the process as defined by the plan and ensuring that resources are available when needed. Resources are formally identified and assigned to process plan elements.

Resources include an adequate number of skilled staff, expense and capital funding, facilities, and tools, techniques, and methods. The interpretation of the term *adequate* depends upon many factors and can change over time. Inadequate resources may be addressed by increasing resources or by removing requirements, constraints, and commitments.

Subpractices

1. Staff the process.

    Ensure that a sufficient and adequate level of human resources is available and appropriately skilled to perform the process.

    Staff responsible for performing process activities may be different from those responsible for evaluating the performance of the process.

    Refer to the Organizational Training and Awareness process area for information about training staff for resilience roles and responsibilities.

    Refer to the Human Resource Management process area for information about acquiring staff to fulfill roles and responsibilities.

2. Fund the process.

    Funding must be earmarked and provided to support the goals and objectives of operational resilience management processes. Funding is an indication of higher-level managers' support and sponsorship of the process.

    At a minimum, funding must be available to support proper oversight of the process. This includes (1) establishing and maintaining an appropriate internal control system for services and related assets and (2) periodic reporting of key indicators and metrics to assess process performance.

    Refer to the Financial Resource Management process area for information about budgeting for, funding, and accounting for operational resilience management processes.

3. Provide the necessary tools, techniques, and methods to perform the process.

GG2.GP4 Assign Responsibility

Assign responsibility and authority for performing the process, developing the work products, and providing the services of the process.

This practice ensures that there is accountability and responsibility for performing the process and ensuring the achievement of expected results throughout the life of the process. The people assigned must have the appropriate authority to act and to perform the assigned responsibilities.

Responsibility can be assigned and tracked through job descriptions, the process plan, or other means, such as performance management (goals and performance reviews).

Refer to the Human Resource Management process area for more information about establishing resilience as a job responsibility, developing resilience-related performance goals and objectives, and measuring and assessing performance against these goals and objectives.

Subpractices

1. Assign responsibility and authority for performing the process.

   Organizations may establish an operational resilience management process group to take responsibility for the overall operational resilience management system, including any specific processes. This group may also formally interface with higher-level managers for the purpose of reporting on organizational progress against process goals as part of the governance process for operational resilience management.

2. Assign responsibility and authority for performing the specific tasks of the process.

3. Confirm that people assigned with responsibility and authority understand it and are willing and able to accept it.

GG2.GP5 TRAIN PEOPLE

Train the people performing or supporting the process as needed.

This practice ensures that the necessary staff have the skills and expertise to perform or support the process. The skills necessary to perform the process are documented in the plan and compared to the available resources. Training needs are identified to address skill gaps.

Appropriate training is provided to the staff who perform the work. Overview training is provided to those who interact with those performing the work.

Refer to the Organizational Training and Awareness process area for more information about training the people performing or supporting the process.

Refer to the Human Resource Management process area for more information about creating an inventory of skill sets, establishing a skill set baseline, identifying required skill sets, and measuring and addressing skill deficiencies.

Subpractices

1. Identify process skill needs.
2. Identify process skill gaps based on available resources and their current skill levels.

3. Identify training opportunities to address skill gaps.
4. Provide training and review the training needs as necessary.

GG2.GP6 MANAGE WORK PRODUCT CONFIGURATIONS

Place designated work products of the process under appropriate levels of control.

The purpose of this practice is to establish and maintain the integrity of the designated work products of the process (or their descriptions) throughout their useful life. Work products of the process must be managed and controlled as operating conditions change and evolve.

The designated work products are specifically identified in the plan for performing the process, along with a specification of the appropriate level of control.

Different levels of control are appropriate for different work products and for different points in time. For some work products, it may be sufficient to maintain version control (i.e., the version of the process work product in use at a given time, past or present, is known, and changes are incorporated in a controlled manner). Version control is usually under the sole control of the owner of the process work product (typically an individual, group, or team).

Sometimes it may be critical for work products to be placed under formal or baseline configuration management. This type of control includes defining and establishing baselines at predetermined points. These baselines are formally reviewed and agreed upon and serve as the basis for further development and use of the process work product.

Additional levels of control between version control and formal configuration management are possible. An identified work product may be under various levels of control at different points in time.

Because change control, version control, and configuration management are fundamental activities in many operational resilience management processes, this generic practice also addresses the processes and practices necessary to establish baseline work products (e.g., developing an asset database) and for performing change control on these work products as the operational environment changes and evolves. In some cases, the management of work products is critical to an operational resilience management process and therefore is included in the specific practices of a process area, ranging from simple change control activities to baseline-driven configuration management. Examples of these practices can be found throughout process areas such as Access Management, Asset Definition and Management, and Incident Management and Control.

Configuration management of technical assets (such as software, hardware, and systems) as traditionally understood in the context of managing information technology is addressed as a specific operational resilience management practice in the Technology Management process area.

GG2.GP7 *IDENTIFY AND INVOLVE RELEVANT STAKEHOLDERS*

Identify and involve the relevant stakeholders of the process as planned.

In this practice, the expected involvement of stakeholders is established, planned, and maintained during the execution of a process.

Stakeholders are involved in various activities in a process. Their roles should be considered in the process plan and could include

- planning
- decision making
- commitments
- communications
- coordination
- review
- appraisal
- requirements definition and documentation
- resolution of problems

The objective of planning stakeholder involvement is to ensure that interactions necessary to the process are accomplished without excessive numbers of affiliated groups and individuals impeding process execution.

In some process areas, the identification and inclusion of stakeholders in the process are critical to process success. In these areas, specific practices or subpractices have been included to address stakeholder involvement, particularly where processes reach extensively into the organization, such as in the Monitoring and Communications process areas.

Subpractices

1. Identify process stakeholders and their appropriate involvement.
   Relevant stakeholders are identified among the suppliers of inputs to, the users of outputs from, and the performers of activities within the process. Once the relevant stakeholders are identified, the appropriate level of their involvement in process activities is planned.
2. Communicate the list of stakeholders to planners and those responsible for process performance.
3. Involve relevant stakeholders in the process as planned.

GG2.GP8 *MONITOR AND CONTROL THE PROCESS*

Monitor and control the process against the plan for performing the process and take appropriate corrective action.

The purpose of this practice is to perform the direct day-to-day monitoring and controlling of the process. Appropriate visibility into the process is maintained so that appropriate corrective action can be taken when necessary. Monitoring and controlling the process involve establishing appropriate metrics and measuring appropriate attributes of the process or work products produced by the process. The metrics and measurements may be qualitative or quantitative as appropriate.

Refer to the Monitoring process area for more information about the collection, organization, and distribution of data that may be useful for monitoring and controlling processes.

Refer to the Measurement and Analysis process area for more information about establishing process metrics and measurement.

Refer to the Enterprise Focus process area for more information about providing process information to managers, identifying issues, and determining appropriate corrective actions.

Subpractices

1. Measure actual performance against the plan for performing the process.
   The measures are of the process, its work products, and its services.
2. Review accomplishments and results of the process against the plan for performing the process.
3. Review activities, status, and results of the process with the immediate level of managers responsible for the process and identify issues.
   The reviews are intended to provide the immediate level of managers with appropriate visibility into the process. The reviews can be both periodic (for example, planned as part of a regular audit of the organization's internal control system) and event-driven.

   Process reviews are likely to concentrate on the effectiveness and efficiency of the internal control system for services and assets, as well as the satisfaction of service and asset resilience requirements.
4. Identify and evaluate the effects of significant deviations from the plan for performing the process.
5. Identify problems in the plan for performing and executing the process.
6. Take corrective action when requirements and objectives are not being satisfied, when issues are identified, or when progress differs significantly from the plan for performing the process.
   New risks that could be introduced or affect the mitigation plans for existing risks should be considered before any corrective action is taken. *(Refer to the Risk Management process area for more information about managing risk.)*

   Corrective actions may include the following:
   - taking remedial action to repair defective work products or services
   - changing the plan for performing the process
   - adjusting resources (people, tools, etc.)
   - negotiating changes to the established commitments
   - securing change to the requirements and objectives that have to be satisfied
   - terminating the effort

If corrective action is required, further analysis may be necessary to identify improvements to the process.

7. Track corrective action to closure.

GG2.GP9 OBJECTIVELY EVALUATE ADHERENCE

Objectively evaluate adherence of the process against its process description, standards, and procedures, and address non-compliance.

The purpose of this practice is to provide assurance that the process is implemented as planned and adheres to its process description, standards, and procedures as evidenced through an evaluation of selected work products of the process. The evaluation must be independent; that is, those directly involved in the performance of the process cannot perform the objective evaluation or render an opinion on adherence.

Activities such as internal and external audits, post-event reviews, and capability appraisals allow the organization to have an independent and objective evaluation of the effectiveness of the risk management process, adherence to the process, and identification of areas of non-compliance.

Objectively evaluating adherence is especially important during times of stress (such as during incident response) to ensure that the organization is relying on processes and not reverting to ad hoc practices that require people and technology as their basis.

GG2.GP10 REVIEW STATUS WITH HIGHER-LEVEL MANAGERS

Review the activities, status, and results of the process with higher-level managers and resolve issues.

As a part of governing the operational resilience management system, higher-level managers are provided with the appropriate visibility into the process.

Higher-level managers include those in the organization above the immediate level of managers responsible for the process. This information is provided to help higher-level managers to provide and enforce policy for the process, as well as to perform overall guidance. (This practice is not performed to help those who perform the direct day-to-day monitoring and controlling of the process.)

Different managers have different needs for information about the process. These reviews help ensure that informed decisions on the planning and performing of the process can be made. Therefore, these reviews are expected to be both periodic and event-driven.

Refer to the Enterprise Focus process area for more information about providing sponsorship to and oversight to the operational resilience management system.

GG3 INSTITUTIONALIZE A DEFINED PROCESS

The process is institutionalized as a defined process.

GG3.GP1 ESTABLISH A DEFINED PROCESS

Establish and maintain the description of a defined process.

The purpose of this generic practice is to establish and maintain a description of the process that is tailored from the organization's set of standard processes to address the needs of a specific organizational unit or line of business. The organization should have standard processes that define the specific operational resilience management capability, along with guidelines for tailoring these processes to meet the needs of a specific organizational unit or line of business, or any other organizationally defined operating division.

Managing the operational resilience management system is an enterprise concern that is typically carried out at the enterprise level, given that it must reflect the strategic and performance objectives for the organization. That said, aspects of the process must be tailorable and adaptable at the organizational unit or line of business level to ensure that appropriate process activities occur throughout the organization.

To achieve consistency of process application, the tailored definition of processes used at local levels must be consistent with and reflect the enterprise philosophy and strategy. This consistency allows the organization to track performance, mitigate risks within defined risk parameters, and derive benefits (e.g., efficiencies, value, and cost savings) at the enterprise level. It also ensures minimal variability as the process is performed across the enterprise, allowing for the sharing of process assets, work products, data, and learning. Otherwise, the execution of process activities at local levels will be inconsistent and variable, resulting in inefficiencies and ineffectiveness of these activities at the enterprise level.

Subpractices

1. Select from the organization's set of standard processes those processes that cover the process and best meet the needs of the organizational unit or line of business.
2. Establish the defined process by tailoring the selected processes according to the organization's tailoring guidelines.
3. Ensure that the organization's process objectives are appropriately addressed in the defined process, and ensure that process governance extends to the tailored processes.
4. Document the defined process and the records of the tailoring.
5. Revise the description of the defined process as necessary.

GG3.GP2 Collect Improvement Information

Collect work products, measures, measurement results, and improvement information derived from planning and performing the process to support future use and improvement of the organization's processes and process assets.

The purpose of this generic practice is to collect information and work products derived from planning and performing the process. This generic practice is performed so that the information and work products can be included in the organizational process assets and made available to those who are planning and performing the same or similar processes. The information and work products are stored in the organization's measurement repository and its process asset library.

Subpractices

1. Store process and work product measures in the organization's measurement repository.

    The process and work product measures are primarily those that are defined in the common set of measures for the organization's set of standard processes.

2. Submit documentation for inclusion in the organization's process asset library.
3. Document lessons learned from the process for inclusion in the organization's process asset library.
4. Propose improvements to the organizational process assets.

APPENDIX B

TARGETED IMPROVEMENT ROADMAPS

Achieving FISMA Compliance

A suggested targeted improvement roadmap[1] for using CERT-RMM to achieve FISMA compliance is provided in Table B.1.

TABLE B.1 Targeted Improvement Roadmap for FISMA Compliance

Required CERT-RMM Process Areas

Category	Process Area	Minimum Required Capability Level	Association with FISMA, NIST Supporting Documents	Notes
Operations	Access Management (AM)	Level 2[2]	FISMA—Select Security Controls FISMA—Implement Security Controls FIPS 200 NIST SP 800-53 NIST SP 800-70 OMB Memorandum M-10-15	Strong connection to Identity Management in CERT-RMM.

Continues

---

1. See page 88 for more information about using CERT-RMM targeted improvement roadmaps.
2. Because of the FISMA emphasis on policies and procedures to support security programs, these process areas are raised to level 2 capability in CERT-RMM, which addresses elements of process capability (such as policy, governance, resources, training, monitoring, and control) that support a "managed" level of operational resilience management. Without FISMA policy requirements, these capability levels could be established at level 1.

TABLE B.1 Targeted Improvement Roadmap for FISMA Compliance *(Continued)*

Required CERT-RMM Process Areas

Category	Process Area	Minimum Required Capability Level	Association with FISMA, NIST Supporting Documents	Notes
Engineering	Asset Definition and Management (ADM)	Level 2	FISMA—Categorize Information Systems FIPS 199 NIST SP 800-60 OMB Memorandum M-10-15	Level 1 specific practices in ADM more broadly cover all asset types—people, information, technology, and facilities—while FISMA is focused on information systems.
Enterprise Management	Enterprise Focus (EF)	Level 1	FISMA—Establish Organizational View NIST SP 800-39 OMB Memorandum M-10-15	Level 1 specific practices in CERT-RMM are more extensive than required by FISMA or NIST 800-39's "organizational view."
Operations	Environmental Control (EC)	Level 2	FISMA—Select Security Controls FISMA—Implement Security Controls FIPS 200 NIST SP 800-53 NIST SP 800-70	EC addresses security controls specifically for *facility* assets. EC also addresses dependencies on public services and public infrastructure (e.g., telecommunications, utilities, emergency management, and first responder services).
Operations	Identity Management (ID)	Level 2	FISMA—Select Security Controls FISMA—Implement Security Controls FIPS 200 NIST SP 800-53 NIST SP 800-70 OMB Memorandum M-10-15	Strong connection to Access Management in CERT-RMM.

Required CERT-RMM Process Areas

Category	Process Area	Minimum Required Capability Level	Association with FISMA, NIST Supporting Documents	Notes
Operations	Incident Management and Control (IMC)	Level 2	FISMA General Requirements NIST SP 800-61 OMB Memorandum M-07-16 OMB Memorandum M-06-19 OMB Memorandum in support of Executive Order 13402 OMB Memorandum M-10-15	Supports FISMA incident management and handling provision.
Operations	Knowledge and Information Management (KIM)	Level 2	FISMA—Select Security Controls FISMA – Implement Security Controls FIPS 200 NIST SP 800-53 NIST SP 800-70	KIM addresses security controls specifically for *information* assets.
Engineering	Controls Management (CTRL)	Level 2	FISMA—Assess Security Controls NIST SP 800-37 NIST SP 800-39 NIST 800-53A OMB Memorandum M-10-15	Level 2 capability for controls management exceeds FISMA requirements and extends to all asset types, not just information systems.
Process Management	Monitoring (MON)	Level 2	FISMA—Assess Security Controls FISMA—Monitor Security State NIST SP 800-37 NIST SP 800-53A OMB Memorandum M-10-15	Supports the process of continuous real-time monitoring.

Continues

TABLE B.1 Targeted Improvement Roadmap for FISMA Compliance *(Continued)*

Required CERT-RMM Process Areas

Category	Process Area	Minimum Required Capability Level	Association with FISMA, NIST Supporting Documents	Notes
Enterprise Management	Organizational Training and Awareness (OTA)	Level 1	FISMA General Requirements	Supports FISMA security awareness and training provision; CERT-RMM level 1 specific practices are more extensive than required by FISMA.
Enterprise Management	Risk Management (RISK)	Level 2	FISMA—Categorize Information Systems FISMA—Implement Security Controls FIPS 199 NIST 800-30 NIST SP 800-60 OMB Memorandum M-10-15	Level 2 capability for risk management exceeds FISMA requirements and extends to all asset types, not just information systems.
Engineering	Resilience Requirements Definition (RRD)	Level 1	FISMA—Categorize Information Systems FIPS 199 NIST SP 800-60	Level 1 specific practices in CERT-RMM are more extensive than required by FISMA.
Operations	Service Continuity (SC)	Level 2	FISMA—Select Security Controls FISMA—Implement Security Controls FISMA—Assess Security Controls FIPS 200 NIST SP 800-53 NIST SP 800-53A NIST SP 800-70	Supports FISMA continuity of operations provision.

Category	Process Area	Minimum Required Capability Level	Association with FISMA, NIST Supporting Documents	Notes
Operations	Technology Management (TM)	Level 2	FISMA—Select Security Controls FISMA—Develop System Configuration Requirements FISMA—Implement Security Controls FIPS 200 NIST SP 800-53 NIST SP 800-70	TM addresses security controls specifically for *technology* assets including software, hardware, systems, and networks.
Operations	Vulnerability Analysis and Resolution (VAR)	Level 2	FISMA—Assess Security Controls FISMA—Monitor Security State NIST SP 800-53A NIST SP 800-37 OMB Memorandum M-10-15	Considered part of FISMA risk management, although it is a separate process in CERT-RMM.

Managing Cloud Computing

A suggested (but not all-inclusive) targeted improvement roadmap for measuring how well the organization is managing the potential risks when using cloud computing services is provided in Table B.2.

TABLE B.2 Targeted Improvement Roadmap for Cloud Computing

Process Areas	Selection Rationale
Asset Definition and Management	Asset Definition and Management (ADM) is focused on the resilience of service-critical assets. Managing the risks from cloud computing means that the organization has processes in place to identify and document assets, establish ownership and custodianship for assets, and link assets to the services they support. The concepts of asset ownership and custodianship are especially important in the cloud computing environment to establish clear lines of demarcation and responsibility for operational resilience.

Continues

TABLE B.2 Targeted Improvement Roadmap for Cloud Computing *(Continued)*

Process Areas	Selection Rationale
External Dependencies Management	In External Dependencies Management (EXD), the organization's process for identifying, analyzing, and addressing the risks associated with the actions of service providers, the formalization of the relationship with such providers, and the ongoing management of provider relationships is established. An external dependency exists when an external entity has access to, control of, ownership in, possession of, responsibility for (including development, operations, maintenance, or support), or other defined obligations related to one or more assets or services of the organization. For cloud computing, managing external dependencies is an ongoing concern over the life of the relationship.
Risk Management	Risk Management (RISK) addresses the organization's cycle for identifying, analyzing, and mitigating operational risk. For cloud computing, this process area is focused specifically on how well the organization identifies, analyzes, and mitigates risk related to all sources and categories of operational risk, such as data privacy, regulatory compliance, and insider threats. This process area seeks to ensure that the organization also has the capability to manage the risk of unmet requirements from providers of cloud computing infrastructure, platforms, or software services.
Resilience Requirements Development	Resilience Requirements Development (RRD) broadly addresses the way in which the organization identifies, develops, implements, and manages resilience requirements to ensure that high-value assets are not disrupted. For cloud computing, resilience requirements form the basis for the selection of appropriate controls for protecting and sustaining assets. RRD ensures the organizational processes for developing the appropriate requirements, informs the process for control selection, and supplies defined requirements for formal agreements with the cloud service provider.
Resilience Requirements Management	Resilience Requirements Management (RRM) addresses the process used by the organization to manage resilience requirements as they change and evolve over time. For cloud computing, the effective management of requirements ensures that an agreed-to set of requirements between asset owners and asset custodians (service providers) is defined and managed. This includes establishing criteria for the evaluation of, acceptance of, and communication about asset requirements between the organization and the cloud computing provider.
Technology Management	Technology Management (TM) addresses the management of operational risk to technology assets. It covers the technology operational life cycle—release management, protecting and sustaining technology assets, interoperability, capacity planning,

Process Areas	Selection Rationale
	and maintenance—and seeks to ensure that potential vulnerabilities and threats related to operating and maintaining hardware, software, systems, tools, and infrastructure (such as failing to control access to technology assets or not performing configuration management) do not pose risk to the integrity and availability of technology assets.
Knowledge and Information Management	Knowledge and Information Management (KIM) is focused on understanding the importance of high-value information to the organization's services. For cloud computing, this process area determines the organization's capability in managing the confidentiality, integrity, and availability of intangible information. This includes implementing strategies to protect and sustain information assets (considering all the ways in which they are stored, transported, transmitted, and processed), such as proper duplication and retention to ensure availability of the information when needed.
Environmental Control	Environmental Control (EC) addresses the process used to manage an appropriate level of physical, environmental, and geographical controls to support the resilient operations of services in organizational facilities. Considerations for cloud computing include understanding the organization's dependence on public services, public infrastructure, and geographic location of data centers where services are performed.
Service Continuity	Service Continuity (SC) addresses the process used to develop, deploy, exercise, implement, and manage plans for responding to and recovering from disruptive events and restoring operations to business as usual. Considerations for cloud computing include ensuring the organization has sufficient capability to determine requirements and oversee continuity of operations for cloud computing services.

Managing the Insider Threat Challenge

A suggested (but not all-inclusive) targeted improvement roadmap for measuring how well the organization is managing the potential threat posed by trusted staff is provided in Table B.3.

TABLE B.3 Targeted Improvement Roadmap for Managing Insider Threat

Process Area	Selection Rationale
Human Resource Management	Human Resource Management (HRM) addresses the management of operational risk posed by the processes for acquiring and severing staff. It covers the employment life

Continues

TABLE B.3 Targeted Improvement Roadmap for Managing Insider Threat *(Continued)*

Process Areas	Selection Rationale
	cycle—hiring, performance management, and termination—and seeks to ensure that potential vulnerabilities and threats related to acquiring and managing staff (such as failing to identify a job candidate's criminal history or past credit problems) do not pose risk to the organization.
People Management	People Management (PM) is focused on minimizing the impact of the lack of availability of high-value staff on the organization's operational resilience. For insider threat, this process area determines the organization's capability in identifying high-value staff (who could intentionally cause damage to the organization) and ensuring proper redundancy and succession planning if these staff members are unavailable for any reason, including termination.
Risk Management	Risk Management (RISK) addresses the organization's process for identifying, analyzing, and mitigating risk. For insider threat, this process area is focused specifically on how well the organization identifies, analyzes, and mitigates risk related to the intentional or accidental actions of trusted staff, including employees and external entities (contractors, etc.).
Vulnerability Analysis and Resolution	In Vulnerability Analysis and Resolution (VAR), the organization's process for identifying, analyzing, and addressing potential threats to high-value assets is established. For insider threat, this process area is focused on the degree to which the organization can specifically identify areas of weakness that can be exploited by trusted staff. This process area also focuses on how well the organization identifies and manages vulnerabilities related to how staff are acquired, trained, deployed, and managed.
Controls Management	Controls Management (CTRL) broadly addresses the way in which the organization identifies, develops, implements, and manages controls (administrative, physical, and technical) to ensure that high-value assets are not disrupted. For insider threat, controls management is focused on managing the controls that specifically prevent trusted staff from intentionally or inadvertently disrupting high-value assets. In addition, this process area seeks to ensure that controls are implemented to manage potential vulnerabilities and threats posed by trusted staff who have special privileges (such as special levels of access to high-value assets).
Access Management	Access Management (AM) addresses the process used by the organization to enable access to high-value assets through the management of access privileges. For insider threat, the effective management of access privileges ensures that trusted staff members are provided only the level of access necessary to perform their assigned job responsibilities and that staff provided with special levels of access are provided those levels only when needed.

APPENDIX C

GLOSSARY OF TERMS

This appendix contains an alphabetical glossary of terms for the CERT Resilience Management Model. The glossary provides definitions based on how the term is used in the context of operational resilience management. For this reason, the definitions provided may differ from those in common use.

For terms that relate directly to a process area, the process area acronym is noted in brackets at the end of each definition. For example, [AM] refers to the Access Management process area.

abuse case See *misuse/abuse case*.

access acknowledgment A form or process that allows users to acknowledge (in writing) that they understand their access privileges and will abide by the organization's policy regarding the assignment, use, and revocation of those privileges. [AM]

access control The administrative, technical, or physical mechanism that provides a "gate" at which identities must present proper credentials and be authenticated to pass. [AM] [KIM]

access control policy (access management policy) An organizational policy that establishes the policies and procedures for requesting, approving, and providing access to persons, objects, and entities and establishes the guidelines for disciplinary action for violations of the policy. [AM]

access management (AM) An operations process area in CERT-RMM. The purpose of Access Management is to ensure that access granted to organizational assets is commensurate with their business and resilience requirements.

access privilege A mechanism for describing and defining an appropriate level of access to an organizational asset—information, technology, or facilities—commensurate with an identity's job responsibilities and the business and resilience requirements of the asset. [AM] [HRM]

access request A mechanism for requesting access to an organizational asset that is submitted to and approved by owners of the asset (with sufficient justification). [AM]

acculturation The acquisition and adoption of a process improvement mind-set and culture for resilience throughout all levels of the organization. [HRM]

adaptive maintenance Maintenance performed to adapt a facility to a different operating environment. [EC]

administrative control A type of managerial control that ensures alignment to management's intentions and includes such artifacts as governance, policy, monitoring, auditing, separation of duties, and the development and implementation of service continuity plans. [KIM]

agreement A legal agreement between the organization and a business partner or supplier. The agreement may be a contract, a license, or a memorandum of agreement (MOA). The agreement is legally binding. Performance measures against the agreement are typically created and documented in a service level agreement (SLA), a secondary agreement that often supports the legal agreement.

appraisal scope The part of the organization that is the focus of a CERT-RMM–based appraisal of current resilience practices. The scope of an appraisal is typically, but not necessarily, the same as the scope of the improvement effort. (See the related terms *model scope* and *organizational scope*.)

area of impact (organizational impact area) An area in which criteria are established to determine and express the potential impact of realized risk on the organization. Typical areas of impact include life and safety of employees and customers, financial, legal, and productivity. [RISK]

asset (organizational asset) Something of value to the organization; typically, people, information, technology, and facilities that high-value services rely on. [ADM]

asset custodian A person or organizational unit, internal or external to the organization, responsible for satisfying the resilience requirements of a high-value asset while it is in its care. For example, a system administrator on a server that contains the vendor database would be a custodian of that asset. [ADM] [RRM]

asset definition and management (ADM) An engineering process area in CERT-RMM. The purpose of Asset Definition and Management is to identify, document, and manage organizational assets during their life cycle to ensure sustained productivity to support organizational services.

asset disposition The retirement of an asset from service, particularly an information asset, commensurate with resilience requirements and information categorization and in accordance with any applicable rules, laws, and regulations. [KIM]

asset inventory An inventory (or inventories) of organizational assets—people, information, technology, and facilities. [ADM]

asset-level resilience requirements Asset-specific requirements that are set by the owners of an asset and are intended to establish the asset's protection and continuity needs with respect to its role in supporting mission assurance of a high-value service. [RRD]

asset life cycle The phases of an asset's life from development or acquisition to deployment to disposition. [ADM]

asset owner A person or organizational unit, internal or external to the organization, that has primary responsibility for the viability, productivity, and resilience of an organizational asset. For example, the accounts payable department is the owner of the vendor database. [ADM] [RRM]

asset profile Documentation of specific information about an asset (typically an information asset) that establishes ownership, a common definition, and other characteristics of the asset, such as its value. [ADM]

assurance case A structured set of arguments and a corresponding body of evidence demonstrating that a system satisfies specific claims with respect to its security, safety, or reliability properties. [RTSE]

attack pattern A design pattern describing the techniques that attackers might use to break a software product. [RTSE]

attack surface The set of ways in which an attacker can enter and potentially cause damage to a system. The larger the attack surface, the more insecure the system [Manadhata 2010]. [RTSE]

availability For an asset, the quality of being accessible to authorized users (people, processes, or devices) whenever it is needed. [EC] [KIM] [PM]

awareness Focusing the attention of, creating cognizance in, and acculturating people throughout the organization to resilience issues, concerns, policies, plans, and practices. [OTA]

awareness activity A means for implementing the awareness approaches that the organization has considered and developed to meet the specific needs of the stakeholder community. Formal awareness training sessions, newsletters, email messages, and posters and other signage are examples of awareness activities. [OTA]

awareness training A means by which the organization can highlight important behaviors and begin the process of acculturating staff and business partners to important organizational resilience goals, objectives, and critical success factors. [OTA]

awareness training waiver See *waiver*.

base measures Data obtained by direct measurement (for example, the number of service continuity plans updated in the last 12 months). [MA]

baseline configuration item A configuration item that serves as the baseline foundation for managing the integrity of an asset as it changes over its life cycle. [TM]

business process A series of discrete activities or tasks that contribute to the fulfillment of a service mission. (See the related term *service*.)

business requirement A requirement that must be met to achieve business objectives. Such requirements establish the baseline for how organizational assets are used to support business processes. [ADM]

capability level An indicator of achievement of process capability in a process area. A capability level is achieved by visibly and verifiably implementing the required components of a process area. (See the related terms *required component* and *process area*.)

capacity planning The process of determining the operational demand for a technology asset over a widely variable range of operational needs. [TM]

change control (change management) A continuous process of controlling changes to information or technology assets, related infrastructure, or any aspect of services, enabling approved changes with minimum disruption. [KIM] [RRM] [TM]

co-location (also collocation or colocation) The act or result of placing or arranging together. In facilities management, co-location refers to the grouping of facilities, the effects of which must be considered in service continuity planning. [EC]

communications (COMM) An enterprise process area in CERT-RMM. The purpose of Communications is to develop, deploy, and manage internal and external communications to support resilience activities and processes.

communications stakeholder A person or group that has a vested interest in being involved in or a beneficiary of the organization's resilience communications activities. [COMM]

compliance (COMP) An enterprise process area in CERT-RMM. The purpose of Compliance is to ensure awareness of and compliance with an established set of relevant internal and external guidelines, standards, practices, policies, regulations, and legislation, and other obligations (such as contracts and service level agreements) related to managing operational resilience.

compliance A process that characterizes the activities that the organization performs to identify the internal and external guidelines, standards, practices, policies, regulations, and legislation to which they are subject and to comply with these obligations in an orderly, systematic, efficient, timely, and accurate manner. [COMP]

compliance knowledgebase A common accessible information repository for compliance data. The repository may include documentation of the compliance obligations and their owners and due dates, the results of compliance and substantive testing of controls, compliance targets and metrics, compliance reports, non-compliance reports, remediation plans, and tracking data to provide status on satisfying compliance obligations. [COMP]

compliance obligations The internal and external guidelines, standards, practices, policies, regulations, and legislation with which the organization has an obligation to comply. [COMP]

condition A term that collectively describes a vulnerability, an actor, a motive, and an undesirable outcome. A condition is essentially a threat that the organization must identify and analyze to determine if exploitation of the threat could result in undesirable consequences. [RISK] (See the related term *consequence*.)

confidentiality For an asset, the quality of being accessible only to authorized people, processes, and devices. [KIM]

configuration item An asset or a series of related assets (typically information- or technology-focused) that are placed under configuration management processes. [KIM] [TM]

configuration management A process for managing the integrity of an information or technology asset over its lifetime. Typically includes change control processes. [KIM] [TM]

consequence The unwanted effect, undesirable outcome, or impact on the organization as the result of exploitation of a condition or threat. [RISK] (See the related term *condition*.)

constellation In the CMMI architecture, a collection of components that are used to construct models, training materials, and appraisal materials in an area of interest (e.g., services and development).

container (information asset container) A physical or logical location where assets are stored, transported, and processed. A container can encompass technical containers (servers, network segments, personal computers), physical containers (paper, file rooms, storage spaces, or other media such as CDs, disks, and flash drives), and people (including people who might have detailed knowledge about the information asset). [KIM]

continuity of operations An organization's ability to sustain assets and services in light of realized risk. Typically used interchangeably with *service continuity*. [RISK] [SC] (See the related term *Service Continuity*.)

controls The methods, policies, and procedures—manual or automated—that are adopted by an organization to ensure the safeguarding of assets, the accuracy and reliability of management information and financial records, the promotion of administrative efficiency, and adherence to standards. [CTRL] [KIM]

controls management (CTRL) An engineering process area in CERT-RMM. The purpose of Controls Management is to establish, implement, monitor, and manage an internal control system that ensures the effectiveness and efficiency of operations through mission assurance of high-value services.

convergence The harmonization of operational risk management activities that have similar objectives and outcomes.

corrective maintenance A process of correcting and repairing problems that degrade the operational capability of facility services. [EC]

cost of resilience An accumulation of expense and capital costs related to providing resilience services and achieving resilience requirements. [FRM]

credentialing A process for identifying, acquiring, and maintaining access for first responders (vital staff members) from governmental authorities. [PM]

crisis An incident in which the impact on the organization is imminent or immediate. A crisis requires immediate organizational action because the effect of the incident is already felt by the organization and must be limited or contained. [IMC]

critical success factors The key areas in which favorable results are necessary to achieve goals. They are both internal and external to the organization. They can originate in the organization's particular industry and with its peers, in its operating environment, from temporary barriers, challenges, or problems, or from the various domains of organizational management. [RRD]

cross-training Training in different roles or responsibilities within the organization, thus preparing staff to accept and perform new roles, however temporary, until a return to business as usual can be accomplished. [PM]

cryptographic controls Encryption of data and information that provides an additional layer of control over information assets by ensuring that access is limited to those who have the appropriate deciphering keys. [KIM]

custodian See *asset custodian*.

defined process A managed process that is tailored from the organization's set of standard processes according to the organization's tailoring guidelines; has a maintained process description; and contributes work products, measures, and other process improvement information to organizational process assets. [OPD] (See the related terms *managed process* and *organization's set of standard processes*.)

deprovisioning The process of revoking or removing an identity's access to organizational assets. [AM] (See the related term *provisioning*.)

derived measures Data obtained by combining two or more base measures (for example, the percentage of risk mitigation plans completed on time in the last 12 months). [MA]

disposition The appropriate and proper retirement of an asset at the end of its useful life. [KIM] [RISK]

encryption policies Policies that govern the use of cryptographic technologies as appropriate or required for each level of information asset categorization. Includes organizational policies that manage the assignment of use, storage, disposal, and protection of cryptographic keys (such as public and private keys). [KIM]

enterprise Synonymous with *organization*.

enterprise focus (EF) An enterprise process area in CERT-RMM. The purpose of Enterprise Focus is to establish sponsorship, strategic planning, and governance over the operational resilience management system.

enterprise-level resilience requirement Resilience requirements that reflect enterprise-level needs, expectations, and constraints. These requirements affect nearly all aspects of an organization's operations. [RRD]

environmental control (EC) An operations process area in CERT-RMM. The purpose of Environmental Control is to establish and manage an appropriate level of physical, environmental, and geographical controls to support the resilient operations of services in organizational facilities.

establish and maintain Whenever "establish and maintain" is used in a specific practice, it refers not only to the development and maintenance of the object of the practice (such as a policy) but to the documentation of the object and observable usage of the object. For example, "Establish and maintain the plan for performing the organizational process focus process" means that not only must a plan be formulated, but it also must be documented, have a process definition, have assigned ownership, and be maintained relative to corrective actions, changes in requirements, or improvements.

event One or more occurrences that affect organizational assets and have the potential to disrupt operations. [IMC] (See the related term *incident*.)

event triage The process of categorizing, correlating, and prioritizing events with the objective of assigning events to incident handling and response. [IMC]

exercise The testing of a service continuity plan on a regular basis to ensure that it will achieve its stated objectives when executed as the result of a disruption or interruption. [SC]

expected component A model component that explains what may be done to satisfy a required CERT-RMM component. Specific and generic practices are expected model components. Model users can implement the expected components explicitly or implement equivalent alternative practices. (See the related terms *informative component* and *required component*.)

external dependencies management (EXD) An operations process area in CERT-RMM. The purpose of External Dependencies Management is to establish and manage an appropriate level of controls to ensure the resilience of services and assets that are dependent on the actions of external entities.

external dependency An external dependency exists when an external entity has access to, control of, ownership in, possession of, responsibility for, or other defined obligations related to one or more assets or services of the organization. [EXD] (See the related term *external entity*.)

external entity An individual, business, or business unit (such as a customer, a contractor, or another group within the same enterprise) that is external to and in a supporting or influencing relationship with the organization that is using a process area. [EXD]

facility Any tangible and physical asset that is part of the organization's physical plant. Facilities include office buildings, warehouses, data centers, and other physical structures. [ADM] [EC]

federation The assembled identity of an object across organizational units, organizations, systems, or other domains where the object has multiple identities. [ID]

financial resource management (FRM) An enterprise process area in CERT-RMM. The purpose of Financial Resource Management is to request, receive, manage, and apply financial resources to support resilience objectives and requirements.

first responder Vital staff trained to conduct damage assessment after a disruption and recommend a path to reestablishing the high-value services of the organization. [PM]

functional monitoring requirements Requirements that describe, at a detailed level, what must be performed to meet the monitoring requirement. Specific infrastructure needs are a type of functional monitoring requirement. [MON]

fuzz testing A means of testing that causes a software program to consume deliberately malformed data to see how the program reacts [Microsoft 2009]. [RTSE]

generic goal A required model component that describes characteristics that must be present to institutionalize processes that implement a process area. (See the related term *institutionalization*.)

generic practice An expected model component that is considered important in achieving the associated generic goal. The generic practices associated with a generic goal describe the activities that are expected to result in achievement of the generic goal and contribute to the institutionalization of the processes associated with a process area.

generic practice elaboration An informative model component that appears after a generic practice to provide guidance on how the generic practice should be applied to the process area.

geographical dispersion The specific and planned dispersion or scattering of physical structures and facilities so that they are not all affected by a single event or incident. [EC]

governance An organizational process of providing strategic direction for the organization while ensuring that it meets its obligations, appropriately manages risk, and efficiently uses financial and human resources. [EF]

high-value assets People, information, technology, or facilities on whose confidentiality, integrity, availability, and productivity a high-value service is dependent. [ADM]

high-value services Services on which the success of the organization's mission depends. [EF] [RRD]

human resource management (HRM) An enterprise process area in CERT-RMM. The purpose of Human Resource Management is to manage the employment life cycle and performance of staff in a manner that contributes to the organization's ability to manage operational resilience.

identity Documentation of certain information about a person, object, or entity that may require access to organizational assets to fulfill its role in executing services. [ID]

identity community The baseline population of persons, objects, and entities—internal and external to the organization—that could be or are authorized to access and use organizational assets commensurate with their job responsibilities and roles. Also, the collection of the organization's identity profiles. [ID]

identity management (ID) An operations process area in CERT-RMM. The purpose of Identity Management is to create, maintain, and deactivate identities and associated attributes that provide access to organizational assets.

identity management A process that addresses the management of the life cycle of objects (typically people, but often systems, devices, or other processes) that need some level of trusted access to organizational assets. [ID]

identity profile Documentation of all of the relevant information necessary to describe the unique attributes, roles, and responsibilities of the associated person, object, or entity. [ID]

identity registration The process of making an identity "known" to the organization as a person, object, or entity that may require access to organizational assets and that may have to be authenticated and authorized to use access privileges. [ID]

identity repository A common accessible information repository that provides a single (or virtual) consistent source of information about organizational identities. [ID]

impact valuation Determines the extent of the impact of operational risk using the organization's risk measurement criteria. [RISK]

incident An event (or series of events) of higher magnitude that significantly affects organizational assets and requires the organization to respond in some way to prevent or limit organizational impact. [IMC]

incident closure The retirement of an incident that has been responded to (i.e., there are no further actions required, and the organization is satisfied with the result) and for which the organization has performed a formal post-incident review. [IMC]

incident escalation The process of notifying relevant stakeholders about an incident that requires an organizational response and involves stakeholder actions to implement, manage, and bring to closure with an appropriate and timely solution. [IMC]

incident life cycle The life cycle of an incident from detection to closure. Collectively, the processes of logging, tracking, documenting, escalating and notifying, gathering and preserving evidence, and closing incidents. [IMC]

incident management and control (IMC) An operations process area in CERT-RMM. The purpose of Incident Management and Control is to establish processes to identify and analyze events, detect incidents, and determine an appropriate organizational response.

incident owner The individuals or teams to whom an incident is assigned for containment, analysis, and response. [IMC]

incident response The actions the organization takes to prevent or contain the impact of an incident to the organization while it is occurring or shortly after it has occurred. [IMC]

incident stakeholder A person or organization that has a vested interest in the management of an incident throughout its life cycle. [IMC]

information asset Information or data that is of value to the organization, including diverse information such as patient records, intellectual property, customer information, and contracts. [ADM] [KIM]

information asset baseline A foundational configuration of an information asset from which changes to the asset can be detected over its life cycle. [KIM]

information asset categorization A process for labeling and handling the sensitivity of information assets, typically based on a categorization taxonomy or scheme. [KIM]

information asset container A technical or physical asset on which information is stored, transported, or processed, or a person who has information or knowledge. [ADM] [KIM]

information asset owner See the related term *asset owner*.

informative component A model component that helps model users understand required and expected components. Informative components can contain examples, detailed explanations, or other helpful information. Subpractices, notes, references, goal titles, practice titles, sources, typical work products, amplifications, and generic practice elaborations are informative model components. (See the related terms *expected component* and *required component*.)

institutionalization Incorporation into the ingrained way of doing business that an organization follows routinely as part of its corporate culture.

integrity For an asset, the quality of being in the condition intended by the owner and therefore continuing to be useful for the purposes intended by the owner. [KIM] [TM]

intellectual property The unique information assets of the organization that are created by the organization and are vital to its success. Intellectual property may include trade secrets, formulas, trademarks, and other organizationally produced assets. [KIM]

internal control system The methods, policies, and procedures used to protect and sustain high-value assets at a level commensurate with their role in supporting organizational services. [KIM] (See the related term *high-value assets*.)

key control indicators Organizationally specific indicators that provide information about the effectiveness of the organization's internal control system. [EF]

key performance indicators Organizationally specific performance metrics that measure progress against the organization's strategic objectives and critical success factors. [EF]

key risk indicators Organizationally specific thresholds that, when crossed, indicate levels of risk that may be outside of the organization's risk tolerance. [EF] [RISK]

knowledge and information management (KIM) An operations process area in CERT-RMM. The purpose of Knowledge and Information Management is to establish and manage an appropriate level of controls to support the confidentiality, integrity, and availability of the organization's information, vital records, and intellectual property.

line of business A logical grouping of organizational units that have a common purpose, such as production of products for a particular market segment.

managed process A performed process that is planned and executed in accordance with policy; employs skilled people having adequate resources to produce controlled outputs; involves relevant stakeholders; is monitored, controlled, and reviewed; and is evaluated for adherence to its process description. (See the related term *performed process*.)

measurement and analysis (MA) A process management process area in CERT-RMM. The purpose of Measurement and Analysis is to develop and sustain a measurement capability that is used to support management information needs for managing the operational resilience management system.

measurement objectives Documents the purpose for which measurements and analysis are done and specifies the kinds of actions that may be taken based on the results of data analysis. [MA]

measures Measurements of the resilience process that may be categorized by obtaining direct measurements (*base measures*) or by obtaining measurements that are a combination of two or more base measures (*derived measures*). [MA]

misuse/abuse case A descriptive statement of the undesirable, non-standard conditions that software is likely to face during its operation from either unintentional misuse or intentional and malicious misuse or abuse. [RTSE]

model scope The parts of CERT-RMM that will be used to guide the improvement effort.

monitoring (MON) A process management process area in CERT-RMM. The purpose of Monitoring is to collect, record, and distribute information about the operational resilience management system to the organization on a timely basis.

monitoring infrastructure The technologies and support services that are needed to support the achievement of monitoring requirements. [MON]

monitoring requirements The requirements established to determine the information gathering and distribution needs of stakeholders. [MON]

monitoring stakeholder A person or group that has a vested interest in being involved in or a beneficiary of the organization's monitoring activities. [MON]

operational constraint A limit imposed on an organization's operational activities. Such a limit can be imposed by the organization on itself or can come from the organization's operating environment (e.g., regulations). [RRD]

operational resilience The organization's ability to adapt to risk that affects its core operational capacities. Operational resilience is an emergent property of effective operational risk management, supported and enabled by activities such as security and business continuity. A subset of enterprise resilience, operational resilience focuses on the organization's ability to manage operational risk, whereas enterprise resilience encompasses additional areas of risk such as business risk and credit risk. (See the related term *operational risk*.)

operational resilience management The direction and coordination of activities to achieve resilience objectives that align with the organization's strategic objectives and critical success factors.

operational resilience management system The mechanism through which operational resilience management is performed. The "system" includes the plan, program, processes, procedures, practices, and people that are necessary to manage operational resilience.

operational resilience requirements Refers collectively to requirements that ensure the protection of high-value assets as well as their continuity when a disruptive event has occurred. The requirements traditionally encompass security, business continuity, and IT operational requirements. These include the security objectives for information assets (confidentiality, integrity, and availability) as well as the requirements for business continuity planning and recovery and the availability and support requirements of the organization's technical infrastructure. [RRD]

operational risk The potential impact on assets and their related services that could result from inadequate or failed internal processes, failures of systems or technology, the deliberate or inadvertent actions of people, or external events.

operational risk taxonomy The collection and cataloging of common operational risks that the organization is subject to and must manage. The risk taxonomy is a means for communicating these risks and for developing mitigation actions specific to an organizational unit or line of business if operational assets and services are affected by them. [RISK]

organization An administrative structure in which people collectively manage one or more services as a whole, and whose services share a senior manager and operate under the same policies. May consist of many organizations in many locations with different customers. (See the related terms *enterprise* and *organizational unit*.)

organization's process asset library A library of information used to store and make available process assets that are useful to those who are defining, implementing, and managing processes in the organization. This library contains process assets that include process-related documentation, such as policies, defined processes, checklists, lessons-learned documents, templates, standards, procedures, plans, and training materials.

organization's set of standard processes A collection of definitions of the processes that guide activities in an organization. These process descriptions cover the fundamental process elements (and their relationships to each other, such as ordering and interfaces) that must be incorporated into the defined processes that are implemented in projects across the organization. A standard process enables consistent development and maintenance activities across the organization and is essential for long-term stability and improvement. [OPD] (See the related terms *defined process* and *process element*.)

organizational asset See *asset*.

organizational impact area See *area of impact*.

organizational process assets Artifacts that relate to describing, implementing, and improving processes (e.g., policies, measurements, process descriptions, and process implementation support tools). The term *process assets* is used to indicate that these artifacts are developed or acquired to meet the business objectives of the organization, and they represent investments by the organization that are expected to provide current and future business value. (See the related term *process asset library*.)

organizational process definition (OPD) A process management process area in CERT-RMM. The purpose of Organizational Process Definition is to establish and maintain a usable set of organizational process assets and work environment standards for operational resilience.

organizational process focus (OPF) A process management process area in CERT-RMM. The purpose of Organizational Process Focus is to plan, implement, and deploy organizational process improvements based on a thorough understanding of current strengths and weaknesses of the organization's operational resilience processes and process assets.

organizational process maturity In models with a staged representation, organizational process maturity is measured by the degree of process improvement across predefined sets of process areas. Since CERT-RMM does not have a staged representation, characterization of organizational process maturity can only be implied by reaching successively higher levels of capability across CERT-RMM process areas.

organizational scope The part of the organization that is the focus of the CERT-RMM deployment.

organizational sensitivity The degree to which access to an information asset must be limited due to confidentiality or privacy requirements. [ADM]

organizational subunit Any sub-element of an organizational unit. An organizational subunit is fully contained within the organizational unit.

organizational superunit Any part of an organization that is at a higher level than the organizational unit. The term *organizational superunit* can also be used to refer to the entire organization.

organizational training and awareness (OTA) An enterprise process area in CERT-RMM. The purpose of Organizational Training and Awareness is to promote awareness and develop skills and knowledge of people in support of their roles in attaining and sustaining operational resilience.

organizational unit A distinct subset of an organization or enterprise. An organizational unit is typically part of a larger organization, although in a small organization, the organizational unit may be the whole organization.

organizationally high-value services See *high-value services*.

people All staff, both internal and external to the organization, and all managers employed in some manner by the organization to perform a role or fulfill a responsibility that contributes to meeting the organization's goals and objectives. [PM]

people management (PM) An operations process area in CERT-RMM. The purpose of People Management is to establish and manage the contributions and availability of people to support the resilient operation of organizational services.

perfective maintenance Maintenance performed by acquiring additional or improved operational capacity. [EC]

performed process A process that accomplishes the needed work to produce work products. The specific goals of the process area are satisfied.

physical control A type of control that prevents physical access to and modification of information assets or physical access to technology and facilities. Physical controls often include such artifacts as card readers and physical barrier methods. [EC] [KIM] [TM]

planned downtime Acceptable and planned interruption of the availability of an information or technology asset, usually as the result of a user- or management-initiated event. [TM]

post-incident review A formal part of the incident closure process that refers to the organization's formal examination of the causes of an incident and the ways in which the organization responded to it, as well as the administrative, technical, and physical control weaknesses that may have allowed the incident to occur. [IMC]

preventive maintenance Preplanned activities performed to prevent potential facility problems from occurring. [EC]

privacy The assurance that information about an individual is disclosed only to people, processes, and devices authorized by that individual or permitted under privacy laws and regulations. [KIM]

privilege See *access privilege*.

problem management The process that an organization uses to identify recurring problems, examine root causes, and develop solutions for these problems to prevent future, similar incidents. [IMC]

process Activities that can be recognized as implementations of practices in the model. These activities can be mapped to one or more practices in process areas to allow the model to be useful for process improvement and process appraisal. (See the related terms *process area*, *subprocess*, and *process element*.)

There is a special use of the phrase "the process" in the statements and descriptions of the generic goals and generic practices. In that context, "the process" is the process or processes that implement the process area.

process architecture The ordering, interfaces, interdependencies, and other relationships among the process elements in a standard process. Process architecture also describes the interfaces, interdependencies, and other relationships between process elements and external processes (e.g., contract management). [OPD]

process area A cluster of related practices in an area that, when implemented collectively, satisfy a set of goals considered important for making improvement in that area.

process asset library A collection of process asset holdings that can be used by an organization or project. (See the related term *organization's process asset library*.)

process capability The range of expected results that can be achieved by following a process. The generic goals and practices define the degree to which a process is institutionalized; capability levels indicate the degree to which a process is institutionalized.

process element The fundamental unit of a process. A process can be defined in terms of subprocesses or process elements. A subprocess can be decomposed further into subprocesses or process elements; a process element cannot. Each process element covers a closely related set of activities (e.g., estimating element, peer review element). Process elements can be portrayed using templates to be completed, abstractions to be refined, or descriptions to be modified or used. A process element can be an activity or a task. [OPD] (See the related term *subprocess*.)

process performance A measure of actual results achieved by following a process. It is characterized by both process measures (e.g., vulnerabilities eliminated before being exploited) and product or service measures (e.g., control system network unavailability due to exploited vulnerabilities).

protection strategy The strategy, related controls, and activities necessary to protect an asset from undesired harm or disruptive events. The protection strategy is relative to the conditions to which the asset is subjected. (See the related term *condition*.)

provisioning The process of assigning or activating an identity profile and its associated roles and access privileges. [ID]

proximity The relative distance between facilities, which is a consideration in co-location and geographical dispersion. [EC] (See the related terms *co-location* and *geographical dispersion*.)

public infrastructure Infrastructure owned by the community in the geographical area that contains a facility. Includes telecommunications and telephone services, electricity, natural gas, and other energy sources, water and sewer services, trash collection and disposal, and other support services. [EC]

public services Services that are provided in the community or in the geographical area that contains a facility. Includes fire response and rescue services, local and federal law enforcement, emergency management services such as paramedics and first responders, and animal control. [EC]

recovery point objective (RPO) Establishes the point to which an information or technology asset (typically an application system) must be restored to allow recovery of the asset and associated services after a disruption. [TM]

recovery time objective (RTO) Establishes the period of acceptable downtime of an information or technology asset after which the organization would suffer an unwanted consequence or impact. [TM]

regulation A type of compliance obligation issued by a governmental, regulatory, or other agency. [COMP]

release build A version of an information or technology asset that is to be released into production; an object in the release management process. [KIM] [TM]

release management The process of managing successive release of versions of information and technology assets into an operations and production environment. [KIM] [TM]

required component A CERT-RMM component that is essential to achieving process improvement in a given process area. Required components are used in appraisals to determine process capability. Specific goals and generic goals are required components. (See the related terms *expected component* and *informative component*.)

residual risk The risk that remains and is accepted by the organization after mitigation plans are implemented. [RISK]

resilience See *operational resilience*.

resilience budget A budget specifically developed and funded to support the organization's resilience activities. [FRM]

resilience management See *operational resilience management*.

resilience obligations An understanding of a commitment, promise, or duty to follow and enforce the resilience requirements of the organization. [HRM]

resilience requirement A constraint that the organization places on the productive capability of an asset to ensure that it remains viable and sustainable when charged into production to support a service.

resilience requirements development (RRD) An engineering process area in CERT-RMM. The purpose of Resilience Requirements Development is to identify, document, and analyze the operational resilience requirements for high-value services and related assets.

resilience requirements management (RRM) An engineering process area in CERT-RMM. The purpose of Resilience Requirements Management is to manage the resilience requirements of high-value services and associated assets and to identify inconsistencies between these requirements and the activities that the organization performs to meet the requirements.

resilience specifications Criteria that the organization establishes for a working relationship with an external entity, which may be incorporated into contractual terms. Typically include the resilience requirements of any of the organization's high-value assets and services that are placed in the external entity's control. Also may include required characteristics of the external entity (e.g., financial condition and experience), required behaviors of the external entity (e.g., security and training practices), and performance parameters that must be exhibited by the external entity (e.g., recovery time after an incident and response time to service calls).

resilience staff Internal or external staff who are specifically involved in or assigned to resilience-focused activities that are typically found in security, business continuity, and IT operations disciplines. [OTA]

resilience training The process and activities focused on imparting the necessary skills and knowledge to people for performing their roles and responsibilities in support of the organization's operational resilience management system. [OTA]

resilience training needs Training requirements related to the skills and competencies required at a tactical level to carry out the activities required for managing operational resilience. [OTA]

resilient technical solution engineering (RTSE) An engineering process area in CERT-RMM. The purpose of Resilient Technical Solution Engineering is to ensure that software and systems are developed to satisfy their resilience requirements.

return on resilience investment (RORI) The return on investment for funding resilience activities. Provides a way to justify resilience costs and provides direct support for the contribution that managing operational resilience makes toward achieving strategic objectives. [FRM]

risk The possibility of suffering harm or loss. From a resilience perspective, risk is the combination of a threat and a vulnerability (condition), the impact (consequence) on the organization if the vulnerability is exploited, and the presence of uncertainty. In CERT-RMM, this definition is typically applied to the asset or service level such that risk is the possibility of suffering harm or loss due to disruption of high-value assets and services. [RISK]

risk analysis A risk management process focused on understanding the condition and consequences of risk, prioritizing risks, and determining a path for addressing risks. Determines the importance of each identified operational risk and is used to facilitate the organization's risk disposition and mitigation activities. [RISK]

risk appetite An organization's stated level of risk aversion. Informs the development of risk evaluation criteria in areas of impact for the organization. [RISK] (See the related terms *area of impact*, *risk measurement criteria*, and *risk tolerance*.)

risk category An organizationally defined description of risk that typically aligns with the various sources of operational risk but can be tailored to the organization's unique risk environment. Risk categories provide a means to collect and organize risks to assist in the analysis and mitigation processes. [RISK]

risk disposition A statement of the organization's intention for addressing an operational risk. Typically limited to "accept," "transfer," "research," or "mitigate." [RISK]

risk management (RISK) An enterprise process area in CERT-RMM. The purpose of Risk Management is to identify, analyze, and mitigate risks to organizational assets that could adversely affect the operation and delivery of services.

risk management The continuous process of identifying, analyzing, and mitigating risks to organizational assets that could adversely affect the operation and delivery of services. [RISK]

risk measurement criteria Objective criteria that the organization uses for evaluating, categorizing, and prioritizing operational risks based on areas of impact. [RISK] (See the related term *area of impact*.)

risk mitigation The act of reducing risk to an acceptable level. [RISK]

risk mitigation plan A strategy for mitigating risk that seeks to minimize the risk to an acceptable level. [RISK]

risk parameter (risk management parameter) Organizationally specific risk tolerances used for consistent measurement of risk across the organization. Risk parameters include risk tolerances and risk measurement criteria. [RISK] (See the related terms *risk tolerance* and *risk measurement criteria*.)

risk statement A statement that clearly articulates the context, conditions, and consequences of risk. [RISK]

risk taxonomy See *operational risk taxonomy*.

risk threshold An organizationally developed type of risk parameter that is used by management to determine when a risk is in control or when it has exceeded acceptable organizational limits. [RISK]

risk tolerance Thresholds that reflect the organization's level of risk aversion by providing levels of acceptable risk in each operational risk category that the organization has established. Risk tolerance, as a risk parameter, also establishes the organization's philosophy on risk management—how risks will be controlled, who has the authorization to accept risk on behalf of the organization, and how often and to what degree operational risk should be assessed. [RISK]

root-cause analysis An approach for determining the underlying causes of events or problems as a means of addressing the symptoms of such events as they manifest in organizational disruptions. [VAR]

scope See *appraisal scope*, *model scope*, and *organizational scope*.

secure design pattern A general, reusable solution to a commonly occurring problem in design. A design pattern is not a finished design that can be transformed directly into code. It is a description or template for how to solve a problem that can be used in many different situations. Secure design patterns are meant to eliminate the accidental insertion of vulnerabilities into code or to mitigate the consequences of vulnerabilities. Secure design patterns address security issues at widely varying levels of specificity, ranging from architectural-level patterns involving the high-level design of the system down to implementation-level patterns providing guidance on how to implement portions of functions or methods in the system [Dougherty 2009]. [RTSE]

sensitivity A measure of the degree to which an information asset must be protected based on the consequences of its unauthorized access, modification, or disclosure. [KIM]

service A set of activities that the organization carries out in the performance of a duty or in the production of a product. [ADM] [EF] (See the related term *business process*.)

service continuity (SC) An engineering process area in CERT-RMM. The purpose of Service Continuity is to ensure the continuity of essential operations of services and related assets if a disruption occurs as a result of an incident, disaster, or other disruptive event.

service continuity plan (business continuity plan) A service-specific plan for sustaining services and associated assets under degraded conditions. [SC]

service level agreement (SLA) A type of agreement that specifies levels of service expected from business partners in the performance of a contract or agreement. In CERT-RMM, SLAs are expanded to include the satisfaction of resilience requirements by business partners when one or more organizational assets are in their custodial care.

service-level resilience requirements Service requirements established by owners of a service such as an organizational unit or a line of business. [RRD] (See the related term *asset-level resilience requirements*.)

service profile A description of services in sufficient detail to capture the activities, tasks, and expected outcomes of the services and the assets that are vital to the service. [EF]

service resilience requirements Resilience needs of a service in its pursuit of its mission. Resilience requirements for services primarily address availability and recoverability but are also directly related to the confidentiality, integrity, and availability requirements of associated assets. [RRD]

services map Details the relationships between a service, associated business processes, and associated assets. [RRD]

shared resilience requirements Requirements that are developed for shared organizational assets, such as a facility in which more than one high-value service is executed. [RRD]

skills inventory or repository A means for identifying and documenting the current skill set of the organization's human resources. [HRM]

specific goal A required model component that describes the unique characteristics that must be present to satisfy the process area. (See the related terms *process area* and *required component*.)

specific practice An expected model component that is considered important to achieving the associated specific goal. The specific practices describe the activities expected to result in achievement of the specific goals of a process area. (See the related terms *expected component*, *process area*, and *specific goal*.)

staff All people, both internal and external to the organization, employed in some manner by the organization to perform a role or fulfill a responsibility that contributes to meeting the organization's goals and objectives. Does not include those in managerial roles.

stakeholder A person or organization that has a vested interest in the organization or its activities. (See the related terms *communications stakeholder* and *monitoring stakeholder*.)

standard process An operational definition of the basic process that guides the establishment of a common process in an organization. A standard process describes the fundamental process elements that are expected to be incorporated into any defined process. It also describes relationships (e.g., ordering, interfaces) among these process elements. [OPD] (See the related term *defined process.*)

strategic objectives (strategic drivers) The performance targets that the organization sets to accomplish its mission, vision, values, and purpose. [EF]

strategic planning The process of developing strategic objectives and plans for meeting these objectives. [EF]

subprocess A process that is part of a larger process. A subprocess can be decomposed into subprocesses or process elements. [OPD] (See the related terms *process* and *process element.*)

succession planning A form of continuity planning for vital staff and/or decision-making managers focused on providing a smooth transition for vital roles and sustaining the high-value services of the organization. [PM]

supplier An internal or external organization or contractor that supplies key products and services to the organization to contribute to accomplishing the missions of its high-value services.

sustain Maintain in a desired operational state.

sustainment strategy The strategy, related controls, and activities necessary to sustain an asset when it is subjected to undesired harm or disruptive events. The sustainment strategy is relative to the consequences to the organization if the asset is harmed or disrupted.

technical control A type of technical mechanism that supports protection methods for assets such as firewalls and electronic access controls. [KIM] [TM]

technology asset Any hardware, software, or firmware used by the organization in the delivery of services. [TM]

technology interoperability The ability of technology assets to exist and operate in a connected manner to meet an organizational goal, objective, or mission. [TM]

technology management (TM) An operations process area in CERT-RMM. The purpose of Technology Management is to establish and manage an appropriate level of controls related to the integrity and availability of technology assets to support the resilient operations of organizational services.

threat The combination of a vulnerability, a threat actor, a motive (if the threat actor is a person or persons), and the potential to produce a harmful outcome for the organization. [RISK] [VAR] (See the related term *condition.*)

threat actor A situation, entity, individual, group, or action that has the potential to exploit a threat. [RISK] [VAR]

threat environment The set of all types of threats that could affect the current operations of the organization. (See the related term *threat*.)

threat motive The reason that a threat actor would exploit a vulnerability or otherwise cause harm. [RISK] [VAR]

unplanned downtime Interruption in the availability of an information or technology asset (and, in some cases, a facility asset) due to an unplanned event or incident, often resulting from diminished operational resilience. [TM]

user Any entity or object to which the organization has granted some form of access to an organizational asset. Typically referred to as an "identity." (See the related term *identity*.)

vital records Records that must be preserved and available for retrieval if needed. This refers to records or documents that, for legal, regulatory, or operational reasons, cannot be irretrievably lost or damaged without materially impairing the organization's ability to conduct business. [KIM]

vital staff A select group of individuals who are absolutely essential to the sustained operation of the organization, particularly under stressful conditions. [PM]

vulnerability An exposure, flaw, or weakness that could be exploited. The susceptibility of an organizational service or asset to disruption. [VAR]

vulnerability analysis and resolution (VAR) An operations process area in CERT-RMM. The purpose of Vulnerability Analysis and Resolution is to identify, analyze, and manage vulnerabilities in an organization's operating environment.

vulnerability management strategy A strategy for identifying and reducing exposure to known vulnerabilities. [VAR]

vulnerability repository An organizational inventory of known vulnerabilities. [VAR]

vulnerability resolution The action that the organization takes to reduce or eliminate exposure to vulnerability. [VAR]

waiver Documentation for staff members who have been exempted from awareness training or other activities for any reason. Such documentation includes the rationale for the waiver and approval by the individual's manager (or similarly appropriate person). Each required course should include criteria for granting training waivers. [OTA]

APPENDIX D

ACRONYMS AND INITIALISMS

ADM Asset Definition and Management (process area)

AM Access Management (process area)

BSIMM Building Security In Maturity Model

CBCP Certified Business Continuity Professional

CIO chief information officer

CISA Certified Information Systems Auditor

CISSP Certified Information Systems Security Professional

CMF CMMI Model Foundation

CMMI Capability Maturity Model Integration

CMMI-ACQ CMMI for Acquisition

CMMI-DEV CMMI for Development

CMMI-SVC CMMI for Services

COBIT Control Objectives for Information and Related Technology

COMM Communications (process area)

COMP Compliance (process area)

COPPA Children's Online Privacy Protection Act

COR cost of resilience

COSO Committee of Sponsoring Organizations of the Treadway Commission frameworks

COTS commercial off-the-shelf

CPA Certified Public Accountant

CSIRT computer security incident response team

CTRL Controls Management (process area)

CVE Common Vulnerabilities and Exposures project

CXO higher-level managers (CEO, CSO, etc.)

DBA database administrator

DRII Disaster Recovery Institute International

EC Environmental Control (process area)

EF Enterprise Focus (process area)

EUDPA European Union Data Protection Directive

EXD External Dependencies Management (process area)

FBI U.S. Federal Bureau of Investigation

FCRA Fair Credit Reporting Act

FERC Federal Energy Regulatory Commission

FERPA Family Educational Rights and Privacy Act

FRM Financial Resource Management (process area)

FSTC Financial Services Technology Consortium

GG generic goal

GLBA Gramm-Leach-Bliley Act

GP generic practice

HIPAA Health Insurance Portability and Accountability Act

HRM Human Resource Management (process area)

HVAC heating, ventilation, and air conditioning

ID Identity Management (process area)

IIA Institute of Internal Auditors

IMC Incident Management and Control (process area)

ISACA Information Systems Audit and Control Association

ISO International Organization for Standardization

ISSA Information Systems Security Association

IT information technology

ITIL Information Technology Infrastructure Library

KCI key control indicator

KIM Knowledge and Information Management (process area)

KPI key performance indicator

KRI key risk indicator

MA Measurement and Analysis (process area)

MCSE Microsoft Certified Systems Engineer

MON Monitoring (process area)

OCTAVE Operationally Critical Threat, Asset, and Vulnerability Evaluation

OPD Organizational Process Definition (process area)

OPF Organizational Process Focus (process area)

ORPG operational resilience process group

OTA Organizational Training and Awareness (process area)

OWASP Open Web Applications Security Project

PA process area

PCI DSS Payment Card Industry Data Security Standard

PDA personal digital assistant

PM People Management (process area)

RFID radio frequency identification

RFP request for proposals

RISK Risk Management (process area)

RMA Risk Management Association

RMM Resilience Management Model

RORI return on resilience investment

RPO recovery point objective

RRD Resilience Requirements Development (process area)

RRM Resilience Requirements Management (process area)

RTO recovery time objective

RTSE Resilient Technical Solution Engineering (process area)

SAMM Software Assurance Maturity Model

SC Service Continuity (process area)

SCADA supervisory control and data acquisition

SCAMPI Standard CMMI Appraisal Method for Process Improvement

SEI Software Engineering Institute

SG specific goal

SLA service level agreement

SOX Sarbanes-Oxley Act

SP specific practice

TM Technology Management (process area)

US-CERT United States Computer Emergency Readiness Team

VAR Vulnerability Analysis and Resolution (process area)

APPENDIX E

REFERENCES

URLs are valid as of the publication date of this book.

Alberts 1999 C. J. Alberts, S. G. Behrens, R. D. Pethia, and W. Wilson, *Operationally Critical Threat, Asset, and Vulnerability Evaluation (OCTAVE) Framework, Version 1.0*, Carnegie Mellon University, Software Engineering Institute, Technical Report CMU/SEI-99-TR-017, 1999. [Online]. www.sei.cmu.edu/library/abstracts/reports/99tr017.cfm.

Allen 2004 J. H. Allen et al., *Best in Class Security and Operations Roundtable Report*, Carnegie Mellon University, Software Engineering Institute, Special Report CMU/SEI-2004-SR-002, 2004. Available upon request from info@sei.cmu.edu.

Caralli 2004 R. A. Caralli, *Managing for Enterprise Security*, Carnegie Mellon University, Software Engineering Institute, Technical Note CMU/SEI-2004-TN-046, 2004. [Online]. www.sei.cmu.edu/library/abstracts/reports/04tn046.cfm.

Caralli 2006 R. A. Caralli, *Sustaining Operational Resiliency: A Process Improvement Approach to Security Management*, Carnegie Mellon University, Software Engineering Institute, Technical Note CMU/SEI-2006-TN-009, 2006. [Online]. www.sei.cmu.edu/library/abstracts/reports/06tn009.cfm.

Caralli 2007 R. A. Caralli et al., *Introducing the CERT Resiliency Engineering Framework: Improving the Security and Sustainability Processes*, Carnegie Mellon University, Software Engineering Institute, Technical Report CMU/SEI-2007-TR-009, 2007. [Online]. www.sei.cmu.edu/library/abstracts/reports/07tr009.cfm.

Caralli 2010 R. A. Caralli et al., *CERT Resilience Management Model, Version 1.0*, Carnegie Mellon University, Software Engineering Institute, Technical Report CMU/SEI-2010-TR-012, 2010. [Online]. www.sei.cmu.edu/library/abstracts/reports/10tr012.cfm.

CMMI Product Team 2006 CMMI Product Team, *CMMI for Development, Version 1.2*, Carnegie Mellon University, Software Engineering Institute, Technical Report CMU/SEI-2006-TR-008, 2006. [Online]. www.sei.cmu.edu/library/abstracts/reports/06tr008.cfm.

CMMI Product Team 2009 CMMI Product Team, *CMMI for Services, Version 1.2*, Carnegie Mellon University, Software Engineering Institute, Technical Report CMU/SEI-2009-TR-001, 2009. [Online]. www.sei.cmu.edu/library/abstracts/reports/09tr001.cfm.

CNSS 2009 Committee on National Security Systems, *Instruction No. 4009, National Information Assurance Glossary*, Revised June 2009.

Deming 2000 W. E. Deming, *Out of the Crisis*, MIT Press, 2000. [Online]. http://mitpress.mit.edu/shared/contact/default.asp.

Dougherty 2009 C. Dougherty, K. Sayre, R. C. Seacord, D. Svoboda, and K. Togashi, *Secure Design Patterns*, Carnegie Mellon University, Software Engineering Institute, Technical Report CMU/SEI-2009-TR-010, 2009. [Online]. www.sei.cmu.edu/library/abstracts/reports/09tr010.cfm.

Economist 2007 Economist Intelligence Unit, "Business Resilience: Ensuring Continuity in a Volatile Environment," The Economist Intelligence Unit, 2007.

FFIEC 2004 Federal Financial Institutions Examination Council, *Outsourcing Technology Services* (IT Examination Handbook), 2004. [Online]. www.ffiec.gov/ffiecinfobase/booklets/outsourcing/Outsourcing_Booklet.pdf.

Imai 1986 M. Imai, *Kaizen: The Key to Japan's Competitive Success*, McGraw-Hill/Irwin, 1986.

Manadhata 2010 P. K. Manadhata and J. M. Wing, *Attack Surface Measurement*, 2010. [Online]. www.cs.cmu.edu/~pratyus/as.html.

McFeeley 1996 R. McFeeley, *IDEAL: A Users Guide for Software Process Improvement*, Carnegie Mellon University, Software Engineering Institute, Handbook CMU/SEI-96-HB-001, 1996. [Online]. www.sei.cmu.edu/library/abstracts/reports/96hb001.cfm. See also www.sei.cmu.edu/library/abstracts/presentations/idealmodelported.cfm.

Mead 2010 Nancy Mead et al. *Master of Software Assurance Reference Curriculum*, Carnegie Mellon University, Software Engineering Institute, Technical Report CMU/SEI-2010-TR-005, 2010.

Microsoft 2009 Microsoft Corporation, *Microsoft Security Development Life Cycle, Version 4.1*, Microsoft Corporation, 2009. [Online]. www.microsoft.com/security/sdl/.

REF Team 2008a Resiliency Engineering Framework Team, *CERT Resiliency Engineering Framework v0.95R*, Carnegie Mellon University, Software Engineering Institute, 2008. [Online]. www.cert.org/resilience/rmm_materials.html.

REF Team 2008b Resiliency Engineering Framework Team, *CERT Resiliency Engineering Framework: Code of Practice Crosswalk, Preview Version, v0.95R*, Carnegie Mellon University, Software Engineering Institute, 2008. [Online]. www.cert.org/resilience/rmm_materials.html.

SCAMPI Upgrade Team 2006 SCAMPI Upgrade Team, *Appraisal Requirements for CMMI, Version 1.2 (ARC, V1.2)*, Carnegie Mellon University, Software Engineering Institute, Technical Report CMU/SEI-2006-TR-011, 2006. [Online] www.sei.cmu.edu/library/abstracts/reports/06tr011.cfm. See also www.sei.cmu.edu/cmmi/tools/appraisals/materials.cfm.

van Opstal 2007 D. van Opstal, *The Resilient Economy: Integrating Competitiveness and Security*, Council on Competitiveness, Washington, DC, 2007. [Online]. http://compete.org.

Westby 2008 J. R. Westby and R. Power, *Governance of Enterprise Security: CyLab 2008 Report*, Carnegie Mellon CyLab, 2008. [Online] www.cylab.cmu.edu/outreach/governance.html.

Book Contributors

BOOK AUTHORS

Julia H. Allen
Senior Member of the Technical Staff
Software Engineering Institute

Julia Allen is a senior researcher on the Resilient Enterprise Management team in the CERT Program at the Software Engineering Institute (SEI). Julia's areas of interest include operational resilience, software security and assurance, and resilience measurement and analysis.

Julia is the author of *The CERT Guide to System and Network Security Practices* (Addison-Wesley 2001) and moderator for the CERT Podcast Series: Security for Business Leaders. She is a coauthor of *Software Security Engineering: A Guide for Project Managers* (Addison-Wesley 2008) and a contributing author to the CERT Resilience Management Model.

David W. White
Senior Member of the Technical Staff
Software Engineering Institute

David White is a senior member of the technical staff on the Resilient Enterprise Management Team in the CERT Program at the Software Engineering Institute (SEI). David has served as product manager and a core member of the CERT-RMM development team since 2006. He has also led numerous projects to assist organizations with their adoption and use of the model, including pilot CERT-RMM appraisal efforts. David is an instructor for the Introduction to the CERT-RMM course and a lead appraiser for the CERT-RMM capability appraisal method. David is also the project manager for the SEI Smart Grid Maturity Model, a management tool that an electric power utility can use to evaluate, guide, and improve its smart grid transformation project. David has bachelor's and master's degrees in engineering from Carnegie Mellon University.

Richard A. Caralli
Technical Manager
Software Engineering Institute

Richard Caralli is the technical manager of the Resilient Enterprise Management Team in the CERT Program at the Software Engineering Institute (SEI). Richard's areas of interest include information assurance risk management, critical infrastructure protection, resilience process improvement, and resilience measurement and analysis. In addition to being the lead architect of the CERT Resilience Management Model, Richard has developed several information assurance risk assessment methods at the SEI, including the OCTAVE Allegro method, and has taught extensively on information security management topics. Prior to joining the SEI, Richard spent more than twenty-five years in information technology positions in industry, primarily in IT auditing. Richard received his bachelor's degree in accounting from St. Vincent College and an MBA from Duquesne University.

INDEX

A

abuse/misuse case, 965, 976
access acknowledgement, 965
access control policy, 965
access controls. *See also* Access Management (AM), 965
  establishing identity community, 452–453
  for information assets, 525–526
  modification management and, 527–528
  overview of, 150–151
  for technology assets, 882–883
  for trusted access. *See* Identity Management (IM)
Access Management (AM)
  achieve specific goals, 161
  assign responsibility for, 165–166
  collect improvement information, 173–174
  correct inconsistencies, 159–160
  defined, 965
  enable access, 152–155
  establish defined process for, 173
  establish process governance, 161–162
  FISMA compliance, 957
  identify and involve relevant stakeholders, 168–169
  insider threats and, 964
  introductory notes, 149–151
  manage and control access, 151–152
  manage changes to access privileges, 155–157
  manage work product configurations, 168
  monitor and control the process, 169–171
  monitoring needs of, 586
  objectively evaluate adherence, 172
  as Operations process area, 57
  periodic review of access privileges, 157–159
  plan the process, 163
  provide resources for, 163–165
  purpose, 149
  related process areas, 151
  review status with higher-level managers, 172
  summary of specific goals and practices, 151
  train people for, 167
access privileges
  assign on basis of identity, 451
  correct inconsistencies in, 159–160
  defined, 965
  deprovisioning identity profiles and, 459–460
  granting, 152–155
  to human resources documents, 440–441
  identify invalid identities, 456–457
  identity management linked to, 449
  manage and control access with, 151–152
  manage changes to access, 155–157
  manage changes to employment status, 430–431
  manage involuntary termination, 432
  overview of, 149–151
  periodic review of, 157–159
access requests
  defined, 966
  enabling, 152
acculturation, 966
achieve specific goals, generic goals and practices, 945
acronyms, used in this book, 989–992
acting phase, process improvement, 82–83
action plans
  for conflict mitigation, 755
  implementing process action plans, 636
  for organizational processes, 634–635
adaptive maintenance
  defined, 966
  of environmental conditions, 285
adherence, objective evaluation of
  Access Management, 172
  Asset Definition and Management, 144–145
  Communications, 206
  Compliance, 238
  Controls Management, 267–268
  Enterprise Focus, 336–337
  Environmental Control, 303
  External Dependencies Management, 377–378
  Financial Resource Management, 408
  generic goals and practices, 953
  Human Resource Management, 444
  Identity Management, 470–471
  Incident Management and Control, 508–509
  Knowledge and Information Management, 546
  Measurement and Analysis, 574–575
  Monitoring, 603
  Organizational Process Definition, 626–627
  Organizational Process Focus, 651
  Organizational Training and Awareness, 682–683
  People Management, 713
  Resilience Requirements Development, 767
  Resilience Requirements Management, 789–790
  Resilient Technical Solution Engineering, 826–827
  Risk Management, 743–744
  Service Continuity, 864–865

1001

adherence, objective evaluation of (*contd.*)
  Technology Management, 911–912
  Vulnerability Analysis and Resolution, 939
ADM. *See* Asset Definition and Management (ADM)
administrative (management) controls
  defined, 966
  at enterprise/service/asset level, 248–250
  for facility assets, 277–278
  for information assets, 519–521
  overview of, 246
  for technology assets, 876–878
agreements
  confidentiality, 429–430
  employment, 420–422
  with external entities, 360–362, 370
  legal, 966
  service level agreements (SLAs), 985
Allen, Julia H., 104–105, 115, 999, xxiii–xxiv
AM. *See* Access Management (AM)
amplifications, process area, 47–48
analysis
  of Compliance obligations, 217–218
  of controls, 250–253
  cost and performance analysis in budgeting, 393–394
  measurement and. *See* Measurement and Analysis (MA)
  of monitoring requirements, 585–587
  of resilience requirements, 755
  risk analysis, 983
  root-cause analysis, 494, 984
  of vulnerabilities. *See* Vulnerability Analysis and Resolution (VAR)
analysis, in incident management
  analyze and triage events, 482–483
  to support response, 485–486
appraisal
  CAM (Capability Appraisal Method), CERT-RMM, 92–94
  capability appraisal in evaluation of adherence, 953
  capability dimension used for, 68
  of organizational processes, 632–633
  scope, 93–94, 966
architecture
  guidelines for resilient software and systems, 801–802
  interoperability standards, 898
  process architecture, 610, 980
area of impact
  business impact analysis, 892
  defined, 966
  limiting organizational impact of incidents, 488–490
assembly guidelines, for Resilient Technical Solution Engineering, 805–807
assessment
  of awareness program, 662–663
  of communications, 192–194
  of controls, 253–257
  of facility asset risks, 280–281
  of information asset risks, 522
  of performance, 425–426
  of risks due to external dependencies, 350–351
  of staff risks, 691–692
  of technology risks, 879–880
  of training program, 670–671
asset custodian. *See* custodians, asset
Asset Definition and Management (ADM)
  achieve specific goals, 134
  assign responsibility, 138–139
  Cloud Computing and, 961
  collect improvement information, 146–147
  defined, 135, 966
  develop resilient software across life cycle with, 107
  as Engineering process area, 56
  establish common understanding of assets, 126–128
  establish defined process, 145–146
  establish organizational assets, 123–124
  establish ownership and custodianship, 128–130
  establish process governance, 135–136
  establish relationship between assets and services, 130–131
  FISMA compliance, 958
  identify and involve stakeholders, 141–142
  introductory notes, 121–122
  inventory assets, 124–126
  manage assets, 132–134
  manage work product configurations, 141
  monitor and control process, 142–144
  objectively evaluate adherence, 144–145
  plan process, 136–137
  provide resources, 137–138
  purpose of, 121
  related process areas, 122–123
  summary of specific goals and practices, 123
  train people for, 140
asset disposition, 966
asset inventory
  creating, 124–126
  defined, 967
  maintaining changes to assets, 133–134
  managing changes to employment status, 430–431
asset life cycle, 37, 794, 967
Asset Management, Engineering, 56
asset owner, 967
asset profile, 967
Asset Resilience Management, Operations, 57
asset-level controls, 248–250
asset-level resilience requirements
  analyze, 755
  defined, 967
  establish, 752–753
  overview of, 748–749
  validate, 756
asset-level risks
  identifying, 723–725
  review and adjust strategies for, 732
assets. *See also* Asset Definition and Management (ADM)
  alternate locations for organizational process, 95–96
  concept of, 30–33
  define required functionality of, 754–755
  defined, 966
  establishing improvement objective with asset scope, 89–90
  facility, establishing resilience-focused, 275
  facility, prioritization of, 273–274
  identifying vulnerabilities, 917–918
  life-cycle, 37, 794, 967
  managing changes to employment status, 430
  objective views for. *See* objective views, for assets
  operational risk as potential impact on, 25–26
  protecting and sustaining, 35–36
  relationships among services, business process and, 27–28
  resilience requirements, 773–774
  resilience requirements for, 33–35
  risks of external entities and, 342
  stress of managing intangible, 22
  traceability of resilience requirements and, 777
assets, technology
  access controls, 882–883
  assign resilience requirements, 875–876
  establish and implement controls, 876–878
  establish resilience-focused, 873–874
  identify and assess risks, 879–880

Index

maintain, 894–895
manage availability of, 890–891
manage capacity of, 895–897
manage integrity of, 881–882
manage interoperability of, 897–899
manage risks, 878–879
mitigate risks, 880–881
perform change management, 887–888
perform configuration management, 883–887
perform release management, 889–890
protect, 874–875
sustain, 891–894
assign responsibility, generic goals and practices, 948–949
assurance case, 967
Assurance for CMMI PRM (Process Reference Model), 109–110
attack pattern, 967
attack surface, 967
attributes, critical attributes of process elements, 609
audits
   for configuration management, 887
   discovery of vulnerabilities, 921
   manage external dependencies, 362
   in objective evaluation of adherence, 953
   perform resilience oversight, 324–325
   for process-compliance, 639
   review enterprise focus plan, 337
   of technology assets, 883–884
authority, assigning
   Access Management, 165–166
   Asset Definition and Management, 138–139
   Communications, 199–200
   Compliance, 231–232
   Controls Management, 261–262
   Enterprise Focus, 330–331
   Environmental Control, 296–297
   External Dependency Management, 370–371
   Financial Resource Management, 402–403
   generic goals and practices, 949
   Human Resource Management, 437–438
   Identity Management, 464–465
   Incident Management and Control, 501–502
   Knowledge and Information Management, 539
   Measurement and Analysis, 569
   Organizational Process Definition, 621
   Organizational Process Focus, 645–646
   Organizational Training and Awareness, 675
   People Management, 706–707
   Resilience Requirements Development, 760–761
   Resilience Requirements Management, 782–783
   Resilient Technical Solution Engineering, 819
   Risk Management, 738
   Service Continuity, 858
   Technology Management, 904–905
   Vulnerability Analysis and Resolution, 933
availability
   attributes of information assets, 514
   defined, 967
   Knowledge and Information Management and, 513
   of measurement information, 564
availability, of information assets
   document organizational and intellectual knowledge of staff, 532–533
   duplication and retention, 531–532
   overview of, 530–531
availability, of staff
   establish redundancy for vital staff, 694–695
   manage, 693–694
   perform succession planning, 695–697
   plan for return-to-work following disruptive events, 700–701
   plan to support staff during disruptive events, 698–700
   prepare for redeployment, 697–698
availability, of technology assets
   maintain technology assets, 894–895
   manage technology capacity, 895–897
   manage technology interoperability, 897–899
   overview of, 890–891
   sustain technology assets, 891–894
awareness activity, 967
awareness materials, 659–660
awareness plan, 657–658
awareness program. *See also* Organizational Training and Awareness (OTA)
   assess effectiveness of, 662–663
   defined, 967
   establish delivery capability, 658–660
   establish needs, 655–657
   establish plan, 657–658
   overview of, 655
   perform activities, 660–661
   records of, 661–662
   waiver. *See* waiver

B

back up, of information assets, 531–532
base measures
   data collection and, 561–562
   defined, 967
   specify, 556
baseline competencies
   comparing skills inventory to, 416
   establishment of, 414–415
baseline verification criteria, acquisition of staff, 419
baselines
   baseline configuration item, 968
   for change management, 887–888
   for configuration management, 887
   identifying and assessing risks, 522
   resilience requirements, 776
   for technology assets, 884
BES (Bulk Electric System), 101–102
BIC-SORT (Best in Class Security and Operations Roundtable), 10–11
BRM (business resilience management), 110–115
budgeting
   benefits of CERT-RMM, 6
   commit funds for operational resilience management, 383–384
   establish financial commitment, 382–383
   establish resilience budgets, 388–389
   establish structure to support financial management, 384–386
   fund resilience activities, 390–391
   perform cost and performance analysis, 393–394
   resolve funding gaps, 388–389
bugs, availability of technology assets and, 891
builds, release management and, 889–890
Bulk Electric System (BES), 101–102
business case
   for adoption of CERT-RMM processes, 81
   commit funds for operational resilience management, 383–384
   for convergence of operational risk activities, 24–25
   fund operational resilience management, 318–319

business continuity plans. *See also* service continuity plans, 839
business impact analysis, availability of technology assets and, 892
business processes
  concept of, 29–30
  defined, 968
  fueled by assets, 30–33
  relationships among services, assets and, 27–28
business requirements. *See also* resilience requirements, 968
business resilience, downtime tolerance and, xvi
business resilience management (BRM), 110–115

C

CAM (Capability Appraisal Method), CERT-RMM, 92–94
capability appraisal, in objective evaluation of adherence, 953
Capability Appraisal Method (CAM), CERT-RMM, 92–94
capability dimension, CERT-RMM
  defined, 68
  understanding capability levels, 68–69
capability dimension, CMMI, 19
capability levels
  connecting to process institutionalization, 69–73
  considerations when establishing targets, 84–85
  defined, 968
  for generic goals and practices, 73
  overlaying ratings on targeted improvement profile, 93–94
  targeted improvement profile, 91–92
  targets for establishing improvement objectives, 90–91
  understanding, 68–69
Capability Maturity Model Integration. *See* CMMI (Capability Maturity Model Integration)
capacity, of technology assets, 895–897
capacity planning, 896, 898
Caralli, Richard A., 1000, xxiii
catalogs
  of external dependencies, 344–347
  of items in process asset library, 614
categories
  of information assets, 517–518, 975
  process areas by, 41–42
  of process components, 42–44
  of risk, 351, 719–720, 727
CERT Resiliency Engineering Framework: Code of Practices

Crosswalk, Preview Version, v0.95R (REF Team 2008b), 13
CERT Resiliency Engineering Framework, v0.95R (REF Team 2008a), 12
certification training, Communications, 201
CERT-RMM (CERT Resilience Management Model)
  audience for, xviii
  benefits to organizations, 5–6
  CMMI models and, 15–18
  CMMI vs., 18–19
  evolution of, 9–12
  influences on, 12–15
  introduction to, xvii
  need for, 3–4
  official release of v1.1, 12
  overview of, 7–8
  process improvement and CMMI models influencing, 8–9
  as process improvement model, 2–3
  purpose of, xvii–xviii
CERT-RMM concepts
  adapting terminology and, 39
  convergence, 23–25
  disruption and stress, 21–23
  elements of operational resilience management, 27–39
  operational resilience management, 25–27
CERT-RMM uses
  for business resilience, 110–115
  diagnosing with, 92–95
  examples, 78–80
  measuring operational resilience, 115–118
  model-based process improvement with, 80–83
  overview of, 77
  planning improvements with, 95–97
  setting and communicating objectives. *See* objectives, setting and communicating
  for software assurance, 104–110
  for utility sector, 99–104
change criteria
  for asset management, 132–133
  for service continuity tests, 852
change management
  for configuration settings, 887
  defined, 968
  for external dependencies, 362
  for identity community, 455–456
  for resilience requirements, 775–776
  for service continuity tests, 852–853
  for technology assets, 887–888
  for work product configurations, 950

channels, communications
  establish and maintain infrastructure for, 190–191
  identify, 188–190
checks, integrity, 562
classes, formal capability appraisal, 92–94
closing incidents, 492–493
Cloud Computing, targeted improvement roadmap for, 961–963
CMMI (Capability Maturity Model Integration)
  CERT-RMM generic goals and practices vs., 73
  equivalent CERT-RMM process areas, 15–18
  evolution of CERT-RMM and, 12–15
  process areas influencing CERT-RMM RTSE, 108, 795
  using CERT-RMM without familiarity with, 13
  why CERT-RMM is not, 18–19
CMMI-ACQ (CMMI for Acquisition) model
  defined, 15
  equivalent CERT-RMM process areas, 17–18
  influencing CERT-RMM, 13
CMMI-DEV (CMMI for Development) model
  defined, 15
  equivalent CERT-RMM process areas, 17–18
  focus of process improvement in, 15
  influencing CERT-RMM, 13
CMMI-SVC (CMMI for Services) model
  defined, 15
  equivalent CERT-RMM process areas, 16–18
  influencing CERT-RMM, 13
codes of practice
  convergence vs., 25
  relationship between CERT-RMM process areas and other, 12–13
coding guidelines, for resilient software and systems, 803
collect improvement information. *See* improvement information, collecting
co-location, 968
commitment
  establish financial commitment, 382–383
  of funds to operational resilience management, 383–384
  to incident management plan, 477
  to resilience requirements, 774–775
  to service continuity plans, 834–835

Index

communication
  of awareness activities, 660
  of changes to resilience requirements, 776
  guidelines and standards, 181–183
  identify relevant stakeholders, 177–179
  identify requirements for, 179–181
  in incident management, 490–492
  in incident response and recovery, 487–488
  measure and assess performance using, 425–426
  of measurement results, 564–565
  of measures, 557
  of objectives. *See* objectives, setting and communicating
  preparing for, 177
  process lessons learned and, 639–640
  to stakeholders, 951
  to stakeholders regarding incidents, 489
  of vulnerability analysis and resolution strategy, 919
communication program
  assessing effectiveness of, 192–194
  assigning staff to, 186–188
  establishing, 185–186
  improving, 194–195
Communications (COMM)
  achieve specific goals, 195
  assign responsibility for, 199–200
  collect improvement information, 207–208
  defined, 968
  deliver, 188–191
  Enterprise Management, 54–55
  establish and maintain plan for, 197–198
  establish defined process, 207
  establish guidelines and standards, 181–183
  establish plan, 183–184
  establish process governance, 196–197
  establish program, 185–186
  identify and assign plan staff, 186–188
  identify and involve relevant stakeholders, 202–203
  identify relevant stakeholders, 177–179
  identify requirements, 179–181
  improve, 191–195
  introductory notes, 175–176
  manage work product configurations, 202
  monitor and control the process, 203–205
  objectively evaluate adherence, 206
  plan the process, 197–198
  prepare for, 177
  prepare for management of, 183
  provide resources for, 198–199
  purpose of, 175
  related process areas, 176
  relationships driving threat/incident management, 58
  review status with higher-level managers, 206
  summary of specific goals and practices, 176
  train people for, 200–201
communications stakeholders, 968
comparison, using CERT-RMM as basis for, 78–79
compensating controls, 247
competitive differentiators, resilience management as, xvi
complexity, operational risk of, 22
compliance
  collection and preservation of evidence and, 482
  converting compliance activities into improvement activities, 6
  defined, 968
  developing program for, 212–214
  evaluating adherence to. *See* adherence, objective evaluation of
  performing resilience oversight, 324
Compliance (COMP)
  achieve specific goals, 227
  analyze obligations for, 217–218
  assign responsibility for, 231–232
  collect and validate compliance data, 219–225
  collect improvement information, 239–240
  defined, 968
  demonstrate extent of satisfaction of obligations, 221–223
  establish defined process, 239
  establish guidelines and standards, 214
  establish obligations for, 215–217
  establish ownership for meeting obligations, 218–219
  establish plan for, 211–212
  establish process governance, 227–228
  establish program for, 212–214
  identify and involve relevant stakeholders, 234–236
  introductory notes, 209–210
  manage work product configurations, 234
  monitor activities of, 225–226
  monitor and control the process, 236–237
  objectively evaluate adherence, 238
  plan the process, 229
  prepare for compliance management, 210–211
  provide resources for, 229–231
  purpose of, 209
  related process areas, 210
  remediate areas of non-compliance, 223–225
  review status with higher-level managers, 238
  summary of specific goals and practices, 210
  train people for, 232–233
compliance knowledgebase, 969
compliance obligations, 969
compliance office, defining and installing, 212
components, model
  defined, 981
  expected components, 43–44, 48, 972
  informative component, 43–44, 48, 975
  numbering scheme, 47–49
  process area component categories, 42–44
  process area component descriptions, 44–47
  process areas and their categories, 41–42
  required components, 43–44, 48, 981
  typographical and structural conventions, 49–51
computer security incident response team (CSIRT), 476
conditions, 969
confidentiality
  access controls and, 525–526
  agreements, 429–430
  attributes of information assets, 514
  defined, 969
  disposal management, 526–527
  encrypt high-value information, 524–525
  Knowledge and Information Management process area and, 513
  of measurement information, 564
  overview of, 523–524
configuration items, 969
configuration management
  defined, 969
  for information assets, 529
  for technology assets, 883–887
  work product configurations and, 950
conflict resolution
  identify and resolve conflicts in service continuity plans, 846
  mitigation action plans, 755

consistency vs. flexibility, 611
constellation, 969
containers
  defined, 969
  managing information asset risk in, 521
contingency plans. *See* service continuity plans
continuity of operations. *See also* Service Continuity (SC), 969
continuous representation, of CERT-RMM structure, 68–69
contracts, with external entities, 360–362
control objectives
  analysis of controls to ensure, 250–252
  assessment process for, 255–257
  defining, 244–246
  establishing controls to meet, 246–248
  identifying and establishing controls, 248–250
  overview of, 244
controls. *See also* monitor and control
  access. *See* access controls
  administrative. *See* administrative (management) controls
  defined, 969–970
  external dependencies management, 361
  for incident management, 506–508
  for information assets, 519–521
  internal, 975
  manage work product configurations and, 950
  revision plan, 732
  for risk mitigation, 732
  for technology assets, 875–878
  for validity and reliability of information assets, 529–530
Controls Management (CTRL)
  achieve specific goals, 257
  analyze controls, 250–253
  assess control effectiveness, 253–257
  assign responsibility for, 261–262
  collect improvement information, 269–270
  define controls, 248–250
  defined, 970
  as Engineering process area, 56
  establish control objectives, 244–246
  establish controls supporting objectives, 246–248
  establish defined process for, 269
  establish process governance, 257–259
  FISMA compliance, 959

  identify and involve relevant stakeholders, 264–265
  insider threats and, 964
  introductory notes, 241–243
  manage work product configurations, 264
  managing changes to protecting and sustaining services and assets, 131
  managing overall internal control system in, 151
  monitor and control process, 265–267
  objectively evaluate adherence, 267–268
  plan process, 259
  provide resources, 259–261
  purpose of, 241
  related process areas, 243
  relationships driving threat/incident management, 58
  review status with higher-level managers, 268
  summary of specific goals and practices, 244
  train people for, 262–263
convergence
  defined, 970
  of operational risk management activities, 23–25
convergence advantage
  of CERT-RMM, 5–6
  defined, 7
coordination communications, 187
corrective measures
  for access privileges, 159–160
  for controls management, 247
  defined, 970
  for enterprise focus, 325–326, 336–337
  for environmental conditions, 285
  for inconsistencies in identity community, 457–459
  monitoring and controlling and, 952–953
  for performance issues, 325–326
cost of resilience, 970
costs. *See also* Financial Resource Management (FRM)
  external dependencies management, 362
  of non-compliance, 222–223
  used to track and document resilience management, 392–393
credentialing, 970
crisis
  defined, 970
  governance, xvi
critical success factors, 970

cross-training, 970
The Crosswalk, 13
cryptography. *See* encryption
CSIRT (computer security incident response team), 476
CTRL. *See* Controls Management (CTRL)
cultural norms, stress of managing globalization risks, 23
curriculum, for training program, 668
custodians
  of access management, 159–160, 168–169
  of asset definition and management, 126–130
  defining, 33
  of environmental control, 296–297
custodians, asset
  conformity to resilience requirements, 778
  defined, 966
  resilience requirements and, 774–775

D

damage control, responding to incidents, 489
dashboard, governance, 324
data analysis. *See also* Measurement and Analysis (MA)
  of measurement data, 562–563
  methods and tools, 559–560
data collection
  collection standards and guidelines, 589–591
  of compliance data, 219–221
  of measurement data, 561–562
  monitoring and, 577–579, 588–589
  of monitoring data, 591–592
  techniques for, 557–559
  vulnerability data collection, 921–922
Data Collection and Logging, Process Management, 58–59
data storage, 563–564
databases
  for change management, 888
  for configuration management, 886
  identify external dependencies, 344–347
  identify vital organizational, 837–839
  incident knowledgebase, 922
  of service continuity plans, 843
Davis, Noopur, 115
defined process
  Access Management, 173
  Asset Definition and Management, 145–146

Communications, 207
Compliance, 239
Controls Management, 269
defined, 970
Enterprise Focus, 337–338
Environmental Control, 304
External Dependencies Management, 378–379
Financial Resource Management, 409
generic goals and practices, 954
Human Resource Management, 445
Identity Management, 471
Incident Management and Control, 510
Knowledge and Information Management, 547–548
Measurement and Analysis, 575–576
Monitoring, 604
Organizational Process Definition, 627–628
Organizational Process Focus, 652
Organizational Training and Awareness, 683
overview of, 72
People Management, 714
Resilience Requirements Development, 768–769
Resilience Requirements Management, 791
Resilient Technical Solution Engineering, 827–828
Risk Management, 744–745
Service Continuity, 865–866
Technology Management, 912–913
Vulnerability Analysis and Resolution, 940
deliver communications
 establish and maintain infrastructure, 190–191
 identify methods and channels, 188–190
 overview of, 188
delivery capability
 for awareness program, 658–660
 for training program, 666–668
Deming, Edward, 80, 82
dependencies
 analyze asset-service, 131
 identify, 837
 manage external. *See* External Dependencies Management (EXD)
 manage on public infrastructure for facilities, 288–289
 manage on public services for facilities, 287
deploy practices, using CERT-RMM as organizing structure for, 79–80

deploy process assets
 incorporate experiences into process assets, 639–641
 monitoring implementation, 639
 overview of, 636–637
 standard processes, 638
deprovisioning identities
 controlling identity management work products, 466–467
 correcting inconsistencies in identity community, 458–459
 defined, 970
 introduction to, 448–449
 involving stakeholders in, 468
 overview of, 459–460
derived measures
 data collection and, 561–562
 data sets for, 563
 defined, 971
 specifying, 556
descriptive statistics, in data analysis, 560
design guidelines, for resilient software and systems, 801–802
detective controls, 247–248
development lifecycle, software and systems, 793
development plans, for resilient technical solutions
 creating, 807–808
 integrating selected guidelines with, 809–810
 monitor execution of, 810–812
 release solutions into production, 812–813
 select and tailor guidelines for, 808–809
diagnosing phase, process improvement
 defined, 82–83
 formal diagnosis using Capability Appraisal Method, 92–94
 informal diagnosis, 94–95
 planning CERT-RMM-based improvements, 95–97
diagnosis of current resilience practices
 formal, using Capability Appraisal Method, 92–94
 informal, 94–95
digital information, stress of managing intangible assets, 22
disciplinary action, for violation of resilience policies, 426–427
disposition (disposal)
 defined, 971
 of information assets, 526–527
dispute resolution, external dependencies management, 362
disruptive events

CERT-RMM control of organizational behavior during, 21–23
identifying staff risks, 691
managing staff availability during, 693
plan for return-to-work following, 700–701
plan to support staff during, 698–700
prepare for redeployment of staff during, 697–698
distribution, of monitoring information, 592–594
DNA, identity's
 defined, 450
 understanding, 447–448
documentation
 in access management, 173–174
 in asset definition and management, 146–147
 of awareness needs, 657
 of changes to process assets, 637
 of changes to resilience requirements, 776
 of commitments to resilience requirements, 774–775
 of commitments to service continuity plans, 834
 of communications, 194, 197, 207–208
 of compliance, 223, 239–240
 of controls management, 245–246, 269–270
 of disciplinary action, 426–427
 of environmental controls, 277, 286–290, 305
 event detection and, 479
 of external dependencies management, 361
 in financial resource management, 388, 392–394, 400
 in human resource management, 419, 422, 435–436
 in identity management, 450–451, 458–459, 462–463
 of improvement information, 955
 of incident analysis, 486
 of incident evidence, 481–482
 incident management plan and, 476
 of inconsistencies in resilience requirements, 778
 of maintenance operations, 895
 of measurement objectives, 555
 post-incident review and, 494
 of return-to-work plan, 700
 of risk measurement criteria, 723
 of scope of vulnerabilities, 917
 of service continuity plans, 840–842

documentation *(contd.)*
    of service continuity tests, 848
    of succession plan, 696
    of support for staff during
        disruptive events, 699
    of training needs, 665
    of vulnerability analysis and
        resolution strategy, 919
downtime
    business resilience and, xvi
    planned, 890, 979
    unplanned, 890, 987
due diligence, performing on candidate
    external entities, 359
duplication, of information assets,
    531–532

E

EC. *See* Environmental Control (EC)
EF. *See* Enterprise Focus (EF)
emergency actions, responding to
    incidents, 489
employment. *See* Human Resource
    Management (HRM)
employment agreements, 420–422
employment status, managing changes to
    manage access to assets, 430–431
    manage impact of position changes,
        428–430
    manage involuntary terminations,
        431–432
    overview of, 427–428
encryption
    cryptographic controls, 970
    of high-value information, 524–525
    policies, 971
Engineering process areas
    ADM. *See* Asset Definition and
        Management (ADM)
    CTRL. *See* Controls Management
        (CTRL)
    defined, 7–8
    model view of, 56
    overview of, 41–43
    RRD. *See* Resilience Requirements
        Development (RRD)
    RRM. *See* Resilience Requirements
        Management (RRM)
    RTSE. *See* Resilient Technical
        Solution Engineering (RTSE)
    SC. *See* Service Continuity (SC)
Enterprise Focus (EF)
    achieve specific goals, 325–326
    assign responsibility for, 330–331
    collect improvement information,
        338–339
    commit funding for operational
        resilience management,
        318–319
    defined, 971

as Engineering process area, 56
establish corrective actions,
    325–326
establish critical success factors,
    310–312
establish defined process, 337–338
establish organizational services,
    312–314
establish process governance,
    327–328
establish resilience as governance
    focus area, 322–323
establish sponsorship, 317
establish strategic objectives,
    309–310
FISMA compliance, 958
identify and involve relevant
    stakeholders, 332–333
identify communications
    requirements with, 180
introductory notes, 307–308
manage work product
    configurations, 332
monitor and control the process,
    333–336
objectively evaluate adherence,
    336–337
perform resilience oversight,
    324–325
plan for operational resilience,
    314–317
plan the process, 328–330
promoting resilience-aware culture,
    319–320
provide resilience oversight,
    321–322
provide resources for, 328–329
purpose of, 307
related process areas, 308
relationships driving threat/incident
    management, 58
review status with higher-level
    managers, 337
summary of specific goals and
    practices, 308
train people for, 331
enterprise level
    monitoring at, 579
    policies, 971
    specifications for external entities,
        353–354
enterprise management, aspects of
    CERT-RMM, 14–15
Enterprise Management process areas
    COMM. *See* Communications
        (COMM)
    COMP. *See* Compliance (COMP)
    defined, 7–8
    EF. *See* Enterprise Focus (EF)
    FRM. *See* Financial Resource
        Management (FRM)

HRM. *See* Human Resource
    Management (HRM)
model view of, 54–55
OTA. *See* Organizational Training
    and Awareness (OTA)
overview of, 41–43
RISK. *See* Risk Management (RISK)
enterprise-level controls
    as administrative controls, 246
    assessing effectiveness of, 253–254
    creating, 248–250
    defined, 242
enterprise-level resilience requirements
    assigning to services, 753–754
    defined, 971
    establishing, 751–752
    identifying, 750
    overview of, 748
entities, creating identities for. *See*
    Identity Management (IM)
Environmental Control (EC)
    achieve specific goals, 290
    assign resilience requirements to
        facility assets, 276–277
    assign responsibility for, 296–297
    Cloud Computing and, 963
    collect improvement information,
        304–305
    control operational environments,
        282–283
    defined, 971
    establish and implement controls,
        277–280
    establish defined process, 304
    establish process governance,
        290–292
    establish resilience-focused facility
        assets, 275
    FISMA compliance, 958
    identify and involve relevant
        stakeholders, 299–300
    introductory notes, 271–272
    maintain environmental conditions,
        285–286
    manage dependencies on public
        infrastructure, 288–289
    manage dependencies on public
        services, 287
    manage facility asset risk, 280–282
    manage work product
        configurations, 298–299
    monitor and control the process,
        300–302
    monitor needs of, 586
    objectively evaluate adherence, 303
    as Operations process area, 57
    perform facility sustainability
        planning, 284–285
    plan for facility retirement, 289–290
    plan the process, 292–293
    prioritize facility assets, 273–274

protect facility assets, 275–276
provide resources for, 293–295
purpose of, 271
related process areas, 272
review status with higher-level managers, 303
summary of specific goals and practices, 272
train people for, 297–298
environments. *See* operational environments
equipment
as critical dimension of organizations, 8–9
service intervals in maintaining, 894–895
errors, availability of technology assets and, 891
escalation. *See* incident escalation
escrow provisions, external dependencies management, 362
establish and maintain, defined, 971
establish defined process. *See* defined process
establish process governance. *See* governance
Establishing and Managing Resilience, Engineering, 56
establishing phase, process improvement, 82–83
evaluation
of external entities, 358–359
form for assessing training effectiveness, 670
using CERT-RMM as basis for, 78–79
event detection
analyzing and triaging events, 482–483
collecting, documenting, and preserving event evidence, 481–482
establishing process for, 478
logging and tracking events, 480–481
monitoring, identifying, and reporting events, 478–479
transitioning from detection to declaration, 484
event logging, in incident management, 480–481
event triage
defined, 971
overview of, 482
events
defined, 971
disruptive. *See* disruptive events
evidence collection, responding to incidents, 489
example blocks, process area
defined, 47–48
typographical and structural conventions, 51

EXD. *See* External Dependencies Management (EXD)
exercises. *See also* test (exercise)
service continuity plans, 971
exit interview process, 429
expected components
defined, 972
overview of, 43–44
summary of, 48
expenditures, optimizing resilience
determine return on investments, 396–397
identify cost recovery opportunities, 397–398
overview of, 394–396
expense requests, funding resilience activities, 391
experience, incorporating into process assets, 639–641
external dependencies, 972
External Dependencies Management (EXD)
achieve specific goals, 365
assign responsibility for, 370–371
Cloud Computing and, 962
collect improvement information, 379–380
defined, 972
develop resilient software across life cycle with, 108
establish defined process, 378–379
establish enterprise specifications for, 353–354
establish formal relationships, 352–353
establish process governance, 366–367
establish resilience specifications for, 355–357
evaluate and select external entities, 358–359
formalize relationships, 360–362
identify and involve relevant stakeholders, 373–374
identify external dependencies, 344–347
identify risks associated with external dependencies, 349–351
introductory notes, 341–343
manage external entity performance, 363–365
manage work product configurations, 373
monitor and control the process, 375–377
objectively evaluate adherence, 377–378
as Operations process area, 57
plan the process, 368
prioritize external dependencies, 348–349

provide resources for, 368–370
purpose of, 341
related process areas, 343
review status with higher-level managers, 378
risk mitigation strategies for external dependencies, 352
summary of specific goals and practices, 344
train people for, 371–372
external entities, 972
external sources, of vulnerabilities, 920

F

facilities. *See also* Asset Definition and Management (ADM) and Environmental Control (EC)
facility assets. *See also* Asset Definition and Management (ADM)
access privileges focusing on, 153
achieve specific goals, 290
assign resilience requirements to, 276–277
assign responsibility for, 296–297
in CERT-RMM, 32
collect improvement information, 304–305
controlling operational environment, 282–283
defined, 972
establish and implement controls for, 277–280
establish process governance for, 290–292
establish resilience-focused, 33–35, 275
identify and assess risk for, 280–281
identify and involve relevant stakeholders, 299–300
life-cycle of, 38
manage work product configurations, 298–299
managing dependencies on public infrastructure for, 288–289
managing dependencies on public services for, 287
monitor and control, 300–302
objective views for, 60–61, 63–64
perform sustainability planning, 284–285
plan for retirement of, 289–290
plan process for, 292–293
prioritization of, 273–274
protect, 35–36, 275–276
provide resources for, 293–295
review status with higher-level managers, 304
risk mitigation strategies for, 281–282
train people, 297–298

Federal Energy Regulatory
    Commission (FERC), 101–102
federations
    correcting inconsistencies in
        identity community, 458
    defined, 447, 972
    of identities, 468
FERC (Federal Energy Regulatory
    Commission), 101–102
financial commitment, establishing
    establish structure to support,
        384–386
    for operational resilience
        management, 383–384
    overview of, 382–383
financial exceptions, in cost and
    performance analysis, 394
Financial Resource Management (FRM)
    account for resilience activities,
        392–394
    achieve specific goals, 398
    assign responsibility for, 402–403
    collect improvement information,
        410
    commit funding for operational
        resilience management,
        383–384
    defined, 972
    Enterprise Management and, 54–55
    establish defined process, 409
    establish financial commitment,
        382–383
    establish process governance,
        398–400
    establish structure to support
        financial management,
        384–386
    fund resilience activities, 390–391
    identify and involve relevant
        stakeholders, 404–406
    introductory notes, 381–382
    manage work product
        configurations, 404
    monitor and control the process,
        406–407
    objectively evaluate adherence, 408
    optimize resilience expenditures
        and investments, 394–398
    perform financial planning,
        386–390
    plan the process, 400
    provide resources for, 400–402
    purpose of, 391
    related process areas, 382
    review status with higher-level
        managers, 409
    summary of specific goals and
        practices, 382
    train people for, 403–404
Financial Services Technology
    Consortium (FTSC), 11

first responders, 972
FISMA compliance, 957–961
flexibility vs. consistency, 611
formal agreements, with external
    entities
    assigning responsibility, 370
    overview of, 360–362
formal relationships, with external
    entities
    establish enterprise specifications,
        353–354
    establish formal agreements,
        360–362
    establish resilience specifications,
        355–357
    evaluate and select external entities,
        358–359
    overview of, 352–353
FRM. See Financial Resource
    Management (FRM)
FTSC (Financial Services Technology
    Consortium), 11
functional monitoring requirements,
    972
funding. See also Financial Resource
    Management (FRM)
    establishing baseline competencies
        to determine, 414
    operational resilience management,
        316–319
    resource provision and, 948
funding, for process areas
    Access Management, 164
    Asset Definition and Management,
        138
    Communications, 199
    Compliance, 213, 230
    Controls Management, 260
    Enterprise Focus, 329
    Environmental Control, 294
    External Dependency Management,
        369
    Human Resource Management, 437
    Identity Management, 463
    Incident Management and
        Control, 500
    Knowledge and Information
        Management, 538
    Measurement and Analysis, 568
    Monitoring, 597
    Organizational Process Definition,
        620
    Organizational Process Definition
        and, 618
    Organizational Process
        Focus, 644
    Organizational Training and
        Awareness, 675
    People Management, 705
    Resilience Requirements
        Development, 760

Resilience Requirements
    Management, 782
Resilient Technical Solution
    Engineering, 817
Risk Management, 737
Service Continuity, 856
Technology Management, 903
Vulnerability Analysis and
    Resolution, 932
fuzz testing, 972

G

general guidelines, for Resilient
    Technical Solution Engineering,
    798–800
generic goals and practices
    applying, 74
    assign responsibility, 948–949
    capability levels related to, 69–73
    collect improvement information,
        955
    defined, 46–48, 972–973
    elaborations, 74
    establish defined process, 954
    establish process governance, 946
    identify and involve relevant
        stakeholders, 951
    manage work product
        configurations, 950
    monitor and control the process,
        951–953
    objectively evaluate adherence, 953
    perform specific practices, 945
    plan the process, 946–947
    process areas supporting, 74–75
    provide resources, 948
    review status with higher-level
        managers, 953
    tags and numbering scheme for, 49
    train people, 949–950
    typographical and structural
        conventions, 50
    understanding, 73
    using practice-level scope, 88–89
geographical controls
    establishing and managing. See
        Environmental Control (EC)
    for operational environment, 283
geographical dispersion, 973
geopolitical shifts, stress of managing
    globalization risks, 23
global economy, stress of managing
    operational risk in, 22–23
globalization, operational resilience
    management and, 2
goals. See also objectives
    establishing resilience through goals
        and objectives, 423–424
    generic. See generic goals and
        practices

measure performance against goals and objectives, 425–426
governance, process
Access Management, 161–162
Asset Definition and Management, 135–136
Communications, 196–197
Compliance, 212, 227–228
Controls Management, 241, 257–259
defined, 973
Enterprise Focus, 327–328
Environmental Control, 290–292
establish corrective actions, 325–326
establish resilience as focus area of, 322–323
External Dependencies Management, 366–367
Financial Resource Management, 398–400
generic goals and practices, 946
Human Resource Management, 433–435
Identity Management, 460–462
Incident Management and Control, 497–498
Knowledge and Information Management, 534–536
Measurement and Analysis, 566–567
Monitoring, 594–595
Organizational Process Definition, 617–618
Organizational Process Focus, 641–643
Organizational Training and Awareness, 671–673
People Management (PM), 701–703
perform resilience oversight, 323–325
provide resilience oversight, 321–322
Resilience Requirements Development, 757–758
Resilience Requirements Management, 779–780
Resilient Technical Solution Engineering, 814–815
risk and crisis oversight and, xvi
Risk Management, 734–735
Service Continuity, 853–855
Technology Management, 899–901
Vulnerability Analysis and Resolution, 929–930
grid modernization, electric power industry, 103–104
guidance, using CERT-RMM as basis for, 78–79
guidelines. *See also* standards
for configuration management, 886
establish tailoring criteria and, 610–612
for handling information assets, 517
for integrated teams, 615–616
for monitoring, 589–591
for resilience, 320–321
for service continuity, 835
guidelines, for resilient technical solutions
identify architecture and design guidelines, 801–802
identify assembly and integration guidelines, 805–807
identify general guidelines, 798–800
identify implementation guidelines, 802–805
identify requirements guidelines, 800–801
integrating selected guidelines with software and system development process, 809–810
select and tailor, 808–809

H

hardware, integrity of, 882
hazards, service continuity planning and, 832
higher-level managers, reviewing with
Access Management, 172
Asset Definition and Management, 145
Communications, 206
Compliance, 238
Controls Management, 268–269
Enterprise Focus, 337
Environmental Control, 304
External Dependencies Management, 378
Financial Resource Management, 409
generic goals and practices, 953
Human Resource Management, 445
Identity Management, 471
Incident Management and Control, 509
Knowledge and Information Management, 547
Measurement and Analysis, 575
Monitoring, 603
Organizational Process Definition, 627
Organizational Process Focus, 651
Organizational Training and Awareness, 683
People Management (PM), 714
Resilience Requirements Development, 768
Resilience Requirements Management, 790–791
Resilient Technical Solution Engineering, 827
Risk Management, 744
Service Continuity, 865
Technology Management, 912
Vulnerability Analysis and Resolution, 940
Highfill, Darren, 99–100
high-value assets
defined, 973
metrics for, 893
high-value information, encryption of, 524–525
high-value services
defined, 973
as focus of CERT-RMM, 29
identify and prioritize, 835–836
identify internal and external dependencies and interdependencies, 837
identify vital organizational records and databases, 837–839
prioritization of technology assets related to, 871–872
resilience requirements for, 33–35
Human Resource Management (HRM)
achieve specific goals, 433
address skill deficiencies, 416–418
assign responsibility for, 437–438
collect improvement information, 445–446
defined, 973
Enterprise Management and, 54–55
establish baseline competencies, 414–415
establish defined process, 445
establish disciplinary process, 426–427
establish process governance, 433–435
establish resilience as job responsibility, 423
establish resilience performance goals/objectives, 423–425
establish resource needs, 413
identify and involve relevant stakeholders, 441–442
insider threats and, 963–964
introductory notes, 411–412
inventory skills and identify gaps, 415–416
manage changes to employment status, 412, 427–432
manage staff acquisition, 418–422
manage staff performance. *See* performance, in staff management
manage work product configurations, 440–441
measure and assess performance, 425–426

Human Resource Management (HRM) (contd.)
    monitor and control the process, 442–444
    objectively evaluate adherence, 444
    plan the process, 435–436
    provide resources for, 436–437
    purpose of, 411
    related process areas, 412
    review status with higher-level managers, 445
    summary of specific goals and practices, 413
    train people for, 439–440

I

icons, process area, 42–43
IDEAL model, 82–83
identify and involve relevant stakeholders. *See* stakeholders, identify and involve
identities
    assign roles to, 453–454
    correct inconsistencies in, 457–459
    creating, 450–451
    defined, 973
    deprovision, 459–460
    establish identity community, 452–453
    manage, 454
    monitor and manage changes to, 455–456
    overview of, 449–450
    periodically review/maintain, 456–457
identity community
    assigning roles to identities, 453–454
    correcting inconsistencies in, 457–459
    defined, 973
    establishing, 452–453
    monitoring and managing changes in, 455–456
    periodic review of, 456–457
Identity Management (IM). *See also* Access Management (AM); Risk Management (RISK)
    achieve specific goals, 460
    assign responsibility for, 464–465
    assign roles to identities, 453–454
    collect improvement information, 471–472
    create identities, 450–451
    defined, 973
    enable access request and approval, 152
    establish defined process, 471
    establish identities, 449–450

establish identity community, 452–453
establish process governance, 460–462
FISMA compliance, 958
identify and involve relevant stakeholders, 467–468
introductory notes, 447–449
manage work product configurations, 466–467
monitor and control the process, 468–470
monitoring needs of, 586
objectively evaluate adherence, 470–471
as Operations process area, 57
plan the process, 462
provide resources for, 462–464
purpose of, 447
related process areas, 449
review status with higher-level managers, 471
specific goals and practices, 449
train people for, 465–466
identity profiles, 973
identity registration, 974
identity repository, 974
IM. *See* Identity Management (IM)
IMC. *See* Incident Management and Control (IMC)
impact valuation, 974
implementation guidelines, for resilient software and systems, 802–805
improvement information, collecting
    Access Management, 173–174
    Asset Definition and Management, 146–147
    Communications, 207–208
    Compliance, 239–240
    Controls Management, 269–270
    Enterprise Focus, 338–339
    Environmental Control, 304–305
    External Dependencies Management, 379–380
    Financial Resource Management, 410
    generic goals and practices, 955
    Human Resource Management, 445–446
    Identity Management, 471–472
    Incident Management and Control, 510–511
    Knowledge and Information Management, 548–549
    Measurement and Analysis, 576
    Monitoring, 604–605
    Organizational Process Definition, 628

Organizational Process Focus, 652
Organizational Training and Awareness, 684
People Management, 714–715
for process areas, 202
Resilience Requirements Development, 769
Resilience Requirements Management, 791–792
Resilient Technical Solution Engineering, 828–829
Risk Management, 745–746
Service Continuity, 866–867
Technology Management, 913–914
Vulnerability Analysis and Resolution, 940–941
improvement mind-set, benefits of CERT-RMM, 6
inappropriate behavior, identifying staff risks, 691
incident closure, 492–493, 974
incident declaration
    analyzing incidents, 485–486
    criteria for, 484–485
    to support response, 483–484
incident escalation
    communications and, 187
    defined, 974
    Incident Management and Control, 487–488
incident life cycle, 974
Incident Management and Control (IMC)
    achieve specific goals, 497
    analyze and triage events, 482–483
    analyze incidents, 485–486
    assign responsibility for, 501–502
    assign staff for, 477–478
    close incidents, 492–493
    collect, document, and preserve event evidence, 481–482
    collect improvement information, 510–511
    communicate incidents, 490–492
    declare events for response planning, 483–484
    define criteria for event declaration, 484–485
    defined, 974
    detect and report events, 478–479
    escalate incidents, 487–488
    establish defined process, 510
    establish process for, 475–476
    establish process governance, 497–498
    FISMA compliance, 959
    identify and involve relevant stakeholders, 504–506
    identify communications requirements, 180

integrate incident handling with
  problem management,
  494–495
introductory notes, 473–475
learn from incidents, 493
log and track events, 480–481
manage work product
  configurations, 504
monitor and control the process,
  506–508
monitoring needs of, 586
objectively evaluate adherence,
  508–509
plan for, 476–477
plan the process, 498–499
post-incident review, 493–494
provide resources for, 499–500
purpose of, 473
related process areas, 475
relationships driving threat/incident
  management, 57–58
respond to/ recover from incidents,
  487–490
review status with higher-level
  managers, 509
summary of specific goals and
  practices, 475
train people, 502–503
translate lessons into strategy,
  495–496
incident owner, 974
incident response
  closing incidents, 492–493
  communication in, 490–492
  defined, 974
  developing and implementing,
    488–490
  escalation of incidents, 487–488
  establishing process for, 487
incident stakeholder, 974
incidents, 974
incomplete process, capability level 0, 70
informal diagnosis, of current
  resilience practices, 94–95
information. *See also* Asset Definition
    and Management (ADM) and
    Knowledge and Information
    Management (KIM)
  access privileges focusing on, 153
  as asset in CERT-RMM, 31–32
  establishing compliance
    knowledgebase or repository,
    220–221
  identifying external dependencies,
    344–347
  life-cycle of, 37
  objective views for, 59, 61
  processing cycle, 529–530
  protecting and sustaining, 35–36
  resilience requirements for, 33–35

information asset baseline, 974
information asset categorization, 975
information asset container, 975
information asset owner, 975
information assets
  defining. *See* Asset Definition and
    Management (ADM)
  definition of, 974
  managing. *See* Knowledge and
    Information Management
    (KIM)
information technology. *See* IT
  (information technology)
informative component
  defined, 975
  overview of, 43–44
  summary of, 48
infrastructure
  for communications, 190–191
  managing dependencies on public,
    288–289
  for monitoring, 588–589
initialisms, acronyms used in this
  book, 989–992
initiating phase, process improvement.
  See also objectives, setting and
    communicating, 82
insider threats, 963
inspections, product release and,
  812–813
institutional knowledge. *See*
  organizational and intellectual
  knowledge
institutionalization
  capability levels and, 68–69
  CERT-RMM as organizing structure
    for, 80
  CERT-RMM generic goals and
    practices, 73–74
  connecting capability levels to,
    69–73
  defined, 975
  defined process. *See* defined process
  managed process. *See* managed
    process
  overview of, 67
  process areas supporting generic
    practices, 74–75
instructors
  for awareness program, 659–660
  for training program, 667
intangible assets, stress of managing, 22
integrated teams, establish rules and
  guidelines for, 615–616
integration guidelines, for Resilient
  Technical Solution Engineering,
  805–807
integrity
  checks, 221, 562
  data analysis and, 561–562

defined, 975
Knowledge and Information
  Management and, 513
of measurement information, 564
integrity, of technology assets
  access controls, 882–883
  overview of, 881–882
  perform change management,
    887–888
  perform configuration management,
    883–887
  perform release management,
    889–890
integrity of information assets
  attributes, 514
  configuration management, 529
  modification management, 527–528
  overview of, 527
  validity and reliability, 529–530
intellectual property
  contrasted with institutional
    knowledge, 532
  defined, 975
  protecting, 513
interdependencies, identify internal
  and external dependencies, 837
internal communications. *See also*
  Communications (COMM),
  186–187
internal control system
  assessing effectiveness of,
    253–254
  defined, 975
  implementing for facility assets,
    277–280
  overview of, 241–242
interoperability
  defined, 986
  of technology assets, 897–899
interviews, to assess effectiveness of
  awareness program, 662
*Introducing the CERT Resiliency
  Engineering Framework:
  Improving the Security and
  Sustainability Processes* (Caralli
  2007), 12
inventory. *See also* repositories
  of assets, 124–125
  of compliance obligations,
    216–217
  maintaining changes to assets and,
    133–134
  of service continuity plans, 843
  of skills, 415–416, 985
  of staff, 688
  of stored data, 564
investigation reports, in establishing
  disciplinary process, 427
investments, resilience
  determining return on, 396–397

1014 Index

investments, resilience (contd.)
  identify cost recovery opportunities, 397–398
  optimize resilience expenditures and, 394–396
involuntary termination of employment
  managing, 431–432
  overview of, 428
IT (information technology)
  evolution of CERT-RMM, 9–12
  managing operational risk for, 23
  as traditional focus of operational risk management, 8–9

J

job descriptions
  creating to reflect base competencies, 415
  developing requisitions for unfilled positions, 417–418
  establishing terms and conditions of employment, 420–422
  incident management plan and, 477
  inserting resilience obligations in, 423
  updating to incorporate missing skills, 417
job-specific verification criteria, 419–420

K

key control indicators (KCIs)
  defined, 975
  performing resilience oversight, 325
key indicators
  establish corrective actions, 325–326
  perform resilience oversight, 325
key performance indicators (KPIs), 325
key risk indicators (KRIs)
  defined, 975
  performing resilience oversight, 325
Knowledge and Information Management (KIM)
  access controls for information assets, 525–526
  achieve specific goals, 533
  assign responsibility for, 538–539
  availability of information assets, 530–531
  categorize information assets, 517–518
  Cloud Computing and, 963
  collect improvement information, 548–549
  confidentiality and privacy considerations, 523–524

configuration management, 529
controls for information assets, 519–521
defined, 975
disposal management, 526–527
document organizational and intellectual knowledge of staff, 532–533
duplication and retention of information assets, 531–532
encrypt high-value information, 524–525
establish defined process for, 547–548
establish process governance, 534–536
FISMA compliance, 959
identify and assess risks, 522
identify and involve relevant stakeholders, 542–543
integrity management, 527
introductory notes, 513–514
manage work product configurations, 541
mitigate risks, 523
modification management, 527–528
monitor and control the process, 543–545
objectively evaluate adherence, 546
as Operations process area, 57
plan the process, 536
prioritize information assets, 516–517
protect information assets, 518–519
provide resources for, 536–538
purpose of, 513
related process areas, 514–515
resilience requirements for information assets, 519
review status with higher-level managers, 547
risk management and, 521
summary of specific goals and practices, 515
train people for, 540–541
validity and reliability of information assets, 529–530
knowledgebase
  for compliance data, 220
  for incident management, 481

L

labor, funding resilience activities, 391
laws
  documenting events and, 481–482
  external dependencies management, 362
  stress of managing operational risk, 23
layering, of controls, 247

learning
  from incidents and events, 493
  integrating incident handling with problem management, 494–495
  lessons learned and communicated, 639–640
  overview of, 493
  post-incident review, 493–494
  translating lessons into strategy, 495–496
learning phase, process improvement, 82–83
legal issues. See laws
libraries, process asset, 613–614
licensing agreements, with external entities, 360–362
life-cycle
  addressing resilience for software assurance, 104–110
  of assets, 794
  integration of resilience requirements in, 797
  resilience of, 36–39
line of business, 976
Lockheed Martin Corporation, using CERT-RMM, 110–115
logs
  asset modification, 883–884
  configuration management, 887
  Incident Management and Control, 480–481

M

MA. See Measurement and Analysis (MA)
maintenance
  adaptive, 285, 966
  of infrastructure, 190–191
  perfective, 285, 979
  preventive, 285, 979
  of service continuity tests, 851
  of technology assets, 894–895
manage work product configurations. See work product configurations
managed process
  as capability level 2, 70–72
  defined, 976
management
  developing operational resilience plan for, 314–316
  identity. See identity management
  of risks due to external dependencies, 349–350
management, preparing for communications
  establish plan, 183–185
  establish program, 185–186
  identify and plan staff, 186–188
  overview of, 183

management, preparing for compliance
  establish guidelines and standards, 214
  establish plan, 211–212
  establish program, 212–214
  overview of, 210–211
managers
  identifying vital, 689
  process governance and, 946
  review with higher-level. *See* higher-level managers, reviewing with
Managing for Enterprise Security, (Caralli 2004), 11
maturity advantage, of CERT-RMM, 7
maturity models
  CERT-RMM objectives vs., 12
  CERT-RMM vs., 18–19
  characteristics setting CERT-RMM apart from other, 113
  raising bar on business resilience, 111–112
measurement. *See also* improvement information, collecting
  for assessing performance, 425–426
  benefits of CERT-RMM, 5–7
  effectiveness of service continuity plans, 851
  establish corrective actions, 325–326
  establish risk measurement criteria, 722–723
  objectives, 976
  of operational resistance, 115–118
  perform resilience oversight, 324–325
  repository, 612–613
Measurement and Analysis (MA)
  Access Management and, 170–171
  achieve specific goals, 565
  align activities with information needs and objectives, 553
  analysis procedures for, 559–561
  analyze measurement data, 562–563, 640
  assign responsibility for, 569–570
  collect improvement information, 576
  collect measurement data, 561–562
  communicate results, 564–565
  data collection and storage procedures for, 557–559
  defined, 976
  establish defined process for, 575–576
  establish objectives, 553–555
  establish process governance, 566–567
  identify and involve relevant stakeholders, 571–573
  introductory notes, 551–552
  manage work product configurations, 571
  measurement results, 561
  measures for, 556–557
  measuring operational resistance using CERT-RMM, 115–118
  monitor and control the process, 573–574
  monitor asset definition and management process, 142–144
  objectively evaluate adherence, 574–575
  plan the process, 567
  as Process Management, 59
  provide resources for, 567–569
  purpose of, 551
  related process areas, 552
  review status with higher-level managers, 575
  store data and results, 563–564
  summary of specific goals and practices, 552
  train people for, 570–571
measurement results
  analyze data, 562–563
  collect data, 561–562
  communicate, 564–565
  overview of, 561
  store data and results, 563–564
measures
  base measures, 556, 561–562, 967
  classes of commonly used, 612–613
  defined, 976
  derived measures, 556, 561–562, 563, 971
  overview of, 556–557
media, distribution methods and, 593
Mehravari, Dr. Nader, PhD, 109–110
memoranda of agreement, with external entities, 360–362
methods. *See also* tools, techniques, and methods
  controls management, 261
  environmental control, 295
  establishing infrastructure for communications, 190–191
  identify communications, 188–190
metrics. *See also* improvement information, collecting; monitor and control
  capacity planning, 896
  for high-value technology assets, 893
  measure and assess performance with, 425–426
  Measurement and Analysis, 551
  for monitoring process, 602
  for operational resistance, 117–118
performing resilience oversight, 324–325
misuse/abuse case, 976
mitigation
  conflict mitigation plans, 755
  for external dependencies, 352
  for facility assets, 281–282
  implement risk strategies, 731
  risk mitigation plans, 729–731
  of risks, 729
  of staff risks, 692–693
  of technology asset risks, 880–881
model components. *See* components, model
model relationships
  model view. *See* model view
  objective views. *See* objective views, for assets
  overview of, 53–54
model scope
  asset scope, 89–90
  defined, 84, 976
  establishing improvement objective with, 87–88
  practice-level scope, 88–89
  resilience scope, 89–90
  targeted improvement roadmaps, 88
model view
  defined, 54
  Engineering process areas, 56
  Enterprise Management process areas, 54–55
  Operations process areas, 56–57
  Process Management, 57–59
model-based process improvement, using CERT-RMM for, 80–83
modification management, for information assets, 527–528
MON. *See* Monitoring (MON)
monitor and control
  Access Management, 169–171
  Asset Definition and Management, 142–144
  Communications, 203–205
  Compliance, 225–226, 236–237
  controls for information assets, 521
  Controls Management, 265–266
  Enterprise Focus, 333–336
  Environmental Control, 300–302
  event detection and, 478–479
  execution of software and system development plan, 810–812
  External Dependencies Management, 375–377
  Financial Resource Management, 406–407
  generic goals and practices, 951–953
  Human Resource Management, 442–444
  for identity changes, 455–456

monitor and control (contd.)
　　Identity Management, 468–470
　　Incident Management and Control, 506–508
　　Knowledge and Information Management, 543–545
　　Measurement and Analysis, 573–574
　　Monitoring, 601–603
　　Organizational Process Definition, 624–626
　　Organizational Process Focus, 649–650
　　Organizational Training and Awareness, 680–682
　　People Management, 711–713
　　performing resilience oversight, 324–325
　　process implementation and, 639
　　Resilience Requirements Development, 765–766
　　Resilience Requirements Management, 787–789
　　Resilient Technical Solution Engineering, 823–826
　　Risk Management, 741–743
　　risks to information assets, 522
　　Service Continuity, 862–864
　　software and systems, 795
　　Technology Management, 909–911
　　Vulnerability Analysis and Resolution, 937–939
Monitoring (MON)
　　achieve specific goals, 594
　　analyze and prioritize requirements for, 585–587
　　assign responsibility for, 597–598
　　collect and record information, 591–592
　　collect improvement information, 604–605
　　defined, 976
　　develop resilient software across life cycle with, 108
　　distribute information, 592–594
　　establish collection standards and guidelines, 589–591
　　establish defined process, 604
　　establish process governance, 594–595
　　establish requirements for, 583–585
　　establishing/maintaining program for, 578–581
　　establish/maintain infrastructure for, 588–589
　　FISMA compliance, 959
　　identify and involve relevant stakeholders, 581–582, 600–601
　　introductory notes, 577–578

manage work product configurations, 599–600
monitor and the control process, 601–603
objectively evaluate adherence, 603
performance of, 587–588
plan the process, 596
as Process Management, 59
provide resources for, 596–597
purpose of, 577
related process areas, 578
relationships driving resilience at enterprise level, 55
relationships driving threat/incident management, 58
review status with higher-level managers, 603
summary of specific goals and practices, 578
train people for, 598–599
monitoring infrastructure, 976
monitoring requirements, 976
monitoring stakeholder, 976
Moss, Michele, 104–105

N

natural disasters
　　availability of technology assets and, 890–891
　　identifying staff risks, 691
NERC (North American Electric Reliability Corporation), 100, 102
non-compliance
　　demonstrating extent of compliance obligation satisfaction, 221–223
　　evaluate adherence to compliance process, 238
　　remediate areas of, 223–225
　　requirements for identifying and documenting risks of, 214
North American Electric Reliability Corporation (NERC), 100, 102
notes, process area
　　defined, 47–48
　　typographical and structural conventions, 51
notification communications, 187
numbering scheme, process areas, 47–49

O

objective views, for assets
　　facilities, 60–61, 63–64
　　information, 59, 61
　　people, 59–60
　　perspectives addressed by, 59
　　technology, 60, 62

objectively evaluate adherence. See also adherence, objective evaluation of
objectives, measurement and analysis
　　aligning needs by objectives, 553
　　establishing, 553–555
　　updating, 559
objectives, setting and communicating
　　capability level targets, 90–92
　　model scope, 87–90
　　organizational objectives, 84–85
　　organizational scope, 85–87
　　overview of, 83–85
　　relating process needs to, 631
　　using CERT-RMM for strategic/operational, 78
objects, creating identities for. See Identity Management (IM)
obligations, compliance
　　analyzing, 217–218
　　assign responsibility for, 231–232
　　collect and validate compliance data, 219–221
　　demonstrate extent of satisfaction with, 221–223
　　developing plan for managing, 211–212
　　establish ownership for meeting, 218–219
　　evaluate adherence to, 238
　　identify and document, 215–217
　　monitor activities, 225–226
　　remediate areas of non-compliance, 223–225
OCTAVE (Operationally Critical Threat, Asset, and Vulnerability Evaluation) method, CERT, 10
off-budget request for funds, process for, 391
off-cycle request for funds, process for, 391
online references
　　CERT-RMM, 12
　　The Crosswalk, 13
　　developing resilient software across life cycle, 108–109
OPD. See Organizational Process Definition (OPD)
open borders, stress of managing globalization risks, 22–23
operational constraints, 976
operational controls, 242
operational environments
　　identifying vulnerabilities, 917–918
　　maintain environmental conditions, 285–286
　　manage dependencies on public infrastructure, 288–289
　　manage dependencies on public services, 287
　　overview of, 282–283

perform facility sustainability
    planning, 284–285
  plan for facility retirement, 289–290
operational objectives
  establish scope of improvement, 84
  using CERT-RMM to support, 78
operational resilience, 976–977
operational resilience management
  applying risk information to,
    731–732
  assets, 30–33
  business processes, 29–30
  CERT-RMM v1.1 introducing
    system of, 12
  as competitive differentiator, xvi
  concept of, 25–27
  defined, 105, 977
  developing program for, 316–317
  governing. See Enterprise Focus
    (EF)
  identifying resilience requirements.
    See Resilience Requirements
    Development (RRD)
  incident management and, 473–474
  life-cycle coverage, 36–39
  managing resilience requirements.
    See Resilience Requirements
    Management (RRM)
  managing risk, 717
  measuring using CERT-RMM,
    115–118
  monitoring and, 577, 583
  resilience requirements, 33–35
  services, 27–29
  strategies for protecting/sustaining
    assets, 35–36
  training and awareness and, 653
operational resilience process group
  (ORPG), 617, 672
operational resilience requirements
  Access Management and, 155–156
  asset disposal and, 526
  for assets. See Resilience
    Requirements Development
    (RRD)
  assign to technology assets,
    875–876
  change management, 131
  Communications and, 179–181,
    183–184
  defined, 977, 982
  driving operational resilience
    through, 33–35
  establishing, 26–27
  for facility assets, 276–277
  identify inconsistencies in meeting,
    778
  for information assets, 518–519
  maintain traceability of, 776–777
  manage changes to, 775–776
  Measurement and Analysis and, 554

obtain commitment to, 774–775
  for software and system
    development, 797
  for software and systems, 800–801
  understanding, 773–774
operational risk
  common problems of, 3–4
  defined, 25–26, 977
  how CERT-RMM solves problems
    of, 5–6
  managing. See Risk Management
    (RISK)
  overview of, 2–3
  to technology assets, 878–881
Operationally Critical Threat, Asset,
  and Vulnerability Evaluation
  (OCTAVE) method, CERT, 10
Operations process areas
  AM. See Access Management (AM)
  defined, 7–8
  EC. See Environmental Control
    (EC)
  EXD. See External Dependencies
    Management (EXD)
  IM. See Identity Management (IM)
  IMC. See Incident Management and
    Control (IMC)
  KIM. See Knowledge and
    Information Management
    (KIM)
  model view of, 56–57
  overview of, 42–43
  PM. See People Management (PM)
  TM. See Technology Management
    (TM)
  VAR. See Vulnerability Analysis and
    Resolution (VAR)
OPF. See Organizational Process Focus
  (OPF)
optimization of resilience
  expenditures/investments
  determining return on resilience
    investments, 396–397
  identify cost recovery opportunities,
    397–398
  optimize resilience expenditures,
    394–396
  overview of, 394
organizational and intellectual
  knowledge, of staff, 532–533
organizational assets. See also Asset
  Definition and Management
  creating identities for access to,
    449–451
  defined, 978
  enable access to, 152–155
  establish common understanding
    of, 126–128
  establish ownership and
    custodianship, 128–130
  establishing, 123–124

inventory assets, 124–126
  manage and control access to,
    151–152
  returning upon departure from job,
    430–431
organizational impact area. See area of
  impact
organizational objectives, 84–85
organizational process assets
  establish measurement repository,
    612–613
  establish process asset library,
    613–614
  establish rules and guidelines for
    integrated teams, 615–616
  establish work environment
    standards, 614–615
  establishing, 608
  set of standard processes, 608–610
  tailoring criteria and guidelines,
    610–612
Organizational Process Definition
  (OPD)
  Access Management and,
    173–174
  achieve specific goals, 617
  assign responsibility for, 620–621
  collect improvement information,
    628
  defined, 978
  establish defined process, 627–628
  establish measurement repository,
    612–613
  establish process asset library,
    613–614
  establish process governance,
    617–618
  establish rules and guidelines for
    integrated teams, 615–616
  establish standard processes,
    608–610
  establish tailoring criteria and
    guidelines, 610–612
  establish work environment
    standards, 614–615
  identify and involve relevant
    stakeholders, 623–624
  introductory notes, 607
  manage work product
    configurations, 623
  monitor and control the process,
    624–626
  objectively evaluate adherence,
    626–627
  plan the process, 619
  as Process Management, 59
  provide resources for, 619–620
  purpose of, 607
  related process areas, 608
  review status with higher-level
    managers, 627

1018 Index

Organizational Process Definition (OPD) (contd.)
  summary of specific goals and practices, 608
  train people for, 621–623
Organizational Process Focus (OPF)
  Access Management and, 173–174
  achieve specific goals, 641
  appraise organizational processes, 632–633
  Asset Definition and Management, 145
  assign responsibility for, 645–646
  collect improvement information, 652
  deploy process assets, 636–637
  deploy standard processes, 638
  determine process improvement opportunities, 630
  establish defined process, 652
  establish process action plans, 634–635
  establish process governance, 641–643
  establish process needs, 631–632
  identify and involve relevant stakeholders, 648–649
  identify improvements to processes, 633–634
  implement process action plans, 636
  incorporate experiences into process assets, 639–641
  introductory notes, 629–630
  manage work product configurations, 647–648
  monitor and control the process, 649–650
  monitor process implementation, 639
  objectively evaluate adherence, 651
  plan and implement process actions, 634
  plan the process, 643
  as Process Management, 59
  provide resources for, 643–645
  purpose of, 629
  review status with higher-level managers, 651
  summary of specific goals and practices, 630
  train people for, 646–647
organizational process maturity, 978
organizational scope
  defined, 978
  overview of, 84–87
organizational sensitivity. See sensitivity
organizational subunits
  defined, 978
  in organizational scope, 86
  planning practice instantiation, 96

organizational superunits
  defined, 979
  in organizational scope, 86
  planning practice instantiation, 96
Organizational Training and Awareness (OTA)
  Access Management and, 164, 167
  achieve specific goals, 671
  assess effectiveness of awareness program, 662–663
  assess effectiveness of training program, 670–671
  Asset Definition and Management and, 137, 140
  assign responsibility for, 676–677
  collect improvement information, 684
  conduct training, 668
  defined, 979
  deliver resilience training, 668–669
  Enterprise Management and, 54–55
  establish awareness delivery capability, 658–660
  establish awareness needs, 655–657
  establish awareness plan, 657–658
  establish defined process for, 683
  establish process governance, 671–673
  establish training capability, 666–668
  establish training needs, 664–665
  establish training plan, 665–666
  establish training records, 669–670
  FISMA compliance, 960
  identify and involve relevant stakeholders, 679–680
  Incident Management and Control and, 510–511
  introductory notes, 653–654
  Knowledge and Information Management and, 548–549
  manage work product configurations, 678–679
  Measurement and Analysis and, 576
  monitor and control the process, 680–682
  Monitoring and, 604–605
  objectively evaluate adherence, 682–683
  Organizational Process Definition and, 628
  Organizational Process Focus and, 652
  perform awareness activities, 660–661
  perform awareness records, 661–662
  plan the process, 673–674
  provide resources for, 674–675
  purpose of, 653
  related process areas, 654

  review status with higher-level managers, 683
  summary of specific goals and practices, 655
  train people for, 677–678
organizational units
  defined, 979
  deploying standard processes to, 638
  in organizational scope, 85–87
  planning practice instantiation, 96
  standard processes tailored by, 607–608
organizationally high-valued services. See high-value services
organizations
  defined, 977
  process asset library. See process asset library
  role in External Dependencies Management, 341–343
  standard processes. See standard processes
ORPG (operational resilience process group), 617, 672
OTA. See Organizational Training and Awareness (OTA)
overhead allocation, funding resilience activities, 391
oversight, resilience
  establish corrective actions, 325–326
  as governance focus area, 322–323
  for operational resilience management program, 317
  overview of, 321
  performing, 323–325
ownership
  of access management, 152, 156, 168–169
  of asset definition and management, 126–130
  of compliance, 231–232
  of compliance obligations, 218–219
  defining, 32–33
  of environmental control, 296–297
  planning and, 946

P

partnerships, operational resilience management and, 2
passwords, access control via, 525
patch management, 889
PDCA (Plan, Do, Check, Act) cycle, 80–81, 82–83
peer pressure, 101–103
people
  as asset. See Asset Definition and Management (ADM), People Management (PM), and Human Resource Management (HRM)
  as asset in CERT-RMM, 31–32

creating identities for. *See* Identity
 Management (IM)
as critical dimension of
 organizations, 8–9
as human resource. *See* Human
 Resource Management (HRM)
life-cycle, 37
objective views for, 59–60
protecting and sustaining, 35–36
resilience requirements for, 33–35
People Management (PM)
achieve specific goals, 701
assign responsibility for, 706–707
collect improvement information,
 714–715
defined, 412, 979
establish defined process for, 714
establish process governance,
 701–703
establish redundancy for vital staff,
 694–695
establish vital staff, 687–690
identify and assess staff risks,
 691–692
identify and involve relevant
 stakeholders, 710–711
insider threats and, 964
introductory notes, 685–686
manage staff availability, 693–694
manage work product
 configurations, 709
mitigate staff risks, 692–693
monitor and control the process,
 711–713
objectively evaluate adherence, 713
as Operations process area, 57
perform succession planning,
 695–697
plan for return-to-work following
 disruptive events, 700–701
plan the process, 703–704
plan to support staff during
 disruptive events, 698–700
prepare for redeployment, 697–698
provide resources for, 704–706
purpose of, 685
related process areas, 686–687
review status with higher-level
 managers, 714
summary of specific goals and
 practices, 787
train people for, 707–709
perfective maintenance
defined, 979
of environmental conditions, 285
perform specific practices, generic
 goals and practices, 945
performance
analysis for funded resilience
 management activities,
 393–394

corrective actions for poor, 325–326
management of staff, 411
managing external entity, 363–365
measuring against plan, 573
measuring and assessing, 425–426
performance, in staff management
establish disciplinary process,
 426–427
establish resilience as job
 responsibility, 423
establish resilience performance
 goals/objectives, 423–425
measure and assess performance,
 425–426
overview of, 411, 422–423
performed processes
defined, 979
managed processes vs., 71–72
overview of, 70
periodic reviews. *See* reviews
physical controls
access control via, 525
defined, 979
at enterprise/service/asset levels,
 248–250
establishing and managing. *See*
 Environmental Control (EC)
for facility assets, 277, 279
for information assets, 519–521
overview of, 247
for technology assets, 876–878
Plan, Do, Check, Act (PDCA) cycle,
 80–81, 82–83
plan the process
Access Management, 163
Asset Definition and Management,
 136–137
Communications, 183–184,
 197–198
Compliance, 211–212, 229
Controls Management, 259
Enterprise Focus, 328
Environmental Control, 292–293
External Dependencies
 Management, 368
for facility retirement, 289–290
Financial Resource Management,
 400
generic goals and practices,
 946–947
Human Resource Management,
 435–436
Identity Management, 462
Incident Management and Control,
 498–499
Knowledge and Information
 Management, 536
Measurement and Analysis, 567
Monitoring, 596
for operational resilience
 management system, 314–317

Organizational Process Definition,
 619
Organizational Process Focus, 643
Organizational Training and
 Awareness, 673–674
People Management, 703–704
remediating areas of non-
 compliance, 224
Resilience Requirements
 Development, 758–759
Resilience Requirements
 Management, 780–781
Resilient Technical Solution
 Engineering, 816
Risk Management, 735
Service Continuity, 855
Technology Management,
 901–902
Vulnerability Analysis and
 Resolution, 930–931
planned downtime, 890, 979
planning CERT-RMM-based
 improvements, 95–97
plans
awareness, 657–658
capacity, 896
control revision, 732
development plans. *See*
 development plans, for
 resilient technical solutions
process actions, 634
risk mitigation, 692–693, 729–731
service continuity, 697–698, 733
succession, 695–697
sustaining technology assets,
 891–894
training, 665–666
plans, financial
defining funding needs, 387–388
establishing resilience budgets,
 388–389
for funding resilience management
 activities, 386–387
resolving funding gaps, 389–390
plans, for disruptive events
staff return-to-work, 700–701
staff support, 698–700
PM. *See* People Management (PM)
policies
change management, 887–888
Compliance, 216
configuration management, 886
Controls Management, 259
developing and publishing for
 compliance, 228
Enterprise Focus, 328
environmental control, 291–292
External Dependency Management,
 367
Financial Resource Management,
 385–386, 391, 399–400

1020 Index

policies (contd.)
   Human Resource Management, 434–435
   identify compliance obligations, 215–216
   Identity Management, 461–462
   Incident Management and Control, 498
   information assets, 518
   internal control, 241–242
   Knowledge and Information Management, 535
   Measurement and Analysis, 567
   Monitoring, 595
   Organizational Process Definition, 618
   Organizational Process Focus, 642–643
   Organizational Training and Awareness, 673
   People Management, 702–703
   release management, 889–890
   Resilience Requirements Development, 758
   Resilience Requirements Management, 780
   Resilient Technical Solution Engineering, 815
   Risk Management, 735
   Service Continuity, 854–855
   sponsoring resilience, 320–321
   standard processes adhering to, 610
   Technology Management, 901
   Vulnerability Analysis and Resolution, 930
post-incident review, 493–494, 979
practice-level scope, 88–90
practices
   damage of evaluation based on, 9–10
   defining CERT-RMM, 14–15
   generic. See generic goals and practices
   limitations of organizations focused on, 9
   organizing structure for deployed, 79–80
   planning instantiation of, 95–96
pre-employment verification of staff, 418–419
preventive controls, 247–248
preventive maintenance
   defined, 979
   of environmental conditions, 285
prioritization
   of candidates for process improvement, 634
   of control objectives, 246
   of data collection/storage, 559
   of external dependencies, 348–349
   of high-value services, 835–836
   of information assets, 516–517
   of measures, 557
   of monitoring requirements, 585–587
   of risk, 727
   of risks, 726
   of staff, 687
   of vulnerabilities, 924–925
prioritization, of technology assets
   establish resilience-focused technology assets, 873–874
   overview of, 871–873
privacy
   access controls and, 526
   attributes of information assets, 514
   defined, 979
   of information assets, 523–524
privileges. See access privileges
problem management
   defined, 980
   integrating incident handling with, 494–495
procedures
   as critical dimension of organizations, 8–9
   for handling information assets, 517
process actions
   establish action plans, 634–635
   implement action plans, 636
   planning and implementing, 634
process architecture, 610, 980
process areas
   ADM. See Asset Definition and Management (ADM)
   AM. See Access Management (AM)
   arranging in model view, 54–59
   by category, 41–42
   in CERT-RMM and CMMI models, 12–15
   COMM. See Communications (COMM)
   COMP. See Compliance (COMP)
   component categories, 42–44
   component descriptions, 44–47
   CTRL. See Controls Management (CTRL)
   defined, 980
   EC. See Environmental Control (EC)
   EF. See Enterprise Focus (EF)
   EXD. See External Dependencies Management (EXD)
   FRM. See Financial Resource Management (FRM)
   generic goals and practices, 950
   HRM. See Human Resource Management (HRM)
   icons, 42–43
   IM. See Identity Management (IM)
   IMC. See Incident Management and Control (IMC)
   institutionalization of. See institutionalization
   KIM. See Knowledge and Information Management (KIM)
   MA. See Measurement and Analysis (MA)
   MON. See Monitoring (MON)
   numbering scheme, 47–49
   OPD. See Organizational Process Definition (OPD)
   OPF. See Organizational Process Focus (OPF)
   OTA. See Organizational Training and Awareness (OTA)
   PM. See People Management (PM)
   RISK. See Risk Management (RISK)
   RRD. See Resilience Requirements Development (RRD)
   RRM. See Resilience Requirements Management (RRM)
   RTSE. See Resilient Technical Solution Engineering (RTSE)
   SC. See Service Continuity (SC)
   selecting for model scope, 87–90
   supporting generic practices, 74–75
   tags, 47–49
   TM. See Technology Management (TM)
   typographical and structural conventions, 49–51
   VAR. See Vulnerability Analysis and Resolution (VAR)
process asset library
   collecting improvement information for communications, 208
   defined, 977, 980
   establishing, 613–614
process capability, 980
process element, 980
process governance. See governance, process
process improvement
   appraisal of organizational processes, 632–633
   CERT-RMM for, 77
   CERT-RMM for model-based, 80–83
   CERT-RMM vs. CMMI focus, 15
   determining opportunities for, 630
   establish organizational process needs, 631–632
   identify improvements, 633–634
   proposals, 641
Process Management process areas
   defined, 7–8
   MA. See Measurement and Analysis (MA)
   model view of, 57–59
   MON. See Monitoring (MON)
   OPD. See Organizational Process Definition (OPD)
   OPF. See Organizational Process Focus (OPF)
   overview of, 42–43

process maturity, 978
process performance, 980
processes
　defined, 980
　definition of. *See* Organizational Process Definition (OPD)
　focus of. *See* Organizational Process Focus (OPF)
production environment, use of CERT-RMM in, 14
profiles, identity
　assigning roles to identities, 454
　correcting inconsistencies in, 458–459
　deprovisioning, 459–460
　establishing, 450–451
　establishing identity community from, 452–453
　plan process for, 462–463
protection, of information assets
　controls for, 519–521
　overview of, 518–519
　resilience requirements, 519
protection, of technology assets
　controls for, 876–878
　overview of, 874–875
　resilience requirements, 875–876
protection strategy
　for assets, 35–36
　defined, 981
　resilience requirements as basis of, 35
protocols, communication, 491
provide resources, generic goals and practices. *See* resources, providing
provisioning
　defined, 981
　establishing identities and, 447
proximity, 981
public infrastructure, 981
public services
　defined, 981
　managing dependencies on, 287
purchase orders, with external entities, 360–362
purchase requests, funding resilience activities, 391
purpose statements
　for process areas, 44, 48
　typographical and structural conventions, 50

Q

quality attributes, in software and system development, 793–794
questionnaires, for assessing effectiveness of awareness program, 662

R

reassignment, of roles and responsibilities, 429
records
　of awareness activities, 661–662
　identify vital organizational, 837–839
　of maintenance operations, 895
　of monitoring information, 591–592
　of training activities, 669–670
recovery plans, service continuity and, 839
recovery point objectives (RPOs)
　availability of technology assets and, 892–893
　defined, 981
recovery time objectives (RTOs)
　availability of technology assets and, 892–893
　defined, 981
redundancy
　availability of technology assets and, 891
　establish for vital staff, 694–695
　succession planning and, 695–697
reference resources, for information in this book, 993–995
references, process area
　defined, 47–48
　typographical and structural conventions, 51
registration, of identities, 450–451
regulations
　defined, 981
　documenting events and, 481–482
　electric power industry and, 101–103
　establish scope of improvement, 84
　managing. *See* Compliance (COMP)
　stress of managing operational risk, 23
related process areas section, 45, 48
relationships
　establish enterprise specifications, 353–354
　establish formal agreements, 360–362
　establish resilience specifications, 355–357
　evaluate/select external entities, 358–359
　identify internal and external dependencies and interdependencies, 837
　model view. *See* model view
　objective view. *See* objective views, for assets
　overview of, 53–54, 352–353
　between process elements, 610
release builds, 981

release management
　defined, 981
　technical solutions released into production, 812–813
　for technology assets, 889–890
reliability
　of information assets, 529–530
　resilience and, 100–101
remediation
　of areas of non-compliance, 223–225
　identifying areas needing compliance, 223
repeatability, of measures, 557
reports
　on communications effectiveness, 194
　on compliance obligation satisfaction, 222–223
　on corrective actions, 326
　on event status, 483
　external dependencies management, 362
　in incident management, 478–479, 486
　on incident status, 491
　logged events and, 481
　post-incident review, 494
　on resilience oversight, 325
repositories
　for compliance data, 220–221
　identity repository, 452, 974
　for processes and work products, 955
　for skills, 985
　for vulnerability information, 922–923, 925, 987
required components
　defined, 981
　overview of, 43–44
　summary of, 48
requirements
　guidelines for Resilient Technical Solution Engineering, 800–801
　validate service continuity plans against, 845–846
requirements, for Monitoring
　analyze and prioritize, 585–587
　establishing, 583–585
requirements, resilience
　developing. *See* Resilience Requirements Development (RRD)
　managing. *See* Resilience Requirements Management (RRM)
　operational. *See* operational resilience requirements
Requirements Development, CMMI process area, 795
residual risk, 981

resilience
  configuration management and, 884–885
  defined, 981, xv
  establish resilience-focused technology assets, 873–874
  identifying vital resilience functions of staff, 689
  inserting obligations in job descriptions, 423
  management. *See* operational resilience management
  reliability and resilience in, 100–101
  requirements. *See* operational resilience requirements
  resilience-aware culture, 319–320
  resilience-focused assets, 275
  scope, 89–90
  of service, 14
  staff and training, 982
  using goals and objectives to support, 423–424
resilience budgets
  defined, 982
  establishing, 388–389
  funding resilience activities, 391
  resolving funding gaps, 388–389
Resilience Requirements Development (RRD)
  achieve specific goals, 756
  analyze resilience requirements, 755
  assign enterprise resilience requirements to services, 753–754
  assign responsibility for, 760–761
  Cloud Computing and, 962
  collect improvement information, 769
  define required functionality, 754–755
  defined, 982
  develop service requirements, 752
  developing resilient software across life cycle with, 107
  as Engineering process area, 56
  establish asset resilience requirements, 752–753
  establish defined process for, 768–769
  establish process governance, 757–758
  for facility asset resilience requirements, 276–277
  FISMA compliance, 960
  identify and involve relevant stakeholders, 763–764
  identify enterprise requirements, 750–752
  introductory notes, 747–750
  manage work product configurations, 763
  monitor and control process of, 765–766
  objectively evaluate adherence, 767
  plan the process, 758–759
  provide resources for, 759–760
  purpose of, 747
  related process areas, 750
  review status with higher-level managers, 768
  summary of specific goals and practices, 750
  train people for, 761–763
  validate resilience requirements, 756
Resilience Requirements Management (RRM)
  achieve specific goals, 778
  assign responsibility for, 782–783
  Cloud Computing and, 962
  collect improvement information, 791–792
  defined, 982
  developing resilient software across life cycle, 107
  as Engineering process area, 56
  establish defined process for, 791
  establish process governance, 779–780
  identify and involve relevant stakeholders, 786–787
  identify inconsistencies in meeting resilience requirements, 778
  introductory notes, 771–772
  maintain traceability of resilience requirements, 776–777
  manage changes to resilience requirements, 775–776
  manage work product configurations, 785–786
  managing change to resilience requirements, 131
  monitor and control the process, 787–789
  objectively evaluate adherence, 789–790
  obtain commitment to resilience requirements, 774–775
  plan the process, 780–781
  provide resources for, 781–782
  purpose of, 771
  related process areas, 772
  review status with higher-level managers, 790–791
  summary of specific goals and practices, 772
  train people for, 783–785
  understanding resilience requirements, 773–774
resilience specifications
  defined, 982
  evaluating/selecting external entities based on, 358–359
  for external dependencies, 355–357
  external dependencies management, 361
resilience training
  delivery of, 668–669
  establish training needs, 664–665
  establish training plan, 665
  materials, 666–667
Resilient Technical Solution Engineering (RTSE)
  achieve specific goals, 813
  assign responsibility for, 818–819
  collect improvement information, 828–829
  create development plans for resilient technical solutions, 807–808
  defined, 982
  developing resilient software across life cycle, 106–107
  as Engineering process area, 56
  establish defined process for, 827–828
  establish process governance, 814–815
  identify and involve relevant stakeholders, 822–823
  identify architecture and design guidelines, 801–802
  identify assembly and integration guidelines, 805–807
  identify general guidelines, 798–800
  identify implementation guidelines, 802–805
  identify requirements guidelines, 800–801
  influenced by CMMI process areas, 108
  integrating selected guidelines with software and system development process, 809–810
  introductory notes, 793–796
  manage work product configurations, 821–822
  monitor and control the process, 823–826
  monitoring execution of development plan, 810–812
  objectively evaluate adherence, 826–827
  plan the process, 816
  provide resources for, 816–818
  purpose of, 793
  related process areas, 796
  release solutions into production, 812–813
  review status with higher-level managers, 827
  select and tailor guidelines, 808–809

summary of specific goals and
    practices, 796
train people for, 820–821
resource needs, establishing
    address skill deficiencies, 416–418
    establish baseline competencies,
        414–415
    inventory skills and identify gaps,
        415–416
    overview of, 413
resources, providing. *See also* Financial
        Resource Management (FRM)
    Access Management, 163–165
    Asset Definition and Management,
        137–138
    Communications, 197
    Compliance, 213, 229–231
    Controls Management, 259–260
    Enterprise Focus, 328–330
    Environmental Control, 293–295
    External Dependencies
        Management, 368–370
    Financial Resource Management,
        400–402
    generic goals and practices, 948
    Human Resource Management,
        436–437
    Identity Management, 462–464
    Incident Management and Control,
        499–500
    Knowledge and Information
        Management, 536–538
    Measurement and Analysis, 567–569
    Monitoring, 596–597
    Organizational Process Definition,
        619–620
    Organizational Process Focus,
        643–645
    Organizational Training and
        Awareness, 674–675
    People Management, 704–706
    Resilience Requirements
        Development, 759–760
    Resilience Requirements
        Management, 781–782
    Resilient Technical Solution
        Engineering, 816–818
    Risk Management, 736–737
    Service Continuity, 856–857
    Technology Management, 902–904
    Vulnerability Analysis and
        Resolution, 931–932
responding to incidents
    declare events for response
        planning, 483–484
    limiting organizational impact of
        incidents, 488–490
    recovery and, 487
response and recovery, responding to
        incidents, 487
responsibilities. *See also* roles

incident management plan and,
        477–478
    linking to identity. *See* Identity
        Management (IM)
    in organizational identity, 448
    periodic review to identify invalid
        identities, 457
    roles vs., 453
responsibilities, assigning
    Access Management, 165–166
    Asset Definition and Management,
        138–139
    Communications, 199–200
    Compliance, 231–232
    Controls Management, 261–262
    Enterprise Focus, 330–331
    Environmental Control, 296–297
    External Dependencies
        Management, 370–371
    Financial Resource Management,
        402–403
    generic goals and practices, 948–949
    Human Resource Management,
        437–438
    Identity Management, 464–465
    Incident Management and Control,
        501–502
    Knowledge and Information
        Management, 538–539
    managing changes to employment
        status, 429
    Measurement and Analysis, 569–570
    Monitoring, 597–598
    Organizational Process Definition,
        620–621
    Organizational Process Focus,
        645–646
    Organizational Training and
        Awareness, 676–677
    People Management (PM), 706–707
    Resilience Requirements
        Development, 760–761
    Resilience Requirements
        Management, 782–783
    Resilient Technical Solution
        Engineering, 818–819
    Risk Management, 737–738
    Service Continuity, 857–858
    Technology Management, 904–905
    Vulnerability Analysis and
        Resolution, 933
restoration plans
    incident response and, 489
    service continuity and, 839
restrictions. *See* access privileges
retention, of information assets,
        531–532
retirement, develop plan for facility,
        289–290
retrieval, of compliance data, 220
return on resilience investment (RORI)

calculation, 396–397
    defined, 983
review status with higher-level
    managers, generic goals and
    practices, 953
reviews
    with high-level managers. *See*
        higher-level managers,
        reviewing with
    monitoring and controlling
        and, 952
    of monitoring processes, 602–603
    in objective evaluation of
        adherence, 953
    periodic of environmental control
        process, 302
    periodic of identities, 456–457
    post-execution review of service
        continuity plans, 851
    sources of vulnerability, 921
revision history, in change
    management, 888
RISK. *See* Risk Management (RISK)
risk
    assessing controls for, 253, 257
    assessment of facility asset, 280–281
    availability of technology assets
        and, 892
    controlling operational
        environment, 282–283
    defined, 983
    defining controls for, 248–250
    due to external dependencies,
        349–350
    governance, xvi
    identifying and assessing external,
        350–351
    identifying related to involuntary
        terminations, 432
    mitigation strategies for external
        dependencies, 352
    mitigation strategies for facility
        assets, 281–282
    of non-compliance, 222
    protecting information assets and,
        518–519
    service continuity planning and, 832
risk analysis, 983
risk appetite, 983
risk category, 983
risk disposition
    assigning, 727–729
    defined, 983
risk management
    focus on high-value services, 836
    incident management and, 475
    interoperability and, 898–899
risk management, for information
        assets
    identify and assess risks, 522
    mitigate risks, 523

1024 Index

risk management, for information assets *(contd.)*
  overview of, 521
  prioritization and, 515–517
risk management, for technology assets
  identify and assess risks, 879–880
  mitigate risks, 880–881
  overview of, 878–879
  prioritization of technology assets, 871
risk management, of staff risk
  identify and assess staff risks, 691–692
  mitigate staff risks, 692–693
  overview of, 691
Risk Management (RISK)
  achieve specific goals, 733
  apply risk information to operational resilience management, 731–732
  assign responsibility for, 737–738
  assign risk disposition, 727–729
  categorize and prioritize risks, 727
  Cloud Computing and, 962
  collect improvement information, 745–746
  define risk parameters, 721–722
  defined, 983
  determine sources and categories of risk, 719–720
  develop risk mitigation plans, 729–731
  Enterprise Management, 54–55
  establish defined process for, 744–745
  establish operational risk management strategy, 720–721
  establish process governance, 734–735
  establish relationship between assets and services, 130
  establish risk measurement criteria, 722–723
  evaluate risks, 726–727
  FISMA compliance, 960
  identify and involve relevant stakeholders, 740–741
  identify asset-level risks, 723–725
  identify service-level risks, 725–726
  implement risk strategies, 731
  insider threats and, 964
  introductory notes, 717–718
  manage work product configurations, 740
  mitigate risks, 729
  monitor and control the process, 741–743
  objectively evaluate adherence, 743–744
  plan the process, 735
  preparing for, 719
  provide resources for, 736–737

  purpose of, 717
  related process areas, 718
  relationships driving threat/incident management, 58
  review and adjust risk-related strategies, 732–733
  review status with higher-level managers, 744
  summary of specific goals and practices, 718
  train people for, 738–739
risk measurement criteria, 983
risk mitigation
  defined, 983
  for external dependencies, 352
  for facility assets, 281–282
  of general risks, 729
  implementing process action plans, 731
  risk mitigation plans, 729–731, 983
  of staff risks, 692–693
  of technology asset risks, 880–881
risk parameters, 984
risk statements
  defined, 984
  developing, 725
  staff risks and, 692
risk taxonomy, 984
risk threshold, 984
risk tolerance
  defined, 984
  overview of, 721–722
  vulnerability analysis and resolution strategy and, 918–919
roles. *See also* responsibilities
  access privileges and, 155–156
  assign for knowledge and information management, 539
  assign to identities, 453–454
  identifying vital staff and, 688
  incident management plan and, 477–478
  linking to organizational identity. *See* Identity Management (IM)
  managing changes to employment status, 429
  organizational process definition process, 621
  periodic review to identify invalid identities, 457
root-cause analysis
  applying to vulnerabilities, 927–928
  defined, 984
  in post-incident review, 494
RORI (return on resilience investment)
  calculation, 396–397
  defined, 983
RPOs (recovery point objectives)
  availability of technology assets and, 892–893
  defined, 981

RRD. *See* Resilience Requirements Development (RRD)
RRM. *See* Resilience Requirements Management (RRM)
RTOs (recovery time objectives)
  availability of technology assets and, 892–893
  defined, 981
RTSE. *See* Resilient Technical Solution Engineering (RTSE)
rules, establish for integrated teams, 615–616

S

safety, work environment standards, 615
SC. *See* Service Continuity (SC)
scalability, of CERT-RMM, 15
SCAMPI (Standard CMMI Appraisal Method for Process Improvement), 92
scope
  of assets and environments, 917–918
  basing improvement objectives on, 84–85
  capability appraisal and, 93–94
  CERT-RMM, 14
  of control assessment, 255–256
  defined, 984
  model scope, 87–90, 976
  organizational scope, 84–87, 978
  of risk assessment, 281
  RORI calculation, 396–397
scorecard, governance, 324
screening, pre-employment, 418–419
secure design pattern, 984
security
  benefits of CERT-RMM, 5
  evolution of CERT-RMM, 10–11
  protection of information assets, 518–519
  protection of technology assets, 874–875
  protection strategy, 35–36
  service continuity plans, 843–844
  work environment standards, 615
SEI (Software Engineering Institute), 8, 9–12
sensitivity
  asset disposal and, 526
  attributes of information assets, 514
  categorize information assets by, 517–518
  defined, 984
  identifying staff responsible for sensitive assets, 690
  organizational sensitivity, 978
service continuity plans
  assign staff to, 842–843
  availability of technology assets and, 891–893

Index

defined, 985
develop and document, 840–842
develop testing program and standards for, 847–848
develop training for, 844
establish change criteria for, 852
evaluate test results, 849–850
execute, 850–851
exercise tests of, 849
identify and resolve conflicts in, 846
identify required plans, 840
identify vital staff, 688
maintain, 851–853
measure effectiveness of, 851
prepare for staff redeployment, 697–698
return-to-work plan, 700
risk mitigation and, 733
store and secure, 843–844
support of staff during disruptive events, 699
technology assets in, 873
validation of, 845–846
Service Continuity (SC)
achieve specific goals, 853
assign responsibility for, 857–858
assign staff to plans, 842–843
Cloud Computing and, 963
collect improvement information, 866–867
controls management using, 243
defined, 984
develop and document plans, 840–842
develop and document test plans, 848
develop operational resilience management plan, 315–316
develop resilient software across life cycle with, 108
develop testing program and standards, 847–848
develop training, 844
as Engineering process area, 56
establish change criteria, 852
establish defined process for, 865–866
establish process governance, 853–855
establish resilience-focused facility assets, 275
establish standards and guidelines for, 835
evaluate test results, 849–850
execute plans, 850–851
FISMA compliance, 960
identify and involve relevant stakeholders, 860–862
identify and resolve conflicts in plans, 846
identify communications requirements with, 180–181
identify high-value services, 835–836
identify internal and external dependencies and interdependencies, 837
identify required plans, 840
identify vital organizational records and databases, 837–839
incident response and, 489
introductory notes, 831–832
maintain changes to plans, 852–853
maintain plans, 851
manage work product configurations, 860
measure effectiveness of plans, 851
monitor and control the process, 862–864
objectively evaluate adherence, 864–865
plan the process, 855
prepare and plan for, 833–835
protect and sustain services and assets, 131
provide resources for, 856–857
purpose of, 831
related process areas, 832–833
relationships driving threat/incident management, 58
review status with higher-level managers, 865
store and secure plans, 843–844
summary of specific goals and practices, 833
test (exercise) plans, 849
train people for, 858–859
validate plans, 845–846
service disruption, 915
service level agreements (SLAs), 985
service profiles, 985
service-level controls
assessing effectiveness of, 253–254
defining, 248–250
service-level resilience requirements
analyze and validate, 754
assigning enterprise resilience requirements to services, 753–754
defined, 985
developing, 752
overview of, 748
service-level risks
identifying, 725–726
review and adjust strategies for, 732–733
services
in CERT-RMM, 14
CERT-RMM not establishing, delivering or managing, 14
concept of, 27–29
defined, 984
establish relationship between assets and, 130–131
focus on high-value, 29
fueled by assets, 30–33
life-cycle of, 38–39
operational risk objectives, 25–27
prioritize external dependencies relative to, 348–349
prioritize information assets relative to, 516
services map, 753
service-support staff, 689
shared resilience requirements, 985
Shewhart cycle, 80
silos, 5
skills
addressing gaps and deficiencies, 416–417
identifying gaps and deficiencies, 416
incident management plan and, 477–478
inventory or repository, 415–416, 985
service continuity plans and, 844
training needs and, 665
skills, training
Access Management, 167
Asset Definition and Management, 138, 140
Communications, 200–201
Compliance, 232–233
Controls Management, 262–263
Enterprise Focus, 331
Environmental Control, 297–298
External Dependencies Management, 371–372
Financial Resource Management, 403–404
generic goals and practices, 949–950
Human Resource Management, 439–440
Identity Management, 465–466
Incident Management and Control, 502–503
Knowledge and Information Management, 537, 540–541
Measurement and Analysis, 570–571
Monitoring, 599
Organizational Process Definition, 622
Organizational Process Focus, 646–647
Organizational Training and Awareness, 677–678
People Management, 708–709
Resilience Requirements Development, 762–763
Resilience Requirements Management, 784–785
Resilient Technical Solution Engineering, 820–821
Risk Management, 739
Service Continuity, 859

skills, training *(contd.)*
  Technology Management, 906
  Vulnerability Analysis and Resolution, 934
SLAs (service level agreements), 985
sociopolitical events, controlling operational environment, 283
software
  architecture and design guidelines, 801–802
  assembly and integration guidelines, 805–807
  errors, 891
  execution of development plan, 810–812
  implementation guidelines, 802–805
  integrating selected resilience guidelines with development process for, 809–810
  integrity of, 882
  monitoring, 795
  releasing resilient solutions into production, 812–813
  resilience guidelines, 800–801
  resilience requirements, 793–794
  stress of managing as intangible asset, 22
  tailoring resilience guidelines using selection criteria, 808–809
software assurance, using CERT-RMM
  about the authors, 104–105
  defined, 105
  overview of, 105–110
Software Engineering Institute (SEI), 8, 9–12
specific goals and practices
  defined, 45–46, 48, 985
  tags and numbering scheme for, 49
  typographical and structural conventions, 50
  using practice-level scope, 88–89
sponsorship. *See also* managers, review with higher-level
  commit funding for operational resilience management, 383–384
  for compliance program, 214, 231
  establish scope of improvement, 84–85
  of identity, 451
sponsorship, for operational resilience management
  commit funding, 318–319
  overview of, 317–318
  promote resilience-aware culture, 319–320
  standards and policies, 320–321
staff
  access controls for, 883–884
  acquisition of, 418
  assigning to service continuity plans, 842–843
  defined, 985
  document organizational and intellectual knowledge of, 532–533
  establish vital, 687–690
  incident response and, 490
  for maintenance operations, 894–895
  managing. *See* People Management (PM)
  for operational resilience management program, 316–317
  personnel services. *See* Human Resource Management (HRM)
  post-incident review, 494
  providing for incident closure, 492
  resource provision and, 948
  training. *See* training people
  training in discovery of vulnerabilities, 923
  verifying suitability of candidates, 418–419
staff, providing
  Access Management, 163–164
  Asset Definition and Management, 137
  Communications, 186–188, 198–200
  Compliance, 229–230
  Controls Management, 260
  Enterprise Focus, 329
  Environmental Control, 293–294, 296–297
  External Dependencies Management, 368–370
  Financial Resource Management, 400–401
  Human Resource Management, 436
  Identity Management, 462–464
  Incident Management and Control, 477–478, 499–500
  Knowledge and Information Management, 537
  Measurement and Analysis, 568
  Monitoring, 596–597
  Organizational Process Definition, 619–620
  Organizational Process Focus, 644
  Organizational Training and Awareness, 674
  People Management, 704–705
  Resilience Requirements Development, 759–760
  Resilience Requirements Management, 781
  Resilient Technical Solution Engineering, 817
  Risk Management, 736–737
  Service Continuity, 856
  Technology Management, 902–903
  Vulnerability Analysis and Resolution, 931–932
staff availability
  establish redundancy for vital staff, 694–695
  managing, 693–694
  perform succession planning, 695–697
  plan for return-to-work following disruptive events, 700–701
  plan to support staff during disruptive events, 698–700
  prepare for redeployment, 697–698
staff risks
  identify and assess, 691–692
  mitigate, 692–693
  overview of, 691
stakeholders
  communicating measurement results to, 564–565
  communicating to regarding incidents, 489
  defined, 985
  distributing collected information to, 592–593
  escalation of incidents for input from, 487–488
  in monitoring processes, 581–582
  for performing resilience oversight, 324–325
stakeholders, identify and involve
  Access Management, 168–169
  Asset Definition and Management, 141–142
  Communications, 177–181, 202–203
  Compliance, 234–236
  Controls Management, 264–265
  Enterprise Focus, 332–333
  Environmental Control, 299–300
  External Dependencies Management, 373–374
  Financial Resource Management, 404–406
  generic goals and practices, 951
  Human Resource Management, 441–442
  Identity Management, 467–468
  Incident Management and Control, 504–506
  Knowledge and Information Management, 542–543
  Measurement and Analysis, 571–573
  Monitoring, 600–601
  Organizational Process Definition, 623–624
  Organizational Process Focus, 648–649
  Organizational Training and Awareness, 679–680
  People Management, 710–711

Resilience Requirements
Development, 763–764
Resilience Requirements
Management, 786–787
Resilient Technical Solution
Engineering, 822–823
Risk Management, 740–741
Service Continuity, 860–862
Technology Management, 907–908
Vulnerability Analysis and
Resolution, 935–936
Standard CMMI Appraisal Method for
Process Improvement
(SCAMPI), 92
standard processes
composition of, 607
defined, 978, 986
defined processes compared
with, 954
deploying, 638
establishing, 608–610
measurement repository for, 612
monitoring implementation of, 639
tailoring and, 611–612
standards. *See also* guidelines
for communications, 181–184
Compliance, 214
for configuration management, 886
establishing standard processes,
608–610
interoperability, 898
managing. *See* Compliance (COMP)
for monitoring, 589–591
for service continuity, 835
sponsoring resilience, 320–321
test service continuity plans against,
847–848
validate service continuity plans
against, 845–846
for work environments, 614–615
statistics, descriptive statistics in data
analysis, 560
Stevens, James, 99–100
storage
of compliance data, 220
of data, 563–564
data collection and, 557–559
of service continuity plans, 843–844
strategic planning
defined, 986
developing operational resilience
management plan, 314–316
establish critical success factors,
310–312
establish organizational services,
312–314
establish scope of improvement, 84
establishing, 309–310
funding operational resilience
management, 383–384
performing resilience oversight for,
323–324

using CERT-RMM to support, 78
strategies
establish operational risk
management strategy, 720–721
establish vulnerability analysis and
resolution strategy, 918–920
implement risk strategies, 731
for protecting/sustaining assets,
35–36
review and adjust asset-level risk
strategies, 732
review and adjust service-level risk
strategies, 732–733
for staff redundancy, 695
translating lessons into, 495–496
strengths and weaknesses, appraisal of
organization, 632–633
stress
causes of in operational resilience
management, 2
CERT-RMM control of
organizational behavior
during, 21–23
managing operational resilience,
25–27
structural conventions, process areas,
49–51
subpractices, process area
defined, 47–48
typographical and structural
conventions, 51
subprocesses, 986
succession planning
defined, 986
perform, 695–697
summary of specific goals and
practices, process areas, 45
Supplier Management, Operations, 57
suppliers, 986
surveys
assess effectiveness of awareness
program, 662
assess effectiveness of training
program, 670
sustain
defined, 986
facility assets, 284–285
information, 35–36
services and assets, 131
technology assets, 891–894
sustainability planning, 285–286
*Sustaining Operational Resiliency: A
Process Improvement Approach to
Security Management* (Caralli
2006), 12
systems
architecture and design guidelines,
801–802
assembly and integration
guidelines, 805–807
execution of development plan,
810–812

implementation guidelines, 802–805
integrating selected resilience
guidelines with development
process for, 809–810
monitoring, 795
releasing resilient solutions into
production, 812–813
resilience guidelines, 800–801
resilience requirements, 793–794
tailoring resilience guidelines using
selection criteria, 808–809

T

tags, process area, 47–49, 50
targeted improvement profile (TIP)
capability level ratings overlaid on,
93–94
overview of, 91–92
targeted improvement roadmaps (TIRs)
for achieving FISMA compliance,
957–961
for Cloud Computing, 961–963
establishing improvement objective
with, 88
for managing insider threats, 963
teams, establish rules and guidelines
for integration of, 615–616
technical controls
defined, 986
at enterprise/service/asset levels,
248–250
for facility assets, 277–279
for information assets, 519–521
overview of, 246–247
for technology assets, 876–878
technical solutions. *See* Resilient
Technical Solution Engineering
(RTSE)
Technical Solutions, CMMI process
area, 795
techniques. *See* tools, techniques, and
methods
technology. *See also* Asset Definition
and Management (ADM) and
Technology Management (TM)
access privileges focusing on, 153
as asset in CERT-RMM, 31–32
assets, 986
identity management and, 448–449
interoperability. *See* interoperability
life-cycle of, 37
managing operational risk of, 23
objective views for, 60, 62
operational resilience management
and, 2
protecting and sustaining, 35–36
resilience requirements for, 33–35
stress of managing operational risk
of, 22
as traditional focus of operational
risk management, 8–9

Technology Management (TM)
  access controls for, 882–883
  achieve specific goals, 899
  assign resilience requirements, 875–876
  assign responsibility for, 904–905
  Cloud Computing and, 962–963
  collect improvement information, 913–914
  defined, 986
  developing resilient software across life cycle with, 108
  establish and implement controls, 876–878
  establish defined process, 912–913
  establish process governance, 899–901
  establish resilience-focused technology assets, 873–874
  FISMA compliance, 961
  identify and assess risks, 879–880
  identify and involve relevant stakeholders, 907–908
  introductory notes, 869–870
  maintain technology assets, 894–895
  manage availability of technology assets, 890–891
  manage integrity of technology assets, 881–882
  manage risks, 878–879
  manage technology capacity, 895–897
  manage technology interoperability, 897–899
  manage work product configurations, 906–907
  mitigate risks, 880–881
  monitor and control, 909–911
  objectively evaluate adherence, 911–912
  as Operations process area, 57
  perform change management, 887–888
  perform configuration management, 883–887
  perform release management, 889–890
  plan the process for, 901–902
  prioritize technology assets, 871–873
  protect technology assets, 874–875
  provide resources for, 902–904
  purpose of, 869
  related process areas, 870
  review status with higher-level managers, 912
  summary of specific goals and practices, 870–871
  sustain technology assets, 891–894
  train people for, 905–906
termination, external dependencies management, 362
termination of employment
  involuntary, 428
  managing impact of position changes, 428–429
  managing involuntary, 431–432
  voluntary, 427
terms and conditions of employment, establishing, 420–422
test (exercise) service continuity plans
  develop and document tests, 848
  develop testing program and standards, 847–848
  evaluate test results, 849–850
  exercise tests, 849
tests
  guidelines for resilient software and systems, 803–805
  release management and, 889–890
Threat, Vulnerability and Incident Management, Operations, 57
threat actor, 987
threat motive, 987
threats. See also vulnerabilities
  defined, 986
  manage insider threats, 963
  monitoring software and systems for, 795
  protecting information assets, 518–519
TIP (targeted improvement profile)
  capability level ratings overlaid on, 93–94
  overview of, 91–92
TIRs. See targeted improvement roadmaps (TIRs)
TM. See Technology Management (TM)
tools, techniques, and methods
  Access Management, 164
  Asset Definition and Management, 138
  Communications, 199
  Compliance, 230
  Controls Management, 260–261
  Enterprise Focus, 329–330
  Environmental Control, 294–295
  External Dependencies Management, 370
  Financial Resource Management, 401–402
  Human Resource Management, 437
  Identity Management, 463–464
  Incident Management and Control, 500
  Knowledge and Information Management, 538
  Measurement and Analysis, 568–569
  for monitoring process, 597
  Organizational Process Definition, 620
  Organizational Process Focus, 644
  Organizational Training and Awareness, 675
  People Management, 705–706
  Resilience Requirements Development, 760
  Resilience Requirements Management, 782
  Resilient Technical Solution Engineering, 817–818
  Risk Management, 737
  Service Continuity, 857
  Technology Management, 903
  Vulnerability Analysis and Resolution, 932
traceability, of resilience requirements, 776–777
tracking
  events in incident management, 480–481
  resilience requirements, 777
training people
  Access Management, 167
  Asset Definition and Management, 138, 140
  Communications, 200–201
  Compliance, 232–233
  Controls Management, 262–263
  Enterprise Focus, 331
  Environmental Control, 297–298
  External Dependencies Management, 371–372
  Financial Resource Management, 403–404
  generic goals and practices, 949–950
  Human Resource Management, 439–440
  Identity Management, 465–466
  Incident Management and Control, 502–503
  Knowledge and Information Management, 540–541
  Measurement and Analysis, 570–571
  Monitoring, 598–599
  Organizational Process Definition, 621–623
  Organizational Process Focus, 646–647
  Organizational Training and Awareness, 677–678
  People Management, 707–709
  Resilience Requirements Development, 761–763
  Resilience Requirements Management, 783–785
  Resilient Technical Solution Engineering, 820–821
  Risk Management, 738–739
  Service Continuity, 844, 858–859
  Technology Management, 905–906
  Vulnerability Analysis and Resolution, 934

training programs. *See also* Organizational Training and Awareness (OTA)
  assess effectiveness of, 670–671
  conduct, 668
  deliver resilience training, 668–669
  establish capability for, 666–668
  establish needs, 664–665
  establish plan, 665–666
  record, 669–670
triaging events, in incident management, 482–483
trusted access. *See* Identity Management (IM)
typical work products, process areas
  defined, 46–48
  typographical and structural conventions, 51
typographical conventions, 49–51

U

unplanned downtime, 890, 987
updating
  measurement and analysis objectives, 559
  process definitions and development plans, 810
  service continuity plans, 846
  vulnerability repository, 925
user IDs, access control via, 525
users, 987
utility sector, CERT-RMM in
  about the authors, 99–100
  grid modernization and transformation, 103–104
  regulation and peer pressure, 101–103
  reliability and resilience in, 100–101

V

validation
  of compliance data, 221
  of resilience requirements, 756
  of service continuity plans, 845–846
validity and reliability, of information assets, 529–530
VAR. *See* Vulnerability Analysis and Resolution (VAR)
verification
  evaluating suitability of candidate staff, 418–420
  managing access to assets during position changes, 430–431
version control, manage work product configurations and, 950
vital records
  defined, 987
  protecting, 513
vital resilience functions, 689

vital staff. *See also* staff, 987
voluntary termination, of employment, 427
vulnerabilities
  analysis and resolution strategy for, 918–920
  analyze, 923–925
  defined, 987
  discover, 921–923
  establish scope of, 917–918
  identify root causes, 927–928
  identify sources of, 920–921
  manage exposure to, 925–927
  monitoring software and systems for, 795
  overview of, 915–916
  protecting information assets, 518–519
  service continuity planning and, 832
Vulnerability Analysis and Resolution (VAR)
  achieve specific goals, 928
  analyze vulnerabilities, 923–925
  assign responsibility for, 933
  collect improvement information, 940–941
  defined, 987
  discover vulnerabilities, 921–923
  establish analysis and resolution strategy, 918–920
  establish defined process, 940
  establish process governance, 929–930
  establish scope of assets and environments to be analyzed, 917–918
  FISMA compliance, 961
  identify and involve relevant stakeholders, 935–936
  identify root causes, 927–928
  identify sources of vulnerabilities, 920–921
  insider threats and, 964
  introductory notes, 915–916
  manage exposure to vulnerabilities, 925–927
  manage work product configurations, 935
  monitor and control the process, 937–939
  monitoring needs of, 586
  objectively evaluate adherence, 939
  plan the process, 930–931
  prepare for vulnerability analysis and resolution, 917
  provide resources for, 931–932
  purpose of, 915
  related process areas, 916
  relationships driving threat/incident management, 57–58

  review status with higher-level managers, 940
  summary of specific goals and practices, 916
  train people for, 934
vulnerability catalogs, 921
vulnerability data collection, 921
vulnerability management strategy, 987
vulnerability notification services, 921
vulnerability repository, 987
vulnerability resolution, 987

W

waivers, 987
White, David W., 999, xxiv
work environment standards, 614–615
work product configurations
  Access Management, 168
  Asset Definition and Management, 141
  Communications, 202
  Compliance, 234
  Controls Management, 264
  Enterprise Focus, 332
  Environmental Control, 298–299
  External Dependencies Management, 373
  generic goals and practices, 950
  Human Resource Management, 440–441
  Identity Management, 466–467
  Incident Management and Control, 504
  Knowledge and Information Management, 541
  Measurement and Analysis, 571
  Monitoring, 599–600
  Organizational Process Definition, 623
  Organizational Process Focus, 647–648
  Organizational Training and Awareness, 678–679
  People Management, 709
  Resilience Requirements Development, 763
  Resilience Requirements Management, 785–786
  Resilient Technical Solution Engineering, 821–822
  Risk Management, 740
  Service Continuity, 860
  Technology Management, 906–907
  Vulnerability Analysis and Resolution, 935
work products, typical
  defined, 46–48
  typographical and structural conventions, 51

The SEI Partner Network:
Helping hands with a global reach.

Do you need help getting started with CERT® Resilience Management Model (CERT-RMM) adoption in your organization? Or are you an experienced professional in the field who wants to join a global network of CERT-RMM service providers? Regardless of your level of experience with CERT-RMM tools and methods, the SEI Partner Network can provide the assistance and the support you need to make your CERT-RMM adoption a success.

The SEI Partner Network is a world-wide group of licensed organizations with individuals qualified by the SEI to deliver SEI services. SEI Partners can provide you with training courses, CERT-RMM adoption assistance, proven appraisal methods, and teamwork and management processes that aid in implementation of the SEI's tools and methods.

To find an SEI Partner near you, or to learn more about this global network of professionals, please visit the SEI Partner Network website at
http://www.sei.cmu.edu/partners

ESSENTIAL CERT® GUIDES

The CERT® C Secure Coding Standard

Robert C. Seacord

ISBN-13: 978-0-321-56321-7

This book is an essential desktop reference documenting the first official release of the CERT® C Secure Coding Standard.

Software Security Engineering

Julia H. Allen, Sean Barnum, Robert J. Ellison, Gary McGraw, Nancy R. Mead

ISBN-13: 978-0-321-50917-8

Drawing extensively on the systematic approach developed for the Build Security In (BSI) Web site, this management guide provides a number of sound practices likely to increase the security and dependability of your software, both during its development and subsequently in its operation.

Managing Information Security Risks: The OCTAVE℠ Approach

Christopher Alberts, Audrey Dorofee

ISBN-13: 978-0-321-11886-8

The OCTAVE approach for self-directed security evaluations, developed at the influential CERT Coordination Center, enables any organization to develop security priorities based on the organization's particular business concerns.

The CERT® Guide to System and Network Security Practices

Julia H. Allen

ISBN-13: 978-0-201-73723-3

The CERT Coordination Center® publishes advisories and develops key security practices, implementations, and tech tips on a timely basis. This essential guide makes these practices and implementations available for the first time in book form.

Secure Coding in C and C++

Robert C. Seacord

ISBN-13: 978-0-321-33572-2

This book covers the root causes of software vulnerabilities and how to avoid them. Drawing on CERT/CC's reports and conclusions, Robert C. Seacord systematically identifies the program errors most likely to lead to security breaches, shows how they can be exploited, reviews the potential consequences, and presents secure alternatives.

For more information on these and other titles in the SEI Series in Software Engineering, visit informit.com/seiseries.

The SEI Partner Network:
Helping hands with a global reach.

Do you need help getting started with CERT® Resilience Management Model (CERT-RMM) adoption in your organization? Or are you an experienced professional in the field who wants to join a global network of CERT-RMM service providers? Regardless of your level of experience with CERT-RMM tools and methods, the SEI Partner Network can provide the assistance and the support you need to make your CERT-RMM adoption a success.

The SEI Partner Network is a world-wide group of licensed organizations with individuals qualified by the SEI to deliver SEI services. SEI Partners can provide you with training courses, CERT-RMM adoption assistance, proven appraisal methods, and teamwork and management processes that aid in implementation of the SEI's tools and methods.

**To find an SEI Partner near you, or to learn more about this global network of professionals, please visit the SEI Partner Network website at
http://www.sei.cmu.edu/partners**